Hellenic Studies 70

KINYRAS

Recent Titles in the Hellenic Studies Series

The Theban Epics

Plato's Four Muses
The Phaedrus and the Poetics of Philosophy

Plato's Wayward Path
Literary Form and the Republic

Dialoguing in Late Antiquity

Between Thucydides and Polybius
The Golden Age of Greek Historiography

Poetry as Initiation
The Center for Hellenic Studies Symposium on the Derveni Papyrus

Divine Yet Human Epics
Reflections of Poetic Rulers from Ancient Greece and India

The Web of Athenaeus

Eusebius of Caesarea
Tradition and Innovations

Homeric Durability
Telling Time in the Iliad

Paideia and Cult
Christian Initiation in Theodore of Mopsuestia

Imperial Geographies in Byzantine and Ottoman Space

Loving Humanity, Learning, and Being Honored
The Foundations of Leadership in Xenophon's Education of Cyrus

The Theory and Practice of Life
Isocrates and the Philosophers

From Listeners to Viewers
Space in the Iliad

Aspects of History and Epic in Ancient Iran
From Gaumāta to Wahnām

Homer's Versicolored Fabric
The Evocative Power of Ancient Greek Epic Word-Making

http://chs.harvard.edu/chs/publications

KINYRAS
THE DIVINE LYRE

John C. Franklin

With a study of Balang Gods
by Wolfgang Heimpel

And illustrations
by Glynnis Fawkes

CENTER FOR HELLENIC STUDIES
Trustees for Harvard University
Washington, D.C.
Distributed by Harvard University Press
Cambridge, Massachusetts, and London, England
2015

Kinyras: The Divine Lyre
   by John C. Franklin
Copyright © 2015 Center for Hellenic Studies, Trustees for Harvard University
All Rights Reserved.
Published by Center for Hellenic Studies, Trustees for Harvard University,
   Washington, D.C.
Distributed by Harvard University Press, Cambridge, Massachusetts, and
   London, England
Production: Kristin Murphy Romano
Cover design: Joni Godlove
Cover illustration: Glynnis Fawkes

First paperback printing (with corrections), April 2017

ISBN 978-0-674-97232-2

EDITORIAL TEAM

Senior Advisers: W. Robert Connor, Gloria Ferrari Pinney, Albert Henrichs,
   James O'Donnell, Bernd Seidensticker
Editorial Board: Gregory Nagy (Editor-in-Chief),
   Casey Dué (Executive Editor), Mary Ebbott (Executive Editor),
   Scott Johnson, Olga Levaniouk, Leonard Muellner
Production Manager for Publications: Jill Curry Robbins
Web Producer: Noel Spencer
Multimedia Producer: Mark Tomasko

On the cover: *Kinyras at Alassa*, by Glynnis Fawkes

The Library of Congress has cataloged the hardcover printing as follows:

Franklin, John, 1964-
Kinyras : the divine lyre / by John Curtis Franklin.
   pages cm. -- (Hellenic studies ; 70)
 Includes bibliographical references and index.
ISBN 978-0-674-08830-6 (alk. paper)
1. Kinyras (Greek mythology) 2. Lyre--History. 3. Music, Greek and Roman--History
   and criticism. I. Title.

ML169.F73 2015
787.7'81909--dc23

2015032440

Κυπρογενῆ Κυθέρειαν ἀείσομαι ἥ τε βροτοῖσι
μείλιχα δῶρα δίδωσιν, ἐφ' ἱμερτῷ δὲ προσώπῳ
αἰεὶ μειδιάει καὶ ἐφ' ἱμερτὸν θέει ἄνθος

  —with eternal gratitude for Glynnis, Sylvan, and Helen

Table of Contents

List of Figures . . . . *xiii*

Preface. . . . . *xix*

Conventions and Abbreviations . . . . *xxv*

INTRODUCTION

1. Kinyras and Kinnaru 1
    Kinyras of Cyprus 1
    The Return of Kinnaru 4
    The Crux. 5
    Plan of This Study and Preliminary Conclusions 7
    Pre-Greek, Greek, and Phoenician Cyprus 10

PART ONE: THE CULT OF KINNARU

2. Instrument Gods and Musician Kings in Early Mesopotamia . . 19
    Divinized Instruments. 19
    Gudea and the Balang-Gods of Ningirsu 26
    Shulgi and the Royal Ideal of Music. 33
    Lovely Lyrics for Inanna. 37
    Music and Seven-Magic 40
    Conclusion. 41

3. The *Knr*. 43
    Jubal: Looking Back from Israel 43
    Identifying the *Knr*. 46
    The Lexical Evidence. 53
    The Problems of Stringing and Tuning 57
    Limits of the Investigation 60

Table of Contents

4. Starting at Ebla 63
    The City and Its Music 63
    Kinnārum and Balang 65
    Lamentation and Royal Ancestor Cult 67
    Divine Lyre at Ebla? 71

5. Mari and the Amorite Age 73
    The City and Its Music 73
    The *Kinnāru* at Mari 76
    The Amorite Connection 80
    Divine Instruments and the Amorite World 83
    Conclusion 87

6. Peripherals, Hybrids, Cognates 89
    The 'Inanna-Instrument' and Hittite Royal Ritual 89
    The Syro-Hurrian Sphere 96
    'Asiatic' Lyres in Bronze Age Egypt 104

7. Kinnaru of Ugarit 113
    The King and His Musicians 113
    More about Kinnaru 119
    Praising Baal 125
    Bow and Lyre in the *Tale of Aqhat* 131
    Rāp'iu, Kinnaru, and the Eternal Power of Music 134
    Silence of Kinnaru 141
    Isaiah and the Lyres of the Rephaim 146
    Conclusion 147

8. David and the Divine Lyre 149
    David, Solomon, and the Ideals of Great Kingship 150
    Musical Management in the First Temple 155
    The *Kinnōr* and the Divine Lyre 158
    King, *Kinnōr*, and the "Spirit of God" 165
    Performing the Divine Lyre 167
    Sweet Psalmist of Israel: David's Lyric Legacy 174

PART TWO: KINYRAS ON CYPRUS

9. Kinyras the Kinyrist 187
The Etymology of Kinyras 187
The Conflict with Apollo 189
Outplaying Orpheus and Thamyris 192
The 'Greek' *Kinýra* 194
"Our *Kenyristḗs* Apollo": Playing the *Kinýra* on Cyprus 203
Lost in Translation:
  Kinýra at the Syro-Levantine Interface 213
Conclusion. 216

10. Praising Kinyras 219
Pindar and the Example of Kinyras 219
The Love of Apollo 226
Singing 'about' Kinyras 231
Caught in the Act: Two Model Shrines 236

11. Lyric Landscapes of Early Cyprus 241
The Current Picture 241
A Lost 'Daughter of Kinyras' in the Cyprus Museum 245
Music, Memory, and the Aegean Diaspora 250
Cypriot Lyres between East and West. 253
Ethnicity and Musical Identity
  in the Cypro-Phoenician Bowls. 258
The Case for Second-Millennium Adaptation of *Kinýra* . . . 272
Conclusion. 276

12. Kinyras the Lamenter. 279
Kinyras and His Cult Family 280
Between Song and Silence 291
The Cypriot Linos-Song 304
Phoinix *Kinyrízōn* 316
Epilogue: The Antinoos Lament from Kourion 318

13. The Talents of Kinyras 321
Great Kingship 321
Metallurge and Potter. 324
Kinyras the Mariner 326
Oilman and Parfumeur 330
The Virtuous Monarch 333
Conclusion. 335

Table of Contents

14. Restringing Kinyras 337
    Aegean Foundation Legends and Epic Homecomings 337
    Kinyras, Dmetor, and the Changing States of Cyprus. 342
    Liar King:
        The Terracotta Fleet and the Curse of Agamemnon . . . 343
    The Unthroning of Kinyras 346
    Kinyras and Pre-Greek Social Topography 349
    Salamis: Euagoras, Teukros, and the Daughter of Kinyras . . 351
    Paphos: Agapenor, Laodike, and the Arcadian Connection . . 359
    Conclusion. 368

15. Crossing the Water 371
    Alashiya and the Mainland Cults. 371
    Importing the Divine Lyre 380
    Music and the Harmonious Realm. 383
    From Divine Lyre to Culture-Hero. 392

16. The Kinyradai of Paphos 401
    Tacitus and the Memories of the Paphian Priesthood 401
    Nikokles and the Kinyrad Legacy 407
    The Kinyradai in Hellenistic and Roman Times 417
    Sons of the *Kinýra* 421

PART THREE: KINYRAS AND THE LANDS AROUND CYPRUS

17. Kinyras at Pylos 427
    Kinyras and the Priests 427
    Naming Kinyras in Greek 432
    Kinyras the Shipwright 436
    A Kinyras Complex. 438

18. The Melding of Kinyras and Kothar. 443
    Kothar and Kinnaru 443
    Philo of Byblos: Khousor and His Retiring Twin. 445
    Étienne de Lusignan: Cinaras and *His* Retiring Twin 452
    The Craftsman-Musician Twins Mytheme 453
    Confounded Lyres?. 456

19. Kinyras, Kothar, and the Passage from Byblos 459
    Kinyras, Kinnaru, and the Canaanite Shift 459
    Lucian: Kinyras at Aphaka 461
    Kinyras and Theias. 466
    Ps.-Melito: Kauthar at Aphaka 468
    Goddess, King, and Copper 473
    The Cypro-Byblian Interface 479
    Ritual Lamentation and the 'Damu' of Byblos 482
    Conclusion. 486

20. Kinyras at Sidon? The Strange Affair of Abdalonymos 489

21. Syro-Cilician Approaches 495
    Aoios and Paphos: Two Cilician Crossings 498
    Solar Gods, Sandokos, and the Syrian Descent. 504
    The Egyptian Detour. 512
    THEIOS AOIDOS: The Lyre-Player Seals 517

APPENDICES

A: A Note on 'Balang' in the Gudea Cylinders. 531

B: Ptolemy Khennos as a Source
    for the Contest of Kinyras and Apollo 535

C: Horace, Cinara, and the Syrian *Musiciennes* of Rome. 537

D: *Kinyrízein*: The View from Stoudios 539

E: The 'Lost Site' of Kinyreia. 545

F: Theodontius: Another Cilician Kinyras?. 549

G: Étienne de Lusignan and the 'God Cinaras' 557

BALANG-GODS 571
    A Study by Wolfgang Heimpel

Bibliography *633*

Index Locorum *715*

General Index *739*

List of Figures

All figures drawn by Glynnis Fawkes unless otherwise noted.

Figure 1   Detail from 'Sea Peoples' reliefs, Medinet Habu, reign of Ramses III (ca. 1184–1152). Drawn from Nelson et al. 1930, pl. 36–37.

Figure 2   'Harp treaty', unprovenanced Mesopotamian cylinder seal, ca. fourteenth century. London, BM 89359. Drawn from MgB 2/2 fig. 108.

Figure 3   'Asiatic' troupe with lyrist, tomb-painting, Beni-Hassan, Twelfth Dynasty, ca. 1900. Drawn from Shedid 1994 fig. 20.

Figure 4   Distribution map of Bronze Age lyres (after DCPIL). Individual images drawn by Bo Lawergren and numbered according to DCPIL figs. 1, 3–5, 8 (used with permission). Other drawings by Glynnis Fawkes are preceded by "Figure," referring to their position in this book.

Figure 5   Distribution map of Iron Age lyres (after DCPIL). Individual images drawn by Bo Lawergren and numbered according to DCPIL figs. 1, 3–5, 8 (used with permission).

Figure 6   Seated/enthroned lyrist with animals. Unprovenanced North Syrian cylinder seal, ca. 2900–2350. Bible Lands Museum, Jerusalem, 2462. Drawn from SAM no. 70.

Figure 7   Musical rite in four registers. Inandık vase, ca. 1650–1550 (Old Hittite). Anadolu Medeniyetleri Müzesi, Ankara. Drawn from photos in Özgüç 1988.

xiii

List of Figures

Figure 8 Ishtar (?) playing harp before Ea. Modern impression of Syro-Hittite seal from Konya-Karahöyük, ca. 1750. Drawn from Alp 1972 pl. 11, no. 22.

Figure 9 Cosmopolitan musical ensemble with 'Asiatic' lyre. Wall-painting from Tomb 367, Theban Necropolis, reign of Amenhotep II (ca. 1438–1412). Drawn from MgB 2/1:30–31 fig. 8.

Figure 10 Two harem apartments with musical instruments. Relief from the Tomb of Aÿ, reign of Akhenaten, ca. 1364–1347. Drawn from Davies 1908 pl. XXIX.

Figure 11 'Kinyrist' celebrating victorious king. Ivory plaque from Megiddo, ca. 1250–1200. Jerusalem, IAA 38.780. Drawn from Mertzenfeld 1954 pl. XXIV–XXV.

Figure 12 Lyre-playing lion king with animal subjects. Ninth-century orthostat relief from Guzana (Tell Halaf). Drawn from Moortgat 1955 pl. 100–101.

Figure 13 Lyrist with animals and tree ('Orpheus jug'). Philistine strainer-spout jug, Megiddo, ca. 1100. Jerusalem, IAA 13.1921. Drawn from Dothan 1982 fig. 21.1 (pl. 61).

Figure 14 Coin of the Bar Kokhba revolt (132–136 CE). Bible Lands Museum, Jerusalem, 5651. Drawn from SAM no. 133–134.

Figure 15 King David with animals. Sixth-century floor-mosaic, Gaza (restored). Jerusalem, IAA 1980.3410. Drawn from SAM no. 72.

Figure 16 Cyprus and the eastern Mediterranean according to the Tabula Peutingeriana. Used by permission of the Österreichische Nationalbibliothek, Vienna.

Figure 17 Lyrist-archer, White Painted krater from Khrysokhou (near Marion), ca. 850–750 (CG III). Collection of the Archbishopric of Cyprus, Nicosia. Drawn from Karageorghis 1980b.

Figure 18 Model shrine with dancers and lyrist. Unprovenanced (seventh century?), Louvre AO 22.221. Drawn from Ridder 1908 pl. 20.106 and CAAC IV pl. LXXVII:9.

List of Figures

Figure 19   Model shrine with lyrist and spectators. Unprovenanced (eleventh–seventh century), Cyprus Museum, Nicosia, inv. B 220.1935. Drawn from Boardman 1971 pl. XVII.1–V.

Figure 20   Map of Cyprus showing distribution of iconography discussed in text.

Figure 21   *Kinyrístria* and dancer. Fourteenth-century Egyptian(izing) faience bowl from Cyprus (unprovenanced). Cyprus Museum, Nicosia, Inv. G63. Drawn from autopsy and Karageorghis 1976a fig. 137.

Figure 22   Female lutenist. Egyptian(izing) faience bowl from near Idalion. New York, MMA 74.51.5074. Drawn from Karageorghis et al. 2000:63 no. 99.

Figure 23   Lyre-player seal, Ashdod, ca. 1000. Jerusalem, IAA 91-476. Drawn from Dothan 1971, pl. XLIX.7.

Figure 24   Juxtaposition of 'western' and 'eastern' lyres. Orthostat relief, Karatepe, ca. 725. Drawn from Akurgal 1962 fig. 142.

Figure 25   Warrior-lyrist. Proto-bichrome kalathos from Kouklia, eleventh century (LCIIIB). Cyprus Museum, Nicosia, Kouklia T.9:7. Drawn from CCSF 1:5, 2:1–3.

Figure 26   Hubbard amphora, Famagusta district, ca. 800. Cyprus Museum, Nicosia, 1938/XI-2/3. Drawn from CCSF 1.8–9, 2.7–9.

Figure 27   Cypriot votive figurines with variety of lyre shapes (scale not uniform). 27a (Cypro-Archaic, unprovenanced) = London, BM 1876/9-9/90, drawn from CAAC IV:I(v)4. 27b (Cypro-Archaic, Lapethos) = London, BM 1900.9-3.17, drawn from CAAC Va:I(xi)i.67. 27c (Cypro-Archaic, unprovenanced) = Cyprus Museum, Nicosia, inv. B192a, drawn from CAAC Va:I(xi)i.71. 27d (Cypro-Archaic, Kourion) = University Museum, Philadelphia no. 54-28-109, drawn from CAAC IV:I(v)3. 27e (Hellenistic, Cythrea), MMA accession no. unknown, drawn from Cesnola 1894, pl. XXXIV no. 282.

Figure 28   Cypro-Phoenician symposium bowl from Idalion, ca. 825. New York, MMA 74.51.5700. Drawn from PBSB Cy3.

Figure 29   'Eastern' lyres in the Cypro-Phoenician symposium bowls, ca. 900–600. Drawn from corresponding photos in PBSB.

List of Figures

Figure 30   'Western' lyres on the Cypro-Phoenician symposium bowls, ca. 750–600. Drawn from photos in PBSB.

Figure 31   Ivory pyxis with lyre ensemble, Nimrud, North Syrian school, ninth–eighth century. Baghdad ND1642. Drawn from Mallowan 1966 fig. 168.

Figure 32   Sixth-century Egyptianizing limestone statue from Golgoi (?). New York, MMA 74.51.2509. Drawn from Aspects fig. 138.

Figure 33   Cypro-Phoenician symposium bowl, before ca. 725. Olympia, Greece. Athens NM 7941. Drawn from PBSB G3.

Figure 34   Statue of female lyre-player with late floral-post lyre, Golgoi, Hellenistic. New York, MMA 74.51.2480. Drawn from Cesnola 1885 pl. cii no. 676.

Figure 35   Myrrha fleeing, putting viewer in position of Kinyras. Roman fresco from Tor Marancio, ca. 150–250 CE, after Hellenistic original. Vatican, Sala delle Nozze Aldobrandine. Drawn from LIMC s.v. Myrrha no. 1.

Figure 36   Próthesis of Achilles, with silenced lyre. Sixth-century Corinthian hydria, Louvre E 643. Drawn from LIMC s.v. Achilleus no. 897.

Figure 37   Lekythos showing dedication of lyre at grave. Berlin 'Antiquarium' no. 3262. Drawn from Quasten 1930 pl. 34.

Figure 38   Enthroned/seated harpist, Sacred Tree, and offering-bearers. Cypriot bronze stand from Kourion (?), thirteenth century. London, BM 1920/12-20/1. Drawn from Papasavvas 2001 fig. 42–47.

Figure 39   Enthroned/seated harpist and harpist devotee. Cypriot bronze stand from Kourion (?), thirteenth century. London, BM 1946/10-17/1. Drawn from Papasavvas 2001 fig. 61–67.

Figure 40   The 'Ingot God', Enkomi, ca. 1250 (LC III). Inv. F.E. 63/16.15. Drawn from Flourentzos 1996:47.

Figure 41   Procession/dance scene. Modern impression of LBA Cypriot cylinder-seal from Enkomi, ca. 1225–1175 (LC IIIA). Nicosia, Cyprus Museum 1957 inv. no. 36. Drawn from Courtois and Webb 1987 pl. 7 no. 23.

List of Figures

Figure 42   Procession/dance scene with possible stringed instrument. Modern impression of LBA Cypriot cylinder-seal from Enkomi Tomb 2. Stockholm, Medelhavsmuseet Inv. E. 2:67. Drawn from Karageorghis 2003:280–281 no. 320.

Figure 43   Limestone head of Kinyrad king, seventh century. Palaepaphos KA 730. Drawn from Maier 1989:378 fig. 40.1.

Figure 44   Paphian coin with 'Apollo' and *omphalós*, reign of Nikokles, ca. 319. Galleria degli Uffizi, Florence. Drawn from BMC Cyprus pl. XXII.11.

Figure 45   Lyrist and bird-metamorphosis. Modern impression of cylinder seal, Mardin (?), ca. 1800. London, BM 134306. Drawn from Li Castro and Scardina 2011, fig. 11.

Figure 46   The Lyre-Player Group of Seals (subset with Lyrist). Drawn variously from images in Boardman and Buchner 1966; Boardman 1990; Rizzo 2007; SAM. For individual references, see 523n182.

Figure 47   Sumerian Bull-headed lyre with 'emergent' bull. Stele-fragment, Lagash, before 2100. Paris, Louvre AO 52. Drawn from MgB 2/2 fig. 45.

Figure 48   David and his musicians. Chludov Psalter, ninth century, Moscow, State Historical Museum, MS D.129, fol. 5v. Drawn from Currie forthcoming pl. 2.

PREFACE

Kinyras has deep roots on Cyprus. He came to the island, I argue, in the Late Bronze Age, when he had already begun to outgrow his musical roots as a Divine Lyre. Already by Homer's time Kinyras had taken on kingship, metal-working, and other typical industries to become the central Cypriot culture-hero. While all Classicists know the metamorphosis of his daughter Myrrha in Ovid, and some may recall brief allusions by Homer, Alkman, Tyrtaios, and Pindar, Kinyras has remained quite obscure otherwise. For the sources, though rich, are widely scattered; Kinyras, like Cyprus, was on a distant horizon of Greek culture.

From an Aegean perspective, that is. That the situation was different on Cyprus itself is shown by a few precious inscriptions, traces of insular traditions collected by Classical and Hellenistic historians and ethnographers, and (indirectly) a rich body of music iconography. I have even been able to show, I believe, that Kinyras persisted as a figure of folklore down into the sixteenth century.[1] Any Cypriot today will tell you at least that Kinyras was an ancient king of Paphos and familiar of Aphrodite. To be sure, this owes more than a little to the renewed prominence he enjoyed in the early twentieth century, when Cypriot intellectuals promoted the island's ancient cultural heroes as worthy counterparts to great figures of the Greek past, and ideas of 'Eteocypriot' identity were encouraged by the British.[2] In this environment Loïzos Philippou (1895-1950), a polymathic lawyer and journalist from Paphos—with which region Kinyras is most prominently connected in ancient sources—founded in the 1930s a Kinyras Club which "contributed to the development of sports in Paphos and to its cultural movement and activity."[3] Today Nea Paphos boasts a Kinyras football

---

[1] See Appendix G.
[2] See 349n65.
[3] I am grateful to Elina Christophorou (whom I quote: communication, September 2015) for providing me with information about Philippou, including his articles on Kinyras and the Kinyradai in the inaugural 1935 volume of his journal ΠΑΦΟΣ ("ΤΑ ΜΥΣΤΗΡΙΑ ΤΩΝ ΚΙΝΥΡΑΔΩΝ", p6-9) and his 1938 *Lecture on Cypriot Poetry*, which emphasized Kinyras' musical dimension (ΔΙΑΛΕΞΕΙΣ ΠΕΡΙ ΤΗΣ ΚΥΠΡΙΑΚΗΣ ΠΟΙΗΣΕΩΣ, ΔΙΑΛΕΞΕΙΣ ΤΟΥ ΣΥΛΛΟΓΟΥ "ΚΙΝΥΡΑ", ΠΑΦΟΣ-ΚΥΠΡΟΥ, 1938, p15-16). Christophorou is gathering further material relating to this phase of Kinyras' reception.

Preface

club, lifeguards association, hotel and restaurant, butcher shop, and a venerable Masonic lodge that on its founding in 1923 looked to Aphrodite's ancient mysteries. In Nicosia there is a Kinyras street, with its Debenhams Kinyras department-store. In the Limassol district a Kinyras Cultural Organization promotes Cypriot music, wine, and perfume. Most appropriate of all, perhaps, is the underwater telecommunications cable named for the mythical king. So modern Cypriot pride has certainly promoted Kinyras. But he did not need to be invented or discovered. Kinyras was always there.

I hope that this book, despite its Cyprocentric focus and special attention to musical matters, will be of more general interest as a detailed case-study of cultural interactions in the eastern Mediterranean. One of the fastest developing frontiers of classical scholarship is the interface between the Greek world and its eastern neighbors. While the standard go-to studies by Walter Burkert and Martin West drew many more and less convincing parallels, they offered fairly tenuous explanations of the mechanisms of 'transfer'.[4] More recent scholarship has called for greater specificity as to chronology, geography, and cultural contexts. Musical evidence is especially promising here, both because much early verbal art was musical; and because the material is relatively abundant, including detailed iconography, literary traditions relating to earlier times, and many documentary sources from the Near East itself.

The basic premise of Ethnomusicology is that musical cultures cannot be studied in isolation from broader anthropological concerns. While I have not engaged very directly with that discipline's literature, my investigation has found many intersections with more general scholarly interests now current in Classics: ethnicity and identity; migration and colonization; cultural interface; early Greek poetics, epic memory, and mythmaking (especially as these transpired on Cyprus); performance criticism; royal ideology and the ritual poetics underpinning traditional authority. And naturally the analysis and collation of classical and ANE material has raised a host of specific philological, linguistic, and iconographical issues—problems not especially characteristic of Ethnomusicology but typical in the emerging field of Music Archaeology and ancient studies more broadly. In hopes of making this work as relevant as possible to those not disposed to work through the complete argument, I have provided a detailed index of topics, and a complete index of sources.

I should confess at once my limited knowledge of the many ANE languages whose texts I have nevertheless had to confront. The study of Kinyras and Kinnaru is necessarily comparative: while divinized instruments are creatures

---

[4] Burkert 1992; EFH.

of the ANE, much of the evidence for Kinyras himself comes from Greek and Roman sources, the connections between which are often far from obvious. Therefore even the most qualified Assyriologist or Ugaritologist would have faced similar challenges—had one pursued the questions that interested me. Fortunately bilingual publication of sources is a fairly general practice in ANE studies, so that training in classical philology often lets one weigh the merits of various interpretive arguments. The shifting historical and cultural systems from which ANE texts emerge are also daunting. But so many useful collections aimed at non-specialists are now available that Classicists can no longer afford to ignore the ANE where relevant. Such disciplinary trespassing added many years to the investigation, and presented countless pitfalls into which I have doubtless stumbled more than once. I can at least claim to appreciate the depth and complexity of the material with which my colleagues in several fields work, and admire the virtuosity with which they do so. I hope they will forgive the wilder surmises of this (increasingly) stout Cortez, overlooking sins of superficiality in favor of what benefits comparative analysis may have brought.

This *méga kakón* has been many years in the making, and I have many debts to record with gratitude. I was introduced to Kinyras in 1997 by J. G. Frazer, and a short but useful notice in West's *East Face of Helicon*.[5] At the time I was a doctoral candidate in Classics at University College London, attempting to connect the early Greek and Mesopotamian tuning traditions.[6] Taking to heart Richard Janko's caution that "Cyprus is not Greece," I used a post-doctoral year as Broneer Fellow at the American School of Classical Studies at Athens (2002–2003) to begin exploring early Cypriot musical imagery and the Aegean settlement of the island. That same year a CAORC Multi-Country Fellowship took me to Cyprus itself, where I first enjoyed the hospitality and resources of the Cyprus American Archaeological Research Institute, under the welcoming directorship of Robert Merrillees. There I stumbled on Kinnaru of Ugarit and began to contemplate the central problem of this study. I also met the great Vassos Karageorghis, then director of the Leventis Foundation, who alerted me to J.-B. Cayla's recent recognition of a *kenyristḗs* Apollo at Roman Paphos.[7] Best of all, I found Glynnis Fawkes, who has provided much inspiration over the years—and the wonderful artwork for this book. A month at the Sackler Library in Oxford during the summer of 2004 led to some preliminary ideas about 'Lyre Gods', including a few pages on Kinnaru, Kinyras, the Kinyradai, and possible

---

[5] See p3–4 and 421–424 below.
[6] See General Index s.v. tuning.
[7] See p205.

Preface

connections with lamentation-singing.⁸ Then during a 2005–2006 fellowship at the Center for Hellenic Studies, where I was meant to revise and expand my dissertation, I budgeted a month to complete my collection of the Kinyras and Kinnaru material, thinking that divinized instruments were an important piece of the puzzle and deserved a chapter's discussion. But the sources proved so numerous, and the problems so fascinating and complex, that I have been chasing the Cypriot Lyre God ever since.

From 2006 I became much occupied with *studiis et rebus honestis* at the University of Vermont, and with starting a family in the American Arcadia. A standard-issue Junior Research Leave (Fall 2008) fleshed out my summer months, letting me collect evidence for an early Cypriot epic tradition and its relationship to the lost *Kypria*.⁹ Though books are never finished, just abandoned, I am very grateful to my enlightened colleagues for letting me hold on to this one when my tenure case came up in 2010; and to my external reviewers for the same long view.

A Research Leave from UVM in 2011–2012 allowed me to take up a fortunate series of fellowships that brought the study to its final stages. As Elizabeth and J. Richardson Dilworth Fellow at the Institute for Advanced Study, I profited especially from discussions with †Joan Westenholz on Mesopotamian lexical texts, as well as Angelos Chaniotis, Glen Bowersock, Heinrich von Staden, Stephen Tracy, Annemarie Carr, Ioannis Mylonopoulos, Emmanuel Bermon, and Gil Renberg. It was at this same time that Anne Kilmer put me in touch with Wolfgang Heimpel, who had undertaken a first survey of Mesopotamian balang-gods in 1998; my request to reprint his list led eventually to the magnificent study with which this book concludes. I am honored that he threw his lot in with mine.

In January, *en route* to the Annual Professorship at the Albright Institute of Archaeological Research, a four-day stop on Cyprus and the kind devices of Ruth Keshishian (Moufflon Books, Nicosia) brought a small flurry of media interest—a spot on national radio, a front-page newspaper story, a lecture at Garo Keheyan's Pharos Arts Foundation—where I had the honor of finally meeting Jacqueline Karageorghis—and an interview by Stavros Papageorghiou for his monumental documentary *The Great Goddess of Cyprus* (Nicosia, 2015).

In springtime Jerusalem I deepened my treatment of ANE material in the magnificent dungeons of the École biblique et archéologique française; and profited from conversations with Sy Gitin, Ann Killebrew, Louise Hitchcock, Jolanta Mlynarczyk, Andrea Rotstein, Miryam Brand, Nick Blackwell, Bill Zimmerle, Emmanuel Moutafov, Eliot Braun, Brendan Dempsey, and Brittany Rudacille.

---

⁸ Franklin 2006a, 2006b.
⁹ Franklin 2014.

Preface

We returned via Cyprus where a month-long CAORC-CAARI Fellowship was highly productive and perfectly timed, bringing me into friendly and productive contact with Jennifer Webb, Bernard Knapp, Joan Connelly, Pam Gaber, Stella Lubsen, Andrew McCarthy, Michael Toumazou, Marvin Kushnet, and especially Robert Walker. In several visits to the Cyprus Museum Glynnis and I discovered the lost 'daughter of Kinyras', discussed in Chapter 11, who makes a crucial contribution to Cypriot lyric history. The Department of Antiquities also granted me permission to examine the Kouklia inscription in which *kenyristés* Apollo appears.[10] This excursion to Paphos was part of a longer, eye-opening adventure up the west coast with Stavros Papageorghiou and Stalo Hadjipieri; these same good friends organized a further excursion to Salamis, the Karpass peninsula, and glimpses of the Syrian horizon. Stavros has remained an invaluable consultant on Cypriot folklore and local geography.[11]

Despite Andrew Ford's friendly exhortation in 2012 to prove myself 'a closer', a further three years—including a normal year's sabbatical at UVM—were needed to bring this book to completion. Hilary O'Shea of the Oxford University Press kindly released me from a contract when the book grew to unmanageable proportions; it was rescued by Greg Nagy, Lenny Muellner, Casey Dué, and Mary Ebbott, who gave it a welcome home in this series. The onerous copyediting, typesetting, and indexing were a positively enjoyable experience thanks to the diligence and expertise of Jill Curry Robbins, Kristin Murphy Romano, Valerie Quercia, Joni Godlove, and Joanna Oh, all of whom improved the book in various ways.

My ideas have been substantially shaped by criticism and feedback from many conference papers and other presentations; I am grateful to all who invited me to speak, most notably at Yale, NYU, The Institute for Advanced Study (Princeton), Leiden, Jerusalem (Albright), Tel Aviv, Washington University, and the International Study Group for Music Archaeology in Germany. I had helpful advice over the years on various ANE languages and philological issues from Mary Bachvarova, Miryam Brand, Vanna Biga, †Jeremy Black, Yoram Cohen, Uri Gabbay, Wolfgang Heimpel, Anne Kilmer, Sam Mirelman, Lisa Nielson, Martin Schwartz, Dahlia Shehata, Stefan Weninger, †Joan Westenholz, Gernot Wilhlem, and Bill Zimmerle. Other valuable suggestions and contributions (some acknowledged in the notes) came from Janet Ambers, Albio Cassio, Armand D'Angour, Ricardo Eichmann, Andrew Ford, Stefan Hagel, Andrew Hicks, Alex Hollman, Thomas Kiely, Timothy Law, Emiliano Li Castro, Barbara Kowalzig, Olga Levaniouk, Pauline LeVen, Sheila Murnaghan, Tim Power, Stelios Psaroudakes,

---

[10] See p205n105.
[11] See p501–502.

Preface

Cemal Pulak, Ian Rutherford, Alexandra von Lieven, †Calvert Watkins, Marek Wecowski, and †Martin West. None of these friends and colleagues is responsible for any unintentional or willful misuse I have made of their expertise and generosity.[12]

For long-term professional support I am deeply indebted to Richard Janko; Anne Kilmer; †Martin West (who quietly saved me from Jude-like obscurity); Greg Nagy, Gloria Ferrari, and other trustees of the Center for Hellenic Studies; Peter Wilson; Eric Csapo, Margalit Finkelberg, Jim Porter, Richard Crocker, and Stefan Hagel (the Lucius Vorenus to my Titus Pullo—or so I like to think); Mark Griffith; Timothy Moore; Ellen Hickmann and Ricardo Eichmann of the ISGMA; Andrew Barker and my colleagues in MOISA (the International Society for Study of Ancient Greek and Roman Music and its Cultural Heritage); and my old pal Armand D'Angour.

Finally I must thank my wonderful colleagues at the University of Vermont for providing us with a great home—Phil Ambrose, Barbara Saylor Rodgers, Robert Rodgers, Bill Mierse, Jacques Bailly, Mark Usher, Brian Walsh, Angeline Chiu, and Jessica Evans.

This book is lovingly dedicated to Glynnis, Sylvan, and Helen, who never quite gave up on it, and shared in many sacrifices and joys along the way.

---

[12] The interesting papers of Manolis Mikrakis came to my notice too late for inclusion, but should be pursued by anyone interested in Cypriot musical history. So too the dissertation on Kinyras by Tsablē (2009), though I am gratified to see that she took on some of my main interpretive points.

CONVENTIONS AND ABBREVIATIONS

To keep the main text as accessible as possible, I have presented all Greek in transliteration (retaining accentuation as several key points depend on this); more specialized philological issues are dealt with in the footnotes, where I have not always translated Greek and Latin.

Following Assyriological convention, Akkadian words are given in italics, Sumerian in expanded spacing, logograms in capital letters, and determinatives in superscript. I have usually not Romanized ancient Greek names; arbitrary exceptions include most place-names.

References to ANE and Greco-Roman sources follow the abbreviations below or are spelled out in full, to be as intelligible as possible for an intended triple audience in Classics, Near Eastern Studies, and (Ethno)Musicology. Specific editions of Greco-Roman authors are given only when the text is questionable, or its numeration seemed to need clarification; commentators are sometimes cited by last name only.

I have not achieved absolute consistency in the use of Roman vs. Arabic numerals, commas and full-stops, etc., though any given source should be treated consistently throughout (except for minor discrepancies with Professor Heimpel's usage in "Balang-Gods"). The treatment of inscription-collections may cause confusion: ICS 94 refers to text 94 in the collection, but ICS:399 to page 399.

All dates are BCE unless otherwise noted. These are mostly conventional, with academic disagreements not affecting the argument unless otherwise noted. For the sake of consistency I have followed Kuhrt 1995 for the ANE (but KH for the Hittites); and the OCD for the Greco-Roman world.

Abbreviations

AEMI	Manniche, L. 1975. *Ancient Egyptian Musical Instruments*. Münchner ägyptologische Studien Heft 34. Munich.
AGM	West, M. L. 1992. *Ancient Greek Music*. Oxford.
AHw	von Soden, W. 1985. *Akkadisches Handwörterbuch*. 2nd ed. 2 vols. Wiesbaden.
AJC	Meshorer, Y. 1982. *Ancient Jewish Coinage*. 2 vols. Dix Hills.
AMEL	Norborg, Å. 1995. *Ancient Middle Eastern Lyres*. Musikmuseets Skrifter 25. Stockholm.
ANET	Pritchard, D. 1969. *Ancient Near Eastern Texts Relating to the Old Testament*. 3rd ed. Princeton.
AOM	Wellesz, E., 1957. *Ancient and Oriental Music*. London.
AP	Hellbing, L. 1979. *Alasia Problems*. Göteborg.
ARAB	Luckenbill, D. D. 1926–1927. *Ancient Records of Assyria and Babylonia*. 2 vols. Chicago.
ARET	Archivi reali di Ebla. Testi. Rome, 1985–.
ARM	Archives royales de Mari. Paris, 1950–.
ARTU	de Moor, J. C. 1987. *An Anthology of Religious Texts from Ugarit*. Leiden.
Aspects	Karageorghis, V. 2006. *Aspects of Everyday Life in Ancient Cyprus: Iconographic Representations*. Nicosia.
AT	Wiseman, D. J. 1953. *The Alalakh Tablets*. London.
BÉ	*Bulletin Épigraphique*, published in *Revue des Études Grecques*.
BIN	Babylonian Inscriptions in the Collection of James B. Nies. New Haven, 1917–.
BM	Museum siglum of the British Museum, London.
BMC	A Catalogue of Greek Coins in the British Museum. 29 vols. London, 1873–1927.
BPOA	Biblioteca del Proximo Oriente Antiguo. Madrid, 2006–.
BT	Epstein, I., ed. 1978. *The Babylonian Talmud*. 18 vols. London.

Conventions and Abbreviations

Bustron	Mas Latrie, R. de 1886. *Florio Bustron: Historia overo commentarii de Cipro.* Collection de documents inédits sur l'histoire de France. Mélanges historiques 5. Paris. Reprinted, with an introduction by G. Grivaud, in 1998 (Th. Papadopoullos, Leukosia; Kypriologikē Bibliothēkē 8).
CA	Powell, J. U. 1925. *Collectanea Alexandrina.* Oxford.
CAAC	Karageorghis, V. 1991–1999. *The Coroplastic Art of Ancient Cyprus.* 6 vols. Nicosia.
CAD	The Assyrian Dictionary of the Oriental Institute of the University of Chicago. Chicago, 1956–.
CAH	*The Cambridge Ancient History,* editions as noted.
CANE	Sasson, J. M., ed. 1995. *Civilizations of the Ancient Near East.* 4 vols. New York.
CAT	Dietrich, M. et al. 1995. *The Cuneiform Alphabetic Texts from Ugarit, Ras Ibn Hani and Other Places (KTU).* 2nd enl. ed. Abhandlungen zur Literatur Alt-Syrien-Palastinas und Mesopotamiens 8. Münster.
CCSF	Karageorghis, V. and J. des Gagniers. 1974. *La Céramique chypriote de style figuré. Supplément,* 1979. 2 vols. Rome.
CDA	Black, J. et al. 1999. *A Concise Dictionary of Akkadian.* SANTAG: Arbeiten und Untersuchungen zur Keilschriftkunde 5. Harrassowitz.
CEWAL	Woodard, R. G., ed. 2004. *The Cambridge Encyclopedia of the World's Ancient Languages.* Cambridge.
Chorograffia	Étienne de Lusignan, *Chorograffia et breve historia universale* (1573); references both by original pagination and section number (§) in *SHC* 10.
CIL	Corpus inscriptionum Latinarum. Berlin, 1863–.
CIS	Corpus inscriptionum Semiticarum. 5 vols. Paris, 1881–1962.
CLAM	Cohen, M. E. 1988. *The Canonical Lamentations of Ancient Mesopotamia.* 2 vols. Potomac.
CPG	von Leutsch, E. L. and F. W. Schneidewin, eds. 1965–1991. *Corpus paroemiographorum Graecorum.* 2 vols. Hildesheim.

Conventions and Abbreviations

CS	Hallo, W. W. and K. L. Younger, eds. 1997–2002. *The Context of Scripture.* 3 vols. Leiden.
CT	Cuneiform Texts from Babylonian Tablets in the British Museum. London, 1896–.
CTA	Herdner, A. 1963. *Corpus des tablettes en cunéiformes alphabétiques découvertes à Ras Shamra-Ugarit de 1929 à 1939.* Mission de Ras Shamra 10/Bibliotheque Archeologique et Historique 79. Paris.
CTH	Laroche, E. 1971. *Catalogue des textes hittites.* Paris.
CUSAS	Cornell University Studies in Assyriology and Sumerology. Bethesda, 2007–.
DCPIL	Lawergren, B. 1998. "Distinctions among Canaanite, Philistine, and Israelite Lyres, and their Global Lyrical Contexts." *Bulletin of the American Schools of Oriental Research* 309:41–68.
DDD	van der Toorn, K. et al., eds. 1999. *Dictionary of Deities and Demons in the Bible.* 2nd ed. Leiden.
DDUPP	Lipinski, E. 1995. *Dieux et déesses de l'univers phénicien et punique.* Leuven.
Description	Étienne de Lusignan: *Description de tout l'isle de Cypre* (1580); references by page number in Papadopoullos 2004, vol. 2.
DGAC	Egetmeyer, M. 2010. *Le Dialecte grec ancien de Chypre. Tome I: Grammaire; Tome II: Répertoire des inscriptions en syllabaire chypro-grec.* Berlin.
DJD	Discoveries in the Judaean Desert. Oxford, 1955–.
DM	Aura Jorro, F. 1985. *Diccionario micénico.* 2 vols. Madrid.
DMG	Ventris, M. and J. Chadwick. 1973. *Documents in Mycenaean Greek.* 2nd ed. Cambridge.
DP	Allotte de la Fuÿe, M. F. 1908–1920. *Documents présargoniques.* 5 vols. Paris.
DUL	del Olmo Lete, G. and J. Sanmartín. 2003. *A Dictionary of the Ugaritic Language in the Alphabetic Tradition.* Leiden.
EA	El-Amarna tablet. See Knudtzon 1907–1915; Rainey 1978; Moran 1992.

Conventions and Abbreviations

EFH	West, M. L. 1997. *The East Face of Helicon*. Oxford.
EGF	Davies, M. 1988. *Epicorum Graecorum fragmenta*. Göttingen.
Emprunts	Masson, E. 1967. *Recherches sur les plus anciens emprunts sémitiques en grec*. Études et Commentaries 67. Paris.
EQ	McAuliffe, J. D., ed. 2001–2006. *Encyclopaedia of the Qurʾān*. 6 vols. Leiden.
ETCSL	J. Black et al., eds. *Electronic Text Corpus of Sumerian Literature* (etcsl.orinst.ox.ac.uk).
ExcCyp	Hogarth, D. G. et al. 1888. "Excavations in Cyprus, 1887-88. Paphos, Leontari, Amargetti." *Journal of Hellenic Studies* 9:147–271.
FGE	Page, D. L. 1981. *Further Greek Epigrams*. Cambridge.
FGH	Jacoby, F. 1923–1958. *Fragmente der griechischen Historiker*. 3 vols. Berlin.
FHG	Müller, C. 1841–1870. *Fragmenta historicorum Graecorum*. 5 vols. Paris.
FM 3	Durand, J.-M. and M. Guichard. 1997. "Les Rituels de Mari." In *Recueil d'études à la memoire de Marie-Thérèse Barrelet* (eds. D. Charpin and J.-M. Durand). 19–78. Mémoires de NABU 4/Florilegium Marianum 3. Paris.
FM 4	Ziegler, N. 1999. *Le Harem de Zimrî-Lîm: La Population féminine des palais d'après les archives royales de Mari*. Mémoires de NABU 5/Florilegium Marianum 4. Paris.
FM 9	Ziegler, N. 2007. *Les Musiciens et la musique d'après les archives royals de Mari*. Mémoires de NABU 10/Florilegium Marianum 9. Paris.
GGM	Müller, C. F. W. 1855–1861. *Geographi Graeci minores*. 2 vols. Paris.
GIBM	Newton, C. T. et al., eds. 1874–1916. *The Collection of Greek Inscriptions in the British Museum*. 5 vols. London.
GMO	*Grove Music Online*, containing updates and emendations to *NG*.
GMW	Barker, A. 1984–1989. *Greek Musical Writings*. 2 vols. Cambridge.

Conventions and Abbreviations

GR	Burkert, W. 1985. *Greek Religion*. Cambridge, Massachusetts.
HBMH	Wellesz, E. 1961. *A History of Byzantine Music and Hymnography*. 2nd ed. Oxford.
HC	Hill, G. F. 1949. *A History of Cyprus, Volume I. To the Conquest by Richard Lion Heart*. Cambridge.
HIOP	Mitford, T. B. 1961. "The Hellenistic Inscriptions of Old Paphos." *Annual of the British School at Athens* 56:1–41.
HKm	Schuol, M. 2004. *Hethitische Kultmusik. Eine Untersuchung der Instrumental- und Vokalmusik anhand hethitischer Ritualtexte und von archäologischen Zeugnissen*. Orient-Archäologie 14. Rahden.
HLC	Barton, G. A. 1905–1914. *Haverford Library Collection of Cuneiform Tablets or Documents from the Temple Archives of Telloh*. 3 vols. Philadelphia.
HMI	Sachs, C. 1940. *The History of Musical Instruments*. New York.
HUS	Watson, W. G. E. and N. Wyatt, eds. 1999. *Handbook of Ugaritic Studies*. Leiden.
I.Kourion	Mitford, T. B. 1971. *The Inscriptions of Kourion*. Philadelphia.
I.Paphos	Cayla, J.-B. 2003. *Les Inscriptions de Paphos: Corpus des inscriptions alphabétiques de Palaipaphos, de Néa Paphos et de la chôra paphienne*. PhD dissertation, Université Paris-Sorbonne.
I.Rantidi	Mitford, T. B. and O. Masson. 1983. *The Syllabic Inscriptions of Rantidi-Paphos*. Konstanz.
I.Thess.I	Decourt, J.-C. 1995. *Inscriptions de Thessalie I. Les Cités de la vallée de l'Énipeus*. Athens.
ICGSL	Moscati, S. et al. 1964. *An Introduction to the Comparative Grammar of the Semitic Languages: Phonology and Morphology*. Wiesbaden.
ICS	Masson, O. 1983. *Les Inscriptions chypriotes syllabiques: Recueil critique et commenté*. 2nd ed. Paris.
IEG	West, M. L. 1989–1992. *Iambi et elegi Graeci ante Alexandrum cantati*. 2nd ed. 2 vols. Oxford.
IG	*Inscriptiones Graecae*. 12 vols. 1873–1939.
IGRom.	*Inscriptiones Graecae ad res Romanas pertinentes*. 3 vols. 1906–1927.

Conventions and Abbreviations

ISMP	Nakassis, D. 2013. *Individuals and Society in Mycenaean Pylos.* Leiden.
ITT	Inventaire des tablettes de Tello conservée au musée impérial Ottoman. Paris, 1910–.
IK	Inschriften griechischer Städte aus Kleinasien. 1972–.
KAI	Röllig, W. and H. Donner. 1966–1969. *Kanaanäische und aramäische Inschriften.* 2nd ed. 3 vols. Berlin.
KAV	Schroeder, O. 1920. *Keilschrifttexte aus Assur verschiedenen Inhalts.* Wissenschaftliche Veröffentlichungen der Deutschen Orient-Gesellschaft 35. Leipzig.
KBo	Keilschrifttexte aus Boghazköi. Leipzig, 1916–.
KH	Bryce, T. 2005. *The Kingdom of the Hittites.* 2nd ed. Oxford.
KN	Linear B tablet from Knossos.
KTU	Dietrich, M. et al. 1976. *Die Keilalphabetischen Texte aus Ugarit, einschliesslich der keilalphabetischen Texte ausserhalb Ugarits.* Alter Orient und Altes Testament 24. Kevelaer.
KUB	Keilschrifturkunden aus Boghazköi. Berlin, 1921–.
KwH	Smith, M. S. 1985. *Kothar-wa-Hasis. The Ugaritic Kraftsman God.* PhD dissertation, Yale University.
Kypris	Karageorghis, J. 2005. *Kypris: The Aphrodite of Cyprus. Ancient Sources and Archaeological Evidence.* Nicosia.
LBW	Lebas, P. and W. H. Waddington. 1870. *Voyage archéologique en Grèce et en Asie Mineure, Vol. III.* Paris.
LIMC	Ackermann, H. C. and J.-R. Gisler, eds. 1981–2009. *Lexicon iconographicum mythologiae classicae.* 8 vols. Zürich.
LJ	Ginzberg, L. 1909–1937. *The Legends of the Jews.* 7 vols. Philadelphia.
LS	Lewis, C. T. and C. Short. 1945. *A Latin Dictionary.* Oxford.
LSJ	Liddell, H. G. et al. 1940. *A Greek-English Lexicon.* 9th ed. Oxford.
LXX	Septuagint.
MAIP	Braun, J. 2002. *Music in Ancient Israel/Palestine: Archaeological, Written, and Comparative Sources.* Grand Rapids.

MgB	Besseler, H. and M. Schneider, eds. 1961–1989. *Musikgeschichte in Bildern*. 4 vols. Leipzig.
MGG	Finscher, L., ed. 1949–1979. *Die Musik in Geschichte und Gegenwart. Allgemeine Enzyklopädie der Musik*. 2nd ed. 17 vols. Kassel.
MgP	Landau, O. 1958. *Mykenisch-griechische Personennamen*. Göteborg.
MMA	Museum siglum of the Metropolitan Museum of Art, New York.
MMAE	Manniche, L. 1991. *Music and Musicians in Ancient Egypt*. London.
MS	Tablet from the Marten Schoyen Collection.
MSG	Jan, K. von 1895. *Musici scriptores Graeci: Aristoteles, Euclides, Nicomachus, Bacchius, Gaudentius, Alypius*. Leipzig.
MSL	Landsberger, B., ed. 1937–2004. *Materialien zum sumerischen Lexikon*. 17 vols. Rome.
MT	Masoretic Text.
MVN	Materiali per il vocabolario neosumerico. Rome, 1974–.
MY	Linear B tablet from Mycenae.
NG	Sadie, S., ed. 2001. *The New Grove Dictionary of Music and Musicians*. 2nd ed. 29 vols. London.
Ni	Tablet from Nippur in the Archaeological Museum, Istanbul.
Nik 1	Nikol'skij, M. V. 1908. *Dokumenty khozjajstvennoj otcetnosti drevnejsej epokci Khaldei iz sobranija N. P. Likhaceva*. Drevnosti Vostocnyja 3/2. St. Petersburg.
NP	Cancik, H. and H. Schneider, eds. 2002–2006. *Brill's New Pauly: Encyclopaedia of the Ancient World: Antiquity*. 15 vols. Leiden.
NPHP	Mlynarczyk, J. 1990. *Nea Paphos in the Hellenistic Period*. Nea Paphos 3. Warsaw.
NRSV	New Revised Standard Version.
OCD	Hornblower, S. and A. Spawforth, eds. 1999. *The Oxford Classical Dictionary*. 3rd ed. Oxford.
OLD	Glare, P. G. W. 1982. *Oxford Latin Dictionary*. Oxford.

Conventions and Abbreviations

OSG	Lightfoot, J. L. 2003. *Lucian, On the Syrian Goddess.* Oxford.
Pap.Oxy.	Grenfell, B. P. and A. S. Hunt, eds. 1898–. *Oxyrhynchus Papyri.*
Paphos	Maier, F. G. and V. Karageorghis. 1984. *Paphos: History and Archaeology.* Nicosia.
PBSB	Markoe, G. 1985. *Phoenician Bronze and Silver Bowls from Cyprus and the Mediterranean.* Berkeley.
PCG	Kassel, R. and C. Austin. 1983. *Poetae comici Graeci.* 8 vols. Berlin.
PDT 1	Çig, M. et al. 1954. *Die Puzris-Dagan-Texte der Istanbuler Archaologischen Museen Teil 1 (1–725).* Annales Academiae Scientiarum Fennicae, Reihe B 92. Helsinki.
PEG	Bernabé, A. 1996–2007. *Poetarum epicorum Graecorum: Testimonia et fragmenta.* 2 vols. Bibliotheca scriptorum Graecorum et Romanorum Teubneriana. Leipzig.
PG	Migne, J.-P., ed. 1857–1887. *Patrologiae cursus, series Graeca.* 161 vols. Paris.
PGL	Lampe, G. W. H. 1961. *A Patristic Greek Lexicon.* Oxford.
PHG	Gabbay, U. 2014. *Pacifying the Hearts of the Gods: Sumerian Emesal Prayers of the First Millennium BC.* Heidelberger Emesal Studien 1. Wiesbaden.
PIW	Mowinckel, S. 1962. *The Psalms in Israel's Worship.* 2 vols. Oxford.
PLG	Bergk, T. 1878–1882. *Poetae lyrici Graeci.* 4th ed. 4 vols. Leipzig.
PMG	Page, D. L. 1962. *Poetae melici Graeci.* Oxford.
PMGF	Davies, M. 1991. *Poetarum melicorum Graecorum fragmenta.* Vol. 1 Alcman Stesichorus Ibycus. Oxford.
PP	Lindgren, M. 1973. *The People of Pylos: Prosopographical and Methodological Studies in the Pylos Archives.* Boreas 3. Uppsala.
PPC	Knapp, A. B. 2008. *Prehistoric and Protohistoric Cyprus: Identity, Insularity, and Connectivity.* Oxford.
Princeton 1	Sigrist, M. 1990. *Tablettes du Princeton Theological Seminary: Epoque d'Ur III.* Occasional Publications of the Samuel Noah Kramer Fund 10. Philadelphia.

Conventions and Abbreviations

PRU 5	Virolleaud, C. 1965. *Le Palais royal d'Ugarit. V: Textes en cunéiformes alphabétiques des archives sud, sud-ouest et du petit palais.* Mission de Ras Shamra 11. Paris.
PTT	Bennett, E. L. and J.-P. Olivier. 1973–1976. *The Pylos Tablets Transcribed.* 2 vols. Rome.
PY	Linear B tablet from Pylos.
RCU	Pardee, D. 2002. *Ritual and Cult at Ugarit.* Writings from the Ancient World 10. Atlanta.
RE	Pauly, A. et al., eds. 1894–1972. *Real-Encyclopädie der classischen Altertumswissenschaft.* 34 vols. Stuttgart.
REG	*Revue des études grecques*
RIH	Tablet from Ras Ibn Hani.
RIME	Frayne, D. and D. O. Edzard, eds. 1984–. *Royal Inscriptions of Mesopotamia. Early Periods.* Toronto.
RlA	Ebeling, E. et al., eds. 1928—. *Reallexikon der Assyriologie und vorderasiatischen Archäologie.* Berlin.
RS	Tablet from Ras Shamra/Ugarit.
RTU	Wyatt, N. 2002. *Religious Texts from Ugarit.* 2nd ed. London.
SAM	Westenholz, J. G. et al., eds. 2007. *Sounds of Ancient Music.* Jerusalem.
SAT	Sigrist, M. 1993–. Sumerian Archival Texts. Bethesda.
SBH	Reisner, G. 1896. *Sumerisch-babylonische Hymnen nach Thontafeln griechischer Zeit.* Berlin.
SCE	Gjerstad, E. et al. 1934–. *The Swedish Cyprus Expedition.* Stockholm.
SEG	Supplementum epigraphicum Graecum. Amsterdam, 1923–.
SF	Deimel, A. 1923. *Die Inschriften von Fara II: Schultexte aus Fara.* Wissenschaftliche Veröffentlichung der Deutschen Orient-Gesellschaft 43. Leipzig.
SH	Parsons, P. J. and H. Lloyd-Jones. 1983. *Supplementum Hellenisticum.* Texte und Kommentare 11. Berlin.

SHC	Wallace, P. W. and A. G. Orphanides, eds. 1990. *Sources for the History of Cyprus.* Albany. Much the same material is collected in Chatzēiōannou 1971–2001, to which *SHC* contains cross-references.
SIAG	Maas, M. and J. Snyder. 1989. *Stringed Instruments of Ancient Greece.* New Haven.
SL	Lipinski, E. 2001. *Semitic Languages: Outline of a Comparative Grammar.* 2nd ed. Leuven.
SOM	Farmer, H. G. 1986. *Studies in Oriental Music.* 2 vols. Frankfurt am Main.
SURS	Clemens, D. M. 2001. *Sources for Ugaritic Ritual and Sacrifice. I. Ugaritic and Ugarit Akkadian Texts.* Alter Orient und Altes Testament 284/1. Münster.
TCL	Textes cunéiformes. Musées du Louvre. Paris, 1910–.
TGF	Snell, B. et al. 1971–1985. *Tragicorum Graecorum fragmenta.* 4 vols. Göttingen.
TH	Linear B tablet from Thebes.
TM	Tablet from Tell Mardikh/Ebla.
TPm	Pardee, D. 1988. *Les Textes para-mythologiques de la 24e campagne (1961).* Paris.
TR	Pardee, D. 2000. *Les Textes rituels.* Paris.
TSA	de Genouillac, H. 1909. *Tablettes sumériennes archaïques. Matériaux pour servir à l'histoire de la société sumérienne.* Paris.
TUT	Reisner, G. 1901. *Tempelurkunden aus Telloh.* Mittheilungen aus den orientalischen Sammlungen 16. Berlin.
UET	Ur Excavation Texts. London, 1928–.
UTI	Gomi, T. and F. Yildiz. 1988–2001. *Die Umma-texte aus den Archäologischen Muséen zu Berlin.* 6 vols. Bethesda.
VS	Vorderasiatische Schriftdenkmäler der Königlichen/Staatlichen Museen zu Berlin. Berlin, 1907–.
W	Tablet from Warka/Uruk.
YBC	Tablet in Yale Babylonian Collection.

Conventions and Abbreviations

YGC   Albright, W. F. 1968. *Yahweh and the Gods of Canaan: A Historical Analysis of Two Contrasting Faiths*. Garden City.

Cultural, Chronological, Linguistic, and Textual:

Akk.	Akkadian
ANE	Ancient Near East(ern)
Ar.	Arabic
Aram.	Aramaic
BA	Bronze Age
Can.	Canaanite
EBA	Early Bronze Age
Ebl.	Eblaitic
EIA	Early Iron Age
ED	Early Dynastic
Gk.	Greek
Hatt.	Hattic
Heb.	Hebrew
Hitt.	Hittite
Hurr.	Hurrian
IA	Iron Age
Lat.	Latin
LBA	Late Bronze Age
LC	Late Cypriot
Lin. B	Linear B
Luw.	Luwian
MA	Middle Assyrian
MB	Middle Babylonian
MBA	Middle Bronze Age
MH	Middle Hittite

Conventions and Abbreviations

MK	Middle Kingdom (Egypt)
Myc.	Mycenaean
N-A	Neo-Assyrian
NE	Near East(ern)
NK	New Kingdom (Egypt)
NK	New Kingdom (Egypt/Hittite)
N-S	Neo-Sumerian
OA	Old Assyrian
OAkk.	Old Akkadian
OB	Old Babylonian
OK	Old Kingdom (Egypt)
Pers.	Persian
Phoen.	Phoenician
P-S	Proto-Semitic
Pun.	Punic
Sum.	Sumerian
Ug.	Ugaritic
WS	West Semitic

Other:

*	reconstructed, hypothetical, or unattested form
|	line division (inscriptions, papyri)
/	verse division
— / ⌣	long/short syllable (verse)
//	phonetic value
√	radical/root
[ ]	1) editorial comment. 2) damaged area of tablet, inscription, or papyrus. 3) false attribution to ancient author (in footnotes, = ps.- in main text)
ca.	circa

Conventions and Abbreviations

col.	column(s)
DN	divine/god name
fig.	figure(s)
fl.	*floruit*/flourished
fr. or F	fragment(s)
κτλ	etc. (in Greek texts)
MS(S)	manuscript(s)
n	note(s)
no.	number(s)
obv.	obverse (of tablet)
p(p).	page(s)
PN	personal name
ps.-	pseudo-
rev.	reverse (of tablet)
Σ	scholion/scholia (to)
s.n.	no name
T	testimonium/a
TN	toponym/place-name
v.l.	variant reading

INTRODUCTION

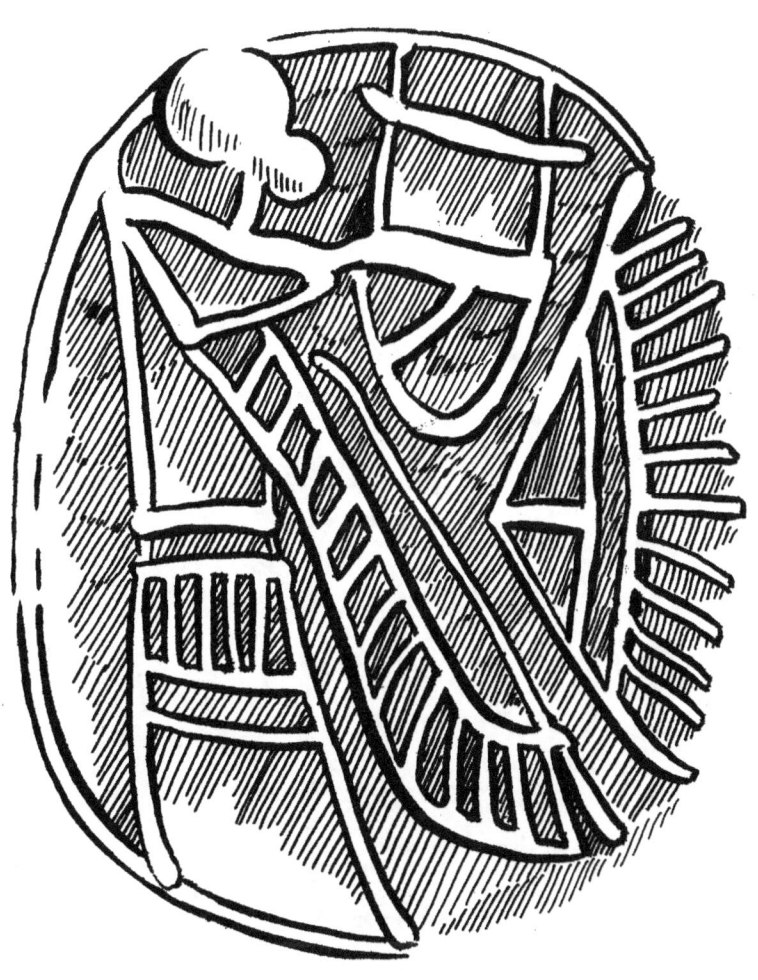

1
Kinyras and Kinnaru
Kinyras of Cyprus

ALREADY FOR HOMER, Kinyras loomed on the eastern horizon, a Great King who treated on equal terms with Agamemnon, sending him a marvelous daedalic breastplate as a friendship-gift:

> Next in turn he donned the corselet round his chest
> Which once Kinyras gave him as a friendship-gift.
> For he had heard a great report on Cyprus—the Achaeans
> Were to sail in ships to Troy—wherefore
> He gave the corselet to him, cultivating favor with the king.[1]

One version of the lost epic *Kypria* told of a broken promise by Kinyras to contribute ships against Troy, and probably how he hosted Paris and Helen on a honeymoon escapade as they evaded pursuit.[2] Alkman describes Cypriot perfume as "the moist charm of Kinyras."[3] Pindar calls him "cherished priest of Aphrodite" whom "golden-haired Apollo gladly loved"; and refers to the "blessed fortune ... which once upon a time freighted Kinyras with riches in

---

[1] Homer *Iliad* 11.19-23: δεύτερον αὖ θώρηκα περὶ στήθεσσιν ἔδυνε / τόν ποτέ οἱ Κινύρης δῶκε ξεινήϊον εἶναι. / πεύθετο γὰρ Κύπρονδε μέγα κλέος οὕνεκ' Ἀχαιοὶ / ἐς Τροίην νήεσσιν ἀναπλεύσεσθαι ἔμελλον· / τοὔνεκά οἱ τὸν δῶκε χαριζόμενος βασιλῆϊ. For this passage, see further p322-323. Other sources relating to this breastplate are Alkidamas *Odysseus* 20-21; Strabo 1.2.32; Themistios *Orations* 4.54a, 16.201c; Eustathios on *Iliad* 11.20, 18.613; Theodoros Hyrtakenos *Anecdota Graeca*, Boissonade 1829-1833 1:263.

[2] [Apollodoros] *Epitome* 3.9, cf. 3.4-5 for Paris and Helen on Cyprus (cf. Proklos *Chrestomathy* 80 = EGF:31.25-27, PEG:39.18-20). This episode was first attributed to the *Kypria* by Wagner 1891:181-182; this was followed by West 2003:72-73, but later rejected as being incompatible with other evidence for 'the poem' and "reflect[ing] no credit on Cyprus" (West 2013:103). But there existed at least two written versions of the *Kypria*, and of course the underlying tradition was multiform (see Franklin 2014:232-240). Moreover, Kinyras as the 'Liar King' can be understood in light of intercity rivalry on Cyprus itself: see p345.

[3] Alkman 3.71 PMGF. See p330.

Chapter One

Cyprus on the sea."[4] Sources from the Hellenistic period onwards, when Cypriot lore entered Greek letters more directly, tell us that Kinyras was first-discoverer of copper and metallurgical operations on the island, and master of other typical industries. Local fourth-century inscriptions show that the Paphian kings traced their descent from Kinyras, and it was said that he built, and was buried in, Aphrodite's great and ancient sanctuary there.[5] His wealth was a byword, rivaling Sardanapalos and Kroisos, and thrice surpassing Midas.[6] And, like these other eastern kings, he underwent a humbling reversal of fortune. One legend held that Kinyras was driven from power by "the Greeks with Agamemnon": this must reflect the Aegean migrations of the twelfth and eleventh centuries, which transformed Cyprus and made it the eastern edge of the Grecophone world.[7] A second catastrophe secured imperishable fame in the western canon, thanks to Ovid: Kinyras was unwittingly seduced by his daughter Myrrha (or Smyrna); she was metamorphosed into the myrrh-tree, anointing her baby Adonis with sappy tears.[8]

These are but highlights of a long and intricate mythological life. Spare traces are widely scattered in poets, historians, philosophers, mythographers, geographers, lexicographers, and church fathers.[9] The relevant sources—never completely assembled—run from Linear B down through the Byzantine period. Some of these are Syro-Levantine traditions that made their way into Greco-Roman authors, and several Syriac texts are also related. Unique information is even found in Étienne de Lusignan, a sixteenth-century Franco-Cypriot historian who has been overlooked in all previous studies of Kinyras, whom he calls "the god Cinara(s)"; some of what Lusignan says is due to his own rationalizing

---

[4] Pindar *Pythian* 2.15–17; *Nemean* 8.17–18. See further Chapter 10.
[5] For the Kinyradai, see Chapter 16.
[6] Tyrtaios 12.6 IEG. See further p322–323.
[7] Theopompos FGH 115 F 103 (Photios *Library* 120a20–22). See Chapter 14.
[8] Ovid *Metamorphoses* 10.298–502. See Chapter 12.
[9] The most concentrated treatments of Kinyras known to me are: van Meurs 1675: 2:105–112; Heyne 1803:323–326; Engel 1841 1:203–210, 2:94–136 (et passim); Movers 1841–1856 1:239–243; ExcCyp:175–185; Hoffman 1896:256–258; Frazer 1914 1:43–52; Drexler, Roscher *Lex.* s.v.; Kroll, RE 11 (1922):484–486; Blinkenberg 1924:31–37; HC:68–69; Dussaud 1950; Heubner 1963–1982 2:30–36; Brown 1965; Kapera 1971; Dugand 1973:198–202; Baurain 1980b; Baurain 1981a; Ribichini 1981:45–57 et passim; Ribichini 1982; Cayla 2001; *Kypris*:14–17, 22–24. The imaginative comments of Ohnefalsch-Richter 1893 (passim) must be treated with great reserve. Panagides 1946, despite its title, has only a brief (and deficient) consideration of Kinyras (139–144). One may also note here two detailed fiction portraits of Kinyras' palace and retainers, and the Achaean embassy: the opera *La Rêve de Cinyras* by Vincent d'Indy and Xavier de Courville (1927); and the short novel ΚΙΝΥΡΑΣ by Panos Ioannides, in *Kronaka II* (1970–1972).

composition, but he does seem to draw several times on the island's conservative oral traditions and/or some lost ancient authority.[10]

As the foregoing sources show—and as C. Baurain emphasized in a fundamental study—Kinyras was already established for Homer and other Archaic poets as the central culture-hero of Cyprus, mythologically linked to the industries and political configuration of the pre-Greek LBA. But two further ideas, seemingly tangential to this dominant paradigm, stand out.

First, several traditions held that Cyprus was not Kinyras' original home, which is variously located in Cilicia, Phoenicia, or Syria/Assyria.[11]

Second, a few sources make Kinyras a musician, or associate him with professional musicians.[12] Commenting on the *Iliad* passage cited above, Eustathios, twelfth-century archbishop of Thessalonica, asserted that Kinyras was named from the *kinýra*.[13] This is the 'Greek' word that in the Septuagint commonly renders Hebrew *kinnōr*, the lyre famous as the instrument of King David.[14] This etymology once seemed plausible to many. In the *Golden Bough*, Frazer astutely compared Kinyras to David:

> If we may judge by his name, the Semitic king who bore the name of Cinyras was, like King David, a harper ... We shall probably not err in assuming that at Paphos as at Jerusalem the music of the lyre or harp was not a mere pastime designed to while away an idle hour, but formed part of the service of religion, the moving influence of its

---

[10] See Appendix G for Lusignan's possible sources and a defense of his authority. I retain Lusignan's 'Cinaras' (deriving from Theodontius in Boccaccio's *Genealogy of the Pagan Gods* 2.50–53) to help differentiate his version of Kinyras from the other traditions to be studied.

[11] 'Syria' and 'Assyria', historically related terms, were rather interchangeable in Gk. usage, and could also embrace Phoenicia (e.g. Strabo 16.1.2). The large geographical range of both derives from the N-A state at its height, and the eventual tendency of its inhabitants to regard themselves as 'Assyrian' regardless of ethnic origin (Parpola 2004). 'Syria' derives from a Luwian truncation current by the eighth century in the Neo-Hittite/Aramaean sphere of North Syria and southeastern Anatolia. The basic studies of Nöldeke 1881 and Schwartz 1931 have been updated, with reference to 'Syria' in the eighth-century Çineköy inscription (Cilicia), by Rollinger 2006 (with earlier controversy).

[12] This material is fully discussed in Chapters 9 through 12.

[13] Eustathios on Homer *Iliad* 11.20. For this passage, and the history of 'Gk.' *kinýra*, see further Chapter 9.

[14] According to modern convention, 'lyre' (< Gk. λύρα) is applied to all ancient instruments having two 'arms' or 'horns' mounted in a resonator, supporting a crossbar or 'yoke' from which strings descend to some form of 'string-holder' at the resonator's base (the terms in Gk. are πήχεις/κέρατα, ζυγόν, and χορδοτόνον respectively). On a 'harp,' by contrast, the strings descend from a single arm affixed to a resonator. The modern terminology goes back to von Hornbostel and Sachs 1914:579–580; see also HMI:463–465. Note, however, that Old English *hearpe* itself denoted what would now be called a 'lyre' (for Anglo-Saxon lyres, see especially the studies of G. Lawson).

Chapter One

melodies being perhaps set down, like the effect of wine, to the direct inspiration of a deity.[15]

But in 1965 J. P. Brown—in an otherwise valuable comparative study of Kinyras and Kothar, the Syro-Levantine craftsman god who plays a vital part in this history—influentially asserted that Eustathios' derivation was anachronistic, an obvious conjecture for a Christian scholar steeped in scripture; he saw "no reason to believe that [*kinýra*] had been adapted from Semitic a millennium earlier to serve as etymology for Kinyras."[16] But this judgment begs the question of Kinyras' own Greekness. Despite Cyprus's close and uninterrupted association with the Aegean from the fourteenth century onwards,[17] the island was always a world apart—and all the more so in the pre-Greek period, to which myth assigns Kinyras.

The Return of Kinnaru

The question was transformed by a discovery from the Syrian coastal city of Ugarit, destroyed shortly after 1200 during the so-called Great Collapse that marked the end of the LBA and saw the Aegean migrations to the eastern Mediterranean (see further below). The 1929 excavations produced a tablet the significance of which was not recognized for several decades, when further finds enabled the restoration of what J. Nougayrol dubbed "le panthéon d'Ugarit."[18] Two new and well-preserved exemplars came to light from the temple district in 1956 and 1961, one in Akkadian with the mixture of syllabic and logographic signs typical of Mesopotamian scribal traditions, the other in Ugaritic and the city's own vowel-free cuneiform alphabet. These were published together in 1968, three years after Brown had discredited the traditional association of Kinyras and *kinýra*.[19]

---

[15] Frazer 1914 1:52–55 (quotation, 52). Others favoring the derivation are Ohnefalsch-Richter 1893 1:216 (opting for a Carian origin [!]: cf. p202); Boscawen 1893–1894:355; also Leaf 1900–1902 1:468; Drexler, Roscher *Lex.* s.v. Kinyras; Evans 1921–1936 2:837–838; Lorimer 1950:465n3; von Kamptz 1956:129–130, 327; Zarmas 1975:10; further references in Baurain 1980a:7n4.

[16] Brown 1965:207–208; followed by Baurain 1980a:8 (who nevertheless took the opposite stance in Baurain 1980b:304); Morris 1992:79–80n26 (apparently); Leukart 1994:215 and n218. The etymology was independently rejected by *Emprunts*:69n2; Chantraine 1968 s.v. κινύρα (Boisacq 1938 was undecided). For Kinyras and Kothar, see further Chapter 18.

[17] See e.g. Iacovou 2006b:32–35.

[18] RS 1.017 (KTU/CAT 1.47), 32: Virolleaud 1929, pl. LXX; Herdner 1963:109–110 (no. 29); TR:291–319, with earlier bibliography; RCU, text 1, col. A. For general discussion of the 'pantheon(s)' see del Olmo Lete 1999:43–86, HUS:305–332, and further below, Chapter 7.

[19] Akkadian: RS 20.024: Nougayrol 1968:42–64 (no. 18). Ugaritic: RS 24.264 + 24.280: Herdner 1978:1–3; KTU/CAT 1.118. Note that preliminary reports had already circulated for a decade: Nougayrol 1957:82–85; Weidner 1957–1958:170; YGC:140–145.

The more informative Akkadian text provided crucial detail. The determinative d(iĝir) (Sum. 'god') appeared throughout, showing that this was a register of thirty-three deities. Many were familiar, like El ('Ilu), Dagan, and Baal (Ba'lu), whose various incarnations begin the list. Some Ugaritic powers were glossed by Mesopotamian equivalents—a typical example of the divine 'translations' that were current in the LBA.[20] Kothar (*Kôṯaru*) for instance was equated with the versatile Ea (patron of music and inventor of the first lamentation-priest, among many other traditional credits).[21] Others were rendered phonetically, revealing their pronunciation more fully than the parallel Ugaritic texts. And at the end came the following:[22]

RS 1.017, 31–33	RS 20.024, 30–32	
uṯḫt	d.dugBUR.ZI.NÍG.NA	Divine Censer (*uṯḫatu*)
knr	d.giški-na-rù	Divine Lyre (*kinnāru*)[23]
mlkm	dma-lik-MEŠ	Divine Kings (*malakūma*)[24]

In the case of the *kinnāru*—an early WS or areal form, cognate with both Heb. *kinnōr* and 'Gk.' *kinýra*[25]—d(iĝir)is followed by a second determinative, giš ('wood'), which in Mesopotamian lexical texts classifies objects made entirely or substantially of wood, including stringed-instruments.[26] So there is no doubt that we are dealing with a physical Lyre that was somehow regarded as Divine.

The Crux

This Divine Kinnaru was promptly hailed as the ancestor of Kinyras by many Semiticists, with W. F. Albright proclaiming that the "ancient derivation [of Kinyras from *kinýra*] ... may now be regarded as certain."[27] Actually Eustathios'

---

[20] For the phenomenon generally, see inter al. Pongratz-Leisten 2011:99–103.
[21] For the relevance of this equation, see further p448–449, 451.
[22] These texts are placed side-by-side, along with RS 24.643, 1–9 (KTU/CAT 1.148), in TR:292–293 (whence the present vocalizations); RCU:14; similarly del Olmo Lete 1999:72–73; RTU:360–362.
[23] For the double -nn-, see p54.
[24] For this identification, and the substantial identity of the Divine Kings and the Rapa'ūma, see Healey 1978; Dietrich and Loretz 1981:235–238; DDD col. 1076–1080 (Puech); TR:311–315; RCU:199. For the Rapa'ūma, see further p135–136.
[25] See further Chapters 3 and 9.
[26] See e.g. Kilmer 1971 passim.
[27] Jirku 1963; Albright 1964:171n47 (quotation); Astour 1965:139n5; Astour 1966:281; Nougayrol 1968:59; YGC:143–144, 147–148; Gese et al. 1970:169; Parker 1970:244n9; Kapera 1972:196; Bunnens 1979:355; Dugand 1973:200; Caquot and Sznycer 1980:16; Baurain 1980b:305–306 (with J.-P. Olivier in n150); Ribichini 1981:48–51; TR:310–311 with other references in n122. The discovery eclipsed a once promising etymology for Kinyras via *el-ku-ni-ir-ša* ('El, Creator of the Earth'), known from a LBA text from Hattusha, with a Phoenician parallel from Karatepe: Otten 1953; cf. Dussaud 1954; Pope 1955:53–54; Picard 1955; Kirst 1956; Redford 1990:827n29. Arguments against: Gese

Chapter One

etymology, although we shall see that it can be traced back to the Hellenistic period and beyond,[28] is now ancillary. A Divine Kinnaru on the Syrian coast—which on a clear day may be seen from Cypriot Salamis and the Karpass Peninsula—demands comparison with Kinyras in its own right.[29] Musical etymology, geographical proximity, and the close political and cultural relations now documented between Ugarit and LBA Cyprus (see below) combine to make *some* connection seem inevitable—especially after S. Ribichini's perceptive reconnaissance in 1982.[30]

But the precise nature of the relationship has remained obscure. What *is* a Divine Lyre? And how could it beget a substantially metamusical Cypriot culture-hero?

A major obstacle is the disparity between the evidence for Kinyras and Kinnaru. The former's mythological domain can be fairly well charted from numerous Greco-Roman sources. But the Divine Kinnaru appears certainly only in a few further 'pantheon texts.' Baurain, while acknowledging that an etymological link between Kinyras and *kinýra* was not in itself implausible, rejected the idea of a 'real' god Kinnaru as "fort excessif," and so declined to extend his study of Kinyras beyond Cyprus and into Ugaritian and other ANE material.[31] This is a common reaction from Classicists, for whom Greek words like *theîos* ('of the gods') or *théspis* ('filled with divine voice')—often applied in early epic diction to singers, their voices, and even their lyres[32]—make it natural to understand 'divine' as simply 'sacred', through association with Apollo, the Muses, or other gods and their cults. Yet these very words have a theological prehistory about which we are largely ignorant, and they may (once) have been more numinous than we suppose.

Be this as it may, divinized cult-objects are a well-attested phenomenon in the ANE and especially Mesopotamia, and these sources must obviously

---

et al. 1970:113–115 and n115; Kapera 1971:133, 136–138; Ribichini 1982:486; Baurain 1980b:305; Baurain 1980a:10.

[28] See p188–189, 280.
[29] Of the studies cited in p2n9, the most well-rounded is Ribichini 1982; Brown 1965 and Baurain 1980b are important and remain very useful, but neither addresses the fundamental issue of the relationship between Kinyras and the Divine Knr; Baurain 1980a:8 and n11, though aware of the recent discovery of Kinnaru, nevertheless considered the connection "périlleux" given the apparent (n.b.) temporal disjunction between Kinyras and κινύρα in Greek sources.
[30] I engage with his results as each point arises.
[31] Baurain 1980b:305 (quotation); cf. Gese et al. 1970:169; contrast Kapera 1971:138–139.
[32] In the Homeric *Hymn to Hermes* the lyre has the "god-filled voice" (θεσπεσίης ἐνοπῆς, 421) traditionally ascribed to singers (cf. θέσπιν ἀοιδήν, 442), and is itself called a "singer" (ἀοιδόν, 25, cf. 38) and "muse" (τίς μοῦσα; 447) who "teaches" (διδάσκει, 484). See further Franklin 2006a:61–62. Note the probable description of Kinyras as *thespésios* (*vel sim.*) in a fourth-century Cypriot inscription: p411.

take priority over Greek literature when seeking illumination for the Divine Kinnaru. Yet Ugaritologists too have tended to see Kinnaru as 'only an instrument', however wonderful. For M. H. Pope, "The mind and mood altering power of music suffices to explain the divinization of the lyre" while "the determinative for wood ... retains touch with reality."[33] Similarly, M. Koitabashi wrote that "the lyre's magical practice for manipulating the god's feelings was a motive for its deification in ancient Ugarit."[34]

These observations are psychologically sensitive and anthropologically relevant. But we are left with a conundrum. Where Kinyras was the center of a rich legendary cycle, the Divine Kinnaru does not certainly (n.b.) appear in any of Ugarit's narrative or 'paramythological' texts (the latter combine myth and ritual[35]). And how *could* a physical object like the *kinnāru* become an actor like the versatile Kinyras?

Yet these problems are not insurmountable. Astarte herself is largely absent from such contexts at Ugarit, though the goddess was of vital importance to the city's royal cult.[36] This parallel becomes all the more relevant given Kinyras' persistent intimacy with 'Aphrodite' on Cyprus. Moreover, Mesopotamian texts provide clear evidence that cult-objects could indeed be personified and take part in mythological narratives; and there is a probable parallel from the Syro-Hurrian world.[37]

In theory, therefore, an historical connection between Kinyras and the Divine Kinnaru is perfectly possible. The real problem is to clarify and specify the historical and cultural conditions which can link these two so seemingly different figures.

Plan of This Study and Preliminary Conclusions

From the foregoing discussion, three broad areas of investigation may be identified, corresponding to the three main Parts of this study.

Part 1, <u>The Cult of Kinnaru</u>, begins by examining the divinization of instruments as a general pattern, especially through the rich Mesopotamian sources (Chapter 2). This will provide a comparative framework for understanding the specific case of Ugarit's Divine Kinnaru, although Kinnaru himself must be seen as epitomizing a much broader and older Syro-Levantine lyric culture. This may be partially reconstructed, after identifying the *kinnāru* itself and defining the

---

[33] M. H. Pope in Cooper 1981:385.
[34] Koitabashi 1998:373–374; cf. Koitabashi 1992.
[35] Classicists may find the term ungainly, but it is established in Ugaritic studies (see TPm).
[36] See p114, 377.
[37] See 26–33, 103; Heimpel, "Balang-Gods," Section 2a.

Chapter One

chronological and geographical limits of the material to be studied (Chapter 3), by examining the earliest sources for the instrument and select cognates, as well as the larger cultural contexts of each attestation. These case studies should be seen as random but representative samples, and are presented in chronological order: EBA Ebla (Chapter 4), OB Mari (Chapter 5), LBA cultures peripheral to the Syro-Levantine heartland of the instrument (Chapter 6), Ugarit itself (Chapter 7), and the Biblical world, with special attention to David (Chapter 8). Part One, as a whole, provides the historical and cultural background, and a collection of parallels, for interpreting Kinyras himself.

In Part Two, Kinyras on Cyprus, I first assess the quality and antiquity of traditions about Kinyras' musicality—obviously essential for conclusively proving some historical connection with the Divine Kinnaru. I show that the Byzantine authors who are our most explicit witnesses were in fact well justified in their belief. A distinctly Cypriot lyric tradition can also be identified, and closely associated with *kinýra*, thanks to J.-B. Cayla's recent recognition of an 'Our *Kenyristés* Apollo' at Roman Paphos (Chapter 9). This musical Kinyras can then be traced back to the fifth century BCE on the island through a close reading of a well-known passage in Pindar's *Pythian* 2 (Chapter 10). To go deeper we must turn to music-iconography and map out the island's 'lyric landscapes', which, it will be seen, are compatible with an early (LBA) arrival to Cyprus of the *knr*[38]—a precondition for the presence of Kinyras himself (Chapter 11). This provides a solid foundation for examining a further, and somewhat elusive, musical aspect of Kinyras—his association with lamentation singing and the Cypriot 'Linos-Song' to which Herodotos refers (Chapter 12). I then review and expand the material which allies Kinyras to the pre-Greek period—both his connections with early Cypriot industries (Chapter 13), and his pivotal role in Aegean migration legends as a cipher for the island's various pre-Greek communities (Chapter 14). These two patterns—the early musical Kinyras and his persistent link with the pre-Greek period—can only be harmonized, I argue, by assuming that a Divine Lyre had been present on Cyprus already in the LBA. I therefore continue by exploring the cultural conditions of the LBA island and its relations with the mainland; what role a Divine Lyre could have played; and how its originally musical powers could have led to secondary, non-musical associations (Chapter 15). I then study the Kinyrad dynasty of historical Paphos, the clearest locus for continuity of the Divine Lyre's cult across the LBA–IA transition (Chapter 16).

If Kinyras and Kinnaru are indeed historically cognate, it is only to be expected that some vestiges are also to be found in mainland traditions. I gather

---

[38] I leave the root unvocalized here, and sometimes elsewhere, to avoid implying a specific source dialect: see further p53–57.

and analyze these extra-Cypriot traces in Part Three, Kinyras and the Lands around Cyprus. I begin by examining the two or more cases of Kinyras as a personal name at Mycenaean Pylos, and argue that these presuppose Kinyras as an established divine figure who had already acquired secondary, non-musical attributes by the thirteenth century (Chapter 17). This leads us to confront Kinyras' relationship with Kothar (Chapter 18). Their fusion presents a particularly challenging aspect at Byblos, but also an opportunity for better understanding the time and circumstances of a Divine Knr's arrival to LBA Cyprus (Chapter 19). I then consider a further possible mainland 'Kinyras' at Sidon (Chapter 20). I conclude by returning to the environs of Kinnaru himself, collecting the traditions that assert a Cilician and/or Syrian origin. These may be seen partly against the Syro-Hurrian cultural heritage of LBA Kizzuwatna—comprising the later Cilicia—and partly eighth-century Phoenician cultural influences in the same region. There is also important music-iconography, especially the well-known Lyre-Player Group of Seals; collectively these present, I argue by way of conclusion, our most comprehensive representation of the Divine Lyre (Chapter 21).

Seven Appendices document and discuss related issues whose treatment would impede the flow of argument in the main text.

Last and far from least comes a small monograph in its own right—an analytical catalogue of Mesopotamian balang-gods (divinized harps or lyres), generously contributed by Professor Wolfgang Heimpel. This work illuminates the breadth and depth of the phenomenon of divinized instruments—I refer to it repeatedly—and will be an important resource for further research.

With Kinyras we are in the unusual position of being able to reconstruct, in broad outline, the complete lifecycle of a mythological figure. Beginning as an instrument of ritual and secular music in the EBA, the Syro-Levantine *kinnāru* was exalted, in emulation of Mesopotamian cult practice, to a Divine Lyre by the second millennium. Coming to LBA Cyprus from one or more mainland locations, Kinyras, as the Greeks would call him, enjoyed a brilliant regal career before devolving into the human king of Greco-Roman myth. But we must always distinguish between Kinyras' treatment in classical literary sources generally, and the situation on Cyprus itself. Ribichini's description of the Divine Lyre as "un modello ormai superato"[39] best applies to the former. We shall see that Kinyras remained numinous on the island much longer than extra-Cypriot sources would suggest.

---

[39] Ribichini 1982:54.

Chapter One

Pre-Greek, Greek, and Phoenician Cyprus

Cyprus, and Kinyras' dominant connection with a specific moment of its history, are at the heart of this study. The Cypriot king mythologically delimits the pre-Greek LBA from the EIA[40] Aegean migrations. The same historical and cultural transition is equally reflected in the disjunction of sources for Kinnaru and Kinyras—the former winning elucidation from ANE texts and iconography especially of the BA, the latter compiled from Greek and Roman authors of later times, often much later. A brief historical sketch is therefore advisable. While the problems of Alashiya and the 'Sea Peoples' are among the most discussed and debated in Cypriot studies, they are still generally unfamiliar to most classicists (this being a period without Greek literary texts). I hope that specialists will not find this sketch too facile, especially as to the archaeological record—which, though of central importance to these questions, is far too complex to address in detail here.[41] My purpose is rather to bring out, in broad strokes, what I deem most relevant to the coming arguments (where I *shall* bring archaeological material to bear as specific issues arise).

It is quite universally agreed that the land of Alashiya, mentioned in ANE texts going back to the nineteenth century, is to be equated with, or located on, Cyprus. There are two decisive points. First, Alashiya is frequently associated with copper in our texts, while Cyprus was the region's premier source of the metal.[42] Second, Cyprus is the only area of sufficient size in which to locate a further Great Kingdom (as it is styled in the Amarna letters) between Egypt, Mitanni, the Hittites, and Ahhiyawa—this last now confidently identifiable as a 'Mycenaean' state in the Aegean, akin to Homer's *Akhai(w)oí*, 'Achaeans'.[43] Conversely, placing Alashiya elsewhere would leave the economically vital island otherwise undocumented.[44] Recent petrographic analysis of Alashiyan

---

[40] I use 'EIA' as a shorthand for the twelfth, eleventh, and sometimes tenth centuries; for this convention, see Iacovou 2006b:28n6.
[41] For an up-to-date overview of sources and issues, and an entrée to the vast library of scholarship, see PPC; Iacovou 2006b; Knapp 2013.
[42] See further p324–326.
[43] For the Ahhiyawa texts, and an up-to-date overview of the issues and secondary literature, see Beckman et al. 2011.
[44] Holmes 1971; Muhly 1972; CAH³ II.2:213–215; SHC 2:1–13; PPC:298–347. A relevant Biblical passage is often undervalued: Genesis 10:4–5 makes 'Elisha' (i.e. Alashiya) son of Javan, from whose sons "the coastland peoples spread." Javan is the eponym for 'Ionians', a blanket ANE term for Greek-speakers (Brinkman 1989). The genealogy, anachronistic in absolute historical terms, appropriately reflects Aegean ascendancy on the IA island, the long-lasting epicenter of Greek in the region (see p204).

diplomatic correspondence with Amarna and Ugarit[45] shows that these tablets' clay-fabric matches samples from the southeastern Troodos—that is, near the actual copper deposits.[46] Alassa and Kalavasos thus become attractive new candidates (versus Enkomi on the east coast, near historical Salamis) for the kingdom's main political center, at least in the fourteenth and thirteenth centuries.[47] A re-evaluation of these sites' importance had already been called for by recent excavation and theoretical models of the social landscape; both were well-situated not only for copper extraction but a "multiplicity of functions" within the island's settlement hierarchy.[48] Nearby Paphos, an important sanctuary already in the LBA, would fit this picture well as the state's main religious center.[49]

That Alashiya comprised much, if not all, of the island is shown by the terms of address used of and by its king in correspondence with Egypt and Ugarit. His freedom to call pharaoh "My Brother" indicates, in the period's diplomatic parlance, his own status as a Great King—that is, politically independent, and controlling a number of lesser polities.[50] Because of this, no amount of regionalism in the archaeological record[51] should be viewed as incompatible with supralocal political control, whatever form that took.[52] The situation in Ahhiyawa may have been comparable, if the traditional portrait of Agamemnon's loose confederation of regional kings is at all accurate. That is, the Great Kings of both Ahhiyawa and Alashiya may have presided over political structures rather less grand and rigidly controlled than the imperial giants Egypt and Hatti. Accordingly they could have been viewed as lesser players. For there does seem to be a slight air of wheedling inferiority on the part of the

---

[45] The Alashiya texts from Amarna are EA 33–40 (SHC 2, nos. 14–22). From Ugarit: RS 20.18, 20.168, 20.238, RSL 1 (SHC 2, nos. 25–28). For the 'new' texts, see Malbran-Labat 1999; Yon 1999; Singer 2006:255.

[46] Goren et al. 2003 (confirming the earlier analysis of Artzy et al. 1976); cf. SHC 2:6; Cochavi-Rainey 2003, 1. Longtime 'Alashiya skeptics' (Merrillees 1987) object that a complete inventory of clay samples is lacking for the eastern Mediterranean (Merrillees and Gilbert 2011); hence some still shy from using the Alashiya texts as evidence in discussing the LBA island (Smith 2009:259–260n27). For an amusing but powerful and concise rejoinder, see Cline 2005.

[47] Goren et al. 2003:248–249; Cline 2005:44.

[48] Knapp 1997:61–62 (quotation): "These two sites most likely controlled directly the mining, production, and transport of copper, were involved in agricultural production (olive oil), and functioned commercially as administrative and trans-shipment points." Excavations at Alassa: Hadjisavvas 1996. Kalavasos: South 1984; Todd and South 1992.

[49] See further p363, 400.

[50] Poetics of brotherhood among Great Kings: Liverani 1990:197–202. Vis-à-vis LBA Cyprus/Alashiya, HC:36–50; AP:38–39, 74; PPC:298–347 passim.

[51] Merrillees 1992; Keswani 1993; Keswani 1996; Iacovou 2006b:31.

[52] See the sensible comments of Goren et al. 2003, especially 251–252.

Chapter One

Alashiyan king towards his Egyptian 'brother.'[53] As to Ahhiyawa, there is the famous case of its ruler erased from a list of Great Kings in a draft of the Hittite treaty with Shaushgamuwa of Amurru (reign of Tudhaliya IV, ca. 1227–1209).[54] Still, Kushmeshusha, the one Alashiyan king now known by name, could address the Ugaritian ruler as "my son," a relationship accepted by the king of Ugarit himself elsewhere.[55] While a politely condescending tone might be adopted by an older but otherwise equal interlocutor, here it was probably justified by Ugarit's status as a Hittite subject-city. Hittite and Ugaritian texts also show that the Alashiyan king could receive deportees, another mark of Great Kingship.[56]

Alashiya was therefore no provincial backwater. Intensive material and economic relations with its neighbors are well documented both archaeologically and textually.[57] Mercantile agents and other royal protégés passed from Alashiya to Egypt and Ugarit (and elsewhere), or resided there for reasons of state and personal interest.[58] The Amarna letters contain many detailed references to the precious materials, finished products, and skilled craftsmen which were bartered and haggled over by the monarchs of Egypt and Alashiya as part of the gift-giving which characterized Great Kingship.[59] New Alashiya letters from Ugarit also confirm the longtime suspicion that, if the Cypro-Minoan script was used for internal records, the royal court also housed scribes who could execute letters in diplomatic Akkadian.[60] Alashiya's scribes were a heterogeneous corps, with Canaanite,[61] Hurrian, and Assyrian dialect elements inflecting the Peripheral Akkadian used in the Alashiya texts, alongside fairly pure Middle Babylonian specimens; one scribe was from Ugarit itself.[62] Looking westward,

---

[53] HC:42.
[54] KUB 23.1 iv.1–7 (CTH 105). See e.g. KH:343–344.
[55] Kushmeshusha (linguistic affiliation obscure: PPC:322) is named in RS 94.2475 (Malbran-Labat 1999:122–123); the other texts are RS 20.238 and 20.168 (restored): Nougayrol 1968:80–83, 87–89 (SHC 2 no. 25, 28).
[56] RS 17.352, 4–11; KUB 1.1+ iii.28–30 and 14.14 obv. 16–22; KBo 12.39 rev. 3'–7' (SHC 2, nos. 23, 34–35, 37); cf. Holmes 1971:427 and references in n18; AP:54, with references in n56. Of course as an island Cyprus was a natural place of exile, as often in the Byzantine period (SHC 7, passim).
[57] See generally PPC; for Alashiya and Ugarit, HUS:675–678 (concise survey).
[58] EA 35.30–36, 39.10–20 (SHC 2, nos. 16, 20); RS 34.152, cf. RS 18.113A = KTU/CAT 2.42 (SHC 2, nos. 29, 47).
[59] For BA gift-exchange, note Strabo's astute description at 1.2.32, and see generally Zaccagnini 1973; Zaccagnini 1983a; Zaccagnini 1987. For Egypt and Alashiya, below p323.
[60] Malbran-Labat 1999. For these texts, see above n45.
[61] I use the conventional 'Canaanite' to denote the Levantine dialects and culture from Byblos southwards (cf. Gelb 1961:42), switching to 'Phoenician' in first millennium contexts (cf. p55). For problematic aspects of this usage, and cautions against over-segregation of 'Canaanite' and 'Ugaritian' in cultural discussion, see Smith 2001:14–18.
[62] Malbran-Labat 1999:122–123; Cochavi-Rainey 2003:2–3, 118–120; PPC:319–320, 322. For regional variation in diplomatic Akkadian of the Amarna age, see Moran 1992:xviii–xxii. For the Ugaritian scribe, RS 94.2177+.

the Cypro-Minoan script implies some interaction with Minoan scribes, with whose own Linear A it is related.[63]

The power and sovereignty of Alashiya waned in the later thirteenth century, with the Hittite kings Tudhaliya IV (ca. 1237–1209) and his son Suppiluliuma II (ca. 1207–1178) claiming dominion over the island following naval victory.[64] Its collapse is to be somehow connected with the chaotic age of the 'Sea Peoples,' the conventional term adapted from inscriptions of the pharaohs Merneptah (ca. 1236–1223) and Ramses III (ca. 1184–1152) for various groups, mainly from the Aegean and western Anatolia, who migrated to the eastern Mediterranean around this time.[65] These movements variously resulted from and/or occasioned the so-called Great Collapse of palatial society in Mycenaean Greece and the Hittite world; the destruction of various Syro-Levantine sites including Ugarit; and, according to Ramses, Alashiya itself:

> The foreign countries, they made a conspiracy in their isles. Removed and scattered in battle were the lands at one time. No land could stand up against their arms, beginning from Hatti; Qode, Karkemish, Arzawa, and Alashiya, cut off (all) at [once] in one [place]. A camp was [pitched] in one place, within Amurru [coastal Syria]; they devastated its people and its land was like what had never existed. They came (on)—(but) the fire was ready before them—on towards Nile-land. Their alliance was: the Philistines [Peleset], Tjekkeru, (Sicelu) Shaklusha, Danu<na>, Washash, lands united. They laid their hands on the lands to the (outer) circuit of the earth, their hearts trusting and confident: "Our plans succeed!"[66]

We may avoid the long-running—but vital—debates about the exact identity and provenance of the several groups mentioned, and the historical accuracy

---

[63] For the affiliation of Linear A and Cypro-Minoan, and the latter's continuity with varieties of first-millennium Cypro-Syllabic, see ICS:34–42; Steele 2013:18–19, 47–51, 93–94, et passim; essays in Steele 2012.

[64] The text is KBo 12.38 = CTH 121; SHC 2 no. 38: Güterbock 1967; AP:53–55, 58; Knapp 1980; H. A. Hoffner in CS 1 no. 175 with references; KH:321–323, whose (low) dating I follow. Another Hittite allegation appears in the *Indictment of Madduwatta* (KUB 14.1 rev. 84–90 = CTH 147; SHC 2 no. 33), now generally dated to the late fifteenth century: Goetze 1928; Beckman and Hoffner 1999:153–160 no. 27; KH:129–136, 380–382; Beckman et al. 2011:69–100. Thutmose III (ca. 1479–1425) may have claimed dominion over Alashiya, although this depends on the disputed interpretation of 'Asiya' as Alashiya (Breasted 1906–1907 2 §402; SHC 2, no. 67–70); moreover, the domestic image projected by the pharaohs was often at variance with political realities.

[65] For a range of up-to-date assessments of these developments, see papers in Oren 2000, Harrison 2008, Killebrew and Lehmann 2012; a good new overview is Cline 2014.

[66] Medinet Habu Inscription, Ramesses III: trans. Kitchen 2008:34; also Edgerton and Wilson 1936:53; ANET:262–263; SHC no. 85.

Chapter One

of Ramses' claim to have prevailed in an epic land-and-sea showdown during the eighth year of his reign—perhaps 1177 (Figure 1). His 'settlement' of the 'vanquished' in his own lands will have included the Peleset and other groups who occupied what now became Philistia—southern 'Palestine', formerly under long-term NK control.[67] This probably also explains the Cypriot cities which appear elsewhere among his triumphs.[68]

It is now understood, however, that Aegean settlement on Cyprus was much more complex and long-drawn than Ramses' inscriptions might suggest, unfolding across the twelfth and eleventh centuries. Various explanatory models have been advanced and continue to be refined.[69] But the outcome of any reconstruction must allow the island's Arcado-Cypriot dialect of Greek—first attested by the famous Opheltas *obelós* (spit) from the Paphos region in the eleventh century,[70] around the same (dramatic) time that the Egyptian official Wen-Amun found that his own tongue was now practically unknown on Cyprus[71]—to emerge as the majority language by the Archaic period.[72] Thus in the Esarhaddon prism inscription (N-A, 673/672) at least half of the Cypriot kings have Greek names, and the same is probably true of others.[73] Even Amathous, where 'Eteocypriot' inscriptions—presumably in one of the island's pre-Greek languages—persisted until the fourth century, had kings with Greek names.[74] Despite this linguistic situation, however, the 'colonial' process can no longer be viewed as unilateral 'Hellenization.' The Aegean influx is practically invisible in the archaeological record, to judge from which there was a fairly general blending by the tenth century, at least as regards material culture (including the

---

[67] Dothan and Dothan 1992:26–27 et passim.
[68] List of Ramses III: Edgerton and Wilson 1936:105–110 (partly dependent upon an earlier monument of Ramses II, though the Cypriot cities are not found there). Those probably attested are Kourion, Salamis, Kition, and Soloi; more doubtful are Marion and Idalion. See HC:49; Snodgrass 1994:169–170.
[69] For a good introduction to the intricate sources and problems, see the papers in Ward and Joukowsky 1992 and Karageorghis 1994. For intervening work, see with much further material PPC:131–297 and Knapp 2013:447–470.
[70] Opheltas *obelós* (ca. 1050–950): Palaipaphos *Skales*, Tomb 49 no. 16: Karageorghis 1980b; Steele 2013:90–97.
[71] CS 1 no. 41 (here p. 93, col. A).
[72] The statement of Iacovou 1999:2—"One need only turn to the archaeological evidence to clarify the process"—may infuriate some, but is ultimately accurate.
[73] ARAB 2:266 §690. Probable equations are Ekistura = Akestor (Idalion), Pilagura = Pylagoras/Philagoras (Khytroi), Ituandar = Eteander (Paphos), Damasu = Damasos (Kourion), Unasagusu = Onasagoras (Ledroi). See further HC:105–107; Mitford 1961a:137; Lipiński 1991; Masson 1992; Iacovou 2006a:318–319; Iacovou 2006b:48.
[74] For Amathous and Eteocypriot, see p349.

Figure 1 Detail from 'Sea Peoples' reliefs, Medinet Habu, reign of Ramses III (ca. 1184–1152). Drawn from Nelson et al. 1930, pl. 36–37.

Chapter One

revealing burial customs).⁷⁵ All the same, we shall see that a distinction between 'Greek' and 'pre-Greek' was sometimes cultivated as late as the fourth century.⁷⁶

Another major trend was underway by ca. 900, with Phoenician groups, led by Tyre and drawn more or less by Troodos copper, settling in various places; Amathous and especially Kition were important early epicenters.⁷⁷ Formal Tyrian political control of Kition, and perhaps elsewhere, probably first emerged in the later eighth century as an extension of Assyrian provincial structure.⁷⁸ The inland sites of Idalion and Tamassos fell to Kition in the early fifth and mid-fourth centuries respectively, while rulers with Phoenician names ruled Salamis periodically under the Persians.⁷⁹ Some kings of Lapethos also had Phoenician names.⁸⁰

This, in very broad strokes, is the historical situation as I understand it. I have elaborated the Alashiyan period most fully, as I consider this the formative age for Kinyras. My treatment of the Aegean and IA Phoenician 'strata' is obviously cursory; but it should suffice as a preliminary framework, into which specific developments can be fit as the argument unfolds.

---

[75] PPC:286–290; Iacovou 2006b:33–42.
[76] See especially p349–351.
[77] Phoenician expansion generally: Bunnens 1979; Lipiński 2004. Cyprus specifically: Gjerstad 1979; Reyes 1994:18–21, 23–26. At Amathous: Karageorghis 1976b:95–97; Reyes 1994:139; Karageorghis 1998, 131–132; Petit 2001; Steele 2013:166–167.
[78] See Smith 2008:261, 264–274 (reprised in Smith 2009), who recognizes that political control of Kition may not have been *continuous* down to the fifth century. The first direct epigraphic evidence for a Phoenician royal-name at Kition is fifth-century: Iacovou 2006b:50.
[79] Iacovou 2006b:50–51; Smith 2008:274–275.
[80] See p339, 510.

PART ONE

THE CULT OF KINNARU

2
Instrument Gods and Musician Kings in Early Mesopotamia

Divinized Instruments

ALREADY IN THE LATE URUK PERIOD (CA. 3300–2900), reverence for cult-objects is implied by the ritual deposition of 'retired' tools from an old temple when a new one was built over it (for example, the Eanna complex at Uruk); the burial of objects including musical instruments and weapons in the 'royal cemetery' of Ur (ca. 2600) may also be relevant.[1] In the so-called Metal List, known from various copies running from Uruk III down to the OAkk. period (ca. 2340–2159), various cult-objects of metal are written with divine determinatives; presumably this is a collection "of items and their deified counterparts," although the precise nature of that divinity is not made clear.[2] God lists going back to Fāra and Abū Ṣalābīḫ (ca. 2600) contain names that indicate an origin in divinized cult-objects, such as crowns, staves, temple-doors, and foundation pegs. Also included are deified offices and professions related to temple administration and society more generally (for example, divine brick-maker, divine shepherd, Lady of the Granaries), as well as 'cultural achievements' like incense, bees' wax, fire, kettle, and torch. We also first find a musical instrument accompanied by the divine determinative (ᵈùb, probably a small kettledrum).[3] In the generation before Sargon came to power (ca. 2340), administrative texts from Lagash document offerings and votive donations to gods and deified objects (statues, steles, and emblems like 'The Bronze Date-Palm'); paraphernalia relating to royal ideology (staves, scepters, chariot); and musical instruments—including the balang (Sum. balaĝ), which in the third millennium at

---

[1] For the material in this paragraph, see Selz 1997, especially 169–177.
[2] See also p580n21.
[3] For the ùb, see also PHG:142 et passim.

least referred to a kind of stringed-instrument, whether harp, lyre, or perhaps sometimes even lute.[4]

Divinized cult-objects could receive offerings of animal sacrifice, spices, oil, fruit, or jewelry.[5] Although these must have been consumed or otherwise processed by cultic personnel, it remains the case that the objects themselves were the intended beneficiaries of the offering-rituals.[6] The great diversity of divinized objects in Mesopotamia strains familiar conceptions of the divine.[7] Apparently there was no essential distinction between 'gods' and those objects we might see as merely representing them, or being otherwise associated. These were not *symbols* of the gods, but *instantiations* of some sort:

> No distinctive feature could be found that functionally separates the divine images proper from cultic objects, including the statues of the ruling elite. They both seem to vary only in their *degree* of religious importance, not in their conceptualization.[8]

> The aura of a god in his temple could so attach itself to the temple, or architectural parts of it in particular, also to implements he used, and to the city which housed the temple, in such a way that these various things also became gods and received offerings as a mark of the fact.[9]

So for all practical purposes, divinized cult-objects *were* gods. A large number of these are attested in god-lists—a subset of lexical text containing accumulated material from various eras—and royal inscriptions from the later third and early second millennia (N-S and OB periods). Especially prominent among musical instruments is the balang; from Heimpel's analysis, it is clear that "most major and many minor master-gods had one or more [balang-gods] as servants."[10]

If offerings to divinized cult-objects were generally small, befitting their status as servant-gods,[11] nevertheless their power was real. It was possible, for instance, to take an oath on one or more musical instruments. The evidence for this comes from *Šurpu* (*Burning*), a series of "incantations, prayers, and

---

[4] For the identity of the balang, see Appendix A and Heimpel, "Balang-Gods," Section 1 (with 9, 11, 12–13, 15, 17f, 20a–20b, etc. for ED III and later evidence of balang-offerings).

[5] Cf. Jean 1931:159; Galpin 1936:65–66; Hartmann 1960:53 and n3, 61–62; MgB 2/2:13, 140; RlA 8:464, 466 (Kilmer, *Musik A I). For offerings to the balang specifically, see references in Sjöberg 1984–, s.v. 1.1.1-2; further material noted by Heimpel 1998a:6–10.

[6] Selz 1997:176–177; cf. Heimpel, "Balang-Gods," Section 2b and 13.

[7] Selz 1997; Selz 2008.

[8] Selz 1997:167 (emphasis added).

[9] Lambert 1990:129.

[10] Heimpel 1998b:4 (quotation). See further Heimpel, "Balang-Gods."

[11] Selz 1997:175.

instructions for magic practices," known from N-A copies, but including older material (for instance several Sumerian incantations known from OB versions).[12] Tablet III contains a long incantation for freeing the participant from the effects of a previously sworn oath that may have been violated unknowingly; accordingly it includes an exhaustive catalogue of oaths that may have been taken.[13] It is in this context that several different musical-instrument oaths are itemized.[14] "It was feared, it appears from this tablet, that the numen inherent in these, once invoked, would stay unbound and afflict the person who had sworn the oath."[15] Although the precise purpose of such oaths is not clear, it is worth noting here a cylinder seal of unknown provenance dating to ca. 1500–1000, interpreted by E. Porada as a treaty agreement; a king shakes hands with a smaller figure, presumably a client ruler, behind whom a musician, of equal stature to the king, plays an upright harp (Figure 2).[16] Presumably the music somehow served to bind the agreement.[17] Note that a number of balang servant-gods are attested for the sun-god Utu, who was associated with law and justice; these bear such apt names as 'Let me live by His Word', 'Just Judge', and 'Decision of Sky and Earth'.[18]

The religious and political importance of divinized instruments is shown by a startling number of official year-names referring to their construction and dedication in major temples. In Lagash ca. 2100, one year of Gudea's reign (perhaps the third) was called "the year in which was fashioned the balang Ušumgal-kalama ('Great Dragon of the Land')."[19] As it happens, this event is

---

[12] Reiner 1958:1 (quotation). The series was cited in connection with Kinnaru by Nougayrol 1968:59. Note that the instruments are not written with divine determinatives. Yet if instruments held such power *without* being divinized, their divinized counterparts will have been all the more numinous. The evidence is therefore relevant.

[13] Reiner 1958:3.

[14] Šurpu III:37 and 88–91. The translation of Reiner 1958:20–21 will serve to illustrate the variety of combinations, although the identification of specific instruments may be questionable. Thus we find an "oath of the cymbals or harp" (37); "oath of the drum and kettledrum" (88); "oath of the timbrel and cymbals" (89); "oath of lyre, harp (*pa-lag-gi*), and timbūtu-harp" (90); "the oath of lute and pipe" (91).

[15] Reiner 1958:55.

[16] London, BM 89359. See Porada 1980; MgB 2/2:102–104 (fig. 108); Collon 1987 no. 665.

[17] Compare perhaps Homer's use of ἁρμονίαι for an agreement between two warriors overseen by the gods (*Iliad* 22.254–255), and the invocation of Κενυριστής Apollo in the loyalty oath to Tiberius at Roman Paphos: see p205.

[18] See Heimpel, "Balang-Gods," 53 III 153–158; cf. V 291 (a balang-servant of Ishtaran, with Heimpel's comments there).

[19] Falkenstein 1966:8; Sigrist and Gomi 1991:317; RIME 3/1:27 (1.1.7, 3); Selz 1997:200n218; Heimpel, "Balang-Gods," 17b. The precise sequence of Gudea's regnal years has not been fully established: RIME 3/1:27.

Chapter Two

Figure 2 'Harp treaty', unprovenanced Mesopotamian cylinder seal, ca. fourteenth century. London, BM 89359. Drawn from MgB 2/2 fig. 108.

treated at some length in the Gudea Cylinders (see below).[20] During the reign of Ibbi-Sin, the last king of Shulgi's line (see below), one year was called "Ibbi-Sin, king of Ur, fashioned the balang Ninigizibara for the goddess Inanna."[21] A divine balang of this same name features in an illuminating lamentation ritual for Ishtar at OB Mari, to be discussed later.[22] Also from the OB period come a handful of further years named after the dedication of divinized instruments.[23]

The creation of a divinized instrument was clearly a momentous event, and must have involved, at all relevant periods, complex rituals comparable to those whereby a god took up its abode in a new or repaired statue.[24] Ethnomusicology provides many parallels for such processes. S. C. Devale, in a seminal synthesis, surveyed material from Africa, the Pacific, and elsewhere for rituals governing various stages in the lifecycle of an instrument, from the several stages of construction through first, subsequent, and last use, with various actions before, between, and after. Construction rituals include offerings to and blessings of the

---

[20] Gudea dedicated another balang to the goddess Bau (spouse of Ningirsu), called "Greatly speaking with the Lady": RIME 3/1 1.1.7.StE iv.12–14; cf. Radner 2005:51 no. 52; Ziegler, FM 9:222 (on 8).
[21] Sigrist and Gomi 1991:329, year 22; Heimpel, "Balang-Gods," 23a1.
[22] See p84–85.
[23] See p83–84.
[24] Lambert 1990:123.

necessary trees, animals, or other materials, or to a culture-hero who invented some essential tool; sacrifice of animals and use of blood or body parts both for the instrument itself, and in appropriate priestly and communal feasting practices; special procedures for releasing an instrument's voice; endowment with a special name describing the instrument's powers; and so on.[25]

The only direct evidence for such construction rituals in Mesopotamia comes from a collection of late texts that document the divinization of the *lilissu*-drum.[26] The 'exemplars'—the various tablets actually contain variations in the ritual[27]—range in date from the N-A period (Assur, Nineveh) down to the Seleucid (Uruk). One of the seventh-century versions, however, is known to have been copied for the library of Ashurbanipal from an older Babylonian tablet. The ritual was thus traditional, if certainly not static.[28] In any case, the *lilissu* texts provide the only hints for imagining analogous rituals of the third and second millennia.[29]

Even a selective summary of the *lilissu* rituals will reveal the astonishing elaborateness of the divinization procedure.[30] The science was performed and guarded by the so-called lamentation-priests (Sum. gala/Akk. *kalû*) whose best-known function was to assuage divine anger and grief through ritual performance.[31] A pure steer, never subjected to yoke or whip, was brought to the temple on a day chosen by careful divination. Offerings were made to Ea, incense burned, and incantations sung. Around the animal were placed twelve god-figurines in a magical arrangement, an actual diagram of which has been found. The figures' positions had cosmogonic and theomachic implications, so that the finished drum would ultimately be strengthened by the renovation of cosmic order.[32] The beast's mouth was washed—an action also attested for the divinization of cult statues, and related to the process of animation[33]—while

---

[25] DeVale 1988. For drum-construction rituals of several African cultures, see Rattray 1923:258–266; HMI:34–36; Nketia 1963:4–16; Blades 1984:57–64.

[26] Thureau-Dangin 1921:1–5; Thureau-Dangin 1922 no. 44–46; Livingstone 1986:187–204; ANET:334–338; Linssen 2004:92–99, 267–282; cf. also Stauder 1970:199–201 and fig. 3a; RlA 8:465 (Kilmer, *Musik A I); Selz 1997:201n215; PHG:118–138.

[27] Linssen 2004:94n495.

[28] See Livingstone 1986:200; Linssen 2004:267, whose study upholds in general the traditional nature of the late ritual texts (167–168); similarly Heimpel, "Balang-Gods," Section 4a §2.

[29] Thus Selz 1997:178–179 assumes that, already in the N-S period, divinization entailed rituals of name-giving, animation, induction to an appropriate cult place, and ongoing offerings and maintenance.

[30] The following account conflates elements from several versions; they are, however, essentially compatible.

[31] For the gala, see Michalowski 2006; Bachvarova 2008; Gadotti 2010; Shehata 2013; PHG; and further p29–30.

[32] Livingstone 1986:201–204; PHG:137–139.

[33] Selz 1997:178.

Chapter Two

Sumerian and Akkadian incantations were sung into its ear through a special tube of aromatic wood. The slaughter was accompanied by further apotropaic lamentation-songs, in which the bull was promised a kind of immortality:

> You are the choice bull, the creation of [the great gods].
> You were created for the wo[rk of the great go]ds ...
> Your hide and your sinew have been assigned to the mystery
>   of the great gods.
> Abide for eternity in the mystery of that god![34]

The victim's heart was extracted, placed in front of the drum, scattered with juniper, and burned. Its skin was removed, treated with flour, beer, wine, fat, alum, and gall-apples, and then applied in many complex steps to a previously prepared drum frame. The rest of the animal was buried.[35] One of the gods to whom offerings were made was Lumḫa,[36] whose name is written in some exemplars as 'Divine Balang' (ᵈBALAĜ).[37] Lumḫa himself was therefore a kind of instrument god, his goodwill needed for the new divinized drum.[38] One should also note the substantial element of seven-magic that underpins the ritual.[39] On the fifteenth day after the drum's completion, it was presented to the temple-god. It was now a Divine Lilissu, and could only be played by the priest to whom it was assigned. Through these procedures, as U. Gabbay has convincingly argued, the bull belonged to both the living and the dead. Its 'heart' survived in the drum itself, which wore its skin, and continued to beat in the beating of the instrument; this was in turn the beating heart of the god to be soothed through ritual lamentation, when the *kalû* would imitate the gestures of mourning.[40]

---

[34] KAR 50 (VAT 8247), trans. Linssen 2004:267–268, obv. 1–12; cf. 278, l.22: "For the great [god]s, guard the divine decrees!"

[35] See PHG:127–128, 138.

[36] AO 6479 II.5, 33–35, III.15, after drum has been made.

[37] For example, KAR 60, obv. 15, N-A, seventh century; in this text the bull is placed in front of Lumḫa while being sacrificed.

[38] Thureau-Dangin 1921:49n13, calls Lumḫa the god of the tympanum, patron of the *kalû*; Linssen 2004:96, treats him as a 'divine harp', but for this period BALAĜ probably represents a drum: see p531, 573.

[39] For the relevance of seven-magic to the larger question of divinized instruments and ritual music, see p40–41. Seven-magic in the *lilissu* texts includes sevenfold offerings in AO 6479 I.17 and 23. Among the twelve divine figurines are the "seven children of Enmešarra" (enumerated at AO 6479 III.3–14), represented by seven heaps of flour (as stated in K 4806, 5–8). These heaps, accompanied by the god-names, are apparently represented in the diagram of O175 reverse, where they have a definite arrangement *vis-à-vis* the bull. See Livingstone 1986:194, 203. The seven gods/heaps correspond somehow to seven "hands" or "handles" (on the drum itself?), and stand in an obscure relationship to the "seven defeated Enlils" who also appear in the diagram.

[40] PHG:79, 173, 177 (mimetic performance of *kalû*); 126, 138, 154 (*lilissu* equated with the divine heart in theological commentaries, and both connected with that of the bull).

The mechanism was thus sympathetic magic: the *kalû* enacted the lamenting god(dess), leading his or her heart to release from anger and grief through the performance of mourning.

A divinized instrument, like other cult-objects, was endowed with a name. This could reflect its physical and conceptual properties, or some aspect of the master-god to whom it was devoted.[41] In either case, the naming ritual endowed the divinized instrument with individual existence.[42] This bears in turn on the capacity of divine objects to enjoy 'personal' relationships with major gods, and hence appear in mythological narratives with them. Thus, for example, in the *Babylonian Erra Myth*, an Akkadian narrative work of the early first millennium,[43] the god Erra's vizier Ishum is perhaps his deified scepter, Ḫendursanga.[44] His seven weapons are definitely anthropomorphized as warriors.[45] Much earlier is the N-S poem *Lugal-e*, telling the adventures of Ninurta.[46] The god's mace Sharur is personified as his advisor, who alerts him in a lengthy speech (24-69) to the existence of a new enemy in the mountains—Azag, who has been chosen leader by that region's plants and stones, the latter represented as warriors.[47] Later as Ninurta carries his mace it "snarled at the mountains" (79). Notable among Sharur's several other actions is his transformation into the thunderbird, flying overhead to spy out the enemy and bring news back to Ninurta (109-150).

The appearance of divinized cult-tools in myth is probably related to their use in ritual. This is well explained by A. Livingstone:

> In Babylonian thinking the distinction between 'ritual' and 'myth' is slight. Statues or symbols used in the rituals were believed *to be* in every sense the deities which we regard them as *representing* ... A ritual in which the statue or symbol of a deity participated was therefore in effect a myth. On the other hand, myths which we would conceive as having happened once in the past were believed by the ancient thinkers to be capable of repetition.[48]

---

[41] See PHG:113-114. For examples of 'conceptual names,' see below and Heimpel, "Balang-Gods".
[42] Selz 1997:178; Heimpel, "Balang-Gods," Section 4b1.
[43] Text: Cagni 1969; English translation: Foster 2005:771-805. Despite the work's late date (Machinist 1983a:221-222), Ḫendursanga himself is known already in the third millennium (Fara; I-II dynasty of Lagash; Ur III): Cagni 1969:138-140 with further references.
[44] Cagni 1969:138-140; Foster 2005:742.
[45] Machinist 1983a:222. As Divine Heptad, RlA 12/5-6:461 (Wiggerman, *Siebengötter A).
[46] *Lugal-e*: ed. van Dijk 1983 = *Exploits of Ninurta*, ETCSL 1.6.2; trans./comm. Jacobsen 1987:233-272. The work has been dated to soon after ca. 2150, due to its allusion at 475-478 to Gudea's building of Ningirsu's sanctuary Eninnu: see van Dijk 1983:1-9; Jacobsen 1987:234.
[47] For the allegory of the stones, see van Dijk 1983:37-47.
[48] Livingstone 1986:169-170 (original emphasis).

Chapter Two

While there is no obvious connection with ritual in the case of Sharur in *Lugal-e*, his very existence was grounded in the *realia* of Ninurta's cult. The closeness of Sharur's mythological relationship to his master-god must have depended on the physical proximity of the mace to Ninurta's statue, which will have been regularly involved in temple rituals. It is likely enough, however, that once such a background was taken for granted, a divinized cult-tool like Sharur could take on a 'life of his own' in the minds of singers and storytellers. Similarly the myth of Erra's seven warrior-weapons presents no overt ritual dimension; yet they are a manifestation of the Divine Heptad, a polymorphous group whose appearance in cult and ritual is otherwise well attested.[49]

This evidence for the ritual-poetic treatment of cult-objects and processes will be important when considering several myths relating to Kinyras and his family.[50]

Gudea and the Balang-Gods of Ningirsu

This fundamental link between ritual and poetics is most clearly illustrated by passages in *The Building of Ningirsu's House*, a work which Gudea of Lagash (ca. 2140–2120), to memorialize his completion of a new temple to the city-god Ningirsu, caused to be composed and inscribed on two large clay cylinders (henceforth Gudea Cylinders). It is a lengthy praise-hymn (zà.mí) describing in great detail the process of construction.[51] Complementary 'documentation' comes from a series of figurative steles, including several scenes of musical performance, which were dedicated at the temple's inauguration.[52] The praise-hymn itself may have been performed on the same occasion.[53] The text, rich in

---

[49] For the *Sebettu* (*vel sim.*), their association with the Pleiades, and other variations, see RlA 12/5–6:459–466 (Wiggerman, *Siebengötter A), with ritual uses at 461 §2 and 464 §4. The bulk of the evidence is from the first millennium (especially N-A contexts), but there are scattered antecedents going back to the N-S period. Classicists will recall here W. Burkert's hypothesis that the myth of the Seven against Thebes derives ultimately from these Seven Warriors (1992:106–114; cf. EFH:455–457), although the pattern of seven against seven suggests Anatolian mediation (for the Hittite doubling of the Divine Heptad, see RlA 12/5–6:466 [Polvani, *Siebengötter B]).

[50] See p280–291.

[51] Text: RIME 3/1:68–101 (1.1.7 CylA/B); ETCSL 2.1.7 (translation followed here, with exceptions as noted); CS 2 no. 155. For the work's genre and title (Gudea Cylinders B 24.17), Suter 2000:277. Pantheon of Lagash: Falkenstein 1966.

[52] Suter 2000:274 et passim. The musical scenes are Suter 2000:ST.9, 13, 15, 23, 53, 54, with discussion on 190–195; for those showing a giant drum, see p532. A proposal by J. Börker-Klähn to restore a bow-harp on a further fragment is unlikely: see Suter 2000:189, with 172 fig. 19a.

[53] Suter 2000:157 and 278, wondering about the audience for the text of the cylinders, notes their reference to the performance of various songs during the construction process, and suggests that the cylinders were a 'draft' for a more polished stele-inscription. Be that as it may, the content of the text and the figurative steles are to a large extent parallel, and sometimes

Instrument Gods and Musician Kings in Early Mesopotamia

sociological and cultic information, brilliantly illuminates the anthropomorphic visualization of cult-objects, slipping easily between material-ritual description and vivid mythological scenes. Thus, at the poem's climax, Ningirsu, arriving at his new 'palace', is accompanied by the functionaries of his divine court—all of whom are 'actually' architectural elements of the temple itself, divinized cult-objects, or cultic personnel masquerading as such.[54]

Once again we encounter Sharur, this time as the mace of Ningirsu; a second weapon is called Shargaz.[55] It is told how Gudea goes to the cedar mountain to make Sharur's shaft—an event that gave its name to yet another regnal year.[56] After Gudea dedicates the mace in Eninnu, it is personified, and Sharur takes up his position; his duties as Ningirsu's 'general' are described in detail.[57] Other cult-objects are made the god's family members. One son, Ig-Alima, is the deified door of the hall of justice; he serves as 'Chief Bailiff' in Ningirsu's court.[58] Ningirsu's oldest son, Šulšaga, is butler to his table.[59] Many such familiar relationships are found in the canonical lamentations,[60] and will be important parallels for approaching Kinyras and his family.[61]

The text is also a key source for understanding divinized instruments, and how ritual music was believed to affect the gods through 'song-acts'.[62] Early in Cylinder A, the goddess Nanshe interprets an ominous dream for Gudea. He is to seek Ningirsu's approval—and with it exact architectural plans—for the temple's construction. Ningirsu must first be made favorably disposed to the king's pleas through the building and dedication of a magnificent chariot. Gudea can then make his request. But it must be 'translated' by the balang Great Dragon of the Land:

---

mirror each other. Thus, for instance, the steles depict ritual musical performances like those mentioned in the text, which in turn alludes to various decorative schemes on steles set up in the temple. Given that "the verbal composition was probably recited in some form at least once" (Suter 2000:279), it is an easy guess that this was during the same set of events that saw the dedication of the steles—i.e., inauguration of the temple.

[54] For this last qualification, see the comments of Heimpel, "Balang-Gods," Section 2a.
[55] Gudea Cylinders A 9.24. For the historical conflation of Ninurta (Nippur name) and Ningirsu (Lagash name), see Jacobsen 1987:233–235.
[56] Gudea Cylinders A 15.19–25. For "The year in which the wood for the Sharur-weapon was made," and a further year-name from the making (or repair) of the mace itself, see Falkenstein 1966:8; RIME 3/1:27 (1.1.7, 6).
[57] Gudea Cylinders A 22.20, B 7.12–21.
[58] Gudea Cylinders B 6.11–23. Cf. Jacobsen 1987:430n22.
[59] Gudea Cylinders B 6.24–7.11.
[60] See e.g. *Elum Gusun* (*Honored One, Wild Ox*) and CLAM:296–297, 314–316.
[61] See p280–291.
[62] Adapting the formulation of Austin 1962. For theoretical considerations of the intersection of 'speech-act' and 'song' in the Hellenic sphere, see *inter al.* Martin 1989 (with illuminating cultural parallels 1–14 et passim); Nagy 1990:30–34.

Chapter Two

> Enter before the warrior who loves gifts, before your master Lord Ningirsu in [his temple] E-ninnu-the-white-Anzud-bird, together with his beloved balang, Ušumgal-kalama, his famous instrument, his tool of counsel (nîĝ-ad-gi4-gi4). Your requests will then be taken as if they were commands;[63] and the balang will make the inclination of the lord—which is as inconceivable as the heavens—will make the inclination of Ningirsu, the son of Enlil, favorable for you so that he will reveal the design of his house to you in every detail.[64]

In Cylinder B, this same balang, along with the rest of the god's accessories, is dedicated in the finished temple—the same event that gave its name to the regnal year. But now the narrative becomes fully mythological as Ningirsu arrives to take up residence. His divine spirit permeates the temple and its sacred parts and contents. Ušumgal-kalama materializes from the balang to be inducted to the office of nar—the 'musician-singer' whose repertoire included songs of divine and royal praise.[65] We are given a clear description of his duties:

> To have the sweet-toned instrument, the tigi-harp, correctly tuned (or 'put in order'[66]), to place the music of the alĝar and miritum, which make the temple happy in Eninnu for the hero, the wise Ningirsu, was his beloved musician-singer (nar), Ušumgal-kalama, going about his duties for the lord Ningirsu.[67]

This balang-god appears as a kind of musical director for the temple orchestra, responsible for the production of celebratory music in times of peace and good order. I shall return to his larger role in the text below.

---

[63] This is translated by Wilson 1996:36, as "(Then) he will receive (even) your most insignificant words as exalted."

[64] Gudea Cylinders A 6.24–7.6. My translations adapted from ETCSL and Jacobsen 1987. Gudea carries out these instructions at A 7.9–8.1.

[65] For the status and organization of nar generally, including the elite offices of "Chief Singer" (nar-gal, a substantially administrative position) and "Singer before the King" (nar lugal, associated especially with the Ur III period), see now Pruzsinszky 2010; Pruzsinszky 2013. The evidence naturally varies from city to city. In the Ur III period there was a 'great academy' (e2 umum gu-la) for royal musicians at Ur itself: Pruzsinszky 2013:35–36.

[66] Wilson 1996:158.

[67] Gudea Cylinders B 10.9–15: translation after Jacobsen 1987 and one by Stephen Langdon in the margin of his copy of Thureau-Dangin 1907, held in the Sackler Library, Oxford. Wilson 1996:159 renders the last line as "(sc. Ušumgal-kalama) passed by the lord Ningirsu with (emblems of the) rituals." Ušumgal-kalama appears further at B 15.19–16.2, for which see below; and B 18.22–19.1, "Ušumgal-kalama took its stand among the *tigi*-harps, the *alu*-lyres roared for him like a storm" (trans. Jacobsen). For these instruments, see 531n1, 532, 575, 606–7n92.

Upon his heels follows a second balang-god—Lugal-igi-ḫuš, the 'Red-Eyed Lord':[68]

> With his divine duties, namely to soothe the heart, to soothe the spirits;[69] to dry weeping eyes; to banish mourning from the mourning heart ... Gudea introduced his balang, Lugal-igi-ḫuš, to Lord Ningirsu.[70]

Although an exact title is not given, the 'Red-Eyed Lord' is clearly a kind of lamentation-priest akin to the gala/*kalû*.[71] In aetiological myth, this figure is associated especially with Inanna; Enki created him either to soothe the goddess's wrath, or to rescue her from the underworld by assuaging its grieving queen Ereškigal.[72] The gala's ritual performances could be sung to self-accompaniment, that of another (Heimpel suggests), or together with a chorus.[73] The several genres of lament used the linguistic mode or register called Emesal, otherwise found of female speech in literary texts and arguably connected with an early tradition of women mourners that was later embraced (co-opted?) by select, 'male' lamenters.[74] This is clearly relevant to certain third-gender qualities long noted for the gala, and that 'his' earliest documented function was lamenting at funerals amidst mourning women.[75] The gala/*kalû* also imitated, in stylized manner, the gestures of female mourning (prostration, torn clothing, breast-beating).[76] Institutionalized lamentation was performed both periodically

---

[68] Falkenstein 1966:82 ("Herr mit dem schrecklichen Blick"); Selz 1997:178 ("Red-Eyed Lord"). The existence of two distinct balang-gods is justified by their separate functions. The lexical collection An:Anum lists no fewer than seven balang-gods of Ningirsu, all otherwise unattested (Heimpel 1998b:5 and "Balang-Gods," Section 2c and 53 V 100–106).

[69] Wilson 1996:159: "to calm the inside, to calm the outside."

[70] Gudea Cylinders B 10.16–11.2. Wilson 1996:160: "His lyre, Lugal-igi-ḫuš, passed by the lord Ningirsu with (emblems of the) rituals."

[71] Cf. also Heimpel, "Balang-Gods," Section 4b2. For the following overview, see PHG:63–64, 70–71, 159–168, et passim. I assume that the detailed first-millennium sources can serve at least as a rough guide to earlier periods. Surviving literary laments: CLAM.

[72] The two narratives are *The Fashioning of the Gala* (BM 29616, balang-composition of OB date): see Kramer 1981; and *Inanna's Descent to the Netherworld* (ETCSL 1.4.1) 228–239. See further Shehata 2006a; PHG:76–78; Heimpel, "Balang-Gods," Section 3b.

[73] PHG:83–84; Heimpel, "Balang-Gods," Section 3b.

[74] See especially Cooper 2006:43–45; approved by Michalowski 2006:49. For the linguistic evidence itself, Schretter 1990. Whittaker 2002 is a good critical review of theories. See also Bachvarova 2008; PHG:68.

[75] The use of 'male' and 'his' are complicated by the third-gender interpretation. See recently, with earlier literature, Cooper 2006:44–45; Gabbay 2008; PHG:67–68. Evidence for the gala's funerary function is early (third-millennium and OB), cf. e.g. Gudea's suspension of funeral rites when purifying the ground for Ningirsu's temple: "corpses were not buried, the gala did not set up his balang and bring forth laments from it, the woman lamenter did not utter laments" (RIME 3/1 1.1.7.StB v.1–4; translation after Cooper 2006:42–43); see further material in PHG:18–19n19.

[76] PHG:79, 172–173.

Chapter Two

('chronic') and as occasion demanded ('acute'). Regular laments, scheduled by day, month, or year within a cultic calendar, were either conducted in front of the god's statue or elsewhere within a temple precinct, depending on the event (including processions to and from sanctuaries).[77] 'Occasional' laments responded to particular situations, and accordingly could be either prophylactic or corrective. Even such a fortunate chance as a royal victory could call for apotropaic lament.[78] Lament was also prescribed for such potentially dangerous transitions as eclipses and the construction or repair of temples, statues, and cult-objects, including musical instruments.[79] Lamentation-priests were also needed for repairing temple walls, gates, and even canals, with the place of performance varying as required.[80]

The activity attributed to Ušumgal-kalama is ad-gi4-gi4, 'return a sound', that is, 'answer' or 'advise'.[81] The same word is applied to Lugalsisa, another 'counselor' of Ningirsu, who was to conduct regular prayers on behalf of Lagash to keep the city in good repair, the king in good health, and his power stable.[82] Considerable external evidence shows that ad-gi4-gi4 typically describes advice or responses from divine sources. The word appears as the name or epithet of several temples or shrines.[83] The balang as 'counselor' is seen in a rich array of material independently assembled by Heimpel and Gabbay.[84] In first millennium god-lists, many minor deities are identified as 'counselors', where the Akk. *mundalku* can be written with the Sum. signs GU4.BALAĜ ('balang-bull'). Their names often incorporate the word balang; refer to musical sound and voice; express some facet of their master-god; or constitute a theophoric sentence describing their counseling services. Some of these GU4.BALAĜ advisors are also found bearing the title ad-gi4-gi4, the word even appearing once as a DN in its own right

---

[77] See PHG Part VII.
[78] Heimpel 1998a:14–16 with parallels; also "Balang-Gods," 42a.
[79] PHG:164n76, 165–166, 173, 180. For the *lilissu* ritual, see p23–25. Dada, a well-documented gala attached to the royal palace in the reigns of Shulgi and Shu-Sin, is also known to have supervised the manufacture and repair of instruments. For Dada, see Michalowski 2006; Mirelman 2010; Heimpel, "Balang-Gods," 54.
[80] Ambos 2004:171–198; PHG: 87, 158, 165–168, 181–182, 187, 272. See further p280–282.
[81] Gudea Cylinders A 7.25. "To which he keeps listening," in the translation of RIME 3/1:73, will yield compatible sense when other evidence for the counseling balang is take into account.
[82] Gudea Cylinders B 8.10–22.
[83] See the five entries for "House of the Counsellor" in George 1993:65–66 (§41–45), which include "the seat of Ennundaĝallu and Ĝanunḫedu, the counsellors of Marduk" in Esagil at Babylon (§41); "seat of Nuska" in the sanctuary of Ningal at Ur (§42); a shrine at Nippur (§44); a sanctuary of Ea (§45). For other shrines of 'counsel' or 'wisdom', see George 1993:89 (§333, 336), 91 (§355–359, 362, 364–365), 129 (§830), 138 (§951); for those of divine 'decisions', 106 (§544, 546–547); cf. perhaps 137 (§943), "House of the Open Ear."
[84] The following points come from Heimpel 1998b; Gabbay 2014 §9–13.

(^{د}ad-gi4-gi4) attached to a balang-god.[85] As Heimpel notes, "this last name is of particular interest as it merges with the function of [balang]-gods as counselors ... It means that all [balang]-gods were understood as counselors of their divine masters."[86] Both Heimpel and Gabbay note the extension of an instrument's physical 'sounding' or 'resounding' (ad-gi4-gi4) to the idea of 'sounding someone out' or being someone's 'sounding board.'[87] But the Sumerian conception is no mere metaphor, as the instruments' ability to communicate with the divine world was regarded as real. As Gabbay sums up:

> The theological image manifested by these references is of the main deities sharing their deliberations with their beloved counselors, the ad-gi4-gi4 deities, also known as GU4.BALAĜ. As counselors (*mundalku*) they are asked for their opinion on different matters, and they answer (Sum. gi4-gi4) with their voice (ad) ... the advisor echoes the god's speech through his counseling and by that calms him.[88]

These astute observations can be fruitfully applied to the Gudea Cylinders. The 'counsels' to be carried out by Ušumgal-kalama and Lugalsisa implicitly refer to modes of divine communication that will be in fact conducted by temple personnel. As presented in the narrative, however, the relationship between a king and his counseling ministers is equally evoked, since Ningirsu's temple is portrayed as a royal court. That a singer or musician should have a king's ear like this, empowered to advise and soothe, may be compared with the influential position of 'Chief Singer', well known from the OB period,[89] and the representation of musicians playing before seated figures (even when these are convivial scenes).[90] There is also young David's service in the court of Saul, where he soothes the "evil spirit" which besets the king.[91]

But if the poem's mythological imagery is converted back to cult realities, one must conclude that *the instrument itself* possessed the power of such counsel. This explains the passage quoted above, describing the balang's communication of Gudea's message to Ningirsu, whose obedience it will compel. The balang is like a herald and translator who speaks directly to the divine mind, otherwise inaccessible to man, with a special hermeneutic language. One may compare a Hittite text that refers to "the sweet message of the lyre, the sweet message

---

[85] Cf. Heimpel, "Balang-Gods," Section 2c.
[86] Heimpel 1998b:5.
[87] Heimpel 1998b:5; "Balang-Gods," Section 2c.
[88] Gabbay 2014 §13.
[89] See p28n65, 74.
[90] See MgB 2/2:52–53 (fig. 28–29, ca. 2600/2450), 54–57 (fig. 32–34, ca. 2600), 60–61 (fig. 36, ca. 2550), 62–65 (fig. 38–39, 41–43, OAkk. period).
[91] See p165–166.

Chapter Two

of the cymbals."[92] In the Bible, too, one finds evidence, quite abundant, for the *kinnōr* as a medium through which gods and mortals can communicate.[93] The god who 'consults' with his balang-servants is a mirror image of the king who seeks divine guidance through the medium of balang-music. Gudea submits his query, and receives his response, through the balang. The respective musings of god and king meet precisely in the instrument, which is thus a kind of hotline between king and divine patron.

Practically speaking, it would seem that any musical counsel a balang was capable of would need to be activated by its player. This assumes that divinized instruments were in fact played, and not merely venerated. This is the case at least with the divinized *lilissu* in first-millennium lamentation rituals.[94] And, after all, Ušumgal-kalama himself is represented as a musician in the Gudea Cylinders. This leads to the circular conception that the balang-god plays the very instrument of which it is considered the spirit. It effectively plays itself, so that all human agency is effaced. Ultimately this seems to imply that the priest-musicians who played such divinized instruments impersonated, or better instantiated, the balang-god, whose epiphany was presumably synchronous with the ritual-performance itself.[95]

A scene of the Gudea Cylinders describes the king's own duties at the temple:

> To see that the courtyard of the E-ninnu will be filled with joy; to see that the ala-drums and the balang will sound in perfect concert with the sim-cymbals, and to see that his beloved balang Ušumgal-kalama will walk in front of the procession, the ruler who had built the E-ninnu, Gudea, himself entered before Lord Ningirsu.[96]

In the future rituals that are imagined here, as in the earlier balang-rite in which he appealed to Ningirsu, Gudea is the sole visible actor. While this might reflect political posturing *vis-à-vis* the temple clergy,[97] it is also consistent with the ideology of the king as a bridge between the human and divine spheres. To all appearances, Gudea will single-handedly supervise the procession of

---

[92] KBo 12.88.5–10; also KBo 26.137, 2: see HKm:203.
[93] See p158–164.
[94] See p24.
[95] There may have been occasions, however, when the instrument itself was the focus of a ritual, without actually sounding. In the Ishtar ritual from OB Mari, a balang is said to be 'placed'—the instrument was heavy—but whether it was actually played is not made clear; it may rather have been the object of lamentation. See further p85, 291–292.
[96] Gudea Cylinders B 15.19–16.2.
[97] Cf. Gabbay 2014 §4 (in another context): "by donating the main instrument which accompanied one of the most important prayers of the temple cult, the king was able to be involved in the ritual and not only the temple and its personnel."

Ušumgal-kalama, and the balang-god will "walk in front." On the mythological level, this evokes a scene of king and balang-god side-by-side—an epiphany in which the cultic agents necessary for bringing it about are eclipsed, and suggesting a 'guardian angel' relationship between Ušumgal-kalama and Gudea, akin to 'presentation scenes' on cylinder-seals of the Akkadian and Ur III periods.[98] But if the scene is imagined on the mundane level, we are still left with Gudea as the leading human agent, escorting his divinized balang at the head of the procession. The two visions suggest a close association between king and balang, perhaps even their identification. Note especially that the king's duties in the passage just given are strikingly reminiscent of Ušumgal-kalama himself, who is to supervise musical rites of just this sort.

Shulgi and the Royal Ideal of Music

The conceit of the king who personally performs complex state rites as a doppelgänger of a balang-god leads naturally to the image of the musician king, and his own enactment or instantiation of divinized instruments. Much relevant material is connected with Shulgi (ca. 2094–2047), second and greatest ruler of the Ur III dynasty, who continued his father Ur-Nammu's ambitious temple-building program and expanded the state's borders to their greatest extent.[99] The issue is caught up with the relatively short-lived phenomenon of divine kingship in Mesopotamia.[100] The first king known to have been proclaimed divine is Naram-Sin of Akkad (ca. 2260–2223); one of his inscriptions describes it as a reward from the gods, petitioned by the people, for quelling the 'Great Revolt.'[101] Divine kingship is next seen flourishing under Shulgi, systematically elaborated the under the political conditions of his time. Shulgi presented himself as the interface between the gods and human society, itself conceived as a terrestrial reflection of the divine realm with its complex hierarchy of powers.[102] This model was inherited by his successors, and at least superficially perpetuated by the Isin dynasty, which set itself up as heir to the Ur III legacy; but by this time

---

[98] E.g. Collon 1987:36; Asher-Greve and Westenholz 2013:199–202, with emphasis on underlying rituals.
[99] Building works of Shulgi and Ur-Nammu: Sallaberger 1999:137–140, 151–152.
[100] For divine kingship, see the lucid account of Michalowski 2008, distinguishing between sacred and divine (41–42).
[101] Bassetki statue: Al-Fouadi 1976; RIME 2 1.4.10; CS 2 no. 90; Kuhrt 1995 1:48–49, 51–52. Great Revolt: Westenholz 1999:51–54.
[102] For the evidence of Shulgi's divine status, Sallaberger 1999:152–156.

the ideology began to wane, "consciously rejected by subsequent generations," and dying out for all practical purposes during the OB period.[103]

One aspect of the Shulgi's divine perfection was his absolute command of music, within an otherwise sophisticated musical culture flourishing under royal patronage.[104] This is well illustrated by passages in his royal praise-hymns—a new genre which arose in connection with divine kingship, and a key source for its conceptions. These poems, cast in the first person, consist almost entirely of ostensible self-praise for the universal perfection of the royal person.[105] The most expansive passage relating to the king's musical abilities is worth quoting in full:

> I, Shulgi, king of Ur, have also devoted myself to the musician's art. Nothing is too complicated for me; I know the depth and breadth of the tigi and the adab, the perfection of music. When I fix the frets on the lute (giššukarak), which enraptures my heart, I never damage its neck; I have established procedures for raising and lowering its intervals. On the [sc. instrument with] eleven tuning-pegs, the lyre (zami), I know the harmonious tuning. I am familiar with the three-stringed instrument (sa-eš) and with drumming on its musical sound-box. I can take in my hands the Mari-lyre (miritum), which brings the house [sc. astonished] silence. I know the finger technique of the horizontal-lyre (alĝar) and the Sabu-lyre (sabitum), royal creations. In the same way I can produce sounds from the King-of-Kish instrument (urzababitum), the ḫarḫar, the zan(n)aru-lyre,[106] the urgula and the dim-lu-magura. Even if they bring to me, as one might to a skilled musician, a lute (gudi) that I have not heard before, when I strike it up I make its true sound known; I am able to handle it just like something that has been in my hands before. If in tuning I tighten, loosen or set [sc. the strings], they do not slip from my hand. I never make the double-pipe sound like a shepherd's instrument, and on my own initiative I can wail a sumunša or make a lament as well as anyone who does it regularly.[107]

---

[103] Quotation: Michalowski 2008:41. For Isin's cultural relationship to Ur, and the promotion of legitimate continuity from Ur in royal hymns and other media, see Michalowski 1983:242–243.

[104] For the royal promotion and organization of music in this period, see the studies cited in n65 above.

[105] Hallo 1963; Klein 1981.

[106] For zan(n)aru—with the double-n guaranteed for Akk. by *Diri* III.043—see further p55, 78–79.

[107] *Shulgi B*, 154–174, trans. adapted from ETCSL 2.4.2.02, partially on the basis of text and commentary in Krispijn 1990 (who attempts some identifications with the catalogue of MgB 2/2). See especially 8–12 for miritum, sabitum, urzababitum, and zan(n)aru. For the first two, which are also found in *Enki's Journey to Nippur* as part of the god's temple orchestra at Eridu (ETCSL 1.1.4, 60–67), see too Hartmann 1960:77–78; cf. Castellino 1972:162–170; Henshaw 1993:84–86. Similar

No doubt a king could be well educated, and really cultivate music. Yasmah-Addu of Mari (crowned ca. 1790) may have studied as a boy with his father's master musician.[108] One of the Hurrian hymns from Ugarit may have been composed by king 'Ammurapi of Ugarit.[109] Psalms were attributed to several Biblical kings.[110] But Shulgi's claims are so extravagant as to be incredible. The essentially symbolic nature of his 'achievements' is revealed by their deliberate recycling in the royal praise-hymns of Ishme-Dagan (ca. 1953–1935), fourth king of the Isin dynasty.[111] At the pinnacle of human society, the king was all things to his people—a living god, the ideal embodiment of civilization and all its arts. His preternatural beauty made the royal shepherd a worthy spouse of Inanna, a new Dumuzi. He was the perfect soldier, the wisest judge, the best diviner, the ultimate scribe—and the ideal musician, of celebratory song and lamentation alike.

Thus, although the royal praise hymns are composed in the first person, there is no compelling reason to believe that the king himself was always, or perhaps ever, the actual composer. (If he were, of course, it would be still more interesting.) The mode of presentation allows any king to compose and perform, at least in spirit, through the mouth of a singer or singers who voiced these songs in the first person. This circular conception is similar to the poetics of divinized instruments considered above.[112] With both, human ministers are effaced, and their offices, actions, and abilities are symbolically co-opted by a higher power—be it god, king, or god-king.

The urzababitum which Shulgi claims to play presents a quite remarkable specimen of the interaction between divinized instrument and divine-king-as-musician. The urzababitum takes its name, for some mysterious reason, from Ur-Zababa, the historical king of Kish whose throne was seized by Sargon the Great.[113] Ur-Zababa himself is found in the OB/MA god-list An:Anum as a balang-deity of Ninurta.[114] The urzababitum is defined elsewhere as "the god Ninurta's

---

boasts are found in *Shulgi C*, segment B, 75–101 (especially 77–78, ETCSL 2.4.2.03); *Shulgi E*, 34–35 (ETCSL 2.4.2.05).

[108] Ziegler 2006b:36.
[109] See p119, 383.
[110] See p178, 383.
[111] See p80–81.
[112] See p30–33.
[113] Could there be a connection here with the obscure but important honorific "King of Kish" which was assumed by several Sumerian rulers of the ED III period and Sargon's dynasty? See generally RlA 5:608–610 (Edzard, Kiš A); Maeda 1981; Kuhrt 1995 2:41–43.
[114] An:Anum I 268 (cited according to Litke 1998). For this god-list, and this entry, see further Heimpel, "Balang-Gods," Section 2c and 53.

instrument" or "Ninurta of music."[115] The specificity of this material makes it reasonable to treat it as a semantic system, despite the disparate dates of the sources. One therefore has a divinized king (Shulgi) who plays ('takes counsel' from) an instrument named after another divinized king (Ur-Zababa), who as the god of the self-same instrument is in turn counselor to a higher master-god—Ninurta, himself the image of the warrior-king.[116] To make matters still more complex, Yasmah-Addu, king of OB Mari, also possessed an (Akk.) *urza-babîtum*, this one probably featuring his *own* name as a theophoric element.[117]

This material lets us glimpse an intricate network of ideas about divinized instruments, the cognitive interaction of instrument and player, and the elaboration of both in the ritual poetics of kingship. Another such case may be a GU4.BALAĜ servant of the moon-god Suen/Sin, called Amar-Suen ('Calf of Suen'); for this is the name of Shulgi's successor (ca. 2046–2038), while Suen/Sin was the patron god of the dynasty.[118] Similarly Ishbi-Erra, first king of the Isin dynasty, dedicated a divinized balang called 'Ishbi-Erra trusts in Enlil'.[119] To judge from its name, this instrument was a servant-god of Enlil. And yet, the incorporation of Ishbi-Erra's own name suggests that the balang was equally an intermediary between the earthly king and his divine counterpart.

These conceptions will be important when considering David, an overt 'lyre-king' serving, praising, and giving voice to Yahweh. And the *kinnōr*-playing David is in turn our best parallel for understanding Kinyras himself—a Divine Lyre lingering on in Greco-Cypriot and Levantine myth, remodeled as an ancient lyre-playing king in the service of 'Aphrodite'.

It is noteworthy that the Shulgi-hymn cited above mentions at least four instruments of 'foreign' provenance and/or associations (the Mari-lyre, the Sabu-lyre, the 'king-of-Kish instrument', and the zan[n]aru).[120] Elsewhere in the Ur III hymns, the Sabu-lyre and Mari-lyre again occur side-by-side, within the larger instrumentarium. These passages suggest that the contemporary court and

---

[115] Ḫḫ 79–80 (MSL 6:123); Ḫg 169 (MSL 6:142); Diri III.49 (MSL 6:119, 15:138): see Falkenstein and Matouš 1934:147 §49; Castellino 1972:166 §166; Heimpel 1998b:6 (translating Sum. nârūti as "music").

[116] As U. Gabbay notes, "It is also not coincidental that the Urzababa instrument is the balang of Ninurta, since this god as hero going out to war was often conceived [as] the mythological mirror image of Mesopotamian kings" (communication, March, 2010).

[117] See further p86.

[118] An:Anum III 51, noted by U. Gabbay (communication, March, 2010); but Heimpel, "Balang-Gods," 53, sees in the name rather "a direct reference to the moon-god."

[119] RIME 4 1.1.1, 13–14; CS 2 no. 92; Radner 2005:56 no. 82; FM 9:222 (on 8); Heimpel, "Balang-Gods," 40.

[120] For identifications, see p34n107, 35–36. For the zan(n)aru (Krispijn's "Anatolian lyre"), see further p78–79.

temple ensembles were deliberately cosmopolitan, with a diversity of instruments representing the cultural horizons of Ur. When the king extends his claim of mastery to instruments "I have not heard before," one imagines musical exotica sent as gifts or tribute, or carried by visiting musicians from beyond Ur's own periphery. Shulgi's international musical vision is therefore an expression of both cultural prestige and political power. It equally alludes to the harmonious peace that his political power has enabled—a portrait of the king at rest from his campaigns, passing his time by enjoying the varied musical delights his efforts have assembled.[121]

Lovely Lyrics For Inanna

We must also glance at the royal hymns that intimate a relationship between the king and Inanna/Ishtar, since here too one sees the conjunction of royal ideology and music-making. The king's position as the goddess's favorite is very ancient. T. Jacobsen sought its roots in the agricultural revolution, interpreting the famous Uruk vase (ca. 3100)—showing Inanna in front of her temple, receiving offerings from a king or priest-king figure—as reflecting some form of hierogamy or 'Sacred Marriage'.[122] That the goddess was royal patroness in the OAkk. period is shown by the inscriptions of Naram-Sin, who evidently "joined the goddess Ishtar-Annunitum as divine city ruler, and possibly as her consort."[123] Ishtar regularly appears as the divine patroness of Sargon and Naram-Sin in the legends that developed around the Akkadian kings.[124] The N-S royal hymns contain many literary reflections of Inanna as the protectress of the king, who assumes the position of Dumuzi, the goddess's ancient, archetypal lover.[125]

---

[121] By contrast, catastrophic situations are marked by the silencing of music; for example, *Ur-Nammu A* (*The Death of Ur-Nammu*, ETCSL 2.4.1.1), 187–188 ("My *tigi*, *adab*, flute and *zamzam* songs have been turned into laments because of me. The instruments of the house of music have been propped against the wall."); so too the ruin of Isin in *The Destroyed House* (Jacobsen 1987:475–477, lines 17–24). For the *Curse of Agade*, see below.

[122] Jacobsen 1975:76, "cultic drama in Mesopotamia as elsewhere has its roots back in 'primitive' society, that is, one based on hunting, herding, or incipient agriculture. Here the drama was a rite of direct sympathetic magic aiming to create fertility."

[123] Quotation: Michalowski 2008:34. Ishtar appears first in the list of gods who supported Naram-Sin's divinization (Bassetki statue: RIME 2 1.4.10; Foster I.c3, cd.

[124] Westenholz 1997:35, 83, 109, 137–139, etc.

[125] The convergence of these themes is seen clearly in *Shulgi X* (ETCSL 2.4.2.24) and *Iddin-Dagan A* (ETCSL 2.5.3.1). Shulgi as shepherd: *Shulgi D* 2, 60, 364; *E* 5, 11; *G* 28–30, 49–53, 60–62; *P* 11–14, 17, 56–66; *Q* 6, 28, 45–48; *R* 41, 67, 84, 89; *X* 9, 37, 40, 53; etc. (these are ETCSL 2.4.2.04, 05, 07, 16, 18, 24, respectively).

Chapter Two

The precise nature and purpose of any actual rites underpinning this ideology at various periods remain disputed. Recent studies downplay the more 'hands-on' interpretations of Frazer and his followers in favor of symbolic rituals tied to regeneration of the land and periodic renewal of royal legitimacy and social order.[126] In any case, the poetic treatment of intimacy between king and goddess remains an observable artifact in its own right, with especially rich material from the N-S and OB periods.

B. Pongratz-Leisten has recently elucidated an important benefit of the king's hierogamous relationship with Inanna/Ishtar. The goddess served as a messenger from Enlil and the assembly of gods, "transferring divine knowledge to the king in order to allow him to partake in the divine plan."[127] When in the OB period hierogamy faded from royal ideology, a close relationship between king and goddess persisted in the venue of prophecy, with Ishtar continuing to function as an oracular go-between. In the present state of evidence, the richest material comes from N-A prophecies, which evince a systematic elaboration of the ideology, with the goddess now interpreted as the 'spirit' or 'breath' of the transcendent god Aššur—the medium by which male and female prophets alike, in an ecstatic state sometimes achieved by lamentative techniques, could consult the divine council, headed by Aššur, and report back to the king by channeling the voice of Ishtar.[128]

Such ideas are compatible with Shulgi's boasts of expertise in omen-reading ("my diviner watches in amazement like an idiot"),[129] and help explain the representation of Inanna as a sort of Muse in the royal hymns. *Shulgi B* makes the king boast that "the protective deity of my power has perfected the songs of my might."[130] The poem's opening verses—"He praises his own power in song"—show that these "songs of my might" are the selfsame royal hymns that Shulgi is represented as having composed and sung.[131] Hence the goddess guides the king's own (real or notional) singing. Another royal hymn represents

---

[126] For an up-to-date survey of approaches formerly and presently taken, see the essays in Nissinen and Uro 2008, especially those of P. Lapinkivi, B. Pongratz-Leisten, and M. Nissinen. Representative recent studies are Cooper 1993; Sweet 1994; Steinkeller 1999; Jones 2003; Lapinkivi 2004. Cf. RlA 4:251–259 (Renger, *Heilige Hochzeit), for cautions about earlier studies, of which one may cite *inter al.* Jacobsen in Frankfort et al. 1946:198–200; Frankfort 1948:295–299; Gurney 1962; Kramer 1963; Kramer 1969:132–133, for the idea of transmission to Anatolia, Greece, and Cyprus in connection with Adonis; Yamauchi 1973; Jacobsen 1975.

[127] Pongratz-Leisten 2008:54–60 (quotation at 60), et passim; further references in Parpola 1997:CIVn237; Jones 2003:291.

[128] Parpola 1997:XVIII–XXXVI, XLVII–XLVIII (with reference to antecedents), et passim. Note that here Ishtar often appears in the role of the king's *mother*.

[129] *Shulgi B* (ETCSL 2.4.2.01),131–149.

[130] *Shulgi B*, 381–382.

[131] *Shulgi B*, 1–10 (quotation at 9–10).

Inanna herself singing an erotic Dumuzi-song to Shulgi, promising "I will decree a good fate for him!"[132] A final gyration elsewhere touches upon the realities of performance and perhaps ritual, while simultaneously removing the king to the divine realm:

> My singers praised me with songs accompanied by seven tigi-lyres. My spouse, the maiden Inanna, the lady, the joy of heaven and earth, sat with me at the banquet.[133]

In this vignette—a striking example of seven-magic combined with music (see below)—the king receives musical offerings, the godly honors he enjoys with his goddess wife, here still a maiden, performed by his royal musicians. Yet once again, by the logic of genre, it should actually be Shulgi who—presumably inspired by Inanna, as in *Shulgi B*—sings about his own musicians. This creates an infinite regrade in which Shulgi embodies the entire musical activity of his court.[134] Subject and object, performer and recipient, merge in a single musical epiphany.

The conceit of the musician-king performing in the 'Sacred Marriage' is also found in a hymn of Iddin-Dagan (ca. 1974–1954), third king of the Isin Dynasty. The poem is devoted exclusively to praising Inanna, and includes a quite erotic description of her union with the king.[135] Again the hymn is presented as sung by the king himself:

> I shall greet the great lady of heaven, Inanna! ... For the young lady I shall sing a song about her grandeur, about her greatness, about her exalted dignity ... Making silver alĝar instruments sound for her, they parade before her, holy Inanna. I shall greet the great lady of heaven, Inanna![136]

The passage is valuable for envisioning the participation of actual cult-musicians. As presented, however, they merely echo and amplify the king's own praises of the goddess. It seems they are to sing the very hymn in which they are themselves so described. Once again, a purposefully circular construction blurs the line between king and musicians, spotlighting the royal performance.

The muse-like role of Inanna in these texts is a suggestive precedent for Aphrodite, who exhibits similar qualities, especially in connection with

---

[132] *Shulgi X* (ETCSL 2.4.2.24), 13–41.
[133] *Shulgi A* (ETCSL 2.4.2.01), 81–83. For the tigi instrument, see p531n1, 575, 606–7n92.
[134] Compare the double harpist imagery on a thirteenth-century bronze stand from Kourion: p388–392.
[135] *Iddin-Dagan A* (ETCSL 2.5.3.1), 181–194.
[136] *Iddin-Dagan A*, 3, 9–10, 35–37.

Cyprus.[137] That the lyre-playing Kinyras was seen as her royal lover is a still more striking parallel. The royal 'takeover' of cult-performances will be seen at Ugarit—where there is also a Singer (or singers) of Astarte active in the royal palace[138]—and still more so with David who, like Shulgi and Iddin-Dagan, outshines his own cult-musicians when leading the Ark to Jerusalem.[139]

Music and Seven-Magic

In early Greek sources, the orderly relations of tunings and rhythms were probably believed capable of inducing or restoring, via sympathetic magic, a similar state in either the natural or social world. Prominent in the sources for Greek musical mysticism is the magical powers of the number seven.[140] Seven-numerology is of course equally ubiquitous in the literature of the ANE. Yet this was not always a mere literary convention, a 'convenient number' signifying totality, or a story-structuring device.[141] I have already mentioned some ritual and cultic aspects of the Divine Heptad.[142] Ritual texts from various times and places show that seven-magic was an important structuring device.[143] We shall encounter examples at Ebla, Ugarit, Emar, and in the Bible.[144] The not-infrequent conjunction of seven-magic and ritual music is to be connected, I believe, with ANE traditions of heptatonic tuning on stringed instruments.[145] This conception goes back, in Mesopotamia, to the OB period at the latest, when a complete tuning cycle was formulated in terms of the (Akk.) *sammû*.[146] Although this was a nine-stringed chordophone (at least in theory), the heptatonic structure of the tuning-system itself is clear.[147] The same perspective is now graphically confirmed by CBS 1766, a neo- or late-Babylonian tablet that visualizes the

---

[137] See Franklin 2014:224–226.
[138] See p114.
[139] See p167–174.
[140] For the wonder-working lyre in early Greek poetics, and the importance of seven-magic, see Franklin 2002b:17–21; Franklin 2006a:52–63.
[141] For the symbolism of seven in the ANE generally, a good source book is Reinhold 2008; for Greece with some discussion of neighboring cultures, Roscher 2003; in Pythagorean cosmology, Burkert 1972a:465–482 et passim.
[142] See p24, 39.
[143] Cf. Wyatt 2001:92–94; Wyatt 2007:54 *vis-à-vis* the Ugaritian ritual texts: "evidently the number seven was of symbolic significance ... no doubt with broad cosmological and ontological echoes."
[144] See index s.v. 'seven-magic'.
[145] Franklin 2006a:58.
[146] For an introduction to these texts, see RlA 8:463–482 (Kilmer, *Musik A I*) with further literature.
[147] From the so-called Retuning Text UET 7/74 (Ur, ca. 1800), as well as CBS 10996 (Nippur, ca. 500–300), which enumerates and names intervals formed from the first seven strings. For these texts, see also p59–60, 97, 119, 392, 451.

Instrument Gods and Musician Kings in Early Mesopotamia

heptatonic tuning cycle as a seven-pointed star; some ulterior, extra-musical purpose seems likely, but remains elusive.[148]

These heptadic harmonic phenomena were surely perceived, from early on, as manifestations of 'sacred seven.' Chordophones especially, and other instruments by extension, were probably seen as structured by, and emitting waves of, sacred seven-ness. This should be borne in mind when dealing with such details as the seven tigi-instruments on which Shulgi's singers sang their royal praises, or much later the gestures of seven-magic in the ritual(s) of *lilissu*-divinization. There is also an archaic tablet from Girsu (Tello, ca. 2400) that records offerings of "seven liters of oil and seven liters of dates for the seven balangs."[149] Similarly, in the *Curse of Agade*, during Akkad's prosperity, "the heart of the city was of tigi-lyres"; but when, after the hybris of Naram-Sin causes Enlil to destroy the city, the survivors try to appease the god, the chief lamentation singer "for seven days and seven nights put in place seven balangs, like the firm base of heaven" (this action is accompanied by lamentative music to percussion instruments).[150] As Heimpel observes, "the motif of the seven balangs ... meant that all festival activity was then pooled in the one great effort to pacify Enlil."[151]

Another half-dozen such examples can be given.[152]

Conclusion

Mesopotamian sources present very rich evidence for the practice and ideology of music in many contexts. The material's abundance varies considerably with time and place through accidents of survival and discovery. I have restricted my discussion to those issues that provide the best parallels for Kinyras, Kinnaru of Ugarit, and Syro-Levantine *kinnāru*-culture generally: divinized cult-tools, their construction and anthropomorphosis in myth; conceptions of musical cognition and communication with the gods through this medium; and royal ideology

---

[148] Horowitz 2006 (*ed. princ.*); Waerzeggers and Siebes 2007 (connecting to musical texts, suggested emendations); Horowitz and Shnider 2009 (collation and verification of some proposed re-readings); Shnider 2010 (suggesting some connection with astronomical and/or divinatory lore).

[149] TSA 1 ix:12–14 (dated to end of first dynasty of Lagash, p. IX).

[150] ETCSL 2.1.5, 34–36, 196–204. Translation after Cooper 1983 and Jacobsen 1987; cf. Heimpel, "Balang-Gods," 43. Discussion: PHG:16–17, 58. For music as symbolizing Agade's prosperity, Cooper 1983:38–39; 238; 252. For the identity of tigi-lyre, see 531n1, 575, 606–7n92.

[151] "Balang-Gods," Section 2c.

[152] Further material: "Balang-Gods," Section 2c and 9, 11, 37, 43; PHG:91, 117, 141, 161n55–56. Probably relevant is the intersection of balang-cult with the lunar calendar. A monthly offering is known from Umma during the Ur III period, made to the 'Balang of the Day-of-Laying', that is, when the moon was invisible before starting again to wax; presumably the occasion called for apotropaic magic. Cited by Heimpel 1998a:6–7 and "Balang-Gods," 28. Cf. Linssen 2004:93 and 306–320 for the kettledrum's use in late Babylonian rituals relating to lunar eclipse.

and self-representation, including ideas of hierogamy. The separate functions of Ningirsu's two balang-gods will also be echoed by the celebratory and lamentative contexts in which Kinyras and the *knr* are found. Mesopotamia is of course a different world from Cyprus and its environs, so one must not expect *exact* parallels. Nevertheless the material considered here will help illuminate many otherwise obscure facets of Kinyras and his mythology.

3

The *Knr*

THE MESOPOTAMIAN MATERIAL, together with the Divine Kinnaru of Ugarit and further evidence from the Hurro-Hittite world, indicates that the divinization of instruments was one facet of an 'international' music culture operative in the BA Near East. Fortunately, the latter enormous subject need not be exhausted here. We may simply focus on the *knr*, for which there is relatively abundant textual evidence and associated iconography. To be sure, this multiform word/instrument does offer an instructive sample of a 'global economy' of music. But it is also the very soul of Kinnaru. So a detailed examination of the instrument's geographical diffusion and cultural position, both practical and symbolic, will illuminate the larger environment from which, I shall argue, Kinyras sailed for Cyprus.

Jubal: Looking Back From Israel

The *knr* was long known best from Heb. *kinnōr*, the famous 'harp'—actually lyre (see below)—of David, with more than forty occurrences in the canonical Old Testament, and many further mentions in the apocrypha, the Dead Sea Scrolls, and Rabbinic literature.[1] The prestigious position which this suggests is paralleled by a wide range of performance contexts, often exalted: sacred psalms, royal praise poetry, triumphal processions and other revelry, musical exorcism, ecstatic prophecy, and even lyric plaints.[2]

The Bible itself, however, is well aware that its *kinnōr* had had a much more ancient past outside of Israel and Judah. The instrument is mentioned in Canaanite/Phoenician contexts, and among the Aramaeans of the patriarchal age.[3] Its invention is appropriately placed in the antediluvian chapters of

---

[1] Sendrey 1969:266–278; Sendrey 1974:169–172; Polin 1974:67–68; MGG 1:1516–1517 (Braun); MAIP:16–17.
[2] For lyric lamentation, see Chapter 12.
[3] Phoenician/Canaanite contexts: Isaiah 14:10–11 (Rephaim, see further p146–147), 23:15–16 and Ezekiel 26.13 (Tyre). Aramaean (Laban story): Gen. 25:20, 31:20, 27; cf. Polin 1974, 16–17. The

Chapter Three

Genesis, where it is attributed to Jubal—a seventh-generation descendant of Cain—as part of a larger family of culture-heroes:[4]

> Lamech took two wives; the name of one was Adah, and the name of the other Zillah. Adah bore Jabal; he was the ancestor of those who live in tents and have livestock. His brother's name was Jubal; he was the ancestor of all those who play the lyre (*kinnōr*) and pipe (*'ūghābh*). Zillah bore Tubal-Cain, who made all kinds of bronze and iron tools. The sister of Tubal-Cain was Naamah.[5]

According to this chronology, the '*kinnōr*' had existed from time out of mind, long before the emergence of 'Israel'—symbolized by Jacob—from the larger popular matrix descended from Noah. The passage incorporates a further chronological indicator: the *kinnōr* arises within a nomadic way of life such as was believed to have characterized the age of the patriarchs.[6] An equally important component of this ancient lifestyle, according to the inclusion of Tubal-Cain, was the working of metals.

This portrait of Lamech's family has often been connected with an Egyptian tomb-painting from Beni-Hassan, dating to the Twelfth Dynasty in the early second millennium (Figure 3 = 4.1j).[7] It shows a seemingly nomadic troupe—men, women, and herd animals—prominent among whom is a man towards the back who carries and plays the lyre. One obvious explanation for his presence is that music is "the provision of the traveller."[8] But there is more. The accompanying text identifies the troupe as thirty-seven "Asiatics of Šwt" (*'3mw n šwt*), led by a ruler with the Canaanite name of Abî-shar, who were bringing a load of the cosmetic *stibium* (antimony) to the owner of the grave, a high-ranking noble

---

    precise relationship between the Biblical Aramaeans and their historical counterpart is somewhat cloudy. See the recent synthesis of Younger 2007. Aram, their eponymous ancestor in the Table of Nations, is an eighth-generation great uncle of Abraham: Gen. 10:22–31, 11:11–26.

[4] Still useful is the discussion of Baethgen 1888:149–151; North 1964:378–383.

[5] Gen. 4:19–22. For *'ūghābh* here see Cassuto 1961 1:236, cf. 235, suggesting a folk etymology connecting 'Cain' (*Qayin*), suffixed to the name of Tubal and referring originally to 'smith' (< *qyn*, 'forge'; cf. YGC:41; North 1964:378), and *qīnā* ('poetic composition' > 'dirge'); cf. Sellers 1941:40–41. Perhaps a similar association implicated *qyn* and *kinnōr*, contributing to the development of a musician-craftsman mytheme; for this wider Syro-Levantine pattern, along with symptomatic variants in the reception of Lamech's family, see Chapter 18.

[6] Cf. North 1964:380, who derives Jubal, Jabal, and Tubal alike from Heb. *yabal*, 'bring in procession', and notes the idea's relevance to both psalmody and caravaneering.

[7] See Newberry 1893:41–72, especially 69, and pl. XXX–XXXI; Shedid 1994:53–65 and fig. 20. Comparison with Jubal and Tubal: Albright 1956:98, 200n7; Ribichini 1981:51 (also noting Kinyras' metallurgical connections); Bayer 1982:32; Staubli 1991:30–35 and fig. 15a; MAIP:77–79; Collon 2006:13.

[8] In the words of Ibn 'Abd Rabbihi (ca. 860–940 CE): SOM 1:9.

The Knr

Figure 3 'Asiatic' troupe with lyrist, tomb-painting, Beni-Hassan, Twelfth Dynasty, ca. 1900. Drawn from Shedid 1994 fig. 20.

named Chnumhotep, in the service of Amenemhet II. Here is early evidence for the circulation of Syro-Levantine lyres beyond their home range. That the instrument is found in a kind of royal context—'accompanying' a king or chieftain—will find parallels at Ebla, Mari, Ugarit, and elsewhere in the Bible. The group is equally prepared for metalworking: they pack anvil, bellows, and tongs. The parallel to Lamech's family is certainly striking—although we shall see that the Biblical portrait is but one example of a more widespread association of music and craftsmanship, which remained a productive mytheme in the Syro-Levantine sphere down into the Byzantine period.[9]

Returning to Jubal himself, it seems significant that he has been lodged in a genealogical context. This device is of course natural for representing the development of civilization; it was equally exploited by Philo of Byblos for his comparable Phoenician history.[10] Yet it probably also acknowledges the early existence of musical 'tribes' or 'guilds' of some sort, with membership at least quasi-hereditary, long before the organization of the First Temple.[11] The evidence for

---

[9] See p453–455.
[10] See p446.
[11] Cf. AOM:289 (Kraeling and Mowry); Cassuto 1961:235–236; PIW 2:80. This is also how Theodore Bar Koni (fl. ca. 800) understood the passage (*Liber scholiorum, Mimrā* 2.97: Hespel and Draguet

Chapter Three

various forms of official musical management in the BA, from Ebla, Mari, and Ugarit—to mention only those that bear most directly on the 'Bible lands'—lets us appreciate the 'accuracy' of Jubal as an ultimate musical ancestor.

We must remember finally the last member of Lamech's family, Naamah. Although she lacks detail here, her siblings entitle us to expect that she too was regarded as some sort of culture-hero. In fact, extra-Biblical sources show that Naamah was the subject of a lively popular tradition, being associated with songs, laments, and an ancient women's practice of frame-drumming—before developing a Rabbinic afterlife as a demonic seductrix.[12] As such, she complements the 'lyre' and 'pipe', which are credited here to Jubal. Together they constitute a full musical range of strings, winds, and percussion, and embrace both male and female musical activity. The overall instrumentation is very close both to the situation at Ugarit and the Cypro-Phoenician symposium bowls.[13]

Identifying the *Knr*

The Bible's memory of an ancient *kinnōr* is confirmed by relatively abundant lexical and iconographic evidence from the wider NE.

The desire to match ancient instrument names with iconographic representations and physical remains goes back to the earliest phases of historical musicology, when the N-A reliefs offered material for speculation well before enough reliable textual evidence had been amassed to support a broader approach.[14] Yet even now, with dozens of instrument finds and scores of representations, secure correlations are often elusive. When one considers the cultural complexity and chronological immensity of the ANE, it becomes clear that the visual evidence, rich as it is, is but a fragmentary sample.

The *knr*, however, is a partial exception to this rule. The word itself, like most ancient instrument names, is of obscure origin.[15] Nevertheless, the Jewish

---

1981–1982 1:116), although his reference to troops of 'Cainite' musical exorcists may be based merely on deduction from e.g. 1 Samuel 10:5–6.

[12] See with sources LJ 5:147–148n45; Utley 1941:422, 445 et passim; Patai 1964:305–307; Scholem 1974:322, 326, 357–358.

[13] See further Chapters 7 and 11.

[14] See *inter al.* Engel 1870; Guillemin and Duchesne 1935; Galpin 1936; HMI; Sachs 1943; Wegner 1950; Stauder 1957; Stauder 1961; Aign 1963; Stauder 1973; Rimmer 1969; Duchesne-Guillemin 1969; Schmidt-Colinet 1981; RlA 6:571–576 (Kilmer, *Leier A); Rashid 1995; AMEL; Braun 1997, with further literature; DCPIL; Duchesne-Guillemin 1999; Dumbrill 2000; MAIP. The quality of these works varies: some are inevitably dated, but even some recent works must be used with caution. Several excellent recent studies bring hope for the future: HKm; Shehata 2006b; Mirelman 2010; Mirelman 2014; Gabbay 2014; Heimpel 2014; PHG:84–154.

[15] As named from the kind of wood typically used in its construction: Behn 1954:54; Brown 1981:401–402. As onomatopoeic: Kapera 1971:134.

kinnōr was clearly not a harp—as rendered in the King James Version—but a kind of lyre.[16] This is seen first in its common translation as *kithára* in the Septuagint.[17] It is also so glossed in several Greek lexical collections.[18] There is no reason to doubt these equations: the basic similarity of the *kithára* to various Syro-Levantine lyres must have been obvious to all educated inhabitants of the eastern Mediterranean, Hellene or otherwise.[19]

This evidence is corroborated by lyres being the most commonly represented stringed instrument in Levantine and North Syrian art, from the third millennium through the first.[20] In the Levant alone, more than thirty representations are known.[21] Most of the evidence was assembled and discussed by A. Norborg in 1995. Soon afterwards, B. Lawergren compared these with examples from the Aegean, analyzing the whole for regional patterns.[22] My Figures 4 and 5 draw upon their work, incorporating Lawergren's drawings (and a few others).[23] I have separated Bronze and Iron Age specimens between the two diagrams, as this best reflects historical patterns in which we are interested, especially the EIA Aegean migrations eastward. Such distribution maps should naturally be used with care. One must allow for some variability in how instruments were depicted, and the randomness of finds. Where an object was made is often not where it was found; and foreign instruments may have been depicted locally for various reasons. Nevertheless, some broad patterns can be detected.

---

[16] For the organological distinction, see p3n14.

[17] Krauss 1910-1912 3:85; Sellers 1941:36-37. The LXX's alternative renderings ὄργανον and ψαλτήριον pose no problem, although the latter attests a distinction of performance technique, since ψάλλειν implies plucking strings with one's fingers, rather than the πλῆκτρον of Greek tradition. But this was not absolute: see p58, 170, 540.

[18] *Suda*, Hesykhios, Photios *Lexicon*, *Anecdota Graeca* (Bachmann 1828-1829) 1:278, *Anecdota Graeca* (Cramer 1839-1841) 4:36.20: κινύρα· ὄργανον μουσικόν, κιθάρα, *vel sim.*

[19] Cf. Josephus' portrait of Jewish Alexandrians as well integrated into the larger Hellenistic culture: *Against Apion* 2.38-42. For the intimate and productive adjacency of Jews and Hellenes in Palestine, see the illuminating discussions of Lieberman 1942; Bowersock 2000:159-174 (especially 165-172).

[20] Its relevance to *knr* long recognized (e.g. Nougayrol 1968:59; Brown 1981:387), the iconographic evidence is most fully collected and analyzed by Lawergren 1993:67-71; AMEL; DCPIL; see also Vorreiter 1972/1973; Eichmann 2001.

[21] DCPIL:51-57; MAIP:xxxii-xxxvi, 18. Representations of Mesopotamian-style upright harps from LBA Cyprus, Alalakh, Egypt, and the Hittite world are only exceptions proving the rule, being explicable in terms of elite displays of cosmopolitanism through imported status symbols: see p90-92, 392. I leave aside the controversial identification of the Megiddo etching (ca. 3300-3000) as a harp rather than early lyre: see e.g. DCPIL fig. 8a; MAIP:58-65, fig. II.6a-7b; SAM:152 no. 116.

[22] DCPIL.

[23] Numbering of individual images follows DCPIL, q.v. for further bibliography and information about each item, if not otherwise given here (also in AMEL). Those labeled "Figure" refer to the same numbered figure in this book.

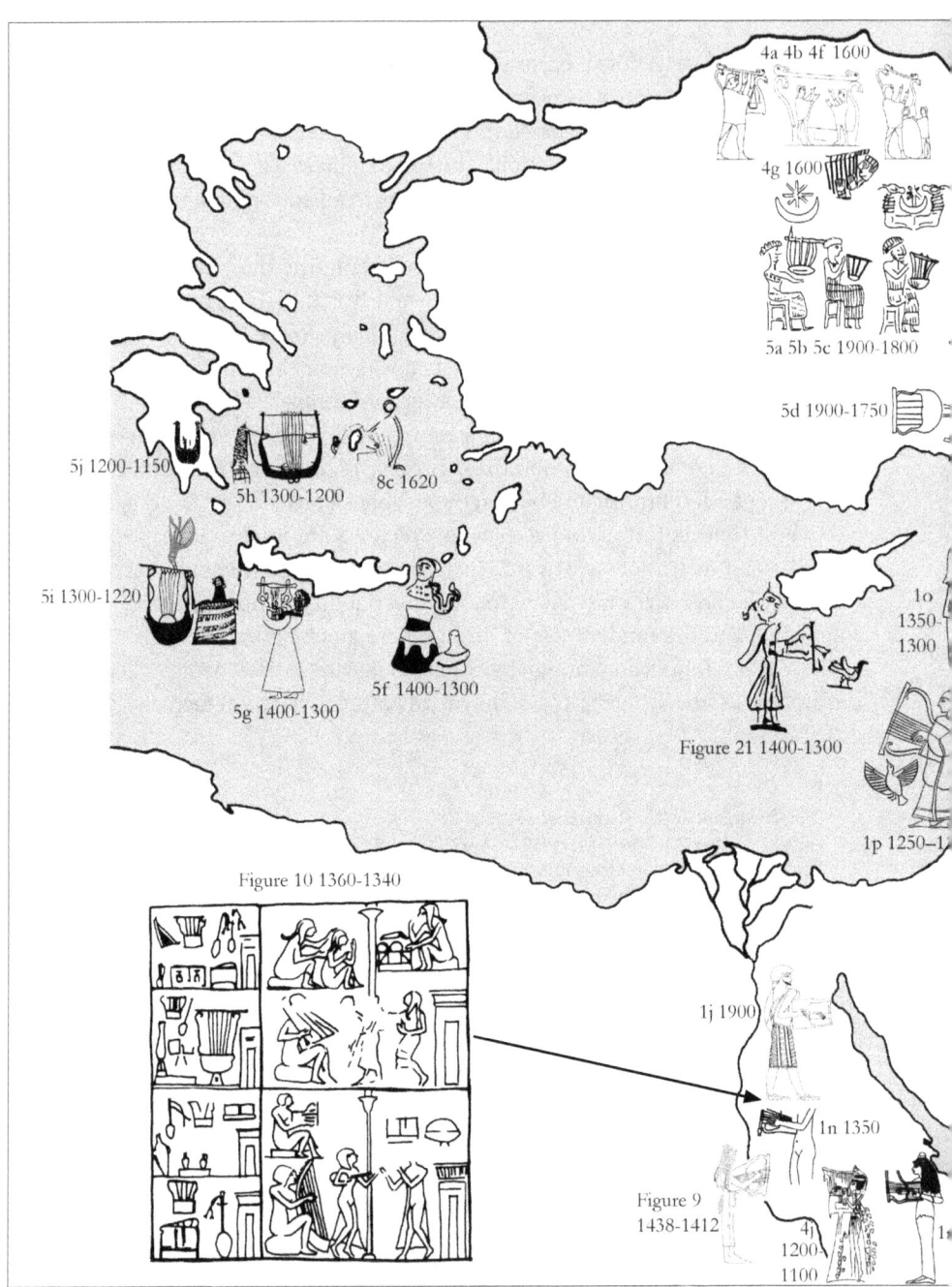

Figure 4 Distribution map of Bronze Age lyres (after DCPIL). Individual images drawn by Bo Lawergren and numbered according to DCPIL figs. 1, 3–5, 8 (used with permission). Other drawings by Glynnis Fawkes are preceded by "Figure," referring to their position in this book.

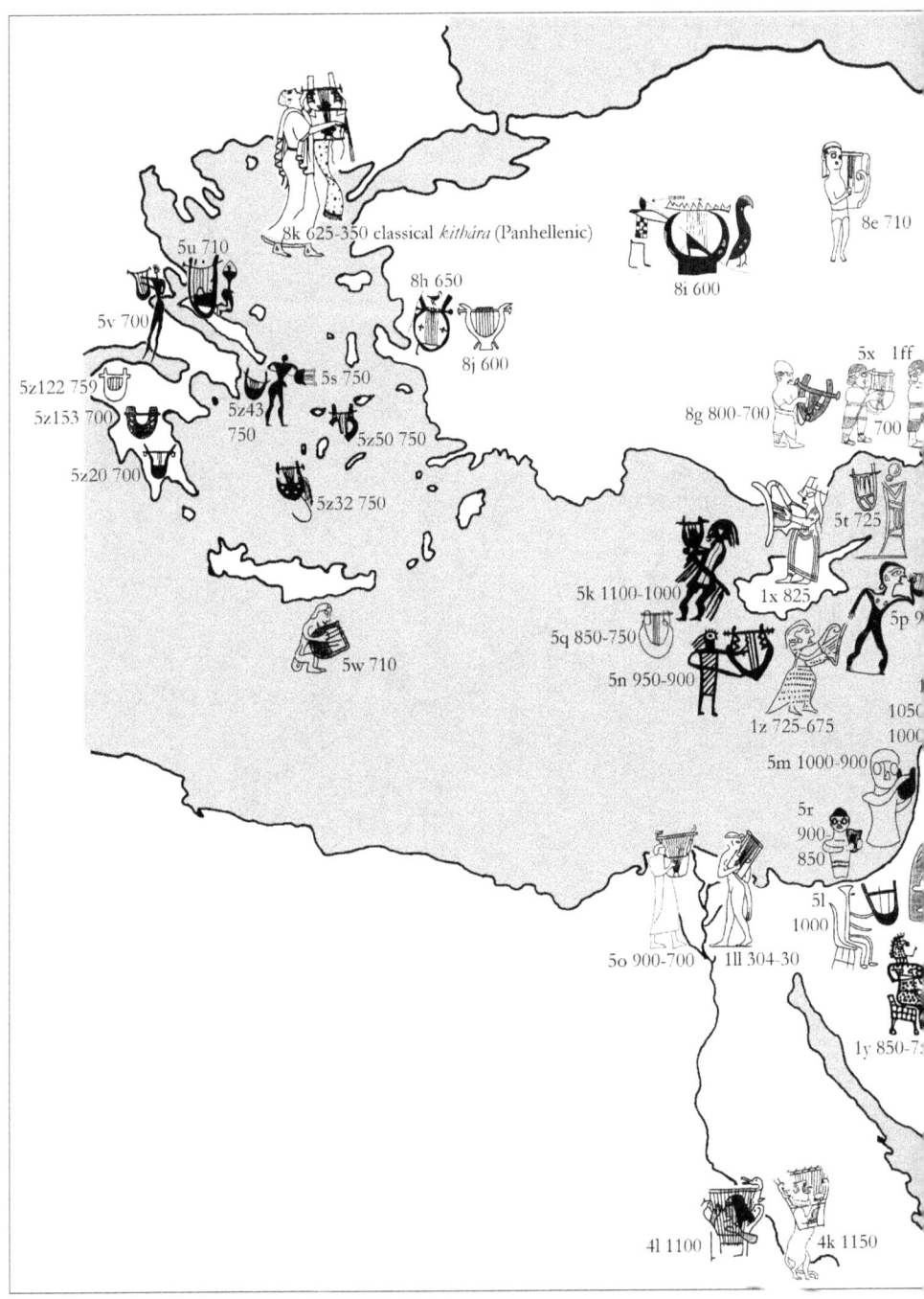

Figure 5 Distribution map of Iron Age lyres (after DCPIL). Individual images drawn by Bo Lawergren and numbered according to DCPIL figs. 1, 3–5, 8 (used with permission).

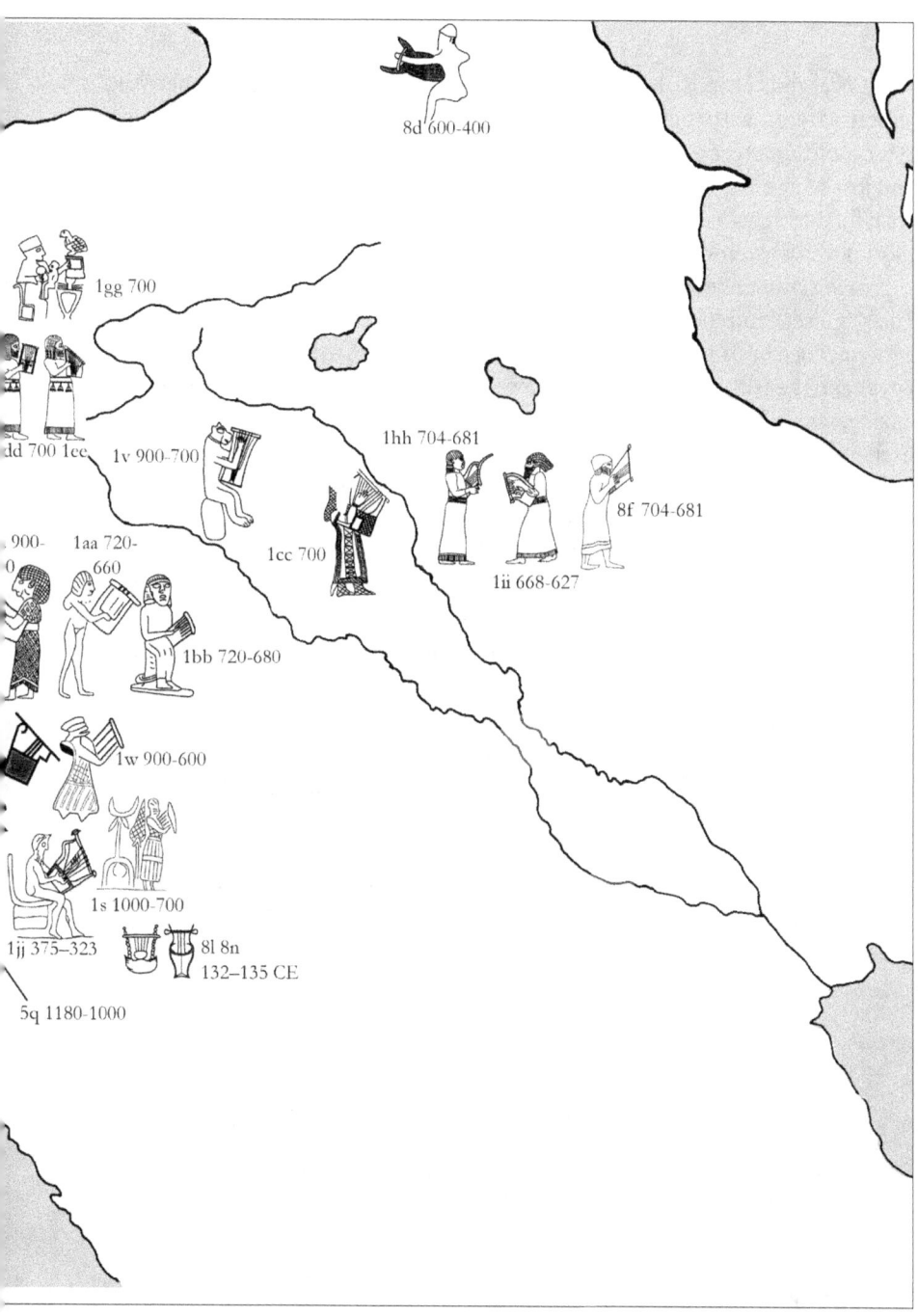

Chapter Three

Lawergren proposed a basic dichotomy (down to about ca. 700) between 'eastern' lyres with flat-based resonators, and round-based 'western' lyres typical of the Aegean.[24] We shall see that this division between East and West, and just where the line should be drawn, concerns Cyprus closely (Chapter 11, with further specimens). For now we shall focus on the 'eastern' lyres, as being most obviously relevant to Kinnaru.

Lawergren divided his eastern lyres into 'thin' (with a substantial 'rectangular' subset) and 'thick', although 'large' and 'small' might be more satisfactory, having a basis in ancient usage.[25] Thick/large lyres are attested both in NK Egypt and the Hittite world, leading Lawergren to posit an unattested Levantine analog, which he would identify with Heb. *nēbel,* often grouped with the *kinnōr* in the Bible (and having an Ugaritic cognate).[26] But perhaps the Egyptian examples are modifications of imported Anatolian specimens, given the 'collecting impulse' otherwise documented for the NK.[27] In terms of scale, the thick/large lyres may be compared with the large bull-lyres of southern Mesopotamia; but despite the third-millennium date of the latter, it is hardly certain that the Anatolian/Egyptian examples derive directly thence.[28]

Thin/small lyres are by far the more numerous, either with outwardly curving arms (often asymmetrical) or a more box-like structure ('rectangular'), and usually held more or less obliquely.[29] Since the earliest representations (third millennium) are concentrated in North Syria, some now see this as a plausible point of origin not only for the Levantine instruments, but even those going back to roughly the same time in Mesopotamia, where they are found alongside harps.[30] Naturally new discoveries could reconfigure the picture. But we should certainly be cautious about the older tendency to see the history of lyres as part of a more general east-to-west 'culture drift' out of Mesopotamia.[31]

---

[24] DCPIL:57–59.
[25] See p90.
[26] DCPIL:43, 55–56. For the *nēbel* problem and sources, see Bayer 1968; cf. NG 3:528–529 (Braun); SAM:170. For a lyric identification, note especially Hesykhios s.v. νάβλα· εἶδος ὀργάνου μουσικοῦ. ἢ ψαλτήριον. ἢ κιθάρα. The status of the *nbl* at Ugarit has been uncertain (Sanmartín 1980:339; Caubet 1994:132; Koitabashi 1998:374; DUL s.v. *nbl*), but now probably does appear in the phrase "by the sound of the *nbl*" in the new Astarte song RIH 98/02 (describing praise of the goddess): see Pardee 2007:31–32; cf. Caubet 2014:176–177.
[27] See p104–111.
[28] Cf. DCPIL:43, "It is hardly a simple Mesopotamian derivative, nor is it uniquely Anatolian."
[29] DCPIL:43–45.
[30] For this proposed revision, RlA 6:581 (Collon, *Leier B); DCPIL:47. Note especially an OAkk. cylinder seal which shows a smaller lyre of rather Syro-Levantine shape, adorned by the slightest of bull-heads: MgB 2/2:64 and fig. 43; SAM:68 no. 22; my Figure 4.1g.
[31] For this view, once standard, see e.g. Hickmann 1961:32–35; MAIP:72–76.

The Knr

Lawergren rightly noted that the earliest attestations of the word *knr* (see below) are roughly coterminous with the distribution of thin/small lyres. Linguistic and organological evidence thus unite for a secure identification of *knr* as 'lyre.'

But we must not be too categorical in our definitions. Given the iconographical fluctuations, which span such a wide geographical and chronological range, *knr* cannot have been the only name ever applied to all of these instruments. A case in point is the *nbl/nēbel*. Conversely, the name *knr* may have been applied to other instruments that do not appear in Lawergren's chart, perhaps even what modern musicologists would distinguish as harps. (Recall the debate over the identity of the early Megiddo etching, ca. 3200–3000.[32]) Such modulations might happen at points of cultural interface, where juxtaposition of traditions could be musically fruitful. This point will be important when we come to consider the situation on Cyprus, especially from the twelfth century onwards, when Aegean and Syro-Levantine traditions interacted within an older insular sphere having its own distinct cultural, and hence musical, identity. The result was a rich range of hybrid phenomena that invite analysis into separate original components, but which are ultimately transcendent and distinctively Cypriot. At the heart of this insular tradition is the Greek-Cypriot word *kinýra*, the interpretation of which, we shall see, calls for some morphological flexibility (Chapter 11).

Within the limitations sketched above, however, it is clear that the word *knr* will have been known with at least generic force throughout most of North Syria, the Levant, and adjacent areas variously from the third or second millennium onwards.[33] This makes it methodologically sound to examine the textual sources as a coherent body of evidence. One must obviously allow for semantic and ideological variations, which will naturally increase with geographical and temporal distance. It is therefore best to privilege the oldest material, as being most relevant for illuminating divinized instruments generally and Kinnaru/Kinyras specifically. Even so, we shall see that important information is sometimes found in quite late sources.

The Early Lexical Evidence

The earliest certain lexical evidence comes from Syria, Mesopotamia, the Levant, Egypt, and Anatolia; it includes administrative documents, ancient lexica, mythological and quasi-ritual texts, and more literary narratives. I present here a

---

[32] See Figure 4.8a; for further references, p47n21.
[33] One may compare the many subspecies of 'guitar' in modern times, noting of course that this word is itself, along with 'zither', 'cithern', etc., but a development of Greek κιθάρα.

Chapter Three

preliminary survey in chronological order, thereby sketching the terrain to be covered in the following chapters.[34]

The oldest known form of the word is *kinnārum*, found at the important North Syrian site of Ebla (ca. 2400), written variously as *gi-na-ru12-um, gi-na-rúm, gi-na-lum*.[35] It was glossed there as Sum. BALAĜ, an important identification given the abundant evidence for the divinization of the balang in early Mesopotamia.[36] Around the same time *kinnārum* found its way, represented as *gi-na-ru12*, into at least one southern Mesopotamian lexical tradition, presumably as a loanword from the west; it appears there alongside the balang and another instrument written with a modified BALAĜ sign.[37] The Eblaite forms still show the mimation (final *-m*), which was largely lost in Northwest Semitic languages during the first half of the second millennium.[38] Eblaite orthography does not distinguish between voiced and unvoiced consonants,[39] but the agreement of later forms shows that the unvoiced *k-* was probably intended. Representation of doubled consonants was also not mandatory by cuneiform convention:[40] at Ugarit (ca. 1250) the word was rendered *knr* in the city's alphabetic cuneiform, and as *ki-na-rù* in the Akkadian practiced by its scribes. But fuller spellings from Mari (ca. 1800), the LBA archives of Alalakh and Emar, and an Egyptian papyrus from the late NK establish geminate *-nn-* as the usual pronunciation.[41]

The early distribution of *kinnāru(m)* has induced many scholars to classify *knr* as a WS word.[42] The situation is complicated, however, by the example from Ebla, since that city's position between East and West Semitic continues to be debated.[43] Some have therefore supposed that *kinnārum* was a P-S word, which

---

[34] Various subsets of the evidence to be considered here were assembled by Spycket 1972:190–191; RlA 6:572–574 (Kilmer, *Leier A); von Soden 1988; Tonietti 1988:119; AMEL:86–87; RlA 8:483 (Tonietti, *Musik A II); Koitabashi 1998:373–374; DCPIL:58–59; Ivanov 1999; MAIP:16–17; HKm:97–98.

[35] *Ebla Vocabulary* §572: Pettinato 1982:264; cf. Fronzaroli 1980:37n6; Krebernik 1983:21; Fronzaroli 1984:141; RlA 6:573 (Kilmer, *Leier A); von Soden 1988; Conti 1990:160; Sanmartín 1991:190; RlA 8:482–483 (Tonietti, *Musik A II).

[36] See Chapter 2, and Heimpel, "Balang-Gods," Section 1a and 4d.

[37] Civil 2010:210 (*Early Dynastic Practical Vocabulary* B_2 = MS 2340+ 22:20'), cf. Civil 2008:99 (suggesting Umma as the tablet's source); Michalowski 2010b:119–120, 122; Heimpel, "Balang-Gods," 4c.

[38] See generally Harris 1939:32–33; ICGSL:96–98 §12.71–72; Sivan 1984:124; SL:280 §33.16; cf. DCPIL:59 and 61n35.

[39] CEWAL:229 (Huehnergard and Woods).

[40] ICGSL:18 §6.2; Sivan 2001:12.

[41] Mari: *ki-in-na-ra-tim* = *kinnārātim* (genitive plural), *ARM* 13 no. 20, lines 5, 7, 11, 16 (cf. p76). Emar: *ki-in-na-ru*: Arnaud 1987 no. 545, line 392' (cf. p78). Alalakh: *ki-in-na-ru-ḫu-li* = ˡúkinnāruḫuli, AT 172.7 (cf. p98). For the *Anastasi Papyrus*, p106. Cf. Huehnergard 2008:138; van Soldt 1991:304.

[42] Caubet 1987:733; von Soden 1988; Koitabashi 1998:373; DCPIL:47; Pentiuc 2001:98.

[43] Diakonoff 1990:29; SL §4.2, 5.2. For Archi 2006:100–101, Eblaite and Akkadian represent two points in a 'Northeast Semitic' dialect continuum.

in Akkadian was displaced by balang or other Sumerian instrument names.[44] And while the trisyllabic structure of *knr* would certainly accord with a Semitic origin, it remains equally possible that this was an adaptation of an older culture-word.[45]

Related to this linguistic puzzle is the inevitable kinship of *kinnārum* with both the *zinar* of Hattian/Hittite tradition, and the *zanaru/zannāru* of Sumerian and Akkadian.[46] This justifies expanding our scope somewhat beyond *knr* itself to include further contextual evidence, especially from the Hittite world, whose ritual texts provide valuable detail on the lyre's use in the royal cult of a LBA society.[47]

That the second syllable of *kinnārum* normally had long $\bar{a}$ is established by Heb. *kinnōr*—the vocalization of which is provided by the MT[48]—since the specific divergence of the two forms must be explained by the so-called Canaanite Shift, whereby P-S $\bar{a}$ developed unconditionally to $\bar{o}$ in both Hebrew and the Canaanite/Phoenician dialects.[49] (Despite the disruptions at the end of the LBA, there is no real cultural break between 'Canaanite' and 'Phoenician': the latter term, reflecting Greek usage, conventionally denotes Canaanite dialects and populations of the first millennium.[50]) It was long known, on the basis of Canaanite words represented in the syllabic Akkadian of the Amarna letters, that the sound change was generally in place by the fourteenth century. Byblos may be taken as the approximate northern limit of this dialect zone, which thus includes the core Phoenician cities of Tyre and Sidon.[51] The OB tablets from Hazor, however, now show that the Shift was already underway, at least in places, some four centuries earlier.[52] Ugarit, while sharing some innovations

---

[44] This seems to be the view of Archi 1987:9; cf. RlA 8:483 (Tonietti, *Musik A II); TR:311n119. Note that one does find Akk. and Ebl. cognates for 'pipes', respectively *embūbu* and *na-bu-bù-um*, presumably < P-S **nbb*: Conti 1988:45–46 (*Ebla Vocabulary* §218); Catagnoti 1989:179n135; Conti 1990:99; RlA 8:482 (Tonietti, *Musik A II).

[45] As a substrate or culture-word, cf. already Ellenbogen 1962:116–117 (writing without knowledge of the Eblaite example); Tischler et al. 1977:578 (rejecting an etymology via Sum. ᵍⁱˢNAR, with determinative realized phonetically, i.e. gišnar > *kinnārum*).

[46] For this issue, see further p78–79, 89–92, 99. '*Zannāru*' is the convenient normalization adopted by Michalowski 2010b:122.

[47] See p89–104.

[48] The Masoretic pointing also indicates gemination of *n* by a diacritical dot (*dagesh*) within the nun.

[49] See generally Harris 1939:43 §17; ICGSL:48–49, 51 (§8.74, 77, 83); Friedrich and Röllig 1970:§71; Sivan 1984:25–34; Garr 1985:30–32; SL:161–162 (§21.9, 12). For a possible 'Phoenician Shift' of $\bar{o}$ > $\bar{u}$, see p273.

[50] See e.g. Edwards 1979:94–98.

[51] Of the examples given by Sivan 1984:25–34, EA 101.25, 114.13, 116.11, 138.6 are from Byblos.

[52] An early second-millennium date, argued tentatively by Gelb 1961:44, and treated cautiously by Sivan 1984:34n1, is endorsed by SL:162 §21.12, noting the vocalization of 'Anat' as *Ḫa-nu-ta* (/'Anōt/) in a theophoric name (versus *Ḫa-na-at* at Mari and *A-na-tu/ti/te* at Ugarit).

Chapter Three

with the Canaanite dialects, resisted this particular development—one of the features that give Ugaritic an archaic appearance[53]—whence we find Kinnaru there.

The comparative evidence thus requires us to assume an early Canaanite form ancestral to Heb. *kinnōr*. Given the present state of excavation in Phoenicia, the evidence for these dialects is largely limited to the representation of Canaanite words in Egyptian sources.[54] But as it happens, Levantine lyres enjoyed a vogue in the NK, following imperial expansion into the region (see Chapter 6). Thus we find a *knr* alongside two otherwise unattested instruments, perhaps exotic, in the *Anastasi Papyrus* (ca. 1200)—a satirical portrait of a libertine scribe given to wild women and music.[55] Although Egyptian writing typically did not indicate vowels, scribes of the MK and especially NK developed a quasi-syllabic system, perhaps under the influence of cuneiform, with supplementary letters serving as phonetic complements (*matres lectionis*) to help represent "foreign names and words, as well as rare or ambiguous Egyptian words and names."[56] Since this system is employed in the papyrus, it is clear that we are dealing with a Canaanite version of *knr*. It is represented in transcription as *kn-nù-rú*—that is, /kinnōru/, /kinnūru/, or somewhere in between.[57]

No certain example of the word has so far emerged from Phoenician inscriptions, neither in the heartland itself, nor in areas of Phoenician/Punic

---

[53] Tropper 1994, with review by Pardee 1997:375; Gordon 1997; Pardee 2008:5, 10. Some PNs and DNs attested at Ugarit which *do* show the $\bar{a} > \bar{o}$ shift "reflect dialects other than that represented by the syllabic transcriptions of actual Ugaritic words": Huehnergard 2008:257n188.

[54] Both in the syllabic cuneiform of the Amarna letters (in which Akkadian was used for international correspondence, including with many Canaanite client-states) and the 'syllabic orthography' described below.

[55] *Papyrus Anastasi* IV: Gardiner 1937:47–48 no. 18, line 12; Caminos 1954:187; Helck 1971:496; the scene is well interpreted by Teeter 1993:88–89. The vignette is reminiscent of a debauched scoundrel in a Sumerian morality tale: Roth 1983; RlA 8:469 (Kilmer *Musik A I).

[56] Albright 1934, especially 12–13 §22–33 (quotation 1); the overall reliability of Albright's method has been upheld by Helck 1989 (with intervening literature in 121n1).

[57] Already Burchardt 1909–1910 2:51 sensibly adduced 'Greek' κιννύρα (*sic*) as the best parallel for this "Old Canaanite foreign-word." The sign-group represented here as *nù* was used to transcribe /nū/, /nō/, and intermediate sounds: Albright 1934:6 (§10), 27n99. Hoch 1994:324n44 reasonably gives *kinnōru*. Albright 1964:171n47 vocalized as *kennūra* with reference to a Phoenician Shift of $\bar{o} > \bar{u}$ (but see p273). Although the first syllable lacks phonetic complement, the general agreement of other forms urges *ki-*, *ke-*, or *kᵉ-*. Thus Helck 1971:523 (no. 253) rendered as *kin-nù-rú*. Note that, while Sivan and Cochavi-Rainey 1992:9, 28 (followed by DUL:451) have *ka-n-nù-rú*, in the updated system of Helck 1989 most signs of the form C+a "can also stand for vowel-less consonants." Earlier transcriptions which did not recognize the 'syllabic orthography' will also be found, perpetuated especially in musicological discussions; cf. DCPIL:61n33, with contribution of O. Goelet.

expansion.⁵⁸ Yet given the numerous Levantine lyres shown on the Cypro-Phoenician symposium bowls (ca. 900–600), one cannot doubt the existence of Phoenician dialect forms like *kinnūr or *kennūr.⁵⁹

I emphasize the Canaanite Shift because such a dialectal form must be the source of 'Greek' kinýra.⁶⁰ I will analyze the abundant lexical and linguistic evidence for this word in due course (Chapters 9 and 11). The question is vital because, despite Ugarit's importance for producing a Divine Kinnaru and rich material for the practical and ideological status of the instrument itself (Chapter 7), the 'shifted' form 'Kinyras' indicates that Ugarit was not the immediate and/or only origin of the legendary Cypriot king. One must give serious consideration to traditions that locate 'Kinyras' at the Canaanite/Phoenician sites of Byblos and possibly Sidon.⁶¹

The foregoing survey outlines the main historical and cultural milieux to be examined. The relevant sources provide generous information about the musical and ritual contexts in which the knr was used, as well as its symbolic potency. It is a likely guess that the Divine Knr embodied this total environment, in various regional incarnations potentially coterminous with the instrument itself. This I believe is reflected in the multiformity of traditions connecting Kinyras with Syria, Phoenicia, Cilicia, and Cyprus. The BA especially will emerge as the time of the Divine Lyre's greatest potency, thanks to the palace and temple systems that supported the divinization of instruments and other cultic tools.

The Problems of Stringing and Tuning

The stringing and tuning of the knr, like that of other ancient instruments, is a thorny issue. It probably differed regionally and even from musician to musician. One may compare the large variation in string numbers and tuning practices in the local traditions of East Africa, where personal preference plays an important role.⁶² This is also suggested by iconographic variety, although one must equally beware the limited reliability of such images: they are not photo-

---

⁵⁸ Van den Branden 1956:91–92, proposed reading 'lyre-players' (knrm) in a fourth-century Phoenician inscription from Kition (Amadasi and Karageorghis 1977 C1, at B7); cf. van den Branden 1968:31 no. 109; followed by Brown 1981:387n13. But this reading was disproven by reexamination of the stone: Peckham 1968:322n4; Masson and Sznycer 1972 ad loc.; Amadasi and Karageorghis 1977:123n3. For the inscription, see also p113. The sequence KNR occurs in several PNs on neo-Punic inscriptions, but these have been interpreted as Libyan/Numidian: see p452n60.
⁵⁹ For the symposium bowls, see p258–272. The Canaanite/Phoenician dialects lost their final case-endings around the end of the second-millennium: see p197n56.
⁶⁰ See p194–204.
⁶¹ See Chapters 19 and 20.
⁶² Owuor 1983:26–27, 31.

Chapter Three

graphs. Nor need regional variations in stringing and tuning be incompatible with shared harmonic conceptions at a deeper level. Consider, for example, the variety of stringing and tuning in modern western instruments, where players nevertheless assume a common tonal apparatus. The same was true of art-music in the Hellenistic and Roman periods, where a single notation and key-system was used by a wide range of professional musicians.[63]

The detailed textual evidence of the Jewish tradition is ambiguous and conflicting. Josephus asserts that the "*kinýra*, fitted out with ten strings, is struck with a pick, while the *nábla*, with twelve tones, is plucked with the fingers."[64] His distinctions are probably too rigid.[65] The Bible itself gives evidence that the *kinnōr* too could be plucked.[66] In one psalm, it is apparently the *nēbel* that is given ten strings, although in another, either or both the *kinnōr* and *nēbel* could be so understood.[67] In the *War Scroll* from Qumran, the *nēbel* apparently has ten strings, since it is to emblazon the standards of ten-men tactical groups.[68]

On these points there arose a tradition of Rabbinic speculation, charting an evolution from the seven strings of David's *kinnōr*, to the eight strings the instrument would assume at the coming of the messiah, to the ten strings of a still more distant future (the aforementioned psalms being interpreted as visions).[69] This must depend in part upon imaginative exegesis and dubious textual readings of known Biblical passages, combined with constructions typical of Hellenistic music historiography.[70] The agreement of the Psalms and the *War Scroll* do give some confidence in the idea of a ten-stringed *nēbel* (if not the *kinnōr*). Yet these texts can hardly be taken as sure evidence for the time of David himself (ca. 1000), much less the earlier *knr*-culture. It is likely enough that further strings were added to Jewish instruments during the life of the Second Temple: such an expansion is well attested for Greek lyres from the later Classical period onwards, and increasing musical sophistication must

---

[63] See now Hagel 2009.
[64] Josephus *Antiquities of the Jews* 7.306: ἡ μὲν κινύρα δέκα χορδαῖς ἐξημμένη τύπτεται πλήκτρῳ, ἡ δὲ νάβλα δώδεκα φθόγγους ἔχουσα τοῖς δακτύλοις κρούεται; varied slightly by Zonaras *Epitome historiarum* 1.116.3.
[65] Note that in Ethiopic tradition it is the *begena*, a sacred lyre associated with David by tradition (see p62n101, 167), which has ten strings; by contrast the *krar* (< **kenar*), used in profane contexts, typically (n.b.) has five or six. See Kebede 1977; MgB 1/10:64–65, 106–109.
[66] 1 Samuel 16:23. This is also implied when the *kinnōr* is rendered as ψαλτήριον in the LXX; note especially Psalms 151:2 (LXX): αἱ χεῖρές μου ἐποίησαν ὄργανον, / οἱ δάκτυλοί μου ἥρμοσαν ψαλτήριον.
[67] Psalms 144:9 and 33:2.
[68] 1Q33 4:5; Vermes 2011:169.
[69] '*Arakin* 13b = BT 16:73–74; also *Midrash Rabbah* Numbers, 15.11 (Freedman and Simon 1983 6:651); cf. LJ 6:262n81.
[70] See e.g. AGM:63–64.

The Knr

have characterized much of the Hellenistic world.[71] Relevant here is the Greco-Roman morphological influence on the lyres of the Bar Kokhba coins and in other musical imagery of the period.[72]

It is quite possible, however, that the Rabbinic attribution of seven strings to David's *kinnōr* reflects a genuine tradition. The number seven enjoys some *a priori* plausibility in the context of ANE chordophone music given the heptatonic-diatonic tunings that are found in the small collection of 'theoretical' texts from Mesopotamia.[73] It is true that the Mesopotamian musical texts per se are products of scribal tradition, being used primarily for educational purposes.[74] Yet there is no reason they should not reflect, at a literate remove, a living tradition of musical practice; after all, the Akkadian terminology found practical application in the Hurrian hymns from Ugarit.[75] When this is taken together with the considerable evidence for musical mobility throughout the ANE in many periods (to be encountered in the following chapters), one has a strong case for supposing that heptatonic-diatonic tunings were also known beyond Mesopotamia and Ugarit. I shall devote a separate study to this problem.[76] Here I raise the issue only occasionally, especially in connection with the appearance of seven-numerology in ritual contexts where music is also involved; and also when considering the appearance of divinized instruments outside of Mesopotamia, since this may well have gone hand-in-hand with the diffusion of musical practice in cult contexts.

Unfortunately, little certain support for a 'heptatonic koine'[77] can be drawn from iconographic evidence. The very low string-counts of the Bar Kokhba coins, for instance, are clearly due to the limited space of the medium.[78] True, where an image is otherwise detailed and apparently precise, one's confidence grows. A good example is the nine-stringed instrument shown on the thirteenth- or early twelfth-century ivory plaque from Megiddo.[79] Here one is tempted to look to the nine-stringed expression of the heptatonic tuning-cycle in Mesopotamia and its adaptation to a kind of schematic harmonic notation in the Hurrian hymns of nearby Ugarit.[80] Yet ANE music-iconography is otherwise so variable

---

[71] See recently the papers in Martinelli et al. 2009; for the astonishing complexity of Hellenistic art music, see now Hagel 2009, especially 256–285 for harmonic observations on the Hellenistic musical documents.
[72] See p180–181.
[73] See p40.
[74] Michalowski 2010a.
[75] See below and further p97.
[76] Franklin forthcoming, revising Franklin 2002c.
[77] For this idea and term, Franklin 2002b; Franklin 2002c:92, 111.
[78] See p180–181 and Figure 14.
[79] See p126 and Figure 11 = 4.1p.
[80] See above.

Chapter Three

that one cannot be certain that the Megiddo plaque's nine-strings are not fortuitous. In any case, one should not expect strict patterns in the iconography. The Mesopotamian tuning system, whatever its diachronic changes, attests an ongoing conceptual resource that could be held in musicians' minds without being strictly deployed on every instrument—just as in our own times the knowledge of intervals, scales, and chords finds many different applications.

All in all, though the question is anything but irrelevant, we may remain agnostic as to the stringing of Jewish and other early lyres, since the *knr*'s attested performance contexts and related ideology are the more urgent evidence for understanding the Divine Kinnaru and Kinyras.

Limits of the Investigation

I have had to abandon many intriguing byways. The decoration of Egyptian instruments with the heads of gods, pharaohs, and animals demands comparison with other ANE material for divinized instruments; but the evidence is so abundant across three millennia, and opens so many philological and conceptual vistas, that even a cursory sketch has proven impractical here.[81]

I closely examine only part of the available iconography, although many specimens would reward further detailed study—for example the fascinating jar from EIA Kuntillet ʿAjrud, which shows a seated female lyrist who may be Asherah, Yahweh's evanescent consort (Figure 5.1y).[82] There is also a remarkable grave-stele from the Neo-Hittite site of Marash, with a goddess holding a lyre on which perches a falcon, possibly symbolizing Ishtar; a small figure, perhaps representing the soul of the deceased, sits on the goddess's lap (Figure 5.1gg).[83]

Knr has further lexical and contextual ramifications in Coptic,[84] Aramaic dialects (Syriac,[85] Palmyrene,[86] Mandaic[87], and perhaps Nabataean[88]), Middle

---

[81] I know of no single study devoted to this question, though much material and useful observations can be found in Schott 1934, 459–461 with references there; cf. Hickmann 1954a; AEMI:80, 107–109 s.v. Animals > heads, Decoration > heads, and Deities. I am grateful to A. von Lieven for initial discussion and references (Sept. 9, 2009).

[82] Bayer 1982:31; Keel and Uehlinger 1998:210–248; DCPIL:55; CS 2 no. 47 with references; Dever 2005:160–167; MAIP:151–154; Burgh 2004:90–91.

[83] See further HKm:73–74 and pl. 14 no. 45, with bibliography.

[84] Coptic: Burchardt 1909–1910 2:51n1; Albright 1927; Albright 1934:47; AOM:273 (Farmer).

[85] Syriac: SOM 2:389 (festive *kennara* in Isaac of Antioch, died ca. 460 CE); Brockelmann 1966:335; Hoch 1994:324; Köhler and Baumgartner 1994–2000:484; DUL s.v. *knr*.

[86] Palmyrene: Levy 1864:105; Farmer 1928:516; Farmer 1929:5; AOM:425 (Farmer); SOM 1:155.

[87] Mandaic: Nöldeke 1875:§104; Brown et al. 1962:490; Brown 1981:387n14.

[88] Nabataean: the Persian Ibn Ḫurdāḏbih (died ca. 912), cited by al-Masʿûdî (died ca. 956), may have attributed the *kinnāra to the Nabataeans (which he says was played like a lute); but the text is

Persian (Pahlavi),[89] Arabic,[90] Old Armenian,[91] Ethiopic,[92] and several Indic and Dravidian dialects.[93] There are, besides, apparent cognates in Caucasian languages, perhaps more directly connected with Hatt./Hitt. *zinar*.[94] The later Aramaic dialects in particular offer fruitful areas for further research. In Syriac, the theological riddles of St. Ephraim (ca. 306-373 CE) about the "lyres of God" seem to 'convert' earlier Aramaean ideas of the *knr*; this transition must also pass through Bardaisan (ca. 154-222), whose biography suggests that he brought together the Aramaean and Hellenistic traditions in the service of early Christian songs later regarded as heretical by Ephraim.[95] In Mandaic texts, one finds a "lyre of lust" paired with pipes and frame-drum, clearly recalling both the ancient ensembles of the Syro-Levantine world, and a recurring pattern of *knr*-playing women—from the scantily-clad *musiciennes* of NK Egypt (Figures 9 and 10) to the *kinnōr*-playing 'harlot' of Isaiah 23:16 and beyond.[96]

There are also the Arabic traditions about djinn who could be conjured by means of music or inspire the songs of musicians; and an instrument's sound could be likened to the voice of the djinn.[97] Such pagan ideas, and related concepts of musical 'enthusiasm,' fueled the Muslim legists in their condemnation of the art.[98]

---

corrupt: Farmer 1928:512, 515-516; MgB 3/2:24; cf. p543n32.

[89] Pahlavi: AOM:425 (Farmer); SOM 1:155-6; Dahood 1966-1970:287; Ivanov 1999:587n15. *Kennar* was used of the Greek constellation Lyra in a lost Pahlavi translation of an astrological work known as the *Liber de stellis beibeniis* (its title in an eventual Latin version); this can be deduced from the ninth-century Arabic translation by Abū Ma'shar, and another in Hebrew: see Bos et al. 2001:85 (Arabic), 118 and 125 (Hebrew). I thank A. Hicks for this reference.

[90] Arabic: AOM:273 (Farmer); Brown et al. 1962:490; Hickmann 1970:63-64, noting oscillation between lute and drum (!); Hava 1964:667; Hoch 1994:324; Köhler and Baumgartner 1994-2000:484.

[91] Armenian: Tischler et al. 1977:578 (as Hittite loanword); Ivanov 1999:587n15.

[92] Ethiopic: *krar*, seemingly dissimilated from **kenar*: Ivanov 1999:587 (cf. SL §17.6: in western Gurage dialects of Ethiopic "non-geminated *n* becomes *r* in non-initial position").

[93] Indic: Mayrhofer 1956-1976 1:209 (Sanskrit, Tamil; deriving Dravidian forms thence); AOM:224 (Bake); Tischler et al. 1977:577-578; Brown 1981:387n17. These are too early to be Arabic imports. The Kinnara gods of Hindu mythology (celestial musicians and choristers) should also be relevant: see e.g. Stutley and Stutley 1977, s.v. Kinnara(s); the interpretation as 'what man?' (*kim* + *nar*-) is a folk etymology (M. Schwartz, communication, April 17, 2014).

[94] Ivanov 1999:587. Note the early (third/second-millennium) archaeological evidence for Caucasian lyre-culture: Kushnareva 2000:103-104, 107-109 pl. I.1, II.2, III.

[95] For Ephraim, see for now Palmer 1993 (an excellent beginning). Bardaisan: Drijvers 1966; Ramelli 2009.

[96] The "lyre of lust" (*kinar šiha*) is found in *Ginzā yamīna* 113:6, 187:18: Drower and Macuch 1963:214 s.v. *kinar, kinara*; Rudolf 1965:390 line 20. For the Egyptian evidence see further p105-111.

[97] Farmer 1929:7 and n9; SOM 1:586.

[98] See SOM 1:7-8 for further references, and 9-33 for the *Unique Necklace* of Ibn 'Abd Rabbihi (ca. 860-940 CE), which responds to the controversy with a more moderate stance.

Chapter Three

Of special interest are the legends and cognitive conceptions of the living lyre cultures of south-coastal Saudi Arabia,[99] Egypt, and East Africa,[100] with the professed connections to Davidic tradition in Ethiopia.[101]

I hope that the present study will provide a useful foundation for the pursuit of all this further material.

---

[99] For the *simsimiyyah* and *ṭambūrah*, Shiloah 1972; Shiloah 1995:147, 162; Braune 1997:48–50, 138; L. A. Urkevich in GMO s.v. Saudi Arabia.
[100] Kebede 1968; Jenkins 1969; MGG 5:1042–1046 (G. Kubik); Plumley 1976; Kebede 1977; MgB 1/10, 64–65, 106–109; Owuor 1983; U. Wegner in GMO s.v. Lyres. 3. Modern Africa, with further bibliography. See also p167, 456n81.
[101] Mekouria 1994.

4

Starting At Ebla

The City and Its Music

THE CUNEIFORM TEXTS of Ebla (Tell Mardikh) have now yielded the word *kinnārum*, nearly a millennium and a half before King David. By ca. 2400, Ebla controlled a sizeable area of upper inland Syria; its dependencies included Karkemish, Alalakh, Hamath, Emar, and Harran.[1] Ebla's political and commercial interests were quite wide-ranging, extending into Mesopotamia (including Kish and Mari) and the Levant (Ugarit, Byblos).[2] Its pantheon included early forms of WS deities (Dagan, Hadda, Rašap) and others from a non-Semitic substrate, most importantly the city-god Kura and his consort Barama.[3] With the possible exception of Ea/Haya,[4] the pantheon is essentially independent of Mesopotamia, and while Ebla was in the orbit of Sumerian scribal culture, the few Mesopotamian hymns and other literary texts found there probably had no cultic use.[5] A possible exception is a collection of Sumerian and Akkadian incantations, which may have stimulated the formation of a comparable local genre.[6]

Publication of the royal archives, spanning some forty-five years and at least three kings—Yigriš-Halab, Yirkab-Damu, and Yiš'ar-Damu—is incomplete.[7] Yet they already reveal a vibrant, cosmopolitan musical world.[8] Numerous

---

[1] Matthiae 1989:259; Stieglitz 2002:215 and n1, 216; Archi 2006:99.
[2] Michalowski 1985; Archi 1988b; Matthiae 1989:256–266; Archi 1997.
[3] Archi 1978–1979; Stieglitz 1990; Archi 1993; Archi 1994; Pomponio and Xella 1997 (87–88, 245–248 for Kura and Barama).
[4] Archi 2006:98.
[5] Archi 2006:98; Tonietti 2010:71–72.
[6] Archi 1993:8. Catagnoti and Bonechi 1998, expanding on the catalog of Michalowski 1992, distinguish Sumerian and Akkadian incantations at Ebla from local Eblaitic ones, as well as Akkadian ones that were 'Eblaitized'; Tonietti 2010:71–72, suggests that "creating a local incantation genre was a programmatic goal of Ebla scribes."
[7] For these archives, their dating, and the kind of information they provide, Archi 1986a; Matthiae 1989:221–298; Archi 1992; Archi 2006:101–109.
[8] The musical evidence spans the entire period of the archive, but becomes more detailed from the reign of Yiš'ar-Damu: see Tonietti 2010:73. See especially the stimulating survey by Biga

63

Chapter Four

singer-musicians (NAR), dancers (NE.DI), and acrobats or 'cult dancers' (ḪÚB) came from other palaces to perform for royal occasions like feasts, wedding celebrations, and religious festivals (temple-musicians per se remain elusive, as no temple archive has been found).[9] Mari, Nirar, Kish, Emar, Tuttul, Nagar, and Aleppo are all attested as sources of musical exchange, with performers often travelling in the train of royal or aristocratic visitors.[10] Local Eblaite musicians active in and about the palace are revealed by repeated appearances in distribution lists.[11] Some have names that suggest an origin outside of Ebla itself.[12] That singer-musicians can be named individually shows the relative prestige that members of this profession might achieve when steadily visible to the world of kings and notables.[13] Some singer-musicians must have traveled in their turn to foreign centers, but such movements remain invisible, not involving palace disbursements on the home end.

A group of some twenty female singers (NAR.MÍ), and a number of dancers, were apparently housed among the royal women, presumably performing within the palace, and perhaps at festivals involving women. There is no evidence to show that they were also concubines, as commonly at OB Mari; but this would hardly be surprising.[14] As to the female mourners who are attested for the funeral of a royal princess,[15] we do not know if this involved more than raw ululation, nor whether there was some overlap with the palace *musiciennes*.

While Sumerian musical titles were regularly used by the scribes of Ebla, it is unclear how far this reflects actual Sumerian musical influence, rather than mere orthographic convention. Still, the regular distinction in the palace archives between 'senior' and 'junior' singers (NAR.MAḪ and NAR.TUR, literally 'big' and 'small' singers) reveals a stratified professional environment comparable to that of Mari and various sites in Babylonia. Clearly defined ranks would have been very practical in a world where regular allocations had to be made to

---

2006, with some references to unpublished material.
[9] Festival and other contexts: Biga 2011:481–482; Tonietti 2010:75–79, 82–83. For the problem of temple musicians, Tonietti 1997; Tonietti 2010:81n69; but cf. Archi et al. 1988:273: "musicians were also active in peripheral towns, in some cases in the temples."
[10] Tonietti 1998; Biga 2006; Tonietti 2010:75–79.
[11] Textile-payments to the NAR were generally done by the group on an annual or biannual basis: Tonietti 1989:118–119; Tonietti 2010:73–74. That they were not monthly, and never involved foodstuffs, has suggested that the NAR did not actually reside in the palace: Biga 2006:30. More recently, however, Biga writes: "À la cour d'Ébla vivaient ... chanteurs" (Biga 2011:490); cf. Tonietti 2010:83 ("attached to the palace").
[12] Tonietti 2010:75.
[13] Cf. Biga 2011:490.
[14] *Musiciennes* at Ebla: Tonietti 1988:115; Archi et al. 1988:273; RlA 8:482 (Tonietti, *Musik A II), noting that the feminine determinative is otherwise unknown in connection with NAR; Biga 2003:65; Biga 2006:26, 28, 30; Tonietti 2010:74–75; cf. Ziegler 2006b:34.
[15] Tonietti 2010:84.

visiting artists, and there was periodic relocation and reintegration of musicians through conquest and gift-exchange. At Ebla it is sometimes possible to follow the promotions, demotions, re-promotions, arrivals, departures, transfers, and deaths of singers over many years.[16] The careers of around fifty Eblaite male singer-musicians (NAR) can be so traced, with clear correspondence between position in list and length of service. One can even observe a nearly 200 percent corporate growth over the period covered by the archives, probably connected with an overall increase in the prosperity of the palace—prior to its destruction by Sargon or Naram-Sin.[17] It also seems that this management structure operated, on a smaller scale, throughout the kingdom.[18]

Kinnārum and Balang

Ebla thus represents a sophisticated, regionally interconnected music-culture prevailing throughout North Syria. It is appropriate that the first attestation of *kinnārum* should come from such an environment. It is found in the so-called *Ebla Vocabulary*, a massive bilingual lexical collection developed during several generations following the introduction of cuneiform to the city.[19] The scribes glossed *kinnārum* with Sum. BALAĜ, quite decisive evidence that, at least in third millennium Babylonia, the Sumerian word could refer to a stringed instrument.[20] This equation cannot be dismissed as scribal confusion.[21] After all, the *kinnārum* was equally known, we saw, to the scribes of ED Mesopotamia, where it was also associated with the balang.[22] Nor can performance context be made the sole basis of these connections, so that the lamenting *lyre* of the west becomes the functional equivalent of the Mesopotamian lamenting *drum*. For BALAĜ appears in another Eblaite text where there is clearly no question of lamentation—a 'BALAĜ-man' (LÚ.BALAĜ) who appears in company with a group of cult-dancers/acrobats (ḪÚB) as recipients of textile disbursements.[23] Elsewhere

---

[16] Tonietti 1988, especially 106–109, 117; Archi et al. 1988:271; Tonietti 1989; Matthiae 1989:283; Catagnoti 1989:176; RlA 8:482 (Tonietti, *Musik A II); Feliu 2003:36; Biga 2006:25–26; Tonietti 2010:74. For Mari, see p73–76.

[17] Tonietti 1988:107–108, who speculates about "un cambiamento della situazione musicale, forse nel tipo di utilizzazione dei NAR.MAḪ"; cf. Tonietti 2010:74.

[18] Cf. Archi et al. 1988:272–273 (temple of Dagan and elsewhere); Tonietti 1988:118; Biga 2006:26; Tonietti 2010:82.

[19] See generally Archi 2006:106–109; Tonietti 2010:70.

[20] See p54, 531; Heimpel, "Balang-Gods," Section 1a.

[21] So DCPIL:58.

[22] See p54; Heimpel, "Balang-Gods," 4c.

[23] LÚ.BALAĜ: ARET 15.1 25 obv. VII.1 (§24): Tonietti 2010:80.

Chapter Four

the instrument of a NAR is a BALAĜ.²⁴ These designations recall the NAR.BALAĜ of Sumerian texts, and Ušumgal-kalama, Ningirsu's balang-god who was not a lamenter but a nar.²⁵ So the scribes' equation of BALAĜ and *kinnārum* was clearly not based on 'genre' alone: they must have seen some organological similarity between the two instruments.²⁶ At Ebla, therefore, the expressions LÚ.BALAĜ and NAR.BALAĜ will mean simply '*kinnārum*-singer'.

Besides the many NAR known at Ebla, palace records attest to the maintenance of another musical class, the BALAĜ.DI. In some texts, they appear as a group of nine.²⁷ Elsewhere, four BALAĜ.DI are specified in connection with a kind of 'cultic chapel' (É.NUN), presumably a dedicated location in which they often operated.²⁸ These BALAĜ.DI are usually interpreted as lamentation-priests, on the basis of early Sumerian usage.²⁹ They are indeed known to have performed in such a context (see below), and this function helps account for the otherwise conspicuous absence from Ebla of Sum. GALA.³⁰ Although the comparative evidence is good as far as it goes, it should not dictate too rigid an interpretation of the BALAĜ.DI's musical character at Ebla itself. It is intrinsically likely, first, that the city's lamentation practices were rather distinct from those of contemporary southern Mesopotamia. Moreover, Sumerian BALAĜ.DI meant originally merely a player of the balang; its application to lamentation-singers is thus a specialized development,³¹ and it is unclear where the Eblaite usage falls along, or branches from, this continuum.

Now the scribes equated BALAĜ.DI with *na-ti-lu-(um)* in their own language.³² This has been plausibly derived from the root *$*nṭl$*, 'raise up', so that BALAĜ.DI/ *nāṭilū(m)* is "he who lifts [sc. the voice]"; a comparable semantic development

---

²⁴ TM 75.2365 rev. XII.17–20; ARET 15.1 23 obv. VII.14–15 (§34). See Archi et al. 1988:273; cf. Tonietti 2010:80.
²⁵ See p28.
²⁶ The appearance of BALAĜ in various compounds in Sumerian lexical texts might suggest a looser usage for a variety of lyres, or even stringed instruments generally: see Krispijn 1990:6–7; Heimpel, "Balang-Gods," Section 1b, 4b.
²⁷ Nine BALAĜ.DI appear in four texts cited by Archi et al. 1988:273; cf. Fronzaroli 1988:12; Matthiae 1989:283; Conti 1990:160; Fronzaroli and Catagnoti 1993:140, 162–163, cf. 171; RlA 8:482 (Tonietti, *Musik A II); Tonietti 2010:80.
²⁸ Tonietti 2010:83, with this translation of É.NUN; for the possible cultic implications of the word, see Conti 1990:118n253 with references. The texts are ARET 12 773 I.1–2 (wool); 874 XIV.11–12; cf. 709 I.3–4 (wool). A further textile disbursement for one BALAĜ.DI is recorded in ARET 3 44 V.1.
²⁹ BALAĜ.DI in Sumerian sources: Hartmann 1960:124, cf. 64; RlA 8:469 (Kilmer, *Musik A I).
³⁰ Noted by Tonietti 2010:85, also suggesting a correlation with the lack of Sumerian names among the NAR of Ebla (by contrast with the Sumerian names borne by the NAR of Mari present at Ebla: Tonietti 1998:89–97).
³¹ Pettinato 1992:277–278.
³² *Ebla Vocabulary* §571: Pettinato 1982:264.

is noted for the Hebrew cognate *nś'*, where the context is lamentation.³³ From here, and the equation BALAĜ = *kinnārum*, it is an easy inference that the BALAĜ. DI of Ebla performed to the lyre; the two entries in the *Ebla Vocabulary* are in fact adjacent. We shall see further evidence in Chapter 12 of lyric lamentation to the *knr*. But since the BALAĜ-*kinnārum* of Ebla was definitely used for *more* than lamentation-singing, clearly the distinction between NAR and BALAĜ.DI relates to their respective functions more than the instruments used. And the BALAĜ.DI of Ebla probably had some broader purview than lamentation alone, to judge from their association with the 'cultic chapel' (É.NUN). Obviously this professional 'segregation' of the BALAĜ.DI from the NAR equally implies some social difference. While it would be rash to draw a hard line between secular and sacred—since NAR could perform at religious festivals, royal weddings, and so on—it does seem likely that the BALAĜ.DI were responsible for the main liturgical functions required by the palace. As such, their range would not have been limited to lamentation.

Lamentation and Royal Ancestor Cult

The one context for which there is any information about BALAĜ.DI performance is a complex series of royal rites attested in three versions. One is evidently a kind of prescriptive template for the other two, which describe specific and slightly varied manifestations relating to the city's last two kings.³⁴ These two are semi-narrative accounts of what actually transpired, although they equally follow a more-or-less fixed sequence.³⁵ The occasion and purpose have been variously interpreted, most often as a royal wedding and/or enthronement.³⁶ The latter idea, at least, is now ruled out by correlations with the textile and metal-distribution tablets, whose chronology, having been established, is incompatible with an accession; nor do these texts give any support to the wedding hypothesis. Biga and Capomacchia have now argued convinc-

---

[33] Fronzaroli 1988:12–13; Fronzaroli 1989; Fronzaroli 1991:33; Fronzaroli and Catagnoti 1993:42. This interpretation is accepted by Conti 1990:160; RlA 8:482 (Tonietti, *Musik A II); Tonietti 2010:83. Pettinato 1992:237, finds this plausible (237), but at 209 gives some credence to the alternative proposal of D'Agostino 1988:79n19 (looking rather to the root *ndr*, attested in Hebrew in the sense of "giurare"). For another interpretation, see Heimpel, "Balang-Gods," Section 3c2.

[34] The texts are TM.75.G.1823+, TM.75.G.1939+, and TM.75.G.1672. See the edition of Fronzaroli and Catagnoti 1993 (ARET 11); also Pettinato 1992, partial edition with alternative reconstruction. Chronology: Fronzaroli 1992:178–183; Fronzaroli and Catagnoti 1993:XI, 21, 72; Biga 2011:487; Biga and Capomacchia 2012:20–22.

[35] Whereas a 'prescriptive ritual' lays out required actions, a 'descriptive ritual' gives an account of "what transpired on special cultic occasions." See the good theoretical discussion of Levine 1983; cf. Levine 1963a:105 (quotation).

[36] Fronzaroli and Catagnoti 1993:XI et passim.

Chapter Four

ingly that, while the ritual sequence may have been executed on, and adapted to, various occasions, the unifying purpose of all three texts is the renovation of royal authority through veneration of the royal ancestors and the regular maintenance of their cult. It may still be, however, that the ritual could be *coordinated* with such occasions as wedding and enthronement, and that such royal themes partially contributed to the ritual's symbolism.[37]

The ritual called for the royal couple to travel to different stations within the kingdom, executing rites and making offerings to various gods and certain of the royal ancestors' divinized shades.[38] The centerpiece was three seven-day ritual cycles undertaken at the mausoleum at Nenaš, where the king and queen took up temporary residence.[39] The actions are enumerated in considerable detail, although the precise timing is not always clear. Included were acts of purification, investment, washing, anointing, and benediction, accompanied at every stage by abundant animal and material offerings, notably to royal ancestors, the Sun, and Kura and Barama—of whom the king and queen were the terrestrial counterparts.[40] Offerings on the seventh day of each cycle were themselves sevenfold.[41]

It is during this long sequence that the BALAĜ.DI lamenters, indispensable to the rites, were called upon to perform.[42] It must have been dramatic. The royal couple, after braving a spooky night in the mausoleum, emerged to sit "upon the two thrones of their fathers" and await the dawn:

> The god Sun rises, the invoker invokes [and] the lamenters (*na-ti-lu*) intone their lamentation—*The Goddess Nintu Who is Angered*.[43] And 'that

---

[37] Biga and Capomacchia 2012 ("rifondazione dei valori sacrali rappresentati dalla coppia regale in rapporto agli antenati del re," 25). For the importance of the queen, and tentative suggestions about hierogamy, Pettinato 1992, with the contribution by P. Pisi, "Considerazioni storico-religiose sulla regalità ad Ebla," 313–341 (complicated by the differing textual reconstruction of Fronzaroli and Catagnoti 1993); cf. Pomponio and Xella 1997:87, 245, 333).

[38] See the account of Fronzaroli 1992.

[39] For the identification of the royal mausoleum, Fronzaroli 1992:173–175.

[40] Fronzaroli 1992:164–165, 180–181; Fronzaroli and Catagnoti 1993:47–48 §85. Three-seven day cycles at the mausoleum itself is made explicit by ARET 11 3 §11–14 (this text is abstracted from ARET 11 2). For Kura and Burama, see Pomponio and Xella 1997:87, 245, 333.

[41] ARET 11 1 §85, 88, 91; 2 §89, 92, 95.

[42] Cf. Biga and Capomacchia 2012:24, emphasizing that all three versions of the text, including its 'handbook' form (ARET 11 3 §12), call for lamentation. The BALAĜ.DI's participation is presumably implied by further allusions to lament elsewhere, if this is the correct interpretation of SI.DÚ: Fronzaroli 1988:13; Fronzaroli and Catagnoti 1993:25 §11. The passages in question are ARET 11 1 §11, line 6 (restored) and §13, line 16 ≈ 2 §16, lines 8, 18. Cf. also ARET 11 1 §32, line 20 (with note on p34 §32).

[43] Fronzaroli and Catagnoti 1993:42 read *ti-'à-ba-nu* here as a derivative of *ḫbn, 'be angered'. But cf. Pettinato 1992:209, who would see rather a reference to song via the corresponding Sumerogram at ARET 11 2 §66, line 22.

which makes to shine' [i.e. aromatic oil[44]] makes its request to do so. [And Nin]tu [makes sh]ine the new Kura, the new Barama, the new king, the new qu[een].[45]

The text appears to preserve the *incipit* of an actual lamentation.[46] The song's character is confirmed by the rite's outcome, since the 'angered' goddess is induced to "make shine" the royal couple. In Sumerian tradition, Nintu was a goddess of childbirth whose powers became associated specifically with the begetting of kings.[47] So this was evidently a kind of symbolic rebirth.

The lamenters are mentioned again soon afterwards, following another series of rites. This time the action is presented in the past tense, apparently indicating not a second performance, but the completion of a sequence that began with the song just discussed:[48]

And the lamenters (*na-ti-lu*) have executed their lament. And [sc. the man of] Harugu[49] recites the benediction. And he (?) sounds the lament of the king three times and of the queen three times.[50]

The importance of this passage lies in the word translated here as "sounds" (*i-a¹ba-ad*). Fronzaroli would read this as /yilappat/ and derive it from the root **lpt* ('touch'), pointing to Akk. *lapātu*, which can be used to describe the playing of a stringed instrument (compare Greek *psállein*).[51] If this is right,[52] it corroborates the argument above that the *kinnārum* was employed in lamentation-singing at Ebla. Admittedly the present performance configuration is hardly clear. With the standing group of BALAĜ.DI apparently excluded, the possibilities envisioned by Fronzaroli are that "the man of Harugu" accompanies either himself in reciting the lament, or the king and queen as they do so.[53] Unfortunately the identity and role of "the man of Harugu" is entirely obscure. And the passage is

---

[44] Fronzaroli 1992:171; Fronzaroli and Catagnoti 1993:25, 42.
[45] ARET 11 1 §63–65 ≈ 2 §66–68 (all translations after Fronzaroli).
[46] Tonietti 2010:85.
[47] See Jacobsen 1973:286–289, 293–295; cf. Fronzaroli and Catagnoti 1993:42 §65. Regarding the Ebalite equivalent of Nintu, Pomponio and Xella 1997:333 write only that "elle était vraisemblablement vénérée comme un variante locale" of similar powers, noting that no equivalent is found in the lexical lists.
[48] For this interpretation, see Fronzaroli and Catagnoti 1993:79 §79.
[49] For this obscure figure, see Fronzaroli 1992:167, 172; Fronzaroli and Catagnoti 1993:35–36 (suggesting that he was a village chief or son thereof).
[50] ARET 11 1 §75–77 ≈ 2 §79–81 ≈ 3 §12.
[51] Fronzaroli 1988:13; Fronzaroli and Catagnoti 1993:45. For the Akkadian usage, CAD s.v. *lapātu*, 1p, 4d; Kilmer 1965:263, 13; RlA 8:464 (Kilmer, *Musik A I).
[52] Note the alternative interpretation of Pettinato 1992:213.
[53] Fronzaroli and Catagnoti 1993:45 §77; cf. Fronzaroli 1988:29–31.

Figure 6 Seated/enthroned lyrist with animals. Unprovenanced North Syrian cylinder seal, ca. 2900–2350. Bible Lands Museum, Jerusalem, 2462. Drawn from SAM no. 70.

so laconic that one should not rule out the further involvement of the BALAĜ. DI. They may have completed the former sequence, but are now employed in a further lament for which only the three key new participants are specified.

What kind of music would be involved in such a mortuary ritual?[54] The appropriateness of lamentation at a *funeral* is self-evident, and is the earliest documented function of the Sumerian GALA.[55] But if the ritual was related to the long-term maintenance of *mortuary* cult, we need not envision only acute grief and continuous ululation. If the *kinnārum* was indeed employed, something more musical—more lyrical—should also be supposed.[56] Probably the lamentation-singing served here, as often in Mesopotamia, a prophylactic function—perhaps securing the good will of the divinized ancestors towards the kingdom's continued prosperity.[57]

---

[54] Following Schmidt 1994:4–12 and Pardee 1996b in connection with Ugarit, 'funerary' refers to one-time rites associated with the death of a king, notably burial and his successor's accession. 'Mortuary' relates to the ongoing maintenance of the royal dead, comparable to the Mesopotamian *kispu* ritual (for which see generally Tsukimoto 1985; for the problematic connection with Ugarit, see with further references Pardee 1996b; TPm:176–178).

[55] See p29.

[56] Compare the Aegean vintage festivals where the lyrist Linos was lamented in what appears to be, as Homer describes it, a quite cheerful occasion: see p308.

[57] Note, however, the arguments of Schmidt 1994 against the currency of 'beneficent dead' in this early period.

The template format of the ritual indicates that this was a traditional procedure, insulated from rapid change by being set down in clay. The ritual was executed for two consecutive kings, and something analogous, if slowly evolving, must have been practiced for many generations. After all, the *Ebla King List* goes back twenty-six generations or more, conceivably to the twenty-eighth century.[58] This list must be associated with eleven further cultic texts in which various divinized kings are named in the contexts of offerings and rituals.[59] Such a royal ancestor cult, enacted by a very small and socially/historically self-conscious group, and limited to occasional but regular performances, might very well enjoy great longevity—on the order of many centuries.[60] Ebla thus evokes a deep historical background for the *kinnāru*'s connections with the royal mortuary cult of Ugarit, a millennium later.[61]

Divine Lyre At Ebla?

No offerings to musical instruments have yet been found in Ebla's economic records.[62] Yet the documents do attest to the veneration of *other* cult-objects: two sheep were offered for the provisioning of the sheath or spear of Rašap of Atanni; sheep for the head and feet of the same god's statue; sheep for the scepters of several gods; and one sheep for a throne (god not specified). Although such objects are not written with divine determinatives at Ebla,[63] the very fact that they received such offerings indicates that Ebla shared with Mesopotamia some conceptions about their potential divinity. Another text apparently relates to bad omens that were believed to result from the improper worship of a divine statue.[64] So one may at least say that the conditions for a divinized *kinnārum* were in place at Ebla, especially given bilateral scribal familiarity with BALAĜ and *kinnārum* between Mesopotamia and Ebla.[65]

It seems quite certain, at least, that the instrument was already considered to possess special powers. This is well illustrated by a cylinder seal in the

---

[58] See Archi 2001; Stieglitz 2002. Cf. also Archi 1986b; Archi 1988a; Biga and Pomponio 1987; Archi et al. 1988:212–215; Matthiae 1989:253; Archi 1993:16; Archi 2006:98.
[59] For the intentional if mysterious patterns of veneration that emerge from these cultic texts, see Stieglitz 2002:220–222.
[60] Cf. Stieglitz 2002:217: "The Ebla archives now extend this royal tradition in Syria back to the first half of the third millennium."
[61] See p134–147.
[62] Biga 2006:30 alluded to a wool-distribution to BALAĜs of the crown prince's palace (TM 75.G.2337 obv. VII 47, reign of Yiš'ar-Damu), but the recipients were actually the BALAĜ.DI lamenters; I thank her for confirming this (correspondence, 10/1/2009).
[63] Pettinato 1979:27–28, 111–112; cf. Baldacci 1992:277; Selz 1997:176.
[64] Fronzaroli 1997.
[65] See p54; Heimpel, "Balang-Gods," 4d and 4e.

Chapter Four

Bible Lands Museum (Figure 6), apparently from North Syria to judge from stylistic parallels, which also indicate a third millennium date.[66] A seated, perhaps enthroned, figure (male?) plays an instrument not dissimilar in shape to contemporary Sumerian lyres, but lacking a bull's-head. In motion before the musician are two animals, perhaps a dog and a lion (or equid). It is a very early example of a motif—lyrist facing or surrounded by animals—which had a long history in the Syro-Levantine sphere.[67] Later parallels suggest that the seal may reflect wisdom traditions associated with lyre-playing and/or the use of lyre-music to symbolize a harmonious realm—the wise and powerful ruler prevailing over the wild forces that threaten social and political stability.[68] Whatever the precise interpretation, the importance of the lyre itself is suggested by its careful rendering and central placement. Well out in front of the musician, in an impossible playing position, the lyre is fully represented, practically independent of its player—an object of interest and significance in its own right.

---

[66] Bible Lands Museum, Jerusalem no. 2462. See with references SAM:110 no. 70, where it is dated ca. 2900–2350 BCE.
[67] Cf. DCPIL:53 and index s.v. 'animals:lyrist and'.
[68] See index s.v. 'order, symbolized by music'.

5
Mari and the Amorite Age
The City and Its Music

THE *KINNĀRU* IS NEXT ATTESTED in the eighteenth century at Mari (Tell Harīri) on the middle Euphrates. The city's massive archive makes it a type-site for the political dynamics and economic complexities of the period. There is rich evidence for an 'international' music-culture, much like that of Ebla or Ur under Shulgi, but currently known in much greater detail.[1] I would stress that, while the larger scope of this study justifies my focus on the *kinnāru* material, these lyres were but one element of Mari's diverse instrumentarium. All the same, the *kinnāru*'s linguistic association with the West gives it a special position *vis-à-vis* the OB city. For this was the so-called Amorite Age, when dynasts of western extraction held power in many Mesopotamian cities—most famously Hammurabi, who ultimately destroyed Mari.[2]

Mari was apparently subject to significant Sumerian musical influence in pre-Sargonic times, to judge from the famous statue of Ur-Nanshe who bore, in addition to the title NAR, both a Sumerian name and professional garb like that worn by singers on the 'Standard of Ur' and elsewhere.[3] This same Ur-Nanshe, earlier in his career, may be among a group of visiting Mariot singers attested

---

[1] This material has been well analyzed in several recent studies by N. Ziegler: FM 4; Ziegler 2006a; Ziegler 2006b; FM 9. Other relevant discussions include: Williamson 1969; von Soden 1988; Malamat 1999; Malamat 2003. For the ED period, see also Tonietti 1998.

[2] See further below. I use 'Amorite' advisedly, well aware of the current debate about the nature of Amorite ethnicity, the degree to which those so described in Mesopotamia (Sum. MAR.TU/Akk. *amurrum*) identified themselves as a coherent group, and so on (recently Miglio 2013:189–197). Nonetheless, the term remains a useful shorthand for discussing cultural and demographic patterns of the period.

[3] Ur-Nanshe: Damascus S 2071, Parrot 1967:88, fig. 127–131 and pl. 45–46; Gelb and Kienast 1990:13–14; Braun-Holzinger 1991:249; FM 9:7–9; RIME 1, 10.12.3. Parallels: MgB 2/2:44–45 (Standard of Ur), 48–49 (fig. 11–12, 17), etc.

Chapter Five

at Ebla, of whom at least nine have names that are recognizably Sumerian, presumably adopted as being professionally appropriate.[4]

The sparse administrative texts of the so-called Shakkanakku period (ca. 2100-1850), which record isolated distributions to singers (NAR), chief singers (NAR.GAL), and songstresses (NAR.MÍ), are clear traces of a lively and stratified music-culture.[5]

But it is the reigns of two later kings—the interloper Yasmah-Addu (ca. 1790-1776) and the restored Zimri-Lim (ca. 1775-1761)—for which we have much material detailing the royal management of music. The texts, which yield abundant evidence for artisan mobility generally,[6] include numerous musical contacts with Karkemish, Babylon, Aleppo, Qatna, Hazor, and elsewhere. The city's musical affairs were directed by a Chief Singer (Akk. *nargallum*), typically a foremost confidant of the king and often appearing among other high officials in the economic documents.[7] Based in a sort of conservatory (*mummum*), his duties included recruiting and training harem musicians (often from war captives),[8] supervising the construction and repair of instruments,[9] organizing musical ensembles and events, and undertaking sensitive diplomatic missions like arranging royal marriages.[10] Zimri-Lim even left his Chief Singer, Warad-Ilishu, in charge of the city while taking the field against Eshnunna.[11] (Compare the unnamed singer whom Agamemnon left in charge of Klytaimnestra at Mycenae.[12]) Enough Chief Singers are attested for other states in contact with Mari for us to conclude that such officials were quite typical of this period.[13] Mari's musical apparatus, if not identical to that of other states, must have been compatible for all practical purposes.

---

[4] Mander 1988:482; Steinkeller 1993:237-238, 240; Tonietti 1988:88-89; Archi et al. 1988:283; Tonietti 1998:91; Archi 2006:98.
[5] Limet 1976:7-9, 36 (dating), 28 (singers), and text-references in index.
[6] Sasson 1968; Durand 1992 passim; Zaccagnini 1983b.
[7] See generally FM 9:7-12, 83-201. As a boy, Yasmah-Addu seems to have been tutored by Ibbi-Ilabrat, the Chief Singer of his father Shamshi-Addu, and, once king of Mari, he appointed his friend Rishiya to the office (FM 9:83-88, 148-149 and n109-110).
[8] FM 9:10-11, 42-43, 168-169, 180-189; Ziegler 2010:119-126. The term 'harem', despite its orientalist connotations, is both convenient and appropriate; for a defense of its use vis-à-vis OB Mari, see FM 4:5-8; for Achaemenid Persia and other ANE contexts, see Llewellyn-Jones 2013:97-102. The distribution lists do not distinguish sharply among queen, secondary wives, royal princesses, *musiciennes*, and a variety of domestic staff. The 'harem' thus comprised all female residents of a palace, not all of whom served as concubines.
[9] FM 4:30n173; Ziegler 2006a:345n6, 348, and n31; FM 9:86, 170, 190-193.
[10] Ziegler 2006a:348; FM 9:11, 86-89, 149-151, 171-175.
[11] FM 9:200-201; cf. 176-179 for a synopsis of Warad-Ilishu's attested activities, which equally show his high standing.
[12] Homer *Odyssey* 3.267-272.
[13] Ziegler 2006a:347n21, citing examples from Shubat-Enlil, Ekallatum, and Karana; FM 9:10.

Mari and the Amorite Age

Although systematic records for male musicians are lacking, there are examples of them receiving land allotments from the king, and other indications of esteem.[14] The management of female musicians, however, may be reconstructed in considerable detail from a series of administrative texts, which, though not completely continuous, span many years. This was a relatively stable, self-sustaining system, with singers maintaining their careers in the face of dynastic change, although naturally the individual was ever vulnerable to royal whim. Thus, while Ilshu-Ibbishu, chief musical instructor under Yasmah-Addu, does not reappear in the records of Zimri-Lim,[15] Rishiya, the Chief Singer under Yasmah-Addu, continued for a time in this office after Zimri-Lim's restoration.[16] Similarly, the same three female music-teachers were apparently active under both kings training harem-*musiciennes*.[17] This helps explain why, despite numerous demotions when Yasmah-Addu's harem was integrated into that of Zimri-Lim, four young girls of the previous regime emerged as full-fledged *musiciennes* in the new.[18] Evidently they had not only come to sexual maturity, but completed their musical training, for which they were duly rewarded.

It is clear that an 'international style' of music was deliberately cultivated, with the foreign and exotic carefully recorded as though important for an accurate inventory.[19] In an age without sound recording, the craving for musical variety was satisfied through the mechanism of royal gift-exchange.[20] In practice this involved the acquisition, training, and trading of players. One set of texts deals with a heavily armed caravan, supervised by Zimri-Lim's Chief Singer, which escorted a group of 'Benjaminite' *musiciennes* to the king of Aleppo.[21] Another tablet refers to the integration of a group of Elamite *musiciennes* into the harem.[22] The need to have a ready stockpile of these 'commodities' accounts for the surprisingly high numbers maintained by the palace—at least 200 in the reign of Zimri-Lim, managed by several dozen Senior *Musiciennes*.[23] Music was

[14] Ziegler 2006a:347; FM 9:20–31.
[15] FM 9:205.
[16] Durand 1988:95–117; FM 4:96; Ziegler 2006a:348n33; FM 9:83, 97 et passim.
[17] FM 4:82–83; FM 9:15–16.
[18] FM 4:12, 35–38.
[19] Ziegler 2006a; FM 9:19–20, 37–41 et passim.
[20] This point was stressed by R. Eichmann in discussion at the 2006 meeting of the International Study Group on Music Archaeology in Berlin.
[21] FM 9:172–175, 194–199 (no. 45–46). For the sense of 'Benjaminite', see p82.
[22] FM 9:120–122 (no. 21).
[23] FM 4:71–72, 78–79, 81–82, 94–96, and n527, 116–118, 120–122; Ziegler 2006a:346–347; Ziegler 2006b:36. Between thirty-two and thirty-five Senior *Musiciennes* (MUNUS.NAR.GAL) are always listed immediately after the royal family, an indication of their high social standing. A main body of Junior *Musiciennes* (MUNUS.NAR.TUR) follows. Next comes a certain Izamu, principal second wife of Yasmah-Addu, who once enjoyed the title 'Servant of the King' and led a group of former wives and singers of the deposed ruler. Some of these were probably Zimri-Lim's own sisters or

thus one of the 'household industries' that contributed to a larger interpalatial economy. Women might even be trained in a specific foreign style: Zimri-Lim committed captives from Ashlakka to a 'Subarian' musical education. From the contemporary Mariot perspective, this probably means Hurrian, so that the Ashlakkans would be cultivating their own traditions for the enrichment of musical life at Mari.[24]

The *Kinnāru* At Mari

This cosmopolitan musical environment is important for fully appreciating the position at Mari of the *kinnāru*, relatively well attested in the city's administrative texts, some of which deal with the building, decoration, and maintenance of musical instruments. A letter to Zimri-Lim from one of his officials is a status-report on a royal order for five *kinnāru*-lyres; two were ready for delivery to the king, while another three were behind schedule.[25] Another text records an allocation of a kind of varnish for two *kinnāru*-lyres.[26] A third, gold given to adorn several instruments, including a *kinnāru*.[27] A fourth mentions a kind of skin or leather allotted for various cult-objects, with several instruments; here two *kinnāru*-lyres are found alongside instruments of foreign provenance or associations.[28] This further attests an openness, at the highest social levels, to

---

cousins, whom Shamshi-Addu had committed to musical training after his acquisition of Mari: FM 4:12n59, 70, 76–79. Ziegler suggests that the giving away of harem *musiciennes* was further motivated by the need to avoid incest (FM 9:15).

[24] FM 9:18, 20, 168–169; Ziegler 2010:16. It seems clear that Ashlakka was in the area known to the Mariots as Subartu; and that while 'Subartu' itself underwent several semantic shifts in different periods (Michalowski 1986; Michalowski 1999), it included for the Mariots the Hurrian zone of the upper Habur triangle: see Finkelstein 1955:2–3.

[25] ARM 13 20.5, 7, 11, 16 = J. Bottéro in Dossin et al. 1964:39, with brief comment on 162; FM 9:72–73 (no. 11); cf. Ellermeier 1970:77; Krebernik 1983:21; HKm:97 and n196. For royal 'audition' of instruments, cf. FM 9:220–221 (no. 53), 6.

[26] ARM 23 180.12 = Bardet et al. 1984:174–175.

[27] ARM 25 547.9 = Limet 1986:171–172 with FM 9:72 and n247. Among the several other instruments mentioned here is an *urzababîtum*, for which see p35–36. For gold and silver adornment, see further Heimpel, "Balang-Gods," 23g, 34c, 42c.

[28] ARM 21 298, lines 16, 20 = Durand 1983:370–371, cf. comments on 367–368, including the mysterious material *šinûntum*. This text is largely duplicated by ARM 23 213 = Bardet et al. 1984:189–191 (*kinnāru* in line 31–32), cf. 140. See also FM 9:71–72n245. The *tilmuttu* is the 'instrument from Dilmun' (Baurain, or the east coast of the Persian Gulf: Howard-Carter 1987). The *paraḫsitu* or *parašitu* is 'the instrument from Marhashi', an area of the Iranian plateau. These instruments have been identified as lyres (or other chordophones) partly on the basis of their adjacency to the *kinnāru* here (they also appear in lexical lists alongside other instruments): Durand 1983:368; cf. Stauder 1970:217; von Soden 1988; FM 4:70n465; Ziegler 2006a:352. Steinkeller 2006:7–10 assembles the textual evidence for the *parašitu* and proposes an identification with the horizontal harps commonly depicted in pre-Iranian art of the region. But note that they appear to be an exclusively female instrument at Mari: FM 9:49.

Mari and the Amorite Age

the blending or juxtaposition of different music-streams, whether in concerted or consecutive performances.

Among the *musiciennes* known to have served members of the nobility outside the royal palace, some are mentioned as playing the *kinnāru*.[29] This is earliest textual evidence for a recurring pattern, from the Levantine lyre-girls of NK Egypt to the female lyre-ensembles of the Cypro-Phoenician symposium bowls, the *kinnōr*-playing 'harlot' of Isaiah, and beyond.[30] Vis-à-vis Mari itself, one may note an unprovenanced terracotta plaque of the OB period which shows a naked woman standing on a pedestal and playing a box lyre with curving arms in nearly horizontal position; before her a man dances and plays a frame-drum (Figure 4.1i).[31]

This plaque's lyre has clear morphological affinities with instruments of Syria and the Levant. Nor is it alone. There are five further OB representations of such instruments, and others from the Ur III and even OAkk. periods.[32] While such lyres must have been current in Amorite traditions,[33] this was probably not an exclusive association; the chronological spread of the material indicates a more general, long-term musical interaction between Syria and southern Mesopotamia. *Kinnāru(m)* must have been one name by which these instruments were known.[34] We saw that the glossing of BALAĜ as *kinnārum* at ED Ebla is mirrored by the roughly contemporary presence of *kinnāru* in Mesopotamian lexical tradition.[35] While the cognate *zannāru* evidently prevailed in southern Mesopotamia during the OAkk. and Ur III periods, P. Michalowski has plausibly suggested that the currency of *kinnāru* at OB Mari may not be due solely to Amorite influence, but represent the same larger regional usage that accounts for *kinnārum* at Ebla.[36]

While *kinnāru* has not yet appeared in the extant portions of any OB lexical text, it most probably was present in some strands of the scribal tradition in this period. This is the readiest explanation for a pair of parallel passages in

---

[29] FM 4:70n465, 221–222 (no. 42.4–5); Ziegler 2006a:347n18; FM 9:41, 50.
[30] See p61, 105–111, 245, 250, 258–272, 302.
[31] Berlin, Vorderasiatisches Museum, VA 7224: MgB 2/2:76–77 fig. 59; DCPIL:44 fig. 1(i); AMEL:60 fig. 21. A suggested connection with Inanna-Dumuzi cult is doubtful: MgB 2/2:76 (following Moortgat); embraced by MAIP:76.
[32] OAkk. cylinder seal: RlA 6:581 (Collon, *Leier B, §2 II.5.a); MgB 2/2:64–65 (fig. 43). Ur III figurine: MgB 2/2:66–67 (fig. 47–48); AMEL:38–39 and fig. 14; DCPIL:44 fig. 1(h). OB material: MgB 2/2:76–77 (fig. 59), 90–91 (fig. 76–77, 80); AMEL:59–60.
[33] HMI:79; Stauder 1961:12–19; AMEL:38–39.
[34] This is implicit in Lawergren's analysis, who in DCPIL includes them among his 'thin lyres', which he connects with *kinnāru* (58–59).
[35] See above p54, 79 and Heimpel, "Balang-Gods," 4c.
[36] Michalowski 2010b:122.

Chapter Five

MB (later second millennium[37]) exemplars of two distinct lexical series, found in areas outside of Babylonia itself.[38] From HAR.ra=*hubullu* (Ḫh),[39] as it was known at the Syrian site of Emar on the upper Euphrates in the fourteenth or thirteenth century, comes the following triad of equations:

Ḫh, Emar[40]

za-anMÙŠ	za-na-ru:	qà-an tá-bi-tum[41]
za-anMÙŠ	ki-in-na-ru	
za-anMÙŠ	ti-in-du-u	

MÙŠ functions here as a logogram, one way of designating the goddess Inanna; the signs ZA.AN are plausibly taken by M. Gantzert as a phonetic gloss of the underlying pronunciation (the first part of *zannāru*).[42] Each of the three entries here was thus considered a variety of 'Inanna-instrument', and closely comparable or akin. One may note here the OAkk. seal, which shows a bull-lyre played before the goddess Inanna/Ishtar.[43] Further permutations of 'Inanna-instrument' (gišza.dInanna, gišzà.mí dInanna, etc.) are known from other Mesopotamian lexical texts, and lyres are commonly so described in Hittite sources.[44] Note that Zannaru also occurs as one of the names by which Ishtar was known in a passage of the *Hymn to the Queen of Nippur* (a MB cento of earlier sources); as Zannaru she was "the wise/skillful goddess" and "honored by Dagan," the latter phrase suggesting a special connection with the middle Euphrates and North Syria.[45]

---

[37] In this usage 'Middle Babylonian' is chronological, not geographical.

[38] I thank †Joan Westenholz and Yoram Cohen for confirming the likelihood of this point (communication, November 2011 and July 2013, respectively).

[39] HAR.ra is now also read/known as ur5-ra: see e.g. Veldhuis 1997:46.

[40] Arnaud 1987 no. 545, lines 391–393' (p. 76); I print the text as it appears in Gantzert 2008, I:102 (Ḫh VI.10–12), also I:118 and II:65 (composite text, entry 4253a–c), where the first two signs are interpreted as a phonetic gloss (see below). Note that the wood determinative is written only at beginning and end of the column: Civil 1989:14. Dating: Pentiuc 2001:10; Civil 2004:5.

[41] Cohen 2010:825–826, has recently reread this 'second gloss' as *qà-an tá-bi-tum* (see CAD s.v. *timbuttu*: stringed instrument), thus correcting *ka-[a]n-da-bi-tu4* in the texts of Arnaud and Gantzert.

[42] I owe this reference to Sam Mirelman (communication, June 2013).

[43] MgB 2/2:64–65, fig. 42. See further Heimpel, "Balang Gods," p574.

[44] For Hittite, see p89–96. Material collected by CAD s.v. *zannaru*; discussions in Sjöberg 1965:64–65; MSL 6:119, 123, n81, 142; Lambert 1982:213; RlA 6:573 (Kilmer, *Leier A); Lawergren and Gurney 1987:41; Krispijn 1990:12; HKm:98.

[45] Lambert 1982 for text and commentary: Zannaru at III.65–68, cf. IV.28, where Inanna is "offspring of Dagan." The most important cult-site of Dagan was at Tuttul, at the confluence of the Euphrates and Balikh rivers; he received state worship at Ebla, and theophoric PNs show that he was venerated throughout northern Syria, including Mari and as far north as Tell Beydar, from at least late pre-Sargonic times onwards: Feliu 2003:8–41. An equation of Zannaru here with the *zannāru* instrument—which could also accord with her being named by and "beloved

Mari and the Amorite Age

Now the scribal traditions of Emar and other cities of the so-called western periphery—including Ugarit—are known to derive from those of OB southern Mesopotamia.[46] But because they also contain a number of local innovations and expansions, it was natural, when our passage of Emar Ḫh was viewed in isolation, to see *kinnāru* as a secondary elaboration of the entry for *zannāru*.[47] But the same sequence has now turned up in a tablet from Assur (Assyria), part of the series Diri = *(w)atru* (a difficult collection of compound logograms) which also derives from an OB tradition of the south:[48]

Diri, Assur[49]
[z]a-an-na-ru	GIŠ.ZA.MÙŠ	*zannāru*
[ ]	[GIŠ.ZA].MÙŠ	*kinnāru*
[ ]	[GIŠ.ZA].MÙŠ	*tindû*

Here too, presumably, ZA is a phonetic gloss, and GIŠ the determinative 'wood'. The agreement of Ḫh and Diri is so close that the passages should be considered duplicates.[50] Although such correspondences are not extensive in OB exemplars of Ḫh and Diri, there are enough "to believe that the two compositions influenced each other" (the direction of influence is unclear in any given case).[51] The simplest conclusion to be drawn from this material is that *kinnāru*, if it did not persist from the third millennium in Mesopotamian lexical tradition, re-entered two or more branches in the OB period thanks to the instrument's currency in the Amorite age. It then 'returned' to the western peripheral cities as part of the scribal tradition, and passed independently northward into Assyria. Whatever the explanation, the probable OB scribal currency of *kinnāru* has interesting implications for the treatment of the Divine Kinnaru in the pantheon texts of Ugarit.[52]

---

of" Ea/Enki—is assumed by CAD s.v.; MSL 6:119, 123, and n81; Sjöberg 1965:64–65; questioned by Lambert 1982:213. I thank †Joan Westenholz for feedback here (2/2011).

[46] Veldhuis 1997:67, 70–71, stressing that the relationships between OB traditions and their MB descendants on the western periphery cannot be precisely determined before the lexical texts from Ugarit are fully published. For the latter, see van Soldt 1995:171–175.

[47] Pentiuc 2001:98; DCPIL:59; Michalowski 2010b:122.

[48] For Diri generally, see Veldhuis 1997:56, 117; Civil 2004:4–6.

[49] Diri III.043–045: I follow the *mise-en-page* of Civil 2004:138. His text as presented is, like a Greek or Latin edition, an editorial composite from several exemplars. See his textual notes on 139 for the reading *ki]n-na-ru* in Assur 11884 (exemplar E: key on 134); cf. 6, "the significant sources for [Diri III] are all M[iddle] A[ssyrian]." The text is in the so-called 1-2-4 format (Civil 2004:4), where the first column is a 'reading gloss' or phonological 'description' of the compound ideogram in column 2; the final column contained the Akk. translation. For lexical text formats, see generally CANE:2305–2314 (Civil).

[50] Cf. Veldhuis 1997:118 (on two other parallels from OB texts of Ḫh and Proto-Diri): "Since the item is repeated three times both in ur5-ra [i.e. Ḫh] and in Proto-Diri we may safely assume that the sections duplicate."

[51] See Veldhuis 1997:118–120.

[52] See p121–122.

Chapter Five

The Amorite Connection

One must in any case assume, on general historical grounds, some integration of Amorite musical traditions into a wider Mesopotamian music-stream. We should therefore examine the broader cultural phenomenon in more detail, as it may further illuminate the position of the *kinnāru* in this time and place, and ultimately perhaps help account for its divinization at Ugarit and elsewhere in the West.

Increasing numbers of Amorite names in Ur III texts indicate a gradual process of infiltration and integration into Mesopotamian society during the late third millennium.[53] In the first centuries of the second, many Mesopotamian cities were controlled by dynasties of Amorite descent. The whole complex process is reflected in several compositions dealing with the god Martu, a Sumerocentric eponym for the Amorite parvenus.[54] In the so-called *Marriage of Martu*, he is presented as a powerful but crude barbarian seeking a bride among the local gentry.[55] His people are mocked for their nomadic ways, eating raw meat, ignorance of the gods and their temples, and the inability to recite prayers.[56] The text's conclusion is broken, but presumably Martu succeeded in his suit, and so at last won a place in polite society. There are also two hymns to Martu, much like those for other Sumerian gods, which seem to show his integration into the Mesopotamian divine order. While keeping his savage power, he is accepted as a son of An, favored by Enlil, and ranked among the great gods.[57] As such he now enjoys the perquisites of civilization, including a 'normal' cult:

> In holy songs musicians sing of him—the dearly cherished one, the god, the man of the hills, renowned everywhere—and promote his name gloriously. Martu, son of An, it is sweet to praise you![58]

These texts make it reasonable to suppose the Amorite adoption or adaptation of Mesopotamian liturgical practices in the course of their acculturation. This inference is supported by the case of Ishme-Dagan, the fourth king of Isin, who, while bearing an Amorite name, promoted a late flowering of Sumerianizing

---

[53] Buccellati 1966, with the problems raised by Michalowski 2011:82–121.
[54] See generally Klein 1997; Pongratz-Leisten 2011:93–94; other texts, in which Amorites are characterized in similar terms as the portrait of Martu to be discussed, are collected in Buccellati 1966:89–95, cf. 330–332.
[55] Ironically, the bride herself seems to have an Amorite name—ᵈAdgarudu < Ashratu, cognate with Athirat: Cross 1973:57; Smith and Pitard 2009:377.
[56] *Marriage of Martu* (ETCSL 1.7.1), 126–141. Römer 1989; Kramer 1990; Klein 1993; Klein 1996.
[57] *Martu A/B* (ETCSL 4.12.1, 4.12.2).
[58] *Martu A*, 57–59, translation ETCSL; cf. Falkenstein 1959:120–140.

literary activity, including more than twenty royal hymns.⁵⁹ In one of these is found a "direct imitation"⁶⁰ of Shulgi's boasts of musical prowess—including expert command of the *zannāru*:

> I have devoted myself to the art of singing, and know the occasions when praise songs are to be sung. That I am eminent in the performance style for ... songs; that I know how to intersperse appropriate words with the accompaniment of the fingers and instruments; that I have mastered the drumsticks, the sa-eš, the sabitum, the ḫarḫar and the zanaru instruments; that I have completely mastered the developed aspects of the art of singing and the recondite points of ... songs— all these things the scholars and the composers of my ... songs have put in my great songs and have declared in my hymns.⁶¹

If such posturing was largely symbolic, it was so within a Neo-Sumerian ideological framework; the important point is its purposeful resurrection by Ishme-Dagan, which he grounded in a real cultural program.⁶²

Similarly the king of Mari continued to promote Sumerian cult-music. We find a music-instructor requesting a gift from the king for teaching his students balang-compositions, while an Ishtar ritual, discussed below, contains cues for a number of Sumerian lamentation-songs.⁶³

The Amorites' own ancestral culture, however, is practically invisible in the archaeological and written record. With the exception of PNs, their language went largely undocumented, since textual production continued to be in Akkadian and literary Sumerian. Nevertheless, the Amorites and their kings evidently maintained a sense of distinct ethnic identity. This may be inferred first from a large corpus of PNs, often theophoric (and so giving limited theological information), or containing words relating to social structure, tribal ancestries, and a semi-nomadic cultural background.⁶⁴ A relatively high proportion of Mariot scribes, carriers of literate Mesopotamian culture, nevertheless bore Amorite names. Constant political relations with the West probably further encouraged the preservation of inherited traditions, and perhaps the mother

---

[59] Römer 1965; Klein 1990:65–67.
[60] Klein 1990:67.
[61] *Ishme-Dagan* A + V, 10–20 (ETCSL 2.5.4.01, 367–377). For the joining of A and V, Ludwig 1990:161–162 with Frayne 1998:7, 9.
[62] For a detailed comparison with Shulgi, and other parallels, see Ludwig 1990:189–200; Klein 1990:72–79; Frayne 1998:20–23. But note also Michalowski 2005:201, et passim on *innovations* in the hymnography of Ishbi-Erra, first king of Isin.
[63] FM 9:237–238 (no. 59); cf. Durand 1992:127; Ziegler 2006a:346, 348, 352; Ziegler 2010:122–123.
[64] Huffmon 1965; Buccellati 1966; Gelb 1980.

tongue, for some part of the OB period.⁶⁵ The case of Zimri-Lim is suggestive: as a young exile he went west to Aleppo and the court of Yarim-Lim, the powerful king of Yamhad who became his father-in-law through interdynastic marriage to the princess Shibtu.

It would hardly be surprising if, in the cosmopolitan musical environment that is clearly seen in the administrative texts, the kings of Mari equally cultivated their Amorite musical heritage. An event of special interest here is the arrival at Mari of a caravan from Hazor carrying three Amorite musicians, for whom Zimri-Lim exchanged three of his own *musiciennes*.⁶⁶ Whether 'Amorite' here has an ethno-linguistic or only a geographical sense is unclear, but it is likely enough to be both.⁶⁷ The text is equally valuable for tying Canaan, otherwise poorly documented in MBA texts, into a larger, cosmopolitan musical world. From the earlier reign of Yasmah-Addu, a letter from the chief musical instructor complains about the quality of Amorite *musiciennes* who had been brought back from a westward military expedition in support of Qatna ("They are all truly cold and old. There's not a single woman among them!").⁶⁸ They were six in number, a small subset of the ninety-four women whose training he managed.⁶⁹ The 'Benjaminite' *musiciennes* sent by Zimri-Lim to Aleppo, mentioned above, are also probably relevant, as the Banu-Yamina was an Amorite tribal group in the area of Mari.⁷⁰ These texts indicate an awareness of Amorite music as something identifiable across a considerable geographical range. It was a distinct strand within the complex web of musical traditions that were brought together and elaborated by the royal courts of Mari, Qatna, Aleppo, and elsewhere.

The fairly prominent position of the *kinnāru* at Mari thus becomes more intelligible. The presence of these lyres among other cult-objects indicates that they were being constructed not solely for novelty entertainment in the harem, but for more lofty roles.

We saw that the Bible, in crediting its *kinnōr*'s invention to Jubal, not only traces it to the distant past, but makes it part of a semi-nomadic lifestyle; and while in isolation this may seem a romantic anachronism, the portrait is generally confirmed by the Beni-Hassan tomb-painting.⁷¹ A comparable intersec-

---

[65] Durand 1992:123–126; Durand 1997 1:39–40.
[66] For this event, Bonechi 1992; Malamat 1999; Malamat 2003; Ziegler 2006a:4; FM 9:19–20.
[67] Cf. FM 9:19–20.
[68] FM 9:217–220 (no. 52.8'–9'), following her translation. For the political background, Charpin and Ziegler 2003:101–102, 124–125.
[69] FM 4 37; cf. FM 9:20, 85n14.
[70] For the Banu-Yamina, see e.g. CANE:1238 (Whiting).
[71] See p44–45.

tion of music-making and a semi-legendary nomadic past may also be inferred behind king-lists relating to Amorite dynasts of Babylon and Assyria.

The *Assyrian King List* famously lists seventeen ancestral "kings who dwelled in tents."[72] This section agrees partially with the *Genealogy of the Hammurabi Dynasty* (*GHD*), where several pairs of cognate rhyming names reveal that the two texts derive from a common heritage of myth-making, and suggest "that this segment of the tradition was originally preserved as some kind of desert chant—perhaps as part of oral epic of early tribal heroes."[73] The ancient 'kings' of these texts are in reality a variety of tribal eponyms—names and relationships that were probably gradually recomposed over the generations to reflect shifting political and social patterns in relations between various Amorite groups and the urban states with which they interacted.[74] One of the names (Ditānu/Didānu) resurfaces at Ugarit as a quasi-deity and seemingly an ancestor of the royal line.[75]

The fluidity of this material would indeed accord with a derivation from some form of oral epic tradition. Numerous ethnographic analogies show that musical accompaniment is often involved in such narrative singing; most common are stringed instruments, which provide in a single convenient package both tonal material and the rhythm essential for structuring verse. Note that the performance medium for the preservation of the *GHD* was royal ancestor cult, internal evidence showing that it was used in the course of a *kispu* ritual, when food and drink were offered to the ghosts of kings past.[76] We encountered something of the sort at Ebla, where I argued for the involvement of *kinnārum*-threnody; similarly at Ugarit I will explore the symbolic importance of the *kinnāru* in royal mortuary cult.

Divine Instruments and the Amorite World

The third-millennium practice of divinizing instruments continued strong in the OB period. Years named after the dedication of *lilissu*-drums are known for Immerum of Sippar (ca. 1845), Itur-Šamaš of Kisurra (ca. 2138), and Iter-Piša of Isin (ca. 1833–1831).[77] An inscription of Warad-Sin of Larsa (ca. 1834–1823) commemorated a *lilissu* (and perhaps also a BALAĜ) "dedicated for his own life

---

[72] ANET:564; CS 1 no. 1.135 (here p. 463).
[73] Finkelstein 1966:112.
[74] See Michalowski 1983:243–246.
[75] Lipiński 1978; HUS:613; RCU:113–114n124.
[76] Finkelstein 1966:113–116; cf. CANE:1239 (Whiting).
[77] See PHG:99–100, with reference to the issue of semantic shift and performance contexts of BALAĜ (see p531, 573); cf. Gabbay 2014 §4.

Chapter Five

and for the life of his father."⁷⁸ Years were also named from the dedication of *ala*-drums by two early nineteenth-century kings, one in the temple of Zababa by Iawium of Kish,⁷⁹ the other in that of Nanna by Manana of Urum/Ilip.⁸⁰

An administrative text from Mari records a large consignment of silver and gold sent to Tuttul, in northern Syria, for decorating 'Ninigizibara'.⁸¹ We saw this name earlier applied to an instrument built and dedicated by Ibbi-Sin of Ur.⁸² Ninigizibara is otherwise well known from Ur III and OB god-lists, where it can appear as a "GU4.BALAĜ advisor of Inanna."⁸³ Animal offerings to Ninigizibara are also attested at Uruk, once "on the occasion of a lamentation rite which accompanied a circumambulation starting from the gate of the Ĝipar," and in a number of other ritual contexts.⁸⁴

Most striking of all, as a comparandum for Kinyras, is a detail in the OB balang-composition (or 'oratorio') Uru'amma'irabi (*That City Which Has Been Pillaged*), in which Inanna lamented the destruction of her city, temple, and the balang Ninigizibara itself, as well as Dumuzi's infidelity and death.⁸⁵ In this work, Ninigizibara seems to be treated as Inanna's husband or lover, "shar[ing] Inanna's bedroom as an intimate partner of the goddess."⁸⁶ Other laments show that it was a trope of these compositions to include the balang, or its hall, among what has been destroyed in a city or temple.⁸⁷

Uru'amma'irabi also featured in a ritual performed at Mari itself during the reign of Yasmah-Addu, which focused on the balang Ninigizibara. This text gives us our most detailed glimpse of how divinized instruments might serve in complex ceremonies, in this case a sequence of lamentation rites involving the

---

⁷⁸ RIME 4 2.13.1002, iii: 4'-9'; PHG:99 (quotation), noting: "Another possibility is that the sequence balaĝ li-li-ìs (zabar) is to be understood as 'balaĝ and (bronze) *lilissu* drum', perhaps indicating that in this period the balaĝ stringed instrument was still used in cult together with the *lilissu* drum." (The same interpretive issue arises with the inscription of Hammurabi discussed on p86–87.) See also Gabbay 2014 §4; Heimpel, "Balang-Gods," 44.

⁷⁹ Simmons 1960:83 (ii); Charpin 1978:28n56, chronology on 40; cf. Mirelman 2014.

⁸⁰ Simmons 1960:76–77 (kk, ll); Charpin 1978:28 (e), chronology on 40; cf. Mirelman 2014.

⁸¹ The text is ARM 25 566 = Joannès 1985:111–112 no. 10; cf. FM 3:47, discussing this goddess's relationship to Dagan at Tuttul; PHG:106; RlA 9:382 (Heimpel, *Ninigizibara); Heimpel, "Balang-Gods," 23g2.

⁸² See p22.

⁸³ Heimpel 1998:10–11; RlA 9:382–384 (Heimpel, *Ninigizibara); Gabbay 2014 §10 and n23 (quotation); PHG:106–107; Heimpel, "Balang-Gods," 23.

⁸⁴ FM 3:47; RlA 9:382–384 (Heimpel, *Ninigizibara, quotation 383), noting several contexts in which Ninigizibara is known from Umma (see Heimpel, "Balang-Gods," 23).

⁸⁵ CLAM:536–603; Heimpel, "Balang-Gods," 47.

⁸⁶ Volk 2006:94, line 14 with PHG:112–113 (quotation), raising the question of Ninigizibara's gender; also Heimpel, "Balang-Gods," Section 2d and 23f.

⁸⁷ See for example *Uruhulake of Gula* (*She of the Ruined City*), a+45, 48 (CLAM:256, 262) and *Abzu Pelam* (*The Defiled Apsu*), 86 (CLAM:55, 60); I thank U. Gabbay for these references (communication, July 2012). See further Heimpel, "Balang-Gods," 49.

king himself.⁸⁸ On the last day of an unnamed month, the goddess's temple was purified and the instrument set up before her. The king and other participants, including lamentation-priests and ensembles of male and female musicians, were carefully arranged around and facing Ninigizibara, which was itself flanked by various cultic symbols.⁸⁹ An elaborate series of rites then unfolded, punctuated by lamentation-singing; the structure of this ritual seems to be informed by the sequence of elements in Uru'amma'irabi itself.⁹⁰ Laments were somehow conjoined with prophecy by an 'ecstatic' (*muhhûm*), although the precise relationship between the two practices is unclear.⁹¹

It may be that Ninigizibara was not actually played in these performances, but was the *object* of song "as a representation of Inanna herself ... in her aspect as a lamenting goddess."⁹² This interpretation would fit nicely with the idea, attested in both Greek and ANE sources, that lamentable situations like war and royal deaths are times when lyre-music should be stilled.⁹³ At the same time, the participating ensembles make it quite certain that instrumental music, including strings, was indeed heard. Thus, while Ninigizibara itself might represent the stilling of music, the ritual as a whole will have used music to reverse the divine mood—the normal function of lamentation singing.⁹⁴ Perhaps sympathetic vibration played a role here, since an unplayed Ninigizibara would still murmur in response to the music of others. Was this seen as evidence that the instrument was indeed alive, had its own voice, and was itself lamenting?

The Mari tablet, which records silver and gold for Ninigizibara, makes it quite possible that, with other texts involving precious metals for musical instruments, we are again dealing with divinized specimens. We saw above that the *kinnāru* is attested in just such a context. Indirect support for the deduction comes from the *urzababîtum* included in the same transaction, which transpired

---

⁸⁸ OB Ishtar ritual from Mari: Dossin 1938; FM 3 2, the name appearing as ᵈNingizippara at i.8', 10' (see comments on 47), also in "Le rituel d'Eštar d'Irradân," FM 3 3 i.21' (cf. p62); FM 9:55-64; Nissinen et al. 2003:80-82 (nos. 51-52), with further literature; cf. PHG:106; Ziegler 2010:126-127.
⁸⁹ Cf. FM 3:48, with the illustration of FM 9:56.
⁹⁰ See FM 3:49-50; FM 9:61 (on ii.19'); PHG:182-183.
⁹¹ FM 3 2 ii.19'-27', and the comparable 3 iii.4'-13', is unfortunately lacunose. See remarks of Durand 1988:386-387; FM 3:50; Nissinen et al. 2003:82n a; FM 9:61, 63-64. Stökl 2012:211-214 rejects a direct link between music and ecstatic prophecy. But key readings are quite uncertain, and the immediate conjunction of musicians and ecstatics in both texts must be *somehow* significant. The instructions may be elliptical, not fully elaborating the stages of 'collaboration' between musicians and ecstatics.
⁹² U. Gabbay (communication, July 2012); cf. also Ziegler's observations on the instrument in FM 9:60 (on i 8'), 62 (on iii, 12, 14, 18, 28). Heimpel, "Balang-Gods," Section 4a, suggests that the instrument was indeed played—an "illogical element."
⁹³ See p41, 291-303.
⁹⁴ See p23-29.

under Zimri-Lim. For another Mari text, this time from the reign of Yasmah-Addu, in referring to a group of instruments ready for royal 'audition,' mentions the incomplete status of an *urzababîtum* whose name incorporates that of the king himself: Samsi-Yasmah-Addu, 'Yasmah-Addu is my Sun'.[95] This must be a divinized instrument. The name, to judge from the parallels, seems to place Yasmah-Addu in the position of a master-god who will be served by the *urzababîtum*.[96] We encountered another such 'King of Kish instrument' in the texts of Shulgi, and one appeared in a god-list as servant of Ninurta; the complex model of 'musical cognition' this implies brings together king, past king, and the divine through the medium of royal music.[97] To find yet another *urzababîtum* in the service of Mari's monarch, and even bearing his own name, raises interesting questions about the intersection of musical ideology and the tradition—that is, the handing down—of royal power.[98] It may even be that Yasmah-Addu's *urzababîtum* is the very one which Zimri-Lim—his successor *from a rival dynasty*—caused to be adorned.

Finally one must note a Babylonian royal inscription relating to the fortieth year of Hammurabi's reign. The king marked his defeat of Zimri-Lim and the destruction of Mari by dedicating two musical instruments and a standard in the Emeslam, a temple of Nergal in Kutha (a day's ride northeast of Babylon):

> Eternal seed of kingship, mighty king, king of Babylon, king of all the Amorite land, king of Sumer and Akkad, when he captured Mari and its villages, destroyed its wall, and turned the land into ru[bble heaps (and) ru]ins, he set up a BALAĜ and a bronze kettledrum (for) holy songs, which please the heart, etc.[99]

We saw two earlier dedications of a BALAĜ, one by Gudea of Lagash, the other by Ibbi-Sin, last of the Ur III emperors. These events were of sufficient political importance to give their names to the year in question. These parallels underscore the gravity of Hammurabi's action, and show this self-consciously Amorite king to be equally a pious perpetuator of Mesopotamian cult practice

---

[95] See FM 9:221–222 (no. 53.7-8), arguing against an alternative interpretation of this name as belonging to a musician. So too U. Gabbay (communication, March 2010): "An *urzababîtum* instrument in Mari is called Samsi-Yasmah-Addu ... surely referring to the king of Mari of this name ... which again shows the connection of this instrument to kings." Cf. Heimpel, "Balang-Gods," p627.
[96] Is the sun god also somehow invoked?
[97] See p35–36.
[98] Cf. p134–141.
[99] Sollberger and Walker 1985; but I follow the text and translation of RIME 4 3.6.11, who read BALAĜ in line 31 (the passage quoted here is lines 23–34).

("king of all the Amorite land, king of Sumer and Akkad").[100] The context also permits reasonable guesses about the significance of the dedication. That this was considered the right gesture to punctuate the king's final triumph over Zimri-Lim is indicated, first, by the text's immediate juxtaposition of the two events. Furthermore, the god Nergal, to whom the instruments are devoted, has already been invoked as "the terrifying king who [goes] at the head of the troops, who annihilates the enemy lands." With Mari's defeat, Hammurabi's long and careful expansionist career reached a successful climax, giving him unrivalled control over the Babylonian heartland and the eastern stretches of the Amorite cultural sphere.[101] The instruments may therefore be seen as a gesture of thanksgiving to Nergal, on the one hand, and a symbol of Hammurabi's New World Order on the other—with the vanquished enemy ushering in an age of peaceful, festive music, and the end of lamentation.

Three key points remain uncertain. First, we cannot be sure that the BALAĜ of this text means 'lyre', for this is the period in which it seems to have made its transition to a kind of drum.[102] It may also be that BALAĜ functions merely as a determinative, qualifying the *lilissu* in some way.[103] Nor can we be certain that this BALAĜ was divinized, although the dedicatory context makes this probable. Finally, it is possible that BALAĜ may conceal some more properly Amorite instrument name, just as it was glossed as *kinnārum* by the scribes of Ebla and in the ED Practical Vocabulary.[104] If one could infer such an equation here, it might be that Hammurabi was expressing his triumph over a rival Amorite king with a gesture that was not only devout from a traditional Mesopotamian perspective, but also symbolically potent within the Amorite cultural continuum.

Conclusion

Amorite integration in Mesopotamia during the Ur III period and OB periods, combined with the continuing sense of Amorite identity across a wide geographical range, together provide a favorable environment for the emergence of a Divine Kinnaru.[105] The Martu texts hint at the assimilation of Amorite

---

[100] Hammurabi bears the title 'king of all the Amorite land' again in RIME 4 3.6.10, 8.
[101] See generally Kuhrt 1995:95–109; van De Mieroop 2005:64–79. RIME 4:344, follows Stol in suggesting that Hammurabi had already assumed the title "King of All the Amorite Land" in his thirty-fourth regnal year.
[102] See p531, 573.
[103] See PHG:99, and above n78.
[104] See p54, 65–67, 79.
[105] Liverani 1971:61 writes of this period: "l'omogeneità delle popolazioni stanziate in Mesopotamia e in Siria (gli Amorrei) e gli ampli rapporti politici e commerciali tra le due aree (come sono esemplarmente documentati dai testi di Mari) rendevano particolarmente agevole il trapasso di idiologie e di procedimenti politico-sociali e religiosi."

Chapter Five

cult to Mesopotamian liturgical practices. Mari, where we can most clearly document Amorite traditions surrounded by ancient Mesopotamian cult practices—including divinized instruments—should be considered a type-site in this respect too. The presence of an ecstatic prophet within the Ishtar/Ninigizibara ritual above is a suggestive case of West-meets-East.[106] So too the lexical equation of *kinnāru* and *zannāru* (probably of OB date, but certainly MB), where their definition as 'Inanna-instrument' surely implies some theological interpretation of the lyre—for typically divine balangs reflected and embodied various facets of their master gods.[107] It should be noted that Byblos, one traditional home of Kinyras, was within the cultural orbit of the Ur III emperors (Chapter 19). The practice of divinizing lyres and other cult-objects may have been generally adopted among the Amorites and other Syro-Levantine kings of the late third and early second millennium as part of a conscious emulation of the ideological and cultural models of contemporary Babylonia. The *kinnāru*'s importance in royal cult—implicit at Ebla and Mari, and more clearly demonstrable elsewhere from the LBA onwards as the following chapters will show—provides a plausible motivation, with the instrument's deep antiquity being matched by that of the royal cults themselves.

---

[106] Cf. FM 3:50: "Cette intervention d'un prophète occidental au sein d'une grande liturgie sumérienne, pour déconcertante qu'elle soit, montre bien à quel degré de syncrétisme on en était arrivé dans la région d'Akkad." For the Amorite dimension of the Mari prophetic texts, see Lemaire 1996.

[107] See Heimpel, "Balang-Gods," passim.

6

Peripherals, Hybrids, Cognates

THIS CHAPTER PRESENTS A SELECTIVE SURVEY of mainly LBA texts and iconography from cultural areas peripheral to, and closely engaged with, the Syro-Levantine linguistic and cultural sphere in which *kinnāru* was at home. From a vast body of more general evidence, I have assembled the material bearing most closely on the Kinnaru-Kinyras question. This investigation helps flesh out a larger background for both Kinnaru of Ugarit and that city's lyre-culture (Chapter 7), and the Syro-Levantine lyric heritage of the Biblical world (Chapter 8). Beyond this, it provides compelling parallels for the diffusion of the *knr* and associated ideas to Cyprus already in the second millennium (n.b.). It also clarifies the cultural motivations that can account for such a development, including various ritual uses to which lyres were put, especially in royal contexts. Finally, it illuminates the processes by which such cult importations transpired; I pay special attention to 'Ishtar'—vitally relevant for Kinyras given the goddess's persistent association with stringed-instruments, and his intimate relationship with 'Aphrodite.'

The 'Inanna-Instrument' and Hittite Royal Ritual

We have seen that both *kinnāru* and *zannāru* were defined as 'Inanna-instrument' ($^{za-an}$MÙŠ, $^{giš.za}$MÙŠ) by Mesopotamian scribes probably already in the OB period.[1] An equivalent expression, $^{giš.d}$INANNA, is well-attested in Hittite sources. That this 'Inanna-instrument' was normally (if not exclusively) a lyre in the Hittite world is established by several sets of overlapping evidence.[2] First, $^{giš.d}$INANNA is the most frequently attested instrument in Hittite texts, while lyres are the most

---

[1] See p77–79.
[2] For the following points, see Laroche 1955:72–73; Sjöberg 1965:64–65; Gurney 1977:34; de Martino 1987 and RlA 8:483–488 (*Musik A III); Özgüç 1988:99; Güterbock 1995:57; AMEL:87; Klinger 1996:229–234; DCPIL:58–59; Ivanov 1999:587–589; HKm:97–106, with further references in n193.

commonly represented in a rich iconographical record.³ Second, the common qualification of the 'Inanna-instrument' as 'large' or 'small' (⁽ᵍⁱˢ·ᵈ⁾INANNA.GAL and ᵍⁱˢ·ᵈINANNA.TUR) may be correlated with the famous Inandık vase, which shows two sizes of lyre (Figure 7, and below). Third, the same size-distinction is reflected in the equivalent Hattic-Hittite terms *ḫun-zinar* and *ippi-zinar*, where the linguistic kinship of *zinar* to both *kinnāru* and *zannāru* is obvious to the eye (though the precise historical-cultural explanation is debated).⁴ It is thus quite certain that ᵍⁱˢ·ᵈINANNA typically means 'lyre', and that *ḫun-zinar* and *ippi-zinar*, though themselves but lightly attested, are regular referents of the Sumerograms.

Still we should not be too categorical.⁵ The Hittites embraced many regional cults, maintaining them with the appropriate liturgies. We hear of those who sang in Hittite, Hattic, Hurrian, Luwian, and 'Babylonian' (that is, Akkadian); some festivals brought together musicians from different parts of the kingdom.⁶ Since Sumerograms can represent various languages, and since ᵍⁱˢ·ᵈINANNA is often found in connection with foreign musicians and/or rites deriving from different ethnic spheres,⁷ the expression must sometimes have designated instruments *not* called *zinar*. In rituals of Hurrian extraction, we shall see, the underlying word was, or at least would once have been, *kinnāru*.

This point bears especially on the position of harps (not lyres) in second-millennium Anatolia, Syria, and the Levant, where they are represented much less frequently than lyres—a sign of some exceptional and/or exotic status. This, when combined with clear morphological sympathies, shows that these instruments were more or less consciously Mesopotamianizing; and that in turn raises questions about the retention and development of associated theological concepts as they passed beyond the two rivers. Representing Syria is a fifteenth-century cylinder-seal from Alalakh, showing a female harper performing with

---

³ See the recent catalogue of HKm with extensive bibliography for each piece.
⁴ See especially Ivanov 1999:588–589, proposing a proto-Luwian adaptation behind the three forms, e.g. WS *ki-* > proto-Luw. *kᵘi-* > *zi-* (whence Hatt./Hitt. *zinar*) > *za-* (Akk./Sum. *zannāru*, this last stage not being fully explicated by the author). The third-millennium date which these developments require could also account for several apparent cognates in Caucasian languages noted by Ivanov (see p61). A Luwian hypothesis does seem promising in view of that language's early 'superstrate' relationship to Hittite (Yakubovich 2010:227–238). But it would remain to explain how a (proto-)Luwian form could have become established in Mesopotamian usage by the OAkk. period. Ivanov is quick to concede that not all forms in *z-* need go back to a single development (palatalization of *k-* before front vowel is a common phenomenon). Note that Gurney's rejection of a Luwian origin for Hatt./Hitt. *zinar* (in DCPIL:59) is not in itself insurmountable, as Hattic prefixes could have been added secondarily (Klinger 1996:230n408).
⁵ Cf. Klinger 1996:233–235, with different emphasis.
⁶ Pecchioli Daddi 1982:339–343; Haas 1994:539–615; CANE:1991 (G. McMahon); de Martino 2002:624; HKm:9–14 et passim.
⁷ Pecchioli Daddi 1982:329–336 passim; HKm:100–106 passim.

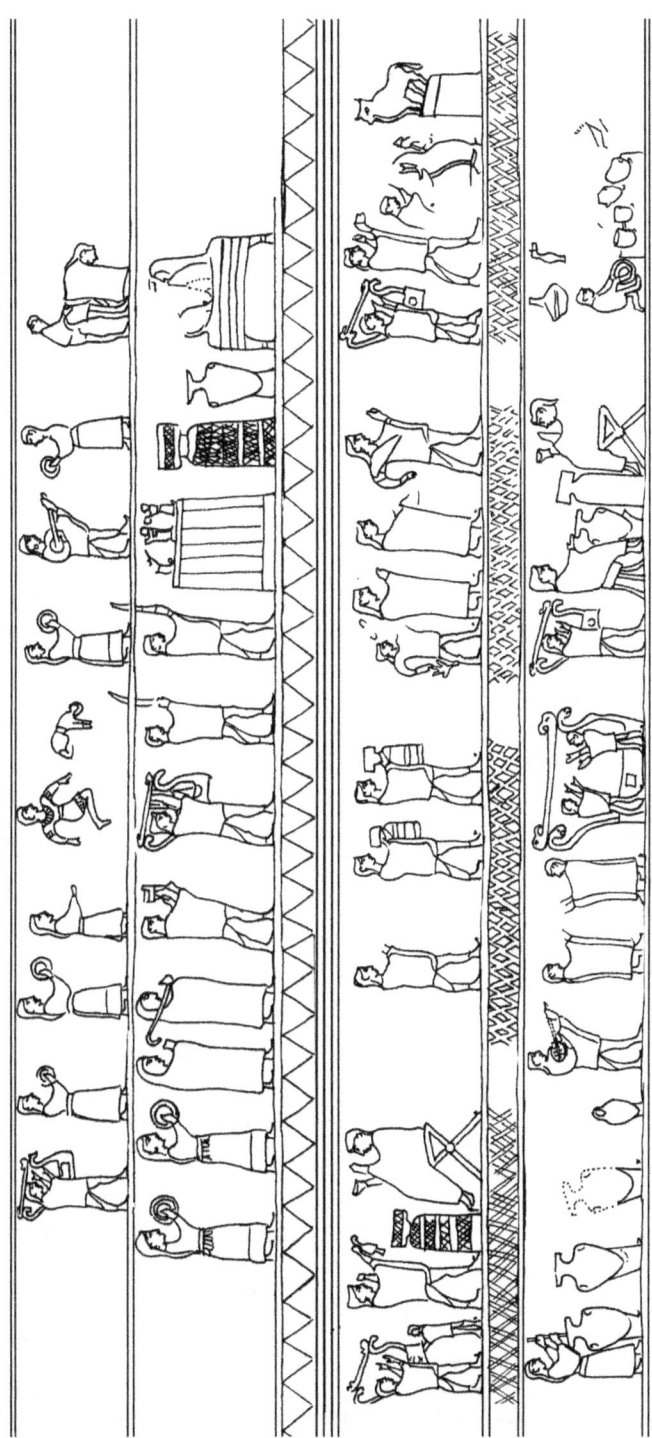

Figure 7 Musical rite in four registers. Inandık vase, ca. 1650–1550 (Old Hittite). Anadolu Medeniyetleri Müzesi, Ankara. Drawn from photos in Özgüç 1988.

Figure 8 Ishtar (?) playing harp before Ea. Modern impression of Syro-Hittite seal from Konya-Karahöyük, ca. 1750. Drawn from Alp 1972 pl. 11, no. 22.

a female drummer and dancer before an enthroned goddess; stylistic parallels corroborate an eastern origin or antecedents for the seal.[8] The numerous angle-harps of NK Egyptian art may be explained as musical imports from Levantine imperial holdings and/or the Syrian diplomatic periphery; at least some of those from the palace of Amarna (Figures 9, 10) probably derive from dynastic marriages with Mitanni (see below).[9] A final example, one of several Anatolian representations, returns us to the question of Hittite scribal usage. This is a Syro-Hittite-style seal of Hittite OK date, from the palace of Konya-Karahöyük, which probably shows Ishtar playing a harp before Ea and his vizier (Figure 8).[10] If so, the instrument would clearly deserve the title 'Inanna-instrument' as much as *zinar*, *kinnāru*, or *zannāru*. In other words, the designation's essential ideas will have been predicated less upon narrow organological distinctions—partly or largely modern—than such factors as performance context and ritual poetics. In practice this means that, when seeking sympathies between Mesopotamian

---

[8] Alalakh cylinder-seal (Antakya 7989): see Collon 1982:74–75 no. 47, dating it to the first half of the fifteenth century, and suggesting parallels for the harp and throne at Nuzi and in Elam; cf. also Collon 1987 no. 664; Caubet 1996:30 fig. 8; RlA 8:489 fig. 2 (Collon, *Musik I B). The two harps in the Nuzi seal which Collon cites from Porada 1947:58, 116 no. 711 do provide a quite exact parallel; comparable forms are found in OB terracotta plaques: MgB 2/2:80–85 fig. 62–70.

[9] Hickmann 1954b:292; Green 1992:219; Manniche 2000:234; Manniche 2006.

[10] Alp 1972:120–121 and pl. 11.22; Esin 2002:514–515, 518 fig. 1, suggesting the OA trading colony at MBA Kanesh as the conduit for such imagery. For the other two images, see HKm:57, 60 with pl. 4 no. 14 (ceramic fragment with relief, sixteenth–fifteenth century), 68 with pl. 10 fig. 31 (terracotta figurine) and 32 (ceramic fragment with relief, thirteenth-twelfth century), 107–108. There are also two episodes in the Hurro-Hittite *Kumarbi Cycle* where Ishtar-Shaushka plays music to seduce (and thus overthrow) monstrous offspring raised by Kumarbi to challenge the storm-god Teshup; one of the instruments, in the *Song of Ullikummi*, is rendered as BALAĜ.DI, but its interpretation as lyre or harp is not secure, most preferring 'drum': CTH 345 (§35–37 in Hoffner and Beckman 1998:60–61). The parallel scene is in *Song of Hedammu*: CTH 348; fr. 11 in Siegelová 1971, with Hoffner and Beckman 1998:54 and 77n14. See further HKm:112–115; Brison 2014:189–194.

and western musical theologies and ideologies, we need not be strictly bound by morphological constraints. These points will be important for understanding a key piece of LBA Cypriot evidence.[11]

Since *ḫun-zinar* and *ippi-zinar* contain Hattic prefixes, it is generally and rightly held that *zinar* itself was borrowed into Hittite from Hattic.[12] This must relate to the integration of Hattian mythology, festivals, cult, and ritual processes into Hittite life after Hattusili I (ca. 1650-1620) transferred his dynastic seat from Kanesh to Hattusha.[13] The long-term impact of Hattic cult-lyric per se is indicated by the Hittite use of *zinar/zinir* to mean 'music' generally; thus, for the Hittites, as doubtless for the Hattians, ritual music was preeminently lyre-music, whatever other instruments may have complemented it.

The early Hattian-Hittite use of large and small lyres is best illustrated by the Inandık vase of the seventeenth or sixteenth century (Figure 7)—a piece which also gives a vivid impression of the potential complexity and grandeur of Hittite music-rituals generally. Various stages of action are presented across four registers involving priests, priestesses, offering-bearers, libation-preparers, acrobats, and musicians—with lyres predominant, but also cymbals and lutes.[14] The whole composition, and the ritual actions shown therein, climax in a scene of explicit sexual intercourse. Here, if anywhere, one might hope to vindicate the kind of 'hands-on' hierogamy once readily imagined by many scholars not so long ago. The objections and cautions raised by more recent critics have certainly done much to refine our understanding of the disparate phenomena traditionally grouped under 'Sacred Marriage', some of which we encountered in connection with Shulgi of Ur.[15] The carnality of the Inandık vase, however, is hard to dismiss completely. Some would see the ritual depicted as a local emulation of contemporary Mesopotamian practice, a royal rite in honor of Inanna/Ishtar or an epichoric equivalent.[16] Others look to an indigenous procreation festival and royal initiation rites.[17] Be this as it may, the scene should be born in mind when considering the connection between Kinyras and Aphrodite in

---

[11] See p383-392.
[12] Wegner 1981:155–156; Güterbock 1995:57; DCPIL:58–59; Ivanov 1999:587–588; HKm:97–106.
[13] See generally Klinger 1996, especially 229–234, 740–754. Ethnomusicologists might see in this an example of "museum effect" (Nettl 1985:28), though 'temple effect' would be better here.
[14] Cf. Özgüç 1988:99. In the ritual text KUB 25.1 rev. v.11–16, the large lyre, while playing together with drum, cymbals, lute, and clapping, appears to be the lead instrument in the hands of a priest-singer: cf. HKm:102.
[15] See p37–40.
[16] Özgüç 1988:92–104 (suggesting the OA trading colony at Kanesh as the locus of transmission, 99); Wimber 2009:7.
[17] Alp 2000:19–20; Brison 2014:195 with references.

Chapter Six

Greco-Roman mythology, and the church-fathers' allegations of orgiastic sexual rites at Paphos.[18]

Hittite texts of the NK show that the *zinar* and other cult-objects enjoyed devotions similar to what is found in Sumerian sources.[19] One example relates to the Festival of the Crocus (AN.TAḪ.ŠUM), a major Spring celebration for the "Sun Goddess of Arinna and the Gods of the Hatti Land," during which king and queen traveled to various temples to oversee a series of appropriate rites, involving at different junctures singers and incantation priests, including lamentations for several forms of Ishtar.[20] The numerous offerings prescribed during the preliminaries at Hattusha itself include the following:

> Next they attend to the [sc. holy] places with liver, w[ine]: once for the Altar ... once for the Throne-God, once for the Window, once for the Inside Chamber, once behind the Hearth, once for the Lyre of the Divinity.[21]

Presumably, this initial offering to the lyre helped ensure the efficacy of the lyre-performances that would transpire during several of the ceremonies. These included, among many drinking and offering rituals for various gods, one at the *ḫešti*, a temple associated with the underworld goddess Lelwani and royal ancestor cult; and a major performance of massed lyres at the 'great assembly'.[22]

Similar procedures are found in other texts.[23] Offerings of sheep, cheese, bread, honey, groats, and libations of wine and beer, are attested for lyres alongside other cult-equipment and temple-furniture.[24] Another ritual, going back to the Hattic cult-stratum, calls for a soothsayer to anoint various utensils of the gods, including lyres, drums, and cymbals, alongside the god's statue itself.[25]

---

[18] See p222 and n15.
[19] The following material is collected in HKm:101–102. For treatment of *loci numinosi* in Hittite temples more generally, see Popko 1978:14–28 (83–84 for musical instruments, suggesting that this was a development of the NK); Haas 1994:262–282 (with subsections on hearth, altar, roof, pilasters, etc.) and 682–684 for cult-music; further references in HKm:102n226.
[20] See generally Güterbock 1960; Haas 1994:772–826; HKm:12.
[21] KBo 4.13 + KUB 10.82 rev. v.4–10; see Haas 1994:779; HKm:101n219.
[22] Haas 1994:780–781, 789–790, 794–795 (at the *ḫešti*, for which see generally 245; Singer 1983–1984 1:112–115; Bachvarova forthcoming, passim), 796, 800 (great assembly), 801–802, 807, 817–818.
[23] KBo 17.74 with offerings to throne, hearth, etc., apparently with lyre accompaniment (the text is damaged): Neu 1970:18–35. KBo 19.128, probably also relating to the AN.TAḪ.ŠUM festival: Otten 1971:8–9. Cf. Popko 1978:23, 83–84.
[24] KBo 4.13 rev. iv.7 (sheep for the 'Lyre of the Divinity of the Father of the Sun God'): Badalì 1991:80 no. 60; for translation see HKm:101. KUB 20.43, 3': Popko 1978:83; *HKm*:101.
[25] KBo 33.167 rev. iv.16'–20'. Another lyre is anointed in KBo 23.42 + 27.119 rev. iv. 24'–25'. This is followed by a Hurrian passage. Cf. HKm:101.

Hittite sources are equally valuable for their comparatively detailed documentation of the cultic use of lyres. One tablet calls for lyre-music, accompanied by drums and cymbals, during a royal ritual connected with the Storm God of Zippalanda.[26] This ensemble predicts the pairing of lyre with frame-drum in several of the so-called Lyre-Player Group of Seals from eighth-century Cilicia (Chapter 21). Another drinking ritual has the royal couple sitting while a priest-singer plays the large lyre.[27] In a third, cymbals are given to the royal couple while lyres and drums continue to play.[28] Others again call for unaccompanied lyre-music.[29]

Several texts bring the lyre into connection with funerary and/or mortuary rituals.[30] One deals with the decoration of a lyre with silver (perhaps sheeting) for such a use.[31] Sometimes lamentation singers ($^{lú.meš}$GALA) are specified as playing the instrument.[32] One ritual calls for drinks for the soul of the dead, with lyre accompaniment.[33] In other cases, however, lyre-music is specifically prohibited.[34] Thus, during a drinking ceremony for the soul of a deceased king or queen, on the second day of the royal funerary rites after cremation and gathering of the bones, the lyre was required to be still.[35] Nor were lyres to sound during a ritual for the death-goddess Lelwani (part of the AN.TAḪ.ŠUM festival).[36]

There was another such prohibition during the KI.LAM ('gatehouse') festival, an autumnal event designed to display "the unity of all parts of the core of the Hittite empire by bringing in regional performers and administrators to the Hittite capital, including male choruses and female choruses of maidens, each ceremonially presenting the results of their labor that sustained the kingdom."[37] Lyres—variously large or small, with and without singing—accompanied royal

[26] KUB 20.19 + 51.87 rev. iv.12'–14': HKm:98. Lyre and drum specified together in what seems to be an entry-ritual: KBo 21.34 ii.9–10: HKm:100.
[27] KBo 20.85 rev. iv.1–5: HKm:98, cf. 102–103.
[28] KUB 56.46+ ii.3'–7': HKm:99, cf. 102.
[29] HKm:99.
[30] HKm:103–104.
[31] KUB 30.25+ KBo 34.68 + KBo 39.4.25: Popko 1978:83; HKm:104.
[32] KBo 11.60 rev. 7'–8', 12'–13', 14'–15': HKm:102, cf. 161–162.
[33] HKm:103–104 with references.
[34] HKm:153–155.
[35] KUB 30.15 + 39.19.17–20 and KUB 30.23 + 39.13 ii.5: see Otten 1958:66, 72; HKm:155. Note that singing to the harp is sometimes specified for other funerary rituals, at least at certain junctures: see with references HKm:107.
[36] HKm:105, 155.
[37] Quotation from Bachvarova forthcoming. For the festival generally, see Singer 1983–1984, with synopsis of events 1:58–64; Haas 1994:748–771; CANE:2666–2667 (de Martino, seeing a "visual parallel" among the musical orthostats of Alaca Hüyük, for which see HKm:66–67 and pl. 9–10 [nos. 29–30]).

Chapter Six

drinking ceremonies in honor of different gods at different junctures (including the 'great assembly'), as well as a procession of cult-objects. But on the second day of the festival there was to be no music at all.[38]

The Syro-Hurrian Sphere

Another major contribution made by the Hattusha archives comes from ritual texts deriving from the Hurrian cultural sphere. These, complemented by sources from elsewhere, especially North Syria, present further parallels for the veneration of cult-objects, including lyres, and illuminate other phenomena relevant to the Kinnaru-Kinyras question.

Hurrian is a non-Semitic, non-Indo-European language with debated affinities. Hurrian-speakers are attested already in the Old Akkadian period (ca. 2340–2159) around the Khabur river valley to the north of Mesopotamia. By the early second millennium, they were spreading westwards through North Syria and as far as the area later known as Cilicia in southern Anatolia.[39] Key evidence comes from Alalakh (Tell Atchana), which in the early second millennium belonged to the kingdom of Yamhad, centered on Aleppo (where Zimri-Lim passed his youthful exile[40]). Although this city was largely Amorite at the time, its onomasticon indicates a major Hurrian cultural presence; within several centuries half the population bore such names.[41] The city was then controlled by the substantially Hurrian kingdom of Mitanni, which emerged in the power vacuum following the Hittite sack of Babylon by Mursili I (ca. 1595). Mitanni came to dominate much of North Syria and southeast Anatolia in the fifteenth and fourteenth centuries, and its cultural influence in the larger region was considerable—including on Cyprus, Ugarit, and Kizzuwatna, an important Hurro-Luwian state that included the later Cilicia. The Hittite annexation of Kizzuwatna occasioned a major Hurrian cultural and religious influx in the fourteenth and thirteenth centuries.[42] Consequently much of what we know about Hurrian culture comes, in this Syro-Hurrian form, from the Hittite archives.

Already the texts of OB Mari, we saw, probably attest Hurrian musical engagement with Mesopotamia and the Amorite world.[43] The same city has produced a collection of Hurrian incantations, which, along with later examples from

---

[38] See Singer 1983–1984 1:74, 103 and n48, with cult-object procession 89–97; Haas 1994:749, 757–758, 760, 762, 764–766; HKm:11, 100, 105, 154.
[39] See generally Wilhelm 1989.
[40] See p82.
[41] Draffkorn (Kilmer) 1959; Dietrich and Loretz 1966:188; Wilhelm 1989:13.
[42] Wilhelm 1989:71; Desideri and Jasink 1990:51–109 passim; KH:111–113 et passim. For the Kizzuwatnan rituals, see Haas and Wilhelm 1974; Miller 2004; Strauss 2006.
[43] See p76.

Ugarit and Hattusha, show that "Hurrian incantatory craft extended ... from the Middle Euphrates through north Syria ... for over at least half a millennium."[44] Further evidence of Hurro-Mesopotamian musical interface comes from the songs of the *Kumarbi Cycle*, as retold in Hittite, which integrate Mesopotamian gods and cosmological elements into an otherwise Hurrian armature.[45]

But the most spectacular evidence of Hurro-Mesopotamian musical hybridity comes from Ugarit—the famous cult-hymns containing schematic representations of harmonic sequences based on the Akkadian terminology for musical intervals that goes back to the OB period or earlier. These terms were strongly Hurrianized through several centuries of oral transmission.[46] Although the hymns themselves were composed in Hurrian, the one complete specimen is addressed to Nikkal (< Ningal), an originally Sumerian moon goddess associated especially with Ur. These complex musical artifacts were more than learned curiosities, since they were archived according to the practical criterion of tuning, and therefore saw active liturgical use at Ugarit.[47] This living tradition explains the not-infrequent appearance of Hurrian hymnic elements embedded in other Ugaritian ritual texts. There is an example of this in one of the tablets that record offerings for Kinnaru (alongside many other gods).[48] So while Ugarit was apparently never a Mitannian vassal, Hurrian cultural influence on the city was nevertheless quite extensive, with Hurrian hymnography vital to "l'aspect lyrique du culte"—whether or not, by the thirteenth century, the actual language was kept alive only by priests and other liturgists.[49]

The Hurrians may seem a world away from Greece. But the *Song of Kumarbi*'s startling and celebrated anticipation of the Hesiodic succession myth, including the castration of Ouranos, vividly illustrates the material's potential relevance to Classicists.[50] While *western* Anatolia is likely to have been a productive

---

[44] Mayer 1996:208; cf. Wilhelm 1989:70–71. At Mari: Thureau-Dangin 1939. For Hurro-Hittite incantations, see below. At Ugarit, p119–120.

[45] Güterbock 1948:132–133; Wilhelm 1989:59–60; EFH:105. The texts are conveniently collected and translated by Hoffner and Beckman 1998. That these were songs is shown by expressions like "I sing" (*išḫamiḫḫi*): see Güterbock 1951:141; Hoffner 1988:143n1, 147; Beckman and Hoffner 1985:23.

[46] Hagel 2005:293n22.

[47] The recovered hymns, so far as we know, were all composed in the *qablītu* tuning. The same organizing principle is seen in the MA song catalogue VAT 10101 (Ebeling 1919 no. 158; Ebeling 1922; Kilmer 1965:267; Kilmer 1971:138).

[48] RS 24.643 = KTU/CAT 1.148, 13–17 (see p120n51). Cf. Pardee 1996a:67, noting the hymnic classification of these verses by Laroche 1968:517–518. It is not certain, however, that this section of the text reflects an organic continuation of the earlier offering rite: TR:789 and n47.

[49] Pardee 1996a:67, 75–76; contrast Mayer 1996:205–206, 209–210. Ugarit and Mitanni: HUS:619–21, 632 and n89 (Singer).

[50] CTH 344; Hoffner and Beckman 1998 no. 14, with further references on p95; ANET:120–121 (*Kingship in Heaven*). Comparison with Hesiod: Güterbock 1948; Walcot 1966:1–26; West

Chapter Six

Aegean interface, for Cyprus we should look rather to Cilicia/Kizzuwatna and coastal North Syria, both before and after the EIA Aegean migrations. Cilicia is the setting, for instance, of Zeus' battle against Typhon, which clearly echoes another early Anatolian myth, the *Tale of Illuyanka*.[51] This Syro-Cilician theater is important for the Kinyras question, because several traditions trace his origin thence (Chapter 21).

The *kinnāru* was certainly current among Syro-Kizzuwatnan Hurrians. An administrative text from fifteenth-century Alalakh records a PN beginning with *Kin(n)ar*[- (the rest is damaged) as a recipient or possessor of a royally owned vineyard.[52] (Compare the use of Sum. balaĝ as a name-forming element, including two cases of temple musicians.[53]) Although any ethnic affiliations of this person are unknown, a roughly contemporary text from the same city puts down an individual's profession as ˡúkinnāruḫuli (*ki-in-na-ru-ḫu-li*). This is a hybrid linguistic formation using the productive Hurrian agent suffix *ḫuli*, and so means 'kinnarist'.[54] The Hurro-Semitic fusion of this word, with its agentival force, echoes the active cultivation of Hurrian hymnography at nearby Ugarit.

A second Hurro-Semitic agent form, ˡúkinirtallaš, occurs in a Hittite lexical text. This must relate to the influx of Hurrian ritual and cult in the NK, since Hittite, we saw, had its own word for lyre, *zinar*. The meaning of ˡúkinirtallaš is established by an adjacent entry, ˡúNAR-*aš*, where the Sumerogram NAR makes the effective meaning '*kinnāru*-singer'; similarly its counterpart in the Akkadian column, if correctly restored as *za-am-ma-]ru*, is simply 'singer'.[55] These correspondences show that lyric accompaniment was often a normal part of song; conversely, a 'kinnarist' (ˡúkinnāruḫuli, ˡúkinirtallaš) was not only a lyre-player, but a lyre-*singer*. This will be an illuminating parallel for the otherwise ambiguous 'singers' of Ugarit, the Cypro-Greek form *kenyristḗs*, and 'Kinyras' himself.[56]

1966:18–31; EFH:279–283, with further literature at 103n120, 279n5; Bryce 2002:222–229; López-Ruiz 2010:84–94.
[51] CTH 321; Hoffner and Beckman 1998 no. 1 (ANET:125–126); [Apollodoros] *Library* 1.6.3, etc.
[52] Dietrich and Loretz 1969a:48, no. 11 (Antakya 67), line 7: *Kinar*[*i?*]; the amount of distribution cannot be read. Cf. Sivan 1984:237.
[53] Balaĝ is well attested as a name-forming element from ED I through the N-S period: Hartmann 1960:165, 169, 182.
[54] Alalakh: AT 172.7: Dietrich and Loretz 1966:192 (defining as "indische Zither") and 203n94; Laroche 1976–1977:148; Foxvog and Kilmer 1979–1988:440; von Soden 1988; DCPIL:58 with 61n29. For the suffix, Wegner 2007:57–58, whose parallels make the translation '*kinnāru*-maker'—sometimes given as an alternative—seem less probable. Of course one and the same person might both make and play the instrument.
[55] KBo 1.52 obv. i.15–16. Hrozny 1917:52n1; Tischler et al. 1977:577–578; von Soden 1988; AMEL:87; Ivanov 1999:585; HKm:98 and n198.
[56] See p115–118, 210–211, 432–435.

Two further Hurro-Hittite texts may bear on Syro-Hurrian *kinnāru*-culture. One belongs to the *Itkalzi* series, royal purification rites deriving from Kizzuwatnan tradition, conducted by a divination/incantation-priest (AZU). The text in question was a ritual for Tašmišari, probably the Hurrian throne-name of Tudhaliya III (ca. 1360–1344).[57] Although largely damaged—the moon-god Kušuḫ is mentioned for some reason—one clause contains signs interpretable as the instrumental case *ki-na-ra-a-i* ('with the lyre'); the next line, from an adjoining fragment, may contain the injunction 'hear!' (Hurr. *ha-a-ši*), though 'salve' is also possible.[58] A musical reading would accord well enough with the larger *generic* context.[59] The second is a liver-omen text from the citadel of Hattusha, again highly fragmentary (Aleppo is mentioned), whose apodosis ('then' clause) contains the sequence *ki-in-na-a-ri*.[60] The divinatory context may make a musical interpretation seem unlikely.[61] Still, not only was Kinyras himself considered a diviner, but the Kinyradai of Roman Paphos (and doubtless earlier) practiced divination by entrails (extispicy)—an art which they believed came to them *from Cilicia*.[62] There are also signs that in third-millennium Mesopotamia extispicy was coordinated with the singing of Emesal prayers/laments.[63]

Even without these two highly suggestive texts, the Hurro-Semitic agent-forms establish Kizzuwatna and North Syria as loci of a Hurrianized *kinnāru*-culture. We may thus presume that, in the many Hittite ritual texts that call for the lyre, those of Hurrian extraction presuppose not Hatt./Hitt. *zinar*, but *kinnāru*; or at least that this would have been true for the Hurrian archetypes from which they descend. In one sense, of course, the semantic distinction was slight, since Hittite scribes must have regarded *kinnāru* as basically synonymous with *zinar* and *zannāru*.[64] But given the Hittite practice of maintaining adopted cults using the appropriate traditional idiom, significant contextual differences probably remained.

---

[57] Haas 1984:6.
[58] KUB 47.40 obv. 10 (Haas 1984:271–274 no. 50, exact find-spot unknown); cf. Ivanov 1999:586n8. I thank G. Wilhelm for his comments on this text (communication, January 2, 2014), and for reference to the adjoining piece, KBo 629 = KUB 45.45 (Trémouille 2005 no. 31), of which he writes: "*ha-a-ši* [in line 2] ... in Bo-Orthographie als Imperativ 'höre!' übersetzt werden kann. (Im Mit[anni]-Brief wird *haš-* nie plene geschrieben; in Bo [Hattusha texts] kann das Verb *haš-* 'hören' mit gleichlautendem *ḫaš-* 'salben' verwechselt werden, das oft plene geschrieben wird.)"
[59] The sister series, *Itkaḫi* (also purification rituals), is characterized by "hymn-like recitations": Wilhelm 1989:72–73.
[60] KBo 33.109 right col. line 6; de Martino 1992:82–83 no. 37.
[61] G. Wilhelm (communication, January 2, 2014), to whom I owe the reference.
[62] Tacitus *Histories* 2.3. See p401.
[63] PHG:171–172.
[64] See p77–79, 89–90.

Chapter Six

As a case-in-point, we may take the so-called *Ritual and Prayer to Ishtar of Nineveh*, an invocational rite that also provides crucial evidence for Ishtar-cult on LBA Cyprus (see Chapter 15). The deity in question, Ishtar of Nineveh, was a Mesopotamianized version of the Hurrian goddess Shaushka. She is invoked in many Hurro-Hittite magical texts against plague and curses, often containing Hurrian incantations and technical terms; and she herself bore the title 'woman of incantations'.[65] These same texts show that singer-musicians were quite constant participants in her cult.[66] Ishtar-Shaushka was also associated with a Hurrian genre of songs called *zinzabuššiya*, named for a kind of bird (perhaps dove).[67] In the *Ritual and Prayer to Ishtar of Nineveh*, immediately after the damaged opening, 'singer-men' ($^{lú.meš}$NAR) are instructed to perform as the priest makes ritual preparations. When his incantation is finished, they play again, with the instruments now being specified as *galgalturi* (cymbals?) and the lyre ($^{giš.d}$INANNA).[68] Given the Hittite lexical conjunction of ^{lú}NAR-*aš* and ^{lú}*kinirtallaš*, we may accept this text as evidence, if only palimpsestic, of Syro-Hurrian *kinnāru*-culture.

The Hurro-Hittite texts are also important for having produced our most detailed evidence for the processes by which cults were transplanted from one place to another—'dividing' a god so that it could take up residence in a new temple while simultaneously remaining in an earlier home. The key witness, recently dubbed *Establishing a New Temple for the Goddess of the Night*, is vital for also attesting the concomitant transfer of cult-music.[69] The Goddess of the Night was regarded as a form of Ishtar, although she equally exhibits local (Hurro-Hittite) features distinct from her Mesopotamian counterpart (notably an infernal aspect).[70] The exact occasion of the text in question is unknown, though some would connect it with Tudhaliya I/II (early fourteenth-century) and a division of the Goddess of the Night of Kizzuwatna-city to establish a double in Šamuḫa.[71] Later Hattusili III (ca. 1267–1237) cloned an Ishtar of Šamuḫa for a new cult at Urikina.[72] While both cases were presumably driven by specific geopolitical motivations, they

---

[65] Literally "the woman of that which is repeatedly spoken": see Beckman 1998:5–6 and n54, n56; Bachvarova 2013:27. Connection with magic: Wegner 1981:55–63.
[66] Wegner 1981:155–156; Beckman 1998:6n73.
[67] Beckman 1998:6 and n70.
[68] KUB 15.35 + KBo 2.9, obv. i.16–18, rev. iv.29–30 (CS 1 no. 65, §3, §16). For the identification of the *galgalturi*, HKm:124–128.
[69] CTH 481: Kronasser 1963 (section numbers used here); Miller 2004:272–312; trans. CS 1 no. 70 (B. J. Collins), q.v. for further references, adding Beal 2002; Miller 2008; Pongratz-Leisten 2011:91–93.
[70] Beal 2002:201–202; Miller 2004:363–396, 438; Miller 2008:69–71.
[71] KUB 32.133 i.1–7: Kronasser 1963:58–60; Miller 2004:312–19, arguing at 357–362 against associating this event with that of the ritual text itself; cf. Miller 2008:68, 70 (quotation).
[72] KUB 21.17 ii.5–8; Beal 2002:198; Miller 2004:360n514, 363–393; Miller 2008:69–70.

must equally represent more general and far-reaching procedures.[73] Thus, while the present text derives from a real occasion, it also envisions other such endeavors in the future ("[When] someone settles [the deit]y separately, for her/it [th]is is the ritual," §32).[74]

Composed by a priest of the goddess (§1), the ritual prescribes in minute detail and at great length the preparation of a near-identical copy of the goddess's statue and all necessary furniture, jewelry, clothing, vessels, and other accessories for her new home (§2-8). There follows a series of rites, offerings, and sacrifices—inflected with considerable seven-magic—designed first to draw the goddess into her old temple and propitiate her; and then persuade her to "divide your divinity, come to these new temples, take an honored place" (§21). The goddess's infernal aspect is shown by offerings in ritual pits, from which she herself is somehow drawn.[75] Her international profile and cultural ancestry, however, is equally evident, fossilized it seems in Hurrian ritual poetics: when invited to her new temple, the goddess is evoked (by "seven roads" and "seven paths") from ancient Mesopotamian and Elamite cult-centers (Akkad, Babylon, Kish/Ḫursagkalamma, Susa, §24).

Crucially, the new goddess's attributa include three beloved musical instruments (§4): a set of *ḪASKALLATUM* (probably an Akkadogram for Hitt. *galgalturi*, cymbals); a set of *ḫuḫupal* (drums? lutes?); and an *arkammi* (probably drum).[76] While these instruments are not written with divine determinatives, they must have enjoyed cult-devotions analogous to the divinized instruments of Mesopotamia and Ugarit. For a number of Hittite ritual texts, deriving from both Hattic and Hurrian cult-practice,[77] document offerings for instruments and anointings with oil.[78] In one salving rite, a soothsayer anoints both the *galgalturi* and *arkammi*.[79] Magical properties are attested for the *ḫuḫupal*, with a remarkable parallel—surely a survival—in the later Phrygian mysteries of Kybele and

---

[73] Cf. Miller 2004:260.
[74] For the historical possibilities of the several attested 'expansions,' see Miller 2004:350–439, leaving the occasion of the ritual text itself "an open question" (437), and seeing the text as the priest's outline for a specific upcoming ritual; but cf. 530 on the Kizzuwatna rituals as "guides for future performances."
[75] For the practice in comparative ANE perspective, see Hoffner 1967; Bachvarova forthcoming.
[76] For possible identifications of these instruments, Güterbock 1995; HKm:108-120, 124-128.
[77] This would seem to suggest that the veneration of lyres and other cult-objects was more widely practiced in Anatolia and North Syria during the second millennium. But cf. Popko 1978:84, noting that it is only in texts of the Hittite NK that instruments are clearly ranked among cult-objects.
[78] See HKm:100-101 and above, p94-95.
[79] KBo 33.167, rev. iv.16'-20'; HKm:101.

Attis.[80] Whether or not the *actual* instruments dedicated to the Goddess of the Night were themselves ever played, rather than simply venerated, their placement in the new temple certainly indicates a parallel transposition of the appropriate cult-music. For when the goddess has come to her new temple, a number of offerings are made to the accompaniment of precisely the *galgalturi* and *arkammi* (§26).

We may reasonably deduce that such formal divisions of gods typically entailed parallel musical transplantations. The dividing ritual presents, *mutatis mutandis*, just the context and combination of elements needed to explain the arrival to Cyprus of a Divine *Kinnāru* beloved of 'Aphrodite'—recalling Kinyras' intimate relationship with the goddess, and the Divine Balang Ninigizibara's treatment as Inanna's counselor and husband.[81]

While no stringed-instrument is specified for the Goddess of the Night, other forms of Ishtar-cult must often have employed chordophone music, given the persistent description of lyres and perhaps harps as 'Inanna-instrument'.[82] Indeed the ᵍⁱˢ·ᵈINANNA is the instrument most frequently attested in Hittite texts, by a wide margin, as the beneficiary of offering and salving rituals. And the evidence for its *use* in ritual—typically royal—is abundant. This clearly privileged position of the ᵍⁱˢ·ᵈINANNA among the Hittites may be compared with the evidently unique divinization of the *kinnāru* at Ugarit.

Also illuminating is the Hurrian veneration of cult-objects more generally, including thrones, footstools, incense-containers and -stands, model temples, and many other things still unidentified.[83] One Hurrian text from Ugarit, which will be important later for its evidence about Alashiyan cult, is a list of gods receiving sacrifice. These include, besides the WS El, Kothar, and several Hurrian deities, two cult-objects used for the preparation and burning of incense.[84] That they were regularly venerated in the Hurrian cult of Kizzuwatna is shown by their recurring appearance in Hurro-Hittite texts relating to the divine-circles

---

[80] The *ḫuḫupal* is central to a ritual text of Luwian extraction which obscurely describes a procedure of filling the instrument with wine and beer (at different stages), filtering it into another *ḫuḫupal*, with the resulting liquid consumed by the god or cult officiants depending on the outcome: KUB 25.37+ = CTH 771; see Güterbock 1995:63–71; HKm:111. Compare Clement of Alexandria *Exhortation* 2.15.3 (Ἐκ τυμπάνου ἔφαγον· ἐκ κυμβάλου ἔπιον, "I have eaten from the drum, I have drunk from the cymbal"); Firmicus Maternus *On the Error of Profane Religions* 18.1.

[81] See p184 and Heimpel, "Balang-Gods," Section 2d and 23f.

[82] Cf. the new Astarte hymn from Ugarit (RIH 98/02), which calls for praise of the goddess "by the sound of the *nbl*": see p52n26.

[83] Haas and Wilhelm 1974:103–115, focusing on those involved with bird offerings/purification rituals.

[84] RS 24.274, 14, 16. Laroche 1968:504–507; SHC 2 no. 65; cf. AP:55. See further p373–374.

(*kaluti*) of the storm-god Teshup, his consort Hepat, and Shaushka-Ishtar.[85] Similarly an offering-list for the cult of Hepat of Aleppo and Hatti and her circle prescribes bread-offerings for the lyre and other cult-objects.[86] These texts present clear parallels to the pairing of Divine Censer and Divine Kinnaru in the Ugaritian pantheon texts.[87] The Hurro-Hittite material, when combined with the importance of Hurrian hymnography at Ugarit, urges us to regard Kinnaru there as locally embodying the lyric dimension of a complex cultural amalgam prevailing in North Syria during and before the thirteenth-century.

Finally, another Hurro-Hittite text arguably provides the most vivid example, outside of Sumerian sources, for the mythological treatment in song of a cult-object. This is the *Song of Silver*, a damaged episode of the so-called *Kumarbi Cycle*.[88] It parallels the *Song of Hedammu* and the *Song of Ullikummi* in that Silver is a son of Kumarbi who challenges the storm-god Teshup; evidently triumphing at first, ultimately of course he must fall to the prevailing world order. The story also exhibits striking parallels with the Greek myth of Phaethon—Silver is a father-less child who, taunted by an age-mate, seeks out his father and ultimately drags the sun and moon down from heaven.[89] That Silver is to be understood precisely as the homonymous metal is supported by the 'elemental' nature of the forces that Kumarbi elsewhere enlists (Hedammu is a sea-monster; Ullikummi is the diorite-man, begotten through intercourse with a rock). V. Haas is thus probably right that the song personifies and mythologizes silver; of various animated, magical metals and stones found in Hurro-Hittite ritual, silver was the cathartic material *par excellence*, used to ward off demons, curses, and sickness.[90] Silver's power over sun and moon may also correspond to aspects of ritual magic.[91] And we saw, in the Assyro-Babylonian *lilissu* ritual, that the positioning and manipulation of god-figurines endowed the proceedings with a cosmogonic dimension, and that such procedures could effectively generate or replay myths.[92]

---

[85] See Laroche 1968:506–507; cf. Laroche 1948:116 (line 13) with note on 118, 122 (line 29). A *kaluti* is a more or less canonical grouping of gods, following a definite sequence and serving as a kind of template for offering rituals: Wilhelm 1989:65.

[86] KBo 14.142 i.20–33: Haas 1994:555; HKm:101.

[87] See p5, 120n53, 121, 124, 283, 512n119.

[88] CTH 364, multiple fragments: see Hoffner 1988; Hoffner and Beckman 1998 no. 16.

[89] See the detailed comparison of James and van der Sluijs 2012.

[90] Haas 1982:167–168, 177; cf. Haas and Wilhelm 1974:38–41; Strauss 2006:179–180.

[91] Control of the sun or moon characterizes magical ability in some Greco-Roman sources: Aristophanes *Clouds* 749–750 with Dover 1968:192; Hippokrates *On the Sacred Disease* 1.69, 1.77 (I owe this reference to A. Hollmann). The darkening or disappearance of sun and moon also characterizes malevolent theophany in Mesopotamian Emesal prayers/laments, which were often performed at liminal moments (eclipse, sunrise): PHG:30, 175–180.

[92] See p25–26.

Chapter Six

The Syro-Hurrian and Kizzuwatnan material seems to present all essential conditions for linking the sacred lyres of ritual to Kinyras the cult-musician of myth, and for connecting this in turn to still older Mesopotamian cult-music practices.[93] While the Hittite archives are valuable generally for their detailed information about lyre-cult in action, the constellation of elements just considered has enhanced probative value, given Syro-Hurrian cultural influence at Ugarit, and the proximity to Cyprus of Cilicia (Kizzuwatna), which one set of traditions saw as Kinyras' original home (see Chapter 21). Some form of Ishtar-cult, quite possibly a specifically Syro-Hurrian strain, provides one (n.b.) likely context for the importation to Alashiya of a Divine Knr—as reflecting an essential performative dimension in the rites of the goddess, who was herself, in some forms, closely allied to the ideology of LBA kingship.[94]

'Asiatic' Lyres in Bronze Age Egypt

Here I shall briefly sketch the history of musical contact between Egypt and 'Asia' during the second millennium, especially the diffusion and purposeful transplantation of Syro-Levantine lyre-culture beyond its home-range, and the factors that account for it. The phenomena were naturally shaped by specific political and cultural forces, notably long-term NK control of Canaan and the unusual modulations of the Amarna Age (fourteenth century). Still the Egyptian material complements the Syro-Hurrian and Hurro-Hittite sources just discussed, for together they circumscribe a larger musical periphery around a Syro-Levantine center. If this circle were completed on a map, it would comfortably include Cyprus. This procedure may seem forced, but it is not unjustified. For we must assume Cyprus' close political and cultural engagement with Egypt, Canaan, Syria, and Anatolia throughout the LBA, even when not explicitly documented—as it often is by texts from Amarna, Ugarit, and Hattusha. The Egyptian patterns can therefore contribute useful approaches for navigating the dire straits of LBA Cypriot music.

Plato caricatured Egypt as a musical Never-never Land where no innovation was ever permitted.[95] But Egyptian interest in foreign music is attested from the earliest times. Already in the OK, while tomb-paintings establish curved-harps, end-blown flutes, double (parallel) clarinets, and sistra as basic to the native

---

[93] See further p280–291, 328–329, 380–383, 392–400.
[94] See further p37–40, 375–383, 473–479.
[95] Plato *Laws* 656e–657f.

tradition,[96] we read of royal patronage of musicians and dancers imported from the south (Nubians and pygmies).[97]

As to musical exchange with the Levant, this goes back at least to the MK, when the Beni-Hassan tomb-painting first depicts a lyre-player—in an 'Asiatic' troupe that confirms the instrument's Levantine origin (Figure 3). While the overtly foreign context of the Beni-Hassan painting might discourage one from inferring any real Levantine musical 'presence' in MK Egypt, this is counterbalanced by a variety of textual sources referring to 'Asiatic' singers and dancers, often in the contexts of cult and festival. Especially notable are the temple archives from Illahun (Sesostris II, ca. 1897–1878, Twelfth Dynasty), with one papyrus listing as many as fifty cult-performers of 'Asiatic' origin (the term could include not only the Levant, but Syria and Mesopotamia).[98] The Beni-Hassan painting has prompted the suggestion[99] that simple rectangular-lyres entered Egyptian life at this time and were gradually elaborated into the instruments with curving, asymmetrical arms of the NK. On this theory, the lovely lyre of the Megiddo plaque (Figure 11 = 4.1p), for instance, would represent an Egyptianizing fashion in the Levant during the period of NK control (with the 'Eastern' lyres of the Cypro-Phoenician symposium bowls following suit[100]). But the comparable, early lyres of the Inandık vase (Figure 7) make the Syro-Levantine sphere epicentral to the elaborate morphology, broadly speaking, and thus its more probable home—although one may certainly allow for synergy with neighboring regions.[101]

The Hyksos period (ca. 1648–1540), when a still-mysterious 'Asiatic' dynasty established itself in the eastern Nile Delta, must have marked a new stage of Egyptian-Levantine musical interaction.[102] As matters stand, however, the great mass of evidence dates from the NK, making it impossible to ignore imperial expansion to the north, initiated in the Eighteenth Dynasty by Thutmosis III (1490–1436), as a major determining factor. The forceful acquisition of Levantine musicians worthy of royal service is proven by a record of Amenhotep

---

[96] HMI:89–95; AEMI:12–17, 36–62 (for the several varieties of curved-harp that developed over time); MMAE:24–37.
[97] von Lieven 2008:156.
[98] Schneider 2003:276–278; cf. MMAE:123, 125; von Lieven 2008:156, 158.
[99] Brown 1981:387–388.
[100] See p258–272.
[101] Cf. the female double-piper who plays before a local (Egyptian? Canaanite?) imperial governor on a fourteenth-century Egyptianizing ivory plaque from Sharuhen, near Gaza (MAIP:95–96, fig. III.15). The eleventh-century (?) *Tale of Wen-Amun* represents the king of Byblos as maintaining an Egyptian songstress, Tentnau, who entertains the title character (CS 1 no. 41; cf. Hickmann 1954b:286; MMAE:126).
[102] Hickmann 1961:33; MgB 2/1:16; *MGG* 5:1042 (Kubik); Helck 1971:496 remains agnostic.

Chapter Six

II (ca. 1438–1412), itemizing many *musiciennes* among the captives of his first campaign:

> Noblemen 550, their wives 240, Canaanites 640, sons of noblemen 232, daughters of noblemen 323, songstresses of the noblemen of all foreign countries 270 with their instruments of pleasure of silver and gold, together 2214.[103]

At nearly fifteen percent of the total, 'songstresses' were clearly desirable booty, deliberately gathered. Doubtless this text represents a more general pattern under other pharaohs. 'Asiatic' musicians will also have attended the various foreign princesses wedded by the pharaohs, for instance those of Mitanni with whose marriages several Amarna letters are concerned.[104]

But NK ethno-musical diversity was not restricted to the royal sphere. Numerous paintings from elite contexts (tomb, domestic, and other) represent banquets, many for the deceased and/or the Feast of the Valley (a celebration of the dead),[105] featuring mainly female musical ensembles that appear to be deliberately cosmopolitan. They play various combinations of Syro-Levantine instruments—lyres, double-pipes, lutes, and Mesopotamian(izing) angle-harps—alongside a contemporary form of Egyptian curved-harp.[106] Representative is a Theban tomb-painting, again from the reign of Amenhotep II (Figure 9).[107] If Syro-Levantine lyres did not catch on in the MK, they clearly did so now; no fewer than six actual instruments, more or less intact, have been recovered, the earliest from sixteenth-century Thebes.[108]

As at OB Mari, imported musicians will have been prized for their ability to provide variety. One must therefore suppose that Syro-Levantine musical traditions were perpetuated within NK Egypt in some form.[109] Accordingly foreign musicians can be indicated by non-Egyptian dress.[110] This also explains the Egyptian retention of the Canaanite loanword represented as *kn-nù-rú* which, though not attested before ca. 1200 (*Papyrus Anastasi*), must be centuries older.[111]

---

[103] Helck 1955:1305; cf. Lawergren 1993:55; von Lieven 2008:158 (translation used here).
[104] Manniche 1989:26; Green 1992:219; Manniche 2000:234.
[105] Manniche 2000:234.
[106] MgB 2/1:30-31 (no. 8, the only angle-harp prior to the Amarna period), 144-145 (no. 118); AEMI:5-6, 31, 80-86, 89-91; MMAE fig. 2, 21, 26, 30-31, 52-54; Teeter 1993:83 (fig. 4-6-8 [sic]). For these ensembles, and for lyres, lutes, and double-pipes as Levantine imports: Hickmann 1961:32-35; Helck 1971:496-498; Manniche 1989:26-27; MMAE:40-56, 125; Teeter 1993:84.
[107] MgB 2/1:30-31 fig. 8; cf. Teeter 1993:80.
[108] For the surviving lyres, see with further references AMEL:128-130.
[109] Helck 1971:496-498; von Lieven 2008:156, 159.
[110] Helck 1971:497; MMAE:91-92; von Lieven 2008:156.
[111] See p56. Another word current in the MK, *dꜣdꜣt*, is sometimes interpreted as 'lyre'; but this is quite uncertain (MMAE:125).

Peripherals, Hybrids, Cognates

Figure 9 Cosmopolitan musical ensemble with 'Asiatic' lyre. Wall-painting from Tomb 367, Theban Necropolis, reign of Amenhotep II (ca. 1438-1412). Drawn from MgB 2/1:30-31 fig. 8.

Several NK texts refer to performances by foreign musicians as part of Egyptian festivals.[112]

Yet the desire to hear exotic music clearly did not entail a complete segregation of foreign and Egyptian practice. In the period's paintings it is often impossible to distinguish between Egyptian and foreign.[113] What do we make of women who play lyres and other Levantine instruments, often alongside Egyptian harps, but wear Egyptian-style hair and traditional Egyptian sheath-dresses, or a variety of other garments fashionable in the NK?[114] Are they acculturated foreigners; natives who have embraced novel fashions; or a mixture of the two? While lyres and angle-harps appear to be shown in mainly convivial scenes, lutes at least, played by men, were sometimes integrated in hieratic contexts, joining the traditional curved-harp.[115]

These trends persisted into the Amarna period, when, however, novel twists were induced by the revolutionary theology of Akhenaten (1364-1347), who proclaimed the Aten or Sun-Disk as sole god, established a new capital at

[112] See with references von Lieven 2008:158.
[113] Von Lieven 2008:159-160.
[114] MgB 2/1:68-71 (nos. 39-41), 78-79 (no. 61); MMAE fig. 27; Teeter 1993 fig. 4-6-8 (*sic*).
[115] MgB 2/1:28-29 (no. 7), 42-43 (no. 20), 82-83 (no. 51), 132-133 (nos. 101-102); MMAE fig. 40. Cf. Manniche 1989:26.

Chapter Six

Akhetaten (el-Amarna), and cultivated an innovative iconography in support. Of the huge number of reliefs originating in the palace and Aten temples (including those at Karnak and Luxor), and further images from officials' tombs, a startling proportion shows musical scenes transpiring in temples and especially around the palace, where a variety of musical ensembles play before the royal family during banquets and festivals.[116] Given the period's novel artistic conventions, and that this is our first detailed view of Egyptian royal life, we often do not know how far iconography reflects musical innovation, even if this seems likely enough in general. This reservation applies for instance to unparalleled details of instrument morphology, and playing positions.[117]

More reliable are the varying details of clothing, hairstyle, and instrumentation, which indicate purposeful diversity in the ethnic and gender makeup of the many ensembles. The general validity of this principle is established by the harem scenes.[118] Figure 10, for instance, shows a schematic suite with guarded doors; its furnishings are dominated by musical instruments, not only reflecting a major aspect of female palace life (as at OB Mari), but equally serving as conspicuous iconographic markers of ethnic diversity.[119] Within six rooms one sees an Egyptian curved-harp, five Syro-Levantine lyres, two Mesopotamian(izing) angle-harps, six lutes, and a 'giant' lyre—apparently introduced in this period, and perhaps best paralleled by the instruments of the Inandık vase (Figure 7).[120] Most have minor variations to enhance the impression of diversity. There is also significant differentiation in their distribution. The women of the 'upper' chamber have long curling hair; two wear three-tiered Levantine robes, and one plays a Mesopotamian(izing) angle-harp; the giant lyre is found in *their* adjoining rooms. Although the lower register also includes Syro-Levantine instruments, as had made their way into earlier NK tomb-paintings, these rooms' Egyptian character is confirmed by the women's hairstyle and an Egyptian curved-harp. The composition clearly represents segregation of the several harem communities. The 'upper apartments' would perfectly suit, for instance, the female entourage of a Mitannian princess.

---

[116] See especially Manniche 1989; MMAE:84–96; Green 1992; Manniche 2000.
[117] Cf. MMAE:88–89.
[118] See the analysis of MMAE:85.
[119] Davies 1908, pl. XXIX, cf. XXVIII (tomb of Aÿ); MMAE:86, fig. 50.
[120] The bull-lyres of Sumer were long vanished. Some posit an unattested Levantine analog (DCPIL: 60n5: cf. p51 above), though NK Hittite cultural influence on North Syria, even before Suppiluliuma I (ca. 1344–1322), may be a sufficient explanation for the Egyptian evidence. There is some variety in how these instruments are shown; the harem's apparently round-based lyre might point to the Aegean or even Cyprus/Alashiya. See Manniche 1971:162–163; AEMI:88–89; Manniche 1989:27; Duchesne-Guillemin 1989 compares the oversized Minoan lyre on the Chania pyxis (Chania XM 2308, Late Minoan III: SIAG:2, 16 and fig. 2b), but it is hard to trust these proportions; MMAE:91–92; Green 1992:218 (Anatolian); AMEL:141–142.

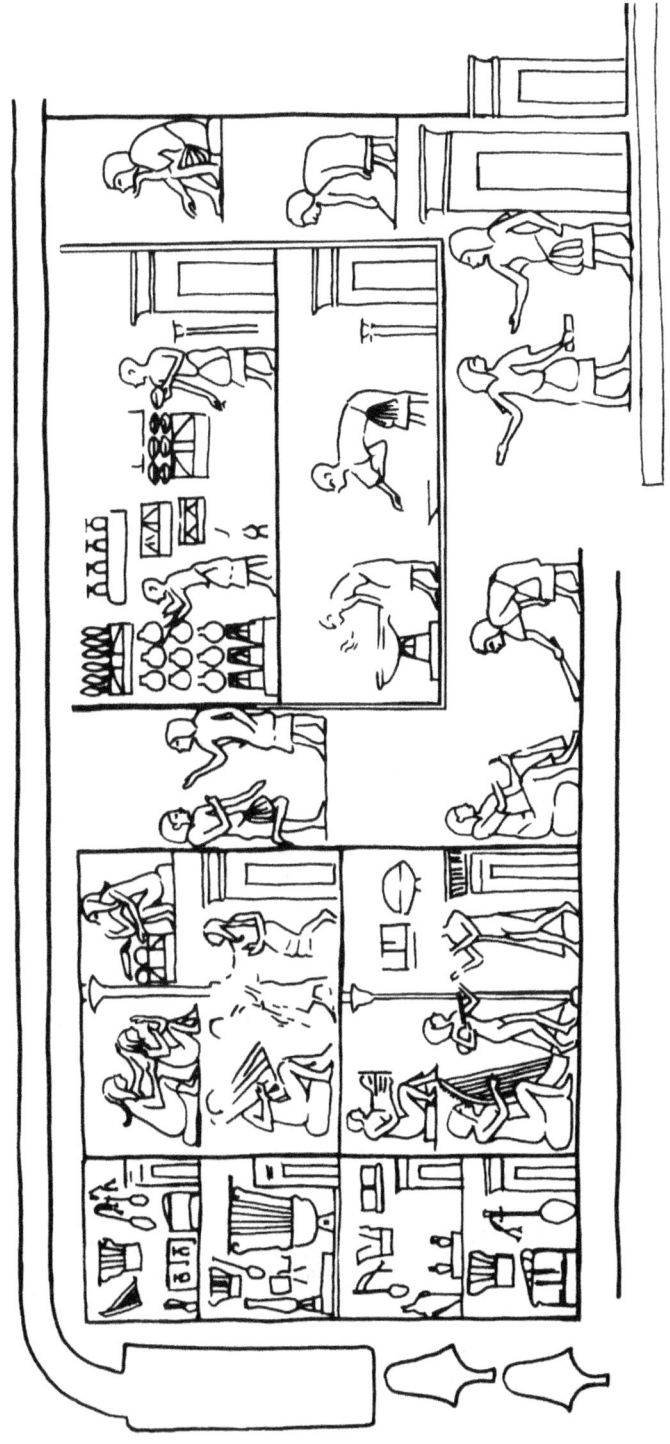

Figure 10 Two harem apartments with musical instruments. Relief from the Tomb of Aÿ, reign of Akhenaten, ca. 1364–1347. Drawn from Davies 1908 pl. XXIX

Chapter Six

Similar diversity characterizes musical scenes set elsewhere in the palace, although now male groups are also found, both Egyptian and foreign. The latter wear conical headgear, long narrow sleeves, the same triple-tiered Levantine robes as women in the foreign harem, and again play (in pairs) the 'giant' lyre.[121] Female Egyptian groups continue the iconography of earlier tomb-paintings with their combination of Asiatic and Egyptian instruments.[122] Some of these groups were probably drawn from the 'Egyptian harem', which exhibits just the same variety.[123]

Such female groups must also have been patronized by earlier pharaohs. But with Akhenaten as the terrestrial embodiment of the Sun-Disk, palace life took on a newly sacred dimension. This is vividly illustrated by the male palace musicians who are always depicted with blindfolds. This detail is clearly reminiscent of the traditional (MK) representation of temple-harpers as actually blind; the latter convention probably had some basis in reality, although it became stereotyped in iconography and literary sources.[124] At Amarna, clearly, male musicians were actually blindfolded, as they are shown *without* blindfolds when not playing. The practice is best explained as 'symbolic blindness' while performing in the presence of the god-king, whose splendor was perhaps overwhelming when hymned as a god.[125] Female musicians, never blindfolded, were apparently better able to withstand his radiance.

This clear collision of musical practice and religious meaning encourages further correlations of theology and music-iconography. Compare the sistra of this period, which lose their traditional Hathor-heads.[126] The cosmopolitanism of Akhenaten's court-music may echo the universalism of the Aten-hymns, which refer to the many languages embraced by the Sun-Disk's domain, and to kings coming from Syria and Kush to venerate him ("Singers, musicians, shout with joy ... in all temples in Akhetaten").[127] While musical diversity must have been cultivated by other Great Kings of the time, Akhenaten evidently made the most of musical forces available from his imperial holdings and royal peers abroad. The foreign *male* musicians are especially diagnostic. Since the massive,

---

[121] MMAE:90.
[122] Manniche 1989:26; MMAE:85.
[123] Although no foreign female groups are certainly identified outside of the harem, these too are likely. In one relief, showing a row of headless musicians with the three-tiered robe worn by foreign men and women alike, other contextual details support a female reading: MMAE fig. 53.
[124] MMAE:100–101.
[125] Manniche 1978; Manniche 1989:30–31; Green 1992:218. Male palace musicians are shown only on blocks from Karnak.
[126] MMAE:86.
[127] Quotation: *Short Hymn to the Aten*, trans. Lichtheim 1973 2:91 (here following Scharff 1922:68). Cf. MMAE:92; Manniche 2000:235. The *Great Hymn* is CS 1 no. 28. Versions of the *Short Hymn*: Davies 1908:25–35.

unwieldy giant lyres will have been cultic instruments in their native traditions (so in the Inandık vase, and like the later Ethiopian *begena*), foreign religious 'lyric' has evidently been repurposed for Aten-worship. This trend could also explain the increased appearance of Levantine lutes—and the new appearance of lyres—in the hands of *men*.[128] Others see here a purposeful gender-blurring, in accord with a larger 'unisex' tendency in Amarna art, whereby Egyptian male ensembles now emulated the convivial female groups of earlier tomb-paintings.[129]

---

[128] AEMI:91; Manniche 1971:156 fig. 2, 161 fig. 9; Manniche 1989:27.
[129] Distinguished only by the lack of double-pipes, which had erotic associations in Egyptian iconography: Manniche 1971:155-156 fig. 1-2; Manniche 1989:26; MMAE:89.

7
Kinnaru of Ugarit

HAVING NOW SURVEYED the lyre-culture of the wider Syro-Levantine sphere, we may now turn to Ugarit, home of the Divine Kinnaru itself. Since Kinnaru does not certainly appear in personified form in any of the city's narrative texts—although I shall suggest several possible cases[1]—we must approach him first through the evidence for the *kinnāru* itself. Not only does Ugarit provide the richest such material for the LBA, the relevant texts provide different perspectives from what was seen at Ebla, Mari, Hattusha, and in Egypt. Whereas Ugarit's economic documents are rather meager in musical matters, a number of ritual, mythological, and paramythological texts considerably illuminate the cultic role and associated symbolism of instruments and music, including the *kinnāru*.[2]

The King and His Musicians

The king's control of Ugarit's economy, in the word's broadest sense, is such that the city seems largely an extension of the royal household.[3] This casts a shadow on the ritual texts too, where the king dominates the action[4] while singers and other cultic actors are only rarely mentioned.[5] This royal bias recalls the sole-officiant pose struck by Gudea, Shulgi, and Ishme-Dagan, and vividly illustrates the religious potency of the king's person. His ritual actions involved and

---

[1] See p130–131, 139–140, 443–445.
[2] General studies of music at Ugarit: Tsumura 1973, 176–178; Caubet 1987b; Koitabashi 1992a; Caubet 1994; Caubet 1996; Koitabashi 1996; Koitabashi 1998; Caubet 1999; Caubet 2014.
[3] HUS:423–439 (Heltzer), 467–475 (Vita).
[4] del Olmo Lete 1999 passim. This point is often and rightly stressed: Xella 1979–1984:473; Pardee 2000:77–78; RCU:57.
[5] See RS 24.250+ = KTU/CAT 1.106.15-17 (Herdner 1978:26–30; RCU:53–56), with discussion of Koitabashi 1996:226–227; Koitabashi 1998:384. Also RS 2.002 = KTU/CAT 1.23.15, 18, perhaps 21, RTU:324–335, with further literature on 324; a *qdš*-priest sings in RS 24.256 = KTU/CAT 1.112.18–21 (RCU:36–38). Further evidence may be found in Clemens 1993:68n21; Koitabashi 1996.

Chapter Seven

induced an occasional quasi-divinization "to bridge the ontological gap when he represented the nation before the gods in the cult."[6] As Pardee puts it:

> It was by this sacred role (or, perhaps, because his royal status already had a sacred aspect to it) that the living king participated in the divine; that is, on the ideological level at least, he served the divine meals in which he and the divinities participated, thus establishing their communion.[7]

Yet while the king's real and extensive participation in liturgy is undoubted, the 'clergy' were obviously indispensable for its detailed execution. It is rather in the economic documents that their vital presence, and that of court-musicians, is best attested.[8]

Palace lists record a 'Singer of Ugarit'—the only musician known by name—suggesting a high official of some sort, comparable perhaps to the Chief Singer of Mari, with his extra-musical organizational and diplomatic duties.[9]

Also attested is a 'singer [or singers] of Astarte' (šr. ʻṯtrt).[10] While Astarte is somewhat elusive in Ugaritian *mythological* texts, she is a definite presence in rituals, including several that govern her entry into the royal palace.[11] She appears to be a "protective goddess to [the] kings of Ugarit, because of her power of breaking enemies."[12] Her 'singer', appearing in a text recording distributions of cloth—probably for the ritual investiture of a divine-statue—suggests a master musician presiding over her cult (the new hymn to Astarte calls for the goddess to be celebrated 'by the sound of the *nbl*').[13] One naturally thinks of the

---

[6] Wyatt 2007:63, 69.
[7] Pardee 2000:77–78.
[8] Such texts rarely make a cult context clear. But as singing is specified in Ugarit's rituals, and there is much comparative evidence for cult-musicians in the ANE, it is generally assumed that singers listed in the city's economic texts were indeed of this kind. See the balanced review of SURS:312-313, concluding that "as *bnš.mlk*, their sphere of service as a group could include both temple and palace."
[9] Singer of Ugarit: RS 19.16 (KTU/CAT 4.609; PRU 5 no. 11), line 37 (*mnn.šr.ugrt*); cf. Caubet 1996:17 ("qui devait marquer l'identité du clan ou de la ville au cours d'une liturgie sociale"); Caubet 1999:13 ("le titre … semble indiquer le caractère officiel, lié à la capitale (ou au royaume) d'Ougarit"); SURS:448–451 ("may actually indicate a singer in the service of the city rather than of its temples," 450); Koitabashi 1998:365–366; McGeough and Smith 2011:331–335; Caubet 2014:182, comparing the Chief Singer of Mari.
[10] Singer of Astarte: KTU/CAT 4.168, 4 (RS 15.82): SURS:313 and n861, 346–348, with references, and 347n1019 for whether a singular or plural should be read; McGeough and Smith 2011:125–126; Koitabashi 2012 (Japanese, English abstract), addressing also the new hymn to Astarte (for a preliminary reading of which see Pardee 2007).
[11] For a current survey see Smith 2015.
[12] Koitabashi 2012:53 (quotation).
[13] RIH 98/02: see p52n26, 102n82.

Kinnaru of Ugarit

relationship between Aphrodite and Kinyras. Alternatively, if a plural reading is correct, one could look to the cult-musicians of the Cypro-Phoenician symposium bowls who lead offering-processions to an Astarte-type goddess. Such scenes would also provide a plausible parallel for the female singers (*šrt*) which some would see in two texts (but there remain contextual difficulties with these readings).[14]

The typical designation of Ugaritian guilds was *bn*—'sons of'—where actual heredity must sometimes have been operative, although a metaphorical sense was probably at least equally common.[15] The construction may be attested for singers (*bn šrm*), although the reading is uncertain.[16] In any case, groups of singers (*šrm*) and cymbalists (*mṣlm*) were certainly included, alongside priests (*khnm*) and diviners (*qdšm*), among the 'king's men' (*bnš mlk*).[17] This term denoted officiants supported by the palace, receiving land and other distributions in exchange for labor, services, and provisioning of goods. Such a corporate status for the singers is illustrated by a tax that they, along with the city's other professional groups, had to pay in fulfillment of a treaty between Ugarit and the Hittite kingdom. Similarly, the singers, like other groups, had to contribute an archer to the city's guard.[18] Some singers apparently—and not surprisingly—resided in the palace itself.[19] That they provided a more secular range of entertainment, in addition to their liturgical duties, is probable,[20] although the two spheres may not always have been sharply delimited.

That cymbalists are distinguished in the economic texts makes us wonder about the other instruments necessary for ritual music. Lyres, double-pipes, frame-drums, and other percussion are variously attested in two 'paramythological' and ritual texts connected with the cult of dead kings.[21] Are these

---

[14] For the bowls, see Chapter 11. The texts in question are KTU/CAT 4.360 (RS 18.050) and KTU/CAT 4.410 (RS 18.250A+B): see PRU 5:105-106 (no. 80, line 12); SURS:438-439, 440-443 (noting for the second text that it is hard to envisage a scenario, "lurid or otherwise," in which some 78 female singers "would be allocated to or levied from so many citizens," 442); McGeough and Smith 2011:246 (treating *šrt* as a TN in the first text) and 276-278 ("archers" in the second).

[15] Levine 1963a:211-212.

[16] RS 2.002 = KTU/CAT 1.23, 2. See Tsumura 1973:24-25, 174-175; Koitabashi 1998:367.

[17] Twelve examples of singers (*šrm*) were known to Heltzer 1982:137n28. For further discussion and sources, see Koitabashi 1998:365-368; HUS:433-436 (Heltzer), 300 (Merlo/Xella); SURS:311-314, 370 and n1121 (rejecting the thesis that *šrm* were instrument-builders, 314 and n864). Note also KTU/CAT 4.399 (RS 18.138), an obscure text that *might* deal with land distribution for singers: McGeough and Smith 2011:269n144.

[18] KTU/CAT 4.610 (RS 19.017): Heltzer 1982:137; Koitabashi 1998:367; HUS:429-430 (Heltzer); SURS:451.

[19] Caubet 2014:181 and n20.

[20] HUS:301 (Merlo/Xella).

[21] See p134-135, 443-444.

other musician categories simply unattested as yet in the administrative texts? This seems unlikely, given the dozen or more occurrences of 'singer(s)'. Rather, 'singer' must imply the use of various instruments—much like Sum./Akk. nar/ *nâru*, with which Ugaritic *šr* was lexically equated.[22] There is a good parallel from the fourth-century temple of Astarte at Kition on Cyprus, where only 'singers' (*šrm*) are listed among the personnel, despite the considerable musical variety implied by the Cypro-Phoenician symposium bowls.[23] Similarly the various musical 'guilds' whose establishment the Chronicler attributes to David are grouped under the general heading of 'singers'; they are to be equipped with 'instruments of song' (*k^{e}lê šir*), which include the *kinnōr*, *nēbel*, and *m^{e}ṣiltayīm* (cymbals).[24] The implications of this are confirmed, and extended, by the Septuagint, where the normal translation of 'singers' is Gk. *psaltōidoí*—a word whose derivation from *psállein*, 'pluck', clearly indicates the primacy of chordophones among the 'instruments of music'.[25] It is quite certain, therefore, that the invisible *kinnāru*-players of Ugarit were reckoned as a subset of singers, and were indeed the singers *par excellence*.[26] Recall the Hittite ritual texts, in which lyre-music is very often specified, with or without other instruments.[27] Here lyre-playing can be described by the same verb used for singing, and in several case both seem to be implied simultaneously.[28] Elsewhere the accompaniment of singing by lyre-music is explicit.[29] Especially illuminating is the lexical equation of Hurro-Hittite ^{lú}*kinirtallaš* with ^{lú}*nar-aš* and Akk. *za-am-ma-]ru*: that is, 'singer' = 'kinnarist'.[30]

One may conclude, therefore, that at Ugarit lyre-players were as vital to the cult as cymbalists (and pipers and other percussionists). But this equally

---

[22] For the equation, Heltzer 1982:137; SURS:312n856 with further references.
[23] Amadasi and Karageorghis 1977 C1, A.6 with comments on 111–112 (superseding KAI 37). The proposal of van den Branden 1956:91–92, to see a payment to 'lyre-players' (KNRM) at B7, has been abandoned: see p57n58.
[24] 1 Chronicles 15:16, 19–21. Noted by Koitabashi 1998:370, cf. 377, concluding that "'to sing' ... which could express singing to the accompaniment of musical instruments, is [equivalent to] the term 'music' in modern times."
[25] For 'singers' = ψαλτῳδοί, a few examples may suffice: 1 Chronicles 15:16 (David appoints τοὺς ψαλτῳδοὺς ἐν ὀργάνοις ᾠδῶν, νάβλαις καὶ κινύραις καὶ κυμβάλοις); 9:33, 13:8; 2 Chronicles 5:12–13; etc.
[26] But there is a counter-example at Psalms 68:25, where singers (*šarîm*) are distinguished from instrumentalists/chordophonists (*nōg^{e}nîm*) and drummers (*tôpēpôt*): noted by Koitabashi 1996:223.
[27] HKm:97–106 passim.
[28] HKm:98, 99–100.
[29] Cf. Popko 1978:83; HKm:100–106 passim.
[30] KBo 1.52 obv. i.15–16: see p98.

confirms that the cymbalists, being separately specified, were a group apart.[31] This may seem surprising, yet there is a striking Biblical parallel.[32] The cymbalists Heman, Asaph, and Ethan, while they and their instruments are subordinated to the general categories of 'singers' and 'instruments of song', nevertheless occupy a lead position in the temple music described by the Chronicler:

> Asaph was the chief, and second to him Zechariah, Jeiel, Shemiramoth, Jehiel, Mattithiah, Eliab, Benaiah, Obed-edom, and Jeiel, with *nēbel*-lyres and *kinnōr*-lyres; Asaph was to sound the cymbals.[33]

A similar hierarchy is elaborated at 15:16–22, where "the singers Heman, Asaph, and Ethan were to sound bronze cymbals,"[34] while the more numerous *nēbel*- and *kinnōr*-players are said to be "kindred of the second order" (18).[35] Even if this material is secondary to the traditions about Davidic music in 2 Samuel,[36] the very peculiarity of the arrangement makes it quite certain that the managerial prominence of cymbalists in I Chronicles perpetuates an ancient regional practice, one form of which was also current at Ugarit. This is confirmed by the archaeological record, with more than twenty actual instruments recovered not only from Ugarit itself, but other LBA sites in Syria, Anatolia, Egypt, the Levant, and Cyprus (n.b.).[37] It might be suggested that their brazen clash served as a call for attention, 'clearing the air' for the sacred songs to follow; or that cymbals were endowed with extra-musical powers, serving as a link between

---

[31] Cymbals (*mṣltm*) are mentioned in two texts: RS 2.[014] + 3.363 = KTU/CAT 1.3 i.18–22; RS 24.252 = KTU/CAT 1.108, 4. For general discussion of cymbalists, including the several pairs of instruments discovered at Ugarit itself (one in 'la maison du Grand Prêtre'), see Caubet 1987a; Caubet 1987b:734, 739–740; Koitabashi 1992b; Caubet 1994:131; Caubet 1996:10; Koitabashi 1998:375; Caubet 2014:175.

[32] Noted by Tsumura 1973:178; Koitabashi 1992b:4: Koitabashi 1996:222.

[33] 1 Chronicles 16:5.

[34] 1 Chronicles 15:19: οἱ ψαλτῳδοί· Αιμαν, Ασαφ καὶ Αιθαν ἐν κυμβάλοις χαλκοῖς.

[35] For Biblical cymbalists, see also 2 Samuel 6:5, Ezra 3:10, 1 Chronicles 13:8, 16:5, Psalms 150:4, etc. The role of Asaph in 1 Chronicles 16:5 could suggest that, in the construction of 15:16–22, Heman and Ethan would preside over similarly constituted but discrete 'orchestras'. This would make good sense in an environment like Ugarit, where multiple cults and locations had to be serviced; this seems to be the sense of 1 Chronicles 25:6 also. At Ezra 3:10, however, it is suggested that Asaph's 'clan' was made up entirely of cymbalists. That the tradition is multiform, however, does not invalidate its individual elements for purposes of historical comparison. The Mishnaic tradition agrees that a single cymbalist played among a varying but much larger number of lyrists: see 'Arakin 10a, 13b = BT 16:54, 72–74, specifying 2–6 *nēbel*-players, nine or more *kinnōr*-players, and 2–12 pipes (*ḥalil*), in varying contexts. For the massed lyres of Phoenician tradition, see Chapter 11.

[36] See Myers 1965:111–112.

[37] Archaeological evidence: Caubet 1987b; NG 3:527–528 (Braun); MAIP:107–112.

Chapter Seven

the orchestra and non-musical ritual gestures.[38] Yet the Chronicler himself describes them as accompanying song, and this is also found in an Ugaritian text to be discussed below. Therefore, whatever other properties cymbals may have possessed, they had a definite musical function. The obvious practical explanation is that cymbals, with a more penetrating sound than the frame-drum, would have provided a fundamental rhythm.[39] As such, they would be appropriate to an orchestral leader, comparable to a conductor's baton. And such a position of leadership would naturally go to a person of higher social status than the players under him.[40]

Whatever the exact explanation at Ugarit, it does seem clear that cymbalists enjoyed a certain prominence within the practical machinery and social stratification of cult-music. And yet the very existence of Kinnaru indicates some key role for the instrument, which alone was deified so far as we know. How can this be reconciled with the idea of cymbalist-leaders?

First, we may draw once more on the Chronicler, noting that, while the cymbalists may have led the music, the music itself was made up, for the most part, of massed lyres (the two types presumably covering different ranges[41]). This was fundamentally lyre-music, therefore, and it is ultimately this that justifies the divinization of Kinnaru. We have seen a comparable situation in Ušumgal-kalama, Ningirsu's balang-god in the Gudea Cylinders, who is treated as a musical director for the full temple orchestra.[42] The lyre-playing David is also crucial here. For despite his traditional appointment of Asaph, Heman, and Ethan to 'lead' with cymbals, he himself was nevertheless the ultimate royal and musical 'leader' of the overall corporation. Thus, the Chronicler says that Asaph and his sons "prophesied under the direction of the king."[43] And while a king might naturally be expected to preside over his servants, David literally takes the musical lead in the procession of the ark (see Chapter 8).

In what follows I shall further explore the intersection of *kinnāru* and royal ideology in the Ugaritian narrative and ritual texts. Kinnaru implies the cultural primacy of the ancestral lyre, with the tradition's depth vividly indicated by the

---

[38] Cf. Kleinig 1993:82–84; Koitabashi 1992b:4. For a good discussion of the 'extra-musical' properties of percussion in ritual contexts, with special reference to Cyprus, see Kolotourou 2005. At Ugarit horns (one instrument is apparently engraved with an Astarte figure: Caubet 2014:178–180 with references) may have played a comparable role as signal instruments, as they did in Hittite and Jewish ritual: see generally Kleinig 1993:79–82; NG 3:529–530 (Braun); HKm:259.
[39] See references in Kleinig 1993:82n3.
[40] Compare the use of cymbals by king and queen in the Hittite drinking ritual KUB 56.46 + vii.3'–7': cf. HKm:99, and above, p95 and n28.
[41] See p52.
[42] See p28.
[43] 1 Chronicles 25:2.

evidence from Ebla. The significance of this emerges still more clearly when one considers that Ugarit, by the thirteenth century, presented a highly cosmopolitan environment. The city's pantheon contained Hurrian and even Anatolian deities alongside WS and Mesopotamian gods,[44] and the Ugaritic onomasticon indicates a Hurrian ethnic heritage for as much as a quarter of the city's population.[45] The musical dimension of this cultural mélange is vividly illustrated by the many Hurrian hymnic elements found in Ugaritian ritual texts, including the famous cult-songs with 'notation', discussed above in connection with the currency of the *kinnāru* among the Hurrians of North Syria and Kizzuwatna.[46] This material shows that the music-culture of Ugarit, both within and without the state cult, must have been very rich and diverse, with multiple strands of tradition of considerable antiquity. It is this total complex, and not just the *kinnāru* itself, which one should see as the domain of Kinnaru. This 'commanding role' also helps explain how a Divine Lyre might mirror the king, as the ultimate authority over the state cult and its musicians. This suggestion is most clearly validated by David and Kinyras. But A. Caubet has attractively proposed that, at Ugarit itself, the *Hymn to Nikkal* was composed by 'Ammurapi, the city's last king, rather than a homonymous scribe (the name appears in the colophon).[47] The hymn may therefore reflect the king's direct involvement in the larger musical life of the palace, which was itself substantially structured around the royal cult.[48]

With this we may turn to the rich evidence of the Ugaritian texts for the role of the *kinnāru* in royal cult.

More About Kinnaru

We may begin by resuming the discussion in Chapter 1 of the tablets in which the Divine Kinnaru is attested.[49] Another tablet mentioning Kinnaru was discovered

---

[44] Del Olmo Lete 1992:62–65; Pardee 1996a:67–70; Mayer 1996:207; HUS:323–326 (del Olmo Lete).
[45] Pardee 2000:79 with chart in HUS:509. Names are of course not a guarantee of ethnicity: naming fashions are known to change due to various acculturative processes. Nevertheless, it remains equally possible that names drawn from a given language reflect a person's ancestry from the original speakers of that language. One may still reasonably wonder to what ethnicity one may best assign a person of Hurrian name who was otherwise completely assimilated to a local culture. Yet modern parallels (e.g. American) show that names (along with songs and dances) are one of the more stable ethnic indicators retained by many groups.
[46] See p97.
[47] Caubet 1999:11, 21; Caubet 2014:181.
[48] Caubet 1999:14: "La musique est pratiquée, par le roi et pour le roi, dans le cadre de manifestations ou de cérémonies dont certaines peuvent être religieuses (chantre d'Astarté) ou sont l'expression d'une identité propre à Ougarit (chantre d'Ougarit)."
[49] See p4–5.

Chapter Seven

in 1961 in one of the two archives of the so-called House of the Hurrian priest—the 'Cella of Tablets', containing texts both ritual and paramythological—as well as thirty clay liver-models (and one lung-model) used for extispicy.[50] The tablet in question (RS 24.643) is written in alphabetic cuneiform, and contains two independent texts, one on either side, each prescribing sacrifices to a slightly different sequence of gods.[51] That on the obverse is somewhat more expansive, beginning with a "Sacrifice for the gods of Mount Ṣapanu," followed by a list of divinities and the offerings received by each (1-12). Then comes a poorly understood Hurrian hymn (13-17) and an 'entry ritual' for calling Astarte-of-the-Steppe (ʿAṯtartu-Šadî) into the royal palace, where she is to be offered sacred garments, wool, perfumed oil, gum, and honey (18-22). The precise relationship among the three sections is uncertain. The opening list of gods corresponds almost exactly, both in selection and order, to the 'pantheon' texts already considered.[52] The ritual specifies that Kinnaru receive a ram—the same offering assigned to most of the other gods.[53]

The practical connection between this ritual and the 'pantheon' texts complicates the latter's original interpretation by Nougayrol as a document of Ugarit's official pantheon.[54] Other sacrificial texts present different divine groupings, and further independent 'pantheon' lists may be interpreted as "liturgical outlines" or "abstractions" of still other rituals.[55] Yet because these are all official documents, and sometimes occur in multiple copies (or near-copies) of prescriptive rituals, they do exhibit a canonical dimension. That is, the 'pantheon' is an emergent property of the corpus, including further lost texts of the same type.

---

[50] This house, along with nine others containing tablet archives, was evidently a private residence, although the ritual texts themselves relate to state functions. For the find-spot, see HUS:48-51 (Pitard) with references.

[51] RS 24.643 = KTU/CAT 1.148. Published Virolleaud 1968:580-584 (no. 9). For detailed discussion see Pardee 1992; TR:779-806; RCU, text 12 (translation used here); RTU:427-429. The first ritual (obverse) spans lines 1-22; the second (reverse) from 23-45: damage in 31-45 may be substantially restored from a new Akkadian parallel, RS 92.2004: see below.

[52] See p5. Cf. Nougayrol 1968:64.

[53] Only the 'big three' who open the list (El, Dagan, and Baal in various hypostases) receive more—both ram and bull. Note that this first section of the text concludes with three unattributed sacrifices, "two bulls, two birds, and a cow" (line 9). It is not clear whether these were destined for the gods as a whole; for Kinnaru himself (which would make him by far the greatest beneficiary of the rite, hence unlikely); or (most probably) for the Divinized Kings, the Censer, and a third god (Šalimu) who, though unnamed in the text, are expected based on the parallel 'pantheon' texts. See Pardee 1988a:138-139; TR:784-785, 792-793; RCU:102-103n38 (inclining towards the third explanation).

[54] Nougayrol 1968:64.

[55] See Pardee 2000:61, 67-68; RCU:11-13.

Kinnaru of Ugarit

The reverse of the tablet just discussed (RS 24.643) contains a second prescriptive sacrifice for a different group of deities, labeled as "The gods of the month Ḫiyyāru" (23-45). Unfortunately, the text is damaged where we would expect to find Kinnaru.[56] Yet the known honorands correspond almost exactly to a further god-list (RS 92.2004) known since 1992, composed in Akkadian and exhibiting telltale check marks from the text's use in a ritual performance.[57] Here the Divine Lyre *does* appear, after the Divine Censer and this time written $^{d.giš.za}$MÙŠ.[58] This sign-group and variants, we saw, meant 'Divine Inanna-instrument', and corresponded to both *zannāru* and *kinnāru* in lexical traditions probably going back to the OB period, represented on the western periphery of Mesopotamia by tablets from Emar and Ugarit.[59] It is therefore quite certain that $^{d.giš.za}$MÙŠ represents Kinnaru, and that he should also be restored in the parallel text RS 24.643. Thus, these texts (along with 26.142[60]) attest a further sacrificial god-grouping independent of the first ritual discussed above (RS 24.643 obverse).[61]

Some scholars have called attention to Kinnaru's lack of a distinct Mesopotamian equivalent in the Akkadian 'pantheon' text RS 20.024. Although *kinnāru(m)* could be identified with Sum. balaĝ already a millennium earlier at Ebla,[62] such a correspondence—if it was still known—may have been less satisfactory when it came to the *kinnāru*'s divine form in the West, as not providing a sufficiently

---

[56] The problem is discussed by TR:784-785, 805 (cf. RCU:24n12, 102n33), who tentatively suggests the restoration of Kinnaru here (line 43 of RS 24.643 [rev.]) on the basis of RS 92.2004.

[57] RS 92.2004: Arnaud 2001:323-326 no. 22, with n2 for the checkmarks; cf. RCU:12-13. A preliminary transliteration was published in TR:795, cf. 789; RCU:17-18.

[58] RS 92.2004, line 37: Arnaud 2001:324. This is also found in RS 26.142, a damaged syllabic version of the same list discovered in 1963 and published by Nougayrol 1968:321-322 no. 170; re-edition with revised line-numbering by Arnaud 1994 (hence the Divine Lyre has moved from line 6 to line 19; cf. TR:795-806 passim. These earlier publications give ᵈGIŠ.ZA.MÍM (whence also in TR:311n121 and RCU:18, drawing on a pre-publication version of RS 92.2004 by Arnaud), but already del Olmo Lete 1992:52n65, read $^{d.\,giš}$ZA.MÙŠ; MÍM is an alternative reading of the same sign, considered "unsicher" by Borger 2004:77 (no. 153). For clarification of this point I thank S. Mirelman; for ZA as a phonetic indicator (pointing to *zannāru*), see p78.

[59] See p77-79. Although most of Ugarit's lexical texts remain unpublished (cf. p79n46), one may note RS 13.53, a section of HAR.ra=*hubullu* containing names of musical instruments: see Veldhuis 1996:28 (I assume that this is what Caubet 1996:133 refers to, citing communication with D. Arnaud). While this small text fragment does not preserve *kinnāru* or *zannāru*, its close parallels with lexical texts from Emar show "that the Middle Babylonian Western lexical texts basically belong to one tradition" (Veldhuis 1996:29; cf. Veldhuis 1997:68-69n218 et passim).

[60] See p121n58.

[61] Note that Nougayrol 1968:321-322, in his edition of RS 26.142 (no. 170), rendered his line 6 as '*zannaru*', while raising the question of its etymological relationship with *kinnāru* (see his note *ad loc.*). This was before the presence of *kinnāru* in the MB lexical texts from Emar and Assur was known (for which, see p77-79).

[62] See p54, 65-67.

Chapter Seven

exact equivalent.[63] With the large number of divinized balangs known from Mesopotamia, each bears its own name, and is in the service of a specific master god.[64] The *kinnāru*, by contrast, was apparently unique, the only instrument so deified at Ugarit. D. Pardee plausibly suggests that cult equipment may have been subject to stricter rules when these pantheon equations were being drawn, and that the scribe wanted to insist on the local character of Kinnaru—that only this instrument could be divinized for service in the Ugaritian cult.[65] This seems right; but there may be more to it.

The Ugaritian scribes would have known that *kinnāru* was a word/instrument of deep antiquity and broad distribution; we saw the same awareness in the Bible.[66] The evidence of Ḫh and Diri shows that, by the thirteenth century and probably the OB period, *kinnāru* could be considered an Akkadian word, alongside *zannāru*.[67] Kinnaru's appearance in the Akkadian god-list RS 20.024 may therefore be evidence not only that no satisfactory equation was available, but that none was needed—that the Divine Kinnaru was current beyond Ugarit, stretching eastward into Mesopotamia. This would be in keeping with my suggestion that the Amorite age was formative for the divinization of the *knr*.[68] One should note here that Greco-Roman sources sometimes distinguish a Cypriot Kinyras from one who is king of Assyria or Syria.[69]

In the cultic texts so far considered, there is nothing that distinguishes Kinnaru and the Divine Censer from other 'real' gods. This was the same in Mesopotamia, where, in addition, cult-objects could be personified and take mythological action. I argued for the same combination in the Hurro-Hittite *Song of Silver*.[70] At Ugarit, one may compare the magical weapons that Kothar makes for Baal's battle against Yamm (Sea) in the *Baal Cycle*. In an embedded incantation ritual, Kothar assigns each a proper name—'May he Drive' and 'May He Expel All'—reflecting the task it must perform in the god's hands.[71] Recall the anthropomorphic talking weapons of Ninurta/Ningirsu, and that in Mesopotamia

---

[63] See already Nougayrol 1968:59.
[64] See Heimpel, "Balang-Gods."
[65] TR:311.
[66] See p43–46.
[67] See p77–79.
[68] See p83–88.
[69] See index s.v. 'Kinyras:(As)syria'.
[70] See p103.
[71] KTU/CAT 1.2 iv.11–27 (RS 3.367). The nature of this scene was identified by Obermann 1947, and has won quite general acceptance: cf. Clapham 1969:106; Baumgarten 1981:166; Smith 1984; KwH:409–410; Morris 1992:87–88; Smith 1994:341–343; Smith in Parker 1997 (translation of the names).

name-giving rituals were important for endowing divinized objects with individual personality.[72]

It is a pity there is not more explicit evidence for the activity of personified cult-objects in Ugaritic poetry. For if Kinyras really originated in a Divine Lyre like Kinnaru, the rich mythological material about him would seem to require some comparable treatment on the mainland. Perhaps this was not especially developed at Ugarit, by comparison with, say, Byblos and/or Kizzuwatna (Cilicia), where Kinyras is sometimes localized (Chapters 19 and 23). But note that a certain Theias ('Divine') is a recurring doppelganger of Kinyras at Byblos.[73] Could the doublet Theias-Kinyras reflect something like the Ugaritic formulation of divine determinative + *kinnāru*?

Recurrent sub-groupings of gods in the Ugaritic sacrificial lists point to a living tradition of theological speculation. D. Pardee has noted a striking parallel between the first five recipients in the second sacrificial text discussed above, and a genealogical sequence in the fragments of Philo of Byblos' *Phoenician History*.[74] Composed in the late first or early second century CE, Philo's work survives mainly in several extensive quotations and paraphrases by Eusebios (ca. 260–339), bishop of Caesarea in Palestine, who exploited it for Christian polemic. Philo claimed to possess the work of an ancient priest, Sankhuniathon, who supposedly lived around the time of the Trojan War according to Philo's quite detailed discussion.[75] While the dating and even existence of Sankhuniathon have been subjected to serious doubt, Philo is likely enough to have had recourse to relatively early writings, not to mention living mythological traditions.[76] It is certainly clear that Philo exercised considerable invention, combining parallel regional traditions to compose a continuous 'history'; and following the Hellenistic model of Euhemeros, he interpreted the Phoenician gods as culture-heroes, mapping the course of civilization as he perceived it. Nevertheless, the Ugaritic texts have substantially refurbished the overall credibility of his raw

---

[72] For the naming rituals, see p23n29, 25. The comparison of Baal's weapons with those of Ninurta/Ningirsu was made by Albright in Ginsberg 1935:328n22; cf. Smith 1994:343.

[73] See further p466–468.

[74] See RCU:23n2, on RS 24.643 (reverse), 23–26. The corresponding gods in Philo (FGH 790 F 2 [15–16, 24]) are Ug. *ilib* ≈ 'Gk.' Elioun; *arṣ w šmm* ≈ Epigeios Autokhthon ("later called Ouranos") + Ge; *il* ≈ Elos a.k.a. Kronos; *kṯrt* ≈ Seven Titanides/Artemides; *dgn* ≈ Dagon. The sequence is not strictly linear in Philo's narrative: the Titanides/Artemides, who answer to the Kotharat goddesses in this position of RS 24.643, 25, are treated by Philo *after* the introduction of Dagon.

[75] For the pedigree of Sankhuniathon (FGH 790 F 1 [20–22] = Eusebios *Preparation for the Gospel* 1.9.20–22), see generally, with earlier bibliography, Lokkegaard 1954; Barr 1974; Oden 1978; Baumgarten 1981:41–62 et passim; Attridge and Oden 1981:3–9; Cameron 2004:157 (comparing it with the Second Sophistic fashion for fabricating pre-Homeric authorities).

[76] See the balanced assessments of Lokkegaard 1954:51–53; Baumgarten 1981:261–268.

material. While there are many inconsistencies with what we find at Ugarit, these may be explained through EIA evolution[77] and/or Philo's synthesis of regional variants. So the structural agreement between his 'cosmogony' and the aforementioned Ugaritian text should indeed reflect, as Pardee argues, a common theological tradition going back to the LBA at least.

It follows that *other* conjunctions of gods in the Ugaritian lists are potentially meaningful, and open to clarification from other sources. Two possibilities relating to Kinnaru must be considered. First is his proximity to the Divine Kings (*mlkm*), that is, the divinized royal ancestors.[78] We have seen a comparable combination with the BALAĜ.DI of Ebla, and I shall argue below that the same pattern underlies the appearance of the *kinnāru* at the head of a musical ensemble in a text connected with Ugarit's royal mortuary cult.[79] The same elements come together in the Kinyradai, the royal dynasty of Paphos, which traced its descent from Kinyras (Chapter 16).

Also remarkable is Kinnaru's adjacency to the Divine Censer. This is not so surprising in itself, since both lyre and incense were obviously important liturgical tools, and are the only divinized objects in the list.[80] We saw from Hurro-Hittite texts, deriving from Kizzuwatna, that both lyre and censer received offerings within larger divine circles (*kaluti*).[81] But the connection may be still more intimate. From Mesopotamia, for instance, we know of two balang-gods called 'Censer' and 'Torch', servants of the fire-god Gibil; presumably the first of these implies some close connection between music and incense-offerings.[82] Aphrodite's sanctuary at Paphos, over which the Kinyradai presided, was noteworthy for its avoidance of animal sacrifice in favor of incense offerings; and this probably underlies the *thyapolía* which is apparently attributed to a Kinyrad priest or priest-king in a fourth-century inscription from Paphos.[83]

Moreover, as W. F. Albright observed, the adjacency of Kinnaru and Censer is "at least a striking coincidence" given the famous myth of Kinyras and Myrrha—the personification of myrrh—to be discussed in Chapter 12.[84]

---

[77] E.g. the association of Khousor with iron, versus Kothar and bronze: cf. p46.
[78] This connection was rightly emphasized by Grottanelli 1981:42.
[79] See p134–146.
[80] Cf. Caquot 1979 col. 1404.
[81] See p102–103.
[82] See Heimpel, "Balang-Gods," 54 II 343–344; cf. 27 for the balang 'cedar-resin'.
[83] See p412–414.
[84] For the myth *vis-à-vis* the Ugaritian pantheon texts: YGC:147n102 (quotation); Gese et al. 1970:169; Ribichini 1981:49n50. Albright's suggestion is strongly supported by Grottanelli 1984:42 and n35: "il parallelo è troppo preciso per non essere significativo"; it signifies "il modus vivendi regale e divino nei suoi aspetti più seducenti." For Grottanelli's interpretation, see further p283.

Praising Baal

The *kinnāru* is mentioned several times in Ugaritian mythological and paramythological texts. Some of these passages, like much of Ugaritian literature, are still imperfectly understood and have occasioned much debate. Their obscurity is due both to the fragmentary state of many texts and to the city's laconic alphabetic script, where the omission of vowels occasions much ambiguity and hinders lexical analysis via cognates in other Semitic languages. The interpretations offered here, largely dependent as they are on the philological work of others, are necessarily provisional. They are, however, informed by much comparative material.

Three mythological vignettes evoke the use of the *kinnāru* in royal praise poetry, seemingly of a narrative nature. Together they attest a formulaic scene, the basic expression of which makes Baal the subject of song.[85] A hymn to Baal depicts him seated in majesty on Mount Sapan (Saphon), enjoying peace after his defeat of Yamm:

> Virgin Anat [washed] her hands ...
> She took her lyre (*knr*) in her hand,
> [She clasped] the bull-shaped instrument[86] to her breast.
> She sang of the loves of valiant Baal.[87]

Almost identical verses occur in two other poems concerning Baal and Anat, so that, although in each case the verse where *kinnāru* is expected has been

---

[85] For type-scene and other aspects of oral-formulaic composition in Ugaritian narrative poetry, see with references Cross 1974:1 and n1; Cross 1998:139–141.

[86] The 'bull-shaped instrument' (*r'imt*) has been explained by reference to the well-known bull-headed lyres of Sumer: RTU:76n36; TPm:151 and n179; Krispijn in Koitabashi 1998:374 (for an alternative derivation, Watson 1996:78). Caubet 1987b:735 rightly cautions that a thousand years separate these from the Ugaritian text, and thinks rather of a *kinnāru* with "outward-curved arms resembling the horns of a bull" (Caubet 2014:177; cf. e.g. the Megiddo plaque: Figure 11 = 4.1p). Smith and Pitard 2009:218–219 suggest that the age-gap with Sumerian bull-lyres "does not preclude the use of a name for a lyre that no longer corresponds to the original form," and go on to make the interesting suggestion that "the unusual word selection might be attributed to the alliteration that it forms with the following word, *l'irth*. This latter term perhaps hints at a Mesopotamian genre of love-poetry known as *irtum*-songs" (this genre employed all seven canonical tunings of the Mesopotamian diatonic cycle: cf. e.g. RlA 8:475 [Kilmer, *Music A I]). Perhaps it is a case of poetic fossilization, an ancient musical world removed to the realm of the gods, the 'epic distance' of Homeric studies? But note that an Egyptian lyre with bull-head *is* known from the Ptolemaic era (temple of Philae): MgB 2/1:34–35 fig. 12; AEMI:89.

[87] RS 24.245 = KTU/CAT 1.101.16-19: *ydh . btlt . 'nt . uṣbʻtʻh⸢ [. ybmt] | l'imm . t'iḫd . knrh . b yd[h . tšt] | r'imt . l'irth . tšr . dd 'al['iyn] | b'l . 'ahbt*. Text and supplements: TPm:119–152, with further literature). Translation is that of RTU:388–390 (hence alternative supplements, with earlier editions and studies noted on 388).

Chapter Seven

destroyed, it may be confidently restored. There remains, however, some grammatical and textual uncertainty about whether it is Anat who sings in both cases, rather than a male minstrel.[88] That the subject is Baal's *loves* may tend to support Anat as the more likely performer, being herself female and his lover (and sister). While a female singer praising a king's deeds of *war* might seem striking from a Greek perspective,[89] the Bible attests a women's tradition of greeting returning warriors, when victorious, with celebratory music—scenes which relate to the pre-monarchic period.[90] Most of the passages specify only frame-drum, which evidently serves as the principal marker of the women's tradition;[91] but those who greet the victory of Saul and David over the Philistines present some greater variety.[92] Such an event may be portrayed on the famous ivory plaque from Megiddo, dated by stylistic criteria to the thirteenth or early twelfth century BCE (Figure 11 = 4.1p),[93] if the lyrist who provides a victory song to a seated king, as prisoners are led before him, is indeed female, as some believe (but this is hardly certain).[94] The birds that flock about may represent the king's own divine favor, and/or an epiphany evoked by the music.

[88] The first is RS 2.[014] + 3.363 = KTU/CAT 1.3 iii.4–5 (*Baal Cycle*); the second is RS 5.180 + 5.198 = KTU/CAT 1.7.22–24. See the discussions of RTU:76–77 n36–37, 149–150n4, 289n176, 390n17; cf. ARTU:8–9 and n39, 248; Smith in Parker 1997:109, 167n54; Smith and Pitard 2009:216–217, noting a vertical wedge in the damaged line 4 which would be consistent with the expected *bydh* from KTU/CAT 1.101.17 (RS 24.245, in which *knr* actually is attested.)
[89] But note that the *aoidós* channels the voice of a female Muse.
[90] Exodus 15:20; Judges 5 (Song of Deborah) and 11:34; 1 Samuel 18:6; Jeremiah 31:4.
[91] See Poethig 1985; Meyers 1991, especially 21–27, elucidating a Canaanite tradition of terracotta figurines of women frame-drum players; cf. Meyers 1993, especially 58–62; Fariselli 2007:26–34. The tradition is well-represented on Cyprus, from an isolated example in the late second millennium (LC III) down to abundant specimens in the IA: see especially Kolotourou 2005:188–195. Doubleday 1999 gives a good survey of ANE evidence (105–111) and the gradual and varied transformation of female musical practice with the advent of Islam (111–134). One should also note the *týmpanon*, which is a regular attribute of the Anatolian goddess Kybele. Its presence in the iconography of Atargatis, the 'Syrian Goddess' of Hierapolis, is due, according to OSG:19, 21, 29–30, 32, to the influence of Kybele in her Hellenized representation; but the ANE parallels indicate deeper indigenous strata.
[92] 1 Samuel 18:6, specifying frame-drums along with *šālišîm*, a much-debated word variously interpreted as sistra, lutes, castanets, triangular harps, or cymbals: see MAIP:41–42 with further references.
[93] Jerusalem 38.780: Megiddo, stratum VIIa. A *terminus ante quem* ca. 1150 is given by a cartouche of Ramses III; yet parallels with horse-representations in Egyptian NK art show that the plaque could be as early as Ramses II, being preserved as an heirloom object: Liebowitz 1967. For further analysis of the scene, Loud 1939:13 no. 2 and plate 4 (gender unspecified); Mertzenfeld 1954 no. 342, 1:88 and pl. XXIV–XXV; Frankfort 1970:270–271; Dothan 1982:152 (treats as male); Moscati 2001:38–39; MAIP:96–97 and fig. III.16 (female; aristocratic status indicated by clothing).
[94] Burgh 2004:134, argues that clear gender indicators are lacking in this representation, noting that the lyrist is dressed like the woman just before the throne (but for the latter's polos); cf. Burgh 2006:89–90. This need not mean, of course, that the figure is *intentionally* ambiguous. One

Figure 11 'Kinyrist' celebrating victorious king. Ivory plaque from Megiddo, ca. 1250–1200. Jerusalem, IAA 38.780. Drawn from Mertzenfeld 1954 pl. XXIV–XXV.

Chapter Seven

In the so-called Baal Cycle, however, we encounter a praise-singer who is unambiguously male, and the subject is non-erotic praise. The scene is a feast following a victory by Baal, probably over Yamm (Sea), although this is still disputed.[95]

> He arose, intoned and sang,
> Cymbals in the Gracious Minstrel's (*n'm*) hands;
> Sweet of voice the hero sang
> About (before?[96]) Baal on the summit of Sapan.[97]

The word *n'm*, variously rendered 'handsome', 'pleasant', 'gracious', or 'good', is often applied to gods or heroes.[98] The present passage, however, is one of several where it seems to have a special musical application. Such an interpretation is made probable here by the evident parallelism of *n'm* with *ġzr ṭb ql* ('the youth, good of voice'), and corroborated by the respective verbal phrases *ybd wyšr … yšr* ('intoned and sang' … 'sang'). (It most naturally follows that there is only one singer, who simultaneously accompanies himself with cymbals: see below.)[99] *N'm* may be applied to another 'youth of good voice' who apparently executes some seven-fold cultic song-act in the enigmatic *Gracious Gods*, a paramythological text of obscure ritual application that many scholars have connected with hierogamy.[100] We shall see *n'm* used of a praise-singer of Baal in the *Tale of Aqhat*, where it is again the subject of the phrase *ybd wyšr* ('intoned

---

may note here the hypothesis of Jirku 1960:69, that there existed a 'Kinaratu' (*sic*) alongside Kinnaru. He wished to see this Kinaratu as the origin of the TN Kinneret (Numbers 34:11; Josh. 13:27): cf. Jirku 1963:211; YGC:144n91. See the rightful cautions of Fritz 1978:43 and n35, noting that another TN once derived from *knr* (Gordon 1965a:421 no. 1274) is no longer viable. Görg 1981:9, refers to Jirku's idea in reading the 'King's daughter' seal (Avigad 1978) as an apotropaic emblem; but this famous piece is probably a forgery: MAIP:161–164.

[95] See Smith and Pitard 2009:101–102.
[96] For the ambiguity of the preposition, see Smith and Pitard 2009:115.
[97] RS 2.[014] + 3.363 = KTU/CAT 1.3 i.18–22: *qm . ybd . wyšr | mṣltm . bd . n'm | yšr . ġzr . ṭb . ql | 'l . b'l . b . ṣrrt | ṣpn*. Text and translation: Smith and Pitard 2009:91–96, changing 'virtuoso' to 'Gracious Minstrel' for consistency with the parallel passages, as translated below. Cf. ARTU:4 ('gracious lad'); RTU:71 ('minstrel'); Smith in Parker 1997:106 ('singer'). For the identification of the figure as a praise-singer in a royal court, versus competing interpretations, see Koitabashi 1996:222–223.
[98] TPm:171; Schmidt 1994:68–69 with references; DUL:613–614, s.v.
[99] Tsumura 1973:177; Koitabashi 1992b:2; Koitabashi 1996:233–234; Koitabashi 1998:370 and n30; B. Zuckerman in Smith and Pitard 2009:113–114. In fact, Koitabashi considers it possible, despite the parallelism, that two different people are involved.
[100] RS 2.002 = KTU/CAT 1.23: a musical interpretation of *n'm* at 17 is made plausible by the phrase *ġzrm g ṭb* at 14 (Watson 1994:5–6, interprets as a singular; others take as plural); singers (*šrm*) are possibly specified at line 22, apparently in the context of liturgical 'instructions'. See with further literature D. Pardee in CS 1 no. 87, especially p278n24; RTU:324, 328 and n19, 23. For a skeptical assessment of the case for a hierogamic cult-drama, and review of the various scholarly positions, see Smith 2008.

and sang'), thus further supporting the idea of a praise-singing type-scene (although in *Aqhat* the *kinnāru* is not specified).¹⁰¹ It appears, therefore, that *n'm* had a specialized application to court- and/or cult-music, approaching the force of a title. This semantic development is often explained by supposing in Ugaritic a convergence of the roots *n'm* and *nġm*, the latter productive of musical words in Arabic.¹⁰² This argument was first made by U. Cassuto, who observed the same phenomenon in Biblical Hebrew,¹⁰³ and elegantly explained the resulting semantic duality: *n'm* was an epithet of something or someone "who made pleasant [or sweet] the songs, one who composed them with sweetness."¹⁰⁴ The most outstanding example, we shall see, is the description of David himself as *nĕʿîm*, where the Ugaritian examples just discussed provide compelling parallels for understanding him as praise-singer of Yahweh.¹⁰⁵ In accord with this semantic duality, I have translated *n'm* as 'Gracious Minstrel', and shall do so consistently below.¹⁰⁶

It is somewhat surprising, in view of the episode in which Anat celebrates Baal to the lyre, and the two parallel scenes in which *kinnāru* is generally restored, that the Gracious Minstrel in the present passage is said to use cymbals. We have seen that cymbalists probably functioned as 'conductors' of larger cult ensembles. It may well be, therefore, that the cymbal-playing *n'm* in the present scene stands for a more complex musical texture. Note that in the parallel passage of *Aqhat*, despite the kindred diction, cymbals do *not* appear.¹⁰⁷ Are they assumed there too, or is the addition of cymbals in the present text an expansion of a more basic episode? Evidently the type-scene permitted of some variety—not surprising given the diversity of musical life at Ugarit itself.¹⁰⁸ In the present case it may be that "the stress falls on the activities offered to

---

¹⁰¹ *Aqhat:* RS 2.[004] = KTU/CAT 1.17 vi.32: see further p131.
¹⁰² For example *naġmat*, 'melody'. Ugaritic typically distinguishes between *'ayin* (ʿ) and *ghain* (ġ), but the correspondences are not absolute, and the latter converged with the former in some cases: thus the proposed collapse of *nġm* and *n'm* is "an unusual but by no means rare equation": Cross 1998:140, with Emerton 1982; cf. Smith 1994:65n126 and more positively Smith and Pitard 2009:114, "It is possible (though irregular) that the two roots had already coalesced in Ugaritic, in which case perhaps the word's range included both senses"; Smith in Parker 1997:166n36.
¹⁰³ The phonetic development of ġ > ʿ occurred unconditionally in Hebrew: ICGSL:44–45.
¹⁰⁴ Cassuto 1961 1:236, 238; cf. Cassuto 1971:111–112; his Biblical comparanda are 2 Samuel 23:1; Psalms 81:2, 135:3, 147:1, and the figure of Naamah in Genesis 4:21 (see further p44, 46); also Sirach 45:9: Sarna 1993:213n8. Cf. Koitabashi 1996:223–224; cf. Tsumura 1973:189–190.
¹⁰⁵ 2 Samuel 23:1. See further p149, 175–178.
¹⁰⁶ Cf. Smith and Pitard 2009:114, whose 'virtuoso' is "an attempt to retain the etymological sense of Arabic *n'm* and B[iblical]H[ebrew] *n'm* operative in the word-field pertaining to music suggested by Arabic *nġm*."
¹⁰⁷ See p131.
¹⁰⁸ For RS 24.252, in which pipes and drums appear together with the *kinnāru*, see p141–146.

the pleasure of Baal and not the figure involved in his service."[109] That is, the details of the music-making are intentionally left somewhat indeterminate, and we are to think broadly of a celebratory ensemble of which only a single detail is provided.

In any event, the Anat scene and its restored parallels show that the *kinnāru* played an important role in praise-singing and festive music generally. Given this, it is a reasonable guess that Kinnaru himself could play the role of *n'm* before Baal, for instance in the passage of *Aqhat* where cymbals are not mentioned.[110] Certainly Baal's praise-singer must be divine, and although Baal's servants and attendants are generally not named either in fragments of the Cycle or in other texts,[111] many scholars have attempted to divine the identity of Baal's singer. U. Cassuto, writing before the 'pantheon' texts had been fully apprehended and dismissing a variety of earlier conjectures, saw in the present passage "one of the gods who was famed as a musician and a singer."[112] M. H. Pope suggested in 1965 that it could be the versatile craftsman-god Kothar, but confessed the lack of unambiguous Ugaritian parallels for his musical nature.[113] While Kothar's putative musicality remains controversial,[114] his status as a magical inventor god and patron of craftsmen might give him a logical claim to the art, and derive some support from the Rāp'iu text (discussed below).[115] Pope did note the attribution of musical abilities to Phoenician Khousor by Philo of Byblos, and this has remained the main support for a musical Kothar.[116] I shall argue, however, that that passage actually derives from an ancient 'brotherly' association between Kothar and the Divine Lyre, perhaps especially at Byblos.[117]

If one is to identify Baal's praise-singer at all, why should he not be Kinnaru himself—the only known musical god attested for the city? This explanation works very well for the scenes featuring the *kinnāru*. It is admittedly awkward in the aforementioned passage with cymbals. But since the type-scene was apparently flexible as to its musical details, we need not expect *kinnāru* and Kinnaru in

---

[109] Smith and Pitard 2009:113.
[110] See p131–132.
[111] Smith 2001:56–58; Smith and Pitard 2009:50–51.
[112] Cassuto 1943 (Hebrew: *vidi* ...); Cassuto 1961 1:236 (quotation), 238, noting proposals by Virolleaud (Mot), Dussaud (Dan'el), and de Vaux (Baal).
[113] Pope and Röllig 1965:296; the identification was approved by Dahood 1963:531.
[114] Proposed musical associations of Kothar: Gaster 1961:161nXIV; Dahood 1963; Pope and Röllig 1965:276; Brown 1965; de Moor 1969:177; Parker 1970:244; TPm:99n105; Clemens 1993:74 and n68. For arguments against, see KwH:441–445, followed by Morris 1992:87–88.
[115] Cf. Parker 1970:244n9; ARTU:188n4; Clemens 1993:74 and n68.
[116] Pope and Röllig 1965:275.
[117] See p445–452 and Chapter 20.

every instance. Moreover, if Kinnaru symbolized the totality of Ugaritian music-making, he himself might have been treated somewhat flexibly when anthropomorphized into the realm of mythological narrative, when he might 'leave' the lyre and become simply a Gracious Minstrel.

Bow and Lyre in the *Tale of Aqhat*

The motif of the royal praise-singer is cleverly developed in the *Tale of Aqhat*. The poem's crisis revolves around the hero's wonderful bow, built by Kothar; he apparently receives it as a coming-of-age gift, representing his arrival to the peak of life and strength—a fitting symbol in this age of chariot-warfare.[118] This weapon is apparently bestowed at a feast, attended by Kothar himself and other gods. Anat is present, and lusts for the bow on first sight. Trying to coax it away, she offers Aqhat the world:

> Ask for life, O valiant hero Aqhat:
> Ask for life and I shall give (it) you,
> Immortality and I shall bestow it on you ...
> Like Baal when he is revived, he is served,
> (When) he is revived, one serves and gives him drink,
> Chants and sings before him—
> A Gracious Minstrel (*nʿm* or *nʿm[n*[119]) [who is?] his servant (?).[120]

Although a lacuna frustrates exact interpretation of the final line quoted,[121] the parallels of diction with the second Baal-celebration scene discussed above

---

[118] Margalit 1989:75; RTU:266n70. The royal potency of archery is not limited to this poem, but reflects a more widespread symbolism in the ANE, going back at least to Naram-Sin. The most vivid depictions from the LBA, the Golden Age of chariot warfare, are found in Egyptian reliefs representing the pharaoh as warrior and hunter; cf. the Egyptianizing, enthroned archer on a cylinder seal from Ugarit (RS 3.041, from perhaps the fourteenth century: Schaeffer 1983:12–13). Archer/chariot scenes are also known from LBA Cyprus: *Aspects*:61–66, fig. 46–53. This background illuminates the bow's Excalibur-like narratological function in the *Odyssey*. The archer-king motif is developed extensively in the N-A reliefs, the bow representing long reach and deadly accuracy (see e.g. Winter 1997).

[119] The lacuna makes it uncertain whether to read *nʿmn* or simply *nʿm*; but these adjectives are effectively synonymous (DUL s.v.), and in any event will be used substantively as the sentence subject (rather than 'with pleasant tune', Parker 1997:61): see below.

[120] RS 2.[004] = KTU/CAT 1.17 vi.26–32: *irš . ḥym . laqht . ǵzr | irš . ḥym watnk . | blmt wašlḥk .|...|...| kbʾl . kyḥwy . yʿšr .| ḥwy . yʿšr . wy[š]qynh | ybd wyšr . ʿlh | nʿm [. . .] ʿnynn.* Translation after RTU:273 and Smith 1994:65 with observations in n125 (changing Wyatt's 'minstrel' and Smith's 'Gracious One' to 'Gracious Minstrel' for consistency with the parallel passages discussed above).

[121] Cf. Smith 1994:65n127, "any suggestion remains most tentative." Some representative variations are Pope 1981:162, "One sings and chants before him / Sweetly [and they] respond"; Parker

strongly support those who see in n'm a reference to the singer rather than the music.[122] The present passage, therefore, should be considered yet another instance of the type-scene in which Baal is the subject of praise-singing.[123] One must then ask why the *Aqhat*-poet has deployed the scene in this secondary context.[124] Without denying other possible levels of meaning,[125] I believe that the present passage and other examples of the type-scene must be treated synoptically as a formulaic system; this will reveal specific emphases developed in each case. In the first passage discussed above, Anat lavishes musical attentions on Baal; in the second and third, it is a Gracious Minstrel (n'm). It is not certain that one arrangement should be preferred as more basic than the other. The majority rule would suggest that it was a Gracious Minstrel, rather than Anat, who was normal. Yet in the third instance (our *Aqhat* passage), it is Anat herself who conjures the image of minstrelsy. Moreover, details in the sequel seem to implicate Anat once again in music-making.

In the goddess's seductive vision, Aqhat will not merely be *like* Baal. He will occupy the god's immortal position, enjoying his eternal feasts of music. But Aqhat condemns Anat's deceit, knowing that, unlike Baal, all men must die. He refuses to yield the bow—unwisely adding a chauvinistic insult that enrages the deadly goddess.[126] Aqhat may or may not recognize the ultimate irony of Anat's proposal. Since the only immortality that mortal kings can enjoy is memorialization in song, her offer of making him eternally sung is tantamount to a promise of death.[127] And that much Anat *can* deliver.

The goddess, infuriated, seeks and wins El's approval to kill the hero.[128] She causes a raptor (the transformed mercenary Yatipan) to strike and slay Aqhat

---

1997:61, "As Baal revives, then invites / Invites the revived to drink / Trills and sings over him, / With pleasant tune they respond"; RTU:273, "Like Baal he shall live indeed! / Alive he shall be feasted, / he shall be feasted and given to drink. / The minstrel shall intone and sing concerning him." See also Herdner 1963:83; Dijkstra and de Moor 1975:187–188; Smith and Pitard 2009:122.

[122] Rightly stressed by Dijkstra and de Moor 1975:187–188 ("absolutely certain"); Pardee in CS 1:347n42 ("difficult to avoid"); Smith 1994:65; RTU:273; Smith and Pitard 2009:122 ("the correspondences ... are unmistakable").

[123] There is indeed some dispute as to whether it is Aqhat or Baal himself who is celebrated at feast here (for Baal, see Clemens 1993:68n19 with further references; Aqhat, RTU:273n110; ARTU:238–239). But that distinction does not affect my argument, for either way Baal-like honors are evoked for Aqhat himself.

[124] Cf. Smith and Pitard 2009:122: "The primary issue is the question of the significance of the correspondence."

[125] See the review of opinions in Smith and Pitard 2009:122.

[126] KTU/CAT 1.17 vi.34–38.

[127] Cf. RTU:273n111: "The hero's name will live on in the lays of the poets. Anat is conjuring up a picture of him being alive to hear them."

[128] KTU/CAT 1.17 vi.45–1.18 i.19.

as he feasts.¹²⁹ Apparently Anat is struck by sudden and deep remorse—all the more powerful for its unexpectedness.¹³⁰ Unfortunately the sequel is obscure, between an exceptionally damaged text and unusual language that hinders restorations based on parallels; consequently "wildly varying" interpretations have been proposed.¹³¹ It does seem clear that Aqhat's bow is broken, whether from falling, snapped by Anat in a rage, or for some other reason.¹³² This would to continue the earlier symbolism: the hero's death is inevitably reflected by the broken weapon, which previously marked Aqhat's attainment of life's full powers. The goddess loses her prize.

Several scholars detect in this section a simile involving a singer, a singer's hands, and a *kinnāru*.¹³³ Perhaps the slain hero's hands are like those of a singer.¹³⁴ Or Anat picks up the broken bow, as a singer would his lyre—"delicately, fastidiously, lovingly."¹³⁵ However it was developed, the juxtaposition of lyre and bow would be quite striking. The two 'instruments' are historically akin, although which came first, if either, is unknown. A poetic symbiosis of bow and lyre is abundantly attested in early Greek poetry, and was already traditional for Homer; it probably reflects the relationship between epic singer and royal patron, and the singer's ability to project 'winged words'.¹³⁶ The current passage, however, would be the earliest such example, a precedent for the Homeric trope.

I suggest that we read the simile in *Aqhat* against Anat's earlier allusion to the musical celebration of Baal. On Anat's offer, bow was to be traded for praise-singing. Upon Aqhat's death, he becomes a subject for lamentation and memorialization; the *breaking* of the bow, symbolizing the *end* of Life, makes such performances necessary. It would be strikingly appropriate, therefore, if Anat is likened to a singer *as she weeps*. The setting is, as originally promised, a feast. But what a feast! According to some scholars, Anat dismembers Aqhat's

---

¹²⁹ KTU/CAT 1.18 iv.14, 19, 30; a feasting context is accepted by RTU, canvassing alternative interpretations in 283n147.

¹³⁰ KTU/CAT 1.18 iv.39; cf. Caquot 1985:94.

¹³¹ See, with further literature, ARTU:247n149; Pardee in CS 1:350n81 (quotation); RTU:287n166; Wright 2001:140 and n1.

¹³² KTU/CAT 1.19 i.5; cf. Caquot 1985:96 (Anat breaks the bow out of spite at not being able to string it); RTU:288 and n170 (breaks by falling to the ground).

¹³³ See del Olmo Lete 1984:125–131 (especially 128n289) with review of debate to date. Some would also see a reference to the *kinnāru*, perhaps another comparison with the bow, slightly earlier at 1.19 i.4: ARTU:247; Wright 2001:141. Note also RTU:266n70, *vis-à-vis* the disputed interpretation of 1.17 v.2.

¹³⁴ ARTU:246.

¹³⁵ RTU:290 and n177, following Cooper 1988:22; cf. Gordon 1965a:421 no. 1274.

¹³⁶ Franklin 2002b:1–5 and p254–255 below for other conflations warrior and poet.

corpse and either eats it herself or feeds it to her birds. Anat may even force Aqhat's mouth open and stuff it with food.[137] On my view, the goddess's revenge is presented both as an inversion of her original proposal to Aqhat, and its ironic fulfillment. The poetic manipulation of the praise-singing topos would thus be brought full circle. In retrieving the bow-become-lyre, Anat would replay her position as *kinnāru*-singer (clearly seen in the first instance of the type-scene above); she would indeed 'sing' of Aqhat, by lamenting him. Yet the hero, as he foresaw, would not attain Baal's immortality—except in song, the poem's own function being to immortalize Aqhat.

This reading, though obviously very speculative, is no more so than others'—all based on such an uncertain text. It has the advantage of establishing mutual coherence between two critical passages of the poem.

Rāp'iu and the Eternal Power of Music

In the last Ugaritian text that mentions the *kinnāru* (RS 24.252), celebratory music and royal immortality are again juxtaposed. It begins with an invocation of Rāp'iu, 'king of eternity', who is invited to drink amidst festive music-making (1-5):

> Now may Rāp'iu, king of eternity, drink,
> May he drink, the god mighty and noble ...
> Who sings[138] and makes music (*ḏmr*)
> With lyre (*knr*) and double-pipe,[139]
> With drum and cymbals,

---

[137] Cooper 1988:21–23; RTU:291–292n185. This would accord with a larger pattern of "infelicitous feasting" which has been detected in the poem: Wright 2001:99–138.

[138] This construction is debated: see below.

[139] The *ṯlb* is identified as a kind of pipe on the basis of Akkadian *šulpu* (de Moor 1969:177; TPm:98; Caubet 1996:15). This is supported by general considerations, double-pipes accompanying lyres in the Cypro-Phoenician bowls and the North Syrian ivory box from Nimrud (see p248). These iconographic sources, augmented by a second Megiddo plaque (MAIP:95, fig. III.16), a statuette from Ugarit itself (Caubet 1996:15, 31 fig. 11) and figurines and plaques from the Levant and Cyprus (Levant: MAIP:133–145 with figures; Cyprus: Meerschaert 1991:190–191; Flourentzos 1992), offer strong support for the suggestion of Koitabashi 1998:375, that *tlbm* in RS 24.257 (see p141) be interpreted as dual (cf. RCU:208n33). The absence of a comparable form in the present text is not necessarily problematic: the Greek double-pipes, conceived as a single instrument, were always designated by the singular αὐλός.

With ivory clappers[140]—
With the goodly companions[141] of Kothar.[142]

The text goes on to invoke Anat under several names ('Lady of kingship, / Lady of sovereignty', etc.) along with other gods, mainly obscure (6–13). A damaged middle section seems to have contained a prayer to Rāp'iu by the king of Ugarit (14–18).[143] The concluding section refers to some such petition, and states that Rāp'iu will exercise his 'power' (ḏmr, 22), 'might', 'paternal care', and 'divine splendor' to ensure that the king will long possess and enjoy these self-same attributes (18–27, with ḏmr repeated at 25). An attractive conjecture, with some basis in the damaged text, is that Rāp'iu is to accomplish this by interceding with Baal on the king's behalf.[144] Yet by a curious sleight-of-hand, the actual delivery of these blessings is entrusted to a group called the Rapa'ūma. Verbatim repetition of the list of royal advantages shows that Rāp'iu and Rapa'ūma are essentially equivalent somehow. Evidently, both serve to link the worlds of men and gods.

After considerable debate about the identity of Rāp'iu, he seems most likely to be a hypostasis of the underworld god Milku (< mlk, 'king'), in his guise as eponymous leader of the Rapa'ūma.[145] Etymologically, Rāp'iu would be the

---

[140] This line has been interpreted by some as referring to cult-dancers: Virolleaud 1968:553; KwH:438-441; ARTU:18'8; Good 1991:159–160; cf. Clemens 1993:73n57. But I am persuaded that a passage in Aqhat (RS 3.322+ = KTU/CAT 1.19 iv.22-31) is, despite heavy damage (KwH:440-441), sufficiently parallel to clarify the present text. Dancers are thus excluded in favor of a further instrument, made of ivory (šn)—with clackers/clappers (rather than castanets) the most promising option, as such instruments have been found at Ugarit: see Caquot et al. 1974:455n't' (sic); Caquot 1976:300; Margalit 1984:166–167; Caubet 1987; TPm:98–99 (tentatively); Margalit 1989:447–448; Caubet 1996:12; del Olmo Lete 1999:187n60; Caubet 1999:15–16; RTU:396; Caubet 2014:175.

[141] Or 'the goodly ones enchanted by Kothar': Margalit 1989:438, following KwH:406–410, 443–445, who proposes for ḥbr Heb. and Akk. cognates relating to wizardry and 'binding': see further p444–445 (noting, however, the reservations of Clemens 1993:74n66). The traditional interpretation of ḥbr as 'companions' goes back to Virolleaud 1968:553; cf. Caquot 1976:299–300; KwH:441 with references. Clemens 1993:73–74, rightly rejects the proposal of Good 1991:156–157, to interpret b ḥbr. kṯr. ṯbm as relating to a further instrument akin to Greek κιθάρα/κίθαρις (hence 'with the beautiful cords of the cithar').

[142] RS 24.252 = KTU/CAT 1.108, 1–5: [hl]n . yšt . rp'u . mlk . 'lm w yšt | ['il] ⌈g⌉ṯr . wyqr ... | ... d yšr . w ḏmr | b knr . w ṯlb . b tp w mṣltm . b m|rqdm . d šn . b ḥbr . kṯr . ṯbm. Text, supplements, and colometry of TPm:75–118 (Virolleaud 1968:551–557 no. 2). Translation after RCU:193–194, with minor adaptations as noted.

[143] TPm:118.

[144] For this interpretation of line 18, see TPm:112–113; RCU:192–193, 206 n14–15.

[145] For Rāp'iu, see inter al. Jirku 1965; Virolleaud 1968:551–557; Parker 1970; Parker 1972; KwH:419–445, 385–396; TPm:84–94; Dietrich and Loretz 1989; Brown 1998:139–141; RCU:204–205n6. The main interpretations are 1) Rāp'iu is the high god El seated in state, with Astarte at his side, and hymned by Baal/Haddu who performs upon the kinnāru (an idea developed by Cross 1973:20–22, 185, "as David sang to old Saul," 21); 2) Baal in the chthonic phase of his cycle; 3) Resheph; 4)

'Healthy' or the 'Health-giving'—the 'Healer' or 'Savior' (< *rpʾ*, 'heal').¹⁴⁶ Most scholars believe that the Rapa'ūma themselves are the shades of deceased kings, whose immortality or divinization is achieved through the rites of royal mortuary cult.¹⁴⁷ They are thus to be equated with the Divine Kings (*mlkm*) who appear in the 'pantheon' texts (next to Kinnaru).¹⁴⁸ Rāp'iu would then be the archetypal ancestor, embodying all dead kings from the beginning of time to the last lord buried. This will explain why both Rāp'iu and the Rapa'ūma possess the same royal qualities, and why *his* actions result in *their* bestowing these powers on the living king.

The text does not contain enough directives to qualify as prescriptive ritual; but it does seem to reflect such a rite at some remove.¹⁴⁹ It bears witness to a reciprocal relationship between the living king and his defunct ancestors. The king perpetuated their memory through rites that ensured that his forebears' royalty, now transmuted to the netherworld, was maintained. In return, the king would enjoy the same status while he lived, and be received in their company upon his death.¹⁵⁰ A rather similar idea is found half a millennium later in an eighth-century Aramaic royal inscription from Sam'al (Zincirli); Panammuwas I envisions one of his sons on the throne, maintaining the royal mortuary cult and praying to Hadad: "May the soul of Panammuwas dine with you, may his soul drink with you."¹⁵¹ This is an important regional parallel for the survival of LBA Cypriot royal ideology via mortuary cult into the IA, notably at Paphos.¹⁵²

The Rāp'iu text has several points of interest for the *kinnāru*. The instrument's seeming association with Kothar will be considered later in connection with the coalescence of that god and the Divine Kinnaru (Chapter 18). Crucial

---

eponym of the Rapa'ūma (no further identification with Milku). As Pardee argues, Milku's dwellings, known from other texts, are the same as those given here for Rāp'iu; while the latter's description as 'king of eternity' (*mlk ʿlm*) is a roundabout allusion to Milku himself and the "atemporality of the afterlife" (RCU:204-205n6).

¹⁴⁶ See various entries in DUL:742-743.

¹⁴⁷ RTU:315-323 provides convenient translations of the *Rpum* texts (KTU 1.20-22). For the main interpretive issues, and enormous bibliography, one may usefully begin from KwH:377-396; Pitard 1992; Schmidt 1994:71-100; HUS:259-269 (Pitard); concise summary in Wright 2001:77-78n27. For connections with the Biblical Rephaim, see review in Shipp 2002:114-126.

¹⁴⁸ For the identification, see p5n24. Cf. Healey 1978:91: "*rpʾum* is simply a special epithet of *mlkm*, the two being not identical in meaning but probably used of exclusively the same group of people."

¹⁴⁹ TPm:118; cf. RCU:193: "In any case, the form of this text is, strictly speaking, neither that of the hymn, nor that of the prayer; rather ... the text would be that of a rite by which the transfer of these powers is effected."

¹⁵⁰ Cf. RCU:206n14.

¹⁵¹ KAI 214.15-22: See Greenfield 1973; Smith 1994:99n194.

¹⁵² See Chapter 16.

here, I feel, is the involvement of the *kinnāru* itself in the royal mortuary cult. The opening verses, given above, present a picture of Rāp'iu in a festive royal setting, where jubilant music portrays "the royal lot in the netherworld as a happy one."[153] The general idea is well paralleled by Egyptian tomb paintings and mortuary steles especially of the MK and NK, where harpers and (in the NK) mixed cosmopolitan ensembles—as well as the song-texts that sometimes accompany them—"conjure up the happiness of the life after death by picturing it in terms of earthly joys."[154]

But there are several uncertainties. First, who is singing? Morphology supports three interpretations, all agreeing that Rāp'iu is antecedent to the relative particle (*d-*, 'who' or 'whom', line 3), but diverging on the precise construction.[155] The relative can be the subject of an active verb, so that Rāp'iu himself is singing to, or with, the instruments (this view is reflected in the translation above).[156] Or the verb can be passive, so that Rāp'iu 'is sung'—hymned or celebrated *by* the instruments (with the players merely implied). Finally, it may be active but impersonal, with Rāp'iu as the object, that is, 'whom one sings' with the various instruments. For some scholars, Rāp'iu as a musician seems undignified, as though he were a mere "court entertainer"; the scenes of Baal being celebrated by his minstrel, discussed above, are offered as the normal arrangement—a god receiving musical offerings, not giving them.[157]

The question is complicated, however, by a wordplay whose importance has been well emphasized by Pardee.[158] In the translation above, where Rāp'iu is said to 'sing (*yšr*) and make music (*ḏmr*)', a musical sense to *ḏmr* is required by its parallel placement with *yšr*, known to mean 'sing'. Consequently scholars derive the word from P-S *zmr*, which produced cognates related to singing in Akkadian, Hebrew, and Arabic.[159] (Although the inherited sound z- normally

---

[153] RCU:205n8.

[154] But there are many permutations of these ideas, and a complex development: see Lichtheim 1945 (quotation, 183); MMAE Chapter Seven. Note also that figurines of musicians were placed in tombs "as servant statues ... intended to entertain the deceased in the underworld": see Leibovitch 1960 (quotation 53), with examples from OK–late NK.

[155] See *inter al.* ARTU:188 (active); TPm:81 (active); Good 1991 (passive); Clemens 1993:68–72 (impersonal, with parallels); Koitabashi 1998:371 (uncertain); RCU:205n8 (active but acknowledges other possibilities); RTU:396 and n9 (impersonal); DUL s.v. *knr* (passive).

[156] Cf. Caubet 1999, 15; DDD col. 914 (Pardee), "musician and diviner"; RCU:205n8; cf. Smith 2001:268n196 (Rāp'iu "leads the musical entertainment").

[157] Good 1991:158; Clemens 1993:65–66 (quotation); RTU:396 and n9.

[158] For the following philological points, see TPm:97–98 (with earlier literature in n88–89), 118; Sivan 2001:21–22; RCU:205n8 ("one of the principal wordplays in this text").

[159] DUL:287; Botterweck and Ringgren 1997–2006:91–98. For P-S z > Ug. z, ICGSL:34 §8.31, 44 §8.60; Pardee 2008:292. Note for instance the *zammārū*, cultic singers of nearby Emar (cf. p171). For musical derivatives of *zmr* in Hebrew, see also Jones 1992:934a (*mizmôr* 57 times in psalms, "probably a label indicating music associated with liturgy and the guilds"); MAIP:35.

Chapter Seven

continued as such in Ugaritic, other examples of a phonetic 'confusion' with ḏ are now known.¹⁶⁰) In the text's climax, however, when we twice find ḏmr among the benefits the Rapa'ūma will bestow upon the king (22, 24), the parallel constructions dictate that it now have a sense like 'power' or 'protection'.¹⁶¹ This must derive from an historically distinct root (P-S *ḏmr), with various derivatives in Arabic and several other cognate languages; these include 'Zimri', attested among the Amorite PNs of Mari (for instance Zimri-Lim), the Canaanite governors of the Amarna texts, and as a royal PN in the Bible.¹⁶² At Ugarit the two roots had evidently become sufficiently homophonous to enable the wordplay in the present text, whose opening and closing sections are thereby closely bound.¹⁶³ This was clearly no gratuitous pun, but a prominent structuring element—even a magical assonance. It establishes an essential equation between 'song' and 'power'.

I suggest the following interpretation. Milku, as Rāp'iu, embodies the 'power' that is a property of the Rapa'ūma; he is the agent who bestows it, or effects its transfer, to the living king. This active relationship with 'power', by its homonymous equation with 'song', supports the view that Rāp'iu himself is the singer in the first part of the text. His song *is* power, power projected precisely through song: the royal line will maintain its position for as long as Milku sings. This would accord, first, with Pardee's idea that festive music is a primary marker of the eternal, blissful condition. Other nuances emerge, however, from the perspective of ritual performance. The text's opening attempts to secure Rāp'iu's good will through an offering of libations; this is expressed paramythologically as an invitation to a ritual symposium that is supposed to mirror the situation at Milku's own palace.¹⁶⁴ It is this offering that, by the principle of reci-

---

[160] For the "apparent confusion of /ð/ [i.e. ḏ] and /z/," see Pardee 2008:292, who compares nḏr/ nzr ('vow') and ḏrʿ/zrʿ ('seed/arm'). These parallels rule out the idea that ḏmr in the present text is merely a scribal error (so Blau and Greenfield 1970:12). They also make it unnecessary to suppose complicated borrowings from other Semitic languages. Lowenstamm 1969:465–466, for instance, argued that Ug. ḏmr and Heb./Arab./Akk. zmr derived from a single P-S root *ḏmr already containing within itself the dual notions of 'song' and 'power'. This involves dismissing Arabic and Syriac zmr, which are normally used to establish a P-S root *zmr (Blau and Greenfield 1970:12), as loanwords from Canaanite (similarly Blau 1977:82–83, suggested that the Hebrew and Aramaic forms were loanwords from Akkadian, with Arabic zmr borrowed in turn from Aramaic).

[161] So already de Moor 1969:179.

[162] Ugaritic ḏmr: DUL:287–288. Zimri- names at Mari: Huffmon 1965:187–188, cf. Buccellati 1966:227; RCU:205n8. Amarna tablets: see index to Moran 1992 ('mayors' of Sidon and Lakiša). Zimri in Hebrew: Numbers 25:14; 1 Kings 16:9–20.

[163] TPm:118; Lewis 1989:51–52.

[164] This is not to insist that the marziḥu was a subspecies of mortuary cult, only that its festive form—to which drinking and music were basic, as seen both here and in the famous polemic of Amos against those who "lie on beds of ivory ... who sing idle songs to the sound of the kinnōr

procity, will secure the god's beneficent actions at the end of the text. The corresponding ritual in real life would have involved an actual musical celebration of the god, itself an offering, and this is doubtless echoed by the description of music in the opening scene. That is, whatever Milku may be *imagined* as doing, one must envision cult-musicians in their usual liturgical roles. Yet this too accords with the equation of 'song' and 'power'. If the cult-honors for Milku and the royal ancestors are continuously maintained, they will maintain the royal line in power. Cult-songs thus *express* Milku's power, both literally and figuratively. The position of Milku, which oscillates between his giving and receiving song, mirrors that of the living king—the notional executant of all royal ritual, yet subject of praise-singing by his own minstrel. (The syntax of line 3 may be intentionally ambiguous for just this reason.)

We may now consider the *kinnāru* itself. It is quite possible that it and the other instruments are imagined here in personified form, so that we are actually dealing with Kinnaru and a band of musical colleagues. I will discuss this possibility further when examining the phrase 'goodly companions of Kothar' against other evidence for the syncretism of Kothar and Kinnaru/'Kinyras'.[165] In any event, it is significant that the *kinnāru* is the first instrument listed. This must reflect its preeminent status within the Ugaritian cult, an idea supported both indirectly by the instrument's prominence in the comparative material, and by the *kinnāru*'s uniquely divinized status in the Ugaritian 'pantheon' texts. Indeed, the juxtaposition there of Kinnaru alongside the Divine Kings (*mlkm*) doubtless has theological significance, reflecting some special connection between lyre and royal cult, and perhaps especially its mortuary aspect.[166] This could accord, for instance, with the instrument's use

---

... who drink wine from bowls" (6:4-7, cf. 5:21-23; Isaiah 5:11-12)—lent itself well to securing divine goodwill. See Pardee 1996b:277-279; cf. RCU:184-185n2. For the *marziḫu/marzeaḥ* generally see *inter al.* Greenfield 1974; Pope 1979-1980; Friedman 1980; King 1989; McLaughlin 1991; McLaughlin 2001; del Olmo Lete in Johnston 2004:315-316.

[165] See p443-445.

[166] For the reasoning, see p123-124. Unfortunately, that Kinnaru and the Divine Kings might receive sacrifices on the same occasion is not confirmed by the two rituals of RS 24.643 (1-12 and 23-45) which correspond to the 'pantheon' texts; for while Kinnaru is honored in one or both, the Divine Kings (*mlkm*) are not listed—although one of the three apparently unassigned offerings of line 9 may indeed have been intended for them (TR:792-793; cf. p120n53). But this still would not corroborate a special relevance to the pairing of Kinnaru and *mlkm*, since they would be but two recipients in a much larger divine group. Note that offerings to the *mlkm* are in any case attested by two other ritual texts: oil-libations in RS 24.266, 25' (KTU/CAT 1.119), and check-marks in RS 94.2518 which indicate the text's use in a sacrificial ritual (TR:680; RCU:102-103n38, 104n52, 200). These have suggested that the omission of Divine Kings from RS 24.643 was intentional after all, the mortuary cult not being relevant to the two occasions comprised by RS 24.643 (TR:303n59). It would then follow that Kinnaru's importance was not *limited* to the mortuary cult (as one would hardly expect anyway).

Chapter Seven

for epic and other poetry in which the dead were memorialized—the practice that lay behind Anat's deceptive offer to Aqhat.

Now if Rāp'iu can be imagined as singing, it seems quite possible that he himself was conceived as playing the *kinnāru*.[167] This could symbolize his, and indeed all past kings', ongoing memorialization in the terrestrial cult, and consequently his 'power' to bless the living king through the medium of his 'song'. There would be a striking parallel in Cypriot Kinyras as archetypal, *kinýra*-playing royal ancestor to the historical kings of Paphos (Chapter 16). There is also the Sumerian chthonic god Ninazu ('Lord Healer'), best attested for the Ur III and OB periods, who was associated especially with the cult of deceased kings at Ur, and with the sites of Enegi and Eshnunna.[168] According to the Enegi temple-hymn, dating to the Amorite Age (OB period):

> Your prince (is) the seed of the great lord, the pure one of the 'great earth', borne by Ereškigalla,
> He who with a loud voice plays the zan(n)aru-instrument, sweet (as) the voice of a calf,
> Ninazu, (who hears) the word(s) of prayer.[169]

Ninazu's other characteristics, which varied considerably with time and place, include associations with lamentation-singing, dying-and-rising gods like Dumuzi, and perhaps healing.[170]

It is also worth noting N. Wyatt's intriguing suggestion of an etymological relationship between Rāp'iu and Orpheus,[171] both apparently lyre-players and health-givers, both connected with the Underworld and resurrection of the dead.[172] One thinks especially of traditions, associated with Lesbos, that the lyre

---

[167] A further objection to seeing Rāp'iu as a "court entertainer" has been that he cannot play all of the instruments simultaneously: Good 1991:158; Clemens 1993:66. But this reading is overly literal. I have already offered arguments in support of Rāp'iu's at least notional performance. If he is leader of the song, he could also play the instrument by which the 'orchestra' is led, just as David leads his own musicians.

[168] See generally Cohen 1993:465–470, especially 469–470.

[169] *Temple Hymns* 14.182–184; trans. Sjöberg and Bergmann 1969:27–28, with discussion at 8–9 and 88–89.

[170] See with sources RlA 9:329–335, especially 332–333 (Wiggermann, *Nin-azu). As son of Ereshkigal, Ninazu could be steward and seal-keeper of the underworld; he is called 'lord of prayers and supplications' (*Shulgi X*, 105–106) and is once lamented alongside Dumuzi and other deceased kings (*In the Desert by the Early Grass*, Jacobsen 1987:59–60). For further connections with lamentation-singing, see PHG:76 and n129. His associations with healing are somewhat elusive.

[171] RTU:395n2.

[172] His consistent mythological connection with Thrace, however, is problematic. Among the innumerable sources for Orpheus, note especially Kern 1922:21–22 (underworld), 25 (magician and healer).

and/or head of Orpheus survived his death, threnodizing of its own accord and carrying on his tradition.[173] His attempt to revive Eurydike recalls the creation of the gala-priest to rescue Inanna from the netherworld.[174]

From much farther afield comes a colorful and illuminating analogy. The remains of lyres have been found in many Anglo-Saxon elite burials, most recently the so-called 'Prittlewell Prince'.[175] Clearly symbolic of the deceased's achievement of memorable deeds, these lyres were also among the possessions a warrior was thought to *need* in the next world. Here there is no clear line between singer and sung. After all, how many princes and kings could really play the lyre—even if Homer presents just this image in Achilles, cheering his heart by singing the 'famous deeds of men' as he ponders whether or not to die young at Troy and achieve 'imperishable fame'.[176]

Silence of Kinnaru

The hypothesis that the *kinnāru* enjoyed a special position in the royal mortuary cult and the ideology of the Rapa'ūma, and that Rāp'iu himself may have been represented as a *kinnāru*-player, must confront the musical details of another Ugaritian text—the maddeningly elusive yet highly suggestive RS 24.257. Though badly damaged, the tablet probably contained a rite connected with the cult of dead kings, since a list of them—originally from thirty-two to fifty-two names, accompanied by divine determinatives—appears on the reverse.[177] The obverse contains repetitions of the following formula:[178]

> [...] and high is his drum
> [...] peoples, for the Gracious One (*n'm*).
>
> [...] and high is the double-pipe
> [...] PR, for the Gracious One (*n'm*).[179]

---

[173] For the post-mortem life of Orpheus' lyre and head, see p140-141 and cf. Power 2010:390-391.
[174] See p29.
[175] The 'Prittlewell Prince' lyre has not been published yet, but other specimens are discussed by Lawson 2004:66-67; Lawson 2006:5-6; Lawson 2008:391-392.
[176] Homer *Iliad* 9.185-189.
[177] RS 24.257 = KTU/CAT 1.113: Virolleaud 1968:561-562 (no. 5); TPm:165-178; RCU:195-210 (text 56A). A parallel king list is RS 94.2518: Arnaud 1998; RCU:203-204 (text 56B). A connection between the tablet's reverse and obverse is supported by Smith 1994:100; Lewis 1989:51-52; RCU:195-201, 203; RTU:399-403, with further references.
[178] The music is mentioned in lines 2, 4, 6, 9-10.
[179] [...] ⌜-⌝ *w rm tph* | [...] *l'umm l n'm* | [...] ⌜w⌝ *rm tlbm* | [...] *pr l n'm*. Text: TPm:165-178. Translation RCU:201-202, changing 'Good One' to 'Gracious One' for consistency with my larger interpretive arguments about the term *n'm*.

Chapter Seven

Pardee, assuming a connection between these mysterious actions and the king list, posits that the text was a "rite characterized by music in favor of the departed kings. One function of each entry, then, would be to state that the king in question had ... joined the Rapa'ūma and become a god."[180]

A principal uncertainty is the identity of the 'Gracious One' (n'm). Given the context, and the word's normal application to gods or heroes like Keret and Aqhat, the most obvious referent should be a king (whether the reigning monarch, or each of his divinized ancestors, remains an interpretive conundrum).[181] And yet, as T. Lewis has stressed, "the weakness of such a view is that it does not justify why l n'm occurs repeatedly among musical instrumentation."[182] This makes it very reasonable to look to the special musical sense of n'm, discussed above, so that 'Gracious One' becomes rather 'Gracious Minstrel'.[183] Yet this need not mean that the text refers only to "various musical instruments which are dedicated to the chief musician."[184] The two positions may be well harmonized by supposing that the king(s) himself is depicted here as a singer/musician. Hence, Pardee attractively suggested that Rāp'iu/Milku, whom he sees as a musician in RS 24.252, is in fact the 'Gracious One' of the present text.[185] On the other hand, Pardee was equally drawn to Wyatt's suggestion that the formula was repeated once for each of the divinized kings in the list of the reverse.[186] Once again the two interpretations need not be mutually exclusive. Each divinized monarch, invoked as 'Gracious One', may be seen as occupying one stage of an eternal royal continuum whose totality is represented by Rāp'iu/Milku. Each king, by virtue of being n'm, is invoked as an instantiation of the eternal musician-king which (on the hypothesis) Rāp'iu/Milku is represented as being in RS 24.252. It must be significant that on the one occasion when David is described as nĕ'îm—a Heb. cognate to n'm—the kinnōr-playing king is on his deathbed, laying out the legacy of his reign.[187]

But if Pardee is right to develop a relationship between the present ritual and the portrait of Rāp'iu/Milku as an underworld musician-king, one must

---

[180] RCU:200, with his most recent, and convincing, arguments that divinized kings are in question here; cf. Pardee 1996b:276.
[181] For a representative sample of interpretations, see Kitchen 1977:133-134, 137 (the reigning king); TPm:169 (Rāp'iu?); Schmidt 1994:68-69 (a god, but does not identify); RTU:400n7, with further, dissenting literature ("the reference is unclear"), and suggesting that the 'Gracious One' may have referred, in each of its presumed repetitions, to a different deceased king.
[182] Lewis 1989:52.
[183] So F. M. Cross in Lewis 1989:52; Smith 1994:100; RCU:201. For n'm, see p128-129.
[184] So Lewis 1989:52.
[185] TPm:171; RCU:201; the idea is given some credence by Smith 2001:268n196.
[186] RCU:201.
[187] See further p148-149, 175-178.

squarely face an organological discrepancy between the two texts.[188] Whereas in RS 24.252 the *kinnāru* appears to occupy a leading position, it is not mentioned in RS 24.257; but its companions—pipes and drums—play a well-defined role, whatever other actions the fragmentary rite may have entailed. Even so, the proposed centrality of the *kinnāru* to royal funerary and/or mortuary ritual is not thereby compromised; the instrument's absence here could be very deliberate, a further case of emphatic treatment. That is, RS 24.257 may present an opposite, but complementary, perspective to the material considered above. The following thoughts may be useful in stimulating argument.

First, one might imagine that each *n'm*, as Gracious Minstrel, is in fact conceived of as a *kinnāru*-player—mirroring Rāp'iu/Milku as underworld musician *par excellence*—to whom pipes and drums pay tribute, just as Kinnaru himself stands out as the only divinized instrument known at Ugarit. Each repetition could thus summon an image of the divinized king enthroned, Rāp'iu-like, and as a lyrist leading the ensemble of instruments that is more fully enumerated in RS 24.252.[189] One may note here the plausible suggestion of S. Ribichini, on the basis of Kinyras' connections with the verb *kinýresthai* ('lament'), that Kinnaru "aveva probabilmente un ruolo specifico nella lamentazione funebre di Baal ed in quella dei sovrani defunti."[190]

Alternatively, one could suppose that the vision of RS 24.257 encompasses not only the blissful enthronement of the divinized kings, but also concisely 'replays' the funerary ritual by which each ancestor originally joined the Rapa'ūma. Such a rite is elaborated in RS 34.126, a "funerary text in poetic form," which accompanied the burial rites and sacrifices for Niqmaddu III, the penultimate king of Ugarit.[191] This text invokes the *Rapa'ūma* (2-10), with two former kings mentioned by name (11-12); calls for mourning of the king's throne, footstool, and table (13-17); invokes the sun-god Šapšu (18-19), who bids the deceased "descend into the earth ... lower yourself into the dust" (19-22), there to join his ancestors among the *Rapa'ūma* (23-26); stipulates a seven-fold

---

[188] The appearance of pipes and drum in both texts was noted by Virolleaud 1968:561 and Kitchen 1977:140. By itself, however, this parallel is rather too general to be significant (so rightly Lewis 1989:51); and in any case the correspondence is only partial. Thus to support the mutual relevance of the texts on the basis of their musical details, one must (ideally) *both* find further specific performative and/or conceptual parallels, *and* account for the apparent absence of the *kinnāru*.

[189] On this interpretation the 'drum' of RS 24.257 might comprise the lesser percussion instruments named in RS 24.252; so too the Cypro-Phoenician symposium bowls show predominantly, but not exclusively, frame-drums for percussion (see p265).

[190] Ribichini 1982:498.

[191] RS 34.126 = KTU/CAT 1.161: Bordreuil and Pardee 1982; Bordreuil/Pardee in Bordreuil 1991:151-163 no. 90; KTU:150-151. See also Levine and de Tarragon 1984; Pardee 1996b:274; RCU:85-88 no. 24 (quotation 87); RTU:430-441; Shipp 2002:53-61.

Chapter Seven

sacrifice to accompany the king's descent (27–30); and orders a final bird-sacrifice to secure good fortune for the new king ('Ammurapi) and the city of Ugarit (30–34).

Now if it is right to suppose an intimate link between king and *kinnāru* in the ideology of a blissful afterlife, it would be quite appropriate for the lyre *not* to be heard during a ritual marking the king's descent 'into the dust'. Its silence would echo the king's death, a royal object to be mourned, like his throne. After arriving in the underworld and being accepted by his deceased forebears, the king would again take his throne, resuming a joyous existence modeled on that which he had pursued in life. The pipe-drum music of RS 24.257 might thus recall an immemorial sequence of royal funerary rites-of-passage, each having issued in a revival of the joyous *kinnāru*, whereupon pipes and percussion reverted to the secondary and tertiary positions they occupy in the Rāp'iu text. The *kinnāru* would thus symbolize the deceased's attainment of eternal kingship: he assumes a new form of power, which, as with Rāp'iu, is envisioned as a life-giving song.

A possible parallel comes from the *Tale of Aqhat*. After mourning his son for seven years, Danel banishes lamenters from his house, and offers a meal and incense to the gods. The next three verses are heavily damaged, but one probably mentioned cymbals and ivory clappers in the same order they appear in the Rāp'iu text.[192] Whatever else may have transpired here, it seems clear that the end of Danel's mourning is marked by a resumption of music. That his actions are relevant to royal mortuary cult, and to be connected with the Rāp'iu text and the rite just discussed, was plausibly suggested by M. Dijkstra.[193]

The foregoing arguments are inevitably tenuous. But the following comparative points should be borne in mind. First there is the topos of grief stilling the sound of music, found already in Sumerian sources.[194] We saw that several Hittite ritual texts prohibit singing and/or lyre-music, including a drinking ceremony to the soul of a deceased king or queen.[195] Conversely, pipe-music played a special role in funerary rituals in many parts of the ANE and Aegean.[196] In the N-A version of the *Descent of Ishtar*, for example, a 'pipe of lapis-lazuli' is mentioned as part of the annual rites for Dumuzi.[197] Osiris was also connected

---

[192] KTU/CAT 1.19 iv.22–31 = RS 3.322+. See above, n140.
[193] Dijkstra 1979:209–210; cf. Dijkstra and de Moor 1975:211.
[194] For instance in the *Death of Ur-Nammu* (*Ur-Nammu A*, ETCSL 2.4.1.1), 187–188: "My *tigi*, *adab*, flute and *zamzam* songs have been turned into laments because of me. The instruments of the house of music have been propped against the wall."
[195] See p95.
[196] For the Aegean, see Chapter 12.
[197] This was noted as a possible parallel to RS 24.257 by Dijkstra 1979:210; TPm:98 ("l'usage du mot *ṭlb* a peut-être bien servi à donner le ton à une cérémonie pour les morts"). As translated by E. A.

with flute-music and funeral rites, and was mourned by Isis.[198] Greek representations of the *Adōniá*, a funereal celebration of Adonis observed by many women in the Classical period and deriving at some remove from the Phoenician sphere, show the use of double-pipes and sometimes frame-drums and clappers (*krótala*); this contrasts with the depiction of Adonis, while alive and in company with Aphrodite, as playing the lyre.[199] Then there are the *gíngras* (or *gíngros*) pipes reported by Athenaios, drawing on late Classical and Hellenistic authorities, as used by the Phoenicians in lamenting Adonis,[200] and an alternative name for Adonis himself; an etymological connection with Kinyras, proposed by W. H. Engel, may be signaled here.[201]

On the other hand, there is equally good evidence from the Aegean and the Syro-Levantine sphere for the use of lyres in more stylized threnodic contexts (Chapter 12). I have already argued for such an interpretation of evidence from Ebla (Chapter 4), and will present more when discussing the 'Greek' word *kinýresthai*, 'threnodize', which must be cognate with both *knr* and Kinyras (Chapter 12). Period cult-lyric threnodies may also be intended in the Cypro-Phoenician symposium bowls, with their temple 'orchestras' of *knr*, pipes, and frame-drum, if these are to be connected with Astarte/'Adonis' cult as many believe.[202] One must also note what the Greeks called Linos-song—a threnodic form for which Herodotos alleges close parallels in Cyprus, Phoenicia, and

---

Speiser (ANET:109): "Wash him with pure water, anoint him with sweet oil; / Clothe him with a red garment, let him *play* on a flute of lapis [or 'let the lapis lazuli pipe play': S. Dalley in CS 1 no. 108, here p. 383]. / Let courtesans turn his mood (rev. 48–50) … (Ishtar speaking) 'On the day when Tammuz comes up to me, / When with him the lapis flute (and) the carnelian ring come up to me, / When with him the wailing men and the wailing women come up to me, / May the dead rise and smell the incense'" (55–58). Of course the 'flute' here aptly reflects Dumuzi's role as shepherd (a very early association illustrated by an OAkk. cylinder-seal showing a seated single-pipe player among herd animals: Collon 1987 no. 675; for another pastoral piper, MgB 2/2:62–63, fig. 40). But for this very reason the instrument is a most appropriate symbol for Dumuzi's fall and rise. There is an ominous scene in a Sumerian version of the myth. When the enraged goddess returns from the underworld and confronts the heedless lover on his throne, her demon assistants "would not let the shepherd play the pipe and flute before her" (*Inanna's Descent to the Netherworld* [ETCSL 1.4.1], 353).

[198] Egyptian sources: Hickmann 1954a:50–52. Also Juba FGH 275 F 16.

[199] Pipes at the *Adōniá*: LIMC s.v. Adonis no. 48, 48b. Adonis with lyre: LIMC s.v. Adonis no. 8 (Attic), 10(?, Attic), 19 (Etruscan mirror), s.v. Myrrha no. 2 (Apulian) = Aphrodite no. 1555. Cf. Servais-Soyez 1984:63, 68.

[200] Athenaios 174f; other sources collected in AGM:92 n56–57; see also GMW 1:262–263. Apparently these instruments enjoyed some novelty value in the Greek symposium and perhaps the theatre, to judge from the comic sources cited by Athenaios.

[201] See further p190n19, 202–204, 299n117. Some would also connect the name *Abóbas*, by which Adonis was known at Perga in Pamphylia (Hesykhios s.v. Ἀβώβας), with Semitic words for pipes like Syr. *abbūba* and Akk. *embūbu* (Movers 1841–1856 1:243; SOM 2:389; AOM:251 [Farmer]; see also p55n44 and 538). But *Abóbas* belongs rather with other sources which offer Ἀῷος (*vel sim.*) as titles of Adonis, via Gk. ἀ(ϝ)ώς/ἠ(ϝ)ώς, 'dawn'. See Lightfoot 1999:184 and further p502 and n46.

[202] Fariselli 2007:20. See further p262, 293, 486.

Egypt. For Linos is a lyrist whose unseasonable death was lamented by lyre-players, who thereby reenacted, and thus effectively resurrected, the object of their lament.[203]

RS 24.257 is not decisively illuminated by any one of these parallels, which do not themselves conform to a single underlying template. But their collective diversity is useful and suggestive, demonstrating purposeful articulations in the use of cult instruments to create musical environments appropriate to specific ritual contexts. Any explanation of RS 24.257 should bear this material in mind.

Isaiah and the Lyres of the Rephaim

That the *kinnāru* may have been 'brought down' by or with the king during his ritual descent to the underworld—and/or in the paramythological representation of that rite—recalls a passage of Isaiah, one of many places in the Bible that mention 'Rephaim'. The precise relationship of the Rephaim to the Rapa'ūma of Ugarit remains controversial, but here especially their essential kinship is clear. The Rephaim are described as "all who were leaders of the earth ... all who were kings of the nations" (14:9).[204] Isaiah predicts the downfall of "the king of Babylon" (in fact probably an Assyrian emperor) and conjures an image of his arrival in the underworld.[205] There the royal shades will be raised from their thrones to greet him thus:

> You too have become as weak as we! You have become like us!
> Your pomp is brought down to Sheol, and the sound of your lyres;
> Maggots are the bed beneath you, and worms are your covering.[206]

Isaiah was clearly familiar with the details of royal ideology going back to the BA in the region: his 'Rephaim' are correctly placed in the underworld, their royal status is ongoing, and they are enthroned.[207] The larger passage parodies a royal dirge both in form and content,[208] and offers a number of parallels to the funerary ritual for Niqmaddu III discussed above. Common elements include the weeping over, or of, inanimate objects; the rousing of the 'Rephaim' to greet

---

[203] See further p308–310.
[204] For other passages, and their link to the Ugaritian Rapa'ūma, see references in p136n147.
[205] For the authenticity of the attribution to Isaiah here, and the identification of the "king of Babylon" with an Assyrian king, perhaps Sargon II, see Shipp 2002:158–162. But the following arguments do not depend on Isaiah's own authorship.
[206] Isaiah 14:10–11. In attributing all of these lines to the Rephaim's speech, I follow the argument of Shipp 2002:129–132, 155–156.
[207] Compare 1 Kings 18, which exhibits detailed familiarity with the ritual procedures and narratives of Baal cult: Ackerman 2001:86–88.
[208] Shipp 2002.

the newly deceased; the king's *katábasis*; propitiatory sacrifices; and proclamation of the new king. Isaiah systematically perverts this agenda: cedar trees celebrate the hated tyrant's death; the Rephaim—themselves disempowered—do not welcome him to their company, but meet him with cold disdain; instead of hailing a successor, his sons are to be slaughtered and the royal line eradicated.[209] Whereas the Rephaim "lie in glory, each in his tomb" (14:18), the "king of Babylon" will not enjoy a proper burial, nor go to a royal resting-place but to the lowest pit (14:15-20): "you are cast out, away from your grave ... / ... like a corpse trampled underfoot" (14:19).[210]

Given the prophet's informed engagement with the ideology of Syro-Levantine royal mortuary cult, his inclusion of the *kinnōr* is surely no accident. Elsewhere in the Bible, and in other ANE literature, joyful music marks a prosperous and orderly realm; its silencing, the opposite.[211] In Isaiah himself, Yahweh's vengeance on Judah's enemies stills "the song of the ruthless" (25:5), and "the noise of the jubilant" who drink to the music of lyre and drum (24:8). The present passage certainly adheres to this pattern. But there seems to be more at work. That the *kinnōr* is the one specific example used to typify royal "pomp" supports two hypotheses developed above, both generally and in connection with the Rāp'iu text. First, that the lyre occupied a leading position in the musical life of the city and its cult: if one instrument is to represent its totality, the *kinnāru/kinnōr* is the most effective choice. The second position is a derivative of the first: the *kinnāru* played a special role in the symbolism of the royal mortuary cult. We should therefore take Isaiah's details quite exactly, and see in the bringing down of "your pomp" and "the sound of your lyres" not only an image of the fallen mighty, but an allusion to the actions and imagery of the same kind of royal funerary rite whose details he has otherwise systematically perverted. This would fit very well with the proposed interpretation of RS 24.257, developed on independent grounds.

Conclusion

Ugaritian texts are notoriously difficult, and this chapter has called for more speculation than elsewhere. But my interpretations have been constrained by the reasonable assumption that the *kinnāru* material is consistent both within itself and with other evidence for cult-music in the city, which offers the most abundant textual evidence for the instrument outside of the Bible. Thus, while

---

[209] Shipp 2002:60-61, 129-163, et passim; cf. also Lewis 1989:40-46.
[210] See Shipp 2002:155-157 for the contrast between burial of the Rephaim and the 'Babylonian king'.
[211] See index s.v. 'order, symbolized by music'; 'silence, ritual'; 'lyres:silence of'.

Chapter Seven

the Divine Kinnaru itself has remained rather elusive, we have gained some idea of the sacred musical life that he epitomized.

8

David and the Divine Lyre

THE IMPORTANCE OF THE *KINNŌR* in early Jewish tradition, and royal ideology specifically, is most fully embodied by David. The Bible and Josephus offer detailed descriptions of musical organization under David (ca. 1005–965) and Solomon (ca. 965–930).[1] Some consider these to be retrojections of the Second Temple's sophisticated musical arrangements back into an imagined Golden Age of the First Temple.[2] Certainly 1 Kings, Chronicles, and Josephus incorporate legendary details, and the Chronicler does rely on the musical organization of his own time to understand the past. Yet the comparative material so far considered strongly suggests that traditions about organized 'guildic' music under David and in the First Temple are built upon an historical core.[3] This would accord with much other material in the books of Samuel and 1 Kings, deriving from sources and traditions—often propagandistic—going back to the times of David and Solomon themselves.[4]

In this chapter I shall argue that the First Temple's sacred musical groups should be understood as imitating and perpetuating royally supported musical guilds of the kind known at Ugarit. The Ugaritic word *nʿm*, which we saw applied several times to royal and/or cultic singers, reappears of David himself—an appropriate designation both for Saul's lyre-playing favorite, and David's later role, when king, of praise-singer for Yahweh himself. The Bible preserves extremely rich evidence for understanding the early theology of the lyre, and for the reworking, within the evolving cult of Yahweh, of older Syro-Levantine ideas about the instrument's powers. I shall argue, indeed, that David

---

[1] 1 Chronicles 6:1-32, 15:16-24, 25:1-31; Josephus *Antiquities of the Jews* 8.94, 176. See generally Engel 1870:277-365; Behn 1954:53-62; AOM:282-312 (Kraeling and Mowry); Wegner 1950:38-44; North 1964; Sendrey 1969; Sendrey 1974:98-103; Polin 1974:49-76 passim.

[2] AOM:291 (Kraeling and Mowry); references in North 1964:373n3; Weitzman 1997:101-102; MAIP:107-108, 115-116.

[3] PIW 2:79-81; de Vaux 1961:382; Myers 1965:111-112.

[4] For compelling arguments against Biblical minimalists and archaeological skeptics, see Halpern 2004, especially 57-72, 208-226.

and Solomon inherited concepts that in Ugarit would have been associated precisely with the Divine Kinnaru. David in particular is our most vivid analogy for Kinyras and his involvement with Cypriot monarchy in the LBA.

David, Solomon, and the Ideals of Great Kingship

The Ugaritian material has already prompted enough Biblical parallels to justify the view that the United Monarchy's musical apparatus grew organically out of a larger cultural matrix, anchored in the palace-temple complexes of the LBA.[5] It is at just this time that Jewish society—at least the higher tier conspicuous in the Biblical narrative—most closely resembles that of other ANE states. The matter is put expressly thus when the Israelites are portrayed as importuning Samuel for a king, "that we also may be like other nations."[6] A king who aspired to be a respected player on the international scene required a royal apparatus equal to his rivals, complete with palace, temple, and all the specialized artisans and functionaries needed to build and staff them. Nebuchadnezzar's sack of Jerusalem in 586 meant dismantling these same institutions.[7] The cosmopolitan standards of royal ideology and cultural attainment that David, Solomon, and their successors strove to emulate can be traced back in part ultimately to the last centuries of the third millennium, when the dynasties of Akkad and Ur III established perennial models of kingship and empire. It is symptomatic that the Hebrew words for palace/temple, throne, and scribe are all ultimately Sumerian in origin.[8]

Solomon especially appears as a Great King in the LBA mold. The wide array of precious gifts he gave and received evokes the erstwhile Club of Powers as known from the Amarna letters.[9] It was largely through such exchanges that he built the First Temple in Jerusalem.[10] Hiram of Tyre gave both materials and labor for the time-consuming project, which lasted seven years—a conventional 'cosmic' number.[11] In return, Solomon sent annual consignments of grain and

---

[5] See p116–119, 129, 146–147. For this view, see especially Albright 1956:125–129; YGC:249–253; cf. de Vaux 1961:382–383; Levine 1963a:211–212; Tsumura 1973:176–178.
[6] 1 Samuel 8:20, cf. 5.
[7] 2 Kings 24:13–25:21.
[8] See Ellenbogen 1962:67, 78–79, 89; Stieglitz 1990:89n52, proposing Ebla as the intermediary for the passage of such terms to the west; Metzger and Coogan 1993 s.v. Temple; Dalley et al. 1998:61.
[9] 1 Kings 10:11–25. For the dynamics of royal gift-exchange, see generally Liverani 1990.
[10] For the controversies surrounding the nature and stature of the First Temple, see Mierse 2012:249–254, 262–267, who convincingly situates Solomon's building program between LBA traditions and the novel political conditions of the EIA.
[11] Fisher 1963:40–41, compares the seven days required for the building of Baal's palace, also from Lebanese cedar: KTU/CAT 1.4 vi.16–33 (= RS 2.[008]+).

oil, payment for the workers, and "twenty cities in the land of Galilee."[12] The use of Lebanese cedar must have been *de rigueur*, its acquisition by conquest or exchange almost a royal rite-of-passage.[13] Clearly the temple was a cosmopolitan construction to rival other states' cult centers—"a royal vehicle to communicate to the widest possible audience the authoritative presence of the ruler who had built it."[14]

Solomon's splendid qualities are effectively a completed checklist in the application for Great Kingship.[15] A roster of subordinate kings and princes, with their lavish diplomatic gifts, demonstrates his status as a Great King,[16] while his occupation of a new imperial center is established by the claim that all the world's kings—and the Queen of Sheba—came to hear his wisdom, which excelled that of "all the children of the east country, and all the wisdom of Egypt":[17]

> He was wiser than anyone else, wiser than Ethan the Ezrahite, and Heman, Calcol, and Darda, children of Mahol ... He composed three thousand proverbs, and his songs numbered a thousand and five. He would speak of trees, from the cedar that is in the Lebanon to the hyssop that grows in the wall; he would speak of animals, and birds, and reptiles, and fish. People came ... from all the kings of the earth who had heard of his wisdom.[18]

It is clear from the pairing of "the east country" with "Egypt" that this Solomonic portrait asserts a new cultural eminence in the Levant, formerly caught between empires. Yet the range of learning sketched here "echoes mainstream Babylonian texts studied by scribes in Mesopotamia and beyond."[19] Solomon's combined achievements, while conceivable perhaps for a single man of leisure, become incredible given the demands of kingship. This portrait is therefore best taken to symbolize the cultural efflorescence claimed for Solomon's reign.

---

[12] 1 Kings 6:37-38, 9:11.
[13] 1 Kings 5, with cedars at 6-10, 18 (acquired through gift-exchange), 6:15-16, 7:2, 9:10-14, cf. 2 Samuel 7:7, 1 Chronicles 17:6, 22:4 (David's provision for "cedar logs without number" acquired from the Sidonians and Tyrians). Cedars in the palace of David: 2 Samuel 7:2; 1 Chronicles 17:1; palace of Solomon: 1 Kings 7:2-3, 11-12. Cedars from Lebanon, paid for by Cyrus the Great, were also used for the Second Temple: Ezra 3:7, 6:4.
[14] Mierse 2012:265.
[15] 1 Kings 4.
[16] The huge menu required for Solomon's men (1 Kings 4:22-28; cf. de Vaux 1961:122) calls to mind the Old/Middle Assyrian text about the retainers of Sargon the Great: Foster 2005:71-75 (§ I.6). For gift-giving, note also 10:23-25.
[17] 1 Kings 4:30, cf. 10:23-25; Queen of Sheba: 1 Kings 10:1-3.
[18] 1 Kings 4:31-34.
[19] Dalley et al. 1998:74.

Chapter Eight

This is remarkably close to Shulgi's self-presentation in his royal praise-hymns.[20] Solomon and Shulgi will be important parallels for the comparably broad portfolio credited to Kinyras. Note especially that Solomon's dossier, like Shulgi's, contains an important musical component. With more than a thousand songs to his credit, Solomon here rivals David himself. This aspect of his wisdom is reflected in the traditional attribution of some Psalms to him, along with David (see below), as well as the Song of Songs, Proverbs, Ecclesiastes, the *Psalms of Solomon*, and the *Odes of Solomon*.[21] The *kinnōr* is close to hand in some of these attributions. Moreover, all four wisemen bested by Solomon in the passage above have primarily musical associations. Ethan and Heman appear elsewhere as leaders of two Davidic musical guilds (see below), so that here Solomon, like Shulgi, outshines his own court's leading lights. Heman, Calcol, and Darda are called "Sons of Mahol"; yet *maḥôl*, as W. F. Albright argued, can equally be taken as a common noun relating to choral activity, making these figures archetypal "members of a guild of dancers or singers—probably combining both."[22] The description of Ethan as an "Ezrahite" is applied elsewhere to Heman, Calcol, and Darda; the designation evidently means 'native/autochthonous', leading Albright to see the four sages as representing an older background of Canaanite music and wisdom traditions.[23]

The artistic and intellectual activity credited to Solomon is predicated on an abundance of peace and prosperity, so that the underlying message is an assertion of power. We have seen similar uses of music in Shulgi's cosmopolitan virtuosity, Hammurabi's dedication of a (presumably divine) BALAĜ following his defeat of Mari, and the divine singer who praises Baal after (probably) his

---

[20] See above, p33–35. For a detailed comparison, Kramer 1991.

[21] *Psalms of Solomon*: PIW 2:118–120. *Odes of Solomon*: e.g. Franzmann 1991:5–7.

[22] Albright 1956:127 and 210n96 ("members of the orchestral guild," deriving *maḥôl* from *ḥwl*, 'to circle'); followed by de Vaux 1961:382 ("sons of the choir"); YGC:251–252 (quotation); for root and other derivatives, see with further references MAIP:39–40; Mazar 2003:126. One may note here the possible appearance of Baal as a dancing god: Baal Marqod, attested in a third-century BCE inscription, and derived from WS √rqd, 'skip/dance' (Sendrey 1969:441; Tubb 2003:121; Mazar 2003:126). But this interpretation has been well challenged by DDUPP:115–116.

[23] Albright 1956:14, 126–129; PIW 2:80–81, 95–97 YGC:250–253. Cf. Cogan 2000:222, "The context suggests that they were non-Israelites." In the heading of Psalms 88, Heman is made an Ezrahite; at 1 Chronicles 2:6 "Zimri, Ethan, Heman, Calcol, Dara" [i.e. Darda] are the "Sons of Zerah," hence all interpreted as 'Ezrahites' by Albright 1956:127 and 210n95 (noting especially Numbers 9:14 and the Septuagint's regular translation of *'ezraḥ* as αὐτόχθων); cf. Cogan 2000:222. Albright (YGC:250 and n125) connected 'Ethan' with several instances of the Ugaritic name 'Atyn, which he vocalized as Attuyana and considered of Hurrian origin; cf. Albright 1956:127. Note also 'Attanu, the "Chief Priest ... the adept" (*lmd . 'atn rb | khnm*), named alongside king and scribe in the colophon of CTA 6.6.54–55, and evidently "the master singer who dictated to the scribe": see Cross 1974:1n1; Cross 1998:139–140.

David and the Divine Lyre

Figure 12 Lyre-playing lion king with animal subjects. Ninth-century orthostat relief from Guzana (Tell Halaf). Drawn from Moortgat 1955 pl. 100–101.

defeat of Yamm, the Sea. Just such a sequence of events is connected by Josephus with David and his *kinnōr*:

> And now, after David had been freed from campaigns and dangers, and enjoying thenceforth universal peace, he composed his odes and hymns to God.[24]

That this vision is no mere deduction by Josephus, but a traditional Syro-Levantine image, is shown by several monuments from the Aramaean sphere. First are two ninth-century orthostat reliefs from Guzana (Tell Halaf), capital of Bit Bachiani during the reign of Kapara, before it came under Assyrian control (by the eighth century).[25] Each shows a slightly different group of animals dancing and playing instruments before a lion, who sits upon a rock— evidently enthroned—and plays a tall rectangular lyre (Figure 12 = Figure 5.1v).[26] This is an image of political stability and lyric control. The same idea is

---

[24] Josephus *Antiquities of the Jews* 7.12.3: Ἀπηλλαγμένος δ᾽ ἤδη πολέμων ὁ Δαυίδης καὶ κινδύνων καὶ βαθείας ἀπολαύων τὸ λοιπὸν εἰρήνης ᾠδὰς εἰς τὸν θεὸν καὶ ὕμνους συνετάξατο.
[25] See RlA 4:54 (Hrouda, *Ḫalaf, Tell) with further references.
[26] Moortgat 1955:95–98 and pl. 100–101; HKm:72 with pl. 14 no. 42 and further references.

found, in negative form, in the eighth-century Sefire steles, to be examined in Chapter 12.[27]

That David and Solomon alike maintained both male and female singers and musicians in the royal household is asserted and implied by the Bible.[28] There is no reason to doubt this. The evidence from Mari, Nuzi, Amarna, and elsewhere confirms that such 'collections' were actively developed.[29] We also have independent documentary evidence from Assyrian sources for the palace musicians, both male and female, maintained by Hezekiah (715–687), who delivered them up as tribute to Sennacherib after the campaign of 701.[30] Presumably, many of Solomon's female musicians were ranked among the three hundred concubines who, with seven hundred wives, made up the royal harem.[31] Although these figures are probably swollen, their reported origins—Egypt, Moab, Ammon, Edom, Sidon, and Hatti—are a realistic reflection of Solomon's political reach: extensive, but not unlimited.

The Mari texts and Amarna reliefs showed that the harem was an important locus of cosmopolitan musicality. The cultural influence of royal women also extended to the religious sphere when they imported native deities to a new home through interdynastic marriage.[32] One may compare the Hittite kings' wholesale adoption of Hurrian and other gods, both from foreign wives and conquered peoples.[33] Solomon is said to have built cult-places for all (!) his wives' gods, famously including the Astarte (Ashtoreth) of Sidon.[34] This phenomenon too is musically relevant, since such transferred deities, we have seen, could be accompanied by the appropriate cult personnel and ritual repertoire.[35] It is quite remarkable, therefore, to find the following legend in the Talmud:

---

[27] See p300.
[28] David: 1 Samuel 19:36; Solomon: Ecclesiastes 2:8, reflecting a traditional view of Solomon, to whom the work was attributed: cf. de Vaux 1961:121–122.
[29] For the ideology, see especially Ziegler 1999.
[30] ARAB 2:143 §312; CS 2:119B. These can be connected with the captive lyrists shown in the emperor's reliefs depicting the siege of Lachish (BM 124947): see *inter al.* PIW 2:80 (interpreting as temple-singers); Rimmer 1969:34; MgB 2/2:122 and pl. 142; Oded 1979:101 and n179; DCPIL:49 (questioning the identification as Judaean); Cheng 2001:74–75; my Figure 5.8f. Hebrew accounts of the events: 2 Kings 18:13–37, Isaiah 36:1–2; cf. Herodotos 2.141.
[31] 1 Kings 11:1–3. See generally de Vaux 1961:115–117.
[32] Liverani 1990:221, 224–225, 274–282.
[33] See e.g. Bryce 2002:135–136 et passim.
[34] 1 Kings 11:4–8. This datum has been important (e.g. Kramer 1963; Kramer 1969:85–106) to the tradition of interpreting the Song of Songs as deriving at some remove from hierogamic ritual—e.g. borrowed during the time of Solomon from Canaanite royal practice, itself more or less influenced by Sumerian/Babylonian archetypes. For this long-contested issue, see recently Lapinkivi 2004:91–98 (developing further parallels with Mesopotamian love-poetry), and especially Nissinen 2008, tracing the history of debate.
[35] See p100–102.

When Solomon married Pharaoh's daughter, she brought him a thousand musical instruments and said to him, "Thus we play [lit. 'do'] in honour of that idol, thus in honour of that idol"—yet he did not forbid her.[36]

According to Rabbinic tradition, Solomon's marriage transpired on the very day the temple was consecrated, which was thereby overshadowed: the delights of Pharaoh's daughter caused Solomon to oversleep, so that the morning sacrifice could not be carried out. From that day forward, it was said, God determined to overthrow Jerusalem. The tale must be related to the Rabbinic rejection of instrumental music following the city's destruction in 70 CE, with an 'original musical sin' traced back to the very founding of the First Temple.[37] Nevertheless, given the evidence from Mari, the legend is doubtless encrusted upon some genuine reminiscence of purposeful musical diversity in the monarchic period, very probably going back to Solomon himself.

Musical Management in the First Temple

A major state needed a system for the training and management of musicians. Traditionally the sacred musical groups were inaugurated by David to accompany the Ark's removal to Jerusalem, and were perpetuated in service before the Tabernacle at its new home.[38] The 'singers' were divided into 'families' by specific instruments: the major groups were strings (*kinnōr*, *nēbel*), cymbals (*mᵉṣiltayīm*), and trumpets (*shofar*).[39] Recall the designation of Ugaritic guilds, including perhaps the singers, as *bn* ('sons of'), and the Bible's representation of Jubal as an ultimate musical ancestor of lyre- and pipes-players.[40] The Bible's implication of existing musical resources on which David could draw is

---

[36] *Shabbath* 56b = BT 2:264.
[37] Cf. LJ 4:128-129, 6:280-281 n12-13 with further references; SOM 1:553-571 (including the more moderate stance of Maimonides).
[38] 2 Samuel 6:5, 15; 1 Chronicles 6:1-32, 15:16-24, 28, 25:1-31; 2 Chronicles 7:6; cf. Josephus *Antiquities of the Jews* 8.94, 176; Zonaras *Epitome historiarum* 1.116.3. The whole matter is well discussed by Kleinig 1993. David's original organization is also invoked by the Chronicler in the context of Hezekiah's reign, as well as Ezra and Nehemiah in describing the restoration of music in the Second Temple: 2 Chronicles 29:25; Nehemiah 12:27-47; cf. Ezra 2:41, 64, 3:10-13.
[39] For the *nēbel*, see p52n26. The use of signal trumpets, for instance, is sure to be very ancient. For the silver instruments of Moses, Numbers 10:1-10; Josephus *Antiquities of the Jews* 3.12. Note that a disbursement of silver to decorate musical horns is found at Ebla: Tonietti 2010:80-81. There are also Egyptian representations from the NK (Myers 1965:113), and actual specimens have been found in the tomb of Tutankhamun (Manniche 1976) and in the Uluburun wreck (ca. 1300: Pulak 1998:205); cf. MAIP:14-16. Note too the Talmudic tradition that there had been in the temple a pipe and cymbals from the time of Moses: *'Arakin* 10b = BT 16:58.
[40] See p43-44, 115.

Chapter Eight

corroborated by the extensive parallelism of the earliest specimens of Hebrew poetry, clearly akin to Ugaritian practice.[41] Such songs are evidently relics of an ancient epic cycle, cultivated at various league sanctuaries.[42] Some form of 'family' musical groups may already have served such sacred sites, and were simply repurposed by David. At such an early date, however, there is no reliable means of distinguishing 'Israelite' music from a Canaanite 'background'. And with Solomon's monumental new temple, it is not improbable that the music of Yahweh's cult would have been 'renovated' in conformity with standards and practices of major Canaanite sanctuaries.[43] We have already seen that two of the musical leaders traditionally appointed by David—Heman and Ethan—probably represent Canaanite traditions of music, wisdom, and dance.[44] They are provided with complete Levitical genealogies by the Chronicler, but these will be later constructions.[45] Even if these figures are entirely legendary, and their founding position in the Chronicler represents an anachronistic insertion—comparable to the traditional attribution of psalms to David and Solomon—they do indicate "that Hebrew temple-music as such" might be recognized "as going back to early, pre-Israelite, sources."[46]

A deeper pre-Davidic musical background is also assumed in Saul's performance with the musical prophets. Samuel foretells that the young king-elect will have a remarkable encounter at Gibeath-elohim ('Hill of God'):

---

[41] E.g. the 'Song of Miriam' (Exodus 15), the 'Song of Deborah' (Judges 5), the 'Oracles of Balaam' (Numbers 23–24), the 'Song of Moses' (Deuteronomy 32), etc. Relative dating schemes for these and other songs have been attempted: see *inter al.* YGC:1–28, 42–52; Freedman 1976. While their methodology might be refined by the development of further criteria, Albright's basic principle remains valid: the Ugaritic texts show that extensive parallelism is an archaic feature of Hebrew poetry. Pardee 1988b, Appendix I (168–192) provides a good overview of trends in research to that date; note especially the call for situating Ugaritic and Hebrew parallelism in a larger, hence more ancient, Semitic context, which should include Aramaic, Akkadian, and other evidence (174–175).

[42] Cross 1973, especially 79–144.

[43] Cf. de Vaux 1961:382, "It is not too bold to think that the first choir of singers for the Temple at Jerusalem was recruited from among non-Israelites." One should recall here the controversial Jebusite hypothesis: the high priest Zadok was retained from a priestly family that had long presided at Jerusalem, and was only later outfitted with an Aaronid genealogy. This idea, elaborated by Rowley 1939, has won, despite vigorous challenges (Cross 1973:207–215, et al.), increasing support (with various modifications): see with further references Jones 1990:25, 40–42, 131–135, 151n35, 154n44; Albertz 1994:129, 295n7–8, with references.

[44] See p152 and n22.

[45] Cf. Cogan 2000:222: "by the time of the Chronicler [i.e. 1 Chronicles 2:6] they were given Israelite ancestry, as grandsons of Judah, taking the 'Ezrahite' to refer to Zerah son of Judah and Tamar."

[46] Albright 1956:128—stressing, however, that this does not itself "prove that David organized the first religious music of Israel." Some of the extant psalms are also ascribed to them: Asaph (12), Heman (1), Ethan (1), and Jeduthun (3). Cf. de Vaux 1961:382; YGC:250.

You will meet a band of prophets coming down from the shrine with *nēbel*, frame-drum (*tof*), pipes (*ḥalil*),[47] and *kinnōr* playing in front of them; they will be in a prophetic frenzy. Then the spirit of the Lord will possess you, and you will be in a prophetic frenzy along with them and be turned into a different person.[48]

The phenomenon of musical prophecy will be discussed below.[49] Here I would emphasize that the ensemble's make-up is not dissimilar to what David's musical 'families' will offer, and which one must posit for Ugarit.[50] This array has been called a 'Canaanite (temple) orchestra',[51] although the Ugaritian texts and north Syrian ivories show that 'Syro-Levantine' would be the better term.[52] The famous cult-stand with musicians from Ashdod is a happy parallel here, given the Bible's statement that there was a Philistine garrison at Gibeath-elohim.[53] The stand's players match 1 Samuel closely: lyre, double-pipes, frame-drum, and perhaps cymbals. (But note that the lyre is round-based, probably reflecting the Philistines' Aegean background.[54]) Similar ensembles are often represented, with minor variations, in the corpus of Cypro-Phoenician bowls (*phiálai*), ranging from the tenth century to the sixth (see further Chapter 11).

David's full musical establishment is said to have been under the management of a certain Chenaniah who "was to direct the music, for he understood it."[55] The exact interpretation of his position *vis-à-vis* the Levitical guilds remains controversial; but some definite musical function is likely given the Septuagint's "Leader of the Singers."[56] While it is elsewhere stated that he and his sons were "officials and judges" *outside* the Temple,[57] this actually resembles the Chief

---

[47] For this instrument, see NG 3:525 and MGG 1:1514 (both Braun). It may be significant, as noted by Sellers 1941:41, that this its first Biblical attestation.
[48] 1 Samuel 10:5-6.
[49] See p161-165.
[50] See p115-118. It is the same ensemble which Isaiah 5:11-12 attributes to the drinking parties of Jerusalem's dissolute inhabitants—those "wild grapes" (5:2, 4) who "do not regard the deeds of the Lord" (5:12). The prophet has apparently redeployed the 'orchestra' appropriate for sacred performances into a profane context, parallel to his larger critique. The passage was understood along similar lines at Qumran, where Isaiah's target was interpreted as the Essenes' sectarian rivals in Jerusalem, "the congregation of Scoffers" (4Q162.6-10: DJD 5:15-16; Vermes 2011:499, with comments on 54, 61).
[51] Bayer 1982:32; Poethig 1985:19, 23-27.
[52] See p134-135, 267-268.
[53] 1 Samuel 10.5. For the cult-stand, see Dothan 1970; Dothan 1982:249-251; Bayer 1982:32; Poethig 1985:23-27; MAIP:166-174; SAM:156-157 (no. 121).
[54] See p250-251.
[55] 1 Chronicles 15:22, cf. 27.
[56] LXX: ἄρχων τῶν ᾠδῶν. A musical function is accepted by the NRSV. For the controversy, see recently with further literature Kleinig 1993:44-51; Leithart 2003:59-62.
[57] 1 Chronicles 26:29.

Singer of such OB states as Mari, whose duties were not exclusively musical, but comprised important civic functions. David himself, in the court of Saul (ca. 1025–1005), had occupied a comparable position. There was not yet an elaborate musical bureaucracy for him to preside over, but he was evidently a royal singer and confidant of the king—at least initially. His catharses of Saul's "evil spirit" suggest something not unlike the purification-priests of Mesopotamian tradition.[58]

David was also remembered as building instruments and instructing the Levites in their use.[59] One recalls the royal order for instruments, including the *kinnāru*, at Mari.[60] Solomon too is called an instrument-builder. Josephus preserves an extra-Biblical tradition in his vivid portrait of forty thousand lyres (*knr* and *nbl*) made of precious woods, stones, and electrum, commissioned for the Levites to sing the Lord's praises.[61]

Summing up, although David is treated in the Biblical narratives as a musical pioneer, his actions make best sense against an older Canaanite tradition of temple music. There is plenty of comparative material to show that the musical organization credited to the First Temple by tradition is inherently plausible, even if the precise numbers and divisions are open to question. Given the royal ambitions of David and Solomon, it is hard to believe that Yahweh would have lacked the sophisticated honors paid to Baal and other gods in the temples of their peers.[62]

The *Kinnōr* and the Divine Lyre

Against this backdrop we may consider the Biblical *kinnōr* and its divine overtones. The Divine Lyre cannot be seen directly. Already in the Davidic period Jewish culture had begun to distinguish itself sharply from its neighbors, despite a shared religious heritage. And the narratives relating to the United Monarchy were shaped by the concerns of later theologians who reworked traditional materials into the forms we now possess. Most familiar perhaps is the anti-monarchic bias of the post-exile period, when the earlier defeat of Israel and Judah, and the destruction of the First Temple, had to be explained; this had a major impact on the recension and canonization of traditional materials.[63] Even

---

[58] 1 Samuel 16:23.
[59] 1 Chronicles 23:5; 2 Chronicles 7:6; 29:26; Nehemiah 12:36; Amos 6:5; Josephus *Antiquities of the Jews* 7.305; Psalms 151:3 LXX.
[60] See p76–77.
[61] *Antiquities of the Jews* 8.94, 176, cf. 7.305; also 1 Kings 10:12, Solomon's lyres from the exotic, still-unidentified *almug* wood (cf. Burgh 2006:24).
[62] Cf. PIW 2:80–81.
[63] An accessible introduction is Friedman 1987.

so, there are many cases where an older Levantine theological environment is more or less evident.⁶⁴ It is perfectly conceivable therefore that beliefs and practices that in the LBA would have been connected to the cult of a Divine Lyre should have found their way into the Bible, albeit in altered form and contexts.

Soon after Kinnaru was discovered at Ugarit, A. Jirku hypothesized that the various magical effects attributed to the *kinnōr*—for example David's purification of Saul's "evil spirit"—would once have been seen as the "Einwirkung des Gottes Kinaru" (sic).⁶⁵ A. Cooper cautioned that "the case for relating the use of the lyre to any purported function of [Kinnaru] is tenuous."⁶⁶ More recently, however, N. Wyatt has given some credence to the idea that the prophetic and exorcistic uses of the Biblical *kinnōr* "may faintly echo the old theology, albeit long reinterpreted."⁶⁷

Since the Biblical portrait of Solomon's wisdom and musicality was evidently formulated in dialogue with Canaanite ideals, we may begin with a remarkable piece of iconographic evidence that is earlier than David himself (as conventionally dated). This is the so-called 'Orpheus Jug', an eleventh-century vase-painting from Megiddo, which brilliantly illustrates the older musical background, giving it a specifically 'lyrical' slant and containing a magical element that accords very well with the idea of a Divine Lyre (Figure 13).⁶⁸ This late Philistine production, combining thematic elements deriving from both sub-Mycenaean (IIIC:1b) and local Levantine tradition, shows a lyrist with animals in three registers—lion, gazelle, horse, fish, dog, bird, crab, and scorpion—all apparently proceeding towards a schematized palm tree, very probably of cultic significance (see below). The iconography of lyrist and animals has been predictably explained by appeal to Orpheus—that is, as an Aegean intrusion due to Philistine settlement in the region during the twelfth century.⁶⁹ Yet such an interpretation could at best tell only half of the story.

In a careful reassessment, A. Yasur-Landau has noted that while strainer-jugs do belong to the repertoire of Aegean symposium vessels, and traces of

---

⁶⁴ See *inter al.* YGC; Smith 1990.
⁶⁵ Jirku 1963.
⁶⁶ Cooper 1981:385.
⁶⁷ DDD col. 912.
⁶⁸ IAA 13.1921, strainer-spout jug, Megiddo stratum VIA, ca. 1100: Loud 1936:1110, fig. 9, 11–12; Rutten 1939:442–443 and fig. 11; Dothan 1982:150–153 and fig. 21.1 (pl. 61); SAM:111 (no. 71). Note the ribbons or bands that hang from the musician's waist and legs, presumably ceremonial and recalling the betasseled lyrist on the roughly contemporary Kouklia kalathos from near Paphos, and a swordsman on a shard from Lefkandi (LH IIIC): Deger-Jalkotzy 1994:21 and 18 fig. 4.3; cf. p255. Yet further non-musicians are so adorned on another Megiddo pot (level VIIA), so that perhaps this element "merely reflects local iconographic tradition" (Dothan 1982:150).
⁶⁹ So already Loud 1936:1110, fig. 9: "suggestive of Orpheus, but from a site more associated with David"; Dothan 1982:150–153.

Chapter Eight

Figure 13 Lyrist with animals and tree ('Orpheus jug'). Philistine strainer-spout jug, Megiddo, ca. 1100. Jerusalem, IAA 13.1921. Drawn from Dothan 1982 fig. 21.1 (pl. 61).

Philistine and Cypriot stylistic elements can be detected in the present example, its narrative imagery and composition find better parallels in LBA Canaan, for instance the motif of palm-tree and ibex.[70] And while the lyrist is preeminent within the animal procession, the composition as a whole is focused on what is generally taken as a Sacred Tree or Tree of Life—itself a Near Eastern motif of deep antiquity and associations with a goddess figure, whence it functions as a symbol of fertility.[71]

What has not been sufficiently stressed in past discussions is the Levantine morphology of the instrument itself.[72] And we have seen that the motif of lyrist with animals goes back to the third millennium in North Syria (it is further attested by two southern Anatolian seals of the early second).[73] In later Jewish and Arabic folklore, too, David and Solomon were often credited with power

---

[70] Yasur-Landau 2008: "The subtle message of the vase is conveyed by referring the owner and his drinking guests to a well-known ANE mythological theme, celebrated for centuries in Canaanite Megiddo: the peaceful demonstration of the power of the goddess, represented by the sacred tree, the unity between man and nature, and music" (225).
[71] So for this piece Dothan 1982:152; Keel 1998:39–40; Yasur-Landau 2008:224–225. For the Sacred Tree motif generally, see Danthine 1937 (fertility, 152–153, 157); Keel 1998; Keel and Uehlinger 1998, 232–236 et pass.; Giovino 2007 (doxographical review with emphasis on Assyrian iconography). For the motif's reception on LBA Cyprus, see p386.
[72] But note Bayer 1982:22–23.
[73] See p153–154, 517–518. Cf. DCPIL:53.

over, and the ability to communicate with, the animal kingdom—persistent traditions that can hardly be fully explained by Philistine or later Hellenistic influence.[74] Given these data, the comparison with Orpheus is superficial at best. The Bible's wise and musical Solomon provides a more immediate parallel,[75] and of course the lyre-playing David.

Without denying the possibility of Aegean musical influence at this time,[76] the great contribution of the Orpheus jug, being somewhat older than the United Monarchy, is to establish the deep antiquity and indigenous nature of ideas in the Biblical narratives. Like David and Solomon themselves, it is an idealized portrait—of the lyrist as Master of Wisdom, whose knowledge and powers included, but were not limited to, 'the music itself'.

A further power shared by the *kinnōr* and the Divine Kinnaru may be inferred by way of the Mesopotamian comparanda: "the ability to enable communication between the spiritual and natural worlds."[77] The Biblical prophets were regarded as couriers relaying the decrees of Yahweh and the divine assembly. Comparison with the Ugaritic texts shows that this role was formerly executed by lesser, 'messenger' deities.[78] Kinnaru himself is not directly attested in that role. Yet music and prophecy are frequently linked in the Bible, especially in connection with the *kinnōr*. The Psalms, many of which were traditionally regarded as the prophetic productions of David, offer several striking expressions of this relationship.

The opening verses of Psalm 49 preserve a crucial first-person, professional perspective:

> Hear this, all you peoples;
> > give ear, all inhabitants of the world,
> both low and high,
> > rich and poor together.

---

[74] See p181–184.
[75] So rightly Mazar 1974:174–182 (Hebrew, *non vidi*), cited by Dothan 1982:152; also approved by MAIP:147.
[76] This may explain the prescription of '*gittith*' for the music of three Biblical psalms (Psalms 8, 81, and 84), which C. H. Gordon interpreted as "the instrument of Gath" (in the Philistine pentapolis). One of these psalms is attributed to David himself, and while this is probably anachronistic, it may well suggest that later generations of psalmodists were prepared to recognize a musical dimension to David's fifteen-month sojourn among the Philistines (1 Samuel 27:1–6). See Gordon 1965b:225; cf. MAIP:39, suggesting "style" of Gath as an alternative. If an openness to Philistine music-culture seems unlikely in view of the Bible's generally hostile stance, one could see this as a case of appropriating the musical symbols of a defeated people, comparing the situation in Shulgi's Ur or NK Egypt: see p36–37, 105–111.
[77] DDD col. 912 (Wyatt).
[78] See Mullen 1980:209–226, 279, 283.

Chapter Eight

> My mouth shall speak wisdom
> > and the care of my heart understanding.
>
> I shall incline my ears to a parable (*māšāl*);
> > and in/on the lyre I shall disclose my dark saying (*ḥîdāh*).[79]

The psalmist goes on to deliver a universalizing meditation on the fragility of life and inevitability of death. But the prelude is readily detached: it is an introductory formula, like the many exhortations to song in other psalms, or the psalmists' repeated invocations of Yahweh to "incline" to their song and so lend them his voice.[80] Psalm 49, however, strikes an unusual note as a singer's glancing self-portrait. He trumpets his public role and ability to command universal attention, before turning inwards to describe his prophetic process through the lyre. What exactly is involved is clarified by a cognate passage in Psalm 78, which, after an almost identical beginning, carries on:

> I will open my mouth in a parable;
> > I will utter dark sayings/riddles from of old,
>
> things that we have heard and known,
> > that our ancestors have told us.[81]

Even if Psalm 49 is relatively late, perhaps post-monarchic,[82] the parallel formulae in Psalm 78 indicate that the lyre-singer is assuming a traditional stance as custodian of an ancient lyric art of prophecy. He both reproduces the often obscure lore of his predecessors, and recasts it in his own terms. While he presents *interpretations* of the "dark sayings," he equally re-riddles what he has received to "disclose" admonitory puzzles of his own.

A key component of the psalmodists' enigmatic pronouncements was the inherited technique of parallelism, which permitted both singer and audience to construct multi-directional and semantically productive correspondences between verse cola. Psalm 49:3-4 itself appropriately exemplifies the technique, schematizing, as A. N. Palmer nicely puts it,

---

[79] Psalms 49:1-4, with translation in 3-4 following the LXX: 'disclose' reflects ἀνοίξω and the literal 'open' of the Hebrew (< √pth), cf. NRSV 'solve', Palmer 1993:377, 'utter'. For this and the other key Hebrew words, notably the range of *māšāl* and *ḥîdāh*, see van der Ploeg 1963:145; Richards 1985:508. The potential relevance of these verses to Kinnaru was noted by Wyatt (DDD col. 912).

[80] While most of the Psalms implicitly fulfill one or both of these functions, the following are notably explicit. Musical exhortations: Psalms 33:1-3, 47:1, 61:1-2, 66:1-2, 81:1-2, 95:1-2, 96:1-2, 98:1-2, 105:1-2, 147:1, 149:1, 150:1-6. Epicletic formulas: 4:1, 5:1-2, 34:1, 77:1, 80:1, 83:1, 86:1, 88:1-2, 89:1, 92:1-3, 101:1, 102:1-2, 116:1-2, 120:1, 130:1-2, 141:1, 142:1-2, 143:1.

[81] Psalms 78:2-3.

[82] So van der Ploeg 1963:138-139.

the contrast between speech and thought, listening and singing, at the same time as it suggests that what is spoken and thought of, listened to and sung, is something which binds together the four words: wisdom, meaning, parable, riddles ... These comparisons encourage the reader to go further and find analogies between the mouth and the lyre, between the heart and the ears ... The psalmist describes not himself, but his mouth, as uttering wisdom ... which the general tenor of his poetry suggests is the wisdom of God ... the reader is led to consider ... that the "I" of the last phrase is that of the source of [the] Psalmist's inspiration, God.[83]

In support of Palmer's view that as the invocation progresses the psalmodist's voice becomes that of Yahweh, note that it is normally the latter to whom the expression "incline the ears" is applied in the Psalms.[84] If this is right, it places the phrase "in the lyre" in a rather more startling light. The emphasis would be less on the *psalmodist* using the lyre and its music to communicate *with* Yahweh, than on Yahweh placing his message into the lyre, from which the singer must attempt to extract it. In doing so, however, Yahweh himself becomes a kind of lyrist, so that the human lyre-prophet is attempting to replicate the song and message that God has devised for him. We are reminded of the balang-god of Ningirsu, visualized as a singer, with his communication to the human realm enabled precisely by the instrument of which he is the spirit.

While parallelistic composition is well known from Ugaritian poetry and early songs embedded in the Bible itself, the aforementioned Psalm verses are uniquely precious for vouchsafing a connection with professional lyric, and explicitly acknowledging the deep antiquity of the tradition. Again we must thank the Orpheus jug for linking the Biblical psalmists with this older cultural milieu. Given this ancient background, one must be struck by the direct invocation of the lyre in Psalm 108 (1–3):

> I will sing and make melody.
>   Awake, my soul!
> Awake, O *kinnōr* and *nēbel*!
>   I will awake the dawn.
> I will give thanks to you, O Lord, among the peoples;
>   I will sing praises to you among the nations.

---

[83] Palmer 1993:377–378, with additional analysis, followed by application to the poetics of St. Ephraim, for whom cf. p61 above.
[84] Cf. van der Ploeg 1963:144.

Chapter Eight

Wyatt is surely right to suggest that these lyre-invocations (the formula is repeated in Psalm 57:8-9) echo "an older usage when minor gods of the pantheon were called upon to glorify their overlord."[85] He quickly concedes that they might also be explained as simple poetic apostrophes. But even if the latter view is correct from a sixth-century or later Jewish perspective, the traditional nature of the verses salvages some heuristic value with respect to the ancient lyric art from which the Psalms descend. And given that a Divine Lyre *is* known to have existed, within an institutional framework that predicts many features of the First Temple, how can one really distinguish between 'simply poetic'—if such an idea is even valid for the earlier period—and a more potent 'ritual-poetic', of which the Psalms present so much other clear evidence? Insofar as the lyrist serves as the mouthpiece of Yahweh, we have a form of divine communication very similar to what we saw of divine instruments in Mesopotamia.

Some of the Davidic musical groups are said to have been appointed expressly to "prophesy" to the music of *kinnōr*, *nēbel*, cymbals, and trumpets—an instrumental range closely comparable to Saul's band of prophets.[86] Yet other passages show that it was the *kinnōr* that was the prophetic instrument *par excellence*. I Chronicles (25:3) attributes to David the appointment of the sons of Jeduthun, who "prophesied with the *kinnōr* in thanksgiving and praise to the Lord." Here "prophesy" seems to cover a broader musical range than the English word might imply, including praise poetry and perhaps the interpretation of sacred songs. These functions are not sharply separated in the Old Testament, where it is precisely praise songs, properly executed, which bring about miraculous results. Two notable illustrations will suffice.

Jehoshaphat, the fourth King of Judah in the ninth century, having received the Lord's word via the prophet Jahaziel that he would be victorious against the Moabites and Ammonites, "appointed those who were to sing to the Lord ... As they began to sing and praise, the Lord set an ambush against the Ammonites, Moab, and Mount Seir."[87] Here apparently praise-singing was needed to cause a prophesied event to come to fruition.

---

[85] DDD col. 912 (Wyatt), adducing the Rāp'iu text as a parallel (for which see p134-135).

[86] 1 Samuel 19:20-24; 1 Chronicles 25:1 ("David and the officers of the army also set apart for the service the sons of Asaph, and of Heman, and of Jeduthun, who should prophesy with *kinnōr*, *nēbel* and with cymbals"), with 1 Chronicles 15:16-24 (David's appointment of musicians from the Levites) and 25:3-6; 2 Chronicles 5:12, 20:21-23. Musical prophecy may be implicit at 1 Samuel 19:20-24; Psalms 49:2-5, with the lyre: see below; Ezekiel 40:44-46. For earlier times cf. Exodus 15:20-21; Deuteronomy 31:19-22 (of Moses). See generally Sendrey 1969:481-489, 507-515; Shiloah 1993:58-59.

[87] 2 Chronicles 20:22-23.

From the next generation comes a striking example of prophecy-in-performance during the campaign of Jehoram, son of Jehoshaphat, against the Moabites, when the united army of Israel, Judah, and Edom was stranded in the wilderness without water.[88] This was seen as a divine ordinance, and the prophet Elisha was summoned to enquire the Lord's purpose. "'But get me a musician,'" Elisha ordered. "And then, while the musician was playing"—the *kinnōr* is clearly implied[89]—"the power of the Lord came on him; and he said, 'Thus says the Lord, I will make this wadi full of pools.'" Here music returns order to a disordered natural world. A sort of sympathetic magic proceeding from harmonic and rhythmic structure is probably implied. But the result was apparently accomplished through channeling divine will.

These passages are remarkable for their relatively precise practical descriptions of the arts of musical prophecy and catharsis. Music is transformative, purifying, but only by evoking through performance the "spirit of the Lord"—on behalf of whom the *kinnōr*-singer not only speaks (the literal sense of 'prophet'), but acts.

While the Psalms provide evidence of lyric communication with the divine, their collection into a psalter, as we have it, tends to obscure their original connections with actual ritual practice.[90] Readers may thus be inclined to regard their lyre imagery as conventional, governed by internal poetics of genre with no 'real' connection to the outside world. The narrative snapshots just considered are a crucial corrective, broadening our conception of the traditional lyrist 'in action'. They provide a further link to the Orpheus jug; its animal-charming scene, though not unparalleled in the Psalms by images of nature echoing the praise of God,[91] clearly emphasizes the practical, efficacious nature of the musician's art. With this we come one step closer to what must have been the purview of Kinnaru in the rich ritual life of Ugarit.

King, *Kinnōr*, and the "Spirit of God"

We have prepared the ground for understanding the *kinnōr*-playing David, not only as a potent symbolic figure in later tradition, but as a royal performer in his own historical drama. I shall now argue that his priestly role and ritual actions, and the legends that developed therefrom, provided a refuge in which

---

[88] 2 Kings 3:13–20.
[89] This was seen by St. Ephraim: *non quodcumque, sed habens harmoniam in chordis designat; ut ex Hebraeo verti posset, cinnaram* (Latin translation: Assemani 1732–1746 1:524 A). Cf. DDD col. 912 (Wyatt).
[90] PIW offered a seminal corrective.
[91] See p178–179.

Chapter Eight

ancient ideas about divinized lyres were able to shelter, and so partially weather the ongoing expulsion of Canaanite cultic elements from Jewish life and the Biblical sources.[92] Besides David's traditional association with the Psalms, to be discussed below, the most important evidence is the use of the *kinnōr* as a structuring device in the Samuel narratives about David's rise to kingship and his takeover of Yahweh's cult.

The Saul episode, we saw, attests the practice of musical prophecy by (soon-to-be) royalty. This ability, apparently in an ecstatic state, is taken as a sign of divine favor, a power given to a rightful king, who is possessed by the "spirit of the Lord." Importantly, however, this is carried out in conjunction with a musical ensemble, apparently necessary for establishing the appropriate mental conditions. One may compare the situation at Hattusha and Ugarit, where ritual performances were executed by kings (and queens) together with cult officials.[93]

As Saul falls from grace, his increasing affliction by an "evil spirit" is balanced by the passage of "the spirit of the Lord" to David, whose ascent to kingship becomes inevitable.[94] This transfer of divine favor is mediated precisely by the *kinnōr*. Because Saul suffers from the "evil spirit"—having lost God's favor—he summons a *kinnōr*-player. Because David plays the *kinnōr* so well, he is summoned.[95] Note that the advice to Saul is generic:

> "Let our lord now command the servants who attend you to look for someone who is skillful in playing the lyre: and when the evil spirit from God is upon you, he will play it, and you will feel better."[96]

On one narratological level, David has already been chosen by God. But from Saul's perspective it is merely a professional *type* that is needed. Evidently, the desired cathartic power was made possible by the *kinnōr* itself, a kind of potential energy that would be released by a "skillful player."[97] David is so qualified,

---

[92] Albright 1940:296-297 and n45 seems to have inferred something very similar even before the recognition of Kinnaru. After noting that Kinyras had absorbed aspects of Kothar (see further Chapter 18), and tersely asserting the accuracy of his name's connection with *kinýra*, Albright wrote: "There are many striking confirmations and illustrations of this derivation, with which I hope to deal later. One of the most remarkable parallels, hitherto unrecognized, comes from Hebrew tradition ... A great deal more can be said on this subject, but it must be reserved for a more suitable occasion." I do not know that he ever presented his ideas in more than desultory remarks (cf. Albright 1964:171n47; YGC:144n91, 147 and n102).
[93] See p93-94.
[94] Cf. 1 Samuel 16:14: "Now the Spirit of the Lord departed from Saul, and an evil spirit from the Lord tormented him."
[95] 1 Samuel 16:14-23.
[96] 1 Samuel 16:16.
[97] Lyre catharses are well-attested in Greek tradition with Orpheus, Pythagoras, etc.: cf. Franklin 2006a:59-60; Power 2010:279-280, 381-385 et pass.; Provenza 2014.

because, as Saul is advised, "the Lord is with him."[98] To us, the phrase clearly implies the transfer of Yahweh's favor to David; to Saul, however, it means only that here was an inspired *kinnōr*-healer. This brilliant ambiguity may go beyond its narratological appeal. For the two planes of meaning neatly intersect, if being an 'inspired kinyrist' was considered a royal virtue—an idea well paralleled by Shulgi, and vital for the question of Kinyras.[99]

The episode of David's selection clearly presents the idea that a ritual lyrist is only effective when divinely empowered. The Bible of course recognizes a single legitimate god. But one may reverse the terms of the relationship: a lyrist is effective only when empowered by *his* god, which in the old theology would have been the patron deity of his own professional duties.[100] One should note here a remarkable Ethiopian legend relayed by a traditional musician, Melaku Gelaw, to A. Kebede:

> God Himself made the *begena* [box-lyre] and gave it to Dawit. "Use this instrument to adorn and praise My name," God said. God tuned the ten strings to the ten forces of goodness and virtue that governed the universe. The inspired Dawit composed his psalms, sang to the greatness and glory of God, and accompanied himself with the *begena*.[101]

Mutatis mutandis, the conception of an inspired performer activating the powers of the *kinnōr* in service to Yahweh strongly recalls the Sumerian material, discussed above, notably the divinized balang, servant to the master-god Ningirsu, whose epiphany is effected through performances conducted symbolically, and perhaps literally, by the king. In the Biblical narrative, playing the *kinnōr* is a kingly virtue. But whereas Saul merely prophesies *among* the musicians, David himself wields the lyre, as though this puts him 'in closer touch' with God. And of course David himself was traditionally prophetic, his medium being precisely the *kinnōr*-accompanied psalm (see further below).

Performing the Divine Lyre

We are now in a better position to appreciate the most magnificent *knr*-performance on record. David astutely expressed his establishment of a new

---

[98] 1 Samuel 16:18.
[99] See p33–37.
[100] Compare especially the Ugaritic PN *$k\underline{t}rmlk$, 'Kothar-is-king', born by a silversmith (RS 19.16 [PRU 5 no. 11], line 32, appearing in the Akkadianized form *kšrmlk*; cf. KwH:62 and 131n71). For Kothar and Kinyras, see Chapter 18.
[101] Kebede 1977:380–381; cf. MGG 5:1032 [G. Kubik]). Note that in Ethiopic tradition the *krar* (< **kenar*) is exclusively secular, "the devil's instrument": see p58n65.

Chapter Eight

capital, and his centralization of political and religious control, through the transfer of the Ark to Jerusalem—"a brilliant maneuver that effectively galvanized the loose confederation of Israelite tribes into a monarchical state."[102] To be epoch-making, this needed to be a stunning public event, a massive display of solidarity unifying the divided tribes behind a new king. The main accounts are 2 Samuel, 1 Chronicles, and Josephus.[103] While the LXX version of 2 Samuel contains material not to be found in the MT, this is not all secondary expansion; for 2 Samuel, especially, the MT is "a poor text, marked by extensive haplography and corruption," with fragments from Qumran showing that the LXX preserves many details omitted by the MT.[104] It is on this older tradition that Josephus also draws.[105] And as it happens, the LXX and Josephus preserve several crucial details about David and his *kinnōr*.

The shared narrative structure for all three is as follows. After David consulted with the country's leading men,[106] and drew up the new musical groups of string-players, cymbalists, frame-drummers, and trumpeters, "the whole people"—some seventy thousand in the LXX—"came together as they had planned."[107] The expression suggests a staged crowd as much as a spontaneous popular movement. The Ark was borne out on a river of sound. Yet not all was clockwork: there was a three-month delay *en route* after a driver tried to stabilize the Ark but was struck dead for his vigilance. After the Lord's anger seemed to abate, David offered appropriate sacrifices, and the whole troupe, now reassembled, set out again with the same pomp. There follows the curious

---

[102] Seow 1989:1.
[103] 2 Samuel 6; 1 Chronicles 15–16; Josephus *Antiquities of the Jews* 7.78–89. For the probable allusion in Psalms 132, see Seow 1989:145–203.
[104] Cross 1998:212 (quotation). See DJD 17:25–27: "The [sc. Qumran] fragments ... confirm most emphatically the usefulness of the Old Greek for the establishment of a more nearly original Hebrew text." Cross 1998:205–212, gives a good review of the 'Old Greek' text's value, especially as a witness to Samuel; cf. also YGC:34–35. Further speculation about the earlier stages and interrelationships of the various textual traditions is best avoided here. For these complex problems, including the theory of the proto-Lucianic recension (whereby the 'Old Greek' text was "revised, with corrections and additions provided to make it conform to the 4QSam text tradition in contemporary Palestine," Ulrich 1978:258), see e.g. the recent overview of Kauhanen 2012:13–23, with extensive bibliography.
[105] Ulrich 1989:93 holds that Josephus did not use 1 Chronicles; material which they share can be explained by assuming that the Chronicler too used a version of 2 Samuel closer to the 4QSam^a/LXX versions than to the MT. Begg 1997, examining David's transfer of the Ark specifically, argues for Josephus' knowledge of the LXX Chronicler, but not the MT. Avioz 2015 now corroborates the historian's use of both LXX and MT (or better MT forerunner): see especially 195–201, with previous literature on the debate (which will no doubt continue). Of course Josephus had his own voice in all this; for his larger exegetical concerns and methods, see inter al. the aforementioned studies of Begg and Avioz.
[106] Josephus *Antiquities of the Jews* 7.78.
[107] Josephus *Antiquities of the Jews* 7.79: συνελθόντος οὖν τοῦ λαοῦ παντός, καθὼς ἐβουλεύσαντο.

David and the Divine Lyre

incident of Saul's daughter Michal, David' wife, who saw the king "leaping and dancing before the Lord; and she despised him in her heart."[108] The ritual closed with sacrifices once the Ark was positioned in the Tabernacle, where David's musical groups would continue to observe the cult.[109] When Michal confronted David for his nudity before his maidservants, and the general indignity of his musical performance, she was afflicted with barrenness—conveniently enough.

The narrative of David's divine favor, which structures our accounts, was probably already being formulated on the ground.[110] It has been well argued, for instance, that the Bible's discontiguous Ark episodes, including its loss to and recovery from the Philistines, once formed a unified narrative produced within the Davidic court to provide theological justification for the new cult-center at Jerusalem.[111] The massive musical procession, with its jubilant atmosphere, is clearly a sort of victory march. S. Mowinckel and others have seen it as modeled on a Canaanite New Year ritual.[112] Similarly, C. L. Seow reads it as a ritual drama with David enacting Yahweh as the triumphant divine warrior; the basic structure reflects (he argues) the influence of Baal mythology on that of Yahweh.[113] Propaganda aside, David's elaborate ritual display seems equally an apotropaic gesture to forestall divine wrath at this intervention in the cultic status quo. David and his advisors probably felt a very real sense of apprehension.[114]

The traditions about the musical nature of the ritual are of considerable interest. The three accounts basically agree on its guildic nature, with massed players of *kinnōr*, *nēbel*, frame-drummers, and other instruments.[115] Apparently the song and dance is executed by these same performers (at least those whose mouths were free). The Chronicler asserts the involvement of Chenaniah, the 'Chief Singer'.[116] Of David's own participation Josephus paints a most vivid picture:

---

[108] 2 Samuel 6:16 (quotation), 20–23; 1 Chronicles 15:29; Josephus *Antiquities of the Jews* 7.85–89.

[109] 2 Samuel 6:13–17.

[110] Cf. Seow 1989:97–104, who also detects a "blatantly clear … propagandistic intent" (102); Halpern 2004:333–340.

[111] Campbell 1975, especially 193–210.

[112] PIW 1:125–130, with Chapter V for the related 'enthronement psalms'; Porter 1954.

[113] Seow 1989, especially 207–209, with review of earlier interpretations on 2–8, arguing that Baal's cult made its impression while the Ark was housed at Qiryat-Yeʻarim for about twenty years.

[114] The incident of the driver, however, is suspicious: it seems designed to demonstrate Yahweh's presence at the dangerous and enormous undertaking, and ultimately, when no further disaster befalls, to confirm the divine approval of David's actions. Seow 1989:97–104 connects Yahweh's wrath and the killing of Uzzah with a "dramatization of … mythological combat," comparing "reenactments of cosmogonic battles … in state-sponsored rituals in Mesopotamia" (99).

[115] There are variants in the tradition: LXX includes double-pipes (ἐν αὐλοῖς, 2 Samuel 6:5) and trumpet (μετὰ φωνῆς σάλπιγγος, 6:15); the MT (6:5) has *mᵉnaʻanʻîm*, interpreted as κύμβαλα in the LXX, *sistra* in the Vulgate, and variously by modern scholars: see MAIP:19.

[116] 1 Chronicles 15:27. See p157.

Chapter Eight

> The king led the way, and with him was the whole multitude, hymning God, and singing every kind of local song, and leading the Ark into Jerusalem with a complex din of instrumental playing and dances and psalms and even of trumpets and cymbals.[117]

More interesting still is his account of the parade's resumption:

> He brought the Ark to his own house, with the priests carrying it, and seven choruses which the king had drawn up leading the way, and himself playing on the *kinýra*.[118]

These details are not purely Josephus' own invention. He is clearly interpreting the Septuagint version, on which he mainly relied, and which here certainly preserves an old form of the tradition.[119] The LXX also has seven choruses, carrying the Ark.[120] The statement that "David struck up (*anekroúeto*) the music" was rightly interpreted by Josephus to mean that he led the procession with his '*kinýra*,' for the verb clearly implies a stringed-instrument.[121] The idea is further supported by the king's position "among harmonized/tuned-up instruments" (*en orgánois hērmosménois*), an expression that foregrounds the ensemble's chordophones.[122] Eusebios espouses the same interpretation, and draws attention to David's position as musical leader of his own musical leaders.[123]

The seven choruses are a striking example of seven-magic in a practical musical context. Indeed, the whole event is buttressed by sevens. A sacrifice of seven bulls and seven rams, mentioned by the Chronicler, corresponds to the

---

[117] Josephus *Antiquities of the Jews* 7.80–81: προῆγε δ' ὁ βασιλεὺς καὶ πᾶν σὺν αὐτῷ τὸ πλῆθος ὑμνοῦντες τὸν θεὸν καὶ ᾄδοντες πᾶν εἶδος μέλους ἐπιχώριον σύν τε ἤχῳ ποικίλῳ κρουσμάτων τε καὶ ὀρχήσεων καὶ ψαλμῶν ἔτι δὲ σάλπιγγος καὶ κυμβάλων κατάγοντες τὴν κιβωτὸν εἰς Ἱεροσόλυμα. 2 Samuel 6:5 states only that "David played," but is more specific as to guildic instrumentation.

[118] Josephus *Antiquities of the Jews* 7.85: τὴν κιβωτὸν πρὸς αὐτὸν μετακομίζει, τῶν μὲν ἱερέων βασταζόντων αὐτήν, ἑπτὰ δὲ χορῶν οὓς διεκόσμησεν ὁ βασιλεὺς προαγόντων, αὐτοῦ δ' ἐν κινύρᾳ παίζοντος (closely followed by Constantine Porphyrogenitos *On Virtues and Vices* 1 [55.16–22, Büttner-Wobst/Roos]).

[119] Josephus and the LXX agree against not only the MT, but the Qumran text, the latter according rather with 1 Chronicles 15:26 (Ulrich 1978:182, 223–259, especially 235–236, 241; Ulrich 1989:88; Kauhanen 2012:34–35).

[120] Wellhausen 1871:169 already saw that the seven χοροί must go back to an early Hebrew text.

[121] 2 Samuel 6:13–14 LXX: καὶ ἦσαν μετ' αὐτῶν αἴροντες τὴν κιβωτὸν ἑπτὰ χοροί ... καὶ Δαυιδ ἀνεκρούετο ἐν ὀργάνοις ἡρμοσμένοις ἐνώπιον κυρίου κτλ. For ἀνακρούω and stringed instruments, see LSJ s.v. κρούω (5), κροῦμα (2), etc. Note also ἀνακρουόμενον at 6:16.

[122] For the special relevance of ἁρμονία and related words (like ἡρμοσμένοις) to stringed-instruments, see Franklin 2003:301, 303–304.

[123] Eusebios *Commentaries on the Psalms*, PG 23:73A: Δαυὶδ, αὐτὸς ἄρχων ἀρχόντων ᾠδῶν, κρατῶν ἐπὶ χεῖρας τὸ ψαλτήριον.

oxen and fatlings, which, according to 2 Samuel, David offers before taking his seventh step after resuming the procession.[124] Such numbers may seem like so much storytelling color, but a detailed prescriptive ritual from LBA Emar in North Syria urges us to give them some credence. This text governs the 'enthronement' of the high priestess of Baal, and contains many heptadic gestures.[125] It is equally important for assigning specific ritual actions to a group of liturgical singers (*zammārū*), notably heading processions every time the scene of action had to change.[126] Musical procession must have been a regular function of temple-singers in many parts of the ANE. Several types of Emesal prayers/laments were used in various processions and circumambulation rites at different periods in Mesopotamia.[127] In Babylonia, a musical corps participated in processional rites during the Akitu-festival.[128] Many musical processions are found in N-A reliefs as well.[129] They are also attested in the Hittite world.[130]

As argued above for Mesopotamian material, seven numerology takes on a special interest in musical contexts, especially those involving stringed-instruments.[131] It is especially suggestive beyond the two rivers, where it furthers the likelihood that the heptatonic-diatonic tone-system was locally known—as indeed it was at Ugarit. Many marginal examples are best not

---

[124] 2 Samuel 6:13; 1 Chronicles 15:26.

[125] Text of the *Installation of Baal's High Priestess*: Arnaud 1986 no. 369, superseded by Fleming 1992 (with new lineation); CS 1 no. 122. While other numbers, 'significant' and otherwise, are present in the ritual, the intentional concentration of sevens is obvious. There is an offering of one ox and six sheep (11, 36–37); "seven dinner-loaves, seven dried cakes" (11); seven and seven ḫamša'u-men eating (12–13); an unknown action lasts seven days (26); seven-fold wine and beer offerings (and some other non-seven offerings) are to be consumed by the seven *qidašu* and *ḫussu*-men (27–28, 38); the priestess is given a "seven-shekel silver *tudittu*-pin as her gift" when enthroned (44); a sacred axe is placed on a statue for seven days (46); various offerings are made over a seven-day period; some are consumed by the "seven and seven ḫamša'u-men" (49–59, cf. 54); each singer receives a share of sacrifice, sheepskins, and a dinner-load and jug of beer for seven days (79–83). Nor is this the only ritual text from Emar that combines seven-magic and song-acts: see Arnaud 1986 no. 388.51–52, 395.2'–4'. Cf. also RlA 12/5–6.464 §5.3 (Wiggerman, *Siebengötter).

[126] Processions in the *Installation of Baal's High Priestess*: lines 8, 29–36, 45, 62–64. Additionally, two hymns were specified (33A, 73); and the singers' share of offerings and their payment were stipulated (79–84). The ritual also involved lamentation, probably for the death of the old priestess (Fleming 1992:173). There are many other references at Emar to the cult performances of singers, especially in connection with sacrificial ritual, as well as to female singers (*zammirātū*): see the discussion of Fleming 1992:92–94, with references; cf. SURS:313n861.

[127] PHG:170–171.

[128] Fleming 1992:93n81; Pongratz-Leisten 1994: 47; Cheng 2001:92n8; PHG:170.

[129] Franklin 2008:198 with references.

[130] E.g. in the KI.LAM festival, Singer 1983–1984 1:62. For Hittite occasions see further CANE 4:2661–2669 (de Martino).

[131] See p40–41.

pressed.¹³² Tending in the right direction is Solomon's transfer of the Ark into the Temple during Ethanim, the seventh month of the year—a replay of David's Ark-procession, again with massed musical praise drawing Yahweh to a new home.¹³³ Much clearer are the pious measures taken by Hezekiah to restore the Temple from neglect in the reign of his father Ahaz (735–715).¹³⁴ Seven bulls, seven rams, seven lambs, and seven male goats were sacrificed. Cult-musicians bore "cymbals, *nēbel*-lyres, and *kinnōr*-lyres," and the music is carefully synchronized with the heptadic sacrifices: "When the burnt offering began, the song to the Lord began also, and the trumpets, accompanied by the instruments of King David … all this continued until the burnt offering was finished."¹³⁵ The music evidently basted the offerings in waves of magical sevenness.

The parallels from Ebla, Emar, Hattusha, Ugarit, and elsewhere for musical parades and the ritual use of sevens make David's Ark-procession perfectly plausible as an historical event, and suggest that the surviving accounts preserve actual details from the occasion, and/or its periodic reenactment in the royal cult.¹³⁶ They amount to, and/or derive from, a descriptive ritual.¹³⁷ One may compare the detailed ritual actions that are incorporated into a text like *Aqhat*.¹³⁸ (By contrast, the Emar ritual is strictly prescriptive.¹³⁹) Yet descriptive rituals need not be mere literary productions. They could also be functional, "quasi-canonical models, or manuals for the operation of the temple cults."¹⁴⁰ That some such account of the Davidic ritual was composed at a near contemporary date would accord with the theory of a unified Ark-narrative, and explain the existence of the Bible's more literary narratives, for which it could have been a source at however many removes. It would also provide an attractive practical explanation for why the ritual actions of Solomon and Hezekiah share three structuring elements with those of David. All three rituals include seven-magic alongside song-acts governing the establishment, building, or maintenance of the cult center. The continuity between these events is made explicit.

---

¹³² For example, that David was selected for kingship after his seven older brothers had been rejected (1 Samuel 16:10) is most simply explained as a narratological device and folklore motif; while it does derive special interest from David's training as a lyrist, the two details are not explicitly connected in the text itself.

¹³³ 1 Kings 8:2; 2 Chronicles 5:3, 11. Cf. PIW 1:174–175 and n176.

¹³⁴ 2 Chronicles 29:21–28.

¹³⁵ 2 Chronicles 29:27–28.

¹³⁶ For the same conclusion on other grounds, see Seow 1989:209. For ritual re-enactment of the Ark-procession, PIW 1:174–175 (thinking rather of saga than a contemporary source for the original event).

¹³⁷ For the term, see p67n35.

¹³⁸ For which see Wright 2001 passim.

¹³⁹ Fleming 1992:70.

¹⁴⁰ Levine 1983:473.

Solomon's completion of the Temple is seen as the fruition of David's own vision; the Levites minister "with instruments for music ... that King David had made for giving thanks to the Lord."[141] Hezekiah's musicians were stationed, says the Chronicler, "according to the commandment of David."[142]

The parallels strongly suggest that David based his actions upon earlier Canaanite rituals, products of the same cultural environment that inspired or dictated his musical reorganization.[143] With this we may consider more closely the musical dimension of David's own performance. The king sings, dances, and plays the *kinnōr* before Yahweh, at the head of all his subjects, in front even of his own priests, musicians, guild leaders, and the Chief Singer himself. As a victory procession for Yahweh, David plays the role of 'royal' praise-singer, not unlike the position he had actually held under Saul. But as a victorious king himself, this was equally his own triumph, so that David assumes a position analogous to that of Yahweh. The ritual is a remarkable practical application of what, in the Sumerian texts, can otherwise appear a rather poetic conceit: the king who excels his own singers, and executes state rituals single-handedly. It also fleshes out the Ugaritian ritual texts, where the king dominates the action, yet the cultic establishment was fully involved.[144] David's performance, I suggest, is as close as we are likely to come to witnessing the Divine Lyre in action. Here more than anywhere the *kinnōr* is a powerful symbol of the king's divine favor. But the practicality of the lyre tradition makes the *kinnōr* more than just a symbol. It was the actual instrument with which to cross the chasm separating human and divine. With it, a king could communicate queries, receive instruction, and channel divine power toward specific ends.

Why does Michal react so strongly against this performance? That she found it unacceptable is important: such a ritual was evidently unprecedented in some way. This should relate to the equal newness, from the Jewish perspective, of David's musical arrangements for the same ceremony. If those were indeed modeled on earlier Canaanite temple-music traditions, David's own performing role may well be of a piece. Clearly he is putting on a mantle of kingship, publically demonstrating divine favor while simultaneously seeking to secure it. His actions will accord with the people's desire that "we also may be like other nations," the request that led to the original appointment of Saul. The popular nature of David's rite is clear: it is repeatedly stressed that "all the people" are present (with "every kind of local song"). In gratifying the crowd to this extent, David goes far beyond any royal display credited to Saul, and thereby shows

---

[141] 2 Chronicles 7:6.
[142] 2 Chronicles 29:25.
[143] See PIW 1:130–136 for further considerations.
[144] See p113–114.

himself to be 'more kingly'. It is therefore appropriate and revealing that it is Michal, the last vital link between David and her deposed father, who objects to these novel royal antics.[145] David, in his rejoinder, takes up the implied contrast with Saul, and asserts that the performance is divinely-approved and his royal prerogative:

> It was before the Lord, who chose me in place of your father and all his household, to appoint me as prince over Israel, the people of the Lord, that I have danced before the Lord.[146]

To conclude, David's *kinnōr* is an integral part of the early narratives about the rise of the United Monarchy. David's entrance in 1 Samuel is motivated by Saul's need to find a *kinnōr*-player. He advances because "the Lord is with him," and no longer with Saul. This power is expressed through the *kinnōr* in David's catharses of Saul and his 'victory procession' for Yahweh. The lyre's ability to serve as a pivotal narratological device derives from the instrument's more ancient potency in the royal cults of the wider region. David is not merely a king who happens to play the *kinnōr*. He is king in large part *because* he plays it, incomparably well. This will be a crucial comparandum for understanding Kinyras of Cyprus.

Sweet Psalmist of Israel: David's Lyric Legacy

It was later believed that both the canonical Psalms and other songs embedded in the Biblical narratives were produced during the United Monarchy. And this is true in many cases, if not of the whole corpus. Although specific attributions to David and Solomon, as well as to their traditional guild-leaders, can never be conclusively verified, some Psalms are clearly of high antiquity.[147] Certain songs may actually antedate their supposed author.[148]

---

[145] Cf. Campbell 1975:138–139.
[146] 2 Samuel 6:21.
[147] See Freedman 1976 generally, with discussion of the early song in 2 Samuel 22 at 75–77; for the latter's transmission history, with the parallel Psalms 18, see McCarter 1984:473–475, with further references. For 2 Samuel 23:1–7, David's swan-song, see p175–178. The attribution of certain psalms to the "Sons of Korah" (2 Chronicles 20:19; Psalms 42, 44–49, 84–85, 87–88) is made more credible by Korah's relative obscurity in the Bible itself; for their Levitical descent, see Numbers 16:1–11 (but cf. 31–33); 1 Chronicles 6:22, 9:19, 9:31.
[148] For Psalms 29, attributed to David, see Freedman 1976:60–61, 96, dating it to the *twelfth* century on stylistic criteria ("repetitive parallelism to an extraordinary extent," 60).

Even the most careful scholars are prepared to support Davidic authorship and/or date in certain cases—like Psalm 132, relating to the Ark-procession.[149] There is also the elegy for Saul and Jonathan in 2 Samuel, quoted from the *Book of Jashar*, a lost anthology of poetry including other purportedly royal productions. The song's antiquity and even authenticity are suggested both by its topical content and the seemingly apologetic instruction that it be disseminated and taught throughout Judah.[150] Such a gesture of public lamentation may in itself be seen as an assertion of kingship, if it was the royal prerogative and duty for a new monarch to raise the lament for the passing of his predecessor—an idea that would fit well with the ritual texts from Ebla and Ugarit relating to royal funerary and/or mortuary cult.[151]

The same contexts could also provide a good home for the famous song, supposedly the dying words of David himself, at the end of 2 Samuel. It begins:

> Oracle of David son of Jesse
> Oracle of him whom ʾĒl exalted,
> Anointed of the God of Jacob,
> Favorite of the Mighty One of Israel (*nĕʿîm zimrat yiśrāʾēl*),
> The spirit of Yahweh spoke through me
> His word was upon my tongue.[152]

Scholars have dated this song variously between David's demise and the late Judaean monarchy, with a strong case for an early origin on the grounds of diction and content.[153] But an absolute date is less vital here than how David is represented. According to the traditional reading of the MT, *zmrt* is to be

---

[149] See generally PIW 2:152-154. The antiquity of Psalms 132, a key text for the later royal cult (PIW 2:174-176), is defended by Cross 1973:94-97 ("reworked only slightly in the later royal cult," 97, with archaic details enumerated in n24) and 232-237 ("our earliest witness to the Davidic covenant ... lore of Davidic date," 232).

[150] 2 Samuel 1:19-27: see McCarter 1984:74, 77, 484 (also supporting the authenticity of the elegy to Abner at 2 Samuel 3:33-34); Cross 1998:137-138 (for typological analysis of its parallelism); Halpern 2004:64.

[151] See p67-71, 134-146.

[152] 2 Samuel 23:1-2, trans. and colometry of Cross 1973:235-236. For the text itself, of which the MT is the best witness, see Mettinger 1976-1977.

[153] Those supporting a Davidic date include Albright 1956:126; Cross 1973:234-237 and n81 (of a piece with Psalms 132); Freedman 1976. McCarter 1984:483-486 lays out and convincingly meets the objections against an early date in dissenting literature, interpreting the psalm's application of solar imagery to the king in terms of LBA Egyptian and Hittite royal usage. In his view (480-481, 483), the presentation of David as prophetic—dismissed as a late feature by some—can be excised as secondary and due to later messianic reinterpretations of the Psalms (cf. e.g. Acts 2:30). Yet the *kinnōr* is found not only in prophetic contexts of the ninth century, but earlier still with Saul and the band of musical prophets.

Chapter Eight

vocalized as *zĕmīrôt*, 'songs' (< P-S √*zmr*, 'sing/play'[154]), while *nĕ'îm* comes from the root *n'm* ('sweet, pleasant, gracious')—whence "Sweet Psalmist of Israel" in the King James Version and its adherents. Now a musical interpretation goes back at least to the Hellenistic period, being reflected in the Septuagint translation, the importance of which to the tradition we have seen.[155] But with modern appreciation of parallelism, it has become clear that the phrase should be equivalent to the description of David as "Anointed of the God of Jacob." Hence, most scholars now abandon a musical reading to vocalize *zmrt* as *zimrāt* and connect it with Semitic cognates relating to 'power' and 'protection' (< P-S √*dmr*).[156] Similarly, *nĕ'îm* is interpreted in terms of the *n'm* which we saw applied to gods and heroes in Ugaritian texts.[157] Therefore, *nĕ'îm zimrat yiśrā'ēl* can be well rendered as 'Favorite of the Mighty One of Israel', 'Favorite of the Defense of Israel', or the like.[158]

This reinterpretation certainly produces a satisfying parallelism with "Anointed of the God of Jacob." Yet this probably does not exhaust its meaning. If the Ugaritic usage of *n'm* is indeed relevant—as is generally agreed—it becomes possible to maintain a musical nuance here on the basis of the word's specialized application to divine musicians, especially the praise-singer of Baal.[159] When this is seen against the casting of David as a *kinnōr*-player in the narratives discussed above, and his ongoing stance as praise-singer of Yahweh in the Psalms, it become hard to avoid taking *nĕ'îm* as akin to the Ugaritic usage, with all its cultic overtones. The Hebrew word may thus mean something very like 'Gracious Minstrel' *in itself*—that is, whether one relates *zmrt* to 'songs' or 'power'.[160] The parallelism with 'Anointed' is not violated by this reading; indeed it accords well with the idea, argued above, that one of David's qualifications for

---

[154] For this root, see p137 and n160.
[155] There, however, one has εὐπρεπεῖς ψαλμοὶ Ἰσραήλ: David *is* the "seemly songs of Israel."
[156] Gaster 1936–1937; Cross and Freedman 1955:243n b; Richardson 1971:261–262; Cross 1973:234n67; Freedman 1976:58, 73; Mettinger 1976–1977:149–151 (treating *zimrāt* as an "intensive plural"); McCarter 1984:476–480.
[157] See p128–129. Cf. Richardson 1971:261; Cross 1998:140, noting that the precise vocalization is uncertain.
[158] This new understanding of *zmrt* has also affected the interpretation of an ancient formula that appears in several Biblical passages. Hence in the 'Song of Miriam' (Exodus 15:2) "The Lord is my strength and song" becomes "strength and might," *vel sim.*; similarly in Isaiah 12:2, Psalms 118:14. For the evidently deep (Canaanite) antiquity of this "fossilized pair of words ... preserved in this set context only," see Lowenstamm 1969:464, the critique of Parker 1971, and further below, p177n161.
[159] See p128–129. The potential of this parallel has been noted by ARTU:4n16; Koitabashi 1996:222; Parker 1997:166n36; RTU:328n19.
[160] Levenson 1985:66, in interpreting *n'm* as 'person granted a favorable omen', rejected 'singer' as lacking in Biblical parallels; but he did not note the Ugaritian ones.

kingship is his power as an inspired lyrist. The reading has the further advantage of accounting for the early musical interpretation of the LXX.

Given all this, it remains worth considering whether Heb. *zmr* was once capable of some semantic ambivalence between 'song' and 'power'—not by virtue of historical linguistics, but ritual-poetic convention.[161] We have seen this precise duality in the Ugaritic text RS 24.252 with its crucial wordplay on *zmr/ḏmr*, whereby the 'song' of Rāp'iu was simultaneously a source of the king's 'power'.[162] The phrase *nĕʿîm zimrat yiśrāʾēl* may therefore imply not only that David was the Gracious Minstrel of the Might of Israel, but that his own power as Yahweh's terrestrial agent derived precisely from his praising of Yahweh in song.

Only on his deathbed is David characterized as *nĕʿîm*, contemplating his role as mouthpiece of Yahweh, god's covenant with his royal house, and the legacy of his own reign. I suggest connecting this with the appearance of *n'm* in RS 24.257, evidently a text relating to the royal mortuary cult of Ugarit, with its eternal, archetypal monarch presiding over a paradisiacal feast of *kinnāru*-led music—quite possibly, I have argued, as the *kinnāru*-player himself.[163] The Rabbinic tradition presents vivid images of David at the eternal banquet that was to follow judgment day—immune to fleshly decay, and with his *kinnôr* leading the angelic host and all his royal descendants and other Israelite kings in singing new hymns to Yahweh, across from whom David was to be enthroned.[164] This

---

[161] Stimulating and provocative suggestions to this effect were put forward by Lowenstamm 1969, vis-à-vis the formula in Exodus 15:2; Isaiah 12:2, Psalms 118:14 (see p76n158). Lowenstamm's argument (465–466) for a single P-S root *ḏmr* containing within itself ideas of both 'song' and 'power/glory' cannot be sustained on linguistic grounds: see p138n160. I also recognize the general validity of the critique by Parker 1971 (cf. Mettinger 1976–1977:150n13). Yet neither study took account of the wordplay on *ḏmr* in RS 24.252 (see p137–139). Such a conflation of 'song' and 'power' seems to underlie the Zimri son of Zerah who has four musical brothers in Ethan, Heman, Calcol, Darda (1 Chronicles 2:6), the Canaanite cultural sympathies of whom were explicated by Albright 1956:127 (cf. p152). Pardee 1988a:142 thinks of folk etymology: "It is quite likely that in popular understanding the onomastic element *zimrî* was 'mistakenly' thought to be related to *zamar* 'make music'." Therefore I am still drawn to Lowenstamm's conclusion that "No translation is likely to render the exact force of the Hebrew words, because their connotations and associations are too deeply rooted in the specific theology of the ancient Canaanite hymnic tradition" (469–470). My analysis of the wordplay on RS 24.252 has led, from an independent angle, to a result very similar to Lowenstamm's conception of the early Hebrew formula: "The noun ... primarily denoting the glory given to God in cultic song, may also be applied to the glory bestowed by the Lord upon those who glorify Him ... The notion of praise in cultic music becomes reduced to that of glory pure and simple. It follows that the pair of words denotes the Psalmist's strength and glory, the source of both he finds in his God" (468).

[162] See p137–139.

[163] See p140.

[164] See sources and discussion in LJ 4:114–116, 6:272–273 n128–129. I thank Miryam Brand for her help with these texts.

Chapter Eight

portrait, although a composite from several late sources, nonetheless exhibits striking sympathies with the Ugaritian Rāp'iu text.

The temporal disparity between the Ugaritian texts and 2 Samuel 23:1 on the one hand, and the late evidence for David as Yahweh's praise-singer in paradise on the other, is of course enormous. Yet the intervening period is at least partially spanned by a living tradition of psalm-singing. Note for instance the bird-headed finials on the instruments of the captive Judaean musicians from the reign of Hezekiah, shown on a relief of Sennacherib (704–681)—a decorative feature going back to the LBA, with parallels from Egypt, Cyprus, and the Hittite world.[165] A fundamental justification for the later attribution of psalms to David must have been the continued importance of the *kinnōr* in the cult. A specific connection with David is seen in those psalms that, when not authentic, nevertheless adopt as a performative stance his persona as *kinnōr*-playing prophet-king, mouthpiece of Yahweh, and thus a kind of divine messenger.[166] This Davidic guise probably arose in the context of the royal rituals by which the House of David maintained its founder's ideological legacy. Although ensemble playing is sometimes specified for various psalms, it is probable that they were equally performed in a Davidic manner—that is, by an individual *kinnōr*-player, or one who led an ensemble, as David was said to have done in the ark-procession. A psalmist who performed such songs in these circumstances will have effectively reenacted the ancient king. This would further explain the traditions of the song-writing Solomon, just as Ishme-Dagan repeated the musical claims of Shulgi.[167] The Qumran texts—whose many psalms, entirely absent from the canonical Psalters (LXX/MT) yet sharing much of their diction, show the tradition flourishing post-exile—include songs attributed to Mannaseh, an otherwise unnamed "King of Judah" (Hezekiah?), and perhaps David himself ('the Man of God').[168]

The traditional reenactment of David seems one of the clearer legacies of the Divine Lyre. The instrument's magical qualities certainly rang on in the

---

[165] BM 124947 (see above, n30). For the point, Sellers 1941:38; Rimmer 1969:34; DCPIL:49; Parallels: see p247 and n27.

[166] Of the psalms attributed to David (Psalms 3–9, 11–32, 34–41, 51–70, 86, 101, 103, 109–110, 122, 124, 131, 133, 138–145), a clearly Davidic persona may be seen in e.g. 144–145, and especially the supernumerary Psalms 151 in the LXX (relating to the victory over Goliath). For 2 Samuel 22/ Psalms 18, see p147n174; for 2 Samuel 23:1-7, p175. This phenomenon provides some justification for those who would translate *nĕ'îm zĕmîrôt yiśrā'ēl* as "Favorite of Israel's Songs": so e.g. Laymon 1971:180.

[167] See p80–81.

[168] 4Q381 fr. 24.4 ('Man of God'), 31.4 ('King of Judah', name lost), 33.8 (Mannaseh). For Psalmody at Qumran: Schuller 1986 (royal ascriptions, 29 and 101); Schuller's introduction to Charlesworth 1997:1 with references.

corpus. In Psalm 98, one finds the same ancient conception represented by the Orpheus jug—the lyrist exercising control over the natural world:

> Make a joyful noise to the Lord, all the earth;
>> break forth into joyous song and sing praises,
> Sing praises to the Lord with the lyre,
>> with the lyre and the sound of melody.
> With trumpets and the sound of the horn
>> make a joyful noise before the King, the Lord.[169]

The universal glorification of Yahweh is itemized in greater detail in Psalm 148, where the *kinnōr*, though not explicitly mentioned, is implied by the parallel of Psalm 98 and the genre itself:

> Praise the Lord from the earth,
>> you sea monsters and all deeps,
> fire and hail, snow and frost,
>> stormy wind fulfilling his command!
> Mountains and all hills,
>> fruit trees and all cedars!
> Wild animals and all cattle,
>> creeping things and flying birds![170]

These Psalms show that the praise-singing lyrist, while but one instantiation of a more cosmic exultation that also included every form of musical celebration,[171] nevertheless plays a privileged role, occupying an intermediate, focusing position between the natural world and the divine object of its praise. It is this power which eventually facilitated David's absorption of Orphic qualities in the Byzantine period.[172]

David's quasi-divine status gradually crystallized with the idea that Yahweh had established an eternal covenant with his line.[173] This eventually gave rise, with the fluctuating fortunes of Israel and Judah, and the interruption of the Davidic royal line, to the idea that the projected messiah would be a second David, even

---

[169] Psalms 98:4–6.
[170] Psalms 148:7–10; cf. 149.
[171] Note Psalm 149:3 and especially the famous instrumentarium of 150, which became a favorite subject of Byzantine musical iconography: see Currie forthcoming and p543–544.
[172] See p193–194.
[173] See e.g. LJ^2 5:451, 459–463.

Chapter Eight

his reincarnation.[174] One musical outgrowth of this is the early Christian trope of Jesus as a lyre-player, which equally incorporated Apollo's role as overseer of cosmic harmony; on the human plane, a devout Christian was a lyre—often *kinýra*—on which Jesus played his divine message.[175]

Another development is seen in the coins of the Bar Kokhba revolt (132–136 CE)—the last Jewish insurrection against Rome, when cultural oppression after the destruction of Jerusalem in 70 CE culminated in Hadrian's new temple to Jupiter on the temple mount (ca. 130). The revolt was led by Shimon, son of Koseva, whose name was reinterpreted as Kokhba to imply fulfillment of the prophecy that "There shall step forth a star (*kokhav*) out of Jacob."[176] The tradition that the prominent sage ʿAqiba (ca. 50–135 CE) was among those who promoted Bar Kokhba as the messiah is probably accurate; and it may be no coincidence that ʿAqiba is the earliest source for the vision of David's eternal throne alongside Yahweh.[177]

One of the rebels' primary gestures of independence was to usurp the imperial prerogative of coinage. Making a political virtue of economic necessity, they withdrew Roman issues from circulation and over-stamped the heads of hated gods and emperors.[178] The Romans themselves had shown that coins were a vital medium for propaganda.[179] Hence, one cannot doubt that the Bar Kokhba coins "bore a clear political message and every detail on them was intentional."[180] The limited repertoire of motifs related to the temple and its tools, simultaneously expressing the nationalist ideal of rebuilding Yahweh's cult center, and supporting the messianic image of Bar Kokhba himself.[181] Prominent among the coin-types are two kinds of lyre, in several variations due to multiple dies (Figure 14). These instruments probably represent *kinnōr* and *nēbel*,[182] albeit in contemporary forms showing the Hellenistic morphological influence one sees

---

[174] Thus Matthew 1:1–17 carefully establishes the Davidic descent of Jesus. Further sources and discussion in LJ 6:272–273; EJ^2 5:451a–454a.

[175] See Halton 1983, and further p209–210. For the link back to David, note e.g. the description of Jesus in Paulinus *Carmina* 20.41–42 as *ille Dauid uerus, citharam qui corporis huius / restituit*, etc.

[176] Numbers 24:17. For the messianic aspect of the Bar Kokhba movement, see with ancient sources Yadin 1971:18–19, 23, 27; AJC:140–142; EJ^2 3:157–159.

[177] This is accepted by Strack 1983:72, who otherwise rejects much of the biographical tradition about ʿAqiba; cf. EJ^2 1:562a–563b. David's throne: *Sanhedrin* 38b (BT 12:245); LJ 6:272n128.

[178] Mildenberg 1984:13–14.

[179] For the sophistication of Roman imperial propaganda via coins, see Noreña 2011.

[180] AJC:141, cf. 137.

[181] Yadin 1971:27; AJC:140–142.

[182] Lyre-coins: Mildenberg 1984 no. 165, 172–186, 196, 201–220, 232–241, 244, 247–249; AJC no. 223a–h, 236, 238–242a, 272–275, 296–299, with discussion at 147–149. For identification as *kinnōr* and *nēbel*, Bayer 1968; RlA 6:580 (Collon, *Leier B); SAM:170–171 (no. 133–134).

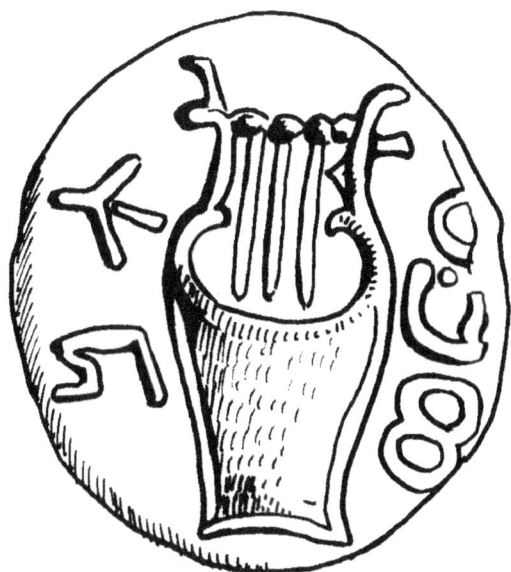

Figure 14 Coin of the Bar Kokhba revolt (132–136 CE). Bible Lands Museum, Jerusalem, 5651. Drawn from SAM no. 133–134.

in many NE lyres of the Roman period.[183] The Bar Kokhba coins thus evoked the liturgical practices associated with David, while promoting a rebuilding campaign.[184] It is tempting to relate these lyre-coins to a Rabbinic tradition that Zedekiah, last king before the Babylonian Exile, and Baruch, the scribe of Jeremiah, had hidden the sacred instruments of the First Temple before its destruction, to be revealed at the coming of the messiah.[185]

The legendary musical powers of David and Solomon persisted through antiquity and beyond in the Jewish, Greek Christian, Syrian Christian, and Arabic traditions alike.

A Jewish legend intended to explain the invocation of the *kinnōr* in Psalm 57:8–9 and 108:1–3 (see above) is attributed to Simeon the Pious in the third century BCE. Here the *kinnōr* is seen as an Aeolian harp, stimulated by a

---

[183] DCPIL:56 ("Neo-Grecian"), cf. MGG 5:1035–1036; also 1:1510 pl. 2 (Braun) for other seemingly Hellenized lyre forms from Akko, Caesarea, Gaza, Samaria, Gadara, Petra, and elsewhere in Jordan.

[184] Recall the musical organization that accompanied the Second Temple's dedication. Cf. AJC:148, with reference to Nehemiah 12:27.

[185] LJ 4:21, 6:411n64.

midnight wind and calling David to his liturgical duties "of its own accord."[186] Here it effectively has a life and a voice of its own, although, given its sympathetic vibration with the natural order, Yahweh is not far away. Similarly Greek Christian hymnographers described David's 'kinýra' as "god-sounding," "god-inspired," and an "animated psaltery ... a kinýra charming souls / Towards god-inspired love."[187] Gregory of Nazianzus, archbishop of Constantinople in the later fourth-century CE, in listing David's youthful virtues, refers to "the power of his kinýra"—the Gk. dýnamis has connotations of 'capacity' and 'potential'—and describes the lyre itself as "even overcoming the Evil Spirit with its enchantment."[188] Nikephoros Basilakes, rhetorician of the early twelfth-century, imagines David both "with the holy spirit, and the kinýra of the holy spirit."[189] Despite the lateness of this source, the 'lyre of the spirit' is an early and well-attested motif, vividly developed in the Syriac theological poetry of St. Ephraim (ca. 307–373).[190]

In Arabic tradition, which incorporated oral lore from Jewish and Christian populations in fable-rich southern Arabia, David remained the paragon of musical ability, as seen from many passages in the *Arabian Nights*.[191] The Quran accepts David as a true prophet whose visions of God are relayed in the Book of Psalms.[192] Mohammed rightly saw that, while David's prophetic songs induced the sympathetic vibration of nature, the source of his power was held to come from beyond the psalmist himself. It was God who:

---

[186] The tale appears in *Berakhot* 3b (BT 1:9–10), where it is given "in the name of R. Simeon the Pious" (cf. Strack 1983:107, identifying with the High Priest Simeon I, ca. 300 BCE); *Sanhedrin* 16a (BT 12:79); *Midrash Rabbah* Numbers 15.16 (Freedman and Simon 1983 6:659): "A harp [i.e. *kinnōr*] hung over David's bed. When the hour of midnight arrived, a northerly wind blew upon it and it played of its own accord. Thereupon David would rise up with his disciples. For they used to occupy themselves with the Torah, toiling and driving sleep from their eyes, studying Torah until the dawn. This is why David said, 'Awake, my glory; psaltery and harp, I will awake the dawn.'" Cf. LJ 4:101.

[187] *Analecta Hymnica Graeca, Canones Januarii*, Day 25, Canon 30 (1), Ode 6.46 (ed. Proiou/Schirò): τὴν θεόηχον κινύραν (referring to the emulation of David by Gregory of Nazianzus); *Canones Decembris*, Day 26, Canon 51, Ode 5.16–17 (ed. Kominis/Schirò): τοῖς μελῳδήμασι / χρώμενοι Δαβίδ, τῆς ἐνθέου κινύρας σου; Ode 8.56–58: ψαλτήριον ἔμψυχον / καὶ κινύρα ψυχὰς θέλγουσα / πρὸς ἔρωτα τὸν ἔνθεον.

[188] Gregory of Nazianzus *Orations* 43 (PG 36:596B): πρὸ τῆς βασιλείας ἡ τῆς κινύρας δύναμις, καὶ πονηροῦ πνεύματος κατεπᾴδουσα.

[189] Nikephoros Basilakes *Orations* 1.608: τὸν Δαυῒδ μετὰ τοῦ πνεύματος καὶ τῆς τοῦ πνεύματος κινύρας. Cf. *Analecta Hymnica Graeca, Canones Novembris*, Day 30, Canon 44, Ode 7.8 (ed. Kominis/Schirò): τὴν κινύραν τοῦ πνεύματος, again of David.

[190] See p61, 210.

[191] SOM 1:75. For the cultural and historical issues which account for Mohammed's familiarity with and use of these legends, see Adang 1996:1–22. For a good survey of sources for pre-Islamic Arabian legend, including the development of David and Solomon, see Norris 1983.

[192] See 17.55, 27.15. For the Quran's engagement with the Psalter specifically, cf. Masson 1958:429.

caused the mountains and the birds to join with David in Our praise. All this We did.¹⁹³

We made the mountains join with him in praise evening and morning, and the birds, too, in all their flocks; all were obedient to him. We made his kingdom strong, and gave him wisdom and discriminating judgment.¹⁹⁴

In the Quran, Solomon speaks with beasts, birds, and insects, and is master of the elements through his command of the djinn. David was credited with similar superpowers by both the Rabbinic and Quranic exegetes.¹⁹⁵ In a tenth-century Arabic source, David can assemble the djinn by means of his 'harp' (mi'zaf).¹⁹⁶ A particularly striking parallel to the Orpheus jug is a legend compiled by al-Tha'labī in the eleventh century from earlier authorities:

[David] would recite the Psalms with seventy melodies so that those with fever would sweat and the unconscious would revive ... Wild beasts and beasts of prey would draw near and be seized by the neck, while birds shielded him from the sun's rays, the flowing water stood still, the wind died down.¹⁹⁷

A similar portrait of Solomon is found in the *Targum Sheni of Esther*, which reached its present form ca. 700 CE:

[The king] had dominion over the demons, spirits and Lilin, and knew the language of each ... and when his heart was merry with wine, he would command the wild animals, the fowl of heaven, and the creeping things of the earth, as well as the demons, spirits and Lilin, to dance before him.¹⁹⁸

---

¹⁹³ 21.79 (trans. Dawood); cf. 34.10.
¹⁹⁴ 38.18 (trans. Dawood).
¹⁹⁵ For the tale of David and the talking frog, see LJ 4:101–102, 6:262–263n84. Quran: see especially 21.81, 27.16–45 (language of birds); 34.12–14; 38.36. The Quranic passages relating to David and Solomon are compared with their Biblical antecedents by Masson 1958:423–436. Much fabulous material is found in the exegetical tradition of the Quran: see Thackston 1978:289–286, 300–308; EQ 1:495a–497b (I. Hass s.v. David), 5:76a–78b (P. Soucek s.v. Solomon); Wheeler 2002:266–279; Brinner 2002:462–468 (David), 491–498 (Solomon).
¹⁹⁶ SOM 1:123 (source: the *'Iqd al-Farīd*).
¹⁹⁷ Brinner 2002:463 (translation), cf. 464 (the mountains answer David's songs); Thackston 1978:289 (the earth laughs and beasts bow down to David upon Solomon's birth).
¹⁹⁸ *Targum Sheni to Esther* 1:3 (translation after Ego 1996). For this work and its dating, see EJ² 19:513b–515a. Naturally individual elements of the targum may represent older traditions.

Chapter Eight

Despite the lateness of these texts, their details go well beyond what is obvious in the Bible itself. Nor can they be dismissed by appeal to later Hellenistic influence. The persistence of these traditions about magical music and David's inspired lyre is best explained as having been reinforced by the widespread and deeply rooted indigenous lyre-cultures whose prestige and power is so vividly epitomized by the cult of Kinnaru at Ugarit—and the rich mythology of Kinyras, to whom we may finally turn.

PART TWO

KINYRAS ON CYPRUS

9

Kinyras the Kinyrist

A FUNDAMENTAL OBSTACLE to connecting Kinyras with Kinnaru of Ugarit, and Syro-Levantine lyre-culture generally, is the relative scarcity and lateness of sources linking him to music. It is therefore best to begin by securing this elusive dimension, which should be the heart of Kinyras. Once that is established, his extra-musical associations can then be explored as special developments.

The Etymology of Kinyras

Homer's mention of Kinyras in *Iliad* 11[1] prompted an impressively learned disquisition by Eustathios in his twelfth-century commentary—our single richest source for the mythical Cypriot king, followed by choppy notices in the Pindaric scholia. One passage especially opens many windows on Kinyras' complex mythology:

> Kinyras ... was a son of Theias, according to some; he was a very wealthy king of Cyprus, who hosted the Achaeans when they came, promising that he would also send necessary supplies to Troy. But they say that after defaulting he was cursed by Agamemnon.[2] [They] also [say] that he perished competing musically with Apollo—<u>because he was an expert in music; which is even why Kinyras was named by derivation from the *kinýra*</u>—while his daughters, fifty in number, leaped into the sea and turned into halcyons.[3]

---

[1] See p1.
[2] I punctuate after Ἀγαμέμνονος following Erbse's treatment of the parallel passage in the Σ.
[3] Eustathios on Homer *Iliad* 11.20 (expanding upon material in the Homeric Σ): ὁ Κινύρας ... Θείαντος ἦν κατά τινας παῖς, βασιλεὺς Κύπρου ζάπλουτος, ὃς παριόντας τοὺς Ἀχαιοὺς ἐξένισεν, ὑποσχόμενος καὶ ἐν Ἰλίῳ πέμψειν τὰ ἀναγκαῖα. φασὶ δὲ αὐτὸν ἀμελήσαντα ἐπικατάρατον γενέσθαι ὑπὸ Ἀγαμέμνονος· καὶ αὐτὸν μὲν ἀπολωλέναι ᾠδικῶς ἁμιλλώμενον τῷ Ἀπόλλωνι ὡς

Chapter Nine

Eustathios has taken the bulk of this passage, somewhat denser than his usual rolling prose, from the corresponding Homeric scholia—one of his principal sources—with mainly cosmetic variations.[4] As often, however, he includes further details, highlighted in my translation. These are crucial: Kinyras was a musician, and took his name from the *kinýra*.[5]

The etymology is not Eustathios' own idea, for we will see it in a second Byzantine source, where the context is proverbial. And elsewhere he offers a parallel derivation of *kinýresthai* ('threnodize'[6]) from *kinýra*. He supports this assertion, raised in a discussion of the Homeric adjective *kinyrḗ* ('mournful'), with a remarkable allusion to professional threnodes:

> *kinyrḗ*: properly of those who sang songs for the dead, using the *kinýra*— which [sc. action] was even *kinýresthai*.[7]

This derivation is too tangential to the Homeric passage, with too many idiosyncratic details, to be *ad hoc* invention; evidently Eustathios had access to a source well-informed about lamentation-singing in some parts and periods of the *kinýra*'s native range. That he is reproducing ancient etymologies is

---

οἷα μουσικῆς τεχνίτην. διὸ καὶ Κινύρης ἐκλήθη παρωνύμως τῇ κινύρα. τὰς δὲ θυγατέρας αὐτοῦ πεντήκοντα οὔσας ἁλέσθαι εἰς θάλασσαν καὶ εἰς ἀλκυόνας μεταπεσεῖν.

[4] For Eustathios' relationship to the scholia, see van der Valk 1971–1987:LIX §70 and n2; Dickey 2007:23–24 with further references.

[5] Note how the added material has slightly disturbed the balance of μέν and δέ in the scholion. It is thus not strictly accurate to conclude that "la conséquence de cette mort pendant le concours justifiait son nom" (Baurain 1980a:7): Eustathios has drawn the etymology from elsewhere (see below).

[6] For this dominant meaning, Σ Homer *Iliad* 17.5: κινύρεσθαι γὰρ τὸ θρηνεῖν; Σ Apollonios of Rhodes 1.292: σημαίνει γὰρ τὸ θρηνῳδοῦσαι; *Suda* s.v. κινυρομένη· ὀδυρομένη, θρηνοῦσα; s.v. κινυρόμεθα· θρηνοῦμεν; Photios *Lexicon* s.v. κινύρεσθαι· ὀδύρεσθαι; Hesykhios s.v. κινύρεσθαι· θρηνεῖν, κλαίειν (he also defines the hapax χλουνάζειν as κινύρεσθαι). With this word I shall mark the upsilon long (*kinýresthai*) to help keep the issue of vocalization in mind.

[7] Eustathios on Homer *Iliad* 17.5: Κινυρὴ δὲ κυρίως ἐπὶ ἀνθρώπων, οἳ κινύραις χρώμενοι ἀοιδὰς ἐπὶ τοῖς κειμένοις ἔμελπον, ὃ καὶ κινύρεσθαι ἦν. The feminine adjective occurs in a simile of a mother-cow standing κινυρή over a newborn calf; the comparison is to Menelaos guarding the fallen Patroklos (Homer *Iliad* 17.4–6). Space prohibits a detailed discussion of the passage and κινυρός itself. Fortunately this omission is not crucial, as the abundant material for κινύρα, κινύρεσθαι, and κινυρίζειν can by itself carry the coming arguments. I would simply state my view (and cf. Lorimer 1950:465) that κινυρός is indeed historically related to these words, as Eusathios and other sources assert, and that the Menelaos/Patroklos passage can be illuminated in light of the threnodic conventions which these words evoke (the cow's cry for its calf is already a trope of Sumerian lamentation poetics: see Heimpel, "Balang-Gods," Section 3c1). Κινυρή is glossed as οἰκτρά, θρηνητική, *vel sim.* in Apollonios Sophistes *Homeric Lexicon*, *Suda*, Photios *Lexicon*, Hesykhios, and *Anecdota Graeca* (Bachmann 1828–1829) s.v. κινυρή, κινυρόν (but Hesykhios also records what are clearly guesses from the Homeric context: ἁπαλή, 'soft, tender'; νέα, 'new, young'; s.v. κινυρόν· λεπτόν, 'slender, weak'; καπυρόν, 'loud'; ὀξύ, 'shrill'); Eustathios and Σ have οἰκτρόφωνος.

corroborated by the trope of Kinyras the Lamenter, present already in one of Ovid's Greek models.[8] Since the derivation of *kinýresthai* from *kinýra* is obviously of a piece with this, *the whole complex can be traced back at least to the Hellenistic period*.[9]

Of course this in itself does not guarantee that the etymologies were correct, as Hellenistic scholars delighted in fanciful lexical associations. But we saw that in the BA Near East the *kinnāru* was sometimes linked to mortuary cult and lamentation; I shall present further such material in Chapter 12, some bearing on *kinýra* itself in Greek sources. It may be objected that a *direct* connection between *kinýra* from *kinýresthai* is ruled out by the differing quantities of upsilon (y/ȳ).[10] But we shall see below that 'Greek' *kinýra* often represents a variety of linguistic cognates from the East, most of which did indeed contain the long second vowel.[11] We may conclude that the ancient impulse to associate all these words was generally justified.

The Conflict With Apollo

I have already noted the faulty cultural assumptions beneath the view of J. P. Brown—writing without knowledge of Kinnaru—that Eustathios' etymology of Kinyras < *kinýra* was a false, Christianizing interpretation.[12] The deficiency of this is still more evident from the larger context of the passage, since it cannot account for the further musical material which Brown did not address—the contest of Kinyras and Apollo.

Eustathios' summary exhibits many details that would appeal to a Hellenistic poet or early imperial mythographer: ethnographic trivia from a marginal locale, aetiological metamorphosis, and etymological wordplay. Besides the derivation of Kinyras from *kinýra* itself, the halcyons are born from a "leap" (*halésthai*) into the "sea," where *thálassan* may conceal a further play on *hála* ('brine') in an anterior source.[13] There was perhaps another pun on Apollo as 'the destroyer' (hence *apolōlénai*).

Yet the contest per se conforms to a well-known and generally older pattern, already found in Homer, relating to Apollo's Panhellenic displacement of or syncretism with epichoric 'rivals'.[14] Especially numerous are the Olympian's

---

[8] See p280–282.
[9] See especially p197n55, 280.
[10] See p188n6, 199–200.
[11] See p213–216.
[12] Brown 1965:207–208: cf. p4.
[13] The halcyon was also known as the ἁλιπορφυρίς: Thompson 1936:46.
[14] See e.g. GR:188–189: "Apollo brings death to Linos, Hyakinthos, and Neoptolemos ... The figure killed in this way is preserved in the divine domain as a dark reflection of the god. Even the

Chapter Nine

musical competitions: the flaying of Marsyas; the thieving young Hermes' threatening new lyre;[15] the killing of Linos for using linen lyre strings, or for putting his own musical ability on a level with the god's.[16] There is also Apollo's takeover of the Cretan deity Paiawon, echoed in his kidnapping of paian-singing priests in the *Homeric Hymn to Apollo*.[17]

So Apollo's contest with Kinyras is readily viewed as a cultural 'confrontation', whether through ongoing commerce between Greece and Cyprus, the transplantation and growth of Apollo-cult on the island itself, or both. And there are other mythological expressions of this encounter, which is *hostile* only in the present case.[18] All such constructions must echo the long-term historical adjacency of Aegean and Cypriot musical traditions, and more specifically their lyric strains.[19] We shall see much further evidence for this in what follows.

Now Kinyras' deception of Agamemnon is elsewhere attested and must derive from the lost epic *Kypria*.[20] But this episode was probably never linked to the contest with Apollo outside of a mythological handbook. In the imaginative reconstruction of C. Vellay, Agamemnon's curse called down *madness* on Kinyras, who thus challenged Apollo and was killed *by the god's arrows*, with his desperate daughters then throwing themselves into the sea.[21] But the italicized material has no basis in the text, and the Greek of the scholion and Eustathios can be punctuated to make a division into two separate myths a natural

---

Olympian god would not be what he is without this darker dimension."

[15] Franklin 2003:295–299.
[16] For Linos, see p306.
[17] *Homeric Hymn to Apollo* 388–544; cf. Burkert 1992:60, 63; Franklin 2006a:59–60. Homer knew a similar dispute between Apollo and Eurytos over archery: Homer *Odyssey* 8.224–228.
[18] See p221, 226–235, 410, 512.
[19] Engel 1841 1:273, 2:109–115, saw here rather a conflict between Phoenician/pipes and Greek/κιθάρα (comparable to Apollo and Marsyas). This interpretation depends upon a proposed etymological connection of Kinyras with the Phoenician γίγγρας-pipes used in Adonis-lament (Athenaios 174f, etc.). The phonetic similarity of Kinyras and Gingras is admittedly striking, and some real connection should perhaps not be ruled out (see further p145, 202–204, 299n117). But recent scholarship has made clear that lyre and pipes were not immemorial enemies; their conflict emerged in the later fifth century, especially in Athens, where the αὐλός spearheaded the so-called New Music, the strong demotic associations of which implicated the instrument in contemporary social struggles (Wilson 1999; Martin 2003; Csapo 2004; Franklin 2013). Engel's view was initially influential: Lenormant 1871–1872:255; Marquand 1887:335, "Kinyras was the personification of Phoinikian music, which was based upon the pipe"; Sayce 1898:264–265, proposing a further collateral form in Cenchreis/Kenkhreis (wife of Kinyras in Ovid *Metamorphoses* 10.435; Hyginus *Fabulae* 58); Roscher *Lex*. s.v. Kinyras (Stoll); HC:68–69 and n5, rather agnostic; Atallah 1966:312–313. It must have entered Cypriot encyclopedias, for the idea has come up in several conversations there.
[20] See p1 and n2.
[21] Vellay 1957:242, perhaps following Wagner 1891:182, *quo terrore perculsae* etc. (of the daughters).

reading.²² Madness and arrows aside, a king's curse provoking a musical contest seems a very tenuous link. Agamemnon's anger finds a more natural sequel in a Cypriot tradition treated by Theopompos, whereby the Mycenaean king and his men drove Kinyras from power.²³ Conversely, the many fatal confrontations between Apollo and upstart musicians strongly suggest that Eustathios' contest was originally a self-standing myth.

Kinyras' musical death and the metamorphosis of his daughters, however, are an organic unit.²⁴ The halcyon's lament was proverbial already for Homer,²⁵ suggesting a connection between Kinyras' ill-fated daughters and the topos of Kinyras 'The Lamenter' (see Chapter 12).²⁶ Note that *kinýresthai* became a Hellenistic mannerism to evoke the plaintive songs of halcyons, swallows, and other sorrowing birds.²⁷ This provides an attractive context for the curious *kinnyrídes*, which Hesykhios glosses as 'tiny little birds'.²⁸ The word is probably a poetic coinage, these creatures being otherwise unknown.²⁹ The feminine plural form, with what may be taken as a patronymic suffix, suggests something very close to 'daughters of Kinyras'.³⁰ In any case, Kinyras' halcyon-daughters probably aetiologized female choruses like those shown on the Cypro-Phoenician bowls, which feature lyres, pipes, frame-drums, and dancers (see Chapter 11). One may compare the metamorphosis of the Pierides, rivals of the Heliconian Muses, into magpies; or the Meleagrides, sisters of Meleager, who, as they lamented their brother's death, were transformed by Diana into guinea hens.³¹ Equally apposite is a fragment of Alkman (ca. 625), seemingly from a prelude to a Spartan maiden-dance, in which the *kitharōidós* imagines himself an aged male halcyon, born along by a young female chorus:

---

²² See n2 and n3 above.
²³ Theopompos FGH 115 F 103. See further p346–348.
²⁴ So rightly Baurain 1980b:304 ("étroitement liée").
²⁵ Homer *Iliad* 9.561–564, etc.: see Thompson 1936:47. For the poetic topos of lamenting birds generally, including halcyons, Levaniouk 1999.
²⁶ See p.289. The halcyon's ocean habitat might also recall Kinyras' own maritime associations: p326–330.
²⁷ See e.g. [Moskhos] *Lament for Bion* 37–44, 46–49 (κινύρατο at 43). Swallows and κινύρεσθαι: *Greek Anthology* 5.237.1 (Agathias Scholasticus); 7.210.5 (Antipatros of Sidon). John Tzetzes, the twelfth-century Byzantine polymath, attests a more upbeat avine association: "the melodious κινύρα" was a nickname for the Iÿnx (Eurasian wryneck), a bird whose parts had many uses in love magic, and was called "an aid to lovers": *Chil.* 11.380, line 582, Οἱ δὲ κινύραν ἐμμελῆ [sc. τὴν ἴυγγα λέγουσι]; cf. 571, ἐρῶσι συνεργόν.
²⁸ Hesykhios s.v. κιννυρίδες· τὰ μικρὰ ὀρνιθάρια.
²⁹ This would account for the lexicographer's generic-sounding definition: he (or his source) was guessing, but had some limited context.
³⁰ Compare the Memnonides, sister-birds who arose from the ashes of Memnon's pyre: [Moskhos] *Lament for Bion* 43; Ovid *Metamorphoses* 13.600–622.
³¹ Ovid *Metamorphoses* 5.294–678; 8.534–546.

Chapter Nine

> O sweet-sounding, holy-voiced maidens, my limbs can
> Carry me no farther. Come now, come—let me be a *kērýlos*,
> Who flies above the blossom of the wave together with the halcyons,
> With fearless heart, a sea-purple sacred bird.[32]

The image of a lyrist surrounded by birds is very ancient; the two elements are conjoined in iconography of the second and even third millennium, in both the Aegean and ANE.[33] These scenes are generally held to represent divine epiphany, whether effected by a musician alone or as part of a larger performance.[34]

I conclude therefore that Eustathios and the scholion present a fusion of two originally independent Kinyras myths, both rooted in archaic mythmaking. But the contest in its present form has passed through Hellenistic or later hands. The halcyon daughters could have appeared in one of the fashionable Hellenistic compendia of metamorphoses—perhaps Boios' *Creation of Birds*.[35] Another more tangible candidate is the *Novel History* of the early imperial wonder-monger Ptolemy Khennos ('The Quail'); I defend this suggestion in Appendix B. The episodes were eventually conjoined by someone wishing to develop a coherent biography of the Cypriot king, though whether they were ever *causally* linked is very doubtful.

Outplaying Orpheus and Thamyris

A second Byzantine source that makes Kinyras a musician is an anonymous epistolary poem, from a thirteenth-century codex but itself somewhat older. The poet flatters a musician-friend, likening him to:

---

[32] Alkman 26 PMGF: οὔ μ' ἔτι, παρσενικαὶ μελιγάρυες ἰαρόφωνοι, / γυῖα φέρην δύναται· βάλε δὴ βάλε κηρύλος εἴην, / ὅς τ' ἐπὶ κύματος ἄνθος ἅμ' ἀλκυόνεσσι ποτήται / νηδεὲς ἦτορ ἔχων, ἁλιπόρφυρος ἰαρὸς ὄρνις. The poet's diction is obscure at several points, but this does not undermine the comparison. For the topos of the aged male halcyon, Thompson 1936:46–51; for the *kērýlos*, 139–140. For the citharodic/choral quality of these verses, see Nagy 1990:352 and Power 2010:202–203 and n44, noting the equally relevant fr. 38 ὅσσαι δὲ παῖδες ἀμέων ἐντί, τὸν κιθαριστὰν αἰνέοντι, "and all the younger girls among us praise the *kitharistḗs*" (trans. Power).

[33] Examples include Figure 4 (1e, 1k, 1p, 1r, 4a–f?, 4j–l, 5e, 5i, 5g, 5o, 5t), 5 (1gg, 8f, 8h–i), 11, 13, 22, 47 (IIa–b). Note that some of my images do not preserve the bird element (for which see DCPIL); in other cases it appears as a feature of the instrument itself.

[34] Cf. Power 2010:25 and n49.

[35] For a convenient list of Hellenistic metamorphoses collections, Cameron 2004:272. Boios' Ὀρνιθογονία: Philokhoros FGH 328 F 214 and the nine credited episodes in Antoninus Liberalis. Ovid contains a large number of bird-transformations, but his treatment of Alcyone followed two other traditions, represented by Nikandros (fr. 64 Gow/Schofield) and Theodoros (SH 750): see [Probus] on Vergil *Georgics* 1.399.

> Some Orpheus or Thamyris or even Kinyras—
> With songs they charmed the trees, the stones, and animals.[36]

These verses, though bland, preciously establish Kinyras as a proverbial musician. Indeed, the rhetorical structure, slight as it is, shows that he was considered the best of the lot. And the company he keeps verifies that Kinyras was a lyre-player. The poet was obviously familiar with the etymology known to Eustathios, which was therefore popular. Dismissing Kinyras' inclusion here as a late, Christianizing artifact would strain incredibly against the cumulative evidence. It may be, however, that his association with *kinýra*—the instrument of David, and a potent Christian symbol—did give him a renewed edge against the lyrists of Greek pagan mythology. Still, any such favor that Kinyras enjoyed must have been equally rooted in living musical traditions going back to pre-Christian antiquity. In the home range of the *knr*, 'Kinyras'—in whatever linguistic guise—will always have stood out from imported Aegean figures, no matter how firmly Hellenistic settlement in the East lodged them in local artistic and literary convention.

At first glance, admittedly, the musical deeds attributed to Kinyras are suspicious. In classical sources, the lyric control of animals and trees is credited not to Thamyris or Kinyras, but to Orpheus—who appears first in the poet's list. Moving rocks is typically associated with Amphion and building seven-gated Thebes, but Orpheus too can move them in Euripides.[37] Later authors sometimes lump Orpheus and Amphion together for their magical music.[38] Our verses are thus something of a pastiche, and one may suspect that the powers of Orpheus and Amphion have been extended to Thamyris and Kinyras by artistic license.

Yet why should we suppose that this lyric pastiche did not equally entail an eastern contribution? David we saw charms beast, bird, and nature, and Solomon had power over animal and mineral.[39] When Constantine Manasses, a twelfth-century chronicler, attributes to David's *kinýra* the power of charming "even stones," it is surely more than conflation with Amphion.[40] One should equally resist bland Orphic interpretations of such images as a sixth-century floor-mosaic from a synagogue in Gaza, where David (tastefully restored) charms snake,

---

[36] *Anecdota Graeca* (Cramer 1839-1841) 4:274.5-6: Ὀρφεύς τις ἢ Θάμυρις ἢ καὶ Κινύρας / ἔθελγον ᾠδαῖς δένδρα, θῆρας καὶ λίθους (for dating, see p265).
[37] Euripides *Iphigeneia at Aulis* 1211-1212; Apollonios of Rhodes 1.26-27; Konon *Narrations* FGH 26 F 1 (45); [Apollodoros] *Library* 1.3.2; Seneca *Hercules Furens* 569-572, *Medea* 228-229; [Orpheus] *Argonautika* 261-262; etc.
[38] Pausanias 6.20.18; Macrobius *Commentary on the Dream of Scipio* 2.3.8.
[39] See p178-179, 182-184.
[40] Constantine Manasses *Chronicle* 4687-4688: τῷ Δαβὶδ ἤχησε ... / ἡ καὶ τοὺς λίθους θέλγουσα καλλιμελὴς κινύρα (ed. Lampsides).

lion, and giraffe with his lyre (Figure 15).⁴¹ True, David is attired as a Byzantine emperor, and his instrument betrays centuries of Greco-Roman influence.⁴² Yet this was still a synagogue; the mosaic's dedicatory inscription is in Greek, but its donors have Jewish names. Hybrid iconography presupposes a receptive partner, and we have seen that the Syro-Levantine 'lyrist with animals' motif goes back to the EBA (Figure 6).⁴³ The mysterious, animal-charming 'kinyrist' of the eleventh-century 'Orpheus jug' holds more than enough eastern promise to account for the thaumaturgical Kinyras of our verses (Figure 13).⁴⁴ Jug and poem are separated by two millennia; but the gulf is largely spanned by the *knr* tradition itself. To 'outplay' Orpheus and Thamyris, Kinyras' musical roots must have been as deep and wide as theirs—and more so in the Byzantine East.

The 'Greek' *Kinýra*

And so we come to the basic conundrum that has caused scholars to reject, as late artifice, Eustathios' derivation of Kinyras < *kinýra*.⁴⁵ This is the apparent disparity between Kinyras' nonmusical qualities in early Greek poetry, and the comparatively late first attestation of *kinýra*, in the LXX translations of the third century. It is often stated or assumed that this word was borrowed directly from Hebrew; many have held that it was coined to translate *kinnōr*.⁴⁶ Admittedly, the most visible subsequent examples are either in overtly Judaic contexts like Josephus, or in Christian writers who might seem to elaborate that tradition.⁴⁷ But this cannot be right.

---

⁴¹ IAA 1980.3410: Ovadiah and Ovadiah 1987:60–62 no. 83, pl. LVIII.1, LIX, CLXXVIII; SAM:112 (no. 72).
⁴² Compare those of the Bar Kokhba coins: p180–181.
⁴³ Note the LXX's supernumerary Psalms 151, where David, in recollecting his youth, juxtaposes his pastoral duties with his instrument-making and psalmistry: "I shepherded my father's flocks. My hands made an instrument, and my fingers tuned this 'psaltery'" (ἐποίμαινον τὰ πρόβατα τοῦ πατρός μου. / αἱ χεῖρές μου ἐποίησαν ὄργανον, οἱ δάκτυλοί μου ἥρμοσαν ψαλτήριον, 1–2).
⁴⁴ See p159–161.
⁴⁵ Those rejecting Kinyras < *kinýra* include, besides Brown 1965:207–208, *Emprunts*:69n2; Chantraine 1968 s.v. κινύρα; Baurain 1980a:11–12; Baurain 1980b:304. Boisacq 1938 s.v. was undecided.
⁴⁶ Muss-Arnolt 1892:127; Lewy 1895:164 ("κινύρα = Hebr... . *kinnōr*"); von Kamptz 1956:129–130, 327 (conditioned by folk etymology with κινυρός); Frisk 1960 s.v.; Brown 1965:207; *Emprunts*:69 (apparently); Chantraine 1968 s.v. ("emprunt à l'hébreu *kinnōr*"); Kapera 1971:133 ("first used in the Septuagint ... to render the Hebrew *kinnōr*"); Dugand 1973:200 (remodeled via κινυρός); Tischler et al. 1977:577; Beekes 2009 s.v. follows von Kamptz.
⁴⁷ Hence the word was not given detailed treatment by E. Masson, who wished to concentrate on pre-Hellenistic borrowings (*Emprunts*:69n2).

Kinyras the Kinyrist

Figure 15 King David with animals. Sixth-century floor-mosaic, Gaza (restored). Jerusalem, IAA 1980.3410. Drawn from SAM no. 72.

One immediate challenge is posed by generic-sounding definitions in ancient lexica—for example, "*kinýra*: a musical instrument; *kithára*"—where there is no obvious reason to exclude extra-Biblical contexts.[48]

Besides, Heb. *kinnōr* could have been rendered much more accurately than '*kinýra*'. The form itself, indeed, decisively places the adaptation well before the LXX. The Semitic originals from which a 'Greek' adaptation could derive would either have preserved the ancient vocalization *kinnār-* which persisted in North

---

[48] *Suda*, Hesykhios, Photios *Lexicon*, *Lexica Segueriana*, *Anecdota Graeca* (Bachmann 1828–1829) s.v. κινύρα· ὄργανον μουσικόν, κιθάρα, *vel sim.*

195

Chapter Nine

Syria, or come from the Canaanite/Phoenician sphere, where *ā* had shifted to *ō* by ca. 1800–1400.⁴⁹ While the original, unshifted vocalization has indeed left a few traces in our sources (see below), the upsilon of *kinýra* cannot have represented *ā* at any point in Greek history. By the same token, the Greek letter can only have corresponded to Semitic *ō* or *ū* prior to the fourth or even fifth century BCE, by which time its original sound—a back closed, rounded vowel of variable length (ŭ/ū)—was already assuming a pronounced fronted quality (like German *ü*) in the Ionic dialect (whose sound values became a point-of-reference when the Ionic alphabet was adapted, via Athens, for use in regional inscriptions beginning in the fourth century).⁵⁰

A third-century Greek adaptation would thus have rendered Phoenician **kinnūr* as **kin(n)our* or even **kyn(n)our*. In fact, the latter form is found in a typically calculated passage of Lykophron, whose *Alexandra* is a Trojan Cycle in miniature—a monstrous display of Hellenistic learning masquerading as the ominous ravings of Kassandra.⁵¹ E. L. Brown argued convincingly that Paris is portrayed as a lyre-playing gadabout *en route* to Sparta, "passing the night by causing the nine-sail expeditionary band to leap-and-prance ... to the accompaniment of the 'eastern lyre' (*pròs kynoûra*)."⁵² This reinterpretation, which after all accords with Homer's own depiction of Paris as a lyrist,⁵³ brings sudden sense to a passage that was already obscure to ancient critics.⁵⁴ But why did

---

⁴⁹ See p55–57.
⁵⁰ Thus Herodotos could already represent the Persian name *Vištaspa* as *Hystáspēs*; conversely the use of omicron + upsilon (OY) to represent /*ū*/ in Boeotian inscriptions by ca. 350 shows that upsilon was no longer suitable: see Allen 1987:66–69.
⁵¹ Fraser 1979 persuasively confirms those critics (going back to antiquity) who would see the whole *Alexandra* as the work of a second Lykophron in the second century BCE (in accord with the description of Rome's power at 1229), rather than by 'the' Lykophron who was active in the early third; see also Fraser in OCD s.v. Lycophron.
⁵² Lykophron *Alexandra* 97–101 with Brown 1981:398–399. Brown's hypothesis treats the noun as third-declension (see below); but his κύνουρα and consistent but unexplained κίνυρα for traditional κινύρα (for -ā, cf. λύρα and κιθάρα) appear to be a lapse.
⁵³ Homer *Iliad* 3.54; Ptolemy Khennos in Photios *Library* 153a1–5; Plutarch *Alexander* 15, *Moralia* 331d; Ailianos *Various History* 9.38; Stobaios *Anthology* 3.7.52; Eustathios on Homer *Iliad* 3.24, 54. While most of these sources are late, the lyre was a standard attribute of Paris in later Archaic and Classical vase-painting: LIMC s.v. Alexandros nos. 9–11, s.v. Paridis Iudicium nos. 9, 13, 17, 20–21, 29, 37–39, 45, etc.; SIAG:38, 52 fig. 16, 104 fig. 9; Gantz 1993 2:569.
⁵⁴ Our only interpretive clue for what Scheer gives as πρὸς κύνουρα (99) is the scholiast's πρὸς τὰς τραχείας πέτρας; but this is easily explained by false inference from Γύθειον as an ἀκρωτήριον τῆς Λακωνικῆς. Brown's hypothesis does seem to be clinched by the bow-lyre imagery of 139–140 (τοιγὰρ ψαλάξεις εἰς κενὸν νευρᾶς κτύπον / ἄσιτα κἀδώρητα φορμίζων μέλη), noting especially that 'plucking' (ψαλάξεις) is atypical of Greek lyre-practice, but known for the *kinnōr* (see p58). Brown's ultimate argument, incidentally, is that Greek *Kynósoura* is a deformation via folk-etymology ('dog's-tail') of a Phoenician name (**kinnūr*) for the constellation Lyra. Add to his dossier that Lyra is called *kennar* in a Pahlavi translation of a Greek astrological work, the *Liber de stellis beibeniis*: see p61n89.

Lykophron adopt what from a contemporary Greek perspective was not only an archaizing phonetic spelling, but at odds with the short upsilon of *kinýra*, which on any account will have been current in the poet's time? As it happens, etymological speculation about *kinýra* and its seeming relations provided considerable entertainment for Alexandrian and other Hellenistic savants.[55] These parallels assure us that Lykophron's *pròs kynoûra* was a willful contrivance; conversely, *kinýra* must have had connotations he wished to avoid. Apart from any possible metrical convenience, the poet may have wanted to defamiliarize the word for poetic effect, enhancing his oriental characterization of Paris. Possibly he intended to present *kinýra* as pronounced in legendary times. On the other hand, long pronunciations of the second syllable would still have been heard in the Semitic dialects of Alexandria and the Levant. That Lykophron cast his coinage into the third declension, rather than the first of *kinýra*, equally accords with *Phoenician and Hebrew forms, which had lost their ancestral final vowels centuries earlier.[56] Remarkably, however, the poet gives his first upsilon its *contemporary* Greek value, as though tipping us off to his anachronistic novelty.[57] But then Lykophron is filled with riddles from start to finish.

---

[55] An explanation of κινύρα through a player's 'moving' (κινεῖν) of its strings (*Suda* s.v.: ἀπὸ τοῦ κινεῖν τὰ νεῦρα) was stretched to account also for κιθάρα and κίθαρις (*Anecdota Graeca* [Cramer 1839–1841] 4:35.13–14: παρὰ τὸ κίω τὸ κινῶ κίναρις καὶ κίθαρις; for κίναρις, see p198), and connected to their ability to 'move', i.e. arouse, love (*Etymologicum Gudianum* s.v. κίθαρις: ἀπὸ τοῦ κινεῖν τὸν ἔρωτα; s.v. κιθαρῳδός: παρὰ τὸ κινεῖν εἰς ἔρωτα τοὺς ἀκούοντας; *Anecdota Graeca* [Cramer 1839–1841] 4:35.10–11: κιθάρα, παρὰ τὸ κινεῖν εἰς ἔρωτα τοὺς ἀκούοντας, ἢ παρὰ τὸ κινεῖσθαι ῥᾳδίως). That these etymologies go back to Hellenistic speculation is confirmed by Apollonios' treatment of κινύρεσθαι (see below) and the pre-Ovidian topos of Kinyras the Lamenter (Chapter 12). Moreover, Lykophron's κυνουρ- as a contrived equivalent of κινυρ- is corroborated by the attempt of Apion (fl. ca. 25 CE) to derive κινύρεσθαι from κινεῖν + οὐρά ('tail') to explain Homer's bovine κινυρή (*Iliad* 17.5) in terms of 'tail-moovements' (Σ Apollonios of Rhodes 1.292 = Apion FGH 616 F 51 = 48 Neitzel: κυρίως δὲ κινύρεσθαί ἐστιν ἐπὶ βοὸς καὶ εἴρηται παρὰ τὸ κινεῖν τὴν οὐρὰν ἐν τῷ μυκᾶσθαι). In doing so, the scholiast says, Apion was "transferring an etymological discovery" by his Alexandrian predecessor Apollodoros of Athens (ca. 180–110), a Homerist disciple of Aristarkhos who had derived ταῦρος ('bull') from τείνειν ('stretch') and οὐρά ('tail'), i.e. in light of a bull's posterior tendencies (Apollodoros FGH 244 F 277: καὶ Ἀπίων δὲ εὑρὼν τὴν ἐτυμολογίαν παρὰ Ἀπολλοδώρῳ ταύτην, ὅτι ταῦρος λέγεται παρὰ τὸ τείνειν τὴν οὐράν, μετέθηκε τὴν εὕρεσιν τῆς ἐτυμολογίας). Hesykhios s.v. κινούρας· τοὺς κακούργους ἵππους (LSJ: "shaking the tail, a sign of weakness in a horse") is presumably related to these efforts.

[56] They are generally represented in the Amarna letters (as also at Ugarit), but occasional omissions indicate a transitional state (Sivan 1984:114–123), as do inaccuracies of representation (Albright 1934:29 §61). The endings were certainly lost well before the eighth century, since it induced further developments complete by that time, as seen in e.g. the Greek letter-name ἰῶτα: the new final syllable of *jád* was lengthened under accent to *jād*, which then became *jōd* under the Canaanite Shift, the influence of which continued to affect such cases of secondary (not inherited) *ā*. See Harris 1936:25 §8, 34–35 §11, estimating an eleventh-century loss; cf. Harris 1939:59–60; SL §21.13, 25.6.

[57] Assuming that the upsilon has been correctly transmitted.

In any case, it is certain that when the LXX represented *kinnōr* as *kinýra*, this was a true translation, using a 'Greek' word that long predated the new Hellenistic settlements that followed Alexander's conquests.[58] It must have been obvious, of course, to all educated Jews, that *kinýra* and Hebrew *kinnōr* were essentially the same word.[59] Yet Hebrew will hardly have been the *direct* source of *kinýra*. We must look to the Greco-Levantine interface more broadly.

O. Szemerényi repeatedly traced Semitic loanwords in Greek to specific periods and source dialects, using vocalization as a key diagnostic.[60] The phonetic and phonemic inventory of an adapting language naturally reshapes the original, and the outcomes are often more than random distortions.[61] But the situation is seriously complicated by unknown and undeciphered intermediaries; crucial missing pieces are Minoan and other pre-Greek languages of the Aegean and Cyprus. The impact of these lost tongues on early loanwords must not be underestimated.

There is sufficient evidence to show that *kinýra* was once but one of several adaptations of *knr* in the Eastern Mediterranean. The Greek lexicographic tradition has preserved a few sparse traces of Syrian (i.e. non-Canaanite/ Phoenician) originals. Thus, alongside Homeric *kítharis* ('lyre-playing' and later 'lyre'), one finds the parallel *kínaris*.[62] It is impossible to say which form was modeled on the other; perhaps they developed side-by-side. Still more striking, Hesykhios has an entry for a verb *kinarýzesthai*, which he defines as "to lament with groaning."[63] The derivation of this remarkable word from *knr* is again justified by the evidence, ANE and Greek alike, for the lyre's association with lamentation (Chapter 12). And the upsilon of *kinarýzesthai* surely echoes the ancient Semitic form *kinnāru(m)*, found at Ebla, Mari,

---

[58] As rightly seen by Albright 1964:171n47; Baurain 1980b:305.
[59] See above, p47 and n19.
[60] Szemerényi 1968 (criticizing the tendency of *Emprunts* to ignore vocalization and trace all loans to Phoenician); Szemerényi 1974; Szemerényi 1981; Szemerényi 1986.
[61] The view of Burkert is too categorical: "foreign words [sc. in Greek] ... are accepted only in perfectly assimilated form as to phonetics and inflexion ... They imitate and go into hiding, adapting themselves to the roots and suffixes of native Greek ... Popular etymology plays its role in metamorphosis; *no rules of phonetic evolution can be established*" (1992:35, my emphasis).
[62] *Anecdota Graeca* (Cramer 1839–1841) 4:35.13–14: κίθαρις· παρὰ τὸ κίω τὸ κινῶ κίναρις καὶ κίθαρις, ἢ παρὰ τὸ κίω, τὸ πορεύομαι ("*kínaris* and *kítharis* come either from *kíō* in the sense of *kínō* ['I move'], or from *kíō* in the sense of *poreúomai* ['I go']"). That κίναρις is as genuine a word as κίθαρις seems guaranteed by the awkward etymological explanation from κινῶ (see n55). One could suppose that an intended κινύρα was influenced by κίθαρις, but this would leave unexplained why κίθαρις was given etymological attention rather than the more obvious κιθάρα.
[63] Hesykhios s.v. κιναρύζεσθαι· θρηνεῖν μετὰ τοῦ γογγύζειν.

and Ugarit.⁶⁴ It is thus potentially quite old in Greek, given the EIA evanescence of inherited final vowels in Aramaic, Phoenician, and Hebrew.⁶⁵

These rare 'unshifted' forms are hard to pinpoint historically. One may think, for instance, of an adaptation from Aramaic during 'Philistine' settlement of the Amuq in the EIA, or a later trade colony like Al-Mina (ca. 800).⁶⁶ An equally attractive candidate is Cilicia, once part of the Hurro-Luwian state of Kizzuwatna in the LBA.⁶⁷ One should note here that Kinyras himself has a Cilician pedigree in several traditions, including one that makes his father Syrian.⁶⁸ Another was adopted—or contrived—by the mysterious Theodontius, a lost source for Boccaccio's *Genealogy of the Pagan Gods* (ca. 1350–1375). But it is probably just a striking coincidence that these authors, followed by Étienne de Lusignan, give the spelling Cinaras rather than Cinyras.⁶⁹

A Syrian musical milieu must also underlie the Cinara whom Horace loved in his youth—an allusion to the Syrian *musiciennes* who became a fixture of Roman streetlife after Pompey annexed the region in 64 BCE (see further Appendix C).

Another notable phonetic variant is the long upsilon of *kinȳresthai* versus the short vowel of *kinýra*, *kinyrízein*, and *Kinýras*.⁷⁰ There are other cases of Semitic loanwords preserving their vowel-length in Greek; there are also exceptions.⁷¹ While *kinȳresthai* normally relates to threnody in Greek sources,⁷² this need not require complete dissociation from *knr*, since the instrument's use in and/or association with ANE lamentative contexts provides the necessary semantic link (Chapter 12). Moreover, while the derivation of *kinýra* from a long-vowel original like **kinnūr* is beyond doubt, it is the long upsilon of *kinȳresthai* that corresponds more closely to the original Canaanite/Phoenician forms.

---

⁶⁴ It will have been readily adapted to a well-defined pattern of Greek verbs that add -ζω to stems in -υ (τονθορύζω, γρύζω, γογγύζω, etc.).
⁶⁵ Cf. p197 and n56 above; Aramaic: SL:270 (§32.24); CEWAL:400 §3.5 (Creason).
⁶⁶ For the fast-developing picture in the Amuq, see the concise synthesis of Hawkins 2009. Al-Mina: Boardman 1980.
⁶⁷ Cf. p96 above. Of course a substantial Phoenician cultural presence in the eighth century is attested by the inscriptions at Karatepe and Çineköy (Hawkins 2000 no. I.1, I.8; Tekoglu and Lemaire 2000). See the survey of Lipiński 2004:109–144.
⁶⁸ See Chapter 21.
⁶⁹ See Appendix F and G.
⁷⁰ Thus Lewy 1895:164 rightly noted that Kinyras cannot be derived *directly* from *kinȳresthai*. For *kinyrós*, see p188n7.
⁷¹ Vowel length preserved: ὕσσωπος, χιτών, σινδών, μνᾶ: see discussions of Szemerényi 1968:194–197; also καυνάκης, Aram. *gōnnakā*. Loss of vowel length: βύσσος (flax and flaxen cloth) versus Akk. *būṣu* and Heb. *būṣ*, cf. Phoen. *bṣ* (*Emprunts*:20–22); μύρρα (myrrh), Ug. *mr* (DUL s.v.), Can. *mu-ur-ra* (EA 269.16), Akk. *murru* (CAD s.v.), Aram. *mūrā*, Heb. *mōr* (cf. *Emprunts*:55; Chantraine 1968 s.v.). Some variations in vowel length are due to metrical utility, e.g. Σῐδόνες/Σῑδῶνος: Homer *Iliad* 23.743, *Odyssey* 15.425; cf. Brown and Levin 1986:78 with further permutations.
⁷² See definitions in n6 above.

Chapter Nine

Thus, we should trust the instincts of sources that connect *kinýra* and *kinýresthai* without batting an eye. Besides Eustathios, note several lexicon entries that are tied to a passage of Apollonios of Rhodes:

Amphikinȳrómenai: Apollonios. *kinȳrómenai*: playing music (*mélpousai*), singing; from the *kinýra*.[73]

For this etymology to work, the short-upsilon *kinýra* must stand generically for one or more ANE cognates that maintained the original long vowel; but such a universalizing usage is well paralleled (see below).

The relevant passage of Apollonios completes a simile that began with a sunny scene of happy, busy bees. These he compares, in a much discussed mood reversal,[74] with the Lemnian women 'whining about' the Argonauts, beseeching them not to leave:

> Thus indeed did they,
> Crying/Crooning (*kinȳrómenai*), pour themselves about the
>   men in earnest
> Saluting each with hands and speeches,
> Imploring the gods to bestow a harmless homecoming.[75]

The contrast between tenor and vehicle is jarring, discordant; many scholars agree with the scholiast that "the comparison is not sound nor harmonious in all respects ... the meadow rejoices and exults, and yet the city is in pain, which is why he says '*kinȳrómenai*'."[76] This straightforward reading is certainly natural, and accords with the earlier scene of Jason's mother lamenting his departure (using the same verb).[77] Yet this makes all the more striking the lexicographers' definition of the word as "singing" and "playing music." The viability of a non-lamentative sense is seconded by another lexical entry—this time with no clear link to Apollonios—which connects *kinýra* itself with a verb *kinýrō*, defined as both "threnodize" and "sing."[78] These 'positive' musical definitions are a kind of *lectio difficilior* that must be explained.

---

[73] Apollonios of Rhodes 1.882–883; *Etymologicum Genuinum* s.v. ἀμφικινυρόμεναι· Ἀπολλώνιος. κινυρόμεναι· μέλπουσαι, ᾄδουσαι· ἀπὸ τῆς κινύρας; much the same entry is found in *Etymologicum Symeonis* and *Etymologicum Magnum* s.v., the latter also with καὶ <κινύρετο>, ἐθρήνει. Μέλπειν often implies lyre-music: LSJ s.v.; Franklin 2003:297.

[74] See the excellent analysis of Clare 2002:179–187, with literature in n16.

[75] Apollonios of Rhodes 1.882–885: ὣς ἄρα ταίγε / ἐνδυκὲς ἀνέρας ἀμφὶ κινυρόμεναι προχέοντο, / χερσὶ δὲ καὶ μύθοισιν ἐδεικανόωντο ἕκαστον, / εὐχόμεναι μακάρεσσιν ἀπήμονα νόστον ὀπάσσαι.

[76] Σ. *ad loc.*: ἡ δὲ παραβολὴ οὐχ ὑγιὴς οὐδὲ εἰς πάντα ἁρμόζεται ... χαίρει καὶ ἀγάλλεται ὁ λειμών, καίτοι λυπεῖται ἡ πόλις, διό φησι κινυρόμεναι.

[77] Apollonios of Rhodes 1.292.

[78] *Etymologicum Gudianum* s.v. κινύρα· κιθάρα, ἐκ τοῦ κινύρω τὸ σημαῖνον τὸ θρηνῶ καὶ ᾄδω.

R. J. Clare has explicated, in the larger Lemnian episode, Apollonios' careful manipulation of emotional expectations, climaxing in the present scene with *kinyrómenai* being "the crux of the entire comparison"; it is "a jolt in itself to realise that lamenting is being compared to rejoicing ... a reflection of the sudden comprehension of the women as their idyllic interlude disintegrates and optimism turns to pessimism."[79] Given Hellenistic interest in *kinȳresthai* and its apparent cognates,[80] it would seem that Apollonios has exploited, in support of his purposefully dissonant simile, a semantic bifurcation between the celebratory and plaintive that was inherent in the word.[81] This reading is supported by several performative nuances that result. Lamentation could be addressed to the gods apotropaically against future misfortune.[82] That is clearly operative here, and later we shall see a *kinýra* used in just this way.[83] But the image of women streaming out of a city equally evokes the ANE custom, attested in the Bible, of greeting victorious, homecoming warriors with celebratory music—just the outcome for which the Lemnian women beseech the gods.[84] This perverted 'coming out' scene neatly reprises the further careful permutation with which the Lemnian sojourn began—when the women, fearing that the arriving Argonauts were enemies, poured forth under arms.[85]

I conclude that Apollonios, like Lykophron, has carefully crafted his passage around an ongoing poetic and scholarly dialogue about *kinȳresthai* and its presumed cognates.

The phonetic discrepancy between forms in *y* and *ȳ* is explicable in regional terms, resulting from parallel adaptations in separate linguistic spheres. Leaving aside many self-conscious literary examples of *kinȳresthai* in Hellenistic and later poetry,[86] the harder demographic evidence of epigraphy indicates the word's popular currency in Anatolian funerary inscriptions of the Roman era.[87]

---

[79] Clare 2002:184.
[80] See p197 and n55 above.
[81] There is a similarly willful mixture of joyous and plaintive context with *kinȳresthai* at 3.259 and 664.
[82] See p30, 279.
[83] See p302-303.
[84] See p126.
[85] Clauss 1993:140–142; Clare 2002:179–181.
[86] The verb, like the adjective *kinyrós*, became a standing resource for Hellenistic authors, and a mannerism in late epic; they regularly refer to, or presuppose, lamentation in mythological contexts. A representative sample includes Kallimakhos *Hymns* 2.20 (see p126); Apollonios of Rhodes, passages already cited and 4.1063; Triphiodoros 430; Nonnos *Dionysiaka* 2.157, 4.199, etc.; Quintus Smyrnaeus 6.81, 7.335, etc; Kollouthos 216.
[87] Three cases are undated but belong to the first centuries CE. The type may be exemplified by SEG 29:1202 (Lydia), an epigram for a Iulianos by his sons and wife, "who has miserable pain in her heart, lamenting your death my youthful husband" (ἥ τε | σύνευνος ἔχου|σα φρεσὶ λύπην |

Chapter Nine

Here *kinýresthai* describes lamentation—or better threnody (see Chapter 12)—by the bereaved when dedicating the stone; by committing this act to an ostensibly permanent medium, a one-time funerary rite was effectively converted into a perpetual mortuary cult.[88] That *kinýresthai* was particularly at home in Anatolia would also help explain a passage in Aristophanes' *Knights* (424 BCE), where the verb describes "lamenting a lyre-pipe concert (*synaulían*), the mode of Olympos" (the legendary Phrygian aulete).[89]

If *kinýresthai* is indeed to be connected with *knr*, as seems inevitable—and note that an Anatolian context could be equally indicated by Lykophron's Paris and even Apollonios' Lemnian women—one might look to the westerly Phoenician expansion along the Anatolian coast in the eighth and seventh centuries, attested by inscriptions in Cilicia and Pamphylia, and other sporadic traces from Lycia and Caria in southwestern Anatolia.[90] Compare the threnodic Phoenician pipes known as *gíngras*, which our sources indicate took special hold among the Carians.[91] The word is also said to be an alternative name for Adonis:

> The *gíngras* is a kind of small *aulós*, mournful and emitting a funereal sound, of Phoenician discovery and suitable for the Carian muse. And the Phoenician language calls Adonis Gingras, and their *aulós* takes its name from this.[92]

It has long been proposed to derive *gíngras* and several related words from *knr*, and to see Adonis-Gingras as a doublet of Kinyras.[93] If this derivation is right,

---

ἀμέγαρτον· / σεῖο | κινυρομένη θάνα|τον θαλεροῦ παρα|κοίτου, 7–13); similarly Calder 1928 319, cf. SEG 6:290 (Gözlu, Galatia); Mitchell et al. 1982 149e (Meyildere, Galatia). Of two examples from Thessaly, one lacks any Anatolian association (Peek 1955 694: Thessalian Thebes, third [?] century CE), but in the second the mother was evidently of Anatolian background, Dounda being a variant of Douda, common in Asia Minor (I.Thess.I no. 43B, Ktiri, third century CE; SEG 28:515). The form κινυραμένη in 5–6 is slightly puzzling: although an aorist is rightly read at [Moskhos] *Lament for Bion* 43 (despite LSJ s.v. κινύρομαι), here the funerary context makes one expect a present participle, as in the three foregoing parallels. Perhaps it is a lapicidal error (note that the cutter erroneously gave the accusative κινυραμένην).

[88] See further p70n54.
[89] Aristophanes *Knights* 9–11 (ξυναυλίαν κλαύσωμεν Οὐλύμπου νόμον. / μυμῦ μυμῦ μυμῦ μυμῦ μυμῦ μυμῦ. / τί κινυρόμεθ᾽ ἄλλως). Μυμῦ obviously imitates the αὐλός, but συναυλία implies an equal lyric component: see p295 and n95.
[90] For Cilicia (Karatepe, etc.): see p252n50. For the Cebel Ires Daği inscription (Pamphylian border), Mosca and Russell 1987 (dating to ca. 625–600); Lipiński 2004:128–130 (ca. 650), cf. 141–143 for a survey of data relating to Lycia and Caria.
[91] See p145n200. Sources for Carian lamenters generally: Reiner 1938:66.
[92] Pollux *Onomastikon* 4.76: γίγγρας δὲ μικρός τις αὐλίσκος γοώδη καὶ θρηνητικὴν φωνὴν ἀφιείς, Φοῖνιξ μὲν ὢν τὴν εὕρεσιν, πρόσφορος δὲ μούσῃ τῇ Καρικῇ. ἡ δὲ Φοινίκων γλῶττα Γίγγραν τὸν Ἄδωνιν καλεῖ, καὶ τούτῳ ὁ αὐλὸς ἐπωνόμασται.
[93] See p145, 190n19, 299n117. The unstable representation of Semitic stops is a known phenomenon: cf. Szemerényi 1968:197; for *g* < *k*, cf. e.g. Gk. γρύψ < Sem. kᵊrūb (Szemerényi 1974:150);

gíngras would constitute yet another epichoric adaptation, presumably localized in Caria if one may trust the sources.[94] Although it would result in a remarkable semantic shift from lyre to pipes,[95] this might be explicable via the poetics of ritual performance.[96]

"Our *Kenyristḗs* Apollo": Playing the *Kinýra* on Cyprus

The Anatolian associations of *kinýresthai* encourage us to seek the origin of *kinýra* and other short-upsilon forms *elsewhere*. Admittedly parts of Anatolia remain poorly documented. Yet one cannot ignore Cyprus as a probable locus for parallel adaptations, since the island was the epicenter of Greek cultural and linguistic interface with Syria and the Levant from at least the twelfth century BCE.[97] This privileged position is reflected in a Cyprocentric conception of the eastern Mediterranean that must equally go back to the EIA migrations. Already for Homer, Menelaos' homecoming route from Troy took him "wandering through Cyprus and Phoenicia and the Egyptian people"—that is, clockwise around what the geographer Strabo, commenting on the passage, called "the lands around Cyprus."[98] The same idea helps account for the description of Paphos as 'the center of the world' (*gês omphalós*), alluding to its far-famed sanctuary, which rivaled Delphi itself.[99] Even after Greek horizons were expanded in the Hellenistic age, the island's cultural prominence was out of proportion to its size; this is well illustrated by the *Tabula Peutingeriana*, a thirteenth-century map going back to a Roman original of later antiquity, with still older antecedents.[100] Here Cyprus, greatly magnified, is the focus of the eastern Mediterranean (Figure 16).[101]

---

the opposite may be seen in καυνάκης/γαυνάκης < Aram. *gōnnakā*, or other Semitic forms (Hemmerdinger 1970:50–51).

[94] For example, with backward shift of accent from Cypro-Phoenician **Kinnýras* leading to syncopation of the second syllable and dissimilation of -*nn*- to -*ng*-?

[95] Brown 1965:207.

[96] For such an interpretation of the Ugaritic text RS 24.257, see p141–146. Further considerations, p291–303.

[97] I am not insisting on an absolute division between Cyprus and Anatolia; if *kinýresthai* may indeed be referred to Phoenician influence, *a fortiori* such a form would be viable on Cyprus itself with its sizeable Phoenician population. As I shall argue, however, the short-upsilon forms go back on the island to the LBA, and would thus be at least a parallel adaptation there: see p272–278.

[98] Homer *Odyssey* 4.81–85 with Strabo 1.2.32 (τὰ περὶ Κύπρον χωρία).

[99] Hesykhios s.v. γῆς ὀμφαλός· ἡ Πάφος καὶ Δελφοί. See further p411, 416.

[100] For the antecedents of the *Tabula Peutingeriana*, see Bowersock 1983:169–186 passim (tracing to Agrippa); Talbert 2010, Chapter 5.

[101] Admittedly this owes something to the mapmaker's narrowing of water-bodies to accommodate land-masses. Nevertheless, the island is given relatively prominent treatment. Like Crete and Sicily, Cyprus features a road network, and only Cyprus and Crete have the word *Insula*

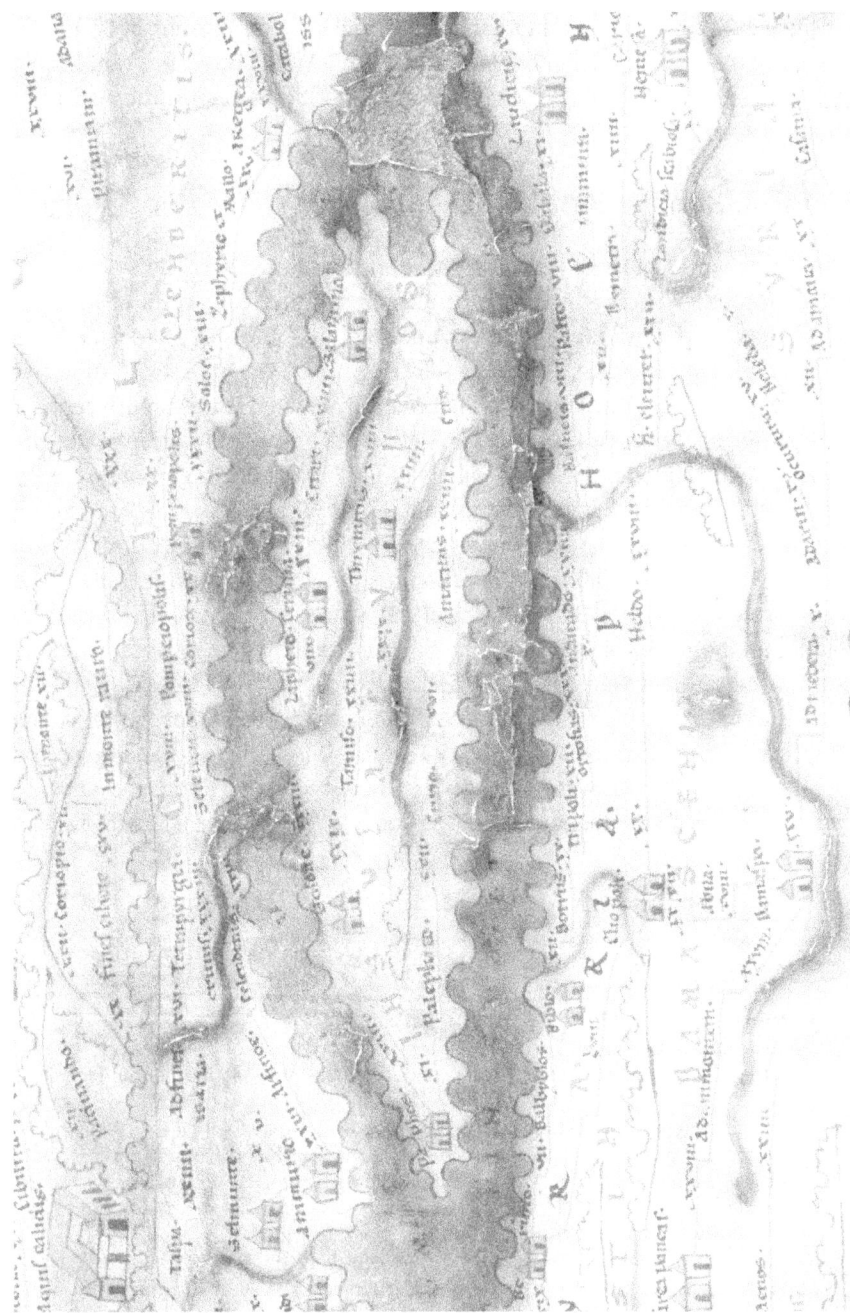

Figure 16 Cyprus and the eastern Mediterranean according to the Tabula Peutingeriana. Used by permission of the Österreichische Nationalbibliothek, Vienna.

The island's central location and large concentration of Greek-speakers provide a compelling explanation for how a specifically Greco-Cypriot form—I mean *kinýra*—could eventually prevail in the Hellenistic koine. Until recently this would have been but an educated guess. It can now be corroborated by evidence from Cyprus itself.

In 1959, a marble slab was discovered in secondary use at a church in the village of Nikokleia, near Palaipaphos. It contains an oath of allegiance to Tiberius, taken by the Community of Cyprus on the Roman emperor's accession in 14 CE.[102] Several gods are invoked as witnesses:

> By our *Akraía*-Aphrodite and our Kore and our *Hylátēs*-Apollo and our *Kenyristḗs*-Apollo and our saviors the Dioskouroi and the island's common *Boulaía*-Hestia and the common ancestral gods and goddesses of the island and the god Caesar, august descendant of Aphrodite, and eternal Rome and all other gods and goddesses ...[103]

When T. B. Mitford first published the stone in 1960, he read Apollo's second cult-title as *Ke[r]ynḗtēn*, connecting it with Keryneia on the north coast. This was not entirely satisfactory: the site is rarely mentioned in ancient sources, and none attests a connection with Apollo.[104] J.-B. Cayla has recently made a vital contribution, perceiving that the correct reading is in fact *Ke[n]yr[i]stḗn*. This I can corroborate from my own examination of the stone.[105]

---

written in full. All other islands, including the larger Sardinia, are represented very schematically. See Talbert 2010:89–90, 108.

[102] For the development of τὸ κοινὸν τὸ Κυπρίων in Cypriot inscriptions, HC:185, 233–234; Mitford 1960c:77–78; HIOP 99 and notes.

[103] Kouklia-Palaipaphos Museum, inv. 85; Mitford 1960c, cf. SEG 18:578; Karageorghis 1960:274 and fig. 53), revised reading by Cayla 2001 (SEG 51:1896) = I.Paphos 151, reprised in Cayla 2005 (SEG 55:1534): [νὴ τ]ὴν ἡμετέραν Ἀκραίαν Ἀφροδίτην κα[ὶ] | τὴ[ν ἡμ]ετέραν Κόρην καὶ τὸν ἡμέτερον Ὑλά|τη[ν Ἀπόλλ]ω καὶ τὸν ἡμέτερον Κε[ν]υρ[ι]στὴν (Cayla 2001: Κε[ρ]υνήτην Mitford 1960c) | Ἀπόλλω καὶ τοὺς ἡμετέρους Σωτῆρας | Διοσκούρους καὶ τὴν κοινὴν τῆς νήσου | Βουλαίαν Ἑστίαν καὶ θεοὺς θεάς τε τοὺ[ς] | κοινοὺς τῆς νήσου πατρῴους καὶ τὸν | ἔκγονον τῆς Ἀφροδίτης Σεβαστὸν Θεὸν | Καίσαρα καὶ τὴν Ἀέναον Ῥώμην καὶ τοὺ[ς] | ἄλλους θεοὺς πάντας τε καὶ πάσας κτλ.

[104] Cf. HC:87.

[105] Cayla 2001:78–79; *pace* Fujii 2013:80. I verified Cayla's observation of a curve consistent with P, not N, in the fifth position. To his upper and lower horizontal strokes, requiring restoration of Σ or Ε instead of Mitford's Η (four letters from the end), I can add that the sloping inner strokes of the Σ are just visible, at certain angles of light, along the left edge of the lacuna (having apparently helped shape the break). I thank the Department of Antiquities for permission to examine the stone at Kouklia on May 25, 2012; and J. Webb, G. Fawkes, and especially R. Walker for additional eyes and discussion. Walker also pointed out that ἡμέτερον κε[ν]υρ[ι]στήν yields a dactylic sequence (on the reasonable assumption that it shares the short upsilon of Zenodotos' κινυρίζειν [see below] and the short-voweled Kinyras himself, both of which are metrically guaranteed).

Chapter Nine

On Cyprus, and especially at Paphos, *kenyristḗs* inevitably evokes Kinyras. It clearly interprets the legendary Cypriot king as a form of Apollo.[106] But what exactly is implied?

As Mitford saw, the qualification of the oath-gods as 'ours' indicates their distinctively Cypriot status. The particular combination of divinities, however, remains obscure, with several being otherwise poorly attested. Mitford speculated that they were intended to represent the island regionally, and although the geographical associations of Kore and the Dioskouroi are too poorly known to permit conclusive demonstration, the hypothesis would accord well enough with the totalizing reference to "the common ancestral gods and goddesses of the island."[107] Cayla uses this pan-Cypriot perspective to explain the surprising absence of such famous Cypriot powers as Paphian Aphrodite and Salaminian Zeus, strongly associated with particular cities.[108] But it is possible that these and other gods were indeed invoked in a lost stone containing the oath's preamble.[109] In any case, while the precise rationale behind the surviving *theoì hórkioi* is still unclear, "Our *Kenyristḗs* Apollo" is a uniquely Cypriot figure.

Any deeper appreciation depends upon determining the meaning(s) of *kenyristḗs*. The word is clearly related to the verb *kinyrízein*, which, though only thrice attested, must once have been more widely current than this would suggest.[110] These two words are most naturally interpreted in light of three exact parallels from the world of lyre-playing, the agent-verb pairs *kitharistḗs-kitharízein*,

---

[106] The certain Κεν- for expected Κιν- is unproblematic, though interesting. Cayla 2001:78–79 (cf. Cayla 2005:229) rightly notes other oscillations of ι/ε in Cypriot inscriptions (e.g. Idalion/Edalion, Kition/Ketion). Because inherited ε becomes ι before ν in Cypriot (e.g. ἰν for ἐν, cf. Bechtel 1921–1924 1:403 §15; Masson 1988a:21; Ruijgh 1988:143; Risch 1988:71, 76), Cayla suggests that Κεν- may be hyperdialectal—an artificial form induced by a desire to create an impression of antiquity (the phenomenon is otherwise attested in Hellenistic Cypriot inscriptions: Steele 2013:150–151, 238–239). That Κεν- should reflect a *genuinely* ancient form is complicated by the agreement of Linear B *ki-nu-ra* (see Chapter 17) and Kinyras in Homer, on the one hand, and the consistent vocalization of *knr* as *kin-* at Ebla, Mari, Ugarit, Emar, and Alalakh. I recognize the potential ambiguity of representing vowels in these early scripts (note that oscillations between *e* and *i* vis-à-vis later Greek forms are not uncommon in Linear B [Risch 1966:154; Ruijgh 1967:71–72], and that an early Cypriot adaptation may have been exceptional. Yet Κεν- could also be a *later* development through the influence of Phoenician, where "short *i* was rather lax and open" (hence Μιλκ-/Μελκ-, etc.): SL §21.13; cf. ICGSL:48–49 [§8.74, 77]. Cf. Lipinski 2004:62, seeing Phoen. influence behind Edalion/Idalion; the same should apply to Kition/Ketion, a largely Phoenician site.

[107] Mitford 1960c:77.

[108] Cayla 2005:228.

[109] Fujii 2013:78–82.

[110] The scribal error of Κινυρίδαι for Κινυράδαι in Σ Pindar *Pythian* 2.27b might point in this direction.

phormiktḗs-phormízein, and *lyristḗs-lyrízein*.[111] *Kenyristḗs* should therefore simply mean 'the *kinýra*-player', and *kinyrízein* 'to play the *kinýra*'.

And yet *kinyrízein* has been almost universally interpreted along different lines. This misunderstanding derives from the earliest attestation, a rhapsodic variant in the *Iliad* championed by Zenodotos (fl. ca. 285), Homeric critic and first librarian of Alexandria; it was later disputed by Aristarkhos of Samothrace (ca. 216–144), who advanced his own preference, which is itself distinct from what has come down in the manuscript tradition. We know of this scholarly issue from Aristonikos, a critic of the Augustan age who mentioned it in his Homeric commentary, along with many of Aristarkhos' other readings, which he often contrasts with those of Zenodotos. The verse in question forms part of Achilles' rebuttal of Phoinix who, as a member of the embassy sent by Agamemnon to soothe the sulking warrior, has just finished his cautionary exemplum about the destructive pride of Meleagros. The three versions are as follows:

> Traditional: Do not confuse my angry-heart (*thymón*) with your lamenting and wailing (*odyrómenos kaì akheúōn*).[112]
>
> Zenodotos: Do not confuse my angry-heart with your *kinýra*-lamenting (*odyrómenos kinyrízōn*).[113]
>
> Aristarkhos: Do not confuse my angry-heart in my breast with your moaning (*enì stḗthessin akheúōn*).[114]

We are told that Zenodotos treated *odyrómenos kinyrízōn* "as if it meant *thrēnôn*"— that is, 'singing a funeral dirge'. One can hardly suppose that Zenodotos did not know what the phrase meant: *odyrómenos*, and the correspondence of *kinyrízōn* with *akheúōn*, guarantee that *kinyrízein* could be at least connected with lamentation. And yet this would be readily explained by the *kinýra*'s use in threnody.[115] According to Aristonikos (evidently reproducing the opinion of Aristarkhos) Zenodotos' variant was "un-Homeric and out-of-character"

---

[111] Adduced with different emphasis by Cayla 2001:80–81.
[112] Homer *Iliad* 9.612: μή μοι σύγχει θυμὸν ὀδυρόμενος καὶ ἀχεύων. Cf. *Iliad* 24.128, *Odyssey* 2.23, 4.100, 14.40.
[113] Zenodotos: μή μοι σύγχει θυμὸν ὀδυρόμενος κινυρίζων.
[114] Aristarkhos: μή μοι σύγχει θυμὸν ἐνὶ στήθεσσιν ἀχεύων.
[115] See Chapter 12.

Chapter Nine

(*parà tò prósōpon*).¹¹⁶ Not all modern scholars have been persuaded by this condemnation,¹¹⁷ but editors have generally preferred the traditional version for its "*parallelismus membrorum* and the accumulation of synonyms," while the variants of Zenodotos and Aristarkhos have been attributed to the Alexandrian desire to avoid such constructions, diversify at the expense of formulaic diction, and increase sentimentality.¹¹⁸ Still, the variant enjoys solid precedents in the formulaic system. *Odyrómenos stenakhízō*, attested four times in the same position, would readily support a substitution of *kinyrízōn* in a lamentative sense without requiring that the two be strictly synonymous.¹¹⁹ Crucial here is the frequent occurrence of *kitharízōn* ('playing the *kithára*') and collateral forms in the same verse-final position, typically preceded by an adverbial expression.¹²⁰

When we come to consider *kinýra*-lamentation in more detail, I shall argue that Zenodotos' variant introduces interesting nuances to the scene.¹²¹ But first we must corroborate this 'lyric' interpretation of *kinyrízein*. Of the word's two other attestations, which Classicists have hitherto overlooked,¹²² it will suffice to present only the earlier here. The second, being quite late (ninth century), raises further historical issues and needs more convoluted argument; it is analyzed in Appendix D.

---

¹¹⁶ Aristonikos Grammaticus, *On the Signs of the Iliad*, 168 Friedlander: μή μοι σύγχει θυμὸν ἐνὶ στήθεσσιν ἀχεύων> ὅτι Ζηνόδοτος γράφει <ὀδυρόμενος, κινυρίζων>, οἷον θρηνῶν. ἔστι δὲ οὐχ Ὁμηρικόν, καὶ παρὰ τὸ πρόσωπον; Σ Homer *Iliad* 9.612: <ὀδυρόμενος καὶ ἀχεύων:> ὅτι Ζηνόδοτος γράφει <ὀδυρόμενος, κινυρίζων>, οἷον θρηνῶν. ἔστι δὲ οὐχ Ὁμηρικὸν καὶ παρὰ τὸ πρόσωπον. Ἀρίσταρχος δὲ <ἐνὶ στήθεσσιν ἀχεύων>. Aristonikos may, however, merely be offering his own interpretation of the divergence (so Duentzer 1848:131 and n62); Aristarkhos' emendations were often not provided with commentary, and Aristonikos displays periodic independence and unreliability *vis-à-vis* his predecessor. See van der Valk 1963 1:537 (on Aristarkhos) and 1:553–592 (Aristonikos' methods).

¹¹⁷ Duentzer 1848:131 and n62, approved Zenodotos' two participles in asyndeton, finding the variant *significantior ... Achilles rem recte auget, Phoenicem monens, ne lamentationibus ipsum fatiget ... Hic asyndeton gradiationem bene indicat. Aristarchos scripturam minus vivide rem describentem recepit.* Cf. Lorimer 1950:465, "it hardly deserves the strictures of Aristarchos."

¹¹⁸ See van der Valk 1963 2:1–37 and 113–118, especially 21 and 113–114 for the present verse (and quotation); cf. van der Valk 1949:104–105.

¹¹⁹ Ὀδυρόμενος στεναχίζω: *Odyssey* 1.243, 9.13, 11.214, 16.195.

¹²⁰ *Homeric Hymn to Apollo* 515 (ἐρατὸν κιθαρίζων), cf. *Homeric Hymn to Hermes* 424 (λιγέως κιθαρίζων), 432 (ἐπωλένιον κιθαρίζων), 455, 510; *Homeric Hymn to Aphrodite* 80 (διαπρύσιον κιθαρίζων). Also *Apollo* 201, *Hermes* 17, 475.

¹²¹ See p316–318.

¹²² Thus van der Valk 1963 2:21, asserts that *kinyrízein* is "not attested in Greek," and that Zenodotos "seems to have coined a new word, derived from κινυρός"; accordingly he interprets *kinyrízōn* as 'whimpering'. The same etymological connection was drawn by Duentzer 1848:131 and n62. So far as I have found, only PGL s.v. κινυρίζω has recognized the word's correct meaning ('make music') *vis-à-vis* the later attestations.

The *Acts of Xanthippe and Polyxena* are a pair of hagiographical romances variously dated between the third and fifth centuries CE, recounting the Christian conversions of the title figures—the wife and sister-in-law of Roman Spain's governor in the time of Claudius.[123] At the relevant juncture, Xanthippe had sneaked out of the house, as her Christ-resisting husband slept, to seek the apostle Paul. Assaulted *en route* by a troop of demons, Paul materialized like a superhero to the rescue, after which he promptly baptized her as a precaution against further mishap. Safely home, Xanthippe pours out praise of Jesus and Paul:

> I desire to keep silent, since human reason makes me afraid, lest I have not the grace of eloquence. I desire to keep silent, and am compelled to speak, for someone inflames and sweetens me within. If I say, I will shut my mouth, (yet) there is someone playing the *kin(n)ýra* in me (*éstin tis kinnyrízōn en emoí*) ... Is it not that teacher that is in Paul ... filling the heavens, speaking within and waiting without, sitting on the throne with the father and stretched upon the cross by man?[124]

Xanthippe's irrepressible inner joy clearly does not support a threnodic sense for *kinnyrízōn*. Some scholars, seeking a parallel with the verb *minyrízein*, suggest a translation like "someone murmurs inside of me."[125] Yet *minyrízein* typically connotes despondency; even its most positive possible sense, 'sing in a low tune, warble, hum', will hardly suit Xanthippe's ebullience.[126] The metaphor must convey the ineffable and intimate—even erotic[127]—exultation with which Jesus fills Xanthippe. For this, thrilling lyre-music would be highly apt. Divine praise-hymns and other celebratory and amatory occasions are well known for the *kinnōr* in the Bible and the *kinnāru* elsewhere in the Syro-Levantine world,

---

[123] Gorman 2003:6–15; debt to Greek novel: Hadas 1953:xiii.

[124] *Acts of Xanthippe and Polyxena* 14 (James 1893:68, cf. 54 for dating): trans. after Roberts et al. 1885–1896 9:209.

[125] So in Roberts et al. 1885–1896 9:209. Leumann 1950:241–243 sought semantic enlightenment from the parallel pairs κινυρός/κινύρεσθαι and μινυρός/μινύρεσθαι and an appeal to the principle of *Reimwortbildung* (see generally Güntert 1914; cf. Frisk 1960 s.v. κινυρός). But his tidy historical scheme (μινυρίζω + μύρομαι > μινύρομαι; μινυρίζω + κινυρός > μινυρός; κινυρός + μινύρομαι > κινύρομαι) assumes that μινυρίζειν and κινυρός are the oldest forms because they alone are in Homer. The inadequacy of this approach is sufficiently shown by the lamentative κιναρύζεσθαι, which must be quite early (see p65n64). Two senses were rightly distinguished by Ptolemy of Ascalaon, Heylbut 1887:402.11–12 = Ammonios *On Similar and Different Words* 321: μινυρίζειν μὲν λέγουσι τὸ ἠρέμα προσᾴδειν, μινύρεσθαι δὲ τὸ θρηνεῖν· τὸ δ' αὐτὸ καὶ κινύρεσθαι.

[126] LSJ s.v.

[127] An erotic reading fits well with the thematic interplay of sexuality, asceticism, Christian conversion, and marital harmony analyzed in this and related works by Gorman 2003:27–44 et passim. Recall the ancient linking of κίθαρις, κιθάρα, and κίναρις with κινεῖν ('move') and erotic arousal (n55 above), and cf. *Analecta Hymnica Graeca, Canones Decembris*, Day 26, Canon 51, Ode 8.57–58 (ed. Kominis/Schirò): καὶ κινύρα ψυχὰς θέλγουσα / πρὸς ἔρωτα τὸν ἔνθεον (of David's lyre).

and are equally attested in Gk. for *kinýra*—Photios defining "musics" as "glad delights as from pipes and *kinýra*, and similar things."[128] This lyric interpretation is corroborated by the *-nn-* of *kinnyrízōn*, which betrays an association with ANE forms like *kinnōr* (see below). In the *Acts of Xanthippe*, therefore, we have one of many illustrations of the Christian 'conversion' of earlier Pythagorean and Platonic ideas of cosmic harmony and the soul as an attunement (*harmonía*).[129] A particularly illuminating parallel comes from Clement of Alexandria (ca. 150–215 CE), who presents Jesus as a new Apollo, Orpheus, Amphion, or Arion—an enchanting "new song" (*kainòn aîsma*) or incantation (*epōidḗ*) to replace the seductive deceptions of pagan liturgical music:[130]

> Tuning this world and this microcosm—I mean man, both soul and body—with the holy spirit, he plucks (*psállei*) this many-toned instrument—man—and sings thereto for God.[131]

Similar ideas relating to the *knr* specifically are found in St. Ephraim's elaboration of the 'Lyre of the Spirit' and the 'Lyres of God'.[132] Jesus is thus playing sweet, passionate music on Xanthippe's 'inner *kin(n)ýra*'.[133]

We must conclude that, while Apollo is not unknown as a lamenting god,[134] his Cypriot epithet *kenyristḗs* meant, first and foremost, the '*kinýra*-player'. This effectively glosses Kinyras himself, showing that this name/word too could entail a sense of agency: 'Kinyras' *is* 'the *kinýra*-player' (see Chapter 17). *Kenyristḗs* also presents an obvious parallel with *kitharōidós* ('*kithára*-singer'), one of Apollo's most familiar guises—reflecting his patronage of professional

---

[128] Photios *Lexicon* s.v. μουσικά· τερπνὰ τὰ δι' αὐλῶν καὶ κινύρας καὶ τὰ ὅμοια = *Anecdota Graeca* (Bachmann 1828–1829) 1:304.
[129] Aristotle *On the Soul* 407b–408a, etc. For the influence of these ideas on early Christian musical thought, HBMH:46–60, 96–97, et passim.
[130] Clement of Alexandria *Exhortation* 1, especially 1.4–5. See Halton 1983; Cosgrove 2006:276–281; Kindiy 2008:138–149.
[131] Clement of Alexandria *Exhortation* 1.5.4.
[132] Palmer 1993, with further parallels from Greek patristic sources. See further p180.
[133] There is considerable further evidence for the trope of Jesus as "the cosmic lyre-player" in early Christian thought: see Halton 1983:184–186 (quotation 184), noting especially Paulinus *Carmina* 20.30–61, where Jesus himself is treated as the lyre of God hung upon the cross (*hanc renovaturus citharam Deus ipse magister, / Ipse sui positam suspendit in arbore ligni*, 51–52, etc.). Byzantine hymnography also developed the idea; note especially the opening of Ode 4 in *Analecta Hymnica Graeca*, Canones Januarii, Day 27, Canon 34 (ed. Proiou/Schirò): "Divine Lyre / Of secret songs, / *Kinýra* of the mysteries of Christ, / Cry faithfully out again, / Sounding with secret mystery" (Ἡ θεία λύρα / τῶν ἀπορρήτων ᾠδῶν, / ἡ κινύρα τῶν μυστηρίων Χριστοῦ / αὖθις κέκραγε πιστῶς, / μυστικῶς ἠχήσασα, κτλ, 3–7).
[134] See p294–295.

lyrists, in whose image he was typically represented.¹³⁵ But the insistence on "*Our* Kinyrist" shows that this Apollo, whatever the immediate reasons for his inclusion in the *theoì hórkioi*,¹³⁶ stands for the full musical range of the island's own lyrical traditions. These used not the *kithára*, not the *phórminx*, not the *lýra*— but the *kinýra*.¹³⁷

The deliberate and traditional character of the epithet, in an official document of Tiberian date, becomes all the more palpable when one considers the long musical engagement of Cyprus with the outside world, and especially the Aegean. The island and its singers helped formulate several Cyprocentric themes that found their way into mainstream Greek epic.¹³⁸ The lost *Kypria*— attributed in ancient sources to either Stasinos or Hegesias/Hegesinos of Salamis—must have contained the 'Cypriot Hosting of the Achaeans', with Kinyras' terracotta fleet.¹³⁹ A lyre-singer Stesandros—or better Stasandros— of Salamis performed 'battles *à la* Homer' at Delphi, apparently in the sixth century; although Athenaios ranks him among historical *kitharōidoí*, he himself probably considered his instrument a *kinýra*.¹⁴⁰

Mainstream Greek genres must also have been increasingly visible on the island with the emergence of international musical celebrities and professional concert circuits from the Classical period onwards.¹⁴¹ Thus, the early fourth century saw Stratonikos—the Groucho Marx of the *kithára*—at Salamis and/or Paphos; while these anecdotes transpire in the royal courts, Stratonikos was

---

[135] While the term *kitharōidós* makes explicit that the lyrist was also a singer, *kenyristés* should not be taken to imply mere instrumental performance. For historically the role of *kitharōidós* evolved from that of the communal, ritual *kitharistés* who accompanied choruses but also sang preludes (*prooímia*)—whence Apollo's other title 'Muse-leader' (*Mousagétas*)—and might also sing epic. This background is reflected in such early formulations as ἀνὴρ φόρμιγγος ἐπιστάμενος καὶ ἀοιδῆς, Homer *Odyssey* 21.406; ἀοιδοὶ καὶ κιθαρισταί, Hesiod fr. 305.2 M-W. See further Franklin 2003:299; Power 2010:201–215 (noting 205n49); Franklin 2011b.

[136] One may recall here the Mesopotamian evidence for oaths sworn on musical instruments, and the LBA seal in which a harp-player apparently accompanies a loyalty oath (see p20–21). Note also the mutually binding pact between two warriors at Homer *Iliad* 22.254–255, where the gods "will be / The best witnesses and overseers of 'accords'" (τοὶ γὰρ ἄριστοι / μάρτυροι ἔσσονται καὶ ἐπίσκοποι ἁρμονιάων); ἁρμονία is literally a 'joint' (e.g. mortise-and-tenon, Homer *Odyssey* 5.247–248, 361–362), but a secondary musical nuance could be equally operative.

[137] One must therefore resist reducing all Cypriot representations of lyrists to 'Apollo κιθαρῳδός', as Karageorghis 1998:114 rightly stresses on more general grounds.

[138] Franklin 2014.

[139] For the attribution, *Kypria* T 3–4, 7–9, 11 EGF; 1, 3, 7–9, 11 PEG. The sources are discussed by Jouan 1966:23. For the Cypriot Hosting, see below p343–344.

[140] Athenaios 638a = Timomakhos FGH 754 F 1 (with Wilamowitz' convincing emendation of Σάμιον to Σαλαμίνιον); see further Franklin 2014:229–231. Zarmas 1975:15 mistakenly makes Timomakhos himself a Cypriot citharode.

[141] For this long-term trend, see now Power 2010.

equally famous for his public recitals.[142] Around the same time, Nikokles I of Salamis is said by Theopompos to have vied with Straton of Sidon in making his court luxurious, bringing citharodes and rhapsodes from Greece, as well as singing- and dancing-girls.[143] Cypriot patronage of dithyramb and tragedy is also attested: Alexander held musical contests in Phoenicia that were made splendid by the lavish expenditures of the island's kings, who competed with each other as executive producers (*khorēgoí*).[144] It is in this same period that Cypriot statuary, as part of the medium's more general assimilation to a Hellenistic koine,[145] shows several lyres which are influenced by the *kithára* in their upper structure, yet maintain the round base of their Cypriot ancestors (Figure 27e).[146] Yet even here such precedents as the Khrysokhou lyrist (Figure 17) and the instrument on the Louvre amphora (Figure 5.5q, tenth or ninth century) make *unilateral* 'Greek influence' a problematic assumption.[147]

Cypriot performers are well attested outside the island during the Hellenistic period, typically as victorious competitors at foreign festivals.[148] An inscription from Nemea, plausibly dated to 323/322, lists several Cypriot kings serving as *theōrodókoi*—that is, hosting the Nemean ambassadors who came to

---

[142] Athenaios 349e-f (Makhon 156–162 [11 Gow]), 352d; cf. HC:145–146. On whether the anecdotes relate to Paphos or Salamis, see Gow 1965:90–91. For Stratonikos generally, see Gilula 2000.

[143] Theopompos FGH 115 F 114 = Athenaios 531a–d; cf. HC:145. Nikokles is also known to have staged choral and musical performances at the funeral of his father, Euagoras: Isokrates 9.1.

[144] Plutarch *Alexander* 29.1-6: ἐχορήγουν γὰρ οἱ βασιλεῖς τῶν Κυπρίων ... καὶ ἠγωνίζοντο θαυμαστῇ φιλοτιμίᾳ πρὸς ἀλλήλους. μάλιστα δὲ Νικοκρέων ὁ Σαλαμίνιος καὶ Πασικράτης ὁ Σόλιος διεφιλονίκησαν (2–3). We also hear of the aulete Dorion (GMW 1:226n138; AGM:54) visiting the court of Nikokreon of Salamis: Athenaios 337e-f.

[145] Connelly 1991.

[146] Cesnola 1894, pl. XXXIV no. 282 (= Myres 1914:359 no. 2254); Monloup 1994 no. 392. Note also Apollo's instrument in the 'Apollo and Marsyas' mosaic, house of Aion, Nea Paphos (Daszewski et al. 1988:66 fig. 32; Michaelides 1992:61 no. 30). This is effectively a '*Kenyristḗs* Apollo'.

[147] The Louvre amphora was so dated by Rutten 1939:436–438, but without stratigraphic information.

[148] These are all from either Paphos or Salamis, the same sites which have produced inscriptions relating to the Artists of Dionysos (see below). A certain Antisthenes of Paphos (ca. 100) is called a μελοποιός ('melody-maker', 'composer'), a word that may well imply stringed-instrument music (for the various subtle contrasts with κιθαρῳδός, see Power 2010:121, 234, 238, 511); but here κινύρα and κιθάρα would be equally possible. Antisthenes is no. 219 in Stefanis 1986, whose other examples include a Paphian trumpeter (σαλπιγκτής) Aristonax (no. 397, early first century; cf. Pouilloux 1976:161); a Paphian 'herald' (κῆρυξ) Zoïlos (no. 1034, early first century); a Salaminian piper (αὐλητής) Onasimos (no. 1947, third–second century); and a 'costumer' (ἱματιομίσθης) from Salamis named Stratokles (no. 2307, second quarter of the third century). Also known are a Cypriot πυθαύλης ('Pythian-piper', cf. LSJ s.v.; AGM:93 and n63) named Publius Aelius Aelianus who won victories at Delphi, Rome, Nemea, Argos, and several other places in the mid-second century CE (*FD* III.1 no. 547); and an anonymous Cypriot πυθαύλης καὶ χοραύλης buried at Rome (Pouilloux 1976:163 and n2, with references).

announce upcoming games.¹⁴⁹ Between the mid-second and early first century, a Cypriot branch of the Artists of Dionysos is attested, seemingly headquartered at Paphos; it was evidently promoted by the Ptolemies to support their dynastic cult during the troubled accessions of this period.¹⁵⁰ In the earliest inscription (ca. 144–131), the only one to give any information about the guild's organization, a citharode Kriton is named president.¹⁵¹ This is the first secure evidence that the word *kithára* was current on the island. Yet one can hardly assume that it had displaced *kinýra*.¹⁵² The Artists of Dionysos were avowedly professional and international in outlook, and therefore cannot represent the totality of popular and cultic music-making on the island.¹⁵³

Lost in Translation: *Kinýra* At the Syro-Levantine Interface

Because Cyprus was the ancient epicenter of Greek in the region, it was the island's *kinýra*, rather than a number of parallel forms having all but disappeared from the record, which prevailed in the Hellenistic koine. That it was then used to render Heb. *kinnōr* is but one conspicuous example of a quite universalizing usage whereby *kinýra* became a blanket term for referring to the lyric cultures of Syria and the Levant. It is still possible, however, to detect linguistic and cultural multiformity behind a number of scribal variants in the transmission of Greek manuscripts, as well as several translation phenomena.

It is not unusual to encounter textual oscillations between *-n-* and *-nn-* in the representation of *kin(n)ýra*, Kin(n)yras, *kin(n)yrós* ('plaintive'), and *kin(n)ýresthai* ('threnodize'). A single *-n-* is metrically guaranteed for all by Greek poetic sources, variously from Homer onwards; they are equally found in prose. It is clear therefore that these forms reflect genuine Grecophone pronunciations. This divergence from *-nn-* in the Near East must be due, like the short upsilon of *kinýra*, to phonetic differences in one or more adapting languages. Nevertheless,

---

¹⁴⁹ Nem. Inv. no. I 85 (stele): Miller 1988; Miller 2004:115.
¹⁵⁰ Aneziri 1994, especially 186–194, with a collection of the nine inscriptions from Paphos and Salamis (the former probably being the guild's headquarters); I.Paphos:386–389, 525 (§17); Anastasiades 2009, especially 200–203; Papantonio 2012:155 (further correlating the Artists with the advent of theaters on the island, in the context of Ptolemaic Dionysos-cult), cf. 344n303; Fujii 2013:18.
¹⁵¹ SEG 13:586; Mitford 1953:135–137 no. 10 with n14; Aneziri 1994 no. 1; Anastasiades 2009:198.
¹⁵² The only other attestation known to me is the mannered κίθαριν of I.Kourion 104 (ca. 130/131 CE), the Antinoos inscription: see p318–319.
¹⁵³ An apt parallel here is the strong conservatism of Cypriot sanctuary architecture in this and later periods. Cf. Snodgrass 1994:171: "The Cypriote preference for the open-air courtyard sanctuary was so strong that, centuries later, it could resist and often defeat the influence of the Greco-Roman columnar temple, which eventually became a commonplace in countries lying to the south and east, as well as the west and north, of Cyprus."

Chapter Nine

spellings in *kinnyr-* were clearly seen as legitimate by many authors and anonymous scribes, for whom an origin or association with Syria or the Levant, when not directly attested, may be reasonably inferred. Especially revealing is the exchange of *kinýra* and *kinnýra* in manuscripts of the LXX, where the Hebraic context helps explain the 'confusion'—or better reverse engineering (and note that such a *kinnýra* was probably regarded as having a *long* upsilon).¹⁵⁴ Elsewhere an eastern provenance may seem likely on biographical grounds, but cannot be certainly established.¹⁵⁵ In Greek metrical works, forms with *n* must generally be preferred.¹⁵⁶ But otherwise there is no reliable criterion for deciding whether an *author* originally intended -*nn*- rather than -*n*-, or if one or the other was introduced by a *scribe*. In every case, however, these variants betray alternative and vital regional pronunciations. In the Byzantine period, there were certainly many bilingual scribes in and from Syria and the Levant (a considerable number of monks left Muslim Palestine for Constantinople in the eighth and early ninth centuries¹⁵⁷).

The great value of these *nn* variants is that they attest a fairly general belief that the several Greek words were etymologically related to Phoen. *kinnūr, Heb. *kinnōr*, etc. In particular I would emphasize that the variant of Ki<u>nn</u>yras for Kinyras¹⁵⁸ echoes the ancient form Ki<u>nn</u>aru at Ugarit. Indeed the principle of the *lectio difficilior* would normally urge us to accept 'Kinnyras' as the 'correct'

---

¹⁵⁴ For example, the variant κιννύραις for κινύραις at LXX 2 Samuel 6:5: see the apparatus of Brooke and McLean 1906–1940 2.1:124.

¹⁵⁵ In a homily falsely attributed to John Chrysostomus (ca. 347–407), a native of Antioch and later archbishop of Constantinople, one finds κιννύρα for κινύρα ([John Chrysostomus] *On the Adoration of the Precious Cross*, PG 62:752.72). Was this anonymous author himself Syrian? The Byzantine historian Nikephoros Kallistos (ca. 1256–1335) apparently used κιννύρα for David's lyre in a hymn to Mary; he was active in Constantinople, but his native home is unknown: *Carmina* 4, stanza 23.3 (text: Jugie 1929–1930). Biographical data: Cross and Livingstone 1997 s.v.

¹⁵⁶ The variant κιννύρονται appears in the Σ to Aiskhylos *Seven against Thebes* 122. An especially interesting case is found in the Laurentian codex 31.16, a fifteenth- or sixteenth-century collection including Aristophanes' *Knights*. In line 11 (for the passage, cf. p202n89 above), κινυρόμεθ' was 'corrected' to κιννυρούμεθ' (*sic*, see the apparatus of von Velsen's 1869 Teubner edition. This manuscript is *not* the same as 31.15, which later editors rely on: I thank Giovanna Rao of the Biblioteca Medicea Laurenziana for confirming this). Was this false emendation metrically motivated, the scribe confused by the initial resolution (τί κινῡρόμεθ' ἄλλως; οὐκ ἐχρῆν ζητεῖν ἔτι; ⏑⏑–⏑⏑–|––⏑–|––⏑–)? Perhaps the copyist thought he saw a quick solution: had he assumed ῠ, his 'correction' would give an initially satisfying iambic metron (⏑–⏑–), but leave the remainder a jumble.

¹⁵⁷ Corrigan 1992:956.

¹⁵⁸ See C. Baurain in Aupert and Hellmann 1984:111n20: two MSS (M and A) of Photios *Library* (the Theopompos fragment on Kinyras [FGH 115 F 103]: see p347), and the Codex Marcianus (Gr. 622) of Hesykhios, which has Κινυράδαι, Κινύρας, κινυρή, and κιννυρίδες. This fifteenth-century manuscript is rather corrupt, probably copied from a tenth-century exemplar in southern Italy; beyond that the trail vanishes (Latte 1953–1956 1:XXIV–XXXIII). But the three forms show that this was no slip of the pen: the copyist thought this a legitimate way to spell these words.

reading, were not 'Kinyras' itself otherwise sanctioned by Greek usage.[159] In fact, neither 'reading' is exclusively correct: 'Kin(n)yras' was at home in more than one linguistic-cultural sphere.

The foregoing scribal variants are symptomatic of the long-term overlap of Greek and Syro-Levantine cultures, which, though a central feature of Greek-Cypriot life from at least the twelfth century BCE, became a much more widespread phenomenon in the Hellenistic period. Given this situation, it is likely that some 'bi-musicality', rather than the mere influence of scripture, underlies Byzantine writers' periodic use of *ki(n)nýra* in contexts where one expects the simple Greek *kithára*.[160] John Tzetzes, the encyclopedic pedant of twelfth-century Constantinople, who was Georgian on his mother's side and at least superficially familiar with a number of other languages, calls Pindar 'the Theban *kinýra*' without missing a beat.[161] Elsewhere Tzetzes replaces *kithára* with *kinýra* in paraphrasing Prokopios.[162] Similarly, Theodoros II, emperor of Byzantine Nicaea (1254–1258), expressed inexpressible Christian joy by rhapsodizing: "Who will take up the *kinýra* of Orpheus? Who will tune it in the manner of Pindar?"[163] There are many other examples of this interchangeability.[164]

In other cases when *kinýra* has won through against *kithára*, further dialectal variety lurks. Forms in *kinnyr-* or *kinnar-* must often have been leveled to *kinyr-* under mainstream literary influence in the Greek East—whether by translators of Syriac writings, bilingual Syro-Levantine authors, and/or later

---

[159] Baurain in Aupert and Hellmann 1984:111n20: "nous ne sommes pas loin de penser qu'elle serait celle [sc. Kinnyras] qu'il conviendrait d'adopter s'il n'y avait pas l'usage consacré."
[160] For the notion of bi-musicality, see e.g. Nettl 1985:73–74.
[161] John Tzetzes *Khiliades* 7.99, line 15: Ἡ Θηβαῒς κινύρα δε—τὸν Πίνδαρόν σοι λέγω, κτλ. Tzetzes apparently dabbled in "Alanic, i.e. Ossetian ... Cuman, which belonged to the Turkic family, Seljuk Turkish, Latin, Arabic, Russian, and Hebrew": Wilson 1983:192.
[162] Prokopios *On the Wars* 4.6.30–31; John Tzetzes *Khiliades* 3.77–88, line 332. For the passage, see further p302–303.
[163] Theodoros II Doukas Laskaris *Epistles* 195.19 (ed. Festa): τίς Ὀρφέως λάβῃ κινύραν; τίς ἁρμόσει κατὰ τὸν Πίνδαρον.
[164] This was already seen in ancient definitions like κινύρα· ὄργανον μουσικόν, κιθάρα (see p195n48 for sources). It also explains random oscillations between κιθάρα and κινύρα in LXX translations of *kinnōr* (twenty and seventeen times respectively: HMI:106–107). Note also 1 Maccabees 4:54 (reconsecrating the temple ἐν ᾠδαῖς καὶ κιθάραις καὶ κινύραις καὶ κυμβάλοις, where κιθάρα stands for Heb. *nēbel*). Similarly [Philo] *Biblical Antiquities* (ca. 100 CE, ed. Harrington 1976), 2:8, where the Biblical invention of Jubal (Iobal) is expanded beyond the *kinnōr* to include *cyneram et cytharam et omne organum dulcis psalterii*. This apparently builds on LXX Genesis 4:21 Ιουβαλ· οὗτος ἦν ὁ καταδείξας ψαλτήριον καὶ κιθάραν, where ψαλτήριον will correspond to κινύραν, as regularly; hence also Augustine *City of God* 15.17.35; similarly in Michael the Syrian's twelfth-century *Chronicle* 1.6 (Chabot 1899–1924 1:10).

copyists of either.¹⁶⁵ Thus, in the Greek works attributed to Saint Ephraim (ca. 306–373 CE), one finds *kinýra* rather than the *kinnār(a)* Ephraim himself would have used in his native Syriac.¹⁶⁶ Philip of Side, in his early fifth century CE *Christian History*, used *kinyrístriai* of the female lyrists, in the temple of the Babylonian Hera, who accompanied the Muses' spontaneous song on the night of Christ's birth (among other portents); here too the cultural setting should imply an underlying Aramaic form.¹⁶⁷ The opposite process would have occurred with Aramaic translations of Biblical books (the targums), where the triconsonantal root *knr* would easily pass out of Hebrew vocalization. There is even a Syriac commentary on 2 Kings, attributed to Ephraim, in which '*cinnara*' is called a *translation* of the Hebrew word.¹⁶⁸ One should be similarly sensitive to the frequent use of Greek *kithára* or *psaltérion* in Christian contexts where it answers to the original *kinnōr* of the Bible.¹⁶⁹ When this is found in texts deriving from the greater Syrian sphere—for instance with Gregory of Nyssa, in Cappadocia (d. after 394)—it is quite possible that the author himself would have used *kinnār(a)* when speaking to his neighbors.

Conclusion

I have shown that *kinýra* and several cognates, along with the instruments so designated, enjoyed a life in the Byzantine world independent of Biblical exegesis.¹⁷⁰ This is the cultural framework within which Eustathios and the anonymous poet still knew Kinyras as a proverbial lyrist, and accepted without question an etymological link with *kinýra* and *kinýresthai*. Because the *knr*'s traditional range, for many centuries, fell largely within Byzantine territory, the burden of proof

---

[165] It is hard to decide whether Greek poets or the LXX exerted the greater influence here. It probably varied regionally and with personal interests. Over the centuries, of course, as the mainstream was progressively Christianized, the 'Biblical' value of *kinýra* must have become increasingly influential.

[166] The accuracy of the traditional attributions to Ephraim of these Greek writings, which purport to be translations of his works, is generally doubtful (Murray 2004:32–33). But the authorship of Ephraim himself is less the issue here than any author's own ultimately Syrian origin, and/or his inspiration by Ephraim himself or his tradition.

[167] The word is absent from LSJ. Philip of Side fr. 3.2 is found in the so-called *Religionsgespräch am Hof der Sasaniden*; the passage in question reads αὐτομάτως αἱ κινυρίστριαι ἤρξαντο κρούειν τὰς κινύρας καὶ αἱ μοῦσαι ᾄδειν. For the Greek text see Bratke 1899; for its inclusion among the fragments of Philip, Heyden 2006. The episode and word are repeated by John of Damascus (ca. 675–749), *Sermon on the Birth of Christ* 9.

[168] In the Latin translation of Assemani 1732–1746 1:524A (comment on 2 Kings 3:15): *ut ex Hebraeo verti posset, cinnaram*.

[169] For *psaltérion*, see p194n43, 215n164, 541 .

[170] For the elusive question of how and when these words/instruments went out of practical (rather than learned) use, see Appendix D.

must be on those who would insist that, when a Christian author writes *kinýra*, he has only the Jewish instrument in mind, or that any symbolism he attaches to it derives exclusively from the Bible. His independence will be especially clear when not simply commenting on scripture, but engaged in his own creative work.

It is certain that the etymology of Kinyras from *kinýra* was no anachronistic Christian construct, but went back into the pagan past, and was long recalled by some in Cyprus and the Syro-Levantine home range of the *knr*. "Our *Kenyristḗs* Apollo," as a recasting of Kinyras, looks back from Roman Paphos upon a distinctively Cypriot lyric art form stretching into past centuries. We must now trace this tradition as far back as possible, and determine the depth and nature of Kinyras' involvement with it. Our first step takes us to the fifth century and the poet Pindar.

10

Praising Kinyras

PINDAR'S *PYTHIAN* 2 contains the most elaborate allusion to Kinyras in early Greek literature, and is our first explicit source for him as a familiar of Aphrodite and Apollo.[1] The latter relationship by itself readily suggests the musical and prophetic abilities credited to Kinyras elsewhere.[2] This natural inference, I shall argue here, is not mistaken, so that Pindar (ca. 518–440) equally becomes our earliest source for a musical Kinyras, while himself presupposing a tradition of untold antiquity.

The poet juxtaposes the Cypriot king with Hieron of Syracuse, an analogy that sheds light on both parties, and so contributes considerably to our understanding of Kinyras as a royal figure. At the same time, the immediate context of the comparison is musical, both figures being the subject of celebratory song. The verses, complemented by scholiastic notices and iconographic evidence, can be pressed to yield further insight about the musical—and specifically lyrical—aspect of Kinyras.

Pindar and the Example of Kinyras

The poem, addressed to Hieron, alludes to a chariot-racing victory of controversial date and location, notwithstanding its traditional Pythian designation.[3] It is a complex work, the tone and meaning of which have occasioned much debate. Ancient allegations of rivalry between Pindar and Bakkhylides induced older scholars to infer a souring of relations between patron and poet, detecting

---

[1] Kinyras is probably understood as Aphrodite's lover here (Woodbury 1978:285n3), cf. Clement of Alexandria *Exhortation* 2.14 (ἡ Κινύρᾳ φίλη κτλ), 2.33 (Ἀφροδίτη δὲ ἐπ' Ἄρει κατῃσχυμμένη μετῆλθεν ἐπὶ Κινύραν κτλ).
[2] So Farnell 1896–1909 4:245.
[3] See Lloyd-Jones 1973:117–118, with reference to the theories and classifications of the Alexandrian scholars (preserved in the Σ) and the extensive secondary literature. The proposed dates range from 477 to 468, with the majority of scholars divided between 470 (Pythian games) and 468 (Olympics).

219

Chapter Ten

discreet reprimands by the latter.⁴ Later fashions discredited this idea as so much biographical fiction; Pindar's decrying of envy becomes a well-developed generic theme—something that eminent men like Hieron inevitably attract.⁵ One's critical stance will color interpretation of the poem's two mythological exempla—Kinyras and Ixion—and their relevance to Hieron. Both relate to *kháris*—that sense of gratitude for a good deed that compels reciprocal action.⁶ Kinyras—who is associated with *kháris* surprisingly often in early sources—is presented concisely as a positive parallel to Hieron himself, and receives his due from those in whom he has aroused gratitude.⁷ Ixion's refusal to requite the favor shown him by the gods negates the motif and is developed at length. Yet Kinyras himself featured in some traditions as a dishonest double-dealer—*kháris* perverted, leading to his kingdom's downfall; moreover, like Ixion, he was a sobering case of "lawless coupling" (*eunaì parátropoi*, 35) "without the Graces" (*áneu Kharítōn*, 42), thanks to his unwitting incest with Myrrha.⁸ Pindar seems to allude to these darker tales in *Nemean* 8, where he declines to elaborate.⁹ It is therefore worth considering whether Pindar chose Kinyras precisely because the theme of *kháris* was ambivalently developed in his mythology. If so, the exemplum could contribute to a larger admonitory program by bridging the wholly positive Locrian maidens (see below) with the wholly negative Ixion. I shall return to this point below.

For now we may concentrate on the more obviously favorable. The relevant verses are as follows:

---

⁴ See e.g. Bowra 1964:135–136 (from the slanderers mentioned in 72–82, 89–92, and the Σ relating to Bakkhylides). The controversy, well reviewed by Gantz 1978, Woodbury 1978, and Currie 2005:258–295, need not be rehearsed here.
⁵ So Lloyd-Jones 1973:126–127, very forcefully. See generally Kurke 1991:218–224.
⁶ For χάρις in Pindar, Bundy 1962:86–91 (on εὐεργεσία); Nagy 1990:65–66n72 ("a beautiful and pleasurable compensation, through song or poetry, for a deed deserving glory ... [*kháris*] conveys both the beauty ('grace') and the pleasure ('gratification') of reciprocity") et passim; Kurke 1991:154–156 ("that force which creates community, which links the victor to the gods, his family, his aristocratic group, and the poet," 155). Χάρις in this poem: Schadewaldt 1928:328–330; Lloyd-Jones 1973:119, 121n72; Bell 1984:5–7; Kurke 1991:98, 111–112.
⁷ Kinyras is connected with χάρις by Homer *Iliad* 11.19–23 (χαριζόμενος, 23), the relationship with Agamemnon being further developed in the *Kypria*'s terracotta fleet episode (see Chapter 14); also Alkman 3.71 PMGF (νοτία Κινύρα χ[άρ]ις), for which see p1, 330.
⁸ For the double-dealing Kinyras, see p343–346; for Kinyras and Myrrha, p282–289. The phrases quoted are used of Ixion and the cloud and the birth of Kentauros. For the contrast of Kinyras/χάρις and Ixion/ἄνευ Χαρίτων, Gantz 1978; Bell 1984:11–14; Brillante 1995:33–34; Redfield 2003:415. For the Kharites/Graces as personifications of χάρις, Nagy 1990:206.
⁹ Pindar *Nemean* 8.19–22, with Σ and Giuffrida 1996:292. Cf. below p223n30.

> Other men have made well-sounding hymns (*euakhéa hýmnon*) for
>   other kings—the reward of virtue. While
> Cypriots' songs (*phâmai Kyprîōn*) often resound around
> Kinyras—whom golden-haired Apollo gladly loved, the
> Cherished (*ktílon*[10]) priest of Aphrodite—driven no doubt by awe-
>   filled gratitude (*kháris*) for one of his friendly deeds,
> You, Deinomenes' son, the maids of Western Locri
> Sing (*apúei*) before the temple (*prò dómōn*), looking out secure from
>   helpless
> Toils of war, because of your great power.[11]

The passage has been closely analyzed for linguistic nuance and historical context in a recent study by B. Currie.[12] Two main questions arise. What did Hieron do to earn Kinyras-like gratitude? And why has Kinyras, of all possible mythical figures, been chosen to mirror the tyrant?

The scholia adduce the infamous episode of the Locrian maidens, otherwise known from Justin's epitome of Pompeius Trogus (Augustan era), who in turn probably drew on fourth-century historical sources: Hieron saved the city of Locri from attack and destruction by Rhegion between 478–476, with the Locrians allegedly vowing to prostitute their maiden daughters to Aphrodite if they prevailed.[13] This passage has been much debated. Currie, attempting to harmonize textual and archaeological evidence, concludes that the vow was indeed made and executed. Hieron should be connected, he argues, with the construction of the Ionic temple, dated to ca. 480–470, which lies just outside of Locri, and a reorganization of Aphrodite's cult there, specifically the institution

---

[10] My translation follows observations by Woodbury 1978 on the nuances of κτίλον (285–286 and n3). Morpurgo 1960, followed by Currie 2005:277–283, interpreted Pindar's κτίλον literally as 'ram', instead of (or in addition to) its derived sense of 'beloved' (cf. Σ 31: κτίλον Ἀφροδίτης οἰονεὶ σύνθρεμμα καὶ συνήθη τῇ θεῷ). This idea was rejected by Lloyd-Jones 1973:119n59, overlooking however the fleece-clad priests mentioned by John Lydus (*On the Months* 4.65, discussed by Currie) who, writing in the sixth century CE, gave an antiquarian description of the old *Adōniá* at Paphos. The details are too abstruse to be pure invention. During a sacrifice of sheep the priests would (apparently) dress in fleeces; wild pigs were also slaughtered, a choice which the author relates to Adonis' death at the tusks of the boar. Note also that early coins from the reign of Euagoras of Salamis, who claimed descent from Kinyras, depict a ram on the reverse: BMC Cyprus:c, cii and pl. XI.8–11.

[11] Pindar *Pythian* 2.13–20: ἄλλοις δέ τις ἐτέλεσσεν ἄλλος ἀνήρ / εὐαχέα βασιλεῦσιν ὕμνον ἄποιν' ἀρετᾶς. / κελαδέοντι μὲν ἀμφὶ Κινύραν πολλάκις / φᾶμαι Κυπρίων, τὸν ὁ χρυσοχαῖτα προφρόνως ἐφίλησ' Ἀπόλλων, / ἱερέα κτίλον Ἀφροδίτας· ἄγει δὲ χάρις φίλων ποί τινος ἀντὶ ἔργων ὀπιζομένα· / σὲ δ', ὦ Δεινομένεϊ παῖ, Ζεφυρία πρὸ δόμων / Λοκρὶς παρθένος ἀπύει, πολεμίων καμάτων ἐξ ἀμαχάνων / διὰ τεὰν δύναμιν δρακεῖσ' ἀσφαλές.

[12] Currie 2005:258–295, with a thorough review of the secondary literature.

[13] Σ Pindar *Pythian* 2.36bc, 38; Justin *Epitome* 21.3.

Chapter Ten

of a festival of deliverance (*sōtēría*) in which the maidens fulfilled their promise and celebrated Hieron in choral-song "before the temple."[14] The crucial point that allies Kinyras and Hieron, he suggests, is the Cypriot king's associations with 'sacred prostitution' at Paphos.[15]

This complex thesis will raise eyebrows in the current critical climate, highly skeptical of all references to 'sacred prostitution' (in various forms).[16] But Currie's reconstruction of a celebratory choral context at Locri can stand.[17] I shall consider in detail below its implications for Cypriot choral-lyric in the cult of Kinyras. But note first that, if the analogy is strictly pressed, we should be dealing with *female* Cypriot choruses—an idea that distinctly resonates with the lyre-playing and dancing women who grace the Cypro-Phoenician symposium bowls.[18] One should also emphasize the traditions of Kinyras as founder of Aphrodite's temple in Paphos, as this is a strong parallel for Hieron's presumed building initiative at Locri.[19]

Let us leave Locri and consider the conjunction of Kinyras and Hieron more generally. The scholia conjecture that, while Kinyras was consecrated as hierophant for the two gods, Aphrodite and Apollo, Hieron's father was responsible for transferring cultic rites from Cyprus to Sicily; or that Deinomenes was himself of Cypriot ancestry.[20] The latter is probably biographical fiction; the former less

---

[14] For a good survey of archaeological work conducted at Locri, and the history and identification of the cult-structures, see Redfield 2003:207–223; cf. Bellia 2012, with references in 21n6.

[15] Following Woodbury 1978, especially 291–292. The main sources for 'sacred prostitution' in connection with Paphos and Kinyras are Christian and polemical. First and foremost is Clement of Alexandria *Exhortation* 2.13.4–5: "The Cypriot islander Kinyras would never beguile *me*—he who dared transmit from night to day the lustful orgies of Aphrodite, eagerly hoping to deify a prostitute, one of his citizens" (Οὐ γάρ με ὁ Κύπριος ὁ νησιώτης Κινύρας παραπείσαι ποτ' ἄν, τὰ περὶ τὴν Ἀφροδίτην μαχλῶντα ὄργια ἐκ νυκτὸς ἡμέρα παραδοῦναι τολμήσας, φιλοτιμούμενος θειάσαι πόρνην πολίτιδα); repeated verbatim by Eusebios *Preparation for the Gospel* 2.3.12, 15; cf. Firmicus Maternus *On the Error of Profane Religions* 10.1.

[16] See now Budin 2008, who argues that all relevant passages constitute so many historiographical myths going back ultimately to Herodotos, who is himself given a liar-school interpretation; Near Eastern references (she holds) have been alleged by those seeking confirmation of Herodotos. Leaving aside the dubious Christian polemics relating to Kinyras (see n15), I am not fully convinced by her account (210–239) of other evidence for Cyprus (Herodotos 1.199.5; Klearkhos fr. 43a Wehrli = Athenaios 515e; Justin *Epitome* 18.5). In particular recall that Klearkhos was himself from Cypriot Soloi (rightly stressed by Currie 2005:283). Moreover Budin's proposed "neutral" translation of Justin (239) leaves unexplained exactly how the dowry money *was* to be earned. For a good response to Budin's treatment of the ANE material—in which Cyprus must be included—see Bonnet 2009.

[17] Bellia 2012:21–22 further relates Pindar's sketch to cultic and performance realities at Locri.

[18] See p258–272.

[19] See Chapter 16.

[20] Σ Pindar *Pythian* 2.27b: διαπορεῖται δέ, τί δή ποτε εἰς τοὺς τοῦ Ἱέρωνος ἐπαίνους τὸν Κινύραν προσῆκται, εἰ μὴ ὅτι ταῖν θεοῖν ἱεροφάντης ἀπεδέδεικτο· Δεινομένους γὰρ υἱεῖς εἰσιν οἱ περὶ τὸν

obviously so.²¹ Modern scholars have pointed out that Kinyras and Hieron were both priest-kings—the latter being hierophant of Demeter and Persephone.²² Others suggest that Hieron, victorious at the Pythian games, could resemble Kinyras in enjoying the favor of Apollo.²³

Certainly the comparison with Hieron guarantees that Kinyras is regarded here as a king. That he is simultaneously priest of Aphrodite confirms the Paphian dynastic legend already for the fifth century (see Chapter 16). Yet the poet's general terms show that Kinyras is envisioned as a pan-Cypriot figure; and it is this island-wide stature that justifies the parallel with Hieron. The Syracusan tyrant, as "lord and master of many well-garlanded cities and an army," dominates his own large island, reproducing a Golden Age like that of Kinyras on Cyprus.²⁴ A scholiast aptly suggests that the Cypriots celebrated Kinyras "either as founder/leader (*arkhēgétēn*) of the island, or as its most fortunate (*eudaimonéstaton*) king and greater than those before him."²⁵

A further point of contact probably relates to Kinyras' proverbial connections with seafaring.²⁶ Pindar's awareness of this dimension is seen in *Nemean* 8, were he parallels the "blessed fortune" of the honorand (Deinias of Aegina) with that which "freighted Kinyras with riches once upon a time in Cyprus on the sea."²⁷ Here the Cypriot king's immense wealth is quite logically linked to seafaring. The same association suits Hieron, who inherited one of the two largest fleets in the Greek world—some two hundred ships at the time of the Persian Wars, built up by Gelon for use against his Sicilian neighbors and

---

Ἱέρωνα τοῦ τὰ ἱερὰ ἐκ Τριοπίου [ἐκ τριοπίας, GQ; αὐτροπίου, EF; ἐκ τριόπου, P; ἐκ τριόπης, C] τῆς Κύπρου εἰς Σικελίαν κομίσαντος ... ἢ οὕτως· εἰσὶν οἱ λέγοντες τὸν Δεινομένην τὸν πατέρα Ἱέρωνος ἀνέκαθεν Κύπριον· διὸ νῦν εὐλόγως γράφων εἰς τὸν Ἱέρωνα μέμνηται Κινύρου. Cf. Σ in Abel 1891: ὁ τοῦ Ἱέρωνος πατὴρ Δεινομένης τὸ ἀνέκαθεν Κύπριος ἦν.

21 The point is obscured by textual corruption (see previous note), as no site called Triopios is known on Cyprus: see Bell 1984:6–7 with literature in n17; Cannavò 2011:419. For other attempts to explain the connection of Deinomenes and Cyprus, see Giuffrida 1996:294–301, with further references.
22 Σ Pindar *Olympian* 6.158a. Bell 1984:6–7 and n17; Currie 2005:283; Cannavò 2011:419. Note Cypriot Aphrodite's identification with Demeter: p287n46, 396n133.
23 Schadewaldt 1928:328; Lloyd-Jones 1973:119–120; Parry 1982:30–32.
24 Pindar *Pythian* 2.58: πρύτανι κύριε πολλᾶν μὲν εὐστεφάνων ἀγυιᾶν καὶ στρατοῦ. For the parallelism between the two islands and rulers, Gildersleeve 1907:258; Schadewaldt 1928:328. For the Golden Age of the blessed, virtuous Kinyras, see further Chapter 13.
25 Σ Pindar *Pythian* 2.27 (Abel 1891): τὸ δὲ κελαδέοντι εἶπεν ἢ ὡς ἀρχηγέτην τῆς νήσου, ἢ ὡς βασιλέα αὐτῆς εὐδαιμονέστατον καὶ μείζω τῶν πρὸ αὐτοῦ γενόμενον.
26 See p326–330.
27 Pindar *Nemean* 8.17–18: ὄλβος ... / ὅσπερ καὶ Κινύραν ἔβρισε πλούτῳ ποντίᾳ ἔν ποτε Κύπρῳ.

Carthaginian rivals.[28] Hieron himself won a famous naval victory against the Etruscans at Cumae in 474, and other such actions may be presumed.[29]

Pindar's two allusions, though concise and disconnected, reveal a consistent view of the Cypriot king. In *Nemean* 8, Kinyras exemplifies "wealth" which is "more stable" for having been "planted with a god's favor." Further details clarify that Aphrodite is the deity in question.[30] The idea is conventional; but when applied to Hieron's own prosperity in *Pythian* 2 it brings further point to the comparison with Kinyras.[31] Hieron's fortune is so great, Pindar claims there, that nobody in ancient Hellas was so exalted in wealth or honor.[32] Similarly, Kinyras was ranked among such wealthy kings of legend as Kroisos, Midas, and Sardanapalos; and even here Kinyras was exceptional since, by one proverb, "Rich was Midas, but thrice as rich Kinyras."[33] In a further popular saying, someone particularly well-to-do was "richer than Kinyras."[34] Pindar's point is therefore that Hieron has achieved and exceeded the highest prosperity known to myth and legend. Yet the poet may include an insurance policy against divine envy by specifying Hieron's peer group as Hellas, whereas Kinyras belonged, like Kroisos, Midas, and Sardanapalos, to its oriental periphery.[35] *They* all experienced catastrophic reversals-of-fortune, so that the wealth of an eastern

---

[28] Herodotos 7.158.
[29] For Gelon's naval program, including probable maneuvers around the battle of Himera in 480, see Dunbabin 1948:419–426.
[30] Kinyras stands at the climax of a sequence of thought that progresses by the following stages: an invocation of "Youth, the herald of Aphrodite's immortal love-encounters" (Ὥρα πότνια, κάρυξ Ἀφροδίτας ἀμβροσιᾶν φιλοτάτων, 1); the "better loves" (τῶν ἀρειόνων ἐρώτων) which one attains by "not straying from due season" (καιροῦ μὴ πλαναθέντα ... ἐπικρατεῖν, 4–5); such loves, the "shepherds of Kypria's gifts" (ποιμένες ... / Κυπρίας δώρων), attended the bed of Zeus and Aigina (6–7); consequently their son Aiakos and all his line (including by implication the honorand) enjoyed the same long-lasting good fortune as Kinyras (7–18). The circuit is closed by Kinyras' own "immortal loves" with Aphrodite (cf. Giuffrida 1996, 292). Given the context of encroaching sexual maturity and the exhortation to age-appropriate decisions, the specter of Kinyras and Myrrha is probably in the background—an ominous reminder of paths not to be chosen: cf. p220.
[31] See Parry 1982:32 on *Pythian* 2.56: τὸ πλουτεῖν δὲ σὺν τύχᾳ πότμου σοφίας ἄριστον ("to be wealthy by the good fortune of one's divine fate is wisdom's best [sc. result *vel sim.*]." Although the sentiment is somewhat obscurely deployed here, its application to Hieron (rather than the poet himself) seems guaranteed by the sequel: see the reading of Lloyd-Jones 1973:121–122. For extra-Pindaric parallels: Henry 2005 *ad loc.*
[32] Pindar *Pythian* 2.58–61.
[33] *Pap.Oxy.* 1795.32 (*Lyrica Adespota* 37 CA): ὄλβιος ἦν ὁ Μίδας, τρὶς δ' ὄλβιος ἦν ὁ Κινύρας. For further sources, p323n10.
[34] Κινύρου πλουσιώτερος: *Suda* s.v. καταγηρᾶσαι; *Appendix Proverbiorum* 4.68.
[35] Differently Currie 2005:293–294, who argues for divine overtones in the poet's treatment of Hieron: "The implications of the simple collocation of Kinyras and Hieron at 15–20 thus seem to have become bolder: now not even Kinyras (or any other hero of myth) could claim to outdo Hieron."

monarch was something better avoided. Thus Kinyras, despite his virtues and prosperity, could equally serve as a conventional admonition about the instability of fortune and the enduring importance of reputation (like Kroisos in *Pythian* 1).[36]

Given Pindar's purposeful contrast between Hellas and the Orient, it is probably significant that he refers to the composition and dispatch of his ode as follows:

> Like Phoenician merchandise this
> Song is being sent beyond the dusky sea.
> Inspect with open mind this Kastor-song on Aeolian strings—
> Greeting with favor this gratitude-gift (*khárin*)
> From my seven-toned lyre.[37]

Poet as navigator and poem as voyage are again conventional ideas.[38] But the ethnographic detail stands out. For Bowra, who considered the work a "poetic letter" rather than a proper choral ode, "Phoenician merchandise" effectively means "on approval."[39] I suggest rather that it takes its point from the earlier Kinyras exemplum, given the Cypriot king's treatment as a virtual Phoenician in some strands of tradition.[40] The poet, in singing of Hieron, does so like the Cypriots who praise Kinyras in a "well-sounding hymn" (*euakhéa hýmnon*). The parallel nature of their activity, resulting logically from the exemplum itself,[41] is emphasized by the poet through well-placed verbal echoes. Pindar's description of his poem as a *kháris*-gift (70) recalls the *kháris* that motivates the Cypriots in their celebration of Kinyras.[42] And since Pindar's own musical *kháris*-gift was a product of "the seven-toned lyre," he implies that the Cypriots also venerated their ancient king through choral lyric. Now in Pindar's later statement "I shall embark on a well-flowered naval-expedition, resounding about your virtue," the phrase *amph' aretâi / keladéōn* clearly echoes the earlier *keladéonti ... amphì*

---

[36] Pindar *Pythian* 1.92–98.
[37] Pindar *Pythian* 2.67–71: τόδε μὲν κατὰ Φοίνισσαν ἐμπολάν / μέλος ὑπὲρ πολιᾶς ἁλὸς πέμπεται· / τὸ Καστόρειον δ' ἐν Αἰολίδεσσι χορδαῖς θέλων / ἄθρησον χάριν ἑπτακτύπου / φόρμιγγος ἀντόμενος.
[38] Kurke 1991:49–61, 198; Segal 1998, Chapter 10, gives a detailed reading of the motif as developed in *Nemean* 5.
[39] Bowra 1964:135–136; cf. Gentili 1992:52.
[40] See p317, 345. Compare Bakkhylides' and Korrina's use of 'Phoenician' to mean 'Carian' (Athenaios 174f), and consider the substantial Phoenician population which had long been present on Cyprus itself.
[41] Cf. Σ Pindar *Pythian* 2.27e: ἡ δὲ ἀνταπόδοσις τοῦ λόγου αὕτη· περὶ μὲν τὸν Κινύραν οἱ τῶν Κυπρίων ὕμνοι, περὶ δὲ σὲ ὁ ἐμὸς καὶ τῶν Συρακουσίων. Similarly Σ 2.32: προευεργετηθεὶς ὑπὸ τοῦ Ἱέρωνος νῦν ἀμείβεται αὐτὸν τοῖς ὕμνοις καὶ ἐγκωμίοις.
[42] Cf. Gentili 1992:52–53, who notes also χαῖρε in 67.

Kinýran, of the Cypriot singers' own praise-songs.⁴³ Yet, whereas *they* can praise their king in their own territory, Pindar's song must be shipped to Syracuse: the "Phoenician merchandise" is thus a virtual Cypriot song dispatched by Pindar—temporarily assuming the guise of a Cypriot lyre-singer—to Hieron, that new Kinyras. The poet's maritime metaphor, reinforced by reference to the "Kastor-song," equally recalls Pindar's treatment of Kinyras in *Nemean* 8, where the king grew wealthy from seafaring: Hieron will be enriched by Pindar's musical 'merchandise'.⁴⁴

The Love of Apollo

That Pindar places himself in the position of a Cypriot lyre-singer executing royal praise calls for closer examination of the Kinyras passage in its own right—that is, divorced from its immediate context and treated as an ethnographic idyll. The poet sketches a vivid cultic scene, evoking the sight and sound of celebration in a few deft strokes. *Pollákis* ('often') shows that Pindar envisages the Cypriot praise-songs (*phâmai*) as an ongoing custom, not a single occasion.⁴⁵ This is given further substance by Kinyras as "priest of Aphrodite" and "beloved of Apollo," which conforms to a pattern of early epichoric 'heroes' who were connected to the cults of female gods and eventually absorbed by male Olympians who wore their names as epithets. The phenomenon brings further point to Apollo's title *Kenyristés*, the preconditions for which were therefore already established in Pindar's own day, and probably before (see below).⁴⁶ The poet thus assumes a sanctuary-setting of Cypriot 'Aphrodite' where Kinyras played a role, just as we find at Classical Paphos (see Chapter 16). This would be a natural venue for the development of cult-narratives, helping account for the rich (if lamentably terse) notices that survive about Kinyras, his family, and

---

⁴³ Cf. 62–63: εὐανθέα δ' ἀναβάσομαι στόλον ἀμφ' ἀρετᾷ / κελαδέων. Also noted by Currie 2005:293, with different emphasis.

⁴⁴ Note too the poet as unsinkable cork (80). The Καστόρειον is evidently to be connected with fr. 105–106: see Gentili 1992, with 54–55 for possible generic nuances of Kastor-song. The Dioskouroi's role as patrons of sailors (GR:213) is probably relevant. Their cult on Cyprus is known from the loyalty oath to Tiberius (see p205). They are also called κιθαρισταὶ ἀοιδοί by Theokritos *Idylls* 22.24 (see p480n126); the fifth-century currency of this detail is seen in a red-figure hydria by the Kadmos Painter (ca. 430–420 BCE: SIAG:74, fig.7), for which, and the Theokritos passage generally, see now Power 2010:282–285.

⁴⁵ See Currie 2005:275 and n84, with Pindaric parallels.

⁴⁶ Cayla 2001:74, with the parallels Erekhtheus + Athena > Poseidon-Erekhtheus; Hyakinthos + Artemis > Apollo Hyakinthios. For Apollo and his rivals, see p189–190.

associates.⁴⁷ The Cypriot king was the center of his own mythological cycle, giving the phrase "about Kinyras" (*amphì Kinýran*) one immediate point.⁴⁸

Admittedly Pindar's *phâmai* does not directly denote a musical form; the word's basic meanings are an 'utterance prompted by the gods' and 'reputation' (that is, what people are saying).⁴⁹ Yet this is linked to the basic function of a praise-poet, whose divinely inspired songs secure such 'fames'.⁵⁰ This explains the parallel construction between the "Cypriots' *phâmai*" and the "well-sounding hymn(s)" (*euakhéa hýmnon*) with which other unnamed singers celebrate their own patrons. So Pindar definitely alludes to a Kinyras song-tradition. It is precisely this which gives the exemplum weight: not only are Hieron's "friendly deeds" worthy of similar praise-poetry, they are great enough to endure the centuries and secure imperishable fame—the essential self-justification of the professional praise-singer.⁵¹

By contrast with Aphrodite, the presence of Apollo adds nothing *essential* to the picture. It is rather a Panhellenizing gloss on Kinyras himself—an alternative expression of the cultural encounter that underlies the fatal musical contest.⁵² Pindar's Apollo, who "loved" (*ephílēse*) Kinyras, emphasizes cultural *sympathies*. One scholiast denies that Kinyras was Apollo's beloved (*erṓmenos*)—an idea perhaps inspired by parallels like Hyakinthos.⁵³ Another states that Kinyras was the Olympian's son—a seemingly banal solution that may nevertheless reflect a specific dynastic construction developed by the Kinyrad kings of Paphos and/or Salamis, integrating themselves into a Panhellenic framework.⁵⁴

---

[47] Farnell 1930–1932 2:122 ("Pindar's statement that Apollo also loved him points to the contemporary prevalence in Cyprus of music associated with Kinuras [sic]"); Bell 1984:6 ("cultic community"); Karageorghis 1988:182n6. Hero-cult as productive of mythmaking: Nagy 1979:304–305 and n4 (*vis-à-vis* Arkhilokhos). For other hero-cults connected with legendary priest-kings, interred within a deity's temple, see Pfister 1909–1912:450–459 passim (for Kinyras/Kinyradai, 295 [as city founder], 303 [as royal ancestor], 452–453); Farnell 1921:17; West 1966:428; Currie 2005:275 and sources in n86.

[48] For Kinyras' family 'cycle', see p280–291 and Chapter 14. Cf. Σ Pindar *Nemean* 8.32c: πολλαὶ οὖν, φησί, περὶ τοῦ Κινύρου καταβέβληνται ἱστορίαι καὶ διάφοροι.

[49] LSJ s.v. φήμη I.1-3; Woodbury 1978:294–297 especially n31; Kurke 1991:124n46.

[50] Cf. Pindar *Olympian* 7.10–12, etc.; of external parallels, note especially Aiskhylos *Suppliants* 694–697: εὔφημον δ' ἐπὶ βωμοῖς / μοῦσαν θείατ' ἀοιδοί, ἁγνῶν τ' ἐκ στομάτων φερέσθω φήμα φιλοφόρμιγξ.

[51] Cf. Gantz 1978:17–18; Bell 1984:6; Currie 2005:284.

[52] See p187, 189–192.

[53] Kinyras appears in Clement of Rome's catalogue of Apollo's lovers (*Homilies* 5.15.2; PG 2:184C–185D): Ἀπόλλων Κινύρου, Ζακύνθου, Ὑακίνθου, Φόρβαντος, Ὕλα, Ἀδμήτου, Κυπαρίσσου, Ἀμύκλα, Τρωΐλου, Βράγχου, †Τυμναίου [i.e. Ὑμεναίου?], Πάρου, Ποτνιέως, Ὀρφέως.

[54] Σ Pindar *Pythian* 2.27a: ἦν δὲ οὗτος Ἀπόλλωνος υἱός. See further p410. Apollo is also Kinyras' father in Σ Theokritos *Idylls* 1.109; Hesykhios s.v. Κινύρας. For the Kinyrad descent of Euagoras of Salamis, see p351–359.

Figure 17 Lyrist-archer, White Painted krater from Khrysokhou (near Marion), ca. 850–750 (CG III). Collection of the Archbishopric of Cyprus, Nicosia. Drawn from Karageorghis 1980b.

Praising Kinyras

A third commentator supposes that Apollo loved Kinyras "either as an archer or as a musician."[55] Neither suggestion grows obviously from the Pindaric text, and one may suspect that the scholiast has simply brought forward bow and lyre as being Apollo's main attributes—an ancient pairing, firmly entrenched in epic diction.[56] Yet the scholion prompts comparison with a remarkable Cypriot vase dated to the ninth or eighth century and discovered near Marion, bordering the kingdom of Paphos to the north (Figure 17).[57] One side shows a lyre-player seated, surrounded by quadrupeds like an Orpheus, and playing an instrument of at least six strings; that he is enthroned is suggested by the chair's monumental proportions. The other side shows him (or a twin?) returning from the hunt, leading a captive bull; he carries a quiver of arrows on his back.

By what name would the painter have known this figure? Bow and lyre make the Classicist think first of Apollo. Yet the Greeks had no monopoly over this ancient idea. We have seen a probable example from Ugarit in the *Tale of Aqhat*.[58] There is also Kinyras' syncretism with Kothar, Aqhat's bow-maker.[59] The bow is besides an attribute of the WS god Resheph, who was equated with Apollo by Phoenician-Cypriots.[60] But a fourth-century bilingual inscription from Tamassos qualifies both Apollo and Resheph as 'Alashiyan', so that we must also assume a pre-Greek, pre-Phoenician figure whose powers overlapped with theirs.[61] The vase vividly illustrates the problem of isolating indigenous gods in the Cypriot iconographic record. It would be no less reckless to suppose that the painter intended Apollo and Apollo alone, than to insist upon seeing only Kinyras here. This situation is familiar from the many exotic titles born by Apollo on Cyprus from the Classical period onwards; for despite the diversity and strangeness of these epithets, the Cypriots themselves were evidently prepared to see one god with many faces.[62] The two that come most readily to mind in the present case

---

[55] Σ Pindar *Pythian* 2.30g (Abel 1891): ἢ ὡς τοξικὸν ἢ ὡς μουσικόν.

[56] Homer *Odyssey* 21.406–411; *Homeric Hymn to Apollo* 131; *Homeric Hymn to Hermes* 515; cf. Herakleitos 22 B 51 DK; Plato *Kratylos* 404e–405d; Kallimakhos *Hymns* 2.42–46; Diodoros Siculus 5.74.5; innumerable later instances, especially in poetry. The two 'instruments' share the same principle of construction; their historical kinship (HMI:56–57) is reflected in Greek vocabulary, both having 'arms' or 'horns', 'yoke', and string (πήχεις/κέρατα, ζυγόν, χορδή). See further Kirk 1954:207–209; Franklin 2002b:2–5; Franklin 2003:297–301.

[57] White painted ware krater (CG III) in private collection, dated ca. 850-750 by Karageorghis 1980b (giving the number of strings as five—but examine them just under the crossbar); stylistically it is very close to SB.1 and SI.1 in CCSF *Supplément*:6–17.

[58] See p131–134.

[59] See Chapter 18.

[60] Lipinski 2009:104–108.

[61] ICS 216. See p372.

[62] Cult-titles of Apollo on Cyprus include (besides *Alasiṓtas*) *Amyklaîos* (see p372n6), *Hylátēs*, *Kaîsar*, *Keraiátēs*, *Kýprios*, *Lakeutḗs*, *Mageírios*, *Melánthios*, *Myrtátēs*. See with further references HC:80–81; Mitford 1961a:116, 134; Glover 1981; Cayla 2005:227n1.

are *Hylátēs* (the 'woodsman'), attested from the fourth century; and of course *Kenyristḗs*.⁶³ And yet the vase is centuries older than the epigraphic evidence for Apollo's insular cult-titles.

The ultimate age of the Olympian's association with Kinyras cannot be determined; Pindar merely provides a *terminus ante quem*. It may have developed very early indeed, if Apollo was imported to the island during Aegean migration in the twelfth and eleventh centuries, when comparisons with pre-Greek divinities will have been quickly drawn.⁶⁴ While Apollo is not attested in Linear B, recent scholarship on his Anatolian background indicates that he was indeed of BA antiquity.⁶⁵ Certainly by the Archaic period Apollo was known on the island. His name is found in a sixth-century inscription fragment from Paphos (Rantidi).⁶⁶ And a seventh-century tripod dedicated by a Cypriot to Apollo at Delphi, along with other contemporary evidence for a Cypriot aristocratic presence there at this time, shows that the Olympian's cult was influential on the island.⁶⁷ The laurel spray and eagles that appear on some fifth-century Paphian coins have been interpreted as Apollonian symbols, and later fifth-century types from Marion seem to show Apollo's head accompanied by the king's name.⁶⁸

Given this early evidence, and Apollo's traditional guise as lyre-player, his identification or association with Kinyras surely goes back into the Archaic period—whether the connection was made by Aegean Greeks seeking to understand the peculiarities of Cypriot cult, Greek-Cypriots under Panhellenizing influence, or both.⁶⁹

---

63 See further p204–213.
64 See generally Dietrich 1978. Apollo *Keraiátēs* ('Horned Apollo') has been adduced as an import, because Apollo was known under such a title in Arcadia (*Kereátas*, Pausanias 8.34.5): see e.g. Karageorghis 1998:32, noting that Apollo was worshipped as a god of sheep and cattle at Kourion by the eighth or seventh century (cf. Hadjioannou 1971:40, also affirmative). Yet there is the counter-example of a cult of Paphian Aphrodite at Tegea, which obviously originated in Cyprus, probably in some kind of reciprocal action following the EIA migrations: see further p364–365. Others would explain *Keraiátēs* in light of the famous Horned God of Enkomi, itself exemplifying a widespread ANE pattern of divine representation: see p396n134.
65 This question will be treated in detail by Bachvarova forthcoming.
66 I.Rantidi 14; ICS 39 (cf. 40–41, 43–44); DGAC:780 no. 237.
67 The evidence for Cypriots at Delphi down into the Roman period is collected by Pouilloux 1976, to which one should add the case of the (sixth-century?) lyre-singer Stesandros/Stasandros (see p211). Apollo *Pýthios* is attested at the sanctuary of Apollo *Hylátēs* at Kourion (I.Kourion 41, late third century BCE). Note also that a connection between Kinyras and Delos may be implied by the myth of 'Melus': see p290.
68 Paphos: BMC Cyprus:lxviii–lxxiv; Marion: BMC Cyprus:lviii and pl. XX.5–6; Head et al. 1911:739.
69 But this need not contradict Cayla's hypothesis that Nikokles of Paphos introduced an Apollo-*Kenyristḗs* alongside Apollo-*Hylátēs* when founding New Paphos in the fourth century: Cayla 2005:235–238; see further p410.

Singing 'about' Kinyras

While the ancient suggestion that Apollo loved Kinyras "as a musician" is in itself too bland to inspire much confidence, another scholiast makes a crucial contribution:

> [Kinyras] was loved by the god because he [Kinyras] was celebrated in song by musicians.[70]

This could hardly have been inferred from the poem alone, for Pindar's "Cypriots' songs" suggests pandemic reverence, not the narrower customs of musicians.[71] But of course the latter group will have been essential in practice. *The musicians' Kinyras is therefore a genuine tradition.* Once this is appreciated, Apollo's affection for Kinyras becomes readily intelligible, just as the scholiast saw.[72] And because Kinyras enjoyed his musical praise in a formal cultic setting, *his honors were akin to those of a god.*

Let us reexamine the passage with this in mind. First, one may read *amphí* in its literal spatial sense ('around, about'), and so interpret the Cypriot praise-songs as those of a festival chorus of traditional circular shape, with 'Kinyras' in the center. In early Greek choral lyric, this was the position typically occupied by the musician, sometimes at an altar, whose playing led the dance.[73] The arrangement is seen in many Cypriot terracotta figure-groups, probably going back to the pre-Greek period.[74] Pindar's allusion to choral space was caught by one scholiast: "The hymns of the Cypriots often dance around (*perí*) Kinyras".[75] Note that *hýmnos* (drawn from the poet's own text) is properly used of divine praise-songs, typically to the lyre in Apollonian contexts; and that *perí* permits

---

[70] Σ Pindar *Pythian* 2.31b: οὐχ ὅτι ἐρώμενος Ἀπόλλωνος ὁ Κινύρας· ἀλλ' ἀγαπᾶσθαί φησιν αὐτὸν ὑπὸ τοῦ θεοῦ διὰ τὸ ἐγκωμιάζεσθαι αὐτὸν ὑπὸ τῶν μουσικῶν. For the musical dimension of ἐγκωμιάζεσθαι, cf. LSJ s.v. ἐγκώμιον, II.2 (ἐγκώμιον, 'laudatory ode'), noting that a group performance (κῶμος), i.e. choral, may also be implied.

[71] Jager 2000:270 (following Zarmas 1975:10–11) states without argument that Pindar considered Kinyras a κιθάρα-player (*sic*), by tacitly combining the Pindaric scholia with Eustathios' etymology of Kinyras < κινύρα, and imputing both ideas to the poet himself. I agree with the overall result; but the treatment of sources here and throughout is cavalier.

[72] Cf. Farnell 1930–1932 2:122.

[73] A circle-dance is often described by χορεύειν + ἀμφί or περί; note also the compounds ἀμφιχορεύειν and περιχορεύειν. A vivid citharodic example is Euripides *Alkestis* 583: χόρευσε δ' ἀμφὶ σὰν κιθάραν, of Apollo; the arrangement is also readily inferred for *Homeric Hymn to Apollo* 194–203. Perhaps the most detailed performative sketch is the much-discussed Pratinas PMG 708 (although this concerns the αὐλός).

[74] See p242.

[75] Σ Pindar *Pythian* 2.27d: χορεύουσι μὲν περὶ τὸν Κινύραν πολλάκις οἱ τῶν Κυπρίων ὕμνοι.

Chapter Ten

the same ambiguity between 'about' and 'around' as *amphí*.⁷⁶ As noted above, Pindar's parallel with the Locrian maidens makes it very likely that female choruses are imagined here, just what one finds in the Cypro-Phoenician bowls, the Hubbard amphora, and other Cypriot representations, where again a circle dance is assumed.⁷⁷

It is equally possible to connect *amphí* + DN with a regular device of early Greek lyre-poetics, describing the god 'about' whom one is singing. Several examples from Homer and the Homeric hymns show that the phrase had general application.⁷⁸ Yet the professional interests of *kithára*-singers (*kitharōidoí*) meant that Apollo was so invoked especially often. This led to the semi-technical expression *amphianaktízein* for the act of calling upon 'Lord' (*ánax*) Apollo at a musical outset—a protocol so standard that *kitharōidoí* became known as *amphiánaktes*.⁷⁹ Such an epicletic force to *amphí* in our Pindar passage is made perfectly possible by *keladéonti* ('resound'), which, referring basically to the production of loud sound, commonly described celebratory singing addressed to god, hero, or man, especially in citharodic contexts.⁸⁰

I suggest therefore that *amphì Kinýran* both gives the *subject* of the "Cypriots' songs," and evokes the lyric environment in which they transpired. This would provide an attractive context for Apollonios of Rhodes' *amphì kinyrómenai*, which several ancient lexica construed as a compound verb, "play music, sing," deriving it "from the *kinýra*."⁸¹ While this word/expression, like the simple

---

76 Ὕμνος developed a special connection with praise of gods and heroes by the Classical period: see especially *Etymologicum Gudianum* s.v. ὕμνος; Furley and Bremer 2001 1:9–14, with Appendix C for the link to lyre-music (cf. e.g. Pindar *Olympian* 2.1: ἀναξιφόρμιγγες ὕμνοι).
77 See p222, 236–237, 256, 262, etc.
78 The construction, which takes both genitive and accusative, may be seen in Homer *Odyssey* 8.267: ἀμφ' Ἄρεος φιλότητος ἀείδειν; *Homeric Hymn* 7.1–2: Ἀμφὶ Διώνυσον Σεμέλης ἐρικυδέος υἱὸν / μνήσομαι; 19.1: Ἀμφί μοι Ἑρμείαο φίλον γόνον ἔννεπε Μοῦσα; 22.1: Ἀμφὶ Ποσειδάωνα θεὸν μέγαν ἄρχομ' ἀείδειν; 33.1: Ἀμφὶ Διὸς κούρους ἑλικώπιδες ἔσπετε Μοῦσαι (Dioskouroi). See further Power 2010:194–195. Pindar usually makes the object praised accusative without preposition: Pindar *Olympian* 1.9–10, 2.2, 6.88, 10.79–81, *Pythian* 11.10, *Nemean* 9.54, *Isthmian* 1.52–54. But the prepositional complement is paralleled by *Pythian* 2.62–63 (κελαδεῖν + ἀμφί + dative) and *Isthmian* 5.47–48 (κελαδεῖν + περί + genitive), and after all accords with the traditional syntax.
79 The key evidence comes from the *Suda* s.v. ἀμφιανακτίζειν, defining it as τὸ προοιμιάζειν. διὰ τὸ οὕτω προοιμιάζεσθαι ("to sing a prelude, from preludes being so sung"). See further Gostoli 1990:49–50; Power 2010:194–195; Franklin 2013:221–222.
80 Cf. Woodbury 1978:294–5n30. For 'positive, citharodic' κελαδέω, a few further examples may suffice: the invocation of Apollo attributed to Terpandros (σοὶ δ' ἡμεῖς ... / ἑπτατόνῳ φόρμιγγι νέους κελαδήσομεν ὕμνους, Terpandros 4 [Gostoli]); Pindar *Olympian* 2.1–2 (Ἀναξιφόρμιγγες ὕμνοι, / τίνα θεόν, τίν' ἥρωα, τίνα δ' ἄνδρα κελαδήσομεν, which gives the range of usual praise-objects), cf. *Olympian* 10.79–81; Euripides *Iphigeneia among the Taurians* 1129, cf. *Herakles* 694.
81 Apollonios of Rhodes 1.882–883; *Etymologicum Genuinum* s.v. ἀμφικινυρόμεναι· Ἀπολλώνιος. κινυρόμεναι· μέλπουσαι, ᾄδουσαι· ἀπὸ τῆς κινύρας; similarly *Etymologicum Symeonis, Etymologicum Magnum* s.v. See further p200n73.

kinýresthai, just as readily connotes 'lament', I have argued that the Apollonios passage is purposefully ambivalent between 'positive' and 'negative' connotations, reflecting the two main performance moods of the *kinýra*.[82] The same duality would readily apply to songs about Kinyras himself, since the Cypriot king, as father of Adonis and many other ill-fated children, was well qualified to bestow or receive lyric-laments (see Chapter 12). Note that Pindar's *keladéonti*, translated above as 'sing', is also found of mournful outcries.[83]

The proposed semantic duality, with the "Cypriots' songs" both *about* Kinyras and performed *around* Kinyras, is harmonized by the lyrist himself who, by singing hymns *about* a god, leads an encircling chorus in bringing that power into the space they circumscribe.[84] (The audience creates a second concentric circle.) It is a mimetic ritual where the performer, in the Aegean, 'played Apollo'—whose most familiar guise, after all, was *kitharōidós*. Such enactments must have been seen as sufficiently magical for *kitharōidoí* like Terpandros and Arion to perform the civic catharses and city-foundation rituals that are surprisingly abundant in Greek legend, music-historiography, and other sources.[85]

Pindar implies a comparable conception of ritual performance on Cyprus, where the distinction between 'Kinyras' and 'kinyrist' vanishes. This idea is corroborated by further implications of "our *kenyristés* Apollo." As Cayla rightly stresses, the epithet adheres to a well-attested pattern of agent-words in -*stēs*/-*stas* or -*dēs*/-*das* and verbs in -*zein* built upon divine names and cult-titles, and relating to cultic societies that celebrated the root-figure. Many such groups

---

[82] See p200–201 and further Chapter 12.
[83] Pindar fr. 128eb.7 (threnodic context); Aiskhylos *Seven against Thebes* 866–870 (ed. Page), especially τὸν δυσκέλαδόν θ' ὕμνον Ἐρινύος ἀχεῖν Ἀίδα τ' / ἐχθρὸν παιᾶν' ἐπιμέλπειν; cf. *Libation Bearers* 609 (of a baby's cry); Euripides *Iphigeneia among the Taurians* 1089–1093 (of the halycon's lamenting song); *Hel.* 371 (formal lament for war-dead); *Cyclops* 489–490 (κέλαδον μουσιζόμενος / ... κλαυσόμενος).
[84] This idea is inherent in the citharodic epicletic formula itself. The basic version associated with Terpandros (fl. ca. 675, and credited with traditional practices of unknowable antiquity) permits two simultaneous readings: 1) Let my heart *for me* again sing *about* the far-shooting Lord; 2) *Round about me* let my heart sing again the far-shooting Lord (ἀμφ' ἐμοὶ αὖτις ἄναχθ' ἑκατηβόλον ἀειδέτω φρήν, Terpandros 2 Gostoli = *Suda* s.v. ἀμφιανακτίζειν). The viability of the second interpretation is confirmed by a skillful Aristophanic pastiche in the parabasis of *Clouds*. The antode begins by invoking Apollo with a spare adaptation of the citharodic formula—"(Be) around for me once again, Lord Phoebus" (*Clouds* 595: ἀμφί μοι αὖτε, Φοῖβ' ἄναξ κτλ)—where the absence of any explicit verb, and the appearance of "*ánax* Phoebus" in the vocative rather than nominative case, requires *amphí* to bear the full weight of invocation with its literal spatial force. The antode's three further invocations (of other junior Olympians) all depend upon this opening construction.
[85] See generally Franklin 2006a, especially 52–62.

Chapter Ten

are found in Classical, Hellenistic, and Roman-era inscriptions.[86] From Cyprus itself one may note *Damatrízein* (glossed by Hesykhios as "to gather in the fruit of Demeter");[87] and the *Basiliastaí* ('Celebrants of the King', perhaps garrison soldiers) attested at Old Paphos and Lapethos in connection with the Ptolemaic ruler cult in the early first century.[88]

A *Kenyristés* Apollo can therefore be not only a *kinýra*-player but "un fidèle de Kinyras, qui honore Kinyras, qui participe au culte de Kinyras."[89] It is no great leap to see this Apollo as embodying the function of the Kinyradai of Paphos.[90] There are strong parallels with various musical 'clans' from the Greek world: 'Musaists' (*Mousaïstaí*) of Rhodes and Macedonia;[91] the Homeridai of Chios and the Kreophylidai of Samos, well-known rhapsode-guilds;[92] and especially lyre-clans like the 'motherless' *Ametorídai* (purveyors of erotic *kithára*-songs in the context of Cretan rites-of-passage),[93] and the Eumolpidai of Eleusis and the Euneidai at Athens.[94] There are also the *Thamyríddontes* (< *thamyríddein = *thamyrízein) of an early fourth-century inscription from Thespiai in Boeotia.[95] These functionaries, probably not a standing body but periodically appointed,[96] clearly evoke Thamyris (or Thamyras), the legendary lyre-singer who was blinded for rivaling the Muses (a myth perhaps representing a competing regional tradition, or epic

---

[86] Besides the Adoniasts and Haliads of Rhodes (Cayla 2001:79–80), there were Ἀπολλωνιασταί, Ἀρτεμισιασταί, Ἀσκληπιασταί, Βακχισταί, Διονυσιασταί, Διοσσωτηριασταί, Διοσκουριασταί, Ἑστιασταί, Πανιασταί, Ποσειδωνιασταί, Πριαπισταί, Σαβαζιασταί, Σαραπιασταί, etc. (LSJ s.v.).
[87] Hesykhios s.v. Δαματρίζειν· τὸ συνάγειν τὸν Δημητριακὸν καρπόν. This verb, which relates to the Cypriot goddess's fertility aspect (see p287 and n46) probably does not predate the influx of Olympian names in the Classical and Hellenistic periods: Karageorghis 1988:191.
[88] ExcCyp 124; HIOP 105; I.Paphos 82; cf. HC:185; Papantonio 2012:154; Fujii 2013:18n31. Other such royal-cult groups are known: Καισαριασταί, Ἀτταλισταί, Εὐμενισταί, et al.: see LSJ s.v.
[89] Cayla 2005:229. Cf. GR 184 for other Apolline cult-titles deriving from festivals or ritual activities the god is imagined as doing (e.g. *Daphnēphóros*).
[90] See p421–424.
[91] Ialysos, Rhodes, third century: Carratelli 1939–1940:165–166 no. 19.24; IG XII.1, 680 (undated); Pieria, Macedonia, early second century: SEG 49:697.
[92] Allen 1924:42–50; Burkert 1972b; West 2001:15–17.
[93] Athenaios 638b, with Chaniotis 2013 §2.3; cf. Power 2010:373n164.
[94] Burkert 1994; Cassio 2000; Power 2010:305, 364–367.
[95] SEG 32:503 (genitive θαμυριδδόντων, line 2), ca. 400–350 BCE. Cf. Cayla 2001:79–80.
[96] The present participle θαμυρίδδοντες (rather than *Θαμυριστᾶν) "indicates a temporary function, probably an office ... they were the presidents of the association's assembly" (A. Chaniotis, SEG 55:562).

competition itself).⁹⁷ They evidently presided over a "hero-cult for Thamyris himself in the valley of the Muses."⁹⁸

This argument for *kenyristḗs* Apollo as "the one who celebrates Kinyras" is not incompatible with a concurrent interpretation as the '*kinýra*-player'.⁹⁹ A kinyrist venerated Kinyras precisely by playing the instrument from which the Cypriot king took his name. The title recalls our attention *to the lyre itself*—just as the Ugaritic pantheon text makes plain, through its determinatives, that Kinnaru's flesh was wood.¹⁰⁰ This conflation accords perfectly with the phenomenon of divinized instruments. One effected the god's epiphany by playing the *kinýra* in the appropriate ritual setting and so assuming the role of *kenyristḗs*—of Kinyras himself. He thereby gives voice to, and receives it from, the instrument, which is thus as central to the celebration as its player. If we seem to have come a long way from Pindar, recall the apostrophe of *Pythian* 1, where the lyre is virtually personified and celebrated for powers one might rather attribute to the lyrist:

> Golden *phórminx*—Apollo's and the dark-tressed
> Muses' joint possession—whom the dance-step heeds, the beginning
>   of festivity,
> And singers obey your signs
> When thrumming you fashion beginnings of chorus-leading
>   preludes.¹⁰¹

Only change *phórminx* to *kinýra* and one arrives at a fundamental aspect of the Cypriot celebrations "about Kinyras" to which Pindar alludes.

---

⁹⁷ Wilson 2009 has argued that this figure's negative treatment by Homer and later authors was generically motivated, with Thamyris representing a rival regional tradition of considerable antiquity, closer perhaps to Aeolic lyric. Ford 1992:90–101 views the contest in terms of agonistic poetics and the singer's relationship to the tradition (represented by the Muses).

⁹⁸ Wilson 2009:51–52 (quotation), with additional evidence for a local cult of Thamyris in n17 (adding Clay 2004:87 and 153, and noting especially Durante 1971–1974 2:202); further observations in Power 2010:208–209. Wilson suggests that the name "probably combined the sense of 'the gatherers' with that of 'Thamyrists'," looking to Hesykhios s.v. θάμυρις· πανήγυρις, σύνοδος ... καὶ ὁδοὺς θαμυρὰς τὰς λεωφόρους and s.v. θαμυρίζει· ἀθροίζει, συνάγει. That *θαμυρίζω may mean 'celebrate the cult of Thamyris' was recognized by P. Roesch (SEG 32:503). For a possible connection with Tacitus' *Tamiradae* of Paphos, see p405–406.

⁹⁹ As Cayla 2001:79, rightly notes.

¹⁰⁰ RS 20.024, 31: see p5.

¹⁰¹ Pindar *Pythian* 1.1–4: Χρυσέα φόρμιγξ, Ἀπόλλωνος καὶ ἰοπλοκάμων / σύνδικον Μοισᾶν κτέανον· τᾶς ἀκούει μὲν βάσις ἀγλαΐας ἀρχά, / πείθονται δ' ἀοιδοὶ σάμασιν / ἁγησιχόρων ὁπόταν προοιμίων ἀμβολὰς τεύχῃς ἐλελιζομένα. For the comparable personification in the Homeric *Hymn to Hermes*, see p6n32. For Kallimakhos *Hymns* 2.18–21, see p318n233.

Chapter Ten

Caught in the Act: Two Model Shrines

The idea of 'Kinyras in performance' becomes much more tangible when confronted with the rich music iconography of Cyprus, which extends our chronological horizons far beyond the literary record. We may begin with two model-shrines showing lyre-players in clear cult contexts.[102] Both pieces are thoroughly Cypriot, incorporating older stylistic elements going back to comparable LBA specimens of both the Levant and Aegean. Their provenance is unknown, with no compelling reason to assume a special Paphian connection.[103] After all, the goddess had many other cult centers throughout the island—Amathous, Kition, Golgoi, Idalion, Tamassos, Lapethos, and Salamis, to cite only the more prominent.[104] The models therefore indicate that hieratic lyre-playing was a general feature of Cypriot cult.

The presence of 'Aphrodite' is especially clear in the first model, from perhaps the seventh century (Figure 18).[105] At the center of this complex composition is a tapering, fenestrated pillar surmounted by birds. Its general shape evokes the aniconic representation of the Paphian goddess that appears on coins of the Roman era (also apparently adorned with birds, perhaps representing sculpted ornaments).[106] The pillar's identification as a 'dove-cote'[107] lets it be confidently linked with 'Aphrodite', whose sacred birds are well known.[108] This conforms to a wider regional pattern, which Lucian also attests for his 'Syrian Goddess' of Hierapolis (Manbog), in whose cult doves were held to be

---

[102] The careful description and initial observations of Boardman 1971 were brilliantly expanded by Mlynarczyk 1983, whose interpretation I develop here.
[103] But note that Mlynarczyk 1983:113–115 does argue for dove-apertures in the architectural remains of the Paphos sanctuary, comparing those of the first model shrine (see below).
[104] For these and numerous minor cult-places, see *Kypris*.
[105] Louvre AO 22.221: Ridder 1908:120–124 no. 106, pl. 20.106 (more intact than presently. He considered the lyrist female, and described the now-lost instrument's shape as trapezoidal, 123); Boardman 1971:40, fig. 4, pl. XVIII.1; Mlynarczyk 1983:111 fig. 2; CAAC IV:III[i]10 and pl. LXXVII:9 (Karageorghis associates with Kinyras); Paleocosta 1998:49–50, pl. V; Dunn-Vaturi 2003:109–110 (dating to late seventh or early sixth century).
[106] See p481n129.
[107] This depends on a close parallel from Kition, another conical structure with apertures attended by birds and now a female figure gazing from a doorway—a feature familiar from many house-shrines of Cyprus and the Levant (Boardman 1971:38 with further references in n2; 39 fig. 1). Two such specimens from Idalion—an important cult-site of the goddess (*Kypris*:179–189)—have rows of apertures on their upper walls, evidently for birds.
[108] Sources for Aphrodite's doves, and at Paphos in particular (cf. Martial 8.28.13, *Paphiae columbae*), are collected and discussed by Blinkenberg 1924:17, 20; Pirenne-Delforge 1994:415–417. For Aphrodite's doves on Paphian coins (Timarkhos and an early Alexandrine): BMC Cyprus:lxxvi-viii and pl. VIII.8–10, pl. XXII.6, 8–9; HC:73.

Praising Kinyras

Figure 18 Model shrine with dancers and lyrist. Unprovenanced (seventh century?), Louvre AO 22.221. Drawn from Ridder 1908 pl. 20.106 and CAAC IV pl. LXXVII:9.

sacred or even divine.[109] On Cyprus, they are linked to Kinyras himself through the aetiological myth of Peleia/Pelia.[110]

Four figures have been placed around the pillar. Three dancers occupy half the perimeter, facing the shrine. Opposite is a lyrist, whose back is to the pillar. Yet he stands so close that his 'interest' in it is clear, and this is reinforced by a cauldron at his side, presumably containing an offering. The configuration has several effects. First, the pillar-shrine is clearly the primary object of adoration. Yet the lyrist himself enjoys secondary focus, since, with his back to the

---

[109] Lucian *On the Syrian Goddess* 14, 33, 54 with comments of OSG:513–514; cf. GR:153.
[110] Servius Auctus on Vergil *Eclogues* 8.37: for this passage, see p290.

Chapter Ten

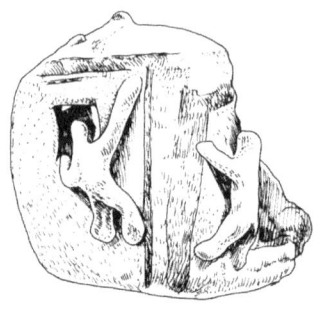

Figure 19 Model shrine with lyrist and spectators. Unprovenanced (eleventh–seventh century), Cyprus Museum, Nicosia, inv. B 220.1935. Drawn from Boardman 1971 pl. XVII.1-V.

dancers, and indeed the pillar itself, they become background for his performance. He controls the viewer's entrance into the cultic circle—a Master of Choral Ceremonies who mediates between 'audience' and god.

The second model has been variously dated between the eleventh and seventh centuries (Figure 19).[111] It is a rounded, rectangular house-shrine, with three windows, damaged door, and missing roof. Against one of the inner walls sits the lyre-player. Near the opposite wall is a broken stump, probably the base of an offerings table. Two rough figures on the outer walls peer through window and door, as though glimpsing a sacred mystery; two more have been lost, and another probably peeked through a vent above.[112] Their collective gaze shows that here too the object of veneration is the shrine itself and the deity for whom it stands.[113] But the composition, like that of the pillar-shrine, serves to isolate the lyrist within a sacred space, which he alone is worthy to enter.

In both scenes then the lyrist is a secondary focus, so that while he is as an intermediary to the divine, his own numinosity must not be underestimated. Boardman aptly applied the Homeric expression 'divine singer' (*theîos aoidós*) to these musicians:

---

[111] Cyprus Museum, Nicosia, inv. no. B 220.1935: Dikaios 1961:205n54 (seventh or sixth century); Boardman 1971, pl. XVII.1-V; Mlynarczyk 1983:111 fig. 1; dated to CG I (ca. 1050–950) in CAAC II:III[LGB] with fig. 69 and pl. XXXVIII; Paleocosta 1998:48–49, pl. IV.1-3; *Aspects*:103–104 no. 78, fig. 90–91 (dated simply CG).

[112] One may note here various sources that refer to the rites of Aphrodite as 'mysteries' (*Kypris*:53–54), although these typically relate to allegations of 'temple prostitution', or may be dismissed as poetic conceit in the context of love elegy (e.g. Ovid *Art of Love* 2.607–608).

[113] No birds are to be seen, though the lost roof would have provided an appropriate perch.

His isolation with the table in the Nicosia model, his place in the de Clercq model and the generally religious association of all the other models mentioned, may lend support to his identification *either as divine* or as an important servant or familiar of the deity ... *The lyre player lacks a name still, but perhaps this too will one day be revealed in the island or the east* (my emphasis).[114]

It was left to Mlynarczyk to connect these shrines with Kinyras and the Paphian kings in their role of "High Priest of the Queen."[115] But we must not forget Boardman's intuition about the lyrist's *own* divinity.

---

[114] Boardman 1971:41.
[115] Mlynarczyk 1983:112-113.

11
Lyric Landscapes of Early Cyprus

PINDAR, SUPPLEMENTED BY THE SCHOLIA and other relevant texts, has established a musical Kinyras some five centuries older than "Our *Kenyristḗs* Apollo" at Roman Paphos. Three initial forays into Cypriot iconography have indicated earlier horizons still, although such pieces, being mute, can never *prove* that 'Kinyras himself' is intended. Nevertheless the abundant visual evidence for early Cypriot lyre culture can hardly be ignored, given its contextual details and deep antiquity. It goes far beyond Greco-Roman literary sources to converge with documentary and iconographic evidence of the larger BA Near East.

Fortunately, Kinyras' very name connotes sympathies with the Syro-Levantine sphere and its musical cultures. This provides a welcome first road-sign for traversing the lyric landscapes of early Cyprus. We shall see that the path from Syro-Levantine lyre morphology to the Cypriot term *kinýra* is not entirely straightforward. But patient exploration will clarify key historical and cultural issues, ultimately establishing the LBA as a viable period for Kinyras' genesis on the island—a proposal that can then be refined in subsequent chapters.

The Current Picture

The general dearth of LBA musical evidence presents a considerable obstacle to satisfactory analysis of the island's ethnomusical history, and especially its transition through the major cultural developments of the first millennium. Conversely, that of the latter period, so much more conspicuous and abundant, is potentially misleading. In fact the earlier material—votive figurines (see below), rattles, scrapers, bronze cymbals, cylinder seals with dance scenes, and two outstanding bronze stands showing harpers—is ultimately quite illuminating for the Kinyras question, and will have to be considered in due course (Chapter 15). But first we must trace the history of lyres specifically, so far as possible.

Ancient Cypriot music iconography has never been completely assembled, thanks to hundreds of first-millennium terracotta- and limestone-votive

Chapter Eleven

musicians in collections around the world (Figure 27).[1] Found in IA sanctuary contexts throughout the island, these figurines include many groups of dancers around a central musician, typically lyre or double-pipes—an arrangement that, I have already noted, resonates clearly with Pindar's portrait of "Cypriot voices around Kinyras."[2] That the medium itself goes back to the LBA is shown by two well-preserved female figurines, one playing frame-drum and the other perhaps clapping, dated to ca. 1450–1200.[3] Some hundred such figurines were also found at the sanctuary of the Ingot God at Enkomi, going back to pre-Greek levels. Although these are so fragmentary that specific instruments cannot be identified, the superabundant IA specimens make it very likely that some or many of them were arranged in circular compositions around a central lyrist or double-piper.[4] This point has been neglected, so far as I have found, in previous surveys of Cypriot music iconography.[5]

Several past studies have focused on a basic morphological dichotomy observable in the IA evidence, which has been linked to Aegean and Phoenician immigration and/or colonization. The two groups are:

1) round-based lyres first attested in an eleventh-century vase painting (Figure 25 = 5.5k: see below), and then regularly in vase painting, votive figurines, and other media; these clearly resemble (n.b.) early Aegean

---

[1] General iconographic surveys: Aign 1963:60–74; Karageorghis 1977:216; Hermary 1989:387–393 (Louvre sculptures); Meerschaert 1991; Karageorghis et al. 2000:148–151 no. 227–237, 239 (coroplastic, Cesnola Collection, including some not in CAAC); *Aspects*:78–84, 101–113, 140–152, 217–218; Fariselli 2007 (Phoenician material); Knapp 2011. Lyres: CCSF 1:33; Monloup 1994:109–112 (female terracottas, Salamis); DCPIL:49–51; Kolotourou 2002; Paleocosta 1998 (lyre-iconography). Double-pipe and other winds: Flourentzos 1992. Frame-drums/percussion: Averett 2002–2004; Kolotourou 2005; Kolotourou 2007. Dance: Lefèvre-Novaro 2007 passim; Fariselli 2010 (Phoenician focus). General studies (use with caution): Zarmas 1975; Jager 2000.

[2] These musician figures may be noted for future research: CAAC, II (Late Cypriot–Cypro-Geometric): A(vi)1–2, GD1–6, LGA[iii]5–7, LGB1, LGC1, LGC9; III (Cypro-Archaic): no. 174; IV (Cypro-Archaic): I[v]1–8, I[vi]1–7, I[vii]1–19, II[iv]5, III[i]1–10 (ring dances); Va (Cypro-Archaic): I[vii]1, I[ix]1–36, I[x]3, I[xi]h.60–66, I[xi]i.67–80, II[xiii]2, 4–5, II[xiv]1–5, II[xv]1–71; Vb (Cypro-Archaic): Ch. VI, 59, Ch. VII, Ch. VIII[i]1–3, VIII[ii]4, VIII[iii]5–54. Many more are in individual museum collections and site publications, including: Myres 1914:338–339 no. 2241–2256 (ring-dances, Cesnola collection); Monloup 1984:134 no. 512–513 (Archaic frame-drummers, Salamis); Yon and Caubet 1988a:4–5 no. 10–12, pl. II (female lyrists, Lapethos); Monloup 1994:109–117 (Classical female lyrists, Salamis); Vandervondelen 1994; SAM:164–166 no. 128–130 (Bible Lands Museum, Jerusalem).

[3] CAAC II:A(vi)1–2 and pl. VII.2–3, dated LC II–III. See also *Aspects*:84 no. 60–61, fig. 70–71; Knapp 2011:122. Both figurines belong to the type "Standing Nude Female Figure with 'Bird' Face."

[4] Figurines from Ingot God sanctuary: Courtois 1971:326–356 (note especially 348, fig. 145); CAAC II:64–65, dating to end of LC III or beginning of CG IA; so too Webb 1999:102–113, especially 112 and Webb 2001, especially 76, 79.

[5] See further p398.

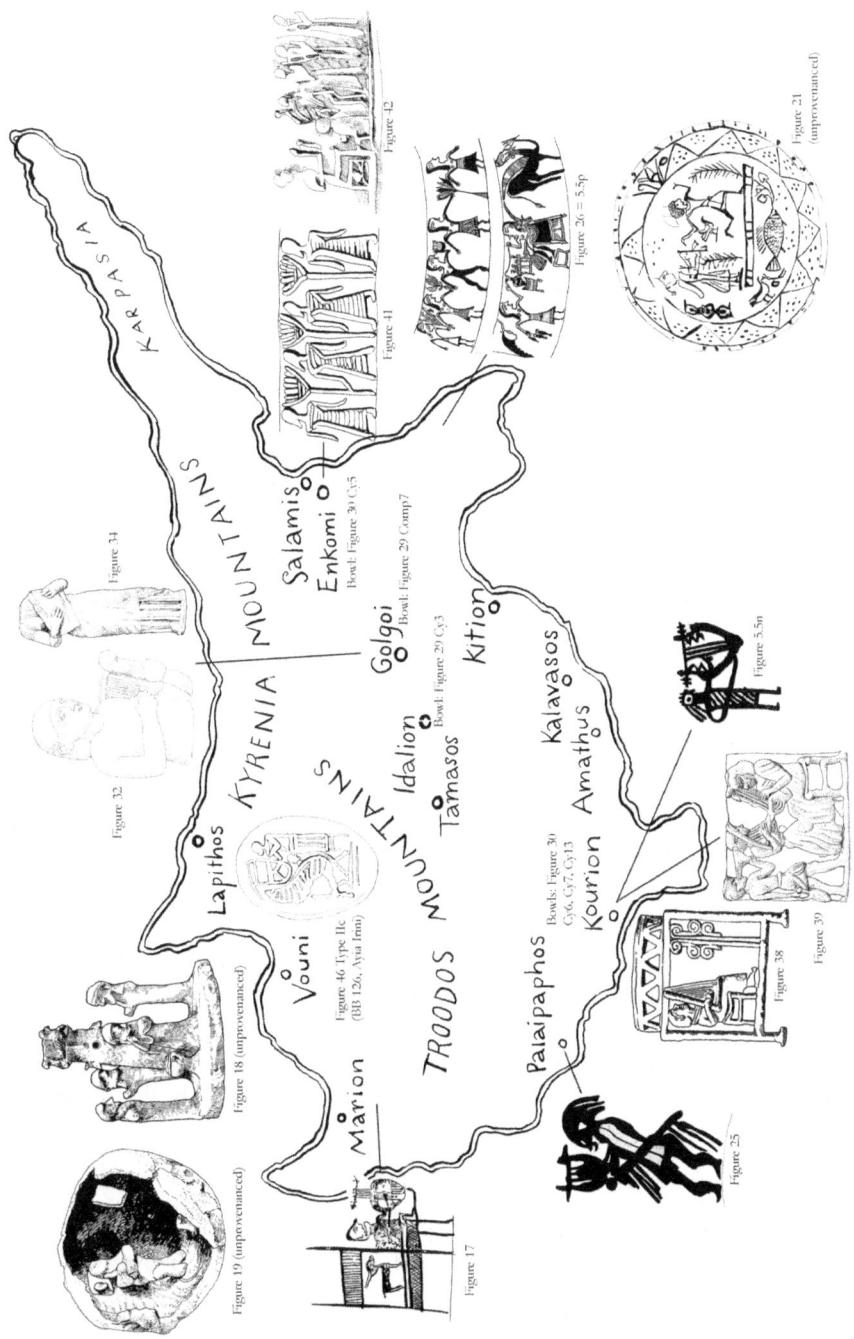

Figure 20 Map of Cyprus showing distribution of iconography discussed in text.

specimens from the LBA to ca. 400 and sporadically beyond (see Figures 4 and 5);[6]

2) flat-based, often asymmetrical lyres appearing in the Cypro-Phoenician symposium bowls (*phiálai*)[7] between ca. 900–600 (Figure 29); these adhere to the Syro-Levantine *knr*-types discussed in Chapter 3 (with Figures 4 and 5).

This apparent coincidence of chronology and morphology was systematically elaborated by B. Lawergren as follows:

> The lyres of Cyprus deserve special mention. Like Palestine [sc. in the Philistine EIA], Cyprus had both Eastern and Western lyres. Round-based lyres flourished ca. 1100–800 B.C.E. ... in the wake of Aegean influences ... The round-based lyres were followed by thin lyres [i.e. *knr*] ... as a result of Phoenician influences beginning ca. 850 B.C.E, but a few Western lyres continued through this period. Strong Greek influences reemerged in the second half of the sixth century B.C.E. ... and a very large number of round-based lyres were represented during the fifth century.[8]

Lawergren tacitly begins from a (presumed) lack of pre-Greek representations, but prudently avoids definite conclusions about the LBA island.[9] Deger-Jalkotzky more boldly suggested that lyres, previously *unknown*, are an ethnic marker of Aegean influx (for her other morphological criteria, see below).[10] Similarly, Maas and Snyder treated the Cypriot lyres as a variety of "Greek stringed instruments."[11] Fariselli, in her valuable recent study of Phoenician music and dance, also assumes a basic contrast between Phoenician and Aegean types in discussing the symposium bowls; but what 'Aegean' means in eighth-seventh century cultural terms, and within the iconographic repertoire of the *phiálai*, is not determined.[12]

Closer investigation shows that the current picture is too reductive.[13] A lyre-less pre-Greek Cyprus is *a priori* unlikely given the many third-millennium

---

[6] This rough terminus reflects the advent of the κιθάρα in its classical form.
[7] *Pi-a-la* (φιάλα) is inscribed on one of the Kourion bowls: PBSB:73 (Cy11); I.Kourion 4.
[8] DCPIL:49, with the East/West dichotomy building on Lawergren 1993.
[9] But "Greek influences reemerged" does imply that the earlier 'western' morphology was absent from the pre-Greek island.
[10] Deger-Jalkotzy 1994, especially 21–22.
[11] SIAG:8, making the point that they are only representations from the Dark Age.
[12] Fariselli 2007:13 n15–16, 19, 23, with further analysis of dance in Fariselli 2010.
[13] This discussion supersedes Franklin 2006a:44–45; Franklin 2006b.

Syro-Levantine and Mesopotamian specimens, especially since second-millennium lexical evidence shows the word *knr* extending beyond the Syro-Levantine heartland (Mari, Assur, Hattusha, Egypt). That the same could be true of LBA Cyprus is supported in a general way by the large percentages of Semitic and Hurrian names born by Alashiyans in texts from Ugarit and Amarna, since various forms of *knr* had been current among these linguistic groups for centuries before the Greek influx.[14] It would fully accord with the pre-Greek island's cosmopolitanism, which, we shall see, finds clear musical expression in the Mesopotamianizing *harps* on the aforementioned bronze-stands (thirteenth-century).[15] These very instruments, admittedly, have been contrasted with the round-based IA lyres in attempting to distinguish two phases of Cypriot ethno-musical history.[16] The Kourion stands certainly do give a vital glimpse of pre-Greek musical conceptions, and bear importantly on Kinyras.[17] Yet it need not follow that lyres per se were a novelty of the IA.

Clearly even a single lucky find could alter the picture significantly. And as it happens, a key piece of evidence has been overlooked. In what follows, I shall present this 'lost daughter of Kinyras,' thus documenting at least one lyric dimension of pre-Greek Cyprus. I next reassess the 'Aegeanness' of the island's round-based lyre-representations. We can then consider the implications of our new evidence and interpretations for understanding, in broad cultural terms, the morphological 'confrontation' seen in the symposium bowls. Finally, we shall see what this material contributes to the linguistic prehistory of the word *kinýra*, thus returning us full circle to Kinyras himself.

A Lost 'Daughter of Kinyras' in the Cyprus Museum

A lovely but broken faience dish, unprovenanced but dated by stylistic criteria to the fourteenth-thirteenth century (LC II), has been on display in the Cyprus Museum for decades (Figure 21).[18] It was tersely described by P. Dikaios in the 1961 guide:

> Remarkable whitish faience bowl covered with blue-green glaze, probably a local imitation of an Egyptian Eighteenth Dynasty prototype. Painted ornamentation on the interior: two human figures, one

---

[14] See p53–55, 98–99.
[15] See p241.
[16] Sherratt 1992:336 (see below).
[17] See p383–392.
[18] Nicosia, Inv. G63; height 4.2. cm, diameter 13.2. The best image known to me is Karageorghis 1976a:178 fig. 137; also Dikaios 1961:153–154 no. 6, pl. XXXIII.5; Peltenburg 1968:303, includes it among his unpublished specimens (vii).

Chapter Eleven

Figure 21 *Kinyrístria* and dancer. Fourteenth-century Egyptian(izing) faience bowl from Cyprus (unprovenanced). Cyprus Museum, Nicosia, Inv. G63. Drawn from autopsy and Karageorghis 1976a fig. 137.

dancing and, to their left, Bes; in the field, conventional trees, below, bird and fish. Fourteenth century B.C.[19]

The bowl belongs to a larger class of "Egyptian or Egyptianizing pieces consist[ing] chiefly of blue green or white shallow bowls ... and scenes with roughly drawn fish, boats, dancing and instrument-playing figures, hieroglyphs, and lotus flowers."[20] They are variously held to be Egyptian imports, Egyptianizing objects from a Canaanite workshop, or local Cypriot imitations

---

[19] Dikaios 1961:153–154.
[20] Foster 1979:50 and n316. By "instrument-playing figures" she must mean the lute-player bowls (see below).

Lyric Landscapes of Early Cyprus

of Egyptian styles and scenes.[21] Some see this elusiveness as their most striking feature, with the more than 130 faience vases and fragments reflecting "the cross currents of cultural influences on the island during this period of eclecticism as no other single body of material does."[22]

Dikaios declined to identify the left-hand figure, whose interpretation is made difficult by several breaks in the bowl.[23] Degradation of the glaze along the shard-edges has endowed them, and hence the join lines, with a darkish color very close to the lines of the figure itself, over which they crisscross confusingly. Nevertheless, patient observation and continual reference to the underside of the dish, where the breaks may be clearly distinguished, enable a confident, if not entirely complete, reconstruction.[24] She is in fact a musician who plays for the dancing figure, while Bes, patron of much professional music, especially involving dance, oversees the performance.[25] She is a '*kinyrístria*', wielding a lyre of Syro-Levantine type.[26]

Parts of the soundbox can only just be detected. Two give away details, however, are quite clear. First is the slight incurve to the arms where they join the crossbar. There is also a largish, bird-head finial on the right end of the crossbar, and perhaps faint traces of another on the left; there are close parallels in Hittite and Egyptian art, one of the latter featuring a lyre-girl with a Bes tattoo.[27] Two tassels are attached to the yoke, like those found on lutes in Akhenaten's harem and Hittite/Neo-Hittite representations.[28] Our lyrist has a

---

[21] See especially Peltenburg 1986:155–161, noting lack of stylistic deviations which might betray Cypriot manufacture; he challenges their critical reception as "poor, local copies of Egyptian work" (Peltenburg 1972:131); Levantine workshop(s) are considered possible, but less likely (contrast Peltenburg 1968:143–151). But certain types *can* be attributed to a Cypriot faience industry: Foster 1979:49–55; Karageorghis et al. 2000:62.

[22] Peltenburg 1972:129.

[23] Cf. Peltenburg 1968:304 (bowl no. 5d): "To the left a female with calf-length billowing robes. She seems to hold something over a papyrus which grows from the boat, but the brown designs are too fugitive here to make it out."

[24] I thank G. Fawkes for sharp observations and drawings during a museum visit on May 17, 2012. The dish is displayed vertically, so both top and bottom may be examined.

[25] Bes and music: Hickmann 1954a:35–38; MgB 2/1:36–39 fig. 15–17; MMAE:48 fig. 26, 57–58 and fig. 32, 110, 116–119 passim, with fig. 72.

[26] For this word, see p216.

[27] Hittite: Inandik vase. Egypt: MgB 2/1:32–33 fig. 9; MMAE:48 fig. 26 (Nineteenth Dynasty, Bes tattoo, bird-finial one end only), 108 fig. 64 (Twenty-First or Twenty-Second Dynasty); HKm, pl. 18 no. 52.1, 52.3-4. Musicians with Bes-tattoos are otherwise known: Hickmann 1954b:276; Hickmann 1954a:37–38.

[28] Egypt: MMAE:86 fig. 50. Hittite/Neo-Hittite: HKm, pl. 4 no. 11 and 15, 7 no. 26, 9 no. 29, 11 no. 35, 12 no. 37–38. With lutes the question may arise whether these tassels are not rather the ends of strings. Even when their position at the end of the neck makes this possible, they are sufficiently long that one must suppose that they have been worked into an adornment (cf. HKm:59). In other cases the tassels come from the middle of the neck.

short cape, paralleled by female musicians on a Cypro-Phoenician symposium bowl and the cognate musical procession/dance scene of a ninth- or eighth-century North Syrian ivory pyxis from Nimrud (Figure 31).[29] She also holds her instrument horizontally, again as usual in Canaanite and NK representations.[30] The exact position of the player's arms, and indeed whether both are shown, have eluded our repeated autopsy and comparison.

This musical reading is corroborated by several closely related bowls. One, said to be from near Idalion, is well preserved and shows another Egyptian(izing) female figure, in diaphanous dress, playing a lute against a background of lotus-blossoms (Figure 22).[31] A very similar dish in Leiden has a lute-girl with a Bes tattoo on her thigh.[32] A third lutenist, from a tomb at Maroni and heavily effaced, may be reconstructed through a close parallel from Egypt itself.[33] While all these scenes are Egyptian(izing), the Levantine lyre shows that the corpus is to be associated specifically with the international musical groups cultivated in the NK.[34] Wherever these bowls were actually manufactured, our *kinyrístria*—or at least her instrument—is ultimately 'from' the Syro-Levantine world.

The cautious will warn that 'pots are not people'—that the dish was perhaps valued for its exotic imagery, and so need say nothing about contemporary Cypriot music. But the dishes' relevance to musical reality is vividly supported by the processed tortoise shells found aboard the fourteenth-century Uluburun wreck.[35] R. Eichmann and S. Psaroudakes have concluded that these were intended for Egyptian-style lutes like those of the faience dishes.[36] The shells corroborate, materially, the circulation of musical technology implied by iconography and the lexical evidence. They join the ship's cargo as a microcosm of LBA palatial exchange—recalling that Cyprus was, if not the ship's origin, at least a major point of call.

Moreover, faience vessels were generally not *mere* exotica on Cyprus, but often employed in local cultic environments—as though ritually efficacious

---

[29] Bowl: PBSB Cy13 (Kourion), where the rightmost musician of a trio (probably double-piper) clearly has the cape; Culican 1982:15 and n6 detected one on the second (lyrist) as well, and noted the Nimrud bowl.

[30] Canaanite: Megiddo, Figure 11 = 4.1p; Kamid el-Loz: DCPIL fig. 1o = my Figure 4.1o. Egypt: MMAE:43 fig. 21, 86 fig. 50, 89 fig. 52, 91 fig. 54 (twice); also Wegner 1950, pl. 7a, 9a–b (the dimensions of 9b being close to our lyrist). The *vertical* position is seen in MMAE:48 fig. 26, 53 no. 30.

[31] New York, MMA 74.51.5074 = Cesnola 1903, pl. CVIII no. 4 = Myres 1914:274 no. 1574 = Karageorghis et al. 2000:63 no. 99. Also Aign 1963:61 fig. 26; Peltenburg 1968:307.

[32] RMO Leiden, inv. AD 14, Eighteenth to Nineteenth Dynasty.

[33] London, BM (18)98.12–1.145, from Maroni, tomb 17: Johnson 1980:24 no. 136, pl. XXVI.136 = Peltenburg 1986:158 no. 35 = Peltenburg 2007, fig. 5b.

[34] See p105–111.

[35] For the wreck generally, see below p326 with references. The shells are unpublished.

[36] I thank Eichmann and Psaroudakes for a group email discussion with C. Pulak (November, 2008).

Figure 22 Female lutenist. Egyptian(izing) faience bowl from near Idalion. New York, MMA 74.51.5074. Drawn from Karageorghis et al. 2000:63 no. 99.

precisely by virtue of their precious qualities. Along with other, often imported luxury items (ivory, glass, alabaster, and ostrich eggs), the vessels "occur most frequently in urban cult buildings, where they probably served as votives and containers of oil, perfume, incense and other substances used in the cult."[37] This pattern of cultic imports provides one motivation for the arrival of the *knr* itself to Cyprus in this international age. Of course, our new *kinyrístria* is just as readily connected with scenes of secular music-making and the collecting of exotic female musicians.[38] But a cultic role for female kinyrists is clearly seen in the Cypro-Phoenician symposium bowls, which, though later, perpetuate LBA guildic traditions (as known from Ugarit).[39] And conquering kings, in taking over the musicians of their vanquished rivals, must often have brought home cult-performers. Recall the foreign musicians employed for religious festivals in second-millennium Egypt, and the pervasive sacral ambience of Akhenaten's

---

[37] Webb 1999:243.
[38] See p75, 105–111.
[39] See p258–272, 273.

Chapter Eleven

palace.⁴⁰ These customs provide, I believe, the best explanation for a myth reported by ps.-Apollodoros: Kinyras' daughters, having offended Aphrodite, slept with foreigners and ended their lives in Egypt.⁴¹

Music, Memory, and the Aegean Diaspora

Our 'lost daughter' is the clearest proof one can reasonably expect that pre-Greek Cyprus was not a lyric blank canvas. Yet by reminding us that the absence of evidence is a risky foundation for historical constructions, she bids us wonder whether she herself represents but one contour of a richer—and perhaps older—landscape that remains as yet otherwise undiscovered. As noted above, it is not unlikely that some of the smashed votive figurines from Enkomi were indeed lyre-players.⁴² And with several LBA cylinder seals showing infinite processions or ring-dances, one readily assumes musical accompaniment that is simply not depicted.⁴³

Now it does seem clear that several IA round-based lyres from Philistia and Cilicia—other areas of the twelfth-century Aegean diaspora—do indicate an Aegean ethnic presence and/or cultural memory.⁴⁴ In the Levant especially, an unambiguous Aegean interpretation becomes much more compelling, given that 'eastern' *knr*-type lyres are otherwise so dominant. I have already mentioned the cult-stand from Ashdod with its 'Canaanite orchestra'—where, however, the lyre is not the Canaanite form one expects.⁴⁵ The piece adds valuable nuance to the monochromatic representation of Philistine religion in the Biblical narratives, which do not distinguish it from the surrounding Canaanite environment.⁴⁶ A tenth-century seal from the same site shows a seated musician

---

⁴⁰ See p107–111.
⁴¹ [Apollodoros] *Library* 3.14.3, with the parallel in Servius Auctus on Vergil *Eclogues* 10.18. See further p504 and n60. Others would connect this myth with traditions of 'sacred prostitution' at Paphos (HC:71n1), but this leaves the Egyptian facet unexplained.
⁴² See p242.
⁴³ See p397.
⁴⁴ Locally produced LH IIIC 'Mycenaean' pottery appears in considerable quantity in Cilicia at this time (most conspicuously at Tarsus, with nearly 900 shards, but at Mersin and Kazanlı as well). This material is often dismissed on the 'pots are not people' argument (e.g. Vanschoonwinkel 1990:190–192). But Birney 2007 has shown that the shapes are consistent with domestic use, not mercantile activity, a conclusion supported by other finds of domestic application. It is therefore clear that there was early Aegean settlement here.
⁴⁵ See p157 and cf. AMEL:99–100.
⁴⁶ See generally Machinist 2000.

Lyric Landscapes of Early Cyprus

Figure 23 Lyre-player seal, Ashdod, ca. 1000. Jerusalem, IAA 91-476. Drawn from Dothan 1971, pl. XLIX.7.

also with round-based lyre (Figure 23),[47] and another such instrument is held by a terracotta figurine from the same site, about a century later.[48]

Equally remarkable musical evidence is found in the reliefs of Karatepe, the eighth-century Cilician site whose inscriptions celebrate the restoration of the House of Mopsos to power over the Danunians in a kingdom called Hiyawa. The latter name is a normal Luwian truncation of Ahhiyawa, and is to be connected somehow with the Aegean/Mycenaean state of this name with which the

---

[47] Dothan 1971 1:138–139, 2:162–163 and fig. 76.1, pl. 69.7; Keel 1997:666–667 and fig. 15, with further bibliography.
[48] Dothan 1971 fig. 62.1, pl. 55.1; Dothan 1982:249 and pl. 35; SAM:159 no. 123.

Chapter Eleven

Figure 24 Juxtaposition of 'western' and 'eastern' lyres. Orthostat relief, Karatepe, ca. 725. Drawn from Akurgal 1962 fig. 142.

Hittites periodically clashed in western Anatolia.[49] The bilingual inscriptions[50] record two forms of the name Mopsos—Luwian Mukšaš and Phoenician Mpš—which exhibit divergent outcomes of a more ancient labiovelar; this allows reconstruction of a name that is indeed found in Linear B texts as *Mo-qo-so* (/Mok^{u}sos/). Whether this is Greek or Anatolian *in origin*, it was certainly at home in the Mycenaean world. The simplest explanation is therefore that the later Greco-Anatolian traditions about the migration of Mopsos/Moxos—to "Cilicia and Syria, even as far as Phoenicia"—do accurately reflect population movements at the end of the LBA.[51] Given this, it is most striking to see, in a banquet scene symbolizing renewed political harmony after civil war, a round-based lyre

---

[49] See above p13n64, 348n63. The Luw. aphaeresis of Ahhiyawa > Hiyawa is already attested in a LBA text (Singer 2006:242–262, especially 251), and recurs in an eighth-century inscription from Çineköy, Cilicia (Tekoglu and Lemaire 2000, especially 968–972).

[50] For the Karatepe texts (KAI 26; ANET:653–654; CS 2 no. 21 and 31), see now W. Röllig in Çambel 1999:50–81 (cf. 108–110) for the Phoenician text (with philological commentary supplementing Bron 1979), and Hawkins 2000 no. I.1 for the Luwian text (with extensive earlier bibliography).

[51] Strabo 14.4.3: τοὺς δὲ λαοὺς μετὰ Μόψου τὸν Ταῦρον ὑπερθέντας τοὺς μὲν ἐν Παμφυλίᾳ μεῖναι τοὺς δ᾽ ἐν Κιλικίᾳ μερισθῆναι καὶ Συρίᾳ μέχρι καὶ Φοινίκης. Whether or not Mopsos was an *historical* individual is another question. Representative recent discussions are Finkelberg 2005:150–152; Jasink and Marino 2007; Oettinger 2008; Hawkins 2009:165–166; López-Ruiz 2009. Most of the primary sources are collected in Houwink ten Cate 1961:44–50.

juxtaposed with a model of Syro-Anatolian type (Figure 24).[52] There seems little doubt that the former derives from Aegean tradition in the region, among the people whose designation "Half-Achaeans" (*Hypakhaioí*) was already obsolete in the time of Herodotos.[53]

These Aegean lyres in diaspora contexts are not merely potent *symbols* of ethnic memory. They were an essential *tool* for its preservation. The Karatepe reliefs powerfully illustrate what is anyway a natural supposition—that Aegean migration deeds were sung not only or even primarily in Greece, but 'on the ground' within and between diaspora communities.

A comparable situation on Cyprus must account for at least some of the many legends about migration to the island after the Trojan War; Teukros at Salamis and the Arcadian Agapenor at Paphos are two of the more compelling examples (see Chapter 14). I shall therefore begin surveying the island's round-based lyres from what is at once the earliest such representation, and that which permits the most viable sub-Mycenaean interpretation. Even here, however, 'Greek' and 'Cypriot' cannot be entirely distinguished. So this case will also serve as an *a fortiori* caution against overly Hellenocentric readings of the abundant later material.

Cypriot Lyres Between East and West

The piece in question is an eleventh-century kalathos from Kouklia/Old Paphos, roughly the same date and place as the Opheltas *obelós* that first documents Greek on the island.[54] In one frame, a warrior with a sword holds a round-based lyre and parades or dances (Figure 25). In another, a man probably sacrifices a goat or ram on an altar by a tree. The vase belongs to a group of eleventh-tenth century pictorial pottery used (among other objects) as status symbols in Mycenaean-style tombs of the period.[55] Figurative painting alternates with geometric decoration; on the whole the lack of *precise* Aegean parallels for their iconographical repertoire makes it best to describe them as 'Cypriot'. Yet a subset contains representations of warrior or hunter figures, armed and engaged in activities described as "macho" or "heroic," and novel with respect

---

[52] HKm 73 and pl. 14–15 no. 43–44. The Syro-Anatolian lyre is well paralleled by an instrument from the Zincirli reliefs: HKm pl. 13 no. 39, and the Hittite precedent in pl. 9 no. 28.3.
[53] *Hypakhaioí*: Herodotos 7.91. Cf. Lanfranchi 2005:482; Oettinger 2008:66n9.
[54] Nicosia, Kouklia T.9:7, proto-bichrome kalathos, LCIIIB: CCSF 1:5, 2:1–3; Iacovou 1988:72 (Cat. no. 29), fig. 66–70. For the *obelós*, see p14.
[55] Coldstream 1989, especially 330–331 (eleventh-century chamber-tombs with long *drómoi* have higher concentration of status symbols than other burial types, and appear in areas of later Greek-speaking kingdoms); cf. Rupp 1985:126–127; Sherratt 1992:330.

Chapter Eleven

Figure 25 Warrior-lyrist. Proto-bichrome kalathos from Kouklia, eleventh century (LCIIIB). Cyprus Museum, Nicosia, Kouklia T.9:7. Drawn from CCSF 1:5, 2:1–3.

to earlier Cypriot iconography.[56] One striking case shows a man drinking from a kylix and holding a figure-eight body shield—an armament that was "uniquely Aegean with a history of apparently potent symbolism," since it had gone out of actual use centuries earlier.[57] Sherrat attractively reads this is "a symbol of a specifically Aegean, Greek-speaking past ... being used to analogise and define the present."[58]

The Kouklia kalathos may well convey a comparable message, resonating with a traditional topos of Greek poetry, and especially epic—the bifurcation and/or conflation of warrior and singer, familiar from Achilles singing *kléa*

---

[56] Sherratt 1992:332–333.
[57] Iacovou 1988:71 (Cat. no. 15), fig. 34; Sherratt 1992:335 (quotation).
[58] Sherratt 1992:336.

254

andrôn on his lyre and Odysseus stringing his bow like an expert lyrist his instrument.[59] This vase is the best evidence we are likely to get of a sub-Mycenaean epic tradition flourishing in Cyprus.[60] Yet its Aegean aspects are not incompatible with Coldstream's apt comparison to "Kinyras himself" on the strength of the vase's Paphian provenance.[61] Sherrat qualified this by stressing stylistic differences from other LBA Cypriot musical representations (the harps on the Kourion stands: see Chapter 15) and the instrument's presumed Aegean morphology. If he "is intended to represent Kinyras," she wrote, "then it is a quite different Kinyras ... the more recognisably Greek version of himself ... the appropriation and transformation of an element of common Cypriot 'history' into something intended to be identified as peculiarly Greek-Cypriot."[62]

While Sherrat's emphasis on hybridity offers a useful way forward for considering Cypriot lyre morphology more generally, note that even her reading begs the question of whether these round-based instruments were, or were not, a novelty of Aegean immigration. S. Deger-Jalkotzy saw a further Aegean marker in the tassels on the Kouklia musician's sword, comparing a similarly adorned weapon on a potsherd (LH IIIC) from sub-Mycenaean Lefkandi on Euboea.[63] Yet much the same streamers grace the lyrist on the eleventh-century 'Orpheus jug' from Megiddo (Figure 13) and another non-musician figure from the same site. Any Philistine/Aegean explanation of the Orpheus jug must account for the even stronger Canaanite elements of its style and iconography. Not least is the *knr*-shape of the instrument itself, which makes this figure more obviously a '*kinyras*' than his counterpart at Old Paphos.[64]

A third Aegean lyre-marker proposed by Deger-Jalkotzky, not found in the Kouklia kalathos, is the 'zigzag' arms of several Mycenaean-Minoan images,[65] and two EIA Cypriot representations. One is on a late tenth-century vase from the necropolis of Kaloriziki (Kourion area), which in another panel shows the

---

[59] Homer *Iliad* 9.189 (with [Plutarch] *On Music* 1145f), cf. 13.730–731; *Odyssey* 21.406–411 (for which see p387 and n99); Terpandros 5 (Gostoli); Arkhilokhos 1 West IEG; Alkman 41 PMGF; Pindar *Olympian* 1.1–12; Euripides fr. 759a.1622–1623 TGF; cf. Plato *Laws* 804d; Plutarch *Lykourgos* 21.4; *Moralia* 238b; etc. For the motif, see further Moulton 1977:145–153; Thalmann 1984:170–184; Goldhill 1991:1–68; Franklin 2003:297–301. It is still found in one version of the medieval epic *Digenes Akrites* (4.396–435, Grottaferrata codex: Mavrogordato 1956): the hero λαμβάνει καὶ κιθάραν ... κάλλιστα δ' ἐπεπαίδευτο ἐν μουσικοῖς ὀργάνοις (397–399), κτλ.

[60] Franklin 2014:214–216.

[61] Coldstream 1989:330–331; cf. Paleocosta 1998:56.

[62] Sherratt 1992:337.

[63] Deger-Jalkotzy 1994:21 and 18 fig. 4.3. This figure did not necessarily carry a lyre.

[64] See p159–161.

[65] Deger-Jalkotzy 1994:18 fig. 4 (cf. already Aign 1963:352); SIAG:16 fig. 2b (Chania), 18 fig. 3b (Tiryns).

Chapter Eleven

same (or similar) figure pouring a libation; together the images indicate a ritual involving music and drinking, whether symposium, funerary rite, or some combination (Figure 5.5n and 20).[66] The other is the famous Hubbard amphora (Famagusta district, ca. 800), a longtime centerpiece of the Cyprus Museum (Figure 26 = 5.5p).[67] Markoe convincingly explicated the funerary symbolism of its scenes, in which the deceased, enthroned amid symbols of death and rebirth, is honored by a lyric choral ritual.[68] This is a striking parallel to the Rāp'iu text from Ugarit, with its *kinnāru*-led musical ensemble regaling the underworld king who is closely associated with royal ancestor cult.[69] The Hubbard vase, with its well-paralleled Syro-Anatolian and Egyptian iconographic elements going back to the MBA, offers little contextual purchase for interpreting the musician's instrument as 'Aegean' rather than 'Cypriot'.

Indeed, two southeastern Anatolian cylinder seals, not noticed by Deger-Jalkotzky, also show lyres with both round base and zigzag arms (Figure 4.5d, 5e).[70] These seals are now dated to ca. 1800, and can no longer be explained through Aegean diaspora.[71] Clearly the combination of round-base and zigzag arms was an early areal attribute spanning the Aegean and eastern Mediterranean.[72] Note too several further third-millennium Syro-Anatolian lyre-representations whose bases are rather indeterminate between round and flat; or which seem flat-based while having slightly zigzag arms (Figure 4.1c, 1e–f, 5a–c). Their relationship to the more rigidly defined ground of 'East' and 'West' is anything but clear.[73] Do they constitute a chronological transition from one to the other? A geographical one? Both? Their temporal and geographic distribution makes it perfectly possible that some at least went by a form of the word *knr*, despite not closely resembling the (mainly second-millennium) instruments we normally associate with that word.[74]

---

[66] Nicosia, Kaloriziki Tomb 11 no. 5: Dikaios 1936–1937:71; Rutten 1939:442; CCSF 1:33, 2:97–98 (no. IX.1).
[67] Hubbard amphora: Nicosia, 1938/XI-2/3: Dikaios 1936–1937; CCSF 1:8–9, 2:7–9.
[68] Markoe 1988.
[69] RS 24.252 = KTU/CAT 1.108. See p134–141.
[70] For these seals and their interpretation, see p517.
[71] Collon 1987:43 no. 148 (correcting Porada 1956:204). The challenge these posed to an exclusively Aegean interpretation was recognized by SIAG:9 (even on the basis of their former dating to ca. 1200).
[72] Li Castro and Scardina 2011; similarly DCPIL:47–49: "The trait began already at Tarsus and Mardin ... before its association with the Aegean, i.e., this trait was integral to round-based lyres at their very their inception."
[73] DCPIL:47, is appropriately agnostic on their affiliation. Li Castro and Scardina 2011:211 (with fig. 13–15) decline to address them as being too vaguely rendered.
[74] I include here the Hattic/Hittite form in z- and cognates: p55, 89–90.

Lyric Landscapes of Early Cyprus

Figure 26 Hubbard amphora, Famagusta district, ca. 800. Cyprus Museum, Nicosia, 1938/XI-2/3. Drawn from CCSF 1.8–9, 2.7–9.

And so while Lawergren's distinction between 'eastern' and 'western' lyre-morphology remains broadly valid, it is not clear just where the line should be drawn. Cyprus falls precisely within the 'disputed' area. If we persist in equating 'western' with Greek/Aegean and 'eastern' with Canaanite/Phoenician, the island becomes a passive matrix for the implantation of foreign lyric identities—an idea not merely politically objectionable, but inherently implausible.

To be sure, there must indeed have been a time when lyres were new to the island. But given the high antiquity of chordophones in the Aegean, Anatolia, and larger ANE, we cannot definitely conclude that lyres first arrived *only* in the fourteenth-century (our 'lost daughter'), or that their morphology was only ever that of the Levant. For all we know, some more rounded shape had been current well beforehand, and even went by a name prefiguring *kinýra*. At this point, all options must be kept open.

Chapter Eleven

While an Aegean musical presence on EIA Cyprus is certainly not to be denied, and an important sub-Mycenaean 'lyric' component is perfectly plausible,[75] the round-based lyres are not as diagnostic as generally supposed. Contextual details of the Kouklia kalathos can indeed confirm an Aegean cultural perspective. But even here we must resist *segregating* Greek from pre-Greek. And the Anatolian seals gravely undermine an Aegeocentric explanation of the IA Kaloriziki and Hubbard lyrists, which are just as likely to perpetuate an old insular tradition with broader areal connections.

We must seriously consider, therefore, whether the round-based lyres of IA Cyprus were in fact, morphologically and culturally, *Cypro-Aegean hybrids*; and whether similar instruments already inhabited the pre-Greek island. This hypothesis solves several problems in a stroke. First, it accounts for the early ubiquity of round-based lyres in the popular medium of votive-figurines.[76] Second, it allows for the rich non-Aegean iconographic and cultic elements in the relevant representations (Hubbard amphora and the pieces discussed in Chapter 10). Finally, while these lyres would no longer be *unambiguous* Aegean ethnic markers, they would remain *compatible* with early Aegean cultural expression in a 'colonial' environment, if other elements justify the reading (Kouklia kalathos).

Ethnicity and Musical Identity in the Cypro-Phoenician Symposium Bowls

Our new *kinyrístria* also complicates the 'eastern' lyres of the Cypro-Phoenician *phiálai*. Did Levantine morphology disappear in the less cosmopolitan EIA, to return with ninth-century Phoenician colonization? Or was there a continuous tradition, as yet unrepresented archeologically? Here the early votive-figurines are again important, but difficult to interpret (Figure 27a–d). Their soundboxes, though roughly-formed with a small band of clay, are on the whole distinctly round. Yet their arms vary between perpendicular (as in Aegean instruments) and divergent (as often with Levantine). Are these differences mere habits of

---

[75] Franklin 2014.
[76] The best discussion known to me of lyre-playing female figures is Monloup 1994:109–117, on those from Salamis. But I disagree with her view that the rounded Cypriot lyres *normally* represent tortoiseshell instruments; the clearer lines of limestone sculpture show that this is generally not the case. Tortoiseshell-lyres are indeed occasionally attested, but most of these are comparatively late; and while examples include votive figurines (e.g. Cesnola 1894, pl. XXXIV no. 285), they are often found in fairly clear Greek iconographic contexts (imported Attic black-figure, white-ground lekythos: Karageorghis 2002a:126 no. 146; limestone statue of Apollo, Salamis, ca. 450: Yon 1974:21–25 (no. 5), fig. 12 and pl. 3; Cesnola 1885, pl. LXXIV, 476–479 (sympotic sarcophagus scene, ca. 500–450) = Myres 1914:226–229 no. 1364 = Karageorghis et al. 2000:204–206 no. 331 = *Aspects*:210–211 no. 208, fig. 224; cf. Karageorghis 2002a:154–155 no. 192; Sophocleous 1985:157 and pl. XXXVII.3-4, with further references.

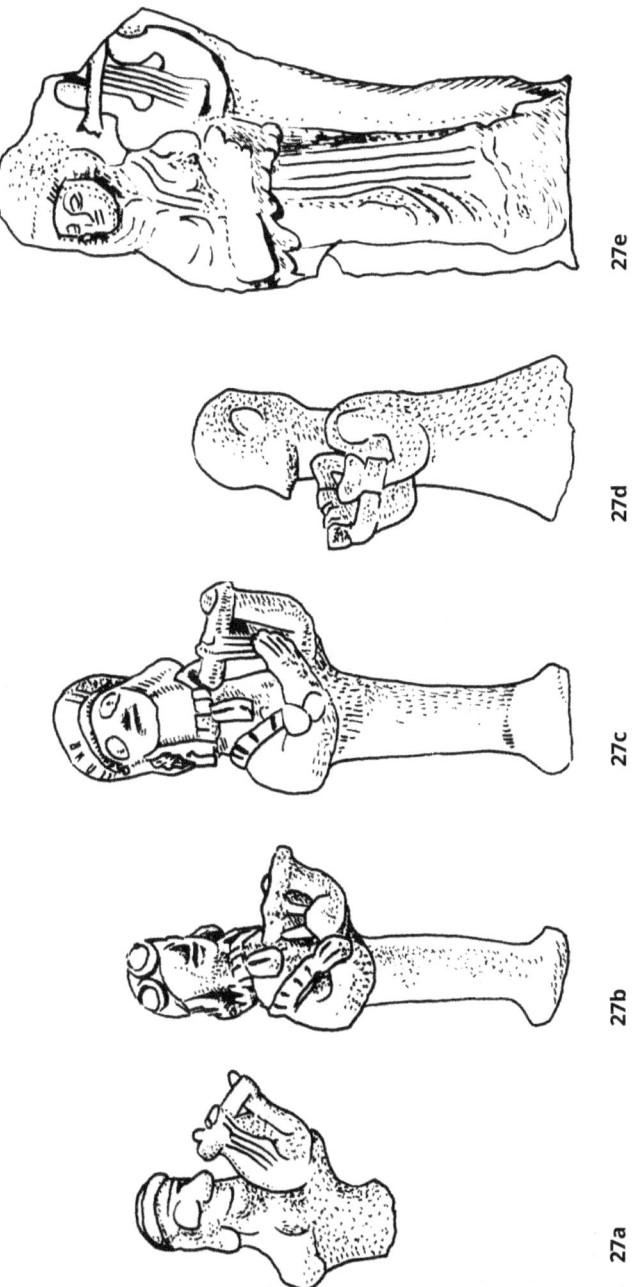

Figure 27 Cypriot votive figurines with variety of lyre shapes (scale not uniform). 27a (Cypro-Archaic, unprovenanced) = London, BM 1876/9-9/90, drawn from CAAC IV:I(v)4. 27b (Cypro-Archaic, Lapethos) = London, BM 1900.9-3.17, drawn from CAAC Va:I(xi)i.67. 27c (Cypro-Archaic, unprovenanced) = Cyprus Museum, Nicosia, inv. B192a, drawn from CAAC Va:I(xi)i.71. 27d (Cypro-Archaic, Kourion) = University Museum, Philadelphia no. 54-28-109, drawn from CAAC IV:I(v)3. 27e (Hellenistic, Cythrea), MMA accession no. unknown, drawn from Cesnola 1894, pl. XXXIV no. 282.

workshop production, or do they reflect significant ethno-musical distinctions? In at least one case a definite squiggle has been introduced, presumably corresponding to the ancient zigzag element discussed above.[77] Other examples, rather indeterminate between round and flat bases, could be dismissed as aberrations of mass production.[78] Coming down to the Cypro-Archaic period, a handful of examples from Lapethos, an area with Phoenician associations, have clearly divergent arms (Figure 27b, c).[79] In other cases, including more carefully crafted votives of the Cypro-Classical period, one does find a few examples with quite rectangular frame, and/or with arms flaring outwards (Figure 27d).[80] All told it would appear that we must allow for ongoing Cypro-Levantine hybrids alongside Cypro-Aegean. Whether these can be pushed back across the period ca. 1200–900 is not entirely clear, though it would not be surprising in light of our new *kinyrístria*.

What *is* certain is that the island had developed distinctive instruments by the ninth-century, when Phoenician colonists brought their own contemporary models, as shown in the Cypro-Phoenician symposium bowls (*phiálai*). These objects, manufactured from ca. 900–600 BCE, have been found far and wide, including Cyprus, Greece (especially Crete), Iraq (Nimrud), Italy (especially Etruria), Iran, and Israel.[81] Despite the lack of examples from Phoenicia itself—excavation has been minimal at most major sites—early production centers must have been located there.[82] It has also been possible, especially by comparison with the Nimrud ivories, to distinguish broadly between Phoenician and North Syrian traditions (in this and other media) on stylistic and technical grounds—with the former more obviously Egyptianizing and favoring more

---

[77] CAAC II:LGA[iii]5, pl. XXXV.5, classified here as CG I (ca. 1050–950), but apparently re-dated in *Aspects*:101 by association with LGA[iii]6, which is moved to CG III (900–750).

[78] CAAC Va:II[xiv]1 and 3; Vb:VIII[iii]19, 21. See also Monloup 1994 no. 406, with comment on 110 about probable distortions introduced by the moulding technique.

[79] See for instance CAAC Va (Cypro-Archaic), female lyrists: I[xi]i.67, 70 and 77 (Lapethos); 71–73 (unknown provenance); Yon and Caubet 1988b:4–5 no. 11, pl. II (female lyrist, Lapethos). An earlier possibility is CAAC II: LGC1, a sidesaddle lyrist-horseman from Palaipaphos-*Skales* (Cypro-Geometric II–III).

[80] Coroplastic examples are CAAC IV:I[v]3, Cypro-Archaic, Kourion, sanctuary of Apollo *Hylátēs*; the lyre, which is carefully rendered, has a flat-base and tapering arms. Also n.b. my Figure 18 (autopsy 7/2015). In limestone, Hermary 1989:388 no. 791 (Louvre AM 2987), Golgoi, female, ca. 575; also 388 no. 792 (Louvre N 3522), female, ca. 550 (note the nearly horizontal playing position, typical of the Levant). Cf. Monloup 1994:111 and n2, possible Syrian influence here and the close parallel of the Canaanite figurine from Kamid el-Loz: DCPIL, fig. 10 = my Figure 4.10.

[81] I follow Markoe's catalogue numbers in PBSB where possible. The literature is enormous. A good doxographic survey is Neri 2000:3–13; cf. Falsone 1988:95.

[82] Falsone 1988.

Lyric Landscapes of Early Cyprus

Figure 28 Cypro-Phoenician symposium bowl from Idalion, ca. 825. New York, MMA 74.51.5700. Drawn from PBSB Cy3.

symmetrical, balanced compositions.[83] There are, however, a number of intermediate examples.[84]

Establishing more precise geographic origins for specific bowls is famously difficult, with many factors in play. Plunder, deportation of craftsman, and willful hybridity underlie the rich, complex evidence from Nimrud. Itinerant/immigrant craftsman and local imitation are often supposed, especially for Crete and Italy/Etruria.[85] And the bowls were subject to wide circulation through the usual

---

[83] Barnett 1939, etc.; Winter 1976:6–11; Falsone 1988:80–81 with references.
[84] Cf. Winter 1987, identifying an intermediate 'South Syrian' style of ivory carving, which she convincingly connects with Aramaean Damascus.
[85] Neri 2000:3–13; Markoe 2003; Falsone 1988:94–95.

Chapter Eleven

mechanism of elite exchange and desire for luxury imports.[86] But some broad correlations are possible between distribution and known historical phases. Winter's vision of an exclusive ninth-century Greco-North Syrian market[87] was clouded by early new finds from Lefkandi (ca. 900) and Crete, which indicate parallel Phoenician activity.[88] It remains the case, however, that the devastations of Sargon (722–705) effectively terminated the older North Syrian trade westward.[89] The more symbiotic Assyrian policy towards the coastal cities enabled the Phoenician schools to continue their development and circulation. This later phase coincides with Phoenician colonial ventures in the West, the regular appearance of bowls in Italy and Etruria, and the use of Spanish silver for the *phiálai*.[90]

It has long been recognized that some portion of the bowls must have been produced on Cyprus.[91] Not only have many been found there, but some depict known items of Cypriot material culture, including ceramic vessels (Figure 28)[92] and wheeled vehicles.[93] Moreover, several contain Greek inscriptions in Cypro-Syllabic script. While inscriptions might be added secondarily to imported bowls, in one case (Cy11, Kourion) the owner's name was clearly engraved at the time of manufacture, accommodated by the surrounding imagery.[94] Last but not least, Cyprus is the only area that has produced finds, in both votive and funerary contexts, throughout the lifecycle of the bowls.[95]

With this we may turn to the substantial subset of bowls containing musical scenes (Figures 29, 30). The basic motif is generally seen as a celebration of Astarte/'Aphrodite',[96] representing a multi-stage festival involving choral song by cultic groups around a divine image.[97] The singers supported by the fourth-century Astarte temple at Phoenician Kition are a much-cited comparandum.[98] One finds various combinations of god, altar, and/or

---

[86] Vella forthcoming.
[87] Winter 1976:11–22; more broadly Winter 1988, especially 356–365.
[88] Falsone 1988:106; Popham 1995; Neri 2000:12; Markoe 2003:211.
[89] Winter 1976:17–20.
[90] Falsone 1988:105–106; Neri 2000:4–5.
[91] Gjerstad 1946; PBSB:6–9; Falsone 1988:94–95.
[92] See Gjerstad 1946:5, 7, diagnosing Cypriot pottery and dress in Cy3 (Idalion, his Proto-Cypriote I class, which otherwise exhibits clear North Syrian stylistic traits: Falsone 1988:96) and Cy5 (Kourion, Gjerstad's Proto-Cypriote III).
[93] Culican 1982:14 (vehicles in outer band of Cy13).
[94] Gjerstad 1946:12–16.
[95] Neri 2000:4–5 with her table.
[96] PBSB:59 (but cf. Winter 1990:241); Neri 2000:4–5; Fariselli 2007:13–14. G3, however, also appears to depict a male deity (PBSB:204).
[97] Fariselli 2007:13 (comparing cultic costumes of Cr7 and G8); Fariselli 2010:14–16.
[98] Amadasi and Karageorghis 1977 C1 (p103–126).

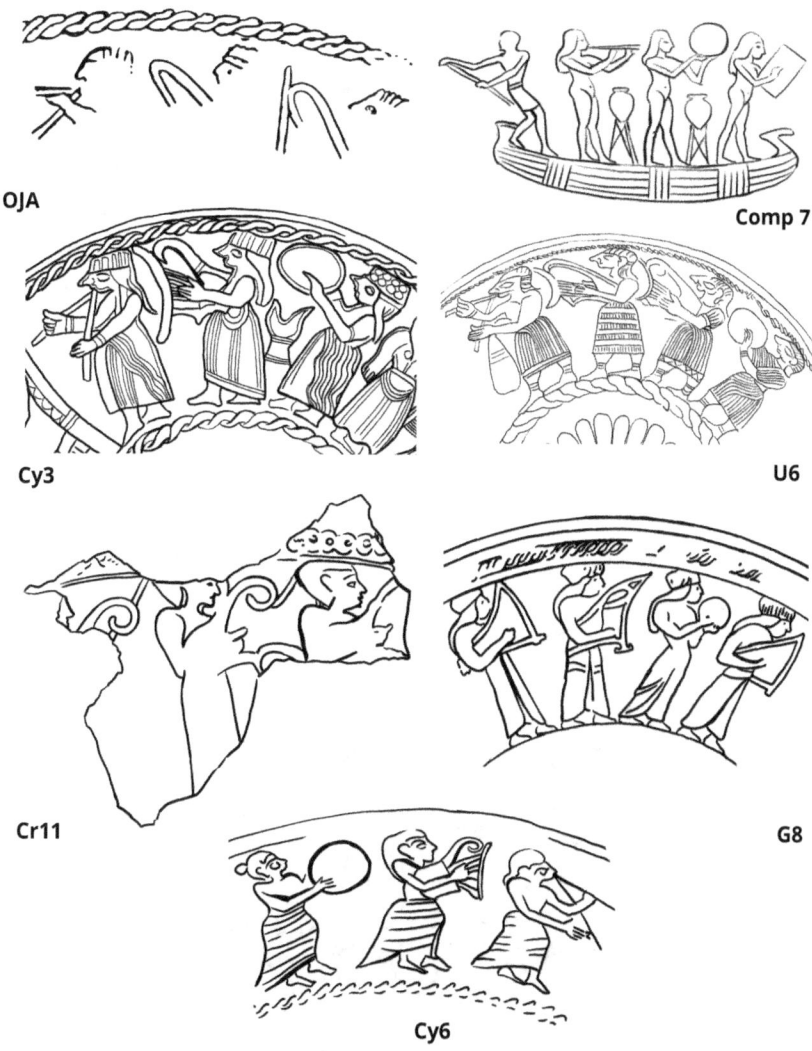

Figure 29 'Eastern' lyres in the Cypro-Phoenician symposium bowls, ca. 900–600. Drawn from corresponding photos in PBSB.

Figure 30 'Western' lyres on the Cypro-Phoenician symposium bowls, ca. 750–600. Drawn from photos in PBSB.

offerings-table (Cr11, Cy3, G3, G8, U6); a procession of usually female[99] musicians; dancers (Cr7, Cy3, G3); dancing musicians (U7, drummers); and offering-bearers (Cr7, Cr11, Cy3?, Cy5, Cy6, Cy7?, G3, U6). All elements are rarely found together (G3?, Cy3); usually the scene is more or less abbreviated.[100] Where the goddess scene merges with royal and/or elite banquet (Cy5, Cy6), a hierogamic reading does seem plausible.[101] That interpretation is more elusive when the context is banquet alone (Cy13, second band), although one might still fall back on 'sacred festival'.[102] Sometimes a fragmentary context makes closer interpretation hazardous (Cy7, Cy13, outer band).[103]

It will be seen from the clearly cultic scenes that the makeup of the 'orchestra' is in principle very consistent, the full complement being lyre, double-pipe,[104] and hand-percussion (usually frame-drum). This combination has clear affinities with Levantine traditions going back to the LBA; compare the musician guilds of Ugarit, the Rāp'iu text, and the musical prophets met by Saul.[105] Considerable variation in the *order* of musicians suggests that this element is insignificant. Emphasis is achieved rather by duplication and omission. Thus U7, by showing only dancing drummers, spotlights this aspect/phase of ritual; but the orchestra is probably implied. From the remaining bowls, it is clear that lyres enjoyed some prominence. As Table 1 shows, lyres alone appear in every other clearly cultic case. Often more than one is depicted, recalling the massed *kinnōr* groups of the Jerusalem temple (and, I shall argue, the *kinyrádai* of Paphos).[106] By contrast, the double-pipe is never certainly

---

[99] As female cult scenes, see e.g. Karageorghis et al. 2000:187–188, on no. 306 (Cy3) = *Aspects*:112–113 no. 84, fig. 97. Their gender is questioned by Burgh 2004:131–133 (on Cy3), who suggests intentional ambiguity; cf. Knapp 2011:125. Karageorghis 1999a:16 believes that, of the two mirrored groups now known to have graced the presumed royal banquet of Cy6, one was female and the other male. Fariselli 2007:11–12n10 notes the male pipers on Cy5 and Cy13 (third band: reclining symposiasts).

[100] Note the suggestion of Fariselli 2010:16 that the offering-bearers of Cy6 are also dancing.

[101] The argument for Cy5 hinges upon Κυπρομέδουσα ('She Ruling Cyprus') over the female figure; with 'king' perhaps over the male: Karageorghis 2002b:156 (with fig. 322), 177. Cy6 depends upon the addition of orgiastic-sympotic imagery: Karageorghis 1993.

[102] Neri 2000:3–4; Fariselli 2010:13–14.

[103] In these two cases, where mythological narratives are suspected, the musical processions may evoke an underlying ritual reality. Marquand 1887:225–226 wished to interpret the scenes of Cy7 as the adventures of Kinyras himself, and its musical element as Adonis-like lament.

[104] Fariselli 2007:11 and n6 would see single-pipes on Cy5 and Cy7. But these are surely double, simply shown in parallel (as often in Greece); this seems guaranteed by Comp7, where the pipes diverge just enough to prove their doubleness. Her final single-pipe example (Cy13, inner band) is more persuasive; but here the exceptional rustic context (played by stable-boy) only proves the rule that the more sophisticated cult-music used *double*-pipes.

[105] RS 24.252 = KTU/CAT 1.108; 1 Samuel 10:5–6. See further p421–424.

[106] See further p134–135, 156–157. Is it significant that no 'western' lyres are duplicated? Or is this due to the late, abbreviated iconography of those particular bowls?

Chapter Eleven

multiplied,[107] and is sometimes omitted altogether. This cannot be coincidence, and we must conclude that lyres were especially prominent in the cult. Recall that the *kinnāru* alone was divinized at Ugarit.

Bowl[108]	Find Spot	Phase[109]	Ensemble[110]	Lyre Type[111]
OJA	Lefkandi	I ca. 900	[?]/L/L/P	E
Comp7	Golgoi, Cyprus	10th century	P/D/L	E
Cy3	Idalion, Cyprus	I ca. 825	D/L/P	E
U6	Luristan (?)	I ca. 825	D/L/L/P	E
Cr11	Mt Ida, Crete	II–III	L/L/L	E
G3	Olympia	II before 725	P/D/L	W
G8	Sparta (?)	II before 725	L/L/D/L	E
Cy6	Kourion, Cyprus[112]	III early 7th	D/L/P	E
Cy7	Kourion, Cyprus	III early 7th	L/P/D(?)	W
Cy5	Salamis, Cyprus	IV later 7th	D/P/L	W[113]
Cy13	Kourion, Cyprus	IV later 7th	?/L/P(?)[114]	W[115]

Table 1. Lyre-Ensembles in the Cypro-Phoenician Symposium Bowls

---

[107] Fariselli 2007 (11 and n6, 12 and n12) would see two pipers in Cy7, seemingly misreading the drawing in PBSB; a photograph (Karageorghis et al. 2000:186–187 no. 305) shows clearly that the leftmost figure has a round-based lyre, as Marquand 1887:326–328 already saw (for its telltale floral decor, see below). Cy13 (second band) *may* have had two pipers; but the following figure is broken, and could have been lyrist or drummer. Even so, the bowl is very late, and we are at some remove from the basic cultic scene; the context is strongly sympotic, which accounts for the oddity of a reclining male piper and seated female drummer in the third band.

[108] By catalogue numbers in PBSB, except for OJA = Popham 1995.

[109] Markoe's dating scheme in PBSB (used here) is, after close inspection, fundamentally compatible with Gjerstad 1946. Both are based on an assumed typological development towards greater complexity. But the reliability of this criterion is partially undermined by the existence of multiple workshops/sub-traditions, some potentially more conservative than others: Culican 1982:22; also the critique of Winter 1990.

[110] Back to front: L = lyre; P = double-pipe; D = frame-drum.

[111] I retain Lawergren's 'eastern' (E) and 'western' (W) without equating 'western' and 'Aegean' (see above).

[112] The 'Kourion' bowls come from Cesnola's notorious horde, suspected of being a sensationalist assemblage by Cesnola himself; but Kourion may still be the *general* area of origin: PBSB:176–177.

[113] The instrument played by the *hetaíra* (?) on the *klínē* is quite ambiguous; but that of the processional orchestra does seem round-based.

[114] See Culican 1982:15.

[115] Fariselli 2007 (17n40) states that Culican 1982:15 detected a distinctly Assyrian character to the lyre in the outer band of Cy13; hence she groups it with other 'eastern' examples (Cr11, Cy3, U6). But Culican's phrase "particularly Assyrian features" applies only to the player—an important distinction. That the lyre is in fact 'western,' as suggested by his drawing, is confirmed by its vertical orientation.

Lyric Landscapes of Early Cyprus

Figure 31 Ivory pyxis with lyre ensemble, Nimrud, North Syrian school, ninth–eighth century. Baghdad ND1642. Drawn from Mallowan 1966 fig. 168.

As it happens, only the lyres exhibit clear morphological variety, between Lawergren's 'eastern' and 'western' types. This evidence has been neglected in previous typological analyses of the corpus, even though "when neighboring cultures share the same symbols yet choose to represent them very differently, those differences should be culturally significant."[116] Conversely musicologists have extracted the organological data from their larger iconographic contexts, without considering how the instruments support, complicate, or contradict prevailing classification schemes. The round-based lyres open analytical areas that evade the binary distinction between North Syrian and Phoenician schools (the instruments of these traditions being apparently too similar to differentiate).[117]

---

[116] Winter 1976:20.
[117] Since minor variations are always attributable to different workshops. But this question may reward closer scrutiny: cf. p268 and n118.

267

Chapter Eleven

Figure 32 Sixth-century Egyptianizing limestone statue from Golgoi (?). New York, MMA 74.51.2509. Drawn from Aspects fig. 138.

Note first that the eastern morphology dominates the early phases of Markoe's typological scheme. With one exception (G3: see below), the Aegean (including Crete) has produced only eastern specimens. Cy3, also with eastern lyre, is again of North Syrian derivation, its instrument strikingly similar to that of the ivory pyxis from Nimrud (Figure 31), although its depiction of Cypriot vessel-forms strongly suggests an insular workshop.[118] Of Phoenician or intermediate style are OJA, Cr11, G8.

---

[118] See p262n92. Nimrud pyxis (ND1642): Mallowan 1966:216, 218 fig. 168; assignment to North Syrian group: Barnett 1935:189. U6 is closely related to Cy3, but travelled to Iran.

By contrast the four 'western' examples (G3, Cy5, Cy7, Cy13) come from phases II–IV, suggesting a secondary development. It can hardly be coincidence that three have been found on Cyprus itself. Here we must accept the sane principle that, "all other factors being equal, a trait or artifact type probably originated somewhere near the center of its distribution."[119] This is confirmed by the presence of *kypriaká* in Cy5 and Cy13.[120] Moreover, the instrument on Cy7 (Figure 30) has a decorative element on one of its arms that must correspond to the floral (papyrus?) detail found on lyres in the more refined limestone statuary of the Cypro-Archaic and -Classical periods—for example an Egyptianizing sculpture (ca. 575) said to be from Golgoi (the arm is topped by a lion or gryphon head: Figure 32).[121] These floral lyres are a vivid indication of a vibrant insular tradition going back to the Archaic period and doubtless beyond,[122] and call to mind early Cypriot singers like Stasinos and Stasandros.[123] Note too that these Cypriot lyres are apparently smaller, by and large, than those in Archaic representations of clear Greek provenance. The same seems true of the Hubbard lyrist, whose instrument might otherwise appear somewhat inexpertly rendered.[124] These impressions are corroborated by countless terracotta votives of the Cypro-Geometric and -Archaic periods, which invariably show quite small instruments. It is thus possible that their pitch-range was often somewhat higher than Greek models.[125] The way they are held is also distinctive, almost 'cradling'[126]

---

[119] L. R. Binford, quoted by Winter 1990:14.

[120] See 262n92–93.

[121] MMA New York inv. no. 74.51.2509 (45.2 cm high): Cesnola 1885, pl. XII; Myres 1914:198 no. 1265; Karageorghis et al. 2000:132 no. 198, where the instrument is misidentified as a triangular harp (also Myres 1914:199 no. 1264; *Aspects*:147); Lawergren 1984:152n4 rightly recognized a round-based lyre with only the front portion sculpted. A comparable αὐλός-player, probably also from Golgoi, was perhaps a companion piece: MMA inv. 74.51.2517; Myres 1914:198 no. 1264; Karageorghis et al. 2000:133 no. 199. A rather similar figure and lyre, but lacking the floral details, is Hermary 1989:284–285 no. 577, also dated to ca. 575.

[122] Note that floral/papyrus motifs are also seen in Egyptian instruments (see AEMI s.v. Decoration>floral); one, dated to the first quarter of the first millennium, is peculiar for its round base, and might be related to the Cypriot instruments: see AEMI:87, 91. Other Cypriot floral lyres: mould-made female figurine, possibly from Lapethos and dated to ca. 600–480 (Karageorghis et al. 2000:148–149 no. 227). Another such figure (tomb, Idalion) apparently held a 'floral-post' lyre; unfortunately the instrument is broken (Cesnola 1894, pl. V no. 29; cf. pl. XXXIV no. 287). An especially interesting example from the Hellenistic period shows the influence of the Greek *kithára* and/or contemporary Levantine specimens: see p278 and Figure 34.

[123] See p211 and further Franklin 2014:229–231.

[124] Cf. SIAG:9: its "size … cannot be taken literally."

[125] Cf. Monloup 1994:111.

[126] This is not to be confused with the term 'cradle *kithára*' (*Wiegenkithara*) which M. Wegner introduced to describe the *shape* of round-based instruments in Attic art ca. 550–400—which apparently perpetuate the earlier so-called *phórminx* even as the flat-based concert *kithára* became

Chapter Eleven

Figure 33 Cypro-Phoenician symposium bowl, before ca. 725. Olympia, Greece. Athens NM 7941. Drawn from PBSB G3.

This clear evidence of local Cypriot preference in the *phiálai* should be compared, and contrasted, with the numerous finds from Italy/Etruria where the cult-music type-scene is strikingly absent.[127] Its retention and development on Cyprus through the final typological phases must be due to the funda-

---

the normal instrument of professionals (Wegner 1949:30–32; cf. SIAG:139). The insufficiency of this as a blanket term was noted by Lawergren 1985:27 et passim (cf. Lawergren 1984) in distinguishing a species common to Attica, Etruria, and (western) Anatolia, which he dubbed the 'cylinder *kithára*' on the basis of the small round discs which appear to be wedged between body and arm-bases. This feature is generally lacking from Cypriot lyres, which accordingly must be recognized as yet another species.

[127] This should be added to the evidence there for local preferences in iconography, adaptation to new materials, and reorientation of use/ideology: synopsis in Neri 2000:3–13, noting e.g.

mental importance there of 'Aphrodite'/Astarte cult.[128] This also accounts for the 'confrontation' of 'western' and 'eastern' morphologies within an otherwise constant iconographic repertoire. For, while the Cypriot and Phoenician versions of the goddess were readily identifiable in broad terms (hence the shared iconography),[129] the respective cultural spheres maintained separate senses of identity (whence the variation of detail).

Undoubtedly the morphological distinction implies complex social perceptions that developed and shifted, on a regional basis, with changing Phoenician political fortunes and other demographic trends. While most such nuances now escape us, they should be recognized as 'known unknowns' that can at least help us frame relevant questions. What should we make, for instance, of Cy6, which, though presenting an 'eastern' instrument, carries a Greek inscription in the Cypro-Syllabic script, while its find location (Kourion) is not especially distinguished as an area of Phoenician settlement? Is it significant that the later typological phases are represented on Cyprus by only a single eastern specimen? Should the presence of an early 'eastern' example at Idalion be connected with Levantine metal-hunting in the Troodos foothills? Should we associate the unusual model from Golgoi with the undeciphered language there?[130] Or does elite exchange render any such regional analysis futile within the island? After all, while the iconographic distinction between contemporary Cypriot and Syro-Levantine lyres is clearly intentional and culturally significant, each bowl enjoyed a life of its own, and there is no practical basis for segregating one ethnicity from another in a bowl's after-market existence. On the contrary, Cy6 suggests a quite general intermingling of Cypriots of all ethnic backgrounds in the context of elite drinking rituals during the eighth and seventh centuries.

The Olympia bowl (Figure 33) is the only 'western' lyre found in Greece itself. But this is no evidence of local manufacture for Aegean Greek consumption. Who would argue this for the other Aegean finds with 'eastern' lyres? Cr11, one should note, contains a Phoenician owner's inscription, and of course we now know that there was an important Phoenician presence on Crete at Kommos. To be sure, the Lesbian poet Alkaios (ca. 600) knew of the 'Phoenician lyre' (*phoínix*, presumably in a sympotic context). But it is precisely the *exotic* nature of both bowl and instrument that best accounts for their presence in the Aegean and the poetics of Alkaios (see further below). The Olympia bowl is

---

emphasis on martial themes and exclusively funerary find-contexts; Markoe 2003:213–215 (materials/media).

[128] For which see generally Karageorghis 1977; Karageorghis 2005.

[129] A third-century Phoenician inscription from Paphos commemorates some dedication to "Paphian Astarte" ( ]'štrt pp[ ): Masson and Sznycer 1972:p81–86; Bonnet 1996:160; Lipiński 2004:106; *Kypris*:42.

[130] See p339, 350.

therefore most economically explained in the same terms, with the exception that it must be traced to an extra-Aegean source where round-based lyres were indeed established. Once again the obvious candidate is a Cypriot workshop. Stylistically the bowl seems to stand midway between the North Syrian and Phoenician schools.[131] That it is inscribed with an Aramaean name is not problematic, given that Cy3, though produced locally, adheres to the North Syrian style (see above). Moreover, the island has produced a number of early (eighth-seventh century) inscriptions in non-Phoenician Semitic languages, attesting "the strong interaction among peoples on the island."[132] The bowl then came through elite circulation to Greece, where the lyre's broad similarity to contemporary Aegean instruments would have made it both exotic and familiar—though of course how it passed from Aramaean hands to its final deposition at Olympia remains a mystery.

Thus, in the symposium bowls too the 'western' lyre-morphology presents a distinctly Cypriot aspect. With their temple-orchestra deployment, these instruments are a world apart from the Aegean. But despite the clear kinship of this performance tradition with the Levant, we need not dismiss its insular manifestation as secondary and derivative; nor assume that it dates only from the Phoenician colonial period. This may well be a mirage of the *phiálai* and novel iconographic fashions. Historical connections with Syro-Levantine cult practice, in my view, must be traced to the LBA (see Chapter 15), although one may allow a syncretic reconvergence in the ninth-eighth centuries.

The Second-Millennium Adaptation of *Kinýra*

The natural implication of our new 'lost daughter' is that one or more pre-Greek forms of the word *knr* was/were already current on the LBA island, and persisted into the IA as Greek-Cypriot *kinýra*. There would remain a certain dissonance between the dominant round-based Cypriot morphology and the Syro-Levantine shapes with which one usually associates *knr*. Some may therefore suspect that both morphology and word disappeared from Cyprus after the LBA, to reappear with Phoenician settlement in the ninth century. Nevertheless, I believe this hypothesis of 'double importation' can be confidently rejected, at least as regards the word.

---

[131] Phoenician: Egyptianizing figures, vertical partition of space (cf. Falsone 1988:101). North Syrian: rendition of god(dess)/offering table motif, and central design (Frankfort 1970:327–328).

[132] Smith 2008:264–266 (quotation), with references. Of course we must remember that eighth-century Cilicia has also produced examples of 'western' lyre-morphology in the Karatepe reliefs (see p251–253) and the Lyre-Player Group of Seals, which present complex interpretive challenges (Chapter 21). Nevertheless, a Cypriot origin for G3 remains the best explanation given the parallels of Cy5, Cy7, and Cy13.

Certainly the symposium bowls leave no doubt that a 'proper' Phoenician dialect form with ū (*kinnūr) was known on Cyprus from at least ca. 900.[133] Accordingly, some scholars believe this was when kinýra first came into Greek,[134] just as Lawergren saw here the first arrival of Levantine lyres to the island. Proponents of these views also connect both 'Gk.' kinýra and Phoen. *kinnūr (as opposed to Heb. kinnōr) with a first-millennium 'Phoenician Shift', whereby the inherited sound of the Canaanite Shift (ā > ō) further developed to ū in various dialects; the evidence for this is a recurrent oscillation between ō and ū in the Assyrian, Greek, and Latin representation of Phoenician words and names.[135]

But neither of these points is decisive. First, the bowls are misleading. Consider that, if one were to judge from iconography alone, the bowls would suggest that ensemble playing was an innovation of the ninth century. But the Rāp'iu text from Ugarit proves that this was not the case.[136] A novelty in artistic representation need not imply a corresponding novelty in what is represented.

Nor can the Phoenician Shift be so rigidly applied. The evidence for LBA Canaanite vocalization is ambiguous, since neither the cuneiform of the Amarna letters (with transcriptions of Canaanite words and names), nor the special semi-syllabic Egyptian orthography used in the second millennium for writing foreign words (especially Canaanite), possessed separate signs for distinguishing ō from ū.[137] Therefore it is impossible to establish an exact value between ō and ū during the LBA, and it may in any case have varied by dialect.

A valuable parallel here is Gk. khrȳsós ('gold'), already attested in Linear B as ku-ru-so. The long upsilon reveals that this was borrowed from a Canaanite dialect form *ḫarūṣ(u), by contrast with Akk. and Ug. ḫurāṣu.[138] The Mycenaean form indicates that the Canaanite sound was closer to ū than ō, since these two values were distinguished in the Linear B syllabary. Even if this word entered Greek indirectly, with an intermediary language introducing an adjustment of ō towards ū, khrȳsós remains a clear case of the sound of the Canaanite Shift

---

[133] See p56–57.
[134] So Neil 1901:8; Albright 1964:171n47: "Greek kinýra ... itself a loan from Phoenician kinnûr"; cf. YGC:144n91.
[135] YGC:144n91. For the phenomenon generally, Friedrich and Röllig 1970 §86; Friedrich et al. 1999:41–42 (§79); Krahmalkov 2001:30–31 §2b (conditioned by stress and syllable-closing).
[136] See p134–135.
[137] SL §21.3 and 21.9; cf. Huehnergard 2008:264.
[138] The Can. form *ḫarūṣ(u) is reconstructible from a PN at Ugarit (ḫa-ru-ṣe-en-ni, with Hurr. suffix: Gröndahl 1967:140; Sivan 1984:228) and vocalization of the Heb. cognate ḫārūṣ. See Szemerényi 1964:53–54 (viewing the reduction of the first syllable in Greek [ḫarūṣ- > χρυσ-] as a post-Mycenaean development, with Lin. B. ku-ru-so representing rather *χυρῡσός); Emprunts:37–38; Szemerényi 1968:195–196; Priebatsch 1980:317; Szemerényi 1981:116; SL §65.6; CAD s.v. ḫurāṣu; DUL s.v. ḫrṣ.

Chapter Eleven

reappearing elsewhere as *ū* already in the LBA. And this makes a contemporary adaptation of *kinýra* perfectly possible.

With *kinýra*, however, the Semitic original's long penultimate vowel has been reduced—this time, certainly, due to the phonetic impact of an adapting language.[139] This would naturally occur in a tongue for which, unlike Greek, vowel length was not phonemic (that is, did not contribute to distinctions of meaning). Such was probably the case with the pre-Greek language(s) of the Aegean.[140] Whether the same was true on pre-Greek Cyprus is unclear, but E. L. Brown has reasonably suggested that *kinýra* could be due to "a mere underdifferentiation of the *o* vowel" in a "Cypro-Minoan model."[141] Cyprus would indeed seem the obvious place for the adaptation, thanks to the prominent position occupied there by Kinyras and now "Our *Kenyristés* Apollo."[142] Is it coincidence that Gk. *mýrrha* has also lost its Semitic vowel-length, and is so closely associated with Kinyras and Cyprus?[143]

Vital support for the LBA chronology proposed here comes from the PN Kinyras (*ki-nu-ra*) at Mycenaean Pylos; I shall explore the contextual details fully in Chapter 17, showing that a derivation from *knr* is indeed probable, and perfectly compatible with the special Cypriot associations I have proposed.

So I find no *positive* linguistic reason to exclude a pre-Greek antecedent of *kinýra* from LBA Cyprus, and good circumstantial evidence to support the hypothesis. Moreover, it can be corroborated by an independent line of argument.

As mentioned above, Alkaios (ca. 600) is our earliest source for an instrument called *phoínix*, 'the Phoenician (instrument)'. This and several related forms (*phoiníkion, lyrophoínix, lyrophoiníkion*) are mentioned by Herodotos, Aristoxenos, the Aristotelian *Problems*, and an array of later historiographical and lexical sources. Some kind of lyre is definitely intended, and the ancient authors draw connections with Phoenicia, Syria, and Libya (presumably *vis-à-vis* the Punic colonies in north Africa).[144] Now a general Greek awareness of Phoenician

---

[139] For the geminate -*nn*-, see p213–214.
[140] Beekes 2009:xx, xxxii §6.2.
[141] Brown 1981:397–398.
[142] Cf. Brown 1981:397–398. Baurain 1980b:11–12 rightly stresses that Eteocypriot must have had a more important impact on 'Greek' Cypriot words than is generally recognized; but obviously I cannot agree with his derivation of 'Kinyras' from a hypothetical Eteocypriot form that was accidentally homophonous with WS *knr*, giving rise in later times to a false etymology from the lyre (8).
[143] See p191n71 and 477.
[144] The surprisingly numerous sources are assembled by AGM:59 (for the accentuation φοίνιξ, vs. φοῖνιξ [LSJ], cf. Naoumides 1968:272; West 1990:7). Those bearing most closely on the present discussion are Alkaios p. 507 Voigt = Campbell 1982–1993, 1 fr. 424A; Herodotos 4.192; Athenaios 637b (Phoenician origin, citing Ephoros FGH 70 F 4 and Skamon FGH 476 F 4); Juba FGH 275 F 15

instruments in the Archaic period is not in itself surprising. The discovery of the bowls in Aegean contexts is but one of many signs of an ongoing Phoenician cultural presence. Besides the stereotyped representation of the Phoenicians by Homer,[145] Sappho's colorful description of Hektor and Andromakhe's arrival at Troy amidst mingling myrrh, cassia, and frankincense—aromatics often imported via Phoenicia—is a good parallel for her countryman Alkaios' familiarity with the *phoínix*.[146] The puzzle is rather that Greek sources never use *kinýra* in an unambiguously Phoenician context. Foreign instruments, admittedly, often received Greek nicknames (for instance *paktís* and *trígōnos*, applied to harps arriving from points east).[147] Nevertheless one would really expect *kinýra* to have been mentioned *somewhere* among the numerous late Classical and Hellenistic sources that attest a general Greek interest in foreign instruments.[148] After all, the Phoenician *nábla(s)*, sibling to the *knr*, enjoyed a vogue in the fourth-century, appearing several times in the fragments of Attic comedy, apparently as a novelty.[149] *Kinýra*, however, is missing even from the long list of foreign instruments drawn up by Aristoxenos around this same time—in which, however, he *does* include *phoínix*![150]

We must conclude therefore that, by *phoínix*, Alkaios and other Greeks meant precisely what a Phoenician would have called **kinnūr*—and not only Tyrians and Sidonians, but Phoenician Cypriots too. The absence of *kinýra* from Phoenician contexts, therefore, is strongly marked, and requires explanation. The word was somehow unavailable for designating the Phoenician instruments with whose name it was nevertheless cognate. Evidently *kinýra*

('Syrian' origin); Hesykhios s.v. λυροφοίνιξ· εἶδος κιθάρας. It is tempting to connect Herodotos' statement that the instrument's arms were made from Libyan antelope horns with the 'eastern' lyres of the Cypro-Phoenician bowls. This could explain first not only the pronounced curls of the arms, but also why they are often asymmetrical and different from bowl to bowl. Admittedly, these curls can be readily fashioned in wood, as one sees in the six surviving Levantine-style lyres from Egypt (see p106). It may still be, however, that finely worked wooden instruments reproduced the lines of more rustic prototypes, just as a Greek concert *kithára*'s curving back sometimes evoked the humble tortoise whose carapace was used in early and amateur lyres.

[145] Winter 1995.

[146] Sappho 44.30. Phoenician link: Herodotos 3.111.2, cf. 3.107.1. For the origins and routes of these spices, Miller 1969:42–47, 102–105 (frankincense and myrrh), 153–172 (cassia/cinnamon).

[147] Similarly one finds κλεψίαμβοι and ἐννεάχορδα in Aristoxenos' list of foreign instruments (fr. 97 Wehrli). By the later fourth century, the Greek formation ψαλτήριον ('plucking instrument') emerged as a generic term for 'harp' (AGM:74, with evidence for harps on 71–73), but could also be used to translate Heb. *kinnōr*: see p47n14, 194n43, 312n188. The Archaic vogue for harps was seemingly stimulated by an Assyrianizing fashion in Lydia: Franklin 2008, especially 197–198.

[148] See especially the important surveys in Athenaios 174a–185a, 634c–637f. For the σαμβύκη, νάβλα(ς), πανδοῦρα, γίγγρας, and variants, AGM:75–80.

[149] *Nábla(s)*: Bayer 1968 (Greek sources, 108–110); AGM:77. Cf. p53, 58.

[150] Aristoxenos fr. 97 Wehrli = Athenaios 182f, reappearing at 636b in a discussion quoted from Phillis of Delos (FHG 4:476 fr. 2).

Chapter Eleven

was already established in the Greek mind with different cultural associations, although of course this lexical situation must itself be sought at the edge of the Canaanite/Phoenician linguistic sphere. The solution to this puzzle is that the Cypriot *kinýra*, though distinct from the Greek *kithára*, was 'Greek enough' not to call for special comment.[151] If it seem strange that Alkaios and others be so attuned to intra-Cypriot organological nuances, consider that the Cypro-Phoenician symposium bowls present just such a careful distinction of Cypriot and Phoenician lyre-types. In other words, any awareness of *Phoenician* lyres in Archaic Greece (Alkaios, *phiálai*) will have been matched, *a fortiori*, by familiarity with models current among *Greek-Cypriots*. This is hardly surprising given the ongoing musical interaction between Cyprus and the Aegean, discussed above.[152]

It follows that *kinýra* was current on Cyprus prior to ca. 900, as already predicted. The round-based instruments whose popular Cypriot character is guaranteed by countless early terracotta votives, many predating the Phoenician colony period—*these* will be the lyres anciently known as *kinýra*.[153] There remains the discrepancy between these EIA Cypriot lyres and the shapes scholars usually associate with *knr*. But semantic/morphological shifts are quite common in the history of instruments. Many lyre names, for instance, persisted unchanged despite the almost universal transition to lutes in late antiquity and the early medieval period.[154] I have also emphasized that LBA Cyprus could easily have housed wider lyric variety than is yet attested, with older insular shapes akin to the traditions of EBA–MBA southern Anatolia and North Syria—the "lands around Cyprus." As I stressed at the outset,[155] we must not be too categorical in assigning *knr* to one particular morphology. Its general applicability to the core Syro-Levantine types of the second and first millennia is of course undoubted. But we do not know how the correspondence of name and shape may have fluctuated along the cultural interfaces of the periphery at different periods.

Conclusion

This investigation, though raising many questions, has reached some definite conclusions. Considerable minor variations in the early iconographical record attest both the internal diversity of the island's lyric culture, and its overall distinctiveness *as* an insular tradition. There is no doubt that Aegean

---

[151] For this 'same yet different' quality of the pair, see further p47n18, 195n48, 215n64.
[152] See p211–213.
[153] *Kinýra* must therefore supersede the "lyre-cithare" used by Monloup 1994, Chapter 3, of Cypriot round-based lyres.
[154] See Appendix D.
[155] See p53.

Figure 34 Statue of female lyre-player with late floral-post lyre, Golgoi, Hellenistic. New York, MMA 74.51.2480. Drawn from Cesnola 1885 pl. cii no. 676.

Chapter Eleven

and Levantine influences were important determining factors. But the island was more than a receptive matrix. While the pre-Greek period remains largely a blank, we must not rule out an early lyric tradition here which had already differentiated itself from the Levant *before* the fourteenth century and our long lost 'daughter of Kinyras'. She, in any case, now makes it as certain as can be that the pre-Greek island had its own lyric tradition(s), and that some form of *knr* was already established in Cypriot usage, being applied to instruments of contemporary Levantine morphology and very possibly earlier insular types. Whether the Aegean influx induced a general transformation from 'eastern' to 'western' morphology, or whether round-based instruments were *already* established on the pre-Greek island alongside Levantine shapes, this pre-Greek lexical forerunner of *kinýra* persisted into the IA as the standard Greek-Cypriot word for 'lyre', being applied to the characteristically Cypriot instruments of the early votives; it thus resisted absolute identification with the models brought by Phoenician colonists ca. 900. Yet, given the vigorous display of contemporary Phoenician tradition in the symposium bowls and the Phoenicians' ongoing cultural presence, one should not be surprised to find traces of Levantine lyre-morphology enduring into later times. I would therefore conclude by noting, besides the occasional votives mentioned above,[156] a particularly exquisite sculpted instrument of the Hellenistic period that maintains the Archaic tradition of floral decoration (Figure 34).[157] One could attribute its flat base to the Greek *kithára's* impact, but that outwardly flaring arms make ongoing Levantine influence equally likely or more so.

---

[156] See p260 and n80.
[157] Cesnola 1885, pl. cii no. 676; Myres 1914:190 no. 1238. For the tradition of floral decor, see p269.

12

Kinyras the Lamenter

IN THE GUDEA CYLINDERS, the 'court' of Ningirsu included two separate balang-gods, one overseeing music to "make the temple happy," the other "to banish mourning from the mourning heart."[1] This dichotomy, reflecting basic aspects of human experience and their musical expression, is also found in the evidence for Kinyras. We have seen that Kinyras was a performing guise for the Cypriot 'kinyrists' who played praise-hymns both in his own honor, and in the service of his master-god, the Cypriot 'Aphrodite.' Now we must consider Kinyras' connections with lamentation-singing, specifically an early Cypriot threnodic tradition using—and sometimes perhaps purposefully eschewing—the *kinýra*.

Those more familiar with the Greek world must recall that in Mesopotamia lamentation-singing was not always a personal affair responding to a specific event like the death of a child or spouse. It was also used to soothe a wrathful or grieving god, both apotropaically and in a crisis. The prophylactic mode was tied to regular calendrical occasions, but could also be dictated by specific events, including the building of temples and creation of cult-objects—two examples relevant to the Kinyras material.[2] The closest analogy in the Greek world, we shall see, are the seasonal threnodies allied to certain festivals and hero-cults.

The first evidence for Kinyras the Lamenter comes from a set of mournful predicaments inflicted on and/or suffered by him and his children. These tragic plights typically yield some substance, object, or process connected with Cypriot cult—a clear indication that we are still a world apart from the Aegean, as was also suggested by the temple-orchestras of the Cypro-Phoenician symposium bowls. We must then assemble material that lets the *kinýra* and its cognates be linked to threnody, as this is the practical medium that must have produced the lamentable Kinyras myths, and to which they allude. This tradition can then be further illuminated by a passage of Herodotos, who refers to lamentation-songs

---

[1] See p26–33.
[2] See p29–30.

Chapter Twelve

of Cyprus, Phoenicia, and Egypt which were essentially 'the same' as the Aegean 'Linos-song', for which we have much and early evidence. When *kinýra*-lamenting has been clarified as far as possible, we can complete our examination of the Homeric variant discussed in Chapter 9, and see what is implied by having Phoinix petition Achilles as though 'lamenting to the *kinýra*'. I close with a note on the lyric threnody for Antinoos from Kourion (ca. 130/131 CE).

Kinyras and His Cult Family

Key evidence linking Kinyras to lamentation comes from Ovid's ever-surprising *Metamorphoses*.[3] Athena, in the weaving contest against Arachne, frames her web with four mythological competitions between mortals and gods, to show "what reward to expect for such mad daring."[4] One alludes to an otherwise unknown 'Cinyras' episode in which the king laments his daughters, who have been metamorphosed into parts of a temple:

> Bereft the corner holds Cinyras;
> And he, embracing temple steps—his own daughters' limbs —
> Is seen to sob while lying on the stone.[5]

Although Kinyras does not weep explicitly (n.b.) in any extant *Greek* author, the very idea depends upon a Greek etymological association of Kinyras with *kinýresthai* and/or *kinyrós*—both of which were connected, one way or another, with *kinýra* in late sources like Eustathios and the lexica.[6] A key contribution of Ovid, therefore, is to guarantee the antiquity of the etymological complex, which accordingly goes back to his Hellenistic models at the latest. Actually we may be quite sure that the essential associations are much older still. For two persistent themes in the mythology of Kinyras' children—angered or grieving gods, and metamorphoses into objects or processes of cult—echo far earlier conceptions relating to the professional functions of ritual lamenters in Mesopotamia.

We may begin by considering the motive and outcome of the transformation just cited. Like Athena's other three scenes, the fate of Cinyras' daughters should result from a specific challenge to divine prerogative. There is no hint about the crime; but the probable Cypriot setting makes 'Aphrodite' most likely to have

---

[3] This passage was noticed by Ribichini 1982:500.
[4] Ovid *Metamorphoses* 6.83–85: *ut ... exemplis intellegat ... / quod pretium speret pro tam furialibus ausis / quattuor in partes certamina quattuor addit*.
[5] Ovid *Metamorphoses* 6.98–100: *Cinyran habet angulus orbum; / isque gradus templi, natarum membra suarum, / amplectens saxoque iacens lacrimare videtur*. As Boccaccio construed the Latin, Cinyras himself is changed to stone: *Genealogy of the Pagan Gods* 2.51; hence Bustron p14.
[6] See p187–189.

been slighted, as with several of Kinyras' other children.⁷ The closest parallel for the actual metamorphosis is also found in Ovid, the Propoetides of Amathous (a city whose connection with Kinyras and Eteocypriot culture we shall see). These girls, having denied the divinity of 'Venus', were made to prostitute themselves until turned 'to hard flint' (*in rigidum ... silicem*) by lack of shame.⁸ This is presumably an aetiology for some feature of the goddess's temple in that city. Scholars have thought variously of betyls, stelai, or a statue-group.⁹ There is to be sure the story of the stony-hearted Anaxarete of Cypriot Salamis, transformed into a statue for refusing the love of Iphis.¹⁰ Yet Lat. *silex* more naturally suggests architectural members, as in the Cinyras episode.¹¹ A further parallel has been sought in the myth that Kinyras' daughters Orsedike, Laogore, and Braisia were forced by an angry Aphrodite—presumably they neglected her cult or vied with her in beauty—to sleep with foreigners, finishing their lives in Egypt.¹² Some would relate both tales to allegations of sacred prostitution on Cyprus,¹³ but this would not account for the second's connection with Egypt, nor is there any mention there of prostitution; I have alternative explanations to offer.¹⁴

---

7   That the second and third exempla concern Juno occasioned the guess (so rightly Bömer 1969–1986 3:34) of ps.-Lactantius Placidus that here too Juno was offended, and that hers was the temple where Kinyras' daughters served as steps (*Summaries of Ovidian Tales* 6.1: *Cinyrae, regis Assyriorum, praeterea filias ob insolentiam ab eadem dea in gradus templi sui lapide mutatas*). This view was followed by Engel 1841 2:127–128, assuming that fifty daughters were in question. Ps.-Lactantius is evidently also the origin of a distinction between Ovid's first Cinyras as "king of the Assyrians" and the poet's explicitly Cypriot second Cinyras. The idea was elaborated by Theodontius (who used ps.-Lactantius elsewhere) and so passed into Boccaccio *Genealogy of the Pagan Gods* 2.51 and Bustron p14; this explains why the first Cinyras was ignored altogether by Étienne de Lusignan (see p559 and n19). Ps.-Lactantius probably took his Assyrian Kinyras from Hyginus, a regular source for the 'Narrator' (Cameron 2004:6–7), even though Hyginus himself was treating the *Myrrha* story, and makes Cinyras son of Paphos despite the 'Assyrian' setting! The distinction of an earlier and later Cinyras probably enjoyed some specious support from the large interval that separates the episodes in Ovid. Yet both are free of the poet's overarching chronological scheme, being embedded in other narratives (Athena's web and the song of Orpheus, respectively).
8   Ovid *Metamorphoses* 10.238–242.
9   HC:80n2, thinking of "some group of statues" at Amathous; *Kypris*:78–79; Papantonio 2012:274 (betyls or stelai).
10 Ovid *Metamorphoses* 14.698–764. A variant on the story is Antoninos Liberalis *Metamorphoses* 39 (from the third-century Hermesianax).
11 See OLD s.v. 1b.
12 [Apollodoros] *Library* 3.14.3–4.
13 Engel 1841 2:127; HC:71 and n1. See also p250n41. It is worth noting that, according to Justin (*Epitome* 18.5), the one-off pre-marriage prostitution of Cypriot maidens was meant to *appease* Aphrodite prior to a life of monogamous modesty.
14 See p250. The ps.-Apollodoros passage is probably also related to a peculiar version of the Adonis tale recorded in Servius Auctus on Vergil *Eclogues* 10.18, where again there is no idea of prostitution: see further p512–516.

Chapter Twelve

A different approach is suggested by the Mesopotamian material discussed in Chapter 2. We saw in the Gudea Cylinders that elements of Ningirsu's temple, and attributa of the god himself, were mythologized as his family members or court intimates (one son, for instance, was the deified door of the hall of justice).[15] To understand how such conceptions begat actual myths, recall A. Livingstone's observation that Babylonian ritual was mythogenic through its use of statues and other embodiments of deity, including divinized cult-objects.[16] The image of Kinyras weeping while lying on and embracing his 'step-daughters' can be explained by the role of ritual lamenters in the fabrication and repair of temples, divine statues, and cult-objects. The purpose of such singing was to avert any divine anger that may have caused a repair to be necessary, or which might be aroused through construction or modification to an existing element. While much lamentation-song transpired on a regularly scheduled basis before a god's statue, repairs called for performance at the location affected (temple roofs, gates, and walls), or at a sacred workshop in the case of statues or cult-objects. Such a background satisfactorily accounts for every certain element of Ovid's otherwise peculiar vignette.

A second myth that fits this pattern, also in the *Metamorphoses*, is treated by Ovid at much greater length. This is the terrible tale of Myrrha (or Smyrna), whose seduction of her father earned Kinyras—here Cinyras—his principal place in the western canon.[17] Once again, cultic aetiology is combined with lachrymosity. But this time the tears are those of Cinyras' daughter.

Myrrha embodies myrrh (Ug./Phoen. *mr*, Gk. *mýrra*), the resinous arboreal sap imported to the Levant from East Africa (Punt) and coastal Arabia from the second millennium onwards, and probably known earlier still in Egypt.[18] It was used for incense-offerings, perfumed-oils for anointing statues and kings, embalming the dead (Egypt), as an additive to wine, and in a variety of medical applications.[19] Myrrh was an important element of Ugaritic ritual,

---

[15] See p27.
[16] See p25.
[17] Ovid *Metamorphoses* 10.298–502; further brief allusions at *Art of Love* 1.285–288 (already emphasizing tears), *Remedy for Love* 99–100, *Ibis* 361. For the tale's medieval and Renaissance reception, see Flinker 1980, discussing allegories of Myrrha as the Virgin Mary (impregnated by the 'father' and begetting Adonis, equated with Jesus). Dryden used the myth for a satirical political allegory of the 'Glorious Revolution' (1688): Lee 2004; also Hopkins 1985.
[18] Groom 1981; Miller 1969:104–105, 108; RlA 8:534–537 (Karg/Farber, *Myrrhe). Lexical material and semantic analysis: *Emprunts*:54–56; Bömer 1969–1986 5:114; CAD s.v. *murru* (but the word was applied to other local aromatic plants in Akk.). The typology and distribution of early censers is being exhaustively treated by Zimmerle forthcoming.
[19] See further *Emprunts*:54–56; Groom 1981:1–21; Ribichini 1981:50; Miller 1969:108; Detienne 1994:6–7, 148n6 with references.

282

where it is the only aromatic explicitly named—an indication of its prestige.[20] The anthropomorphosis of Myrrha suggests that myrrh too was once divinized in a still unknown mainland pantheon—for instance Byblos, where the myth is often located (Chapter 19). A strong parallel for this is the Divine Censer of the Ugaritian pantheon texts, immediately adjacent to the Divine Kinnaru.[21]

For Frazer the myth's incest motif derived from early attempts to control matrilineal royal succession.[22] Bömer saw here rather a reflection of the Paphian princesses' duties in the cult (not necessarily sexual), over which their royal father presided as high priest.[23] Capomacchia argues that the incest motif simply reflects Greek ideas of the Orient as a place where normal behavior is inverted.[24] This may be, but specific ritual contexts or theological constructs relating to myrrh itself must have helped shape the myth. Thus Grottanelli, shifting the focus to Myrrha and the perfumed Adonis, rightly looks to royal salving rites like those attested in Hittite, Egyptian, and Biblical sources, incense offerings in royal ancestor cult, and the use of myrrh in royal burials (including an epigraphic example from fifth-century Byblos).[25] A further suggestive analogy is found in a N-A mystic ritual enacting the descent of Tammuz to the underworld: one section defines the substances used as body parts of the "kidnapped god", with myrrh called his semen.[26] Myrrh's aphrodisiac uses must be relevant.[27]

Given Kinyras' connection with the perfumed oil industry, the Cypriot Myrrha was probably linked with *mýron*—oil infused with myrrh, frankincense, cassia, and/or saffron.[28] This was used among other things for smoke-offerings, as must have featured in the Kinyrad cult of Old Paphos with its bloodless altar of

---

[20] See RCU:275, restoring myrrh in RS 1.003.20 (KTU/CAT 1.41) from RS 18.056.22; also RS 13.006.5. These are respectively texts 15A, 15B, and 30 in RCU.

[21] See p5, 103, 121, 124.

[22] Frazer 1914 1:43–44. See p174.

[23] Bömer 1969–1986 5:113.

[24] Capomacchia 1984.

[25] Grottanelli 1984, with reference to Adonis' associations with perfume (for which see Detienne 1994), Jeremiah 34:5 (incense and laments for dead kings), anointing imagery in the Song of Solomon, etc.; the Byblian inscription is discussed on p. 55.

[26] For *The Rites of Egašankalamma*, see Livingstone 1989:95–98 (no. 38); cf. also Jacobsen 1975:72–73. The relevant passage is rev. 5–20, with myrrh in 13. Note also the closing formula at 20, which shows that this was a *mystic* ritual: "[Secret lore of the great gods. An initiate may] show it [to another initiate]; the uninitiated may not see it." The esoteric symbolism was thus formulated by a priestly clique for practical application.

[27] Fulgentius *Mythologies* 3.8 (citing Petronius). Myrrh appears in erotic contexts also in Proverbs 7:17; Song of Songs 5:13.

[28] Cf. Σ Lykophron *Alexandra* 829: μύρραν ... ὅθεν καὶ τὸ μύρον καλεῖται. For the elusive etymological relationship between these words, see Frisk 1960 s.v. μύρρα; Chantraine 1968 s.v. μύρον (folk etymology).

Aphrodite,[29] and provides apt employment for the perfumed-oil-worker (*mu-ro-wo-ro-ko* = *myroworgós*) of a sixth-century inscription from the nearby sanctuary of Rantidi.[30] In a remarkable travesty of Kinyrad icons, Antiphanes, the fourth-century comic poet, puts *mýron* in another context—describing a Paphian king as smeared with "scented-oil from Syria" so that, as he dined, sacred doves would hover about and fan him with their wings.[31] Dramatic epiphany!

The story of Myrrha/Smyrna was known in Greece from at least the fifth century, when it was treated by Panyassis, the epic poet and kinsman of Herodotos, who made the father Theias king of 'Assyria'—Kinyras' doppelganger normally connected with Byblos.[32] Some would see the Kinyras version of the tale behind the sexual struggle of Kinesias (= Kinyras) and Myrrhina (= Myrrha) in Aristophanes' *Lysistrata*,[33] but I find this unlikely. Kinyras did feature in the lost poem on lamentable romantic predicaments by Antimakhos of Colophon (fl. ca. 400), and this may have touched upon Adonis' tearful conception.[34] A tragedy of unknown authorship, in which both Kinyras and Myrrha died, was playing at the Macedonian royal court when Philip was assassinated in 336.[35] Kleitarkhos cited the Theias/Byblos version of the myth in connection, presumably, with Alexander's Phoenician campaign,[36] and the tale, with or without Kinyras, remained popular throughout Hellenistic and later times.[37]

---

[29] See p413. Myrrh and other 'spices' in smoke-offerings: Porphyry *On Abstinence from Animal Food* 2.5.3–5 = Theophrastos *On Piety* fr. 2 Pötscher (584A Fortenbaugh); cf. Detienne 1994:38–39.

[30] Mitford 1961b:13–14 no. 6.1, with discussion and parallels (including -ϝοργός compounds in Lin. B); SEG 20:225; I.Rantidi 2.1; DGAC:768 no. 171.1.

[31] Antiphanes fr. 200 PCG (= Athenaios 257d), especially 5–9: ἐρριπίζετο / ὑπὸ τῶν περιστερῶν ... / δειπνῶν ὁ βασιλεύς ... / ... ἠλείφετο / ἐκ τῆς Συρίας ἥκοντι τοιούτῳ μύρῳ. This passage is discussed by Grottanelli 1984:48–49, arguing for its relevance to Syro-Levantine royal ritual beneath the caricature. For Aphrodite's doves, see p238 and n108.

[32] Panyassis fr. 22ab EGF = fr. 27 PEG = [Apollodoros] *Library* 3.14.4. For Theias at Byblos, see further p466–468.

[33] Ahl 1985:218–223; Detienne 1994:63–64.

[34] Since Antimakhos "with lamentations filled his sacred / scrolls" (Hermesianax 7.45–46 CA: γόων δ' ἐνεπλήσατο βίβλους / ἱράς), his account of Adonis as son of Kinyras (fr. 92 Matthews 1996) must have treated his death and lamentation.

[35] *Tragica Adespota* 5d TGF; Josephus *Antiquities of the Jews* 19.94; Suetonius *Caligula* 57. Discussed by Tsablē 2009:237–243. From around this same time comes an Apulian red-figure pelike, showing Aphrodite and Demeter competing for Adonis in the main register, and perhaps Myrrha and her nurse on the neck: LIMC s.v. Myrrha no. 2.

[36] Kleitarkhos FGH 137 F 3; Stobaios *Anthology* 40.20.73. See p492.

[37] For the version of Theodoros (SH 749), see below n43. The story was also treated by the Cypriot ἱστορικός Xenophon (*Suda* s.v. Ξενοφῶν), for whom see further Appendix G. Other sources: Σ Theokritos *Idylls* 1.109; Lykophron *Alexandra* 828–830 (Byblian setting, see Σ ad 829, 831); for Cinna, see below; Lucian *On Dancing* 58; Antoninos Liberalis *Metamorphoses* 34 (from Panyassis? Nikandros? Papathomopoulos 1968: ix–xix, 146–148); [Apollodoros] *Library* 3.14.4; Hyginus *Fabulae* 58, 242, 251, 271, cf. 248, 275; Nemesianus *Cynegetica* 26–29; Servius Auctus on Vergil *Eclogues* 10.18, *Aeneid* 5.72; Nonnos *Dionysiaka* 13.460, 32.30, 220, 42.346, 48.267; Hesykhios s.v.

Figure 35 Myrrha fleeing, putting viewer in position of Kinyras. Roman fresco from Tor Marancio, ca. 150–250 CE, after Hellenistic original. Vatican, Sala delle Nozze Aldobrandine. Drawn from LIMC s.v. Myrrha no. 1.

Cinna, drawing perhaps on Parthenios, introduced the story, with Cinyras, to Rome. His *Zmyrna*, a neoteric *tour-de-force* nine years in the making (ca. 65–56)—coinciding with the Roman takeover of Cyprus (58)—was so recherché, and sufficiently popular, that a commentary was produced by Crassicius Pansa in Augustan times.[38] That the majority of certain artistic representations of Myrrha are from the Roman period may owe as much to Cinna as to Ovid (Figure 35).[39]

As it happens, one of the *Zmyrna*'s few fragments mentions the heroine's tears, predicting the central role of this motif in Ovid.[40] This element must have been traditional, sap-drops being so described by botanical writers as early as Aristotle and Theophrastos—doubtless adapting a popular usage of considerable antiquity.[41] This and other details from Cinna's masterpiece presented Ovid with intertextual opportunities too good to squander; like the poet of the Vergilian *Ciris*, he engaged with the *Zmyrna* closely.[42] But Ovid was never slavish, and may have incorporated elements from one or more other versions available in the fashionable transformation-anthologies of the Hellenistic period.[43]

μυρίκη; Cyril of Alexandria *Commentary on Isaiah* 2.3 (PG 70:440C); Fulgentius *Mythologies* 3.8; *Mythographi Vaticani* 1.60.

[38] Nine-years: Catullus 95; Quintilian *Institutio Oratoria* 10.4.4; Servius Auctus on Vergil *Eclogues* 9.35. Pansa's commentary: Suetonius *On Grammarians* 18. See further Wiseman 1974:48; Bömer 1969–1986 5:111–112; Wiseman 1985; Courtney FLP:218–220, 306. That Cinna was in turn alluding to an Adonis poem by Parthenios is suggested by Catullus' mention, in praising the *Zmyrna*, of the Satrachus/Setrakhos, a rarely attested river with which Parthenios also dealt (the name otherwise appearing only in Lykophron *Alexandra* 448; Nonnos *Dionysiaka* 13.459): see Lightfoot 1999:183 on her fr. 29 (SH 641), and below p500–501.

[39] Atallah 1966:48; LIMC s.v. Myrrha no. 1, 4–5 (= Adonis 3–4), ca. 70–250 CE.

[40] Cinna fr. 6, 8 Courtney FLP.

[41] The tears of Myrrha/Smyrna may often be implicit in descriptions of myrrh as 'tears' of sap: Σ Homer *Iliad* 19.5; Aristotle *Metaphysics* 388b18, 389a14 (cf. Alexandros of Aphrodisias *ad loc.*, *Commentary on Aristotle's Metaphysics* 3.2, p220.22); Theophrastos *History of Plants* 4.4.12, 7.6.3, 9.1.2, 4 (with perhaps an allusion in Porphyry *On Abstinence from Animal Food* 2.5.1–2 [= Theophrastos *On Piety* fr. 2 Pötscher, 584A Fortenbaugh], but cf. 2.6.4); Posidonius FGH 87 F 114; Diodoros Siculus 2.49.2; Ovid *Art of Love* 1.285–288; Seneca *Hercules Oetaeus* 196; Columella *On Agriculture* 10.1.1; Dioskourides *On Medical Material* 1.24.1, 64.1, 66.1; Plutarch *Moralia* 384b; Arrian *Anabasis of Alexander* 6.22.4; Antoninos Liberalis *Metamorphoses* 34.4; Oribasios *Collectiones medicae* 12Σ35, 57; Fulgentius *Mythologies* 3.8; Paul of Aegina 7.3.10. Note also Pindar fr. 122.3 = Athenaios 574a, of frankincense.

[42] For quotations and allusions to Cinna's version in [Vergil] *Ciris* (e.g. 238–240), see Lyne 1978:39–44, 185–186 et passim. Lyne shows that Cinna is the common source for ideas and diction shared by Ovid's Myrrha and the *Ciris*. We may deduce, for example, that Cinna's heroine fled to Arabia, given Ovid's *palmiferos Arabas Panchaeaque rura relinquit* (10.478) and the nurse's allusion at *Ciris* 237–238: *ei mihi, ne furor ille tuos invaserit artus, / ille Arabae Myrrhae quondam qui cepit ocellos*. For further such proposals see Thomas 1981:371–373. For Cinna's legacy generally, see Wiseman 1974:56–58.

[43] An attractive candidate here is Theodoros, who dealt with transformations in epic verse (*Suda* s.v. Θεόδωρος). Relatively little is known about him (Forbes Irving 1990:240; RE 5 [1934], 1809

Ovid has Myrrha driven by a Fury to fall in love with her father, who exemplifies all that is good and noble. The poet elaborates Myrrha's inner torment, harping on the continual tears that determine her transformation.[44] The fatal opportunity comes when the girl's mother Cenchreis[45] is absent, and abstinent, at a nine-day festival of 'Ceres'.[46] A conniving nurse successfully proposes to Cinyras an anonymous tryst with a beauty she describes as just his daughter's age, and very similar in looks.[47] Cinyras is all-too-willing. With a possible reminiscence of Aeneas' *katábasis* to Anchises,[48] the nurse leads Myrrha in darkness to her father's chamber. For Cinyras it was fun while it lasted. But overcome with curiosity on the final night, he discovers his mysterious partner by lamp-light and, enraged, whips out his sword (with an Ovidian double-entendre).[49] Myrrha flees and "wanders through the palm-bearing plains of Arabia and the districts of Panchaea" and finally the Sabaeans—that is, through the historical and legendary lands from which myrrh came, or was believed to.[50] Half dead, half alive, she begs the gods for release. Her prayers answered, Myrrha is

---

[18]). But his collection contained a version of Kinyras/Myrrha (SH 749 = [Plutarch] *Moralia* 310f = Stobaios *Anthology* 4.20.71), and we are told that Ovid, in treating the myth of (H)alcyon (*Metamorphoses* 11.410-748), combined the versions of Theodoros and Nikandros: [Probus] on Vergil *Georgics* 1.399 (SH 750: *in altera sequitur Ovidius Nicandrum, in altera Theodorum*). For Ovid's sources in the *Metamorphoses* more generally, see Cameron 2004:268-274.

[44] Ovid *Metamorphoses* 10.360 (*suffundit lumina rore*); 361-362 (*Cinyras ... flere vetat*); 387 (*tum denique flere vacavit*, of the nurse); 406 (*lacrimantem*); 419 (*lacrimisque ... obortis*); 500-501 (*flet tamen, et tepidae manant ex arbore guttae. / est honor et lacrimis* etc.); 509, tears in childbirth (*lacrimisque cadentibus umet*); 514: *Naïdes impositum lacrimis unxere parentis* (baby Adonis anointed with his mother's tears).

[45] For speculation about this name, Engel 1841 2:126-127 (extension of the mythology binding Cypriot and Saronic Salamis); similarly Stoll in Roscher *Lex.*:1190; Bömer 1969-1986 5:113-114.

[46] Ovid has the women robed in white, offering grain-wreaths as first fruits, and nine days chaste. This setting is unique (Frazer 1914 1:43n4 looked to Theodoros), but has a genuine Cypriot flavor. A decree from Amathous (n.b.) records a sacrifice to Aphrodite for the fertility of crops (GIBM 4:2 975; HC:78), which can be connected with Hesykhios' reference to a fruits-offering for Aphrodite in the same city (s.v. κάρπωσις· θυσία Ἀφροδίτης ἐν Ἀμαθοῦντι) and to 'Demeterizing' on Cyprus more generally (s.v. Δαματρίζειν· τὸ συνάγειν τὸν Δημητριακὸν καρπόν. Κύπριοι). A high priestess of Demeter for the island is also known, her cult-center probably at New Paphos (Mitford 1990:2182, with LBW 801). A temenos of Demeter and Kore is attested at Kourion (fourth century: I.Kourion 6), and "our Kore" is invoked in the loyalty oath to Tiberius (see p205). Cf. Apuleius *Golden Ass* 11.2, where Ceres, Venus, and Paphos appear among the many names by which the Queen of Heaven (*regina caeli*) was known. There is also the myth that Adonis was shared by Aphrodite and Persephone for six months each: Σ Theokritos *Idylls* 3.48, cf. Σ 1.109; [Apollodoros] *Library* 3.14.4; Hyginus *Astronomica* 2.6; Ailianos *On the Nature of Animals* 9.36.

[47] Antoninus Liberalis *Metamorphoses* 34 calls the nurse Hippolyte: cf. Papathomopoulos 1968:146.

[48] Dyson 1998-1999.

[49] For the sexual word play, see Ahl 1985:223.

[50] Ovid *Metamorphoses* 10.476-480. For the (semi-)legendary treatment of the spice-lands, Detienne 1994:5-36.

transformed into the myrrh-tree; the baby Adonis, busting out at end of term, is anointed with his mother's sappy tears.

Although Ovid's two Cinyras scenes are obviously unrelated, the poet used the first to preview his greater attraction. "Embracing temple steps, his own daughters' limbs" and "lying on the stone" would readily assume an incestuous flavor for readers primed by Cinna. And while Kinyras himself does not lament in the Myrrha episode, the earlier vignette makes ironic his request that she not weep during their lovemaking. The mournful Kinyras is also implied by the description of Myrrha as *virgo Cinyreïa* ('Cinyreian maiden'), where the patronymic clearly suggests Gk. *kinyrós* ('mournful').[51] Being a child of Cinyras means 'familiarity' with tears and mourning.

Several variants in the Myrrha tale may be noted. According to Servius, Myrrha was driven to seduce her father by the "anger of the Sun" (no further details are given).[52] This may be related to the sun's imagined role in the production of myrrh,[53] or perhaps one of Kinyras' semi-solar lineages (Chapter 21). For Hyginus, Myrrha's obsession was brought about by her mother's boast that her daughter was lovelier than Venus; after the affair the anguished Cinyras, here king of 'Assyria', kills himself.[54] Elsewhere Aphrodite is angered by Myrrha/Smyrna's claim to have better hair.[55] Vaguer sources agree that Myrrha's lust was caused by some failure to honor the goddess.[56] Every case involves divine

---

[51] Ovid *Metamorphoses* 10.369.
[52] Servius Auctus on Vergil *Eclogues* 10.18. Krappe 1941-1942, in an outmoded solar reading of the myth (spurned by Atallah 1966:50), suggested a connection between Kinyras' double Theias (see p466-468) and Theia, wife of Hyperion and mother of Helios, Selene, and Eos (Hesiod *Theogony* 371-374, cf. 134-135). But 'Theia' is a rather bland name, perhaps coined by Hesiod for its rhyme with Rheia in 135 (West *ad loc.*).
[53] Fulgentius, after telling the tale of Myrrha without naming her father, proceeds to read it as an allegory for myrrh production; Myrrha's infatuation for her father is her love of the Sun, since he is "father of all things" (*Mythologies* 3.8; resumed by Boccaccio *Genealogy of the Pagan Gods* 2.52). Cf. Groom 1981:143-146; Detienne 1994:6-9.
[54] Hyginus *Fabulae* 58, 242 (who follows Ovid in naming the mother Cenchreis, and in making Kinyras son of Paphos); the same motive is found in [Lactantius Placidus] *Summaries of Ovidian Tales* 10.9. Kinyras also kills himself in the anonymous Hellenistic tragedy (see p284) and in Antoninos Liberalis *Metamorphoses* 34.4.
[55] Σ Theokritos *Idylls* 1.109. This may explain the mirror held by Myrrha in the fourth-century vase mentioned in n35 above.
[56] Aphrodite's anger was mentioned by Theodoros (SH 749); [Apollodoros] *Library* 3.14.3-4 (κατὰ μῆνιν Ἀφροδίτης οὐ γὰρ αὐτὴν ἐτίμα; but note that Smyrna appears here as the daughter not of Kinyras, but Theias, for whom see p466-468); cf. Hyginus *Fabulae* 251 *voluntate Veneris*. Ovid *Metamorphoses* 10.311-314 blames the episode on a Fury; the possibility of divine anger is broached at 396-399. The use of magic to soothe the gods in [Vergil] *Ciris* 258-262 is probably based on a scene in Cinna's *Zmyrna*: see Lyne 1978 *ad loc.* Detienne 1994:64 seeks the offense in Myrrha's spurned suitors, but both Ovid and Antoninus Liberalis make it clear that her rejection of them is due to a *preexisting* love for her father.

anger and a tearful outcome. But a final variant, probably original to Cyprus and perhaps late and popular, linked Myrrha not with myrrh but myrtle (*mýrtos*), a plant often associated with Aphrodite and not obviously tearlike.[57]

Several other familiars of Kinyras may be connected with cult-objects or processes, although the motifs of divine anger and tearfulness are not always so clearly emphasized as with Myrrha or Kinyras and his temple-step daughters.

The myth of Pygmalion, Cypriot king and sometimes Kinyras' grandfather or father-in-law, is clearly relevant. His love for a statue—either brought to life by Aphrodite, or of the goddess herself—must reflect the divinization of cult images, a practice known throughout ANE history. Some form of hierogamy is also suggested by versions in which Pygmalion lay with the statue itself.[58] These thematic similarities may have inspired Ovid to devise the succession Pygmalion-Paphos-Cinyras, not attested in any other ancient source.[59]

We saw that a wrathful Apollo destroyed Kinyras in a musical contest, leading to the metamorphosis of the king's daughters into halcyons. This I suggested aetiologized threnodic female choruses like those that appear in the Cypro-Phoenician bowls.[60] Note that birds chased from a temple, or a city destroyed through a god's anger, are a common image of Mesopotamian Emesal prayers/laments.[61]

A possible son Amaracus, connected with perfume-making, was metamorphosed into marjoram; according to Étienne de Lusignan he too—like Adonis, Myrrha, and 'Cinaras'—was "numbered among the gods." This tale, as scantily preserved, does not mention an angered or grieving divinity (Lusignan's version is euhemerizing); rather it is the boy's 'confusion' or 'shame' that ends in his transformation. But the link between Amaracus and Kinyras is not certainly ancient.[62]

A final group of myths relates to the death of Kinyras' son Adonis, and the annual lamentations instituted as a result. The father-son relationship itself reflects an aspect of ritual poetics (see below), though we now shift from occasional lamentation (construction of temples, cult-objects) to periodic, calendrical performances. Whether on Cyprus such laments were exclusively tied to Adonis is another question, for Kinyras is not attested as his father before

---

[57] Servius Auctus on Vergil *Aeneid* 5.72 (cf. 2.64: *Paphiae ... myrtus*); cf. Detienne 1994:63.
[58] The statue as Aphrodite herself, with which Pygmalion lays: Philostephanos *FHG* 3.31 fr. 13 (from the Περὶ Κύπρου); Arnobius *Against the Pagans* 6.22. Aphrodite brings statue to life: Ovid *Metamorphoses* 10.243–297. Divinization of statues in the ANE: Matsushima 1993.
[59] See further Appendix F.
[60] See p191.
[61] PHG:32.
[62] See p331–332.

the later fifth century.⁶³ Adonis himself is a complex figure, equally localized at Byblos—with and without Kinyras—where his death and rebirth shaped an annual ritual cycle involving death, lamentation, and perhaps a kind of resurrection (see Chapter 19). Of the innumerable sources, the most relevant here, found in Servius, aetiologizes not only Aphrodite's establishment of Adonis-laments, but her sacred apples and doves.⁶⁴ All of these elements are integrated into Kinyras' family circle:

> This is the story about how the apple-tree (*melus*) took its name in Greek (*mêlon/mâlon*). A certain Melus, born in the island of Delos, forsook his homeland and fled to the island of Cyprus where at that time Cinyras was king, having Adonis as his son. Cinyras bade Melus be a friend to his son, and when he saw that Melus was of a good nature, gave him one of his relatives to marry, called Pelia [< Gk. *Péleia*], who was herself a devotee of Venus. From them was born [sc. another] Melus, whom afterwards Venus, being gripped by love for Adonis, ordered to be raised among her altars as if he were the son of her beloved. But after Adonis was killed by the wound from the boar, the senior Melus, unable to endure his grief for the death of Adonis, hung himself from a tree and so ended his life. It is from this man's name that the apple-tree is so called. And his wife Pelia died in turn by hanging herself in this tree. Venus, driven by pity for their death, established perennial mourning (*luctum*) for Adonis, turned Melus into the fruit-tree of his own name, and transformed his wife Pelia into a dove. As to the younger Melus, who alone survived of Cinyras' line, when Venus saw that he had reached manhood, she ordered him to gather a band of men and return to Delos.⁶⁵

---

⁶³ Adonis as son of Kinyras: Plato Comicus fr. 3 PCG (with Athenaios 456a); Antimakhos fr. 92 (Matthews 1996, with comments on 256–257) = [Probus] on Vergil *Eclogues* 10.18 = 102 IEG. Other sources include Σ Theokritos *Idylls* 1.109; Σ Dionysios the Periegete 509 (FGH 758 F 3a), where the mother is Thymarete; Ailianos *On the Nature of Animals* 9.36; [Apollodoros] *Library* 3.14.3, with mother Metharme. For Thymarete and Metharme (doublets), see p497–498, 512.

⁶⁴ Aphrodite is shown holding apples from the Archaic period onwards: LIMC s.v. Aphrodite no. 61, 89, 172, 237, etc. Doves: see p236 and n108.

⁶⁵ Does the passage between Cyprus and Delos that begins and ends this myth reflect some communication between the cults of Kinyras and Delian Apollo (cf. Engel 1841 2:129)? Are Delo/Delum errors for Melo/Melum (see Thilo's *ap. crit.*)? The story concludes: "And he [the younger Melus], after reaching the island [Delos] and making himself master of the situation there, founded the state of Melos. And when he first ordained that sheep be shorn and cloth be made from their wool, it was right that they be called *mêla* from his name (since sheep are called *mêla* in Greek)." Servius Auctus on Vergil *Eclogues* 8.37 (ed. Thilo): *unde melus graece traxerit nomen, fabula talis est: Melus quidam, in Delo insula ortus, relicta patria fugit ad insulam Cyprum, in qua eo tempore Cinyras regnabat, habens filium Adonem. hic Melum sociatum Adoni filio iussit esse, cumque eum videret esse*

The recurrence in these tales of an angered or grieving Aphrodite is striking in view of the Mesopotamian charter-myth that Enki created the lamentation priest (gala/*kalû*) to assuage Inanna's grief.[66] It can hardly be coincidence that Kinyras is the personification of the *knr*, defined as the 'divine Inanna-instrument' in second-millennium Mesopotamian scribal tradition; and that versions of this instrument, including the Cypriot *kinýra*, are associated with lamentative contexts (see further below). While Kinyras' role as Aphrodite's priest and lover accords with the Mesopotamian pattern of cult-objects as familiars of their master-god, there is an analogous relationship between Kinyras and his *own* cult-object children. He is the hub of a miniature myth-cycle, the king within whose 'realm' their metamorphoses transpire. These relationships should require, by the Mesopotamian parallels, that *Kinyras himself be a god*, even if his own worship was subordinated to the goddess. This 'second-in-command' status must reflect the controlling role of kinyrists in the cult, as is also implied by the title Kinyradai at Paphos.[67]

Between Song and Silence

Ovid's portrait of Kinyras weeping suggests not only the posture of a lamentation *priest*, but a grieving *god* who himself needs calming. Here we must recall the remarkable Ishtar ritual and lamentation 'oratorio' Uru'amma'irabi, performed at OB Mari and focused on the divinized balang Ninigizibara—which is called the goddess's spouse or lover.[68] The balang somehow represented Ishtar as she mourned for, among other things, the death of Dumuzi and the destruction of her balang.[69] If Ninigizibara was not itself played, as Gabbay suggests, this would suit the divine mood and the conceit of the instrument's loss; in this scenario, the balang was rather the *target* of song by lamentation priests and groups

---

indolis bonae, propinquam suam, dicatam et ipsam Veneri, quae Pelia dicebatur, Melo coniunxit. ex quibus nascitur Melus, quem Venus propterea quod Adonis amore teneretur, tamquam amati filium inter aras praecepit nutriri. sed postquam Adonis apri ictu extinctus est, senex Melus cum dolorem mortis Adonis ferre non posset, laqueo se ad arborem suspendens vitam finit: ex cuius nomine melus appellata est. Pelia autem coniux eius in ea arbore se adpendens necata est. Venus misericordia eorum mortisducta, Adoni luctum continuum praestitit, Melum in pomum sui nominis vertit, Peliam coniugem eius in columbam mutavit, Melum autem puerum, qui de Cinyrae genere solus supererat, cum adultum vidisset, collecta manu, redire ad Delum praecepit. qui cum ad insulam pervenisset et rerum ibi esset potitus, Melon condidit civitatem: et cum primus oves tonderi et vestem de lanis fieri instituisset, meruit ut eius nomine oves μῆλα *vocarentur; graece enim oves* μῆλα *appellantur.*

[66] See p29.
[67] See Chapter 16. Recall the apparent use of lyre-music during offerings to cult-objects in one Hittite text: p94n23.
[68] See p291.
[69] See p291–292, and Heimpel, "Balang-Gods," Section 2c, 2d, 4a, 23f.

of male and female musicians. In any case, the ritual would lead the goddess herself back from dolorous silence, with Ninigizibara somehow effecting this in the divine realm.

These remarkable oppositions of song and silence in ritual and/or ritual poetics provide an ancient real-world background for examining the relationship between the lamenting Kinyras trope and the actual role of the *kinýra* in threnody. Eustathios, we saw, states plainly that the verb *kinýresthai* referred to singing songs "over/for the dead" (*epì toîs keiménois*) using the *kinýra*.[70] But what exactly is envisioned? And is this more than guess work?

In the Greek world, funeral rites consisted of three stages: *próthesis*, the laying-out and preparation of a body for burial; *ekphorá*, carrying the body to the gravesite; and the actual interment. A principal ceremony of *próthesis* was indeed the singing of laments, which our sources divide into two types. *Góoi* were spontaneous yet patterned wailings in which the deceased's nearest kin, especially female, articulated grief and anger about their loss and dark future.[71] These were interspersed with, and sometimes responded to, *thrênoi*—more formal songs by professional threnodes.[72] The *locus classicus* for this dichotomy is the funeral of Hektor in the *Iliad*:

> And alongside [Hektor's body] they set singers (*aoidoús*),
> Leaders of dirges (*thrénōn exárkhous*) who [sing] sorrowful song;
> They began to sing the dirge (*ethréneon*), and the women added
>   their groans.[73]

Homer goes on to give us lengthy stylized representations of the *góoi* of Hekuba, Andromakhe, and Helen,[74] while the songs of threnodes are left to the

---

[70] Eustathios on Homer *Iliad* 17.5 (for the Greek text, see p188n7). Recall that any linguistic kinship between *kinýra* and *kinýresthai* must be indirect, given their quantity-difference in the second syllable; Eustathios is following the 'umbrella' usage of *kinýra*: see p213–216.

[71] Reiner 1938:8–61, especially 53–56. Iconography indicates an unbroken if evolving tradition going back to the LBA. See Alexiou 2002:4–23 passim; cf. GR:192; Burke 2008, stressing however that the Mycenaean material is not monolithic, and exhibits greater variety than Archaic representations.

[72] Reiner 1938:4–5, 8–9; Alexiou 2002:10–14; Nagy 1979:36n103, 112, 170–177; Garland 2001:29–30; Holst-Warhaft 1992, 111–112; Olivetti 2010, 1–71 (further magical nuances of *góos*). Battlefield conditions account for the lament of Patroklos by Achilles and the Myrmidons (Homer *Iliad* 23.12-13), who must replace female next-of-kin: Holst-Warhaft 1992:108–110. For the tradition of female lamentation specifically see, besides Alexiou and Holst-Warhaft, Lardinois 2001; Dué 2006, especially 30–46; papers in Suter 2008.

[73] Homer *Iliad* 24.720-722: παρὰ δ' εἷσαν ἀοιδοὺς / θρήνων ἐξάρχους, οἵ τε στονόεσσαν ἀοιδὴν / οἳ μὲν ἄρ' ἐθρήνεον, ἐπὶ δὲ στενάχοντο γυναῖκες. There is some uncertainty as to syntax and readings (Diehl 1940:112–113), but the sense is clear. See the analysis of Reiner 1938:8–11 with further references.

[74] Nagy 1979:112.

imagination. It is grammatically clear that these specialists were male; and *aoidoí* and *exárkhoi* indicate that they were probably lyrists.[75] But the *Odyssey*'s description of Achilles being mourned by Nereids and Muses, whose performances correspond to *góoi* and *thrênoi*, respectively, strongly suggests that threnodes could also be female.[76] This was true in the Biblical world,[77] and is supported by Sappho's Adonis fragments.[78] It may well also be that the female groups of the Cypro-Phoenician symposium bowls should be related to 'Adonis' lamentation in the cult of Astarte/'Aphrodite'.[79] Pindar and Simonides, who composed *thrênoi*, were of course male lyrists, though whether these particular songs were accompanied by the instrument is another question. One of the more informative sources on these points is Lucian's satirical *On Funerals*, which, though so much later, is broadly compatible with Homer. Here the 'expert in dirges' (*thrḗnōn sophistḗn*), certainly male, acts as a kind of 'choral producer' (*khorēgós*); he leads with his own songs, drawn from a large repertoire of 'ancient misfortunes' (*palaiàs symphorás*), which were punctuated at certain intervals by the family's own outbursts.[80] This scenario agrees with the laments for Hektor, and the Muses' "alternating threnody with beautiful voice" at Achilles' funeral.[81] *Thrênoi* and *góoi* were thus an integrated performance; the former were truly musical (*mélos* in Lucian), drawing on 'chronic' mythological repertoire to provide a framework for the expression of 'acute' personal grief.

---

[75] Reiner 1938:8, 61–62 (apparently) and Alexiou 2002:12 rightly considered these threnodes male; thus οἵ τε and οἳ μέν are contrasted with γυναῖκες; Holst-Warhaft 1992:205n40 argued anyway for a female interpretation, but while ἀοιδός is sometimes used of women in later poetry (LSJ s.v. 2), this is unparalleled within Homer. Homer's ἀοιδός normally (but not invariably) implies a lyre-singer (not excluded by Reiner 1938:67n5). Ἔξαρχος suggests the same: Athenaios 180d states that "'leading off' was proper to the lyre" (τὸ γὰρ ἐξάρχειν τῆς φόρμιγγος ἴδιον), and discusses passages from Homer, Hesiod, Arkhilokhos, and others. But the verb is also used of Achilles, Thetis, and Andromakhe as they 'lead off' γόοι (Homer *Iliad* 18.51, 316 [cf. 23.12]; 24.723).

[76] Homer *Odyssey* 24.58–61 with Pindar *Isthmian* 8.56–62 and Nagy 1990:36n103, 204. Cf. Reiner 1938:56–59 for the limited evidence of professional female mourners in the Greek world (though his emphasis here is on *góoi*).

[77] Jeremiah 9:17, 20; cf. Holst-Warhaft 1992:205n40.

[78] Lardinois 2001. Another γυνὴ ἀοιδός sings an Adonis-song in Theokritos *Idylls* 15.100–143.

[79] Marquand 1887:336. The same trio of pipes, lyre, and frame-drum appears in Isaiah 5:11–12 in (probably: McLaughlin 2001) the context of *marzeaḥ*. In his commentary on the passage, Basilios of Caesarea (fourth-century CE) interprets the music as threnodic (Reiner 1938:68n3), but with a twist makes its target the feasters themselves (*Commentary on Isaiah* 5.155 Trevisan = PG 30:373).

[80] Lucian *On Funerals* 20: ἀλλ' ὅμως οἱ μάταιοι καὶ βοῶσι καὶ μεταστειλάμενοί τινα θρήνων σοφιστὴν πολλὰς συνειλοχότα παλαιὰς συμφορὰς τούτῳ συναγωνιστῇ καὶ χορηγῷ τῆς ἀνοίας καταχρῶνται, ὅπῃ ἂν ἐκεῖνος ἐξάρχῃ πρὸς τὸ μέλος ἐπαιάζοντες ("The simpletons wail themselves and, summoning some expert in dirges who has collected many ancient misfortunes, employ him as a fellow actor and a choral-producer of their folly, adding their 'Alas!' to the melody however he directs them to").

[81] Homer *Odyssey* 24.60–61: ἀμειβόμεναι ὀπὶ καλῇ / θρήνεον.

Chapter Twelve

Notwithstanding Lucian's valuable testimony, our understanding of the threnodic tradition is rather obscured by sixth- and fifth-century legislation instituted in several cities, including Solon's Athens, aimed at curbing the political influence of clans by limiting the public visibility of funeral rites and the political potential of heroizing the dead.[82] Henceforth at Athens *próthesis*, the principal occasion for *góoi*, was to be conducted indoors and by close family only, without the assistance of professional threnodes. Iconographic and literary evidence shows clearly that pipers normally accompanied funeral *processions*,[83] but there is now little firm evidence for lyric threnody during *próthesis*.[84] Two vase paintings have indeed been cited in support of the practice, but in both cases the lyre is *held* by a mourner, not actually played.[85] The significance of this is quite clear in the famous scene of the Nereids or Muses mourning Achilles: the lyre is *the hero's own instrument*, now silenced (Figure 36).[86] In the second case the lyre is held, appropriately, by a *paidagōgós*.[87] These images are to be connected rather with the tragic trope that occasions of death and war are 'lyre-less' (*ályros*)—lacking the festive ease-of-mind normally associated with lyre-music and choruses.[88] The idea is well illustrated by a Corinthian black-figure plate: a man is laid out in a shroud, with his lyre suspended above.[89]

On the other hand, there is considerable evidence for lyric lamentations in extra-Athenian mythological contexts. Ovid has Apollo weeping in an aetiology for the Hyakinthos festival at Sparta; he will ever remember his beloved with lyre-songs (a choral context is probably assumed).[90] Ovid also has Apollo mourn his son Linos "with reluctant lyre" in the elegy for Tibullus.[91] Orpheus with his lyre moved the underworld to tears, from human shades to the very Furies.[92]

---

[82] See Holst-Warhaft 1992:114–119.
[83] Quasten 1930:196; Reiner 1938:67–70; AGM:23; Garland 2001:32, 142 (note to p. 30).
[84] Cf. Reiner 1938:66–67.
[85] Quasten 1930:196–198; countered by Reiner 1938:68–69.
[86] Sixth-century Corinthian hydria, Louvre E 643: LIMC s.v. Achilleus no. 897; SIAG:38, 51 fig. 15a.
[87] See Quasten 1930:196n4.
[88] For tragic and other sources, including the words *akítharis* and *ákhoros* ('danceless'), see GMW 1:68n38, 73n69; SIAG:80. Lyre and εὐφροσύνη: *Homeric Hymn to Hermes* 449, 480–482, etc.
[89] New York 06.1021.26: Vermeule 1979:209 fig. 31; SIAG:37, 50 fig. 14e. The deceased is often interpreted as a dead poet, quite unnecessarily.
[90] Ovid *Metamorphoses* 10.196–219, especially 204–205: *semper eris mecum memorique haerebis in ore. / te lyra pulsa manu, te carmina nostra sonabunt* ("You will always be with me, and cleave to my mindful lips. / You our hand-struck lyre will sing, you our songs"); choral dances for Hyakinthos are mentioned by Euripides *Helen* 1469–1470. Grave-offerings for Hyakinthos in connection with Apollo cult at Amyklai: Pfister 1909–1912:451–452, 492.
[91] Ovid *Amores* 3.9.23–24 (*invita ... lyra*). Other instances of Apollo lamenting, with no lyre mentioned, are Apollonios of Rhodes 4.611–618 (among the Hyperboreans); [Moskhos] *Lament for Bion* 26 (Apollo and Bion); Ovid *Metamorphoses* 10.141–142 (Apollo and Cyparissus).
[92] Ovid *Metamorphoses* 10.40–49.

Kinyras the Lamenter

Figure 36 Próthesis of Achilles, with silenced lyre. Sixth-century Corinthian hydria, Louvre E 643. Drawn from LIMC s.v. Achilleus no. 897.

Upon his own death, the natural world, over which he had power while alive, wept for him; and his lyre itself as it drifted down the Hebros "sang some tearful plaint" of its own accord—like a thing still living.[93] That these intimations of lyric lament represent real traditions of deep antiquity is confirmed both by the evidence for Linos-song (see below), and the Minoan funerary or mortuary ritual on the Hagia Triada sarcophagus, where sacrifice and libation are accompanied by male piper and lyrist, among otherwise female participants.[94] This scene gives historical depth to the proverbial expression "concert (*synaulía*) of Olympos"—referring to lamentation music, and as we saw the earliest context for the verb *kinýresthai*—since Gk. *synaulía* could involve both pipes and strings.[95]

---

[93] Ovid *Metamorphoses* 11.44–53 (quotation 52: *flebile nescio quid queritur lyra*); cf. especially Lucian *The Ignorant Book-Collector* 11; also Phanokles 1.11–22 CA; [Nikomakhos] *Excerpts* 1 (MSG:266). Further sources, bringing the head and/or lyre to Lesbos, are collected by Pfister 1909–1912:213n213.

[94] Haghia Triada sarcophagus and procession fresco (LM IIIA1): Paribeni 1908; Evans 1921–1936 2:834–838; Long 1974, 38; Burke 2008, 76–80.

[95] For Aristophanes *Knights* 8–12, see p220; cf. Σ *ad loc.* (ξυναυλία λέγεται ὅταν κιθάρα καὶ αὐλὸς συμφωνῇ) and *Tragica Adespota* 53 TGF. Also *Suda* s.v. Ξυναυλίαν πενθήσωμεν, Οὐλύμπου

Chapter Twelve

Lamentation customs will naturally have varied by culture and period, and there is no more reason to believe that *thrênoi* were *always* lyric productions than there is to exclude the instrument entirely, despite the undoubted prevalence of pipes in funereal settings. Nevertheless the foregoing material does present a significant dichotomy. The 'lyreless grief' of real situations is expressed through *góoi*, especially by female kin. The lyric laments relate to mythological figures and archetypal sufferings; their subject matter was still 'lyreless grief', but regarded from a commemorative future—often in a recurring festival, and composed and/or led by male lyrists (hence the lamenting Apollo). Here are the "ancient misfortunes" of Lucian's threnodic repertoire. Such themes will have set a present tragedy in more general historical perspective, praising the deceased and introducing him to the heroic dead. *Thrênoi* were thus immortalizing, equally appropriate for subsequent memorials, often annual (a probable occasion for the *thrênoi* of Pindar and Simonides).[96] From here one passes easily to various forms of hero-cult, including those for which lyric lament is definitely attested (Hyakinthos, Linos).[97] The genre was inherently forward-looking, promising a return from lyreless grief. This is colorfully illustrated by a threnodic fragment of Pindar, who describes the afterlife (for the fortunate) as a perpetual banquet with games and lyre music.[98] Many such scenes are found in funerary reliefs of the Classical period, and this was not unlike the message of Orphism, with its lyre-playing prophet.[99] This also explains the dedication of lyres at gravesites, or of lekythoi with images of lyres (Figure 37).[100] Some

---

νόμον; Eustathios on *Iliad* 19.129; Theodoros Metokhites *Philosophical and Historical Miscellanies* p. 304 Müller: ξυναυλίαν ὀλοφυρομένους Ὀλύμπου νόμον, ὡς ἡ κωμικὴ παροιμία (cf. Dindorf 1835–1838 3:292); cf. Theophylaktos Simokates *Epistles* 32 (p. 19.1 Zanetto). Olympos' association with mournful/funerary music is otherwise well-attested: Aristoxenos fr. 80 Wehrli; Ovid *Metamorphoses* 6.392–394; [Plutarch] *On Music* 1136c; Pollux *Onomastikon* 4.78–79: νόμοι ... Ὀλύμπου ἐπιτυμβίδιοι, cf. 4.72–75 passim for the mourning αὐλός more generally (γοερόν, γοῶδες, θρηνῶδες); cf. Reiner 1938:71–72. One also finds συναυλία in threnodic contexts without mention of Olympos: Aiskhylos *Seven against Thebes* 835–839: ξυναυλία δορός ("concert of the spear") with ἔτευξα τύμβῳ μέλος ("I framed a melody for a tomb," 835); Philostratos *Imagines* 1.11.3; Libanios *Orations* 61.20; Gregory of Nazianzus *Orations* 14 (PG 35:873B); Gregory of Nyssa *Against Eunomios* 11 (PG 45:865D; 3.9.25 Jaeger); Synesios *Epistles* 4.14. See further sources in LSJ s.v.; Pearson 1917:39; Michaelides 1978 s.v.

[96] See with ancient sources Reiner 1938:4–5, 62–63. For Pindar and Simonides, Kurtz and Boardman 1971:202; Nagy 1979:170–177.

[97] See Pfister 1909–1912:497–498 for a catalogue of hymnic offerings relating to hero-cult. Some of these occasions must have involved stylized lyric lament. Plutarch *Aratos* 53 specifies that songs were sung to the *kithára* by the Artists of Dionysos for Aratos' hero-cult; while the event in question was treated as a festival of σωτηρία, a connection was presumably made with the death of the 'hero'.

[98] Pindar fr. 129, especially 6–9.

[99] Cf. Garland 2001:70–71 with discussion of *Totenmahl* scenes from ca. 400–280.

[100] See Garland 2001:115–116, 119, 170 (note to p. 119) with references.

Figure 37 Lekythos showing dedication of lyre at grave.
Berlin 'Antiquarium' no. 3262. Drawn from Quasten 1930 pl. 34.

festivals played out just such a return from lyreless grief to joyous life. The Adonis-rites at second-century CE Byblos, for instance, began with heartfelt wailing and threnodies, but culminated with acclamation of the hero's resurrection.[101] The women of Elis lamented Achilles at the start of the Olympic games.[102] These occasions were sanctioned pretexts for lamenting one's own woes, focused through mythological exempla.[103] The transition of mood must often have been marked by shifts in musical 'mode' and instrumentation: solemn pipe-dirges could be followed by more sentimental lyre threnodies, cathartically closing a complex ritual cycle.[104]

In such threnodic contexts Eustathios' *kinýra*-lamenters must find their place. For the ancient lexica are generally agreed that *kinýresthai* meant not simply 'wail', but 'sing a *thrênos*'.[105] Eustathios' *epì toîs keiménois* should therefore refer not only to songs *over* the dead (during *próthesis*) but *for* the dead and *buried* (a common sense of *keîmai*). This will also explain the presence of *kinýresthai* in grave inscriptions.[106] There is a telling passage in the *Epitaph for Bion* (ca. 100), where the Memnonides lament (*kinýrato*) their brother while flitting "around the tomb."[107] Although this poem is highly mannered, its accumulation of mythological misfortunes, both stock and exotic, must mimic threnodic convention.[108]

The poetics of lyric threnody will also explain the apparent contradiction between Eustathios' assertion that *kinýresthai* was the activity of *kinýra*-threnodes, and the common use of *kinýresthai* in literary and/or mythological contexts that are *ályros*. Lest one suspect that Eustathios has made his own false deduction, precisely the same paradox underlies Ovid's Kinyras, prostrate and weeping for his daughters—an image which remains underappreciated until one sees Kinyras as 'the kinyrist', since the emotional plight and physical posture are antithetical to lyre-playing. The same opposition is assumed by passages that

---

[101] Lucian *On the Syrian Goddess* 6.
[102] Pausanias 6.23.3.
[103] Note Homer's clear psychological explanation at *Iliad* 19.301–302.
[104] Such a progression may explain, for instance, the Euripidean chorus which envisions Alkestis commemorated at the Spartan Karneia—which featured an important and early citharodic competition—with "many melodies ... / to the heptatonic mountain / Tortoise ... also in lyreless hymns" (Euripides *Alkestis* 445–447). See further Franklin 2012:748–753.
[105] For definitions of *kinýresthai*, see p188 and n6.
[106] See p201–202.
[107] [Moskhos] *Lament for Bion* 43: ἱπτάμενος περὶ σᾶμα κινύρατο Μέμνονος ὄρνις. For the Memnonides, see p191n30.
[108] Note also its adaptation of the lyreless theme to Bucolic conceits at 51–56 and 116–126. Although one cannot sing while piping, genre requires both Bion and the lamenting poet to be (pan)pipers, not lyrists. Thus, the poet would be an Orpheus-of-the-pipes to fetch Bion back, but lacks the skill; the superior Bion will be the Orpheus—charming Persephone with his pipes to resurrect himself (i.e. his poetry is immortal).

pointedly call Adonis 'son of Kinyras' at the moment of his death, and so elicit threnodic overtones.[109] This is best illustrated by a poignant sepulchral epigram of the *Greek Anthology*, where a bereaved father, addressing the infernal ferryman, casts his son as an Adonis: "Give your hand to the son of Kinyras as he mounts the / boarding-ladder, black Kharon, and receive him."[110] Through this allusion the father himself becomes the Lamenter. Much the same idea is found in an epigram of Ausonius.[111] These passages are evidently literary reflections of a threnodic trope.[112] Of particular interest is Bion's *Lament for Adonis* (ca. 150–100), which, by describing as *kinýresthai* Aphrodite's mourning for the 'son of Kinyras', assumes an etymological link between the Cypriot king and threnody.[113]

It remains the case that *kinýresthai* often seems to mean something more like *góos*—personal expression of raw grief, with no overt lyric context.[114] But there is a close parallel in the blurring of *thrênos* and *góos* (and derivatives) in tragic usage. That development is sometimes attributed to decreased awareness of formal distinctions due to the anti-threnodic legislations mentioned above.[115] But this is not convincing, as professional threnody persisted for centuries in other parts of the Greek world. A better explanation comes from the realities of ritual performance itself. *Thrênos* would naturally grow to encompass *góos* since it incorporated the latter formally, and yet was itself, from the perspective of the bereaved, but a vehicle for it.[116] Exactly this development lets us reconcile *kinýresthai* as defined by Eustathios via *kinýra* with its commonly attested usage. One must emphasize that, leaving aside the word's many mannered literary occurrences, its use in actual epitaphs gives no compelling reason to reject lyric threnody as the background context.[117]

---

[109] Besides the examples to be discussed, note *Greek Anthology* 7.407.7 (Dioskourides) Κινύρεω νέον ἔρνος ὀδυρομένη Ἀφροδίτῃ ("Aphrodite weeping for the young scion of Kinyras"); cf. *Greek Anthology* 5.289.8 (Agathias Scholasticus), a girl weeping for her lover compared to Persephone and Adonis. Adonis as 'son of Kinyras' also appears in an epitaph for a slain gladiator: see p335.

[110] *Greek Anthology* (Zonas of Sardis) 7.365.3-4: τῷ Κινύρου τὴν χεῖρα βατηρίδος ἐκβαίνοντι / κλίμακος ἐκτείνας δέξο, κελαινὲ Χάρον.

[111] Ausonius *Epigrams* 62.7 (*Persephonae Cinyreius ibis Adonis*), cf. *Letters* 14.42-43 (*Cinyrea proles* / ... *Veneri plorandus Adonis*).

[112] Cf. Wypustek 2013:121-124, who would identify Ausonius at least as representing a "no longer existing epigram tradition that heroised the deceased by identifying them with the abduction of Adonis by Persephone" (124).

[113] Bion *Lament for Adonis* 42: πάχεας ἀμπετάσασα κινύρετο, μεῖνον Ἄδωνι ("throwing up her arms, [Aphrodite] wailed 'Adonis, stay!'"); 91: αἱ Χάριτες κλαίοντι τὸν υἱέα τῶ Κινύραο (the chorus of Graces laments the "son of Kinyras").

[114] The two senses are also juxtaposed in several lexicon entries: see p188n6.

[115] Alexiou 2002:10-14.

[116] Cf. Reiner 1938:6; Olivetti 2010:109, 124-133.

[117] See p201-202. Alternatively one might seek a special semantic development whereby *kinýresthai* effectively meant 'act as Kinyras when lamenting', thus eschewing lyre-music. Here if anywhere one might validate Gingras—said to be an alternative name for Adonis deriving from the

Chapter Twelve

I have argued that the tearful Kinyras embodies a necessary abnegation of *kinýra* music. That this idea goes far deeper than Ovid himself, and is not merely a Hellenistic literary contrivance, is guaranteed by a persistent oscillation between song and silence in ANE sources relating to the *knr*.

The Sefire steles, dating to the mid-eighth century and discovered near Aleppo, offer a precious glimpse of Old Aramaic and its traditional literary figures. The text is a treaty between Mati'el of Arpad and a nearby rival, Bar-Ga'yah, and contains numerous curses for whoever breaks its conditions. In one of these, the silencing of lyre-music epitomizes the desolation inflicted on Arpad if unfaithful:

> Nor may the sound of the *kinnār* be heard in Arpad; but among its people [sc. let there rather be] the din of *affliction* and *the noi*[*se of cry*]*ing* and lamentation.[118]

There is a similar musical stipulation in the N-A vassal treaty between the same Mati'el and Assurnerari V (754–745), this time combined with a typical agricultural curse: "may his farmers not sing the harvest song in the fields."[119] The *knr* is not specified, but we must recall Herodotos' testimony about a kind of seasonal 'Linos-song' in the Cypro-Levantine region (see further below).

Much the same motif—an afflicted people whose *kinnōr* is silenced—occurs in several Biblical passages, in both Jewish and Phoenician contexts.[120] Most famous is Psalm 137:

> By the rivers of Babylon—there we sat down and there we wept when we remembered Zion.
> On the willows there we hung up our lyres ...
> How could we sing the Lord's song in a foreign land?[121]

---

dirge-pipes used to lament him—as a derivative of *knr*, as some propose (see p201–202). The interpretation of such a Gingras as a kind of Adonis would parallel the father-son construction of Kinyras-Adonis attested elsewhere: see p312–316.

[118] Stele I, A 29–30: KAI 222; Dupont-Sommer and Starcky 1958:20, with comments on 45–46 (cf. Greenfield 1965:15); Fitzmyer 1995:45 (translation used here), cf. 87; Hoftijzer and Jongeling 1995:520.

[119] Parpola and Watanabe 1988:11; cf. ANET:533 (the detail does not emerge in ARAB 1:267 §756). This might suggest that the curse against the *kinnār* in the Sefire stele as due to the influence of N-A imperial rhetoric, since such peripheral responses are otherwise well documented (for comparison of the Sefire texts with Hittite and Assyrian treaties, Fitzmyer 1995:162–166). Yet the Jewish parallels establish its traditional nature, and in any case the Assyrians' own loyalty oaths apparently derive from second-millennium Syro-Anatolian conventions, coming by way of "Aramaic intermediaries" (Tadmor 1982:145).

[120] Besides the following passages, note also Isaiah 24:8; Revelation 18:22.

[121] Psalms 137:1–4.

This lyreless silence responds to the captors' demand for a "song of Zion." We have seen other cases of taking over an enemy's musicians, including the Judaean lyrists given up by Hezekiah to Sennacherib.[122] Psalm 137 reminds us that such deportations not only provided the victor with musical variety, but denied the vanquished the adornments of peace, power, and (with vassal treaties) fidelity.[123]

This agreement of IA Jewish and Aramaean tradition on the symbolic force of the *knr* indicates their common inheritance of a more ancient idea prevalent in the BA Syro-Levantine sphere. We have seen its positive form—the *knr* epitomizing a harmonious realm that makes joyous music possible—in King David and the lion-lyrist of eighth-century Guzana (Tell Halaf), and I shall argue for such a view of Kinyras on LBA Cyprus.[124]

Psalm 137 also returns us to the question of lyric lament, for here too is the tension between *real* lyreless grief and its appearance as a *motif* within a predominantly lyric genre (Hebrew psalmody). The same paradox informs a willful dissonance in Isaiah's oracle about the destruction of Moab: "In the vineyards no songs are sung ... Therefore my heart throbs like a *kinnōr* for Moab."[125] Moab's silent vineyards and the undoing of its harvest are obviously akin to the curse of the Mati'el-Assurnerari treaty; but the prophet himself, at a safe remove, can envision this as a subject for plaintive lyre-song. These texts support lyric interpretations of various penitential and sorrowful Psalms, and even David's laments for Saul, Jonathan, and Absalom—despite the lyreless narrative contexts in which they are embedded.[126] According to a ninth-century Arabic treatise, "David ... had a stringed instrument (*mi'zafa*). When he recited, he played on it and wept, and made [others] weep."[127] This might be dismissed as late guesswork, but that the Dead Sea Scrolls explicitly refer to a "*kinnōr* of lamentation" with which to mourn the sinfulness of man, which has brought about present evils. Once delivered, god's righteousness will be praised with "the *kinnōr* of salvation" and other joyful instruments.[128] This imagery surely reflects real performance modes, even if instruments were not employed for psalmody at Qumran itself (as is sometimes suggested[129]).

---

[122] See p106, 154.
[123] Conversely, a top priority of the Jewish restoration was reestablishing music in the new temple: Nehemiah 7:1, 67, 73, 12:27–47. Cf. Sellers 1941:34, 37.
[124] See p152–154 and Chapter 15.
[125] Isaiah 16:10–11.
[126] 2 Samuel 1:17–27, 18:33.
[127] Al-Mufaḍḍal ibn Salama, *Kitāb al-malāhī* (*Book of Instruments*). See Robson and Farmer 1938:5–6.
[128] 1QH-a col. XIX (formerly XI), 22a–23, supplemented by 4Q427 (4QH-a) 1:4–5: DJD 29:89–90; cf. Vermes 2011:249.
[129] For this issue, see Werner 1957:26–28.

An especially sophisticated treatment of these tropes is found in Isaiah's oracle about the destruction of Tyre:

> From that day Tyre will be forgotten for seventy years, the lifetime of one king. At the end of seventy years, it will happen to Tyre as in the song about the prostitute:
>
>> Take a lyre, go about the city, you forgotten prostitute!
>> Make sweet melody, sing many songs, that you may be remembered.[130]

Following the traditional idea, the kingdom's restoration is heralded by the resumption of the *kinnōr* (or rather **kinnūr*, given the Phoenician context). But the prophet introduces a new inversion of the *knr*'s royal symbolism by combining it with another conventional motif, the idolatrous city as a 'harlot'; the royal instrument is thus cast unclean into the streets.[131] The conflation probably pivots on the use of female lyrists in cult, as we saw in the Cypro-Phoenician symposium bowls. Note too how the prostitute's embedded song in itself suggests a plaintive mode, as would be appropriate in the repertoire of such a *kinyrístria*—comfort for her own troubles, and suitable for certain sympotic moods. This intuition is corroborated by the corresponding passage of the Isaiah Targum, one of the Aramaic translations of scripture that emerged during the Second Temple period and incorporated much additional material, both innovative and traditional. This expanded version reads:

> *Your glory has been overthrown, cast out to a province,* the city *that was as a* harlot *is rejected!* Turn your lyre *to lamentation and your music to keening, that you might be remembered.*[132]

While "Turn your lyre to lamentation" might by itself be interpreted as 'Put down your lyre and lament instead', this is excluded by the original context, which unambiguously envisions the 'harlot' singing to the lyre.

Greek sources have also preserved traces of the plaintive *kinýra*.[133] It is found in Tzetzes' retelling of an anecdote about Gelimer, last Vandal king in Africa

---

[130] Isaiah 23:15–16.
[131] Cf. *Kelim* 15 (BT 17:75) on the ritual purity of the Levitical *kinnōr* versus the instruments "of song," i.e. popular ones prone to impurity.
[132] Translation: Chilton 1990:46 (changing 'harp' to 'lyre'), with expansions indicated by his italics; cf. xiii–xxviii for the Targums generally; also Alexander 1992:322–323.
[133] Two MSS of Hesykhios (AS) include οἰκτρά ('lamentable, piteous') in defining κινύρα, though perhaps this was detached from a definition of the adjective κινυρός. Another odd jumble, presumably truncated, is *Suda* s.v. κινύρα· κινυρόμεθα, θρηνοῦμεν.

(530–534), who defiantly bade the besieging Byzantine commander: "send me a *kinýra*, Belisarios ... that I may sing sad songs of my ill-fortune."[134] In the Byzantine poetic version of the *Alexander Romance*, the famous Theban aulete Ismenias abases himself before the Macedonian conqueror, hoping to turn him from anger to pity—and so save the city—by threnody:

> [sc. Ismenias] began to accompany / a pitiable melody ... / ... [and] himself to speak to the *kinýra*, / thinking, through pipes, singing, and threnodies, / to lead Alexander round to mercy ... he began to play (*psállein*), amidst the pipes, the following for the king: / "Having seen that your power is the greatest, Alexander / we revere it as like to a god."[135]

The poet solved a logical conflict that was variously treated in other recensions. How can a piper simultaneously play a dirge and deliver a speech? Ismenias was wrenched from his historical profession, and made to sing his pleas while playing a *kinýra* alongside other anonymous (!) auletes.[136] The very violence of this revision shows that *kinýra* was willfully interpolated as being a true instrument of threnody. And note the strikingly appropriate context: one of lamentation's essential purposes in the ANE—soothing an angry god—is clearly implied. Ismenias' petition is effectively an apotropaic version of the city-lament—that ancient genre reflected in literary transmutations from Sumer down to the Biblical *Lamentations*, and even the Fall of Troy in Greek epic.[137]

---

[134] John Tzetzes *Khiliades* 3.77–88, lines 332–333: κινύραν, Βελισάριε, στεῖλον μοι ... / ... ὡς τραγῳδήσαιμι τὸ βαρυσύμφορόν μου, replacing κιθάρα in Prokopios *On the Wars* 4.6.30–31: χαῖρέ μοι, ὦ φίλε Φάρα, καί μοι κιθάραν τε καὶ ἄρτον ἕνα καὶ σπόγγον δεομένῳ πέμπε.

[135] *Historia Alexandri Magni*, recensio Byzantina poetica (cod. Marcianus 408, ed. Reichmann), 2264–2268: ἤρξατο καὶ μέλος / ἐλεεινὸν προσφθέγγεσθαι ... / ... αὐτὸς λέγειν μετὰ κινύρας, / νομίζων, διὰ τῶν αὐλῶν, μελῳδιῶν καὶ θρήνων, / εἰς οἶκτον τὸν Ἀλέξανδρον προσαγαγεῖν κτλ; 2273–2275: ἤρξατο ψάλλειν μετ' αὐλῶν τῷ βασιλεῖ τοιαῦτα. / Κράτος τὸ σόν, Ἀλέξανδρε, τὸ μέγιστον ἰδόντες, / ἰσόθεον σεβόμεθα κτλ.

[136] Recension α, 1.46a1–9 (ed. Kroll), has Ismenias both play the pipes and beseech Alexander, consecutively. Ismenias also appears in recension β (ed. Bergson), compelled to pipe while Thebes is destroyed (1.27.10); the petition to Alexander comes rather from an anonymous piper (τις τῶν Θηβαίων αὐλῶν μελῶν ἔμπειρος ἄνθρωπος, 1.46.29), whose speech is a single line ('Ἀλέξανδρε βασιλεῦ μέγιστε, νῦν πείρᾳ μαθόντες τὸ σὸν ἰσόθεον κράτος σεβόμεθα, 1.46.36–37)—a variant of which merely *introduces* Ismenias' speech in the Byzantine poetic recension. Recension γ (ed. Parthe) again has an anonymous piper (46.38–53), while ε (ed. Trumpf) gives a rather different petition scene involving an aulete named Demokeus (12.6). For the interrelationships of these texts generally, see Stoneman 2008:230–232, 244.

[137] Mesopotamian city-laments are collected in CLAM. Fall of Troy as an extension of ANE/Anatolian city-laments: Bachvarova 2008.

Chapter Twelve

The Cypriot Linos-Song

We must conclude that Syro-Levantine *knr*-players, like Greek lyric threnodes, cultivated a lamentative mode that took lyreless grief as its subject matter. The deep antiquity of the tradition is indicated by the BALAĜ.DI lamenters of Ebla and their service in the royal mortuary cult.[138] Also relevant, I suggested, are scenes of the underworld gods Rāpʾiu and Ninazu, featuring the *kinnāru* and *zannāru*, respectively.[139] The purposeful opposition of song and silence was perhaps central to the Ninigizibara ritual at Mari, and we saw lyres variously silent and sounding in Hittite funerary and/or mortuary rites.[140] One should also recall the rich tradition of Egyptian funerary harp-songs (see further below).

Clearly then, the Hellenistic topos of Kinyras the Lamenter is a late reflection of a much more ancient art of lyric threnody. This may be readily connected with Cyprus, given Kinyras' dominant associations with the island. But any insular tradition must be contemplated against a larger regional backdrop coterminous with the *knr* itself. Crucial here is a passage from Herodotos' Egyptian logos:

> [The Egyptians] cultivate ancestral customs, adding nothing else ... there is one song, the Linos—who is much sung (*aoídimos*) in Phoenicia, Cyprus, and elsewhere. Although his name varies with each people, he happens to be the same figure whom the Greeks call Linos when they sing the song. So while there are many other Egyptian matters which amaze me, one is certainly this: where did they get *their* Linos-song? And they have clearly been singing this song forever. But in Egyptian Linos is called Maneros. The Egyptians said that he was the only son of the first king of Egypt, and that after he suffered an untimely death he was honored by them with these threnodies, and that this was their first and only song.[141]

---

[138] See p67–71.
[139] See p140.
[140] See p84–85, 95–96.
[141] Herodotos 2.79 (ed. Legrand): Πατρίοισι δὲ χρεώμενοι νόμοισι ἄλλον οὐδένα ἐπικτῶνται ... ἄεισμα ἕν ἐστι, Λίνος, ὅς περ ἕν τε Φοινίκῃ ἀοίδιμός ἐστι καὶ ἐν Κύπρῳ καὶ ἄλλῃ, κατὰ μέντοι ἔθνεα οὔνομα ἔχει, συμφέρεται δὲ ὡυτὸς εἶναι τὸν οἱ Ἕλληνες Λίνον ὀνομάζοντες ἀείδουσι· ὥστε πολλὰ μὲν καὶ ἄλλα ἀποθωμάζειν με τῶν περὶ Αἴγυπτον ἐόντων, ἐν δὲ δὴ καὶ τὸν Λίνον ὁκόθεν ἔλαβον [τὸ οὔνομα]. Φαίνονται δὲ αἰεί κοτε τοῦτον ἀείδοντες. Ἔστι δὲ αἰγυπτιστὶ ὁ Λίνος καλεόμενος Μανέρως. Ἔφασαν δέ μιν Αἰγύπτιοι τοῦ πρώτου βασιλεύσαντος Αἰγύπτου παῖδα μουνογενέα γενέσθαι, ἀποθανόντα δὲ αὐτὸν ἄωρον θρήνοισι τούτοισι ὑπὸ Αἰγυπτίων τιμηθῆναι, καὶ ἀοιδήν τε ταύτην πρώτην καὶ μούνην σφίσι γενέσθαι. Cf. Pausanias 9.29.6–7.

The antiquity of Egyptian culture is a commonplace of Classical historiography, and Herodotos elsewhere makes Egypt the source of Greek customs of unknown but deep antiquity.[142] He seems inclined to do so here.[143] Certainly the historian, and any native informants, rightly regarded lamentation-singing as extremely ancient. Despite Herodotos' description of the Egyptian, Phoenician, Cypriot, and Greek versions as 'the same', his admission of different identities for the lamented subject acknowledges substantial regional variation. Rather than dismiss his comparisons as facile and naïve, we should credit the historian with perceiving significant parallels in what he heard, or heard about—in performance practice, calendrical occasion, aetiological narratives, and so on.

To be sure, Maneros himself is probably a chimera of Greek historiography and/or folk belief. When the Egyptian funerary harp-songs were first studied, Herodotos was often invoked. But the texts of this complex tradition, already well developed by the MK, offer no confirmation of the historian's aetiological narrative.[144] Indeed Plutarch, in his *On Isis and Osiris*, says that some denied that *manerôs* was a man's name at all, but was rather a kind of sympotic toast.[145] Yet even this idea has proven a dead end, eluding any convincing Egyptian etymology—although it does at least approach the subject matter of the harp-songs, many of which draw on the imagery of feasting while emphasizing the transience of life, and offering visions of the afterlife.[146]

Nonetheless, Maneros, whatever his origin, enjoyed a revealing career in the Greek imagination. Later authors compared him to the subjects of other regional lamentation traditions, for instance in Anatolia.[147] He was also treated as a "first inventor of music" (Plutarch), and an "inventor of farming and student of the Muses" (Pollux).[148] These texts introduce an interesting complication, contradicting Herodotos' statement that the Maneros-lament was the Egyptians' "first and only" song. Rather, it implies, lamentation was invented *upon the death of the first musician*. This idea has much in common with the lyreless motif discussed above, and brings us to the Greeks' very similar view about Linos-song proper.

---

[142] Herodotos 2.48–49.
[143] But note the opposite reading of Pausanias 9.29.7–9, who makes Greece the source of *all* Linos-song, including the Maneros-lament.
[144] Lichtheim 1945:178–180.
[145] Plutarch *Moralia* 357e–f.
[146] See the collection in Lichtheim 1945.
[147] See Pollux *Onomastikon* 4.54–55 for the Mariandynoi (the 'Bormos' song: cf. Athenaios 619f = Nymphis FGH 432 F 5), and Phrygians.
[148] Plutarch *Moralia* 357e: τὸν δ' ἀδόμενον Μανερῶτα πρῶτον εὑρεῖν μουσικὴν ἱστοροῦσιν; Pollux *Onomastikon* 4.54–55: ὁ Μανέρως γεωργίας εὑρετής, Μουσῶν μαθητής.

Chapter Twelve

Here, fortunately, we are much better informed, as was Herodotos himself.[149] We may reasonably hope that the material for Greek Linos-song, which is after all the basis of the historian's comparisons, can illuminate the Cypriot tradition to which he alludes—all the more so given the important Aegean contribution to the island's IA culture. The crucial point of contact is that Linos—like Kinyras, but unlike Maneros, so far as we know—was a lyre-player. Their respective mythologies present many suggestive parallels, though naturally one cannot expect exact correspondences: the absence of any single canonical myth about Linos' death shows that all such tales are secondary to the ritual practice of lyric lamentation per se. In one set of tales, Linos was killed *with* the lyre by Herakles, his frustrated pupil.[150] Another has Apollo slay him for using linen strings, or for putting his music on a level with the god's own—Kinyras' own mistake in the myth discussed in Chapter 9.[151] In all variants, Linos' death is the constant to which the laments respond.[152]

The interpretive key is a Hesiodic fragment that establishes the lyric, threnodic, choral character of Linos-song, and shows that it was already widespread, hence long traditional, by the seventh century:

> Ourania then bore Linos, her much-loved son—
> He's the one all men lament (*thrēneûsin*) who are
> Singers and lyrists (*aoidoì kaì kitharistaí*), in banquets and choruses
>   (*en eilapínais te khoroís te*):
> Starting and ending by calling out "Linos!"[153]

"Banquets and choruses" may seem an odd setting for *thrênoi*, but these were proper not only to festivals but funerary rites.[154] 'Starting and ending from Linos' rings true as a professional and distinctly lyric detail, echoing the epicletic formulas of the *Homeric Hymns* and confirming that Homer's threnodes at Hektor's funeral are indeed male lyrists.[155] The ascription of Linos-song to

---

[149] For sources and discussion, see Roscher *Lex.* s.v. (Greve); Pfister 1909–1912:194–195, 220; RE 13 (1926), 715–716 (1, Abert); Reiner 1938:109–113; AGM:28–29, 45–46; Stephens 2002; PEG II/3:XI–XIII with literature; Olivetti 2010:141–186; Power 2010 index s.v. "Linus."

[150] Pausanias 9.29.9, citing a Theban myth of a second Linos, son of the other; [Nikomakhos] *Excerpts* 1 (MSG:266).

[151] Linen strings: Philokhoros FGH 328 F 207 (Σ Homer *Iliad* 18.570). Rivaling Apollo: Pausanias 9.29.6–7 (Ἀπόλλων ἀποκτείνειεν αὐτὸν ἐξισούμενον κατὰ τὴν ᾠδήν).

[152] Stephens 2002:16–17.

[153] Hesiod fr. 305 M-W (= Σ Homer *Iliad* 18.570 = PEG T 2): Οὐρανίη δ' ἄρ' ἔτικτε Λίνον πολυήρατον υἱόν· / ὃν δή, ὅσοι βροτοί εἰσιν ἀοιδοὶ καὶ κιθαρισταί, / πάντες μὲν θρηνεῦσιν ἐν εἰλαπίναις τε χοροῖς τε, / ἀρχόμενοι δὲ Λίνον καὶ λήγοντες καλέουσιν.

[154] Note, for instance, Ammianus Marcellinus 19.1.10–11.

[155] Note also Σ Homer *Iliad* 18.570: φασὶ δὲ αὐτὸν (sc. Λίνον) ... τιμᾶσθαι ὑπὸ ποιητῶν ἐν θρηνῴδεσιν ἀπαρχαῖς. Cf. the remarks of Power 2010:210n58.

"all singers and lyrists" shows that this was a fundamental, ancient repertory item. Hesiod's universalizing assertion may well imply the same international perspective as Herodotos—an awareness that lyric threnody was a general practice in and beyond the Aegean. Important here is the report that Sappho sang of "Oito-Linos together with Adonis"; this is presumably related to her fragments of lyric lament for the latter, but in any case is early evidence for the threnodic tendency to compile "ancient misfortunes."[156] A similarly international outlook probably underlies the mother-son relationship of Ourania-Linos in Hesiod, since 'Ourania' is regularly applied to Aphrodite in her Cypriot and NE manifestations, while the Cypriot goddess could be invoked as a kind of Muse in her own right.[157] Although the attribution of mystical books to Linos (and similar figures) is relatively late,[158] Linos would not have become the target of forgers without the traditional reputation attested by another Hesiodic fragment, which calls him "learned in all kinds of wisdom." This recalls the connection between lyrists and wisdom traditions in the ANE.[159]

Hesiod's allusion to professional Linos-threnodes is fleshed out by the evidence for regional Linos cults.[160] In the grove of the Muses on Helicon, Pausanias relates, there was an annual rite in which Linos was revered before sacrifices to the Muses were conducted.[161] Note the order of offerings: celebration of the Muses—and hence other gods—depended upon efficacious music, so the performance itself was first secured by appeal to the demigod lyrist. The Thebans, Pausanias continues, had once maintained a monumental grave to Linos,[162] and the Homeric scholia preserve phrases from a traditional Linos-song said to have been inscribed there.[163] Two further Linos-tombs in the temple of

---

[156] Sappho 140b = Pausanias 9.29.8: Σαπφὼ ... Ἄδωνιν ὁμοῦ καὶ Οἰτόλινον ᾖσεν (Pausanias, after commenting on Oitolinos, refers to a form of Linos-song by the Athenian Pamphos). Sappho's Adonis fragments are 140a, 168.

[157] Franklin 2014:224–226, adding Sappho's hymnic invocations of Aphrodite (Nagy 2007).

[158] West 1983:55–67.

[159] Hesiod fr. 306 M-W (PEG T 3): παντοίης σοφίης δεδαηκότα (cf. Allen 1924:130–131). Note the similar language applied to Hermes' lyre at Homeric Hymn to Hermes 482–484, where the instrument is represented as a teacher to its player: "Whoever, learned in skill and wisdom, enquires of her, she teaches, uttering all sorts of things pleasing to the mind" (ὅς τις ἂν αὐτὴν / τέχνῃ καὶ σοφίῃ δεδαημένος ἐξερεείνῃ / φθεγγομένη παντοῖα νόῳ χαρίεντα διδάσκει). For this passage, see further Franklin 2006a:61–62.

[160] For Linos, Pfister 1909–1912:489, cf. 213–214 for Orpheus; Farnell 1921:23–30; Power 2010:208n55. These cults provided patterns for the veneration of deceased *historical* poets: Farnell 1921:367; Clay 2004; Kimmel-Clauzet 2013.

[161] Pausanias 9.29.6: τούτῳ κατὰ ἔτος ἕκαστον πρὸ τῆς θυσίας τῶν Μουσῶν ἐναγίζουσι.

[162] Pausanias 9.29.8–9; Philokhoros FGH 328 F 207.

[163] See sources in PMG 800 (*Carmina popularia* 34); Philokhoros FGH 328 F 207.

Apollo *Lýkios* at Argos are mentioned by Pausanias,[164] and there was another on Euboea.[165] Eleutherna on Crete also claimed to be his homeland, and still another Linos is found among the fifty sons of Lykaon, the primeval Arcadian king.[166] The distribution of this material, taken together with the testimony of Hesiod and Sappho, shows that Linos-song goes back in various epichoric forms to the BA.

This is corroborated by Homer himself, who includes, among the images on the shield of Achilles that typify a peaceful city and orderly cosmos,[167] a cheerful vintage scene:

> Maidens and unmarried youths, light at heart,
> Bore the fruit, as sweet as honey, in wickerwork baskets.
> A boy in their midst, with clear-sounding lyre, played it
> Soulfully, singing for them a lovely Linos-song (*línon d' hypò*
>   *kalòn áeide*)
> With elegant voice—while the youths, stamping time all together,
> With singing and shouting were following, feet skipping.[168]

We need not doubt the ancient belief that this scene depicts Linos-song.[169] True, the setting is not lugubrious. But threnody could be highly stylized and enjoyable outside of actual funerals, on occasions of more holiday humor. Compare the Adonis festival represented by Theokritos, where the 'lament' is closer to a concert, and the event much anticipated.[170] Homer's harvesters, in one or more choruses, feel a pleasant yearning at the lyrist's moving performance (*himeróen kithárize*).[171] Together they savor the bittersweet of waning light and another

---

[164] One Linos was said to be the son of Apollo and Psamathe, the other was the famous poet: Pausanias 2.19.8. For Linos myth and ritual at Argos, Farnell 1921:26–29.

[165] Diogenes Laertios 1.4; Pfister 1909–1912:220.

[166] Eleutherna: Stephanos of Byzantium s.v. Ἀπολλωνία: ... κγ´ Κρήτης, ἡ πάλαι Ἐλεύθερνα, Λίνου πατρίς (noted by Power 2010:373n164); Arcadia: [Apollodoros] *Library* 3.8.1.

[167] Hephaistos' inclusion of earth, heaven, sea, sun, moon, and constellations (18.486–492) makes the shield a microcosm of the natural cycles that dominate human culture. See generally Hardie 1985.

[168] Homer *Iliad* 18.567–572 (PEG T 1): παρθενικαὶ δὲ καὶ ἠίθεοι ἀταλὰ φρονέοντες / πλεκτοῖς ἐν ταλάροισι φέρον μελιηδέα καρπόν. / τοῖσιν δ' ἐν μέσσοισι πάϊς φόρμιγγι λιγείῃ / ἱμερόεν κιθάριζε, Λίνον [v.l. λίνος: v. infra] δ' ὑπὸ καλὸν ἄειδε / λεπταλέῃ φωνῇ· τοὶ δὲ ῥήσσοντες ἁμαρτῇ / μολπῇ τ' ἰυγμῷ τε ποσὶ σκαίροντες ἕποντο. For μολπή as 'song and dance', typically to lyre-music, see Franklin 2003:296.

[169] Σ Homer *Iliad* 18.570; Pausanias 9.29.7.

[170] Theokritos *Idylls* 15 with Power 2010:63.

[171] For the scene's choral quality, cf. Nagy 1990:352–353. The expression ῥήσσοντες ἁμαρτῇ / ... ἕποντο is a clear indication of dance: note especially the similar language in the choral-lyric scene of *Homeric Hymn to Apollo* 514–517. Power 2010:210 suggests interpreting the Linos-song

year gone—primeval feelings, which, one must concede to Frazer, found widespread poetic and musical expression in ancient agrarian calendars.[172]

Homer's lyre-singer is a 'youth' (*páïs*) with 'elegant voice' (*leptaléēi phōnêi*), a description perfectly appropriate for Linos himself before any of his untimely deaths. One should therefore still entertain a variant rejected by Aristarkhos but championed by Zenodotos, who preferred nominative *línos* for accusative *línon*. The reading, in Zenodotos' view (or so Aristarkhos understood him), yielded not 'he sang (of) Linos', but the 'linen(-string) sang'.[173] This interpretation was probably correlated with myths of Apollo killing Linos for using linen strings, and the *aílinos*-song of loom-workers.[174] But the variant may be more pregnant than the ancient critic(s) appreciated. For if one can follow Aristarkhos (as most scholars do) in taking accusative *línon* as 'Linos[-song]', the nominative variant can equally be read as 'Linos' in apposition to *páïs*. This would produce a performative picture much like what I have proposed for Kinyras on other grounds:

> A boy in their midst, with clear-sounding lyre, played it
> Soulfully, and [sc. as] Linos sang for them
> With delicate voice.

Even on the traditional reading, Homer's description shows that the youthful, delicate-voiced lyrist is somehow *enacting* Linos. In this circular mimesis the musician, by hymning and invoking his semi-divine counterpart, becomes a *theîos aoidós*—the 'godly singer' who is visited with 'god-uttered song' (*théspis aoidḗ*) through devotion to the appropriate divinity. This musical interface between human and divine was canonically expressed, in Greek tradition, as

---

here as "a *prooimion* to the choral *molpê*"—that is, an epicletic opening-hymn as the harvesters set down their baskets and get into choral formation.

[172] Olivetti 2010, troubled by the apparent dissonance, would derive the threnodic opening *aílinon* (see below) from ἔλινος ('vine'), attractively resegmenting *Iliad* 18.570 from κιθάριζε, λίνον to κιθάριζ' ἔλινον (177–182); this, she argues, created a need to explain λίνον in Homer's text, which led to creation of a personal Linos, perhaps by ps.-Hesiod himself (143–145). But I feel this relies on too rigid a relationship between fixed texts, and cannot account for the widespread and early Linos traditions implied by the Hesiodic fragment and cultic evidence. Athenaios 619c, citing Aristophanes of Byzantium, states that that the Linos-song could be sung on joyous occasions, noting Euripides *Herakles*, where Apollo "cries '*aílinon*' in happy song-dance (αἴλινον μὲν ἐπ' εὐτυχεῖ / μολπᾷ), driving the beautiful-toned *kithára* with a golden pick" (348–351).

[173] Σ Homer *Iliad* 18.570 (via Aristonikos): παρὰ Ζηνοδότῳ 'λίνος δ' ὑπὸ καλὸν ἄειδε'. ὁ δὲ Ἀρίσταρχος βούλεται μὴ τὴν χορδὴν λέγεσθαι, ἀλλὰ γένος τι ὕμνου τὸν λίνον. ὥσπερ εἰ ἔλεγεν παιᾶνα ᾖδεν ἤ τι τοιοῦτον. The semi-technical and invertible ὑπὸ καλὸν ἄεισε/ἄειδε (Homer *Odyssey* 21.411; *Homeric Hymn to Hermes* 54, 502) supports either reading: Franklin 2003:300–301. Kallimakhos may allude to the issue: Stephens 2002:19.

[174] Loom-workers: Athenaios 681d, citing the sixth-century Epikharmos; cf. *GMW* 1:276n76. Linen-strings: p190, 306.

Chapter Twelve

a patronage relationship with Apollo and/or the Muses.[175] But the Homeric Hymns show that in practice there was more flexibility, since the deity invoked for inspiration is normally that to whom the hymn itself is addressed. G. Nagy, in a detailed reading of Sappho, has demonstrated much the same relationship with Aphrodite, the poet petitioning her divine patroness for assistance, and being 'overcome' in performance by the goddess, with whom she engages in dialogue.[176] This is precisely what I propose for Linos, Kinyras, and the lyrists who venerated them. Much the same relationship, we saw, was developed for divinized instruments in the ANE, and between the Biblical psalmodists and Yahweh. An important difference, however, is that Linos is dead. He is literally *ályros*, his music stilled. The performing lyrist makes Linos and his lyre live again, 'reviving' an ancient power through the ecstasy of song and dance.

This suggests a similar interpretation of Pindar's "Cypriot voices around Kinyras." In Chapter 10, I analyzed that passage in terms of praise-singing, but this is equally compatible with a threnodic reading, since *thrênos* itself could be encomiastic.[177] After all, Pindar's Kinyras illustrated great men's reputations *after death*, and Kinyras' grave at Old Paphos clearly indicates a kind of mortuary cult.[178] Pindar's plural *phâmai* will readily encompass the lamentable tales that after all are rather prominent in Kinyras' mythology. Cypriot *kinýra*-singers might thus have commemorated his death at the hands of Apollo, his suicide following the seduction by Myrrha, or even his defeat by Agamemnon (a kind of city-lament?). They could also win him back from grief over his various unhappy children.

The traditional cry *aílinon*, understood by the Greeks as 'Ah, Linos!', is often thought to derive from a Semitic phrase 'Alas for us!'. The idea is plausible, though not universally accepted.[179] Certainly Linos himself must be a back-construction from *aílinon*, which would have given poets free range for tragic aetiologies. While *aílinon* occurs in many threnodic contexts with no clear allusion to Linos-song per se, other cases seem relevant. In Euripides' *Helen*, the heroine, stranded in Egypt, calls for "Libyan lotus-pipes, panpipes, or lyres

---

[175] See especially Hesiod *Theogony* 94–95.
[176] Nagy 2007.
[177] Cf. Aristokles of Rhodes *On Poetry*, quoted in Ammonios *On Similar and Different Words* 178: θρῆνος ... ὀδυρμὸν ἔχει σὺν ἐγκωμίῳ τοῦ τελετήσαντος.
[178] See p419.
[179] For the Greek interpretation, Pindar fr. 128c5–6 (PEG T 4); Pausanias 9.29.8. For the proposed WS etymology from *'ai lānu, 'alas for us', Farnell 1921:24; Brown 1965:208n2; Hemmerdinger 1970:42; Rosól 2013:157; cf. EFH:262, suggesting rather a connection with Ialemos (another figure of Greek lament) and the WS god Lim (cf. Zimri-Lim).

(*phórmingas*)" to help lament her "'Ah-Linos!' woes" (*ailínois kakoîs*).[180] This confirms the existence of lyric threnodies and Herodotos' assertion that a kind of Linos-song was known in Egypt (though possibly Euripides is himself alluding to the historian). In the *Orestes*, Euripides again associates the cry *aílinon* with eastern threnody, this time in an Anatolian context. The Phrygian eunuch, in a campy showpiece set to eerie double-pipe melodies,[181] begins his account of events inside Agamemnon's palace as follows:

> Ah Linos! Ah Linos! (*aílinon aílinon*)—As barbarians say
> At the start of a lament (*arkhàn thrḗnou*)—
> Alas!—in Asiatic voice, when
> Blood of kings is poured to earth by swords—
> The iron swords of Hades.[182]

While the poet's genius is certainly on display—the ensuing exchange with Orestes is larded with amusing orientalist slurs—the Eunuch's description of *aílinon* as the formal "start of a lament" confirms the Hesiodic testimony that threnodes (lyre-singers in the fragment) began and ended by invoking Linos. By the play's own terms, of course, we are dealing not with stylized, calendrical lament, but one undertaken at a definite moment.[183] But this too fits with the threnodic use of such "ancient misfortunes."[184]

Herodotos' treatment of Maneros-song suggests that the historian would have viewed the lament of father for son as an intelligible mythological and performative stance for 'Linos-song' too.[185] This is echoed by the royal context of Euripides ("blood of kings"), whose generalizing terms equally imply an ancient tradition. The arrangement is attested for Linos himself, who in Ovid is

---

[180] Euripides *Helen* 167-178, especially 175-176—a difficult passage. Despite the variety of Helen's imagined musical landscape, the realities of tragic performance required *aulós* accompaniment for her song. Euripides exploits this situation by soon having the chorus describe Helen's song as a "lyreless elegy" (*ályron élegon*, 185). Compare Euripides *Medea* 190-200, where the chorus stresses the inability of festive lyre-songs to cure mortal woes.

[181] This was explicated by M. Griffith, "How Should Phrygian Slaves Sing (in the Athenian Theater)?," at the conference *Music in Greek Drama: History, Theory and Practice*, May 28-29, 2011, University of California, Santa Cruz.

[182] Euripides *Orestes* 1395-1399: αἴλινον αἴλινον ἀρχὰν θρήνου / βάρβαροι λέγουσιν, / αἰαῖ, Ἀσιάδι φωνᾶι, βασιλέων / ὅταν αἷμα χυθῆι κατὰ γᾶν ξίφεσιν / σιδαρέοισιν Ἅιδα.

[183] The eunuch laments the destruction of Troy and his own enslavement—another literary adaptation of city-lament. His song also prepares the way for Orestes' own anticipated spilling of royal blood.

[184] Compare the situation in Ammianus Marcellinus 19.1.10-11, where female mourners at an actual royal funeral are compared to devotees (*cultrices*) of Aphrodite lamenting Adonis.

[185] Though not invariably, as this does not fit Homer's vignette.

mourned by his father (Apollo) with 'reluctant lyre'.[186] Here, in different mythological and performative terms, is a doublet of Homer's vintage scene—the lyrist-singer commemorating the lyrist-of-song.

A remarkable parallel for father-son threnody comes from an Arabic source, Hisham ibn al-Kalbī (died ca. 819–821), who records a tradition about Lamk, the Biblical Lamech. After Lamk's young son (unnamed) died, he hung the body in a tree so that "his form will not depart from my eyes until he falls in pieces." When only thigh-, leg-, foot-, and toe-bones remained, Lamk modeled these parts in wood to form soundbox, neck, pegbox, and pegs, respectively, added strings for his son's sinews, and so invented the lute in his image (by now lutes had generally displaced lyres: see Appendix D). "Then he began to play on it and weep and lament, until he became blind; and he was the first who sang a lament."[187] The *instrument* as an *embodiment* of the dead son, who thus achieves a kind of immortality in musical memory and indeed physical form as he is held by the lamenting father, is most suggestive vis-à-vis divinized instruments. Although the son is not named, and dies at the age of five, it is surely significant that it is precisely Lamech's son (Jubal) who in the canonical tradition invents the lyre (*kinnōr*).[188] Unfortunately, the ultimate antiquity and ethnic affiliation of the present tale are unclear; in the reception of Biblical stories, the musical inventions of Lamech and his family were widely adapted to local cultural conditions.[189] Nonetheless, the myth, being utterly independent of Greek tradition, is vital for its corroboration, in an ANE context, of chordophonic lamentation-singing and a father-son charter-myth. We should also recall here David's lament for Absalom.[190]

Although Herodotos declines to identify the mythological subjects of Phoenician and Cypriot lament, one name he and other Greeks would certainly have offered was Adonis. The unofficial celebration of annual Adonis festivals (the *Adōniá*) was by now a fixture of women's popular culture in Athens and elsewhere.[191] And Herodotos will have known Kinyras as Adonis' father in some versions of the myth. It is assumed only slightly later by the Athenian comic poet Plato (fl. ca. 420–410), whose *Adonis* contained a silly but intriguing oracle warning

---

[186] Ovid *Amores* 3.9.23–24.
[187] Robson and Farmer 1938:9 (translation here). Note Lamech's song at Genesis 4:23–24, "uniformly singled out by critics as the earliest surviving sample of Israelite rhapsody" (North 1964:379).
[188] Genesis 4:21. LXX has ψαλτήριον καὶ κιθάραν. For this and other variations, see p215n164.
[189] See p454–455 and n76. The motif of blindness of course recalls the tradition of Egyptian harpers: see p110.
[190] 2 Samuel 18:33.
[191] For the *Adōniá*, see Alexiou 2002:55–57; GR:258; Winkler 1990:108–209; Holst-Warhaft 1992:99–103; Detienne 1994:99–101 et passim.

Kinyras of his son's impending death.¹⁹² Antimakhos of Colophon (fl. ca. 400) paired Kinyras and Adonis soon afterwards.¹⁹³ That both authors conjoin Kinyras and Adonis in the context of the youth's death cannot be an accident: they consciously avoided Phoinix ('The Phoenician'), the more canonical Hesiodic father.¹⁹⁴ This shows that Kinyras was already understood as The Lamenter, and Herodotos very probably had Kinyras-Adonis in mind when he alleged that Cypriot and Phoenician lamentation was 'the same' as the songs for Linos and Maneros.¹⁹⁵ Like Maneros' father, Kinyras is a primeval king and Adonis a fallen prince; if the analogy can be pressed, Kinyras becomes the fountainhead of Cypriot music, the original and most characteristic form of which was lyric threnody.

But since both Kinyras and Adonis were lovers of Aphrodite, the two also appear to be mythological doublets of a sort.¹⁹⁶ Note that Adonis is often portrayed with a lyre in the Classical period.¹⁹⁷ While this does suit his youth and the erotic context—Aphrodite also appears in these scenes—there is more to it. First there are Aphrodite's muse-like properties, especially clear on Cyprus.¹⁹⁸ Moreover, given the lyre's symbolism in the funerary scenes discussed above, Adonis' instrument must equally mark the life he is soon to lose, with the lyreless grief and divine laments that follow. This is confirmed by the lyre's *absence* in contemporary scenes showing Adonis-laments, which feature rather double-pipes and frame-drums or *krótala*.¹⁹⁹ I have suggested that much the same organological dichotomy may be seen in Ugaritic ritual and paramythological texts of the royal ancestor cult.²⁰⁰

---

¹⁹² Plato Comicus fr. 3 PCG (Athenaios 456a): "Plato in his Adonis, saying that an oracle was given to Kinyras about his son Adonis, has: 'O Kinyras, king of Cypriots, shaggy-assed men, / To you was born a son, the most beautiful and marvelous / In the human race; but two gods will destroy him— / She who is driven by secret oars, and he who drives'. He means Aphrodite and Dionysos; for both loved Adonis" (Πλάτων δ' ἐν τῷ Ἀδώνιδι χρησμὸν δοθῆναι λέγων Κινύρᾳ ὑπὲρ Ἀδώνιδος τοῦ υἱοῦ φησιν· ὦ Κινύρα, βασιλεῦ Κυπρίων ἀνδρῶν δασυπρώκτων, / παῖς σοι κάλλιστος μὲν ἔφυ θαυμαστότατός τε / πάντων ἀνθρώπων, δύο δ' αὐτὸν δαίμον' ὀλεῖτον, / ἡ μὲν ἐλαυνομένη λαθρίοις ἐρετμοῖς, ὁ δ' ἐλαύνων. λέγει δ' Ἀφροδίτην καὶ Διόνυσον· ἀμφότεροι γὰρ ἤρων τοῦ Ἀδώνιδος).
¹⁹³ See p284.
¹⁹⁴ Hesiod fr. 139 M-W = [Apollodoros] *Library* 3.14.4.
¹⁹⁵ It may even be that Herodotos used the more familiar Kinyras-Adonis material to flesh out a tale for Maneros. One might make a similar point about Herodotos' account of sacred prostitution at Babylon.
¹⁹⁶ Atallah 1966:313.
¹⁹⁷ See p145.
¹⁹⁸ See p307.
¹⁹⁹ See p145.
²⁰⁰ See p141–146.

Chapter Twelve

The historical implications of this Kinyras-Adonis doublet are somewhat elusive, thanks to the vanishing nature of Adonis himself, who, as S. Ribichini showed, originated at the Hellenosemitic interface as a half-understood pastiche of Levantine religious life.²⁰¹ This generic quality is reflected in his very name, which must derive from WS *'dn* ('lord'); this has proven difficult to pin to a specific mainland god, though the Baal of Byblos is one probable reference.²⁰² Adonis' death while hunting does appear to recycle a Levantine mytheme.²⁰³ His pairing with Kinyras the Lamenter must also echo some early Levantine cult practice. Annual lamentations are famously attested at Roman Byblos for a god of the so-called dying-and-rising type who at that time was identified with Adonis/Tammuz, while his father, called Kinyras and Kauthar, was said to have lamented him at Aphaka (see further Chapter 19).

It seems likely that the Greek concoction of Adonis should be connected especially with Cyprus, where many sources locate him.²⁰⁴ The appropriate cultural conditions are probably best traced to IA Aegean settlement there, followed by ninth-century Phoenician colonization. Yet Kinyras himself, as I shall show in the following chapters, was by then an ancient fixture of Cypriot life, rooted in the pre-Greek period. This suggests an historical-cultural explanation for his pairing with Adonis, since mythological relationships can encode the juxtaposition and/or coalescence of distinct cultures and analogous features thereof.²⁰⁵ One figure assumes a senior or dominant role, the other a junior or subordinate one, depending on specific historical and sociological conditions. Greater mythological 'age' may reflect only relative antiquity or importance within a given geographical sphere and/or cultural perspective that is dominant in some respect. I have already interpreted Kinyras as the son or beloved of Apollo along such lines.²⁰⁶ Given that musical syncretism, a phenomenon well known to ethnomusicology, occurs precisely around the most compatible features of two traditions,²⁰⁷ Cypriot Kinyras would naturally have become secondarily associated with the Phoenician cult-music which underlies the large **kinnūr* ensembles of the symposium bowls and the 'singers' maintained

---

²⁰¹ Ribichini 1981; papers in s.n. 1984. See also Dussaud 1945:366; Dietrich 1978:6; DDUPP:90, 97–98.
²⁰² See the review in Mettinger 2001:124–126 with references.
²⁰³ Such an accident is recorded by Philo of Byblos for his 'Elioun': FGH 790 F 2 (15): ἐν συμβολῇ θηρίων τελευτήσας ἀφιερώθη. Cf. Baudissin 1911:76; Lightfoot 2004:79. Grottanelli 1984:38 compares the death of Aqhat while hunting.
²⁰⁴ See sources in Baudissin 1911:81–82.
²⁰⁵ For a comparable historical reading of Kinyras-Adonis on more general (i.e. nonmusical) grounds, cf. Atallah 1966:313–315; Baurain 1980b:10.
²⁰⁶ See p226–230, cf. 410.
²⁰⁷ See Nettl 1985:20–23 with further examples and literature.

by Astarte's temple at Kition.[208] Indeed, 'secondarily' does some injustice to the situation, if indeed the Cypriot Kinyras himself originated in Syro-Levantine practices of the BA. It would be a case rather of insular divergence and reconvergence with cognate Canaanite/Phoenician ideas.[209] The father-son pairing of the doublets Kinyras-Adonis would thus express this historical stratigraphy within the island, in addition to reflecting, presumably, the father-son motif that was evidently fairly typical of lyric-threnody traditions in the region.

Another advantage of this scenario is that, while Adonis is most helpful for corroborating Kinyras as The Lamenter, it allows the ancient king to be connected with further lamentation subjects in the pre-Phoenician period. This lets us explain the diverse tales with which this chapter began—Kinyras' other lamentable children, their wide-ranging connection with cult-objects and processes, and angered and grieving gods to soothe, especially 'Aphrodite'. There are also the several obscure names recorded as alternative Cypriot designations of Adonis, including Pygmaion,[210] Kirris,[211] Gauas, and Ao or Aoios.[212] The 'Aphroditos' who was honored at Amathous and elsewhere on the island recalls the gender-bending dimension of Astarte/Ishtar, and perhaps transgendered lamentation-priests (Sum. gala, Akk. *kalû*, surely related to the *gálloi* of Kybele cult).[213] Also relevant is the report that, again at Amathous, "Adonis was

---

[208] See p116.
[209] Here one should note the lamentation scene, evidently through dance, on the sarcophagus of Ahiram of Byblos (KAI 1). Though Ahiram probably dates to the tenth-century, the sarcophagus itself goes back perhaps to the thirteenth-century (Frankfort 1970:271–272) and was repurposed. Cf. Fariselli 2010:17, comparing this scene to Herodotos' Phoenician 'Linos-song'.
[210] Hesykhios s.v. Πυγμαίων· ὁ Ἄδωνις παρὰ Κυπρίοις. This clearly relates to the Cypriot or Cypro-Phoenician god *pmy*, already attested in the Nora Stone from Sardinia (KAI 46). See DDUPP:297–306; Dupont-Sommer 1974:84. For the royal name Pumayyaton at Kition, see p244, 358.
[211] *Etymologicum Magnum* s.v. Κίρρις; Hesykhios s.v. Κίρις; cf. HC:70n2; Atallah 1966:315.
[212] For these last names, see p498–503.
[213] Hesykhios s.v. Ἀφρόδιτος, citing Theophrastos and Paion of Amathous: FGH 757 F 1; cf. Aristophanes fr. 325 PCG; Catullus 68.51–52; Macrobius *Saturnalia* 3.8.2; Photios *Lexicon* s.v. Cf. Karageorghis 1988:195; *Kypris*:110–112 with further references, including the bisexual Adonis of Photios *Library* 151b5-7. For ANE parallels, see Asher-Greve and Westenholz 2013, index s.v. gender > amalgams and gender > ambiguous. For Sum. gala/Akk. *kalû* see p29–30. The connection with 'Gk.' *gálloi* has not yet been fully elucidated, but the Hittite ritual material assembled by Taylor 2008 provides a convincing cultural/chronological link. Of classical sources, note especially Lucian's description of the parallel Attis: "He left off from the male lifestyle, and exchanged it for a female form and put on womanly clothing; and ranging through the world he carried out the rites and told about his sufferings and sang of Rhea" (βίου μὲν ἀνδρηίου ἀπεπαύσατο, μορφὴν δὲ θηλέην ἠμείψατο καὶ ἐσθῆτα γυναικηίην ἐνεδύσατο καὶ ἐς πᾶσαν γῆν φοιτέων ὄργιά τε ἐπετέλεεν καὶ τὰ ἔπαθεν ἀπηγέετο καὶ Ῥέην ἤειδεν, *On the Syrian Goddess* 15).

honored as Osiris; though Egyptian, the Cypriots and Phoenicians made him their own"[214]—for Osiris himself was an object of ritual lamentation.[215]

Phoinix *Kinyrízōn*

Having established the existence of lyric threnody to the *kinýra*, we may resume and complete our analysis of the phrase *odyrómenos kinyrízōn*, which, according to Aristonikos, Zenodotos wished to read at *Iliad* 9.612 "as if it meant 'singing a threnody' (*thrēnôn*)."[216] The phrasing implies that the sense of *kinyrízōn* was being somehow stretched. I showed that this word must mean, basically, 'play the *kinýra*', and suggested that secondary connotations of lamentation arose from the instrument's performance contexts. With *odyrómenos kinyrízōn* working together naturally as single phrase,[217] Achilles' rebuke of Phoinix effectively mimes pathetic violin-music to a would-be sob story:

> Do not confuse my angered-resolve with this moaning to the *kinýra* (*odyrómenos kinyrízōn*).

Zenodotos was quite right that the expression, which parallels the Homeric description of epic poetry as "singing and lyre-music,"[218] was equivalent to *thrēnôn*. But it alludes to a distinct performance reality with colorful connotations.

Achilles' metaphor takes on special meaning given that an important use of ANE lamentation was to win back the affections of a wrathful 'vanishing god'—in this case, the hero's withdrawal with its catastrophic reversal for the Greeks. Phoinix himself makes this comparison, telling Achilles to give over his wrath, as even gods bend to incense-offerings, libations, and burnt victims.[219] His cautionary tale of Meleagros involves a wrathful hero who eventually came around to save a city, but too late to enjoy the goodwill gifts *he* was offered.[220]

---

[214] Stephanos of Byzantium s.v. Ἀμαθοῦς· πόλις Κύπρου ἀρχαιοτάτη, ἐν ᾗ Ἄδωνις Ὄσιρις ἐτιμᾶτο, ὃν Αἰγύπτιον ὄντα Κύπριοι καὶ Φοίνικες ἰδιοποιοῦνται. While Amathous maintained a recognizably Eteocypriot character until at least the Hellenistic period, the city was also home to a substantial Phoenician contingent (see p16). It was presumably the latter who introduced Osiris, who was interpreted as a version of Adonis at Byblos (Parthenios fr. 42 and Lucian *On the Syrian Goddess* 7, with Lightfoot's comments on both; Stephanos of Byzantium s.v. Βύβλος).

[215] Frazer 1914 2:12.

[216] See p207–208.

[217] See the parallels in p208n120.

[218] See e.g. Homer *Iliad* 13.731 (κίθαριν καὶ ἀοιδήν), cf. *Odyssey* 1.159, 21.406 (ἀνὴρ φόρμιγγος ἐπιστάμενος καὶ ἀοιδῆς); Hesiod fr. 305.2 M-W (ἀοιδοὶ καὶ κιθαρισταί); *Homeric Hymn to Hermes* 432 (πάντ' ἐνέπων κατὰ κόσμον, ἐπωλένιον κιθαρίζων).

[219] Homer *Iliad* 9.497–501.

[220] The exemplum is treated in detail by Nagy 1979:103–111.

Agamemnon's own bribes are extraordinarily rich. But only if Achilles accepts them, Phoinix says, will "the Achaeans honor you like unto a god."[221]

Moreover, *odyrómenos kinyrízōn* yields vivid ethnic nuances when directed against Phoinix, whose name means simply 'the Phoenician'.[222] To be sure, this particular Phoinix, son not of Agenor but Amyntor, is not otherwise connected with Phoenicia.[223] But that merely sharpens the sting. Achilles is ordering Phoinix to pull himself together, and not act the Phoenician—a people generally represented by Homer as dishonest sneaks.[224] There are more ominous overtones too. In Hesiod, Adonis' father is also Phoinix.[225] And Homer has consistently characterized Phoinix as a surrogate father to Achilles.[226] Phoinix himself uses this as leverage for his petition: "I made you my son, god-like Achilles / That you might someday protect me from unworthy calamity."[227] Reading *odyrómenos kinyrízōn* lets Achilles take up all of these points. For Achilles' own death is inevitable, once he has accepted Agamemnon's peace terms and a return to battle. Against Phoinix' claim of the protection due a father, Achilles implies that the old man, in attempting to win him over by acting the *kinýra*-lamenter, will find himself in the position of a Phoenician king mourning a prince who has died unseasonably. Here one must remember the lamentations connected to hero-cults of Achilles.[228] Finally, recall the tradition that Phoinix—that is, the Phoenician king—invented the *gíngras*-pipes for lamenting Adonis.[229]

---

[221] Homer *Iliad* 9.114–161; 603: ἶσον γάρ σε θεῷ τίσουσιν Ἀχαιοί.

[222] My interpretation of the name need not exclude concurrent possibilities (e.g. Mühlestein 1981:91 associates with φοινός + ἱκέτης, with reference to Phoinix' backstory of blood-crime and his beseeching of Achilles), especially if κινυρίζων is a secondary accretion.

[223] Edwards 1979:68n64. But the story of his stepmother trying to seduce him has ANE parallels. For sources, see Gantz 1993:618; comparisons are drawn by Astour 1965:144–145; Brown 1968:166–168; EFH:373; Brown 1995:65–70.

[224] Winter 1995.

[225] Hesiod fr. 139 M-W = [Apollodoros] *Library* 3.14.4.

[226] See Mühlestein 1981:89 for the internal evidence. This role was apparently quite consistent in epic, judging from notices about Phoinix in the *Kypria* and the *Nostoi*. According to Pausanias (10.26.4 = *Kypria* fr. 16 EGF, 21 PEG), in the *Kypria* it was Phoinix who gave Achilles' son the name Neoptolemos (reflecting Achilles' own youth when entering the war). According to Proklos' summary of the *Nostoi*, Phoinix dies during the homeward journey of Neoptolemos, who, after burying him, is reunited with his grandfather Peleus (Proklos *Chrestomathy* 277 = EGF:67.23-24, PEG:95.15–16)—the surrogate father being now dispensable.

[227] Homer *Iliad* 9.485–495 (quotation at 494–495: ἀλλὰ σὲ παῖδα θεοῖς ἐπιείκελ' Ἀχιλλεῦ / ποιεύμην, ἵνα μοί ποτ' ἀεικέα λοιγὸν ἀμύνῃς).

[228] The case of Elis was mentioned above. Lykophron alludes to similar mourning rites at Croton (*Alexandra* 859). In an annual Thessalian mission to honor the grave of Achilles in the Troad, the grieving Thetis was propitiated with a hymn before landing (Philostratos *On Heroes* 53.10). Cf. Pfister 1909–1912:498; Farnell 1921:208–209; Nagy 1979:9, 114, 116–117; Dué 2006:41. There was also a cult to Achilles at Sparta by the late Geometric period: Ainian 1999:11 with references.

[229] Pollux *Onomastikon* 4.76; cf. p145, 190n19, 202–204, 299n117.

Chapter Twelve

If we follow Aristarkhos in rejecting *odyrómenos kinyrízōn* as un-Homeric, we must at least recognize that this was an inspired interpolation. But the phrase is so strikingly appropriate that I am tempted to see it as original. *Kinyrízōn* would readily fall afoul of Aristarkhos, being otherwise alien to the lyre-vocabulary of epic, with its general preference for *phórminx*. But this begs the question of whether or not Homer intended some special lyric effect; for singers would naturally take professional interest in parallel 'lyric' traditions. The blinding of Thamyris seems to be an offhand allusion to—and hostile dismissal of—a competing lyric genre.[230] Pejorative cross-generic implications may also inform the poet's occasional use of *kítharis* and *kitharízein*.[231] Homer's favorable treatment of Linos-song equally acknowledges a parallel lyric tradition distinct from his own epic art.[232] Indeed, the scene of Linos-song on Achilles' shield may be more than incidental color. The poet portrays Achilles as a beautiful young lyrist, singing *kléa andrôn* (when Phoinix arrives) and meditating on his basic crisis of whether or not to be epic—his choice between immortality in song (*kléos áphthiton*), or singing about others at his tent.[233] These parallels make it quite possible that Homer could have indulged in such genre-play with *odyrómenos kinyrízōn*. And after all, he was familiar with Kinyras himself.[234]

Epilogue: The Antinoos Lament From Kourion

I close this examination of Cypriot lyric threnody, which has necessarily relied heavily on comparative data and systematic considerations, with a welcome inscription from Kourion. It records a threnodic tribute to the late Antinoos, Hadrian's beloved, who, after drowning in the Nile in 130 CE, was deified by the emperor and given cult-honors far and wide, often complete with temples, priesthoods, festivals, competitive games, and music.[235] While Antinoos was identified with Osiris in Egypt, the Kourion hymn takes the appropriate form

---

[230] See p234–235.
[231] Franklin 2011b.
[232] Stephens 2002:13–14.
[233] Homer *Iliad* 9.189, 413. Kallimakhos at least seems to have drawn a direct connection between Linos and Achilles in a typically dense passage of his *Hymn to Apollo*, where *kinýretai* is used of the laments by Thetis, and the god's lyre itself is the object of praise-singing: "Even the sea keeps quiet, when singers celebrate / His *kítharis* or bow, the instruments of Lykoreian Phoibos. / Nor does mother Thetis bewail (*kinýretai*) Achilles with "Ah Linos!" (*Aílina!*) / When she hears 'hiè paiêon hiè paiêon!'" (*Hymns* 2.18–21: εὐφημεῖ καὶ πόντος, ὅτε κλείουσιν ἀοιδοί / ἢ κίθαριν ἢ τόξα, Λυκωρέος ἔντεα Φοίβου. / οὐδὲ Θέτις Ἀχιλῆα κινύρεται αἴλινα μήτηρ, / ὁππόθ' ἰὴ παιῆον ἰὴ παιῆον ἀκούσῃ).
[234] One could also seek a parallel in κινυρή at *Iliad* 17.5, the Homeric status of which was unchallenged by the ancient critics.
[235] Lambert 1984:184–197.

of an Adonis-lament. Its diction is predominantly lyric; the poet invokes Apollo as *lyroktýpos* ('ringer of the lyre'), and says of his own performance: "For you I rouse the *bárbita* [baritone-lyres], for you the *kítharis* / by the altar-side."[236] Given Hadrian's injunction that Antinoos was to be "mourned as a son,"[237] the poet, as mourner of Antinoos-Adonis and (at least notional) lyric threnode, is probably assuming, or at least alluding to, the traditional image of Kinyras the Lamenter. That Greek lyre-names are used here, rather than *kinýra*, accords both with the non-Cypriot identity of the honored and the dedicator (seemingly a high-ranking official), and the progressive Hellenization of Cyprus in preceding centuries.[238] But *kenyristḗs* Apollo at Tiberian Paphos indicates that such a threnody, elsewhere on the island, could probably still have been performed by a *kinýra*-player.

---

[236] I.Kourion 104 (ca. 130/131 CE); Lebek 1973; SEG 53:1747bis: λυροκτύπος, 9; σοὶ] βάρβιτα, σοὶ κίθαριν δονῶ | παρὰ βωμόγ, 10–11. Mitford also proposed [τοῦτο τὸ κιθάρι]σμα in line 5, but this is rather unsure. Against his reading [αἰνοῦ]μεν Ἄ[δ]ωνιν ὑπὸ χθόνα πα[τρίδ'] | [ἀποφ]θίμενον Ἀντίνουν λέγε μοι (7–8), Lebek (110) would supplement as [θρηνοῦ]μεν (5) based on a new metrical analysis; the passage becomes 'we mourn Antinoos, an Adonis' (110n12), not 'as we sing Adonis, tell me of Antinoos'.

[237] Clement of Alexandria *Exhortation* 4.49.2: τί δὲ καὶ ὡς υἱὸν θρηνεῖσθαι προσέταξας;

[238] See p211–213.

13

The Talents of Kinyras

OUR ANALYSIS OF CYPRIOT ICONOGRAPHY and the prehistory of *kinýra* (and associated music) is compatible with the idea that Kinyras could go back to the pre-Greek island in some form. And after all, our best evidence for divinized instruments is of BA date, from Kinnaru of Ugarit on back to third-millennium Mesopotamia. And, as it happens, while the fifth-century Pindar is our earliest literary source for a *musical* Kinyras, the bulk of Greco-Roman notices, from Homer onwards, do connect him with the pre-Greek LBA, which was evidently remembered as a kind of Golden Age.[1] The material may be divided into two parts. The first, to be collected and contextualized in the present chapter, links Kinyras to Cypriot industries, which, though pursued throughout the IA, greatly flourished in the LBA, the age of Alashiya. The second group (Chapter 14) confirms and extends this view by connecting Kinyras to the island's pre-Greek population(s), whence he is variously encountered in Aegean migration legends.

Great Kingship

The first point which allies Kinyras closely to LBA Cyprus is that many sources regard him as king over the whole island.[2] A political structure of comparable extent and duration did not reappear after the fall of Alashiya until the island came under Ptolemaic control.[3] True, Euagoras of Salamis aimed for island-wide power and influence in the late fifth century, and even won some ephemeral

---

[1] This was recognized by Gjerstad 1944; Gjerstad 1948:429–430; Dussaud 1950; Kapera 1971:132; Baurain 1980b:291–301, 303n134; Baurain 1981a:24n4; Loucas-Durie 1989.
[2] Island-wide kingship is the most natural reading of Homer *Iliad* 11.20 (with Σ and Eustathios; cf. Baurain 1975–1976:535; but *contra* Lorimer 1950:31n5), where Cyprus is mentioned, not Paphos; so too Pindar *Pythian* 2.13–20 with Σ; cf. Plato Comicus fr. 3 PCG (βασιλεῦ Κυπρίων); Σ Lykophron *Alexandra* 831; Σ Dionysios the Periegete 509 (FGH 758 F 3a); Clement of Alexandria *Exhortation* 2.13.4 with Σ (but *Exhortation* 3.45.4 connects Kinyras with Paphos), *Miscellanies* 1.21.132; Servius Auctus on Vergil *Eclogues* 10.18; *Suda* s.v. καταγηρᾶσαι; Hesykhios s.v. Κινύρας.
[3] But note that Alashiya did not necessarily control the *whole* island: see p11.

Chapter Thirteen

holdings in Phoenicia. Yet this exception proves the rule, since Euagoras himself found it expedient to pose as a descendant of Kinyras in support of his pan-Cypriot pretentions.[4]

Kinyras' status as a Great King is already assumed by Homer, for whom the Cypriot monarch, sending Agamemnon the corselet of *Iliad* 11, treated on equal terms.[5] As Eustathios and the scholia rightly suggest, the verb *kharizómenos* ('cultivating favor'), with its connotations of reciprocity, shows that the *thṓrax* was no "penalty for not serving" (unlike the magical horse Aithe with which Ekhepolos of Sicyon bought his freedom from Troy—Ekhepolos acted "under compulsion" since Agamemnon was "his own king").[6] Gift-giving of course remained a fundamental practice in the IA Aegean. But Agamemnon's clear and traditional characterization as a Great King ("lord of many islands") justifies seeing Kinyras' breastplate as an epic memory of the exchange networks of the LBA 'Club of Great Powers'—to which, after all, both Alashiya and Ahhiyawa belonged.[7] Despite Homer's ample description, the corselet is not, like the shield of Achilles, so elaborate as to defy all reality—although in the real world something this ornamental would have been for ceremonial display rather than battle.[8] The poet's ecphrasis includes details reminiscent of Canaanite workmanship; its precious materials—gold, tin, and enamel (*kýanos*)—are all attested as palatial commodities in the Mycenaean world, where the word *thṓrax* itself was also current.[9]

Agamemnon's daedalic *thṓrax* shows that Homer already knew the Cypriot king both as a famous metallurge (see below) and proverbially wealthy. The riches of Kinyras are mentioned already by Tyrtaios (ca. 650), who pairs him

---

[4] See further p351–359.
[5] Homer *Iliad* 11.19–23. See p1.
[6] Eustathios on Homer *Iliad* 11.20–23 (cf. Σ): ὁ Κινύρης θώρακα ἔδωκε ... «χαριζόμενος βασιλῆϊ», καὶ δώροις οὕτως οἰκειούμενος τὴν Ἑλληνικὴν φιλίαν καὶ οὐ δήπου διδοὺς εἰς ποινὴν ἀστρατείας, ὡς ὁ τῷ Ἀγαμέμνονι ὑποτελῶν Σικυώνιος Ἐχέπωλος (= *Iliad* 23.296–297) τὴν ὑμνουμένην Αἴθην τὴν τοῦ Ἀγαμέμνονος ἵππον ἐξ ἀνάγκης αὐτῷ ὡς οἰκείῳ βασιλεῖ δέδωκεν, ἵνα μὴ στρατεύσηται; for the point, Wagner 1891:182.
[7] For Agamemnon's status, see especially Homer *Iliad* 12.100–108 (quotation 108), which prepares the Catalogue of Ships; cf. 3.187. For LBA gift-exchange as relevant to the Kinyras episode, Dussaud 1950:58; Baurain 1980b:291–301; Morris 1992:6–8, 104; Morris 1997:610.
[8] Homer *Iliad* 11.24–28, with H. Catling in Buchholz and Wiesner 1977:78–79.
[9] PY Sh 736 (*to-ra-ke*, θώρακες) = DMG no. 296 (general discussion, 375–381). For Kinyras' corselet as reflecting LBA Cypriot and/or Canaanite industry: Webster 1964:102–103; Brown 1965:204; Kapera 1972:192; H. Catling in Buchholz and Wiesner 1977:78–79; Baurain 1980b:295–298; Loucas-Durie 1989:119; Morris 1992:8–9; Morris 1997:610. Baurain 1975–1976:535 would even connect its decorations with snake symbolism of second-millennium Cyprus. D'Acunto 2009:157–158, on the other hand, explains the ecphrasis in terms of eighth- and seventh-century Cypro-Phoenician workmanship. Homer was of course familiar with contemporary Phoenician metalwork (*Iliad* 23.740–750, *Odyssey* 4.615–619 = 15.115–119, cf. 15.425).

with Midas; according to the proverb, "rich was Midas, but thrice as rich Kinyras"; elsewhere he is ranked alongside Kroisos and Sardanapalos.[10] This facet of Kinyras echoes the large and varied treasures—fine cloth, horses, chariots, ivory, ebony, gold, and "very great quantities of silver"—which the Alashiyan kings received from Egypt in exchange for mountains of copper.[11] Cyprus also heads Homer's catalogue of lands from which Menelaos reestablished his fortune after Troy.[12] Eustathios, discussing the Agamemnon-Kinyras passage, says that Cyprus's wealth and general prosperity were bywords.[13]

Kinyras' proverbial wealth epitomizes a portfolio of other traditions associating him with industries which flourished on LBA Cyprus.[14] Not all products documented in the Alashiya texts, or in the archaeological record, are connected with Kinyras in literary sources. He has no legendary involvement, for instance, with worked ivory, fine cloth, or faience. Yet this is itself significant: these latter industries were not peculiar to Cyprus, but more widely cultivated (and ivory had to be imported).[15] Kinyras' dominant associations are rather with metallurgy and the sea, those archetypal Cypriot activities. But this rule was not hard and fast since, as we shall see, he was also connected with the perfumed oil industry, pottery, and building materials.

It should be signaled here that Kinyras' nonmusical powers are one sign that he underwent early syncretism with Kothar, the Syro-Levantine craftsman god. I shall treat this complex problem, with collateral phenomena from the mainland and Mycenaean Pylos, in Chapters 17, 18, and 19.

---

[10] Proverbial wealth: Tyrtaios 12.6 IEG; Pindar *Nemean* 8.17–18, cf. Σ Pindar *Pythian* 2.27 (Abel 1891), εὐδαιμονέστατον; Plato *Laws* 660e; *Pap.Oxy.* 1795.32 (*Lyrica Adespota* 37 CA): ὄλβιος ἦν ὁ Μίδας, τρὶς δ' ὄλβιος ἦν ὁ Κινύρας; Diogenianos 8.53 (1.316 Leutsch/Schneidewin); Dio Khrysostomos 8.28; Lucian *Professor of Public Speaking* 11.9; Julian *Epistles* 82; Libanios *Epistles* 503.3, 515.4, 571.2, 1197.5, 1221.5, 1400.3, *Orations* 1.273, 25.23, 55.21, 63.6, cf. 47.31; *Suda* s.v. καταγηρᾶσαι, Σαρδανάπαλος; Eustathios and Σ Homer *Iliad* 11.20 (ζάπλουτος); Thomas Magister *Anecdota Graeca*, Boissonade 1829–1833 2:212. Note also Ovid *Metamorphoses* 10.299 (*inter felices Cinyras*) and 400 (*fortuna*). Cf. Kapera 1972:192; Baurain 1980b:301–303.

[11] EA 33–40 passim (quotation 35.43, trans. Moran).

[12] Homer *Odyssey* 4.81–89.

[13] Eustathios on Homer *Iliad* 11.21: οἷα δὲ ἡ Κύπρος εἰς πλοῦτον καὶ λοιπὴν εὐδαιμονίαν, αἱ ἱστορίαι δηλοῦσιν; cf. Eustathios on Dionysios the Periegete 508–509; Vergil *Aeneid* 1.621–622: *opimam /... Cyprum*.

[14] Cf. Kapera 1972:193–194; Baurain 1981a; Loucas-Durie 1989.

[15] That is not to say that the LBA Cypriot versions of these industries were not distinctive: For Alashiyan ivory-work (EA 40.7-8, 13–14), with an 'international style' combining Aegean, Levantine, and Egyptian elements, see PPC:268–272. Fine cloth (EA 31, 34; Hittite texts: SHC 2 no. 39–40; Ezekiel 27:7) was produced by most or all LBA palaces; but note the lovely clothes with which the Graces regularly dress Aphrodite at Paphos in Greek epic (though the motif per se probably derives from traditions about Astarte/Inanna: Richardson 1991).

Chapter Thirteen

Metallurge and Potter

With some four million tons of slag produced during Cyprus's premodern history, the copper industry's long-term impact on the island's physical landscape, settlement patterns, and social organization was profound.[16] Alashiya is first definitely attested ca. 1900 in the *Old Assyrian Sargon Legend*, discovered among the texts of the Assyrian merchant colony at Kanesh in central Anatolia. It is claimed as a conquest by the Old Akkadian emperor Sargon (ca. 2340), who had by now become a figure of legend, his historical exploits variously expanded and adjusted to suit local horizons.[17] There can be little doubt that mainland interest in Alashiya was already driven by the island's rich copper deposits. Alashiyan copper is mentioned in eighteenth-century economic texts from Mari, Babylon, and Alalakh.[18] This is also when evidence mounts for extracting and processing around the copper sources of the Troodos, where Near Eastern imports now begin to appear.[19] Copper-interests also dominate correspondence between Alashiya and Egypt in the fourteenth-century Amarna letters, clearly driving the other commodities exchanged.[20] That the copper trade peaked at this time explains the appearance of monumental ashlar buildings at many sites (especially in the thirteenth century).

It has been well observed that Kinyras' metallurgical associations preserve an early cultural stratum of island-wide significance—older, that is, than the Paphian dimension which the historical Kinyradai emphasized, and which became conventional (as shown by many and later extra-Cypriot sources).[21] To be sure, Paphos was itself a site of LBA metalworking.[22] But the traditions indicate a pan-Cypriot focus. The elder Pliny states that "the first discovery of copper/bronze was in Cyprus,"[23] and lists the metallurgical inventions associated with Kinyras, alongside the working of clay:

---

[16] Cypriot copper industry: Catling 1963; Muhly 1986; Knapp 1986; Knapp 1988; Muhly 1989; Keswani 1993; Muhly 1996; Knapp 1997; Steel 2004:166–168.
[17] For text, translation, and previous literature, Alster and Oshima 2007; also Foster 2005:74. For the historical circumstances that produced such a work, Westenholz 2007; Westenholz 2011; Bachvarova forthcoming; more generally Michalowski 1993:89–90.
[18] SHC 2 no. 2–9 (Mari), 10–13 (Alalakh), 32 (Babylon). There is also a possibly relevant Ebla text (no. 1).
[19] SHC 2:5; Knapp 2006; Knapp 2011:252.
[20] Alashiyan copper: EA 33.16–18, 34.18, 35.10, 36.5–7, 12–14, 37.9, 40.7–8, 13–14; bronze workers: 35.14–15, 35.37.
[21] Baurain 1980b:303n134; cf. Baurain 1981a:24n4. For the Kinyradai, see Chapter 16.
[22] Cf. Karageorghis in Karageorghis and Masson 1988:36.
[23] Pliny *Natural History* 34.2.2: *in Cypro, ubi prima aeris inventio* (connected with the Kinyras passage by Heubner 1963–1982 2:35). Pliny often discusses Cypriot copper and related processes elsewhere: see SHC 1:140–155 passim.

Cinyras, son of Agriopa,[24] invented clay tiles[25] and copper mines—both on the island of Cyprus—and likewise tongs, hammer, crowbar, anvil.[26]

For once a *prôtos heuretḗs* sounds a realistic note, since in a monarchic society ultimate control of mines and production processes will have rested in a single pair of royal hands.

This rich little catalogue of metallurgical inventions is otherwise unparalleled in surviving ancient sources. It reappears, however, in Étienne de Lusignan, who, while elsewhere acknowledging Pliny as an authority,[27] adds several independent details. His 'Cinaras' has now also discovered the mining of gold; and his clay-working abilities have expanded from tile-making to bricks, bowls, and other shaped vessels. Lusignan connects these further industries specifically with Tamassos and Lapethos, where he states they were still cultivated in his own day.[28] Now the *tegulae* of Pliny and Lusignan's pottery (*vasi fittili*) would converge neatly in the single Greek word *kéramos*; but while Pliny's dependence

---

[24] Agriopa is otherwise unknown in connection with Kinyras (Étienne de Lusignan has 'Agrippa' [!], perhaps a typographical error: *Chorograffia* p13a [§28]). While Agriopa would seem to stand in the place of a father, Heyne 1803:324–325 considered this Kinyras' mother, and it is noteworthy that an Agriope/Argiope is several times elsewhere connected with mythical lyre-heroes—appropriately if the name means 'clear-voiced' (cf. Καλλιόπη)—either as the wife of Orpheus (Hermesianax 7.2 CA) or the nymph-mother of Thamyris via Philammon of Delphi (Pausanias 4.33.3; [Apollodoros] *Library* 1.3.3). See already Engel 1841 2:124; Movers 1841–1856 2:275 and n50a. Alternatively, one might think of the Argiope who was known to Pherekydes as the daughter of the Nile, married by the Phoenician king Agenor: Σ Apollonios of Rhodes 3.1186 (= Pherekydes FGH 3 F 21); cf. Roscher *Lex.* s.v. no. 3.

[25] *Tegulae* can refer to both roof and wall tiles (OLD s.v.). Baurain 1980a:9 wished to interpret *tegulae* as *formae*, i.e. molds for molten bronze ("au risque de donner un sens nouveau à ce mot"), thereby discrediting the parallel drawn by Brown 1965:203 with the anonymous brother of Khousor in Philo of Byblos, who invents bricks (πλίνθοι); yet these are credited to Kinyras himself by Étienne de Lusignan (see below and further p452–453). But note that Gk. πλίνθος can also refer to metal ingots (LSJ s.v. II.2).

[26] Pliny *Natural History* 7.56.195: *tegulas invenit Cinyra, Agriop<a>e filius, et metalla aeris, utrumque in insula Cypro, item forcipem, martulum, vectem, incudem.*

[27] *Chorograffia* p. 2 (§1). Lusignan's debt to Pliny is also clear from his making this (younger) 'Cinaras' the son of 'Agrippa'.

[28] *Chorograffia* p. 13a (§28), of 'Lapithus': "In questa fù primamente ritrovata l'arte di far li vasi di terra, & li coppi, & anchora dura, ritrovata da Cinara, figliuolo di Agrippa"; p. 14a (§37), of 'Tamasse': "il rame [sc. fù primamente ritrovato] da Cinara figliuolo di Agrippa"; p. 20 (§72): "Cinara dunque fù il primo inventore in Cipro del rame & dell'oro; & primo inventore di far li coppi, & altri vasi fittili nella città di Lapitò; nella quale anchora persevera quell'arte"; p. 87 (§590): "Cinaria [*sic*] figliuolo di Agrippa fù il primo, che ritrovò l'oro & il rame in Cipro" (here iron is attributed to "Damneo & Selmente di generatione hebrei"). From the *Description*, p. 28, of Lapethos: "Cinare fils d'Agrippe y trouva premierement l'invention de faire la brique"; p. 80, of Tamassos: "Cinare fils d'Agrippe fut le premier inventeur en cette ville de la mine d'or, comme il avoit esté en Lapithe inventeur de la confection de la bricque"; p. 468: "[sc. Cinara] trova en Cypre un mine d'or & d'airain."

on a Greek source is undoubted (Eratosthenes?), how could such information come down to Lusignan? (I shall contemplate his possible sources further in Appendix G.)

"The talents of Kinyras," a curious proverb used of fair and scrupulous dealings, probably also relates to the Cypriot copper industry and specifically the 'oxhide' ingots that were the standard form for raw copper distribution in the LBA.[29] The scale of this trade was dramatically revealed by the fourteenth-century Uluburun shipwreck, discovered in 1982 off the southwestern coast of Turkey.[30] Its cargo is a microcosm of the LBA palatial macroeconomy, and included—besides the processed tortoise shells for lutes already mentioned[31]—ebony, faience, ivory, amber, gold, terebinth resin, and coriander, along with other materials and goods of wide-ranging provenance (Cypriot, Canaanite, Mycenaean, Egyptian, Nubian, Baltic, Babylonian, Assyrian, Kassite). But the ship's main haul was raw metals: 354 ingots of copper and some forty more of tin, the majority of oxhide shape. Because the cargo is mixed, the point-of-origin remains uncertain. But Cyprus was at least a major port of call, providing all the copper (as indicated by lead isotope analysis).[32] This fact, and the huge quantity involved—eleven tons—make it quite certain that this stage at least of the ship's voyage was directly sponsored by an Alashiyan king. This would also accord with the dominance of Cypriot pottery on board.[33]

Kinyras the Mariner

In any case, it is clear from the Amarna letters and Ugaritic texts that ship-building, shipping, and timber were major Alashiyan industries.[34] This was intimately related to the metals trade, since wood was needed for smelting and the ships that carried oxhide ingots. The extent and depth of these activities is vividly suggested by Eratosthenes, as paraphrased in Strabo's description of Cyprus:

---

[29] Makarios 7.100 (CPG 2:214–15, cf. 653): Τὰ Κινύρου τάλαντα· ἐπὶ τῶν τὸ ἴσον καὶ τὸ δίκαιον φυλαττόντων; cf. Blinkenberg 1924:32. For the equation of ingot and talent, see Muhly 1979:95; Knapp 2011:250, noting however that the actual weight of oxhide ingots excavated in the eastern Mediterranean "varies considerably, from 21–39 kg."
[30] Bass 1986; Pulak 1998; Karageorghis 2002b:30–34.
[31] See p248.
[32] Muhly et al. 1980.
[33] Karageorghis 2002b:33 ("a royal trade mission on behalf of the king of Alashiya"); cf. Pulak 1998:220.
[34] Shipping interests and agents are implicit in all Alashiyan commercial transactions (royal and otherwise) with the mainland (see e.g. EA 39.10–20, RS 18.113A, 18.119). But export of ship-building timbers is also specified: EA 35.27–29, 40.7–8, 16–20.

The Talents of Kinyras

Eratosthenes says that of old, when the plains ran riot with growth so that they were covered with thickets and could not be farmed, the [island's] metal-resources were of some assistance, since people would cut down trees for the smelting of copper and silver. Moreover, he says, there was the building of fleets, since the sea was already being sailed without fear and in force.[35]

Eratosthenes seems to allude to a Cypriot popular memory of a time when the island's ships 'commanded' the seas. Similarly, Cyprus appears in the ancient thalassocracy-lists, immediately before Phoenicia and Egypt.[36] There have been various attempts to match this list's sea-powers with historical epochs; that of Cyprus is often placed in the ninth or eighth centuries.[37] Such analyses are inevitably undermined by the list's obvious artificiality, especially for the alleged sea-powers of earlier times. For the LBA, in particular, the thalassocratic model has been well challenged; still, it is certain that Cyprus played a key role in LBA trade between the Aegean, the Levant, and Egypt.[38] If the Cypriot 'thalassocracy' rests on any genuine tradition, the 'historical precedence' of Cyprus over Phoenicia makes it quite possible that this reflects some popular memory of Alashiyan maritime activity. Eratosthenes certainly envisioned a very early horizon for "the sea being sailed in force."

In later times too, of course, Cyprus was renowned for its seamanship and shipbuilding.[39] The legendary Assyrian queen Semiramis was said by Ktesias (fl. ca. 400) to have used Cypriot, Phoenician, and Syrian shipwrights to build a fleet

---

[35] Strabo 14.6.5 (Eratosthenes fr. III B 91 Berger, 130 Roller): φησὶ δ' Ἐρατοσθένης τὸ παλαιὸν ὑλομανούντων τῶν πεδίων ὥστε κατέχεσθαι δρυμοῖς καὶ μὴ γεωργεῖσθαι, μικρὰ μὲν ἐπωφελεῖν πρὸς τοῦτο τὰ μέταλλα δενδροτομούντων πρὸς τὴν καῦσιν τοῦ χαλκοῦ καὶ τοῦ ἀργύρου, προσγενέσθαι δὲ καὶ τὴν ναυπηγίαν τῶν στόλων ἤδη πλεομένης ἀδεῶς τῆς θαλάττης καὶ μετὰ δυνάμεων κτλ (the passage goes on to describe a custom of granting land to any who would clear it). See also Diodoros Siculus 2.16.6; contrast Theophrastos *History of Plants* 5.8.1, who states that the Cypriot kings tended the forests and allowed the trees to grow to great heights.

[36] Eusebios *Chronicle* 1:225 Schoene = Diodoros Siculus 7, fr. 11; for other authorities and analysis, Miller 1971. Note also Eustathios on Dionysios the Periegete 508–509, where the island's wealth is connected with its sea-power: "The Cypriots are the most blessed/richest of islanders; and they too are said to have ruled the seas one fair time" (ὀλβιώτατοι δὲ νησιωτῶν οἱ Κύπριοι· λέγονται δέ ποτε θαλαττοκρατῆσαι καιρόν τινα καὶ αὐτοί).

[37] Myres 1906:120–122 thought of the period before Sargon claimed control of the island, i.e. 742–709; cf. CAH² III.1:532; HC:103–104, with further references in n4; for Miller 1971:112–113, 128–129, 170–171 the position of Cyprus was keyed to that of Phoenicia, as being the logical antecedent to the island's 'conquest' by Pygmalion, which she ties to the 'Tyrian annals' (see p407n45) and the Phoenician colony period.

[38] Knapp 1993; Iacovou 2006b:33 (Cypro-Minoan signs on Mycenaean pottery suggest Cypriot involvement in the shipping of Mycenaean wares).

[39] Strabo 14.6.5; Pliny *Natural History* 7.56.209.

with which to assault India.⁴⁰ An inscription of Sennacherib (704–681), indeed, states that the Assyrian emperor used captive Cypriot and Phoenician sailors in his sixth campaign against Elam (694), sending them down the Tigris from Nineveh.⁴¹ There were also major Cypriot contingents at various times in the fleets of Persia, Alexander the Great, and the Ptolemies.⁴²

But the Cypriots must have been mariners since the island's first settlement in the seventh millennium. Two clay vases in the shape of boats, with figures of sailors and birds attached around the edge, have been dated to the MBA.⁴³ A number of other ship models, both merchant and war, are known from the LBA and especially Cypro-Archaic period, attesting a continuous artistic tradition, which obviously parallels this dominant aspect of island life. Many examples have been found in the necropolis of Amathous.⁴⁴ For some scholars, these vessels merely reflect the lifetime occupations of the tombs' inhabitants. Others see them as symbolizing a voyage to the next world, perhaps under Egyptian influence (model ships have also been found in Mesopotamian tombs).⁴⁵ These explanations may work for burial contexts. But what are we to make of further examples from the *harbor* of Amathous? Cesnola first compared these to the tradition that Kinyras deceived Agamemnon with a fleet of clay ships, which he cast into the sea.⁴⁶ The custom is so unusual, and its coincidence with the tale so perfect, that here surely we have a Greek or Greek-Cypriot literary reflection on a distinctive practice of pre-Greek culture—recalling that the Eteocypriot language long endured at Amathous, whose inhabitants were held to be "the remnants of Kinyras' men."⁴⁷

But what do the sunken ship-models mean? V. Karageorghis reasonably suggested that sailors submerged them apotropaically to ensure a safe voyage⁴⁸— an idea that could also account for those from the necropolis, with death seen as a hazardous voyage.⁴⁹ Nor should we overlook the use of model boats in Hurrian

---

40   Ktesias FGH 688 F 1b = Diodoros Siculus 2.16.6.
41   ARAB 2:145 §319.
42   HC:119–122, et passim.
43   CAAC I:IV[WHP.IV]21–22; *Aspects*:49–50 (no. 30).
44   Terracotta ships from Amathous: Murray et al. 1900:112–114, fig. 164 no. 10, 12, 16–20, 22, 24 and fig. 165 no. 6; CAAC IV:II[vi]1–11; *Aspects*:185–189 no. 176–181.
45   See CAAC I.189, canvassing with further references the different interpretations, and rejecting the symbolic afterlife voyage (again *Aspects*:49). For possible Egyptian influence, see also Kapera 1970:50–51. Mesopotamia: Strauss 2006:204 and n66.
46   For the episode itself, see p1n2 and p343–346. Cesnola 1877:4–5; Ohnefalsch-Richter 1893 1:217; Kapera 1966; Kapera 1969; Kapera 1970; Kapera 1971:132; Kapera 1972:194.
47   Theopompos FGH 115 F 103. See further p346–348.
48   *Aspects*:185.
49   Compare Odysseus' voyage to the underworld in *Odyssey* 11. For the idea in ancient and modern Greek folk-tradition, see Alexiou 2002:190–193; more impressionistically, Vermeule 1979:179–209.

and Mesopotamian purification rituals. These carried away, into the sea (often symbolically) and from the eyes of the gods, impurities arising from curses, oaths, and perjuries (note that Kinyras is the 'liar-king' only in this episode).⁵⁰ One of the texts, known as the *babilili*-Ritual, derives from the same Kizzuwatnan 'workshop' that produced *Establishing a New Temple for the Goddess of the Night*.⁵¹ It is a royal ritual, addressed to an Ishtar-type (Pirinkir), and contains some twenty-five incantations in Akkadian (West Peripheral, but deriving from an OB tradition) for calling upon the goddess. They were to be sung by a ˡᵘNAR, which in Syro-Hurrian tradition, we saw, would be a 'kinnarist'.⁵² This real-world material from the LBA helps us see how Kinyras, though rooted in ritual music, could grow extra-musical associations.

Other links between Kinyras and the sea include Pindar's reference to the "blessed fortune ... which freighted Kinyras with riches once upon a time in Cyprus-on-the-sea."⁵³ A character named Kinyras in Lucian's *True History* is made the son of a Cypriot sailor called Skintharos: this Kinyras is of considerable interest, because he plays a Paris-like role in an alternative abduction of Helen.⁵⁴ 'Kinyras' also appears as a typical mariner's name in two tasteful epigrams by Julian of Egypt (sixth century CE), both referring to a humble old fisherman who has retired.⁵⁵ In the first, Kinyras devotes his nets to the nymphs—a considerable sacrifice, as these are his only possessions of value. His expertise is made clear in the second: the fish will rejoice, because the sea is now liberated. This aged 'Kinyras' appears to be a type, recalling the 160-year lifespan that Anakreon attributed to the royal Kinyras in a lost poem.⁵⁶ Proverbial longevity, incidentally, might be taken to reflect the great historical antiquity of Kinyras.⁵⁷ And the lowly status of Julian's Kinyras seems a pointed inversion of the legendary Cypriot king's fabulous riches.

---

⁵⁰ See Strauss 2006:201–204.
⁵¹ See p100–102.
⁵² See p116. The *babilili*-Ritual (CTH 718): Beckman 2002a; Strauss 2006:189–215 (201–204, model-boat [KUB 39.71++ rev. iv.9–21]; 192, music [KUB 39.71++ obv. ii.18–30, cf. HKm:167–168]); Beckman 2010, especially 110; Beckman 2014.
⁵³ Pindar *Nemean* 8.17–18. For this passage, see above, p223–224.
⁵⁴ I shall discuss this episode in Franklin forthcoming.
⁵⁵ *Greek Anthology* 6.25, 26 (Julian of Egypt). Cf. Brown 1965:206.
⁵⁶ For Anakreon, see Pliny *Natural History* 7.48.154 (cf. notes to Anakreon 361 PMG).
⁵⁷ Note also Kinyras' role as the father of the Laodike married to Elatos son of Arkas—five mythological generations before Agapenor led the Arcadians to Cyprus: see p365–366. Baurain 1975–1976:540n1 attractively connected Kinyras' reported old age with his BA antiquity (cf. Ribichini 1982:496). Later he saw it as a contamination with Tithonos and/or Arganthonios due to his parallel appearance with them in proverbs (Baurain 1980b:308n153). These views are not necessarily incompatible. Ribichini 1982:497–498n71 would connect Kinyras' longevity with the traditions of his mantic powers, citing Nestor, Teiresias, and Glaukos as parallels.

Chapter Thirteen

Several indirect marine connections may also be suggested. First is the myth that Kinyras' fifty daughters were metamorphosed into halcyons (seabirds).⁵⁸ The role of Aphrodite and Astarte as patronesses of sailors—the former's cult-titles include *Eúploia* ('Good Sailing') and *Einalía* or *Pontía* ('Marina')—is one of several interests Kinyras shares with the goddess he served.⁵⁹ Finally the fish that appears on one of the lyre-player seals is perhaps worth noting.⁶⁰

Oilman and Parfumeur

The Spartan (or Lydian) poet Alkman (ca. 625), in an otherwise spare fragment, refers to perfume as the "moist charm of Kinyras."⁶¹ This elaborate periphrasis links Kinyras to another Cypriot industry stretching back to the LBA. Oil generally, and perfumed oil specifically, are mentioned in connection with Cyprus in Linear B, Ugaritic, and Egyptian sources.⁶² Scented oils were exchanged between the kings of Alashiya and Egypt.⁶³ A large oil distribution to an Alashiyan is attested at Ugarit, and an excavated depot there contained some thousand flasks for the scented salves of Cyprus.⁶⁴ On the island itself, the massive ashlar warehouse at Kalavasos (Building X) could store as much as 50,000 liters of oil in six-foot-high terracotta jars (recall that Kinyras also invented clay vessels).⁶⁵ That Cypriot oil-processing was, like copper, under divine protection is suggested by industrial facilities associated with several sanctuary sites.⁶⁶ There is a parallel from Mycenaean Pylos, where one unguent boiler is qualified as

---

⁵⁸ See p187–191.
⁵⁹ Aphrodite's connection with the sea, and Cyprus, is fundamental in Hesiod *Theogony* 188–200; she is invoked as Κύπρις for a safe voyage in Sappho 5.18 (but the old supplement in line 1 is now known to be incorrect). Aphrodite *Eúploia* is attested on a coin from Knidos already in the seventh century: Head et al. 1911:615–616. Further evidence for Aphrodite *Eúploia*, *Einalía*, *Pontía* in Farnell 1896–1909 2:687–691; Pirenne-Delforge 1994:433–437; Budin 2003:21–23; *Kypris*:223–224; cf. GR:153.
⁶⁰ No. 113quater in Buchner and Boardman 1966. For the general relevance of these seals, see p517–527. But note the use of fish in purification rites like the *babilili*-Ritual (CTH 718): Beckman 2002a:39; Strauss 2006:199–201. For this text, see further p329.
⁶¹ Alkman 3.71 PMGF: νοτία Κινύρα χ[άρ]ις (cf. Gallavotti 1976:56n9); Pliny *Natural History* 13.2.4–18 passim.
⁶² Collected in SHC 2. Ugaritian and Egyptian sources: Helck 1971:415–416, 421; Muhly 1972; AP:41–42, 53; Baurain 1980b:303n135; Knapp 1991:37–40; SHC 2 no. 86–87; HUS:677 (Singer).
⁶³ EA 34.24, 50–51, 35.25.
⁶⁴ RS 18.42 = KTU/CAT 4.352 (SHC 2 no. 53); Roaf 1990:147.
⁶⁵ South 1984:15–16, dating the site to LC IIC (ca. 1325–1225); Todd and South 1992:195; Hadjisavvas 1992:235; Hadjisavvas 1993; Keswani 1993:76–77; Muhly 1996:45; Knapp 1997:66–67.
⁶⁶ See Hadjisavvas 1992.

'Potnian',⁶⁷ and Cypriots apparently collaborated in the perfume industry there.⁶⁸

Cypriot scents continued strong into the IA. Besides Alkman, Greek epic regularly has Aphrodite slathered in perfumed oils by her graceful handmaidens at Paphos.⁶⁹ Furthermore, as we saw, Kinyras is persistently linked to aromatics by his daughter Myrrha, the personification of myrrh (Chapter 12). We may also deal here with the perfumer Amaracus (to give the Latin form we find), metamorphosed into marjoram (Gk. *amárakos*). Our oldest source for the tale is Servius:

> Amaracus: This prince⁷⁰ was a perfume-maker who, by chance slipping while he was carrying unguents, made a greater scent from their confusion; whence the best unguents are called *amaracina*. Afterwards he was turned into *sampsucum* [Gk. *sámpsoukhon*], which is now also called *amaracus*.⁷¹

The verse of the *Aeneid* to which this notice was attached relates to Venus' abduction of Ascanius, whom she hides "in the high groves / of Idalion, where soft *amaracus* exhaling / with flowers and sweet shade embraces him."⁷² Servius and other commentators often attached gratuitous aetiologies where not really justified by the original text. Here, however, Vergil's intentionally ambiguous syntax and diction, which permit both concrete and personified readings (note especially *adspirans complectitur*), strongly suggest that he is indeed alluding to the Amaracus tale. If so, it would readily imply, given the setting of Idalion, that Amaracus himself was a Cypriot prince. It then becomes quite possible that he was the son of Kinyras himself.

---

⁶⁷ The text is PY Un 249. But note that this worker is somewhat anomalous in that he (apparently) worked at the palace, not one of the regional sanctuaries or shrines that were engaged with industrial work: see Lupack 2007:56; Lupack 2008b:119; Nakassis 2013:342.

⁶⁸ The relevant texts (KN Fh 347, 361, 371, 372) relate to the ethnics *ku-pi-ri-jo* (*Kýprios*) and *a-ra-si-jo* (*Alásios*). See the convenient resume in Gallavotti 1976:55–56 (comparing Kinyras); Shelmerdine 1985:49, 137–138. For the dual ethnics, see further below, p435–436.

⁶⁹ Homer *Odyssey* 8.360–366 (cf. *Iliad* 14.172–174, of Hera in an Aphrodisiac context, with Janko's note *ad loc.*, citing a Pylian tablet [Fr 1225] which records an allotment of oil for Potnia); *Homeric Hymn to Aphrodite* 59–62; *Kypria* fr. 4.1–6 EGF/PEG; Nonnos *Dionysiaka* 33.4–8.

⁷⁰ Servius' *regius puer* echoes the description of Ascanius himself at *Aeneid* 1.677–678.

⁷¹ Servius Auctus on Vergil *Aeneid* 1.693: *Amaracus: hic puer regius unguentarius fuit, qui casu lapsus dum ferret unguenta, maiorem ex [unguentorum] confusione odorem creavit: unde optima unguenta amaracina dicuntur. hic postea in herbam sampsucum versus est, quam nunc etiam amaracum dicunt.*

⁷² Vergil *Aeneid* 1.692–694: *dea tollit in altos / Idaliae lucos, ubi mollis amaracus illum / floribus et dulci adspirans complectitur umbra.*

Unfortunately, this idea is not confirmed by any extant ancient source; the few other notices are clearly dependent upon Servius.[73] Nevertheless, Amaracus as the son of Kinyras achieved some currency after it was presented matter-of-factly by the Italian humanist Julius Pomponius Laetus ('Sabinus') in his commentary on Vergil (1487–1490).[74] That it was his own deduction, and not drawn from some lost work, is indicated by his reference to Pliny, who states that "the best and most fragrant *sampsuchum* or *amaracum* is in Cyprus."[75] It was certainly an inspired guess, and may even be right.[76] Pomponius was presumably the source for Étienne de Lusignan, whose version may nevertheless be given as being our most expansive version of the tale, with details otherwise unparalleled. Here 'Amaraco', who "gave himself to making ointments," is called a son of "the god Cinaras" and a "Chirurgien"; he too, we are told, came to be numbered among the gods. Having perfected a recipe, he was bringing it to his father "in an alabaster vessel" (probably Lusignan's own elaboration of Pliny[77]) when he dropped the batch:

> He did not want his father to know about it, but could not hide it, because the scattered scent gave off more odor than before. And so, being thrown into confusion, the poets say that he was turned into an elder-tree[78] in a grove in the city of Idalion. But we say that, through shame, he did not let himself be seen anymore, and pretended to have been turned into that tree.[79]

---

[73] *Mythographi Vaticani* 1.34, 2.182; Isidore *Origines* 4.12.8, 17.9.14.

[74] The earliest edition I have been able to consult is Pomponius Laetus 1544:286.

[75] Pliny *Natural History* 21.93.163: *sampsuchum sive amaracum in Cypro laudatissimum et odoratissimum*; cf. Dioskourides *On Medical Material* 3.39.1 σάμψουχον· κράτιστον τὸ Κυζικηνὸν καὶ Κύπριον; etc. For the varieties that grow on Cyprus, see Hadjikyriakou 2007. Ancient references to such perfume: LSJ s.v. ἀμάρακον, ἀμαράκινος; OLD s.v. *amaracus*.

[76] Van Meurs 1675 2:107–108 approved it with some reserve, noting that he could find no ancient authority. Engel 1841 2:125–126 treated is as established.

[77] Cf. Pliny *Natural History* 13.19 (*unguenta optime servantur in alabastris*), and 36.60.

[78] Lusignan has reinterpreted *sampsucum* as *sambucum* (the closest variant in Thilo's *ap. crit.* is *samsucum* [BH]).

[79] *Chorograffia* p. 21 (§76), cf. 19a (§66). The name is given here as 'Amaruco', 'Amarucq' in the parallel passage of *Description* (p. 38a), where he is also "Chirurgien." For the form 'Cinaras,' see further p3n10, 199, 554–555, 560.

The Virtuous Monarch

Kinyras' multifaceted role as a Cypriot culture-hero contrasts strongly with the 'liar king' tradition that was developed in one branch of Grecophone epic.[80] The virtuous Kinyras was clearly the dominant paradigm.

Kinyras' virtues are further reflected in the names of his children. In Greek mythology, names often reflect the deeds or qualities of a father or grandfather. Odysseus, Telemakhos, Neoptolemos, and Megapenthes are a few ready examples.[81] Such speaking-names were also used to help structure myth. There is a clear and extensive example in the legend of Battos, founder of Cyrene.[82] Similarly, the drama of Achilles and Patroklos is encoded in their names.[83] If one may detect this principle at work in Kinyras' family, a son Oxyporos would celebrate the 'Swift-Passage' of Cypriot ships.[84] A father called Eurymedon, 'Wide-Ruler', could evoke the competitive territorialism, by land or by sea, chariot or ship, of the Great Kings.[85] Daughters like Orsedike, Laodike, and Laogore should endow their father respectively with 'Rousing Justice', 'Justice for the People', and the ability to 'Assemble the People' (and perhaps 'Speak to the People').[86] Unfortunately, we lack any narrative treatment of these figures that could give them the life one sees in the Battos myth—though I shall attempt to reconstruct a lost tale that featured Orsedike, Laogore, and a third sister Braisia (see Chapter 21).

---

[80] See p1n2, 343–346.
[81] According to Homer *Odyssey* 19.407–409, Odysseus' maternal grandfather, "having been angry with many people (πολλοῖσιν ... ὀδυσσάμενος), chose his name accordingly. Telemakhos, the 'far-fighting', reflects Odysseus' prowess with the bow, and/or his reluctant departure for Troy immediately after his son's birth. Similarly Neoptolemos was so called because his father Achilles was still 'young' when he went to 'war' (Pausanias 10.26.4). Megapenthes, son of Menelaos by a slave woman, refers to his father's 'great suffering': Homer *Odyssey* 4.10–12, 15.103; [Apollodoros] *Library* 3.11.1.
[82] Herodotos 4.154.1–155.1. Following the analysis of Chaniotis 2013, Battos was the son of the virtuous Phronime ('Prudence'), whose wicked stepmother induced the girl's father—Eteoarkhos, the 'True King' of Oaxos (on Crete)—to do away with his daughter. A 'righteous' Theran merchant, Themison, was commissioned to do the deed, but he outwitted his oath and delivered her to the 'renowned' Theran notable, Polymnestos, by whom Phronime bore Battos, the 'stammerer'.
[83] Nagy 1979:102–115.
[84] Oxyporos: [Apollodoros] *Library* 3.14.3; Σ Dionysios the Periegete 509. For this figure, see further p497–498, 504, 512–513, 515 .
[85] Father Eurymedon: Σ Pindar *Pythian* 2.28. The name is born by many disparate figures of Greek mythology. But note the two Homeric charioteers (*Iliad* 4.228, 8.114, 11.620; cf. Hainsworth *ad loc.*), recalling the common royal pose as chariot-lord in the LBA. Poseidon is also said to be 'wide-ruling'—an equally appropriate association for Kinyras the mariner (Pindar *Olympian* 8.31). But the name may rather indicate connections with southern Anatolia: see p489.
[86] Orsedike and Laogore: [Apollodoros] *Library* 3.14.3. Laodike: see p359–368.

Chapter Thirteen

Kinyras recurs in other sources as a paragon of virtue. Pindar, we saw, refers to the "beloved deeds" or "friendly acts" that earned him celebration in Cypriot song, the "reward of virtue."[87] In *Nemean* 8, when Pindar alludes to Kinyras' maritime riches, it is a positive and pious example: his blessed wealth was so long-lived because it was "planted with a god."[88] A lost Hellenistic tragedy about Kinyras and Myrrha will have portrayed the king in noble terms, to achieve a sufficient reversal-of-fortune (as prescribed by Aristotle).[89] Ovid's Myrrha describes her father as "pious and mindful of propriety,"[90] and this will have been a feature of Cinna's earlier treatment in the famous *Zmyrna*.[91]

A virtuous Kinyras is also attested in extra-Cypriot contexts. Besides the 'one good man' of Cilicia in an epigram in the *Greek Anthology*, and Abdalonymos the 'last of the Kinyradai' at Sidon,[92] there is also a "certain slave, Cinyras by name," who appears in Dictys of Crete as a member of Acastus' household—slain by Neoptolemos during the hero's extended homecoming. While this Cinyras displays no clear connection to the Homeric figure, his description as "very faithful" (*perquam fidus*) is perhaps in keeping with other traditions about the Cypriot king's virtues (it is notable that this otherwise unimportant character is named at all).[93]

An admirable Kinyras is also implied by the use of 'Kinyras' as a PN.[94] In three epigraphic examples, unsurprisingly, there is insufficient context to corroborate this.[95] Clearer is a funeral inscription from Cos (Roman imperial

---

[87] Pindar *Pythian* 2.14–17 with Σ; cf. Woodbury 1978:286. See above, p221.
[88] Pindar *Nemean* 8.17: σὺν θεῷ γάρ τοι φυτευθεὶς ὄλβος ἀνθρώποισι παρμονώτερος.
[89] For sources, see p284n35.
[90] Ovid *Metamorphoses* 10.354–355: *pius ille memorque est / moris*.
[91] This may be deduced from the pseudo-Vergilian *Ciris*, where one finds a more extensive portrait of a good king, loved by the gods for his plentiful sacrifices and adornment of temples ([Vergil] *Ciris* 524–526). See Lyne 1978:39–45 for this poet's debt to the *Zmyrna*, and the principle that themes shared by the *Ciris* and Ovid's account of Myrrha will go back to Cinna; see also p286n42.
[92] See p497 and Chapter 20.
[93] Diktys of Crete *Journal of the Trojan War* 6.8: *servus quidam Cinyras nomine perquam fidus* (127.4–5 Eisenhut). The text is corrupt—the MSS and Σ offer Cymirias, Tymiras, and Cyranas (see Eisenhut's apparatus)—but the reading Cinyras does seem most plausible.
[94] *Suda* s.v. Κινύρας· ὄνομα κύριον. This probably explains *Etymologicum Gudianum* s.v. κινύρα· κιθάρα ... καὶ κύριον ὄνομα, although one should the maenad ΚΙΝΥΡΑ who appears on an Attic red-figure vase amidst typically adorned pairs of dancing maenads and silens; her partner is ΚΙΣΣΟΣ (Warsaw Nat. Mus. 142458, ca. 440). There seems no particular reason to interpret her name as the instrument (Κινύρα); hence Beazley read Κινυρά, although the context suggests not 'mournful' but 'crooning' (Beazley 1928:61–64, on the names and vase generally; pl. 29.2 and 30 for vase; LIMC s.v. Kinyra).
[95] The name is found in a commemorative inscription in a cave on Acrocorinth (IG IV 382: ἐμνήσ[θη] Κινύρας | τῆς θρεψά[σης] | Ἐπιφανείας, undated); indirectly as a patronymic adjective (Κινυραίου, genitive) in a list of names in a proxeny decree from Thessaly (Kierion), dated ca.

period), commemorating a gladiator "Zeuxis, a.k.a. Kinyras."⁹⁶ It was common practice for gladiators to assume or be assigned performing names, typically an internationally recognized mythological figure who matched the image he wished to project, probably often for his style of fighting or other physical abilities. Names implying power, victory, and glory, are also frequent.⁹⁷ 'Kinyras' has seemed an odd choice to some.⁹⁸ His virtuous and kingly associations are probably relevant. But gladiators named after famous loverboys (Hyakinthos, Narkissos, Hylas, Patroklos, and Adonis) equally suggest Kinyras' legendary beauty.⁹⁹ And since all of these youths died (or disappeared) tragically young, their names would be doubly effective with the professional threat of death ever-present. This suggests some connection between Zeuxis' performing name and the trope of Kinyras the Lamenter (Chapter 12).¹⁰⁰

Conclusion

Kinyras is consistently associated in Greco-Roman sources with industries typical of Alashiya/LBA Cyprus. While these same activities continued into the IA, this was a period of political fragmentation, hence smaller-scale operations. A *fortiori* the Kinyras traditions, which present him as the fountainhead of these activities, should relate first to the Golden Age of Cypriot popular memory.

The various 'Kinyrases' found in extra-Cypriot contexts, like those for whom a Cypriot setting is not explicit (for instance, Julian of Egypt's fisherman), nevertheless usually resonate with *the* Kinyras. They should not be dismissed as irrelevant for understanding the Cypriot legends.¹⁰¹ Since their sympathies go well beyond what is found in the portraits of Homer and Ovid, they must reflect a broader, multiform tradition of which Cypriot Kinyras is merely the

---

187-168 (I.Thess.I no. 15, line 5); and of a Roman freedman working as a public scribe (CIL 6 1826, no date). See also below p537n2.

⁹⁶ Herzog 1899 no. 133, 2-3: Ζεύξει | τῷ καὶ Κινύρᾳ.
⁹⁷ See generally Robert 1940:297-307; Cameron 2004:230-231.
⁹⁸ Cf. Robert 1940:44, 191, 299.
⁹⁹ For the beauty of Kinyras, *Greek Anthology* 16.49 (Apollonides)?; Lucian *Professor of Public Speaking* 11.9; Hyginus *Fabulae* 270; cf. Lucian *A True Story* 2.25 (μέγας ὢν καὶ καλός), where this underworld Kinyras, by abducting Helen, clearly draws on his epic counterpart. Kinyras' beauty is shared with his son Adonis: Heubner 1963-1982 2:35. The superhuman beauty of Theias, Kinyras' doublet beginning with Panyassis (see p466-468), was mentioned by Kleitarkhos FGH 137 F 9 (Stobaios *Anthology* 40.20.37); Σ John Tzetzes *Exegesis of Homer's Iliad* 435.5-15 Papathomopoulos. The beauty of Cyprus's ancient 'god-men', including 'Cinaras', is stressed by Étienne de Lusignan: *Chorograffia* p. 28a (§157).
¹⁰⁰ Compare the epitaph-song erected by an 'Odysseus' for his gladiator friend, whose beauty he compares to Hyakinthos or "Kinyras' beautiful son Adonis" (Κινύρου καλὸ[ν] | υἱὸν Ἄδωνιν): SEG 17:599 = Peek 1955:1 no. 815, 4-5; Antalya, Pamphylia, second-third century CE.
¹⁰¹ As does Baurain 1980a:9-10.

Chapter Thirteen

dominant example. The two types of material are after all linked by traditions that saw Kinyras as an immigrant to Cyprus from various parts of the mainland (see Part 3).

14
Restringing Kinyras

THIS CHAPTER FURTHER DOCUMENTS Kinyras' fundamental connection with pre-Greek Cyprus. I shall examine traces of popular narratives featuring the Cypriot king and his family which variously mythologized Aegean settlement in the eastern Mediterranean during the LBA–IA transition, and the evolving relationships between the new Greek-speaking communities and the pre-Greek and later Phoenician groups with whom they shared the island.

Aegean Foundation Legends and Epic Homecomings

The Cypriot music-iconography examined in Chapter 11 provides a practical context for a number of Aegean migration and foundation legends, some of which must have been treated in narrative song.[1] Unfortunately, what remains is little more than terse references and passing allusions.[2] Some are found in, or may be reasonably posited for, lost cyclic poems like the *Kypria* and the *Nostoi*. Others are fragments, often unidentified, of historical and ethnographic works from the Classical, and especially Hellenistic, periods (Hellanikos, Eratosthenes, Philostephanos, et al.), extracted by lexicographers or placed in 'secondary use' by poets (Lykophron, Nonnos), geographers and periegetes (Strabo, Pausanias), historians (Diodoros), biographers (Plutarch), or mythographers (ps.-Apollodoros).[3]

---

[1] Cf. Franklin 2014:219–221, and p250–253.
[2] Various subsets of the sources are collected and discussed by Engel 1841:210–229; Gjerstad 1944; Gjerstad 1948:428–429; CAH³ II.2:215–216; Khatzēiōannou 1971–2001 1:46–67; Fortin 1980; Maier 1986b; Vanschoonwinkel 1994; Franklin 2014:219–221.
[3] We know of Κυπριακά by Hellanikos (FGH 4 F 57, 756 F 1), Palaiphatos of Abydos (FGH 44 T 3), Kreon (FGH 753), and Timomakhos (FGH 754 F 1-2); there were Περὶ Κύπρου by Philostephanos (FHG 3:30 fr. 10-14), Alexandros Polyhistor (FGH 273 F 31), and a certain Androkles (FGH 751 F 1; some would emend to Menandros [of Ephesus]: FHG 4:448 fr. 7; cf. Fraser 1979:335n2; note that Menandros dealt with relations between Tyre and Kition: FGH 783 F 4). Asklepiades of Cyprus (FGH 752) wrote a Περὶ Κύπρου καὶ Φοινίκης. Amathous was the subject of works by Eratosthenes (FGH 241 F 25: see below, p546) and Paion of Amathous (FGH 757). The *Suda* reports

Chapter Fourteen

Moreover, the underlying myths are of varying quality, not all deserving the label 'tradition'. As E. Gjerstad clearly demonstrated in a seminal article:

> They may be purely fictional or reflect later logographic speculations and political propaganda, but they may also be more or less clear records of an historical tradition. It is the task of the historian to distinguish the valuable material from the worthless, thus bringing forth the historic evidence.[4]

The basic accuracy of this assessment cannot be doubted; and while one may question how conclusively Gjerstad has executed the historian's task on specific points, his analysis remains admirably thorough and sensitive, despite many subsequent revisions of detail to his fundamental historical synthesis of 1948.

The plasticity of such myths has been well exposed by I. Malkin's study of Odysseus' "returns" from Troy—substantially remolded, and largely developed, during ninth-century "proto-colonization" to the West. The hero's route, and the relationships established along the way, were continually reformulated by Greek colonists, merchants, and local communities to create a "common, mutually comprehensible world," typically in the venue of drinking rituals (*symposia*).[5]

On Cyprus, a comparable diachronic process, beginning several centuries earlier, will have obscured the facts of immigration, with history continuously reimagined throughout the IA. In particular, one can observe the impact of the Aeolic-Ionic epic tradition, which assigned various homecoming adventures (*nóstoi*) to the Greek heroes returning from Troy. This development, in which Cypriot migration figures were integrated into the emerging Panhellenic cycle, should be placed in the ninth or eighth centuries, parallel in many respects to the "returns of Odysseus." This is not due to the spread of Homer per se, since the textualized *Iliad* and *Odyssey* did not attain canonical status until the later seventh or sixth century, to judge from the evidence of vase-painting.[6] Rather, it reflects Cypriot (re-)integration with a larger Grecophone storytelling world. Homer's poems themselves, however, must still be dated early on linguistic grounds, let us say the later eighth century.[7] Given this, it is most significant that Homer himself assumes a developed tradition of 'Eastern Wandering', from

---

a Cypriot ἱστορικός named Xenophon as an author of a Κυπριακά (s.v. Ξενοφῶν = FGH 755): for this controversy, see p565–567. Of course many other works contained information about Cyprus, and other Cypriot or Cyprus-based authors (like Demetrios of Salamis: FGH 756 F 1) will have discussed the island. See further Engel 1841 1:3–11.

4   Gjerstad 1944:107.
5   Malkin 1998 (quotation 157; "proto-colonization" is also his term).
6   See with further references Franklin 2014:227–229, 232–233.
7   Janko 1982.

a stop by Paris and Helen at Sidon *en route* to Troy, to the post-Troy wanderings of Menelaos, which take him to "Cyprus and Phoenicia and the Egyptian people."[8] A shared poetics developed precisely around the position of Cyprus on the eastern edge of the Hellenic world.[9]

It is perhaps easiest to apprehend the structural variations that underlie the Cypriot 'founders' by beginning with those that are most clearly artificial and aetiological in nature. Litros (< Ledroi) and Lapethos (< Lapethos), for instance, are known only from the highly mannered epicist Nonnos (ca. 400 CE), and were perhaps invented by him for the occasion; nor does he draw any clear connection with Aegean migration.[10] The population of Classical Lapethos was quite heterogeneous, even its kings bearing Greek and Phoenician names alike.[11] The foundation of Idalion was attributed to a certain Khalkanor, whose name betrays an aetiological connection with metalworking at the site (and perhaps nearby Tamassos).[12] Idalion itself is explained in terms of an oracle that suggests an eastward metal-hunting venture: Khalkanor was to build his city where he 'saw' (*id-*) the 'sun' (*[h]álion*) rising.[13] The foundation of Golgoi by a certain Golgos is equally artificial, and his Sicyonian origin remains puzzling—all the more so given the undeciphered pre-Greek language attested there.[14]

Both Golgos and Khalkanor—the latter depending upon *Greek* etymology—attest a desire for connection with an 'Achaean' past, which, though artificially expressed, may nevertheless be symptomatic of real, if dim, historical

---

[8] Homer *Odyssey* 4.83. See for now Franklin 2014:221–222n23, 231. I shall deal with the poetics of 'Eastern Wandering' more fully in Franklin forthcoming.
[9] See Franklin 2014:221–224 et passim.
[10] Nonnos *Dionysiaka* 13.432–433.
[11] Seibert 1976:19–23; Greenfield 1987:395–396; Maier 1985:35 stresses the inadequate factual basis beneath repeated scholarly assertions of dynastic changes at Lapethos due to fifth-century Persian interventions. Lapethos is called a Phoenician city by [Skylax] 103 (GGM 1:78). Honeyman 1938:289 suggested that 'Lapethos' derives from a pre-Greek TN, given its divergent representation in Greek and Phoenician; but the correspondence of Gk. θ/Phoen. š is now known to be normal (Lipiński 2004:62).
[12] HC:87n2.
[13] Stephanos of Byzantium s.v. Ἰδάλιον, πόλις Κύπρου. χρησμὸς γὰρ ἐδόθη … ὅπου ἴδοι [sc. ὁ Χαλκήνωρ] τὸν ἥλιον ἀνίσχοντα, πόλιν κτίσαι, κτλ. The tale is repeated by Étienne de Lusignan *Chorograffia* p. 16a (§42), who attributes it to the time "before the gods existed."
[14] Stephanos of Byzantium s.v. Γολγοί· πόλις Κύπρου, ἀπὸ Γόλγου τοῦ ἡγησαμένου τῆς Σικυωνίων ἀποικίας. Cf. Gjerstad 1944:121. Sicyon *is* represented in the Catalogue of Ships: Homer *Iliad* 2.572. Or should we look instead to Eusebios' primeval Sicyonian dynasty (Schoene 1967 1:173)? Étienne de Lusignan assigns the foundation to Pygmalion, here a Sicyonian (*Description* pp. 34–34a, 38, 91a–92); it is unclear how this squares with his being the son of Cilix (see further Appendix F)! For the Golgoi tablets, see p350.

recollections.[15] These figures were presumably inspired by emulation of other Cypriot cities for which such claims were better grounded, that is, those whose ctistic legends betray no clear ulterior motive through association with Homer and/or some powerful mother-city. Kourion's claim to have been an Argive settlement, for instance, could be open to doubt because of the close mythological connection between Argos and Mycenae.[16] It may still be, of course, that the Kourion tradition did have some historical basis. After all, the island's Arcado-Cypriot dialect indicates that the majority of immigrants came from sites in the pre-Doric Peloponnese. *A priori* it is quite likely that some groups will have come from the heartland of Mycenaean power. The point is simply that, in a case like this, it is harder to isolate the trustworthy.

By contrast, two migrations are more convincing for the very obscurity of the connections proposed. Lykophron, after giving considerable detail about Teukros, Agapenor, and the sons of Theseus (see below), briefly mentions a fourth and fifth Cypriot founder. These are Praxandros and a band of Laconians from Therapna (connected with Lapethos by Strabo), and Kepheus with Achaeans from the minor sites of Olenos and Dyme.[17] The poet, while making these figures part of the post-Troy homecomings, nevertheless describes them as "not lords of a naval host, but a nameless scattering (*sporaí*)."[18] They are presumably "nameless" because they are not found in Homer's Catalogue of Ships. Probably these were genuine Cypriot traditions, available to Lykophron through the ethnographic work of Eratosthenes and Philostephanos.[19]

With Akamas and Demophon at Soloi, however, the epic framework of post-Troy wandering was apparently exploited for fifth-century propaganda.[20]

---

[15] See especially Herodotos 7.90, reporting Cypriots' claims to know their origins—though here too history and myth are blended.

[16] Herodotos 5.113; Strabo 14.6.3. While 'Argives' (Ἀργεῖοι) is used flexibly in Homer, a narrower connection with the Mycenaean royal house may be seen at *Iliad* 1.30, 79, 119, 2.107–108, 3.82–83, 11.154–155, etc.; according to [Apollodoros] *Library* 2.1.2, Argos named the Peloponnese after himself.

[17] Lykophron *Alexandra* 586–591, with Σ 586 (= Philostephanos FHG 3:31 fr. 12); Strabo 14.6.3. Étienne de Lusignan calls Praxandros 'Pixando' (*Chorograffia* p. 36 [§180]), and places his origin in Thessaly, presumably for an etymology of Lapethos from the Lapiths.

[18] Lykophron *Alexandra* 586–587 οὐ ναυκληρίας / λαῶν ἄνακτες, ἀλλ' ἀνώνυμοι σποραί. A similar 'scattering' is found in Herodotos 7.91, of the followers of Amphilochos and Kalkhas (Οἱ δὲ Πάμφυλοι οὗτοί εἰσι τῶν ἐκ Τροίης ἀποσκεδασθέντων ἅμα Ἀμφιλόχῳ καὶ Κάλχαντι); this is reprised by Strabo 14.4.3 (τινὰς δὲ σκεδασθῆναι πολλαχοῦ τῆς γῆς), where it anticipates the diaspora of Mopsos (for which cf. p252).

[19] Lykophron's sources: Fraser 1979, especially 335–341, seeing Eratosthenes as primary (his geographical work, the *Amathousia* [cf. p546], and perhaps the *Hermes* [cf. p505]), Philostephanos as secondary; cf. Pirenne-Delforge 1994:327.

[20] Akamas, Demophon, and Phaleros at Soloi: Lykophron *Alexandra* 494–534; Strabo 14.6.3; Plutarch *Solon* 26; cf. [Apollodoros] *Epitome* 6.17.

An earlier stratum has the sons of Theseus return to Athens after the war. But Gjerstad convincingly argued that they—along with their fellow countryman 'Phaleros' (an eponym for Phaleron, a departure point for Athenian naval expeditions)—reflect Athenian imperial interests and military endeavors on Cyprus, between the defeat of the Persians at Mykale (479) and the death of Kimon in the siege of Kition (449/448).[21] Solon's anecdotal involvement with Soloi probably also took on its principal features at this time.[22] Akamas' grandson 'Khytros' (< Khytroi) may be similarly understood.[23] Nevertheless, since there does seem to have been Aegean settlement in the region of Soloi at the end of the LBA,[24] a late political myth like this could take on specious substance by repurposing local memories.

Some figures, however, do represent genuinely ancient traditions. Teukros and Agapenor, associated with Salamis and Paphos, respectively, may be confidently associated with historical population movements from western Anatolia and the Peloponnese for reasons, to be discussed below, that overcome any suspicion raised by their incorporation into the epic *nóstoi*. That these are the two best-attested Cypriot migration legends must relate to the prominence of Salamis and Paphos on the island itself, and hence their greater visibility within early Panhellenic horizons.

As it happens, both Teukros and Agapenor have connections with Kinyras and his family. We thus arrive at the central question of this chapter. In the treatment of Kinyras, one would predict both local Cypriot traditions of potentially sub-Mycenaean antiquity, and a modulation in the ninth or eighth century under the stimulus of Aeolic-Ionic epic. We have already seen evidence of the latter with Kinyras' brief cameo in the *Iliad*, where he appears as an esteemed guest-friend to Agamemnon—a fellow Great King.[25] A more ancient Kinyras, I have argued, is found in the rich traditions that make him an all-around culture-hero for the island and its ancient industries (Chapter 13). In both cases, Kinyras is presented in a positive light. But his virtues and talents did not go wholly uncontested. Another stream of tradition made Kinyras a traitor to the Greek cause, who had to be punished accordingly (see below). More middling, 'hybrid' perspectives are found at early Paphos and fifth-century Salamis, where the royal dynasties presented themselves as descendants of the legendary king.

---

[21] Gjerstad 1944:120–121. For the political situation, see HC:121–125.
[22] For which see HC:117.
[23] Khytroi and Khytros: Xenagoras FGH 240 F 27 (= Harpokration *Lexicon of the Ten Orators* and Stephanos of Byzantium s.v. Χύτροι); Gjerstad 1944:120.
[24] Fortin 1980:26–35.
[25] See p1, 322.

Chapter Fourteen

I shall develop specific historical explanations for each of these strains, arguing that Kinyras was a kind of historical boundary stone delimiting Greek and pre-Greek perspectives within the evolving social landscape of IA Cyprus, even when the two populations are indistinguishable in the material record. Ultimately this ethnic, national function of Kinyras will permit further inferences about his own early history upon the island (Chapter 15).

Kinyras, Dmetor, and the Changing States of Cyprus

After Kinyras' brief mention in the *Iliad*, Homer tells us nothing more about him. Instead Odysseus, lying to Antinoos about how he fell into beggary, claims that he was captured while marauding the coast of Egypt and handed over to a certain "Dmetor son of Iasos, who ruled Cyprus by force."[26] Dmetor is envisioned as commanding the whole island.[27] Eustathios was puzzled by this:

> If Kinyras was king of Cyprus in the *Iliad*, he is no longer, but the Dmetor who is named seems to have been king.[28]

Eustathios' suggestion remains the most economical interpretation of the Homeric data. The alternative, to view the *Odyssey* poet as using a different frame of reference than the *Iliad*, is not merely uneconomical but discouraged by Homer's own generous clues. For *Dmḗtōr* means 'Subduer', and is even so defined by the immediate sequel: "who ruled in Cyprus by force." This is proof enough, were it needed, that Dmetor is no historical figure. Yet he may still have an historical *dimension*. Both his name and its gloss show that the *Odyssey* poet recognized an early Greek conquest scenario on Cyprus. That Dmetor exerted his rule "by force" naturally implies a hostile native population, which in turn suggests that his kingdom was recently established. This might be reading too much into a single name, were it not for other mythological examples of Achaean heroes establishing kingdoms on Cyprus just after the fall of Troy— only a few years of dramatic time before the action of the *Odyssey* (Odysseus was the last hero home).

---

[26] Homer *Odyssey* 17.442–443: αὐτὰρ ἔμ' ἐς Κύπρον ξείνῳ δόσαν ἀντιάσαντι, / Δμήτορι Ἰασίδῃ, ὃς Κύπρου ἶφι ἄνασσεν.

[27] Ἀνάσσειν takes the dative of peoples ruled, but typically genitive of a place within which and over which one holds supreme power, including islands: Homer *Iliad* 1.38, 452 (Τενέδοιό τε ἶφι ἀνάσσεις, of Apollo), 6.478, *Odyssey* 4.602; Hesiod fr. 141.16 M-W; *Homeric Hymn to Apollo* 181 (Delos), *Homeric Hymn to Aphrodite* 112 (all Phrygia).

[28] Eustathios on Homer *Odyssey* 17.442–443: εἰ δὲ Κινύρας ἐν Ἰλιάδι Κύπρου ἦν βασιλεύς, ἀλλ' ἐκείνου μηκέτ' ὄντος ὁ ῥηθεὶς Δμήτωρ βασιλεῦσαι δοκεῖ (expanding the blunter statement of a scholiast *ad loc.*: Κινύρου ἀποθανόντος Δμήτωρ ἐβασίλευσε Κύπρου).

Dmetor thus concisely embodies a traditional convention that Cyprus, in a post-Troy *nóstos*, should be a Kinyras-free zone.[29] Kinyras and Dmetor symbolize the island's two storytelling 'states'. The transition between them, one may suppose, could be uncompressed and developed at will, as normal with formulaic themes. But of course this need not mean that *only* Dmetor figured in tales of post-Troy Cyprus.

Another possible lead is Dmetor's patronymic, *Iasídēs*, 'son of Iasos' (or descendant), if this is more than an on-the-fly invention. Iasos recurs in mythological constructions of the Argive royal house, either as the son of Phoroneus and father of Argos (Hellanikos), or as the son of Argos himself (ps.-Apollodoros).[30] *Iasídēs* may therefore symbolize not simply a Greek conquest of Cyprus, but one in which 'Argos'—broadly understood—played a central role. There is also the Iasos whom ps.-Apollodoros places in the Arcadian royal house as the son of Lykourgos—that is, in the 'disempowered' branch that descends from the eponymous Arkas via his younger son Apheidas.[31] This Iasos' brother was Ankaios, father of Agapenor, the Paphian migration hero (see below); this would make Dmetor and Agapenor first cousins. Of course one need not insist on any such precise relationship. But Homer's *Iasídēs* may well suggest a specifically Peloponnesian background to Dmetor and his power over Cyprus.

Liar King: The Terracotta Fleet and the Curse of Agamemnon

The political relationship between Kinyras and Agamemnon was more fully elaborated in what Eustathios calls the 'Cypriot Hosting of the Achaeans' (*Kypriakḕ xenía tôn Akhaiôn*). Our knowledge of this tale comes from three authors, who yield four closely related tellings.[32] They speak variously of an Achaean embassy to Cyprus and a broken promise by Kinyras to contribute ships for the expedition against Troy. According to ps.-Apollodoros:

---

[29] Cf. the astute comments of Serghidou 2006:171–173.
[30] Hellanikos FGH 4 F 36; [Apollodoros] *Library* 2.1.3. Cf. HC:88.
[31] [Apollodoros] *Library* 3.9.2.
[32] Alkidamas *Odysseus* 20–21; [Apollodoros] *Epitome* 3.9; two versions in Eustathios on Homer *Iliad* 11.20. While the earliest text is the fourth-century Alkidamas, this is clearly a fashionable sophistic exercise comparable to the revisionist encomia of Helen by Gorgias and Isokrates, and Gorgias' *Defense of Palamedes* (Gorgias DK 82 B 11 [Helen], 11a [Palamedes]; Isokrates 10; I assume the Gorgianic works are authentic: Untersteiner 1954:95; Segal 1962:100, 136–137n10 with further references). Alkidamas' 'Defense of Kinyras' only makes sense as systematically correcting a traditional epic episode that cast the Cypriot king in a negative light, shifting all blame to Palamedes. I shall deal more fully with the interrelationships of these texts, and the episode's position within a larger tradition of Eastern Wandering, in Franklin forthcoming. See for now Franklin 2014.

> Menelaos went with Odysseus and Talthybios to Kinyras in Cyprus, and tried to persuade him to join the battle. But he [Kinyras] made a gift of a breastplate[33] for Agamemnon, who was not present; and vowing to send fifty ships, he sent one, which [name lost] the son of Mygdalion commanded. And molding the rest out of clay, he launched them into the sea.[34]

This tale must have featured in some version of the lost *Kypria*, which dealt with events leading up to the Trojan War.[35] We have also seen that, incredible though it seem, Kinyras' terracotta fleet must somehow allude to an Eteocypriot tradition of terracotta ship-models stretching from the Archaic period back to the MBA.[36] The episode is implicitly aetiological, but is the aetiology fundamental or incidental? That is, did the ritual give rise to the story of Kinyras' treachery, or merely embellish it?

The "son of Mygdalion" is eccentric and puzzling. The name is reminiscent of 'Pygmalion', which some would change the text to read—an easy emendation—recalling the tradition that Kinyras married a daughter of Pygmalion.[37] On this hypothesis, the "son of Mygdalion" becomes Kinyras' brother-in-law, a plausible enough arrangement. Or should the more difficult reading prevail? Since 'Pygmalion' is a Hellenic representation of a Canaanite/Phoenician divine and/or royal name like Pumayyaton, one can find equal support for Mygdalion in Milkyaton, a name born by a fourth-century king of Kition and himself the father of a Pumayyaton.[38] Several alternative attempts at a Semitic etymology for Mygdalion may also be noted.[39]

---

[33] The text has the plural "breastplates."
[34] [Apollodoros] *Epitome* 3.9: Ὅτι Μενέλαος σὺν Ὀδυσσεῖ καὶ Ταλθυβίῳ πρὸς <Κινύραν εἰς (suppl. Wagner)> Κύπρον ἐλθόντες συμμαχεῖν ἔπειθον· ὁ δὲ Ἀγαμέμνονι μὲν οὐ παρόντι θώρακα[ς] ἐδωρήσατο, ὀμόσας δὲ πέμψειν πεντήκοντα ναῦς, μίαν πέμψας, ἧς ἦρχεν … ὁ Μυγδαλίωνος, καὶ τὰς λοιπὰς ἐκ γῆς πλάσας μεθῆκεν εἰς τὸ πέλαγος.
[35] See p1n2, 211n139.
[36] See p328.
[37] Emendation: Wilamowitz-Möllendorff 1900:535n1; West 2003:72–73. Kinyras and the daughter of Pygmalion: [Apollodoros] *Library* 3.14.3; see further p498, 504.
[38] KAI 32–33, cf. 34, 39, 41; for the new inscription, see p357. The proposal of Cross 1972 to see a similar pairing in the Nora Stone (Sardinia, ca. 800; KAI 46) has not been generally followed; most would see in *pmy* of line 8 a reference to the Cypriot/Phoenician god Pummay (whence Hesykhios s.v. Πυγμαίων· ὁ Ἄδωνις παρὰ Κυπρίοις). See Amadasi 1967:86; Lipiński 2004:236n52, 240. Phonological considerations indicate that the Pygmaion/Pummay (corresponding to the theophoric element in 'Pygmalion') goes back on Cyprus to a borrowing from Canaanite, i.e. *before* ninth-century Phoenician colonization: Cross 1972:18; Brown 1981:390n31. For Pygmaion and Pygmalion, see further p315 and n210.
[39] Lewy 1895:238; Kapera 1971; Kapera 1972:197–199.

Either way, the "son of Mygdalion/Pygmalion" is an authentic Cypriot touch. Important enough to rate a mention, he is a faint trace of a more developed portrait of Kinyras' court. He equally imparts a Cypro-Phoenician flavor, as does making Kinyras himself a faithless foreigner, since Homer usually represents Phoenicians as sneaky dealers.[40]

The Liar King clearly expresses a more general cultural confrontation between Greek and non-Greek. But the opposition is not a simple geographical one between Cyprus and the Aegean; for the virtuous Kinyras appears in Homer, Alkman, and Pindar, and he was promoted by the Kinyrad kings of Paphos who nevertheless bore Greek names (Chapter 16). The Liar King is therefore likely to derive from a specific regional tradition *within Cyprus*, which, unlike Paphos—where the episode is set[41]—stood to gain by denying Kinyras' virtues and emphasizing his un-Greekness. The obvious candidate here is Salamis. First, this is the city for which an epic tradition is best attested. Salamis appears in an invocation of Aphrodite in one of the lesser Homeric hymns.[42] There is also the hexametric oracle, attributed to the legendary Cypriot prophet-singer Euklees, which purports to predict Homer's birth "in a field ... / outside of very-wealthy Salamis."[43] At least two Salaminian singers are known by name, Stasinos and Stasandros.[44] To the former (or alternatively to Hegesias or Hegesinos of Salamis) was attributed the *Kypria*, some version of which remains the most likely home for the terracotta fleet on other grounds.[45] I suggest therefore that the Liar King served the interests of the Salaminian royal house, undermining the island-wide prestige the Paphian Kinyradai enjoyed as high priests of Aphrodite's temple.[46]

With or without Salamis, an insinuation of Phoenician sneakiness may have been useful at certain points in the island's history when a sense of Hellenic identity waxed especially strong here or there. This leads to an important detail added by Eustathios: that Kinyras, "after defaulting" on his promise, "was

---

[40] I owe this observation to G. Fawkes. Homer's Phoenicians: Winter 1995; cf. Morris 1997:612.
[41] Eustathios on Homer *Iliad* 11.20.
[42] Aphrodite is "ruler of well-founded Salamis / And Cyprus on the sea" in *Homeric Hymn* 10.4. An early 'epic environment' has often been suggested on the basis of the royal tombs at Salamis: Karageorghis 1967:117–124; CAH² III.3:60–62; Karageorghis 1999b. Cf. also Nonnos *Dionys.* 13.463: ἀειδομένην Σαλαμῖνα.
[43] Pausanias 10.24.3: ἐπ' ἀγροῦ ... / νόσφι πολυκτεάνοιο ... Σαλαμῖνος. This oracle accords with Hellanikos FGH 4 F 5b, where Εὐκλέης appears as the grandson of Orpheus, and thus a distant ancestor in a continuous line down to Homer. His name appears in a slightly different form in Pausanias (cf. 10.12.11, 10.14.6). For this important figure, see further below and Franklin 2014:227–228.
[44] See p211.
[45] See p1n2, 211n139.
[46] Note that inscriptions to the Paphian goddess have been found at Khytroi, Golgoi, Ledroi and Keryneia: HC:87; NPHP:70 and n20; *Kypris*:167, 198, 200. For the Kinyradai of Paphos, see Chapter 16.

cursed by Agamemnon."⁴⁷ Though Eustathios himself offers no clear sequel, Agamemnon's curse is very probably to be connected with a remarkable tradition recorded by Theopompos, to which we now turn.

The Unthroning of Kinyras

Theopompos, active in the fourth century, ranks alongside Herodotos, Thucydides, Xenophon, and Ephoros as one of the most important Classical historians.⁴⁸ He traveled and lectured widely in the Greek world, making considerable use of local traditions.⁴⁹ An understandable desire to include everything he collected accounts for his proneness to tangents. The fifty-eight volume *Philippika*, dealing with the history of Philip of Macedon and the generations preceding his rise to power, was so replete with ethnographic, historical, and mythological digressions that their excision by Philip V (ca. 238–179) reduced the work to a mere sixteen books.⁵⁰ The original version, however, apparently survived down to the ninth century when it was read by Photios, with the exception of four books he reports as lost.⁵¹ He also mentions a certain Menophanes, who believed that a fifth volume too—Book 12—had fallen from the tradition. Yet Photios himself had this very book in hand, and luckily felt impelled to epitomize it for posterity. We may therefore be sure that he has represented the original structure quite faithfully, even if the severity of his cuts may obscure the relative emphases of the original topics.⁵²

Book 12 dealt with the career of Euagoras I (ca. 435–374), the brilliant, swashbuckling king of Salamis who walked a long and dangerous tightrope on

---

⁴⁷ Eustathios on Homer *Iliad* 11.20: φασὶ δὲ αὐτὸν ἀμελήσαντα ἐπικατάρατον γενέσθαι ὑπὸ Ἀγαμέμνονος. Eustathios' version is cited more fully on p187.
⁴⁸ Flower 1994.
⁴⁹ Theopompos FGH 115 F 25–26 and T 28a, with discussion of Flower 1994:18–19, cf. 201.
⁵⁰ Photios *Library* 121a35–41 (FGH 115 T 31). Cf. Flower 1994:29 and 160–165 on Theopompos' essentially Herodotean digressive technique. Cicero (*On the Laws* 1.5) refers to the "countless tales" of both authors (*et apud Theopompum sunt innumerabiles fabulae*); these included, besides the legends of Kinyras and Mopsos (see p252 and below), the myth of Midas and Seilenos (FGH 115 F 75).
⁵¹ Photios *Library* 120a6–14.
⁵² His epitome closes with the strong declaration ἃ μὲν οὖν ὁ ἠφανισμένος Μηνοφάνει δωδέκατος λόγος περιέχει ταῦτά ἐστιν (120b17–18). Against Photios' claim in the prologue to have made his summaries solely from memory, T. Hägg, by comparing the extant *Vita Apollonii* of Philostratos with its epitome, showed that Photios sometimes worked with open book: episode sequences are repeated exactly and in detail, with even a textual problem taken over (Hägg 1973, especially 218; Hägg 1975:195–204). When Photios is indeed recollecting, sequences are slightly jumbled and extraneous material mistakenly inserted. Had he epitomized Book 12 of Theopompos so, one would expect an unbroken account of Euagoras' career. Instead, it is 'interrupted' by the 'digressions' on Kinyras and Mopsos; and the obscure daughters of Mopsos would hardly have been recalled by name.

the Persian periphery. He grew up while Salamis was controlled by a usurping Phoenician dynasty; a further coup ca. 415 by another Phoenician adventurer—Abdymon (or Abdemon) of Tyre and/or Kition[53]—caused Euagoras to flee to Cilician Soloi. Returning several years later with a picked band of fifty followers, he regained his throne in a daring night attack.[54] Consolidating his position, he went on to enjoy a long reign in which he aimed at, and briefly glimpsed, fairly general control of Cyprus and even several Phoenician cities including Tyre, before Persia cut back his little empire to Salamis itself.[55]

How Theopompos related his Euagoras narrative to the career of Philip is not immediately clear. One likely point of contact is Euagoras' involvement in the Battle of Knidos (394), since this was relevant to the history of hegemonic struggles in Greece itself.[56] In any case, Theopompos included two curious mythological digressions that are but tersely noticed by Photios. One was on Mopsos, whom the historian tied to ethnic conflict between Greeks and barbarians in Caria (the Meliac War, ca. 700) and probably Pamphylia.[57] He also described, immediately after recounting Euagoras' surprise upset of Abdymon,

> the manner in which the Greeks with Agamemnon occupied (*katéskhon*) Cyprus, driving off the men with Kinyras, of whom the Amathousians are the remnants.[58]

One's immediate reflex, conditioned as we are by the usual Homeric version of events, is to understand "the Greeks with Agamemnon" as a group who had fought beside the Mycenaean king *at Troy*, but then went on to Cyprus *by themselves* while he went home to Klytaimnestra.[59] By this view, *hoi sỳn Agamémnoni* would be an elliptical reference to other, better-attested migration legends

---

[53] Theopompos FGH 115 F 103: Ἀβδύμονα ... τὸν Κιτιέα ταύτης ἐπάρχοντα; Diodoros Siculus 14.98: Ἀβδήμονα τὸν Τύριον.

[54] Isokrates 9.30-32; HC:126–127.

[55] See generally RE 6 (1907), 820–828 (8); Spyridakis 1935; HC:125–143. The source for Euagoras' Phoenician possessions is Diodoros Siculus 15.2.4: ἐκυρίευε ... κατὰ δὲ τὴν Φοινίκην Τύρου καί τινων ἑτέρων.

[56] For the battle and Euagoras' role, see Xenophon *Hellenika* 4.3.10-12; Diodoros Siculus 14.39; HC:130–131; Maier 1985:39–40. Flower 1994:165 suggests that Theopompos' treatment of Cyprus, Egypt, and Asia Minor served as background to Philip's intended conquest of Asia.

[57] The key evidence linking Theopompos FGH 115 F 103 (Photios *Library* 120b8-13) to the Meliac War is a Hellenistic inscription from Priene: FGH 115 F 305 and Hiller von Gaertringen et al. 1906 no. 37. See the discussion of Huxley 1960; cf. Huxley 1966:22.

[58] Theopompos FGH 115 F 103 (Photios *Library* 120a20-22): ὄν τε τρόπον παρὰ δόξαν Εὐαγόρας τῆς Κυπρίων ἀρχῆς ἐπέβη Ἀβδύμονα κατασχὼν τὸν Κιτιέα ταύτης ἐπάρχοντα· τίνα τε τρόπον Ἕλληνες οἱ σὺν Ἀγαμέμνονι τὴν Κύπρον κατέσχον, ἀπελάσαντες τοὺς μετὰ Κιννύρου [sic] ὧν εἰσὶν ὑπολιπεῖς Ἀμαθούσιοι· ὅπως τε ὁ βασιλεὺς Εὐαγόρα συνεπείσθη πολεμῆσαι. For the viable alternative spelling 'Kinnyras', see p214–215.

[59] So Baurain 1984:111.

like Teukros, Agapenor, and their bands of followers. Such further figures are certainly well *encompassed* by the expression. Yet the more natural reading of the Greek makes Agamemnon himself lead the showdown.[60]

We must therefore recognize, startling though it be, a tradition of the island's invasion by the Mycenaean king, accompanied by some portion of the returning Greek host.[61] And there is a remarkable parallel: according to medieval Cypriot tradition, the Greek expedition against Troy gathered not Aulis but Paphos, as it was from here—not Sparta—that Helen had been abducted![62] Such Cyprocentric variants obviously originated on the island itself, enduring into the fourth century and well beyond despite their inconsistency with the Panhellenic narrative of Homer.

R. Dussaud once suggested that Theopompos' myth reflected an historical breach of etiquette between Mycenae and Alashiya, precipitating a Greek takeover of Cyprus at the end of the LBA.[63] Writing before the discovery of Kinnaru at Ugarit, Dussaud supposed that Kinyras was an actual Alashiyan king, and envisioned a Mycenaean rout of his followers; fleeing from Enkomi (which Dussaud regarded as the Alashiyan capital), they settled in Amathous and Paphos.[64] Since Kinyras was in all probability *not* an historical individual, Dussaud's 'rout of the Kinyradai' must remain overly literal; and his political geography may be too specific. Nevertheless, if Kinyras was indeed a kind of royal persona in LBA Cyprus, as I shall argue (Chapter 15), the fate of the island *would* be very neatly mythologized as a decisive confrontation with Agamemnon.

---

[60] Thus, for example, in Neanthes FGH 84 F 31 (191), οἱ σὺν Εὐρυμένει is soon varied as τὸν μὲν Εὐρυμένην καὶ τοὺς σὺν αὐτῷ. The context is also clear in Philostephanos FHG 3:30 fr. 1: τῶν σὺν Μόψῳ ἀφικομένων. Other comparable and unambiguous expressions are e.g. Lucian *A True Story* 2.26: τοὺς δὲ ἀμφὶ τὸν Κινύραν; Eustathios on Dionysios the Periegete 11: οἱ περὶ τὸν Μενέλαον. Further parallels: Herodotos 5.58; Hellanikos FGH 4 F 31; Xenophon *Anabasis* 1.2.15, etc. Photios himself has Ἀδελφιὸς καὶ οἱ σὺν αὐτῷ, *Library* 12b30; Ἄτταλος καὶ οἱ σὺν αὐτῷ, 72a33. As a counterexample one might cite Xenophon *Anabasis* 4.1.1, οἱ σὺν Κύρῳ ἀναβάντες Ἕλληνες, where Cyrus is already dead; yet the aorist participle clarifies that σὺν Κύρῳ was true *in the past*. Without such qualification, we must assume the presence of Agamemnon.

[61] Agamemnon's direct agency is rightly accepted by Stiehle 1853:73–74; Cesnola 1877:4–5; Wagner 1891:182; HC:68; Gjerstad 1948:428–429; Kapera 1969; Kapera 1971:132; Kapera 1972:192; Dussaud 1950:58; Shrimpton 1991:90–91; Flower 1994:163.

[62] Reported by John Adorno (1470): "Helena while she was on her travels was captured at the temple [sc. of Venus at Paphos]" (SHC 8:173). There is a variant in Ludolf of Suchen (after 1350), *De itinere terrae sanctae liber* (Mas Latrie 1852–1861 1:211–212; SHC 8:169): *In hoc templo primo de perdicione Troye tractatum est, nam Helena tendens ad templum istud in via capta est* ("It was in this temple [of Venus at Old Paphos] that counsel was first taken regarding the destruction of Troy. For Helen was captured *en route* while journeying there"). Cf. Hogarth 1889:190.

[63] Recall that some conflict between Alashiya and Ahhiyawa is attested by the *Indictment of Madduwatta* (KUB 14.1 rev. 84–90 = CTH 147); but this is now dated to the fifteenth century: see p13n64.

[64] Dussaud 1950:58; cf. Baurain 1980b:299–300; Baurain 1984:111.

Kinyras and Pre-Greek Social Topography

The Theopompos fragment unambiguously links Kinyras to the island's pre-Greek population, and offers Amathous as its principal 'stronghold'. The city's partially non-Greek character is confirmed by ps.-Skylax, who called the Amathousians autochthonous.[65] As late as the fourth century (Theopompos' own day) the Amathousian kings, despite their Greek names, commissioned political and funerary inscriptions in the undeciphered language conventionally known as Eteocypriot—which, in bilingual settings, even enjoyed "la place d'honneur" ahead of the Greek.[66] That Amathous was not founded until ca. 1100 need not conflict with the tradition of pre-Greek 'origins'; compare the roughly contemporary transition from LBA Enkomi to nearby 'Teukrid' Salamis.[67] The city's indigenous orientation will also explain its description as the (or a) "most ancient city of Cyprus," and the (obviously erroneous) view that the island was originally called *Amathousía*.[68]

There must also have been communities outside of Amathous, of whatever size, that maintained some sense of pre-Greek identity. Ps.-Skylax, after calling several sites Greek, and Lapethos Phoenician, states that "there are also other non-Greek-speaking (*bárbaroi*) cities in the interior."[69] While this can certainly include further Phoenician centers (Idalion; Kition is on the coast), it could equally embrace other pre-Greek groups within the *póleis*. Several Eteocypriot inscriptions have been found at Paphos, with probably another from Kourion.[70] At least a hundred more examples, interpretable as neither

---

[65] [Skylax] 103 (GGM 1:78): Ἀμαθοῦς αὐτόχθονές εἰσιν. This and the following material is treated with undue skepticism by Reyes 1994:13–17 and Given 1998, despite the latter's excellent account of how the British colonial authority promoted the 'Eteocypriots' to undermine the Enosis movement. See the responses to Given by Petit 1999; Egetmeyer 2010; Steele 2011; Steele 2013:101 and n9.

[66] ICS 190–196 (quotation p207); DGAC:580–590; Steele 2013:99–172. The case for Eteocypriot as a late Hurrian dialect is renewed by Fournet 2013; for Hurrian as the/a language of the LBA Cypro-Minoan tablets, see p440n110.

[67] For Salamis, see p354. Cf. Papantonio 2012:281, "Such an autochthony legend could reinforce the anteriority of the Amathousians in Cyprus, and the mythological precedence of the local dynasty over the other *Basileis*."

[68] Herodian *De prosodia catholica* 242.34 Lentz (Ἀμαθοῦς πόλις Κύπρου ἀρχαιοτάτη, cf. Stephanos of Byzantium s.v. Ἀμαθοῦς) and p. 294.4 (Ἀμαθουσία. οὕτως ἐκαλεῖτο ἡ Κύπρος), cf. Pliny *Natural History* 5.35.129. Note also Étienne de Lusignan *Chorograffia* p. 9 (§12), where an indigenous horizon still older than 'pre-Greek' is envisioned: "Amathus was an ancient city, built before the gods came to the island." That these "descendants of the gods" ruled on the pre-Greek island is shown by e.g. p. 36 (§180), on Paphos (cited below, p561).

[69] [Skylax] 103 (GGM 1:78): εἰσὶ δὲ καὶ ἄλλαι πόλεις ἐν μεσογείᾳ βάρβαροι.

[70] Paphos: DGAC no. 123, 148–149, 249; Egetmeyer 2010:72–73; Steele 2013 no. EC 19–22, cf. pp. 119–120. Kourion: ICS 183; DGAC no. 10; Steele 2013 no. EC 23.

Chapter Fourteen

Greek nor Phoenician, have been found elsewhere on the island.[71] Of course, those who self-identified as neither Greek nor Phoenician need not themselves have been ethnically homogeneous: the Alashiyan onomasticon shows that the LBA island was already quite diverse.[72] Some hold, for instance, that a number of undeciphered inscriptions from Golgoi represent a pre-Greek language distinct from 'Amathousian'.[73]

But these ethnic and linguistic intricacies in no way invalidate Kinyras' function as a totalizing symbol of the pre-Greek island. And his connection with Amathous justifies extending this idea to his various toponymous relations. Kinyras is the trunk of a family tree whose roots and branches include a father Paphos and mother Paphos/Paphia; a mother Amathousa; sons Marieus (< Marion) and Koureus (< Kourion); and Kypros, either a son or daughter (the name is masculine in form, but islands are normally feminine).[74] It is probably significant that that these figures, in an arc Marion-Paphos-Kourion-Amathous, are concentrated in the southwestern part of the island; when the points are connected on a map, the area includes Alassa (with Kalavasos nearby) and the main distribution of Eteocypriot inscriptions.

The multiform clan of Kinyras neatly 'opposes' the Aegean migration legends. It does not follow, of course, that Greek and pre-Greek communities were always or ever strictly segregated. Thus, Aegean foundations appear side-by-side with Kinyras or his family at several sites (Paphos, Salamis, Kourion, and elsewhere).[75] It is unclear whether these Kinyrad toponyms were generated by pre-Greek communities, by the island's Grecophone element, were fabricated by early ethnographers like Hellanikos, or some combination. Probably

---

[71] Steele 2013:100–101.
[72] See p440.
[73] Egetmeyer 2010, 71, 73–74; Egetmeyer 2012; cf. Steele 2013:110–111; Fournet 2013:26–30.
[74] Son/Daughter Kypros: Philostephanos FHG 3:30 fr. 11; Istros FGH 334 F 45; Herodian *De prosodia catholica* 204.4 Lentz; Stephanos of Byzantium s.v. Κύπρος; Eustathios on Dionysios the Periegete 508–512; Constantine Porphyrogenitos *On the Themes* 1.15. Father/mother Paphos/Paphia: Σ Pindar *Pythian* 2.27a (father Paphos), 2.28 (mother Paphia or perhaps 'a Paphian nymph'; of course 'Paphia' was an epithet of the goddess herself); Ovid *Metamorphoses* 10.297–298 (Paphos, apparently feminine); Σ Dionysios the Periegete 509 (father Paphos); Hyginus *Fabulae* 242, 270, 275 (father Paphos); Theodontius in Boccaccio *Genealogy of the Pagan Gods* 2.50–51 had father Paphos, apparently misinterpreting Ovid (whence Bustron and *Chorograffia/Description*): see p499. Son Koureus: Herodian *De prosodia catholica* 200.2 and 358.19 Lentz; Stephanos of Byzantium s.v. Κούριον. Mother Amathousa: Herodian *De prosodia catholica* 242.34 Lentz; cf. Stephanos of Byzantium s.v. Ἀμαθοῦς. Son Marieus: Stephanos of Byzantium s.v. Μάριον. These sources are conveniently tabulated in Baurain 1980b. There is another probable reference to Paphos as the father of Kinyras in lines 4–13 of *Pap.Oxy.* 2688 (early third century CE): see further p499n30.
[75] That is, Agapenor versus the Kinyradai at Paphos (cf. p359–368); Teukros and the daughter of Kinyras at Salamis (see below); Argives versus Koureus son of Kinyras at Kourion. Presumably something similar is implied by Kinyras' associations with Lapethos and Tamassos (see p325), and perhaps indirectly with Idalion through his son 'Amaracus' (p331–332).

most lacked any real mythology (although an inventive poet or historian might weave them together, as did Nonnos; there is also the quasi-narrative treatment of 'Cinaras' and 'Curio' in Étienne de Lusignan).[76] They remain valuable nonetheless as ethno-historical ciphers.

A final topographical connection, which has presented a puzzle since antiquity, is the 'Cinyria' mentioned by Pliny as an abandoned site of uncertain location. I discuss this in Appendix E.

Salamis: Euagoras, Teukros, and the Daughter of Kinyras

We must now consider why Theopompos included Agamemnon's unthroning of Kinyras in recounting the career of Euagoras. This was surely not gratuitous detail, but integral to the logic of his narrative.[77]

Kinyras' defeat by Agamemnon, it has been suggested, made Cyprus "legitimately part of the Greek world" and "explains, if it does not justify, Euagoras the Greek's claim to legitimate rulership over that of Abdymon, whose name sounds distinctly barbarian."[78] That Theopompos himself developed such a polarized vision of Greeks versus others is not unlikely, given his treatment of Mopsos and the Meliac War in the same book.[79] And such a philhellenic Euagoras is found in Isokrates, whose eulogy of the king is decidedly anti-Persian in tone.[80]

Yet the traditional view that philhellenism was central to Euagoras' *own* political agenda (as opposed to Isokrates') has been well challenged by F. G. Maier, exposing as largely factoidal the assumption, omnipresent in older histories, that fifth-century Cyprus saw a general showdown between Greek-Cypriots and a Persian-Phoenician axis.[81] That idea is rather at odds with our current understanding of the island's ethnic complexity and the fairly general dispersal and mutual acculturation of its three (or more) populations.[82] Cypriot kings of all backgrounds, Maier contends, generally acted in their own interests, and this

---

[76] Nonnos *Dionysiaka* 13.432–463. For Étienne de Lusignan, see Appendix G.
[77] Not only did it survive the epitomizer's cuts, but, as Shrimpton 1991:91 points out, the digression ("if digression is the correct word") differed from others in not falling at a natural narrative break.
[78] So Shrimpton 1991, quotations from 73 and 91; similarly Baurain 1984:112.
[79] See p347.
[80] See e.g. Isokrates 9.19–20 (addressed to Nikokles I, 374–ca. 360). One may note here the biographical tradition that makes Theopompos a student of Isokrates; but Flower 1994:42–62 argues that this is a Hellenistic fiction.
[81] Maier 1985.
[82] Seibert 1976.

sometimes led *incidentally* to confrontations between Greek- and Phoenician-Cypriots, and, following the Ionian revolt, with the Persians.[83]

The point is well taken. Nevertheless, we should not dismiss all ethnic distinctions on the island as meaningless. The very fact that communities cultivated legends about their past shows that such affiliations mattered to them. Such beliefs could therefore be politically exploited; and if this were to coincide with the interests of a Cypriot king, why would he have hesitated to do so?

I would like to take a middle position and argue that both tendencies—ethnic openness, and political rivalry articulated along ethnic lines—were variously operative in Euagoras' bid for power and influence, and that Kinyras had an important role to play therein. A key passage comes from Diodoros:

> [Euagoras] tried to make the whole island his own. Mastering some of the cities by force, adding others by persuasion, he soon gained leadership over the rest. But the men of Amathous, Soloi, and Kition, resisting under arms, sent ambassadors to Artaxerxes king of the Persians for help.[84]

The resistance of largely Greek-oriented Soloi clearly illustrates Maier's principle of ethnically indifferent self-interest. But it can hardly be coincidence that Amathous and Kition were the island's two sites with the most pronounced non-Greek cultural orientation (note that Amathous had not joined in defecting from Persia after the Ionian Revolt).[85] And once war was drawn along these lines, an aspect of ethnic disharmony may well have presented itself, even if political expediency played the leading part.[86] Kition served the Persians as their main naval base on the island, and the city probably flourished accordingly; no doubt this would perfectly suit its kings' own aggressive ambitions. Still, this privileged position may have been due not only to Kition's important harbor, but to its cultural ties with the mainland, making it somehow more familiar and manageable in Persian eyes. Similarly Phoenician/Tyrian political control of Kition had probably emerged in the late

---

[83] Cf. Seibert 1976:26.
[84] Diodoros Siculus 14.98: ἐπεχείρησεν ἅπασαν τὴν νῆσον σφετερίσασθαι. τῶν δὲ πόλεων ἃς μὲν βίᾳ χειρωσάμενος, ἃς δὲ πειθοῖ προσλαβόμενος, τῶν μὲν ἄλλων πόλεων ταχὺ τὴν ἡγεμονίαν παρέλαβεν, Ἀμαθούσιοι δὲ καὶ Σόλιοι καὶ Κιτιεῖς ἀντέχοντες τῷ πολέμῳ πρέσβεις ἀπέστειλαν πρὸς Ἀρταξέρξην τὸν τῶν Περσῶν βασιλέα περὶ βοηθείας.
[85] Cf. Tuplin 1996:75–76 (Amathous "is a case history which discloses that it is not simply ridiculous to think Cypriot politics and international relations to have had some ethnic component").
[86] So rightly Tuplin 1996:76 §4(a).

eighth century under Assyrian patronage.[87] It was here that Sargon erected his stele (ca. 707).[88]

Such intra-Cypriot issues might be dismissed as irrelevant to the interpretation of Theopompos himself, who was free to develop whatever historical framework he wished; on this view, Kinyras could enter his narrative as mere ornamentation, with no immediate connection to the realities of Euagoras' career. Yet a crucial datum, preserved uniquely by Pausanias (second century CE), makes it quite likely that Theopompos' Kinyras digression was intended to illuminate propaganda of the Salaminian king himself. Pausanias, it should be emphasized, drew regularly on Theopompos, and his familiarity with the book in question is shown by his discussion elsewhere of Mopsos' expulsion of the Carians from Colophon.[89] This makes it very probable that Theopompos is also his source for the passage we are about to examine.

Pausanias, in his tour of Athens, refers to a statue of Euagoras, also known to Isokrates.[90] This the Athenians erected in gratitude for the king's role in brokering a Cypro-Phoenician naval contingent, under the command of Konon who was in exile at his court, to support the Athenian fleet against the Spartans at Knidos:

> Near the stoa stands Konon and his son Timotheos, and Euagoras, king of the Cypriots, who caused the Phoenician triremes to be given to Konon by King Artaxerxes. He acted as an Athenian (*hōs Athēnaîos*), since he traced his ancestry back to Salamis via Teukros and a daughter of Kinyras.[91]

With the victory at Knidos, Euagoras and his sons were awarded front-row seating at Athenian festivals in perpetuity. Euagoras had previously been granted Athenian citizenship (his friendly relations with the city are attested by inscriptions from ca. 410).[92] This accounts for *hōs Athēnaîos* in our passage. But Pausanias also shows that Euagoras' honorary citizenship, though spurred by

---

[87] For further observations on the relationship with Persia, see Smith 2008:261, 264–278.
[88] Sargon stele: ARAB 2:102 §186; Reyes 1994:24, 51, with further literature.
[89] Pausanias 7.3.1–2 must derive from Theopompos' use of the Mopsos legend in connection with the Meliac War: see p347n57.
[90] Isokrates 9.57.
[91] Pausanias 1.3.2: πλησίον δὲ τῆς στοᾶς Κόνων ἕστηκε καὶ Τιμόθεος υἱὸς Κόνωνος καὶ βασιλεὺς Κυπρίων Εὐαγόρας, ὃς καὶ τὰς τριήρεις τὰς Φοινίσσας ἔπραξε παρὰ βασιλέως Ἀρταξέρξου δοθῆναι Κόνωνι· ἔπραξε δὲ ὡς Ἀθηναῖος καὶ τὸ ἀνέκαθεν ἐκ Σαλαμῖνος, ἐπεὶ καὶ γενεαλογῶν ἐς προγόνους ἀνέβαινε Τεῦκρον καὶ Κινύρου θυγατέρα.
[92] Isokrates 9.54; cf. Demosthenes 12.10. The relevant inscriptions are IG I³ no. 113 (SEG 34:24), ca. 410; IG II² no. 20 (ca. 393/392) no. 716. Cf. HC:128–129, 131.

his benefactions (he is *euergétēs* in the inscriptions), was nevertheless grounded in a quasi-legal appeal to his alleged Teukrid ancestry, via a daughter of Kinyras (probably the Eue or Eune or Eunoe mentioned as Teukros' bride elsewhere).[93] This must also be why Isokrates emphasizes Euagoras' Teukrid descent, to which he attributes the virtues of the Salaminian royal line and the king's admirable achievement in restoring it to power.[94]

Teukros, as an eponym of the 'Teukrians', is a multiform figure involved in a bewildering array of very early legends that connect him especially with the Troad and migrations thence. Homer's Teukros is apparently but one special development.[95] An eponymous relationship between Teukros and the Tjekkeru of the Sea Peoples inscriptions remains very seductive,[96] given that Salamis arose in the eleventh century after several generations' decline at Enkomi.[97] The contemporary (?) *Tale of Wen-Amun* paints a comparable picture, with the Tjekkeru pursuing the title character between Byblos and Cyprus, where Egyptian is no longer understood.[98] There is also Vergil's picture of political disorder on Cyprus shortly after the Trojan War: Teukros was permitted to settle there by the grace of 'Belos', king of Sidon, who was in the process of ravaging the island.[99] Although clearly fictional in most respects, the atmosphere this passage evokes—war, hostile immigration, and political decentralization—is also 'right' to some extent, at least as a generalized popular memory. It is worth noting that Belos is sometimes made ruler of Egypt—in ps.-Apollodoros, for example, he is the son of Poseidon and the Egyptian princess 'Libya', while his twin brother Agenor moves to Phoenicia—probably reflecting popular recollection of NK expansion in the Levant.[100] Such a Belos, giving Teukros a place on Cyprus, would remind one of Ramses III's 'settlement' of the Philistines, and his claimed conquest of Cypriot cities.[101]

An Athenocentric wrinkle was eventually introduced to the story. For Homer, Teukros was the half-brother of Ajax—sharing a father in king Telamon of Salamis in the Saronic Gulf, but having for his mother Hesione, daughter of

---

[93] Σ Lykophron *Alexandra* 450: Τεῦκρος … ἐλθὼν ἐν Κύπρῳ Σαλαμῖνα κτίσας ᾤκησε καὶ γήμας Εὔην τὴν Κύπρου Ἀστερίαν ἐγέννησεν, with variants in Scheer's *ap. crit*. This identification, requiring minor emendation (τὴν Κινύρου or τὴν Κινύρου τοῦ βασιλέως Κύπρου, *vel sim*.), goes back to Engel 1841 2:125; cf. Stoll in Roscher *Lex*. s.v. Kinyras col. 1191; Cayla 2005:230.
[94] Isokrates 9.18-19.
[95] See Gjerstad 1944:114-120 with further references.
[96] Gjerstad 1944:119-120; Giuffrida 1996:285. For the inscription, see p13.
[97] Salamis: Karageorghis 1969:21. For the gradual abandonment of Enkomi, Webb 2001.
[98] *CS* 1 no. 41. Cf. above p14.
[99] Vergil *Aeneid* 1.619-622: *Atque equidem Teucrum memini Sidona venire / finibus expulsum patriis, nova regna petentem / auxilio Beli; genitor tum Belus opimam / vastabat Cyprum, et victor dicione tenebat*.
[100] [Apollodoros] *Library* 2.1.4.
[101] See p14.

Laomedon of Troy. In the Catalogue of Ships, Ajax stations twelve vessels alongside the Athenian phalanxes; a scholiast asserts that this was an interpolation by Solon (fl. ca. 600) to support the Athenian claim on Salamis, which was disputed with Aegina.[102] Later still, it seems, comes the story of Telamon banishing Teukros for failing to avenge Ajax' death at Troy. Wandering east, Teukros came by various routes to Cyprus, landing by tradition at the 'beach of the Achaeans' on the Karpass peninsula, and so founded Salamis.[103] Gjerstad attractively argued that Teukros' exile from Saronic Salamis grew from Athenian diplomatic relations with Cypriot Salamis, following Athenian intervention on the island after the Ionian Revolt (much as Akamas, Demophon, and Phaleros were linked with Soloi and Khytroi).[104] It remains slightly puzzling, however, that Pindar would present this version of events in a poem for an *Aeginetan* recipient.[105] It may be that the mythological link between the two Salamises is earlier and more complex than appears.[106]

However the Teukrid link between Saronic and Cypriot Salamis arose, it is certain that Euagoras, in using the 'Athenian Teukros' to promote his cause, was sensitive to the political advantages of mythical genealogy. It is therefore reasonable to suppose that he made comparable use of the "daughter of Kinyras." But to what end? One must consider her potential appeal to two broad audiences, Athenian and Cypriot.

A maternal descent from Kinyras would seem, *prima facie*, to have little claim on Athenian affections. And yet a kind of 'Athenian Kinyras' is indeed found in two sources, partially cognate, which trace the Cypriot king's ancestry back, through extraneous local traditions, to Kephalos son of Herse, daughter of Kekrops—that is, to the legendary royal house of Athens.[107] As these texts belong otherwise to a group allying Kinyras to Cilicia, I shall present them separately

---

[102] Homer *Iliad* 2.557–558; Σ Homer *Iliad* 2.494–877: Σόλων τὴν Σαλαμῖνα Ἀθηναίοις ἀπένειμε διὰ τὸ "Αἴας δ' ἐκ Σαλαμῖνος ἄγεν δυοκαίδεκα νῆας."

[103] Aiskhylos *Persians* 895; Pindar *Nemean* 4.46–47 with Σ; Euripides *Helen* 144–150; Isokrates 9.18; [Aristotle] *Peplos* (fr. 640 §8 Rose); Klearkhos fr. 19 Wehrli (= Athenaios 256b), a Cypriot native; Lykophron *Alexandra* 450–478; *Parian Marble* A 26; Vergil *Aeneid* 1.619–622; Strabo 14.6.3 (with 'beach of the Achaeans' as the landing place of Teukros); Tacitus 3.62; Pausanias 1.3.2; Nonnos *Dionysiaka* 13.461–462; John Malalas *Chronography* 5.29 Thurn. Sources in Chavane and Yon 1978:33–91; cf. HC:85. Herodotos 7.90 is also relevant. A good account of the evidence is Gantz 1993:694–695.

[104] Gjerstad 1944:119–120.

[105] Pindar *Nemean* 4.46–47.

[106] Engel 1841 2:126–127 speculated on deeper links between the myth cycles of Saronic and Cypriot Salamis.

[107] Σ Dionysios the Periegete 509 = FGH 758 F 3a; [Apollodoros] *Library* 3.14.3. The Athenian dimension of these constructions was recognized by Engel 1841 1:183–186, 2:130–133; Robert 1883:441; Baurain 1975–1976:525; Baurain 1980a:9; Baurain 1980b:282.

in Chapter 21. The important point here is that Euagoras, by backing a Kephalid descent for Kinyras, could have supported his Teukrid claim to Athenian citizenship—with a good dose of sophistry—on both sides of the family (a live issue since Perikles' citizenship law of 451).[108] Moreover, the version of ps.-Apollodoros presents potential points of contact with Euagoras' career and propaganda. The mythographer has Kinyras cross "with a host" from Cilicia to Cyprus, found Paphos, and marry Metharme, daughter of Pygmalion.[109] Just such a crossing launched Euagoras' own career (noting that Cilicia too had traditions of Achaean and Teukrid settlement[110]). The dynastic link to Pygmalion may also be significant (see below).

An Atthidographic source for the 'Athenian' Kinyras has long been suspected.[111] Hellanikos (ca. 480–395) has been suggested, though no reasons have been given.[112] It is a good guess,[113] but equally probable is Phileas, an Athenian geographer contemporary with Hellanikos, who treated the connection with Cyprus of a certain Aoios son of Kephalos; for this same Aoios is elsewhere brother of Paphos and uncle of Kinyras (see further Chapter 21).[114] It is perhaps hard to understand how such mythological concoctions could be made to carry any real political weight. Yet the pioneering synthesis of local myth with public inscriptions and archives by late fifth-century antiquarians will have seemed like cutting-edge historical science to many.[115] Under these conditions, an astute politician might readily turn such 'discoveries' to good account—just as Solon had exploited Homer to join Salamis to Athens.

---

[108] Aristotle *Constitution of the Athenians* 26.3; Plutarch *Perikles* 37.2–5.

[109] [Apollodoros] *Library* 3.14.3.

[110] Ajax son of Teukros was said to have initiated a hereditary Teukrid priesthood at Olbe: Strabo 14.5.10; cf. 14.5.8, Cilician Soloi founded by Achaeans and Rhodians.

[111] This was supposed by Robert 1883:441.

[112] Giuffrida 1996:292n51.

[113] The Lesbian historian, who must have traveled widely in collecting material for his regional histories (Dionysios of Halicarnassus *On Thucydides* 5.1), composed a *Kypriaka*, the one certain fragment of which relates to Pygmalion's founding of Karpasia—close to where one might naturally land when crossing from Cilicia (see p345 and n3, with Chuvin's proposed connection of [Apollodoros] *Library* 3.14.3 and Hellanikos FGH 4 F 57). Hellanikos, whose later career was much occupied with fabricating an Athenian past, was a master of devising early genealogies out of legendary materials and tailoring them to local interests (Franklin 2012). A hitherto unnoticed Cypriot example should be registered here: Hellanikos, in making Euklees/Euklous older than Homer in an ultimate descent from Orpheus, probably followed an insular tradition for the Cypriot prophet-poet of this name (Hellanikos FGH 4 F 5b). Finally, the time of Hellanikos' professional activity substantially overlaps Athens' alliance with Euagoras.

[114] *Etymologicum Genuinum* s.v. Ἄῷος; *Etymologicum Magnum* s.v. Ἄῷος (*sic*); Σ Dionysios the Periegete 509 (GGM 2:450) = FGH 758 F 3a.

[115] Criticism of their methods was not long in coming from some quarters: see for instance Philokhoros FGH 328 F 92 on Hellanikos.

However Euagoras may have presented matters to his Athenian allies, a professed Kinyrad ancestry will necessarily have carried greater weight on Cyprus. And since the island was itself ethnically heterogeneous, the 'daughter of Kinyras' will have spoken differently to different groups.

It must remain possible that earlier Salaminian kings had already Kinyradized their Teukrid ancestry for reasons now obscure. But if I am right that the Liar King portrait of Kinyras stems from regional rivalry between Paphos and Salamis in the Archaic period,[116] a Teukrid family relationship with Kinyras must have been a later development. It would then be most economical to suspect that Euagoras himself was responsible, both because he was clearly prepared to exploit ancient history, and because it is for him that the Kinyras connection is actually named. And, as it happens, a plausible political explanation has recently come to light.

A Phoenician inscription discovered at Larnaka/Kition in 1990 records a victory by king Milkyaton, in the first year of his reign (perhaps 392/391), over "our enemies and their Paphian allies (*w'zrnm hppym*)."[117] It is quite certain that these enemies are the Salaminians, given that the date falls squarely within the decades of Euagoras' expansionist undertakings, and that Kition is known to have resisted him by force. The real surprise is to find Paphos, about which virtually nothing was known for this period, in the position of Euagoras' most noteworthy ally.[118] Clearly this was one of the cities he won over through "persuasion"; indeed the inscription suggests that the *hēgemonía* with which Diodoros credits Euagoras should be interpreted rather loosely, at least as regards Paphos.

This alliance might very well have been underpinned by a newly 'discovered' dynastic marriage between Teukros and the Kinyrad house. It was quite usual for political alignments to be expressed by grafting mythological limbs to family trees.[119] And yet it will have been an embarrassment, on my hypothesis, that Kinyras had once been smeared by Salaminian singers as a Liar King. Is it mere coincidence that Alkidamas presented his whitewashing 'Defense of Kinyras' right around this time?[120] While the tongue-in-cheek tone of that work

---

[116] See p345.
[117] Yon and Sznycer 1991:799–800 et passim; Yon 2004:201 no. 1144 with further references, cf. 142 no. 180; Lipiński 2004:94–95 and n331.
[118] The root sense of the Phoenician word is 'help': see Krahmalkov 2000:363–364.
[119] This can be seen, for instance, in the Lydian royal line, where the intrusion of Belos and Ninos represented the client relationship with Assyria in the seventh century; the alleged descent from Herakles probably reflects alliance with Sparta in the sixth: Burkert 1995:144–145; Franklin 2008:195.
[120] See p343n32. A. Chaniotis compares the roughly contemporary rehabilitation of Minos as a wise lawgiver, apparently connected with the publication of the *Laws of Minos* by Kharon of Lampsakos (communication, December 19, 2011).

Chapter Fourteen

hardly suggests propaganda, it would read well as a satiric response, following contemporary literary fashions, to some recent public visibility of Kinyras in Athens. Euagoras' prominence there imposes itself as a promising stimulus.

Diodoros' account of Euagoras prevailing over the Cypriot cities through persuasion or force indicates a two-stage policy in which he first attempted to win over *all* his insular peers by appealing to the political, economic, ethnic, or other ideological interests of each. Only when that failed would it be worth resorting to arms. One should therefore consider how Euagoras may have hoped that a claim of Kinyrad ancestry would 'persuade' not only Paphos, but the other cities as well. The explanation, I suggest, is that he wished to balance the Greek associations of his Teukrid ancestry with an appeal to other Cypriot populations. If the intensity of ethnic rivalries on the island has been overemphasized in the past, nonetheless for a king who aimed at island-wide control the value of cultivating universal appeal is obvious. Indeed Euagoras' hybrid heritage may have been designed precisely to *promote* ethnic harmony, not the reverse. That Theopompos specifically dealt with the Amathousians as descendants of Kinyras' men may even echo some of Euagoras' rhetoric in trying to win that city over. A Cypro-Phoenician aspect would also be seen in Kinyras' marriage into the house of Pygmalion, who clearly resonates with the dynastic names of Kition (Milkyaton's son was Pumayyaton). Kinyras/Pygmalion might have served Euagoras equally well in his ephemeral holdings on the Phoenician coast, given the traditions of 'Kinyras' at Byblos and perhaps Sidon (Chapters 19 and 20).

Kinyras would also have admirably reflected Euagoras' ambition to control the whole island, being remembered as the last king to have done so.[121] Note that many of the virtues that Isokrates ascribes to Euagoras can be paralleled with those attributed to Kinyras, which, I shall argue, perpetuate a memory of Alashiyan ideology.[122] Even if this is largely coincidental—wise and benevolent rulers are bound to share many characteristics[123]—one may at least say that Kinyras, as such a figure, would contribute positively to Euagoras' pedigree and public image.

To conclude, on Cyprus itself Euagoras will have balanced any philhellenism he may have felt personally, or projected to his Athenian allies, with a more inclusive appeal to the island's ancient traditions. This was evidently partially successful (Paphos and elsewhere), but in the end he could not overcome the

---

[121] But recall the possible tradition of 'Argive' overlordship associated with the figure of Dmetor (p342–343), seconded by the elaborations of Étienne de Lusignan (see p558n8, 561n32), and perhaps related somehow to Agamemnon's invasion of the island.
[122] See p381–383.
[123] Isokrates lavished similar praise on Nikokles I in the *Ad Nicoclem* (Isokrates 2).

political and/or ethnic disinclinations of Soloi, Amathous, Kition, and whatever other cities he was obliged to assail. Theopompos' digression on the showdown of Kinyras and Agamemnon was probably intended to illuminate both the Kinyrad and Teukrid branches of Euagoras' family tree—but perhaps especially the former, which will have been less immediately intelligible for an extra-Cypriot readership. Euagoras himself, however, is unlikely to have made *divisive* use of the Kinyras and Agamemnon myth, which would hardly have endeared him to Amathous, Paphos, or Kition. I suggest, therefore, that Theopompos inserted the Unthroning of Kinyras on his own initiative to explain the 'daughter of Kinyras' and provide 'historical' background for the arrival of Teukros himself. Nor is it unlikely that his account of the "men with Agamemnon" dealt with other migration figures—Agapenor, for instance.

Paphos: Agapenor, Laodike, and the Arcadian Connection

Agapenor appears in Homer's Catalogue of Ships as the king of Tegea who led an Arcadian contingent to Troy. These mountain-bound landlubbers, lacking a fleet of their own, sailed in ships on loan from Agamemnon.[124] Such participation would naturally imply that Agapenor was one of Helen's suitors, and we find him duly listed as such by ps.-Apollodoros.[125] Yet everything else we know about him concerns his migration to Cyprus.[126] The main ancient source is Pausanias (n.b.), who states all-too-briefly that the storm that scattered the returning Greeks drove the Arcadian squadron to the island, where Agapenor founded (New) Paphos and the temple to Aphrodite at Old Paphos.[127] The cryptic Lykophron does nothing to clarify matters, although he includes one point of considerable interest. It is only in Étienne de Lusignan that we find any further detail. I will discuss both of these passages below.

It might be suggested that Agapenor himself did not enter Cypriot legend before the island's exposure to the mainstream epic tradition. But this is the wrong way around. An epichoric bid for Panhellenic integration would not have used such an obscure figure; rather:

---

[124] Homer *Iliad* 2.603–614; cf. Thucydides 1.9; Pausanias 8.1.3; [Apollodoros] *Epitome* 3.12.
[125] [Apollodoros] *Library* 3.10.8.
[126] [Aristotle] *Peplos* (fr. 640 §30 Rose); Lykophron *Alexandra* 479–493; Strabo 14.6.3; Pausanias 8.5.2 (see next note), 8.53.7; [Apollodoros] *Epitome* 6.15; cf. Herodotos 7.90 (Arcadians, Agapenor not mentioned).
[127] Pausanias 8.5.2, where Πάφου οἰκιστής must correspond to Nea Paphos by contrast with ἐν Παλαιπάφῳ τὸ ἱερόν.

> The Arcadians are there [in the Catalogue of Ships] because they must be given a place in this (late!) Panhellenic pageant ... The Homeric treatment is embarrassing ... the Arcadians obviously know nothing about ships and sailing ... [Agapenor] never takes part in any fighting: his presence at Troy is completely otiose.[128]

Here then is our clearest evidence of an early Cypriot migration legend that became known outside of the island, and earned a glancing notice in the Catalogue. One may guess that this is because the Paphian royal house enjoyed a comparatively high international profile in the Archaic period, thanks to its world-famous sanctuary.

The antiquity of the legend is confirmed by Agapenor's Arcadian origin itself. This, given the kinship of the Cypriot dialects with those of historical Arcadia and the earlier Mycenaean of Linear B, must be essentially 'right', at least as a symbol of *general* population movement.[129] That Paphos is the area in which the island's Arcado-Cypriot dialect is first attested (ca. 1050–950) is at least a striking coincidence.[130]

So Agapenor was a genuine and early Cypriot legend. More elusive is his position *vis-à-vis* the historical kings of Paphos, who proclaimed their descent from the pre-Greek Kinyras by the fifth century (Pindar) and probably well before, yet bore Greek names already in the seventh.[131] True, the monumental inscriptions of Archaic Amathous show that Greek royal names could coexist with public professions of pre-Greek identity.[132] And yet the connection in local legend of Amathous with the "remnants of the men around Kinyras" should equally imply a belief—at least in Amathous (Theopompos) and probably elsewhere (Lusignan: see below)—that Kinyras' line had *lost power* at Paphos, whose historical kings were therefore not 'really' Kinyradai. And that Agapenor established his own dynasty at Paphos would be, after all, a natural inference from the legend, well paralleled by Teukros at Salamis.

An overlooked source here is Étienne de Lusignan, who offers a more expansive version of events than Pausanias:

---

[128] A. Cassio (communication, February 2012). I thank him for his useful discussion of these points.

[129] 'Arcadian' in these traditions may be shorthand for 'culture and language of the pre-Doric Peloponnese surviving only in Arcadia, whose linguistic and cultural affinities with Cyprus were still recognized'. But for Agapenor's specific link to Tegea, see further below.

[130] Cf. Voyatzis 1985:161; Coldstream 1989:331; Pirenne-Delforge 1994:326; Hall 1997:135–136. For the Opheltas *obelós*, see p14.

[131] See further p407–409. The first named Paphian king, found in the Esarhaddon prism inscription (673/672), is 'Ituandar' = Etewandros: ARAB 2:266 §690 (cf. above p14).

[132] See p349.

> Agapenore stopped in the area of Paffo, and there he was crowned king. He banished from the kingdom the kings who had descended from the gods; then he built a city called Paffo, in memory of the old royal city. The banished descendants of the gods, however, moved to the city of Curias [Kourion] and reigned there and in other Cypriot cities.[133]

As always with this remarkable historian, it is hard to know what has found its way from a lost ancient source, what from oral tradition, and what is his own imaginative interpretation or extrapolation (see Appendix G). But the present passage, on the whole, seems to have some ancient or traditional basis. Lusignan's portrayal of Agapenor as a conquering king could be seen as heavy-handed historicism, were it not for the 'rout' of the former royal line, which cannot be dismissed so easily. The historian makes clear elsewhere that Paphos was the kingdom of "the god Cinaras," father of 'Curio' (< Koureus < Kourion), whom in turn he makes the father of a younger, mortal 'Cinaras'.[134] Even if this use of genealogy to disambiguate two Kinyrases is probably Lusignan's own invention, his 'rout of the Kinyradai' is essentially what we find in Theopompos. And yet these two rout scenarios, though obviously cognate—and geographically quite compatible—are not identical: Lusignan overlooks Amathous, which is not even mentioned, to account for Kourion—midway between Paphos and Amathous (and not far from Limassol, where Lusignan was vicar from 1564-1568[135])—and "other Cypriot cities."[136] So here too, I suggest, is a genuine popular tradition, about an explicitly Greek 'takeover' of the Kinyrad dynasty at Paphos. Note that elsewhere Lusignan specifies that Agapenor's descendants continued to rule at Paphos.[137]

Of course Lusignan's larger history is larded with artificial, anachronistic, and erroneous elements. Given a conquering Agapenor, there is little justification for building a new "Paffo in memory of the old royal city." That this is a piece of Lusignan's own illogic is suggested by his appeal elsewhere to earthquake damage as an explanation for the Arcadian's new foundation.[138] Or perhaps he depends here on medieval tradition, since numerous historical earthquakes at

---

[133] Étienne de Lusignan *Chorograffia* p. 36 (§180).
[134] *Chorograffia* p. 20a (§71, 73, cf. *Description* pp. 38a-39). See further Appendix G.
[135] Grivaud in Papadopoulos 2004 2:iv.
[136] Lusignan's failure to mention Amathous suffices to show that he has not simply adapted the Photian epitome (see p346) for his own purposes.
[137] *Chorograffia* p. 6a (§6).
[138] *Description*, p. 15a.

Chapter Fourteen

Paphos are attested over the centuries, and they had a major impact on popular imagination.[139]

Ultimately, however, Agapenor's association with Nea Paphos seems to go back to an historically false 'tradition' promoted in the Classical period. For this city was not formally founded until the late fourth century, when it was walled by Nikokles II (died ca. 310; henceforth 'Nikokles'); nor has it produced much evidence of habitation earlier than the Archaic period—although tombs from Iskender, on the outskirts of Ktima (upper New Paphos), may go back to the tenth century.[140] This 'new Agapenor' is found in both Strabo and Pausanias.[141] T. B. Mitford plausibly suggested that Agapenor was purposefully redeployed to New Paphos at the time of Nikokles' foundation, as a means of separating two putative royal lines.[142] If so, Agapenor's landing and first settlement was probably said to be at this harbor, while Kinyras was associated with Old Paphos, where Nikokles himself held sway—the last of the Kinyrad kings, as it would prove (see Chapter 16). It is probably relevant that Nikokles promoted at least three cult-sites for Olympian deities at Nea Paphos.[143]

And yet *any* official use of the Agapenor legend presupposes his royal status, which is also assumed by the Catalogue of Ships. *A priori* then there must have existed traditions connecting Agapenor to *Old* Paphos. A trace of this 'old Agapenor' is found in Pausanias, who credits him with founding not only the new city, but also Aphrodite's ancient sanctuary.[144] If Pausanias did indeed draw on Theopompos for Euagoras' descent from a daughter of Kinyras, as I have argued, the historian could well have been his source also for the 'old' Agapenor—storm-tossed founder and temple-builder—and it would follow that Theopompos made Agapenor's position at Paphos agree with the larger theme of Kinyras' unthroning.

---

[139] Earthquakes that affected Paphos are recorded for 15 BCE, 77/76 CE, 332, and the twelfth century; another destroyed Salamis in 322, while some of the eight shocks documented for Antioch between 458–561 are likely to have been felt on Cyprus. See HC:232, 245, 279n4, 311. These events are mentioned very often in ancient, and especially Byzantine, sources, as one can see by going through the texts in SHC. Note e.g. John Adorno (1470): "Paphos that now is almost destroyed" (SHC 8:173).

[140] *Paphos*:20; NPHP:67–85.

[141] See p359n126. Lusignan acknowledges Strabo as a source elsewhere, although he also makes the unparalleled assertion that Strabo himself had been a student of the Cypriot historian Xenophon: see further p564–567.

[142] Mitford 1960b:198.

[143] See p409.

[144] See p359 and n127 above.

Restringing Kinyras

There can be no doubt that the alternative tradition of the sanctuary's consecration by Kinyras goes back to the Paphian dynasty itself.[145] But how does this square with the 'old Agapenor'? The dual tradition must be somehow related to the historical meeting of Greek and pre-Greek at Palaipaphos. But what exactly is implied? Karageorghis and Maier explained it thus:

> The first Achaeans did not forcibly impose their rule upon the city but settled there after peaceful negotiations ... The apparent contradiction between Cinyras and Agapenor conceals a complex historical situation: the existence of a pre-Greek Cypriote city and the impact of the first Achaean colonists. As regards the Sanctuary, Cinyras in a similar way may represent an already established fertility cult, Agapenor its adaptation by the Greeks through the building of a monumental shrine.[146]

This harmonizing approach clearly has merit, even if one questions the specific scenario proposed—as Maier himself did only two years later, stressing the lack of clear archaeological criteria, and arguing that the sanctuary's monumentalization actually antedates the Greek influx.[147] The lack of Aegean architectural elements shows in any case that the outward image of the cult continued unbroken.[148] Thus whatever the ethnic orientation of those who held power in the EIA, it is likely that the older royal apparatus remained at least superficially intact, just as the Kinyrad tradition asserts. As M. Iacovou writes:

> It is more than likely that [the Kouklia and Kition sanctuaries] continued to fulfill their original role. Monumentality defines power and, in the case of the Cypriot sanctuaries, it embodies the strength to control an economy traditionally based on the production and exchange of metal resources.[149]

Given such a scenario of Aegean adaptation to Cypriot cult and royal ideology,[150] a stray detail in Lykophron's otherwise inane treatment of Agapenor

---

[145] See p401–406.
[146] *Paphos*: 79–80, 101. Similarly Gjerstad 1944:110–112; Maier 1983:229n6; Voyatzis 1985:154; Karageorghis 1998:32.
[147] Maier 1986b. The Paphian cult per se was of course much older: Heubner 1963–1982 2:34; Masson 1973:113; Maier 1974; J. Karageorghis 1977:30, 223–224; Maier 1979:234; Fortin 1980:37; CAH² III.1:514; *Paphos*:81–102; Maier 1986a:313; Karageorghis 1998:32–33; Webb 1999:63–64; *Kypris*:26–29.
[148] Cf. Iacovou 2005:132.
[149] Iacovou 2005:132; cf. Iacovou 2006b:46.
[150] This has seemed plausible to Karageorghis 1980a:122–123; Fortin 1980:35–39, 44; Voyatzis 1985; Maier 1986b. A similar situation *vis-à-vis* Aegean settlement in North Syria and Philistia is suggested by the stories of Mopsos/Moxos and Askalos—respectively drowning and marrying

Chapter Fourteen

takes on new importance—recalling that the poet drew upon Cypriot traditions via lost works of Eratosthenes and Philostephanos. Kassandra predicts that Agapenor "will dig for copper and ... mine every pit with his pick."[151] This has a realistic ring, since the island's mineral resources must have been a major draw for Aegean settlement (recall Khalkanor seeking the rising sun at Idalion).[152] Given the LBA institutions of sacred metallurgy centered on the sanctuaries of the goddess, Agapenor here seems to be playing, or rather perpetuating, a truly Cypriot royal role: one may detect a 'Kinyradized' Agapenor, given Kinyras' own legendary status as a metallurgical pioneer (Chapter 13). I have already contemplated a rather similar Greco-Cypriot fusion in the warrior-lyrist of the Kouklia kalathos.[153]

Given the persistent and awkward tension between a tradition of Arcadian kingship on the one hand, and the maintenance of a Kinyrad royal pose on the other, it is unsurprising that the evidence for Agapenor is relatively scarce, and that he was seemingly 'banished' to New Paphos. Nevertheless, the need to accommodate Arcadians within a Paphian royal framework has left several traces in legends about two women named Laodike.

Pausanias follows his terse notice of Agapenor's voyage with this statement: "at a later time Laodike, born of Agapenor, sent a *péplos* to Athena Alea at Tegea."[154] Pausanias had before him a garment purporting to be this relic, which bore the following inscription:

> This *péplos* is Laodike's: she devoted it to her Athena,
> To her wide-spaced fatherland, from Cyprus most divine.[155]

The verses are no older than the fourth century, the robe they graced probably replacing an older one destroyed by fire in 394 BCE.[156] Later, Pausanias, in describing the sacred structures of Tegea, credits the same Laodike with

---

a local woman, one of whom is definitely a goddess-figure, Atargatis. Mopsos/Moxos: Xanthos FGH 765 F 17a = Athenaios 346e, cf. Mnaseas FHG 3:155 fr. 32. Askalos: Xanthos FGH 765 F 8 = Nikolaos of Damascus FGH 90 F 18 = Stephanos of Byzantium s.v. Ἀσκάλων. Cf. Finkelberg 2005:158, "Xanthos' story seems to imply that Mopsos was regarded as the founder of the cult of the 'Askalon goddess'."

[151] Lykophron *Alexandra* 484–485: χαλκωρυχήσει καὶ ... / ... δικέλλῃ πᾶν μεταλλεύων γνύθος (cf. Σ).
[152] Coldstream 1994:145; Iacovou 2006a; PPC:285. Khalkanor: see p339.
[153] See p253–255.
[154] Pausanias 8.5.3: χρόνῳ δὲ ὕστερον Λαοδίκη γεγονυῖα ἀπὸ Ἀγαπήνορος ἔπεμψεν ἐς Τεγέαν τῇ Ἀθηνᾷ τῇ Ἀλέᾳ πέπλον. For the local Arcadian goddess Alea, who began to be identified with Athena in the Archaic period, see Jost 1985:368–385.
[155] Pausanias 8.5.3: Λαοδίκης ὅδε πέπλος· ἑᾷ δ' ἀνέθηκεν Ἀθηνᾷ / πατρίδ' ἐς εὐρύχορον Κύπρου ἀπὸ ζαθέας.
[156] Roy 1987.

founding there the temple "of Aphrodite, called Paphian"; and he carefully notes that Paphos was Laodike's own home.[157] Of course, even a votive *péplos* predating 394 can never have been 'old enough'. But this does not prevent its being an authentic relic of an older mythmaking process, deriving ultimately from cultural memories of connections between Cyprus and Arcadia, even Tegea itself.[158] The diffusion of 'Aphrodite' cult must indeed have involved such westward ventures; yet it is quite striking that, despite the internationally renowned sanctuary at Paphos, nowhere in Greece besides Tegea was the goddess qualified as Paphian.[159] It is crucial that Arcadians of the Classical period had no difficultly believing in such early connections with Cyprus, just as some Cypriot communities claimed Arcadian origins.[160]

Ps.-Apollodoros cites another Arcadian legend involving a Laodike who also appears in the royal lineage, but much earlier—married to Elatos, son of the eponymous Arkas, and elder brother of Apheidas; "these sons divided up the land, but Elatos wielded all the power."[161] Quite remarkably, this Laodike is said to be a *daughter of Kinyras*. This must make her a native of pre-Greek Cyprus, since Elatos lived five generations before Agapenor's arrival to the island. Observe the deep antiquity this assigns to Kinyras, recalling his proverbial old age.[162] There is a curious paradox here. No doubt there were sporadic marriages between Greeks and Cypriots throughout the LBA. But in a mythological genealogy involving eponymous figures—Arkas, Amyklas, Stymphalos, and others—marriage to a 'daughter of Kinyras' should symbolize a quite general intermingling of Arcadian and Cypriot populations. Yet such a situation only makes sense *following* Aegean immigration to Cyprus, and only *on* the island—the more logical arrangement of Teukros and the daughter of Kinyras; or of Diodoros' *South Pacific* scenario for the Dryopes, who, "sailing to the island of Cyprus, and 'mixing it up' (*anamikhthéntes*) with the locals, settled there."[163] It appears, therefore, that with

---

[157] Pausanias 8.53.7, cf. 8.5.2.
[158] See the good discussion of Pirenne-Delforge 1994:328–329.
[159] Gjerstad 1944:111 is surgically incisive: "It is possible to explain the legend of Agapenor's foundation of Paphos without reference to the temple of the Paphian Aphrodite in Tegea, but it is absolutely impossible, so far as I see, to explain that a temple of the Paphian Aphrodite existed on the Greek mainland, *only* in the remote inland country of Arcadia and *only* in Tegea, if we do not bring this fact into relation with the legend of the Tegean king Agapenor's foundation of Paphos. We may thus infer that the legend is primary, the temple secondary in their mutual relations." (The historical sequence Gjerstad goes on to develop, however, is rather inconclusive.) Jost 1985:148 is also open to seeing a genuine tradition behind Laodike's foundation, although she is agnostic as to its date.
[160] Herodotos 7.90.
[161] [Apollodoros] *Library* 3.9.1: οὗτοι τὴν γῆν ἐμερίσαντο, τὸ δὲ πᾶν κράτος εἶχεν Ἔλατος.
[162] See p329.
[163] Diodoros Siculus 4.37.2: εἰς Κύπρον τὴν νῆσον πλεύσαντες καὶ τοῖς ἐγχωρίοις ἀναμιχθέντες ἐνταῦθα κατῴκησαν. The generalizing masculine τοῖς ἐγχωρίοις is counteracted by the sexual

Chapter Fourteen

Elatos and the daughter of Kinyras, the fusion of Greek and Cypriot culture has been exported back up the migration path and pushed into the deep past.[164] Note that diasporas do often involve cyclic returns to the homeland.[165]

The two Laodikes, despite their considerable differences, must be mythological doublets. Both embody cultural relations between Cyprus and Arcadia, expressed at the royal level. Both involve movement *from* Cyprus to Arcadia, against the flow of the historical migrations. While Agapenor's daughter could be imagined as *sending* the *péplos* back to Athena (so Pausanias), she would certainly have to return herself to build a temple to Paphian Aphrodite. That deed is much more logically assigned to the other Laodike, who *did* move from Cyprus to Arcadia: the 'immigration' of a daughter of Kinyras, priest-king of Aphrodite, would perfectly mirror the 'importation' of the Paphian goddess herself (historically cults were indeed transferred by dynastic marriages[166]). Still, that Agapenor's daughter might conceivably return to her fatherland is itself significant, since it allows for just the kind of continuing contacts that one must anyway suppose to account for the interdependence of Arcadian and Cypriot legends.

Both Laodikes may therefore be connected to the cult of the Cypriot goddess, whether explicitly (Agapenor's daughter) or implicitly (Kinyras' daughter). It must be significant that this most Cypriot of institutions, fundamental to political legitimacy at Paphos, is connected in both cases with a woman subordinate to an Arcadian king. This seems a powerful symbol of the appropriation and internalization of Cypriot royal ideology. 'Laodike' itself—'Justice for the People'—points in the same direction, as do Kinyras' other mythological children with such speaking-names.[167] Since all of these have *Greek* etymologies— and note that 'Kinyras' itself has a semi-Hellenic appearance[168]—they represent a cultural sharing of the ideas they express. But Laodike is unique among Kinyras' children for illustrating this 'translation' in the context of a dynastic marriage.

M. Finkelberg has identified a recurring pattern in Greek mythology whereby princes marry into other royal houses while successive generations of princesses/queens remain in place; this seems to reflect a widespread pre-Greek custom, also operative in Anatolia, whereby a king's power was contingent

---

connotations of ἀναμιχθέντες; indeed one might well emend to ταῖς ἐγχωρίοις.
[164] Cf. Engel 1841 2:125.
[165] PPC:49–50 et passim. For Cyprus itself, note that in one variant Teukros tried to return home after Telamon died: Pompeius Trogus in Justin *Epitome* 44.3. There is also the case of the Gerginoi (Athenaios 256b–c): see p457–458.
[166] See p154.
[167] See p333.
[168] See p432–436.

on a female line.[169] A similar point was made long ago by J. G. Frazer, vis-à-vis the myth of Kinyras coming to Paphos from Cilicia and marrying Metharme, daughter of Pygmalion.[170] Finkelberg argues that the practice led to the existence of double and even triple male dynastic lines, in order both to respect and control the hereditary female succession (she detects an historical example in the troubled royal successions of the Hittite OK). Could the dual kingship traditions at Paphos—Kinyradai and Agapenor, Kinyradai and Tamiradai[171]—reflect such a pattern?

In any case, marriage into a local royal establishment is one likely way that Aegean immigrant kings or chieftains renovated their power within their new insular environment, achieving royal legitimacy in the pre-Greek theological context of the goddess's cult.[172] For Agapenor, such a scenario comes only if one may 'pool the resources' of the two Laodikes. Such a procedure is not completely gratuitous, given the nature of mythological doublets; we have already seen that the two Laodikes 'traded' certain attributes. In other words, 'Laodike' was a multivalent figure for whom we have but two 'samples'. Her full mythological potential can be mapped by 'multiplying' the samples and redistributing the results between Agapenor and Elatos, the two Arcadian kings with whom they are connected. The results for Agapenor are as follows:

1. If Agapenor marries Laodike, and Laodike = Kinyras' daughter, then Agapenor marries Kinyras' daughter;

2. If Laodike = Kinyras' daughter, and Agapenor = Laodike's father, then Agapenor = Kinyras;

3. If Agapenor = Kinyras, and Laodike is Kinyras' daughter, then Agapenor/Kinyras marries *his own* daughter.

Is it coincidence that these gyrations not only connect Agapenor to Kinyras' family line, and indeed make a Kinyras of him, but also generate the most famous episode of Kinyras' own mythology—an incestuous union with his daughter?[173] Frazer saw in the myth of Myrrha/Smyrna a reflection of ritualized incest allowing continuous patrilineal control of an otherwise matrilineal royal line.[174]

---

[169] Finkelberg 1991; Finkelberg 2005:65–108.

[170] Frazer 1914 1:41–42: "These legends seem to contain reminiscences of kingdoms in Cilicia and Cyprus which passed in the female line, and were held by men, sometimes foreigners, who married the hereditary princesses." Frazer includes here Kinyras' father Sandokos, who immigrates from Syria to marry Pharnake: see p504.

[171] For the latter juxtaposition, see p401–406.

[172] Cf. Finkelberg 2005:88, "the position of the queen can be satisfactorily accounted for if we assume that she was priestess of the goddess of the land," etc.

[173] See further p282–289.

[174] Frazer 1914 1:43–44.

Chapter Fourteen

Be this as it may, it remains significant that both Laodikes' attested attributes concern the intersection of Arcadian and pre-Greek Cypriot kingship.[175] That this is precisely the crisis of Agapenor *vis-à-vis* the historical Kinyradai of Paphos cannot be accidental. It is all the more curious that, while Elatos' marriage to Laodike 'Kinyradizes' the main branch of the Arcadian royal line, yet his nephew, the emigrant Agapenor, is excluded. While much remains uncertain, the multiform 'Laodike' does attest a tradition of mythological reflection upon these issues. 'She' certainly belongs to the 'old' Agapenor, and may indeed be very early, since the problem of accommodating Aegean dynasts to the Cypriot establishment must go back to the twelfth and eleventh centuries.

Conclusion

The material analyzed here and in Chapter 13 derives from of a multiform mythmaking tradition going back to sub-Mycenaean times on Cyprus. Not every sample is equally old: specific historical developments induced various modulations over time. Taken as a whole, however, the simple existence of such legends is clear evidence that many of the island's communities maintained and cultivated a distinct sense of Greekness down through the centuries—a striking contrast to the thoroughly hybrid material record. But of course there must also have been extensive intermarriage with the pre-Greek population, whose contribution to IA Cypriot culture can hardly be overstated.

Greek ctistic and trade ventures of the ninth and eighth centuries caused some of the early Cypriot legends to be reinterpreted in more mainstream epic terms. Yet the 'Greek colonization of Cyprus' is no mere epic construct or scholarly fantasy. It is firmly rooted in ancient traditions, some of which are very early indeed (Agapenor and Teukros). It is a question rather of what is meant by 'colonization'.[176] The Aegean immigrants' common lot as parvenus probably intensified a sense of Greekness within the island's already multiethnic culture.[177] Ironically, these 'Greek-Cypriots' were (and are) regarded as distinctly 'Cypriot' to Greeks of the Aegean. And, of course, on Cyprus itself there must have been numerous wrinkles in degree of acculturation, depending on such considerations as class and the variable demographics of each community.

Kinyras came to serve as a common mythological reference point for pre-Greek, Greek-Cypriot, and Cypro-Phoenician communities alike in their shared

---

[175] In the case of Agapenor's daughter, the connection with pre-Greek kingship is implicit in her efforts on behalf of Paphian 'Aphrodite'.
[176] For this crux, see recently Iacovou 2008.
[177] For this phenomenon outside of Cyprus, see Hall 1989 (65 and n37, 73 on Lydia); Morris 1992:362–386; Georges 1994:76–114; Raaflaub 2000, with further literature in n7; Burkert 2004:11.

Restringing Kinyras

and sometimes contested history. Naturally, Greeks and pre-Greeks will have been at their most distinct at the time of heaviest Aegean immigration. And it was precisely this moment that was replayed in the various tales of Kinyras and the Achaeans. While Cypriot exposure to the Greek epic cycle may account for Kinyras' encounters with Agamemnon, Menelaos, Odysseus, and Talthybios, it does not explain his dominant image as a pre-Greek culture-hero, which takes precedence. This virtuous, Golden Age Kinyras, however much the Paphian kings may have promoted him, was not theirs alone, but a tenacious contribution by pre-Greek communities generally to IA Cypriot mythmaking. It is all the more striking, therefore, that Kinyras unanimously symbolized the *disjunction* of cultures. This is also why Kinyras must have been introduced *before* the ninth-century Phoenician colonial ventures.[178] To be sure, Phoenician-Cypriots may have rightly insisted that 'Kinyras' was *originally* at home in the Levant before ever coming to Cyprus.[179] But while this might account for myths about Kinyras crossing to the island, and his mythological co-ordination with Pygmalion, *it is insufficient to explain his ubiquitous association with the pre-Greek island*.[180] The epicenter of any historicizing interpretation must be the assumption that Kinyras was already established as a potent figure on Cyprus *at the time of Aegean immigration*.

---

[178] Kinyras as a first-millennium Phoenician import: Drexler, Roscher *Lex.* s.v. Kinyras; HC:69 (ambivalent); Lorimer 1950:208; Bunnens 1979:354–356. The phonology of Kinyras/*kinýra* provides no definite support for this view: see p272–276.

[179] It would be fair to say, therefore, that Kinyras, perhaps like Pygmalion, stands for Canaanite cultural presence on the LBA island: cf. Kroll, RE 11 (1922):484–486; Baurain 1980b:278.

[180] Cf. Engel 1841 1:203: "Sein Name ist phönikisch. Das ist aber auch das einzige Phönikische an ihm geblieben, und wurde in der Mythenbildung gänzlich vergessen."

15
Crossing the Water

I HAVE NOW SHOWN that the evidence for a musical Kinyras is much more extensive than previously realized; that this was not a secondary accretion, but an early and essential dimension; and that his erstwhile divinity echoed into the Roman period as "Our *Kenyristés* Apollo." We have also seen that his multifaceted reflection of pre-Greek Cyprus in IA myth implies that he was somehow established prior to Aegean immigration. So far as I can see, these findings can only be reconciled by accepting that:

1. Kinyras is at heart a Divine Lyre, akin to Kinnaru at LBA Ugarit and very probably other cognates on the mainland; and that:

2. This Divine Lyre was imported by one or more Cypriot cities in the LBA, from one or more specific origins and/or in a more general emulation of mainland culture. He then lingered on into the IA to be used differently by different communities at different times.

My phrasing shows that many specifics remain to be considered. What material is there in the Alashiya texts and other contemporary documents to support and elucidate the proposed importation of a mainland god? Why was a Divine Lyre imported at all? How and when did it develop so many nonmusical attributes and powers? What evidence is there in LBA Cypriot music iconography for the kinds of ideas associated elsewhere with divinized instruments and musician-kings? How and when did this 'Kinyras' come to symbolize the island's pre-Greek culture in its entirety? I shall address each of these questions in turn.

Alashiya and the Mainland Cults

That a Kinnaru-like figure could have been imported to LBA Cyprus finds good general support in the island's cosmopolitan outlook at this time, and close political and cultural engagement with its mainland periphery—NK Egypt, the Hittite Empire, and especially Hurro-Luwian Kizzuwatna/Cilicia, and Syro-Levantine

Chapter Fifteen

sites like Ugarit and Byblos in the core area of *knr*-culture. The relevant material includes clear evidence for ongoing cultic and theological engagement between island and mainland.

In one of the Amarna letters, an unnamed Alashiyan king explains why he has sent Pharaoh only 500 talents (?) of copper. "Behold, the hand of Nergal is now in my country; he has slain all the men of my country, and there is not a (single) copper-worker." As Nergal is a Mesopotamian underworld god associated with war, death, and plague, the king seems to mean that a plague or war has struck his kingdom (one of his queens also died).[1] But 'Nergal' itself is a conventional Akkadian calque used in international communication, so that a corresponding local figure must be assumed—one of many examples of the period's supralocal theological outlook.[2] We may reasonably suppose, *a fortiori*, that this unnamed Alashiyan god was equally seen as a form of Resheph—the Syro-Levantine god connected with war and bringing and averting disease and other disasters—since Resheph was himself early on glossed as Nergal at Ebla, Ugarit, and elsewhere. As a neighboring god, Resheph is also more likely to have had an actual cult on Cyprus, as he did in NK Egypt.[3] Note that the Cypriot Ingot God (see below) is of the smiting type often associated with BA representations of Resheph.[4] Related to this puzzle is a famous bilingual inscription from the sanctuary at Tamassos (ca. 375), where Apollo, also associated with plague, was given the Greek title *Alasiṓtas* (spelled syllabically), thus masking a pre-Greek god.[5] The corresponding Phoenician text gives "Resheph *'lhyts*," where the epiclesis is modeled on the Greek.[6] Here too it is unclear whether we are dealing with *three* originally distinct DNs, with the Alashiyan one implied or forgotten; or whether the latter already bore a form of the name Resheph in the LBA, and

---

[1] EA 35.10–15, 35–39: Schaeffer 1971:509–510; AP:21–37; Moran 1992:107–109 (with defense of "talents" in n2); SHC 2 no. 16; PPC:320.

[2] Hadjioannou 1971:37–40; AP:21–23; Moran 1992:108n3. Similarly, while Nergal is often mentioned in the Amarna letters and Ugaritian and Hittite documents, he need not have been actively worshipped in these places. For theoretical observations on the interplay of "deities in their local and supra-regional aspect," see Pongratz-Leisten 2011:89–93 et passim.

[3] So Dietrich 1978:16–17; DDUPP:187–188. For Resheph as Nergal at Ebla, Ugarit, etc., and his cult in LBA Egypt, see Stadelmann 1967:56–76; Lipiński 2009:23–27, 79–81, 161–221 et passim.

[4] Lipinski 2009:139–160, especially 145–146.

[5] Cf. Dietrich 1978; Glover 1981:148.

[6] ICS 216 (*a-la-si-o-ta-i* = Ἀλασιώτα, line 4); further discussion in Masson 1973:117–119; cf. Hadjioannou 1971:41; Schretter 1974:151–173; AP:22, 25–26; DDUPP:188; SHC 2 no. 122; Lipinski 2009:231–233. That the Phoen. title is secondary is shown by the correspondence of -*ts* with Gk. -τας. Conversely, Apollo Ἄμυκλος (dat. *a-mu-ko-lo-i*) is probably an *interpretatio Graeca* of Resheph Mikal in a third-century inscription from Idalion (ICS 220 = KAI 39, with comments to 38; DGAC:247–248). Others argue for a connection between Laconian and Cypriot cult: Dietrich 1978; GR:51, 145; Lipiński 1987b:95n27 with further references, eclipsing Stadelmann 1967:52–56; Lipiński 2004:64; Lipiński 2009:232–235.

was then distinguished from his mainland namesake by immigrant Phoenicians of the first millennium.[7]

The same Amarna letter contains another illuminating detail—the Alashiyan king's request for an 'eagle-diviner', presumably to help counter the "hand of Nergal."[8] Whether this diviner (Akk. *šā'ilu*) sought guidance from bird-flight, or conducted lustration rituals through avine sacrifice or some other abuse, is uncertain.[9] But clearly Alashiya participated in the international circulation of scientific knowledge and cultic technique that is otherwise well documented between the Great Kings of this period. One may note here several Cyprocentric variants of the myth of the Egyptian king Bousiris: in one he is advised by the Cypriot *mántis* Phrasios to counter a nine-year famine by sacrificing strangers to Zeus (Phrasios himself became the first victim); in another version Pygmalion is the adviser.[10] A well-known parallel from within the Amarna letters is the statue of Ishtar of Nineveh, which the Mitannian king Tushratta sent twice to Amenhotep III.[11] The purpose of these missions is unclear, but obviously the presence of the divine statue was somehow efficacious; and it will have been accompanied by appropriate personnel, including cult-musicians to judge from Hurro-Hittite ritual texts involving this goddess.[12]

One should also note here a divinatory liver-model found at Ugarit and rather ambiguously inscribed as "belonging to '*Agp-ṯr*, when he acquired the young man from the Alashiyan."[13] The underlying transaction and relationships are obscure. But it confirms the circulation of esoteric knowledge generally, and liver-divinization specifically, between LBA Cyprus and the mainland. Recall the association of the Kinyradai with extispicy, and the priestly tradition that the art was imported from Cilicia.[14]

Several further texts bear on the acculturation or syncretism of Cypriot and mainland divinities. From Ugarit comes a Hurrian list of gods receiving

---

[7] Resheph is first directly attested on the island via ostraka and inscriptions in the fifth century. So on the hypothesis he would have been reintroduced during the Phoenician colonial period (perhaps like 'Kinyras' himself: see p369). Cf. Stadelmann 1967:52.
[8] EA 35.26.
[9] For various parallels, especially from Hurro-Hittite sources, see AP:23, 29–37; Strauss 2006:199. For the range of the *šā'ilu*, notably the reading of dreams and incense, see CAD s.v.
[10] Cypriot Phrasios: [Apollodoros] *Library* 2.5.11. Pygmalion: Servius Auctus on Vergil *Georgics* 3.5. Hyginus *Fabulae* 56 gives 'Thrasius', now son of Pygmalion and himself brother of Busiris. The common denominator of these variants is mantic relations between Cyprus and Egypt, even if the Cypriot setting itself is secondary (so HC:66).
[11] EA 23; Moran 1992:61–62; Beckman 1998:2–3.
[12] See Wegner 1981:156 and further below.
[13] RS 24.325 (KTU/CAT 1.141): Dietrich and Loretz 1969b:173–174; SHC 2 no. 64; Baurain 1980b:291; PPC:320.
[14] See p401–406.

Chapter Fifteen

sacrifice, beginning with El; alongside Kothar-wa-Hasis and several Hurrian deities (including Kumarbi and Teshup) is a little geographical triad of "the god of Alashiya, the god of Amurru, the god of Ugarit."[15] It sounds as if the three were seen as analogous—presumably the lord of each local pantheon. This text, whatever the occasion of the underlying rite, is vital evidence that the state cult of Alashiya was seen as a distinctive system, and yet was equally incorporated into a larger theological community spanning island and mainland. If the "god of Alashiya" could be honored at Ugarit, the reverse must also have been true. This is an important parallel for Kinnaru and Kinyras.

The international profile of Alashiyan cult is further seen in another Ugaritian text, seemingly from the harbormaster to the king and dealing with a sale of ships. The official reassures him that "I myself have spoken to Ba'al ⌈Ṣaphon⌉,[16] to the eternal Sun (Šapšu), to Astarte, to Anat, to all the gods of Alashiya."[17] It is generally agreed, from the final phrase, that one of the parties to the transaction (a merchant?) was an Alashiyan. But how to account for the juxtaposition of these specific divinities? Should "all the gods of Alashiya" be taken in *apposition* to Ba'al, Shapsh, Astarte, and Anat, so that these Semitic figures become representatives of the Alashiyan pantheon?[18] ('Ba'al' *is* a theophoric element in several Alashiyan PNs.[19]) A second suggestion—that the Ugaritian official has used local Semitic names to refer to their Alashiyan equivalents—would require such extensive functional correspondences between the two pantheons that some *de facto* syncretism of Alashiyan and Semitic divinities would have to be supposed.[20] Or are "all the gods of Alashiya" simply *conjoined* to the Semitic gods, so that the Ugaritian and Alashiyan parties to the transaction are both divinely represented?[21] This seems the readiest interpretation: it is only natural that, in an Ugaritian document, local gods be named and foreign powers treated generically. But even this interpretation would hardly prevent one or more Syro-Levantine gods from being recognized on Alashiya itself in

---

[15] RS 24.274 = Laroche 1968:504–507; SHC 2 no. 65; cf. AP:55.
[16] For the restoration, see HUS:678.
[17] RS 18.113A,6–8: PRU 5 no. 8; KTU/CAT 2.42; cf. Muhly 1972:207; AP:55; Knapp 1983 (superseding Lipiński 1977); SHC 2 no. 47; PPC:181, 320. *Nmry* in line 9 is usually understood as referring to Amenhotep III (Nebmare); but Singer (HUS:678) has attractively reinterpreted this line as invoking a supreme Alashiyan god, "the blessed/strong one, king of eternity"—noting the seemingly chthonic character this would imply, and suggesting as a possible parallel the description of Rāp'iu in RS 24.252, 1 (for which see p134–135); cf. PPC:320.
[18] Lipiński 1977:213; Webb 2003:17.
[19] For these theophorics, Astour 1964:245–246 (e.g. *Be-e[l]-š[a]-am-m[a]*, 'Baal-inspires-dread'); cf. Knapp 1983:40.
[20] Karageorghis and Karageorghis 2002:273; Budin 2003:133–134.
[21] Muhly 1972:207; HUS:678 (Singer).

some hybrid form. At the very least, the text reinforces the impression that the Cypriot and mainland gods were intimate neighbors.

Of the deities named in the previous text, Astarte and Anat are especially important given Kinyras' intimate alliance with Aphrodite in our sources. Either goddess could inform the Aphrodite *Énkheios* ('of the Spear') known on the IA island.[22] Other mainland powers who seem to share attributes with the historical Aphrodite are the Syrian Ishara, resembling "the bridal aspect of Ishtar"; and Asherah, whose maritime associations equally recall Baalat Gebal (the 'Lady of Byblos') and Isis.[23] Of course, any such analysis of Aphrodite must equally account for the island's own Great Goddess, whose cult goes back to the Chalcolithic period.[24] Figurines in clay and steatite show that Paphos was a key site long before its monumentalization in the thirteenth century.[25] Thus, in contemplating the influence of a mainland goddess on the island one must look to syncretism and theological reinterpretation. While the EIA must not be ignored as a fertile time for syncretic developments under Aegean and Phoenician stimuli,[26] the interpretation of local goddesses as forms of Ishtar/Astarte is a richly documented phenomenon of the LBA.

One example bearing directly on the Alashiya question is the so-called Ishtar of Nineveh, a form of the Hurrian Shaushka who was hybridized with Inanna/Ishtar in third-millennium northern Mesopotamia, apparently in the Old Akkadian period.[27] She was then brought westwards in the MBA through Hurrian infiltration of North Syria and southeastern Anatolia, emerging (for instance) as the patroness of the fourteenth-century Mitannian king Tushratta. After the Hurrianized kingdom of Kizzuwatna (Cilicia) was integrated into the Hittite kingdom during the early fourteenth century,[28] Ishtar of Nineveh entered the state cult there, where she joined some twenty-five regional goddesses who could be labeled with the logogram IŠTAR.[29] Her legacy is also

---

[22] Hesykhios s.v. Ἔγχειος· Ἀφροδίτη. Κύπριοι. Cf. Karageorghis 1988:195. Martial Aphrodite: Farnell 1896–1909 2:653–655; Pirenne-Delforge 1994:450–454.

[23] See Budin 2003:202–206, 274–275 (quotation), suggesting a special connection with Ishara at Alalakh. For the maritime Aphrodite, see p330. For Baalat Gebal, see p463–486.

[24] Karageorghis 1977; Dietrich 1978:16–17; *Kypris*:11–12 and 34 (Paphos), 198 (Khytroi).

[25] See p363.

[26] For eleventh-century Cretan iconographic influence in the 'goddess with upraised arms', see e.g. Budin 2003:275; *Kypris*:78.

[27] For the history and geographical range of Ishtar of Nineveh, see Wegner 1981; Beckman 1998; cf. Bachvarova 2013 with further literature.

[28] For this development, Wilhelm 1989:30–31; KH:150–151.

[29] Since the majority of these were connected with towns and mountains in North Syria or southeastern Anatolia, they may be "hypostases of a single divine archetype." See Wegner 1981:157–195 with Beckman 1998:3–4 (quotation) and n39; cf. Bachvarova 2013:24 and n5.

seen at thirteenth-century Ugarit, where an Astarte-of-the-Hurrian-Land ('Aṭtartu-Ḫurri) was venerated; and she was evidently the dynastic patron of Shaushgamuwa of Amurru (south of Ugarit).[30]

The goddess is linked to Alashiya in the Hittite *Ritual and Prayer to Ishtar of Nineveh*.[31] The purpose of the ritual, which derives from the MH period and Hurrian incantatory practice, was, in time of plague, to entice Ishtar of Nineveh—using "trails of edibles converging on the offering site"[32]—back from whatever foreign land she was lurking in, and thus restore the royal family to health and the natural world to abundance. After the goddess's statue has been appropriately prepared, the diviner-priest (ˡᵘHAL) is instructed to work through a long catalogue of lands according to a fixed epicletic formula ("O Ishtar ... [if you are in Nineveh] then come from Nineveh. If you are [in] R[imuši, then come from Rimuši]," etc.).[33] Alashiya occurs midway through this litany. To be sure, we seem to have a "boilerplate list of names" intended to encompass most of the known world.[34] Hence a very similar (though slightly smaller) catalogue, which also includes Alashiya, appears in another Hittite evocation rite addressed to the Cedar Deities.[35] Nevertheless, many of the places are indeed known to have hosted cults of 'Ishtar' in various guises (including Astarte)—Nineveh, Mitanni, Ugarit, Amurru, Sidon, Tyre, and Canaan, to name the more obvious. There is therefore no *a priori* reason to doubt that Alashiya too housed a goddess identifiable as Ishtar.[36] Also valuable is I. Wegner's observation that Aphrodite's birth and arrival to Cyprus, as told by Hesiod, is embedded in a succession myth of ultimately Hurrian extraction.[37]

The presence of some form of Ishtar cult on LBA Cyprus is corroborated by a fragmentary Hittite treaty with Alashiya of late date (perhaps from the reign of Tudhaliya IV, ca. 1245–1215).[38] After the enumeration of divine blessings that

---

[30] For Hurrian Ishtar at Ugarit, see Herrmann 1973; Wilhelm 1989:51; indices to RCU, and p. 275 for Egyptian usage of 'Hurrian land' to refer to North Syria and southern Anatolia.

[31] KUB 15.35 + KBo 2.9 = CTH 716: Sommer 1921, especially 95; Archi 1977; SHC 2 no. 42; CS 1 no. 65 (whence the title used here). M. Bachvarova, whom I thank for introducing me to this text, points out that the some versions of the ritual contain Hurrian ritual phrases (Haas and Wegner 1988:376–380, nos. 84, 85).

[32] G. Beckman in SHC 2 no. 42.

[33] For the ˡᵘHAL, Wegner 1981:155.

[34] Beckman 1998:5n57.

[35] KUB 15.34 i.48–65 = CTH 483; SHC 2 no. 41.

[36] Cf. Wegner 1981:155, 204–207. One might quibble that the text guarantees only a Hurro-Hittite perspective, the proposition not being necessarily intelligible in Alashiya itself. But this is belied by the evidence already considered for the neighborly theological relations between Alashiya and its mainland neighbors.

[37] Hesiod *Theogony* 188–200. Cf. Wegner 1981:205. That Hesiod's Aphrodite travels *eastwards* from Kythera will then be a Hellenizing innovation.

[38] KBo 12.39; CTH 141; Steiner 1962:134–135; Otten 1963:10–13; SHC 2 no 37.

Alashiya will receive from honoring her duties (these include reporting military threats and housing and extraditing Hittite exiles as required), a damaged clause calls for placing the tablet "before Ishtar." As G. Beckman points out, this is "significant for the religious history of Alashiya, because the Hittites insisted that such documents be placed in the temple of the chief deity of their vassals."[39] It should follow that not only did the *Hittites* recognize a form of Ishtar on the island, but that this perception was shared by the treaty's Alashiyan participants.

Nearby Ugarit provides another example of multiple Ishtars coexisting.[40] Besides the Astarte-of-the-Hurrian-Land ('Aṯtartu-Ḫurri) mentioned above, the pantheon texts list an unmarked Astarte, and a further Astarte-of-the-Steppe ('Aṯtartu-Šadi) who perhaps symbolized the dynasty's pre-urban, Amorite past.[41] Recall that while Astarte is elusive in Ugaritian mythological texts and PNs, she was nevertheless important in the royal cult; an 'entry ritual' designed to lure the goddess to the royal palace seems to have contained a Hurrian hymn, and Kinnaru was one recipient of offerings.[42] Astarte-of-the-Steppe is also found in an edict from the reign of Ammistamru II (mid-thirteenth century) whose two brothers, after receiving their inheritance and a sentence of exile to Alashiya, were made to swear by the goddess no longer to challenge him or his descendants.[43] It has been suggested that Astarte-of-the-Steppe was invoked here as being a divinity *shared* by Ugarit and Cyprus,[44] though a status as dynastic patroness would seem to suffice. But one may at least assume that the princes, like others exiled to Alashiya, brought with them their own religious beliefs; they are thus a microcosm of cultic communication between island and mainland.

And so it is hard to avoid agreeing with J. Karageorghis that "at some point ... there must have been some kind of syncretism between oriental and Cypriot religions."[45] This has been equally inferred from the late LC II Cypriot goddess-figurines, going back to the fifteenth century, which exhibit close stylistic sympathies with contemporary mainland figurines, especially of North Syria, while equally maintaining inherited Cypriot features.[46] More general support can be sought in Cypriot sacred architecture of the fourteenth and thirteenth

---

[39] G. Beckman in SHC 2 no. 37; cf. *PPC*:321. The clause in question is obv. 19: see Steiner 1962:135 (not in the text of Otten 1963:10–13).
[40] Smith 2015:74–77.
[41] See indices to RCU, with Pardee's suggestion on 275.
[42] RS 24.643 (KTU/CAT 1.148), obverse. See further p120.
[43] RS 17.352; Nougayrol 1956:121–122 (no. 55); SHC 2 no. 23; Beckman and Hoffner 1999 no. 35; cf. PPC:320–321.
[44] S. Budin in PPC:321.
[45] Karageorghis and Karageorghis 2002:273.
[46] Karageorghis 1977:72–85; CAAC II.3–16; Budin 2002:319–320; Webb 2003:15–17; Budin 2003:140–145, 274; PPC:176.

centuries, which exhibits strong sympathies with mainland sanctuary design; Enkomi, Kition, Palaipaphos, Myrtou, Ayia Irini, and Athienou all hosted "free standing rectangular structures located in or beside an enclosed temenos, the latter serving to isolate the building and act as an area of cult activity in its own right."[47]

Several later traditions, all difficult to evaluate, allege early Cypriot cult- or city-foundations instigated from mainland sites. Herodotos reports a Cypriot belief that 'Aphrodite Ourania'—that is Astarte/Ishtar—had been imported to the island from Ascalon, held to be her oldest cult-site.[48] But as the latter detail is no doubt incorrect and due to local pride at Ascalon, and because this was a locus of Philistine settlement in the EIA, the tradition may present a special Aegean aspect and be of limited value for the pre-Greek period.[49] Possibly the Father of History conflated a specific Ascalonite claim with a *general* Cypriot awareness that their goddess had an early continental aspect. Pausanias at any rate gives an account evidently designed to correct Herodotos, in which Ourania is (in one sense rightly) traced to 'Assyria' (here Mesopotamia), while the inhabitants of Paphos and Ascalon *share* the distinction of next oldest cult centers.[50]

An apparently independent tradition was entered by Eusebios for the year 1425 of his lost *Chronicle*. This held that Paphos, along with Melos, Thera, and Bithynia, was 'founded' (*condita/ektísthē*) either by 'Phoinix'—a standard Greek eponym for 'Phoenicia', by which we must also understand 'Canaan'[51]—and/or in connection with the abduction of Europa and the search for her by Kadmos 'the Phoenician'.[52] The *exact* date of course has no real value, as Eusebios and the

---

[47] Webb 1999:157–165; Webb 2003:17 (quotation).
[48] Herodotos 1.105. The identification of Aphrodite/Ourania with Astarte is also made by Philo of Byblos FGH 790 F 2 (31): τὴν δὲ Ἀστάρτην Φοίνικες τὴν Ἀφροδίτην εἶναι λέγουσι; Pausanias 1.14.7. For Astarte at Ascalon, cf. 1 Samuel 31:10.
[49] Cf. Brown 1965:214: "We might conjecture ... that when the Philistines took over the Semitic goddess of Ascalon, they began to adapt her into a form which would be more acceptable to other Aegean peoples ... They might then have exported the new version of the cult back along the Phoenician island-settlements which marked their invasion route, and where the old version had already been established." See also Blinkenberg 1924:30n* (sic).
[50] Pausanias 1.14.7: "The worship of Ourania was established among the Assyrians first of men, and after them among the Paphians out of the Cypriots, and out of the Phoenicians those who inhabit Ascalon; and the Kythereans learned to honor her from the Phoenicians." Herodotos himself elsewhere (1.131) subscribed to an Assyrian (and Arabian) origin for the goddess (under respective local names), crediting them with introducing her to the Persians. Pausanias probably rationalized the two passages (Blinkenberg 1924:30).
[51] See p55.
[52] The relevant section is preserved by Saint Jerome, Synkellos, and the twelfth-century *Chronicle* of Michael the Syrian. Helm punctuates Jerome's text as *Melus et Pafus et Thasus et Callista urbes conditae Bithynia condita a Foenice, quae primum Mariandyna vocabatur*, clearly construing the sites prior to Bithynia as Phoenician colonies (Helm 1984:48b = Schoene 1967 2:34). This was also the view of HC:69 and n6 (who however evidently errs in giving the year as 1415 and crediting

earlier Greek chronographers on whom he drew introduced many distortions in rationalizing their sources—which were myths and legends far more often than documents. But the Trojan War serves as one major anchor for all such constructions, so that this 'foundation' was definitely seen as predating the Aegean migrations to Cyprus.[53] To dismiss completely a LBA setting for these 'Phoenician foundations' because of their association with Phoinix or Kadmos would beg the question of what cultural realities underlie those myths. While Thasos and Thera are perhaps more readily connected with *Iron Age* Phoenician trade and settlement,[54] S. Morris has argued compellingly that those pursuits were "a revival, or survival, of Late Bronze Age Canaanite maritime trade"; of Levantine influence in the cult installation at Mycenaean Melos (Phylakopi), she writes that "appreciating these discoveries requires suspending the separation of Bronze and Iron Ages."[55] In any case, the tradition of an early 'Phoenician foundation' at Paphos need not stand or fall with the other sites named; and there is certainly plenty of archaeological evidence from thirteenth-century Paphos for regular trade and cultural contact with the Levant.[56]

These multiform traditions at least represent more general memories of cultural commerce between island and mainland in the LBA, even if the complex lines connecting specific sites were largely effaced. One may recall here an alternative pre-Troy 'Phoenician' legend: according to Vergil, 'Belos' of Sidon had extended his power into Cyprus before Teukros came seeking a new home.[57] Specific traditions may nevertheless sometimes preserve historical content. Given that Paphos was rightly believed to have stood before the coming of the Greeks, should we not equally contemplate some Levantine 'ctistic' venture

---

Byblos specifically—though for Melos at least one may note Herodian *De prosodia catholica* 89.20 Lentz: οὕτω δὲ καὶ ἐκαλεῖτο Μῆλος μία τῶν Κυκλάδων ἀπὸ τῶν Βυβλίων Φοινίκων). Synkellos is closely parallel (Μῆλος καὶ Θάσος καὶ Ἀλκισθὴ ἐκτίσθησαν καὶ Πάφος. Βιθυνία ἐκτίσθη ὑπὸ Φοίνικος, ἡ πρὶν Μαριανδηνὴ καλουμένη, 185.14 Mosshammer), although the punctuation here associates Phoinix only with Bithynia. A solution to the syntax may be sought in Michael the Syrian, who, by including the Rape of Europa, introduces (and probably preserves) the necessary motive: "A cette époque, furent bâties les villes de Mélos, Paphos, Thasos, et Kalistés. L'enlèvement d'Europe eut lieu. Bithynia fut bâtie par Phénix" (3.8, Chabot 1899–1924 1:45). This is synchronized with the age of Moses.

[53] For the Trojan War was a chronographic boundary, and the various ancient calculations, see Burkert 1995.

[54] Edwards 1979:182–184. A connection between Kinyras and the Thasian TN Κοίνυρα, said by Herodotos 6.47 to be near the Phoenician mines, was suggested by Salviat 1962:108n7; G. Dossin in Salviat and Servais 1964:284. But this seems very doubtful.

[55] Morris 1992:110–111, 124–149 et passim (quotations 110, 125); Edwards 1979:187–191 was prepared to accept a stratum of LBA 'memories' in the Kadmos myth, though would commit to no specific detail.

[56] *Paphos*:50–71. Hill dismissed the idea of LBA 'Phoenician colonization' (HC:69 and n6), but the archaeological record has deepened substantially since.

[57] Vergil *Aeneid* 1.619–622: see p354.

Chapter Fifteen

here? It would be natural to associate this with the monumental new sanctuary of the thirteenth century, and posit a reinterpretation of the goddess in terms of an international Ishtar-type.[58] Moreover, as I shall argue in Chapter 19, Kinyras' foundation of the cult, which the Paphian priesthood regarded as a *fama recentior*, is in startling agreement with legends in Syriac sources relating to Byblos, a city with which Kinyras is often connected.

Importing the Divine Lyre

Given Kinyras' intimate relationship with Aphrodite, his arrival to Cyprus is readily intelligible in connection with the importation of an Ishtar-figure. This would explain why at Paphos, for instance, Kinyras enjoyed cultic devotions *within* the goddess's sanctuary, while the city's Kinyrad kings served as high priests of their 'Queen' (*Wánassa*).[59] This hypothesis is well supported by material explored in Part One. We saw Hurro-Hittite sources illuminating the mechanism of cult-transfer through the ritual 'division' and transplantation of a god together with all its *attributa*—including sacred musical instruments, representing the cult's own ritual-music requirements. As it happened, our best evidence concerned a form of Ishtar—evidently one of the most international deities.[60] There was also much evidence connecting Ishtar to stringed instruments, with *kinnāru*, *zannāru*, and *zinar* all defined as the 'Instrument of the Divine Inanna' ($^{giš.d}$INANNA and variants) in and before the LBA.[61] And we saw that the divinized balang Ninigizibara was described as Inanna's spouse in an OB balang-composition.[62] Here we have all the necessary ingredients for a Divine Lyre crossing to LBA Cyprus as an integral part of 'Ishtarizing' the Cypriot goddess.

For the crucial question of how a Divine Lyre could engender so rich a mythological cycle as Kinyras enjoyed, we saw clear examples in Mesopotamian texts (*Lugal-e*, Gudea Cylinders, *Babylonian Erra Myth*), and probably the Hurro-Hittite *Song of Silver*, of mythological narratives spun around anthropomorphized objects and materials of cult and magic. In all of these, the narratological

---

[58] I leave aside the vexed question of the (seemingly inevitable) linguistic kinship of 'Astarte' and 'Aphrodite' (Dugand 1974, especially 91–98; Karageorghis 1977:111–113, 227; for phonetic difficulties, other theories, and earlier references, see GR:408n18; West 2000). The Mycenaean royal title *Wánassa* ('Queen') for the Cypriot goddess (see below) would certainly accord with the existence of an Astarte-figure ('Queen of Heaven', in later Gk. *Ouranía*) at the time of Mycenaean immigration. But these points should not be pressed, as 'Queen' is a natural honorific, and 'Aphrodite' itself is not attested on the island before the Classical period.
[59] See p380, 382n70, 407.
[60] See p100–102.
[61] See p77–79, 89–90.
[62] See p84 and Heimpel, "Balang-Gods," 23f.

role of the personified item reflected the real-world position or function of the item itself. I have also argued that the same pattern underlies the several lamentable metamorphoses that afflicted Kinyras' family members, resulting in cult-objects and processes (Chapter 12). We are thus justified in seeking further correspondences between the mythology of Kinyras and the realia of lyre-cult, particularly the intersection of both with Astarte/Ishtar/Inanna and her function as a royal patroness.

It is perfectly conceivable that, in importing some form of 'Ishtar' cult, LBA Cypriot kings equally emulated the performance practices and ritual poetics of one or more continental neighbors, the latter themselves influenced by Mesopotamian archetypes.

Shulgi and his successors had presented themselves as ideally able to conduct state rituals. David is depicted as doing so in the Bible, Saul verges on such abilities, and Solomon is distinctly Shulgi-like in his superhuman attainments, which include song-writing and the construction of instruments.[63] If a royal ceremony be viewed as a single act, the king (or queen) is its protagonist. Supporting roles like liturgical music—as clearly laid out in the Inandık vase—might then be logically subsumed in the royal performance. Compare the Ugaritic texts, where singers and other cultic agents, though undoubtedly present, are virtually invisible. Even in Hittite rituals, which give much more *practical* information, the cultic hierarchy remains rather obscure.[64] Recall that David led the leaders of his musical guilds and even his own Chief Singer.[65] The intermediate material from Ebla, Mari, and Ugarit is of a different kind, but the *kinnāru(m)* is consistently found in regal contexts. So too the $^{giš.d}$INANNA in Hittite ritual.

These texts, I argued, adumbrate an ancient standard that the *kinnōr*-playing David consciously emulated. Despite later theological revisions, David remains our most vital and illuminating parallel for understanding the interplay of cult-object and mythological persona embodied by Kinyras. David's rise to power in 1 and 2 Samuel is structured around his ability to play upon his *kinnōr*. He is qualified to be king *precisely because he is an inspired 'kinyrist'*—able to effect spiritual catharses, establish political harmony, and communicate with the divine. Like Kinyras, David was a (would-be) temple-builder, a lyre-playing priest-king, a sometime lamenter, and both song-subject and performing role for later psalmists.[66]

---

[63] See p33–37, 80–81, 151–152, 158, 167–174.
[64] Collins 2007:158–159.
[65] See p169–170, 173.
[66] See Chapter 8.

Chapter Fifteen

I submit that one or more LBA Cypriot kings predicted David in presenting themselves as the 'lyre-player' king—*as* Kinyras. Where David is an historical figure dressed in legendary garb, Kinyras is the legend who clothes one or more historical figures. These two realms, the historical and the ideal, are bridged by the Divine Lyre itself, since such cult-objects were simultaneously material and mythogenic.[67] Its essential, original connection with royal ritual music will have made the Divine Lyre a welcome transplant to Alashiya, helping its state cult meet international standards. Associated ritual functions, to judge from the comparative material, could have included celebratory processions, ritual lamentation, and royal ancestor veneration on a Syro-Levantine model—a practice that in the Levant belongs preeminently to the BA,[68] although its survival and evolution can be traced at IA Paphos (Chapter 16).

As the Mesopotamian and Biblical parallels indicate, divinized instruments enabled a monarch to communicate with, and give voice to, the instrument's master god.[69] For Gudea, this was Ningirsu; for David, Yahweh. For the Alashiyan king, it will have been the Ishtarized Cypriot goddess. 'Kinyras' was probably envisioned as her inseparable, lyre-playing consort, uniquely qualified to sing and do the royal deeds and songs she loved. As Frazer suggested over a century ago, his stance as Aphrodite's priest-lover probably reflects some hierogamic relationship between king and goddess.[70] Obviously relevant is the early Mesopotamian concept that a king enjoyed his position by the grace of Inanna/Ishtar, with whom in Neo-Sumerian royal poetics he enjoyed an intimate, sexualized relationship.[71] A recurring motif is his preternatural beauty, by which, as a new Dumuzi, he wins the Divine Queen; similarly Kinyras, like Adonis, was famed for his beauty,[72] as were David and Solomon (the latter cultivating Sidonian Astarte).[73] While it is unclear how such hierogamic ideologies corresponded to underlying ritual systems, the Inandık vase graphically warns against wholesale denial of the sexual rites that scholars once commonly assumed.

---

[67] See p25, 282.
[68] DDUPP:452–453.
[69] See p25–37, 161–165.
[70] Frazer 1914 1:49. It is perhaps significant that the queens of Paphos, like the goddess herself, bore the title *Wánassa*—although the same was true of the king's sisters: Aristotle fr. 526 Rose (from the *Constitution of the Cypriots*) = Harpokration *Lexicon of the Ten Orators* and *Suda* s.v. ἄνακτες καὶ ἄνασσαι· οἱ μὲν υἱοὶ τοῦ βασιλέως καὶ οἱ ἀδελφοὶ καλοῦνται ἄνακτες, αἱ δὲ ἀδελφαὶ καὶ γυναῖκες ἄνασσαι· Ἀριστοτέλης ἐν τῇ Κυπρίων πολιτείᾳ.
[71] See p37–40.
[72] Beauty of Kinyras: p335n99. Cf. *Shulgi A* (ETCSL 2.4.2.01), 15, "I am Shulgi, who has been chosen by Inanna for his attractiveness", and p35, 37–40.
[73] See p154.

Any or all of the aforementioned contexts could have entailed at least notional, and perhaps literal, musical performances by the king himself. I have argued that for Mesopotamian rulers, as for David and Solomon, dedication to music symbolized the peaceful leisure that resulted from establishing a harmonious realm. A. Caubet's suggestion that the Hurrian *Hymn to Nikkal* from Ugarit was composed by king 'Ammurapi himself[74] is perfectly plausible given the traditional attribution of psalms to David, Solomon, Mannaseh, and perhaps Hezekiah.[75] Even as a monarch was praised by his own court singers, he himself could praise the gods in song—especially his divine patroness, who upheld her protégé's terrestrial office. Note that the Hittite king, in presiding over the state's complex religious hierarchy, served nominally as high priest in the cult of Ishtar-Shaushka.[76] An especially striking model for Kinyras as lyre-singer and priest of 'Aphrodite' is the 'Singer(s) of Astarte' (*šr. 'ṯtrt*) who was/were housed in the palace of Ugarit.[77] Remember that in Ugaritic usage 'singer' must often have implied *kinnāru* accompaniment.[78]

Also important here is Kinyras' role as a diviner, given Ishtar's muse-like function as a source of divine knowledge in royal prophecies, a conception going back at least to the OB period in Mesopotamia. The Paphian Kinyradai conducted extispicy within the cult of Aphrodite, who presumably guaranteed its efficacy (Chapter 16). A *kinnāru* may also appear in a Hurrian liver-omen text.[79] While the N-A royal prophecies make no mention of music,[80] an ecstatic prophet featured in the Ishtar ritual from OB Mari focused on Ninigizibara.[81] And of course the Bible provided abundant evidence for *kinnōr*-prophets—preeminently David—as mouthpieces of the divine.[82]

Music and the Harmonious Realm

On the basis of comparative material and systematic considerations, I have posited a LBA Cypriot ideology of the musician-king who oversees a peaceful, powerful kingdom under the protection of the goddess, whom he praises, and with whom he communicates, through song.

[74] See p119.
[75] See p152, 174, 178.
[76] Wegner 1981:148–150.
[77] RS 15.82, 4 (KTU/CAT 4.168): see further p114.
[78] See p114–118.
[79] See p99.
[80] Although the structure of these texts (essentially 'end reports') is hardly conducive to inclusion of such details. For this corpus, see recently Stökl 2012:103–152, 211–215; for the special role of Ishtar, Parpola 1997:XVIII–XXXVI, XLVII–XLVIII et passim.
[81] See p85.
[82] See p161–165.

Chapter Fifteen

These ideas are startlingly corroborated by the exalted and allusive symbolism of two well-known, four-sided bronze stands prominently displayed in the Cyprus Room of the British Museum. Many such stands (and tripods) have been found at sites in Cyprus, the Levant, and the Aegean—unsurpassed masterpieces of second-millennium bronze-work.[83] Their sides were filled with openwork decoration (*ajouré*) exhibiting a variety of subjects. Although they come from contexts as late as the eighth century, dating is complicated by the heirloom effect; stylistic parallels in other media show that these stands reached the peak of their development rather in the pre-Greek thirteenth century, with iconographic forerunners on Cyprus as early as the fifteenth.[84] Recent technical analysis by G. Papasavvas has proven that these objects originated on Cyprus itself, were purposefully exported, and eventually inspired local imitations (notably on Crete where the metallurgical technique was also borrowed).[85] While the stands are thus "uniquely Cypriot artifacts," they were "produced under mutual, hybridized influences bearing the stylistic and iconographic imprint of the Aegean and the Levant."[86]

The first of the two musical stands shows a seated robed figure playing a harp of Mesopotamian type.[87] He occupies the left side of the panel and faces a tree (Figure 38).[88] Each of the other three panels has the tree, repeated exactly, beside a further figure; but here the tree is always on the *left* of the frame, and the figures also face leftwards. Proceeding rightwards—as the musician himself faces—one comes first to an ingot-bearer. Next is a figure who carries two mysterious, long rope-like objects over his shoulder, which R. D. Barnett dubbed "cup and two napkins." (Are these bolts of fine cloth? Sails? Nets? Soutzoukos?) A final figure holds two jugs, or perhaps bundles of fish or dates.

For Barnett, the tree united the four scenes, and was their focus: it was a Sacred Tree, celebrated by all four figures.[89] H. Catling, accepting that the

---

[83] Catling 1964:203–211; Papasavvas 2001; Papasavvas 2004.
[84] Karageorghis and Papasavvas 2001:348–352. For the first stand discussed below with its ingot-bearer before a tree, Knapp 1986:87 has pointed to antecedents in Cypriot pottery and glyptic of the fifteenth and fourteenth centuries: see images in his fig. 2 (eight seals variously from Kourion, Enkomi, and Hala Sultan Teke).
[85] Papasavvas 2001; Karageorghis and Papasavvas 2001:343–348; Papasavvas 2004; cf. PPC:272–274, noting that molds for the *ajouré* figure-work have been discovered on the island.
[86] PPC:274.
[87] For its shape, cf. MgB 2/2:80–85 fig. 62–70 (OB); 102 fig. 108 (Kassite seal, fourteenth century); 126 fig. 145 (N-A); 130 fig. 147 (N-A); 136–138 fig. 151–152 (N-A, 'Elamite orchestra').
[88] London 1920/12-20/1 (height 12.2 cm.; ring diameter 9.4): Catling 1964 no. 34 (205–206 and pl. 34 a-d); Matthäus 1985 no. 704 (314–315 and pl. 100, 102); Papasavvas 2001 no. 23: 239–240 and 351–352, fig. 42–47; *Aspects*:82 no. 58, fig. 68.
[89] Barnett 1935:209: "We are actually shown the male divinity of the tree ... in the process of being worshipped"; Hübner 1992:123.

Figure 38 Enthroned/seated harpist, Sacred Tree, and offering-bearers. Cypriot bronze stand from Kourion (?), thirteenth century. London, BM 1920/12–20/1. Drawn from Papasavvas 2001 fig. 42–47.

repeated tree made the four sides a coherent composition, countered that it need only indicate an outdoor setting.[90] The two interpretations could come together in a sacred grove (a known locus of dance-rites in Archaic Cyprus).[91] There is in any case every reason to accept that this is a Sacred Tree, that ancient motif that came to the island via Mitannian(izing) glyptic, and remained a frequent motif in LBA Cypriot seals and other media.[92] The Sacred Tree's symbolism of fecundity is clearly appropriate here, given the three figures and the variety of products they carry. Barnett is therefore probably right that the Tree is the ultimate focus of the celebration, and so the intended recipient of the harper's song. Recall the 'Orpheus jug' from eleventh-century Megiddo, where again a Sacred Tree was the focus of musical celebration, this time by a 'kinyrist'.[93] In both cases, a goddess is probably symbolized.[94] We shall see precisely this combination of elements again in the Lyre-Player Group of Seals, with their winged lyrists, from eighth-century Cilicia (Chapter 21).

As Catling rightly stressed, however, another symmetrical element must be equally significant: the musician *confronts* the other figures. Given this composition, he asked, "could it not be the musician to whom the offerings are brought?"[95] The musician is further differentiated from the 'porters' by being seated, clearly indicating some higher status. The harper thus serves as a secondary focus of the composition, much like the lyrists in the model shrines discussed above—an intermediary agent of the higher divinity embodied by the Sacred Tree.[96] One thinks of Inanna/Ishtar in her role as royal patroness.[97]

The stand apparently combines the motif of the seated king or god receiving offerings with music as an index of the prosperous and well-ordered state.[98]

---

[90] Catling 1964:206. *Aspects*:82 notes both possibilities.

[91] For this view of the circular space at the temple of Apollo *Hylátēs* (Kourion), see with parallels Hübner 1992; for the one on Yeronisos, Connelly 2011:334–338. The same idea has been advanced for the Idalion *phiálē* (PBSB, Cy3: Figure 29 above): see Tubb 2003. For LBA Canaanite parallels, Mazar 2003.

[92] Mitannian Sacred Tree: Collon 1982:13, 78. Cypriot reception in various media: Danthine 1937:195–209; Porada 1981:27; Meekers 1987 (a typological study of 144 cylinder seals and one impression from LBA Cyprus, distinguishing four stages in the transformation of the Mitannian glyptic version); Webb 1999:272 (scenes of tree-adoration). For the Tree's broader ANE contexts, see p160n71 with references.

[93] See p159–161.

[94] Keel 1998:40: "All of these [sc. offerings on the stand] can be understood as sacrifices and gifts for a goddess or her temple." Gaber forthcoming includes the present tree among other evidence for the diffusion of Inanna iconography from Mesopotamia and its persistence and evolution in appropriate contexts in the Levant and Cyprus.

[95] Catling 1964:206

[96] See p236–239.

[97] See p37–40.

[98] See index s.v. 'order, symbolized by music'.

Whether or not it portrays some specific occasion, the offerings are a generalized picture of plenty. (Compare Homer's portrait of the ideal king, under whose rule a kingdom flourishes—unlike Ithaca, which awaits the return of its lyrist-king.[99]) The idea is reinforced by the distribution of produce around the stand—this, with the central Tree and musician, suggests something rather like the center and periphery of modern theory. The Hittite KI.LAM festival, with its regional offerings and musical celebrations symbolically renewing the kingdom and its ruler, is a very suggestive parallel.[100] In any case, the imagery has inevitable political overtones. It is therefore surely significant that the musician is a *controlling* element of the composition, while being himself subordinate to the most fully centralized element, the Sacred Tree.

Even if the harper is 'only' a celebratory musician, he can still readily symbolize the harmonious working of royal power, just as the porters represent the fecundity that results. Yet this is but the mirror image of a king who advertizes his flourishing regime by assuming a musician's stance, as did Shulgi, Ishme-Dagan, David, and Solomon.[101] There is every reason, indeed, to believe that the harper is *enthroned*. The same sort of double-value is exploited to good effect in many other ANE scenes where one cannot distinguish between royal and divine recipients of gifts. As Catling put it, there is "no telling whether he is divine or human, or even whether he is but an intermediary for the god or prince to whom the fruits of land and sea are brought as gifts."[102] Yet it may

---

[99] Odysseus, still disguised as a beggar, compares the good repute of his faithful Penelope to that of "some faultless king, who, fearing god and / Holding sway among mighty and many men, / Upholds justice. And the rich dark earth brings forth / Its wheat and barley, and the trees teem with their fruit; / Herds steadily produce, and the sea gives up its fish— / All from his kindly leadership—and the people flourish under him" (*Odyssey* 19.109–114). While the passage adheres to the 'Ruler's Truth' of Indo-European tradition (Watkins 1995:85; Martin 1984:34–35), similar concepts characterized LBA royal ideologies of the ANE; in that age of Great Kingship the Mycenaean *wánax*—not an Indo-European word—is likely to have been defined by a fusion of Indo-European, Pre-Greek/Minoan, and ANE concepts (see papers in Rehak 1995). It is therefore relevant that when Odysseus reveals himself through the trial of the bow he is compared to a lyrist (21.406–413). Recall the lyre-player (with Minoanizing instrument) who looms so large in the Throne Room fresco at Pylos (LH IIIB2–IIIC: Lang 1969:79–80 and pl. 27, 125–126), the climax of a procession scene, beginning in the adjacent room(s), which depicts some kind of religious ritual and feast overseen by the king—illustrating "the ruler's direct association both with the festival calendar and with an explicit ideology of divine protection and sound rule": McCallum 1987:140–141 (quotation), cf. 70–71, 109–124, 144–145; Palaima 1995b:132–133; Shelmerdine 2008:83–84.
[100] See p95. Cf. Bachvarova forthcoming, who, comparing the KI.LAM festival, interprets a number of Linear B tablets from Thebes as relating to a harvest festival, involving the convergence of regional labor-groups upon the capital (distributions are recorded for winnowers, builders, basket-carriers, shepherds, fullers, leather workers, textile workers).
[101] See index s.v. 'royal ideology:king as musician'.
[102] Catling 1964:207.

Chapter Fifteen

be this very ambiguity that is the scene's most important element. The harper may slip between musician, musician-king, musician-god, or king who serves as a musician-god to the still higher master-god(dess) in the Tree. Such multiple registers, simultaneously operative, would closely resemble what we saw with the balang-gods of Mesopotamia. And the same patterns seem to be illustrated by the Lyre-Player Group of Seals, which are probably the clearest surviving images of a Divine Lyre (Chapter 21).

Whatever the exact intention, the stand is important for attesting on Cyprus, *already in the pre-Greek period*, an ideologically-charged conjunction of music, metal, and kingship—all three important mythological attributes of Kinyras.

The second stand is open to a complementary interpretation.[103] Its main (upper) panels show, in order, a lion, a sphinx, a chariot and driver (with another figure flying through the air above), and two musicians attended by a server or offerings-bearer (Figure 39). These instruments have been erroneously called lyres, but they too are harps of Mesopotamian inspiration—with rounder angles than on the first stand, but essentially identical to each other (though slight variations accommodate other elements of the scene).[104] Again the four images work together, perhaps "a procession and a ritual feast which includes music and drinking."[105] Here too the seated musician faces all other figures; he is evidently the focus of the composition and the occasion and/or ideology it illustrates.[106] Clearly the symbolic treatment of chordophonic music-making on the previous stand was not unique, but part of a coherent iconographical repertoire on thirteenth-century Cyprus.

The present stand, however, emphasizes power and prestige over plenty. Mycenaean kraters with chariot-racing scenes are frequently found in elite

[103] London 1946/10-17/1 (height 31 cm; ring diameter 15.5): Catling 1964 no. 36, 208–210 and pl. 35 a-6 (musicians in d); Matthäus 1985 no. 706 (316–318 and pl. 103–104); Papasavvas 2001 no. 28, 242–243, 359–360 fig. 61-67 (musicians in 61, 64); *Aspects*:83 no. 59 fig. 69.

[104] Compare especially MgB 2/2:102 fig. 108 (Kassite seal, fourteenth century); 106 fig. 114–115 (NB). The mirroring of the two instruments was recognized by Catling 1964:209; so too Coldstream 1986:13, but calling both lyres; the standing figure's instrument is considered a lyre in *Aspects*:83, followed by Knapp 2011:123. The opposing perspectives are admittedly confusing, but close inspection of the left-hand figure reveals the harp's horizontal bar passing over the player's arm. The rounded material below each instrument's bar must represent the excess string-lengths treated decoratively; there are Mesopotamian parallels for this from the OB (MgB 2/2:88 fig. 75), Kassite (102 fig. 108), and N-A periods (122–123 and fig. 141, 126–127 and fig. 145, 130 and fig. 147, 136–139 and fig. 151–153), although none of these shows the strings gathered and tied off near the corner of the frame, as is apparently done here. I thank S. Hagel for helpful discussion of these points.

[105] Papasavvas 2001:243; *Aspects*:83 (quotation).

[106] So rightly Coldstream 1986:13; D'Albiac 1992:288.

Figure 39 Enthroned/seated harpist and harpist devotee. Cypriot bronze stand from Kourion (?), thirteenth century. London, BM 1946/10-17/1. Drawn from Papasavvas 2001 fig. 61-67.

Chapter Fifteen

Cypriot burials from the fifteenth through thirteenth centuries (LC II).[107] Sphinxes are an equally potent image. The most frequent monster in the corpus of stands, sphinxes enjoyed a long tradition in Cypriot iconography from the LBA into the Archaic period. They are found in various media—glyptic, ivory, gold, bronze, ceramic—and despite stylistic evolution are consistently connected with royal or divine figures and Sacred Trees.[108] A striking parallel are the 'cherubim', lions, and trees that adorned the (much larger) wheeled-stands built for Solomon (by Cypriot artisans?).[109] But the better analogy for our purposes is the juxtaposition of lyrist and sphinx in some of the eighth-century Lyre-Player Group of Seals, including one from Ayia Irini, near Morphou (Figure 46, Type IIc).[110] As C. D'Albiac remarks, "It is tempting to think that the memory of strange beings accompanied by a Lyre Player lingered at Paphos."[111]

Also of interest is the representation of *two* musicians, one seated and presumably enthroned, the other standing and facing him. This composition as a type—that is, in its normally nonmusical contexts—indicates reverence of and/or offerings to a king by his subjects, or to a god by a royal, hieratic, or other devotee. The stand's introduction of mirrored musical performance recalls the oscillations in Mesopotamia between musician-kings and balang-gods. Here again is the 'confusion' of musical performance by an actual officiant, and the (notional?) musicality of royal and/or divine figures. And of course the standing figure may himself be a king, performing before a god upon whom is projected this selfsame image of musician-king.[112]

---

[107] Keswani 1989:61, 65; Steel 1998, especially 291–292; PPC:196–197; Wijngaarden 2002:154–155; Bachvarova forthcoming ("Cyprus as a Source of Near Eastern Epic: An Overview").

[108] Cypriot sphinxes: Dessenne 1957:78–81, 154–160, 192–194, 198–199; Markoe 1988:21–22 (Syro-Phoenician antecedents and funerary associations); D'Albiac 1992; Webb 2001:75, noting two votive examples from the sanctuary of the Ingot God at Enkomi (Sols II–I); *Aspects*:110.

[109] 1 Kings 7:27–37.

[110] SCE 2 pl. CCXLV no. 2180; Buchner and Boardman 1966:35 no. 126; Reyes 2001:69, cat. 75, fig. 98.

[111] D'Albiac 1992:289. This seal-design is stressed by D'Albiac 1992:289–290 as a key example of the IA continuity of complex iconography, along with the Hubbard amphora (see p256).

[112] A remarkable coincidence should be signaled here. From some angles (e.g. Papasavvas 2001, fig. 64 and our Figure 39), a minute face appears below the arm-end of the right-hand instrument, suggesting a parallel with the heads of gods and pharaohs which graced Egyptian harps by the MBA (cf. p60); while these were affixed *above* the arm, a ceramic fragment with relief from Hattusha does show a harp-arm with such an ornament beneath (probably the head of a bird or quadruped: HKm:68 and pl. 10 no. 32; the curve of the arm is also similar). But the face/head on the Cypriot stand is probably illusory, as shown by an x-ray image kindly undertaken by J. Ambers and T. Kiely of the British Museum (who also arranged for preliminary observations and photography by S. Mirelman on my behalf). One sees, in a standard photograph, that the leftmost string of the instrument is, along much of its length, rather puffy; but the x-ray, penetrating corrosion to the underlying features of greater density, shows the thin string-line as originally intended. The top end disappears altogether in the x-ray, showing that here corrosion was more severe, bulging out to yield a fugitive face.

Crossing the Water

Thus, both stands, with differing emphases, adhere to a symbolic system—one that is, moreover, consistent with what has been established for Kinyras. This was acutely perceived already by N. Coldstream, with whose observations we may best conclude:

> A large robed figure, seated on a throne and approached by another male figure, also robed and playing the lyre … We are reminded of the central figure in Cypriot legend, the semi-divine Kinyras … also remembered as a musician who played his lyre in the presence of the gods … [sc. the first stand] seems to confirm that the seated musician is indeed a god … receiving the offerings brought by his worshippers.[113]

Although the ideology of both stands accords very well with a 'Kinyrad' interpretation, an organological complication must be confronted. It would have been most convenient if the musicians were given some form of Syro-Levantine lyre. Instead we find Mesopotamian(izing) harps. Yet this is not a fatal problem. Actually it is quite suggestive.

First, for all we know these harps *were* locally called *knr* in the generic sense of 'stringed instrument'.[114] We saw that several Sumerogrammic expressions meaning 'Inanna-instrument' embraced a variety of chordophones, including lyres and probably harps: in other words, precise morphology was less essential than ritual function and conceptualization.[115] If the Sacred Tree on the first stand does indeed symbolize a goddess, its harp would have been readily viewed as an 'Inanna-instrument'.

Second, recall that in the Gudea Cylinders the balang-god's *function* was, like an orchestra conductor, to supervise and coordinate the performance of *all* instruments. I have argued that Kinnaru played such a role on the basis of his unique divinization at Ugarit, where—as the ancestral lyre of the region—he presided over a complex environment of cultic music deriving from the convergence of several cultural traditions across many centuries.[116] Similarly, Shulgi and Ishme-Dagan claimed to play virtually all instruments—including the *zannāru*.[117] Thus, *any* musical scene with divine and/or royal significance is potentially relevant to the Kinnaru-Kinyras question. One may partially compensate for the 'missing lyre' by comparing the cosmopolitan musical ensembles of NK Egypt, in which both Mesopotamian(izing) harps and Syro-Levantine lyres and lutes

---

[113] Coldstream 1986:13.
[114] See p53, 256–257.
[115] See p77–79, 89–90.
[116] See p118.
[117] See p33–37, 80–81.

are juxtaposed. Such harps are found again at Alalakh and among the Hittites, in both cases an exotic addition to strong local lyre traditions.[118]

Finally, it is very possible that when these upright harps came west from Mesopotamia—evidently in the early- to mid-second millennium—associated conceptions were also imported. Two implications must be entertained. First, the classical Mesopotamian tonal system may have played an important role in this international musical world—as is already suggested by the Hurrian hymns from Ugarit.[119] Second, the harps may imply a parallel spread of divinized instruments and the associated ideology. The stands may therefore portray Cypriot monarchs emulating a Mesopotamian model of royal music-ideology going back ultimately to the likes of Shulgi and Ishme-Dagan.[120] As with the expression ^{giš}d Inanna, we must remain flexible as to organology, since the ideas might easily be transferred from one instrument to another more local one—namely the *knr*.

From Divine Lyre To Culture-Hero

Both stands present music as the controlling element of a larger symbolic system. This is already a startling 'prediction' of Kinyras, as an originally musical figure who subsumed further nonmusical functions. But the parallel is all the more striking for the ingot-bearer of the first stand, given the metallurgical Kinyras of legend. This strongly suggests that a metamusical Kinyras goes back in some form to the thirteenth century (at least); and the same conclusion is urged by independent evidence from Mycenaean Pylos (Chapter 17). This brings us to the puzzling disjunction between the versatile Kinyras of IA Cypriot myth and the powers and associations that can be reconstructed for a Divine Lyre *à la* Kinnaru of Ugarit.

I have argued that the Divine Lyre's importation to Cyprus was one aspect of a more general theological engagement with the mainland, especially as concerned royal cult and its patronage by 'Ishtar'. This context, I submit, can also illuminate the expansion of Kinyras, whose totalizing function as a culture-hero goes well beyond the usual type of *prôtos heuretḗs*, the legendary inventor of some *one* cultural pursuit.[121] The royal hymns of Shulgi and Ishme-Dagan proclaimed the king's superhuman perfection in all civilized arts; similar ideas were applied to Solomon. Like Shulgi, Kinyras established standard measures and ensured that they were scrupulously upheld ("talents of Kinyras"). Both

---

[118] See p90–92.
[119] See p97, 119.
[120] See p92–93.
[121] Kleingünther 1933.

were expert diviners.¹²² The ideal king also built and restored temples. Gudea built the house for Ningirsu; Shulgi's father Ur-Nammu initiated ziggurats at Ur, Eridu, and Nippur, and restored Inanna's complex at Uruk; similar works for Inanna and other gods are attested for Shulgi and Amar-Suen. Although these were historical projects by historical figures, their promotion entailed aspects of mythmaking, as seen clearly in the Gudea Cylinders. It is in keeping with this that Gudea, Ur-Nammu, and Shulgi all assumed the guise of master builder and brickmaker in poetry and/or iconography.¹²³ Just so, legend held that Kinyras built Aphrodite's great sanctuary at Paphos, and invented both bricks and tiles.¹²⁴ As the ideal of royal perfection accounts for the metamusical Kinyras, so it explains the musical powers of Shulgi, Ishme-Dagan, David, and Solomon. Shulgi claimed expertise in both celebratory song and lamentation, and both were practiced by David. We saw the same dual musical function with Kinyras (Chapters 9, 10, and 12).

But how does this interpretation of Kinyras as a metamusical artifact of Alashiyan royal cult and ideology harmonize with the obviously *popular* character attested by IA Cypriot legend—without which, after all, we would have no evidence for Kinyras at all? This gap could be spanned if the idea was publically projected and instituted with sufficient vigor to become rooted in popular thought.¹²⁵ Such an impulse is clearly seen in the N-S inscriptions and iconography, although the Ur III kings were eclipsed in long-term popular memory and myth by their predecessors Sargon and Naram-Sin of Akkad. A better parallel for Kinyras in this respect is David, whose perennial legends preserved pieces of period propaganda—his *kinnōr*-playing among the most tenacious. The proposal is given further substance by two sets of LBA iconographic evidence—cylinder seals and votive figurines—which attest musical performance in the service of

---

¹²² Shulgi: p35, 38. Kinyras: Chapter 16.
¹²³ Ur-Nammu: RIME 3/2 1.1.2-8; CS 2 no. 138C; cf. Michalowski 2008:35. Shulgi: RIME 3/2 1.2.1-34; CS 2 no. 139B. Amar-Suen: RIME 3/2 1.3.3-9, 1.3.14-17; CS 2 no. 140A. Inscribed figurines bearing baskets of bricks on their heads have been discovered in foundation deposits, as well as vast numbers of bricks stamped with royal names: Ellis 1968:23-25 (et passim), and fig. 19-20, 22-25 ('peg-wizards' of Gudea, Ur-Nammu, Shulgi, and Rim-Sin of Larsa bearing baskets on heads, from Lagash, Nippur, Uruk, and Ur, respectively). Gudea is also described as a brickmaker, and carrying a mortar basket on his head, in *The Building of Ningirsu's House* (ETCSL 2.1.7): Gudea Cylinders A 5.2-10, 6.6-8, 18.10-19.2, 20.24-21.12.
¹²⁴ Bricks/tiles: see p325 (these inventions also underlie the complex Khousor, Kinyras' alter ego in later Phoenicia: see Chapter 18). Temple-builder: Tacitus *Histories* 2.3, and further below, p401.
¹²⁵ Cf. Papantonio 2012:54-69 for good theoretical arguments against the idea that ideology and power simply "flow[s] from the top to the bottom of society"; rather it is "dialectically related to the different sets of resources, material (i.e. technology, artefacts) or non-material (i.e. knowledge, rank). In this respect, power and change operations usually can work on the basis of societal reproduction and transformation rather than clash and confrontation" (57-58).

Chapter Fifteen

state cult at a fairly popular level. This material is particularly relevant to the metamusical Kinyras for its connection with metallurgy—his most prominent secondary attribute.

It is certainly startling to think that a legendary priest of Aphrodite and hieratic 'kinyrist' could be credited with metalworking. But recall the industrial use to which lamentation singing and other music was put in Mesopotamia.[126] Conversely, the conjunction of metal-processing facilities and cult sanctuaries at Enkomi, Kition, and other Cypriot sites reveals a systematic sacralization of the LBA copper industry. Evidently metallurgy was seen as a kind of magical art, its geological basis and human development both ultimately in divine hands.[127] This is the readiest explanation of the famous 'Bomford Goddess', a female bronze figurine of unknown Cypriot provenance and probably twelfth-century or earlier date, who stands upon an ingot.[128] H. Catling associated her with a then-recent sensation from a sanctuary at Enkomi—the so-called Ingot God, who also surmounts an ingot (Figure 40).[129] Though found in an assemblage of items dated to the late twelfth or early eleventh century, stylistic criteria show that the Ingot God—akin to the smiting-god type of BA Syria and the Levant—is actually rather older.[130] G. Papasavvas has demonstrated, through technical analysis of the seam between ingot and feet, that the former was added at a relatively late stage, transforming a Levantine type into a distinctively Cypriot idol—embodying and upholding, through a combination of martial and metallurgical attributes, state control of metallurgical production and distribution.[131] Now J. Webb has persuasively argued that a second chamber—the west adyton,

---

[126] See p24, 30.

[127] Sacred/magical metallurgy: Frontisi-Ducroux 1975:35–82 passim; Karageorghis 1976b:57, 73–76; J. Karageorghis 1977:97–117; GR:47, 153; Knapp 1986; Dalley 1987; Loucas-Durie 1989; Morris 1992:87–88, 112; Blakely 2006. There is a parallel from Mycenaean Pylos, where a number of bronze-workers are qualified as 'Potnian', that is, 'of the goddess' (in the Jn series: see Lupack 2007:56; Lupack 2008b:114–119). But note that only about six percent of bronze-workers known from the Pylian records are so qualified (Lupack 2008b:118).

[128] This idea was first formulated by Catling 1971. Two closely comparable examples are in the museums of Nicosia and Kouklia (Palaipaphos), but since the base of each is broken away the original presence of an ingot is uncertain: Karageorghis 2002b:96 no. 194.

[129] Schaeffer 1965; Courtois 1971; Schaeffer 1971:505–510, with pl. I–VII. For these remarkable figures, find-contexts, and ideology, see *inter al.* Masson 1973; Karageorghis 1977:97–117; Knapp 1986; Karageorghis 1998:32–33 and fig. 8–9; Webb 2001; Papasavvas 2011:61–62, noting significant stylistic deviations from the smiting-god type.

[130] Muhly 1980:156–161; Knapp 1986:86–89 ("long been revered ... cared for and protected by both the elites that fostered their worship and the producers who carried it out," 87); Papasavvas 2011:65. Resheph and the smiting-god type: Lipiński 2009:139–160, especially 145–146.

[131] Papasavvas 2011:63–65, suggesting that the original figurine goes back to an earlier cult-structure (Sols V–VI [LC IIC]), while the attachment of the ingot, with its fairly crude artisanship, belongs to the period that immediately preceded the town's abandonment by the eleventh century.

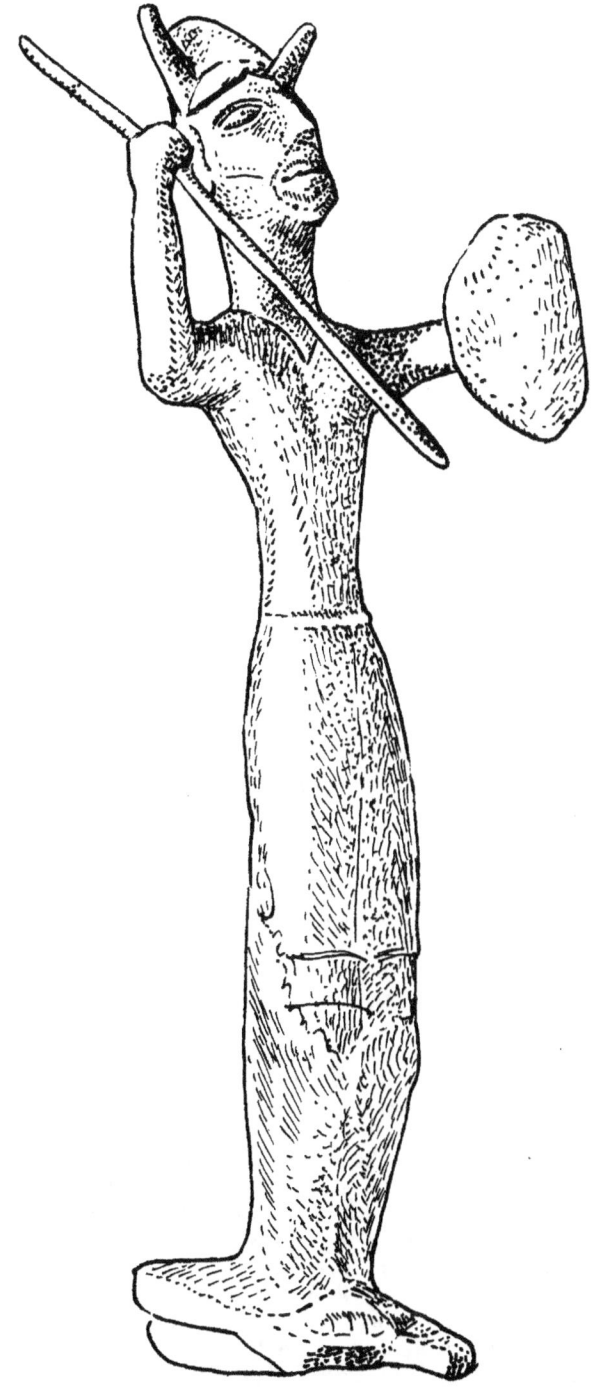

Figure 40 The 'Ingot God', Enkomi, ca. 1250 (LC III). Inv. F.E. 63/16.15. Drawn from Flourentzos 1996:47.

Chapter Fifteen

whose cult-figure is lost—must once have housed a divine consort for the Ingot God, analogous to the Bomford Goddess.[132] These analyses lend strong support to Catling's hypothesis that Cypriot metallurgy was a sacred industry governed by a divine couple—the goddess who guaranteed the fecundity of the mines, and the god who controlled and protected the industrial processes.[133]

What either would have been called in this period cannot of course be verified.[134] Yet Aphrodite's epithet *Kythéreia,* which many have seen as a feminine version of the name Kothar, provides a probable way forward.[135] The pairing of Kothar and *Kythéreia* (or rather a pre-Greek forerunner of the name[136]) would also conform to the well-attested ANE pattern of male and female divine couples sharing a name. Yet the hypothesis that a form of Kothar was present on Cyprus in the LBA—whether as a local interpretation of an indigenous smith-god, or in some more active guise—potentially returns us to Kinyras, as the two figures were eventually syncretized, most clearly on Cyprus itself. We shall return to these issues below (Chapters 18 and 19).

Whatever their names, the Ingot God and Bomford Goddess, along with the metallurgical workshops at sanctuaries and the first stand discussed above, all exemplify a larger program of "copper production and divine protection" going back to the fifteenth century and represented by a wide range of further material (not restricted to Enkomi). This includes miniature votive ingots and elaborate, seemingly ritual scenes on cylinder seals whose iconographic repertoire

---

[132] Webb 1999:102–113 and Webb 2001.

[133] Cf. Budin 2002, emphasizing sexuality and power over fertility both for the Bomford Goddess and Aphrodite more generally. Her point is well taken, though she herself acknowledges (319) that it is precisely in the iconography of the *Cypriot* goddess that a fertility aspect may be identified (LC II kourotrophos figurines); and if this slips away from later iconography, still Aphrodite is often associated with fertility especially in Cypriot contexts: *Kypris*:226–228 et passim. In early Greek poetry, see especially Hesiod *Theogony* 194–195 and *Homeric Hymn to Aphrodite* 69–74. Recall too that the Cypriot goddess was sometimes interpreted as Demeter/Ceres: see p287n46. For the 'fertility' of Cypriot metals, cf. Ovid *Metamorphoses* 10.220 (*fecundam Amathunta metallis*) and 531 (*gravidam Amathunta metallis*).

[134] Schaeffer 1971 argued that the Ingot God, whatever his Cypriot name, had already been associated with Mesopotamian Nergal and/or WS Resheph; the basis was EA 35, containing the Alashiyan king's apology to Pharaoh for his inability to send copper (for this text, see p372–373). Dalley 1987 sees a parallel in the Sumerian fertility goddess Ninhursag, also patroness of copper smelting, who by the early second millennium had been paired in North Syria with Nergal, identified with the WS Resheph (see p372). Dussaud 1954 interpreted as Kinyras the famous 'Horned God', also from Enkomi (Dikaios 1962, with fig. 18–22; Dikaios 1969–1971:197–199, 527–530, pl. 139–144; Karageorghis 1998:30 and fig. 7), and often connected with the island's 'horned Apollo' (Apollo *Kereátas*: see p230n64).

[135] Brown 1965:216–219; EFH:56–57, eschewing the alternative interpretation of Burkert 1992:35, 190.

[136] See p476–479.

likewise features bronze ingots.[137] J. Webb has persuasively argued that cylinder seals—appearing in the fifteenth century under the stimulus of Mitannian glyptic, but soon developing a distinctive Cypriot idiom[138]—were a pervasive and effective medium for the dissemination of state ideology on the island, with specific iconographic registers targeted at different tiers of the hierarchy through which copper production was managed and controlled. Members of the higher echelon sported unique, complex, and exquisitely executed scenes using an internationally oriented symbolic repertoire. 'Middle management' was favored with simpler, repetitive designs that exemplified obedience to authority and maintenance of the status quo.[139]

This latter category includes fairly numerous scenes of infinite processions or ring-dances—indistinguishable performance modes given the circularity of the medium (Figure 41).[140] The dancers typically move against a backdrop of trees, perhaps a sacred grove. Such performances would naturally entail musical accompaniment, which we must assume is simply not shown. This may help explain the numerous clay rattles that have been found in mainly LBA tombs.[141] K. Kolotourou has rescued these finds from obscurity by stressing the subtle, yet potentially profound, psychological and sociological effects of collective rhythmic performance.[142] Moreover, several bronze cymbals going back to ca. 1200–1150[143] may be confidently connected with state cult; using valuable material and needing laborious manufacture, these instruments must derive from higher levels of 'musical management', as was seen at Ugarit and in the Bible.[144]

Two cylinder seals of the procession/dance group show a figure carrying an object interpreted by some as a stringed instrument (Figure 42).[145] Unfortunately

---

[137] See especially Knapp 1986.
[138] Porada 1948:196 et passim.
[139] Webb 2002, developing ideas in Courtois and Webb 1987; Webb 1992; Webb 1999:262; cf. PPC:153–154.
[140] Procession/dance scenes: Schaeffer 1952, pl. VII.1, 3–5; further references in Courtois and Webb 1987:76n249, 78n253; Webb 1999:272.
[141] Buchholz 1966; Buchholz 1990.
[142] Kolotourou 2005; Kolotourou 2007. Knapp 2011:122 has rightly noted that ubiquitous explanations of such finds in terms of goddess-cult are often facile and lacking in contextual support. A number of incised scapulae found in clear ritual contexts have also been interpreted as rhythmical instruments, though others see them as divinatory devices (both ideas could be right): see with references Webb 1999:249–250, doubting the musical interpretation ("predominantly if not exclusively associated with ritual and in particular with urban cult buildings of LC IIC-LC III"). Parallels are known from several Levantine sites: MAIP:94, 176; Caubet 2014:178.
[143] Catling 1964:142–146; Knapp 2011:122, with references.
[144] See p115–118.
[145] Aign 1963:60 with fig. 25. First seal: Schaeffer 1952, pl. VII.4; Webb 1999:272–273 fig. 87.2. Second seal, from Enkomi Tomb 2 (inventory no. E 2:67), Late Cypriot I-II: SCE 1:474 no. 67 and pl. LXXVI no. 67 ("From the left approaches a procession of four adorers. The first of them holds a lyre");

Chapter Fifteen

Figure 41 Procession/dance scene. Modern impression of LBA Cypriot cylinder-seal from Enkomi, ca. 1225–1175 (LC IIIA). Nicosia, Cyprus Museum 1957 inv. no. 36. Drawn from Courtois and Webb 1987 pl. 7 no. 23.

the identification is rather uncertain. In the second of these, illustrated here and dated ca. 1600–1200, the object *may* be a harp akin to those of the second Kourion stand discussed above, elongated to fit into the scene; it is held in an impossible playing position, but *could* be seen as an offering to the seated king or god.

Nevertheless, a chordophonic aspect to metallurgical cult-music is quite plausibly inferred from the hundred or so broken figurines found in the sanctuary of the Ingot God, where their placement around the west adyton indicates that it was his female consort who was the primary focus of worship[146]—an important point given Kinyras' subordination to Aphrodite. As already mentioned, these figurines probably included choral groups around central lyre- and pipe-players.[147] They seem to go back to the main pre-Greek phase of the sanctuary (Sol III, LC IIIB), although they continued to be devoted (Sols II–I)—even as the sanctuary was gradually abandoned during the population shift to Salamis by the eleventh century.[148]

Both the glyptic dance-scenes and the presumed musical figurines from Enkomi indicate the musical enactment of state ideology at a popular social

---

Karageorghis 2003:280–281 no. 320 (lyre or fan), with comments of D. Collon (fan, comparing Collon 1987 no. 270).
[146] Webb 1999:102–113 and Webb 2001.
[147] See p242.
[148] Webb 2001:76–79. For the locations of the figurines, see Courtois 1971:326, fig. 140bis.

Crossing the Water

Figure 42 Procession/dance scene with possible stringed instrument. Modern impression of LBA Cypriot cylinder-seal from Enkomi Tomb 2. Stockholm, Medelhavsmuseet Inv. E. 2:67. Drawn from Karageorghis 2003:280–281 no. 320.

level, specifically in the context of metallurgical cult. This in turn provides both a real-world context for the blending of associations embodied by Kinyras, and a mechanism for elements of a symbolic system to persist across the period in which Aegean immigration unfolded. Such continuity-despite-change is paralleled by the late career of the Ingot God himself, who was carefully cached in a ritual, which, it seems, officially terminated the sanctuary's use.[149]

A more precise understanding of the historical circumstances behind the Divine Lyre's arrival and evolution is considerably hindered by the disputed problem of the island's political configuration in the LBA, which was probably not static. Several scenarios may be suggested.

First, and to me most plausible, is that an expanded, metamusical Kinyras was already a more-or-less island-wide phenomenon by the thirteenth century. This may have been through the Divine Lyre's use in a centralized cult at a time when all or most of Cyprus was under the control of a single royal house, say, hypothetically, in the fifteenth century under Enkomi; or in the fourteenth and thirteenth centuries (the time of Alashiyan correspondence with Amarna and Ugarit), with central power located perhaps near Alassa and/or Kalavasos.[150] Whatever the exact political arrangements in Alashiya, the close proximity of Ugarit and its diplomatic relations with Alashiya impose themselves as

---

[149] Webb 2001; Papasavvas 2011:64.
[150] See p10–11.

Chapter Fifteen

exemplary, although Syro-Hurrian material deriving from Kizzuwatna and North Syria also presents many suggestive parallels. With the later thirteenth century, one must allow for the possibility of political fragmentation and fleeting Hittite control.[151] Yet even here one could suppose regional inheritances of an earlier Alashiyan ideology, so that Kinyras might maintain a supralocal profile. In other words, at this stage Kinyras may have represented kingship *on* the island, rather than *over* it.

Alternatively, one may look to a specific regional Kinyras of the LBA who then became generalized in the IA. Here one must think first of Paphos, with which Kinyras is so commonly connected. The attractive hypothesis that Paphos was the principal sacred site of a state centered around Alassa, whose name is clearly related to Alashiya, needs further investigation.[152] Be this as it may, IA Paphos was one of the most conspicuous sites of cult continuity, and the goddess's most internationally renowned sanctuary. The Paphian kings could therefore rightly claim inheritance of LBA ideology and traditions; because their kingship depended on the grace of the goddess, they 'played the part' of Kinyras in carrying out the duties of her cult, and called themselves his descendants (as we shall see in the next chapter). Following this hypothesis, Kinyras would then have become a magnet for collective memory, widely accepted by the island's various ethnic groups as a figurehead of pre-Greek times. As other IA kings vied with Paphos in establishing rival ideologies, competing claims of Kinyrad ancestry might be advanced, or the virtuous Kinyras undermined; I have argued for both developments at Salamis, at different stages.[153]

On any historical scenario, Kinyras must be seen as a product of the LBA, deriving from the self-image projected by one or probably more Cypriot kings to their subjects. The original Kinyras resided at the intersection of royal ideology and sacred lyre-cult—that is, in the execution of liturgical music in the contexts of state ritual. After the 'Great Collapse', the old ideology rang on in popular memory under his name. His original attributes were best preserved at Paphos, to which we now turn.

---

[151] See p13.
[152] See p11, 363.
[153] See p345.

16

The Kinyradai of Paphos

EVIDENCE FROM AND RELATING TO PAPHOS especially lets us pick up the thread of Kinyras' cult in the Classical period, and follow it down until later antiquity. Here the two broad patterns explored above—the social and political manipulation of Kinyras as a cultural icon, and the maintenance of his ancient role as a hieratic servant of the goddess—overlap most fully. And ultimately Paphian traditions, preserved at the sanctuary itself, may help us track Kinyras back to his mainland origin(s).

Tacitus and the Memories of the Paphian Priesthood

In 69 CE, the future Roman emperor Titus, on his way to Judaea to carry out the siege of Jerusalem for his father Vespasian, stopped at Paphos to consult with the sanctuary's divination-priest about his own career prospects (the wise Sostratos gave a positive forecast).[1] Tacitus, in mentioning this voyage, includes a digression on the history of this most famous cult-site of Aphrodite:

> There is an ancient tradition (*vetus memoria*) that Aerias was the founder of the temple, although some maintain that this was the name of the goddess herself [i.e. *Aeria]. A more recent report (*fama recentior*) holds that the temple was consecrated by Cinyras, and the goddess herself, after being born in the sea, was driven here; but that the art and science of divination was imported, and the Cilician Tamiras introduced it; and that it was so arranged that the descendants of each family would direct the rituals. Before too long, however, the foreign line gave up the science which it had itself brought in, so that the royal line [sc. of Cinyras] might not be without some distinction over the newcomers: only the Kinyrad priest is consulted.[2]

---

[1] Also Suetonius *Titus* 5. Cf. HC:233; Mitford 1990:2180.
[2] Tacitus *Histories* 2.3: *Conditorem templi regem Aeriam vetus memoria, quidam ipsius deae nomen id perhibent. fama recentior tradit a Cinyra sacratum templum deamque ipsam conceptam mari huc*

401

Chapter Sixteen

In the *Annals*, Tacitus again states that Aerias first built the Paphian temple, which was held to be the island's oldest. Aerias, he says, was the father of Amathus, who had gone on to consecrate the temple to "Amathusian Venus." Third in age was the temple to Jupiter at Salamis, established by Teukros.³

This scheme for the Cypriot temples, in which Paphos holds pride of place both chronologically and (*vis-à-vis* Amathous) by mythical genealogy, belongs to Tacitus' catalogue of Greek sanctuaries that in 22 CE had to defend their authenticity before Tiberius, who was investigating rampant abuses in the granting of asylum. To be 'reaccredited', the various states were required to send "charters and ambassadors" to establish their legitimacy; and many, according to Tacitus, "put their trust in ancient superstitions."⁴ The emperor upheld the status of all three Cypriot sanctuaries, and the citizens of Paphos erected a stele proclaiming their gratitude and hailing Tiberius their savior.⁵ The outcome, for Paphos at least, was probably a foregone conclusion, since this was the provincial seat of the emperor cult,⁶ and the Julio-Claudians traced their descent from Venus herself. The latter point had been emphasized by the Community of Cyprus in their loyalty oath to Tiberius upon his accession just eight years earlier (14 CE)—the same occasion on which they invoked "Our *Kenyristḗs* Apollo."⁷

When the evidence of the *Histories* and the *Annals* is combined, and one recognizes the leading role enjoyed by Paphos in the historical construction—which as it happens is broadly correct—it becomes clear that Tacitus' material derives substantially from the Paphian priesthood itself. It is a précis—perhaps even a partial transcription—of their official report before the investigating tribunal, available to the historian through senate archives.⁸ We are therefore dealing with a specifically Paphian understanding of Kinyras.⁹

---

adpulsam; sed scientiam artemque haruspicum accitam et Cilicem Tamiram intulisse, atque ita pactum ut familiae utriusque posteri caerimoniis praesiderent. mox, ne honore nullo regium genus peregrinam stirpem antecelleret, ipsa quam intulerant scientia hospites cessere: tantum Cinyrades sacerdos consulitur.

3   Tacitus *Annals* 3.62: *exim Cyprii tribus delubris, quorum vetustissimum Paphiae Veneri auctor Aerias, post filius eius Amathus Veneri Amathusiae et Iovi Salaminio Teucer, Telamonis patris ira profugus, posuissent.*

4   Tacitus *Annals* 3.60: *placitum ut mitterent civitates iura atque legatos ... multae vetustis superstitionibus ... fidebant.* The mythological basis of these petitions is discussed by Cameron 2004:226–227.

5   ExcCyp 6; IGRom 3:941; I.Paphos 148.

6   Mitford 1990:2182.

7   See p205.

8   For Tacitus' use of the *Acta senatus* generally, see Talbert 1984:326–364 (329 for the asylum petitions). While the so-called *Senatus consultum de Cn. Pisone patre* (Eck et al. 1996) illuminates the historian's creative departure from official records, it is less revealing about his use of the *Acta* themselves (see Talbert 1999; Damon 1999). I see no reason why Tacitus should have distorted the diplomatic record in the present case.

9   Pirenne-Delforge 1994:332–333 suggests that only Aerias was mentioned in the official report, and that Tacitus himself has introduced the familiar tradition of Kinyras. But Kinyras' appearance

Some of what Tacitus relays is familiar from other sources, in particular Kinyras' association with kingship, divinatory arts, and of course the goddess and her sanctuary.[10] The details of Aerias and Tamiras, however, are quite unparalleled.

'Aerias' permits two interpretations. Most scholars have looked to Lat. *aer, aeris* ('air', from Gk. *aḗr, aéros*), seeking a correspondence with Gk. *Ouránios* or *Ouranós*.[11] This would make him a sky- or storm-god like Baal or Zeus, and a male counterpart to Aphrodite Ourania, as later Greek sources often called the goddess when acknowledging her NE background.[12] Because Tacitus adds that "certain people consider this the name of the goddess herself" (that is, *Aeria),[13] some scholars dismiss Aerias as a misunderstanding or a fiction "assez tardif"—that is, a back-construction from Ourania.[14] Of course, the pattern of 'Mr. and Mrs. Sky' has ancient precedents in the Near East, beginning with Sumerian Anu and Inanna.[15] And it is generally recognized that this pattern is reflected in the coupling of Zeus and Dione, who appear unexpectedly as Aphrodite's parents in *Iliad* five—a book containing several other unusual features of a Cypriot cast.[16]

Nevertheless, I prefer the alternative proposal to connect *Aerias* and **Aeria* with Lat. *aes, aeris*, 'copper' or 'bronze'.[17] This would arise readily from reinterpretation of the goddess's epithets *Kýpris* and *Kypría*, since the adjective *kýprios*, passing into Lat. as *cyprius*, was commonly applied to copper by the time in question (Lat. *cyprium aes* or just *cyprium*, whence Eng. 'copper').[18] While the etymology itself would be late, it would have been grounded in ancient and accurate traditions about the central importance of copper to the island—which

---

here is inextricably involved with the Tamiradai, and the very obscurity of the latter shows that they, like Aerias, must derive from the official report.

[10] See p21–323, 363.

[11] The manuscript variant *Uranium* was indeed read by Alciatus (hence the "Uranie Roy" of *Description*, p. 16), but this is clearly a gloss: ExcCyp:176; HC:69n5; cf. Baurain 1980b:290; Pirenne-Delforge 1994:311 (skeptical of the equation); Currie 2005:276n90 (noting that *Ouránios* and *Aérios* are elsewhere attested as epithets of Zeus).

[12] Farnell 1896–1909 2:629–631. See further p378.

[13] Note that ἀερία (presumably 'airy' or 'misty') is reported as a former name for Cyprus (and several other places) by Hesykhios s.v. (ἀερία· ὀμίχλη, παρὰ Αἰτωλοῖς. Θάσον τε τὴν νῆσον, καὶ Αἴγυπτον, καὶ Λιβύην, καὶ Κρήτην, καὶ Σικελίαν, καὶ Αἰθιοπίαν, καὶ Κύπρον οὕτως ἐκάλουν). Can all of these places be imagined as especially 'airy' or 'misty'?

[14] Blinkenberg 1924:31.

[15] Black and Green 1992 s.v. Inana, "derived from a presumed Nin-ana, 'Lady of Heaven'"; also s.v. An for Antu as wife of Babylonian Anu.

[16] Zeus and Dione: Burkert 1992:97–98; EFH:361–363 and further literature in n36. For Dione-Aphrodite and Cyprus cf. also Theokritos *Idylls* 15.106, 17.36; Dionysios the Periegete 508–509. For *Iliad* 5, see Cassio 2012 §4–5. Note too that Aphrodite is apparently paired with Zeus in several late fifth century coins from Marion, and fourth-century examples from Paphos: BMC Cyprus:lx-xi and plates (Marion), lxxix and pl. VIII.12–13 (Paphos); cf. *Paphos*:205.

[17] Pirenne-Delforge 1994:331–333 and n121–122.

[18] LSJ s.v. κύπριος; LS s.v. Cyprus II A–B; OLD s.v. Cyprius.

was itself sometimes called *aerosa* for just this reason.[19] Its key early role in the cult of the goddess herself, we saw, is vividly illustrated by the Bomford Goddess, who has a close male counterpart in the Ingot God; and this coupling may be reflected in Aphrodite's epithet *Kythéreia*, which many would see as a female counterpart to Kothar, the Syro-Levantine craftsman-metals god.[20] This latter idea finds compelling independent support in ps.-Meliton, who knew a myth of 'Hephaistos' (i.e. a metals god) controlling Cyprus before the intervention of a Kauthar-Kinyras figure (see Chapter 19). Admittedly, it would be quite astonishing for the Paphian priests of the Roman era to have maintained an "ancient memory" of a LBA metal-god. But Aphrodite's great sanctuary at Paphos, if anywhere on the island, will have been a locus of early oral traditions, and may even have maintained written records from the LBA into the IA.[21]

Tamiras is equally obscure.[22] Hesykhios contains an entry for *Tamirádai*, defined as "certain priests in Cyprus."[23] Possibly the lexicographer depends solely on Tacitus, but note that the plural form is not found in the historian himself, nor is Paphos specified. It is not clear from either source whether these Tamiradai were still active, but it sounds as if not.

Several etymologies, none entirely convincing, have been proposed for the Tamiradai. Movers suggested a link with Thymarete, the daughter of Pygmalion whom Kinyras married after emigrating from Cilicia in one tradition (if so, the named has obviously been Hellenized).[24] The syllabic sequence *Tu-mi-ra*, which occurs in an Eteocypriot inscription from Amathous and may be a DN, has been thought relevant.[25] Others point to the Hebrew *tamar*, 'date-palm', and suggest a connection with Sacred-Tree cult both on the island and in the Levant.[26] One

---

[19] Paulus Diaconus *Epitome of Festus* 18.23 (Lindsay): *Aerosam appellaverunt antiqui insulam Cyprum, quod in ea plurimum aeris nascatur* (also in Étienne de Lusignan *Chorograffia* p. 2a [§1], "Erosa," *Description* p. 2a, "Aereuse"). The datum goes back to the Augustan period (Verrius Flaccus, whom Festus had himself epitomized in his *On the Meaning of Words*) or beyond; despite Paul's general terms, the 'usage' probably had no popular life outside of poetry and technical writers (Pliny *Natural History* 34.2.2–4 is relevant).

[20] The idea is entertained favorably by *Kypris*:136. See further p476–479.

[21] One must suppose a continuous literate tradition in parts of Cyprus to explain the kinship of the Cypro-Minoan script and later, regional varieties of Cypro-Syllabic: Iacovou 2006b:31–32, 36–39; M. Egetmeyer in Steele 2012:107–131.

[22] RE 4 (1932), 2138; Heubner 1963–1982 2:34, 36.

[23] Hesykhios s.v. Ταμιράδαι· ἱερεῖς τινες ἐν Κύπρῳ. Cf. Neumann 1961:36.

[24] Σ Dionysios the Periegete 509; cf. [Apollodoros] *Library* 3.14.3. See Movers 1841–1856 2:237 and n32, 275n50a; GGM 2:450, *ap. crit.* For these texts, see further Chapter 21.

[25] This was proposed by Power 1929:162–163; rejected by Neumann 1961:36. The inscription is ICS 194 (line 4); cf. Egetmeyer and Hintze 1992:201; DGAC:581 no. 5; Steele 2013 no. EC 3.

[26] Tamiradai < *tmr*: Power 1929:162–163; Dugand 1973:199, following Astour 1965:137 in comparing the episode of Tamar's disguised seduction of her father-in-law Judah (Genesis 38:12–30) with Myrrha's of Kinyras, and noting the correspondence of both female names with that of a tree;

might then think of the harper who sings before the sacred tree on the bronze stand discussed above.[27] But these vague ideas do not account for the special Cilician connection of the Tamiradai. A seventh-century Phoenician inscription from Cebel İres Daği, in Rough Cilicia, contains the consonantal sequence TMRS, apparently a TN; this has seemed promising, but gives little purchase.[28] Slightly more tangible is a proposed connection with *dammara-*, a word of perhaps Luwian or Hurrian origin, which in Hittite sources designates temple-personnel, both male and female, charged with the care of grain; but the absence of overlapping function with the Tamiradai remains problematic.[29]

A final possibility is that Tamiras is somehow cognate with Thamyris/Thamyras.[30] We have seen that a cultic group known as Thamyrists (*Thamyríddontes*) was active in fourth-century Thespiai (Boeotia), evidently tracing their descent from the musician who in Homer's hands was blinded by the Muses.[31] Unfortunately, their function remains largely obscure, frustrating comparison with the entrails-inspection of the Tamiradai. The hypothesis would offer a quite exact parallel to the Kinyradai in their self-presentation as descendants of a legendary lyrist. It would remain to explain how an evidently Aeolic lyre-tradition might find a cognate in early Cilicia and Cyprus. Still, an EIA Aegean/Achaean presence in Cilicia now seems beyond doubt.[32] Note that a further tradition of royal priesthood links Cilicia and Cyprus: the Salaminian lineage was implicated in a local Cilician tradition, whereby Ajax son of Teukros founded a dynasty and hereditary priesthood at Olbe.[33] There is also the term *akhaiománteis*—'Achaean priests' or 'Achaean prophets'—defined by Hesykhios as "those who hold the sacred office of the gods in Cyprus."[34] The word connotes an ultimately extra-Cypriot origin, and thus potentially deep antiquity; unattested in the island's inscriptions, it may have been long obsolete by the Classical period.[35] It is therefore worth considering whether the Tamiradai represent some reflection, at the hieratic level, of a cultural encounter between Aegean

---

Heubner 1963–1982 2:34 suggests that Tamira was the pre-Greek name of the Paphian goddess herself.

[27] See p383–388.
[28] Mosca and Russell 1987:9.
[29] Neumann 1961:36–37.
[30] Movers 1841–1856 2:275 and n50a; Ohnefalsch-Richter 1893 1:252; contra RE 4 (1932), 2138. The presence of *i* versus *y* is unproblematic, given the early fronting of Greek *ŭ/ū* (see p196). For 'confusion' of *t* and *th* in a second-third century context, Allen 1987:24.
[31] SEG 32:503: see p234.
[32] See p250n44.
[33] Strabo 14.5.10. Cf. Gjerstad 1944:116.
[34] Hesykhios s.v. ἀχαιομάντεις· οἱ τὴν τῶν ... θεῶν ἔχοντες ἱερωσύνην ἐν Κύπρῳ.
[35] Cf. Karageorghis 1988:193: "un nom assez révélateur pour les prêtres ... qui évoque leur lointaine origine et leurs dons divinatoires."

Chapter Sixteen

immigrants and a Paphian religious and royal 'establishment' in the twelfth and/or eleventh centuries, with an older Kinyrad ideology eventually prevailing.[36] We saw a comparable duality in the competing myths that attributed the foundation of Paphos to either Kinyras or Agapenor, where again it was the Kinyrad apparatus that maintained the upper hand.[37]

The composite, layered nature of the Paphian priests' 'memories' is striking. It is crucial, I believe, that Kinyras was presented as a secondary stratum *by the priests themselves*. The Paphians may be suspected of being motivated in part by a desire to surpass the other Cypriot sanctuaries in a bid for antiquity; for while the Amathousians obviously attributed to 'Amathous' the foundation of their temple in reporting to the Roman senate, the Paphians advanced Aerias as the *father* of Amathous.[38] Now 'Amathousa' is also found in some sources as the mother of Kinyras.[39] If the Amathousians placed any emphasis on this point, Kinyras would not have given the Paphians the oldest claim. Nor would traditions about Agapenor.[40]

Whatever the Paphian priests' motivation or basis for promoting Aerias, their profession that Kinyras was a relative 'latecomer' must be essentially correct, if Kinyras is rooted in a Divine Lyre of mainland origin(s). This should be added to other traditions that connect Kinyras variously with Byblos, Syria/Assyria, Cilicia, and perhaps Sidon (see further Part Three).[41]

---

[36] Baurain 1975–1976:531–532 rightly saw the juxtaposition of Tamiras and Kinyras as a simple mythological rationalization to explain an historical fact of two priestly families presiding in the cult of Aphrodite. But the question remains: why should there ever have been a dual priesthood at all?

[37] See further p360–368.

[38] See Pirenne-Delforge 1994:332–333.

[39] For Kinyras and Amathous, see p346–350. Mother Amathousa: Herodian *De prosodia catholica* 242.34 Lentz; cf. Stephanos of Byzantium s.v. Ἀμαθοῦς. The genealogy of Kinyras as son of Paphos or Paphia (Σ Pindar *Pythian* 2.28; Σ Dionysios the Periegete 509; Hyginus *Fabulae* 275) would also make him secondary to the foundation of the city and cult.

[40] See p359–368.

[41] For Neumann 1961:36 and Heubner 1963–1982 2:34, Kinyras, though featuring in the *fama recentior*, represents an autochthonous tradition (versus the imported Tamiradai). But while Kinyras clearly symbolizes pre-Greek Cypriot culture in many sources (see Chapters 13 and 14), this need not contradict the persistent traditions of his external origin. It is simply a question of relative chronology, historical and/or mythopoeic: Kinyras must only antedate the *Greek* cultural layer of Cyprus.

Nikokles and the Kinyrad Legacy

Of the ancient kings of Paphos, twelve are known by name, the earliest in the Esarhaddon prism inscription (N-A, 673/672 BCE).[42] Archaic statuary shows the Paphian kings in priestly costume, a clear enough indication that they already served as high priests in the seventh century (Figure 43).[43] This assumption accords well with the religious conservatism implied by the Classical inscriptions, in which one finds the formula "King of Paphos and Priest of the Queen"—using an old Mycenaean royal title for the goddess (*Wánassa* or *Ánassa*).[44] Such a pairing of king and goddess, we have seen, is a royal posture of deep antiquity, attested already in third-millennium Mesopotamia. That this was a LBA survival at Paphos, rather than an IA innovation, is supported by Astarte's role as royal protectress at Ugarit and elsewhere (Chapter 15). The same idea endured among the IA Phoenician kings: those of Sidon and Tyre served as priests of the goddess, while tenth-century Byblian inscriptions portray the goddess as kingmaker and guarantor of the ruler's life and power.[45]

This environment makes it easy to believe that the Kinyrad identity of the royal house was equally traditional. For the fifth century, we have seen, it is

---

[42] See p14n73, p360n131.

[43] See Maier 1989:380–386, detecting significant Egyptian and Assyrian influences in the iconography and dress; yet his suggestion (386) that the Paphian conception of sacral kingship comes therefore from those quarters—that is, quite recently—is unnecessary (Maier 1996:130 is more tentative on this point). The Paphian kings, while maintaining an ancient ideology, could merely have adapted their regalia to the prevailing political climate and attendant fashions. Indeed, the mélange of Assyrianizing and Egyptianizing elements argues against any single foreign source. We are seeing rather a peripheral response to imperial power, a phenomenon otherwise well documented for the N-A period. The Sargon stele from Kition attests an Assyrian ideological presence on the island in the late eighth century (cf. p353). Echoes of N-A imperial diction, recycled to express anti-Assyrian sentiments, are found in Hebrew literature deriving from the period (Cohen 1979, especially 38–47; Machinist 1983b, with further references in 729n29; Machinist 1993:98; Patzek 2003:71–74). Similarly, some Phoenician inscriptions reveal stylistic affinities with the N-A royal inscriptions and annals: Amadasi 1982. For Lydia's responses to Assyrian ideology, see Franklin 2008.

[44] Ὁ ἱερεὺς τῆς ϝανάσσας (also ἱερής, *i-ye-re-se*): ICS 4.1, 6.1, 7.4, 16.2, 17.4, 90.2, 91.7 = DGAC: 730 no. 4, 732–733 no. 1–2, 735–736 no. 8–9, 594–595 no. 1–2. Cf. ExcCyp:186–187; Blinkenberg 1924:31–32; Baurain 1980b:283n26; *Paphos*:157; Maier 1989:376–377; *Kypris*:136, 40–42.

[45] For Ugarit, see p114–115. Sidon: KAI 13.1–2 (Tabnit I, late 6th, "Priest of Astarte, king of the Sidonians, son of Eshmunazar, priest of Astarte, king of the Sidonians") = CS 2 no. 56, cf. KAI 14 (Eshmunazar I) = CS 2 no. 57; also the kings named 'Straton' (i.e. Abdastart), Grainger 1991:22–23, 30 et passim. For Ithobaal of Tyre and royal theophoric names with 'Astarte', see the 'Tyrian Annals' (Aubet 1993:27–28) in Josephus *Against Apion* 1.106–127 (Menandros of Ephesus FGH 783 F 1). Cf. Bunnens 1979:356; Maier 1989:386 and n34; DDUPP:451–452 (with comments on Plutarch *Moralia* 357b). Byblos: KAI 5–7, 10 (Baal, not Baalat, is now read in KAI 4: Bonnet 1993; Mettinger 2001:140); ANET:656; CS 2 no. 32; DDUPP:72.

Figure 43 Limestone head of Kinyrad king, seventh century. Palaepaphos KA 730. Drawn from Maier 1989:378 fig. 40.1.

corroborated by Pindar, with Kinyras as "the beloved priest of Aphrodite."[46] It has been suggested that Homer's brief portrait of Kinyras as a Great King who sends a friendship gift to Agamemnon is evidence that he had not yet taken on a hieratic dimension.[47] But the perception of Kinyras could naturally have been different in and out of Cyprus, and from one genre to the next. Homer's context of royal gift-exchange would not have especially encouraged the inclusion of priestly detail. On the other hand, as I have argued elsewhere, Kinyras was probably Aphrodite's agent in a lost branch of epic that dealt with the heroic wanderings of Paris and Helen in the eastern Mediterranean.[48]

In the current state of evidence, it is only the city's last king, Nikokles II (died ca. 306), for whom we have any detailed information, including on-the-ground epigraphic evidence of the Kinyrad legacy.

That Nikokles was an energetic and ambitious ruler is shown by a little corpus of royal inscriptions documenting an impressive building program.[49] He evidently (re)founded and presumably walled Nea Paphos, the harbor of which could accommodate a large fleet.[50] He also built a monumental new temple to Artemis *Agrotéra* ('The Huntress');[51] expanded an existing shrine to Hera;[52] consecrated an oracular hypogeum to Apollo *Hylátēs*;[53] and probably constructed defensive walls around Old Paphos in the turmoil that followed the death of Alexander.[54]

This evidence is clear "proof of an explicit cultural and religious policy of the king."[55] One thrust of Nikokles' program, with its building projects on behalf of Olympian gods, was probably to present himself as 'more Greek' than his prede-

---

[46] Pindar *Pythian* 2.17. See Chapter 10.
[47] Homer *Iliad* 11.19–28: see p1, 322. This point is made by Maier 1989:377, 387n5; Baurain 1980b:305; similarly Baurain 1981a:24n4 would see Kinyras' connection with Aphrodite as a secondary, post-BA development.
[48] See for now Franklin 2014:232–240, and cf. p1, 338–339 above.
[49] The sources for Nikokles are collected and discussed by Mitford 1960a; Mitford 1960b:200–205; Spyridakis 1963:143–154; Michaelidou-Nicolaou 1976; ICS 1–3, 6–7, 90–91; *Paphos*:222–226; NPHP:67–85 et passim; I.Paphos:39–45; Cayla 2005; DGAC:594–595 no. 1–2, 729–730 no. 1–2, 732–733 no. 1–2, 767 no. 166.
[50] *Paphos*:224, 245n6, 231.
[51] Artemis *Agrotéra*: ICS 1; SEG 18:586, 20:251; DGAC:728–729 no. 1. Mitford 1960b:200–205 saw this goddess as an Arcadian import (cf. Pausanias 8.32.4) whose worship remained 'rustic' until the new temple was built.
[52] Hera: Mitford 1960b:203 no. 5; ICS 90; DGAC:594 no. 1.
[53] Apollo *Hylátēs*: ICS 2–3; DGAC:729–730 no. 2–3; Mlynarczyk 1980; Papantonio 2012:227.
[54] The walling mentioned on the 'Altar of Nikokles' is generally referred to Old Paphos: ExcCyp 46; Mitford 1960b:203 no. 2, cf. 198n5; HIOP 1 (dating it to ca. 321); I.Paphos 1; cf. Gesche 1974:112; *Paphos*:210 (archaeological evidence for rebuilding); NPHP:70–71; Cayla 2005:238 (argues for New Paphos).
[55] NPHP:68.

cessors.⁵⁶ Inscriptions in the old Paphian syllabary were now complemented by alphabetic and digraphic texts.⁵⁷ J. Mlynarczyk has suggested that Apollo was made the father of Kinyras at this time, integrating the Paphian royal line into a Panhellenic framework.⁵⁸ The goal would be, presumably, to anchor his dynasty more firmly in 'international divinity', since Kinyras, though he must have remained numinous on Cyprus itself, especially at Paphos, was probably not so recognized beyond the island. J.-P. Cayla would also attribute Apollo's epithet *Kenyristēs* to Nikokles, comparing the king's cultivation of Apollo *Hylátēs*.⁵⁹ Alternatively, the title, which effectively absorbs Kinyras, may be a theological revision deriving from the Ptolemaic takeover of the royal cult (see below).

Nikokles' modernizing agenda notwithstanding, his inscriptions show clearly that he maintained the ancient customs of his house—presiding over the state cult as "Priest of the Queen," and ruling together with her in some sense. It was this that justified his interventions in the sacred landscape: his priestly status was "not only evidence of his actual role in the cult of the goddess, but also *proof* of the legality of his secular power."⁶⁰ Whether other Cypriot kings exercised such sacral kingship in the Classical period is less certain, since a comparable double titulary is so far unparalleled.⁶¹ Yet there is suggestive evidence at least for Salamis⁶² and Kourion,⁶³ and it would not be surprising if

---

⁵⁶ Cayla 2005:235–238.
⁵⁷ Mitford 1960b:201–203; NPHP:68; Cayla 2005:235.
⁵⁸ NPHP:70.
⁵⁹ Cayla 2005:235–238; cf. p409. This may be right. But Pindar, clearly implying Kinyras' involvement with the Paphian cult by the fifth century, is enough to disprove Cayla's tentative earlier connection with the *fama recentior*: "un ensemble de légendes secondairement greffées ou artificiellement ravivées au début de l'époque hellénistique aurait doublé puis supplanté une tradition plus ancienne" (I.Paphos:38).
⁶⁰ NPHP:70 (her emphasis).
⁶¹ Maier 1989:379–380.
⁶² For Salamis, note especially the invocation of *Homeric Hymn* 10.4–5—χαῖρε θεὰ Σαλαμῖνος ἐϋκτιμένης μεδέουσα / εἰναλίης τε Κύπρου, "Hail, ruler of well-founded Salamis / And Cyprus on the sea." Here again, as at Paphos, the goddess is a kind of queen; when this is combined with the acknowledgement of her island-wide dominion, it reads like a regional counterclaim to the Paphian kings and their control of the goddess's great sanctuary (see p345). For Euagoras' Kinyrad claim, see p351–359. Aphrodite appears on Salaminian coins from at least the reign of Euagoras II (ca. 361–351) down to the end of the kingdom (BMC Cyprus:ciii–cxiv passim; HC:143n3 and 147n3); her status as city-goddess is indicated by the battlemented crown (*pólos*) on the coins of Euagoras II (BMC Cyprus, pl. XXIV.10–11), much like the (later) issues of Nikokles of Paphos (see below) and perhaps his father Timarkhos (BMC Cyprus:lxxvi and pl. VIII.8). At Salamis, Markou 2006 argues that the beardless, earringed, and becrowned figure that appears on the reverse of Aphrodite portrays the king as the priest of the goddess.
⁶³ On the Cypro-Phoenician bowl Cy6 (featuring a musical ensemble with Phoenician-type lyre: Figure 29) are two Greek inscriptions in Cypro-Syllabic script. That above the reclining male figure has been interpreted as 'king'; many readings have been proposed for the one above the reclining female, but Κυπρομέδουσα, 'Ruling over Cyprus', is perhaps most attractive. This has

the conception were fairly common in varying forms on the island, given how generally the goddess was venerated.

Intimately connected with Nikokles' official position as deputy of the goddess was his claim of Kinyrad ancestry. This is proven by an inscription discovered in 1953. Two elegiac couplets, paleographically dated to the last quarter of the fourth century, were carved on the base of a statue of the king, dedicated to Paphian 'Aphrodite' by an admirer at Ledroi (modern Nicosia):

> I[n] the Ledrians' precinct of P[aphia, a scion of glorious]
> Fathers, Arkhaios, [admiringly erect]ed [sc. a statue of]
> Timarkhos' son, the Paphians' [outstanding king]—
> Nikokles, of div[ine-speaking] Kinyras [descendant].[64]

Despite considerable damage to the stone, T. B. Mitford rightly asserted that his exemplary supplements must convey the sense closely.[65] The inscription is supremely important for establishing that later literary traditions of a Kinyrad monarchy at Paphos were in fact historically founded. While Mitford's the[spesíou ('div[ine-speaking') is not certain, some word with the element 'divine' remains highly probable given the known theta, metrical constraints, and the need to find an appropriate epithet for Kinyras.[66] *Thespésios*, a formation that must go back to the second millennium, meant originally 'proclaimed by a god'.[67] Epic diction uses it of such 'ominous' sounds as exalted music (including the lyre) and extends it to other awesome phenomena.[68] Note also Euripides' description of Delphi as the "divinely-singing (*thespiōidón*) center of the world," recalling

---

been taken as an epithet of the goddess, and hence the composition as reflecting some form of royal hierogamy. See Karageorghis 2002b:156 (with fig. 322), 177, with references.

[64] Λεδρίων ἐ[ν] τεμένει Π[αφίας ἶνις περιφήμων] | Ἀρχαῖος πατέρων ἔστ[ασ' ἀγασσάμενος] | υἱὸν Τιμάρχου Παφίων [βασιλῆα φέριστον], | Νικοκλέα Κινύρου θε[σπεσίου πρόγονον]. For text and supplements, see Mitford 1961a, 136–138 no. 36; SEG 20:114 (these publications read Λεδρίωι, not Λεδρίων (so the *PHI Greek Inscriptions* online corpus): the general sense is not affected); ICS:399. Identification of Ledroi: Mitford 1961a, 136–138; ICS:229–232.

[65] Mitford 1961a:137.

[66] One could also think of words with θει-, e.g. θειοπρόπου, θειολόγου.

[67] Athematic compounds containing **thes-* ('god') predate Linear B, which gives *te-o*, reflecting **thehós* or *theós*, not the ancestral **thesós*: Billigmeier and Dusing 1981:13; Beekes 2009 s.v. θεός, θεσπέσιος.

[68] Chantraine 1968 s.v.; Frisk 1960 s.v.; Ford 1992:180–197. Some illuminating musical examples: Homer *Iliad* 2.599–600 (of Thamyris): αὐτὰρ ἀοιδὴν / θεσπεσίην ἀφέλοντο καὶ ἐκλέλαθον κιθαριστύν; cf. 1.328, 8.498; *Odyssey* 12.158 (of the Sirens); Hesiod *Theogony* 31–32; Sappho 44.26–27 (μέλος ἄγν[ον ... / ἄχω θεσπεσία); Alkaios 130.34 (ἄχω θεσπεσία γυναίκων); *Homeric Hymn to Hermes* 420–421 (ἰωὴ / θεσπεσίης ἐνοπῆς, of Hermes' lyre); Pindar *Nemean* 9.7, cf. Pindar fr. 52g.1 (μαντευμάτ[ω]ν τε θεσπεσίων), of prophecies. Often of nonmusical sound: Homer *Iliad* 23.213, etc. (ἠχῇ θεσπεσίῃ, formulaic).

that Paphos also styled itself as *gês omphalós* (see below).[69] A *thespésios* Kinyras would be a most appropriate source—always alongside the goddess herself, of course—for the Paphian kings' priestly and mantic authority.

A statue-base found near Old Paphos contains a second inscription, which, though infuriatingly damaged, must relate to Kinyras. Composed in hexameters, and paleographically dated to the late fourth or early third century, this remarkable text gives a glimpse of a Kinyrad king or priest contemplating his own cultic persona. The recent supplements of S. Follet and J.-B. Cayla improve those of I. Nicolaou as to syntax and letter spacing, and more clearly bring out the divinatory dimension that seems required both by *hieròn nóon* ('sacred mind', 3) and the Kinyrad context. The dedicant's name clearly commenced the second verse; I propose to read "Nikokles, king" (*Nikokléēs basileús*), which is metrically appropriate and well supported by other inscriptions from his reign.[70] The text might thus be:

> This statue, a gift for [P]aphian [   ],
>   [King Nikokles placed, me]morial of the cultic duty
>   (*thyapolías*)
>   [whereby he learned the god]s' sacred purpose (*hieròn nóon*), through
>   [god-sent/divine-voiced] customs
>   Celebrating the arts of the line of [Kiny]ras.[71]

---

[69] Euripides *Medea* 668: ὀμφαλὸν γῆς θεσπιῳδόν; Hesykhios s.v. γῆς ὀμφαλός· ἡ Πάφος καὶ Δελφοί.

[70] Νικοκλῆς βασιλεύς (or Νικοκλῆς Παφίων?). The form Νικοκλῆς, as well as the title βασιλεύς, is indicated by the syllabic inscriptions (*ni-ko-ke-le-ve*: see references in n49). The combination -κλ- makes position both in the alphabetic Altar of Nikokles inscription (εὐρύχορος πόλις ἅ[δε τεᾶι, Νικόκ]λεες, ὁρμᾶι: for references, see n54) and the Ledroi dedication (Νικοκλέα Κινύρου); the latter also parallels the proposed synizesis of -εη- in the second foot, which is further facilitated by the contemporary waning of digamma: cf. *pa-si-le-o-se*, βασιλῆος (rather than *pa-sí-le-wo-se*), in ICS 17.1; DGAC 166.6 (both from Old Paphos). Mitford suggested a comparable restoration in the digraphic Artemis Agrotera inscription: Νικοκλῆς Παφίων βασιλεὺς] υἱὸς Τιμάρχου (Mitford 1960b:200–205; ICS 1).

[71] Nicolaou 1964 23a and pl. XXI 23a (with suggestions of Webster); cf. SEG 23:639; BÉ 79:483; I.Paphos 64. Nicolaou's published text reads: –⏑⏑–⏑⏑–Π]αφίαι γέρας εἰκόνα τάνδε | –⏑⏑–μ] νᾶμα θυαπολίας | –⏑⏑–]ων ἱερὸν νόον ἤθεσι τέχνας | –⏑⏑–Κινύ]ρα κλειζόμενος γενεᾶς. Proposed supplements: 1. Καλὸν ἔθηκε θεᾶι Π]: Webster; θῆκ' Ἀφροδίται τᾶι Π]: S. Follet/Cayla, I.Paphos:200n432—2. Νικοκλῆς βασιλεύς (vel Παφίων): *coni. ego* (*v. supra*); μ]νᾶμα: Webster—3. πατρῴοις σῴζ]ων: Nicolaou (νάον: err. BÉ 79:483)—4. εἶναι τῆς Κινύ]ρα: Nicolaou; θεσπεσίοις Κινύρ]α: S. Follet/Cayla:200n432. Cayla's objection to two nominative participles in asyndeton (I.Paphos:201) in verses 3–4 leads to his relative clause at the start of 3. If, however, one prefers to develop Nicolaou's view that ἤθεσι has lost an epithet in 3 (his πατρῴοις), verse 4 could have held one for Κινύ]ρα, e.g. θεσπεσίω. Cayla's proposal to take τέχνας as the object of κλειζόμενος (in the sense 'celebrating') is graceful and quite persuasive. But if one would follow Nicolaou in seeing verse 4 as a self-contained clause, the interpretation of κλειζόμενος as middle is perhaps less satisfying than a passive, which would indicate popular *recognition*. Cf. IG IX.1 880 (Corfu, ca.

Much is uncertain. But given the dedicant's reference both to blood-descent (*geneâs*, 4) and devotional activity before the goddess (*thyapolías*, 2), Nicolaou's *Kiný*]*ra* (genitive) in verse four must be right, the Kinyradai being the only hieratic lineage certainly known for historical Paphos.[72] Although Nikokles always bears the title "Priest of Wanassa" in the dedicatory inscriptions that are certainly his, those relate to his civic activities as a builder. The present text would deal rather with his duties in the goddess's cult. The king's construction projects were themselves cultic ventures in that he acted by divine approval; yet his status as the goddess's agent was itself due to his Kinyrad descent. So, in the dedicatory texts "Priest of Wanassa" is a kind of shorthand, otiose in an inscription that details the king's priestly duties.

If, however, one follows Cayla in dating to the early third century, the inscription will reflect rather the transition to mere priestly Kinyradai in the post-monarchic period—presumably a high priest's celebration of the cult's alleged perseverance in the Kinyrad line, despite the Ptolemaic takeover (see below). This would certainly be interesting. But a monarchic context seems rather more likely if one accepts J. Mlynarczyk's argument that the statue originated not in the temple at Palaipaphos, but "an unknown sanctuary in the vicinity of the *Zephyria* cape."[73]

That *thyapolía* refers to divinatory sacrifice—a natural implication of the word itself—is corroborated by the striking *hieròn nóon*, whether construed as "his art's sacred intention" (Nicolaou) or "the mind of the gods" (Cayla).[74] Given Tacitus' statement that at Paphos "it is prohibited to pour blood over the altar; the burnings-altar (*altaria*) is kindled only with prayers and pure fire,"[75] *thyapolía* could well indicate the incense rites implied by many sources, especially a fourth-century Paphian coin with Aphrodite before a *thymiatérion*.[76] But since Tacitus himself also says that the Kinyradai inspected the entrails of victims

---

100 BCE–100 CE): ἴσθι δ᾽ ὡς πατρὸς | Ἀθηνίωνος οὖν ταφῇσι κλήζεται; IG XII.3 1190 (Melos, n.d.): πατρὸς κλ[η]ζομένα Δαμα<ι>ν[έ]του, ἐκ δέ γε μητρὸς | Κλεισφύσσας.

[72] Cf. J. and L. Robert, BÉ 79:483 ("N. conjecture avec vraisemblance ... Il nous semble que le vers 3 s'entendrait de l'art divinatoire de Kinyras et de ses descendants"); SEG 23:639 ("recte, ut videtur"). Genitive in -ᾱ, rather than -αυ, is otherwise attested on Cyprus: see Perpillou 1978:296–297.

[73] NPHP:114.

[74] I.Paphos:201. Cf. LSJ s.v. θύω; Chantraine 1968 s.v. θύω 2.

[75] Tacitus *Histories* 2.3: *sanguinem arae obfundere vetitum: precibus et igne puro altaria adolentur*. Cf. Mitford 1990:2180.

[76] Paphian incense: Homer *Odyssey* 8.362–363 (βωμὸς θυήεις); *Homeric Hymn to Aphrodite* 58–59 (but this is formulaic and used of other temples, e.g. *Homeric Hymn to Demeter* 385); Vergil *Aeneid* 1.416–417. Coin: BMC Cyprus:lxxiv-v and pl. VIII.7, noting Hesykhios s.v. κιχητός· <εἰς> ὃ ἐμβάπτεται ὁ λιβανωτός. Κύπριοι; cf. HC:72 and n5–6. Note also the "perfumed-oil-worker" (*mu-ro-wo-ro-ko* = μυροϝοργός) in a sixth-century inscription from Old Paphos: I.Rantidi 2.1 (cf. p280n30). Theophrastos regarded plant offerings as far more ancient than blood sacrifice; but his history

Chapter Sixteen

brought by consultants, this must remain a possible context for the inscription.[77] While extispicy must have transpired away from the main altar, the goddess was probably still implicated in the outcome.[78] But perhaps *thyapolía* refers to *all* dimensions of Kinyrad priestly technique, and the ongoing maintenance the goddess's cult.[79] Given a musical Kinyras, the "arts of his line" may well encompass some lyric dimension—even in a divinatory context. Recall the Hurrian liver-omen text that seems to contain *kinnāru*, and of course the Biblical evidence for lyre-prophecy.[80] A record of cult expenditures from OB Larsa may also imply use of a balang during an incense offering.[81]

When one balances Nikokles' modernizing tendencies with the conservative and distinctly Paphian expressions of piety just discussed, it seems clear that this was no culturally insecure, provincial conformist, but a proud and astute political player who wished to perpetuate and magnify his ancient house. His actions must be seen against the chaotic events following Alexander's death in 323. That the Paphian king should be caught up in the wars of succession was inevitable, since Cyprus was rich in resources and key to naval supremacy in the eastern Mediterranean. In 321, Nikokles joined with Nikokreon of Salamis and the kings of Soloi and Amathous in backing Ptolemy against Perdikkas, the latter supported by Marion, which withstood an initial siege.[82] Nikokles evidently considered himself a partner, not a menial. For soon after Alexander's death, between 323–319, Nikokles issued a notorious Alexandrine on which he inserted, in miniscule characters, his own name within the mane of a lion-skin worn by Herakles—"a furtive kind of assertion of independence."[83] Equally significant is his rewalling of the old city.[84] There is also a syllabic inscription, still poorly understood, which seems to be a kind of loyalty oath, related perhaps to Nikokles' consolidation of forces against impending crisis.[85]

---

of sacrificial practice is a kind of Golden Age myth: Porphyry *On Abstinence from Animal Food* 2.5 = Theophrastos *On Piety* fr. 2 Pötscher (584A Fortenbaugh).

[77] Paphian extispicy is confirmed by Khariton 8.2.8–9.
[78] So Robert/Robert, BÉ 79:439.
[79] Nicolaou 1964:213 interprets this difficult verse as "Preserving in ancestral customs the sacred intentions of his art."
[80] See p99, 161–167.
[81] PHG:70 and n69; Heimpel, "Balang-Gods," 27.
[82] Arrian FGH 156 F 10 §6, from his work on the Successors (Τὰ μετὰ τὸν Ἀλέξανδρον); cf. HC:156–157.
[83] HC:164 (quotation) and references in n42, with pl. V.4a; Gesche 1974:113–122; Michaelidou-Nicolaou 1976:26, making a convincing case for the death of Alexander as a *terminus post quem*; the *terminus ante* is given by the Damanhour hoard: NPHP:71–72.
[84] See n54.
[85] Masson 1980; ICS 8 (cf. p394); DGAC:767 no. 166.

The Kinyradai of Paphos

Figure 44 Paphian coin with 'Apollo' and omphalós, reign of Nikokles, ca. 319. Galleria degli Uffizi, Florence. Drawn from BMC Cyprus pl. XXII.11.

As other Cypriot kings resumed issuing autonomous coins—perhaps ca. 319 with the death of the regent Antipater and the deepening political chaos—Nikokles' mint produced a type bearing a powerful patriotic message (Figure 44).[86] On one side was the goddess with battlemented crown, perhaps trumpeting his new fortifications.[87] For the reverse, Nikokles adapted a Greek type which was fairly common in the fourth century—Apollo sitting on the *omphalós* and holding either bow or lyre.[88] Although the lyre-variant could have had special resonance for a Kinyrad king, and the pairing of bow and lyre was as ancient on Cyprus as in Greece,[89] for this coin Nikokles opted to use the archer—an appropriately martial image for his troubled times. Clearly this Apollo stands in some sense for the king himself, or his royal line. Nikokles could simultaneously demonstrate Olympian piety to a Greek audience,[90] and advance a claim

---

[86] *Omphalós* coin: BMC Cyprus:lxxix-x and pl. XXII.10-11. Interpretation: Wace 1902–1903:215; HC:165; Gesche 1974:111n29 (political gesture); Michaelidou-Nicolaou 1976:27; Masson 1968; NPHP:82-85 and pl. I.3 (suggesting a connection with Nikokles' promotion of Apollo *Hylátēs*); Masson 1991:65-68 (argues, against Hill, for authenticity of all exemplars).

[87] ExcCyp:187; BMC Cyprus:lxxvi; HC:164.

[88] See the catalogue in Wace 1902–1903:215-216. The type later became almost an escutcheon of the Seleucids, who traced their descent from Apollo (cf. p495). For the question of whether some specific historical circumstance links the Paphian and Seleucid motifs, see BMC Cyprus:lxxx; NPHP:82-85; Masson 1991:68 and n55.

[89] See p229–230.

[90] Masson 1991:68.

of religious autonomy. For Paphos, like Delphi, was known as the "navel of the earth" (*gês omphalós*).[91] It is not known how early this precise designation was applied to the city, and it was probably a deliberate echo of the Delphic claim. The essential idea, however, must have been very ancient, grounded in the immemorial prestige of Aphrodite's great sanctuary—as important a cult center for Cyprus and environs as Delphi was in Greece. It is thus quite possible that the island-wide *panḗgyris* described by Strabo goes back to Nikokles' reign, if not beyond. This would certainly provide one strong motivation for the king's monumentalization of New Paphos, whence began the ten-mile procession to Old Paphos with which the festival began in Strabo's day.[92] In any case, Nikokles' *omphalós* coin symbolized his kingdom's religious authority, and insinuated that Paphos was its own political center, not someone else's periphery. It was a potent assertion of sovereignty.

Nikokles' proud gestures must have alarmed Ptolemy, and perhaps especially the founding of New Paphos.[93] But Nikokles was still of his party between 315–312 as Ptolemy put down the Cypriot allies of Antigonos—Kition, Lapethos, Keryneia, and Marion, destroying the last-named and deporting its population to Paphos—its southern neighbor—where it helped fill Nikokles' new foundation (as confirmed by a sudden swelling in the archaeological record).[94] Only two years later, however, Nikokles and his house suffered the famous catastrophe that is colorfully related by Diodoros and Polyainos.[95] Ptolemy, suspecting the Paphian king of negotiating with Antigonos, who was reaching the height of his powers, dispatched two henchmen to surround the palace and demand that Nikokles kill himself. This he did after protestations of innocence fell on deaf ears. According to Diodoros:

> Axiothea, Nikokles' wife, hearing of her husband's death, cut the throats of her own virgin daughters, so that no enemy might possess

[91] Hesykhios s.v. γῆς ὀμφαλός· ἡ Πάφος καὶ Δελφοί.
[92] Strabo 14.6.3. That Nea Paphos was not formally founded until Nikokles, and that it emerged as the administrative capital under the Ptolemies (see p409), would certainly suit a late development (cf. HC:76–77; Mitford 1990:2179). Yet given the antiquity and importance of the sanctuary itself, some pilgrimage custom could have been quite ancient; Old Paphos in any case had its own anchorage (*hýphormos*, Strabo 14.6.3).
[93] Gesche 1974:112.
[94] Diodoros Siculus 19.59.1, 19.62, 19.79.4–5. See HC:159–160; Mitford 1960b:198n6, 204; Mitford 1961a:93; NPHP:72 and n37.
[95] A long-standing controversy, based on confusion in the ancient sources, sometimes assigns the episode rather to Nikokreon of Salamis, whose death is placed in the previous year. HC:161n1 (with further references) supported Nikokreon, but acknowledged "room for some doubt." But persuasive arguments in favor of Nikokles were made by Gesche 1974 and NPHP:72–73; cf. Michaelidou-Nicolaou 1976:24–25. Mitford wished to have Nikokles executed in 306 when Demetrios Poliorketes took Cyprus: Mitford 1960b:198–199 and n6; Mitford 1961a:137.

them, and exhorted the wives of Nikokles' brothers to seize death with her ... The brothers of Nikokles, after barring the doors, set the house on fire and killed themselves. And so the royal house of Paphos ... was undone.⁹⁶

The falling-out of Ptolemy and Nikokles has been convincingly related to the settlement of the 313/312 campaign: while Nea Paphos was awarded only the deported inhabitants of Marion, Nikokreon of Salamis was given the lands and revenues of the other defeated cities, and made *stratēgós* of Cyprus to boot. But after Nikokreon himself died in 311/310 under unknown circumstances, confrontation with Nikokles was a logical follow-up to the suppression and killing of other Cypriot kings:

> Nikokles' activity within his kingdom was too dynamic, his authority as priest-king and descendant of the divine Kinyras was too great, his treasury presumably full, finally the strategic qualities of the kingdom and primarily of the newly founded Nea Paphos too apparent for Ptolemy not to desire to remove a potential ally of Antigonus.⁹⁷

The Kinyradai in Hellenistic and Roman Times

Even if Nikokles' family was not as thoroughly eradicated as Diodoros and Polyainos assert, Ptolemy will hardly have tolerated a Kinyrad heir of any standing to continue as Priest of the Goddess, a position of such great and ancient moral authority in the region.⁹⁸ Yet the cult of the goddess had to go on, and the divination-priests in Tacitus' day, we saw, did maintain a claim of Kinyrad descent. The intervening history, and the nature of Ptolemaic restructuring, is far from clear. The island was now subject to a military governor (*stratēgós*), a position of great distinction and strategic importance given to the highest dignitaries of

---

⁹⁶ Diodoros Siculus 20.21.2–3: Ἀξιοθέα δὲ ἡ γυνὴ τοῦ Νικοκλέους ἀκούσασα τὴν ἀνδρὸς τελευτὴν τὰς μὲν θυγατέρας τὰς ἑαυτῆς παρθένους οὔσας ἀπέσφαξεν, ὅπως μηδεὶς αὐτῶν πολέμιος κυριεύσῃ, τὰς δὲ τῶν ἀδελφῶν τῶν Νικοκλέους γυναῖκας προετρέψατο μεθ' αὑτῆς ἑλέσθαι τὸν θάνατον ... οἱ τοῦ Νικοκλέους ἀδελφοὶ συγκλείσαντες τὰς θύρας τὴν μὲν οἰκίαν ἐνέπρησαν, ἑαυτοὺς δ' ἀπέσφαξαν. ἡ μὲν οὖν τῶν ἐν Πάφῳ βασιλέων οἰκία ... κατελύθη. The version of Polyainos *Stratagems* 8.48 is better still, though longer.
⁹⁷ NPHP:73.
⁹⁸ So rightly NPHP:73–74. Contrast ExcCyp:187–188: "The Ptolemies kept possession of the island, the dethroned Cinyrads retained the priesthood"; similarly Mitford 1961a:137; *Paphos*:239; Papantonio 2012:344.

the Ptolemaic court, including members of the royal family.[99] But the Paphian cult itself was apparently governed by a "Leader of the Kinyradai" (*ho arkhòs tôn Kinyradôn*). This title is attested in an inscription from the reign of Ptolemy IV Philopator (221-205), recording the dedication of a statue of his daughter by a certain Demokrates son of Ptolemy.[100] Demokrates' patronymic does not prove a direct Ptolemaic intervention in the priestly succession—the name became generally popular in this period—but it hardly suggests continuity of the royal line. Yet presumably the Leader of the Kinyradai did carry on at least some of the old king's priestly duties.[101] These would have included extispicy (Tacitus) and probably incense offerings to the goddess. Hierogamic gestures, although depoliticized, may well have continued at the level of agrarian magic and ritual poetics. Kinyras, through Aphrodite and his children (Adonis, Myrrha, et al.), could thus survive in some of his ancient roles.

A Leader of the Kinyradai (or equivalent) must have continued to preside over the Paphian cult even after, in the reign of Ptolemy V Epiphanes (204-181), he was technically outranked by the military governor who henceforth added "High Priest of the Island" to his title.[102] The principal reason for this innovation, which mirrors a development in the contemporary Seleucid satrapies, was probably to increase tax revenues from the island's temples, of which Old Paphos boasted the wealthiest.[103] This is also when New Paphos seems to emerge as the island's administrative capital.[104]

---

[99] For Cyprus under the Ptolemies, and the various data regarding Paphos, see HC:158-211 passim (especially 164-165, 167, 179-180); HIOP:2 et passim; also *Paphos*, 223-224; Mitford 1990:2178-2182; Papantonio 2012.

[100] Ἀφροδίτηι Παφίαι· | Δημοκράτης Πτολεμαίου | ὁ ἀρχὸς τῶν Κινυραδῶν | καὶ ἡ γυνὴ Εὐνίκη | τὴν ἑαυτῶν θυγατέρα | Ἀρίστιον ("For Paphian Aphrodite; Ptolemaios' son Demokrates, Leader of the Kinyradai, and his wife Eunike [sc. have dedicated this statue of] their daughter Aristion"): LBW 2798; HIOP 32; I.Paphos 66; cf. ExcCyp:249, 260. See also comments of Ribichini 1982:494; *Paphos*:239; Masson 1986:455-456 (with a photograph of the stone in fig. 1); Masson 1988b:64n8. Ἀρχός, while virtually absent from prose, is epigraphically attested in various parts of the Greek world; although still unconfirmed in Linear B, it was evidently an ancient rival to the more familiar ἄρχων, and Masson inclines to see it as a genuine inheritance on Cyprus: Masson 1986:455-456, expanding an earlier discussion in ICS:98; cf. HIOP:p13. For a second example of ἀρχός from Paphos, see n126.

[101] Cf. Hogarth 1889:3-4.

[102] The first of many attestations is an inscription (HIOP 40; I.Paphos 9), probably dating to 197 BCE, of Polykrates of Argos, son of Mnasiadas, who evidently became *stratēgós* on the accession of Epiphanes: Πολυ[κτράτης ... | ὁ στ[ρατηγὸς καὶ ἀρχιερ]εὺς τῆς νήσου.

[103] HIOP:40 suggests that Polykrates himself (above note) may have assumed the position of high priest in order to safeguard revenues for his young master against conflicting interests in the Egyptian court; cf. HC:175 (with further references in n1), 183-184, 186.

[104] NPHP:121-122.

One of the first of these governor-priests was Ptolemy of Megalopolis, who had been a courtier of Ptolemy IV Philopator before assuming the Cypriot *stratēgía* under Epiphanes in 197.[105] To him we owe a brief but precious glimpse of the archaeological landscape of Old Paphos a century after the monarchy. He wrote an apparently muck-raking account of his former patron's reign, of which only four fragments remain. By a lucky chance, one of these relates to Kinyras and the Kinyradai. The passage was tapped by Clement of Alexandria and Arnobius for tirades against pagan temples, which they interpreted euhemeristically as tombs of bygone mortals now wrongly venerated. For both, Kinyras concludes a list of legendary figures believed to be interred in the temple precincts of major gods.[106] Kinyras was apparently unique, and so the more outrageous, for being buried with "his whole family—indeed his whole family line"; and Ptolemy guaranteed his information, according to Arnobius, "on the authority of letters" (*litterarum auctoritate*). What does this mean? One reasonably assumes that Ptolemy wrote about the Kinyradai after his appointment to the governorship, in which case he could have made his "declaration" on the authority of his own eyes, rather than by appeal to some earlier historian or ethnographer. This strongly suggests that he referred to epigraphic evidence in the sanctuary itself, akin to the inscriptions discussed above.[107] And there must have been something that was displayed as *the tomb of Kinyras himself*.[108] Since Clement and Arnobius cite their examples to illustrate customs of pagan worship, it should follow that Kinyras received such attentions at Paphos—that his sepulcher doubled as a kind of shrine within the temple precinct. When one considers that vestiges of Cypriot cult lingered on into the Medieval period at various ancient sites,[109] such activity is perfectly possible for Paphos in the second century BCE, when Ptolemy was writing—and even the second or third CE, with Clement.[110]

In the troubled reign of Euergetes II Physkon (146–116), the inscriptions attest what appears to be a new designation, "The Priests of Paphian

---

[105] Polybios 18.55.6–9, cf. 15.25.14–15. He succeeded Polykrates: HC:187.

[106] Ptolemy of Megalopolis FGH 161 F 1 = Clement of Alexandria *Exhortation* 3.45 (Πτολεμαῖος δὲ ὁ τοῦ Ἀγησάρχου ἐν τῷ α΄ τῶν περὶ τὸν Φιλοπάτορα ἐν Πάφῳ λέγει ἐν τῷ τῆς Ἀφροδίτης ἱερῷ Κινύραν τε καὶ τοὺς Κινύρου ἀπογόνους κεκηδεῦσθαι, repeated verbatim by Eusebios *Preparation for the Gospel* 2.6.6) + the paraphrase of Arnobius *Against the Pagans* 6.6 (*Agesarchi Ptolemaeus de Philopatore quem edidit primo Cinyram regem Paphi cum familia omni sua, imo cum omni prosapia in Veneris templo situm esse lit(t)erarum auctoritate declarat*). Cf. Pfister 1909–1912:303, 452–453.

[107] Presumably, Arnobius has used *litterae* to gloss γράμματα in Ptolemy, in which case the plural can indicate multiple inscriptions. For this sense of γράμμα, LSJ s.v., II.d., and often epigraphically.

[108] Blinkenberg 1924:35; Heubner 1963–1982 2:35.

[109] See p563–564.

[110] Clement probably drew this and his other examples from a mythographic handbook.

Aphrodite."[111] Yet this need not mean that Kinyradai had ceased to exist: the title may only be an umbrella term for several groups of cult functionaries, of whom the Kinyradai remained one. Alternatively, 'Kinyradai' itself may once have had this collective force,[112] but was phased out of official use for some reason. Perhaps the old royal connotations were now felt to be potentially subversive, at odds with the Ptolemaic ruler cult itself.[113]

When Ptolemy IX Soter II (Lathyros) established a quasi-independent kingdom on the island in 106/105, the old *stratēgía* became obsolete, and with it apparently the position of "High Priest of the Island."[114] At Paphos a *mantiárkhēs* is now twice attested: such an officer must have overseen divination, personally conducting it as the occasion demanded—for illustrious visitors like Titus, for instance—and was perhaps the equivalent of High Priest.[115] Whether he also counted himself a Kinyrad—as Tacitus would suggest—is unclear; if so, 'Leader of the Kinyradai' had presumably fallen out of formal use.

On the death of Lathyros in 80, a bastard ascended the Cypriot throne; it was this Ptolemy who, when in 58 Cato the Younger offered him the high priesthood of Paphian Aphrodite if he would stand down, famously preferred suicide to demotion. This confirms that the temple then had its own high priest (whether *mantiárkhēs*, *hagétōr*,[116] or some other title), and shows that the position had maintained enough of its ancient regal prestige to be "the best equivalent for royal power which [Cato] could offer."[117]

Under the Empire the title High Priest (*arkhiereús*) is definitely attested in 212, and is probably to be restored in an inscription of the earlier first century

---

[111] Οἱ ἱερεῖς τῆς Παφίας Ἀφροδίτης: HIOP 70 (ca. 142–131) = I.Paphos 19, etc. This is also when the *stratēgós* assumed the third title of 'naval commander' (*naúarkhos*), with the loss of Ptolemaic sea-power in the Aegean and the fleet's consolidation on Cyprus (HC:197).

[112] One might seek such a generalizing sense in Hesykhios s.v. Κινυράδαι· ἱερεῖς Ἀφροδίτης (perhaps a modernizing gloss reflecting οἱ ἱερεῖς τῆς Παφίας Ἀφροδίτης, rather than a lexicographer's vague stopgap).

[113] Note the Βασιλισταί ('Celebrants of the King') who are attested in the reign of Ptolemy IX (see p234). It may be relevant that Cyprus had already edged towards being a self-contained kingdom on several occasions around this time. See HC:193 and n3 for the disputed episode of Eupator (152/1), son of Ptolemy VI Philomētor; 196 for the two year 'retreat' of Ptolemy VIII Euergetes II and his family on the island (131/130–129).

[114] HC:198–202; HIOP:38–39.

[115] HIOP 103–104; I.Paphos 72–73; cf. *Paphos*:244 ("a leader of the priests of Aphrodite"); Mitford 1990:2180 and n20–21.

[116] Hesykhios' definition of ἀγήτωρ as "the priest in Cyprus who leads the offerings of Aphrodite" (ὁ τῶν Ἀφροδίτης θυηλῶν ἡγούμενος ἱερεὺς ἐν Κύπρῳ) finds epigraphic confirmation at Paphos ca. 105–188, and somewhat earlier at Amathous: see ExcCyp 105; HIOP 99 (ἡγητορευκότων, line 4); I.Paphos 79; cf. Blinkenberg 1924:33.

[117] Plutarch *Cato the Younger* 35; quotation Hogarth 1889:3–4 (closely followed by Frazer 1914 1:43); cf. Mitford 1990:2180; HC:204–208; *Paphos*:157, 244.

CE.[118] This, with the contemporary testimony of Tacitus, shows that a continuous Kinyrad self-identity is not incompatible with periodic changes in official nomenclature. This is confirmed by the *Kinýrarkhos* (or *Kinyrárkhēs*) who appears in a heavily damaged inscription from the reign of Antoninus Pius (138–161 CE).[119] The title clearly recalls "Leader of the Kinyradai" from four centuries earlier—an "archaistic revival, perhaps merely honorific, of which the purpose eludes."[120]

The temple hierarchy was clearly not immune to diachronic development, perhaps especially as to titulary. Whereas 'Leader of the Kinyradai' in a third-century BCE context may very well suggest the highest officer in the cult, apparently in Antonine times the *Kinýrarkhos* was distinct from the High Priest.[121] Presumably, then, the Kinyrarch led but one of the temple's colleges, the activity of whose members is indicated by the root *kinyr-*. The implications of this must be pursued next.

Sons of the *Kinýra*

Although the precise relationship between the old kings and the Kinyradai who operated thereafter (under one name or another) is elusive, one important issue can be pinpointed. The titles "Leader of the Kinyradai" and *Kinýrarkhos*, along with Tacitus, show that the Kinyradai were not only a royal and/or priestly 'lineage going back to Kinyras'—a natural interpretation of the patronymic suffix[122]—but equally a coeval priestly cohort. For the monarchy one might try to harmonize these diachronic and synchronic senses by supposing that the larger royal family constituted the Kinyradai, from whose ranks the priesthood was drawn. This seems probable enough; but it does not completely account for the post-monarchic period with its interruption of the royal line. Nor is it credible to divorce completely the synchronic and diachronic senses, assigning one kind of Kinyradai to each period. For even if one regards 'Kinyradai' per se as a

---

[118] Mitford 1990:2180–2181.
[119] The stone is now lost. See ExcCyp 101; SEG 40:1365 (cf. 1319); I.Paphos 181. This obscure inscription was ultimately interpreted as the dedication of a son to his Kinyrarch father by Mitford 1990:2181n21, who would read: [ὁ ἀρχιερεὺς Ἀφρο]δίτης | Διονυσό[δωρος vv τὸν δεῖνα] Διονυσίου | Κινύραρ[χον, εὐεργέτην τοῦ δή]μου, φιλοτειμίας | καὶ φι[λοστοργίας χάριν], τὸν πατέρα. For earlier alternatives, see ExcCyp:249; Mitford 1947:229n121. Cf. HIOP:13; Masson 1986:455–456.
[120] Mitford 1990:2181–2182, who continues "but this text stands isolated in a period from which nothing else concerning the priesthood of Aphrodite survives." Similarly, HIOP:13.
[121] Unless the two are mere incidental variants.
[122] Cf. Σ Pindar *Pythian* 2.27b: "This is the Kinyras, [sc. beginning] from whom the Kinyradai in Cyprus have dedicated themselves to the goddess" (ὁ δὲ Κινύρας οὗτός ἐστιν, ἀφ' οὗ οἱ ἐν Κύπρῳ Κινυρίδαι [sic] τῇ θεῷ ἀνιέρωνται).

titular contrivance of the Ptolemies, stressing the legitimacy of cult continuity despite the loss of monarchy, yet an analogous body of priests must already have existed, whose activity would have to be well described by the new label, if new it was.

Fortunately, the word itself permits further inferences. As M. L. West pointed out, the Greek patronymic suffix can yield not only 'Sons of Kinyras' but 'Sons of the Lyre', corresponding exactly to the normal WS designation of professional 'guilds', with their claims of common descent.[123] This interpretation is highly plausible within a larger NE context; recall the royally sponsored groups examined in Part One (Ugarit, Bible) and the lyre-orchestras of the Cypro-Phoenician symposium bowls (Chapter 11). 'Leader of the Kinyradai' and 'Kinyrarch' would then simply designate the ranking *kinýra*-player of a larger college. Nor is this incompatible with the divination duties Tacitus attributes to the Kinyradai: the Biblical material, we have seen, attributes various ritual, 'magical' powers to the *kinnōr* and its players, including forms of prophecy, which go well beyond the simply musical. This scenario would also explain how the Kinyradai continued so readily after the fall of Paphos, since they need never have been *limited* to the royal family.

The paradox of Kinyradai as both 'cultic lyrists' and 'royal dynasty descended from Kinyras' may be neatly resolved by supposing that the kings of Paphos, in presiding over state rituals as "Priest of the Queen," did so effectively *as* Leader of the Kinyradai (*vel sim.*).[124] This deduction is perfectly compatible with the conclusions reached in other chapters on different grounds—that Kinyras was a kind of royal performing role, and that *kinýras* itself means basically '*kinýra*-player'.[125] It may be that a separate 'lead kinyrist' was already operative in royal Paphos—a kind of Chief Singer as at Mari or under David—who oversaw the execution of practical liturgical matters, while the king, though active as high priest of the goddess—and so notional leader of her cult—did not trouble himself with the detailed management of the Kinyrad priests.[126] Still, the comparanda from Ugarit and Hattusha show that, while royal cult performances were essentially honorary, some real participation was necessary. And

---

[123] EFH:57. Cf. above p115, 155.
[124] As suggested by Ribichini 1982:494.
[125] See p380–383, 392–393, 432–436.
[126] An ἀρχός (*a-ra-ko-se*) named Satrapas(?) has been found in a syllabic inscription of the later fourth century. Apparently a religious functionary within the court of Nikokles, he describes himself as "mouthpiece of the goddess" (ὁ[(μ)φι]ϝοχεῦσι τᾶς ϝανά[σ(σ)ας], and helped develop the oracular hypogeum to Apollo *Hylátēs* near Nea Paphos: Mitford 1960a; ICS 2–3; Masson 1988b:64; NPHP:77–79, 113; DGAC:729–730 no. 2–3. Whether he was more or less equivalent to the later ὁ ἀρχὸς τῶν Κινυραδῶν is impossible to say (but note the interesting speculations of Mitford 1960a:6; Cayla 2005:236).

since the Paphian king was himself of professed Kinyrad descent, he would necessarily act as the 'Lead Kinyrad' of his generation, whoever else may have conducted more quotidian tasks, musical or otherwise.

The Kinyradai, considered diachronically as a royal dynasty, also recall the royal mortuary cult of Ugarit—where the king's ancestors were divinized, and the *kinnāru* was apparently a symbolic marker of eternal, blessed kingship. One might therefore see the Paphian kings as somehow incarnating Kinyras in successive generations.[127] West's view that Kinyras "is nothing but the mythical eponymous ancestor of the Kinyradai," though right in one sense, does not account for the deep antiquity, and materiality, of Kinnaru and the Mesopotamian balang-gods. There are indeed clear examples of eponymous ancestors being secondarily derived from group names (Homer himself is now often suspected); but the opposite process, a group taking their name from an established figure, is equally well attested.[128] To be sure, a Divine Kinnaru must ultimately be a professional projection—an exaltation by hieratic lyre-players of their own religious authority, social status, and venerable tradition. But such a gesture, to account for Kinnaru at Ugarit, will antedate the Kinyradai of historical Paphos by so many centuries that they themselves were perhaps unaware of Kinyras' 'artificial' origin, regarding him in all sincerity as an ancient demigod priest-king whose duties to the goddess they perpetuated. Such a 'dwindling' may be paralleled by divine figures of Linear B reappearing as minor characters in Greek mythology (when not disappearing altogether).[129] Yet it does seems clear, from "Our *Kenyristés* Apollo" and the other evidence so far considered, that the lyric Kinyras remained rather numinous down to the Classical period, and even to the time of Tiberius.

To conclude, we must seriously entertain the possibility that the Kinyradai of Paphos—as a royal lyric clan—go back in one form or another to the pre-Greek

---

[127] Cf. Cayla 2005:239: "le souverain kinyrade était l'incarnation du parèdre de la Souveraine, la *Wanassa*."

[128] Thus, against the 'lyric' Eumolpos < Eumolpidai or Ametor < Ametoridai (see p234) one may place the Asklepiadai (the medical clan of Kos who made Asklepios their ancestor) and the Talthybiadai (heralds of Sparta, from Agamemnon's herald: Herodotos 7.134; cf. Chaniotis 1990:94–95). For Homer as a fictional eponym of the Homeridai, see *inter al.* Durante 1971-1974 2:185–204.

[129] The goddess Ipemedeja, for instance, is known from a Pylian offerings tablet (PY Tn 316 = DMG:172), where she appears in company with Poseidon. In the post-palatial decline, she lost her privileges, whether suddenly or gradually—there is no cult attested for her in later historical sources—but lingered on in epic memory as Iphimedeia, the mother of Otos and Ephialtes by Poseidon (Homer *Odyssey* 11.305–308). See further Gérard-Rousseau 1968:116–118, with entries for other vanished palatial gods like Dopota, Tiriseroe, Manasa, and Dirimijo; cf. MgP:259; DMG:288; GR:43.

Chapter Sixteen

LBA. This idea, which will seem far-fetched when considering only the city's few and relatively late historical inscriptions, becomes much more compelling once one's horizons are expanded by the systematic considerations explored in this and previous chapters. After all, the goddess's cult operated continuously across the LBA–IA transition, and must have been appropriately staffed throughout.

PART THREE

KINYRAS AND THE LANDS AROUND CYPRUS

17
Kinyras At Pylos

IMPORTANT EVIDENCE FOR A BA KINYRAS comes from an unexpected quarter: Mycenaean Pylos. Although the texts present 'Kinyras' as a PN, not DN, the contexts are consistent with the attributes of *the* Kinyras. This material, I shall argue, indicates that by the thirteenth century Kinyras—as the Greeks would call him—had already outgrown his musical roots and begun to develop into the metamusical figure he was on historical Cyprus.

Kinyras and the Priests

The first attestation is in a tablet from the so-called Northeast Building (NEB), excavated in 1957 by M. Rawson and C. W. Blegen, and belonging to the final phase of the 'Palace of Nestor' at Pylos. Long interpreted as a workshop for chariots and leather goods,[1] recent reassessment of its tablets and the associated small-finds has established the NEB's broader function as a "storage facility and administrative clearinghouse that managed the collection and subsequent disbursal of livestock, various goods, raw materials, and groups of workers."[2] The NEB was home to as many as seven scribes who recorded its diverse transactions in semi-archival documents that were eventually transferred to the central Archives Complex (AC).[3]

The Qa series of tablets, recovered from the NEB, is the largest single group outside the AC itself.[4] The twenty-four single-line, leaf-shaped tablets associate various individuals with the distribution (or perhaps receipt[5]) of from one to five

---

[1] Blegen et al. 1966 1:299–325; doxographic review in Bendall 2003, with references in 181n1.
[2] Hofstra 2000; Bendall 2003; Lupack 2008a: 467 (quotation), 471.
[3] Bendall 2003:197–203. For scribal administration at Pylos, and the interrelationship of the AC and other areas, see Palaima 1988:172–189; Palaima and Wright 1985.
[4] For the exact find-positions and contents of the NEB's series (mostly from room 99), see Tegyey 1984:68–75; Palaima 1988:79, 155 fig. 20, 213; Bendall 2003:198–199, 201–224. Two tablets (Qa 1259, 1441) were found outside the NEB, presumably scattered during destruction of the site: Palaima 1988:79, 213; Melena 2000–2001:377.
[5] Cf. Bendall 2003:212–213.

Chapter Seventeen

units of an unknown commodity.[6] The latter is designated by the ideogram *189, consisting of *44 (KE) in a rectangular frame, probably giving the first syllable of the item's name. This is most plausibly interpreted as some form of 'honor-gift' (*ke-ra*, *géras*), but the material reality and occasion are both unknown.[7] A recent argument for the hides of sacrificial animals is attractive, but inconclusive.[8] The entries do not follow a single fixed formula, but exhibit at least four patterns.[9] Because of this variability, some tablets elude definite interpretation when they contain words not otherwise known, and/or when a word can be interpreted as PN *or* title.[10] The following table is based upon the re-edition with new joins by J. Melena, towards his forthcoming corpus of the Pylos texts in *The Palace of Nestor IV*.[11] Omitting tablets too damaged to be illuminating,[12] I have arranged the entries first by formula, where clear, and then by amount of *189, both known and presumed by analogy; the righthand column transliterates and translates only PNs and descriptors (where possible).[13] 'Kinyras' comes at the end among the tablets of uncertain formula:

---

[6] Qa series: Blegen and Lang 1958:183-184, 190-191, pl. 46-47; PTT 1:221-222; Melena 2000-2001:380-384. Contextual discussions: Palmer 1963:371-373; Gérard-Rousseau 1968:34, 108, 190; DMG:484-485 (with illustration of *189, also PTT 2:150); Chadwick 1975:450-451; PP 2:42, 54-55, 94-95; Tegyey 1984:73; Palaima 1988:79-80; Killen 2000-2001; Bendall 2003:212-213; Lupack 2007:57; Lupack 2008a:483-484; ISMP:139-140.

[7] Blegen and Lang 1958:191 initially suggested 'hospitality gifts' (*ke-se-ne-wi-ja*, *xeinḗïa*), but most of the recipients must have resided at or around Pylos itself, to judge from the general omission of TNs (PP 2:55); and the three who do bear TNs all resided within the kingdom, two in the Hither Province. Palmer 1963:371-373 thought of "some sacrificial substance," comparing the appearance of KE in the Ma and Na tablets (cf. 300-313); Chadwick (DMG:484-485) suggested "some kind of textile (a ceremonial robe?)."

[8] See Melena 2000-2001:380-384, proceeding from PY Un 1482, concerned with leather products, in which the ideogram *189 is preceded by *ke-ra-e-we*; this he interprets as **gerahḗwes*, a plural formed from *géras* with the agent-suffix *-eús* (i.e. 'things bestowing honour', *vel sim.*). But see the critique of Killen 2000-2001, who reinterprets as 'horn-worker', and would similarly connect KE with a derivative of *kéras*, 'horn'.

[9] For various attempts to establish categories: see Blegen and Lang 1958:191; Palmer 1963:372; DMG:485; Tegyey 1984:73; Palaima 1988:79; Melena 2000-2001:383n16; Bendall 2003:212-213.

[10] Thus Qa 1294 and 1304 are often analyzed as PN + TN, but Melena 2000-2001:383n16 rightly notes that Title + TN remains possible (but for *pu-ti-ja* in 1294, see below). Note that the third example of a TN (Qa 1290) is certainly Title + TN.

[11] Melena 2000-2001.

[12] Qa 1302, 1309, 1310, 1311, 1312, 1441. In Qa 1291, 1305, and 1306 a PN is likely, but no further context survives; for possible identifications, Melena 2000-2001:283; ISMP:192-193, 216, 241-242, 411.

[13] Transliteration of PNs follows ISMP, q.v. for references.

The Qa Series

PN alone

1297	a-pi-a₂-ro		*189	5	Amphihalos
1292	]e̞-ke-ri-ja-wo[14]		*189	2	Enkherr'awon

PN + Title

1295	qe-re-ma-o	po-qa-te-u	*189	2	Kʷelemahos the Diviner(?)
1300	i-]je-re-ja		*189	2	... the Priestess:
1303	ke-i-ja	i[-je-re-ja]	*189	2	Keheia the Priestess:[15]
1289	ka-wa-ra	i-je-re-ja	*189	[	*Ka-wa-ra* the Priestess
1296	a-o-ri-me-ne	i-je-re-u	*189	[	Ahorimenes the Priest
1298	ne-qe-u	e-da-e-u	*189	1	Neikʷheus the 'Shriner'(?)
1299	ka-e-se-u[16]	po-ti-ni-ja-wi-jo[17]	*189	1	Kaheseus the Potnian
1308		]pa̞-ke-u[18]	*189	1	... the Sacrificer

Title + TN

1290	i-je-re-u	se-ri-no-wo-te	[*189		The Priest at *Se-ri-no-wo*[19]

PN + TN

1294	pu-ti-ja	a-pu₂-we	*189	1	Pythia(s) at *A-pu₂*[20]

Uncertain Formula

1304	a-te-ra-wo[21]	ka-ra-do-ro	[*189		*A-te-ra-wo* at Kharadros[22]
1259[23]	de-ka-ta̞	ri̞-ma[24]	*189	1	Deiktas(?) the *ṛi-ma*(?)
1293		]m̞e̞-nu-a₂	*189	1	See below
1301	ki-nu-ra	me-nu-a₂	*189	[	See below

---

[14] Melena 2000–2001:283 includes this man among his ambiguous cases; but ISMP:243 and n176 convincingly identifies him with the well-known *e-ke-ra₂-wo* (see below).

[15] Or 'Priestess from *ke-e*': Chadwick 1975:450. See also PP 2:56; Tegyey 1984:73; Melena 2000–2001:283; ISMP:282 and n271.

[16] PN at Mycenae: MY Ge 602.4 (DMG:228, 485).

[17] The reading of PTT 1:221. Melena 2000–2001:383, without comment, gives *po-ti-ni-ja-we-jo*, the more usual alternative attested elsewhere (PP 2:124).

[18] Melena 2000–2001:383 considers this ambiguous between PN/Title. But it seems clear from the shape of the fragment that the original tablet extended far enough left that a lost PN must be supposed. Compare its hand-copy with, for instance, that of Qa 1300 (Blegen and Lang 1958, pl. 47).

[19] For this TN, Palmer 1963:372; DMG:149, 581; DM s.v. *sa-ri-nu-wo-te*.

[20] In the Hither Province: DM s.v. *a-pu₂-de*.

[21] Attested only here. Considered ambiguous by Melena 2000–2001:383n16; taken as a PN by DMG:485; ISMP:216 and n109 tentatively suggests a compound in -λαος (making a PN much more likely).

[22] In the Hither Province: DM s.v.

[23] Joined with Xa 1335 (Hand 15, NEB): Melena 2000–2001:377.

[24] A hapax: for textual/interpretive issues, see Melena 2000–2001:377.

Chapter Seventeen

As a general principle, confidence in the identification of homonymous individuals depends upon their appearance in overlapping contexts.[25] Of the five PNs in the Qa series that are otherwise attested at Pylos, four—Amphihalos, Neik^{u}heus, Enkherr'awon, and Pythias—can be securely identified with homonymous individuals appearing, among a larger group of Pylian elite, in a cluster of prosopographically interdependent texts concerned with (among other things) landholding, payments or disbursements of gold, and positions of military authority (including the famous o-ka set, dealing with a 'coast-guard').[26] Neik^{u}heus and Enkherr'awon in particular were major landholders, the latter possessing as much in the district of Pakijane as all other known tenants combined.[27] If Enkherr'awon was not the king (*wánax*) himself, as some hold, he was at least "a man of the highest rank in Pylian society."[28]

Thus, despite some ambiguities, the Qa series clearly deals with "persons of consequence."[29] Its aristocratic character is further revealed by the high concentration of religious personnel among its entries. Two priests (1290, 1296) and two priestesses (1289, 1300) are itemized, with a third priestess plausibly restored (1303). Another figure is qualified as "Potnian" (Qa 1299, *po-ti-ni-ja-wi-jo*), thus serving the goddess Potinija/Potnia ('Queen/Lady') in some capacity.[30] These figures support cultic interpretations of other entries. Some kind of divination-priest, oracle-singer, or 'ritual purifier' is probably meant by *po-qa-te-u* (1295).[31] Neik^{u}heus bears the title *e-da-e-u* both here (1298) and elsewhere; this has been interpreted as *hedaheús, 'man of the abode (of the deity)'.[32] The broken]*pa-ke-u* of Qa 1308 can be taken as *sphageús*, 'sacrificial slaughterer'.[33] *Pu-ti-ja* (1294) too might be read as a cult-title (*Pythía*),[34] although this is more probably the same name and person attested elsewhere as a smith and military officer.[35] Still, the PN 'Pythias' may itself have carried cultic connotations: there are other examples of Mycenaeans whose names reflect their professions (see below).

---

[25] For the basic methodology and associated problems, PP 2:13, 177–204 et passim; ISMP:31–72.
[26] PP 2:190–193; ISMP:117–124, 139–140; cf. Franceschetti 2008b:314n27.
[27] At least 1,000 fig trees and 1,100 vines (Er 880): ISMP:319–320.
[28] Bendall 2003:212. As *wánax*: DMG:265, 454; Chadwick 1975 (quotation 453); PP 2:150–155; Palaima 1995b:134–135. Further bibliography on the controversy, Nakassis 2012:1n2; ISMP:244n181.
[29] The elite nature of the series was soon appreciated: Palmer 1963:372; DMG:485 (quotation); Chadwick 1975:451.
[30] For the title, PP 2:125.
[31] DMG:485 (quotation), comparing φοιβάζω ('prophesy') and suggesting **phoig^{u}asteús*, cf. Chadwick 1975:451; Melena 2000–2001:383n16, follows suit with *phoibateús (i.e. **phoig^{u}ateús*), noting Hesykhios s.v. φοιβητεύειν· χρησμῳδεῖν.
[32] DM s.v. *e-da-e-u*; Melena 2000–2001:383n16. Other possibilities: PP 2:42. For this man's other attestations (certain and possible), Lupack 2008b:77–78; ISMP:139, 319–320.
[33] Lupack 2008a:483.
[34] Melena 2000–2001:383n16.
[35] Palmer 1963:372; ISMP:90, 139–140, 355.

Enkherr'awon is implicated in other religious contexts elsewhere, contributing half the food for a feast of Poseidon, and allocated aromatics alongside deities and religious officials.[36] Moreover, the scribe who wrote all but three tablets of the Qa series (Hand 15)[37] also composed Un 219, a list of commodities assigned to various gods and religious functionaries.[38] It seems that this scribe's special purview was "allocations to the religious sphere."[39] It has been suggested indeed that the personnel of the Qa series be connected somehow with a cultic-industrial interpretation of the NEB itself as a shrine of Potnia Hippeia—a natural patroness for a complex whose concerns included chariot construction and maintenance.[40]

Be this as it may, the Qa series itself is clearly connected with the cultic sphere. It is quite remarkable, therefore, to find the entry *ki-nu-ra me-nu-a$_2$* in 1301. Because *me-nu-a$_2$* also appears in 1293, and there is no certain case of an individual appearing twice in the series, it is generally assumed that *me-nu-a$_2$* is a title, and that consequently *ki-nu-ra* should be read as a PN—Kinyras.[41] The PN interpretation is well supported by a second attestation of *ki-nu-ra* at Pylos, where it must indeed be a PN (see below). Moreover, another tablet containing entries in the form PN + title has *me-nu-a$_2$* preceded by just enough space for the restoration of *ki-nu-ra*.[42]

Nevertheless, as with many other problems in Linear B texts, one must appreciate the provisional nature of this conclusion. First, it cannot be proven that the same person is *not* referred to in both Qa 1293 and 1301, since

---

[36] The texts are Un 718 and Un 219: DMG:282–283; Palmer 1963:259–260; PP 2:152–155; Chadwick 1975:451–452; Nakassis 2012:15; ISMP:243.

[37] For the identifying characteristics of Hand 15 and 33, see PTT 2:14, 16; Palaima 1988:79–80, 96. Qa 1307, formerly assigned to Hand 33 who also wrote 1289, 1300, 1305 (PTT 1:222), has now been transferred to Hand 15 by Melena 2000–2001 on the basis of a new join.

[38] Un 219 (from the AC): Palmer 1963:259; its personnel: Olivier 1960:122–125. Connection with Hand 15/Qa series: Tegyey 1984:73; Palaima 1988:79n106.

[39] Lupack 2008b:128n359. The second scribe (Hand 33), known only from this series, wrote Qa 1289 and 1300, the two that certainly mention priestesses; conceivably this scribe had a special connection to female cult personnel: Tegyey 1984:79; Palaima 1988:80; Franceschetti 2008a:314n24.

[40] See Lupack 2008a and Lupack 2008b:120–129, building on suggestions of Tegyey 1984:75–79. The argument hinges on interpretation of An 1281, recording (in part) assignments of manpower for Potnia Hippeia; and the traditional identification of room 93 as a shrine.

[41] Blegen and Lang 1958:191; Gallavotti 1961:166–167; Morpurgo (Davies) 1963:148; DMG:485, 554; Chadwick 1975:451; Gallavotti 1976:56.

[42] Aq 218.14 (DMG:177): see Gallavotti 1961:167; PP 2:94–95, 193, noting that the restoration is supported by the appearance of *ne-qe-u* in Aq 64.14, which with Aq 218 constitutes a 'diptych' (DMG:422–424; ISMP:118) belonging in the text-cluster noted above (see n26). But this interpretation is complicated by other entries in the form PN + patronymic-genitive: Ruipérez 1956:158–159.

Chapter Seventeen

double-records in small sets are not unparalleled.[43] Next, while Palmer's understanding of *me-nu-a₂* as a TN is generally rejected,[44] its interpretation as a title still lacks decisive etymological support. The word, with its probable graphic variant *me-nu-wa*,[45] is often read as *Miny(h)as or *Miny(w)as with reference to the Minyans (*Minýai*), legendary inhabitants of Boeotian Orkhomenos; but their obscure mythology offers no clarification.[46] A proposed linguistic link with Minos is equally unilluminating.[47] More promising, given the other entries in the Qa series, is a connection with *mēnýein*, to 'disclose what is secret, reveal'.[48]

But any interpretation of *me-nu-a₂* as a title must still confront its unambiguous use as a PN at Knossos, and perhaps Pylos itself.[49] While vacillation between PN and title is a known phenomenon,[50] this makes it equally possible in principle that *ki-nu-ra*, though a PN elsewhere at Pylos, could nevertheless be a *title* in Qa 1301.[51] And even if it is a PN in the Qa series, one would still need to contemplate its etymology, since the PN might in itself have professional implications.

Naming Kinyras in Greek

That the PN 'Kinyras' was already known in LBA Greece accords first with the divergent dialect forms of later sources.[52] The general agreement of the earliest

---

[43] PP 2:94–95.
[44] Palmer 1963:144, 372, on the parallel of *pu-ti-ja a-pu₂-we* in Qa 1294.
[45] See Ruijgh 1967:56, for phonological discussion.
[46] Gallavotti 1961:166–167; Ruijgh 1962:68; DMG:187, 485; Gallavotti 1976:56. Fluctuation of *e/i* is not uncommon in Mycenaean: see p206n106.
[47] For these and other interpretations see the extensive bibliography in DM s.v. *me-nu-a₂* and *me-nu-wa*.
[48] LSJ s.v. See Cataudella 1971:195–196, interpreting broadly as 'judge' (discussing An 724), with a secondary sacerdotal dimension implied in the Qa series.
[49] As PN at Knossos: KN Sc 238, V 60, Xd 7702; Ruijgh 1967:56 and n46; Olivier et al. 1973:122; DM s.v. *me-nu-wa* 2). Parallelism does suggest that in Aq 218.14 (DMG:177–178) *me-nu-a₂* is a title (Ruijgh 1967:56 and n46, although here too Palmer 1963:144 saw a TN). *Me-nu-wa* in PY An 724.2 (DMG:187, perhaps a list of exemptions from rowing service) is ambiguous, the analogous position in lines 5 and 7 being PN and title, respectively: Lejeune 1958:260n14; MgP:82, 172; DMG:485; Killen 2008:170–171.
[50] PP 2:209 and further below.
[51] Nor is it entirely certain that anything preceded]mẹ-nu-a₂ on Qa 1293: for shape of the tablet's lefthand edge, compare (in Blegen and Lang 1958) Qa 1290, 1295, 1304, 1298; for spacing of single-word + quantity of *189, Qa 1292, 1297.
[52] The Ionic nominative Κινύρης is found in Homer (*Iliad* 11.20); Κινύρας should be shared by other dialects, and is so attested (cf. Eustathios on *Iliad* 11.20: ὁ Κινύρας κοινῶς ἢ Δωρικῶς ἢ καθ' Ὅμηρον Ἰωνικῶς ὁ Κινύρης). The Attic or Atticizing genitive Κινύρου (Plutarch *Moralia* 310f, etc.) is also frequent, but Alkman has the Doric Κινύρα (3.71 PMGF); this is also implied for the seventh-century Spartan Tyrtaios in Plato's paraphrase (*Leg.* 660e) of fr. 12.6 IEG (= Stobaios *Anthology* 4.10.1), and should be restored in a fourth-century Paphian inscription (p411). The

authorities also encourages us to ignore the other possible phonetic renderings of the Pylian evidence—namely /Kinnýras/, /Kinýras/, /Kinnŷras/—permitted by the ambiguities of Linear B, which distinguished neither vowel length nor double consonants.[53]

'Kinyras' is also consistent with Mycenaean name-forming patterns.[54] First, it joins the group of single-stem PNs that constitute seventy-five percent of those studied by O. Landau.[55] Of these, names in -ās are well represented at 3.7% of the total, ahead of many other suffixes (if well behind 6.4% in -tās and 11.2% in -eus).[56] According to the scheme of A. Leukart, -ās originally connoted adherence to a social group; but already by the Mycenaean period it was rather more general, appearing with a variety of nominal and adjectival stems.[57] Leukart grouped 'Kinyras' with adjectival nicknames like *E-ru-ta-ra* (*Erythrās*, 'Ruddy'), seeing its root as *kinyrós* ('plaintive') rather than *kinýra* ('lyre') on the grounds that the former is found already in Homer, while the latter is "a late-attested Semitic loan-word"; but oddly enough he was open to deriving from *kinýra* the later attested examples of 'Kinyras' in the eastern Mediterranean.[58]

And yet—leaving aside the possible etymological relationship between *kinyrós* and *kinýra*,[59] and the complication of supposing two independent etymologies for what is surely a single PN—we have seen that the supposed lateness of *kinýra* is illusory; it derives rather from an early culture-word, very probably established on LBA Cyprus in some pre-Greek form.[60] That *kinýra* was not commonplace in pre-Hellenistic Greek is no argument against its currency, or at least peripheral presence, in the Mycenaean world. Consider that *phórminx*, the normal Homeric word for lyre, is unattested in Linear B; yet *lýra*,

---

conventional Homeric/Ionic version of the Tyrtaios verses has the Ionic genitive Κινύρεω, implying an earlier Κινύραο in the Aeolic phase and so on back to the LBA (it is found as an archaism in Bion *Lament for Adonis* 91 and Nonnos *Dionysiaka* 13.451).

[53] While *Kinnýras* is indeed attested, this reflects the reintroduction of the original double-n by a Syrian or Levantine scribe for whom such forms as ki̱nnōr were still a living concern: see p214–215.

[54] The basic study is MgP; see also DMG:96–97; Bartoněk 2003:399–418.

[55] MgP:239–243.

[56] MgP:240–241.

[57] Leukart 1994:147–157, 204–235. Note that Linear B does not represent terminal -s, so that in principle some names of this pattern may actually have ended in -ā rather than -ās (cf. MgP:242; DMG¹:84, 93–94). But the assumption of first-declension nominative masculines in -ās is justified by Myc. genitives in -āo, which probably arose secondarily to disambiguate the new nominatives from earlier genitives in -ās: DMG:400; Risch 1974.

[58] Leukart 1994:215 and n218. For the Cilician Kinyras, see p496–512.

[59] See p188 and n7.

[60] See p272–276.

Chapter Seventeen

long considered a seventh-century novelty,[61] has now surfaced (indirectly) at Mycenaean Thebes.[62] So different lyre-names could easily have been used in different parts of the LBA Aegean, or side-by-side within different generic contexts. When this is combined with post-palatial disruptions, lexical discrepancies between LBA and later usage are only to be expected.[63]

There is no reason, therefore, not to place 'Kinyras' among the more numerous PNs in *-ās* that contain *nominal* stems.[64] *Ki-nu-ra* would thus be 'man of the *kinýra*', equally intelligible as PN and/or title. This interpretation is well paralleled by other Mycenaean PNs. For the addition of *-ās* to a concrete noun, compare for instance *E-ke-a* = **Enkhé(h)as*, < *énkhos*, 'spear'.[65] A still closer parallel is *Ma-ke-ra* = **Makéllas*, < *mákella* ('mattock').[66] There are besides other PNs (of various formations) plausibly derived from musical instruments, including *a-wo-ro* (*Aulṓn*) and *ru-ro* (*Lýros*).[67] PNs from professions are also common, with

---

[61] Arkhilokhos 54.11, 93a.5 IEG; Alkman 140 PMGF (κερκολύρα); Sappho 44.33, 103.9, 208; Alkaios 307c; Stesikhoros 278.2 PMGF; [Homer] *Margites* fr. 1.3 IEG; *Homeric Hymn to Hermes* 422.

[62] The new tablet is TH Av 106.7, where *ru-ra-ta-e* ('two lyrists') has been interpreted as the dual of a deverbative noun **λυρασταί* (< **λυράζω*, against the later λυρίζω/λυριστής—itself but slightly attested: Pliny *Letters* 9.17.3; Artemidoros *Interpretation of Dreams* 4.72): see Aravantinos 1996; Younger 1998:18n42; Aravantinos et al. 2001:29–30, 176–178; Aravantinos et al. 2002:82–83. Others opt for a denominative **λυράτας*: Melena 2001:30–31; Meier-Brügger 2006:115.

[63] For this general point, cf. Franklin 2011a; Franklin 2011b. It may even be that *lýra*, rightly regarded as a "technical loanword from the Mediterranean area" (Beekes 2009 s.v.), was itself cognate with *kinýra*—a regional transformation via some pre-Greek Aegean language, for instance Minoan. This was suggested by M. Schwartz (communication, April 2012). The question needs further investigation, but preliminarily several suggestive phenomena, seen by Beekes as betraying the influence of pre-Greek upon later 'Greek' words, may be noted: interchange of νν/ν and λλ/λ (xviii §5.8); absence of velar in initial position (xxix §5.10); alternation of λ/ν (e.g. νίτρον/λίτρον, xviii §5.7a); possible lack of phonemic distinction in vowel length (xx, xxxii §6.2); note also xxix §5.13, where possible "secondary developments either in Greek or perhaps already in the original language" include κμ- > μ- (κμέλεθρον/μέλαθρον). One hypothetical sequence: Can. **kinnō/ūr(a)* > Eteocypriot and/or Aegean pre-Greek *kin(n)ýra* (with loss of second-syllable length) > Aegean pre-Greek **knýra* > **nýra* > Myc./Gk. λύρα.

[64] Leukart 1994:210–213.

[65] KN V 831.1; MgP:46, 174, 209; Leukart 1994:210, with further examples 210–213. The PN *O-re-a₂* (PY Ep 705) = Ὀρέ(h)ας, < ὄρος, 'mountain, hill' (MgP:174, 209) is considered analogous to Kinyras by DGAC:355; but for Leukart 1994:205 the idea of *place* predominates in that word, constituting a transitional semantic stage between *-ās* as connoting membership in a social group, and the more general constructions involving nominal and adjectival roots.

[66] KN V 831: MgP:235, 242; Leukart 1994:210.

[67] *A-wo-ro*: KN B 800.3, cf. *Aulṓn* in Pausanias 3.12.9. *Ru-ro*: PY Sn 64.4, cf. the obscure Lyros son of Aphrodite and the lyre-playing Ankhises ([Apollodoros] *Library* 3.12.2). Another possibility is *tu-pa2-ni-ja-so* (KN Db 1279, a shepherd) = **Τυ(μ)πανιασ(σ)ος*, < τύμπανον, 'frame-drum' (well attested Semitic cognates include Ug. *tp*: cf. DUL s.v. which notes Heb. *twp*, Aram. *twp*, Arab. *duff*); but the name could be an ethnic (< Τυ[μ]πανέαι, in Triphylia, Peloponnese). For these PNs, see MgP:18, 236; further references in DM s.v.

some born by people working in the associated field.[68] Others reflect cult-activity.[69] These patterns all neatly converge in the PN 'Kinyras' as '*kinýra*-man' or 'kinyrist'.[70]

There are good ANE parallels for this interpretation. Sum. balaĝ, equated with *kinnārum* at Ebla (ca. 2350), is found both as a PN-element and in the agent word balaĝ.di.[71] We saw a PN built on *Kin(n)ar*[- at LBA Alalakh, and Hurro-Semitic agent-forms at both Alalakh and Hattusha.[72] These hybrids, inherently *practical*, reflect a living music-culture in diffusion, and generally support the idea that the Mycenaean world could constitute the western margin of Syro-Levantine lyre-culture—even if this was only secondarily or superficially through contact with Cyprus and Cypriots.[73] *Ki-nu-ra* as a title in Qa 1301 would establish a greater depth of exposure than as a PN; but with the hieratic context, a man called 'Kinyras' could still have executed a function akin to his name. Given Lupack's hypothesis of a cultic-industrial character to the NEB and some direct involvement by the people of the Qa series, it is worth recalling the 'industrial' contexts in which Mesopotamian lamentation-singing is attested.[74]

That 'Kinyras' conforms to Greek word-building rules need not exclude special Cypriot connotations. Besides the ethnic character of *kinýra* itself (Chapters 9-12), and that already for Homer 'Kinyras' and Cyprus were indissolubly associated,[75] *Kýprios* (*ku-pi-ri-jo*) and *Alásios (*a-ra-si-jo*) are well attested at Pylos and Knossos as PNs or as TN-adjectives describing the destination or origin of various commodities, with the contexts often relating to typical

---

[68] Examples from MgP:204–207 and 235–236 include several aptly named shepherds: *Ko-ru-no* (PY Cn 131.4, 719.9) = *Κόρυνος, cf. κορύνη, 'shepherd's staff'; *Ke-to-ro* (KN C 954.1) = *Κέντρος, cf. κέντρον, 'goad'; also Ke-to (KN Da 1134) = *Κέντωρ. Other PNs from professions are *A-ko-ro-ta* (KN Mc 4459, MY Go 610+) = Ἀγρότης, 'Hunter' (or 'Landowner'); *Ta-mi-je-u* (PY Jn 310.3, a smith) = *Ταμιεύς, cf. ταμίας, 'dispenser'; *A-ke-ro* (PY Jo 438) = Ἄγγελος, 'Messenger' (cf. Plutarch *Pyrrhos* 2). Further examples: PP 2:95 and n4, 208–210; Bartoněk 2003:402–403.

[69] MgP:212–213: *Tu-si-je-u* (PY An 19.7, warrior) = *Θυσιεύς, 'Offerer', < θύω, θύσις; *A-wa-ta* (PY An 340) = *Ἀρϝά-τας, 'Priest'/'Pray-er', < ἀράομαι; *Ma-ti-jo* (KN X 1024.1) = Μάντιος (cf. Homer *Odyssey* 15.242).

[70] Cf. Franklin 2006a:47; Franceschetti 2008a:313–314, 316.

[71] Hartmann 1960:124; cf. p65–70.

[72] See p98.

[73] An instrument on a MM IIB prism-seal, variously interpreted as harp or lyre (Younger 1998:76 cat. 56, pl. 23.4; Crowley 2013:221, E184a), has a flat base and curling arms, which *might* be taken to show Levantine morphological influence; but the earlier Cycladic harps seem more relevant (AGM:70–71). One of the Minoan hieroglyphs (MM II–IIIA) rather more closely resembles a lyre of Levantine type (Olivier et al. 1996, sign no. 58 [#053.aB, 053.e]; Aign 1963:37 and 351; Younger 1998:79–80, cat. 67, pl. 25.2a-b); but cf. SIAG:219n3.

[74] See p24, 30.

[75] Gallavotti 1976:56.

Cypriot industries.[76] One Kyprios at Pylos was a bronze-worker who received an allotment of the metal.[77] Another is associated with alum, a versatile mineral of which Cyprus was a source.[78] Other instances involve oil and perfumed-oil making, an important industry for both LBA Pylos and Cyprus (recall Alkman's "moist charm of Kinyras").[79] These words, which one way or another indicate significant commercial and cultural interactions with Cyprus, are Greek in formation with Cypriot and/or Cyprocentric roots.

Kinyras the Shipwright

The page-shaped Vn tablets are not a coherent ancient series, but a modern grouping of texts lacking any ideogram and written by a variety of hands; most come from Room 8 in the AC.[80] Vn 865 is a list of twelve PNs after the heading *na-u-do-mo*.[81] Line 7 contains]*nu-ra*, the final two syllables of a trisyllabic PN. C. Gallavotti's supplement *ki-*]*nu-ra*, Kinyras, is the only restoration possible from words/PNs otherwise attested in Linear B,[82] and is generally accepted.[83]

Was this Kinyras the same or a different man than the *ki-nu-ra* of Qa 1301? Their identification finds no associative *prosopographical* support (that is, no other PN from Vn 865 reappears elsewhere alongside one from the Qa series). Evaluation of the alternative criterion—*contextual* overlap between Vn 865 and the Qa tablets—depends upon understanding the heading *na-u-do-mo*. The underlying word is clearly *naudómos (see below). Given the list structure, it must be either nominative plural introducing the following PNs, or dative singular describing the person to whom the other men are somehow assigned. Since the latter are individually named—a sign of social prominence—one may safely conclude that this is a list of *naudómoi, not laborers assigned to one *naudómos.[84]

---

[76] See MgP:27, 219, 76, 227; Bubenik 1974; Gallavotti 1976 (comparing Kinyras on 56); Baurain 1980b:303n135; Shelmerdine 1985:49, 137–138; Knapp 1985:238; Himmelhoch 1990–1991; Palaima 1991:280–281, 290–295; Cline 1994:130; Nikoloudis 2008:48. That Cyprus should have been known by two names at once is not problematic: see Knapp in SHC 2:11–13.
[77] Jn 320.3.
[78] Un 443.1.
[79] See p330–332. Pylos' perfume industry: Shelmerdine 1984; Shelmerdine 1985.
[80] PTT 1:257, 2:64; Palaima 1988:177–179, 217; ISMP:143.
[81] PTT 1:256.
[82] Judging from the indices of Lejeune 1964:31 and Olivier et al. 1973:296.
[83] Gallavotti 1961:166; Morpurgo (Davies) 1963:148; PP 1:68, 2:95; PTT 1:256 (the under-dots suggest that the editors reexamined the text in light of Gallavotti's suggestion, but there is no comment in the apparatus); DMG:554; Gallavotti 1976:56; ISMP:139–140, 291 (restoration treated as certain).
[84] Palaima 1991:287–288 with contribution of R. Stieglitz.

Kinyras at Pylos

As to the meaning of *naudómos*, two views are viable on orthographical and morphological grounds: '(temple)-builder' (cf. *na[w]ós*) and 'shipbuilder' (< *naûs*).⁸⁵ The minority favoring 'temple-builder' has advanced good arguments and responses, but the majority analysis does seem clinched by two further texts. A second Pylian tablet attesting *na-u-do-mo* is one of a large group recording exemptions from payments of flax to the palace.⁸⁶ Such concessions were evidently granted to those whose professional activity was important to the state; others enjoying this flax exemption include hunters and bronze-workers, where one may think of nets/snares and undershirts for bronze corselets.⁸⁷ While builders might perhaps employ flax-products (textiles, cords), the large amounts involved—fifty units, the highest in the series—tally better with naval needs like sails and ropes (whether or not Pylos was in a state of emergency in the months before its destruction).⁸⁸ The tablet also contains the final syllable of a TN that permits restoration as *ro-o]wa̧*, the probable port of Pylos.⁸⁹ Finally, in a damaged tablet from Knossos, *na-u-do-mo* appears with the word *e-to-ro-qa-ta* and the ideogram *181, which has the shape of a loop.⁹⁰ This is most convincingly interpreted as **entrok*ʷ*atás* and connected with several later Greek words from the same root referring to the 'thongs' through which oars passed (perhaps of flaxen rope at this time).⁹¹

We may conclude, therefore, that the Kinyras of Vn 865 is indeed a shipwright.⁹² There being thus no obvious contextual overlap with the Qa series,

---

⁸⁵ Shipbuilders: Palmer 1963:435; DMG:298; PP 2:100; Palaima 1991:287; further references in DM s.v., 1–2. Temple-builders: Petruševski 1955:400; Stella 1958:50 and n119; Stella 1965:97; Billigmeier and Dusing 1981:14 and n14; DM s.v., 3. Montecchi 2011:172 objects on orthographical grounds, expecting rather **na-wo-do-mo*; but Billigmeier and Dusing 1981:13–14 demonstrated the viability of an athematic form in *nau-/naü-*. Gallavotti 1976:56 allowed both possibilities.

⁸⁶ Na 568: DMG:298–299; PP 2:100; Palaima 1991:287–288 (quotation). The tablets of the N- series (Na, Ng, Nn: DMG:295–301) are concerned with the ideogram SA, whose identification as some form of flax is guaranteed by Nn 228, which contains *ri-no* (λίνον) in its heading: Webster 1954:15; Robkin 1979:469.

⁸⁷ Na 248, 252: Webster 1954:15; Palaima 1991:287–288.

⁸⁸ Webster 1954:15; Palaima 1991:287–288. No emergency: Palaima 1995a.

⁸⁹ Palaima 1991:287–288; DM s.v. *ro-o-wa*.

⁹⁰ KN U 736.2.

⁹¹ Palmer 1955:39; Heubeck 1958:121–122; Melena 1975:53–59; Palaima 1991:295–296; Montecchi 2011:172. The parallels are Hesykhios s.v. ἐντροπῶσαι· ἐνδῆσαι and ἐντροπίδες· ὑποδήματα; τροπός (already Homer), τροπωτήρ and τροπόω (LSJ s.v.).

⁹² There remains the observation of Billigmeier and Dusing 1981:14 and n14 that the name of one **naudómos*, *sa-mu-ta-jo*, is also found as a bronzesmith in Jn 389. The equation of these men is considered "tenuous" for lack of overlapping context by Nakassis (ISMP:372, accepting **naudómoi* as shipbuilders). But bronze-working could supply the necessary intersection, since *ka-ko na-wi-jo* (χαλκὸς *νάϝιος) in Jn 829 is better interpreted as 'temple-bronze' than 'ship-bronze' (Leukart 1979; Hiller 1979; Billigmeier and Dusing 1981:14 and n14); whether this relates to sacred metallurgy (Lupack 2008b:34–43 et passim) is another question.

Nakassis considered the basis for identifying *ki-nu-ra* in Qa 1301 and Vn 865 as merely "tenuous."⁹³ Of course an individual might indeed be involved in two different spheres.⁹⁴

A Kinyras Complex

When Kinnaru of Ugarit came to light, the Kinyras(es) of Pylos attracted renewed attention, with several scholars supporting the derivation both of the Pylian PNs and the mythological Kinyras from the root *knr*.⁹⁵ But the real question here has hardly been recognized: what is the precise relationship between the Kinyras of myth and the homonymous Pylian(s)?

C. Baurain rejected the idea of a 'real' god Kinnaru as "fort excessif."⁹⁶ Hence, while admitting that the Myc. PN was very probably derived from *knr*, Baurain denied that the mythological Kinyras grew from a hieratic musical seed. That *ki-nu-ra* appeared in the priestly Qa series was rendered insignificant, he argued, by Kinyras the shipwright ("une mise en garde contre des implications religieuses trop précises").⁹⁷ On this view, the Kinyras of myth, while his name did indeed mean '*kinýra*-man', simply possessed an ordinary Mycenaean PN like many other heroes.⁹⁸ Consequently, his priestly dimension would have to be a special Cypriot innovation, specifically of Paphos and the Kinyrad dynasty. But this idea is now fatally undermined by the extra-Paphian evidence for hieratic lyre-culture on the island and its culmination in "Our *Kenyristḗs* Apollo."

One might try to compromise with Baurain by admitting that a person named (or entitled) '*kinýra*-man' would find a natural place among the Pylian priests without any necessary reference to the mythological Kinyras; the latter would then bear this same, 'ordinary' Mycenaean PN because it best described the divine, lyre-playing figure whom Aegean Greeks found ensconced on the island in (and before) the twelfth century. And what better place than Cyprus for a Mycenaean usage to persist? Such a survival would be all the more probable if *kinýra* was itself modeled on an originally Cypriot adaptation of a Canaanite

---

⁹³ ISMP:139–140, 291.
⁹⁴ And Nakassis himself seems to identify the two Kinyrases after all at ISMP:140.
⁹⁵ Astour 1965:139n5 (approved in Hemmerdinger's review, REG 81 [1968]:216); Kapera 1971:139; Baurain 1980b:305–306.
⁹⁶ Baurain 1980b:305; cf. Gese et al. 1970:169; contrast Kapera 1971:138–139.
⁹⁷ Baurain 1980b:305–306, "Au vu de PY Vn 865, cette possibilité devient caduque ... Il faut donc admettre que ... Κινύρας était un anthroponyme connu à Pylos et que son attribution ne paraissait pas liée à des considérations religieuses."
⁹⁸ For parallels, see MgP:262–267; DMG:103–105.

form, as I have argued.⁹⁹ But then the specter of *the* Kinyras would rise again, given the early attestation of Kinnaru at Ugarit.

Moreover, while Baurain would use the shipbuilding Kinyras to discredit a connection between the mythical Kinyras and *ki-nu-ra* in Qa 1301, we must remember that the Cypriot king was himself associated with maritime matters. As Baurain himself conceded in a footnote, referring to the terracotta fleet, "nous ne pouvons nier que Kinyras est aussi lié à une étrange historie de bateaux."¹⁰⁰ But this is a serious understatement, for Kinyras' naval persona was as well developed as the priestly/mantic/musical (see Chapter 13). So Vn 865 cannot be used to eliminate the mythical Kinyras from discussion of the Pylian evidence.

We must therefore seriously consider whether the Pylian Kinyrases have as their namesake *the* Kinyras—a Divine Lyre who, having acquired secondary, metamusical attributes *by the thirteenth century*, was lending his name to ordinary mortals (and their children), especially those with appropriate professional interests. This question must be asked whether we are dealing with one or two separate names at Pylos—and for that matter whether the *ki-nu-ra* of Vn 865 was shipwright or temple-builder, since the latter was yet another role played by Kinyras.¹⁰¹

Contemplating this possibility raises further onomastic issues. While theophoric PNs are not especially common in the Mycenaean world, we do find *De-wi-jo* (< Zeús, gen. Diwós), *A-pa-i-ti-jo* (< Háphaistos), *A-re-i-jo* (< Árēs?), and several others.¹⁰² These are typically adjectival constructions, but the quasi-agent formation proposed for Kinyras may be compared with *Di-wi-je-u* (= *Dieús*, < Zeús).¹⁰³ The attested Mycenaean theophorics are mostly single-stemmed—as would be Kinyras—rather than compounds roughly comparable to the familiar Semitic 'sentence-names'. In at least three cases (all soldiers), the individual's profession is relevant to the god whose name he bears (Zeus, Enyalios).¹⁰⁴

So a theophoric etymology for Kinyras is paralleled from within Linear B. Yet if the underlying divine-element (*knr*) was indeed of Cypriot, and ultimately Syro-Levantine, extraction, we should not restrict our view to *Mycenaean* onomastics. After all, non-Greek PNs, born by resident foreigners or fashionable

---

⁹⁹ See p55–57, 195–196, 272–276.
¹⁰⁰ Baurain 1980b:306n150.
¹⁰¹ See p363.
¹⁰² PY An 519.10, KN L 588.1, PY An 656.6. See further MgP:211–212.
¹⁰³ PY An 656.9.
¹⁰⁴ *De-wi-jo* (PY An 519.10); *Di-wi-je-u* (PY An 656.9, a *hequétas* or military 'follower'); *E-no-wa-ro* (Py An 654.14) = *Enýalos, cf. *E-nu-wa-ri-jo* (KN V 52.2), Ἐνυάλιος (later an epithet of Ares: Homer *Iliad* 17.211, etc.). See MgP:211–212.

in the Aegean, are not uncommon in Linear B, and clearly attest the multicultural nature of the Mycenaean world.[105] These include, besides the pre-Greek Aegean PNs one expects, a fair few paralleled in Hittite sources and by Hurrian PNs from Alalakh.[106] The latter are especially suggestive: besides the aforementioned PN with the root *kin(n)ar-* from that city, a number of resident Alashiyans are attested at Alalakh in the eighteenth and fifteenth centuries.[107] One Alashiyan from Alalakh bears the single-stem name *A-la-ši-ia*, confirming that Mycenaean *A-ra-si-jo* is a genuine Cyprocentric PN, not just a Hellenocentric ethnic nickname.[108] Hurrian PNs are the most numerous after Semitic in the diverse Alashiyan onomasticon (compiled from, besides the Alalakh texts, Ugaritic, Hittite, and Egyptian sources).[109] Nor is it unlikely on general grounds that at least some Cypro-Minoan tablets record a Hurrian dialect.[110]

The Alashiyan PNs equally include Anatolian, Egyptian, and other unidentifiable (presumably indigenous) specimens. Despite divergent interpretations of specific PNs and the often loose relationship between a PN's linguistic affiliation and the ethnic identity of its bearer, Alashiya was clearly as multicultural as Ugarit and Alalakh, and of a quite similar mixture.[111] The proposed LBA derivation of *kinýra*/Kinyras from (ultimately) a *Canaanite* dialect finds circumstantial support in six or seven Canaanite PNs, both single-stemmed and theophoric-sentences, in the Alashiya texts. There was also one or more Canaanite-speakers among the scribes who produced those from Amarna,[112] while the cuneiform sign-shapes in the new Alashiya texts from Ugarit seem to show Tyrian influence.[113]

---

[105] Nikoloudis 2008.
[106] See MgP:268–273.
[107] Alashiyans at Alalakh: SHC 2 no. 10–13; PPC:318–319. For the PN, see p98. A remarkable toponymic legend, surviving into the Hellenistic period, recalled how a king 'Kasos' (Mount Kasios) married a Cypriot princess called Kittia (Kition) or Amyke (the Amuq), who brought a Cypriot entourage with her to Syria: Pausanias of Damascus FHG 4:469 fr. 4. See Movers 1841–1856:205–206; HC:32.
[108] AT 385.2; Astour 1964:242.
[109] Alashiyan PNs: Astour 1964 (cf. Astour 1965:139n5, 51n1); Carruba 1968:25–29; Knapp 1979:257–265; Knapp 1983:40; SHC 2:7–8; PPC:318–323. The probably Indo-Iranian *E-šu-wa-ra* of RS 20.19 may be included among the Hurrian PNs for cultural reasons, such names being famously born by the Mitannian kings.
[110] Masson 1974:47–55; Faucounau 1994; for an agnostic critique of these and other proposed decipherments, Knapp and Marchant 1982; PPC:322; Steele 2013:9–97. The same proposal has been made for the later Eteocypriot tablets from Amathous and elsewhere: see p349n66.
[111] Cf. Knapp 1983:40.
[112] Cochavi-Rainey 2003:2–3, 118–119; PPC:322.
[113] Malbran-Labat 1999:121, 123.

We must also cast a glance at Ugarit. Canaanite PNs are found here too, north of the Canaanite dialect zone proper.[114] Alashiyans resident in Ugarit are also well attested.[115] Nor is the use of occupational designations (naturally single-stemmed) uncommon in Ugaritic PNs; especially suggestive are the PNs 'Singer' (*šr*) and 'Priest' (*khn, kmry*).[116] Also important are several theophoric PNs incorporating the craftsman god Kothar, one of which is professionally relevant (*kšrmlk*, 'Kothar-is-king', a silversmith).[117] The simple form is also attested as a PN, from an Amorite king *Kwšr* in the Execration Texts (ca. 1900) of MK Egypt, to 'Khauthar' in a third-century CE tombstone from Hama, an Aramaean area of Syria.[118] The special significance of these Kothar-PNs will emerge in the next chapter, when we study that god's coalescence with Kinyras.

The foregoing catalogue, though somewhat scattershot, shows that a PN like 'Kinyras', in some pre-Greek prototype, is perfectly conceivable on pre-Greek Cyprus.

I find, therefore, that the Kinyras(es) of Pylos are best explained on the hypothesis that Kinyras already existed as a complex, metamusical figure on Cyprus by the thirteenth century. I have already sketched the cultural conditions under which such an expansion of a Divine Lyre's powers could have occurred, and suggested that just such a development underlies the contemporary Kourion stands, where monarchy, music, metals, and other elite symbols are brought together in coherent, 'significant' compositions.[119] These conclusions about the Mycenaean evidence are not so alarming when it is seen within a larger Cypro-Near Eastern framework. After all, Kinnaru probably had a substantial prehistory to find himself in the pantheon of thirteenth-century Ugarit. Despite the deep antiquity these hypotheses entail, the chronological pieces of the puzzle actually fit together very well.

---

[114] See p55.
[115] Resident Alashiyans at Ugarit: SHC 2:36–40; PPC:319; McGeough and Smith 2011:38–40 (the census text RS 11.857 = KTU/CAT 4.102, listing thirty households).
[116] Astour 1964:245; Gröndahl 1967:28–29.
[117] *Kšrmlk* (RS 19.16, 32 [PRU 5 no. 11]) is the Akkadianized form of *kṯrmlk*, also attested. The other names are *ku-šar-a-bi* ('Kothar-is-my-father'), *abdi-ku-ša-ri* and *ʿbdkṯr* ('Servant of Kothar'), and *bin-ku-ša-ri* ('Son of Kothar'). See with references Gröndahl 1967:79, 84, 152; Kinlaw 1967:299; KwH:62–63 and 131n70–71.
[118] See p167n100, 443n2.
[119] See p383–392.

18

The Melding of Kinyras and Kothar

THIS CHAPTER CONFRONTS THE ISSUE of Kinyras' extra-musical qualities, which he regularly assumed on Cyprus, and which already seem to inform the Kinyras(es) of Pylos and the Kourion stands, both in the thirteenth century. I refine and develop the position, taken by J. P. Brown and others, that Kinyras was productively implicated in a syncretic relationship with the WS craftsman god Kothar.[1] I argue that on some parts of the mainland, the Divine Knr was sometimes absorbed by Kothar. On Cyprus, however, Kothar was himself absorbed by Kinyras. I reserve for separate discussion in Chapter 19 the traditions allying both Kinyras and 'Kauthar' to Byblos.

Kothar and Kinnaru

We encountered Kothar at Ugarit as a beneficiary of state sacrifice, the armorer of Baal, and maker of Aqhat's marvelous bow.[2] He also appeared in the Rāp'iu

---

[1] For Kothar generally, Albright 1940:296–297; Gaster 1961:161–163; YGC:135–137; Gese et al. 1970:147–148 et passim; Xella 1976; KwH; Morris 1992:79–100 et passim; Morris 1998; DDD col. 913–915 (Pardee).

[2] 'Kothar' will refer both to the god as a wider Syro-Levantine figure and to his specific manifestation at Ugarit (context should make the difference clear); for the form, see n12. I reserve 'Khousor' (Gk. Χουσώρ) for the complex Phoenician culture-hero presented by Philo of Byblos (see p445–452), probably with special Byblian associations. 'Kauthar' will apply to the cognate figure in ps.-Meliton (Chapter 19). Note that the vocalization of Ug. ktr as Kôtharu (/kōθaru/), which entails taking Arabic *kawtar as cognate (KwH:51–80), is not always accepted; Huehnergard 2008:141 considers it "by no means certain," noting that otherwise the Ugarit-Akkadian ku-šar-ru (RS 20.123+ = Nougayrol 1968:248 (no. 137 IVa.19) will equally permit /kūθaru/ or /kŭθaru/. Yet the latter form is in any case ruled out by Philo's Χουσώρ (see n12 below), which establishes the long quantity of the first syllable. And the Greek spelling ΧΑΥΘΑΡ in a third-century CE tombstone from Hama, Syria (Lassus 1935:33 no. 14), an Aramaean area, definitely favors the Arabic form's relevance to the reconstruction (as realized already by Albright 1938:593; cf. Brown 1965:199; KwH:77; S. Weninger, communication, May 2012); for the old diphthongal value is clearly indicated by Greek αυ, itself still diphthongal at this time (Allen 1987:79–80). It may still be, however, that at Ugarit ku-šar-ru does reflect something closer to /kūθaru/ than /kōθaru/ (cf. p273–274).

Chapter Eighteen

text (RS 24.252.2–5), where the eponymous 'king of eternity' either sang, or was celebrated,

> With *kinnāru* and pipes,
> With drum and cymbals,
> With ivory clappers,[3]
> With the goodly companions of Kothar.[4]

The parallelistic structure of the overall passage is clearly indicated by the repeated conjunction (*b*, 'with').[5] Hence, the expression translated here as 'goodly companions', whatever its exact meaning, must belong to the musical atmosphere, and so most plausibly designates the ensemble as a whole.[6] This may imply some personification of the instruments, so that it is actually Kinnaru, in the first position, who leads the group, just as Ningirsu's balang-god presided over his temple-orchestra.[7] Consider too that only the instruments are named, not players; and yet players are needed if the instruments are to sound. This ambiguity is just what we have seen with the divinized instruments of Mesopotamia. If this interpretation is right, it would be welcome evidence that Kinnaru could indeed feature in (para)mythological contexts—something one expects on the basis of the Sumerian and Syro-Hurrian treatment of divinized cult-objects on the one hand, and Kinyras' numerous appearances in Cypriot and Greek mythology on the other.[8]

In any case, the *kinnāru* and other instruments are apparently somehow subordinated to Kothar. Various cultic nuances may escape us, but one likely explanation is ready to hand: they were *created* by the divine craftsman. Recall that Kothar also made magical weapons for Baal, endowing them with proper names through a special ritual.[9] Nor is this idea incompatible with M. S. Smith's interpretation as 'the goodly ones bound/enchanted by Kothar', detecting connotations of 'magical binding' in *ḥbr* (traditionally "companions"),

---

[3] For this interpretive issue, see p135n140.
[4] See p135, with text and comments.
[5] Good 1991:156–157; Clemens 1993:73.
[6] For those who interpret line three as referring not to another instrument but to cult-dancers (see p135n140), the "goodly companions of Kothar" will follow suit by parallelism: cf. Clemens 1993:73n57: "pair of instruments (x2); personal participant (x2)." Yet even this line of thinking is not incompatible with a musical Kothar, since both instruments and 'Kothar-dancers' would obviously comprise an integrated performance.
[7] N. Wyatt (DDD col. 912) seems to envisage such a possibility, citing the passage in connection with Psalms 57:8–9 (cf. p164) as evidence of "an older usage when minor gods of the pantheon were called upon to glorify their overlord."
[8] Cf. p6–7, 25–33, 103, 122–123.
[9] See p122.

since in Mesopotamia definite ritual procedures governed the construction of cult-objects, their investment with divinity, and their dedication to sacred service.[10]

RS 24.252 is the one Ugaritic text that seems to attest a significant connection between Kothar and music.[11] Yet the *kinnāru*'s divinization in that city surely means that Kothar was not the only or primary musical god there, despite the lack of unambiguous evidence for a personified treatment of Kinnaru.

Philo of Byblos: Khousor and His Retiring Twin

When Kothar was discovered in the Ugaritian texts, he was soon recognized as the ancestor, and helped clarify the early nature, of the Khousor who is mentioned by two late Phoenician authors surviving only in fragments—Mokhos of Sidon and Philo of Byblos.[12]

For Mokhos, reinterpreting his cosmogonic traditions under the stimulus of Hellenistic philosophy, Khousoros (*sic*) was "the first opener" and "the power of mind, since it first distinguishes indistinct nature."[13] He enjoys a very exalted position as son of "Oulomos, the God who has been Thought." 'Oulomos' is related to Heb. *'ôlām* ('Everlasting'), an epithet of Yahweh, with an Ug. cognate used of El.[14]

---

[10] See p23–25.
[11] Support for a musical Kothar has also been sought from the Kotharat, the seven 'skillful' goddesses who preside over marriage and conception rituals, arguably as songstresses (Margalit 1972). But this still would not guarantee a musical sense for Kothar himself, as one can suppose independent semantic developments of √ktr. Dahood 1963 argued well for an allusion to Kothar in Ezekiel 33:32, so that "you are like a singer of love-songs" becomes "skillful with reed-pipes" ("a Kothar on the pipes"?); cf. Cooper 1981:386.
[12] The 'Greek' orthography (Χουσώρ) reflects normal Phoenician phonetic developments. The long *ô* of Kothar resulted from the monophthongization of P-S *aw* (see n2), and then underwent further development to *û*, whence it is represented by Gk. ου (since υ/ῡ, having narrowed to /ü/ or /ǖ/ by the later fifth century, was no longer appropriate: see p196). As to the final syllable, after the loss of final short vowels in Phoenician, accented *a* was lengthened to *ā* and then to *ō* (by the same process which had produced the Canaanite Shift of *ā* > *ō* in the second millennium, still exerting its influence: Harris 1936:25 §8, 34–35 §11; Harris 1939:59–60; SL §21.13, 25.6). The stages of development are thus *Kawṯaru > *Kôṯaru > *Kû/ôšár > *Kû/ôšā́r > *Kûšṓr > 'Gk.' Χουσώρ (cf. KwH:79–80). Initial *k-* can be represented by Greek χ from the Hellenistic period.
[13] Mokhos of Sidon (Tyre? cf. Baumgarten 1981:148n33) FGH 784 F 4, preserved by Damaskios, a Syrian Neo-Platonist of the fifth–sixth century: Χουσωρὸν ἀνοιγέα πρῶτον ... τὴν νοητὴν δύναμιν ἅτε πρώτην διακρίνασαν τὴν ἀδιάκριτον φύσιν, *On First Principles* 125c (1.323 Ruelle); also in Attridge and Oden 1981:102–103. See generally Barr 1974:47–49 (undermining the equation of Khousor-'Opener' and Ptah advanced by Hoffman 1896:253–254 and YGC:193–196).
[14] Οὐλωμὸς ὁ νοητὸς θεός. See Cross 1973:18; Attridge and Oden 1981:104n7; Barr 1974:48–49).

Chapter Eighteen

The account by Philo of Byblos (ca. 100 CE)—partially preserved by Eusebios (ca. 260-339), bishop of Caesarea—is comparatively conservative, and so more informative about the traditional attributes of Kothar/Khousor.[15] Philo collected and combined material from the several Phoenician cities, and it is often not clear, no doubt intentionally, where a given tradition originates.[16] The relevant passage is part of a long genealogy of culture heroes who map the perceived course of civilization, beginning with a mythical foundation of Tyre, but wending its way towards a vaguely Byblian conclusion. It is difficult to know, therefore, whether Philo's Khousor stems from one or the other city, or is more generally representative of Phoenicia.[17]

Khousor appears after the invention of huts, skins for clothing, the taming of fire, the first maritime adventure (on a log), and mastery of hunting and fishing:

> And from them [sc. Hunter and Fisher] were born two brothers, the discoverers of iron and how to work it, of whom the one (*tháteron*), called Khousor, cultivated the verbal arts (*lógous*) and incantations (*epōidás*) and divination (*manteías*). And this one is known as Hephaistos, though he also discovered fishhook, bait, fishing-line, and raft, and was first of all men to sail. Because of this they revered him even as a god after his death; and he was also called Zeus Meilikhios. And some say that his brother[18] had the idea of walls made from bricks.[19]

---

[15] For the character of Philo's work and sources, see p123.

[16] See Philo of Byblos FGH 790 F 1 (21); cf. Lokkegaard 1954:53.

[17] But see p472. Note that Philo's later treatment of Sydyk and Misor and their children appears to double some of his Khousor material: see p510-511.

[18] We must follow Clemen 1939:50 (so tacitly Brown 1965:203; Baumgarten 1981:169) in emending to the singular (τοὺς ἀδελφούς > τὸν ἀδελφόν: see text in next note). The phrase θάτερον τὸν Χουσώρ clearly implies a pair of brothers and that a second will indeed be discussed, as is the case throughout the larger narrative; the traditional plural reading would require us to suppose three (or more) brothers, of whom only Khousor is named. The corruption may have arisen from the following accusative plural τοίχους, with the glossing of Khousor as both Hephaistos and Zeus Meilikhios in the relatively long intervening stretch making a careless scribe lose track of brotherly pairs (A's reading αὐτῶν, "their brothers," will have followed suit). Just possibly Khousor's brother was in fact named, but has fallen from the text, through cavalier abstraction by Eusebios or in transmission; but the text reads smoothly. Some would connect Khousor's anonymous brother with the 'Craftsman' (Τεχνίτης) who comes soon afterwards (Clapham 1969:108); but this figure has a named brother of his own (Γήϊνος Αὐτόχθων). Τεχνίτης may however be a doublet of Kothar deriving from Philo's conflation of regional Phoenician variants (Attridge and Oden 1981:84n170).

[19] Philo of Byblos FGH 790 F 2 (11) = Eusebios *Preparation for the Gospel* 1.10.11-12: Ἀγρέα καὶ Ἁλιέα ... ἐξ ὧν γενέσθαι δύο ἀδελφοὺς σιδήρου εὑρετὰς καὶ τῆς τούτου ἐργασίας, ὧν θάτερον τὸν Χουσώρ λόγους ἀσκῆσαι καὶ ἐπῳδὰς καὶ μαντείας. εἶναι δὲ τοῦτον τὸν Ἥφαιστον, εὑρεῖν δὲ καὶ ἄγκιστρον καὶ δέλεαρ καὶ ὁρμιὰν καὶ σχεδίαν, πρῶτόν τε πάντων ἀνθρώπων πλεῦσαι. διὸ καὶ ὡς θεὸν αὐτὸν

As Hoffman first pointed out in 1896, this dossier overlaps strikingly with what is credited to Kinyras.[20] Another vital sympathy, he emphasized, is that Kinyras is father of Adonis, a role played by Kauthar in ps.-Meliton (see Chapter 19). Brown was able to expand the comparison on the basis of Kothar's profile in the Ugaritian texts.[21] Following Hoffman and Brown, I assembled further evidence in Chapter 13 for Kinyras' nonmusical attributes, three broad areas of which, we now see, are closely paralleled by Philo's Khousor: Kinyras discovered metals and metallurgical tools, promoted seafaring, and invented roof- and/or wall-tiles. I may now add several further comparisons. Kothar too—the Ugaritian god, that is, versus Philo's Khousor—had a maritime dimension, as a kind of divine steersman or protector of sailors invoked in a poem of the *Baal Cycle*;[22] and indirectly through his overseas home on Crete in Ugaritian epic, symbolizing maritime palatial trade networks in daedalic luxury items and technologies.[23] Kothar was, like Kinyras, a builder, constructing palaces for Baal and other gods—Kinyras built Aphrodite's temple—and both worked in precious materials.[24] Kinyras and Kothar are both credited with intricate decorative schemes involving animal figuration.[25] Both are also armorers: Kinyras makes and/or supplies Agamemnon's breastplate(s), Kothar designs the weapons with which Baal subdues Sea, and delivers Aqhat his priceless compound bow.[26] It is tempting to link Kothar the bowyer with the otherwise quite stray report in the

---

μετὰ θάνατον ἐσεβάσθησαν. καλεῖσθαι δὲ αὐτὸν καὶ Δία Μειλίχιον· οἱ δὲ τὸν ἀδελφὸν [Clemen, see n18: τοὺς ἀδελφοὺς MSS] αὐτοῦ [A: αὐτῶν] τοίχους φασὶν ἐπινοῆσαι ἐκ πλίνθων.

[20] Hoffman 1896:256–258.
[21] Brown 1965. But his unawareness of Kinnaru led him to endorse the comparison of Kinyras with *el-ku-ni-ir-ša* (El, Creator of the Earth), now obsolete (cf. p5n27), and to reject the etymology of Kinyras < κινύρα (cf. p4, 189).
[22] RS 2.[009] + 5.155 = KTU/CAT 1.6 vi.51–53. Kothar's conjunction with the sea is clear in this text, although the exact interpretation is debated: see RTU:145 and n126 with further references.
[23] Kothar's homes in Crete (Caphtor) and Egypt: RS 3.361 (KTU/CAT 1.1 iii.1, 18–19); RS 3.346? (1.2 iii.2–3); RS 2.[014]+ (1.3 vi.14–16). For further evidence connecting Kothar and the sea, KwH:105–118; cf. Brown 1965:204; DDUPP:109. Kothar as a totalizing figure of second-millennium trade with the Aegean and Egypt: Morris 1992:93 et passim; Morris 1998; note especially the startling discovery of Minoan frescoes at Avaris and elsewhere: Bietak 2005, etc. The interpretation of Kothar as 'fisherman of Athirat/Asherah' (see Baumgarten 1981:167, 200), and so a close connection with the 'Lady of the Sea' (DDUPP:72; OSG:14 with references in n25), has been abandoned: see Smith and Pitard 2009:377.
[24] Kothar as palace-builder: RS 3.361? (KTU/CAT 1.1 iii.27–28); RS 3.346 (1.2 iii.7–11); RS 2.[008]+ (1.4 v.41–vi.38). See generally Gaster 1961:161nXIV; Gordon 1966:22–23, 48–49, 58–60, 63–64 (somewhat out-of-date); Gese et al. 1970:148; Baumgarten 1981:169–170; KwH:218–250, 310–350; Morris 1992:83–84.
[25] Kinyras and Agamemnon's breastplate: Homer *Iliad* 11.24–28; see p1, 322–323. Kothar's gift for Athirat: RS 2.[008]+ (KTU/CAT 1.4 i.23–43).
[26] Baal's weapons: RS 3.367 (KTU/CAT 1.2 iv.11–15); Aqhat's bow: RS 2.[004] (KTU/CAT 1.17 v.10–28, vi.20–25).

Chapter Eighteen

Pindaric scholia that Apollo loved Kinyras for being an archer.[27] Finally, we have seen that in early Greek poetics, Kinyras was proverbially wealthy and often connected with *kháris*—a display of generosity that results in beholden friendship. This too may echo Kothar, since the root *ktr*, the basic idea of which was 'build/work', led secondarily in Semitic languages to associations with success, prosperity, and abundance.[28] Note that Philo glosses Khousor as Zeus Meilikhios (the 'mild' or 'gracious').[29]

The sympathies of Khousor and Kinyras, already undeniable, become quite remarkable when one considers Philo's attribution of *lógoi*, *epōidaí*, and *manteîai* to Khousor. Although these powers can be paralleled to some extent for Kothar in the Ugaritian texts,[30] they accord much better with what one expects of a Divine Lyre, both on the basis of Mesopotamian and Hurro-Hittite parallels for divinized instruments, and the performance contexts known for the *kinnāru* itself.

Khousor's appearance early in the development of civilization, culminating in the invention of writing by Taautos (< Thoth), encourages us to understand *lógoi* in pre-literate, performative terms as 'the artistic use of language'. After all, even in the literate cities of the LBA Levant, traditions of poetry and liturgical music must have remained basically oral, notwithstanding the Hurrian hymns with musical 'notation'.[31] *Lógoi* comfortably embraces the full verbal range needed in cult and court: ritual prescriptions, praise-hymns, laments, epic poetry or other narrative song.[32] Such powers go well beyond the known realm of Kothar.[33]

A similar point may be made about *epōidaí*, 'incantations'. True, Kothar recites spells while making Baal's weapons, a procedure befitting metallurgy as a kind of magic.[34] The Mesopotamian Ea/Enki, whom the scribes and theologians of Ugarit equated with Kothar, has been invoked as a parallel here, since he

---

[27] Σ Pindar *Pythian* 2.30g (Abel 1891): see p226.
[28] See especially KwH:51–80, convincingly upholding the relevance of Arabic cognates, including *kawṯar*, 'abundant goodness'; so too SL §29.9.
[29] For Kothar as Zeus Meilikhios, see Baumgarten 1981:168–169; contrast KwH:113–114.
[30] For scenes in which Kothar appears to be prophetic, see Smith 1994:336. For incantations, see below.
[31] See p97.
[32] The Greek does not support the idea that λόγους ἀσκῆσαι here is *defined* by καὶ ἐπῳδὰς καὶ μαντείας (KwH:443: "the 'verbal arts' of Khousor ... do not include music, but 'spells and prophecies'"). Λόγοι are a separate category—various forms of poetry that (as typically in the ancient world) will have had a musical aspect.
[33] KwH:442–445 rightly emphasized the tenuous basis for supposing a musical Kothar; cf. Brown 1965:206; Good 1991:157 ("it remains puzzling that the Ugaritic texts do not place Kothar in a musical context apart from [RS 24.252]").
[34] See p394n127. Cf. Obermann 1947:208; Gaster 1961:161–163; KwH:119.

was credited with divination, magic, and an array of other cultural inventions, including music.[35] Yet it is not clear how far Ea's musicality per se is paralleled by Ugaritian Kothar (versus Philo's Khousor), whose association with musical instruments in RS 24.252, I have suggested, is due mainly to his magical craftsmanship.[36] And the Greek word *epōidaí* has considerably wider connotations than what is attested for Kothar.[37] The word's root, *aoidḗ*, means 'song', with *epi-* ('upon') distinguishing simple song from the efficacious singing of ritual acts.[38] Herodotos, for example, uses the word of the Magi's theogonic singing during Persian sacrifices; according to the mysterious *Derveni Papyrus*, the Magi's "incantation has the power to banish interfering spirits."[39] Plato refers to itinerant diviners (*mánteis*) who claimed to compel the gods through "sacrifices and *epōidaí*."[40] Other applications of *epōidḗ* included healing and purification.[41] Highly relevant for the question of Kinyras/Khousor are authors who treat ritual lamentation as a type of *epōidḗ*, notably in the context of Adonis-cult.[42]

Divinatory arts (*manteîai*) would also be most appropriate for a Divine Lyre, recalling Kinyras' guise of priest and prophet, still cultivated by the Paphian Kinyradai in the Roman period.[43] And Philo's plural invites further parallels—the

---

[35] Kothar as Ea: RS 20.024, 15; RS 20.123+, IVa.19, etc.: Nougayrol 1968:44–45 (no. 18), cf. 51; 240–249 (no. 137). Cf. Clapham 1969:107; Gese et al. 1970:98–99, 147; Lichtenstein 1972:104n57, 110; Baumgarten 1981:166; SURS:861 and n1116 with further references. Ea is invoked in various incantations from Ugarit, but is not unique in this: SURS:1020–1021.

[36] See p444–445.

[37] Caquot 1976:300 rightly understood ἐπῳδαί broadly—"chants (ou des incantations)"—but anachronistically retrojects this to Kothar himself.

[38] The 'Getty hexameters' contain much relevant language: text in Faraone and Obbink 2013, 10–11 (note especially lines 1, 6, 23–24).

[39] Herodotos 1.132.3 (μάγος ἀνὴρ παρεστεὼς ἐπαείδει θεογονίην, οἵην δὴ ἐκεῖνοι λέγουσι εἶναι τὴν ἐπαοιδήν); *Derveni Papyrus* col. 6.1–11 (ἐπ[ωιδὴ δ]ὲ μάγων δύν[α]ται δαίμονας ἐμπο[δὼν] γι[νομένο]υς μεθιστάναι, 2–3, ed. Kouremenos et al. 2006). I assume that the papyrus speaks of Persian Magi specifically (for the issue, Lightfoot 2004:103; Kouremenos et al. 2006:166–168 with references), although apotropaic and cathartic incantations were of course more widely spread in the ANE.

[40] Plato *Republic* 364b; cf. *Symposium* 202e. Plato exploits the overlap between singing and incantation in the *Laws*, when his Athenian, after a discussion of the positive psychagogic effects of a proper musical education for children, realizes that "what we call songs (ᾠδάς) now appear in fact to have been incantations (ἐπῳδαί) for the soul" (Plato *Laws* 659d–e, following Bury's text in the Loeb edition).

[41] Sources in AGM:32 (beginning with Homer).

[42] Sophokles *Ajax* 582: θρηνεῖν ἐπῳδάς; Bion *Lament for Adonis* 91, 94–95: αἱ Χάριτες κλαίοντι τὸν υἱέα τῷ Κινύραο … χαὶ Μοῖραι τὸν Ἄδωνιν ἀνακλείοισιν, Ἄδωνιν, / καί νιν ἐπαείδουσιν ("The Graces beweep the son of Kinyras … the Moirai too invoke 'Adonis, Adonis', / and sing incantations over him").

[43] Tacitus *Histories* 2.3–4; Clement of Alexandria *Miscellanies* 1.21. See Chapter 16. Cf. Hoffman 1896:256; Brown 1965:204. Extispicy in the hands of a Divine Lyre may conjure a rather grotesque image. But recall that the slaughtering of a bull for making the divinized *lilissu*-drum was governed by a highly elaborate series of ritual actions and incantations (see p23–26). Hermes'

coercive communication with Ningirsu through the divinized balang in the Gudea Cylinders; the ecstatic song-acts of *kinnōr*-prophets in the Old Testament; or the hexametric oracles of the Delphic priests.⁴⁴

Thus, the overlap between Khousor's powers and what is attested for Kothar at Ugarit is only very partial. Yet all three abilities would suit a Divine Lyre very well.

Philo's musicalized Khousor indicates that in one or more traditions Kothar took over the territory of a more musical 'junior brother', whose very name he eclipsed. A reciprocal tendency may be glimpsed in Philo's assignment of iron-working not only to Khousor but to his anonymous sibling. The latter is further associated with the technique of wall-building from bricks—the closest parallels being Pliny's attribution of *tegulae* to Kinyras, and of bricks, clay vessels, bronze, and gold to 'Cinaras' by Étienne de Lusignan.⁴⁵ While some would explain Philo's pair of builder-brothers through Kothar's dual name at Ugarit (Kothar-wa-Hasis, 'Clever and Wise'⁴⁶), Khousor's mantic/musical skills and the Kothar-like qualities of Kinyras show that the situation is more complex.⁴⁷ The Ugaritic texts reveal that divine couplings were a rather flexible phenomenon in the thirteenth century; of the thirty-three pairs enumerated by J. C. de Moor, seventeen featured gods who appeared elsewhere in different combinations.⁴⁸ Some were clearly *ad hoc* juxtapositions. He concluded that: "combinations of the type *X w Y* meant nothing more at first than bringing two deities who were thought to be somehow related closely together. At this stage they kept their individuality." Later such 'assimilations' came to be regarded as the "double-barreled name of one divine being"; this is seen sometimes already at Ugarit, where for instance Kothar-wa-Hasis can be referred to in the singular. Also relevant is that a divine pair was sometimes called collectively by its first member; for instance 'Anatu and 'Aṯtartu (*'nt w 'ṯtrt*), who are often paired,⁴⁹ are

---

invention of his divine-voiced (see p6n32, 411n68) lyre involved eviscerating a turtle, flaying a cow, and disemboweling a sheep: *Homeric Hymn to Hermes* 39–51 (handwashing is not mentioned).

⁴⁴ See p26–33, 161–165.
⁴⁵ Pliny *Natural History* 7.56.195; *Chorograffia* p. 13a, 14a, 87 (§28, 37, 590); *Description* pp. 27a, 30a, 224a. See p325.
⁴⁶ So Clapham 1969:108; KwH:83–84, 170. I retain for convenience the conventional vocalization of ḥss; but note the further considerations in van Selms 1979:741; KwH:85–90.
⁴⁷ It may well be, however, that Kothar's dual name invited conflation with another god, better-defined than 'Hasis', as a means of better differentiating the two 'brothers'. And doubtless a Divine Knr would be considered 'wise'.
⁴⁸ For the following points, see de Moor 1970:227–228.
⁴⁹ Smith 2015:49–5, 57, 64–65.

The Melding of Kinyras and Kothar

once 'the Two 'Anatu-goddesses'.[50] One may compare the Dioskouroi, who were sometimes just 'the Castors'.[51]

These patterns suggest various routes by which Kothar and a Kinnaru-figure may have coalesced. While Kothar and Kinnaru were evidently distinct at Ugarit, this need not have been universally true in the Levant, about the specifics of whose cults and mythology we remain largely ignorant, especially for the second millennium. If Kothar were himself represented as a *knr*-player somewhere, he could have assumed a byname akin to Kinyras (the 'lyre-player'), and taken on such musical powers as one sees with Philo's Khousor. Or Kothar and a musical brother could have been known eventually as simply 'the Kothars'. It is certainly understandable that the great craftsman-inventor might absorb such a sidekick like a parasitic twin. Even at Ugarit, the Rāp'iu text suggests a 'familiar' relationship between Kothar and *kinnāru*/Kinnaru, the former apparently enjoying the more prominent position. The wide-ranging and abundantly attested[52] Kothar may have been a sort of 'immediate superior' to Kinnaru at Ugarit and elsewhere. His equation with Ea may also have been a factor, since at Ugarit at least local gods who were identified with international counterparts (Sumero-Babylonian, Hurrian) achieved greater prominence in the state cult.[53] Kinnaru, by contrast, stood out for lacking a heteronymous counterpart in the Akkadian versions of the pantheon texts.[54] Recall that Enki/Ea *created* the lamentation-priest (gala) to calm the anguished Inanna.[55] An 'Ea-Creator' string is also attested in the Akkadian version of the Mesopotamian tonal system, which somehow underlies the Hurrian hymns from Ugarit.[56] Here, potentially, is an important link between Kothar-as-Ea and Kinnaru-as-lyre-tradition.[57]

Despite the sporadic illumination provided by the Ugaritian texts, there is no particular reason to suppose that Philo's musicalized Khousor is a *direct* diachronic development of Ugarit's Kothar. We know enough about first-millennium Phoenician cults to be sure that there was considerable diversity from city to city in the LBA too.[58] I have already argued, on the basis of the Kinyras(es) of Pylos and the thirteenth-century Cypriot stands, that a metamusical Kinyras

---

[50] De Moor 1970:228 and n75.
[51] For 'the Castors', Pliny *Natural History* 10.121 (noted by Brown 1965:206).
[52] KwH:51 collected forty-five instances.
[53] SURS:1105–1112.
[54] But see p121–122.
[55] See p29.
[56] See p59, 97.
[57] One may note here the application of carpentry metaphors for the tuning process in both Akkadian (*pitnu*) and Greek (*harmonía*, the phonology of which reveals its Mycenaean pedigree): Franklin 2002b:2, 9, 15; Franklin 2002a:677 (with n26 for Akkadian *pitnu*); elaborated in Franklin 2006a:55n42.
[58] DDUPP passim.

had emerged by this time on the island. Whether this development was original to Cyprus, or had earlier roots in a mainland city other than Ugarit—for instance Byblos—will be considered in Chapter 19.

Étienne De Lusignan: Cinaras and *His* Retiring Twin

While Khousor's absorption of a musical brother is understandable, the reverse, as one has with Kinyras, is more surprising. And it is quite remarkable how the two processes mirror each from island to mainland. It is of a piece with this that, while 'Kinyras' persisted as a Grecophone PN,[59] the element *knr* is not certainly attested in Canaanite or Phoenician/Punic PNs, nor at Ugarit[60]—although we did see a fifteenth-century example from nearby Alalakh.[61] Kothar/Khousor exhibits the opposite distribution. Absent from inscriptions and texts not stemming from Syria and the Levant, Khousor's longevity and popular appeal is clear from Amorite and Ugaritian PNs going back to the MBA and LBA, respectively,[62] and Neo-Punic and Aramaean PNs enduring to the third century CE.[63] The early names especially suggest that Kothar was regarded as a kind of king and/or patron of kings.[64] Here is another parallel with Kinyras.

A still more remarkable inversion is found in Étienne de Lusignan who, we saw, echoes the metallurgical inventions that Pliny assigned to Kinyras, yet adds a number of independent, Kotharesque details, including bricks, bowls, and other shaped vessels.[65] Recall that Philo attributes bricks to Khousor's unnamed

---

[59] See p334–335.
[60] See Pardee 1988a:139n87 for gods in the Ugaritian pantheon texts who are absent from PNs. In the Punic sphere, a KNRSN, son of B'LŠLK may be attested as a member of a *marzeaḥ*, dedicating a temple at Maktar, Tunisia (first century CE): KAI 145.40, with the reading going back to Février 1956 (who considered it "douteux" [30], but compared "libyque KNRSN" in Chabot 1940-1941 no. 232). A KNRD'T appears in KAI 139.1 (gravestone inscription, Chemtou, Tunisia, n.d.); the certainty of this reading is affirmed by Chabot 1918:296–301, but the name, vocalized as "Kanradât," is taken as Libyan/Numidian.
[61] For Alalakh, see p98.
[62] Amorite royal name *Kwšr* in the Execration Texts of MK Egypt (ca. 1900): Sethe 1926:46–47; Albright 1940:297 and n47; Goetze 1958:28; YGC:136n65. Amorite PNs at Mari: Gelb 1980:131; KwH:58. Ugaritian names: Gröndahl 1967:152; KwH:62–63.
[63] Phoenician/Punic: Hoffman 1896:254–255; Benz 1972:131, 336; Brown 1965:201; KwH:74, 77; DDD col. 914 (Pardee); Krahmalkov 2000:244; DDUPP:109–111. For 'Χαυθαρ' at Hama, Syria, see p443n2.
[64] Besides the Amorite king *Kwšr* of the Execration Texts (see n62), there is the Ugaritian theophoric PN *ktrmlk*, 'Kothar-is-King' (see p167n100 above); and King Kushan-rishathaim of Aram-naharaim (Judges 3:8, 10), rendered as Khousarsathom or Khousarsathaim in LXX, and Khousarsathos in Josephus *Antiquities of the Jews* 5.180.3, 183.2 (Hoffman 1896:256–258; but see Pardee, DDD col. 914–915).
[65] See p325.

brother. But the most startling detail in Lusignan's whole ancient Cypriot history is his assertion that

> The god Paffo [Paphos] ... had two sons, Cinaras and another; the latter was not numbered among the gods.[66]

Once again, no extant Classical source mentions a brother for Kinyras.[67] Fraternal pairs, we have seen, were a traditional mythological construction in the region; but they are not otherwise prominent in Lusignan's account. The historian will hardly have invented an anonymous non-entity who plays no role in the ancient Cypriot dynastic sequence in which his 'Cinaras' looms large, and is otherwise so artificially contrived.[68] We are very fortunate indeed that Lusignan bothered to include this point, which must be a vestige of something significant. That he himself felt this way is shown by the later *Description*, which, though containing rather less ancient material, still troubles to mention Paffo/Paphos and his two sons before again discussing only Cinaras.[69] Unless one supposes that Lusignan's source for this 'retiring twin' was some ancient source now lost, he must have drawn on the island's conservative oral traditions. In either case, I conclude that he attests a Cypriot version of the same process that informs Philo—the fusion of Kinyras and Kothar, with a record kept 'in the family' through an anonymous twin.

The historical and cultural circumstances behind this melding of Kinyras and Kothar have remained elusive.[70] Clearly the phenomena are geographically conditioned, with complementary outcomes on Cyprus and the mainland. Yet the two were never fully sundered. This "insularity and connectivity" of Cyprus will be especially important for understanding the interchangeability of Kinyras and Khousor/Kauthar at Byblos as late as the third century CE.[71]

The Craftsman-Musician Twins Mytheme

The melding of Kothar and Kinnaru appears to be a special instance of a more general Syro-Levantine pattern. Philo's long sequence of 'brotherly pair' culture-heroes probably perpetuates an early Canaanite mythological device,

---

[66] *Chorograffia* p. 20 (§68): "Questo Dio Paffo regnando, hebbe dui figliouli, Cinara, & un' altro; ilquale non è numerato fra li Dei."
[67] Our Lusignan passage answers Baurain 1980a:9, who criticized Brown 1965 for failing to produce a sibling for Kinyras to parallel Khousor and his brother.
[68] See Appendix G.
[69] *Description* p. 38: "Cestuy [sc. Paphe] eut deux enfans (*sic*)."
[70] Cf. Parker 1970:244n9: "Exactly when and where Kinnar/Kinyras [*sic*] took over other attributes of Kothar must remain a matter for speculation."
[71] The phrase quoted is that of Knapp, PPC.

Chapter Eighteen

also seen in Cain and Abel, and perhaps the Ugaritic divine pairings.[72] The most conspicuous musical example is in Genesis, where Lamech's son Jubal was the mythological ancestor of lyre- and pipe-players, while his half-brother Tubal-Cain was "instructor of every artificer in brass and iron."[73] Here too, as with Kinyras/Khousor, is a surprising conjunction of music and metalworking, once more in a fraternal relationship. Its projection into the deep past finds startling circumstantial support at Beni-Hassan (Figure 3 = 4.1j, ca. 1900).[74] Popular etymology may also have played a role.[75]

Lamech and his children were particularly mutable in the NE reception of Biblical stories. Because the family was responsible for much early culture, they were often adjusted to fit local traditions, and we find many changes to their discoveries, especially the musical.[76] I have already discussed the remarkable variant in which Lamech invents lamentation and the lute at a stroke.[77] The treatment of Jubal and Tubal-Cain shows that the brothers' names and roles were highly unstable, yielding phenomena very similar to the melding of Kinyras and Kothar. Theodore Bar Koni, for example, the eighth-century Nestorian exegete from Kashkar in southern Mesopotamia, introduces Cainan and Tubal-Cain as a pair of metallurgists:

> Some say that Cainan and Tubal-Cain, who were of the family of Cain, were the first who invented the three tools of the art of working in iron—the anvil, hammer, and tongs ... It is said that "Jubal was the father of all who play lyre and pipes," because the Cainites had bands

---

[72] Brown 1965:206; Baumgarten 1981:141. Ugarit: de Moor 1970:227–228; KwH:81–84; del Olmo Lete 1999:82. Lokkegaard 1954:60–61 proposed that Philo represents a trend "for dividing or specializing the gods according to the splitting up of society in new trades and guilds following the demands of advancing culture and more refined art." But his numerous pairs are probably due more to combining regional variants into a master scheme.

[73] Genesis 4:22. See p43–46.

[74] See p44–45.

[75] For possible associations between *qayin* ('smith'), *qīnā* ('composition, dirge'), and *kinnōr*, see p44n5. D'Angour 2011:64–84 now proposes connecting the Greek myth of Kaineus with √*qyn* ('forge'), interpreting him as 'Spear-Man' and parallel to Kinyras as embodying a Levantine cultural practice.

[76] For Syriac, Persian, and Arabic sources, see Budge 1886:29 and n5 (see below); Farmer 1929:6–7; Robson and Farmer 1938:9 and n4; MgB 3/2:24; SOM 1:10–11, 153; also Jacobson 1996:303 vis-à-vis Tubal-Cain in Philo Judaeus. In the Armenian commentary on Genesis attributed to St. Ephraim, Jubal is connected exclusively with the lyre tradition; pipes are traced rather to the wife of Tubal; Horace's *ambubaiae* and their relations (*Satires* 1.2.1: see Appendix C) make this more interesting than "an inner Armenian corruption or misunderstanding of the Syriac" (Mathews 1998:55 and n111). Similarly, Michael the Syrian (twelfth century), crediting Jubal with both *kinnōr* and *kithára*, eliminates pipes (*Chronicle* 1.6: Chabot 1899–1924 1:10).

[77] See p312.

who played the pipes to make evil spirits flee so that they would not affect people.[78]

Here the metalworking Tubal-Cain has been bifurcated and endowed with a twin. Bar Koni then reverts to the Biblical account by quoting the 'original' verse about Jubal; but note that Jubal is not called the brother of Tubal-Cain, who after all already has Cainan. Since this second metalworking sibling is apparently a local innovation, it is perfectly possible in principle that the family's musical contributions were equally reworked, and yet are masked here by the Biblical quotation.

This speculation is well justified by a parallel passage in the *Book of the Bee*—a sort of theological rumination on various 'historical' topics drawn from Biblical legend by Solomon of Akhlat, bishop of Basra (Iraq) in the early thirteenth century. While the first part of his account is taken over verbatim from Bar Koni (hence the ellipsis below), the metalworking twins go on to share credit for musical inventions, *while Jubal has now disappeared*:

> Cainan [Tubal?] and Tubal-Cain ... constructed all kinds of musical instruments, harps, and pipes. Some say that spirits used to go into the reeds and disturb them, and that the sound from them was like the sound of singing and pipes.[79]

There is a telling 'error' here. The *Book of the Bee* first follows Bar Koni in naming the brothers Cainan and Tubal-Cain. But in its musical sequel quoted above—which contains several deviations from Bar Koni, including the relocation of "evil spirits" from the patients into the pipes themselves—the brothers reappear as Tubal and Tubal-Cain. There is no way to decide the 'correct' reading. One might suggest that 'Tubal' is a mistake for 'Jubal', but this would still leave Tubal-Cain partaking in both metals and music; and given the novel pairing of Cainan and Tubal-Cain, an error of Tubal for Jubal would itself be symptomatic of the mutability of the brothers' names and relationships.

These texts present striking parallels with Philo's Khousor and Lusignan's Cinaras, and strongly suggest that the reception of Tubal and Jubal was shaped by a wider mythological pattern—the craftsman-musician mytheme—with pagan mythology leaving its imprint as in a palimpsest.

---

[78] Theodore Bar Koni *Liber scholiorum*, Mimrā 2.97: the first part of my translation comes from Budge 1886, since the passage was taken over verbatim into the *Book of the Bee* 19; the second part is after Hespel and Draguet 1981–1982 1:116.

[79] *Book of the Bee* 18: translation from Budge 1886; cf. Budge 1927:79–80.

Chapter Eighteen

Confounded Lyres?

The last issue bearing upon Kinyras and Kothar is potentially the most crucial, since it concerns a comparable crossover in lyre terminology and morphology, apparently at the Greek and Syro-Levantine linguistic and cultural interface.

In 1938, soon after Kothar was resurrected at Ugarit, H. L. Ginsberg proposed connecting *kítharis* and *kithára*—common Greek words for lyre-playing and lyre, respectively, and of no certain etymology—with the Sem. √ktr from which Kothar also came.[80] The words' triconsonantal shape would certainly accord with a Semitic origin. But a *direct* derivation is made unlikely by the lack of any certain lyre-name from this root in Semitic languages, where *knr* was so productive and persistent.[81] An *indirect* etymology via some special semantic development, however, has seemed possible to some. J. P. Brown, while exploring the sympathies between Kinyras and Kothar, noted that Ginsberg's suggestion

> would lead to the neat hypothesis (which unhappily goes beyond the evidence) that the *kinnōr* [sic] was Kothar's instrument, and that both words went into Greek as *Kinyras, kitharis*, but with reversed meaning.[82]

It must be stressed that Brown was not proposing to derive *kithára* from *knr*, as has sometimes been thought.[83] Such a suggestion, once made by K. von Jan, was already rejected by H. Lewy in 1895, and has thus mostly remained out of play (but see below).[84] Brown's proposal was rather a chiasmus whereby under mutual

---

[80] Κίθαρις < *ktr*: Ginsberg 1938:13; Nougayrol 1968:51. The potential parallel of Kinyras/*kinýra* and 'Kauthar'/*kithára* was first noted, so far as I have found, by Lenormant 1871–1872:255n1 in connection with the dual tradition at Aphaka (for which see Chapter 19).

[81] The proposal of Good 1991:156–157 to see such an instrument in RS 24.252, 5 (KTU/CAT 1.108), rather than the god Kothar, was refuted by Clemens 1993:73–74 (cf. p135n141). There remains the *kissar*, applied to some traditional lyres of East Africa (Plumley 1976). But this word probably derives from Greek κιθάρα under Hellenistic-Egyptian influence (versus *krar* < **kenar*: see p58n65). Lyres per se, however, are probably older in the region: cf. Athenaios 633f on the harplike instrument played among the 'Troglodytes' (reported by the Hellenistic explorer Pythagoras: AGM:76n126). The *begena*, a last surviving 'giant lyre', is attributed to the Israelite tradition and associated with David (p58n65, 167). See further Kebede 1977:380; MGG 5:1042–1043 (G. Kubik); K. Wachsmann and U. Wegner in GMO s.v. Lyres, §3 Modern Africa, with bibliography.

[82] Brown 1965:207.

[83] So apparently Morris 1992:79–80n26. And beware Braun's confusing statement in MAIP:146 (punctuation and capitalization preserved): "The root of the word itself, *knr*, appears frequently [sic!] in divine names such as *kinýras*, [[*kinnaraas* [sic!], *kuthar*]]." The same hodgepodge appears in MGG 1:1516.

[84] Jan 1882:5, 35n142; Lewy 1895:164 (whence Rosól 2013:181). The idea is perpetuated by Hoch 1994:324 and in n45; but his further argument, that the modification of *kinnāru* to κίθαρις (sic) must have preceded the Canaanite Shift (whence no **κίθορις or **κίθωρις), does not follow in any case since the hypothetical borrowing could have been *at any point* from an 'unshifted' dialect in North Syria. See further below.

semantic influence, each root, *knr* and *kt̲r*, would have produced both a god- and instrument-name, but with opposite outcomes in 'Greek' and Levantine areas:

	Lyre	God/Hero
'Greek'	kithára	Kinyras
Levantine	kinýra/kinnōr	Kothar

Remember that for Brown, without knowledge of the Divine Kinnaru, Kinyras was but a hero of Greek mythology. Yet the phenomenon of divinized instruments—a god invested in a cult-object—might offer a way through the maze.[85] With this, the lines of symmetry are rearranged:

Root	Lyre	God
knr	kinnāru/kínaris/kinýra	Kinnaru/Kinyras
kt̲r	kithára/kítharis	Kothar

When one considers that Kothar and Kinyras were variously confounded in Phoenicia and Cyprus; that Syro-Levantine and Cypro-Aegean lyre-types coexisted on Cyprus probably from the time of Aegean immigration in the twelfth century, and certainly by the ninth (Chapter 11); and that it is precisely on Cyprus, the eastern rim of the early Greek linguistic continuum, that Kinyras most conspicuously survived in an expanded form that incorporated Kothar-like powers—under these very particular circumstances, it would be remarkable indeed if the mirror-image lyre-terminology were accidental.

Nevertheless, accident it may be. A development of Sem. *nn* or *n* to Gk. *th* is not inconceivable perhaps via some Anatolian channel (given a certain lability between dentals and liquids in Hittite, Lydian, and Carian).[86] This problem needs further investigation.[87] Preliminarily, one may note that an interchange of *n* and *th* in a Cypro-Anatolian context is seen with the city of Gergitha in the Troad; according to tradition, this was once called Gergina and was founded by one of the Gerginoi—a kind of secret police in Cypriot Salamis descended from

---

[85] This can also answer the reservation of KwH:77: "Ginsberg's proposal is plausible, but it assumes a thematic transmission from the PN to the name of an instrument. This transmission cannot be verified." And the melding of Kothar and a Divine Knr would accommodate his later remark at 145n137: "Against Ginsberg's proposal, there is no indication from Ugaritic as to why a word for 'lyre' should develop from the PN Kothar and not a different musical instrument (why not a tool?)."

[86] Heubeck 1959:24–27; Heubeck 1961:19–21.

[87] I have found no exact parallels in Melchert 1994, although the simplification of geminates in Lydian (e.g. /nn/ > /n/: p340, cf. 372 §9) would be relevant.

Chapter Eighteen

prisoners brought by Teukros, who in a later generation returned to the Troad.[88] Any underlying historical reality is obviously obscure.[89] But on circumstantial evidence, western Anatolia is a plausible environment for the entry of *kítharis*, *kithára*, and *(en)kitharízein* into Aeolic/Ionic epic diction, where they exist marginally alongside *phórminx* and its relations.[90] And the early Greco-Lesbian tradition maintained that the *kithára* was formerly called 'Asiatic' because of its association with Lydia—that is *Así(w)a*, Hitt. *Aššuwa*.[91] Given the 'unshifted' forms *kínaris* and *kinarýzesthai*,[92] one might posit a development via some North Syrian channel, with or without Cyprus as an intermediary. Recall that some of the earlier 'Cypro-Phoenician' symposium bowls with lyre-ensembles are actually of North Syrian workmanship, and that these workshops were active and even dominant in the ninth/eighth-century Aegean markets.[93]

---

[88] Athenaios 256b–c.
[89] HC:86n2.
[90] Note the Trojan context of Homer *Iliad* 3.54.
[91] Franklin 2010:20–22; Franklin 2012:745–746.
[92] See p198–199.
[93] See p262.

19

Kinyras, Kothar, and the Passage From Byblos
Kinyras, Kinnaru, and the Canaanite Shift

ONE COULD BE CONTENT WITH EXPLAINING Kinyras' arrival to Cyprus simply through the island's proximity to the mainland, and a general emulation of its neighbors' institutions. But in this and the following chapters, I shall attempt to trace more specific geographical connections. One will naturally think first of Kinnaru and Ugarit. This is certainly well justified by the city's known political relationship with Alashiya, and the indications of their theological common ground (Chapters 1, 15). And while Ugarit itself was destroyed ca. 1200, leaving not even its name, a more general association of Kinyras with coastal North Syria and Cilicia is indeed well supported by several traditions (Chapter 21).

But there is a complication. The forms *kinýra* and Kinyras must derive from originals in the Canaanite dialect zone. This terminated well south of Ugarit, with its northern limit approximately Byblos.[1] And that very city, as it happens, is connected with Kinyras by several Greco-Roman authors. This chapter will consider the complex question of how directly these sources reflect real cultural traditions at Byblos. Are they *representations* of Byblian legends in Greek or Greco-Cypriot terms, no deeper than Hellenistic settlement in the Levant? Or do they stem from some older history shared between island and mainland, in which some form of 'Kinyras' was more intimately involved?

We have seen that the coordination of comparable regional divinities has a long history in the ANE (Chapters 6, 15). Greek-Cypriots lived such patterns long before Herodotos offered his equations of Olympian and 'barbarian' gods. And for communities of the Hellenistic and Roman East, divine juxtapositions were not just intellectual exercises, but a familiar dimension of popular religious life.

---

[1] See p55–56, 195–196, 272–274.

Chapter Nineteen

Of course, the ministers of various cults will have had a special, professional interest therein, leaving plenty of room for artifice.[2]

Symptomatic of this later period are hybrid myth-clusters, two of which, found in Syriac sources, contain further important evidence for the complex interaction of Kothar and Kinyras. In Chapter 18, I discussed their melding in rather general geographical terms, and suggested that it need not have developed uniformly throughout the region. We now come to consider how the phenomenon may have unfolded at Byblos, which one Syrian author envisioned as the realm of king 'Kauthar', who came to control Cyprus itself.[3] This same Kauthar is represented by Lucian and other classical authors as Kinyras. The situation is further complicated by Theias—a doppelganger of Kinyras known only as father of Myrrha/Smyrna when the terrible tale is set at Byblos.[4]

Before beginning, it must be stressed that a Cypro-Byblian Kinyras would not prevent a separate Divine Lyre from having been known on LBA Cyprus in a dialectal and conceptual form closer to Kinnaru of Ugarit. We may be dealing with parallel phenomena connecting different Cypriot and mainland cities/regions—let us say hypothetically Ugarit (and/or Kizzuwatna) and Enkomi/Salamis, versus Byblos and Paphos. Alternatively, a more or less monolithic pan-Cypriot, Alashiyan 'Kinyras' may nevertheless have been referred to with some dialectal variety—as would befit the LBA island's cosmopolitan population.[5] Later Greco-Roman sources show that the Canaanite/Phoenician-derived 'Kinyras' generally prevailed in the IA. For Cyprus this would be readily explained by dialectal pressure during the Phoenician colonial period. But since

---

[2] Exemplary studies include Teixidor 1977; Millar 1993 (cases in Part II); Dirven 1999 (Palmyra/Dura Europos); OSG (Hierapolis and parallels); papers in Kaizer 2008; Aliquot 2009 (the Lebanon).

[3] I follow Albright 1940:296 in the English spelling 'Kauthar'. Ps.-Meliton's text (see below) presents *kwtr*, where *w* is a *mater lectionis* which normally reflects either $\bar{o}$ or $\bar{u}$. Without the benefit of the comparative evidence, especially Arabic *kawṯar* (see p443n2), Cureton rendered the name "Cuthar"; E. Renan opted for "Cyther" (in Pitra 1854:XLII, cf. Cureton 1855:iin1). While the diphthong *aw* was typically monophthongized in the Aramaic dialects, it could be preserved in Syriac when not resulting in a doubly closed syllable (in which case it was reduced to *û* or *ô*, respectively, in western and eastern Aramaic): Brockelmann 1899:28 §60; ICGSL:55 §8.101; SL 175 §22.10. But the spelling ΧΑΥΘΑΡ at third-century Hama, Syria clearly reflects the old diphthongal value (see p443n2). Greek θ, on the other hand, was by now often fricative (Allen 1987:23–26). Ps.-Meliton's *kwtr* lacks the diacritical dot that would usually let one distinguish between a plosive or fricative value for *t* (Brockelmann 1899:10 §10). But while the P-S interdental fricative *ṯ* (/θ/) developed to *t* in Aramaic dialects by the mid-first millennium BCE (ICGSL:29 §8.18), in Syriac the dental and other plosives were eventually (re)spirantized after vowels (Brockelmann 1899:22 §42; SL §13.8). It must be this consideration that caused Cureton to give "Cuthar," which is happily corroborated by the Greek spelling at Hama.

[4] The corruption 'Thoas', found in a codex of Apollodoros and [Probus] on Vergil *Eclogues* 10.18 (see comments of Matthews 1996:256–257), occasionally persists in modern scholarship.

[5] See p440–441.

'*kinýra*' itself can mask considerable cultural and dialectal variety,⁶ the same may well have been true of 'Kinyras' in Syro-Cilician traditions—although of course Cilicia itself was subjected to considerable Phoenician influence by the eighth century.

Lucian: Kinyras At Aphaka

Lucian of Samosata was a literary phenomenon of the second century CE, who, though Syrian by birth, became one of the great Greek stylists. His *On the Syrian Goddess* is a fond homage to Herodotean ethnography, centered on the customs, rites, festivals, and myths connected with the cult of Atargatis at ancient Manbog—Hierapolis, as it was redubbed in the Hellenistic period—near Aleppo in North Syria.⁷ This goddess was variously interpreted as "the Assyrian Hera," Rhea, or Derketo, and details of her statue reminded Lucian of Athena, Aphrodite, Selene, Artemis, Nemesis, and the Fates.⁸ Modern scholars see her as combining elements of Astarte, Anat, and Asherah.⁹ The narrator asserts that he himself is an "Assyrian" or "Syrian," and a devotee of the goddess.¹⁰ His information comes, he says, both from autopsy and, for more ancient material, the priests themselves. When he asked them how old the sanctuary was, and the identity of the goddess,

> Many tales were told, of which some are sacred (*hiroí*), some well-known (*emphanées*), and some distinctly fabulous (*mythṓdees*); others again were un-Greek (*bárbaroi*)—though some were in agreement with the Greeks.¹¹

This may seem a generic bid for readers' faith, following the dubious example of Herodotos in Egypt. But it is now well established that the work, despite its whimsical tone, is rich in evidence for Syrian religious history.¹² The clergy of Hierapolis, and the other Syro-Levantine holy sites that Lucian visited, will have had standing repertoires of tales with which to regale and illuminate pilgrims

---

⁶ See p213–216.
⁷ The work's authorship and basic ethnographical authenticity—allowing for Lucian's amusing emphasis on the bizarre and grotesque—has been well defended by Oden 1977:41–46 et passim; OSG:184–221, cf. 205–207 for Lucian's ethnicity and its special relevance to religious matters.
⁸ Lucian *On the Syrian Goddess* 1, 14–15, 32.
⁹ Oden 1977:58–107; OSG:13–15 (for the form 'Atargatis'), et passim.
¹⁰ *On the Syrian Goddess* 1, 60. For the terms 'Assyria' and 'Syria', see p3n11.
¹¹ Lucian *On the Syrian Goddess* 1, 11 (πολλοὶ λόγοι ἐλέγοντο, τῶν οἱ μὲν ἱροί, οἱ δὲ ἐμφανέες, οἱ δὲ κάρτα μυθώδεες, καὶ ἄλλοι βάρβαροι, οἱ μὲν τοῖσιν Ἕλλησιν ὁμολογέοντες κτλ), 60.
¹² See n7 above.

Chapter Nineteen

and other tourists.[13] This medium would permit the persistence of quite ancient mythological elements, whether through oral or written tradition. Evidently the priests of Manbog still knew the Sumerian flood-hero Ziusudra, whom they rendered as 'Sisythes' and equated with the Greek Deukalion.[14] The tale of Stratonike and Kombabos, developed by Lucian as an embedded 'novella',[15] also has deep roots. 'Kombabos' must take his name from Kubaba, the Great Goddess most famously associated with nearby Karkemish, who was also interpreted as a form of Ishtar/Astarte (hence 'Stratonike').[16] Kombabos' self-castration aetiologizes the *gálloi*, familiar to Classicists as priests of Kybele, but surely connected at some remove with the transgendered, lamenting gala-priests of Sumerian tradition.[17]

No doubt such tales could be adjusted to suit visitors of different ethnicities. A lyre-playing god at Hierapolis, for instance, was presented to Lucian as 'Apollo', but was otherwise regarded as a form of Babylonian Nabu or 'Orpheus'. In fact, both labels probably mask an older Syrian divinity connected with the region's *kinnāru*-culture.[18]

Lucian himself mentions Kinyras, though not in connection with Hierapolis but Byblos. The work begins with a brief history of religion, Lucian alleging in good Herodotean manner that the Egyptians were "first to conceive of gods, establish temples and sacred precincts, and assign festivals"; nevertheless, "there are also temples in Syria which are nearly contemporary with those in Egypt, most of which I have seen."[19] Lucian mentions briefly the sanctuary at Tyre; relates the

---

[13] For the close connection between mythology and tourism of ancient sites in this period, see Cameron 2004:234–235 et passim.

[14] This depends P. Buttmann's proposed correction, widely accepted, of Δευκαλίωνα τὸν Σισύθεα for τὸν Σκύθεα (*On the Syrian Goddess* 12). Such late knowledge of Ziusudra is supported by fragments of two Hellenistic authors of Babylonian lore, though the forms they give are closer to the original (Ξίσουθρος, Berossos FGH 680 F 4; Σίσουθρος, Abydenos FGH 685 F 2b–3b). Note also the several reservations of Lightfoot (e.g. Scythian associations of Deukalion) and her argument that Lucian followed a *Jewish* flood account (OSG:340, 342–343). Still, most of Lucian's details *can* be found in the various Mesopotamian versions known to us (Oden 1977:24–36; CANE:2344–2347 [B. B. Schmidt], with a useful comparative table); parallels in the Rabbinic tradition (OSG:339–340) may themselves reflect general ANE influence.

[15] OSG:384–402.

[16] For Kombabos/Kubaba see OSG:384–402 (note especially Hesykhios s.v. Κύβαβος· θεός). For 'Stratonike' as reflecting Ishtar/Astarte, compare 'Straton' of Sidon (p489–493) et al., and cf. Oden 1977:36–46 and DDUPP:106—though both believe that Kombabos should be connected rather with Humbaba, known from the *Epic of Gilgamesh* as guardian of the cedar forest and servant of Ishtar (rightly refuted by Lightfoot).

[17] For this problem, see p315 and n213.

[18] See further p495–496.

[19] *On the Syrian Goddess* 2.

Sidonian Astarte temple to the Greek myth of Kadmos and Europa; and admits to not having visited Heliopolis-Baalbek.[20]

This sequence culminates in a disquisition on Byblos (that ultimately emphasizes the still greater stature of Hierapolis).[21] Lucian's Byblian Aphrodite is Baalat Gebal, Lady of Byblos. Worship of this goddess goes back to the third millennium, when she was already considered a form of Ishtar/Astarte (see further below). By the MBA (or earlier) she was recognized in Egypt and associated with Hathor.[22] In Hellenistic and later sources, both Syriac and Greco-Roman, Baalat Gebal was variously equated with Aphrodite Ourania, Isis, Dione, and of course Astarte.[23]

Lucian's Byblian detour contains his famous description of annual Adonis-laments:

> They say that the boar's deed against Adonis happened within their territory. And each year, as a memorial of his suffering they beat themselves and sing threnodies and carry out his rites and institute great sufferings for themselves throughout the land. But after they have beaten themselves and left off their wailing, they first sacrifice to Adonis as though he were someone dead; but afterwards, on the next day, they tell a myth that he lives, and send him on his way up into the open air.[24]

The signal for this mourning, Lucian says, was given by the nearby Adonis river—the modern Nahr 'Ibrahim which, with spring storms, washes reddish soil down from Mount Lebanon.[25] This phenomenon was interpreted as Adonis' blood, though another Byblian offered a plausible natural explanation. Lucian's investigation of the matter explains his next step, where we suddenly stumble upon Kinyras:

> But I also climbed up into the Lebanon, a day's journey from Byblos, having learned that there was an ancient temple of Aphrodite in that

---

[20] *On the Syrian Goddess* 3–5.
[21] *On the Syrian Goddess* 6–9.
[22] DDUPP:67–68, 70–72.
[23] DDUPP:70–79; Bonnet 1996:19–20.
[24] *On the Syrian Goddess* 6: λέγουσι γὰρ δὴ ὦν τὸ ἔργον τὸ ἐς Ἄδωνιν ὑπὸ τοῦ συὸς ἐν τῇ χώρῃ τῇ σφετέρῃ γενέσθαι, καὶ μνήμην τοῦ πάθεος τύπτονταί τε ἑκάστου ἔτεος καὶ θρηνέουσι καὶ τὰ ὄργια ἐπιτελέουσι καὶ σφίσι μεγάλα πένθεα ἀνὰ τὴν χώρην ἵσταται. ἐπεὰν δὲ ἀποτύψωνταί τε καὶ ἀποκλαύσωνται, πρῶτα μὲν καταγίζουσι τῷ Ἀδώνιδι ὅκως ἐόντι νέκυι, μετὰ δὲ τῇ ἑτέρῃ ἡμέρῃ ζώειν τέ μιν μυθολογέουσι καὶ ἐς τὸν ἠέρα πέμπουσι κτλ. I leave aside the issue of 'sacred prostitution'.
[25] See Jidejian 1968:124; for the river in the civic topography and mythical imagination of Byblos, Aliquot 2009:58–61.

place, which Kinyras had established. I saw the temple, and it *was* ancient.[26]

Despite the terseness of this little epilogue, it is clear from his preceding discussion of the Adonis that Lucian is now talking about ancient Aphaka (modern Afqa) at the river's source, twenty kilometers up.[27] There, according to other accounts, the goddess embraced Adonis for the first time, or the last after his boar-wound.[28] Kinyras must therefore function here as the father of Adonis, and the 'Aphrodite' temple must relate somehow to Adonis-laments (see below). As Lucian does not bother to explain any of this, he clearly has no ulterior rhetorical motive—strong evidence that he did indeed make the journey.

Lucian's wording indicates that he learned of the temple, and its attribution to Kinyras, from informants in Byblos itself—whether from popular legend or the local priesthood is unclear, although the latter is perfectly probable (as at Hierapolis). One must wonder, however, whether 'Kinyras' was a Hellenizing substitute provided for Lucian's edification (like the Hierapolitan 'Apollo'), since Kinyras was well known to Greek-speakers as Adonis' father.[29] Or whether Lucian himself introduced Kinyras for his readers, just as he used 'Aphrodite' for Aphaka's ancient goddess—whom in another work he calls simply "the goddess of [Mount] Lebanon."[30] Either way one might dismiss the entire scenario as having been falsely transferred from Cyprus into Byblian territory, with Kinyras masking a local figure.

As it happens, two further figures *are* named as the father of Adonis/Tammuz at Byblos—Theias and Kauthar. Before turning to their claims, however, let us beware the kneejerk assumption that Kinyras is an *interpretatio Graeca*. After all, his very name betrays Syro-Levantine roots. The same may said of 'Aphrodite', whose linguistic kinship to Astarte seems inevitable.[31] Adonis too, though known to us through a Greek lens, has a Semitic etymology and ultimately derives from Levantine theology and cult.[32] In principle therefore it is

---

[26] *On the Syrian Goddess* 9: Ἀνέβην δὲ καὶ ἐς τὸν Λίβανον ἐκ Βύβλου, ὁδὸν ἡμέρης, πυθόμενος αὐτόθι ἀρχαῖον ἱρὸν Ἀφροδίτης ἔμμεναι, τὸ Κινύρης εἵσατο, καὶ εἶδον τὸ ἱρόν, καὶ ἀρχαῖον ἦν.

[27] This has long been recognized: Frazer 1914 1:28–30; Drexler, Roscher *Lex.* s.v. Kinyras; Brown 1965:198; Aliquot 2009:258.

[28] *Etymologicum Magnum* s.v. Ἄφακα· Σύρων μὲν ἐστιν ἡ λέξις· δύναται δὲ καθ' Ἑλλάδα γλῶσσαν, εἰ δεῖ τὸ δημῶδες εἰπεῖν ῥῆμα, περίλημμα, περιλαβούσης τὸν Ἄδωνιν τῆς Ἀφροδίτης ἐκεῖ ἢ τὴν πρώτην ἢ τὴν ἐσχάτην περιβολήν.

[29] Cf. Ulbrich 1906:85. In this region and period Kinyras may have been more canonical than Hesiod's Phoinix, for whom see p313.

[30] Lucian *The Ignorant Book-Collector* 3. DDUPP:105–108 suggests that the 'Aphrodite' of Aphaka may not have been identical with the Byblian goddess.

[31] See p380n58.

[32] See p314.

perfectly possible that the 'Kinyras' of Aphaka thinly masks a homonymous Canaanite/Phoenician cousin; that this figure was himself glossed as Theias and/or Kauthar; and that here we may be dealing precisely with what Lucian called "barbarian tales agreeing with the Greeks."[33]

Aphaka is certainly a promising locale for the persistence of a BA mytheme. Mountainous regions tend to be culturally conservative (Arcadia, Vermont). The site was clearly regarded as very ancient in Lucian's time. It has not been systematically excavated, though the present ruins, of the Roman period, do show traces of an earlier structure.[34] While early archaeological evidence for Canaanite/Phoenician mountaintop shrines is at present quite limited, going back only to the EIA,[35] the divine treatment of mountains in the LBA is well known—illustrated for instance by Mount Kasios, a local home to the Hurrian storm-god Teshup and Ugarit's Baal (as Hazzi/Saphon), and connected with Adonis himself in one tradition.[36] The Bible also regularly associates early Baal worship with 'high places'.[37] So the absence of an early built structure at Aphaka would be no argument against much older traditions there.[38]

Aphaka's conservatism is indicated by its cultic tenacity in later centuries. The temple's destruction was ordered by Constantine (306-337) in his sweeping attacks on pagan worship;[39] if it was rebuilt under Julian (361-363),[40] there was presumably another demolition under Theodosios (379-395).[41] Even so, Zosimos refers to ongoing pagan veneration in the late fifth or early sixth century, describing a lamplike fire in the sky and a kind of water-divination whereby votive objects thrown into the pool were accepted if they sank (a recipe for success).[42] The church erected above the old temple, also implying

---

[33] Cf. Ulbrich 1906:86: "Die mythologische Figur des Kinyras kann man, wenn sie auch früh in den hellenischen Sagenkreis einbezogen wurde, als die letzte Spur der Erinnerung an die alte, phönizische Zeit betrachten."

[34] Krencker and Zschietzschmann 1938:56-57, with further references. See also OSG:328-331; Aliquot 2009:258-259.

[35] Aliquot 2009:19-20.

[36] Cf. DDUPP:83. Adonis and Kasios: Servius Auctus on Vergil *Eclogues* 10.18 (see further p514).

[37] Aliquot 2009:21-23.

[38] Cf. DDUPP:105-106; Elayi 2009:201.

[39] Jidejian 1968:129-130. Among the early Christian authors who attest the emperor's action, Eusebios stands out for his vivid portrait of an orgiastic sexual culture (*Life of Constantine* 3.55.1-3 = *In Praise of Constantine* 8.5-9).

[40] Baudissin 1911:363n1; Teixidor 1977:155n38.

[41] Jidejian 1968:130.

[42] Zosimos *New History* 1.58. The fifth-century Sozomenos (*Ecclesiastical History* 2.5.5), corroborating Constantine's action, adds interesting detail about the pagan cult that confirms Zosimos' emphasis on the importance of the waters: the prayers of adorants would call down a celestial fire into the Adonis (which was channeled into a sacred pool, as can be seen in the remains).

cult memory,⁴³ eventually succumbed to earthquake and landslide, leaving the place a picturesque ruin of luscious description.⁴⁴ Yet the river is still thought to have healing properties, and would-be or worried mothers—Christian and Muslim alike—hang strips of cloth and other offerings on a tree near the ancient walls. It is called Seiyidet Afqā after the 'The Lady of Aphaka' whose husband was killed while hunting—a clear vestige of very ancient myth.⁴⁵

It is not improbable, all told, that the Kinyras of Aphaka—by whatever name he was known locally in Lucian's day—was a figure of deep antiquity.

Kinyras and Theias

Kinyras' associations with the region are not limited to Aphaka. We may deduce from *On the Syrian Goddess* that Lucian would have accepted Kinyras as father of Myrrha, when he holds up the tale as best representing Phoenicia in a well-rounded pantomime's international repertoire.⁴⁶ Lucian's Kinyras of Aphaka was thus king of Byblos and its hinterland. This view of Kinyras' domain is corroborated by Strabo, for whom Byblos was his "royal seat (*basíleion*)" and "a sacred city of Adonis."⁴⁷ Eustathios adds an important qualification: Byblos was Kinyras' "most ancient capital (*basíleion arkhaiótaton*)."⁴⁸ Elsewhere he asserts that Kinyras was the son of Theias ('Godlike, Divine').⁴⁹ But this is probably a simple rationalization of two parallel figures. For Theias is elsewhere always the Byblian father of Myrrha/Smyrna. He and Kinyras are thus practically twins, distinguished only by the latter's association with Byblos *and* Cyprus.

---

[43] Krencker and Zschietzschmann 1938:59; Donceel 1966:232, noting also a 'Byzantine pillar' (reuse?) engraved with a cross.

[44] Note especially Frazer 1914 1:28–30.

[45] Renan 1864:297; Curtiss 1903:174; Paton 1919–1920:55–56 and fig. 1 ("To this saint vows are made both by Metawilehs and Christians, and sick people are brought to be cured by lying beside the water."); Albright 1940:299; Jidejian 1968:130; Teixidor 1977:155n38. G. Fawkes saw cloth-strips in 2002.

[46] Lucian *On Dancing* 58.

[47] Strabo 16.2.18: Βύβλος, τὸ τοῦ Κινύρου βασίλειον, ἱερά ἐστι τοῦ Ἀδώνιδος. It has been inferred from the sequel—ἣν τυραννουμένην ἠλευθέρωσε Πομπήιος πελεκίσας ἐκεῖνον—that Kinyras was the name of the tyrant deposed by Pompey: Frazer 1914 1:27–28 (whence Thubron 1987:170); BMC Phoenicia:lxii; Bömer 1969–1986 5:113. This is certainly wrong: Kinyras is mentioned in a clearly mythological context (Adonis), and an anonymous antecedent for ἐκεῖνον is readily inferred from ἣν τυραννουμένην. This was rightly seen by Brown 1965:205n4; Jidejian 1968:110; Baurain 1980a:286n39.

[48] Eustathios on Dionysios the Periegete 912: Ἡ δὲ Βύβλος ... Ἀδώνιδος ἱερά, Κινύρου βασίλειον ἀρχαιότατον.

[49] Eustathios on Homer *Iliad* 11.20 (cf. Σ).

Panyassis, our earliest authority for the Myrrha myth, made Theias a king of Assyria.[50] Similarly for Hyginus, *Kinyras* was an Assyrian king.[51] Still others call Adonis Assyrian.[52] Frazer saw in such descriptions "a well-founded belief that the religion of Adonis, though best known to the Greeks in Syria and Cyprus, had originated in Assyria or rather Babylonia"; *Adonî* ('My Lord'), he believed, was merely the title taken by Tammuz—that is, Mesopotamian Dumuzi—when his cult spread to the Canaanite/Phoenician world (see further below).[53] But caution is needed here. It may be that "King of the Assyrians" was in some authors a willfully vague reference to the exotic and distant Orient.[54] Besides, in Greek usage '(As)syria' can include Phoenicia,[55] and Antoninus Liberalis (following Panyassis?) is usefully specific in locating the Theias tale on Mount Lebanon— note his oread wife Oreithuia—and calling him son of Belos, a normal Greek representation of Baal.[56] This mountainous setting obviously implies Aphaka, so here too Theias meets Kinyras.

The twinning of Kinyras and Theias naturally led to confusion. Lykophron alludes cryptically to Myrrha in making Byblos a stop in Menelaos' long search for Helen.[57] He goes on to mention "the tomb of goddess-wept Gauas," an obscure and allegedly *Cypriot* name for Adonis, "slain by the Muses."[58]

---

[50] 'Assyrian' Theias: Panyassis fr. 22ab EGF = fr. 27 PEG = [Apollodoros] *Library* 3.14.4, cf. p284 above; [Probus] on Vergil *Eclogues* 10.18: [sc. *Adonis filius*] ... <ut Panyassis ait,> Thiantis, qui Syriam Arabiamque tenuit imperio (for supplements, see Matthews 1996:256–257, following West; Cameron 2004:205–206); Σ John Tzetzes *Exegesis of Homer's Iliad* 435.5–15 Papathomopoulos. Ps.-Probus' inclusion of Arabia in the realms of Panyassis' Theias has probably been influenced by Ovid; ps.- Apollodoros mentions only 'Assyria'.

[51] 'Assyrian' Kinyras: Hyginus *Fabulae* 58, 242, 270; Boccaccio *Genealogy of the Pagan Gods* 2.51.

[52] Adonis as son of Theias and Myrrha/Smyrna, hence an (As)syrian prince: [Apollodoros] *Library* 3.14.4 = Panyassis fr. 22ab EGF = fr. 27 PEG; Kleitarkhos FGH 137 F 9 (= Stobaios *Anthology* 40.20.73); Σ Lykophron *Alexandra* 829, 831; Σ Oppian *Halieutika* 3.403, 3.407; *Anecdota Graeca* (Cramer 1839–1841) 4:183.15. Bion calls Adonis an "Assyrian lord" (Ἀσσύριον πόσιν): *Lament for Adonis* 24. Lucian refers to the tale of Myrrha/Smyrna as τὸ Ἀσσύριον ἐκεῖνο πένθος (*On Dancing* 58). Myrrha/Smyrna, daughter of Theias, is rejected as mother of Adonis by *Etymologicum Magnum* s.v. Ἄδως; for this tradition, see p502.

[53] Frazer 1921 2:86n1; cf. Langdon 1931:351; Greenberg 1983:171.

[54] Such an impulse is seen in the tale's treatment by Cinna and Ovid, who bring Myrrha to Arabia and even the fabulous Panchaea. See p287.

[55] See e.g. Herodotos 2.116–117 and above p3n11.

[56] Antoninos Liberalis *Metamorphoses* 34, with comments of Matthews 1974:122–123 (arguing for his dependence on Panyassis).

[57] Lykophron *Alexandra* 828–830: ὄψεται δὲ τλήμονος / Μύρρας ἐρυμνὸν ἄστυ, τῆς μογοστόκους / ὠδῖνας ἐξέλυσε δενδρώδης κλάδος κτλ ("he will see wretched / Myrrha's mighty city—Myrrha whose hard birth-/pains an arboreal branch delivered").

[58] Lykophron *Alexandra* 831–832 (τὸν θεᾷ κλαυσθέντα Γαύαντος τάφον / ... μουσόφθαρτον) with Σ: Γαύας δὲ ὁ Ἄδωνις παρὰ Κυπρίοις καλεῖται ("Adonis is called Gauas among the Cypriots"), fancifully etymologized as γῆ + αὔεσθαι ("for the dead are dried out in the earth," Γαύας ἐτυμολογεῖται ὁ νεκρὸς παρὰ τὸ γῇ αὔεσθαι· οἱ γὰρ νεκροὶ τῇ γῇ ξηραίνονται). See further Atallah 1966:306.

A scholiast here, referring to popular ambivalence about the location of these tales, proposes *two* youths named Adonis, one the son of Kinyras on Cyprus, the other son of Myrrha and Theias of Byblos. A scholion to Dionysios the Periegete attempts a different compromise: Kinyras, though king of *Cyprus*, nevertheless sent the body of Adonis to *Byblos*, where it was buried by the river that took his name.⁵⁹ Whether this riparian setting implies Aphaka or a tomb in Byblos itself is not clear, though the former is not improbable.⁶⁰

Evidently Kinyras and Theias are two names for one and the same figure. Despite Theias' exclusive connections with Byblos, it is Kinyras, with his Canaanite/Phoenician etymology, that would seem to have the greater claim to authenticity, Theias being a transparently Greek formation. Was Theias introduced, by Panyassis or someone else, to disambiguate the famous Cypriot Kinyras from a Byblian namesake? I have suggested that 'Theias' might correspond roughly to the divine determinative that accompanies Kinnaru at Ugarit.⁶¹ One should also recall the Greek idea of the *theîos aoidós*, the 'divine singer' who is endowed with *théspis aoidḗ*, 'god-uttered song'; and the epithet *thespésios*, which Kinyras may bear in one Paphian inscription.⁶²

Theias has also been taken to gloss El ('God'),⁶³ the WS pantheon head. But Theias' position as son of Belos in Antoninus Liberalis would suggest rather an interpretation in terms of divine kingship and covenant metaphors—just as the rulers of Ugarit replicated on earth the kingship of Baal.⁶⁴ On this view, Theias and Kinyras could be neatly reconciled as a lyre-playing king under divine patronage and at the head of a royal line. The semi-divine David, 'son' of Yahweh, is close to hand, and Kinyras occupied just such a position *vis-à-vis* the Kinyradai of Paphos.

Ps.-Meliton: Kauthar At Aphaka

Whatever Theias' precise relationship to Kinyras, his Greek etymology keeps us at arm's length from Byblian realities. More intimate insight is promised by

---

⁵⁹ Σ Dionysios the Periegete 509 (FGH 738 F 3a). For the scholiast's comments here, containing further rare information about Kinyras encountering Egyptians on Cyprus, see further p512–516.

⁶⁰ The location of Adonis' tomb is a matter of scholarly debate, some following ps.-Meliton to place it in Aphaka (Renan 1864:296–297; Krencker and Zschietzschmann 1938:60; Servais-Soyez 1977:41–43), others seeking a site in Byblos itself (references in Aliquot 2009:60 and n132–133).

⁶¹ See p123.

⁶² See p6, 411–412.

⁶³ Redford 1990:827n28.

⁶⁴ See generally Cross 1998:3–22.

the 'Kauthar'—a Syrian form of 'Kothar'—who appears as king of Byblos in a key Syriac text—the *Apology* attributed to Meliton, second-century bishop of Sardis.

In 1843, more than three hundred Syriac manuscripts were acquired by H. Tattam from the convent of St. Maria Deipara in the Nitrian Desert—Wadi El Natrun, northwest Egyptian delta.[65] This monastery was particularly rich in early texts, thanks to the 250 codices that Abbot Mushe of Nisibis brought back in 932 from a five-year journey to Baghdad; a large proportion, acquired from centers of learning in North Syria and Mesopotamia, including Edessa, antedated the seventh century.[66] It was most likely one of these that holds ps.-Meliton's treatise.[67] The traditional ascription is now universally rejected; but the work itself, a hortatory Christian polemic addressed to an "Antoninus Caesar," does apparently date to the late second or third century CE.[68] Publication by W. Cureton in 1855 raised an initial flurry of interest, with its new evidence for Syro-Levantine religion.[69] The author uses this material, along with blander fare from Greco-Roman myth, to support his euhemerizing argument that the gods were in origin but particularly illustrious kings and queens—a provocative stance *vis-à-vis* Roman emperor cult.[70] This "remarkably frustrating text," after languishing in obscurity for many decades, has attracted renewed attention of late.[71]

Among ps.-Meliton's illustrations is a dense little narrative relating to Aphaka—a tangled romance of Syro-Levantine, Mesopotamian, Hellenic, and Cypriot figures:

> The people of Phoenicia worshipped Balthi, queen of Cyprus, because she fell in love with Tammuz, son of Kauthar king of the Phoenicians, and left her own kingdom to come and dwell in Gebal [Byblos], a fortress of the Phoenicians. At the same time she made all the Cypriots subject

---

[65] Cureton 1855:i; White 1932:456 and n3.
[66] The main purpose of Mushe's expedition was to appeal to the Caliph al-Muqtadir for remission of a tax upon the bishops and monks of Egypt: White 1932:337–338; Brock 2004:16–17.
[67] British Museum Additional Manuscripts 14658. For the text, Cureton 1855:41–51, with the passage in question (fol. 178a col. 2) on 44; also Otto 1872:426. Cureton dated the MS to the sixth or seventh century on palaeographic grounds (i). It is not among the sixty that carry definite acquisition notes (hence its absence from the catalogue of White 1932:443–445). But very few of the MSS acquired before or after Mushe are older than the eighth century, whereas a high proportion of his are; it is therefore "very likely that ... other very early manuscripts ... belong to the collection" (Brock 2004:17).
[68] For general discussion, including the questions of its original language(s) and sources, see with further references Quasten 1951 1:246–247 and Lightfoot 2004:76–82 et passim (also Lightfoot 2009). Both argue for Syriac as the original language.
[69] See the detailed retrospective of Ulbrich 1906:70–77.
[70] For the particularities of ps.-Meliton's euhemerism, see Lightfoot 2004:69–73, 81–82, 90.
[71] Millar 1993:243 (quotation), 477–478. See now especially Lightfoot 2004.

to king Kauthar; for before Tammuz she had been in love with Ares, and committed adultery with him. Hephaistos her husband caught her, and came and slew Tammuz in Mount Lebanon while he was hunting wild boar.[72] From that time Balthi remained in Gebal, and died in Aphaka where Tammuz was buried.[73]

Cureton promptly saw that Kauthar here was analogous to Kinyras—king of both Byblos and Cyprus, father of Tammuz (corresponding to Adonis: see below), with Balthi evoking in equal measures Baalat Gebal and (as "Queen of Cyprus") the Cypriot 'Aphrodite'.[74] G. Hoffman went on in 1896 to connect Kauthar with Khousor in Philo of Byblos and Mokhos of Sidon, noting other sympathies between those figures and Kinyras, as discussed in Chapter 18.

Further assessment of Kauthar's presence in ps.-Meliton, and his relationship to both Kinyras and the Cypriot 'Queen', must confront several interrelated issues. How much of the material is genuine tradition, rather than the author's own imagination and store of learning?[75] And to what extent is he presenting *interpretationes Syriacae* at variance with his ostensibly Cypro-Byblian scenario? For 'Balthi', like 'Kauthar', is a distinctly Syrian linguistic formation.[76] Tammuz is frequently equated with Gk. 'Adonis' by authors of the early Syrian church, implying a fairly general popular identification at the Levantine/Syro-Mesopotamian interface by Roman imperial times.[77] It is therefore possible in principle that all three names calque heteronymous Phoenician figures, and that the entire myth is a Syro-Mesopotamian fantasy with little connection to Byblian or Cypriot tradition.

Fortunately ps.-Meliton is controlled by an alternative version, also in Syriac, from Theodore Bar Koni in his late eighth-century commentary on Ezekiel. Of the famous allusion to women lamenting Tammuz outside the Jerusalem temple (8:14–15), Bar Koni wrote:[78]

---

[72] Textual corruption here led to E. Renan's startling Latin translation *Cyniram* (?) *vero vertit in aprum* (so in Pitra 1854:XLIII); for the issue, see Cureton 1855:90 (Renan "altogether wanders from the meaning").
[73] [Meliton] *Apology* (Cureton 1855:44.12–22, adapting his translation).
[74] Cureton 1855:90; Otto 1872:467n159; Hoffman 1896:256–258; Ulbrich 1906:86–87; Albright 1940:296–297; Albright 1964:171; Pope and Röllig 1965:296; YGC:147–148; Brown 1965:198; Gese et al. 1970:148; Ribichini 1981:51–52.
[75] Cf. Ulbrich 1906:86.
[76] Cureton 1855:90; DDUPP:73; Lightfoot 2004:90.
[77] See the judicious assessment and cautions of Baudissin 1911:94–97 (beginning from Origen *Selecta in Ezechielem* PG 13:797D–800A: Τὸν λεγόμενον παρ' Ἕλλησιν Ἄδωνιν, Θαμμούζ φασι καλεῖσθαι παρ' Ἑβραίοις καὶ Σύροις κτλ); cf. Ribichini 1981:185–188.
[78] For Bar Koni, see p454.

Kinyras, Kothar, and the Passage from Byblos

This Tammuz, they say, was a shepherd and he loved a woman who was very famous for her beauty. She was from the island of Cyprus; her name was Balthi, her father's was Herakles, her mother's Ariadne, and her husband was Hephaistos. Now this woman fled with Tammuz, her lover, to Mount Lebanon; it is indeed she who is also called Astarte, a name which her father gave her on account of her [text corrupt]. Her father lamented over her for seven days in the month of [Ṭabit], which is the second of *kanoun* [January]. They cooked some bread on the ground and ate it, which even now is called 'cake of Bet Ṭabit' by the pagans. Now Hephaistos followed her to Mount Lebanon, and Tammuz met and killed him; but a boar gashed Tammuz himself, and he died. His paramour, out of love for Tammuz, died of grief over his body. Her father, learning of her death, lamented during the month of *tammouz* [July]. His parents also wept for Tammuz: these are the tears that the impious weep, and the Hebrew people imitated them.[79]

Bar Koni, by expressing obviously cognate material in somewhat different mythological terms, guarantees that the myth was not contrived by ps.-Meliton himself. We must at least suppose an anterior source, though whether Kauthar himself was found there, or introduced by ps.-Meliton, is not immediately clear.[80] The specific aetiology adduced by Bar Koni, as well as his sequel on the goddess's cult statue, seem to look beyond Byblos to a broader Mesopotamian and North Syrian religious milieu.[81]

Nevertheless, the identification of Balthi's parents as Herakles and Ariadne establishes a genuine Cypriot aspect to the myth,[82] and this encourages us to pursue the simplest solution—that Balthi and Kauthar were ready dialectal variants for transparent Byblian cognates.[83] There is obviously no problem in taking

---

[79] Theodore Bar Koni: *Liber scholiorum*, Mimrā 4.38, cf. 11.4; translation after Hespel and Draguet 1981–1982 1:263–264; cf. 2.214.

[80] There is further related material in several other Syriac sources. These include the ninth-century Biblical commentator Ishoʿdad of Merv, who contains the same points of interest I shall emphasize in Bar Koni; but both lack Kauthar. The connections between these texts, and anterior sources, await full explication. See Baudissin 1911:75–76; Leonhard 2001:52–54, 72–73, 82, 221; Lightfoot 2004:74–75, 86–91 with references.

[81] Cf. Lightfoot 2004:88. The late persistence of Tammuz-lament is attested by Isaac of Antioch for the fifth century (2.210 Bickell; cf. Baudissin 1911:95–97), while an Arabic source reports it for the Sabians of Harran in the tenth (Chwolsohn 1856 2:27; Baudissin 1912; cf. Langdon 1935:120; Greenberg 1983:171).

[82] Herakles corresponds to the Phoenician Melqart on Cyprus and elsewhere in the Phoenician/Punic world: DDUPP:291. For the myth of Theseus and Ariadne at Amathous, Paion FGrH 757 F 2 with *Kypris*:107; cf. Lightfoot 2004:89n117.

[83] Cf. Baudissin 1911:74.

Chapter Nineteen

Balthi as Baalat Gebal, whom Philo of Byblos himself Hellenized as *Baaltís*.[84] True, 'Balthi' could just as readily describe the Cypriot goddess, who was known as 'Queen' (*Wánassa*) on the early island.[85] But that divine honorific is common enough, and any such distinction between Cyprus and Byblos is neutralized by the myth itself, which allies Balthi to both places, with the latter her ultimate home. Of course this does not free us from addressing the special Cypriot dimension that ps.-Meliton and Bar Koni both assign her.

A similar reading of ps.-Meliton's Kauthar as Phoen. Khousor, though ready to hand, is considerably complicated by the latter's interchangeability with Kinyras. The problem presents many subtle facets.[86] But I see four main possibilities, of which only one is really satisfactory. First is that Kauthar and Kinyras both correspond to some third Byblian figure; but here surely we may apply Ockham's Razor.[87] The second and third scenarios are complementary: either Kauthar is linguistically cognate with the Byblian 'original' (Khousor), and was glossed as Kinyras by Lucian; or Kinyras is linguistically cognate with the Byblian 'original' (*Kinnūr vel sim.*), and was glossed as Kauthar by ps.-Meliton. Now a Byblian Khousor is inherently likely. It is not that ps.-Meliton somehow outweighs Lucian, who was himself from Syria.[88] But the idea is strongly corroborated by the roughly contemporary testimony for a Phoenician Khousor in Philo of Byblos, combined with that author's own Byblian identity.[89] And we shall see that several further points favor a Byblian Khousor. Even so, a Byblian Khousor will not resolve the problem, for it remains the case that some were prepared to call this figure Kinyras. And if this was true outside of Byblos, some Byblians must also have been aware of the equation, if only peddlers of *hieroì lógoi*. We must therefore support a fourth permutation—that the Byblian figure was variously known by both names, and that Kinyras and Kothar were somehow doublets in a Byblian context. And, after all, Kinyras is linked to Byblos by a *handful* of Greco-Roman sources, while only ps.-Meliton speaks for Kauthar.

A key point favoring the reality of a Byblian Kinyras is the prominence of lamentation in all this material. Besides Lucian's crucial account of the annual

---

[84] Philo of Byblos FGH 790 F 2 (35).
[85] Lightfoot 2004:89. Cf. p441 above.
[86] See Lightfoot 2004:89–91, leaving the problem as a *non liquet*.
[87] Gk. 'Theias' could gloss a Kinyras-figure just as aptly as a Kothar, recalling the royal associations of both (Kothar in theophoric names, Kinyras in mythology: see p321–323, 407).
[88] Cf. Millar 1993:247: "The fact of having been written in Syriac did not necessarily prevent Christian analyses of pagan cults in Syria from representing the same concatenation of confused and incompatible elements as Lucian himself reveals"; Similarly Lightfoot 2009:399: "The use of Syriac *ipso facto* certainly does not imply a closeness to local realities that is somehow unavailable to speakers of a classical language; as much account has to be taken of literary fashioning with ps.-M[eliton] as it does with Lucian and Philo of Byblos."
[89] See p445–452.

'Adonis' rites, the classical myths' emphasis on the tears of Aphrodite obviously aetiologizes such ritual performances. Bar Koni envisions three separate occasions for lament—by Balthi's father, by Balthi herself, and by Tammuz' father *and* mother. Ps.-Meliton is not explicit, but his statement that Balthi "died in Aphaka where Tammuz was buried" parallels her death of grief there in Bar Koni. These passages imply ritual lamentation at Aphaka itself, not just Byblos proper; and this in turn clarifies Lucian's attribution of the temple to Kinyras.[90]

Of course ps.-Meliton would have called Aphaka the work of Kauthar, who as the bereaved father would also be well justified in lamenting Tammuz/Adonis. A lamenting Kauthar can be supported by the 'incantations' (*epōidaí*) of Philo's musicalized Khousor, which in turn consolidates Khousor's own association with Byblos.[91] Even so, this grieving Kauthar would return us ultimately to Kinyras the Lamenter, since the mourning of father for son was a common threnodic theme (Chapter 12). It is precisely this performative stance, indeed, that can explain the otherwise jarring genealogical subordination of Adonis—that is, the Byblian Baal (see further below)—to the lesser Kinyras and/or Kothar.

I conclude from this initial comparison that, despite slightly different terms and a superficially Syro-Mesopotamian perspective, ps.-Meliton and Bar Koni do indeed reproduce a genuinely 'Cypro-Byblian' mytheme that invites closer analysis, both of its internal structure and external sympathies. In pursuing this, we shall be justified in treating the ancient vacillation between Kinyras and Kauthar/Khousor as a valid heuristic tool.

Goddess, King, and Copper

We may begin with a further proof of Kinyras' essential compatibility with ps.-Meliton's Kauthar: whereas Strabo and Eustathios saw Byblos as an *ancient* part of Kinyras' realm, ps.-Meliton presents Cyprus as a *novel* addition to Kauthar's. These conceptions must be cognate. But whereas the classical authors give no further context for the Byblian Kinyras, ps.-Meliton's Kauthar tale implicates a Cypriot king 'Hephaistos', whose kingdom passes under Byblian control through Balthi's affair with Tammuz. This Cypriot Hephaistos—shared by Bar Koni and thus fundamental to the myth—has deep Cypriot roots beneath a partly Hellenized surface. For the Olympian smith-god is conspicuously absent from the early island, thanks to the ancient prestige of an indigenous metallurge like the Ingot God.[92] This figure was effectively wedded to the Cypriot

---

[90] Even if a 'tomb of Adonis' was displayed in Byblos itself (see n60 above), Lucian refers to lamentation rites "throughout the land" (ἀνὰ τὴν χώρην).
[91] See p448–452.
[92] Borgeaud 1975.

goddess herself through shared ingot iconography and his-and-hers adyta in the sanctuary at Enkomi, with 'his' metallurgical facilities housed within 'her' realm.[93] By contrast, the pairing of Hephaistos and Aphrodite has no basis in *Aegean* cult, it being rather Ares with whom the goddess typically received joint worship.[94] So Homer's famous tale of their adultery—exposed by Hephaistos, with the goddess's chastened return to Paphos—is an artificial satire on Aphrodite's cultural gyrations between Greece and Cyprus, where indeed a smith-god husband would cherish her return.[95] By the logic of Homer's narrative this should be Hephaistos; but cultural realities require us to infer an unnamed Cypriot counterpart.

This is precisely Hephaistos' role in ps.-Meliton and Bar Koni. But here the marital escapade moves eastward, merging with a very old motif of distinctly Mesopotamian aspect—the faithless goddess—that was rooted in divine patronage of actual sovereigns. In two Neo-Sumerian epic tales (preserved in later copies/versions), royal ascendancy is marked by securing the 'love' of Inanna, who abandons a rival king.[96] Hence the famous scene in the *Epic of Gilgamesh*, where the hero taxes Ishtar with her history of broken lovers.[97] We saw a similar alliance of myth and royal ideology in the Hittite *Ritual and Prayer for Ishtar of Nineveh*, where it was feared that the goddess had defected to one of the many other royal cult-centers that claimed her—of which one was Alashiya itself.[98]

This pattern ultimately shaped Aphrodite, whose many paramours included (besides Ares and Hephaistos) Ankhises, Phaethon, Adonis, and Kinyras himself.[99] Her promiscuity provided fuel for Christian attacks, and ps.-Meliton himself was clearly so motivated.[100] That he interpolated Homer's Ares for good measure would explain the inorganic complication of Hephaistos' discovery leading to the death not of Ares but of Tammuz; this suggestion is corroborated by the absence of Ares from Bar Koni's version, where Hephaistos plays

---

[93] See p394–395.
[94] Ares/Aphrodite: Farnell 1896–1909 2:622–623, 653–655, 700–703; GR:220. This latter pairing must itself reflect original attributes of the eastern goddess, who in Mesopotamian tradition unites war and love in a single figure. See *Kypris*:136 for the possible correspondence between Ares and the Ingot God, whose smiting pose is as striking as his ingot-base.
[95] Homer *Odyssey* 8.359–366. See Franklin 2014:223–224; cf. Burkert 1993:153; EFH:57.
[96] *Enmerkar and the Lord of Aratta* (ETCSL 1.8.2.3), especially 25–32, 102–104, 227–235; *Lugalbanda and the Anzud Bird* (ETCSL 1.8.2.2), especially 290–321, 345–356.
[97] *Epic of Gilgamesh* vi.24–79: ANET:84. The passage is discussed by George 2003, 1:472–474.
[98] See p376.
[99] Cf. e.g. Clement of Alexandria *Exhortation* 2.33: Ἀφροδίτη δὲ ἐπ' Ἄρει κατῃσχυμμένη μετῆλθεν ἐπὶ Κινύραν καὶ Ἀγχίσην ἔγημεν καὶ Φαέθοντα ἐλόχα καὶ ἤρα Ἀδώνιδος κτλ.
[100] Cf. Lightfoot 2004:86.

Kinyras, Kothar, and the Passage from Byblos

the war-god's sometime role of homicidal cuckold.[101] But in a striking twist, Bar Koni's Hephaistos is himself slain before Tammuz falls to the tusk.

I conclude that the myth presents a distinctly Cypriot and/or Cypro-Byblian fusion of two ideologies that derive from the BA: the divine protection of royal copper-production, and political ascendancy represented by the love of Inanna/Ishtar/Astarte. With Balthi's defection, the island passes from a Cypriot metallurge to a Byblian, represented as Hephaistos and Kauthar, respectively. Whereas Kauthar's relevance to Bar Koni's aetiologies of lament is not immediately obvious, he is perfectly qualified for the current context. This representation of 'ancient history' becomes quite tangible when one recalls that the trade in copper, and control thereof, was the single most important factor structuring Cyprus's internal political organization and its relationships with the outside world, from the early second millennium down through the Aegean and Phoenician colonial movements (Chapter 1).

Now if we had no reason to consider Kinyras and Kauthar/Khousor doublets, we might reasonably expect ps.-Meliton and Bar Koni to have named their ancient Cypriot king not Hephaistos but Kinyras. After all, Kinyras had long been known as the island's ancient metallurgical monarch (Homer) and beloved of Aphrodite (Pindar). While epichoric myths were often converted into Olympian currency, this principle was not consistently applied by ps.-Meliton, as shown by his Kauthar and several other figures. And since Kinyras and Kauthar/Khousor *do* appear to be doppelgängers—most obviously in the present Byblian context—ps.-Meliton's Hephaistos must represent an *indigenous* metal-smith whose control of Cyprus antedates that of Kauthar/Kinyras.

This conclusion is corroborated by its startling agreement with the report of the Paphian priesthood, discussed in Chapter 16. There an "ancient memory" (*vetus memoria*) of Aerias/Aeria—interpretable as 'Mr. and Mrs. Copper'—was contrasted with a "more recent legend" (*fama recentior*) of Kinyras and Aphrodite.[102] This unexpected harmony can hardly be coincidence; it is of a piece with the complementary Greco-Roman and Syrian views of Byblos' dominion under Kinyras/Kauthar. We are dealing with cognate myths, and our analysis of ps.-Meliton and Bar Koni must expand accordingly to embrace the *hieroì lógoi* of Paphos. One immediate benefit is that we can flesh out Tacitus' spare epitome of the Paphian report. That the priests saw Kinyras as not merely *secondary* to their cult, but a parvenu from the mainland, is a ready deduction from his immigration in other sources (Chapter 21). And whereas Tacitus otherwise seems to

---

[101] For sources and discussion, see Ribichini 1981:108–123.
[102] See p401–404.

link Aerias and Kinyras only through relative chronology, ps.-Meliton lets us suppose a causal relationship of geopolitical aspect between the two 'strata'.

This neat convergence strongly suggests that the insular and mainland traditions derive from a shared historical reality of considerable depth. One might try to see here, for example, the breakdown of centralized control on Cyprus at the end of the LBA (= Hephaistos), followed by Phoenician pursuit of copper in the EIA (= Kauthar/Kinyras). But this is not deep enough. So far as we know, it was not Byblos, but Tyre, that dominated the Phoenician colonial movement.[103] And as I have argued on independent grounds, any historicizing interpretation of Cypriot Kinyras must start from his pre-Greek presence.[104] While metal-hungry kings of IA Phoenicia would certainly have had their own reasons to promote a cult of Kothar/Khousor, for them too the industrial superpower of Alashiya will have loomed large in legend. And if there was one Levantine god as likely as Astarte to come to LBA Cyprus, it was Kothar.

A crucial issue here, raised above in connection with the Ingot God and Goddess,[105] is the epithet *Kythéreia*, which Aphrodite bears in Greek epic and beyond.[106] It has long been recognized that this word, with its short epsilon (*Kythĕreia*), cannot derive directly from the island Kythera (*Kýthēra*), despite ancient sources, beginning with Hesiod, that assert or imply just this (one would otherwise expect *Kythḗreia*).[107] West, reviewing the issue, nevertheless urged that "the two words must be related, but perhaps not in that way," and approved those who would see in *Kythéreia* a female counterpart of Kothar, presumably his consort.[108]

Now the form itself, A. Cassio has recently shown, is a relatively late epic concoction.[109] That it derives specifically from Cypro-Aegean interaction in the Orientalizing Period (ca. 750–650) finds good general support in our evidence for the Cypriot engagement with 'Homeric' epic at this time, culminating most

---

[103] But note "the gods of Byblos" in a fragmentary fourth-century votive inscription from Larnaka tēs Lapethou: Honeyman 1938 (line 9), with comments on 296–297; HC:99–100n6, 182n1; Greenfield 1987; Michaelidou-Nicolaou 1987:337.
[104] See p368–369.
[105] See p404.
[106] Homer *Odyssey* 8.285–288 (cf. Franklin 2014:223–224); *Homeric Hymn* 10.1 (Κυπρογενῆ Κυθέρειαν); Sappho 140a (lament for Adonis); Ovid *Metamorphoses* 10.717–720; Manilius *Astronomica* 4.579–581; Nonnos *Dionysiaka* 3.109–111. Cf. Brown 1965:216–219.
[107] Hesiod *Theogony* 192–193.
[108] Gruppe 1906 2:1359; Brown 1965:216–219; GR:152–153; EFH:56–57 with further references.
[109] Cassio 2012 §3: an "artificial bardic creation ... devised ... so to speak in cold blood, and at a late stage"; he sees it as patterned after the equally artificial Gk. *eupatéreia*, which appears in the same verse-end position. See further his contextual arguments.

notably in the episodes that were excised from the *Kypria* by the fifth century.[110] The epithet's special connection with the island is established by the tenth Homeric hymn, where the goddess is invoked not as Aphrodite but rather "Cyprus-born *Kythéreia* ... she who rules well-founded Salamis / and Cyprus-on-the-Sea"—obvious signs of a Cypriot singer and/or performance setting.[111] Yet such on-the-ground cultic realities equally require *Kythéreia*, though a seventh-century neologism in the Aegean, to refer to some older religious reality on Cyprus itself. Kythereia will not have materialized from thin air.

A 'female Kothar' is not without Levantine parallels. The linguistic kinship of Kothar and the Kotharat goddesses of Ugaritian and Canaanite/Phoenician tradition is undoubted, though how their spheres intersected is unclear.[112] The Kotharat typically appear as a group; but Philo of Byblos, who calls them 'Artemides', singles out one as the spouse of Sydyk—the 'Just', our most likely prototype for Sandokos, Kinyras' father in ps.-Apollodoros.[113] Philo also knew a Khousarthis who "brought to light the theology of Taautos [Thoth] which had been hidden and concealed in allegories"—a description less like Philo's own Khousor than that of Mokhos—though how this female Kothar might mesh with Cypriot 'Aphrodite' is hardly obvious.[114] Finally, there is the "Assyrian *Kythéreia*" of Nonnos, whose Byblian context could further corroborate the connection with Byblos of both ps.-Meliton's Kauthar and Philo's Khousor.[115]

The proposed association of Kythereia and Kothar raises two linguistic issues that help us focus the historical view. First is the discrepancy between the short upsilon of *Kythéreia* and the long *ô* of Kothar (< P-S *aw*). Here a plausible explanation is at hand in the changes one may expect at a linguistic interface.[116] That such a mutation could occur precisely on Cyprus is supported by the short upsilons of both Kinyras and Myrrha (versus the long vowels of Semitic cognates).[117]

---

[110] See generally Franklin 2014 and above p1, 211.

[111] *Homeric Hymn* 10.1, 4. The association is also clear at *Hymn* 6.18.

[112] For the Kotharat, see above p445n11; Margalit 1972:55 (resumed in Margalit 1989:285–286); Selms 1979:73–74; KwH:466–472; DDD col. 915–917 (Pardee), with earlier literature.

[113] [Apollodoros] *Library* 3.14.3. For Philo's Artemides as the Kotharat, see YGC:143; Baumgarten 1981:204, 227. Cf. below p123n74, 510.

[114] Philo of Byblos FGH 790 F 10: θεὸς Σουρμουβηλὸς Θουρῶτε ἡ μετονομασθεῖσα Χούσαρθις ἀκολουθήσαντες κεκρυμμένην τοῦ Τααύτου καὶ ἀλληγορίαις ἐπεσκιασμένην τὴν θεολογίαν ἐφώτισαν. Cf. Brown 1965:215; YGC:138–139n73; Selms 1979:744; Attridge and Oden 1981:104n4; Baumgarten 1981:68–74 for Philo's understanding of Taautos.

[115] Nonnos *Dionysiaka* 3.109–111.

[116] By contrast the false *Kythéreia* < *Kýthēra* supposes an internal Greek development, whatever the anterior etymology of *Kýthēra* itself.

[117] See p199n71, 274.

Chapter Nineteen

The second issue concerns the Semitic interdental fricative *ṯ* in *kṯr*/Kothar. This sound could only have emerged as the Greek theta of *Kythéreia* if the underlying adaptation went back to at least ca. 1300, and probably rather earlier.[118] The correspondence of Semitic and other ANE fricatives/laryngeals with early (LBA) Greek aspirates (*th*, *ph*, *kh*) still lacks a comprehensive study, but H. Y. Priebatsch showed that the Greek aspirates could indeed have a spirant quality in the LBA, or at least represent such sounds in loanwords. That quality was typically lost in the EIA, reappearing only in later centuries.[119]

This situation brings the island of Kythera back into the discussion, since it was already so named by the fifteenth century, when it appears in an Egyptian 'itinerary' text and somewhat later as an ethnic designation at Mycenaean Pylos.[120] It is true that traditions of Phoenician settlement on Kythera—including the island's sanctuary of Aphrodite Ourania and the eponymous Kytheros son of Phoinix—might be sufficiently explained by EIA trade expeditions.[121] Yet a deeper connection between Kythera and Kothar is well supported by the god's persistent link to Minoan Crete in Ugaritic legend—"Kaptara is his royal house, Egypt is the land of his inheritance." Kothar's international realm here

---

[118] By this time the twenty-two letter Proto-Canaanite alphabet shows that "the three interdentals [ṯ, ḏ, ṱ] ... merged in Canaanite with dental and palato-alveolar fricatives" (Harris 1939:40–41; SL §13.7, quotation). After the merger, P-S *ṯ* would have yielded *s* in Greek, hence Ug. *Kṯr*/'Gk'. Χουσώρ; cf. σίγλος ('shekel')/Ug. *ṯql*, Pun./Heb. *šql*, Akk. *šeqlu* (*Emprunts*:34–37); σάκκος ('coarse cloth' > 'sack/garment')/Akk. *šaqqu*, Imperial Aramaic *šqq* (*Emprunts*:24–25, where Phoen. *šqq is assumed the source).

[119] See Priebatsch 1980. Note e.g. the famous problem of Gk. Ἀχαιοί/Hitt. Aḫḫiyawa (329), and Gk. χρυσός ('gold' = *ku-ru-so* in Lin. B., which lacks separate signs for aspirates)/Can. *ḥarūṣ(u)* (329–330). Albright's objection to the derivation of Kythera from *kṯr* (YGC:136n65) is no longer relevant. He insisted that the name would have to go back improbably far to the third millennium, believing that *ṯ* was already pronounced *š* by the early second millennium because of its representation in the Sethe execration texts and Akkadian documents of Ugarit. But these correspondences are now attributed to unequal phonetic inventories in the relevant scripts/languages, and it is generally accepted that the interdental was still pronounced at Ugarit (Segert 1984 §34.27; KwH:80; Gordon 1997:51; Pardee 2008:292; Huehnergard 2008:230–231). It may, however, have been a conservative, literate/official usage: occasional interchanges of *ṯ* and *š* hint at coalescence (SL §13.6), and some tablets using the twenty-two letter script have been found (Gordon 1997:49). This would support a rather earlier date for a link between Kothar and Kythereia and/or Kythera than the Ugaritic texts themselves.

[120] *Ktir* is found on an inscribed statue base from the reign of Amenhotep III (ca. 1403–1364) in a list of other Aegean TNs—perhaps "an itinerary describing a route (or a specific voyage) to mainland Greece and Crete": see with further references EFH:6 and n12, 57n238; Cline 2007:194 (quotation). For Lin. B *ku-te-ra* (nominative plural, 'women of Kythera'), see Nikoloudis 2008:47 (PY A- series).

[121] Herodotos 1.105.3 (temple of Aphrodite); Stephanos of Byzantium s.v. Κύθηρα, νῆσος ... ἀπὸ Κυθήρου τοῦ Φοίνικος; repeated by Eustathios on Homer *Iliad* 10.269; Eustathios on Dionysios the Periegete 498. Further evidence and discussion: Morris 1992:79–80n26 (connection with Kothar is "attractive"), cf. 135n142; Lipiński 2004:176–178; Dugand 1973:245–247 arrives at a different etymology.

Kinyras, Kothar, and the Passage from Byblos

symbolized the LBA palatial trade network, one strand of which reached from Crete via Ugarit to Mari and Babylon, through which the Minoans secured tin for making bronze.[122] One might even speculate that Ug. 'Kaptara' itself derives from Kothar, at an earlier linguistic stage than he is found in the Ugaritic texts (< *Kawtar*-?). A cuneiform inscription found on Kythera—relating to Naram-Sin of Eshnunna (ca. 1712–1702 BCE) in far-off Babylonia—helps compensate for the lack of contemporary Levantine material on the island, where a Middle Minoan presence is however well documented.[123]

Whatever the case with Kythera, Cyprus will have been as central as Ugarit itself to that city's mythological vision of Kothar's domain. This follows first from simple geography and the region's seasonal sailing routes.[124] It is clinched by the island's dominant international position in the production and working of copper (Chapters 1, 14). The whole situation is perfectly exemplified by the Uluburun wreck.[125]

Material record, historical context, linguistic considerations, the iconography of the Ingot God and Goddess—faced with this combination of evidence it is hard to doubt that some form of Kothar was active on LBA Cyprus, an importation parallel to Ishtar/Astarte herself (Chapter 15), and that this echoed on in the Greco-Cypriot epithet *Kythéreia*. We need not assume that a separate male *Kyther(os) still existed in the seventh century, as Kothar could have been 'internalized' as an aspect of the goddess—as of Kinyras himself—centuries earlier. On the other hand, given the island's substantial Phoenician population, some conscious conceptual link between goddess and Kothar/Khousor may indeed have persisted into historical times.

With this we return to our crux—the melding of Kinyras and Kothar, and how this transpired between Byblos and Cyprus. In what follows, I shall attempt to account for all data so far presented, and incorporate our hypothetical Byblian Kinyras/Kothar into the larger picture of BA royal cult-music and divinized-instruments explored in Part One.

The Cypro-Byblian Interface

I have now made independent cases for the presence of both a Kothar and a Divine Knr in one or more pantheons of LBA Cyprus—a perfectly credible idea given their official co-existence at nearby Ugarit. A third investigation explored,

---

[122] Primary texts, discussion, and further references in Strange 1980:83–87, 90–93, 101–102; Cline 1994:120–128; cf. Morris 1992:92–95, 98, 100, 102, et passim.
[123] Weidner 1939; Lipiński 2004:176–178.
[124] For which see Murray 1995.
[125] See p326.

Chapter Nineteen

in the thirteenth-century bronze stand from Kourion, the conjunction of music, metalworking, and goddess-worship in a royal context (Chapter 15). A fourth set of evidence, from the roughly coeval Pylos tablets, seemed to imply a meta-musical Kinyras with Kothar-like seafaring skills (Chapter 17). This converging material, I believe, indicates that some Kotharization of Kinyras—firmly established as a metallurgical king already for Homer—was underway on Cyprus by or before the thirteenth century.

We are left needing to explain how a mirror image—a Kinyradized Khousor—could arise in Phoenicia, specifically at, or at least including, Byblos. Given the early horizons sketched above for Cypriot Kinyras, it would seem that he and the Byblian Kinyras/Khousor were parallel regional developments of a specific Canaanite tradition in which Kothar and the Divine Knr were unusually intimate *already in the LBA*. A likely guess is that they were treated as mythological brothers, whence the vestigial siblings known to both Philo and Étienne de Lusignan.[126]

We must evidently posit a specific cult importation from Byblos to Cyprus at some pre-Greek historical juncture. This agrees well with our argument of Chapter 15—that the 'immigration' of Kinyras was connected with a theological reinterpretation of the Cypriot goddess in terms of a mainland Astarte figure. We need only add some form of Kothar, or Kotharization, to the formula. Such a 'moving goddess' is after all just what we find in ps.-Meliton and Bar Koni. In both, Balthi, despite the deep (EBA) antiquity of the Byblian goddess herself, begins the story as queen of Cyprus. (Compare Hesiod's account of Aphrodite's birth, where the goddess is wafted from the Aegean and Kythera to what was in fact her home at an earlier stage of development, Cyprus).[127] There are several significant elements here. The original *independence* of the Cypriot 'queen', who then moves eastward, is mirrored by the dramatic displacement of Byblian 'Balthi' *to Cyprus*—thus a kind of *westward* movement. (The latter trajectory is also implied by the figure of 'Kypros', daughter of 'Byblos', in a fragment of Istros.[128]) This structure implies a mutual assimilation of historically distinct divinities.

---

[126] See Chapter 18. Brown 1965:206–207 compared Kothar and Kinyras with the Dioskouroi, as being two sets of twins, both pairs associated with the sea. A special Cypriot version of the twins ("our Dioskouroi") is seen in the loyalty oath to Tiberius (see p205). There is also Theokritos' description of them as "horsemen kitharists" (ἱππῆες κιθαρισταί, *Idylls* 22.24), which recalls the Cypriot terracottas of horse-riding lyrists: CAAC II:III[LGC]1, cf. [LGC]9; *Aspects*:89 no. 67 and fig. 76 (ca. 750), 91–92 no. 69, fig. 79, with references (ca. 800–750). But Theokritos receives a quite different and attractive explanation from Power 2010:282–285.
[127] Hesiod *Theogony* 191–193.
[128] Istros FGH 334 F 45. See further p515–516.

Kinyras, Kothar, and the Passage from Byblos

The Cypriot Goddess and Baalat Gebal, as known from later times, do have some resemblances. Both cults were of deep antiquity, dominating their respective territories. Aniconic representations were prominent at both sites, and though such 'betyls' were not unique to Byblos, their archaic quality suits the scenario envisaged here.[129] The Lady of Byblos, like other forms of Astarte and Aphrodite herself, was a protectress of sailors.[130] She was also a royal patroness.[131] For Philo of Byblos, the goddesses were closely related. His Byblian Baaltis is 'Dione'; linguistically a female 'Zeus', Dione most famously appears as Aphrodite's mother in an eccentric episode of the *Iliad*, much discussed recently for its Near Eastern and Cypriot sympathies.[132] But, while this could potentially imply that Baaltis was older than her Cypriot counterpart, in Philo himself Dione is the *sister* of Aphrodite, with whom he equates Astarte; Rhea, probably a form of Asherah, is the third triplet, all being wives of Kronos, that is 'Elos' or El.[133]

But none of these correspondences is definitive. They represent the same ongoing 'collation' of regional deities that was so well attested for the LBA (Chapter 15). Those early phenomena, often induced by on-the-ground religious juxtapositions and cult transfers, make it quite possible that our Cypro-Byblian myth ultimately does reflect some religious reality of that time. Unfortunately, we know very little about specific relations between BA Cyprus and Byblos. The latter's early history is fairly dark outside the narrow window of its fourteenth-century subjection to Egypt; Cyprus is darker still. One Amarna text from Rib-Hadda, the king/'governor' of Byblos, does mention sending a certain Amanmashsha to Alashiya; but the mission's purpose is not stated.[134] Alashiya also follows Byblos in the eleventh-century (?) itinerary of Wen-Amun; the context is the turbulent period of the Sea Peoples, but it is implied that

---

[129] The Temple of Obelisks at Byblos goes back to the MBA (DDUPP:67, 77–79, with further references in n83). The famous stone of Paphos (Tacitus *Histories* 2.3, with Heubner 1963-1982 *ad loc.* for other ancient descriptions; also ExcCyp:179) is generally attributed to the BA (*Paphos*:99–100 and fig. 83). It is shown in many variations on Roman coins from Augustus to Caracalla/Geta (BMC Cyprus:cxxvii–cxxxiv and 73–87 *passim* and pl. XIV.3, 7–8, XV.1–4, 7–8, XVI.2, 4, 6–9, XVII.4–6, 8–10, XXVI.3, 6; Head et al. 1911:746; Blinkenberg 1924:7–17 with figs; HC:74; *Paphos*:84, fig. 65–67, 103 fig. 87; Gaifman 2012:169–180). A very similar conical stone is represented on a Byblian coin from the reign of Macrinus (ca. 217–218 CE): BMC Phoenicia:102 no. 36 (pl. xii, 13); cf. Millar 1993:277; DDUPP:76 with references in n68. Aniconic stones within temples are also shown on imperial-era issues from Emesa (sanctuary of Heliogabalos) and Seleucia Pieria in Syria: Price and Trell 1977:168–170; Gaifman 2012:177–178 with references. It is impossible to verify if the 'black stone' displayed at modern Kouklia as Aphrodite's image is indeed that (Gaifman 2012:179–180).

[130] DDUPP:72. For Aphrodite, see p330.

[131] See p407n45.

[132] See p403n16.

[133] Philo of Byblos FGH 790 F 2 (22, 35). Cf. Baumgarten 1981:200–201; DDUPP:74–75.

[134] EA 114. Cf. HC:43; AP:51; Moran 1992:190n12.

such a route was once normal.¹³⁵ But that is hardly surprising given the island's proximity.

Nevertheless, we can be sure that regular official relations did exist, and that these revolved precisely around the copper trade. The enormous quantity of bronze excavated from second-millennium levels of Byblos shows that the city was a major manufacturing center.¹³⁶ Moreover, state control, as on contemporary Cyprus, is indicated by another Amarna letter that refers to the Byblian king's production and supply of bronze weapons to both Egypt and Tyre.¹³⁷ This industry must have involved the Byblian monarchs in close dealings with their cupreous insular peers. Since royal control and divine protection of copper is otherwise well documented for LBA Cyprus (Chapter 15), it is easy to imagine this ideology—and associated cult practices—being extended to, or adapted by, the island's partners in the metals trade. This, I suggest, is the best context for ps.-Meliton's myth, and full justification for Kauthar's starring role.

Ritual Lamentation and the 'Damu' of Byblos

At the same time, a Byblian proto-Kinyras of LBA date—and a lamenting father of Adonis/Tammuz—should imply significant exposure to Mesopotamian theological concepts and practices, since the divinization of instruments and other cult objects evidently originated in EBA Babylonia (Chapters 2, 5, and 6). As one probable environment for the spread of such ideas I identified the increasing involvement of Amorite and traditional Mesopotamian cultures during the Ur III and OB periods. This would make Kinnaru of Ugarit and the proposed Byblian Kinyras parallel regional manifestations at the western end of a cult-music continuum.

While Byblos' early religion is nearly as obscure as its political history,¹³⁸ several points are noteworthy here. First, while the city enjoyed close cultural relations with Egypt for much of the Bronze Age,¹³⁹ its engagement with Syria and Mesopotamia was just as early and longstanding. Southern Mesopotamian influence on the city's material culture can be traced back to the EBA, while its temples and other public buildings show that Byblos avoided the collapse of the southern Levant ca. 2400–2000 (EBA IV), sharing rather in the urban apogee

---

¹³⁵ CS 1 no. 41.
¹³⁶ Falsone 1988:80 ("indubbiamente uno dei maggiori centri produttori di bronzo di tutto l'antico Vicino Oriente").
¹³⁷ EA 77 with Liverani 1997.
¹³⁸ For a general introduction, see DDUPP:67–114.
¹³⁹ There was probably a hiatus during the First Intermediate Period, ca. 2180–2140: cf. Helck 1971:38.

of Syrian sites like Ebla—the archives of which attest regular commerce with Byblos.[140]

In the Ur III period, two economic texts from Drehem (ancient Puzrish-Dagan, one of Ur's major redistribution centers) document diplomatic relations between Amar-Suen (ca. 2046–2038) and a Byblian king—Ibdâdi or Abd-(H)addi (Eb-da-di3)—alongside other Syrian monarchs (of Ebla, Mari, and Tuttul).[141] These tablets were once taken as evidence for Ur's political control of Byblos, but this idea has been discarded with further understanding of the state's provincial administration.[142] Nevertheless, they remain precious indicators of cultural contact at the royal level. And several cuneiform inscriptions have been excavated at Byblos itself, one from the Ur III period (see further below) and two of OB or MB date.[143]

The fourteenth-century Amarna letters show Mesopotamian scribal culture firmly ensconced in the Byblian royal court. This in itself need not imply any theological influence. But a detail in one letter does indeed support the idea. This is a petition from the aforementioned Rib-Hadda, who begs pharaoh to protect the cult-property of a deity rendered as "my DAMU" (ᵈDAMU-*ia*).[144] Scholars have differed as to whether DAMU refers to the Sumerian god of that name,[145] or is a scribal gloss for a local Byblian deity. In his recent reassessment, T. Mettinger argues persuasively for the latter, identifying the underlying figure as the Baal of Byblos, consort of Baalat Gebal—attested in a tenth-century inscription, and probably "the living god" of another Amarna letter.[146] This Baal of Byblos must be the storm-god Haddu, whose cult is attested by the theophoric element in Rib-Hadda's own name, and that of the aforementioned Abd-(H)addi.[147]

---

[140] Saghieh 1983:129–132 et passim; Genz 2010:207, 211–212; Arnaud 2010:167–168.
[141] Amherst (Pinches 1908) 82 rev. 19, with the parallel discussed by Sollberger 1959/1960:121–122; cf. DDUPP:68.
[142] The older interpretation was based on the Byblian ruler's designation as en5-si, as the title en-si2 was used of Ur's provincial governors. It is now known to have been applied also to foreign monarchs; only the emperor was lugal. See with references Saghieh 1983:131; Steinkeller 1987:36–37; Michalowski 2009:19–20.
[143] Dossin 1969.
[144] EA 84.33. Arnaud 2010:175 proposes to reread ᵈDAMU-*ia* as ᵈ*Da-mu-az*⸢, that is, Tammuz/Dumuzi; but this would not resolve, only displace, the interpretive problem posed by DAMU (see below).
[145] So Schroeder 1915; cf. Ribichini 1981:189–192.
[146] Mettinger 2013:137–145, 217–219, with the doxographic review of dying-and-rising god skeptics in Chapter 1, and a convincing refutation of Na'aman 1990, who saw in ᵈDAMU-*ia* a reference to the city's *goddess*. For the new reading of Baal in KAI 4, Bonnet 1993; DDUPP:89; Mettinger 2013:140. For the 'living god' of Byblos (EA 129.51), see also Moran 1992:211n23; for a further possible attestation in a late third-millennium Egyptian *Pyramid Texts*, see Redford 1990:826; Mettinger 2013:144–145 with references in n166.
[147] See DDUPP:79–80.

So far, so good. But one must still explain why Baal/Haddu was glossed as 'Damu' rather than say ᵈIŠKUR, used elsewhere of storm-gods. Damu, associated with the annual cycle of plant life, is one of several Mesopotamian figures who fall in their youthful prime—much like Dumuzi, with whom Damu was eventually assimilated, Dumuzi himself being connected rather with pastoralism.[148] The precise character of these gods' death and any return has been debated since Frazer; Mettinger, while carefully eschewing monolithic, transhistoric definitions, has forcefully revived the idea that these and several other figures were truly 'dying-and-rising' gods. Storm-gods, by contrast, do not normally die, as is well illustrated by Yahweh (for the Baal of Ugarit, see below).[149] The same discrepancy is illustrated by Adonis, whose name, it has long been recognized, must derive from Semitic *'dn* ('lord'). This honorific is attested for a number of Syro-Levantine gods, apparently including the Byblian Baal himself.[150] Yet Adonis, with the noteworthy exception of his predilection for mountainous areas, does not resemble a storm-god. Beautiful young lover of the goddess, haunter of the countryside, his untimely death, her lament, a seasonal return to life, dividing the year between his earthly lover and the queen of the underworld—this is a distinctly Dumuzi-like portfolio.[151]

And so I believe Mettinger is right to suggest that the Byblian 'Baal-Damu' is a hybrid due to Mesopotamian influence on the city's royal cult:

> The proximity of Adon(is), Damu, and Dumuzi should alert us to the possibility that Byblos was a site where Adon(is) was part of a syncretistic development in which he adopted features originally connected with the Sumerian and Akkadian myths of journeys to the Netherworld.[152]

The most tangible and appropriate vehicle for a focused importation of such ideas, as well as their survival into IA myth, is a cult of royal ancestors, akin to the 'Rephaim' of Ugarit.[153] Such developments would have to be placed rather

---

[148] RlA 2:115–116 (*Damu, Ebeling); Black and Green 1992 s.v. Damu.
[149] Mettinger 2013:144, 207, 218, 220.
[150] See with earlier references Loretz 1984; Mettinger 2013:125–126, 140–141 (citing Bordreuil 1977 for 'Adonis' [*'dn*], alongside the goddess herself, in a tenth-century Byblian inscription).
[151] Smith 2001:117–118; Mettinger 2013:218–219. The Byblian cult-myth of Adonis' return, as described by Lucian, can hardly be dismissed as emulation of Christian theology. For those who have held this desperate position, and a convincing refutation, see Mettinger 2010:26–29, 135–136, 153–154, 217–218.
[152] Mettinger 2013:144; cf. Ribichini 1981:190; Smith 2001:117–118.
[153] This context was rightly emphasized by Ribichini 1981:192–197, 202; cf. Grottanelli 1984:36–38 et passim. For Ugarit, see Chapter 7.

early, quite possibly well before Rib-Hadda's letter and Baal's death and return in the Ugaritian Baal Cycle—for which Mettinger posits a parallel "reception in Ugarit of the *descensus* mytheme from the cults of Mesopotamian Dumuzi."[154] For the zenith of Damu's cult was the Ur III or OB periods, when he was honored especially at Ur, Isin, Larsa, and Girsu.[155] Dumuzi enjoyed an equally deep antiquity, being known at Mari for instance already in pre-Sargonic times.[156]

Mettinger's hypothesis, I suggest, can equally explain the Byblian Kinyras, whom we wish to connect with Levantine cultic practices under some Mesopotamian influence. Damu, like Dumuzi, was a subject of lamentation-singing in the Ur III and OB periods, when both were involved in the ritual poetics of royal cult, including the mortuary.[157] Both are also associated with divinized instruments. We saw that Dumuzi featured thematically in lamentations performed at Mari with or in the presence of the divinized balang Ninigizibara, servant to the mourning Ishtar.[158] These passages clarify the attestation of a balang counselor-god for Damu himself in the god-list An:Anum.[159] Kinnaru of Ugarit, we saw, may be approached along similar lines.[160] (As more general *chronological* support one should recall that Egyptian instruments with gods' heads are well attested in the MK.[161])

Our hypothesis requires that the lamentations of historical Byblos perpetuate a traditional practice going back to the Bronze Age. This idea, inherently plausible given contemporary ANE parallels, can now be supported by a cuneiform text of Ur III date from Byblos itself. The tablet was originally interpreted as a sign-list executed by a scribe-in-training.[162] The further inference, that Byblos was already well within the orbit of Mesopotamian elite culture, with "literate administrative personnel," remains reasonable.[163] But D. Arnaud has now shown that the text is in fact a dedicatory inscription relating to some restoration of the temple and/or cult of the Byblian goddess.[164] Though the larger context is damaged, several important details survive.

---

[154] Mettinger 2013:218, cf. 220 for Zechariah 12:11 ("On that day the mourning in Jerusalem will be as great as the mourning for Hadad-rimmon in the plain of Megiddo"). For further evidence of Damu at Ebla (?), Ugarit, Sidon, and Tyre, see DDUPP:190–192.
[155] See n148.
[156] Mettinger 2010:201 and n87.
[157] See Cohen 1993:465–481; Smith 2001:113; PHG 37 and n143, 147, 183, 197n31.
[158] See p64 and Heimpel, "Balang Gods," Section 2c, 4a§5; 23b, 23f, 47a.
[159] Heimpel, "Balang Gods," 53 V 168; cf. PHG:113.
[160] See especially p134–146.
[161] See p60 and n81.
[162] Dossin 1969, especially 245–248; cf. Saghieh 1983:131; Dalley et al. 1998:15, 17.
[163] Genz 2010:211.
[164] Arnaud 2010:164–174 (*Eš6-tar2*-eš3 at reverse 3).

First, the goddess is explicitly called 'Ishtar' (*Eš6-tar2*-eš3)—very early confirmation of classical authors that identify Baalat Gebal as Astarte. We should not be too categorical, of course, since Hittite and Ugaritian sources show that many regional goddesses could be considered forms of Ishtar. But this fact is itself significant for its implications of supralocal theological thought.

Second, the text itemizes several appurtenances of the goddess's cult. These include not only a bed—presumably for processions involving the cult image—but a female singer (mi2-nar), and a female player of the 'balang' (mi2-balaĝ-ti, or munus balaĝ-di3, as Heimpel reads the signs).[165] Arnaud rightly connects these cult-musicians with ritual lamentation, given the common association of balang and lament in Mesopotamian contexts.[166] Yet 'balang' itself need not refer narrowly to a Sumerian instrument of that name; more probably it masks a local counterpart. That this was precisely *kinnārum*—so vocalized in Byblos at this early date—is a ready guess given the same lexical equation at Ebla (Chapter 4) and the many parallels for female *knr*-players in the region—like the later lyre-players who play for a goddess on the Cypro-Phoenician symposium bowls (Chapter 11). Remember that Bar Koni attributes lamentation of Tammuz not only to his father but his *mother*, and that in Mesopotamian laments Dumuzi was variously mourned as the goddess's spouse, son, and brother—a range that "reflects the reality of women crying over their dead husbands and children."[167] While 'balang' is not written with a divine determinative in our text, we can at least say, on the basis of the parallels, that this instrument was the sacred property of the goddess, dedicated to use in her cult.[168]

Circumstantial evidence therefore indicates that by the late third millennium Byblos hosted a cultic environment that is consistent with the eventual emergence of a Byblian 'Kinyras'.

Conclusion

I propose that Kinyras, Kauthar, and Theias are three names for a single complex Byblian figure in whom a Kothar was fused with a Divine Knr independent of Ugarit. While this 'Kinyras' was 'confused' with Kothar at Byblos, the opposite outcome transpired on Cyprus, where Kothar was more severely effaced. This resulted in a curious inversion whereby Cypriot Kinyras could be seen as originating in Byblos, while others saw Byblian 'Kauthar' extending his reign over Cyprus. This mirrored distribution, I have argued, reflects a specific

---

[165] Cf. Heimpel, "Balang Gods," Section 3c1.
[166] Arnaud 2010:173.
[167] PHG:37–38.
[168] See p101–102.

cult-connection between island and mainland in the pre-Greek period. While Alashiya is already attested textually in the nineteenth century, the material record shows clearly that Cyprus' great cosmopolitan age began rather later. The historical 'moment' between Byblos and Cyprus, if such there was, might be related to the 'founding' of Paphos by 'Phoinix', which Eusebios dated to 1425. This tradition, I have suggested, may be connected with monumentalization of the goddess's sanctuary towards the end of the pre-Greek period.[169] A specific link here with Byblos would explain the structural agreement between ps.-Meliton and the *fama recentior* of the Paphian priesthood.

---

[169] See p363.

20

Kinyras At Sidon?
The Strange Affair of Abdalonymos

THIS CHAPTER ADDRESSES A CURIOUS PROBLEM that may entail a further mainland 'Kinyras', this time at Sidon. Abdalonymos—'Servant of the Gods' in Phoenician (Abd-elonim)—was said to be an impoverished member of the Sidonian royal house, installed by Alexander as king of that city in 333–332 after deposing 'Straton' (that is Abdastart III) following the battle of Issos.[1] He is epigraphically attested and appears in several further Alexander episodes.[2] A sarcophagus from the royal necropolis of Sidon, showing a battle-scene in which Alexander is accompanied by a Companion in Persian dress, is usually thought to have been dedicated by him, or to contain his remains.[3] How long he reigned is unknown, but he will have been deposed by one of Alexander's successors before the end of the fourth century.[4]

Despite his realness, however, our accounts of Abdalonymos' promotion have a fablelike quality, tending towards the moral that kings owe their position to Chance, and keep it by Virtue. The basic story must go back to Kleitarkhos, the early and colorful Alexander-historian who favored reversals-of-fortune.[5] It is told, with cosmetic variations, by Plutarch and the so-called vulgate authors who followed Kleitarkhos—Curtius Rufus, Diodoros Siculus, and Justin in his

---

[1] See generally Lane Fox 1980:184; Green 1991:246; Heckel and Yardley 1997:143. Clearly the variant forms Balonymos (Diodoros), Aralynomos or Alynomos (Plutarch), and Abdellonymos (Pollux *Onomastikon* 6.105) result from textual corruption (cf. Hammond 1983:119), as well perhaps as variations in rendering the Phoenician name. The etymology of 'Alynomus' attempted by Ribichini 1982:496n67 is thus unnecessary.
[2] See Lane Fox 1980:184.
[3] Grainger 1991:61–62; Palagia 2000:188–189, plausibly noting that Abdalonymos, as a parvenu, would have had good reason to portray himself at Alexander's side. But for a new reading of the monument, see Heckel 2006.
[4] Grainger 1991:61–62; Palagia 2000:186.
[5] Hammond 1983:43, 113, 119.

epitome of Pompeius Trogus.⁶ Curtius Rufus and Justin correctly place the events at Sidon, an agreement that indicates that this was true of Kleitarkhos too. Diodoros moves the tale to Tyre—perhaps for reasons of dramatic pacing—but his identification of the deposed king as Straton betrays Sidon as the original location.⁷

Unexpectedly, however, Plutarch transfers the tale to Paphos, and applies it there to the last of the Kinyradai. This concise version, which otherwise contains all essential features, may be quoted in full:

> And again in Paphos, when the reigning king was clearly unjust and wicked, Alexander cast him out and began seeking for an alternative, since the race of the Kinyradai seemed to be waning and giving out. But there was one, after all, who they said still survived—an obscure pauper of a man, maintaining himself carelessly in some garden.⁸ Those who had been sent for him arrived, and he was found drawing water for his garden beds. He was really shocked as the soldiers laid hold of him and ordered him to march. And when he had been brought in his cheap garments to Alexander, he was proclaimed king and assumed the royal purple, and became one of the so-called Companions. His name was Abdalonymos.⁹

Some scholars have suspected the influence of Persian or other ANE folktale patterns, a rags-to-riches kingship along the lines of Sargon, Moses, David, or Cyrus the Great.¹⁰ One may also see the imprint of Hellenistic moral philosophy,¹¹ especially in the version of Curtius Rufus, where Abdalonymos recalls the old man of Vergil's *Georgics*—a natural Epicurean whose well-tended garden makes

---

6 Diodoros Siculus 17.47.1–6; Curtius Rufus 4.1.16–26; Plutarch *Moralia* 340c–e; Justin *Epitome* 11.10.8–9.
7 Hammond 1983:43; Grainger 1991:34.
8 Diodoros includes the colorful touch that Abdalonymos was working as a hired laborer: ἔλαβεν αὐτὸν ἔν τινι κήπῳ μισθοῦ μὲν ἀντλοῦντα (17.47.4).
9 Plutarch *Moralia* 340c–d: πάλιν ἐν Πάφῳ, τοῦ βασιλεύοντος ἀδίκου καὶ πονηροῦ φανέντος, ἐκβαλὼν τοῦτον Ἀλέξανδρος ἕτερον ἐζήτει, τοῦ Κινυραδῶν γένους ἤδη φθίνειν καὶ ἀπολείπειν δοκοῦντος. ἕνα δ' οὖν ἔφασαν περιεῖναι πένητα καὶ ἄδοξον ἄνθρωπον ἐν κήπῳ τινὶ παρημελημένως διατρεφόμενον. ἐπὶ τοῦτον οἱ πεμφθέντες ἧκον, εὑρέθη δὲ πρασιαῖς ὕδωρ ἐπαντλῶν· καὶ διεταράχθη τῶν στρατιωτῶν ἐπιλαμβανομένων αὐτοῦ καὶ βαδίζειν κελευόντων. ἀχθεὶς δὲ πρὸς Ἀλέξανδρον ἐν εὐτελεῖ σινδονίσκῃ βασιλεὺς ἀνηγορεύθη καὶ πορφύραν ἔλαβε καὶ εἰς ἣν τῶν ἑταίρων προσαγορευομένων· ἐκαλεῖτο δ' Ἀβδαλώνυμος. For the corrupt variants of his name, see n1.
10 Lane Fox 1980:184; Hammond 1983:43.
11 Cf. Hammond 1983:119.

him more fortunate than a king. Abdalonymos' poverty is due to his essential probity; he goes about his work blissfully ignorant of the events rocking Asia.¹²

According to the more detailed accounts of Curtus Rufius and Diodoros, Alexander bade Hephaistion recruit a suitable replacement for Straton. When Hephaistion offered the position to a guest-friend (or two), it was declined on the grounds that the appointment should be made from the royal stock; Abdalonymos was then put forward. All accounts focus on his surprise at being suddenly seized, clad in royal purple, and enthroned, before becoming a favorite in Alexander's Companions. A genuine member of the royal house may well have been necessary to secure public goodwill and cultic approval; and a relatively disempowered scion would make a more reliable client-king.¹³

But how on earth did this tale become connected with Paphos and the Kinyradai?¹⁴ Plutarch himself may not be responsible for the error. In treating Alexander, he often relied on the various fabricated documents (letters, diary) that in later Hellenistic times filled public appetite for new or better information about the great conqueror.¹⁵ This complex process would provide ample opportunity for the development of a spurious moralizing anecdote. Still, the tale's attachment to Paphos cannot have been random, and calls for some explanation.

Alexander is not known to have set foot on Cyprus personally. All the Cypriot kings, going over to Alexander after Issos and contributing ships for the siege of Tyre, were indemnified for having served the Persians under compulsion.¹⁶ A famous catastrophe was already on record for Nikokles and the whole royal family in 310/309 after Alexander's death.¹⁷ But the ancient controversy about whether the disaster befell Nikokles of Paphos or Nikokreon of Salamis arose

---

[12] Curtius Rufus 4.1: *Causa ei paupertatis sicut plerisque probitas erat. Intentusque operi diurno strepitum armorum, qui totam Asiam concusserat, non exaudiebat.*

[13] Scholars have attempted various historical explanations. For Lane Fox 1980:382, Abdalonymos' insulation from the decadence of the court made him a kindred spirit to Alexander ("just the oriental to see something congenial in Asia's new and unexpected king"). Green 1991:246 sees a calculated dramatic move designed to establish an unfailingly loyal client-king. Grainger 1991:34 suggests that Abdalonymos was purposefully excluded from the court by his royal relations, and even from the city limits.

[14] The Paphian version was accepted as factual by Frazer 1914 1:42–43; Ribichini 1982:496. While HC:152 rightly saw it as fabulous, that cannot completely discredit the historicity of the Sidonian version (see below). NPHP:26, though considering it a myth, gives credence to Paphos as the proper locale since the decadence of the Paphian kings became a topos in the fourth century: see Athenaios 255c–257d, who cites both Antiphanes fr. 200 PCG and Klearkhos of Soloi fr. 19 Wehrli; cf. *Paphos*:205.

[15] See e.g. Powell 1939; Pearson 1955.

[16] Arrian *Anabasis of Alexander* 2.20.3.

[17] Diodoros Siculus 20.21.2–3; Polyainos *Stratagems* 8.48. For this episode's rightful location at Paphos, see p416n95.

very early, being reflected already in the *Parian Marble* (inscribed in 264/263).[18] The transfer of the conflagration to Salamis may have left a vacuum in some minds as to what became of the famous Kinyradai at Paphos. But why should the particular tale of Abdalonymos have filled this gap? One would hardly expect a member of the Paphian royal house to have a good Phoenician name.[19]

An alternative hypothesis should therefore be contemplated—that Kleitarkhos connected the Sidonian royal house to 'Kinyras', using the name as the most appropriate 'Greek' gloss for the city's dynastic ancestor. This is made quite possible in principle by the evidence for Kinyras at Byblos (Chapter 19). H. Lewy boldly suggested long ago, without reference to the present problem, that Agenor, the mythical king of Sidon whose son Kadmos pursued Europa westwards, was a linguistic doublet of Kinyras.[20] While 'Agenor' does have a clear Greek etymology ('very manly'), one might plead folk remodeling. Also worth noting are Kadmos' association with the lyre, and his well-toned wife Harmonia.[21] An appropriate Sidonian royal cult is also ready to hand: the Astarte whose name was piously born by Straton/Abdastart and his predecessors, who served as her priests—a distinctly Kinyras-like role.[22] As it happens, Kleitarkhos also discussed the tale of Myrrha, presumably in connection with Alexander's Phoenician campaign.[23] Although he followed Panyassis in making her father Theias and locating the myth at Byblos,[24] this would be understandable if he connected Kinyras rather with Sidon in explicating the affair of Abdalonymos.

---

[18] *Parian Marble* B 17 (FGH 239).

[19] While Greek and Phoenician royal names alike appear at Lapethos (p339, 510), the explanation for them remains open; and the known Paphian royal names are all Greek.

[20] Lewy 1895:226. Astour 1965:139n5, though agnostic on this point, nevertheless (p. 308) interpreted Kynortas—one of the pre-Dorian kings of Sparta, brother of Hyakinthos (Pausanias 3.1.3; [Apollodoros] *Library* 1.9.5, 3.10.3)—as '*knr*-player'; and even connected Kynortion and Myrtion, the names of two peaks above the sanctuary of Asklepios at Epidauros (Pausanias 2.27.7), with Kinyras and Myrrha. Both ideas, though approved by Dugand 1973:200–202, are highly doubtful.

[21] Nonnos has him pretend to have surpassed Apollo on the instrument; his alleged punishment is not the usual death, but the breaking of his strings (*Dionysiaka* 1.485–505), and he is rewarded with marriage to Harmonia, herself with lyric associations (2.663–666). For Harmonia, see Franklin 2006a:55 and n42; but note that I no longer hold to my interpretation there of [Nikomakhos] *Excerpts* 1 (MSG:266): instead of Ἀχαιοὺς δὲ ὑπὸ Κάδμου τοῦ Ἀγήνορος παραλαβεῖν (suggested by R. Janko), I would revert to Jan's ὑπὸ Κάδμον in MSG. In other words, the Achaeans did not receive the lyre 'from Kadmos' (which would contradict the passage's earlier assertion that Orpheus first received it from Hermes), but 'in the time of Kadmos' (a sign that the passage comes from an early chronographic source, perhaps Hellanikos: see for now Franklin 2003:302n12; Franklin 2012:747).

[22] See p407n45.

[23] Kleitarkhos FGH 137 F 3 (= Stobaios *Anthology* 40.20.73) with Jacoby in RE 11 (1922), 638. Cf. p284.

[24] See p284.

Kinyras at Sidon?

Another line of evidence that may be relevant relates to Euagoras I and the self-styled Kinyrad dynasty of Salamis.²⁵ At the height of his power, Euagoras controlled Tyre and several other Phoenician cities.²⁶ I have argued that his Kinyrad posture was meant to have broad appeal on Cyprus, including to its Phoenician communities; if so, it could have availed equally well in his mainland possessions.²⁷ His son or grandson, Euagoras II, was expelled from Salamis, probably during the revolt against Persia in 351. Persian support for his restoration there was eventually undermined by court slander, but Diodoros tells us that he was assigned a mainland kingdom, and good numismatic evidence indicates that this was precisely Sidon. Ruling poorly for only a few years (ca. 344–341), he was compelled to flee; it is not clear whether he alienated his own citizens, crossed the Persians, or both. He was succeeded there by Straton who ruled for about ten years before being put down by Alexander.²⁸ Meanwhile, Pnytagoras, apparently grandson of Euagoras I, had followed Euagoras II at Salamis; he was among the Cypriot kings who sailed into Sidon with 120 ships for Alexander's expedition against Tyre.²⁹ Could Alexander have agreed to reestablish the Salaminian dynasty in the city? In this case, 'Abdalonymos' might be seen as a throne-name designed to present a native aspect, and his humble origin a means of obscuring the scheme.

A Sidonian Kinyras, in any form, would provide a ready stimulus for the displacement of the tale to Paphos, with which most Aegean Greeks will have associated *the* Kinyras. When the story's rags-to-riches appeal gave it a popular life of its own, it would gladly wander from Sidon and come to its more obvious home, whose last kings, rightly or wrongly, were as famed for decadent power as Straton himself.³⁰ The moral thrust of the story presupposes an essential enduring righteousness of the royal line, when not corrupted by despotism and luxury, which is quite in tune with the virtuous Kinyras examined in Chapter 13. On this point, at least, Kinyras is a plausible prior cause for the story in any of its forms.³¹

---

²⁵ See p346–347, 351–359.
²⁶ Diodoros Siculus 15.2.4; HC:135–136; cf. p347.
²⁷ See p535–359.
²⁸ Diodoros Siculus 16.46.3; HC:146–147 and n3.
²⁹ Arrian *Anabasis of Alexander* 2.20.3. For Pnytagoras' relationship to Euagoras, see HC:143n3.
³⁰ See n14 above.
³¹ Cf. Ribichini 1982:496: "La distinzione tra il prestigio del ricchissimo sovrano 'del tempo del mito', e la miseria del timido e povero suo discendente 'dei tempi reali' non poteva essere più chiaramente delineata."

21
Syro-Cilician Approaches

KINNARU OF UGARIT, I have argued, was probably but one regional manifestation of a more widespread pattern. Kinnaru himself, of course, belongs to a Syrian milieu. We also saw that material from the Hurrian sphere, stretching across Syria and into Cilicia/Kizzuwatna, documents both its second-millennium *kinnāru*-culture, and divinization of cult tools and objects (see Chapter 6).

This background can help explain the curious oracular statue, enrobed and bearded, which Lucian saw beside the throne of 'Helios' at Hierapolis/Manbog.[1] This was presented to him as 'Apollo', but Lucian emphasizes its departure from typical Greek representations; the priests maintained that it was undignified to portray the god as a youth (an imperfect state).[2] One thinks of the bearded 'Apollo' who, seated or enthroned, plays an asymmetrical *knr*-type lyre on two fourth-century (Persian-era) Samarian coins.[3] Other Syrians will have regarded the Hierapolitan 'Apollo' as Nabu, the Babylonian scribe-god and son of Marduk whose cult flourished especially in the Neo-Babylonian period (626–539).[4] Nabu's identification with Apollo was promoted especially by the Seleucids, harmonizing the former's importance in the Babylonian royal cult with their own alleged descent from the Olympian.[5] Ps.-Meliton confirms that Hierapolitan 'Apollo' could indeed be called Nabu in Lucian's time; yet this very passage—described by F. Millar as "a salutary warning as to the impossibility of arriving at a 'true' definition of the nature of Near Eastern deities"[6]—simultaneously reveals that 'Nabu' itself was not a fully satisfactory label to the priests:

---

[1] See p462.
[2] Lucian *On the Syrian Goddess* 35–37.
[3] See Figure 5.1jj above; DCPIL:45 and fig. 1jj with references; SAM:118 no. 78.
[4] See generally Pomponio 1978; RlA 9:16–29 (Seidl and Pomponio *Nabû A and B).
[5] Dirven 1999:130–131; OSG:456–466; Bounni 1981:108; Erickson 2011:57–59.
[6] Millar 1994:243.

Chapter Twenty-One

> But touching Nebo, which is in Mabug, why should I write to you; for, lo! all the priests which are in Mabug know that it is the image of Orpheus, a Thracian Magus.[7]

When Lucian's 'Apollo' and ps.-Meliton's 'Orpheus' are read together, it becomes clear that the Hierapolitan god was depicted *as a lyre-player*.[8] Such a Nabu is corroborated by explicitly labeled representations from Palmyra and Dura Europos, which, while sometimes exhibiting iconographical influence of Apollo *kitharōidós*, equally contain many native Syrian elements, including instrument morphology.[9] Some are qualified as *Nbw qnyt*, which scholars have variously interpreted as 'Association of Nabu', 'Nabu the Citharode', or 'Nabu's Lamentation'.[10] And yet, though 'Nabu the lyrist' was clearly a popular conception in the region, this appears to be a local innovation, as Babylonian sources do not obviously connect Nabu with music, much less the lyre.[11] The problem needs further investigation,[12] but preliminarily it would seem that, in parts of Roman Syria, Nabu absorbed an indigenous, oracular, lyre-playing god; his name was displaced or forgotten, and he could be variously calqued as Apollo or Orpheus. This must be the same figure whom the Sabians of Harran venerated as the prophet 'Orâfî' (< Orpheus).[13]

In what follows, I shall argue that Syrian and Syro-Hurrian *kinnāru* culture has also left its imprint on several mythological traditions tracing Kinyras to North Syria and Cilicia. These complement, rather than contradict, Kinyras' Byblian, and perhaps Sidonian, connections discussed in Chapters 19 and 20. And whereas with Byblos one must question whether Kinyras was a secondary accretion through his association with Adonis, the present material makes Adonis himself seem ancillary. While the geographical orientation of these sources is

---

[7] Ps.-Meliton *Apology* 44.34–36, trans. after Cureton 1855.
[8] Dirven 1999:130n17; OSG:456–457; Lightfoot 2004:99 and n174 ("The discovery of representations of Nebo in the form of Apollo Citharoedus has borne out Clermont-Ganneau's conjecture that the god's identification as Orpheus is most probably visual, and rests on the image of a god wielding a lyre"; cf. Clermont-Ganneau 1885–1907 3:212–216, "Orphée-Nébo à Mabboug et Apollon"). For the apparently incompatible description by Macrobius *Saturnalia* 1.17.66–68, see Bounni 1981:11 with references.
[9] Baur and Rostovtzeff 1929–1952 7/8:266; Ingholt et al. 1955 no. 237, 301–302, 310; Du Mesnil du Buisson 1962:230, 285–287 and fig. 176, 566–567; Pomponio 1979:228; Bounni 1981 pl. II.2–3, III.1–2; Dirven 1999:128 and pl. VII.
[10] See Ingholt et al. 1955:43 ('Association of Nabu'); Milik 1972:159–160 ('Nabu the Citharode'); Du Mesnil du Buisson 1962:286 ('La lamentation de Nébô', proposing a connection with Nabu's laments for Marduk in Babylonia ("allusion à un rite des fêtes de Nîsan"), 567.
[11] Cf. Pomponio 1978:226–228, 230.
[12] Cf. Lightfoot 2004:76, 78–79, 98–105.
[13] Chwolsohn 1856 1:780, 800–801.

unambiguous overall, they present many puzzles, often insoluble. It is all the more welcome, therefore, that Cilicia has produced our most compelling iconographic evidence for a Divine Lyre—the so-called Lyre-Player Group of Seals, an analysis of which will appropriately conclude this study.

We have already seen one oblique link between Kinyras and Cilicia in the Tamiradai, the obsolete priestly order that yielded divination rights to the Kinyradai of Paphos.[14] Another connection is offered by an elegiac couplet in the *Greek Anthology*:

> All Cilicians are bad men. But among the Cilicians is
> One good man, Kinyras—though Kinyras too is Cilician.[15]

These verses, traditionally assigned to Demodokos of Leros (late sixth century BCE), are now considered a post-Archaic, slavish imitation of the poet's two authentic fragments.[16] Those are very close in structure and thought, but feature Milesians and Lerians instead of Cilicians.[17] This makes it uncertain whether Kinyras appears here for any special legendary associations with the region, or has just been plugged into the formula as a handy PN. The couplet does at least suggest the currency of the PN in Cilicia, and may well relate to the 'Virtuous Kinyras' discussed in Chapter 13.

More revealing evidence comes from two mythographic passages that share a basic framework, beginning with a descent from the Athenian hero Kephalos and leading to Kinyras' marriage with Pygmalion's daughter on Cyprus. The Kephalid genealogy is managed quite differently in each text, with the integration of disparate epichoric material presenting many interpretive challenges. But the unique names of Pygmalion's daughter (Metharme or Thymarete, obviously variants) and Oxyporos, her son with Kinyras, show that this much of the two constructions is cognate; and that in turn permits a degree of comparative analysis that implicates a third text, bearing on what may be called the Egyptian Detour.

The origin of these Kephalid genealogies is obscure and probably complex. The presence of Kephalos himself, however, presumably originates in fifth-century Athenian political interests in Cyprus and Cilicia, perhaps finding mythographic expression in one or more Atthidographers.[18] We have already

---

[14] See p402–406.
[15] *Greek Anthology* 11.236 [Demodokos] = fr. 3 PLG/IEG: Πάντες μὲν Κίλικες κακοὶ ἀνέρες· ἐν δὲ Κίλιξιν / εἷς ἀγαθὸς Κινύρης, καὶ Κινύρης δὲ Κίλιξ.
[16] See PLG 2:67; FGE:39–40. West points out that καὶ ... δέ is post-Archaic usage.
[17] Demodokos fr. 1–2, especially 2 (καὶ τόδε Δημοδόκου. Λέριοι κακοί· οὐχ ὁ μέν, ὃς δ' οὔ· / πάντες, πλὴν Προκλέους—καὶ Προκλέης Λέριος).
[18] See p355–356 and n113.

seen that other Athenocentric myths were linked to Akamas, Soloi, and Khytroi, and pondered how Euagoras of Salamis may have profited from an 'Athenian Kinyras'.[19] So I shall concentrate here rather on what happens in the genealogies *after* Kephalos.

Aoios and Paphos:
Two Cilician Crossings

The first passage is a scholion attached to a verse of Dionysios the Periegete's *Description of the World* (second century CE), where Cyprus is described as "the lovely land of Aphrodite, daughter of Dione."[20] At first sight, the scholiast's comments seem rather gratuitous:

> Hyon the Egyptian settled this [island] when it was called Kerastis ['Horned']²¹—Hyon whose son Kettes died with no male heir (*ápais*).²² But Kephalos, son of Pandion and Herse, settling in Asia, did have sons—Aoios and Paphos. The latter, crossing to Cyprus, founded the city named after him, and begot Kinyras; Kinyras held sway over the island alongside Pygmalion, whose daughter Thymarete he married, and begot Oxyporos and Adonis; after Adonis died at the tusks of a boar, [Kinyras] put it about that he had been abducted by Aphrodite, and sent him off to be buried at Byblos in Phoenicia, beside the river which is called Adonis.²³

We shall leave aside for now the introductory Egyptian myth, its possible relationship to what follows, and the marriage into Pygmalion's family—these

---

[19] See p340–341.
[20] Dionysios the Periegete 508–509: Κύπρος ... ἐπήρατος αἶα Διωναίης Ἀφροδίτης. The *v.l.* ἄστυ (for αἶα), appearing in the scholia, Eustathios' commentary, and many MSS, can be applied to islands in epic diction; αἶα is thus generally favored as *difficilor lectio* (retained by Lightfoot 2014). In any case, αὐτήν shows that the scholiast's comments apply to the whole island. But note that Ovid (*Metamorphoses* 10.220–237) locates his Cerastae at Amathous specifically (see below).
[21] Κεραστία is usual (see p516 below), but for Κεραστίς cf. Nonnos *Dionysiaka* 5.614, 13.441, 29.372. For the meaning, see p135.
[22] For this sense of ἄπαις, cf. LSJ s.v. For its significance in the present myth, see below. Note that both 'Hyon' and 'Kettes' are emendations (of υἱός and Κέλτης, respectively) based on the parallel in Servius Auctus on Vergil *Eclogues* 10.18: see further below.
[23] Σ Dionysios the Periegete 509 (GGM 2:450) = FGH 758 F 3a: Κεραστὶν αὐτὴν καλουμένην ᾤκισεν Ὕων Αἰγύπτιος, οὗ υἱὸς Κέττης ἄπαις τελευτᾷ. Κέφαλος δὲ ὁ Πανδίονος καὶ Ἕρσης εἰς τὴν Ἀσίαν οἰκῶν ἔσχε παῖδας Ἀῷον καὶ Πάφον, ὃς διαβὰς εἰς αὐτὴν πόλιν κτίζει Πάφον, οὗ υἱὸς Κινύρας προσέσχε τὴν νῆσον καὶ Πυγμαλίων Φοίνιξ, οὗ θυγατέρα Θυμαρέτην γαμεῖ Κινύρας, καὶ ποιεῖ Ὀξύπορον καὶ Ἄδωνιν, ὃν ὑπὸ συὸς ἀποθανόντα λέγει ἔπεισεν ὡς ἥρπασται ὑπὸ Ἀφροδίτης, καὶ πέμψας ἔθαψεν ἐν Βύβλῳ τῆς Φοινίκης παρὰ ποταμόν, ὃς Ἄδωνις καλεῖται.

discussions require supplementary material from the second passage—and begin by examining Aoios and Paphos. Presumably their mother is to be understood as Eos, the Dawn goddess, well known for her loving abductions of beautiful mortals, including Kephalos. But the abduction motif itself has evidently been suppressed. This is suggested both by Kephalos' 'settling in' (*oikôn*) Asia—potentially embracing Syria or even wider horizons, although a special connection with Cilicia will emerge below—and the euhemerizing version of Adonis' death, which treats tales of divine abduction as deliberate falsehoods and misunderstandings. This may also be why Pandion features here as Kephalos' father, not Hermes (as in the second passage to be considered).[24]

As to 'Paphos', this is only one of several genealogical constructions connecting Kinyras to the city of that name. A Pindaric scholion makes Kinyras' parents Eurymedon and a Paphian nymph (or the 'nymph Paphia').[25] Eurymedon, if it is not a speaking-name,[26] could indicate autochthonous connections with southern Anatolia, as there was a Pamphylian river so called, and a region near Tarsus in Cilicia.[27] If this is the right approach, it would imply some crossing to Cyprus, either by Kinyras or Eurymedon himself, since the nymph-bride suggests a local Paphian birth (for both her and her son). An alternative Paphian mother is probably to be found in the 'Paphos' whom Ovid makes the offspring of Pygmalion and his ivory beloved. Although this child's gender is obscured by variant readings, a female Paphos is more likely on our current understanding of the textual tradition.[28] A male interpretation is found in Medieval mythographers like Theodontius and Boccaccio, who not unreasonably assumed that Ovid intended a dynastic sequence Pygmalion > Paphos > Kinyras (see Appendix F, G). And, indeed, a *father* Paphos was evidently the norm. Besides the Dionysian scholion—obviously independent of Ovid—Paphos is probably given as Kinyras' father by another Pindaric scholion.[29] Then there is an early third-century CE papyrus of 'Greek Questions', in which Paphos, unambiguously male, is called *mētropoleítēs*, citizen of the 'mother city'—a designation Paphos enjoyed *vis-à-vis* the rest of Cyprus in the Roman period.[30] Clearly the question assumed

---

[24] But the variant was itself traditional: a fifth-century vase by Douris shows Eos pursuing Kephalos as Pandion stands by (Getty Museum 84.AE.569, noted by Gantz 1993 1:238).
[25] Σ Pindar *Pythian* 2.28: υἱὸς δὲ Εὐρυμέδοντος καὶ Παφίας νύμφης. Remember that 'Paphia' is a title of the goddess herself.
[26] See p333.
[27] Stephanos of Byzantium s.v. Εὐρυμέδων· ποταμὸς Παμφυλίας καὶ τόπος κατὰ Ταρσόν. Cf. Engel 1841 2:124; Baurain 1980a:280n13.
[28] Ovid *Metamorphoses* 10.297–298: see comments of Bömer 1969–1986 *ad loc*. The issue hinges on *de quo* versus *de qua* in 297, and *hac* in 298.
[29] Σ Pindar *Pythian* 2.27a: ἦν δὲ οὗτος Ἀπόλλωνος υἱός, ἢ Πάφου κατὰ ἐνίους.
[30] *Pap.Oxy*. 2688 lines 4–13, with Π]άφου τοῦ μητροπολείτ[ου υἱός in 6, where υἱός ('son'), if correct, will refer to Kinyras (see below). The unusual sense of μητροπολείτης here is clarified by the

that Paphos himself founded the city. If the text has been rightly supplemented with a reference to his son, it attests an otherwise unknown episode in which Kinyras steals something from Aphrodite and takes it to his house; the goddess comes, sees it in his hand, and seduces him in mortal guise. This explained some Paphian cult-practice involving "garlands of roses." Adonis' metamorphosis into the rose (through his blood) was presumably a parallel aition.[31]

Returning to the passage at hand, the scholiast tells us nothing about Aoios, and one wonders if this was true in his source; for this obscure and remarkable figure is something of a doublet to Paphos, and quite probably older. It is, after all, not Paphos, but Aoios, whose name means 'He of the Dawn' or 'The Eastern One' (< Gk. aṓs/ēṓs),[32] that is the more natural son of Eos. By a lucky chance, two ancient lexica preserve crucial material collated by some benevolent scholar of refined tastes.[33] Here we learn that Aoios was made son of Kephalos and Eos by the early Athenian geographer Phileas (fl. ca. 425–400), who further stated that Aoios was the first king of Cyprus and gave his name to a mountain there, from which ran two rivers, the Setrakhos (or Satrakhos) and the Aplieus.[34] Presumably, the idea that Aoios was an old name for Adonis, and that the Cypriot kings were his descendants, also goes back to Phileas.

The lexicographer went on to note an allusion by Parthenios (first century BCE), who called the Setrakhos 'Aoios' with reference to the river of this name that ran underground at the Corycian Cave in Rough Cilicia, where Typhon was supposed to be buried.[35] Evidently, Parthenios had the Cilician Aoios resurface on Cyprus, and he probably made this the meeting place of Aphrodite

---

intercolumnar Σ to *Pap.Oxy.* 3000: ἡ νῆσος Κύπρος, ἡ μητρόπολις Πάφος, lines 1–3 (see note of Parsons/Lloyd-Jones *ad loc.*; for this text, see further below). The editor tentatively suggests Aristotle's *Constitution of the Cypriots* as a source for the story (Aristotle fr. 526–527 Rose). For Paphos = Cyprus, Servius/Servius Auctus on Vergil *Georgics* 2.64 (*Papho insula*); for this usage of Roman provincial capitals, OCD s.v. *mētropolis* (b).

[31] Bion *Lament for Adonis* 65–66; Servius Auctus on Vergil *Eclogues* 10.18.
[32] See Chantraine 1968 s.v. ἕως; Lightfoot 1999:184.
[33] *Etymologicum Genuinum* s.v. Ἄῳος and *Etymologicum Magnum* s.v. Ἄῳος (sic), which may be amalgamated here after Lightfoot 1999:118 (Parthenios fr. 29, q.v. for textual variants; cf. SH 641): Ἄῳος· Ποταμὸς τῆς Κύπρου. Ἄῳος γὰρ ὁ Ἄδωνις ὠνομάζετο, καὶ ἀπ' αὐτοῦ οἱ Κύπρου βασιλεύσαντες. Ζωΐλος δὲ ὁ Κεδρασεὺς (v. *infra* n48) καὶ αὐτὸν ἀπὸ τῆς ἑαυτοῦ μητρὸς κληθῆναι· τὴν γὰρ Θείαντος θυγατέρα οὐ Σμύρναν ἀλλ' Ἄῳαν καλεῖσθαι (v.l. καλοῦσι). Φιλέας δὲ πρῶτον βασιλέα Ἄῳον, Ἠοῦς ὄντα καὶ Κεφάλου, ἀφ' οὗ καὶ ὄρος τι ὠνομάσθη Ἀῴϊον· ἐξ οὗ β′ ποταμῶν φερομένων, Σε<τ>ράχου καὶ Ἀπλιέως, τὸν ἕνα τούτων ὁ Παρθένιος Ἄῳον κέκληκεν ἢ διὰ τὸ πρὸς τὴν ἠῶ τετραμμένην ἔχειν τὴν ῥύσιν, καθώς φησιν ὁ Παρθένιος· Κωρυκίων σεύμενος ἐξ ὀρέων, ἀνατολικῶν ὄντων· δύναται δὲ οὕτως καλεῖσθαι, καθ' ὃ ἡ Κιλικία Ἄῳα πάλαι ὠνομάζετο.
[34] For Phileas, see Gisinger in RE 19 (1938), 2133–2136 (6).
[35] Parthenios fr. 29 Lightfoot.

and Adonis (to judge from what must be an allusion in Nonnos).³⁶ Lightfoot's conclusion that Parthenios was "offering a learned etymology" for the Cypriot river is inherently plausible; but the parallels she assembles for underground rivers—the Nile was thought to surface at Paphos, and it was foretold that the Pyramus, also in Cilicia, would one day come forth on the island—show that the poet was working with multiform folk-beliefs. This best explains why "Paphian Zeus" was invoked in an epigram (ca. 150-200 CE) commemorating the dedication of Pan and Hermes statues at the Corycian Cave itself, "where the Aoios flees in its invisible channels."³⁷ These verses, despite their later date, are hardly dependent on Parthenios, but an independent sample of the traditions on which Parthenios himself drew.

The epigram's invocation of Paphian Zeus; the conjunction of mountain and river in Cilicia and Cyprus alike; the naming of the Cypriot peak Aoios (or Aoion), 'Son of the Dawn' or 'The Eastern One', source of Cypriot kingship—all of this recalls the Levantine and Anatolian association of mountain peaks with a storm god who functions as royal patron, whom the king serves as high-priest.³⁸ Here we see the force of Aoios' equation with Adonis, a parallel manifestation of the same pattern—notwithstanding the latter's special connections to Byblos and Mount Lebanon, and the distinctive myths the Greeks developed about him.³⁹ Within Anatolia itself, note for instance the image of the Hittite King Tudhaliya IV (ca. 1245-1215) at the rock-sanctuary of Yazılıkaya, shown bestriding a pair of peaks, "probably indicating his association with the divine mountain from which he had taken his name"; in the procession of gods there, "the Sun-god is dressed exactly like the monarch ... only the presence of the winged disk above his head distinguishes the deity from the king."⁴⁰

It may be relevant that Cypriot folk-tradition identifies a 'Baths of Aphrodite' on the north side of the Akamas peninsula, where Anatolia first comes into view when going north from Paphos. At this *locus amoenus*, it is said, the goddess met Adonis (much as in Nonnos).⁴¹ Stavros Papageorghiou recalls a conversation in the early 1970s between some villagers—one may have been a douser—who were discussing how to find waters for irrigation. Some claimed that "rivers from Turkey run under Cyprus and this would solve the water problem in the island

---

36 Nonnos *Dionysiaka* 13.456-460. For sources and discussion, including the 'Satrachus' as it resurfaced in Catullus and probably Cinna (cf. p286n38 above), see Meineke 1843:279-282; Hicks 1891:240-242; Leigh 1994; Lightfoot 1999:181-185.
37 Hicks 1891:240-242 no. 24.2-3: ἐν γαίης βένθεσιν ... / ... ὅθ᾽ Ἀῶος (sic) ἀφενγέσι ῥεύμασι φεύγει.
38 Cf. p465.
39 For Adonis and Mount Kasios, see p465, 514.
40 Beckman 2002b:18.
41 For the spot, and ancient references to 'baths' of the goddess, see *Kypris*:72-73.

permanently."⁴² I do not know that this is said of the Baths of Aphrodite—it may be—but this need not be the ancient Setrakhos for the parallel to be significant. Still, it is worth emphasizing that, while Nonnos does *connect* the Setrakhos with Paphos (whence modern scholars tentatively identify it with the Diarrhizos at Kouklia⁴³), the poet's Cypriot geography is otherwise quite loose; and in the present case he very possibly relied on Parthenios himself.⁴⁴ For either poet, a vague 'Paphos' may have sufficed for such an Aphrodite-scene. And the Baths *are* comfortably within Paphian horizons: remember that nearby Marion was traced back to Marieus, son of Kinyras.⁴⁵

However Parthenios may have manipulated the material, it is certain that 'Aoios' is an old name in the region, being attested in various dialect forms and with special connections to southern Anatolia and Cyprus. It is found as *Abṓbas* at Perga in Pamphylia, and perhaps Ao and Gauas in Cyprus.⁴⁶ The identification with Adonis was made by the fifth century; besides Phileas, we know that Panyassis (ca. 470) called Adonis *Ēoíēs* in treating the tale of 'Assyrian' Theias and Smyrna (located at Byblos).⁴⁷ A certain Zoïlos, probably from Cedasa south of Tyre,⁴⁸ presumably had Panyassis in mind when he says that Aoios himself "was so called from his own mother; for the daughter of Theias was named not Smyrna but Aoia."⁴⁹ The entry in Hesykhios for *aoîa*, defined as "trees cut and dedicated to Aphrodite by the [temple] entrances, as Hegesandros (?) reports," must also be relevant.⁵⁰ Bearing in mind the artificial, Hellenocentric nature of

---

42 Communication, July 25–26, 2014. He continues: "The whole thing excited my fantasy ... I still remember a dream I saw when I was sixteen ... entering a kind of a cave ... wandering in an underground world by car where rivers were running everywhere. My dad who was driving told me that all these rivers come from Turkey." The conversation took place in Psimolophou, near Nicosia.
43 HC:7–8.
44 Cf. Lightfoot 1999:183.
45 Stephanos of Byzantium s.v. Μάριον.
46 Hesykhios s.v. Ἀβώβας· ὁ Ἄδωνις ὑπὸ Περγαίων. For Gauas, cf. p467n58. See further Meineke 1843:281–282 (comparing Γαύας and Aeolic αὕως, Boeotian ἅας); RE 1 (1894), 2656–2657 s.v. Ao (Dümmler); Lightfoot 1999:184.
47 Hesykhios s.v. Ἠοίην· τὸν Ἄδωνιν, Πανύασις (fr. 25 Kinkel, Matthews = fr. 22c EGF, PEG, to be connected with fr. 22ab EGF = fr. 27 PEG = [Apollodoros] *Library* 3.14.4). For the probable Byblian setting, cf. p467.
48 For this emendation of Κεδρασεύς (n33 above), see RE 10A (1972), 714–715 (13); FGH 758 F 7.
49 See n33. The reading καλεῖσθαι, which I prefer, makes this part of Zoïlos' own comments, and lets us restrict Theias to Byblos, where all other sources place him (see p466–468). The variant καλοῦσι ('they call') could be a gloss by the etymologist himself, but it is then unclear just who called Smyrna this; the Cypriots presumably (Meineke 1843:279), but this raises problems for Theias. Cinna may have alluded to Smyrna as Aoia: *te matutinus flentem conspexit Eous / et flentem paulo vidit post Hesperus idem* (Servius Auctus on Vergil *Georgics* 1.288 = Cinna fr. 6 Courtney FLP).
50 Hesykhios s.v. ἀοῖα; cf. FGH 758 F 9.

Adonis himself,⁵¹ and the Greek etymology of Aoios, it seems likely that Aoios arose during the EIA Aegean diaspora as a Grecophone term for various gods of the Baal type, and/or the kings in whose image Baal was created.

Aoios' most frequent connections are with Cilicia. The area as a whole is said to have been called Aoia (probably poetic),⁵² and Hesykhios tells us that the Cilicians were called Aoioi either from a river which flowed through the area (the Aoios, obviously) or "from Aoios the son of Kephalos."⁵³ This dual entry brings us full circle to the scholiast's Kephalid Aoios, and encourages us to view hero and river as largely the same (like the Adonis river at Byblos). There is an obvious parallel between the Cilician river's resurgence on Cyprus (Parthenios) and the hero's own crossing to the island (clearly implied by the scholiast's location of his birth in 'Asia', on the one hand, and the strong Cypriot connections asserted by Phileas on the other). This deduction is confirmed by a precious, though meager, notice preserved in Isidore of Seville (ca. 600 CE), who mentions an "Aeos (*sic*) son of Typhon" as founder Paphos.⁵⁴ (Boccaccio brought this passage to the attention of King Hugo IV of Cyprus, and noted the conflict with Pygmalion > Paphos in Ovid.⁵⁵) The lucky mention of Typhon guarantees that a *Cilician* Aoios is in view, and connects him precisely to the Corycian Cave. The monster's 'fathering' of a river is paralleled by a Syrian version of the Typhon myth, localized at Antioch: the monster's slaughter by Zeus engendered a river, probably the Orontes.⁵⁶ Phileas is likely to have presented some such Cypriot immigration scenario; for while the geographer clearly treated Aoios' insular associations in some detail, Anatolian matters dominate his other fragments (nearly half).⁵⁷ An immigrant Aoios also seems to have induced textual corruption in one MS of the Dionysian scholia.⁵⁸

Given all this material, it is remarkable that the scholion credits not Aoios, but Paphos, with the passage to Cyprus and the city foundation there. Paphos appears to have displaced his brother, who was nevertheless kept in the family.

---

[51] See p314.
[52] See n33.
[53] Hesykhios s.v. Ἄῳοι· ... Κίλικες ἀπὸ Ἀῴου τοῦ Κεφάλου <ἢ> τοῦ παραρέοντος ποταμοῦ (text: Meineke 1843:281).
[54] Isidore *Origines* 15.1.48: *Aeos Typhonis filius Paphum*, with an obvious emendation (Lightfoot 1999:184).
[55] Boccaccio *Genealogy of the Pagan Gods* 4.23.
[56] Eustathios on Homer *Iliad* 2.780–785: noted by Lightfoot 1999:182.
[57] Phileas fr. 7–12 Gisinger (see n34).
[58] See *ap. crit.* to GGM 2:450 (reading of I, in which Κεραστὶν αὐτὴν καλουμένην is followed by εἰς ἣν Αἰὸς (*sic*) ὁ υἱὸς Αἰγυπτίου ᾤκησεν. This corruption was doubtless stimulated by Aoios in line 35; but its specific form (εἰς ἥν) implies some definite idea about the deeds of 'Αἰός'; emendation to Ἀῷος is again easy, but note the form's potential relevance to Isidore, whose *Aeos* should go back ultimately to a (the same?) corrupt Greek text.

Chapter Twenty-One

Solar Gods, Sandokos, and the Syrian Descent

Kinyras' second Kephalid genealogy is a much more elaborate construction found in ps.-Apollodoros, who duly placed it among his Athenian legends—though otherwise the material is startlingly unorthodox:

> The son of Herse and Hermes was Kephalos, whom Eos fell in love with and abducted. Sleeping with him in Syria, she gave birth to a son, Tithonos, whose son was Phaethon. *His* son was Astynoos, and Astynoos' son was Sandokos. Sandokos went out from Syria into Cilicia and founded the city of Kelenderis, and marrying Pharnake[59] the daughter of Megassares, the king of Hyria, he begot Kinyras. Kinyras, arriving with a host, founded Paphos in Cyprus, and marrying there Metharme, daughter of Pygmalion king of the Cypriots, begot Oxyporos and Adonis, and besides these his daughters Orsedike and Laogore and Braisia. But these, sleeping with foreign men through the anger of Aphrodite, ended their lives in Egypt. And Adonis, while still a youth, was, through the anger of Artemis, wounded by a boar and died while hunting.[60]

Preliminarily we may notice Kinyras' three daughters and their Egyptian grooms, whom I shall propose below to identify with Hyon and his brothers in the first text above. For now we shall concentrate, as before, on the elements of Kinyras' descent from Kephalos.

Ps.-Apollodoros' genealogy can be seen in part as an expansion of what the scholiast gave, without implying any immediate *textual* dependence. While they diverge in whom they make founder of Paphos (Paphos and Kinyras,

---

[59] Muncker corrected R's Θαινάκη to Φαρνάκη from *Suda* s.v. καταγηρᾶσαι (Κινύρας δέ, ἀπόγονος Φαρνάκης, βασιλεὺς Κυπρίων); this also permits emendation of Hesykhios s.v. Κινύρας (Φαρνά†) and *Appendix Proverbiorum* 4.68 (Φάρμη†). See Roscher *Lex.* s.v. Pharnake (Höfer); RE 19 (1938) s.v. Pharnake (Kroll). The elaborate dynastic inferences of Engel 1841 2:123 were thereby negated.

[60] [Apollodoros] *Library* 3.14.3 (Wagner): Ἕρσης δὲ καὶ Ἑρμοῦ Κέφαλος, οὗ ἐρασθεῖσα Ἠὼς ἥρπασε καὶ μιγεῖσα ἐν Συρίᾳ παῖδα ἐγέννησε Τιθωνόν, οὗ παῖς ἐγένετο Φαέθων, τούτου δὲ Ἀστύνοος, τοῦ δὲ Σάνδοκος, ὃς ἐκ Συρίας ἐλθὼν εἰς Κιλικίαν, πόλιν ἔκτισε Κελένδεριν, καὶ γήμας Φαρνάκην (Muncker [v. *supra*]: Θαινάκην R) τὴν Μεγασσάρου τοῦ Ὑριέων (Hercher [v. *infra*]: τοῦ Συρίων R) βασιλέως ἐγέννησε Κινύραν. οὗτος ἐν Κύπρῳ, παραγενόμενος σὺν λαῷ, ἔκτισε Πάφον, γήμας δὲ ἐκεῖ Μεθάρμην, κόρην Πυγμαλίωνος Κυπρίων βασιλέως, Ὀξύπορον ἐγέννησε καὶ Ἄδωνιν, πρὸς δὲ τούτοις θυγατέρας Ὀρσεδίκην <καὶ> Λαογόρην καὶ Βραισίαν. αὗται δὲ διὰ μῆνιν Ἀφροδίτης ἀλλοτρίοις ἀνδράσι συνευναζόμεναι τὸν βίον ἐν Αἰγύπτῳ μετήλλαξαν. Ἄδωνις δὲ ἔτι παῖς ὢν Ἀρτέμιδος χόλῳ πληγεὶς ἐν θήρᾳ ὑπὸ συὸς ἀπέθανεν. The variants Σάνδακος, Κελλένδεριν, Μεγεσσάρουν, Θανάκην, and τῶν Συρίων βασιλέα, which Wagner reported in his *ap. crit.*, lost any probative value after Diller 1935, refining Wagner 1894:XIII, showed that all extant MSS depend on R (Par. 2722).

respectively), this difference is relatively insignificant for contemplating structural sympathies between the lineages, since the scholion was itself internally divided on the issue (so to speak), with Paphos evidently displacing Aoios as founder. Indeed, it is Aoios who provides the more obvious thematic link to ps.-Apollodoros, the first part of whose genealogy is dominated by figures with solar associations (Kephalos, Tithonos, Phaethon). At the same time, their obviously purposeful concatenation makes one wonder how best to approach the lineage—as a whole, in segments, or as individual links. Let us examine each element in turn.

Hermes, who 'replaces' Pandion at the head of the line, is not certainly paralleled as an ancestor of Kinyras. But a fairly likely vestige has been supposed at the end of the *Hermes* of Eratosthenes (ca. 285–194), the last two columns of which have left the merest mutilated scraps in a papyrus of ca. 25 BCE–25 CE.[61] Fortunately, a few scholiastic comments between the column margins reveal bits of subject matter. Cyprus and Paphos (the city) were definitely mentioned, as was the legend that Aphrodite's sanctuary was never rained upon; and there is a possible allusion to Adonis-cakes.[62] This is an unexpected conclusion for a work about Hermes, but Parsons noted that "the range of such a poem is unpredictable," speculating that Eratosthenes traced the god's descendants down to Kinyras and the building of Aphrodite's temple. The suggestion is certainly attractive, as no other link is known between Hermes and Paphos. Even if this is right, of course, the poet may not have followed the precise genealogy found in ps.-Apollodoros.

The mythographer continues with the traditional abduction motif that we missed in the scholion. But now we are awash in mythographic method; the three quasi-doublets Kephalos, Tithonos, and Phaethon are arrayed practically like the lists of comparable figures seen in Hyginus.[63] One expects Phaethon to be the son of Kephalos and Eos, as Hesiod has it; instead Tithonos, himself normally a target of Eos' affections, has intruded.[64] Thus, Phaethon, who in Hesiod's vision was abducted by Aphrodite to serve in her temple, now takes the place of Memnon, king of Aithiopia. We need not pursue these multiform myths in further detail: clearly some mythographer has chained together figures associated with the Sun and/or Dawn, and so the semi-mythical East. Like Aoios, each of these figures might aptly be called 'He of the Dawn'. And as Aoios reflects aspects of Levantine kingship, so the goddess-abduction theme

---

[61] *Pap.Oxy.* 3000 (ed. P. J. Parsons); SH 397.
[62] Intercolumnar Σ lines 1–3, 6–8, 13–17, with Parson's notes *ad loc.*; SH 397 with notes.
[63] For this mythographic device, see Cameron 2004:238–249.
[64] Hesiod *Theogony* 986–991 (Eos and Kephalos, Aphrodite and Phaethon); Euripides *Hippolytos* 454–455 (Eos and Kephalos). For Kephalos, see further sources in Gantz 1993 1:36, 238.

has recently been read as (at least partially) an *interpretatio Graeca* of a recurring element of ANE royal ideology—"the exaltation of the king's soul into the sky—annually during his life and permanently after his death—in order to conjoin with a celestial goddess in a *hieròs gámos*."[65] Van der Sluijs and P. James have also emphasized ps.-Apollodoros' Syro-Cilician milieu in their persuasive comparison of the more familiar Phaethon myth—his disastrous outing on the chariot of his father, the Sun—with the Hurro-Hittite *Song of Silver*.[66]

Kinyras' solar ancestors here have been connected with Herodotos' statement that Cyprus was home not only to Greeks and Phoenicians, but a third group—presumably reflecting the pre-Greek island—who were "from Aithiopia."[67] Note too that one version of the Kinyras-Myrrha myth was motivated not by Aphrodite, but by an angered Sun.[68]

Astynoos, who follows Phaethon, is entirely obscure.[69] That his name—'mind of the city' or 'protecting the city' (if one reads *Astynó<m>os*)—has no obvious solar associations may suggest that we have entered a new segment of construction. But the link is perhaps intelligible if the solar figures do reflect ideals of ANE kingship and hence governance. Recall the traditional association of Justice with the all-seeing Sun, an idea famously illustrated by Hammurabi's receipt of his kingship symbols from Shamash on the stele recording his laws.[70] This is one of several indications that the honorific 'My Sun' or 'My Sun God', attested

---

[65] See van der Sluijs 2008, focusing on Phaethon and Aphrodite (quotation, 244).

[66] James and van der Sluijs 2012; see above p103. This interpretation can coexist with the I-E aspects of Phaethon exposed by Nagy 1973.

[67] Herodotos 7.90: οἱ μὲν ἀπὸ Σαλαμῖνος καὶ Ἀθηνέων, οἱ δὲ ἀπὸ Ἀρκαδίης, οἱ δὲ ἀπὸ Κύθνου, οἱ δὲ ἀπὸ Φοινίκης, οἱ δὲ ἀπὸ Αἰθιοπίης, ὡς αὐτοὶ Κύπριοι λέγουσι. It is not certain how far all of these assertions should be attributed to Cypriot tradition, despite the historian's appeal to "the Cypriots themselves." The Athenian link at least was a relatively recent fiction (see p340–341). These Cypro-Aithiopians were linked with ps.-Apollodoros already by Heyne 1803:324; Movers 1841–1856 1:251. A different approach is taken by Petit 1998 (cf. Petit 1999, 115–116), who looks to Amathous' fifth-century political alignment with Persia, and myths that connect Perseus to 'Aithiopia' and make him an eponym of Persia. Personally I suspect that the whole idea originates with a fifth-century logographic interpretation of Homer *Odyssey* 4.83–84, where Menelaos' wanderings took him to Κύπρον Φοινίκην τε καὶ Αἰγυπτίους ἐπαληθείς, / Αἰθίοπάς θ' ἱκόμην καὶ Σιδονίους καὶ Ἐρεμβούς. Cypro-Aithiopians would be generated by correlating the three countries of the first verse with the three peoples of the second. A likely culprit is Hellanikos, on whom Herodotos sometimes drew (Franklin 2012:7n20, 20–22) and who composed a *Kypriaka* (FGH 4 F 57, 756 F 1); this would explain why he located the much-debated Eremboi in Egypt (4 F 154a).

[68] See p288.

[69] Heyne 1803:324 left him in silence. The curious speculations of Engel 1841 2:133 (q.v.) were not taken up by Stoll in Roscher *Lex.* s.v., who merely noted the passage.

[70] CS 2 no. 131 ("I am Hammurabi, king of justice, to whom the god Shamash has granted the truth," trans. Roth); also 107A; RIME 4 3.6.2, 3.6.12, etc. See Beckman 2003:18. Cf. EFH:20 for comparison with Greek Helios.

for Hittite kings as early as the fifteenth century—well before the famous usage of the Amarna Age pharaohs—grew from ideas current in Mesopotamia during the early second and even late third millennium.[71] Note that a handful of balang-gods, bearing judicial names like 'Judge of Sky and Earth', are attested as servants of Utu (the Sumerian counterpart of Shamash).[72] Remember too the lyre-playing god that stood next to the throne of 'Helios' at Hierapolis.[73]

Returning now to ps.-Apollodoros, Sandokos and his deeds—the foundation of Kelenderis, marriage to Pharnake daughter of Megassares—must constitute an organic unit. This is shown both by the general obscurity of all the figures involved, and their geographical associations. These begin from the vague East implied by Eos and her descendants and adequately embraced by 'Syria',[74] from which Sandokos sets out for Cilicia.[75] This trajectory strongly supports Hercher's emendation, whereby Megassares becomes king not of "the Syrians" but "the Hyrians."[76] Hyria, not far from Kelenderis in Rough Cilicia, is thought by many to be the site of Ura, an important port under the Hittite Empire that traded extensively with Ugarit (it was eventually reincorporated as Seleucia Tracheia ca. 300).[77] Megassares is obscure.[78] Pharnake has been variously seen as a Persian 'intrusion' (given names like Pharnakes, Pharnos, Pharnabazos, etc.), and/or a Seleucid one (the fortress on the Orontes, which Seleukos refounded as

---

[71] Beckman 2003.
[72] See p21 and Heimpel, "Balang-gods," 53 III 153–158.
[73] See p495.
[74] Compare the varying locations connected with Memnon (Egypt, Syria, Susa).
[75] For Kelenderis, see RE 11 (1922), 138 (2) (Ruge). Brown 1965:205n3 suggested a connection between Sandokos and the Baal *Krntryš* who is mentioned in the Karatepe inscriptions as having been settled in Azatiwatas' new foundation (KAI 26 A.II.19–20, III.2–3, C.IV.20; *Krntryš* as Kelenderis is still supported by DDUPP:83). The corresponding Luwian text gives the thunder-god Tarhunzas (see Hawkins 2000 *ad loc.*).
[76] Early editors (e.g. van Meurs 1675 2:107; Westermann 1843), looking to descriptions of Kinyras as 'King of Assyria' (Hyginus *Fabulae* 58 etc.), read here γήμας Φαρνάκην τὴν Μεγασσάρου τὸν Συρίων βασιλέα ἐγέννησε Κινύραν *vel sim*. Hercher 1851:573 argued that the obscure Megassares called for further qualification, and his proposal accords well with the archetypal reading of R (τοῦ Συρίων βασιλέως). Because P (containing Συρέων, to which Hercher appealed) is now an invalid textual witness (see n60), one might equally entertain Ἰσαύρων for Συρίων (cf. e.g. Strabo 14.5.1), yielding a similar geographical connection.
[77] See Jasink 2001:603–605; Jasink forthcoming. For the sources relating to trade with Ugarit, see Beal 1992:66n6 and 7 (but identifying Ura with Kelenderis).
[78] Movers 1841–1856 1:77, 240–241 suggested a connection with Magos, father of Misor and Sydyk in Philo of Byblos (see below), and thence a Semitic etymology as 'priest of fire'; approved by Rochette 1848:216–217n3. Many aspects of Movers' interpretation of the larger passage are now outdated; I cannot judge this particular as yet.

Chapter Twenty-One

Apamaea, was formerly called Pharnake).[79] But for neither idea does the passage give much purchase.

As to Sandokos himself, there are two schools of thought. Already in 1877 E. Meyer connected him with the Sandas (Sandes, Sandon, Sandan) whom a handful of classical sources treat as a hero or god associated especially with Cilicia, Cappadocia, and Lydia; he is shown on terracotta reliefs and coins from Hellenistic and Roman Tarsus, and is found as a theophoric element in many PNs in these regions.[80] Ammianus Marcellinus (fourth century CE) knew a tradition that Tarsus was founded not by Perseus, but by Sandan—"a wealthy noble, setting out from †Aethio."[81] Some would read *Aithiopia* here, a kind of parallel for Sandokos leaving Syria. But this emendation is hardly certain, and would seem to conflict with Sandas' probable Cilician/Luwian origin.[82] While Sandas is not lacking further Syro-Phoenician associations, these are evidently secondary.[83] This is indicated first by Stephanos of Byzantium's entry on Adana, the ancient royal seat of the House of Mopsos/Hiyawa in Cilicia.[84] Here 'Sandes' is a son of Gaia and Ouranos—thus a Titan, brother to an eponymous Adanos and two further Cilician figures, Ostasos and Olymbros, along with the more familiar Kronos, Rhea, and Iapetos.[85] This portrayal of Sandas as an 'Elder God' was dramatically confirmed by PNs in documents of the OA colony at Kanesh (ca. 1900),[86] and fourteenth/thirteenth-century Luwo-Hittite and Hurro-Hititte texts.[87] The most informative of the latter corroborates Sandas' Cilician associations. This is the Zarpiya ritual, named after a divination-priest (^{lú}A.ZU) of Kummanni—probably in later Cappadocia, but once capital of Kizzuwatna. The ritual, calling on Sandas repeatedly, was to be performed "If the year (is) bad,

---

[79] Movers 1841–1856 2/2:237 and n85; Tuplin 1996:75 and n179. For the site, see RE 1 (1894), 2663–2664 (Benzinger).

[80] For this interpretation of Sandokos, see Movers 1841–1856 1:240; Meyer 1877:737; Höfer in Roscher *Lex.*, s.v. Sandas (p324); Gjerstad 1948, 429. For an up-to-date bibliography and survey of the known and possible iconography of Sandas, see LIMC s.v. Sandas (Augé); also NP s.v. Sandon. Most of the classical sources were collected by Höfer in Roscher *Lex.* s.v. Sandas.

[81] Ammianus Marcellinus 14.8.3: *Tarsus ... hanc condidisse Perseus memoratur ... uel certe ex †Aethio* [v.l. Aechio] *profectus Sandan quidam nomine uir opulentus et nobilis.*

[82] See Roscher *Lex.* s.v, Sandas:320 (B), and below n93. Even if the emendation is on the right lines, one could still think of an Anatolian location, cf. [Zonaras] *Lexicon* s.v. Αἰθιόπιον ... χωρίον Λυδίας.

[83] Classical sources give some evidence of cult presence in Syria/Phoenicia, and he may have had Kubaba, the state god of Karkemish, as a consort in the Kizzuwatnan period. Some have held that he features as a theophoric element in some Persian PNs: see Roscher *Lex.* s.v. Sandas p329. Kubaba: NP s.v. Sandon:954 (Kammenhuber 1990:191 is agnostic for BA).

[84] See p251–253.

[85] Stephanos of Byzantium s.v. Ἄδανα ... ἔστι δὲ ὁ Ἄδανος Γῆς καὶ Οὐρανοῦ παῖς, καὶ Ὄστασος καὶ Σάνδης καὶ Κρόνος καὶ Ῥέα καὶ Ἰαπετὸς καὶ Ὄλυμβρος.

[86] Kammenhuber 1990:191.

[87] Sources in Kammenhuber 1990:191–193.

(and) there is constant dying in the land."⁸⁸ He is invoked as "Divine Šantaš, King" or "Sun of Heaven," and represented logographically as Marduk (ᵈAMAR. UD).⁸⁹ The ritual includes an invocation of the deified ancestors and the god Ea to partake in offerings; a choir of virgin boys to sing in Luwian; and a "quasi-bilingual Luwian hymn" to be "conjured" by the "Lord of the House" (probably a priest).⁹⁰ The reason for the identification of Šantaš and Marduk, and his description as 'Sun of Heaven', though not entirely clear,⁹¹ support his interpretation as a war god and pantheon-head.⁹² That he was equally connected with the agrarian cycle is suggested both by the context of the Zarpiya ritual, and an annual 'burning-man' ceremony attested down into Roman times, which was also a basis for the general identification of Sandas with Herakles from the Hellenistic period onwards.⁹³

The competing interpretation of Sandokos, going back to J. P. Brown in 1965, was recently revived and strengthened by James and van der Sluijs.⁹⁴ Brown proposed to derive Sandokos from Sem. √ṣdq ('righteous') on the strength of the Sydyk who appears among the culture-heroes of Philo of Byblos, who renders him in Greek as 'Just' (díkaion).⁹⁵ Sydyk's twin, not noted by Brown, is Misor, which should mean 'Fair'.⁹⁶ At that time it was debated whether Philo's Justice Brothers went back to true Canaanite/Phoenician deities, or were abstractions of a later age. But in 1968 the pair was discovered as Ṣdq Mšr in an Ugaritic text, evidently a prayer for blessing from a long list of gods, nearly all grouped in twos.⁹⁷ This confirmed the theophoric character of the element ṣdq in PNs, of which there are Amorite, Ugaritic, Biblical, and Phoenician examples, including

---

[88] The text is KUB 9.31. See Schwartz 1938, whose composite, continuous lineation I follow (the quoted prescription is lines 102–103); more recent bibliography cited by Kammenhuber 1990:192.

[89] His name is spelled out as ᵈša-an-ta-aš LUGAL-uš at 84; 'Sun of Heaven' at 63 and 92; ᵈAMAR.UD at 34, 36, and 55.

[90] Lines 64, 71–74, 82–83, 91–93, 95.

[91] Kammenhuber 1990:192.

[92] Schwartz 1938:349; NP s.v. Sandon.

[93] Pyre-festival at Tarsus: Dio Chrysostomus 33.47 (under name of Herakles); at Hierapolis (unnamed): Lucian *On the Syrian Goddess* 49, cf. OSG ad loc. An agrarian function has often been supported by the perhaps seventh-century rock relief at Ivriz (on the Taurus), showing a god with grain and grapes (NP s.v. Sandon); but the identity of this deity is disputed: LIMC s.v. Sandas (p. 664).

[94] Brown 1965:205n3; James and van der Sluijs 2012:247.

[95] The passage is Philo of Byblos FGH 790 F 2 (13): Μισὼρ καὶ Συδύκ, τουτέστιν εὔλυτον καὶ δίκαιον.

[96] For Philo's problematic definition of Μισώρ as εὔλυτον ('easily solved'), see Baumgarten 1981:175 ("circuitous at best"); DDUPP:113 ("Philon se méprenne sur le sens précis").

[97] RS 24.271 = KTU/CAT 1.123 (Virolleaud 1968:584–586 no. 10) = RCU no. 47 ("A Prayer for Well-Being"): ṣdq mšr are invoked in line 14 (vocalized ṣidqu mêšaru by Pardee).

Chapter Twenty-One

a fifth-century king of Lapethos, on Cyprus, called Ṣdqmlk, 'Sydyk-is-king'.[98] This last name points to the special associations of ṣdq and mšr with Canaanite/Phoenician royal ideology.[99] Already a tenth-century Byblian inscription describes Yahimilk as 'just king' (mlk ṣdq) and 'righteous king' (mlk yšr, < mšr).[100] Similar applications are found in Biblical contexts, typically in connection with the justice of Yahweh.[101] Cognate ideas in Mesopotamia, going back to the OAkk. period, are connected with the pair Misharum and Kittum, who sometimes belong to the divine retinue of the sun-god Shamash; though ṣdq is 'replaced' here by Kittum, Ṣdq's own solar associations are seen in the expression "Sun of Righteousness" in the Hebrew prophet Malachi.[102]

Although no specific attributes have yet materialized for Ṣdq in Ugaritic texts, there are some relevant notices in classical sources deriving from the Syro-Phoenician sphere. Philo places his Sydyk and Misor later in the same stretch of culture-heroes that earlier included Khousor and the unnamed brother whom I would interpret as an evanescent 'Kinyras'.[103] The two sections appear to be doublets in part, probably due to Philo's harmonization of parallel regional variants. But evidently he did not understand Sydyk's and Misor's ancient attributes very well.[104] Their puzzling discovery of salt has been variously explained (always looking to royal and juridical ideals).[105] Misor's son Taautos (< Thoth) is credited with inventing the alphabet, echoing Khousor's *lógoi*. Sydyk's children are unnamed but compared to the Dioskouroi and other Greek brother-sets; they invented ships and sailing (again recalling Khousor and his brother),[106] while their own unnamed sons discovered the medicinal use of herbs and (again like Khousor) incantations (*epōidaí*).[107] Later, in speaking of Beirut, Philo adds that Sydyk was father, by one of the Kotharat goddesses (whom he calls 'Titanids' or 'Artemids'), of 'Asklepios'—a Greek calque that also suggests medical and incantatory skills.[108] Yet when Sydyk's eight sons are

---

[98] See examples in DDUPP:112–113; Liverani 1971:58, 63 (Amorite, Ugaritic). For Ṣdqmlk of Lapethos, Masson and Sznycer 1972:98–99 (no. 111).
[99] See discussion and material in Liverani 1971:55–57; DDUPP:112–114.
[100] KAI 4.6–7; also 10.8–9 (Yehawmilk, Byblos, Persian era).
[101] See sources in Liverani 1971:66–70; Baumgarten 1981:175n193; DDUPP:113 and n348.
[102] For the correspondence of Ṣdq Mšr and Misharum/Kittum, see Liverani 1971:58–62; Baumgarten 1981:176 (noting Malachi 4:2, followed by James and van der Sluijs 2012:247); DDUPP:113.
[103] See p445–452.
[104] Cf. Liverani 1971:70–71; Baumgarten 1981:177.
[105] Liverani 1971:71; Baumgarten 1981:176; DDUPP:114.
[106] Philo of Byblos FGH 790 F 2: πρῶτόν τε πάντων ἀνθρώπων πλεῦσαι (11) and πρῶτοι πλοῖον εὗρον (14).
[107] Philo of Byblos FGH 790 F 2 (13).
[108] Philo of Byblos FGH 790 F 2 (25). For Asklepios' incantations, Pindar *Pythian* 3.47–53; cf. Watkins 1995:537–539 (from an Indo-European perspective).

united at the climax of Philo's account, they are cited not for doctorly virtues, but wordcraft. The deeds of Kronos/El, Philo says, were recorded "by the seven sons of Sydyk—the Kabeiroi—and the eighth son, their brother Asklepios," at the behest of Misor's son Taautos.[109] The commemoration and celebration of the world order through scribal arts are appropriately attributed to descendants of the Just-and-Righteous Brothers; but this equally echoes the *lógoi* of Khousor (and the exegetical activities of Khousarthis, his female counterpart).[110]

Broadly compatible material appears in a Photian epitome of Damaskios (fl. ca. 515-540 CE), who, speaking of Beirut, confirmed that 'Sadykos' was the father of the Dioskouroi/Kabeiroi, with Asklepios an eighth. But here we are given Asklepios' Phoenician counterpart, 'Esmounos'—that is, Eshmoun, whose cult is best attested for Sidon.[111] The glossing of Eshmoun as Asklepios implies that Sydyk/Sadykos could be understood as Apollo, and this is confirmed by Pausanias, who reports a quarrel he had with a Sidonian at the shrine of Asklepios in Achaea. This tiresome tourist maintained the superiority of Phoenician religious knowledge, and offered an allegorical interpretation of Asklepios as air and his father Apollo as the sun.[112] He was clearly translating Sadykos/Sydyk and Eshmoun into Greek terms, and in so doing provides important confirmation of Ṣdq's ancient solar associations.[113]

Let us now consider the relative merits of Sandokos' two paternity suits. Against the *prima facie* similarity of Šantaš and Sandokos (especially given a PN like Sandokes, satrap of Cyme during Xerxes' invasion), one may place the form Saḏykos of Damaskios, and the Greek rendering of the Heb. priestly title Ṣāḏōq (< √ṣdq) as Saddouk and Saddoukaîoi (with dissimilation of *dd* to *nd* readily paralleled in Imperial Aramaic).[114] Both Šantaš and Ṣdq enjoy the BA antiquity of Kinnaru/Kinyras. Both have the solar associations that would explain Sandokos' integration into the lineage of ps.-Apollodoros; but the credentials of Ṣdq are rather stronger and clearer here. Astynoos/Astyno<m>os, evidently reflecting ideas of civic justice, also seems more immediately relevant to Ṣdq; recall that Kinyras had daughters called 'Orsedike' ('Upright Justice'), Laodike ('Justice for the People'), and possibly Eunoe ('Benevolence').[115] But Šantaš as a Marduk-like city-god (Tarsus) might also support such ideas. While Sandas

---

[109] Philo of Byblos FGH 790 F 2 (38): ταῦτα δὲ (φησί) πρῶτοι πάντων ὑπεμνηματίσαντο οἱ ἑπτὰ Συδύκου (Mras: Συδὲκ BO, Σύδου A) παῖδες Κάβειροι καὶ ὁ ὄγδοος αὐτῶν ἀδελφὸς Ἀσκληπιός.
[110] For Khousarthis, see p477.
[111] Damaskios *Life of Isidore* fr. 348 Zintzen.
[112] Pausanias 7.23.7-8.
[113] See Baumgarten 1981:228-231.
[114] James and van der Sluijs 2012:247 and n15 with K. Jongeling.
[115] [Apollodoros] *Library* 3.9.1 (Laodike), 3.14.3 (Orsedike). Eunoe is a possible correction at Σ Lykophron *Alexandra* 450: see p354n93.

seems a good match for Sandokos' foundation of Kelenderis and alliance with Ura/Hyria, one wonders why the more traditional Tarsus was not mentioned instead. And Sandokos' departure *from Syria for Cilicia* is certainly better suited to Ṣdq. The geographical trajectory might be mapped, for instance, onto Ugarit's relations with Ura/Hyria; or IA Phoenician penetration of Cilicia—noting that ṣdq appears as a royal virtue of Azatiwatas in the Phoenician texts at Karatepe (ca. 725–700), while an inscription from Cebel Ires Daği (ca. 650) "even indicates that judicial records were written in Phoenician."[116] That both Ṣdq and Kinnaru were divinized at Ugarit also makes Ṣdq the more promising archetype for Sandokos, while what little we know of Sadykos/Sydyk from Phoenician-derived sources is broadly suggestive of Kinyras/Kothar-like qualities. Finally, the Greco-Phoenician equation of Sadykos and Apollo may well explain why, for Hesykhios, it was not Sandokos but Apollo who partnered with Pharnake to produce Kinyras.[117]

Weighing everything up, the case for deriving Sandokos from Ṣdq does seem rather stronger than that for Šantaš. But the evidence is hardly decisive. Whichever interpretation is followed—assuming that one or the other is indeed correct—Sandokos' presence in the solar lineage is intelligible, and Kinyras is endowed with solid Syro-Cilician associations. Ps.-Apollodoros thus presents a Kinyras who is structurally equivalent to both Aoios and Paphos—a Cilician immigrant to Cyprus who then founds Paphos.

The Egyptian Detour

While the Dionysian scholiast and ps.-Apollodoros diverge on Kinyras' precise Kephalid descent, their agreement on his union with Pygmalion's family, and the son Oxyporos who is otherwise unparalleled, shows clearly that here at least the accounts depend upon the same unique tradition.[118] Their names for Pygmalion's daughter—Thymarete and Metharme—are obviously variants of a single figure, again known only from these passages. Whether either form is original we cannot say, though Thymarete more readily yields an appropriate etymology—'pleasing the heart' (cf. *thymarḗs, thymarḗstē*) being likely in itself as a bride's name, and a nice complement to Kinyras as a musical god/hero.[119]

---

[116] For ṣdq at Karatepe, KAI 26 A.I.12–13. See further Lipiński 2004:139–140 for the judicial use of Phoenician, and 109–144 passim for Phoenician cultural influence in southern Anatolia generally.
[117] Hesykhios s.v. Κινύρας· Ἀπόλλωνος καὶ Φαρνάκης παῖς, βασιλεὺς Κυπρίων.
[118] The variant Oxyparos is to be rejected (see FGH 758 F 3a). For Oxyporos, cf. above p333.
[119] Note the gloss in Apollonios Sophistes *Homeric Lexicon* s.v. θυμαρέα· θυμάρεστον, καὶ θυμῆρες τὸ ἀρέσκον τῇ ψυχῇ. But an etymology of Metharme from Gk. ∨ar- ('fit, join' > 'tune') is perhaps not impossible, and this too could provide an appropriate musical nuance (cf. ἁρμή, μεθαρμογή, etc.). Finally, given the juxtaposition of Kinnaru and the Divine Censer at Ugarit, one might

Given the uniqueness of Oxyporos and Thymarete/Metharme, we are justified in asking whether the three further daughters in ps.-Apollodoros—Orsedike, Laogore, and Braisia—are equally integral to this version of Kinyras' family, or merely tacked on from a separate myth or myths. The latter would seem likely enough but that our Dionysian scholion is the only other source that implicates Kinyras in Egyptian affairs. One must consider, therefore, whether the two Cypro-Egyptian scenarios are mutually illuminating. I believe they are.

When the scholion is taken by itself, there is no obvious connection between the colonization of Kerastis/Cyprus by Hyon and his brothers, on the one hand, and the Kephalid material that follows. That these two events are indeed related, however, emerges from an extract of Donatus' fourth-century commentary on Vergil, preserved in the collection attributed to Servius.[120] After a more-or-less conventional version of Cinyras and Myrrha, Donatus/Servius launches into an unusual variation of the Adonis myth.[121] This *alter ordo fabulae* begins as follows:

> The brothers †Epiuotasterius and Yon set out from Egypt for Cyprus and there found wives. From their union(s) Celes was born, who had a daughter Erinoma. This girl, since she was overly chaste and for this was cherished by Diana and Minerva, began to be hated by Venus.[122]

So Thilo's standard text of 1887. Some decades earlier, however, F. C. Movers had seen that this passage was akin to the Dionysian scholion, where the restoration 'Hyon' was indicated by the 'Yon' of Donatus/Servius; similarly, the divergent

---

wonder whether 'Thymarete' conceals some connection with words like *thymiáō* ('burn incense') and *thymiatḗrion* ('censer'). The child Adonis might then correspond to the divinized kings, who adjoin Kinnaru and Censer in the pantheon texts (see p5, 103, 121, 124, 283).

[120] Servius Auctus on Vergil *Eclogues* 10.18. For the relationship of Servius to Donatus, see Cameron 2004:188.

[121] For a detailed discussion, but from another angle, see Fontenrose 1981:170–172.

[122] Thilo's text (for the whole episode) is: *est etiam alter ordo huius fabulae: ex Aegypto †Epiuotasterius et Yon fratres ad insulam Cyprum profecti sunt atque ibi sortiti uxores. ex quorum genere Celes procreatus est, qui habuit Erinomam filiam. haec cum esset nimiae castitatis et hoc a Minerva et Diana diligeretur, Veneri esse coepit invisa. quae cum puellae castitati insidiaretur, in amorem eius inpulit Iovem. quem dolum postquam Iuno animadvertit, ut fraudem fraude superaret, petit a Venere, ut in amorem puellae Adonem inflammaret. quem posteaquam nulla fraude sollicitare in eius amorem potuit, obiectis quibusdam nebulis, ipsum Adonem in penetrale virginis perduxit. ita pudicitia puella per vim et fraudem caruit. sed hanc Diana miserata circa Cisseum fluvium in pavonem mutavit. Adonis vero ubi cognovit se amatam Iovis vitiasse, metuens profugit in montis Casii silvas ibique inmixtus agrestibus versabatur. quem dolo Mercurii monte deductum cum aper, quem fabulae Martem loquuntur, vehementer urgeret et ab Adone vinceretur, repente fulmen Iuppiter iecit et Adonem morti dedit: sed cum Venus illusum sibi et mortem amati Adonis saepe quereretur, Mercurius miseratus imaginem Adonis, ut vivere crederetur, ad suos reduci fecit; Iuno autem a Iove petiit, ut Adonis in lucis patriis aevum degeret. tum Diana puellae Erinomae formam pristinam reddidit, quae tamen ex Adone Taleum filium procreavit et cum viro permansit.*

'Celes' (Servius) and 'Keltes' (scholion) indicated an original 'Kettes'.[123] This is clearly an eponymous founder for Kition.[124] The corrupt 'Epiuotasterius' must conceal two separate figures.[125] Movers, reading Epivius, Asterius, and Hyon, saw these brothers as representing the island's Egyptian, Phoenician, and Greek cultural influences, respectively.[126] This explanation for Hyon, at least, is attractive: though a Greek 'father' of Phoenician Kition may seem jarring, it would be paralleled by Javan and his son Kittim in the Table of Nations.[127] And his marriage to a daughter of Kinyras would then present an ethnic structure akin to the weddings of Teukros and Elatos.[128] But Hyon's Egyptian origin in the tale complicates any such Aegean interpretation.

The curious fact that Donatus/Servius specifies but a single *daughter* for Kettes—Erinoma—suddenly clarifies the scholiast's *ápais*: Kettes is not 'childless' (so Movers), but 'without male heir'.[129] The relevance of this to the scholiast's Kephalos > Paphos > Kinyras comes from the sequel in Donatus/Servius. Offended by Erinoma's chastity, Venus makes Jupiter fall in love with her, while Juno seeks revenge by convincing Venus (strangely enough) to have Adonis smitten by the girl too. Adonis rapes Erinoma, whom the pitying Diana then transforms into a peacock; fleeing the wrath of Jupiter, the young hunter crosses over not to Mount Lebanon as one might expect, but the wooded Mount Kasios in Syria—a most interesting epichoric variant, as this had been sacred to Ugaritian Baal and Hurrian Teshup (as Saphon and Hazzi, respectively). Mercury sends a boar that lures Adonis into the open, and Jupiter's thunderbolt does the rest. In a baroque catastrophe, the laments of Venus and blandishments of Juno

---

[123] Movers 1841–1856 2/2:204 and n3; *ap. crit.* to GGM 2:450.
[124] A different eponym is found in Eustathios on Homer *Iliad* 10.409: πόλις Κίτιον, κληθεῖσα οὕτω, φασίν, ἀπὸ Κιτίου γυναικός τινος. For -tt-, cf. the legendary Cypriot princess Kittia (Pausanias of Damascus FHG 4:469 fr. 4; HC:32; and above p440n107), and Kittim son of Javan in the Table of Nations (Genesis 10:3–4); further oscillations noted by Movers 1841–1856 2/2:204n3.
[125] Movers 1841–1856 2/2:204n3 and GGM 2:450 suggest *Epivios et Asterius et Yon*; the third term of Thilo's *Ephialtes Asterius Echion* vel *Aethion* must be ignored. Note that an Asterias or Asteria was the child of Teukros and Kinyras' daughter Eue/Eune/Eunoe: see p354n93.
[126] Movers 1841–1856 2/2:204–205 (connecting Asterius with Astarte).
[127] Gen. 10:3–4. 'Hyon' would therefore be, effectively, 'Ionians', the standard ANE term for 'Greek' (< Ἴωνες < Ἰάϝονες; see e.g. Brinkman 1989). While υ for ι is not problematic in a Hellenistic or later source, one would wonder why the more obvious Ἴων was not exploited. Still, Movers may be right that 'Hyon' was drawn from a collateral NE form (though not necessarily Heb. 'Javan'); cf. e.g. Hiyawa for Ahhiyawa at Karatepe (see p251–252). But note too that a 'Hyon' is found as a variant for Hyas in Hyginus *Fabulae* 248, a list of Adonis-like figures who died of boar wounds: Roscher *Lex.* s.v. (Crusius).
[128] See p350–359, 365–366.
[129] One might think here of Karageorghis' view that Kition was abandoned ca. 1000–850, except that Smith 2009 has now shown continuous habitation. But one could still look to the interruption of relations with Egypt in the EIA, as reflected for instance in the *Tale of Wen-Amun*. For the abundance of Egyptian faience vessels at LBA Kition, see Smith 2009:9 with references.

persuade Jupiter to revive Adonis, while Diana returns Erinoma to human form. The baffled couple, reunited as in a New Comedy, reign together on Cyprus and have a son named 'Taleus', perhaps another corrupt eponym (< Idalion? Tamassos?).

Leaving aside the artificial and excessive recombinations of traditional mythemes, the tale's ultimate resolution brings together the lines of Hyon and Kinyras—an alliance that can explain the seemingly abrupt transition from one house to the other in the Dionysian scholion. And with this, we return full circle to the Cypro-Egyptian weddings in ps.-Apollodoros. For the unique Thymarete/Metharme and Oxyporos make it seem inevitable that the three daughters of Kinyras who end their lives in Egypt are the very Cypriot brides whom the Egyptian brothers win in the cognate account of Donatus/Servius. It is striking that brides and brothers alike were all individually named. If this connection is right, it would follow that Kinyras was already established on the island when the Egyptians arrived. True, ps.-Apollodoros says that Kinyras' daughters ended up in Egypt, whereas the action of Donatus/Servius seems to unfold mainly on Cyprus and in Syria. But the marriages of the Egyptian brothers themselves are barely addressed, apart from the daughter Erinoma; and the river where she lives as a peacock—*Cisseum fluvium*—was indeed probably in Egypt.[130] Admittedly, the synchronism of generations would be slightly awkward, with Adonis the great-uncle of Erinoma (Hyon + daughter of Kinyras > Kettes > Erinoma). But this is hardly insurmountable given the many far-fetched relationships and developments otherwise involved—not to mention Kinyras' ripe old age (160 years in Anakreon).[131] I believe therefore that our three passages preserve traces of a single original account, independently epitomized and variously recombined with other material (for all three differ substantially in how they handle the most famous element—the death of Adonis).[132]

I would even propose a specific source: the *Colonies of the Egyptians* by the Hellenistic historian Istros (ca. 250–200), an associate of Kallimakhos and himself probably from Paphos.[133] That this work followed Egyptian ventures to Cyprus specifically is guaranteed by one of our few notices, which shows that Istros told how the island got its historical name:

---

[130] A Kisseus was one of Aigyptos' sons by the naiad Kaliadne ([Apollodoros] *Library* 2.1.5), Aigyptos itself being a Homeric name for the Nile (*Odyssey* 4.477, 581, 14.258, 17.427; cf. Arrian *Anabasis of Alexander* 5.6.5).

[131] So Anakreon: see p329.

[132] Mythological constructions were often loosely combined in the Hellenistic handbook tradition, and thence by Donatus/Servius and other scholiasts: see generally Cameron 2004.

[133] For his Paphian origin, asserted by his contemporary the biographer Hermippos and the most plausible of those proposed, see *Suda* s.v. Ἴστρος; OCD s.v. Ister.

> Cyprus was named after Kypros the daughter of Kinyras, or the daughter of Byblos and Aphrodite, as Philostephanos says in his *On Islands* and Istros in his *Colonies of the Egyptians*.[134]

The parallel syntax shows that Philostephanos offered one explanation, Istros another; and that it was Istros who made Kypros the daughter of Byblos and Aphrodite. This too fits the hypothesis, as Kypros is not one of Kinyras' children in either the scholion or ps.-Apollodoros. If we are on the right track, several further inferences become possible. First, Hyon and his brothers would have come before the account of 'Kypros', since at the time of their colonial venture the island was called Kerastis/Kerastia. Whether this was ever more than a nickname or poetic epithet is doubtful; but it invited considerable Hellenistic speculation.[135] That Istros progressed from Kerastis/Kerastia down to 'Cyprus' would also explain why Dionysios' mention of *Kýpros* triggered the scholiastic notice about Kerastis/Kerastia—although the train of thought is not carried through, at least in the scholion's present form. We must also assume that Kypros, daughter of Byblos and Aphrodite, somehow came to the island, perhaps through dynastic marriage; in any case, this must be added to the traditions linking Byblos and Cyprus (Chapter 19). This suggests, alongside Kettes/Kition, that Istros presented the island's Phoenician element as overlaid on an older Egyptian stratum. One should recall that Adonis and Osiris were eventually identified at both Amathous and Byblos,[136] and that one mythographic stream traced Phoenician figures like Agenor back to Egypt.[137] Possibly, Istros was encouraged to develop this angle as a reflection of the Ptolemaic political circumstances under which he wrote.[138]

---

[134] Constantine Porphyrogenitos *On the Themes* 1.15 = Philostephanos FHG 3:30 fr. 11 = Istros FGH 334 F 45: Κύπρος ἐκλήθη δὲ ἀπὸ Κύπρου τῆς θυγατρὸς Κινύρου, ἢ τῆς Βύβλου καὶ Ἀφροδίτης, ὡς Φιλοστέφανος ἐν τῷ Περὶ νήσων καὶ Ἴστρος ἐν Ἀποικίαις Αἰγυπτίων ἱστόρησαν; also found in Herodian *De prosodia catholica* 204.4 Lentz; Stephanos of Byzantium s.v. Κύπρος. Note also Eustathios on Dionysios the Periegete 912 for an attempt to explain "Byblos" as "some general."

[135] Lykophron (*Alexandra* 447) implies that Cyprus was so called before the Trojan War and Greek immigration. According to a scholion here, Xenagoras (FGH 240 F 26) referred Κεραστία to the island's many ἐξοχαί—headlands (HC:13) or mountain peaks. Androkles (= Menandros of Ephesus? Cf. p337n3) is also cited for the theory that horned-men once inhabited the island (FGH 751 F 1). This idea clearly informs Ovid's Cerastae, transformed into bulls for sacrificing human guests on the altar of Zeus at Amathous (*Metamorphoses* 10.220–237). Modern scholars have suggested a connection with the horned-god statuettes from Enkomi, or bull-masked priest figurines from Amathous itself (*Kypris*:80). Cyprus as Kerastia is also mentioned by Eustathios on Lykophron *Alexandra* 447; Pliny *Natural History* 5.31.35; Stephanos of Byzantium and *Etymologicum Magnum* s.v. Κύπρος, Σφήκεια. See further Engel 1841 1:18–20.

[136] See above, p315–316. Parthenios fr. 42 and Lucian *On the Syrian Goddess* 7, with Lightfoot's comments on both; Stephanos of Byzantium s.v. Ἀμαθοῦς (cf. p316n214 above) and Βύβλος.

[137] [Apollodoros] *Library* 2.1.4.

[138] Cf. Engel 1841 1:7.

Syro-Cilician Approaches

THEIOS AOIDOS:
The Lyre-Player Group of Seals

We have now surveyed the principal ancient sources that connect Kinyras with Syria and/or Cilicia (for Theodontius/Boccaccio, see Appendix F). All the material, more and less traditional, has come to us through at least one pair of mythographic hands, from the fifth century onwards. Sometimes regional variants were stitched loosely together in rough cultural chronography (the Kephalid descents, Pygmalion); or they were elaborated as in a mythological romance (the Egyptian Detour). The cumulative effect should convince us that, outside of Cyprus, 'Kinyras' lived parallel lives in both Syria and Cilicia. This is not surprising given the confluence of several factors: Kinnaru of Ugarit and probably other regional Syrian cognates; the Syro-Hurrian adstrate in Cilicia/Kizzuwatna; the persistence of Hittite royal ideology in the Neo-Hittite states; and Phoenician influence in IA Cilicia. It also corroborates the suspicion that Kinnaru and other such Syro-Cilician 'Kinyrases' were, like their Cypriot cousin, actors in popular mythology.[139]

Although we have not been able to penetrate very far beneath these sources, archaeology provides a considerably deeper foundation. While analyzing Cypriot lyre-morphology I noted two MBA seals, from Tarsus (Cilicia) and perhaps Mardin (southeastern Turkey), showing an early combination of round-base and zigzag arms that complicates interpretation of similar Cypriot instruments as merely 'Aegean'.[140] We may now consider the actual subject matter of the seals. In both, the lyrist is among animals; as with the Megiddo jug, any Orphic interpretation[141] must yield to third-millennium Syro-Levantine parallels (of course, one may still derive Orpheus himself from the same milieu).[142] The seal from Mardin (?) is of particular interest for our subject (Figure 45 = 4.5e). Its top register is a row of birds streaming out in front of the lyrist, as though projected from his instrument and even echoing its shape. As Li Castro and Scardina have perceived, not only does the musician himself have birdlike features, but the stream of birds, as it comes around the cylinder seal, feeds back into his head from behind.[143] This creates an Escher-like metamorphosis, an infinite musical *ékstasis*, or epiphany, through lyric performance.

---

[139] See p7, 113, 131, 380–381, 444.
[140] The seals are 1) Adana Archaeology Museum 35.999 (Tarsus): Porada 1956:400, fig. 35; cf. 235, 394; 2) British Museum 134306 (probably from Mardin): Rimmer 1969:28 and pl. VIIIa; Collon 1987:43 no. 149. Both seals well discussed/illustrated by Li Castro and Scardina 2011:208–211, fig. 11–12.
[141] Goldman 1935:537–538; Porada 1956:204.
[142] See p71–72, 159–161.
[143] Li Castro and Scardina 2011:209 (with 210, fig. 11): "a row of standing birds that suddenly changes into the head of the sitting creature ... the head and neck of a bird coming out from beyond the

517

Chapter Twenty-One

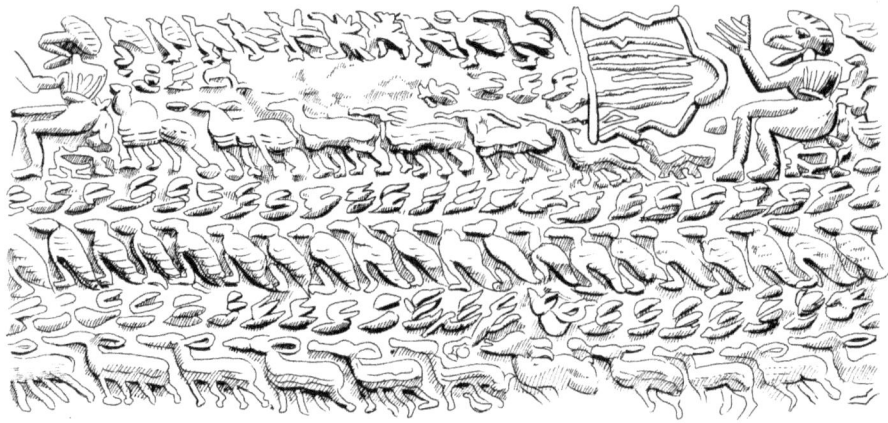

Figure 45 Lyrist and bird-metamorphosis. Modern impression of cylinder seal, Mardin (?), ca. 1800. London, BM 134306. Drawn from Li Castro and Scardina 2011, fig. 11.

Jumping forward a millennium, we come to the well-known Lyre-Player Group of Seals, which collectively offer, I believe, the clearest representation of a Divine Lyre in its several aspects. After establishing Cilicia as the seals' most probable point-of-origin—this has not been universally recognized—we shall examine their find contexts and functions, and finally the iconographic system of the prominent specimens with lyre-players. These are inextricably allied to the remainder of the Group through further shared motifs, to be considered as needed.

The Group was first identified by C. Blinkenberg in 1931, who described fourteen specimens from Lindos (Rhodes) and another thirty-one from various collections; he rather acutely detected a blend of Cypriot and 'late Hittite' elements, and made several observations still generally accepted: the seals were the product of a single workshop operating over a limited period in the eighth century.[144] E. Porada named the Group in 1956 when discussing two examples from H. Goldman's excavations of EIA Tarsus, along with fifty-two parallels, including further specimens from Syria, Phoenicia, Cyprus, and Greece.[145] The seals' repertoire of motifs is very wide, but among the figural examples lyre-players, in

---

yoke and recalling the outline of the instrument's upper arm."

[144] Blinkenberg 1931 1 col. 161–168 ("une branche de l'art hittite tardif qui a subi des influence chypriotes," 168), 172–173, 2 pl. 18 no. 521–534 and A–L. Blinkenberg's basic propositions (1 col. 165) have been followed by Buchner and Boardman 1966:58; Boardman 1990:10; Rizzo 2007:40.

[145] Porada 1956.

various type-scenes, predominate (14.5 percent of the current total). Porada, specifying a later eighth-century date, defined the style more closely, appreciating its "assured economy of means," with the "alternation of hatched and plain areas produc[ing] a pleasant variation" and "a noticeable vertical and horizontal accent in the composition."[146] She argued for an origin on Rhodes, then apparently central to the distribution, and producing the greatest single concentration. She supported this with the valuable observation—still largely unappreciated—that the round-based lyres of the seals could be morphologically Aegean.[147] Having committed herself to the Rhodian hypothesis, Porada acknowledged in a postscript five further examples from Cilicia that had come to her attention, and suggested that these were made locally under Rhodian influence.[148]

The picture expanded considerably with G. Buchner's excavations of Pithekoussai on Ischia (Italy), the site of an early Euboean colony (founded ca. 775). The necropolis initially produced thirty-eight examples in twenty-nine tombs, the closed contexts verifying Porada's later eighth-century dating (ca. 740–720). The new specimens were published in 1966 by Buchner and J. Boardman, with further parallels bringing the total corpus to 162, and Italy and Etruria now well represented.[149] The inland distribution of some seals in Syria argued against a Greek source, while the closest iconographic and stylistic parallels were in the Neo-Hittite sphere; this, along with elements of N-A influence, indicated an origin in North Syria or Cilicia, with the latter especially favored by clear sympathies in the Karatepe reliefs.[150] The large numbers from Pithekoussai were explicable via Greek, and especially Euboean, trading ventures to the region (Tarsus, Al-Mina), otherwise well documented.[151]

In 1990, Boardman augmented the collection with fifty-eight further specimens and now promoted a North Syrian over Cilician origin from the distribution as newly understood.[152]

But the balance shifted decisively in 2001 when H. Poncy and others published thirty-five new examples from the Adana museum, so that Cilicia now rivaled Ischia as the single most productive region. The publishers also pointed out that the dark red and greenish serpentine commonly used for the seals is abundant in the Cilician plain.[153] When this is combined with Buchner's and

---

[146] Porada 1956:186.
[147] Porada 1956:200–204. The idea was mentioned but trivialized by Buchner and Boardman 1966:50.
[148] Porada 1956:206n66.
[149] Buchner and Boardman 1966. The Pithekoussai examples were fully published in Buchner and Ridgway 1993, who added three new examples (lacking lyre-players).
[150] Cf. Boardman in Muscarella 1981:166 ("probably Cilicia").
[151] Buchner and Boardman 1966:60–62. Euboean routes: Boardman 1980.
[152] Boardman 1990, especially 10–11.
[153] Cf. also Buchner and Boardman 1966:42.

Boardman's iconographic analysis, and the fact that the only known sphragistic use is documented at Tarsus,[154] the seals' Cilician origin is now beyond reproach. Their dating would fit with the prosperous reign of Urikki of Que/Hiyawa,[155] prior to the Cilician revolt following the death of Sargon in 705—the culmination of which in Sennacherib's destruction of Tarsus (696) would explain the seals' sudden disappearance. The Cilician setting can also account, as North Syria will not so well, for their Aegean-style lyres, given the Aegean background of Urikki's 'House of Mopsos' and the 'Half-Achaeans' (*Hypakhaioi*) of Cilicia; the Karatepe reliefs also show such an instrument, purposefully juxtaposed with one of Syro-Anatolian design.[156]

In 2009, M. A. Rizzo, unaware of the new Cilician seals, published thirty examples from the sanctuary of Athena at Ialysos (Rhodes), adding an Appendix of thirty-three further parallels not known to Boardman.[157] Embracing (casual) observations by I. Winter, Rizzo emphasized the seals' Phoenician sympathies—these had never been denied[158]—and rightly noted that their distribution in Italy, Etruria, and Greece adhered to patterns of Phoenician trade.[159] All of this caused her to revert to Porada's Rhodian hypothesis, modified to include a Phoenician workshop on the island. But this cannot be maintained against the new Cilician seals. First, these match the Rhodian specimens in simple numbers. Second, as P. Scardina rightly notes in a balanced reassessment, Phoenician stylistic elements are perfectly intelligible in Cilicia, which enjoyed a substantial Phoenician presence and influence at this time.[160] This will equally account for the seals' western distribution, including Rhodes itself; the island's steady commerce with Cilicia is reflected in the contemporary ceramic record and traditions of Rhodian 'foundation' at Cilician Soloi and probably Tarsus itself.[161]

A few further seals have since come to light,[162] and some fifty more from Pithekoussai await publication.[163] More will surely appear. But the current

---

[154] Porada 1956:186; Buchner and Boardman 1966:61; Boardman 1990:10; Scardina 2010:69.
[155] Poncy et al. 2001:11.
[156] See above, p252–253. For this point, Franklin 2006a:45; Franklin forthcoming (as from 2009); Scardina 2010:70.
[157] Rizzo 2007, following the preliminary description of Martelli 1988.
[158] Porada 1956:195–196; Buchner and Boardman 1966:60; Boardman 1990:11.
[159] Rizzo 2007:40, following Winter 1995:267n39.
[160] Scardina 2010:70; so already Boardman 1990:11. Cf. above, p199n67, 202n90, 252n50.
[161] Soloi: Strabo 14.5.8. Bing 1971:103–104 plausibly argued for Lindians at Tarsus on the basis of Eusebios' account (Schoene 1967 1:35) of Sennacherib building a temple of 'Athenians' (i.e. of Athena) there soon after its capture/destruction in 696, and the importance of Athena's cult at Lindos.
[162] SAM no. 23a-c, f; Rizzo 2008–2009; Cerchiai and Nava 2008–2009 (but see n183 below).
[163] Buchner and Boardman 1966:62 Postscript; Rizzo 2007:71–72.

corpus of 345 separate images (some seals are four-sided) presents a sufficiently representative sample for confident analysis.

We saw that the primary function of seals—as a form of identification—is attested for the Group by an impression from Tarsus. As Boardman pointed out, however, these were "very much a ... bazaar product," requiring perhaps ten minutes each to make.[164] Therefore, not much evidence for sphragistic use is to be expected from elite contexts. Probably from the start, these seals also served an amuletic function, as commonly in the ANE from earliest times.[165] This helps explain what may otherwise seem a dramatic contextual shift in Cyprus, Greece, and Italy. In the first two areas, our seals are usually found as votive offerings in coastal sanctuaries.[166] This distribution naturally coincides with the routes by which the seals themselves were carried; perhaps some were dedicated for safe voyages, again an apotropaic function.[167] The Italian and Etrurian finds show that the seals were indeed worn, since silver mountings are sometimes found.[168] Many specimens come from tombs, especially on Ischia where they normally appear in graves of the young. This context especially has suggested an amuletic use.[169] That is probable enough, though we may equally suspect a fad at work given the narrow period of manufacture, the downmarket buyership, and Pithekoussai's position in the Euboean trade network; as Boardman noted, the entire collection could fit in a single sack.[170] The seals' attractive designs were clearly popular, and this will have fueled production.[171] Note that, as with the Cypro-Phoenician symposium bowls, the seals' round-based lyres will have presented a familiar-yet-exotic aspect to Greek customers.[172]

Turning to the actual imagery, Porada proposed that, in accord with ANE ideas, their "designs were meant to secure for the owner the protection of the deities whose symbolic animals or monsters, whose worship or ritual or whose very image appears in the seal designs"; in particular the images of birds and lions—especially one with a goddess standing on a lion—suggested some form of the 'Syrian Goddess'.[173] Buchner and Boardman, observing the random distribution

---

[164] Buchner and Boardman 1966:58; Boardman 1990:10 (quotation).
[165] Porada 1956:198. See generally Collon 1987:113, 119; CANE 3:1600–1601 (Pittman).
[166] Boardman 1990:10.
[167] Rizzo 2007:39–41.
[168] Buchner and Boardman 1966:42–43; Boardman 1990:10.
[169] Buchner and Boardman 1966:22–23; Boardman 1990:9–10.
[170] Boardman 1990:10.
[171] Porada 1956:198; Buchner and Boardman 1966:11.
[172] See p272.
[173] Porada 1956:198, noting especially B1 44 (her fig. 12). But while the individual elements of this seal can mostly be paralleled by others in the Group, its overall style is quite different, and it may well come from a different workshop.

of seal-motifs in the Ischia burials, concluded that amuletic properties adhered to the seals per se (by virtue of their stone).[174] Doubtless the large repertoire of motifs was in part commercially motivated (something for everybody). But this need not invalidate Porada's sensible suggestion (even apart from the possibility that the seals were repurposed at Pithekoussai). As variable as the seals' designs are, the great majority adheres to a single underlying iconographic system. Thus, any one specimen could potentially invoke the 'meaning' of the whole.

The Group is characterized by a tendency towards abbreviation—of more complex scenes from which one or a few elements might be extracted for a given seal; and of the elements themselves, which can appear in shorthand form, making room for other details.[175] The latter pattern is most conspicuous with the Sacred Tree, which in its fullest form includes volutes and palmette foliage, and can be flanked by detached palmettes. This provides the interpretive key for the free-floating palmettes and volutes that are otherwise common.[176] When all such forms are taken together, the Sacred Tree emerges as the Group's primary motif (in 45 percent of the corpus).[177] Appearing variously within its orbit are sphinxes or gryphons, quadrupeds (deer and goats), birds (the seals' second most common element at 43 percent), worshippers both human and divine, besides winged sun-disks and the occasional ankh.[178] That the Tree stands for a goddess, as often in ANE art, is confirmed by one example where the Tree's position between worshippers is taken by the goddess herself.[179]

The iconography is certainly eclectic, and Boardman was reluctant to assign it much concrete religious meaning.[180] But as D. Collon reminds us of ANE seals generally, "what we too often tend to regard as a haphazard collection of filling motifs had the purpose of involving as many deities and beneficent powers as possible on behalf of the seal owner."[181] The Lyre-Player Group's dynamic range recalls the Cypro-Phoenician bowls—if one viewed them with a periscope. Indeed the bowls are a vital parallel. For their thematic material is equally wide-ranging, with scenes of daily life and the decorative treatment of elements from several traditions; but as we saw, this mélange does not negate the religious

---

[174] Buchner and Boardman 1966:22.
[175] Buchner and Boardman 1966:58; Boardman 1990:8.
[176] Buchner and Boardman 1966:56.
[177] Thus corroborating the analysis of Buchner and Boardman 1966:57.
[178] Human figures: Buchner and Boardman 1966 nos. 90, 160; two winged figures flanking the Sacred Tree as in N-A reliefs: no. 147.
[179] Buchner and Boardman 1966 no. 41c: lowest register of a three-tier seal; the middle is occupied by enthroned lyrist, table, and frame-drummer (my Type IIIc).
[180] Boardman 1990:10 ("an amalgam of borrowed and native religious motifs without any very specific significance").
[181] Collon 1987:119, cf. 170.

connotations of the frequent musical cult-scene, which persisted throughout the bowls' lifecycle on Cyprus, part of their home territory (Chapter 11). The seals that feature lyre-players assume a rather similar backdrop. I have analyzed this subset into several Types, which I rank in order of the apparent importance of the Lyre-Player himself (see Table 2 and Figure 46). I say 'apparent', and now use a singular, capitalized 'Lyre-Player', because all Types, I propose, participate in a single iconographic subsystem that may be deduced from them collectively, with each Type taking its meaning from the others.

Type	Motif	Exemplars[182]
I	Standing Winged Lyrist, Sacred Tree	2
IIa	Standing Lyrist, Sacred Tree, Bird	3
IIb	Standing Lyrist, Bird	12
IIc	Standing Lyrist, Sphinx/Gryphon	3
IId	Standing Lyrist, Bird, Devotee (?)	1
IIIa	Enthroned Lyrist, Sacred Tree	5
IIIb	Enthroned Lyrist, Drinking	2
IIIc	Enthroned Lyrist, Table, Female Drummer	3
IIId	Enthroned Lyrist, Female Drummer	8
IIIe	Enthroned Lyrist, Fish	1
IIIf	Enthroned Lyrist, Devotee (?)	1
IVa	Standing Lyrist, Sacred Tree, Female Drummer	1
IVb	Dancing Lyrist, Female Drummer, Ankh	1
IVc	Standing Lyrist, Piper, Drummer Trio	5
Va	Seated Figure, Standing Lyrist, Two Devotees	1
Vb	Seated Figure, Trio, Devotees	5
Vc	Seated Figure, Lyrist and Piper, Devotees	1

Table 2. Typology of Lyrists in the Lyre-Player Group of Seals.

[182] Numbers according to the following publications: A (Adana) = Poncy et al. 2001. BB = Buchner and Boardman 1966. B2 = Boardman 1990. I (Ialysos) = Rizzo 2007. IAP = Rizzo 2007 Appendix. SAM (see Abbreviations), Bible Lands Museum, not including two catalogued in B2. Type I: A1; B2 164. IIa: BB 9; IAP 11, 23. IIb: A2, 6; BB 7–8, 45, 89, 137; B2 120^5; IAP 7, 10; Rizzo 2008–2009, fig. 2; SAM 23f. IIc: BB 88, 126; B2 113^5. IId: A5. IIIa: A7–8; BB 118; I 6; SAM 23a. IIIb: B2 163; I 5. IIIc: BB 41 (middle register), 125; SAM 23c. IIId: A3; BB 114, 139a; B2 113bis, 113ter; IAP 12, 14; SAM 23b.

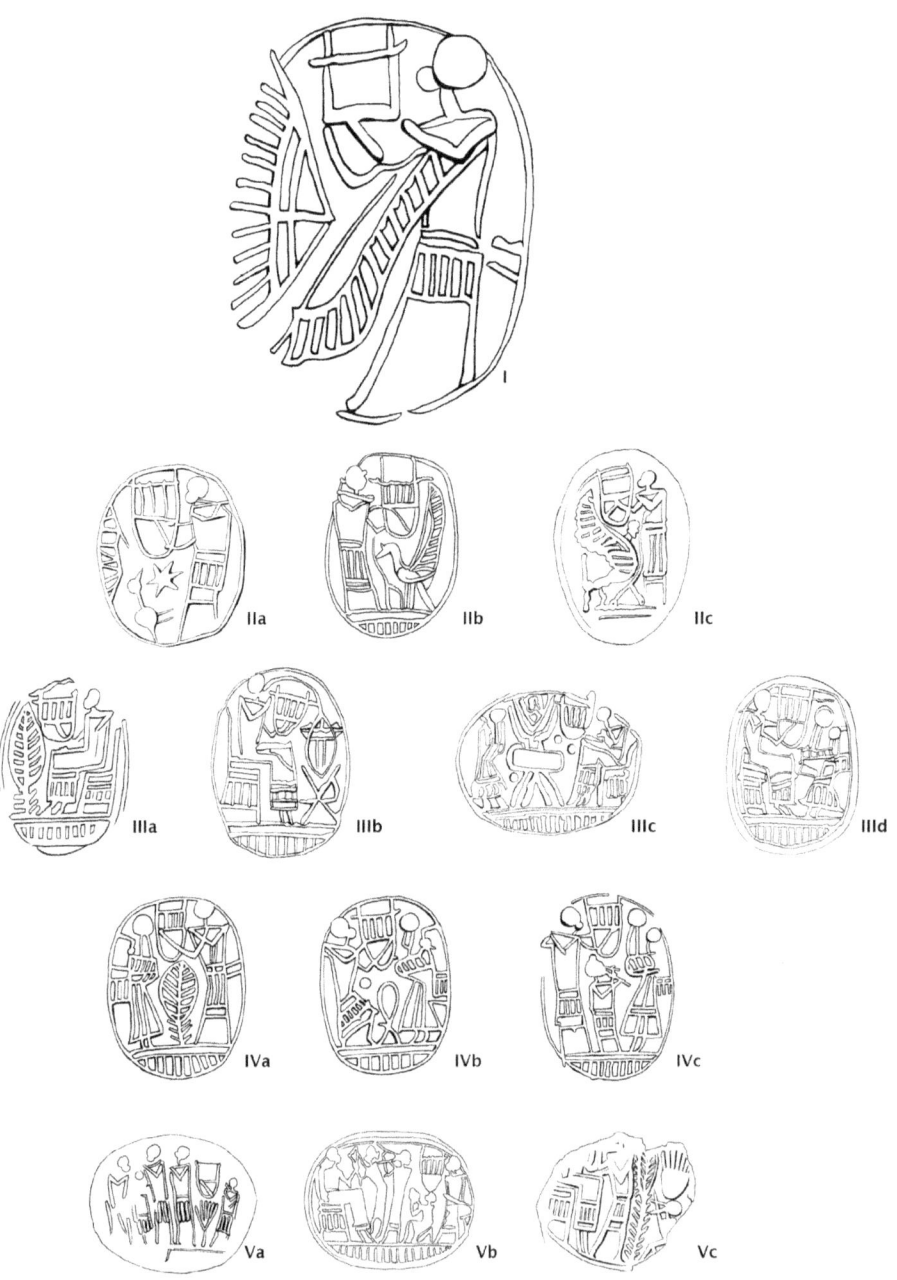

Figure 46 The Lyre-Player Group of Seals (subset with Lyrist). Drawn variously from images in Boardman and Buchner 1966; Boardman 1990; Rizzo 2007; SAM. For individual references, see p523n182.

What may be regarded as the full cult-scene is found only occasionally. In several variations (Types Va–c), it shows an enthroned figure attended by musicians and other devotees, sometimes with an offering.[183] This is clearly a form of the ritual banquet so common in ANE art; and here as elsewhere one cannot distinguish between human and divine beneficiaries.[184] The ambiguity is reinforced by the identical clothing of the seated figure and the winged gods in other specimens.[185]

As with the Cypro-Phoenician bowls, where lyrists predominate despite considerable variation in the ensembles' makeup, the Lyrist in our seals is the only musical constant; he appears alone (Va), with a double-piper (Vc), or with the standard Syro-Levantine trio of lyre, pipes, and frame-drum (Vb). The same favoritism applies in Type IV, but now the focus narrows to the cult-scene's musical dimension. The full trio/orchestra can be shown (IVc), or just the Lyrist and frame-drummer (IVa–IVb). The latter—reminiscent of Hittite ritual texts calling for lyre and drum together[186]—leave room for an abbreviated Sacred Tree, and reveal the ultimate center of the celebration, thus explaining the apparent precedence of musical performance per se over the enthroned listener of Type V.

This conclusion is corroborated by Type III, which presents a startling shift. For the throne is now occupied by the Lyre-Player himself, who is thus drawn into the human-divine borderland this seat entails. The mutual coherence of Types III and IV is shown by the pivotal and frequent IIId, where the Lyrist again faces a female frame-drummer, but is now the clear focus of her performance—a striking prediction of Pindar's Cypriot choruses around Kinyras. That the seated Lyrist is one-and-the-same as the enthroned figure of Type V's full cult-scenes is shown by the other variations in Type III, which implicate him in the banquet. He drinks through a straw from a large vessel (IIIb), an ancient Mesopotamian motif relatively scarce by now, but seen on the roughly contemporary Hubbard amphora (Figure 26 = 5.5p).[187] The feast- or offerings-table can appear between the Lyrist and the frame-drummer (IIIc), reiterating the connection of her

---

IIIe: B2 113quater. IIIf: B2 165. IVa: I 3. IVb: I 4. IVc: A4, 11; BB 103, 161; I 2. Va: B2 120ter. Vb: BB 162; B2 62quater, 120bis, 167 (? see n183 above); IAP 1. Vc: BB 115.

[183] The fullest certain scenes are B2 62quater, 120bis, and IAP 1. Boardman 1990:8 regarded the Seyrig seal (B2 167) as most complete; but this seal's attribution to the Group is rightly questioned by Scardina 2010:68 and n20, along with the recent find from Monte Vetrano (Salerno)—another complex lyre-and-drinking rite (Cerchiai and Nava 2008–2009, fig. 8b), but with none of the defining stylistic feature of the Lyre-Player Group. Of course these further seals are still of great interest as representing parallel workshops within closely related traditions.

[184] Porada 1956:198; Buchner and Boardman 1966.

[185] Buchner and Boardman 1966:44, 57.

[186] See p95.

[187] This comparison was made by Boardman 1990:8–9.

performance with the larger rite, while maintaining the Lyre-Player's twofold role as both singer and song-recipient. A puzzling variant shows the Lyrist with a fish (IIIe, image unavailable); I have noted its potential relevance to Kinyras the Mariner.[188] In a final permutation, the enthroned Lyrist adores the Sacred Tree (IIIa): whatever honors he himself receives are passed on through his own performance to this higher power. The same connection is illustrated by the lower register of seal BB 41c (Type IIIc), an explicit scene of goddess worship.[189] This dual focus is precisely what we saw in the first Kourion stand—an enthroned musician who mediates between his celebrants and a Sacred Tree standing for a Goddess.[190]

With Type II we return to the standing Lyrist of Type IV. But now the exalted status granted by Type III is maintained through the Lyre-Player appearing by himself and along with winged familiars. Most common (IIb) is a bird, that ancient companion of lyre scenes—and indeed lyre-morphology—in the ANE and Aegean, typically suggesting divine inspiration and epiphany through music.[191] This idea is not invalidated for our seals by the bird's appearance in other groupings; that the bird itself stands for divinity is shown by specimens where it takes the place of goddess or Tree as the object of adoration.[192] This reading of the Lyrist-bird conjunction is corroborated by the inclusion of a devotee in one variant (IId[193]) and the Sacred Tree in another (IIa). Similarly exalted tones are roused by the gryphon or sphinx who accompanies the musician in Type IIc. These creatures, we saw, had a deep history in Cyprus attending Sacred Trees and royal or divine figures; one was seen on the second Kourion stand with the two harpers—standing and enthroned, face-to-face.[194]

The Lyre-Player, progressively assimilated to royal and divine registers in Types IV, III, and II, achieves full apotheosis in Type I. This is represented by only two precious exemplars, unknown when the seals were first studied.[195] Again the Lyrist stands before the Sacred Tree, but now magnificently winged.[196] He is a fully fledged divinity in his own rite.

The oscillation between seated and standing lyre-players had already suggested to Porada the possibility that "in these scenes the lyre player is no

---

[188] See p330.
[189] See n179 above.
[190] See p383–388.
[191] See p126, 178, 192, 247. Anent these seals, Scardina 2010:69. For Mesopotamian lexical evidence connecting birds and instruments, including the balang, see now Mirelman forthcoming.
[192] Buchner and Boardman 1966:12–13, 152, etc.
[193] The published image was too small for inclusion in our Figure 46.
[194] See p388–391.
[195] One was first published by Boardman in Muscarella 1981:166.
[196] Buchner and Boardman 1966:4, 48, 147.

ordinary mortal or even a priestly musician but the god Apollo."[197] Buchner and Boardman were more cautious about the seated musician: "the other lyre-players seem not to be divinities, and there is no lyre-player god, Greek or eastern, with both a bird and a sphinx as familiars."[198] Both statements were shaped by the search for the seals' origin: 'Apollo' would support Porada's Rhodian hypothesis, but undermine the Cilician/North Syrian analysis. True, Buchner and Boardman include the qualification "Greek or eastern" in their agnostic declaration. But what 'eastern lyre-player god' could they have named *at all*—with or without bird and sphinx? For that was before Kinnaru had risen again from Ugarit. The Type I seals change the picture completely, as Boardman himself later recognized:

> The role of the lyre player, as recipient of attention or himself an attendant, is ambivalent ... We were reluctant to accord him divine status. Now, however ... he is found winged and the possibility of his divinity has to be entertained.[199]

But even this is surely too cautious. Boardman himself went on to compare the Cypriot cult-shrines we examined in Chapter 10, which he had previously connected with the Homeric expression "divine singer" (*theîos aoidós*). Then too he had puzzled over the identity of this eastern Lyre God, hoping his name might one day be discovered.[200]

There should now be little doubt that the seals' winged Lyre-Player is closely akin to Kinnaru of Ugarit and Kinyras of Cyprus. By whatever name he was known to the artisan and his apprentices who cut the seals, these remarkable images provide a welcome and solid basis for the literary traditions of a Syro-Cilician 'Kinyras'. They give us our clearest representation of a Divine Lyre. That the instrument is never shown alone is consistent with the vital role of performance in summoning the divine. But the lyre itself *is* effectively spotlighted as the common ground in all five Types—from the cultic musicians of V–IV, through the royal lyrists of III, and the increasingly numinous II and I. At the climactic epiphany, the Divine Lyre stands before his Goddess, serving her in song—embodying all cult performers and the lyrist-king himself. Here is the very essence of Kinyras.

---

[197] Porada 1956:200.
[198] Buchner and Boardman 1966:50.
[199] Boardman 1990:7, 10.
[200] See p238–239.

APPENDICES

Appendix A
A Note on 'Balang' in the Gudea Cylinders

THE BALANG WAS THE USUAL INSTRUMENT of the gala's song. But the description of Ušumgal-kalama in the Gudea Cylinders shows that, in the third millennium at least, a balang could also appear in the hands of the nar.[1] The identity of the balang has long been controversial. But it is now quite certain that this word, of perhaps onomatopoeic origin, originally denoted a stringed instrument (before undergoing a notorious semantic shift to 'drum' by or in the OB period, perhaps due to changes in performance practice).[2] Crucial is the equation of balaĝ with *kinnārum* in early lexical texts from Ebla and Mesopotamia (ca. 2400).[3] Gabbay has advanced new arguments for identifying the early balang as a kind of lyre on a triple basis of iconography, the expression GU4.BALAĜ ('balang-bull'[4]), and the shape of the BALAĜ sign itself, which he derives from the bull-lyre prominent in Sumerian art of the third millennium.[5] But debate continues: Heimpel now counters with an attractive defense of the older curved-harp identification, again proceeding from iconography and

---

[1] See p28; cf. Shehata 2006a:120 and n8; Gabbay 2014 §11n31; PHG:103 on the expression nar.balaĝ: "According to my understanding, the tigi and the balaĝ were the same type of instrument (at least originally), the difference between them being their cultic context: the balaĝ was associated with the repertoire of the gala, and the tigi (written with the signs BALAĜ and NAR) with the repertoire of the nar." For several other Sumerian terms containing the element balaĝ, without necessarily referring to the gala, see PHG:82n4. For comparable evidence from Ebla, see p65–67.

[2] The basic sources and issues may already be found in Hartmann 1960:52–67. See now Gabbay 2014, especially §2–5; PHG:67–68, 98–102, 153–154. Onomatopoeic origin: Selz 1997:195n153; Heimpel 1998b:2; Gabbay 2014 §2n7; Heimpel, "Balang-Gods," 4g.

[3] I stressed the evidence from Ebla in Franklin 2006a:43n8; see further p54, 65–67.

[4] The order of signs makes the translation 'balang-bull' preferable to 'bull-balang' (W. Heimpel, communication, October 10, 2013).

[5] Gabbay 2014 §2, and PHG:92–98. Bull-headed lyres have often been identified by scholars as zà.mí (see the review of Lawergren and Gurney 1987:40–43 and the problems raised there); but Gabbay notes that, while the Akkadian equivalent *sammû* is well-attested in the first millennium, bull-lyres have all but disappeared (§2n9). Bull-lyres: MgB 2/2:28–35, 38–41, 44–45, 50–51, 60–61, 64–67, all with figures.

531

Appendix A

sign-evolution.⁶ Of course we must beware of projecting modern organological distinctions onto ancient perceptions; the morphological difference between 'lyre' and 'harp', as defined by von Hornbostel and Sachs, may have been less significant than performance functions.⁷ Consequently, the analyses of this book do not stand or fall with one identification of balang or another.

Of course, one may still question the meaning of balang in the Gudea Cylinders, which one might suppose are late enough to have used the word in its secondary sense. Thus, some would identify Ušumgal-kalama with the giant drum shown several times in the steles, an apparent prominence that would well fit (the argument goes) the balang-god's importance implied by his year-name.⁸ But S. Mirelman has now shown that the giant drum, both here and in the Ur-Nammu stele, is in fact the á-lá.⁹ This instrument, too, is featured in the cylinders, being played for instance in a group that accompanies the making of bricks.¹⁰ The relevant steles may therefore show the instrument as part of the building process, rather than the bestowal of gifts during the temple's inauguration.¹¹ Moreover, the giant drum's visibility is counterbalanced by another stele-fragment from Lagash showing a typical bull-headed lyre (Figure 47).¹² It is surmounted by a smaller bull—a visual echo that seemingly "anime l'objet d'une sorte de vie."¹³ Stylistic considerations indicate that this stele is rather

---

6 Heimpel 2014; "Balang-Gods," Section I.
7 See further p3n14, 90–93, 391–392.
8 Suter 2000:ST.9, (p. 350), 13 (p. 358), 54 (p. 386). The image is connected with the balang by Jean 1931:159; Black 1991:28 and n39; Suter 2000:193 and Civil 2008:100 follow Black in considering balang unambiguously a drum in the time of Gudea (98n138); but note that Black himself was "at a loss" to explain the lexical evidence from Ebla (see p54, 65–67). It might also be felt that the name 'Great Dragon of the Land' is more appropriate to the sound of a giant drum than a lyre. Yet PHG:113–114 includes Ušumgal-kalama among those balang-gods who bear names that reflect properties of their master-god, since Ningirsu is "often portrayed as a snake (ušum)."
9 Mirelman 2014, arguing from the huge size and weight indicated by textual sources. Moreover, as Mirelman notes in a postscript, the á-lá is often connected with the si-im (e.g. both are found in the 'balang-hall' of Eninnu: Gudea Cylinders A 28.18); and since the latter's identification as cymbals in Ur III and later texts is secured by their occurrence in pairs and being made of copper and bronze (Mirelman 2010), one may identify as á-lá and si-im, respectively, the giant drum and cymbals that are paired in the Ur-Nammu and Gudea steles (Gudea: Suter 2000:ST.54, cf. p191; Ur-Nammu stele: MgB 2/2:72–73 (fig. 54–55); Suter 2000, figures on pp. 245–259).
10 Gudea Cylinders A 18.18. It appears also at A 28.18 (in the 'balang-hall'); B 15.20 (among the instruments governed by Ušumgal-kalama); B 19.1, accompanying Ušumgal-kalama when Gudea goes into Eninnu to sacrifice).
11 For the former view, see Mirelman 2014, under "Performance Contexts. a) Building rituals"; the latter is espoused by Suter 2000:190–195.
12 de Sarzec 1884–1912 2, pl. 23 (discussed 1:219–220); MgB 2/2:66–67 (fig. 45); Suter 2000:ST.10 (p. 352).
13 The quotation is from de Sarzec 1884–1912 1:220, whose observation avails even if the second bull represents a physical feature. Another such 'double-bull' lyre is shown on a stamp-seal

Figure 47 Sumerian Bull-headed lyre with 'emergent' bull. Stele-fragment, Lagash, before 2100. Paris, Louvre AO 52. Drawn from MgB 2/2 fig. 45.

Appendix A

earlier than Gudea's own building program.[14] Nevertheless, there are significant sympathies with the iconography and poetics of the Gudea steles. An upper register shows a procession of figures carrying building and measuring tools, presumably on their way to a construction site.[15] They are preceded by a ruler, whose role is thus comparable to that of Gudea as royal overseer. So here the bull-lyre has all the associations that have been thought to make the giant drum of the Gudea steles worthy of identification with Ušumgal-kalama. Note too the 'Hall of the Balang'(part of the temple of Ningirsu), which the Gudea Cylinders liken to the sound of a 'roaring bull'—an apt description if the balang was in fact the bull-lyre.[16]

All told, therefore, one is well justified in supposing that the balang-gods of Ningirsu were indeed stringed instruments.[17]

---

found at Falaika in the Persian Gulf, now in the Kuwait Museum: Barnett 1969:100–101 with fig. 1 and pl. XVIb; RlA 6:580 (Collon, *Leier B).

[14] See Suter 2000:184–185, suggesting it might show a governor of Lagash during the period of Akkadian rule.

[15] Suter 2000:264.

[16] Gudea Cylinders A 28.17; George 1993:63 §4; RlA 8:468 (Kilmer, *Musik A I); Heimpel 1998b:4 and 15n8; Gabbay 2014 §13n37. Another "Chamber of the balang" is found as a shrine of the god Gula in a cultic lament, later qualified as "Chamber of the Princely balang": George 1993:85 §293, 708; cf. RlA 8:468 (Kilmer, *Musik A I).

[17] See also Heimpel's argument that Ušumgal-kalama was a *lute*: "Balang-Gods," Section 1b.

Appendix B

Ptolemy Khennos as a Source for the Contest of Kinyras and Apollo

THE *NOVEL HISTORY* (*KAINḔ HISTORÍA*) by the early imperial wonder-monger Ptolemy 'The Quail' Khennos is known mainly from a terse epitome by Photios, but was equally available to Eustathios, who reproduces a dozen episodes in fuller detail without naming his source (n.b.).[1] That Eustathios could have seen further material *not* mentioned by Photios is made possible by Tzetzes, who knew an episode absent from the epitome.[2]

In keeping with its title, the *Novel History* collected unorthodox myth-variants, especially tangential Homeric back-stories and parallel realities. While some of these were pure invention complete with bogus source citations,[3] others were genuinely rooted in and/or inspired by epichoric traditions.[4] Several episodes involving Apollo and Aphrodite—including an androgynous Adonis beloved of both—point clearly to Cyprus, where in the late Classical and Hellenistic periods these gods were the go-to Olympians for calquing a wide variety of local figures.[5] Ptolemy also reveled in etymologies—including a wordplay on *háls, halós*, 'salt/sea', as I have also proposed for Kinyras' halcyon-daughters—and etymology-driven aetiology, for instance the object-hero Korythos, inventor of the helmet (*kórythos*).[6] And he had a decided interest in local music trivia: the invention of the obscure *skindapsós* (lute? lyre?) by a legendary Skindapsos, another object-hero; accounts of musical conflicts and contests—Apollo and Marsyas, the Pythian citharodic event, Odysseus winning

---

[1] Photios *Library* 146a40–153b29. See van der Valk 1971–1987:CIX § 111–112; Chatzis 1914 (with the versions of Photios and Eustathios in parallel); Cameron 2004:135.
[2] Ptolemy Khennos fr. 1 (Chatzis 1914:46, cf. XLI) = John Tzetzes *Khiliades* 8.195, lines 368–380.
[3] For a clear case, see Cameron 2004:137–142.
[4] This view is often taken by Tomberg 1968, e.g. on the Adonis material (see next note) and on the 'piping Odysseus' (193–194, with the further observations of Power 2012).
[5] Photios *Library* 146b41–147a2, 151b5–7, 153a11–23, with comments of Tomberg 1968:194–195n144, 197n150, 150–151n5, respectively.
[6] Photios *Library* 150a12–19 (goofing on Homer *Odyssey* 11.134, Odysseus' death ἐξ ἁλός), 147b34–36. See further Tomberg 1968:94–99.

Appendix B

an *aulós* competition in Etruria (recently discussed by T. Power); and a whole section "On who composed songs for which cities."[7]

The contest of Kinyras and Apollo would fit perfectly into this portfolio. Following the hypothesis we would then suppose that Eustathios fleshed out the notice in the Homeric scholia by restoring further details from direct consultation of Ptolemy, notably the derivation from *kinýra* of Kinyras and *kinýresthai* (in connection with the hero's daughters mourning his death?).

---

[7] Skindapsos: Photios *Library* 152b20–25 (for the instrument, SIAG:185–186; AGM:60); Marsyas: 149a5–8; Pythian contest: 153a1–5; piping Odysseus: 152b32–36, with Power 2012; songs/cities: 148a410–411.

Appendix C
Horace, Cinara, and the Syrian *Musiciennes* of Rome

HORACE ALLUDES SEVERAL TIMES to a certain Cinara whom he loved in his youth, and her untimely death. She may of course be partly or largely poetic fiction, like other lover-muses of Roman elegy. This role she most clearly fulfils at the start of *Odes* 4.1, when the poet, returning to lyric after a hiatus, pretends to have lost what power he had "in the reign of good Cinara."[1]

The name, most uncommon, has been connected with Gk. *kínara* ('artichoke') and its aphrodisiac properties.[2] Without excluding this as a possible secondary association, a musical interpretation is ineluctably urged by Cinara's counterparts in the elegiac corpus. These are modeled on foreign courtesan-musicians, thus conveniently embodying romance, poetic inspiration, and neoteric exoticism in a single source. A lyric identity is implied for Catullus' Lesbia, who evokes the tenth muse Sappho; while Tibullus' Cynthia and Propertius' Delia allude to the lyre-loving Apollo and Artemis. Horace himself elsewhere mentions a certain "Chia, trained in plucking" and a "Thracian Chloe, expert on the *cithara*" (who nevertheless pales beside Lydia, who made him happier than a Persian king).[3]

While Cinara lacks a straightforward geographical name, the required foreign association is vividly supplied by the Syrian lyre that she must incarnate. Compare the *musiciennes* called *sambŷkai* ('arched harps', cf. Aram. *ṣabbekā*, Akk. *sammû*) who entered Greco-Roman life in the Hellenistic period.[4] Horace's

---

[1] Horace *Odes* 4.1.3–4 (*bonae / sub regno Cinarae*), cf. 4.13.21–23, *Epistles* 1.7.28, 1.14.33. See Johnson 2004:29; more generally Putnam 1986:33–42 for the 'loving-muse' motif, but focusing on the invocation of Venus.

[2] Or still more obscurely the tiny island of Kinaros in the Dodecanese: for both see Coletti 1996–1998 and Johnson 2004:229n88 with references. A *paedagogus* called Cinarus is epigraphically attested at the second-third century CE Rhegium: Buonocore 1989:65–66; Hutchinson 2006:78. One of Aeneas' companions appears variously as Cinyrus, Ciniris, or Cunarus at Vergil *Aeneid* 10.186: see Roscher *Lex*. s.v. Kinyros.

[3] Horace *Odes* 4.13.7 (*doctae psallere Chiae*); 3.9.9–10 (*Thressa Chloe ... citharae sciens*).

[4] AGM:75–77.

Appendix C

interest in Syrian music-girls is otherwise attested by the *ambubaiarum collegia* ("colleges of pipers") who head his appealing list of artistic low-lifes to whom the late piper Tigellius was so generous; that the *ambubaiae* certainly took their name from an ancient Semitic word for double-pipes (Akk. *embūbu*, Ebl. *na-bu-bù-um*) is a strong parallel for seeing 'Cinara' as also embodying a Syrian instrument.[5] Another Cinara is found in Propertius and mentioned by his Babylonian Horus in the context of poetic inspiration.[6] Even if this is no more than an allusion to Horace, it confirms both the generic nature of 'Cinara' herself, and the proposed eastern interpretation. Recall the *kinyrístriai* who were said to be resident in the temple of the Babylonian Hera.[7]

Such *musiciennes* must have come to Rome especially after Pompey's annexation of Syria in 64 BCE. Juvenal, a century after Horace, looks back on the flood of Syrian music-girls who prostituted themselves around the Circus, playing the very instruments that are illustrated in the ensembles ('colleges') of ninth/eighth-century Syrian and Cypro-Phoenician art (Figures 29, 31): double-pipes, frame-drums, and "horizontal strings" (*obliquas / chordas*)—an unambiguous allusion to Syro-Levantine playing technique.[8] One should recall Isaiah's *kinnōr*-playing 'harlot' of Tyre, the 'lyre-of-lust' (*kinar šiha*) in Mandaean tradition, and so on.[9] Another Syro-Levantine lyre known in Roman life at this time was the *nablium* ('little *nábla*'), which Ovid advised would-be courtesans to take up.[10]

Thus, while the 'biography' of Cinara remains obscure, a Syrian lyric identity accords perfectly with the poetic conventions and cultural realities of Horace's time.

---

[5] Ambubaiae: Horace *Satires* 1.2.1; cf. Suetonius *Nero* 27; Petronius *Satyricon* 74.13. For the Akk. and Ebl. forms, see p55n44, 201n145. A Mandaean legend features a group of six *ambūbi*, maidens raised as a piping ensemble in the palace of Hirmiz Shah: Drower 1937:394–396.
[6] Propertius 4.1.99–102. Cf. Hutchinson 2006 *ad loc*.
[7] See p216.
[8] Juvenal *Satires* 3.62–65: *iam pridem Syrus in Tiberim defluxit Orontes / et linguam et mores et cum tibicine chordas / obliquas nec non gentilia tympana secum / vexit et ad circum iussas prostare puellas* ("The Syrian Orontes has long since descended the Tiber / And with it hauled its language and customs and its / Strings Aslant, with the piper, its native drums too / And girls compelled to sell themselves around the Circus").
[9] Isaiah 23:15–16; cf. p60, 302.
[10] Ovid *Art of Love* 3.315–316.

Appendix D
Kinyrízein: The View from Stoudios

I HAVE ARGUED THAT *KINYRÍZEIN* meant first and foremost 'play the *kinýra*'.[1] This is corroborated by the word's third and latest attestation—in a passage of Theodoros, Abbot of the monastery of Stoudios (Constantinople) in the first years of the ninth century.

Tired of seeing his monks giving themselves to worldly pleasures about the place, Theodoros exhorts them to ascetic devotion, calling for continuous adherence to the community program:

> Let us forsake our pleasures (*thelḗmata*) ... Let me not find anyone chatting at random, or smiling, or playing the *kinýra* (*kinyrízonta*), or singing chants (*troparízonta*) ... For there is a proper time for every action. Is it time for chatting? Chat. Time for silence? Be silent. Time for Psalm-singing (*psalmōidías*)? Sing your Psalms (*psálate*).[2]

One might try to construe *kinyrízonta* here as untimely 'complaining', by contrast with the "chatting" and "smiling" that immediately precede. Yet a musical meaning is equally supported by the adjacent *troparízonta*, which refers to the singing of *tropária*, hymnic prayers often inserted after Psalm-verses, and forming part of Matins and Vespers by the fifth century.[3] Moreover, *kinyrízonta* and *troparízonta* would neatly correspond, rhetorically, to the exhortation *psálate*. But what exactly is implied by the antithesis?

In medieval Christian usage, *psállein* regularly means simply 'to sing psalms' of the Davidic canon. In earlier centuries, however, it also described 'private' religious compositions. C. H. Cosgrove has recently shown that dinner parties and symposia, key loci of private performance in the Greco-Roman world,

---

[1] See p206–210, 316–318.
[2] Theodoros of Stoudios *Great Catechism* 91 (651.3-19 Papadopoulos-Kerameus 1904): καταλείψωμεν πάντα τὰ θελήματα ἡμῶν ... καὶ μὴ εὕροιμί τινα ὡς ἔτυχε λαλοῦντα, ἢ προσγελῶντα, ἢ κινυρίζοντα, ἢ τροπαρίζοντα ... καιρὸς γὰρ τῷ παντὶ πράγματι. καιρὸς λαλιᾶς; λαλήσατε. καιρὸς σιγῆς; σιγήσατε. ψαλμῳδίας; ψάλατε.
[3] HBMH:171–179. Cf. PGL s.v. τροπάρι(o)ν: "any metrical composition sung in church services."

continued for early Christians as a venue for the musical expression of religious feelings.[4] The validity of such performances was grudgingly conceded by Clement of Alexandria and other church fathers,[5] who otherwise campaigned against the use of instruments in the liturgy itself—these being associated with popular spectacles and festivals patronized by pagan deities.[6] Their concessions, in accommodating lyre-music specifically, perpetuate ancient ideas about the instrument's salubrious properties (versus the unsettling *aulós*).[7] This early 'Christian lyric' finds its semantic diapason in *psállein* itself, which literally refers to plucking a stringed instrument with the fingers—a technique sometimes specified for the *kinnōr/kinýra*, versus the plectrum usually used for the *kithára*.[8] The same conjunction of instrument and technique is also assumed in Gk. *psaltḗrion* (Lat. *psalterium*), which often translates Heb. *kinnōr* (when *kinýra* itself is not used).[9] It is no accident, therefore, that the well-known Christian hymn with musical notation, from the late third century, is in the Hypolydian *tónos*—one of the basic citharodic keys—and spans the typically 'lyric' range of an octave.[10]

Such 'private' compositions, whose free texts opened the door to heretical sentiments, were condemned for liturgical use by the Council of Laodicea (360 CE), which allowed only hymns based on the canonical psalms; that this edict was only partially successful is indicated by the renewed strictures of the Council of Braga (563 CE).[11] While the general trend was to exclude instruments from the liturgy (except for the organ),[12] private devotional poetry must have continued.

---

[4] Cosgrove 2006:260–265, 282.
[5] See especially Clement of Alexandria *Tutor* 2.4.43: Οὗτος ἡμῶν ὁ κῶμος ὁ εὐχάριστος, κἂν πρὸς κιθάραν ἐθελήσῃς ἢ λύραν ᾄδειν τε καὶ ψάλλειν, μῶμος οὐκ ἔστιν, with a literal (not allegorical) reading of this and other passages well defended by Cosgrove 2006:260; cf. John Chrysostomus *Exposition of Psalm 41* (PG 55:158, 15–17).
[6] See e.g. Clement of Alexandria *Tutor* 3.11.80, *Exhortation* 2.15.3, 2.24.1, 12.119.2–120.2; cf. HBMH:94–97.
[7] Cosgrove 2006:260–261.
[8] In the LXX, *psállein* and cognates almost always reflect some form of Heb. *zmr* ('sing/play') in contexts clearly involving stringed instruments (Botterweck and Ringgren 1997–2006:97). Both plucking and picking are attested for the *kinnōr*, with the difference probably relating to performance contexts. When David soothes Saul, plucking is in order (1 Samuel 16:23; Josephus *Antiquities of the Jews* 6.166: ψάλλειν ἐπὶ κινύρᾳ), cf. 6.168. When he transports the Ark, the greater force of a pick was desirable (Josephus *Antiquities of the Jews* 7.85: ἐν κινύρᾳ . . . κροτοῦντος), cf. 7.306 (τύπτεται πλήκτρῳ, contrasted with the νάβλα(ς), which τοῖς δακτύλοις κρούεται); David has a plectrum in the Gaza synagogue mosaic: see p193–194.
[9] See e.g. Augustine *Confessions* 3.8.32, *City of God* 15.17.35, etc.; and further below, n14. Note also Augustine's comparison of *cithara* and *psalterium* in *Commentary on Psalm 32, Sermon* 1.4–5 (with a typically allegorical spin), which shows that he did not fully understand the Biblical *kinnōr*.
[10] AGM:324–326; Pöhlmann and West 2001 no. 59; Hagel 2009:318.
[11] HBMH 147.
[12] Quasten 1930:166–172, 244, et passim; McKinnon 1968.

It seems counterintuitive to reject as pure allegory the opening verses of the ninth hymn by Synesios, bishop of Ptolemais (ca. 370–413), with its invocation of a 'clear-sounding lyre' (*lígeia phórminx*), several fond and well-informed allusions to the history of lyric, and its Anacreontic meter so suitable for sympotic music-making.[13] Augustine (354–430) describes how, upon his mother's death, "Euodius snatched up a *psalterium* and began to sing a psalm, to which we, the whole house, gave the responses." The incipit of Psalm 101 follows; but *psalterium* here must refer to an instrument, not a psalm-book or Psalter (the word can mean both), for these were surely known by heart.[14] That the context is not liturgical but domestic strengthens the argument, since the aforementioned sources for 'Christian lyric' all relate to devotional music *outside of the church itself*. And given that Euodius' performance was at the bedside of the deceased, one must recall Eustathios' definition of *kinýresthai* as singing "over the dead when they were laid out, using the *kinýra*."[15]

With all this in mind we may return to ninth-century Stoudios, a major center of hymnography at that time.[16] Given the correspondence of *psaltérion* to *kinýra*/*kinnōr*, Theodoros' *kinyrízein* may simply be synonymous with *psállein*, 'sing Psalms'. But a more literal lyric reading seems equally possible. The abbot's exhortation—"let us abandon our pleasurable urges (*thelḗmata*)"—stands at the climax of a sermon against "the works of shamefulness," which distract one's mind from godly pursuits. These include, preeminently, such popular entertainments as "theaters, recitals, horse-racing shows, pantomimes, double-pipe concerts, music generally, [and] instrumental performances."[17] While Theodoros is obviously reprising early debates over the proper function of music in Christian life, clearly this was not a dead issue in his own time. The ongoing impingement of secular music on the monastic world is further seen in illuminated manuscripts that represented Old Testament musical scenes,

---

[13] Synesios *Hymns* 9.1–15. Cf. HBMH:150–152.

[14] Augustine *Confessions* 9.12.25: *psalterium arripuit euodius et cantare coepit psalmum. cui respondebamus omnis domus: misericordiam et iudicium cantabo tibi, domine.* Augustine's famous sympathetic discussion of liturgical singing (*Confessions* 10.33) permits no definite conclusion about instrumental accompaniment.

[15] See p188.

[16] Hymnography at Stoudios: HBMH:229–234; Lemerle 1986:140. According to the second *Life*, Theodoros' monks included "top calligraphers and sacred-psalmists, composers of *kontákia* and songs, first-rate poets and readers, melodists and cultivators of singing" (σοφώτατοι καλλιγράφοι καὶ ἱεροψάλται, κονδακάριοί τε καὶ ᾀσματογράφοι, ποιηταί τε καὶ ἀναγνῶσται πρώτιστοι, μελισταί τε καὶ ἀοιδοπόλοι, PG 99:273C). Note also the detailed evaluation of Theodoros' musical 'program' and its theological rationale in the first *Life*, PG 99:167B–C.

[17] Theodoros of Stoudios *Great Catechism* 91 (648.12–16): τὰ τῆς αἰσχύνης ἔργα, θέατρα, ἀκούσματα, θεάματα ἱπποδρομικά, ὀρχηστικά, αὐλητικά, μουσικά, ὀργανικά, κτλ.; 651.3–4: καταλείψωμεν πάντα τὰ θελήματα ἡμῶν.

Appendix D

especially those associated with David and his temple musicians, in present-day musical terms.[18] Even when the illuminations present historical fantasies,[19] contemporary secular music clearly provided raw ingredients.

The contrast drawn by Theodoros in our first passage is therefore, at the least, between canonical psalms performed in due season, and singing them and other liturgical chants between times for self-gratification.[20] But I consider it more probable that *kinyrízonta* refers quite literally to the use of instruments, not of course in the liturgy itself, but in off-hours; and that, while the offending monks' subjects were no doubt mainly devotional, some more secular strains, against which Theodoros rails, occasionally crept in. The full force of the contrast between *kinyrízonta* and *psálate* would then be "sing only canonical psalms, only at the proper time—and get rid of that lyre!"

This reading of *kinyrízonta* obviously requires the word *kinýra* itself to have remained current, kept alive perhaps by its Biblical connotations. The idea needs some defense given that lyres became generally obsolete during the transition from antiquity to the Middle Ages, when various kinds of lute (and later 'bowed lutes') came to dominate.[21] This was the culmination of a long-drawn process in the Greco-Roman world. While lutes were known in Mesopotamia from the third millennium, and in the Levant from at least the second, it was only in the Hellenistic period that they really entered the Greek sphere.[22] Conversely, Greek lyre-morphology and terminology moved eastwards.[23] Both trends follow from the demographic revolutions occasioned by Alexander and his successors. This was also the era in which Greek art-music had become increasingly complex and chromatic, driven by developments in the *aulós*.[24] While lyres reacted with additional strings, lutes offered ready and pipe-like advantages, notably facility

---

[18] This is well argued by Currie forthcoming.
[19] McKinnon 1968.
[20] A similar polemic against the vulgarization of sacred song is found in Isidore of Pelusium *Epistles* 1.90 (PG 78:244D–245A, fifth century).
[21] 'Lute' here refers generically to instruments with a neck/fingerboard. For the general obsolescence of Greco-Roman lyres by the sixth century, cf. MGG 5:1036 (Lawergren).
[22] ANE/Egyptian evidence: Eichmann 1988; RlA 6:515–517 (Collon, *Leier B); MGG 5:942–951 (Eichmann). Greco-Roman: Higgins and Winnington-Ingram 1965, especially 68–69; SIAG:185–186; AGM:79–80.
[23] For Hellenistic morphological influence in the NE, see p180–181, 194. Apollo *Kitharōidós* as a calque, p210–211, 462, 495–496. *Kithára* is used in the second–third century CE Syriac *Odes of Solomon* (6.1, 14.8, 26.3); even if these come from Greek originals (Franzmann 1991:3 with references), it would remain significant that this word resisted translation. An undated Nabataean inscription from Jebel Ethlib (Mada'in Saleh, Saudi Arabia) may identify a certain Zaïdu as a '*kitharista*' (CIS 2 268; reading disputed by Jaussen and Savignac 1909–1920 1:217–218). The ninth-century (?) Syrian rhetorician Anton of Tagrit also uses the Greek word in his musical discussion: *Rhetoric* 5.10 (trans. Watt 1986:45.30–48.22).
[24] See now Hagel 2009.

Kinyrízein: *The View from Stoudios*

of modulation and sustainable tones (through tremolo).[25] The lute's progress can be traced iconographically. In late antiquity, one sometimes finds 'lutes' played in an upright, lyre-like position.[26] The body-shapes of several 'Coptic' and other lutes, from the third to ninth centuries CE, are also distinctly lyre-like.[27] In Byzantine iconography, King David gradually came to be represented as a lute- or fiddle-player.[28] The eventual triumph of the lute class can be seen in widespread semantic shifts, with Gk. *lýra*,[29] *kithára*,[30] *bárbitos*,[31] and Heb. *kinnōr* all eventually coming to denote lutes and/or fiddles. Similarly, several Medieval Arabic sources compare the *kinnāra* to other types of lute, not lyre.[32]

This evidence makes it perfectly likely that *kinýra* could still be current in ninth-century Constantinople. Even then, however, the word need not have referred exclusively to a form of lute or a lyre-lute hybrid: a ninth century illuminated manuscript from Constantinople—perhaps Stoudios itself—shows David holding what is essentially a rectangular lyre (Figure 48).[33] There are many

---

[25] Note that Nikomakhos *Manual of Harmonics* 4 (MSG 243.15-17) includes *phándourous* (v.l. *pandoúrous*, i.e. the *pandoúra*) among instruments that are midway between winds and strings (μέσα δ' αὐτῶν καὶ οἷον κοινά); cf. Higgins and Winnington-Ingram 1965:65-66.

[26] See e.g. MgB 2/5:130-133 no. 75-78 (sarcophagus-reliefs from Italy).

[27] Coptic lutes: see Eichmann 1994, pl. 23 et passim; MGG 5:951 fig. 7 (Eichmann). Several seeming lyre-lute hybrids are found in illustrated manuscripts of the ninth century (e.g. Utrecht Psalter, ca. 830; San Paolo Bible, ca. 875; Vivian Bible, ca. 846), although how far they reflect musical realities (of their own or an earlier period) and/or a true fossilization of lyre-morphology, is debated: Behn 1954:155 with pl. 91; Eichmann 1994:111-112; Burzik 1995:223-224 fig. 50-52, 241-250 and fig. 61-63 et passim.

[28] For an excellent and well-illustrated survey, see Currie forthcoming; further material in Maliaras 2007.

[29] That *lýra* had made the transition by the ninth century is shown by the Arab historian Al-Mas'ûdî (died ca. 956) who, citing a brief account of Byzantine musical instruments by the Persian Ibn Ḫurdāḏbih (died ca. 912), describes it as having five strings, and equates it with the *rabâb* (SOM 2:536, 538; Farmer 1928:512).

[30] *Kithára* of course eventually produced 'guitar'—the meaning it bears in modern Greek—seemingly by way of Ar. *qīṭārah*, which in a tenth-century source is called a Byzantine instrument and equated with the *ṭunbūr*: see Eichmann 1994:111-113, discussing the word's still obscure history in Arabic; also SOM 1:272; Hickmann 1970:67; Shiloah 1995:81.

[31] Persian *barbaṭ*, also a kind of lute, must derive from Gk. *bárbitos*, perhaps by way of the Ghassanid kingdom of the Byzantine era as Farmer suggested: SOM 1:86, 155 (cf. 129), 2:107-108; MgB 3/2:24, 26 et passim; Shiloah 1995:7.

[32] See SOM 2:161, where the frequent confusion of later Medieval authorities suggests the word's obsolescence in general Arabic usage by the eleventh or twelfth century (it does not appear in the *Arabian Nights*: SOM 1:85). Ibn Ḫurdāḏbih (died ca. 912) may also have mentioned a Nabataean **kinnāra* and compared it to other lutes; but the form in the text is corrupt (Farmer 1928:512, 515-516; cf. MgB 3/2:24). The Indian *kinnarî* is also of the lute-type (AOM:224 (Bake).

[33] Chludov Psalter, Moscow, State Historical Museum MS D.129, fol. 5v: see Currie forthcoming:3 and pl. 2. Corrigan 1992:124-134, discusses the provenance of the Chludov Psalter, reviewing the case for Stoudios; for this important scriptorium and the problems of identifying its manuscripts, Lemerle 1986:141-145.

Appendix D

Figure 48 David and his musicians. Chludov Psalter, ninth century, Moscow, State Historical Museum, MS D.129, fol. 5v. Drawn from Currie forthcoming pl. 2.

further examples.[34] If some contemporaries would have called these *psaltérion*, remember that *psaltérion* itself often translates the *kinnōr* of scripture; and its evolution from earlier lyres is clear.[35] Nor should such 'psalteries' be dismissed as complete historical fantasies; they are clearly cognate with the instruments still known in much of the Middle East that go under variations of Ar. *qānūn*. (This word is derived, ironically, from Gk. *kanṓn*, which originally designated the lute-like monochord used by harmonic theorists from the fourth century BCE onwards.[36])

One way or another, Theodoros' *kinyrízonta* is amenable to the musical reading the parallel passages make us expect.

---

[34] Maliaras 2007, fig. 1, 3, 9, 23–24, 26, etc.; Currie forthcoming:4 and pl. 4.
[35] See for instance MgB 2/5:102–103 no. 57. Compare also the evidence for the *epigóneion*: AGM:78.
[36] See now generally Creese 2010.

Appendix E
The 'Lost Site' of Kinyreia

PLINY THE ELDER, in his list of fifteen Cypriot cities, states that "there was once also Cinyria, Mareum, and Idalium."[1] A *Kinýreion* was also mentioned in the *Bassarika* attributed to Dionysios the Periegete (second century CE) in a passage listing the Cypriots who supported Dionysos' conquest of India, which included "those [sc. who held] *Kinýreion* and lofty *Krapáseia*."[2] On the basis of this pairing P. Chuvin seeks to locate *Kinýreion/Kinýreia* on the Karpass (the long peninsula stretching towards Syria).[3] A similar association is found in the late epicist Nonnos (fl. ca. 400 CE), whose *Dionysiaka* alludes to the poem just discussed in the same context.[4] Here the foundation of *Kinýreia* is explicitly attributed to Kinyras and is mentioned just before the site of Ourania—mentioned by Diodoros Siculus as being on the Karpass.[5]

---

[1] Pliny *Natural History* 5.35.130: *fuere et Cinyria, Mareum, Idalium*. Pliny's source is not clear. He has just cited Timosthenes, Isidorus, Philonides, Xenagoras, and Astynomus variously for the island's size and its alternative names. But his stated authorities for this book (enumerated in book 1) include Eratosthenes: see below.

[2] [Dionysios the Periegete] fr. 2 Heitsch (= Stephanos of Byzantium s.v. Καρπασία): ἠδ' ὁπόσοι Κινύρειον ἰδ' αἰπεινὴν Κραπάσειαν [sc. ἔχον]. Stephanos collects and discusses several versions of the word.

[3] Chuvin 1991:96 (followed by DGAC:355). To support this he would connect the myth that Kinyras crossed to Cyprus from Cilicia and married Metharme, daughter of Pygmalion ([Apollod.] *Library* 3.14.3: see p504), to a fragment of Hellanikos' *Kypriaka*, which records Pygmalion as the founder of Karpasia (FGH 4 F 57 = Stephanos of Byzantium s.v. Καρπασία· πόλις Κύπρου, ἣν Πυγμαλίων ἔκτισεν, ὡς Ἑλλάνικος ἐν τοῖς Κυπριακοῖς). The Karpass would indeed be a natural landing from Cilicia (cf. p553). But note that ps.-Apollodoros specifically has Kinyras go first to Paphos, and *then* marry the daughter of Pygmalion.

[4] This is shown by the distinctive form Κραπάσεια at 13.455; compare also 13.444 οἵ τ' ἔχον Ὑλάταο πέδον with [Dionysios the Periegete] fr. 1 Heitsch: οἵ τ' ἔχον Ὑλάταο θεοῦ ἕδος Ἀπόλλωνος, and the mention of Tembros and Erythrai. Cf. Chuvin 1991:96.

[5] Nonnos *Dionysiaka* 13.451–452: οἵ τε πόλιν Κινύρειαν ἐπώνυμον εἰσέτι πέτρην [v.l. πάτρην] / ἀρχεγόνου Κινύραο ("Those who [sc. held] the city Kinyreia—the still eponymous fatherland [or rock] of / Ancient-born Kinyras"). For Ourania, see Diodoros Siculus 20.47.2 (Demetrios Poliorketes seizes it and marches upon Salamis); cf. Chuvin 1991:96. But note that Nonnos goes on to name Paphos immediately after *Krapáseia*, which undermines his location of *Kinýreion/a* by

Appendix E

But these delicate attempts to locate *Kinýreia/on* may be unnecessary. Pliny, our oldest authority, apparently had no inkling where his *Cinyra* was. Therefore his source did not say. For all we know, ps.-Dionysios, knowing no more than Pliny, merely joined it with *Krapáseia* for the sake of alliteration. Nonnos, following ps.-Dionysios, probably has no independent value; he may have joined *Kinýreia* and Ourania purely because of Kinyras' associations with Aphrodite.

The answer may well lie in a different direction. 'Cinyria' could simply have been an obsolete or poetic designation for an existing city: Pliny himself has just cited several Greek authorities for 'former' names of Cyprus, some of which are clearly poetic or popular wordplays—for instance *Amathusia* and *Cryptos* ('hidden'). An easy guess, given the tradition recorded by Theopompos,[6] is that Amathous had once been known as *Kinýreia*, perhaps in popular or poetic usage. This fact was then recorded by some Hellenistic geographer in an ambiguous context so that Pliny, finding no extant Cypriot city of the name, and knowing that the kingdoms had been terminated by Ptolemy, assumed that 'Cinyria', like Marion, had been destroyed.[7] A likely source is Eratosthenes, known to be one of Pliny's authorities for the book in question, and to have written a work on Amathousian lore.[8]

C. Baurain has even hypothesized that *Kinýreia* was once an *official* name for Amathous. This depends upon an emendation and rereading of the Esarhaddon prism inscription,[9] whereby the otherwise unidentified site of *nu-ri-ja* can be effectively restored as *Kinýreia*.[10] This, he argues, would be best equated with Amathous—a major city at the time, yet not otherwise mentioned in the text's list of kings and kingdoms. The name will have fallen from use, Baurain suggests,

---

geographical association. *Kypris*:75 points out that the variant πέτρην could aptly describe the dramatic acropolis of Amathous.

[6] Theopompos FGH 115 F 103: see p346–348.

[7] For Marion, see p416. For the conquest and absorption of Idalion by Kition in the second half of the fifth century, see HC:125; Maier 1985:34.

[8] Eratosthenes' *Amathousia*: Hesykhios, *Suda*, s.v. Ῥοίκου (or Ῥύκου) κριθοπομπία (FGH 241 F 25). Or could *Kinýreion* simply refer to a Kinyras-shrine, such as one should assume for Palaipaphos (see p419)?

[9] ARAB 2:266 §690.

[10] Baurain 1981b. This requires accepting a sequence of (simple) scribal errors: first, that the preceding sign, read as the determinative URU ('city'), has displaced KUR ('land'), which appears twice elsewhere in this inscription (applied to the Elamites and Gutians: Borger 1956:58, "Episode 19"); second, since KUR can also have the phonetic value of *kin*, (one must suppose) that a second such sign was lost by haplography. The original text would therefore be KUR < KUR, i.e. = *Kîn>nu-ri-ja*. Each step of this reconstruction is straightforward, but some may doubt the cumulative effect.

through some process of synoecism or refoundation, when 'Amathous' was promoted. The hypothesis is certainly seductive.[11]

One should note here the report of Étienne de Lusignan that Amathous was fortified by Semiramis after her husband Ninos, king of the Assyrians, conquered the island.[12] Much of what we know about Semiramis comes from a fragment of Ktesias (fl. ca. 400), who was attached to the Persian court. According to Diodoros' summary, Semiramis made use of Cypriot shipwrights.[13] From this it is a fair and ready inference that the island was among Ninos' wide-ranging conquests. But the fortification of Amathous is not in any ancient source I have found, and does not seem the sort of thing Lusignan would have invented himself. It is, however, something Ktesias could well have mentioned—especially given his diplomatic mission from Artaxerxes to Euagoras I, just before the struggle in which Amathous held aloof from the Salaminian king's party.[14] Could it refer to an actual Assyrian garrison presence on the island—not of course in the legendary past of Ninos, but during the N-A period to which his exploits are best referred?[15] In any event, how a Ktesian detail could have come down to Lusignan is not clear (see Appendix G).

Finally, one may note that Lusignan, though he confessed ignorance about the location of 'Cinaria' in the *Chorograffia*, connects it with a village called Gendinar in the *Description*.[16] He was presumably motivated by the names' similarity. Where Gendinar was located, however, is not clear. No other source mentions it, and it has been considered one of several lost or unidentifiable villages mentioned by Medieval or early modern sources.[17] But it is quite possible that Lusignan has simply given a divergent rendering of a known toponym, or that the intended form was incorrectly typeset. The closest match would seem

---

[11] Baurain's idea is reprised in Aupert and Hellmann 1984:12 and n7, 115, 117; Jasink 2010:154-155 ("cannot be discarded"); cf. Iacovou 2006b:48; Papantonio 2012:281. It is rejected by Masson 1992:29; treated skeptically by DGAC:355. Lipiński 2004:62, 75 argues that *nu-ri-ja* is Marion, explicable as represented to the Assyrians by Phoenician intermediaries; but cf. Masson 1992:29. The question is complicated by the identification of Qartihadast, which many would equate not with Kition but Amathous: see Smith 2008:273, 276-277 (for whom Kition itself is absent from the inscription as not being independent in Assyrian eyes).

[12] *Chorograffia* p. 9 (§12): "[sc. Amathous] fù edificata dalli Asiirij, quando era soggetta alla Monarchi degli Assirii" (cf. *Description* pp. 20a, 91). The legend is repeated by Kyprianos, archbishop of Cyprus, in his Ἱστορία χρονολογικὴ τῆς νήσου Κύπρου (1788). These passages are collected in Aupert and Hellmann 1984:49, 51-53.

[13] Ktesias FGH 688 F 1b = Diodoros Siculus 2.16.6.

[14] Ktesias FGH 688 F 30 = Photios *Library* 72b20-42; cf. HC:130 and above p352.

[15] Cf. Reyes 1994:55 (skeptical).

[16] *Chorograffia* p. 17 (§43), *Description* p. 33a. See further p560 and n2.

[17] Grivaud 1998:252 (taking over a typographical error in Lusignan, so that 'Cinarie' appears as 'Cinavie').

Appendix E

to be the fortress Kantara—which as it happens is in the Karpass (it was rendered Candara by other early French authors).[18]

---

[18] Grivaud 1998:87.

Appendix F

Theodontius: Another Cilician Kinyras?

ONE FURTHER AND QUITE PECULIAR Cilician connection for Kinyras is found in Boccaccio's *Genealogy of the Pagan Gods*. This massive and impressive synthesis, many years in the making (ca. 1350–1375), was undertaken at the behest of King Hugo IV of Cyprus (abdicated 1358). The work remained generally influential for centuries,[1] though its original Cypriot commission probably enhanced its impact on the island's first ancient histories, by Florio Bustron and Étienne de Lusignan in the sixteenth century (see Appendix G). The relevant section derives—at second- or thirdhand via Boccaccio's mentor Paul of Perugia, and probably a certain Barlaam, Paul's own consultant on Greek matters[2]—from Theodontius, a mysterious mythographer whom Boccaccio cites some 200 times for "the debris of a curious and very mixed tradition."[3] Here I shall identify the problems raised by Theodontius' Cilician genealogy of 'Cynara(s)' and offer several suggestions about its genesis.

The essential material is as follows:

> Theodontius says [that Cilix] ... occupied territories not very far away, naming the region after himself, leaving behind two sons there, namely Lampsacius and Pygmalion ... Lampsacius, as Theodontius says and Paul after him, was the son of Cilix and succeeded him as king. Other than this I could not find anything about him ... When [Pygmalion] was young he was driven by the glory of his ancestors, whom he heard had advanced westward and occupied even the shores of Africa; so he

---

[1] Pade 1997:149; Solomon 2011:x–xiii.
[2] Boccaccio gives a forthright description of his sources at *Genealogy of the Pagan Gods* 15.6. For Paul's own work, and his relationship with Boccaccio, see with further references Pade 1997:150–153; Carlucci 2009:401–403. But note that Theodontius was probably still available in some form after Boccaccio: Pade 1997:160–162.
[3] The Theodontius fragments were collected by Landi 1930; for a balanced recent assessment, see Pade 1997. Quotation: Seznec 1953:222.

Appendix F

assembled a Cilician army, mustered the Phoenicians, prepared a fleet, and brought his forces to your Cyprus, most serene king ... Of course, as Ovid testifies, etc.[4]

From here Boccaccio pivots into a euhemerizing summary of Ovid's Pygmalion and the statue, their son (sic) Paphos, and Cinyras, Myrrha, and Adonis. It is clear that Boccaccio was still following Theodontius in linking Cilix to Pygmalion and his descendants, since he reverts briefly to Pygmalion and Paul when discussing Paphos:

Paphos, as Theodontius says, was the son of Pygmalion by an ivory mother. When he succeeded Pygmalion as king, he named the island of Cyprus Paphos after himself. But Paul says that he constructed only a city named after himself. He wanted this city to be sacred to Venus, and after constructing a temple and an altar there, he sacrificed to her for a long time with only incense.[5]

Now Kilix/Cilix, son of Phoenician Agenor and brother of Kadmos, is well attested from Herodotos onwards as the eponymous settler of Cilicia.[6] But Lampsacius, whose name should make him eponymous founder of Lampsacus in the Troad, is otherwise unknown. Nor is there any ancient parallel for Pygmalion as son of Cilix. Where did these ideas come from?

M. Pade has recently confirmed the general view that Theodontius was active between the seventh and eleventh centuries; while she would still entertain an eighth or ninth century *floruit* during the 'Campanian Renaissance', she inclines to a rather later date.[7] Our understanding of Theodontius' sources is fairly limited. He is thought to have known Hesiod, Pausanias, ps.-Apollodoros, Hyginus, ps.-Lactantius Placidus, the D-scholia to the *Iliad*, and the scholia to Pindar and Apollonius of Rhodes.[8] This dossier is sufficient to explain Boccaccio's reference to "certain Greek codices" in which Theodontius found material, without positing further, lost sources.[9] Boccaccio also tells us outright that Theodontius used the Vergilian commentary of Servius (the augmented

---

[4] Boccaccio *Genealogy of the Pagan Gods* 2.47–49 (trans. after Solomon).
[5] Boccaccio *Genealogy of the Pagan Gods* 2.50 (trans. Solomon). Solomon 2013:242 and 442n24 thus errs in suggesting that it was Boccaccio himself who incorporated the Ovidian sequence, with Theodontius' Cilix > Pygmalion merely a useful launching point.
[6] For sources and variants, see Edwards 1979:23–29.
[7] Pade 1997, refining Landi 1930:18–20; Seznec 1953:220–222.
[8] Pade 1997:155.
[9] Boccaccio *Genealogy of the Pagan Gods* 13.1.

version of the seventh or eighth century, Servius Auctus).[10] One diagnostic passage shows that Theodontius exercised fairly free reign with this material, making deductions from and creatively combining discontiguous elements.[11] Some of Boccaccio's cosmogonic scheme, including perhaps the notorious Demogorgon, came via Theodontius from 'Pronapides', a probably late antique or early Byzantine work published under the name of Homer's legendary teacher.[12] Theodontius is probably also Boccaccio's source for four of his five 'fragments' of the Atthidographer Philokhoros (ca. 340–263/2).[13] One is a mere paraphrase of St. Jerome's translation of Eusebios' *Chronicle*,[14] but Theodontius is once named as an intermediate source, and this is probably true of the remainder. Nevertheless, it is quite certain that Philokhoros himself had not been directly available for many centuries, and V. Costa has recently argued that here too, in many cases, Theodontius creatively manipulated citations of Philokhoros that are otherwise still known.[15] None of this inspires much confidence in the older idea that Theodontius preserved strands of ancient tradition now otherwise unrepresented.

Let us next consider the relevant material on internal evidence. Lampsacius is certainly baffling. Boccaccio noted that he could discover nothing else about him, and probably Paul had extracted everything he found in the Theodontian passage. If he truly is the eponymous figure his name suggests, why was Cilicia tied to Lampsacus of all possible places? If this were somehow to reflect fifth-century Athenian strategic interests in both regions, one might then think again of Philokhoros, two of whose alleged fragments do treat Anatolian matters in mythological terms; but as these come, one each, from Boccaccio and Natale Conti, they are doubtful parallels.[16] Or is Lampsacius a single vestige of a more systematic treatment of Anatolia via further unparalleled sons of Cilix? This is surely multiplying complications beyond necessity. And Lampsacius is most

[10] But note the possible complication that Theodontius himself may be cited in Servius Auctus on Vergil *Aeneid* 1.28: *Theodotius, qui Iliacas res perscripsit*. Costa 2004:118 accepts this testimony as a *terminus ante quem*, though he would date the compilation of Servius Auctus somewhat later than usual (see e.g. OCD s.v.), i.e. the ninth or tenth century.
[11] See Pade 1997:153–154, cf. 160.
[12] Pade 1997:158–159.
[13] Optimistic assessments by Landi 1930 and Lenchantin 1932; Jacoby included them doubtfully in FGH; gravely undermined by Costa 2004.
[14] Pade 1997:156–158.
[15] Costa 2004:117–132. The same is true, Costa argues (133–147), of the Philokhoros 'fragments' in the *Mythologiae* of Natale Conti (1568), also reluctantly included by Jacoby.
[16] Philokhoros FGH 328 F 226 (Boccaccio *Genealogy of the Pagan Gods* 4.20), war between Rhodians and Lycians and metamorphosis into frogs. Costa 2004:126–127 points out that the episode cannot be confidently linked to any known title of Philokhoros; but this objection is hardly conclusive. F 228 (from Natale Conti) concerned the sons of Phineus, who was variously brother or uncle of Kilix/Cilix: Edwards 1979:26–27.

Appendix F

suspicious for lacking the essential quality of an eponymous hero. For rather than migrate from Cilicia to found Lampsacus, he *remains* in Cilicia and inherits his father's throne!

We must seriously consider, therefore, whether the form 'Lampsacius' has been correctly transmitted. That this is a corruption of Sandokos (> *SANDOCUS* > *SANDACUS* > *LAMPSACIUS*), who we saw was indeed a king of Cilicia, seems not especially likely on paleographic grounds.[17] Rather more attractive, I suggest, is a corruption of *Sampsuchus or *Sampsachus. Some such form may have been devised by Theodontius as the putative 'true' name for Amaracus, the perfumer who was metamorphosed into marjoram—Gk. *amárakos*, which was originally known, according to Servius who tells the tale, as *sámpsoukhon*.[18] That Servius describes Amaracus as a 'royal prince' (*regius puer*) without naming his father would naturally create a genealogical opportunity for inventive mythographers; Pomponius Sabinus, we saw, called him a son of Kinyras—not implausibly, but evidently without ancient authority.[19] Theodontius, a creative genealogist who was prepared to manipulate Servian material (see above), could well have came up with his own solution. Cilix may seem an odd choice of father, but he has another culture-hero son in Pyrodes who, Pliny says, discovered starting fires with flint.[20] The error of *LAMPSACIUS*, paleographically simple,[21] would then be due to Boccaccio himself. Boccaccio confessed that it had been many years since as a youth (*iuvenculus*) he had taken his Theodontius material from Paul "with more greed than comprehension"; moreover, his notes were no longer always legible.[22] This hypothesis would also explain why Amaracus is otherwise absent from Boccaccio, who elsewhere relied on Theodontius for Servian material.[23]

---

[17] Ps.-Apollodoros, to whom Theodontius perhaps had access (Pade 1997:155), makes Sandokos a migrant to Cilicia from Syria, and not a son of Cilix. The textual variant *Sándakos* is found, but only as a late corruption: see p504n60.

[18] Servius Auctus on Vergil *Aeneid* 1.693 (*sampsucum . . . quam nunc etiam amaracum dicunt*). See further above, p331–332. By way of illustration, Thilo's *ap. crit.* to Servius records these textual variants: *sampsucum, samsucum, sampsuchum*, and *samsacum*.

[19] See p332.

[20] Pliny *Natural History* 7.198: *ignem e silice Pyrodes Cilicis filius*.

[21] Many medieval bookhands would permit confusion of 'l' for (elongated) 's,' and (open) 'a' for 'u': Thompson 1893 Chapter XVIII.

[22] Boccaccio *Genealogy of the Pagan Gods* 15.6: *ex illo multa avidus potius quam intelligens sumpsi, et potissime ea quae sub nomine Theodontii apposita sunt*. This clear account of his reliance on Paul makes it fairly certain that the reference to illegibility (*Genealogy of the Pagan Gods* 10.7: *quaedam alia referat* [sc. *Theodontius*] *litteris a lituris deletis legisse non potui*) applies to his own (or Paul's) notes, and need not imply that Boccaccio himself had seen Theodontius at first hand, as sometimes thought: see Pade 1997:151. For some other consequences of Boccaccio's youthful haste, see Carlucci 2009:309–405.

[23] Boccaccio *Genealogy of the Pagan Gods* 2.14 and 10.11 with Pade 1997:154 and 164n45.

Theodontius: Another Cilician Kinyras?

Several potential objections may be met. First, while it is not clear that Theodontius himself joined Pyrodes to 'Lampsacius' and Pygmalion as sons of Cilix—Boccaccio cites only Pliny here—Theodontius' engagement with Pliny is elsewhere indicated.[24] Note especially that Boccaccio added Pyrodes in a revision to the section that first cites Theodontius for Lampsacius and Pygmalion.[25] Second, Boccaccio found no trace of the original Amaracus story attached to 'Lampsacius'; but Paul may have seen a passage in which Theodontius simply noted the genealogical connection he proposed, while recounting the actual tale elsewhere. Third, while the metamorphosis of Amaracus would seem incompatible with an accession to the throne, this could have been managed with the euhemerism to which Theodontius was prone. Finally, ancient sources offer no special connection between *amárakos/sámpsoukhon* and Cilicia; the best varieties of the plant, according to Pliny, were found in Mytiline and especially Cyprus.[26] But this may not have bothered a Theodontius, more concerned with tying up loose ends.

The foregoing scenario has the further attraction of avoiding an otherwise unknown tradition to which Theodontius somehow had access. But of course this is not inconceivable, especially given the great variety of mythographic handbooks, now all but lost, that circulated until late in the Roman period.[27] And if one believes that 'Lampsacius' has indeed been correctly transmitted, he is surely too geographically specific and abstruse *not* to be an ancient relic. The question remains open.

Turning to Pygmalion and his progeny, the simplest explanation is that Theodontius expatiated on the sequence he found in Ovid. But several issues must be noted. First, the link between Pygmalion and Cilix. A Cilician crossing for Pygmalion has been inferred from a fragment of Hellanikos' *Kypriaka*, who credits him with founding Karpasia, just opposite Cilicia.[28] This *might* imply a father Kilix/Cilix. Ovid himself did not integrate Pygmalion into any genealogical system; his tale is free-floating within the song of Orpheus. Is this because Ovid himself found no father for him in the handbooks he often consulted? Or was he simply concerned here, as often, to juxtapose thematically similar material, since the tales of Pygmalion and Kinyras shared a Cypriot setting and

---

[24] Boccaccio *Genealogy of the Pagan Gods* 2.54 (Pliny cited), *Genealogy of the Pagan Gods* 3.19 (Theodontius and Pliny).
[25] Boccaccio *Genealogy of the Pagan Gods* 2.47. See Solomon 2011:784n16, with explanation of textual history at 775–777.
[26] Pliny *Natural History* 13.10, 21.163.
[27] See generally Cameron 2004.
[28] Hellanikos FGH 4 F 57 = Stephanos of Byzantium s.v. Καρπασία. See further above, p113n356, 545n3.

Appendix F

centered on abnormal erotic passions?[29] Ovid's treatment, in either case, will have encouraged later scholars to divine Pygmalion's ancestry. Such attempts will certainly have been made long before Theodontius. As it happens, the question "Who *was* Pygmalion?" is found in a satirical epigram by Philip of Thessalonica (first century CE), where it typifies the pedantic pursuits of 'thorn-gatherers'.[30] Even so, Theodontius may still have devised his own solution in support of his own grand design, which gave Boccaccio his infrastructure for the early history of Egypt, the Levant, Cilicia, and Cyprus; this included, it should be noted, an account of a 'second Pygmalion', brother of Dido.[31]

While Theodontius' direct dependence on Ovid is probably betrayed by his making Paphos the *son* of Pygmalion—reflecting Ovidian textual corruption—one must recall that the more general tradition did in fact make Paphos male.[32] The idea that Paphos gave his/her name to the whole island reflects Roman-era administrative usage, and is already found in Ovid himself.[33] The idea that Paphos practiced only incense offerings, however, seems to go against Ovid, who has Pygmalion already offering blood-sacrifice to Venus.[34] Perhaps Theodontius took the idea from Tacitus' description of the Paphian sanctuary's bloodless altar, drawing a contrast with the extispicy of the Kinyradai.[35] If the sanctuary was founded by Paphos, as Theodontius held, the customs of Ovid's Pygmalion could be disregarded.

One final issue must be contemplated. If Theodontius did indeed have recourse to some ancient source, no longer extant, which gave Kinyras a Cilician genealogy akin to those considered in Chapter 21, could he have found there the form 'Cynaras'—that is, *Kin(n)áras*—whence it passed into Boccaccio, Florio Bustron, and Étienne de Lusignan (see Appendix G)? In principle, it is perfectly possible that, while Kinyras himself was alive in the popular imagination of antiquity, a parallel dialectal form like *Kin(n)áras* maintained some currency in North Syria and/or Cilicia.[36] But this derives little support from Theodontius himself. Apart from the source-critical issues already raised, there was considerable orthographical fluidity in the medieval treatment of classical names. Almost every conceivable variation—Cyniras, Cynras, Ciniras, Cinera, Cynera,

---

[29] For this compositional principle in the *Metamorphoses*, see Cameron 2004:285.
[30] *Greek Anthology* 11.347.4: τίνος ἦν Πρωτεὺς καὶ τίς ὁ Πυγμαλίων. Cameron 2004:305 and n6 understands the latter phrase as 'Who is Pygmalion [sc. the son of]?'
[31] Boccaccio *Genealogy of the Pagan Gods* 2.2–59 passim ('second Pygmalion' at 59).
[32] See p499.
[33] Ovid *Metamorphoses* 10.295: *illa Paphon genuit, de qua* [v.l. *quo*] *tenet insula nomen*. A male Paphos in such a role is certainly attested in the third century CE: see p499–500.
[34] Ovid *Metamorphoses* 10.270–273.
[35] See p413–414.
[36] See p198–199.

Theodontius: Another Cilician Kinyras?

Cynara, and Cinaras—is found in the manuscript tradition of Ovid.[37] A revealing parallel is the form 'Phyllara'—that is, Philyra, mother of the centaur Kheiron—which Boccaccio gives when again drawing on Theodontius. Because Kheiron invented irrigation, according to Theodontius, he was called the 'son of Philyra.' This presupposes an etymology of the traditional Gk. *Phillyrídēs* ('son of Philyra') as *phílydros* ('water-loving').[38] In other words, though Philyra has come to us as Phyllara, the whole discussion depends upon the original Gk. form—a quite exact parallel to Cinyras/Cynaras.

To conclude, Theodontius' Cilician Kinyras must be treated with great reserve. He is probably a mere artifact of the mythographer's secondary elaboration of Ovid. Still, not every detail in his account, so far as we can reconstruct it from Boccaccio, can be so easily explained. It remains possible, if unlikely, that some elements—notably 'Lampsacius' and the link between Cilix and Pygmalion—did drift across Theodontius' transom from the ancient mythographic tradition.

---

[37] See the *ap. crit.* of Magnus' 1914 edition.
[38] Boccaccio *Genealogy of the Pagan Gods* 8.8 (*Phyllare dictus est filius, quasi Phyllidros*) with Pade 1997:155–156.

Appendix G
Étienne De Lusignan and 'the God Cinaras'

MORE THAN ONCE I have cited the sixteenth-century Franco-Cypriot historian Étienne de Lusignan, arguing for some independent, traditional authority behind several of his unique notices.[1] These included metallurgical and ceramic inventions attributed to his 'Cinaras',[2] with associated topographic details; an anonymous brother, whom I connected with some form of Kothar/Khousor; Agapenor's displacement of the Paphian dynasty to Kourion rather than the Amathous of Theopompos; and the idea that Amathous was fortified by the legendary Assyrian king Ninos.[3] We must now examine Lusignan's credentials more closely for how ancient material may indeed have come to him—whether through oral tradition, a written source now lost, or some combination. But we cannot give all his unique notices equal weight, since some are readily explained as deductions and concoctions from extant authorities and historiographical first principles.

Étienne, born 1527/1528, was a descendant of the royal house established on Cyprus by Guy de Lusignan in 1192, following Saladin's capture of Jerusalem in 1187. Growing up during the time of Venetian control (1489–1571), he was bilingual in Italian and Greek, perhaps 'reacquiring' French only later in life. A Dominican friar and, from 1564–1568, vicar of Limassol, near ancient Amathous and Kourion, Lusignan sailed for Italy just before the Ottoman invasion of June 1570—clearly with good reason. His first decade of exile was consumed in ransoming family and producing two universal histories of his homeland.[4] The

---

[1] For convenience I use the French form that appeared with his *Description*. In fact he was christened Jacques, and assumed the name Étienne/Stephanos upon entering the Dominican order. He is 'Estienne' in the Italian *Chorograffia*. For this and the following details of his life, see G. Grivaud in Papadopoulos 2004 2:iii–xiv, rendering obsolete the remarks of HC 3:1147.

[2] Lusignan normally uses 'Cinara' (*Chorograffia*) or 'Cinare' (*Description*). 'Cinaras', though found in but a single passage of the *Description* (p. 224a), can hardly be a typographical error: it reveals the historian's mind at work, and I have adopted it to help differentiate Lusignan from his predecessors (see below).

[3] See p325–326, 360–362, 452–453, and 547.

[4] For both texts, Papadopoulos 2004.

Appendix G

Chorograffia et breve historia universale was completed 1570–1573, but Lusignan must have begun his researches some years earlier on the island itself. This treatise, with its detailed discussion of recent centuries and physical resources, was intended to rouse western interest in reclaiming the island. But it also presented the most comprehensive account of Cypriot prehistory since antiquity itself.[5] Unfortunately the work was marred by numerous typesetting errors, many of which also escaped Lusignan's errata, where he lamented the adverse conditions in which he labored.[6] Five years of further effort led to the more lucid and expansive *Description de tout l'isle de Cypre* (*sic,* 1580). But this revision gave a much reduced account of antiquity, with, for example, details about Cinaras hacked out—as if no one would be interested!

A thorough source-analysis of both works is needed. The present discussion of Cinaras and his family may serve as a preliminary case study. This material constitutes a single module in a complex archaeology that tried to harmonize Biblical authority,[7] the chronology of Eusebios/Jerome, and a variety of discordant classical sources. The resulting confusion of periods, peoples, and events is "quaintly garbled" to say the least.[8] Other absurdities arose from textual problems and/or a poor grasp of paleography.[9]

Lusignan names Jerome, Vergil, Strabo, Pliny, Horace, Ovid, Justin, and Plutarch as sources for the *Chorograffia*; Aristotle, Pausanias, and Diogenes Laertios were added for the *Description*. Most of his statements, however, lack explicit attribution, "so as not to bore my readers."[10] Some data lacking from his acknowledged authorities can be plausibly traced to less glamorous works. Stephanos of Byzantium and Herodian, for instance, are the only extant sources for a Koureus, son of Kinyras, who reappears in Lusignan as 'Curio' or 'Curion' (see further below).[11] Yet these same works contain relevant material *not* found

---

[5] For ancient analogs, see p337 and n3.
[6] *Chorograffia* pp. 123a–124 (§610–611).
[7] The first Cypriot settler is Cethin/Kittim—eponym of Kition in the Table of Nations. See *Chorograffia* p. 2 (§1), p. 10 (§15), cf. p. 28a (§157), p. 35 (§180), *Description* pp. 1–1a, p. 39a.
[8] Quotation: HC 3:1147. As an illustration, Lusignan envisioned a 140-year period of early Argive (*sic!*) dominance, beginning in 1572 with the island's capture by 'Crassus' (presumably the Krias(s)os of [Apollodoros] *Library* 2.1.2 and Eusebios' *Chronicle* [1:177 Schoene]) from the Assyrians who had conquered it in the time of 'Nino' (Ninos). See *Chorograffia* p. 12a (§22), p. 27 (§47), pp. 19a–20 (§67, Pygmalion), p. 35a (§180); *Description* pp. 37a–38.
[9] For instance 'Agrippa' for probably Argiope/Agriope (see p325 and n24)—unless this is a typesetting error.
[10] *Chorograffia* p. 91 (§608), "per non generare fastidio alli animi delli Lettori."
[11] Herodian, Lentz *Gramm. Gr.* 3.1 pp. 200.2 and 358.19; Stephanos of Byzantium s.v. Κούριον; *Chorograffia* p. 17 (§43), p. 19a (§66), p. 20a (§71); *Description* p. 38a. That Lusignan knew Courio from Stephanos is likely since he also has the story of 'Calcenore' (Khalkanor) at Idalion (*Chorograffia* p. 16a [§42]), for which Stephanos is the only authority I know (for the episode, see p339).

in Lusignan, raising questions about the nature of his engagement.[12] The historian's appetite was clearly voracious, and he seems likely to have incorporated everything he found. But one may doubt the completeness of the manuscripts or editions from which he worked, in an age with few indices.

Boccaccio's *Genealogy of the Pagan Gods*, produced under the patronage of Hugo IV of Cyprus two centuries earlier—and well served in Lusignan's time by Bandini's comprehensive index[13]—provided Lusignan with an authoritative foundation for his historical construction. That Boccaccio's Cypriot material enjoyed quasi-official status is indicated by Florio Bustron's *Historia de Cipro*, which appeared a decade or two before Lusignan's own work (ca. 1565).[14] In his opening essay on antiquity, Bustron took over the unique dynastic sequence of Cilix > Pygmalion (emigrating from Cilicia) > Paphos > Cinara that Boccaccio had himself adopted from the mysterious Theodontius (who expanded Ovid: see Appendix F).[15] Bustron kept the eccentric spelling 'Cinara' against the Cinyras/Kinyras of all classical sources,[16] and maintained the distinction between an Assyrian and Cypriot 'Cinara'.[17] He also reproduced, verbatim, Boccaccio's statement that "of this Cypriot Cinara we have nothing beyond one crime" (the famous incest with 'Mirra').[18]

When Boccaccio's and Bustron's confession of ignorance is set against Lusignan's own relatively detailed treatment of Cinaras and his line, it becomes clear that the younger historian saw here an opportunity to flesh out the island's historical record.[19] Yet he wished to supplement his predecessors, not supplant them, for he too maintained the Theodontian sequence Cilix >

---

[12] Lusignan has no knowledge of Marieus, another son of Kinyras according to Stephanos s.v. Μάριον. While he might have taken Curio from Herodian (200.2 and 358.19), he does not cite Herodian's testimony that Kinyras' mother was Ἀμαθοῦς (242.34; cf. Stephanos s.v.). Similarly, Stephanos cites Hellanikos (FGH 4 F 57) for the idea that Pygmalion founded Καρπασία (s.v.), whereas Lusignan confesses that he has no knowledge about this ancient site (*Chorograffia* p. 12 [§20]), nor is he aware of the further material about 'Cinaria' (i.e. Κινύρειον) in Stephanos' entry (for which see p547n3).

[13] Solomon 2011:ix–x.

[14] For Bustron's prominent public career, and the date and character of this work, see Grivaud's introduction, pp. vii–xii.

[15] The name appears in Bustron p. 12 as *Thedosio* (A) or *Theodotio* (Paris). Mas Latrie saw here a corruption of *Tolomeo*, since Bustron had just stated that he would follow Ptolemy's geographical sequence. But Boccaccio and 'Theodontio' are among the authorities listed in Bustron's preface (p. 7).

[16] Bustron p. 12.

[17] Boccaccio *Genealogy of the Pagan Gods* 2.51; Bustron p. 14. The idea derives from ps.-Lactantius Placidus: see p281n7.

[18] Boccaccio *Genealogy of the Pagan Gods* 2.269 (*Ex hoc autem Cynara Cyprio preter scelus unum non habemus*); Bustron p. 14 ('Di questo Cinara ciprio non havemo altro che una sola sceleratezza').

[19] Lusignan's insular focus explains why he does not mention an Assyrian Cinaras.

Appendix G

Pygmalion > Paphos > Cinara(s).[20] Lusignan even took pains, in discussing the lost site of Kinyreia/Cinyreia mentioned by Pliny—whom he names as his source—to change it to 'Cinaria'.[21] He must have regarded the Theodontian spelling 'Cinara(s)' as an authoritative antiquarian detail.

Theodontius and Boccaccio exerted a second decisive influence on Lusignan's elaboration of Cinaras and his line. Theodontius had promoted the Trojan War as an important historical boundary in a euhemeristic critique of pagan religion, otherwise familiar from Church Fathers and many medieval authors. So too Boccaccio, by way of apology for his fascination with ancient mythology, reminded Hugo of

> this foolishness of the ancients by which they fancied themselves the offspring of divine blood ... Nor was Cyprus, worthy splendor of our king, immune from this malignancy ... It raged during the era of the heroes ... lasting even until the ruin of proud Ilium, for we remember reading that during the Trojan War certain sons of divinities fell.[22]

This idea reappears in Lusignan's 'god-kings' or 'god-men' (*Re Dei* and *dei huomini*), a line of preternaturally beautiful rulers whom "the people were virtually forced to revere and adore," until their reign was interrupted by the intrusion of 'Agapenore' and other veterans from Troy.[23] Lusignan clung to this construction in both his works, despite problems raised by inconsistent traditions that he nevertheless wished to integrate.

A key problem was how to rationalize Adonis as successor to Cinaras' throne—a not unreasonable idea asserted by Boccaccio and Bustron[24]—with

---

[20] See *Chorograffia* pp. 19a–21 (§67–76) and p. 35a (§180). An erroneous translation of the latter passage in SHC 10:48 has Lampsacio take Pygmalion's place in emigrating to Cyprus and founding the royal line: *caveat lector*.

[21] Cinaria appears in his list of Cypriot cities at *Chorograffia* p. 6 (§4); cf. p. 17 (§43), "Cinaria era città fabricata da Cinara ... non sappiamo il luogo, dove l'habbia fabricata: & se di quella sia più vestigio, & che fusse città Plinio la testificata." At p. 20a (§72) the name is given as 'Cinerea'; is the second *e* a relic of the Greek spelling *Kinýreia* (see p454), or just a typographical error? Étienne is otherwise consistent in rendering Greek *υ* as Italian *i*: e.g. *Cipro*/Κύπρος, *Ciro*/Κῦρος, *Cirenaica*/Κυρηναϊκή, etc.

[22] *Genealogy of the Pagan Gods*, Preface 1.4–5, 10 (trans. after Solomon).

[23] *Chorograffia* p. 28a (§157): "Re Dei ... li popoli erano quasi costretti di riverire & adorare essi semidei," etc.

[24] Boccaccio *Genealogy of the Pagan Gods* 2.55: "There was therefore an Adonis, King of Cyprus and husband of Venus, who I think was taken from Venus by a boar or some other death, because in imitation of her tears the ancients had a[n] annual custom of lamenting the death of Adonis." Cf. *Chorograffia* p. 20a (§69–70, 73), *Description* p. 39. This idea was not without ancient parallels (for Servius Auctus on Vergil *Eclogues* 10.18, see p513–515), although Lusignan's assertion that 'Mirra' was pardoned and returned to Cyprus with Adonis is unique.

Curio(n), another son unearthed by Lusignan himself.[25] One still senses his frustration with the dilemma. Observe first how he structures his introductory list of famous Cypriots through the use of 'divine determinatives':

> We will talk about the gentiles first, namely: the god Pygmalion, the god Paffo, the god Cinara, the goddess Mirra, the god Adonis, the goddess Venus, the god of love <Cupid>,[26] Curio, Amaruco, Cinara ...[27]

The startling appearance of a 'god Cinaras' here quickens one's pulse with hopes of die-hard Cypriot folklore. Not impossible, perhaps. But a more prosaic explanation imposes itself: all of Lusignan's 'gods' come from the sequence of tales in Ovid's *Metamorphoses* (whence Theodontius, Boccaccio, and Bustron). Pygmalion was well suited to lead these self-styled 'god-men' because of his ivory statue-turned-queen ('Eburne').[28] Adonis too finds a natural place as the partner of Venus/Aphrodite—a favorite target of Christian polemicists, who treated her as a beautiful woman or even prostitute divinized by Kinyras.[29] Cupid too, of course, was well known as a god.

The pointedly *non*-divine status of Curio and Amaruco (both sons of Cinaras), and a second, younger Cinaras (son of Curio) definitely segregates these figures. That this relates precisely to Agapenor's expulsion of the royal line from Paphos is shown by Lusignan's continuous account, later in the *Chorograffia*, of "those who have dominated Cyprus." Here the historian, after discussing Pygmalion and Paffo, states that "Cinara followed next in the kingdom; and other of their descendants; and they held royal power for around 300 and some years."[30] Probably this three-century interval covers not Cinaras' own descendants,[31] but the entire dynasty from Pygmalion down to a generation or two after the Trojan War.[32] In any case Lusignan, with no mention of Adonis, immediately goes on

---

[25] See p350n74, 361, 558n11.
[26] The text reads "il Dio d'Amore Curio." Cupid is obviously missing, cf. Lusignan's discussion at pp. 20a–21 (§74–75). This makes Curio the first figure not qualified as "Dio."
[27] *Chorograffia* p. 19a (§66).
[28] See *Chorograffia* p. 19a–20 (§67). According to Clement of Alexandria, Pygmalion's statue was of Aphrodite herself (*Exhortation* 4.57.3, citing Philostephanos FHG 3:30 fr. 13).
[29] Clement of Alexandria *Exhortation* 3.45; Arnobius *Against the Pagans* 6.6. Cf. *Chorograffia* p. 20a (§74) and above p222n15, 474.
[30] *Chorograffia* p. 35a (§180): "Seguitò poi nel Regno Cinara, & altri loro descendenti, & tennero quel regno in circa 300. & tanti anni."
[31] So the translation of SHC 10:48.
[32] The early chronology at *Chorograffia* p. 35a (§180) presents several conflicting dates, whether Lusignan's own faulty calculations, typesetting errors, or both. The archaic conquest by 'Crassus' and the Argives is dated to 1572 BCE, and lasted ca. 140 years, i.e. to ca. 1432. Pygmalion's date of 1459 must therefore be his birth, his Cypriot conquest imagined at the age of ca. 28. Since Lusignan dates the Trojan War to 1166, and at *Description* p. 213a makes the interval between

Appendix G

to Agapenore who "banished from the kingdom the kings who had descended from the gods"; they "moved to the city of Curias and reigned there and in other Cypriot cities."[33] That these exiles are Curio and Cinaras II is clear from Lusignan's account elsewhere of their foundations.[34] The conspicuous omission of Adonis here is of a piece with Lusignan's statement, in the earlier entry dedicated to Curio, that this son of Cinaras "succeeded to the kingdom of his father" and founded Kourion "to make himself a name."[35] These scattered passages, when reassembled like this, show clearly that Lusignan at one point envisioned a dynastic sequence Cinaras > Curio > Cinaras II.

Clearly Lusignan was struggling with discordant source material, with traces still visible thanks to the adverse conditions of the *Chorograffia*'s composition and publication. But he refused to abandon Curio and Cinaras II in the *Description*, and even attempted some further definition. Amaruco, Curio, and Cinaras II were now all granted divine status, as one might reasonably expect for descendants of 'the god Cinaras'.[36] But there is a vital geopolitical qualification: Curio and Cinaras II were considered gods only in the cities that they had founded.[37] This revision does nothing to clarify the relationship between Adonis and Curio. Rather it reinforces the idea that Greek immigration after Troy was a cultural watershed, while still allowing some continuity of pre-Greek identity outside of Paphos.

There is obviously some artifice here. Curio/Koureus was probably never more than a cardboard eponym that Lusignan mined from Herodian or Stephanos. The younger Cinaras, Curio's heir, must also be concocted. But several justifications were ready to hand. First, the distinction in Boccaccio/Bustron between an Assyrian and Cypriot Cinyras could have suggested that

---

Pygmalion and Troy 336 years, it seems clear that the 300+ years (and "they held royal power") must refer to the entire line of Pygmalion down to a generation or two beyond Troy, enough to accommodate Curio and Cinaras II (see below). Yet at *Description* 224a Cinaras II is dated to 1000 BCE, well past the Trojan War. Perhaps this reflects Cinyras' 160-year lifespan in Pliny (*Natural History* 7.48.154), near the passage about the Cypriot king's discovery of copper (which Lusignan knew). In any event, the various data seem somewhat incoherent.

33   *Chorograffia* p. 35–36 (§180).
34   *Chorograffia* p. 7–8 (§9–10), p20a (§71–72).
35   *Chorograffia* p. 20a (§71): "Curio … successe nel Regno del padre, & per farsi nominare fabricò due città [i.e. 'Curi' and 'Corinea']." Compare also p. 8 (§10), where Curio's foundation is mentioned and he is called "brother of the god Adonis," but there is no attempt to clarify the regnal situation.
36   For Amaruco, see p331–332.
37   *Description* p. 38a: "Curion, fils du Roy Cinare, bastist … deux villes … Curi, & Corinee, les habitans desquelle l'ont nombré au rang des Dieux. Cinare, fils de Curion, qui estoit fils de Cinare, succeda à son pere aux villes de Curi & Corinee, & edifia d'abondant ceste autre, nomme (*sic*) de son nom Cinarie: des habitans desquelles il a esté aussi mis au rang des Dieux."

this was a recurring, even dynastic name.³⁸ Second, Ovid's Cinyras must have seemed quite different from Pliny's, who was a metallurgical inventor, and son not of Paphos but 'Agrippa' (*sic*).³⁹ Faced with this, Lusignan preserved the metallurgical Cinaras but wished to discard Pliny's problematic paternity.⁴⁰ This was necessary if Cinaras II were to continue the royal line, an idea that I believe was motivated by a desire to accommodate insular tradition. For it is this same Cinaras II whom Lusignan credits with further crafts *not* found in Pliny; he associates these arts with—quite unexpectedly—Tamassos and Lapethos, where, he says, they were still practiced.⁴¹ This appeal to present conditions strongly suggests that local craftsman maintained professional traditions about Kinyras. Of course *they* would have insisted that this was *the* Kinyras. Lusignan, I propose, harmonized his models' Ovidian account with Cypriot tradition by creating Cinaras II, thus accommodating two seemingly different figures while side-stepping Pliny's 'Agrippa'. Note too how Cinaras II, as the end of the royal line, maintains Kinyras' traditional position as a kind of cultural terminus.

If it seems incredible that Kinyras could have survived so long in Cypriot folklore, consider that fourteenth- and fifteenth-century travelers were entertained with remarkable variants on the Trojan War cycle, whereby Paphos became the site of Helen's abduction and the gathering of the expedition against Troy.⁴² Recall that Kinyras himself had featured in episodes of the Trojan cycle.⁴³ Such memories are consistent with the long-lasting impact of pagan cult on the island's Christian landscape. Many basilicas and churches were built on or near ancient sanctuaries.⁴⁴ The Cypriot goddess was sometimes fused with Mary as the Panaghia Aphroditissa.⁴⁵ Lusignan himself alludes to signs that reverence for the old goddess still lingered.⁴⁶ Stones of the sanctuary at Old Paphos were still anointed in the name of the Panaghia, along with other fertility rituals, as late as the 1890s.⁴⁷ Comparable are the island's rag-bushes, often associated with wells or pools believed to have healing properties, that are adorned by women wishing for husbands or babies, and those who are ill and have sick children or

---

³⁸ See p559n17.
³⁹ But note that the original was perhaps Kinyras' *mother* (if Argiope/Agriope): see p325n24.
⁴⁰ *Chorograffia* p. 20a (§72): "Questo Cinara ... alcuni dicono, che era fligliuolo di Agrippa; ma di qual Agrippa non sappiamo."
⁴¹ See p325–326.
⁴² Ludolf of Suchen (after 1350): SHC 8:169; John Adorno (1470): SHC 8:173. For these passages, see p348 and n62.
⁴³ See p1, 343–345.
⁴⁴ *Kypris*:228.
⁴⁵ Frazer 1914 1:36; *Kypris*:228.
⁴⁶ *Description* pp. 92–92a: "Mesme de nostre temps sa memoire n'est encore abolie," etc.
⁴⁷ Hogarth 1896:179–180; Frazer 1914 1.36.

relatives.[48] The best known is at *Petra tou Romiou* near Old Paphos, where the ancient goddess was given by the foam. These great rocks, in one medieval tradition, were interpreted as missiles against the Saracens, thrown by the legendary Digenes defending his Queen—'*Righena*', a ubiquitous figure of Cypriot folklore who inherited many features of the island's goddess.[49] But Aphrodite's traditional birth endures at Chrysorogiatissa, whose monks have a legend that their sacred image of the Virgin was carried to Paphos by the waves.[50]

I have argued that Lusignan's displacement of the Paphian line to Kourion must also have a traditional basis, being essentially compatible with Theopompos' report that the Amathousians were the remnants of Kinyras' men, yet expressed in different terms.[51] That Lusignan maintained the line Cinaras > Curio > Cinaras II in *both* his works, against the dominant paradigm Cinaras > Adonis established by his predecessors, suggests some deeper authority to which he felt beholden, notwithstanding his own active role in developing these figures. I conclude that Theopompos and Lusignan, despite their widely divergent dates, present parallel manifestations of regional Cypriot lore. This idea is strengthened by the mutual proximity of the places in question (Paphos, Amathous, Kourion). Lusignan, as vicar of Limassol, would have been ideally positioned to learn any such legends in the area.[52]

We should resist a strict distinction between 'ancient sources' and 'oral tradition'. After all, the former were often originally based on the latter. And the testimony of ancient authors could itself feed back into oral tradition. An obvious locus for this is the island's Orthodox clergy, the primary conservators of ancient literature. And where would texts touching Cyprus better survive than on the island itself? In assessing this suggestion, and its relevance to Lusignan's early research, one must bear in mind that fourteenth-century Cyprus saw a major efflorescence of manuscript production. This movement is now difficult to appraise. Of the nine hundred or so manuscripts known to have been copied on the island, only a third still reside there. And there must have been many more. Some were donated by pilgrims to other monasteries of the Orthodox

---

[48] The exact number of rag-bushes is naturally unknown. Durrell 1959:47 saw one in Keryneia that Turkish Cypriots hung with votives. Grinsell 1990 collected nine examples. Aupert 2000:37 adds the grotto of Ayia Varvara (Amathous).
[49] *Kypris*:136, 10, 73, 228–229; cf. Karageorghis 1998:123.
[50] Hogarth 1896:179–180; Frazer 1914 1.36.
[51] Theopompos FGH 115 F 103. For this argument, see p360–362.
[52] Note that ca. 1564 he engaged in archaeological investigation of tombs at Kouklia and Limassol: Grivaud in Papadopoulos 2004 2:v.

world, and so vanished. Many more were removed by humanist collectors of the fifteenth century, with further losses under the Ottomans.[53]

Under these conditions, it is quite conceivable that Lusignan was exposed to ancient learning now lost, if only through discussion with his Orthodox peers.[54] One is therefore struck by Lusignan's terse statements about a certain Xenophon:

> Liminea [i.e. Limenia] was an inland city according to Strabo; and one must give credence to Strabo because he was a student of Xenophon, the philosopher and Cypriot historian.[55]

This Cypriot Xenophon appears again, in Lusignan's list of famous Cypriots, as "a philosopher and historian, though where he was from, and when he lived, we do not discover; however, he was from Cyprus."[56] By the *Description*, Lusignan had apparently learned a bit more: he now states that Xenophon was from Salamis, taught others beside Strabo, and wrote several works (still unnamed).[57]

Given Xenophon's description as both a philosopher and teacher of Strabo, one must suspect some confusion here, by Lusignan or an informant, with the Peripatetic Xenarkhos, whose lectures Strabo says he attended.[58] But this cannot be the whole story. Even if one supposes some textual corruption (I find no such variant in the editions), the geographer clearly states that Xenarkhos was from Seleucia in Cilicia. Any attempt to override this with a Cypriot origin would therefore have required some external motivation.[59]

As it happens, another Cypriot Xenophon was known to the *Suda*:

> Xenophon: Cypriot, an historian (*historikós*); [sc. wrote] *Kypriaka*; and this too is a collection (*historía*) of erotic topics—about Kinyras and Myrrha and Adonis.[60]

---

[53] See the overview in Constantinides and Browning 1993:11–38.
[54] Cf. Grivaud in Papadopoulos 2004 2:vi: "D'autres liens avec le monde orthodoxe peuvent être avancés puisque Jean, frère aîné d'Étienne, intègre le clergé régulier orthodoxe au couvent d'Antiphoniti et, au titre de hiéromoine, se présente à l'élection pour le siège épiscopal de Solia."
[55] *Chorograffia* p. 17 (§45, referring to Strabo 14.6.3): Liminea era città, secondo Strabone mediteranea (*sic*); & si deve dar fede à Strabone, perche fù discepolo di Xenofonte Filosofo, & Historico Cipriotto; similarly *Description* p. 33a.
[56] *Chorograffia* p. 19a (§66), p. 22 (§87), "Xenofonte filosofo & historico: ma di che luogo, & quando fù non ritroviamo; però fù di Cipro."
[57] *Description* p. 42a: "Xenofon, Philsophe & Historiographe Salaminien, a esté precepteur de Strabon Historiographe & autres, & a escrit quelques oeuvres."
[58] Strabo 14.5.4.
[59] The same reservation would apply to Xenophon of Lampsacus, on whom Strabo drew.
[60] *Suda* s.v. Ξενοφῶν· Κύπριος, ἱστορικός. Κυπριακά· ἔστι δὲ καὶ αὐτὰ ἐρωτικῶν ὑποθέσεων ἱστορία περί τε Κινύραν καὶ Μύρραν καὶ Ἄδωνιν (= FGH 755).

Appendix G

"This too" refers to a further pair of Xenophons who also wrote *erōtiká*—one the familiar Ephesian novelist, another from Antioch.[61] Because the three entries are so similar, it is often held that a single Xenophon gave rise to spurious doubles through his stories' geographical settings.[62] By this argument, Xenophon of Antioch would have the greatest claim to authenticity, the other two being explicable by the Cypriot context of Kinyras, Myrrha, and Adonis, and the extant *Ephesian Tale* (a *Babylōniaká* is less obviously connected with Antioch). One could then suppose that the bogus Cypriot Xenophon was adopted by Lusignan or some other patriot wishing to elaborate the island's glorious past.

But this hypothesis, though it seems reasonable enough in isolation, creates as many problems as it solves. First, I have found no clear sign that Lusignan used the *Suda* otherwise. One would certainly expect him to have credited his elusive Xenophon with a work about Kinyras, had he seen notice of it. And what becomes of the claim about Strabo? Are we to believe that Lusignan (or someone else) combined a stray dictionary entry with a careless or willful distortion of the geographer's reference to Xenarkhos, without taking over any further biographical details? Similarly, one might suggest that Lusignan's characterization of Xenophon as a philosopher derives from combining the *Suda* with one of the several Xenophons listed by Diogenes Laertios.[63] But how then did Strabo enter the picture? These attempts to explain away Lusignan's Cypriot historian and philosopher start to seem rather strained.

We should therefore entertain the possibility of a real Cypriot Xenophon who wrote about Kinyras, Myrrha, and Adonis—tales that would certainly appeal to a native islander. Just what form this would have taken is unclear, although the *Suda*'s terms *historikós* and *historía* would be consistent with a mythological romance.[64] Might this not be Diogenes Laertios' fifth Xenophon, described as "having busied himself with mythological wonders"?[65] The context of Kinyras

---

[61] *Suda* s.v. Ξενοφῶν, Ἀντιοχεύς, ἱστορικός. Βαβυλωνιακά· ἔστι δὲ ἐρωτικά. Then: Ξενοφῶν, Ἐφέσιος, ἱστορικός. Ἐφεσιακά· ἔστι δὲ ἐρωτικὰ βιβλία ι΄ περὶ Ἀβροκόμου καὶ Ἀνθίας· καὶ Περὶ τῆς πόλεως Ἐφεσίων· καὶ ἄλλα.

[62] Rohde 1914:371–372; Lavagnini 1950:145–147; Kudlien, RE 18/2 [1967]:2058.

[63] Diogenes Laertios 2.59.

[64] See the overview of Cameron 2004:90–93 for ἱστορία as covering "historical, geographical, mythological, or even scientific information" (quoting D. Russel), with a mythographic sense coming to predominate in early Imperial times. Cf. Lightfoot 1999:257 and 261: "One would very much like to know how Myrrha's sinful passion for her father was treated in the romance by Xenophon ... Did it alter the relationship so that it was no longer incestuous? Did it rationalize it or mitigate it in some way? Did it domesticate Myrrha in the same way the *Ninus* romance domesticates Semiramis? If so, how did it deal with the metamorphosis and the birth of Adonis?"

[65] Diogenes Laertios 2.59: πέμπτος μυθώδη τερατείαν πεπραγματευμένος. For this Xenophon see Rohde 1914:371–372n1; RE 18/2 [1967] 2089 [12]). If he was a contemporary of Demetrios of Magnesia—whom Rohde believed to be Diogenes' source here (cf. 2.57)—he would have been the right age to teach Strabo. But others see Diogenes' fifth Xenophon as the Lampsacene: cf. NP s.v.

and Adonis would also give a good home to a free-floating report in Athenaios: "the Phoenicians, as Xenophon says, used to use *gíngras*-like double-pipes, a span in length, making a high, wailing sound."[66] This instrument is nowhere mentioned by the Athenian Xenophon, nor the Ephesian; accordingly editors have challenged the text.

Could some of Lusignan's unique Kinyras material derive from Xenophon, if not directly—the historian knew little about him—but via some earlier interaction of written and oral tradition? Local lore might well have preserved the name of a famous Cypriot 'historian', philosopher, and perhaps teacher of Strabo.

Xenphon [8]. A further Cypriot Xenophon was high-priest (*arkhiereús*) and *stratēgós* of the island ca. 168–163 or after 124 BCE: SEG 20:200; NP s.v. Xenophon [7]. But this would be too early for Strabo.

[66] Athenaios 174f: γιγγραίνοισι γὰρ οἱ Φοίνικες, ὥς φησιν ὁ Ξενοφῶν, ἐχρῶντο αὐλοῖς σπιθαμιαίοις τὸ μέγεθος, ὀξὺ καὶ γοερὸν φθεγγομένοις. For these pipes and their connection with Adonis, see p190n19, 202, 317. As Barker (GMW 1:262n11) notes, γιγγραίνοισι is a poetic form.

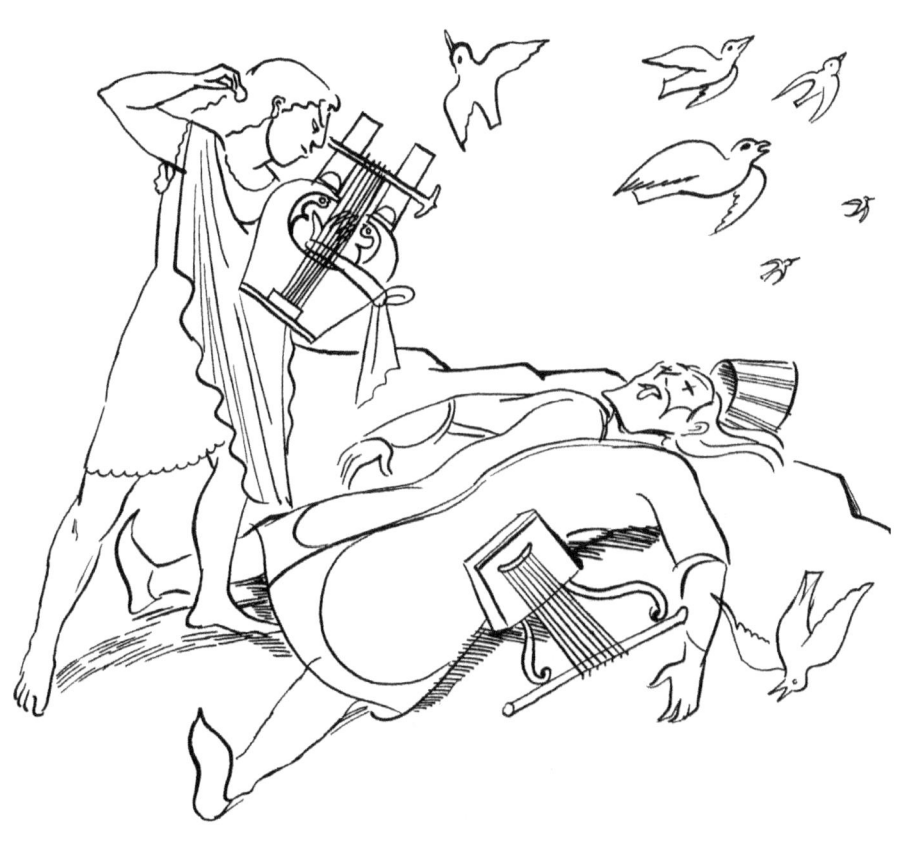

Balang-Gods

WOLFGANG HEIMPEL

Introduction[1]

IN HIS 1997 ESSAY "The Holy Drum, the Spear, and the Harp: Towards an Understanding of the Problems of Deification in Third Millennium Mesopotamia," Gebhard Selz found that the items in his title and other 'cultic objects' were deified by providing them with a name, animating them with the magic of the mouth-washing ritual, and assigning them a cult place and offerings, with the result that their divine nature was the same as those of the images of the gods.

I treat here only the "harp," actually a type of harp that I call the Balang-harp. My initial interest in the topic were the names and functions of the Balang-harp servant-gods that are found in large numbers in the god-list An:Anum (the first line and the modern title of a seven-tablet bilingual list of gods) and my belief that the balang instrument was indeed a harp, and not a drum as widely claimed. Pursuing these two interests and becoming aware of the great variety of uses of the word balang, I attempt in the following to define them and see how they relate to each other. The problem of deification that interested Selz is treated in further detail.

References to entries of the Catalogue are underscored.

---

[1] I could not have done much without the bibliographical help of John Carnahan and copies of searchable scans of needed books from Jay Chrisostomo. I thank them both for it. I also thank Uri Gabbay for letting me use his *Pacifying the Hearts of the Gods* (PHG) years before it was published. He also made numerous observations on an earlier version of this study. Antoine Cavigneaux and Farouk ar-Rawi have graciously allowed me to quote from their unpublished transliteration of an OB text of Uru'amma-irabi.

1 Balang Instruments

1a Neither Drum Nor Lyre

A pictograph of the archaic texts shows a bow dissected with three or four straight lines, a simple but unmistakable representation of a harp (see Section 1d). The pictograph was replaced in the cuneiform stage of script of the Early Dynastic period (ED) by sign BALAĜ. That the cuneiform sign was in fact a replacement of the pictograph of a harp is shown by comparing the archaic and ED versions of the same list of words, where the sign BALAĜ takes the place of the harp pictograph.[2] An image of a harp that would have been represented by the cuneiform sign was not found, which allowed the possibility that it was a harp no more.

Before the publication of the archaic word lists, Cohen argued that the word balaĝ, which is written with the sign BALAĜ—and here rendered phonetically as "balang"—designates a drum.[3] He noted that the balang instrument had a hoop (*kippatu* 52) just like the drum *alû*. Indeed, pictorial representations of ancient Mesopotamian harps make it highly unlikely that they were fitted with a hoop. Cohen noted further that texts called er2-šem3-ma—'tears of the shem', an instrument that is indeed a drum—formed the last part of compositions called balang: "It seems rather unlikely that a composition composed for the drum would then be chanted to a harp." Yes, but the tears of the shem drum were performed *after* the much longer part that was performed with the Balang-harp. Cohen also quoted a ritual that instructs the lamenter (gala) to take the 'hand' of a kettledrum (lilis), bring it before the gods, and perform a balang composition. That was a good argument at the time.

Gabbay (PHG:98–102) has now treated the relationship between balang and lilis and found that the latter supplanted the former as an object of royal dedications to gods and as the central instrument in performing balang compositions. He also noted a case where the lilis kettledrum built and dedicated by an OB king is identified in writing as 'kettledrum' (*li-li-sa-am*) or 'bronze balang' (BALAĜ.ZABAR, 44). Indeed, a 'bronze balang' appears already in a text from the Ur III period (35) and may be a kettledrum. As argued below, the lute as a cultic instrument could also be called a balang. That may also be the case of the kettledrum called the 'bronze balang'.

As regards the balang instrument that is no kettledrum, Gabbay found the first and so far single textual proof that it was indeed a chordophone, an unpublished OB text containing the phrase "to slice the strings of the adviser"

---

[2] Archaic 2 and ED 4a. Cooper 2006:41n6.
[3] Cohen 1974:31.

(PHG:96 with n140). Balang-gods, a category of servant-gods discussed below, were called "adviser" of the god they served, so the strings of the adviser would be the strings of the instrument of the balang servant-god.

In the god-list An:Anum (53), the title of balang servant-gods was written with the logogram GUD.BALAĜ, where GUD is the logogram for the bull. ED pictorial representations and finds of the remains of lyres show that their resonator was formed to resemble a bull [e.g. Figure 4, Figure 47—JCF]. Bull lyres are depicted typically in scenes of feasting; in the words of Michalowski, they were "an iconic symbol of elite entertainment in banquet scenes, and in similar representations of status-affirming conviviality."[4] Gabbay points to the picture of an OAkk. cylinder seal that shows the cult scene of a lyre-player before the seated image of the goddess Ishtar in her warlike aspect with weapons emerging from behind her shoulders.[5] Boehmer interprets the scene as a musical performance meant to soothe the warlike Ishtar.[6] Gabbay builds on this interpretation, describing the scene as a "musical performance" that "is ... intended to soothe Inanna's raging heart, which is the exact role of the performance of Emesal prayers in their musical context, and thus it is not unlikely that the scene may belong to the world of the gala [i.e. lamenter]." Boehmer's interpretation is debatable. Several OAkk. representations of Ishtar with weapons emerging from behind her shoulders are the common offering scenes. The famous seal of Adda (Boehmer no. 377) shows Ishtar standing as morning-star over the mountainland and above the sun-god emerging from below the horizon. This leads me to interpret the representation on the seal Boehmer no. 385 as a musical performance before the morning-star Ishtar. That performance would belong to the world of the temple-singer who celebrates her appearance that announces the coming light of day. Gabbay (2010) adopts Boehmer's interpretation and proposes to strengthen the connection of the scene with the world of the lamenter by associating the musician sitting behind the lyre-player with the image of a chief lamenter on a stone bowl from Assyrian Nimrud who stretches out two objects in his hands that Gabbay interprets as sistrum and drum. I see in the object the stem and flower of a lotus plant. Lotus flowers were a pictorial motif adopted from Egypt in Assyria at the time. They are held in the hands of persons elsewhere in Assyrian art (Bleibtreu 1980:116–120). The object in the other hand of the chief lamenter can hardly be the percussion instrument on the knees of the sistrum player. Only two forward tips clearly separated by empty space are preserved.

---

[4] Michalowski 2010a:219.
[5] Gabbay 2010:25 and fig. 2 = MgB 2/2:64–65 fig. 42.
[6] Boehmer 1965 no. 385.

I believe that the musician with sistrum and percussion instrument on his knees is a singer (nar) because these two instruments are held by a jackal in the famous animal ensemble that decorated one of the bull lyres found in the ED royal tombs of Ur. The head of a jackal served as pictograph of the Sumerian word for the singer (nar), about which more is said below in Section 3a.

The lyres and other instruments deposited in the ED royal tombs were probably not connected to the mourning of the deceased (as suggested by Selz and Gabbay).[7] While the balang instrument was put up and played for this purpose at burials (22), the objects buried in the royal graves of Ur thematize afterlife, not death. The precious lyre with the representation of an animal ensemble was surely a cherished possession in the lifetimes of the deceased and believed to keep entertaining in afterlife, so the lyres in burials are still examples of Michalowski's characterization of items of elite entertainment.

The remaining argument in favor of identifying the balang instrument with a lyre is an entry in an ED lexical text from Ebla in Syria where the sign BALAĜ is translated with *kinnār*, the Akkadian and West Semitic word for the lyre (4d). The translation must be evaluated in connection with document 4c, an unprovenanced, but surely Mesopotamian, ED IIIa vocabulary containing a section listing six musical instruments. Two instruments were written with the sign BALAĜ, one with a modified BALAĜ sign, another with the logogram sequence AL.HUB2, the fifth har-har, known also from later texts as a musical instrument, and the last *ki2-na-ru12*, the ED spelling of *kinnār* "lyre." It appears that the sign BALAĜ wrote two words designating two instruments, the modified BALAĜ sign a third instrument, possibly tigi, modified differently in later periods as NAR.BALAĜ, BALAĜ.NAR, and E2.BALAĜ, and finally *ki2-na-ru12*, the lyre, as still another instrument.

It is interesting that the word for lyre in 4c is written syllabically. Perhaps there existed no logogram for it. The reason for the equation of BALAĜ with *kinnār* in Ebla is unknown. The lyre in ED Northwestern Syria could have been an instrument used in cult. Or the balang instrument in Ebla was the lyre of a temple singer, and thus a cult instrument.[8] However the equation is understood, the following section shows that we have to reckon with instruments written with the balang sign that are not harps, and the lyre—including the lyre on the seal Boehmer no. 385—could be one of them.

---

[7] Selz 1997:170; Gabbay 2010:25.
[8] Cf. Franklin, p65–67.

Wolfgang Heimpel

1b Balang Lute

Kilmer and Collon (RlA 6:512–517, *Laute) proposed that the instrument called "voice-making/speaking wood" in standard Sumerian ĝiš-gu3-di/de2, mu-gu3-di in Emesal Sumerian, was a lute.[9] It was a popular instrument according to pictorial representations of ribald entertainment (MgB 2/2 no. 81–84 and page 92). A lute was the instrument of the singer Urur as shown on his seal (MgB 2/2 no. 38). It was played before a god as shown on an OAkk. seal (MgB 2/2 no. 39). Great Dragon of the Homeland was a "balang" instrument (17b) that was called the "famous lute" (17a). As a person, the balang was "the beloved singer" of his master-god Ningirsu (17c). While walking in procession from the residence of Gudea, the governor of the province of Lagash, to the temple of Ningirsu that Gudea had just renovated (17d), he would have played a lute, not the Balang-harp that needed setting up before playing it (see Section 1d below).

1c ED Harps in Pictorial Representations

Beginning with ED III, various harps are known from pictorial representations. All are bow harps. One type is small enough to be held with one hand and played by its player standing or walking. The upper end of the neck extends beyond the connection point of the outer string, the tip reaching more or less above the head of the male player (MgB 2/2 page 54 [more] and no. 32–35 [less]); short upper ends may result from space limitation. In one case, a donkey plays the harp walking on his hind legs. Another follows him playing claves (MgB 2/2 no. 30).[10]

Another type is a harp the size of an upright person. Two such harps are depicted on a three-tiered seal of the wife of an ED III ruler of Mari. The harp in the middle band appears to have a foot. They are played by women and

---

[9] The lute is discussed from various angles in the papers of ICONEA 2011 [see also Appendix D—JCF]; Krispijn 2011, for instance, believes that the instrument "giš-gu3-di must have had a wider meaning before (the second millennium), since the translation 'lute' does not fit the context" of the Gudea passage (17a). "It must have been a prestigious cultic instrument and not the foreign and increasingly popular folk music type lute." Compare the representation of a lute on an archaic seal in the Uruk style, which is the topic of the article of R. Dumbrill in the same publication. Gabbay rightly objects to Kilmer's connection with the Arabic word for the lute as argument for the identification of the instrument. In my view, the association of the singer Urur with a lute on the OAkk. seal Boehmer 1965 no. 497 is an argument in favor of the identification, considering that the balang servant-god Great Dragon of the Homeland was a temple-singer.

[10] These instruments are often called 'clappers'. Rashid calls them "Klangstäbe," that is claves, and identified them with sickle-shaped copper-blades from ED Kish (MgB 2/2:48 and no. 16). I believe that the 'small sickles' in document 20c represent a smaller variety of the rather long ED claves.

accompanied by women playing claves.¹¹ A similar harp is depicted on a lapis-lazuli seal that was found in the grave of a queen in the royal cemetery of Ur (MgB 2/2 no. 29). The upper end of that harp ends in a circular knob and from the lower end extends a slightly curved narrow engraved line that may be a foot as one might expect for an instrument of that size. The harp was played by a woman. Opposite her stands a woman accompanying her with claves, or so it seems. It must have been difficult to engrave the hard stone, causing thin lines and shallow relief.

A different harp is shown on an early OAkk. cylinder seal (MgB 2/2 no. 44). The upper end of the neck curves back, forming a wide bend. At its upper end, it flares out to form a flat-topped knob. It is played by a woman in front of a god coming back from the hunt.¹²

1d The ED Balang Sign

The archaic pictograph of the Sumerian word balaĝ is the image of a bow harp. Stauder (RlA 4:115, *Harfe) illustrates the then-known examples from the two archaic phases of script, Uruk IV and III. The references for the archaic sign in Englund and Boehmer 1994 include three signs showing four strings.¹³ The least abstracted form shows that the upper end of the instrument's neck was extended in a straight line above the upper connection point of the outermost string (MgB 2/2 no. 27 and 1).

The earliest post-archaic form of the balang sign dates from an early phase of the succeeding ED period when the pictographic character of the archaic script gave way to more abstract forms as the drawing of lines, so ill-fitted to the medium of moist clay, was more and more replaced by impressing wedges. A partly pictographic and cuneiform balang sign is found on a tablet from Ur (3). The sign shows the neck of the harp bending back sharply above the upper connecting point of the outer string and ending in a longish straight line.¹⁴

Written sources of the ED period become more numerous and with wider geographical spread in period ED IIIa. The balang sign of this period is complex and differs radically from the earlier forms. The numerous variants of the sign are drawn by Deimel 1922:6 and quoted as LAK 41.¹⁵ They are the prototypes

---

[11] Marcetteau 2010:67, with a drawing of the editor Beyer. See also the contribution of Collon in the same publication on pages 50–51.

[12] According to Braun-Holzinger not Ninurta/Ningirsu (RlA 9:522, *Ninurta/Ningiru B §2); perhaps Pap-ule-gara. See the last line of a hymn to this god (Foster 1993 1:73).

[13] W6776, c; W6882, f; W5696, ao. Stauder pointed out a harp with four strings and seven plugs at their upper ends (see Hartmann 1960:22n1).

[14] The strings are intersected at a right angle by a central line, perhaps the lower arm of the player.

[15] Some examples are shown in photographs in Krispijn 2010.

of the later fully cuneiform balang sign. The sign LAK 41 takes the place of the archaic balang sign in the ED version of the list of persons Lu2 A (2 and 4a). Parallel lines in the center of the sign suggest strings, but their proper attachment is not shown, and the overall form and details of the sign are not matched by any Mesopotamian pictorial representations of harps of any period. That a harp is represented at all is confirmed by a scene of a plaque from Susa from the same time.[16] It forms a clear match with the sign LAK 41 (Heimpel 2014). At the time, Susa had close ties with Mesopotamia. Such plaques are well attested in the Diyala area where Elamite and Mesopotamian cultures meet. They were used to frame a peg protruding from the door jamb that served as anchor for a rope attached to the door that was slung around it to keep the door closed (Zettler 1987). The plaques show secular scenes, the principal figure probably being the master or mistress of an upscale house for which the plaque was made. Other objects found together with the plaque also demonstrate the cultural tie between Susa and Mesopotamia at the time (Marchesi and Marchetti 2011:82–83). Cuneiform was written there, too, including the ED version of the list Lu2 A.[17]

The Susa harp was a large instrument, its neck reaching from the bottom of the resonator to a point behind and slightly above the head of the seated player. At the bottom, the neck disappears inside the resonator. A foot is not visible, but can be expected for an instrument of that size. The high and fairly thick resonator was fastened to the lower neck. It was probably a cylinder, not a box, because hoops were part of the Balang-harp (52); this answers one argument against identifying the balang instrument with a harp (Cohen 1974). The neck emerges from the resonator and continues for a little less distance than the resonator's height and bends to a point under the left armpit of the player to form the bow that frames the strings. On the right shoulder of the player, it recurves, forming a wide semicircle, and ends behind and slightly above the player's pate. At the upper end, the neck of the instrument flares and forms a flat surface similar to the otherwise quite differently shaped OAkk. harp MgB 2/2 no. 44.

The general form of the ED IIIa balang sign is similar, though some details are not. The neck of the instrument of the sign gains in girth toward the bottom and forms the resonator. Close to the lower end is a horizontal line that may mark the upper end of a stand. The wide recurved bow at the upper end of the neck of the Susa harp is clearly marked in the sign, but much smaller and tighter. The two groups of parallel straight lines may be the strings, with the

---

[16] Pelzel 1977 with earlier literature.
[17] MSL 11:9.

lower group not reaching the other end of the bow and the upper group being the upper ends of strings beyond the point of fastening.

The Susa harp was played by a seated man with the strings between neck and player. All other representations of harp playing from the early periods show that the neck was between player and strings.

1e Features of Balang-harps

The harp shown on the Susa plaque is a type that matches the balang instrument. Both were large. The Balang-harp was "set up" (gub) before being played (17e, 20c, 22, 47a), carried from place to place by harp carriers (balaĝ-il2), and "repositioned" from its place in its home temple to various locations on a procession route including other cities (10). Bull hide (36 and 41), black he-goat hide (41), kid hide (46), or just hide (48) was issued for Balang-harps, surely to cover their resonators.

The recurved uppermost section of the neck of the Balang-harp would have been called the 'grapple-hook' (ĝešba), otherwise used in wrestling.[18] The grapple-hook (23a3) and perhaps other parts of the neck were plated with silver (24) and gold (23g2, 42c), and the instrument as a whole was often called 'shining' as a result.[19] The grapple-hook is mentioned in the name or epithet of a balang servant-god of Ningirsu in An:Anum V 102 (53): 'Dragon of the Outback-Grapple-hook of House Fifty'. The grapple-hook seems to have been so characteristic of the harp that the harp itself could be so called. The Ur III tablet PDT 1 456 records the expenditure of a silver ring as present for the son of a singer (nar) "for having played a grapple-hook" (mu gešba in-tag-tag-a-še3).[20]

The harp also had an 'eye', probably an opening in the resonator (23a3), and a mysterious tooth/teeth/nose/mouth (KA) of the left 'wood piece' (42b).

A single reference (35) attests a "bronze balang," probably a kettledrum that was occasionally so called (see Section 1a).

1f Balang-harp

The lack of Mesopotamian pictorial representations of the type of harp that corresponds to the ED IIIa balang sign and the similar Susa harp was probably

---

[18] The Akkadian equivalent of the Sumerian word ĝešba is umāšu. The meaning 'grapple-hook' was proposed by AHw, s.v. The plating of a gešba shows that 'wrestling (match)' cannot be the only meaning of the word (as claimed by Rollinger, RlA 13:6–16, *Sport und Spiel).

[19] The adjective ku3 is translated in Akkadian as ellu 'shining' (42a, line 44), which is standard qualification of silver. Selz uses the conventional translation of ku3 as 'holy'.

[20] I owe this interpretation to U. Gabbay.

caused by the use of this instrument in mortuary cult (22). Depicting it would have raised the specter of death.

That was not the case in ED Susa where a similar kind of harp was used for elite entertainment, much like the bull lyre in contemporaneous Mesopotamia. While the general design of the large harp was identical in Susa and Mesopotamia, it clearly played different roles in Elamite and Mesopotamian cultures.

2 Balang Names and Balang-gods

There are numerous attestations of positioning Balang-harps at cult places in ED IIIb administrative documents (9–14). The word balang was written without divine determinative and names of the instruments are not recorded in administrative documents. I found one harp-god name in such documents of the OAkk. period (15). Many names are found in texts of the Ur III period. They were written without the divine determinative in the province of Lagash, and with the determinative in sources outside of that province.

The sign of the determinative is the pictograph of a single star. With few known exceptions, it precedes names of gods, so its presence or absence is important for the question of deification.[21]

2a Temple-servants, Divine and Human, in the Ur III Period Temple of Ningirsu in Girsu, the Capital of the Province of Lagash

The Babylonian temple mirrored an elite household. The divine master and mistress of a temple commanded a staff of servants who cared for their every need. An instructive source is the description of a temple renovation by Gudea, ruler of the province of Lagash of the third dynasty of Ur at the end of the third millennium BCE. It is written in Sumerian with the partly syllabic and logographic cuneiform writing of the time. Due to its length and good preservation, the text has been studied much and translated repeatedly. While problems of

---

[21] The pictograph also writes the word 'god' (diĝir in Sumerian and il3 in Akkadian), and the syllable /an/. It is sometimes not clear which value applies. A salient example comes from an ED list of knives that includes sections where pairs with and without the single star appear. There is a 'copper bread knife' and a 'copper bread knife' preceded by the single star and so on. Selz 1997:170–171, following an idea of A. Westenholz, understands the single star as divine determinative. Englund and Nissen 1993:34 found in the archaic metal list also entries with the single star. They suggested that the utilitarian objects in the list were made of copper and the addition of the single star is short for an-na 'tin'. In my opinion, that is certainly also the case in the ED list quoted by Selz. The document would then gain importance for the early development of bronze in the time from archaic Uruk III to ED, and lose relevance for the topic of deification of 'cultic objects'.

translation persist, it represents the best available textual source for the architecture and function of a city-god's temple for this period.

After completion of the renovation, Ningirsu, master of the temple, moved from temporary quarters into his newly made quarters. Moving the image of the god had to be done with the utmost care so it would not be upset.[22] Yet, as Gudea describes it, Ningirsu arrived as a gust of wind and his wife Baba moved to her wing in his temple (she had her own separate temple nearby) flowing stately like the Tigris river—a drastic difference from what actually happened ("fully mythological" as Franklin calls it).[23] The next day Gudea woke Ningirsu with a breakfast in the bedroom suite, and Ningirsu assumed his role as master of the household by reviewing, in the courtyard, the heads of the temple departments "passing before him with their duties."

The review of the temple-servants is described more as a fully actual review than a mythological process. Plough animals in the province of Lagash were also made to pass the reviewer in single file (Heimpel 1995:120). Most but not all names of the temple-servants are preceded in writing by the divine determinative. The divine determinative is found typically for the same gods whose image and house are attested in contemporaneous administrative documents. It is therefore significant that house and image are not attested for the servants whose names are written without the divine determinative. They are the second general, the butler of the bedroom suite, the deer-keeper, and the two balang servants. One might imagine that the two balang could have been a lute with a name and a Balang-harp with a name that were carried around; but this is hardly a solution for 'Lord Deer'. Whether goatherd (as Jacobsen interprets the difficult passage describing him and his duties) or deer-keeper, he was not an object, and lacking the divine determinative in writing, and image or temple in administrative documents, he must have been the human temple-servant in charge of providing the dairy products for the meals of Ningirsu. The balang servants could thus have been the singer (nar) and lamenter (gala) of the temple who carried their instruments with them. The Balang-harp of the lamenter Fierce-faced King would actually have been carried by a harp carrier (4g, 10). The only case for a "house" of a harp-god is 23d3.

The following table lists the servants and whether they are marked with (+) or without (-) the divine determinative. In the "occupation" column, the first identification is that of Jacobsen 1987, the second mine:

---

[22] Accidents while moving images of gods happened and were considered ominous. One example: "when Marduk in exiting or entering Esagila falls down and comes to rest on the ground, the dead will rise, end of rule" (Sallaberger 2000:232).

[23] See p28.

dd?	Name	Translation	Occupation
+	Ig-alima	Bisondoor	High Constable / Chief Bailiff
+	Shul-shaga	Youth of Heart	Butler / Sanitarian
+	Lugal-kurdub	King Mountainland Drubber	Marshal / General
-	(Kurshunaburu)	Mountainland Bird in Hand	Vice Marshal / Second General
+	Lugal-sisa	Straight King	Vice Regent / Adviser
-	Shakkan-shengbar		Private Secretary / Butler of Bedroom Suite
+	Kindazi	Good Barber	Valet de Chambre
+	En-signun	Lord ?	Equerry
-	En-lulim	Lord Deer	Goat Herd / Deer Keeper
-	Ushumgal-kalama	Great Dragon of the Homeland	Bard / Balang-Singer
-	Lugal-igi-hush	Wroth-faced King[24] / Fierce-faced King	Elegist / Balang-Lamenter
+	7 twins of Baba	-	Handmaidens
+	Gishbare	The One Taking out the Plow -	Farmer
+	Lamma-enkud-e-gu2-eden-na	Angel Tax-Collector of Steppe Bank	Fishery Supervisor
+	Dimgal Abzu	Great Post of Groundwater	Herald of Steppe Bank
+	Lugal	King	Guard of Holy City

[24] Jacobsen 1987:434n36: "The 'wroth-faced king' suggests that it would come into play when Ningirsu's face was glowering, the god still full of the wrath of battle."

2b No Servant-gods in a Comprehensive List of Food and Drink allocations to Gods of a Temple

Records of the OB administration of the Ninurta temple Eshumesha in Nippur list recipients of food and drink allocations of the entire temple household as follows (+ = presence, - = absence of divine determinative):[25]

- \+   (Standing) Ninurta (image) in larger house.

    (Sitting Ninurta images) in throne house and sedan-chair house.

    (Armed Ninurta image) in Igishugalama.[26]
- \+   (Images of 6 major gods) Nusku, Sin, Enki, Inana, Ishkur, Utu.
- \+   (Images of the 12 minor gods) Nin-Girgilu, Nergal, Nintinuga, Damu, Ninshubura, Ninsun, Baba, Nin-Isina, Nin-Kirimasha ("Lady Kidnose"), Shulpae, Shuzi'ana, Nin-Nibru.
- \-   9 statues: the larger, breastkid (a statue depicting an offerer bringing a kid in his arms), (former king) + Ishme-Dagan, the three of them, (former king) + Sin-Iqisham, the four of them.
- \+   (Images of 11 gods) Ningishzida, Ninsi'ana, Nanay, Kalkal, Martu, Pabilsag, Enanun, Ninshenshena, Lulal, Numushda, Ennugi.
- \-   Weapon Seven-headed club.
- \-   Main gate.

The three balang-gods of Ninurta of Eshumesha that are listed in An:Anum (I 268–270) were not allocated food and drink. However, eleven human temple-servants receiving food and drink from the temple (Sigrist 1984a:173) do include a chief lamenter (gala mah) and chief singer (nar-gal). They would have performed the duties of the balang servant-gods.

---

[25] Sigrist 1984a:140.
[26] George 1993 no. 524. The weapon 'Fifty-headed Stick' was stationed in Igishugalama and Ninurta determined destinies there (Heimpel 1996:21–22 with fig. 3). The corresponding place in Gudea's ground plan of the Eninnu of Ningirsu was the most protruding of the three gates of the east side of the temple. George's proposal to identify it with the cella of Ninurta in his Nippur temple means that the gate led straight to the cella at the west side with the rising sun greeted by Ningirsu/Ninurta looking at the mountain land to check whether it was necessary to move out on a military expedition (one of his principal functions).

2c Balang-harp Servant-gods in God-lists

Servant-gods may already occur in the long ED IIIa god-lists from Fara, so possibly ᵈmuhaldim-zi-Unug ('Good Cook of Uruk') and others mentioned by Krebernik 1986:165. There are two candidates for a Balang-harp god name, ᵈAb2-er2-ša4 ('Tear-crier Cow'), sharing the first element with Ab2-he2-nun, the harp-goddess of Nin-KI.MAR (20); and ᵈNin-er2(-ra) ('Lady of tears').[27]

The OB forerunner of An:Anum TCL 15 10 lists the names of several servant-gods, without identifying their occupations. According to their listing in An:Anum, the forerunner lists butlers (lines 72, 164, 185, 394), caretakers (53–54, 141–144), attendants (167), doorkeepers (101–102), and two balang-gods—A-ru6 and Ur(sic)-a-ru6 (93–94), the balang-gods of Damgalnuna (wife of Enki) in An:Anum II 315–316.

The earliest exemplars of An:Anum belong to the Kassite period, the first phase of the Late period.[28] It is the single best source for the number and variety of servant-gods, and especially balang servant-gods, of the major temple households of Babylonia. The master-gods are listed according to their rank in the Babylonian pantheon. Listed after each master-god are the names of family members and servant-gods. Renger, treating the servant-gods as an example of household staff, counted forty occupations (RlA 4:436–437, *Hofstaat A). Some were particular to their master-gods. For example, only Enlil had a slaughterer, reflecting the large number of live meat-animals brought for slaughter to the supreme temple of the land. Only Inana had a troupe of five translators, in line with her international character. Only the sun-god had a runner, who carried, at the speed of light and over far distances from the ever moving position of his master, numerous answers to oracle inquiries and legal matters. Other servant-gods were employed by several master-gods. For example, both Enlil and Baba had a housekeeper (agrig), and many master-gods with large temples had butlers, caretakers, attendants, and door-keepers.

Balang-harp servant-gods are by far the most numerous group of servant-gods in An:Anum. This remarkable feature could result from the bias of an author or redactor who was a lamenter, as indicated by document 54.

A master-god could have several balang servant-gods. The moon-god had eight; the sky-god An and war-god Ningirsu seven; the mother goddess, the weather-god, and the sun-god six; none had five, two four, and one three. The

---

[27] In both names, IGI.A is interpreted as equivalent to A.IGI er2 'tear'. IGI.A is logogram for uhhur2 'foam,' but 'Lady Foam' and '... foam Cow' seem unlikely. See Krebernik 1986:191 and 198.

[28] See Veldhuis 2000:79–80 and Lambert in RlA 3:475 (*Götterlisten).

remaining twenty-three balang-gods either came in pairs or as singles. These numbers do not mirror the hierarchy of the master-gods themselves, but rather the level of apprehension about a master-god's tendency to be absent; divine absence threatened the well-being of the community, and called for Balang-harp and lamenter to bring absent gods back for their and the community's good.[29] The moon- and sun-gods disappeared frequently, and the heaven-god An seemed always distant.

The plurality of harp-gods of one and the same master-god has a further aspect. Some names of harp-gods coincide with names of festivals, indicating that an individual balang-god went into action on a specific occasion. The clearest examples are two of the seven harp-gods of An. One is named after the constellation One-Acre-Star whose appearance marks the beginning of the year (53 I 79). Another is named after the festival 'Sitting Gods' when all the gods come together (53 I 75). At the Sitting Gods festival, the oratorio was performed whose lyrics are known from the balang composition Elum Gusun (CLAM 1: 272–318).[30] The Balang-harp and balang-goddess Ninigizibara participate in the oratorio Uru'amma'irabi in which Inana laments the death of her husband Dumuzi (47a). A search for further links between Balang-harps and their corresponding servant-gods and particular oratorios should be fruitful, but has not been attempted here.

A particular feature of balang instruments is their not-infrequent appearance in groups of seven (documents 9, 11, 37, and 43).[31] Document 43 describes an attempt to pacify Enlil when his rage had already caused the destruction of the kingdom and the city of Akkad. One Balang-harp was not enough to pacify him. It was attempted with seven, the number whose magic made it more than seven times one.[32] Against the background of major temples having several festivals with so many oratorios and so many balang instruments, the motif of the seven balangs also meant that all festival activity was then pooled in the one great effort to pacify Enlil. Document 9 lists allocations of oil to a 'large balang', or 'chief balang', in second position after an up-drum, and at the very end a group of seven balangs. Document 11 also mentions a group of seven balangs close to the end of a list of allocations of food. This group of balangs belongs to the temple of Nin-MAR.KI in the province of Lagash. The position of the groups of seven balangs in documents 9 and 11 indicates a low rank among the cultic

---

[29] Löhnert 2009:55–58.
[30] The operatic nature of the performance is described by Ziegler (FM 9:55–64) on the basis of an OB ritual of the performance of Uru'amma'irabi from Mari.
[31] See also Franklin, p41.
[32] See Franklin, p40–41.

institutions of the temples of Nanshe and Nin-MAR.KI. The function of the seven-magic in these cases is unclear.

Balang-gods were given the title GUD.BALAĜ in An:Anum, a term translated as *mumtalku* 'the one with whom one takes counsel, confidant' in KAV 64 II 17. The same function was expressed in Sumerian with the title ad-gi4-gi4, literally 'sound repeating', in conventional translation 'adviser', or as we might say 'sounding board'.

Gabbay (PHG:103–109) pointed out that the designation GUD.BALAĜ is restricted to An:Anum, not attested as Sumerian word, and probably a logogram of ad-gi4-gi4 'adviser'. He quotes in favor of his understanding An:Anum II 94–95: ^{d}ad-gi4-gi4 = ŠU ('same pronunciation', that is, adgigi), ^{d}MIN (that is, ^{d}ad-gi4-gi4) GUD.BALAĜ (written GUD.BALAĜ) ŠU ('same pronunciation'). The gloss MIN indeed points to a pronunciation adgigi. Gabbay further provides an improved reading of An:Anum V 17–18 where the balang-gods of Ninsun and Lugalbanda are listed as divine 'advisers' (^{d}ad-gi4-gi4) rather than as GUD.BALAĜ.

Michalowski 2010a:221–222 notes that the sign BALAĜ actually writes two words, balaĝ and gud10, and interprets GUD.BALAĜ as ^{gud}gud10 (see 4g). It is indeed tempting to read the sign BALAĜ as balaĝ when the instrument is meant and gud10 when it is the balang servant-god. Yet Ningirsu's temple-servant Fierce-faced King in Gudea Cylinders B is said to be 'his balang' (balaĝ-ĝa2-ni) where the spelling rules out a reading gud10. The use of the word balaĝ to designate the lamenter may go back to the archaic period (1 and 2).

The following table gives the numbers of balang-gods and other common types of servant-gods in An:Anum. With caretakers and attendants, the name of the temple rather than that of the master-god was preferred.

Master-god	Balang-gods #	Butler sukkal[33]	Caretaker udug[34]	Attendant gub-ba	Door-keeper i3-du8	Temple
Nanna	8	1		4		
An	7	3+1				
Ningirsu	7			5		Eninnu
Dingirmah	6	1	1	3	4	Emah
Ishkur	6	1				
Utu	6+5[35]	5+1		1	2	Ebabbar
Baba	4		3			
Enki	4	0+2			8	
Ninurta	3	1	1	1		Eshumesha
Damgalnuna	2	2				
Enlil	2	0+1	9	2	2	Ekur
Gibil	2	1				
Gula	2	3	5	5	1	Egalmah
Inana	2			2		
Lugalmarad	2					
Manungal	2	1	2			
Marduk	2	5	2		2	Esagila
Ningal	2	1				
Ningublaga	2					
Ninshubura	2					
Nissaba	2					
Ashgi	1					
Damu	1					
Ishtaran	1	1				
Ninlil	1		1			
Ninkimar	1					
Ninsun	1					
Nusku	1		1			
Panigara	1	1				

[33] 'Chief butler' (sukkal-mah) after +.
[34] For the translation 'caretaker' see Heimpel 2009:138–139.
[35] KAV 64, lines 12–18 of the last two columns of the reverse, lists five names of 'secondary balang' (balaĝ us2, translated as BALAĜ re-du-u2) of Utu.

Master-god	Balang-gods #	Butler sukkal	Caretaker udug	Attendant gub-ba	Door-keeper i3-du8	Temple
Sadarnuna	1					
Tishpak	1	1				
Zarpanitum	1					
	85	33	25	23	19	

2d Gender of Balang-gods

The names of balang-gods show that they were thought to be male or female. Balang-gods serving female master-gods have female names and balang-gods serving male master-gods have male names. Three exceptions are one female balang-god each of the male master-gods Enki, Utu, and Nanna.

A fourth possible exception is Ninigizibara, the balang servant-god of Inana. Gabbay (PHG:112) points out that BM 38593, a Late version of the balang composition Uru'amma'irabi, translates the name Nin-igi-zi-bar-ra into Akkadian as 'whom (masculine suffix) the Lady (= Inana) regarded well'—and further that this balang-god is called Inana's husband (23f, but see Section 4a5, 'my husband'). The maleness of Ninigizibara does fit the short form Igizibara, which was used for the harp-god in records from Ur III Umma and is attested as a masculine PN in the ED and Ur III periods.[36] Gudea calls himself Igizibara of Nanshe in Statue B II 10–1 (RIME 3/1 1.1.7.StB). Yet maleness is contradicted by 23h and 23i where the element nin of the full name Ninigizibara is given in Emesal Sumerian as gašan 'lady'.

Gender-revealing names are presented in the following tables:

---

[36] CUSAS 23 5 (probably Umma ED IIIb), DP 624 I 5–6 (Girsu ED IIIb) and HLC 32 I 11 (Girsu Ur III).

Masculine Names	Master-god and Gender	Documentation
Fierce-faced King	Ningirsu (m)	18
Ishbi-Erra Trustee of Enlil	Enlil (m)	40
Bull Calf of Sin	Nanna (m)	53 III 51
Grand Dragon Nanna	Nanna (m)	53 III 52
Judge of Heaven and Earth	Utu (m)	53 III 154
Just Judge	Utu (m)	53 III 156
Youth of His Mighty Rising	Shamash (m)	53 KAV 64 IV 14
Good Man	Ningirsu (m)	53 V 105
The One from Before	Ishtaran (m)	53 V 291

Feminine Names	Master-god and Gender	Documentation
Lady Conversing Grandly with An	Baba (f)	19
Lady Occupying the Palace	Gula (f)	24
Lady Aruru	Dingirmah (f)	53 II 97
Lady Prayer of An	Zarpanitum (f)	53 II 259
Festival Lady	Enki (f)	53 II 310–311
Eagle Queen	Nin-KI.MAR (f)	53 III 85
Cow of His Risen Heart	Shamash (m)	53 IV 13
Lady Heaven's Bolt	Inana (f)	53 IV 74
Cow Wealth Praise	Ninsun (f)	53 V 18
Great Lady	Gula (f)	53 V 186
Lady of Plenty	Gula (f)	53 V 187
Lady (ga-ša-an) Aru	Damgalnuna (m)	53 V 315

The advising function of balang-gods agrees with their gender distribution and the main characters of oratorios. A woman rather than a man is typically the better confidant to console, soothe, and commiserate a goddess, and a male adviser can better deal with the rage of a god.

3 Human Functionaries Exercising the Duties of Balang-gods

Gudea's list of non-divine and divine temple-servants includes a description of their duties *vis-à-vis* their master. The Balang-harp servants advised, pacified, and entertained their masters. Who were the human temple-servants that performed the duties of the Balang-harp temple-servants and Balang-harp servant-gods?

3a The Singer

The pictograph of a canine head in archaic texts identifies the singer (1). This is shown by the archaic ancestor of Lu2, the oldest version of a list of signs for words that designate persons and professions. The list includes this pictograph in register 105 (2). From later lexical texts we know that the cuneiform sign that developed from the canine head pictograph wrote thirteen words, among them 'fox, jackal' (ka5-a); animal and common PN; 'false' (lul); 'singer' (nar); and one name of a god, Dunga—the god of singers.[37] This combination of meanings reflects the melodious howling of the jackal and the capacity of the fox to deceive.[38]

Singers serving in a divine household are attested in Ur III administrative documents.[39] The balang temple-servant Great Dragon of the Homeland was a singer (17c). He played the lute, an exemplar built by Gudea to entertain Ningirsu. He also managed musical performances in the courtyard and in the bedroom suite. In the latter, he played, or oversaw play with, two more instruments, the 'hoe-setter(?)' (al-ĝar), and the 'Marian' (miritum), possibly the 'Mari harp' listed in an ED lexical text (4b). Great Dragon's duty was further to make sure that joyous music was played in the courtyard (17c). At the musical performance for the inauguration of the renovated temple, he led the drums into the courtyard (17d). He also took care of the tigi instruments (17c). In addition to being a singer and lute-player, he acted as a kind of musical director.[40] The lack of divine determinative indicates that Great Dragon of the Homeland was a human singer. He might have had his own normal PN, but in relationship to the master-god his professional name was 'Great Dragon of the Homeland'.

---

[37] MSL 14:468–469 (lines 118–137) and Civil 2010:12–13 (lines 241–253).
[38] Gabbay 2010 and Collon in RlA 14:142 (*Trommel und Pauke) translate 'jackal'. AHw, CAD, and CDA only 'fox'. The jackal, who likes to live close to human settlement and would have been a more common presence—not the fox (who prefers uninhabited areas)—engages in melodious howling. The Arabic cognate also designates both canids (Lane 1980:338, "ṭa'lab: the fox, canis vulpes of Linn., but in the dialect of Egypt the jackal, canis aureus").
[39] The best source is the administrative record from the province of Lagash published by Gelb 1975, which lists the singers and lamenters of the divine households of the province. Even the households of the servant-gods in Ningirsu's temple, Igalima and Shulshagana, had a singer.
[40] See Franklin, p28. In the temple of Nanshe in Nina, a city in the territory of Lagash, the chief singer played a horn (20c).

3b Lamenters

In an archaic record of persons, the jackal-head pictograph, serving as sign of the word nar 'singer', is followed by the pictograph of a roundharp (1). The same sequence is found in the archaic version of the list of persons Lu2 (2). In the ED IIIa version of that list, the pictograph of the roundharp is no longer found, nor is the sign of the Balang-harp. The place after the singer is taken by two pictographs, UŠ and DUR2. The first designates maleness in its various aspects. The rather abstract pictograph appears to depict an ejaculating penis. The second pictograph writes the words for buttock, sitting, farting, excrement, and wet.

The combined signs write the Sumerian word gala, 'lamenter'. Steinkeller 1992:37 proposed that the combination of meanings that characterize the lamenter are penis and buttock, so that the proper rendering of the sign would be GIŠ3.DUR2 rather than the conventional UŠ.KU. It is difficult to think of another meaningful combination of the two signs. The gala would accordingly have been someone who practiced anal intercourse.[41]

It was the lamenter whom the god of wisdom, Enki, created to extricate the goddess Inana after she was killed in an attempt to add the netherworld to her dominion. The lamenter entered the netherworld and succeeded to gain the trust of its queen Ereškigal by commiserating with her suffering body and mind. In turn, she allowed him the choice of a gift, for which he selected the revival and return of Inana. Sexual activity could resume.[42]

In his visit to the netherworld, the lamenter proved he could manipulate its queen. This would have enabled him to alleviate the destiny of the dead in the netherworld. "When a body was interred, the lamenter set up the balang, elicited tears" (22a). He would have elicited the tears of those present, commiserated with their sense of loss, and exercised his influence on the queen of the netherworld for a good treatment of the deceased in her realm.

Did the lamenter play the Balang-harp that he had set up? Document 22b shows that the lamenter *and* a harpist collaborated at a mourning rite. That was also the case of oratorios where the harp was played by the harpist, not the

---

[41] The Mesopotamian attitude to male homosexuality was "positive appreciation" (Wiggermann, RlA 12:418, *Sexualität A). Apart from homosexuality, anal intercourse with a woman was practiced in order to prevent pregnancy (CAD s.v. *nâku* 3, cited by Wiggermann). For recent discussions of the sexuality and anatomy of the 'third gender' of the lamenter, see Gabbay 2008; Shehata 2009:82–83; Gabbay PHG:67–68.

[42] Michalowski 2006, limiting himself to Ur III administrative documents, finds the very same dichotomy in the nature of the lamenter, which he expresses as "love" and "death," "marriage option" and "military option." The connection with death was the temporal induction of a soldier to serve as lamenter in battle deaths, the connection with marriage might have been the lamenter's instruction of the couple about matters of sexuality.

lamenter. The only statement that the lamenter played the Balang-harp is the Late period document 51 whose Sumerian text and Akkadian translation are not trustworthy. The lamenter was connected with the Balang-harp in oratorios and burial rites as master of ceremony.

The suru was a particular type or designation of lamenter.[43] He is attested already in document 13 from ED IIIb Girsu where the expenditure of beer for the suru and Balang-harps, set up in different places, is recorded. In this case, the suru could not have impersonated the Balang-harp. Perhaps the beer was destined for the harpist who was not the suru.

3c Harpists

In ED pictorial representations, men played the portable roundharp (MgB 2/2 no. 32, 34, 35) and women the large roundharp with foot (MgB 2/2. no. 29 and Marcetteau 2010:69–70). An OAkk. seal (MgB 2/2 no. 44) shows a woman playing a portable roundharp with recurved neck before a god. The female harpists are accompanied by two female musicians with claves, and so is a donkey playing a portable roundharp (MgB 2/2 no. 30). The horizontally held angle-harp that arrived in the OB period was played by women and men.

In OAkk. texts, all harpists (balaĝ-di) appearing in administrative documents were women.[44] On the other hand, a harpist with masculine name Dada is attested in an ED IIIa text (6) and two Akkadian translations of the Sumerian term balaĝ-di are masculine active participles (see p594).

3c1 Female Harpists (balaĝ-di)

Krecher 1966:162n467 observed that the lamenting goddess in an oratorio addresses a harpist, for example "I am displaced from the house, my tears (flow) without end. Oh harpist, I am displaced from the house, my tears (flow) without end" (CLAM 520 A+2-3), or "the cattlepen destroying day, the sheepfold shredding day! Oh harpist, the day when the intent of its heart is not found" (VS 2 12 I 7-8). The harpist must be a woman in this scenario. In the performance of the oratorio, she played the harp and sang. An OB pictorial representation shows a singing female harpist.[45] Her words would have been mostly the words of the goddess, repeated in commiseration and not repeated in script. In two cases, actual answers of the harpist are included in the lyrics of an oratorio:

---

[43] The sign sur9, the word by itself, and as part of the name of the instrument alĝarsura is treated in Veldhuis 1997–1998.

[44] RIME 2.1.4.54; Molina 1991:142–145 = P101667; MAD 1 (Gelb 1952) 232; 303; 336; OIP 104 (Gelb et al. 1989–1991), 43. + MAD 1 54 and 55 rev. IV 7; OIP 104, 44 rev. II' 4'–6'.

[45] Schmidt-Colinet in RlA 12:505 (*Sänger, Sängerin B) with a precise drawing by C. Wolff.

(1) Sherida, the wife of the sun-god, addresses her harpist (Wilcke 1973):

The northwind in my face, the cold days have arrived here. Oh harpist, the northwind in my face, the cold days have arrived here.

The harpist answers:

Lady of this city, my lady Sherida, amber, gentle woman! Oh my lady, lady of Whitehouse ... the mountains will block the wind for you.[46]

(2) In another oratorio (Römer 1983), the city-goddess of Isin laments that an enemy defiled her and her temple on the instigation of An and Enlil. She left her city while her city called for her to stay, giving up responsibility for her temple and city to the enemy. The harpist answers:

How was it destroyed? How was it entirely destroyed? How could you yourself defile it? How could you destroy it, how could you entirely destroy it? Oh Lady, how could you entirely destroy your abode, how defile it?[47]

The harpist in the first case consoles with a rational argument; in the second she tells the lamenting goddess to blame herself. Both actions fit an adviser.

Two additional statements round off the advising role of female harpists. Shehata 2009:94–97, treating the role of harpists, quotes lines 65–66 of the composition *A Man and His God* (ETCSL 5.2.4) where a harpist is asked to act on behalf of the lamenting man: "Is not my sister a harpist of sweet sounds? Let her speak to you [the personal god] in tears of my deeds that have brought about my ruin."[48]

Lines 68–69 of the *Nippur Lament* describe the reaction of harpists to the lament of a personified temple: "Like a cow separated from its calf, the house emitted bitter cries about itself, was tear-stricken. The harpists, those of sweet sounds, answer its words in tears like nursemaids singing a lullaby."[49]

According to the first statement, the harpist can soften the heart of the personal god enraged about the deeds of his human client. In the second, she is compared to a nursemaid who can put a baby to sleep. Clearly the female

---

[46] im kur-ra igi-ĝa2 u4 še18-bi ma-te balaĝ-di im kur-ra igi-ĝa2 u4 še18-bi ma-te nin uru2-ba ga-ša-an-mu su2-ra2-aĝ2 munus ša6-ga a ga-ša-an-mu nin gu-la ga-ša-an e2-bar6-bar6-ra ... im hur-saĝ-e mu-un-ši-ĝar-re.

[47] a-gim i3-gul a-gim i3-gul-gul ni2-zu a-gim mu-un-pe-el, nin ama5-zu a-gim i3-gul-la ni2-zu ‹a-gim mu-un-pe-el›.

[48] nin-mu balaĝ-di lu2 ad du10 na-nam niĝ2-ak šu-hul du11-ga-mu er2-ra ha-ra-ni-ib-be2.

[49] e2-e ab2 amar-bi ku5-ra2-gim ni2-bi-še3 ur5 gig-ga im-ša4 SIG7.SIG7 i3-ĝa2-ĝa2 balaĝ-di lu2 ad du10-ga-ke4-ne ummeda u5-a di-gim mu-bi er2-ra mi-ni-ib-bal-bal-e-ne.

harpist is seen as adviser of her divine mistress. She impersonates the Balang-harp servant-goddess in the role as adviser.

Franklin alerts me to the recent treatment by Arnaud 2010:164-174 of a long known, mostly Sumerian cuneiform inscription from Byblos with Ur III sign-forms. This curious document concerns the restoration of the cult in the temple of Ishtar of Byblos. Its lines are arranged vertically, as in monumental inscriptions of the Ur III period; but the signs are horizontally oriented, as in later periods. The section that Arnaud recognizes as a description of the temple's former state mentions a female singer and female harp player (munus nar munus balag-di3), presumably belonging to the original temple staff.

3c2 Male Harpists

As mentioned already, the only male balang-player appearing in an administrative record known to me is in document 6.

Not all male balang temple-servants had something to do with the Balang-harp. Great Dragon of the Homeland was a singer, lutist, and director of musical entertainment for his divine master. That may also be the case of some of the male balang-gods for whom we have no information beyond the name. The late version of the list of persons Lu2 includes the equation lu2 balaĝ-di = ZA-ri-ru (MSL 12, 134:175). The Akkadian word is a masculine active participle of three Akkadian verbal stems with none of the known meanings fitting a harpist.[50]

The Eblaite translation of balaĝ-di, *na-ṭi3-lu-um*, is also a masculine active participle. In the comment to document 4d, I translate the Eblaite word as Akkadian 'observer' and link it with the Sumerian 'observer' (igi-du8) who acts together with the Balang-harp to soften the impact of, and divert, an oncoming storm (29). His interactions with the storm-god are called 'confrontations' (gaba ri). According to the Sumerian equivalence 'harpist' for the 'observer', it was he who played the harp. He would have impersonated the harp-god as adviser. The use of the word 'confrontation' shows that his adviser role involved strength.

4 Ontology

4a Sumerian Ontology

Perhaps the most revealing passage for the many things a balang is said to be comes in the form of a string of designations with which Inana laments the loss of her Balang-harp Ninigizibara in the oratorio Uru'amma'irabi (23f). It entails the illogical element of Inana lamenting the loss of her Balang-harp while that

---

[50] *sarāru* 'to be false', *ṣarāru* 'to flash, drip, twinkle'; *zarāru* does not seem to exist.

very harp accompanies and responds to her lament. Otherwise, the designations provide a veritable ontology that sets apart and unifies Balang-harp, advising servant-god, and lamenter. The literary form frames the string of designations between the balang instrument and the Balang-harp servant-god, so we can expect that the whole string of designations was meant to itemize the aspects of one and the same thing or concept ("entity" in Selz's terminology).

1. 'The junior', or 'impetuous Balang-harp'.

The meanings of Sumerian ban3-da include 'young' and 'younger' as age designations, and 'junior' as rank designation. The latter could contrast with Inana's more important Balang-harp god Ninigizibara. That would be Ninme'urur who is Inana's other adviser and Balang-harp mentioned next to Ninigizibara in the same text (23). Another meaning of ban3-da is 'impetuous', von Soden's "ungestüm" in AHw s.v. *ekdu*. An incantation describes a breed bull mounting a cow as *ekdu* (BAM [Köcher 1963–1980] 3 248 III 19). If that meaning applies, it could hardly refer to the female Ninme'urur.

2. 'My bellowing aurochs'.

According to the Late ritual for covering a kettledrum—the instrument that eventually took over the role of the Balang-harp—the spotless black hide of a bull never touched by goad or stick became the drum head and its vibrations on the drum the transformed heartbeat of the killed bull turned kettledrum-god.[51] I assume that this Late ritual already existed earlier in some form and was applied to the leather covering of musical instruments with bull hide resonators used in cult. The use of bull hides for Balang-harps is attested in administrative records (36, 41, 42b) and the Balang-harp is called a bull (comment to 4g, 21, 49b). Its sound was the transformed bull's vocalizations.

From bull to god was a small gap to jump in Mesopotamian culture: anthropomorphic gods carried horns on their headgear, betraying an original bovine nature. According to the ritual, it happened by way of the death of the bull. It was important that it was not a working animal, not touched by goad or stick in the ritual, even less touched by civilization in the OB version of the oratorio Uru'amma'irabi an undomesticated aurochs bull.

3. 'The shining Balang-harp'.

'Shining' is the standard characterization of the sheen of silver and refers here to silver plating the neck of the Balang-harp (see note to 42a).

---

[51] Gabbay (PHG:124–128).

4. 'My lapis lazuli'.

Gold and silver for decorating Balang-harps is attested (23g, 34c, 42c); lapis lazuli is not. This stone was part of the inlays framing the sound box of ED lyres. The statement 'my lapis lazuli' must serve for the time being as sole indication that also the Balang-harp was decorated with lapis lazuli.

5. 'My husband'.

There does not appear to be a reasonable linguistic way around understanding 'my husband' as describing the relationship of the Balang-harp god with his mistress Inana. This seems to confirm Gabbay's proposal that Ninigizibara was male, yet the Emesal form gašan for standard Sumerian nin indicates a female (see Section 2d). The context of the lament of Inana is the start of the dry season when her other husband, Dumuzi, departs on his way to eventual death. According to the plot of the oratorio, he was abducted by the same enemy that took her harp. Not many lines after calling Ninigizibara her husband, Inana laments his loss, without calling him her husband, and then the loss of her husband Dumuzi, including in her words the longing for making love with him. The literary form of the lines makes it clear that the status of husband and the wish of making love with him is restricted to Dumuzi (see the comment to 23f). This leaves me doubting the textual tradition. One of the sources writes instead of the expected mu-ud-na-zu ('your husband') mu-ud-nu-bi, which is enigmatic and as *lectio difficilior* the more likely to be authentic.

6. 'My adviser'.

This expresses the service of the balang servant-god for Inana.[52]

7. 'My great suru'.

The word suru designates a priest who is classified as lamenter (gala).[53] A suru priest and a Balang-harp set up in the city center received beer according to an ED IIIb document (13). Balang-gods of the weather-god Adad are named 'Great Suru' and 'Day of the Suru' in An:Anum (53 III 260 and 261). By virtue of being a balang servant-god of the male weather-god, the suru should be male, which again favors Gabbay's argument for the maleness of Ninigizibara.

8. 'My adviser Ninigizibara'.

The last designation identifies the harp servant-god whose name is preceded by the divine determinative.

---

[52] See Section 2c and Franklin p30–33.
[53] See Section 3b.

Different aspects that are separated here were explicitly merged elsewhere. The Balang-harp and the corresponding balang servant-god were merged by making a function of the harp-god that of the instrument: 'his advising instrument' (niĝ2 ad-gi4-gi4-ni, 17a). The balang servant-god is 'fashioned' (23a1). The (neck) of the harp-god is treated with fish-oil (23a2). The grapple-hook and eye of the harp-god is plated with silver (23a3). The harp-god Ninigizibara is 'set up' in 47a.

On the other hand, the instrument and the suru lamenter are recorded to have received drink separately (13).

4b Rationalization

To call this section 'Rational ontology' would be presumptuous for me. I will simply describe what I believe is the reality behind the identifications of instrument, instrument god, and human temple-servant. Two epistemological problems are the identification of instrument and person, and the deification of the person.

4b1 Identifications

The instrument was personalized as result of being named.[54] When Gudea planned the renovation of the temple of Ningirsu, he was advised to keep the god happy in temporary quarters with the gift of a chariot and "his beloved balang, Great Dragon of the Homeland" (17a). The name already existed, the instrument did not, so the name was traditional. Beginning in the OB period, kings, not tradition, named the instrument (40). Judging by the lack of the divine determinative, Gudea's Great Dragon of the Homeland was no deity.[55] He should have been the incumbent temple singer, who assumed the name of the instrument when exercising his functions. With the name of the instrument he would have received the history of his particular office, including the care for the musical entertainment of the divine master of the temple, traditional dress, and perhaps a dragon mask.[56]

The mutual dependency of musical instrument and player would have been the link of identity. Great Dragon of the Homeland was, so to speak, the 'first

---

[54] Cf. Franklin, p25.
[55] See p590.
[56] Many singers are attested in Girsu in Ur III records. There is one Lu-Nanshe, chief singer (nar-gal), who appears as father of a witness in two court cases (Falkenstein 1956 no. 113 and 161). The first case is about prebends in the temple of Ningirsu, so the witnesses were likely clerics, as Falkenstein states. The case was decided in the fortieth year of Shulgi, which means that the chief singer could have been appointed by Gudea. So it is possible that Lu-Nanshe impersonated the Great Dragon of the Homeland.

lute' in musical performances. Without its player, the lute could not 'advise' Ningirsu, and without his instrument, Great Dragon of the Homeland could not do so either.

Fierce-faced King presents us with a different situation. His particular duties identify his profession as lamenter. But instead of giving him that title, he is called Ningirsu's "balang," which may either be the instrument, or the designation of the lamenter as attested in archaic texts and the ED IIIa version of the list of person Lu2 A (1, 2, 4a). Lamenters do not appear to have played the Balang-harp themselves (see Section 3b), so their identification with the instrument rests on their mutual dependency at burial ceremonies and performance of oratorios. Lamenter and Balang-harp—albeit played by a harpist—each needed the other.

4b2 Deification

The word balang is at all periods written without the divine determinative. There are exceptions in Ur III administrative records (25, 26, 28). Still, the general lack of the determinative indicates that neither the instrument nor its named personification was deified in Old Akkadian (15) and the province of Lagash in the early Ur III period.

The deification of the personification outside of Lagash in the Ur III period could have resulted from introducing the magic of turning a bull, whose hide covered the resonator of the instrument, into a god in the Ur III period (see Section 4a §2). Alternatively, it emerged more indirectly from the intellectual climate that was also responsible for the widening importance of the cult of the deified king in the Ur III kingdom. Another motive could have been the expectation of increased prestige, and income, of the players and managers of balang instruments—the temple singers, lamenters, and harpists.

Catalogue

For periods up to and including Ur III, full documentation of meaningful references was the goal. A selection of OB (after 2000) and Late (post-OB) documents follows. The order is basically chronological, but I list under a single number documents about one and the same balang-god, and lexical entries from various periods. All dates of documents are BCE.[57]

---

[57] P000000 is the text number in cdli.ucla.edu.

Archaic Uruk IV (before 3000)

<u>1</u> W 9656,aa = P001443. Englund and Boehmer 1994:94 (transliteration), pl. 89 (copy), and MgB 2/2 no. 27 (photo). List of persons belonging to the household of a lord (en).

> 5 male princes, 2 male ?, 1 mountain ? ?, 5 ?, two registers broken, 3 singers, 4 balang, (total) 120 [+n]. The lord [ ].[58]

The sign ZATU 672 is attested only on Uruk IV tablets, the very similar sign NAR on Uruk III tablets and later. Both signs depict the head and neck of a canid with long, erected ears. The lower end of neck is treated differently. ZATU 672 in W 9311,f is followed by -a, which is likely Ka5-a 'Fox' or 'Jackal', a common Sumerian PN. If the sign NAR = nar = 'singer' and ZATU 672 = ka5 in ka5-a 'jackal', and if the singer and the jackal are two words written with one sign, then ZATU 672 and NAR are variants of one and the same sign.

Archaic Uruk III (ca. 3000)

<u>2</u> Archaic Lu2 105–106 (Englund and Nissen 1993:16–17).
> Great singer (nar-gal), great balang (balaĝ-gal).

ED I/II (ca. 2700), Text From Ur

<u>3</u> UET 2 3:1–2 = P005577.
> List of recipients of kids. The first two recipients received two kids. The name of the second includes the word balang.[59]

ED IIIa (ca. 2600)

<u>4</u> Lexical texts.

<u>4a</u> ED Lu2 A 77–78 (MSL 12:11).
> Great singer (nar-gal), great balang (balaĝ-gal).

<u>4b</u> ED Practical Vocabulary from Ebla and Abu Salabikh 205–211 (Civil 2008:39; Michalowski 2010b:119).
> "Balang-type emarah, balang, Tilmun balang, Mari balang, flute, ? reed, BUR2-type balang."[60]

---

[58] [2? +] 3N1 NUNa Uša, 2N1 ERIN Uša, 1N1 EZENc ZATU 632b KURa, 5N1 DARA3b, 3N1 ZATU 672, 4N1 BALAĜ, 2N34 [ ] ENa [ ]. (ZATU: Green and Nissen 1987).
[59] 2 maš2 ama-UR5a?:ERIMb2:DU:UD, 2 (maš2) balaĝ-SI:DI (= balaĝ si-sa2 or balaĝ-di SI?).
[60] emarah balaĝ, balaĝ, balaĝ dilmun, balaĝ Ma-ri2^{ki}, gi-di, gi-tag, BUR2-balaĝ.

4c ED Practical Vocabulary MS 2340+ XXII 15'–20' (Civil 2010:210).
   BALAĜ, modified BALAĜ, Harhar, BALAĜ, lyre (ki2-na-ru12).[61]

4d Vocabulario di Ebla 571–572, MEE 4 (Pettinato 1982):264.
   "(Sumerian) Harpist (= Akkadian) seer, BALAĜ = lyre."[62]
   The conventional transliteration of the word for lyre is *gi-na-ru12-um*. The sign GI was used to write /ki/ elsewhere in Ebla texts, and the Hebrew word, *kinnōr* begins with /k/. The word *na-ṭi3-lu-um* has been understood to mean 'to raise one's voice'.[63] In Akkadian, it means 'to raise one's eyes, observe', and at Mari is also as substantive, 'observer'. An observer (igi-du8) working with the balang instrument, used to control weather-storms, is attested in Ur III texts (29, cf. Section 3c2).

4e OB version of the ED bird list 101 and 110 (YBC 4613:26 and 35), Veldhuis 2004:220–222 and 345.
   bi2-za-gu3-balaĝ-kar-gir5-za-na^{mušen} and u5-bi2-za-gu3-balaĝ-di-kar-gir5-za-na^{mušen}
This bird name is written in many different ways. The literal meaning is unclear. One element is 'balang voice' (gu3-balaĝ). The unusual length of the name suggests a remarkable bird. Perhaps it is the Eurasian bittern (*botaurus stellaris*) of the heron family. The large bird is often called a bull or cow because part of the mating call sounds like the bellowing of cattle, for example Hungarian *bölömbika* 'bellowing bull', Spanish *avetoro* 'bullbird', German *Rohrbrüller* 'reed bellower', *Kuhreiher* 'cow heron' and many more bovid designations. The Sumerian expression "its porch of the balang was a princely sounding bull (21)" may refer to the fact that the cover of the soundbox was a bull hide rather than to the actual cattle-like sound. Yet the bovidity of the bittern may also refer to the mock attacks of the bird when it puffs up its considerable plumage, lowering its head, and opening its also considerable beak.[64]

4f OB MS 2645 IV 33, Civil 2010:191–192.
   'Sound-of-balang' (ad-balaĝ-ĝa2mušen) is a bird name.
   Civil suggests that this is one part of the decomposed name of document 4e.

4g OB Proto-Ea 202–203 (MSL 14:40).

---

[61] balaĝ, BALAĜxGAN2-*tenû*, AL:HUB2, BALAĜ, har-har, *ki2-na-ru12*.
[62] balaĝ-di *na-ṭi3-lu-um*, BALAĜ *ki2-na-ru12-um*. Cf. Franklin, p66–67.
[63] See Tonietti 2010:83.
[64] A vivid description is found in Brehm 1911–1920 1:163–164.

Pronunciations bu-lu-un and gu-ud/gu2-ud/gu-du of the sign BALAĜ. Selz 1997:195n153 suggested an onomatopoetic 'blang' as pronunciation of what is conventionally transliterated as balaĝ. Bu-lu-un may indeed have been pronounced 'blong' or similar. Michalowski 2010a:221-222 considers the word gu-ud/gu2-ud/gu-du = gud10 and suggests that the term GUD.BALAĜ could be understood as ᵍᵘᵈgud10, "possibly an archaizing late creation that has no equivalent in earlier phases of the Sumerian language, and has as such nothing to do with the balag." I believe the word "bull" was written with the balang sign when it designates a balang-god.

<u>4h</u> OB Proto Lu2 641–644 and 651–662 (MSL 12:56–57).

> Singer, great singer, balang singer, string singer, [eleven further entries of special singers], snake charmer, great snake charmer, lamenter, chief lamenter, little lamenter, royal chief lamenter, royal lamenter, royal mobile lamenter, ? lamenter, mother of tears, balang, of balang, balang carrier.[65]

The position of the snake charmer belongs with the singers rather than the lamenters as shown by the Ur III text BM 014618 (Gelb 1975:57 and 60–61).

<u>5</u> ED IIIa SF 70 = P010663 (MSL 12:13).
List of professions.
Registers 1–11: "bishop, carpenter, leather worker, jeweler, smith, lapidary, mat weaver, balang-player (balaĝ-di), 'bull player' (gu4-di), singer (nar), builder," etc.; lamenter (gala) not included.

<u>6</u> WF (Deimel 1924) 107 = P011065.
List of recipients of bread, among them Dada, 'the balang-player man' (Da-da lu2 balaĝ-di).

<u>7</u> SF 47 III 6–8 = P010632 (MSL 12:14).
List of professions:
"Singer man, festival/song man, balang BUR2 man."[66]

---

[65] nar, nar-gal, nar balaĝ, nar sa, … muš-lah4, muš-lah4-gal, gala, gala-mah, gala-tur, gala-mah lugal, gala lugal, gala lugal-ra-us2-sa, gala ma-da-ab-us2, [am]a er2-ra, balaĝ, b[al]aĝ-ĝa2, [ba]laĝ-il2.

[66] lu2-nar, lu2-ezen/šir3, lu2 BUR2-balaĝ.

Post ED IIIa, Provenience Unknown

<u>8</u> Volk 1988.
PN1 lamenter, PN2, PN3, PN4, PN5, barley consumers, balang. Distribution of shares.[67]

ED IIIb (ca. 2500)

From records of the state archive of the kingdom of Lagash. The references for balaĝ from these records are summarized in Selz 1995:103–105.

<u>9</u> The wife of Lugalanda, ruler of the state of Lagash, traveled annually from her residence in Girsu to the city of Lagash and on to the city of Nina during month VIII (November) at the occasion of the Malt-Eating festival; she offered fat and dates in Lagash, and then in Nina for Nanshe, her pantheon, holy places, and the recipients listed below. Offerings on day one of the month of Malt-Eating of Nanshe: one liter of oil and dates each to gods and various sacred institutions, ending with "silver up(-drum), 'large balang', copper datepalm, stele, statue of Ur-Nanshe, statues inside the house, the eight of them, (and) balangs, the seven of them."[68]

<u>10</u> Similar records from three consecutive years of expenditures of food, for annual journeys of the ruler's wife from Girsu to Lagash and Nina. The occasion was called "it is (expenditures) of the balang carrier having been repositioned" (balaĝ-il2 e-ta-ru-a-kam). The translation 'repositioned' is assured by the corresponding passive form (ba-ta-ru-a-ne) that designates laborers who had been moved from one to another work place (Nik 1 90). Balang carriers are also attested in later lexical lists of professions.[69] The recipients in <u>10b</u> include temples and gods in Lagash and a mortuary installation (ki-a-naĝ), presumably also in Lagash, on the first day. A chief lamenter (gala-mah) is listed as recipient of barley in the final section without indication of a particular day (Selz 1995:103–104).

<u>10a</u> DP 167 dated Urukagina 2 = P220817.

---

[67] Lugal-an-za3-še3 gala, Gala-x, Ur-e2-tur, Me-na-ŠE3, [U]r-^dEn-ki, [l]u2 še gu7, ([x])balaĝ ha-la.
[68] ub5-ku3, [g]al:balaĝ, ĝišimmar urudu, na-ru2-a, alan Ur-^dNanše, alan e2 ša3-ga 8-ba-kam, balaĝ 7-ba-kam. TSA 1 IX 1–14 Lugalanda 2 = P221362; DP 53 IX 7–17 Lugalanda 3 = P220703; Nik 1 23 rev. II 1'–9' Lugalanda 6 = P221730 (minor differences not indicated). Selz 1995:103 and 189–198; Marchesi and Marchetti 2011:232–234.
[69] balaĝ-il2 na-aš2 ba-lam-gi (MAOG 13/2 [Meissner 1940]: 44–48, pl. 4 II 28') and balaĝ-il2-il2 (OrNS 70 [Taylor 2001], 210–211 II 33').

The steward Shul-utul-Men brought bread and beer to Nina and to Lagash "when Shasha, wife of Urukagina, king of Lagash, had repositioned the balang in Nina. (Year) 2."[70]

<u>10b</u> VS 14 93 Urukagina 3 = P020108.
List of cereals expended for the major gods of the territory of Lagash, holy places, and a chief lamenter (gala-mah). "(Responsible for the expenditure was) the administrator Puzur-Mama of Shasha, wife of Urukagina, king of Lagash, when the balang carrier was repositioned in Nina. (Year) 3."[71]

<u>10c</u> VS 14 118 Urukagina 4 = P020134.
"The scribe En-ig-gal brought it (fish), when the governor had repositioned the balang carrier. Year 4."[72]

<u>11</u> DP 55 undated = P220705 (Selz 1995:103).
A group of seven balangs (see <u>9</u>) belonged to the temple household of Nin-MAR.KI, city-goddess of Gu'aba.[73] Expenditures of flour, beer, and fish went to four major and two minor gods; eleven 'places' (ki), among them steles and statues; and in last position "the balangs, the seven of them" (balaĝ 7-ba-kam) and two Enki sanctuaries in the countryside.

<u>12</u> Expenditures at the occasion of a journey of the wife of the governor of Lagash to an Abzu. The term abzu designates the cosmic realm of the groundwater ocean and a type of sanctuary of the water-god Enki. The particular Abzu mentioned in the following texts was one of five such sanctuaries in the territory of Lagash.[74] It was located on the bank of a river and named Circle Side (Da-niĝin2). The name may refer to a layout that allowed circumambulation of a waterhole believed to be bottomless.

<u>12a</u> Nik 1 148 Lugalanda 5 = P221917.
Baranamtara (wife of Lugalanda, governor of Lagash), while staying at the Abzu of the river bank, offers two rams and a male lamb to Enki of Circle Side and a kid to the sanctuary Antasura on day one, two rams for Enki of Circle Side on day two, and "1 kid for the balang on day three" (1 maš ĝišbalaĝ u4 3-kam).

---

[70] Ša6-ša6 dam Uru-ka-gi-na lugal Lagaš^{ki}-ka-ke4 Sirara^{ki}-na balaĝ e-ta-ru-a.
[71] Puzur4-ma-ma agrig Ša6-ša6 dam Uru-ka-gi-na lugal Lagaš^{ki}-ka-ke4 Sirara^{ki}-na balaĝ-il2 e-ta-ru-a-kam 3.
[72] En-ig-gal dub-sar-re2 ensi2-ke4 balaĝ-il2 e-ta-ru-a mu-de6 4.
[73] The reading of the name of the goddess is not assured. For it and the goddess generally see RlA 9:463–468 (Sallaberger, *Nin-MAR.KI).
[74] Selz 1995:121–124.

<u>12b</u> DP 66 Urukagina 4 = P220716.

Expenditures for Shasha (wife of Urukagina, governor of Lagash) on the occasion of the festival of malt-eating of Ningirsu,[75] among them for the Abzu of Circle Side on day one (IV 3) and the Antasura as well as 'a new balang' (balaĝ gibil) on day three (rev. II.1–3).

<u>13</u> VS 14 75 Lugalanda 6 = P020090 (Selz 1995:104).

Record of beer expended to a type of lamentation-priest called Suru (sur9) and for Balang-harps.[76] "The Suru drank, the Balang set up in city center drank, the Balang set up in Fierce Water drank."[77]

<u>14</u> VS 27 55 Enentarzi 5 = P020371.

Record of use of pine lumber: "One extra large piece of pine for the arch of the gate of the balang."[78]

Old Akkadian Period (ca. 2350)

<u>15</u> CUSAS 13 156 Adab undated = P329186.

List of deficits of fat incurred by priests of several gods, including a certain Namahani for the balang Nin-PA.[79] Nin-PA, perhaps Nin-gidri ('Lady Scepter'[80]), is not attested as PN. Namahani is probably the lamenter (gala) of TCBI 1 [Pomponio et al. 2006] 99 = P382351.

<u>16</u> Two of seven attestations of female harpists (balaĝ-di). Male harpists are not attested in this period.

<u>16a</u> RIME 2.1.4.54

Inscription on door plaque from Girsu:

"Son of Naram-Sin the Strong, Nabi-Ulmash governor of Tutu. Lipush-Ja'um, harpist of Sin, his daughter."[81]

<u>16b</u> List of agricultural plots? Molina 1991:142–145 (photo P101667).

---

[75] Of presumably the tenth month: Selz 1995:236.
[76] For the lamenter Suru, see <u>23</u>f.
[77] sur9-de3 e-naĝ, balaĝ ru-a ša3-uru-ka-ke4 e-naĝ, balaĝ ru-a a-huš-ke4 e-naĝ.
[78] 1 ĝišu3-suh gal-gal sig7-igi ka2 balaĝ-ka-še3.
[79] la2-i3 7 1/3 sila3 i3 ĝišbalaĝ Nin-PA Nam-ha-ni.
[80] As suggested by Cavigneaux and Krebernik, RlA 9:480 (*NIN-PA).
[81] DUMU dNa-ra-am-dSu'en da-nim Na-bi2-ul3-maš ENSI2 Tu-tuki Li-pu-uš-ia3-a-um BALAG.DI dSu'en DUMU.MUNUS-su2.

"[PN, the female] harpist stayed at the house of female harpists."[82]

Ur III Period (ca. 2112–2004)

I Inscriptions of Gudea of Lagash and References From administrative Texts.[83]

Ia Balangs With Names:

<u>17</u> Great Dragon of the Homeland (Ušumgal-kalam-ma).

Ušumgal and its Akk. equivalent *bašmu* designates a monstrous venomous snake that is associated with Marduk and several other gods (Wiggermann 1992:166–169). On the other hand, 'Great Dragon' is also an entry of a type of person or profession in line 99 of the archaic list Lu2 A (Englund and Nissen 1993:17). It is a frequent element in Sumerian PNs throughout early Babylonia. A servant-god, the vizier of the Mungoose divinity Nin-kilim, is called 'Great Dragon' (An:Anum V 40).

<u>17a</u> Gudea Cylinder A 6.24–25 (RIME 3/1:73).

Gudea, governor of the territory of Lagash, was visited in a dream by Ningirsu, city-god of the capital Girsu. The governor went to consult with the goddess Nanshe, a dream interpreter and Ningirsu's sister. She told him that her brother wanted him to rebuild his temple. Gudea should make Ningirsu a gift of a chariot and "his beloved balang, Great Dragon of the Homeland, the famous lute, the thing that advises him."[84] The two presents would keep the god happy during his stay in temporary quarters.[85]

<u>17b</u> RTC (Thureau-Dangin 1903) 201:7' = P216974.

"Year when the balang Great Dragon of the Homeland was fashioned."[86]

<u>17c</u> Gudea Cylinder B 10.9–15 (RIME 3/1:94).

The inauguration of the renovated temple included a review of the twenty-three servant-gods of Ningirsu's temple household. They passed in line before the seated image of the master-god Ningirsu. Great Dragon of the Homeland was the tenth in line. He is described as Ningirsu's 'beloved singer' (nar), his duties the management of the musical instruments tigi, bringing joy to the courtyard,

---

[82] [PN MUNUS B]ALAĜ.DI *in* E2 MUNUS BALAĜ.DI *ta2-ku8-un*.
[83] For the date of Gudea in the Ur III period, specifically the reign of the second Ur III king Shulgi, see Wilcke 2011.
[84] BALAĜ ki-aĝa2-ni Ušumgal-kalam-ma ĝiš gu3-di mu tuku niĝ2 ad-gi4-gi4-ni.
[85] See also Franklin, p27.
[86] mu balaĝ Ušumgal-kalam-ma ba-dim2-ma.

and spreading a good atmosphere throughout the temple with the help of the musical instruments alĝar and miritum that entertained Ningirsu in his bed chamber Good House (e2-du10-ga). Balang music in the bed chamber of the moon-god Nanna of Ur is attested in line 441 of the OB text Lamentation over the Destruction of Sumer and Ur.[87]

> With the tigi, the good instruments in good order,[88] with the courtyard of House Fifty filled with joy, with making pleasant House Fifty for the hero of ear,[89] for Ningirsu with alĝar and miritum, the instruments of Good House, with these, his divine powers, passes his beloved singer Great Dragon of the Homeland before lord Ningirsu.[90]

17d Gudea Cylinder B 15.19–16.2 (RIME 3/1:97).
Gudea makes his first visit of the renovated temple of Ningirsu:

"With joy having filled the courtyard of House Fifty, with the balang of the art of the singer, his beloved balang Great Dragon of the Homeland, having walked at the head of (the drums) sim (and) ala, does Gudea, the governor who built House Fifty, enter before lord Ningirsu."[91]

17e Gudea Cylinder B 18.22–19.1 (RIME 3/1:98).
The first offering in the renovated temple was an occasion for musical performance: "(Gudea) placed Great Dragon of the Homeland among(?) the tigi, let the ala [a large drum], a storm, roar for Ningirsu."[92]

---

[87] Michalowski 1989:64.
[88] Jacobsen 1987:434 translates the verb si sa2 *ad hoc* as 'correctly tune', Klein 1981:194, line 54, as 'sweetly play,' Krispijn 1990:3 as 'korrekt spielen'.
[89] The repetition of the dative suffix is unusual, and so is ĝeštug as genitive of a personal designation. Jacobsen 1987 translates "for the warrior with ear (for music)," Edzard (RIME 3/1) "to the listening."
[90] ti-gi4 niĝ2-du10-ge si sa2-a-da kisal e2-ninnu hul2-a sig9-a-da al-ĝar mi-ri2-tum niĝ2 e2-du10-ga ur-saĝ ĝeštug(PI.TUG2)-a-ra ᵈNin-ĝir2-su-ra e2-ninnu du10-bi ĝa2-ĝa2-da nar ki-aĝ2-a-ni Ušumgal-kalam-ma en ᵈNin-ĝir2-su-ra me-ni-da mu-na-da-dib2-be2.
[91] kisal e2!-ninnu-[k]e4 hul2-a sig9-a-da si-im<<-da>> a2-la2 balaĝ nam-nar šu-du7-a balaĝ ki-aĝ2-ni Ušum-gal-kalam-ma saĝ-ba ĝin-na-da ensi2 e2-ninnu mu-du3-a Gu3-de2-a en ᵈNin-ĝir2-su-ra mu-na-da-an-ku4-ku4. For attempts to make sense of <<da>> see PHG:143n578. si-im a2-la2 is found in Gudea Cylinders A 18:18 and *Shulgi D* 366. The reading si-im-da balaĝ in *Shulgi E* 101 is in error. The source Ni 4519 II' 8 has clearly si-im balaĝ, the source TCL 15 14 III 17 si-im ba[laĝ], where the first part of the sign balaĝ is copied as if it were -da.
[92] ušumgal-kalam-ma ti-gi4-a mu-gub a2-la2 u4-dam šeg12 mu-na-ab-gi4. The phrase ti-gi4-a mu-DU has been translated differently—Falkenstein and von Soden 1953:180: "Den Drachen des Landes Sumer, die Pauke, brachte er (mu-tum2);" Jacobsen 1987:441: "Ushumgalkalamma took its stand among the tigi-harps;" RIME 3/1:98 (Edzard): "The (harp) Dragon-of-the-Land he

17f Amherst (Pinches 1908) 17 = P100855.

This administrative record from Girsu, dating from the 25th regnal year of Shulgi, lists expenditures of beer, bread, and soup for households of servant-gods in the "new house of Ningirsu," among them "the balang Great Dragon of the Homeland."

18 Fierce-faced king[93] (Lugal-igi-huš)

Passing before Ningirsu in line behind Great Dragon of the Homeland (17c) was Fierce-faced King, the second balang in Ningirsu's household. His duty was pacification of Ningirsu, specifically at his return from victory over the inimical mountain land, which he achieved on behalf of the king of gods Enlil. According to the literary text "The Return of Ninurta to Nippur," the god's demeanor and the frightful appearance of his trophies and weapons cause anxiety among the gods as he approaches Nippur (Cooper 1978:26–27). The name 'Achieving his Triumph' (^{d}U3-ma-ni sa2-di) of a balang of Ninurta in An:Anum I 269 may refer to his triumph over the mountain land. Fierce-faced King is listed in An:Anum V 97–98 together with Great Dragon of the Homeland as one of five attendants of House Fifty, the temple of Ningirsu.

Gudea Cylinder B 10.16–11.2 (RIME 3/1:94):

> With having soothed the inside, with having soothed the outside, with having wept and ...[94] tears, with having spent sighs from a sighing heart, with having ... when his (Ningirsu's) wave-like risen, Euphrates-like scouring, flood-like ... ing heart had liquefied the lands inimical to

---

joined with the kettledrum(?) (mu-gub)." The parallel passage of 20c writes mu-ni-DU, where -ni- corresponds to the locative –a of tigi. This favors gub 'to stand' rather than tum2 'to bring'. Gabbay (PHG:110) translates "Ušumgalkalama was placed as (literally on) the tigi," basing his translation on the assumption that tigi is the balaĝ of the singer (nar): "The tigi and the balaĝ were the same type of instrument (at least originally), the difference between them being their cultic context: the balaĝ was associated with the repertoire of the gala, and the tigi (written with the signs BALAĜ and NAR) with the repertoire of the nar. Thus, some of the instruments referred to as balaĝ in texts are probably to be identified with what literary and lexical texts usually regard as tigi. For example, Great Dragon of the Homeland is not the balaĝ instrument that is usually associated with the gala, but rather the balaĝ instrument that is usually associated with the nar and is often referred to as tigi(2) (written NAR.BALAĜ or BALAĜ.NAR) [PHG:103]." I believe the translation 'as' for 'literally on' does not agree with the functions of the Sum. locative and that NAR.BALAĜ or BALAĜ.NAR need not be interpreted on the semantic level as 'balaĝ of the nar'. The tigi instrument has been understood as percussion or string instrument. Krispijn 1990:3 argues for identification with a lyre. If the phrase tigi-a gub means 'to place among the tigi' it implies plurality of tigi instruments.

[93] Also translated as 'Red-eyed King', which would be a good description of a lamenter (the name was, however, quite common in Ur III sources and not limited to lamenters).

[94] Bauer 1967:229 proposes that sig stands for sig7 on the basis of the entry er2 sig7-me in the context of burial rites in an ED IIIb text.

Enlil, with having ... his [heart] returned to its banks, with these, his sacred powers, passes his balang—it is Fierce-faced King—before lord Ningirsu.[95]

<u>19</u> Lady Conversing Grandly with An (Nin-an-da-gal-di, see <u>25</u>)
Gudea Statue E IV 12–14 (RIME 3/1:44).
Gudea renovated the temple of Ningirsu's wife Baba, furnishing it with a seat from which to pronounce her judgments, a treasure chest, and a balang:

He fashioned for her the balang Lady Conversing Grandly with An[96] and set it up for her in her mighty house.[97]

<u>20</u> Cow of Plenty (Ab2-he-nun and Ab-he-nun).[98]
The identity of Ab2-he-nun and Ab-he-nun is confirmed by the association of the latter with lamenters in documents <u>20a</u> and <u>20b</u>. Cow of Plenty is probably a harp-god of Nin-KI.MAR. A fairly common PN in Girsu is Ur-(^{d})Ab-he-nun with (Gomi 1981:183 no. 197 etc.) and without (Snell 1986:205 no. 66 etc.) divine determinative. The genitive is occasionally expressed in writing, for example Ur-ab-he-nun-na in ITT 2 736, and a rare writing of the double genitive Ur-^{d}Ab-he-nun-ka 'Hound-of-Cow-of-Plenty' in ITT 5 6795. The divinity ^{d}Ab-ir-nun of ED IIIb Girsu texts may also designate a balang-god. It is associated with the silver up-drum and so are a 'person' (lu2) of the silver up-drum and a 'person' of ^{d}Ab-ir-nun, presumably the players of these instruments. The references are treated by Selz 1995:133–134. The name could mean 'Cow of Princely Aromatic', which compares well with the balangs named Cedar Aroma (<u>27</u>, <u>30</u>). Other 'cow instruments' are treated in PHG:109–112 where the opinion that these were instruments fashioned with cow hides as opposed to bull hides

---

[95] ša3 huĝ-ĝa2-da bar huĝ-ĝa2-da er2 igi pa3-da er2 sig-da ša3 a-nir-ta a-nir ba-da en-na ša3 ab-gim zi-ga-ni i7 buranuna-gim luh-ha-ni a-ma-ru-gim sa-ga-ka-ni kur gu2-erim2-ĝal2 ^{d}En-lil2-la2-ka a-gim u3-mi-ĝar-ĝar [x x (x)] gu2-be2 gi4-a-ni a x su3-da balaĝ-ĝa2-ni Lugal-igi-huš-am3 en ^{d}Nin-ĝir2-su-ra me-ni-da mu-na-da-dib-be2.
[96] The term gal-di, literally 'to speak great', has positive and negative connotations (Attinger 1993:511–512). The ED IIIb Girsu names A-da-gal-di, Ses-da-gal-di, En-da-gal-di, and ^{d}Inana-^{na}-da-gal-di, where the collocutors of the named person are father, brother, ruler, and a goddess, suggest an intimate relationship. The semantic relation with the Akk. translation of gal-di, tizqaru 'exalted,' is unclear. Foxvog 2011:76–77 translates "Excels with (thanks to) the father/brother." See also PHG:104. For the short name An-da-gal-di, see <u>25</u>.
[97] balaĝ Nin-an-da-gal-di mu-na-dim2 e2-mah-na mu-na-ni-gub.
[98] The reading of the sign hi as hi, transliterated elsewhere as du10 or šar2, is confirmed by the Akk. loan word i-he2-nun-na-ku from Sum. i3-he-nun, designation of the top quality cow fat. See RlA 8:196 (M. Stol, *Milch(produkte) A).

is rightly rejected (see 36). The name of a balang of Shamash is 'Cow of his risen heart' (Ab2-ša3-ila2-na) in An:Anum IV 13.

20a SAT 1 256 no year, month III, Girsu = P131365.

Record of expenditure of flour and drink for the deity Cow of Plenty (^{d}Ab-he-nun), a courtyard where the instrument was presumably played, an unclear destination, and lamenters (gala-me).

20b BPOA 1 182 no date, Girsu = P206136.

Record of expenditure of drink for the temple of Nin-KI.MAR, flour and drink for Cow of Plenty (^{d}Ab-he-nun), the 'house Plant of Life' (e2 u2 nam-ti), and another unclear destination.

20c Nanshe Hymn 39–47 (Heimpel 1981).

The OB text of the hymn describes in much detail the working of the temple household of Nanshe in Nina during the time of Gudea when it was surely composed.[99] It includes a description of the New Year festival in Nina. The musical arrangement of the occasion is described in unusual detail. The governor of Lagash in person placed the Balang-harp Cow of Plenty "on, at, among, next to," or any other location with respect to one or more tigi instruments. The harp occupies here the same place as Great Dragon of the Homeland with respect to tigi (17e). Claves in the form of copper sickles accompany the 'holy song' (šir3-ku3) that praises the temple.[100] Line 45 is probably the song's incipit, as first lines of praises often start with the verbal na-form.[101] The chief singer (nar gal) plays the ibex horn. Being the chief implies other singers and instrumentalists playing Cow of Plenty, silver balang, tigi instruments, and claves. (Cow of Plenty shares the second part of its name with the balang of Gula, Lady of Plenty: 40.)

> Gudea, governor of Lagash, placed Cow of Plenty 'on, at, among'
>   the tigi,
> placed the shining balang at its/their side.
> While the holy song, a song of harmony, was sung to her,
> small copper sickles were praising the house.

---

[99] This is confirmed by the fact that the name of the balang-goddess is written without the divine determinative as attested for other balang-gods in the inscriptions of Gudea.

[100] Civil 1987b proposed to read ^{urudu}kin-tur, understanding it as a musical instrument made of copper and called 'frog' kin-tur^{ku6}, but claves in form of sickles are attested (MgB 2/2:48 with fig. 15–16; see also Section 1c above).

[101] The form is commonly understood as affirmative. I understand it as a negative rhetorical question prompting an affirmative answer of the audience.

The chief singer was playing the ibex horn before her.
'Has not the temple been granted divine powers?'
he sang about the princely divine powers in the holy song about the house of Sirara.
The dream interpreter brought the first fruits before her.[102]

20d Hymn to Hendursanga 19–20 (Attinger and Krebernik 2005:38).

Another function of the Cow of Plenty was to entertain Nanshe, or to relieve her anxiety, as she traveled by boat to visit the god Hendursanga. See also 34b.

"The silver boat in which the lady, mother Nanshe sails for you—in it (?) plays for her Cow of Plenty."[103]

Ib Balangs Without Names:

21 Gudea Cylinders A 28.17–18.

Among descriptions of parts of House Fifty was a porch on which the balang was placed, possibly a shaded elevated platform overlooking a courtyard and close to the gate leading to it.[104] "Its porch of the balang was a princely-sounding[105] bull, its courtyard holy prayer, shem and ala (drums)."[106]

22a Gudea Statue B V 1–4 (RIME 3/1 1.1.7.StB).

The city was cleansed in preparation for construction of the temple of Ningirsu. Women were not used as porters during that time, the use of whips

---

[102] gu3-de2-a ensi2 Lagaš^{ki}-a-ke4 ab2-he-nun tigi-a mu-ni-gub balaĝ ku3 da-bi-a mu-ni-gub šir3-ku3 šir3 ha-mun-na mu-un-na-du12-a urudu-gur10-tur-re e2 im-mi-i-i a2 dara3 nar-gal-e šu mu-na-ab-tag-ge e2 abzu-ta me nam-ta-ba e2 Sirara^{ki}-ka šir3-ku3-ba me-nun-ba mu-un-du12 ensi-ke4 ne-saĝ-ĝa2 mu-na-an-tum2.

[103] in-nin9 ama ^{d}Nanše ma2-gur8 ku3 ša-mu-ra-ab-diri-ga ša3(?)-ba(?) Ab2-he-nun mu-na-du12-am3.

[104] The porch of the balang could have been the 'porch of Baba' (a-ga ^{d}Ba-ba6), which is described as 'heart-soothing place' (ki ša3 kuš2) in Gudea Cylinder A 26.12. Gabbay 2013:228n10, quotes the Late Babylonian text SBH 50a:18, in which parts of a temple are lamented in anticipation of their destruction, among them ma balaĝ-ĝa2 gu4 gu3-di:nun x-[-mu] with the explanation ĝa2 ba-la-aĝ2-ĝa2 al-pu [ ] du10-x- [x]. ga2 is the standard Sumerian equivalent of Emesal Sumerian ma. The OB version (CT 36 BM 096691 rev. III 7) writes ka2 balaĝ-ĝa2 am-gim du7-du7-mu, "my gate of the balang butting like a wild bull." If all readings are genuine, the Balang-harp was stationed in a porch (a-ga) by a gate (ka2). A balang-gate is mentioned in 14. Porches and gates are repeatedly mentioned together in the description of the temple of Ningirsu (Heimpel 1996:18–20). The existence of a 'balang-house,' for which see PHG:93, does not seem to be assured. e2-balag-e in TUT 287 is the name of a gala priest, É.BALAG-gi4 in PDT 1 545 according to Sallaberger 1993 1:142n668, perhaps writing for tigi.

[105] The standard translation of the substantive nun is 'prince'. The adjective denotes a positive, but not yet clearly defined, quality.

[106] a-ga balaĝ-a-bi gu4 gu3-nun di kisal-bi šud3-ku3 si-im a2-la2.

was disallowed, mothers barred from striking their children, and balang laments at burials not enacted: "The hoe was not employed at the cemetery of the city, a body was not interred. The lamenter did not set up a balang, did not elicit tears."[107]

22b ITT 2 893 = P110763.

Record of expenditures, including beer and bread received by lamenters and harpists, and flour for nine days when a balang was placed 'over the ghost'(?) at 'the place of mourning for the king'.[108]

Ur III Period (ca. 2112–2004)

II Ur III administrative Records (dated according to Reign Year Month Day):

IIa Balangs With Names:

23 Ninigizibara, Ninsigarana (ᵈNin-si-gar-an-na), and Ninme'urur (ᵈNin-me-ur4-ur4), were the balang servant-gods of Inana.

Ninigizibara is widely attested, in Babylonia in the cities Uruk, Umma, Isin, and Larsa, and on the Middle Euphrates in the cities Mari (see 47) and Tuttul (23g, Durand and Kupper 1985:111). The name of the harp-god was Igizibara in Umma. A lamenter (gala) in Ur III Girsu had the professional name Ur-ᵈIgi-zi-bar-ra (MVN 8 179 I 11).[109]

Ninsigarana and Ninigizibara are listed as the two balang-gods of Inana in the Emesal Vocabulary (23i). The name Ninsigarana means 'Lady Heaven's Bolt'. Cavigneaux and Krebernik (RlA 9:488–489, *Nin-siĝar-ana) list the few attestations in Ur III records, the most informative document being 23b2. They propose that the form of the instrument is likened to the bolt of the name. I believe the name refers to the role of the harp servant-god to relieve the anxiety caused by the departure of Inana as planet Venus when the planet disappeared at the onset of conjunction. It was believed that a gate had to be opened and closed as the stars and planets passed the horizon.

Ninme'urur is associated with Ninigizibara in the Isin god-list (23e) and in the oratorio Uru'amma'irabi, where she is mentioned next to Ninigizibara as one of the two advisers of Inana (RlA 9:470–471 [Cavigneaux and Krebernik, *Nin-me-urur]). The gender of Nin-me'urur is female according to the writing NIN ga-ša-an-me-ur4-ur4 in Uru'amma'irabi (kirugu XX, line 11). In the Late Babylonian version (BM 38593 I 17–18), Inana laments the loss of Ninigizibara

---

[107] ki-mah uru-ka al nu-ĝar adda ki nu-tum2 gala-e balaĝ nu-gub er2 nu-ta-e3.

[108] gala balaĝ-di-ne šu ba-ab-ti ... balaĝ i3-dim-ma gub-ba u4 10 la2 1-kam ki-hul lugal.

[109] For more detail on Ninigizibara see Sallaberger 1993; RlA 9:382–384 (Heimpel, *Ninigizibara); Volk 2006; PHG:106n224, 112–113.

and "my lamenter of the house, Ninme'urur, the face that watches the mountain land."[110] Perhaps the harp Ninme'urur was believed to be lamenting Inana's absence while watching the eastern mountains in wait for the planet's appearance as morning star.

In the OB list of gods SLT (Chiera 1929) 122 II 25–26, Ninigizibara is followed by an 'adviser' (^{d}Ad-gi4-gi4), the common epithet of balang-gods. This may refer to Ninsigarana or Ninme'urur.

23a Ninigizibara and Igizibara in Ur III.

23a1 Year-name Ibbi-Sin 21.
"Year when Ibbi-Sin ... fashioned the balang Ninigizibara for Inana."[111]

23a2 MVAG 21, 22 FH 5 Umma, Amar-Sin 1 = P113033.
Expenditure of fish-oil for the preservation of divine images, statues, and (the neck of the harp) Igizibara, written with divine determinative.

23a3 Princeton 1 523 Umma Amar-Sin 4 X = P127212.
Receipt of "9 3/4 shekels of silver for plating the grapple-hook (and) eye of Igizibara."[112]

23b Ninigizibara in rituals according to records from Ur III Umma.
The beginning of the dry season was celebrated during the first month of the year as withdrawal leading to the ultimate death of the god Dumuzi. The goddess Nin-Gipar, an Inana image in the temple of the city-god of Umma, was brought out 'to the head-grass (u2-saĝ)'.[113] In the same month, Nin-Ibgala, the local Inana figure, 'went' to the nearby city of Zabala to join lamenting the death of her husband Dumuzi. She was accompanied by her balang Igizibara.

23b1 SA (Jean 1923) 129 Amar-Sin 5 I = P128740, Tavolette (Boson 1936) 346 Amar-Sin 6 I = P132131, UTI 3 1885 Amar-Sin 8 I = P139904, UTI 4 2563 = P140582.
Food for Nin-Gipar 'having gone out to the head-grass', as well as for Nin-Ibgala and Igizibara going to Zabala.

23b2 MVN 1 42 Šu-Sin 5 I = P113075.

---

[110] gala e2-a gašan me ur4-ur4 muš3-me kur-še3 i-bí ma-al-la-mu. Volk 2006:105 translates "mein *Abbild*, dessen Aufmerksamkeit beständig auf das Fremdland gerichtet ist."
[111] mu Ibbi-Sin ... ^{d}Nin-igi-zi-bar-ra balaĝ ^{d}Inana-ra mu-na-dim2.
[112] 10 gin2 la2 igi 4 gal2 ku3 ŠU.DIM4^{ba} igi ^{d}Igi-zi-bar-ra ĝa2-ĝa2-de3.
[113] The term u2-sag was first understood to designate early grass. Sallaberger 1993 1:233–234, noting that this does not fit the season, suggested a translation 'high grass'.

Expenditures of flour for the temple of the city-god Shara and his wife Ninura; the deity of Ibgal (diĝir Ib-gal), otherwise called 'Lady of Ibgal'; Ninsigarana, the balang-god of Inana; and a deified musical instrument called 'Harmony Wood' (ᵈGiš-ha-mun). While the date in the first month coincides with the time of the journey to Zabala of the previously listed records, the association with Ninsigarana and the absence of the journey to Zabalam indicate a different cultic context. Note also the difference of the name: Igizibara is paired with Nin-gipar in 23b1 and 23c, Ninigizibara with the deity of Ibgal here.

23c BPOA 6 1176 Umma Šu-Sin 3 = P292368.

King Shu-Sin offered in the temple of the city-god Shara small cattle to Shara, Manishtusu—a statue of the divinized former king of Akkad—and Igizibara. The reason for this offering is not given. Perhaps the balang Igizibara was played as part of the cult of the dead Old Akkadian king.

23d Records from the central royal distribution center Puzrish-Dagan (Drehem) of expenditures for Ninigizibara in Uruk in connection with the absence of the planet Venus venerated as Nanaya.

The fact that the expenditures fall in the same month of two consecutive years means that the two events are not linked with actual inferior and/or superior conjunctions of the planet with the sun. The 'disappearance place' would be the ecliptic at the western horizon.

23d1 BPOA 7 2870 Drehem Šulgi 35 I = P303662.

Small cattle for the Gipar, the sanctuary in the house of Nanaya in Uruk, 'things of the disappearance place of Nanaya' (niĝ2 ki-zah3 ᵈNa-na-a), and for Ninigizibara.

23d2 Schneider 1932 58 Drehem Šulgi 36 I = P101353, Sallaberger 1993 1:221. Expenditures of lambs and kids by the governor of Uruk in Uruk:

> 1 lamb the sanctuary, 1 kid ᵈMuš-a-igi-ĝal2, 1 kid Ninigizibara, 1 kid circumambulation lament of Gipar gate (er2 niĝin2-na ka gi6-par4-ra), 1 kid prayer of the day 'Rise ye up!' (siskur2 u4 zi-ga-ze-na-a), 1 lamb 'disappearance thing' (niĝ2-zah3) of Nanaya of the palace.

23d3 SET (Jones and Snyder 1961) 42 Drehem Šulgi 37 V = P129452.

Expenditures of large and small cattle, among them one kid for the 'house' of Ninigizibara in Uruk and two kids for the *gerrānum*-lament of the house of Belat-Suhnir (for *gerrānum*, see 45).

23e List of gods from OB Isin A II 11/ B II 14–A II 13/ B II 16 (Wilcke 1987:94).
ᵈNin-igi-zi-bar-ra, ᵈNin-me-ur4-ur4, ᵈNin-he-nun-na. For Ninhenuna see 42. Here, balang-goddesses of Inana and Gula are grouped together.

23f Oratorio Uru'amma'irabi, OB version from Tell Haddad (col. III 9–12). Inana laments the loss of her two Balang-harps and their gods:

> The impetuous balang, my bellowing aurochs, the shining balang, my husband, my lapis lazuli, my adviser, my great suru, my adviser Ninigizibara.[114]

VS 2 32 I 11–14 contains the answer of the harpist:

> Your impetuous balang, the bellowing aurochs, / your lapis lazuli mu-ud-nu-bi shining balang, your adviser, your great suru, / the adviser, your Igizibara.[115]

The late version of these lines in the seventeenth tablet of Uru'amma'irabi is treated by Volk 2006. He understands the designation 'my husband' (mu-ud-na-mu) as an expression of the close relationship between Inana and Ninigizibara, translating 'Auserwählter'. Gabbay (PHG:112–113), noting the grammatical male gender of the translated name Ninigizibara in this version, does not exclude understanding this balang-god as male and sexual partner of Inana (see Section 2d).

The overall context of the passage is Inana's lament about the abduction of her husband Dumuzi and removal of her prized possessions. Later in the text, Inana utters her wish that the enemy return her shining balang Ninigizibara and her husband Dumuzi (IV 18–21), longing to lie with him.

> The enemy shall return my shining balang, shall (return it) in my house, shall return the shining balang, my Ninigizibara.

> The enemy shall return my husband. He shall lie in my pure lap ... return my husband Ama'ushumgalana. He shall lie in my pure lap.[116]

---

[114] balaĝ ban3-da am mur-sa4-a-mu balaĝ ku3 mu-ud-na-mu za-gin3-na-mu ad-gi4-gi4-mu Sur-DU-e gal-mu ad-gi4-gi4 ᵈNin-igi-zi-bar-ra-mu.

[115] balaĝ ban3-da am mu-ru-um-šu-a-zu / balaĝ ku3 mu-ud-nu-bi za-gin3-zu / ad-gi4-gi4-zu sur-ru-ga-zu / [a]d-gi-gi ᵈIgi-zi-bar-ra-zu. sur-ru-ga-zu stands for sur9-gal-zu. Syllabary B II 285 (MSL 3:147) sur-ru = SUR9 = *surrû*.

[116] kur2-re balaĝ-ku3-mu tu15-mu-ub-gi4-gi4 e2 ĝa2-a tu15(-mu-ub-gi4-gi4) balaĝ-ku3 ᵈNin-igi-zi-bar-ra-mu tu15-mu-ub-gi4-gi4 kur2-re mu-ud-na-mu tu15-mu-ub-gi4-gi4 ur2-ku3-ĝa2

23g1 For Ninigizibara in Mari rituals see 47.

23g2 ARM 25:566. "(Memorandum) about sending to Tuttul 4 pounds (2kg) of silver and 5 shekels (41.67g) gold for work on Ninigizibara."[117]

23h Balang composition of Inana CT 36, 35 BM 96933 I 8 (A) and Kramer 1987, BM 96680, lines 342, 351, and 406 (B).

Inana is called ga-ša-an Igi-zi-bar-ra in A and ga-ša-an ᵈIgi-zi-bar-ra in B. The reading of A is also found in the Late text MMA 186.11.3509 9a': ga14-ša-an Igi-zi-bar-ra (Maul 2005:79). The reading in B indicates as meaning 'lady of Igizibara', which reflects her relationship as mistress of her servant balang-divinity.

23i N-A copy of Emesal vocabulary I 88–89 (MSL 4:9). Lady Bolt of the Sky (Ninsigarana) and Lady Well Regarded (Ninigizibara in women's Sumerian and standard Sumerian), the two balang-gods of Inana.[118]

24 Lady Occupying the Palace (ᵈNin-e2-gal-e-si).

AUCT 1 (Sigrist 1984b) 969 Drehem Amar-Sin 3 VI = P103814. Record of the royal gift of a silver mirror for the goddess Gula of Umma and silver for her balang Ninegalesi. The name of the balang-goddess refers to the temples of Gula that were called Palaces (e2-gal). The verb si(g) means 'to fill', with the direct object of the English verb corresponding to the Sumerian locative-terminative. It is often difficult to know what exactly is meant. Obviously the harp does not literally fill the palace. Perhaps the verb describes here the sound of the instrument that fills the space of the temple.[119]

25 (= 19) and 26 Greatly talking with An (ᵈBalaĝ An-da-gal-di) and Divine Powers from Pure Heaven (ᵈBalaĝ Me-an-ku3-ta).

SAT 1 198 Girsu Amar-Sin 1 III = P131307. Record of expenditure of fattened small cattle as offerings, including two fattened kids as offerings for the two balang-gods. An-da-gal-di of the text is short for Nin-an-da-gal-di, attested

---

tu15-nu2 ĝa2-e (. . .) mu-ud-na-mu ᵈAma-ušumgal-an-na tu15-mu-ub-gi4-gi4 ur2-ku3-ĝa2 tu15-nu2.

[117] aš-šum 4 ma-na ku3-babbar u3 5 gin2 ku3-GI ša a-na ši-pi2-ir ᵈNin-igi-zi-bar-ra a-na Tu-ut-tu-ulᵏⁱ šu-bu-lim.

[118] [ᵈ]gašan-si-mar-an-n[a] ᵈNin-si-ĝar-an-na [ᵈgaša]n-i!-b[i2-zi-bar-ra] ᵈNin-igi-zi-bar-ra 2 GU4. BALAĜ ᵈInana-ke4.

[119] Cf. the opinion of Selz 1997:202n222 that the verb describes "aptness of the subject to be fit for his/her duty."

as balang-god of Baba (19). Variation of the name with and without initial Nin 'lady' is also found in case of the name Ninigizibara (23).

IIb Balangs Without Name But Description of Function:

27 Cedar-resin Balang of Baba (balaĝ šim ĝišeren ᵈBa-u2).

TUT 112, fragment of a large tablet from Girsu, records in IV 11' expenditure of beer for this balang, and MVN 22 121 of Šulgi 37 XI expenditure of wool. Brunke and Sallaberger 2010:49 give examples for the exceptional use of cedar wood for the manufacture of furniture, but it is unlikely that the long curved and recurved neck of the Balang-harp could have been made of soft cedar wood. The neck could have been treated with cedar-resin (see 23a2). The city-goddess of Gu'aba, another city in the province of Lagash, also had a cedar-resin Balang (30).

A cedar-resin balang appears in a much treated and discussed OB record of cult expenditures in Larsa, fully edited and treated anew in Westenholz and Westenholz 2006:3–81.[120] It includes a word read there qu2-tur4, for which W. Sallaberger proposed the reading ᵏᵘšbalaĝ. Löhnert 2009:68n312 commented on the context: "Während der am Abend stattfindenden Zeremonie Öffnen des Hauses, wenn die Gottheit eintritt, erhalten (die Klagesänger) Substanzen für Rauchopfer und das Kohlebeckenritual; allerdings wird hier mit der Neudeutung W. Sallabergers auch das Balag Instrument erwähnt." Gabbay (PHG:70 with n. 69) proposed a different interpretation: Lamenters "took part in the performance of a Balag during a cultic act involving cedar incense."

28 'Balang of the Day of Laying' (balaĝ u4 nu2-a), that is, the day of invisibility of the moon. The moon's absence was apparently feared despite its regular and predictable occurrence.[121] In Umma, this balang belonged to the household of the goddess Nin-Ibgala, an Inana-figure hailing from Lagash and venerated in Umma. A Girsu record of skins left over from small cattle offerings lists five skins from offerings to the divine balang (ᵈbalaĝ), or 'balang-god' (diĝir-balaĝ) for as many months of the year Šulgi 39, and twelve skins for the full year of Šulgi 40 (TCL 5 5672). This would have been the balang of the day of laying.

---

[120] II 57: i-na ᵏᵘšbalaĝ šim-ĝišeren a-na ki-nu-nim [ ] | III 3–4: šu-ti-a gala-meš i-na ᵏᵘšbalaĝ [ ] a2 u4-te-na [u4 17-kam] | IV 25–29: 4 sila3 i3-giš a-na ša-ra-pi-im 3 sila3 [zi3]-gu ½ sila3 šim-hi-a i-na ᵏᵘš[balaĝ] šim ĝišeren a-na ki-nu-nim ... dabin ... zi3-gu [...] šu-ti-a gala-meš i-na ᵏᵘšbalaĝ šim-ĝišeren 1 sila3 i3-ĝiš i3-šeš4 (EREN) ni-ri-im | VII 19–22: šu-ti-a gala-[meš] i-na ᵏᵘšbalaĝ [ ] a2 u4-te-na u4 20-kam.

[121] Cf. the opinion of Selz 1997:178 that the day of invisibility "alludes to a mourning-ritual in which the harp played a part."

29 'Balang of the storm' (balaĝ u4-da). SAT 2 166 Umma Šulgi 37 XII = P143367; ITT 2 1021+1022 III' 22' date broken, Girsu = P110891.

Records from Umma mention an 'observer' (igi-du8) as recipient of small cattle for prayer offerings described as 'having confronted the storm' (u4-da gaba-ri-a). As pointed out by Sallaberger,[122] two of these records replace the word u4 with ᵈIškur, the name of the weather-god, confirming that u4 means 'storm', not 'day', in this context. The confrontations with the weather-god would have typically taken place in spring when thunderstorms form in the area and threaten the barley harvest. The ritual of confrontation was performed in specified field areas. The observer (igi-du8) appears as responsible for the expenditure for balaĝ u4-[da] in the tablet fragment ITT 5 6916 from Girsu. He would have identified which field area was located in the path of an oncoming storm and confronted it with the balang that would calm the weather-god down. Among the balang servant-gods of the weather-god in An:Anum, 'Storm of the Suru lamenter', 'X his Thunder', or 'He Roars' (53 III 261, 263–264) may have been used for the purpose. For a possible link with the Eblaite word for harpist, see 4d.

30 ITT 3 4977 Girsu no year XI = P111073.

The text records the expenditure of beer and flour for the goddess Nin-KI. MAR and 'cedar-resin Balang, the balang of the storm in the house of Ninmar' (balaĝ šim-eren balaĝ u4-da ša3 e2 ᵈNin-marki). For another cedar-resin balang see 27.

31 'Balang of the Storm, house (and) city encircled' (balaĝ u4-da e2 uru niĝin-na).

The ritual involving this balang took the form of a circumambulation of the temple and the city, as detailed in TCT 1 (Lafont and Yildiz 1989) 796. The circumambulation included offerings at the east and west gates of the Holy City of Girsu, 'tears', and remuneration for the actions of lamenter (gala) and observer (igi-du8). The observer would have determined that a storm threatened the entire city of Girsu. If he corresponds to the 'seer' in ED Ebla, he played the harp.[123] The lamenter could have sung a song such as CT 15, 15–16 of the type 'tears of the drum of Ishkur' (er2-šem3-ma ᵈIškur), which describes the god as riding a storm that causes his mother Ninlil to take fright and the king of gods, Enlil, to duck. Enlil then acknowledges the power of Ishkur's thunder, lighting, and hailstones, and asks him to use it against a rebel land. Ishkur obeys, emerges from his temple pacified, his thunderstorm having moved away. According to

---

[122] Sallaberger 1993 1:266 and 2:163.
[123] See Section 3c2.

HLC 23 = P109901, the chief lamenter (gala-mah) Utu-Bara was responsible for flour expended for the Balang-harp.

See further Sallaberger 1993 1:297 and 2 Tab. 105; Heimpel 1998; Gabbay 2013:235–239.

<u>32</u> 'Balang of the storm, facade toward Uruk house' (balaĝ u4-da igi e2 Unu{ki}-še3).

The location is the west gate of the Holy City of Girsu (Heimpel 1996:20). The balang appears to be directed against a storm approaching from the west, but not deemed a threat for the entire city. Sallaberger 1993:Tab. 105; Gabbay 2013:236n36 understands igi e2 Unu as a location outside Uruk.

<u>33</u> 'Balang of bathing' (balaĝ a-tu5-a).
BPOA 7 1792, Umma, Amar-Sin 6 = P292088.

Record of expenditures of flour for the "Balang of bathing at the festivals, the three of them" (balaĝ a-tu5-a ezen 3-a-ba). These were the festivals of the fourth, eighth, and eleventh months. Sallaberger 1993:239 demonstrated that the bathing of Shara, the city-god of Umma, was the central cult act of these festivals and that it was associated with 'heart cooling' (ša3-te). The latter was effected by a balang, as this newly published text shows. The procedure of bathing a divinity is described by Sallaberger 1993:192: the image in its cella is disrobed, water is poured over it as part of the life-restoring ritual called 'washing of the mouth', and the image is then newly clothed. The manipulation of the image brought with it the danger of enraging the divinity, which was counteracted by the sound of the balang.

IIc Balangs Without Name But Known Master-god:

<u>34a–35</u> Balang of Nanna and Ninsun. Sigrist 1999:132–138 Drehem Amar-Sin 2 XI = P200532.

Record of offerings for the ghost of king Shu-Sin, netherworld divinities, and ghosts, as well as offerings of kids for the balangs of the moon-god Nanna and Ninsun on day sixteen in Ur (rev. II 10–11), and for the balang of Ninsun again on day seventeen (rev. IV 22'–23').

<u>34b</u> BPOA 7 2856 Drehem Amar-Sin 4 XII = P303644.

Record of royal offerings of small cattle at the occasion of the harvest festival for the moon-god Nanna, the boat on which Nanna had come from Ur to the festival house Akiti, and for a balang. The balang may have entertained the moon-god and relieved his anxiety on the boat trip. See also <u>20d</u>.

34c UET 3 298 Ur = P136617.

A smith receives 1/3 pound 8 ½ shekels minus 15 grains (189.6g) gold for plating a balang of Nanna.

35 UET 3 282 = P136599 (PHG:93n111, and 102n178).

Receipt, of the administrator of the temple of Ningal, of cream, cheese, raisins, honey, dates for regular offerings (sa2-[du11]), regular monthly cult expenses (niĝ2-dab5), and a bronze balang (balaĝ UD.K[A.BAR]). The record is sealed by the steward in the temple of Ningal, the wife of the city-god in Ur. While the sign for bronze is not fully preserved, there are no easy alternatives. Possibly the 'bronze balang' was in fact a kettledrum.[124]

36 Balang of Ninura
    TCL 5 5672 V 16 and VI 9 Umma = P131743.

The text registers two bull hides to be used for the balang of Ninura, the wife of the city-god of Umma.

37 NATN (Owen 1982) 824 Nippur = P121521.
    The seven balangs of Nin[ ] receive a fattened ram.[125]

38 Princeton 1 99 Drehem Šulgi 47 I 28 = P126788.

Record of offerings in Uruk, among them small cattle for the gate of the residence of the En priest (ka2 gi6-par3-ra) of Inana, a balang, and Aratta. Cavigneaux 1998 read aratta (LAM!xKUR.RU), which would mean that there existed in Uruk a physical presence of the city Aratta, the prehistoric antagonist of Uruk. He notes that Aratta is mentioned repeatedly in the oratorio Uru'amma'irabi.

39 UTI 4 2849 = P140868 (PHG:102n179).
    "2 cured hides and 1/3 pound of glue—balang of the chief lukur priestess covered."[126]

OB and Late Period Sources

40 Ishbi-Erra-Enlilda-Nirgal. RIME 4 1.1.1.

The king of Isin dedicates a balang to Enlil in Nippur. Unlike in earlier times, the king's name appears in the name of the balang instrument.

---

[124] See Section 1a above.
[125] 1 udu-niga gu4-e us2-sa balaĝ imin ᵈNin-[ ].
[126] 2 kuš u2-hab2 1/3 ma-na sze-gin2 balaĝ lukur-gal si-ga.

For Enlil, king of lands, his king, did Ishbi-Erra, strong king, king of the land, fashion a mighty balang to/for ... the heart. For (prolongment of) his life he dedicated it. That balang's name is 'Ishbi-Erra Enlil's Trustee'.[127]

<u>41</u> Inana Ishbi-Erra. BIN 9 445 Ishbi-Erra 25 = P236455.

[1] old balang (named) Inana Ishbi-Erra was supplied (for repair) with a 1/5 m² piece of cured bull hide, and the requisite 3/10 m² piece of black billy-goat hide and 42g of glue. Responsible [for making sure that the supplies were used for the repair] was PN, the chief lamenter.[128]

The balang that had been named and presumably commissioned by Ishbi-Erra was already 'old' (sumun) in the king's lifetime. 'Inana Ishbi-Erra' does not belong to any name type; probably the real name was longer, and abbreviated in the administrative context. The harp would have belonged to the Inana cult in Isin.

<u>42</u> Lady of Plenty (Nin-Henuna).

Nin-Henuna was the second balang of Gula, city-goddess of Isin, according to An:Anum V 187. She is listed in the OB god-list from Isin together with Nin-me-ur4-ur4 and Nin-igi-zi-bar-ra, the balang-gods of Inana (<u>23e</u>). See Cow of Plenty, Ab(2)-he-nun-na (<u>20</u>).

<u>42a</u> *Nin-Isina's Journey to Nippur* lines 42–48.

A song for Gula under her name Lady of Isin (ᵈNin-Isina) celebrates the rise of the city of Isin to first rank among the cities of Babylonia after the fall of the Ur III kingdom, recounting the city-goddess's triumphant return from a visit with Enlil who had bestowed on her a good fate for her city. Her husband Pabilsang welcomed her back. The king was there, too, and the music struck up. The returning Lady of Isin was praised and the lamenters pacified the highest ranking gods, An, Enlil, Enki, and Ninmah, perhaps because they were feared to be upset about the move of rule over Babylonia to Isin.

---

[127] balaĝ-mah ša3 tu-x-da mu-na-an-dim2 nam-ti-la-[ni-še3] a mu-na-ru balaĝ-ba ᵈIš-bi-er3-ra ᵈEn-lil2-da nir-ĝal2 mu-bi-im. Civil 1987a on the sign -x-: "Neither the meaning nor the traces favor -ud-. Perhaps it is to be read tu-[u]h for du8."

[128] [1] ĝⁱˢbalaĝ-sumun ᵈInana ᵈIš-bi-Er3-ra kuš gu4-u2-hab2-bi 1/3 (gin2) ba-a-si kuš maš2-gal gi6-ga 1/2 (gin2) še-gin2-bi 5 gin2 ĝiri3 Lu2-IGI.KU gala-mah.

The text is a MA copy of an OB Sumerian text with imperfect Akkadian translation. Wagensonner 2008 identified an OB fragment, recopied the Late (MA) tablets, and provided an up-to-date translation and comments.

42 Her beloved shining[129] balang, Lady of Plenty, [ ],
43 ... ly intones the holy song, a praise full of love,
44 plays for her the shining up(-drum), the shining balang.
45 Sum. text: The ... lamenter rises before her, Nin-Isina,
    Akk. text: The lamenters with that prayer to Ninkarak
46 so that An, Enlil, Enki, (and) Ninmah be appeased.[130]
47 After the exalted lady is made to feel good in her dwelling in Egalmah,
48 the king slaughtered a bull for her, and many rams in addition.[131]

42b BIN 9 433 (Ishbi-Erra 19) = P236443. Quoted by A. Cavigneaux and M. Krebernik in RlA 9:378, *Nin-hinuna.

"5 shekels (3 m²) cured bull-hide (for) peg tooth/teeth/nose/mouth (KA) of the left 'wood' of Ninhenuna."[132]

42c BIN 10 75 (Ishbi-Erra 14) = P236619.

"Gold decoration[133] was applied to Ninhenuna."[134]

43 *Curse on Akkad* 199–204.

---

[129] *ellu* 'light, shining' describes the sheen of silver and here probably the sheen of silver plating of the instrument. The same translation is found repeatedly (CAD s. v. *balaggu*). UET 3 1476 lists among silver smiths two persons titled ᵍⁱˢbalaĝ-tuš-a (see PHG:84).

[130] The intransitive form *nuhhu* indicates that the mentioned gods are the subject. Gabbay (PHG:18) points out that gods were routinely solicited to help pacify the heart of a fellow god and translates accordingly.

[131] 42. Sum.: balaĝ-ku3 ki-aĝ2-ĝa2-ni ᵈNin-he-nun A[N   ] Akk.: *ba-lam-ga el-la ša i-ra-am-mu* ᵈNin-he-nun A[N   ] / 43. Sum.: šir3-ku3 za3-mi2 la-la ĝa2-la-ni gu3 nun mi-ni-[ib-be2] Akk.: *za-ma-ri* KU3.MEŠ *ta-ni-ta ša la-la-a ma-la-a-at i-x-x-x* / 44. Sum.: ᵏᵘˢub-ku3 balaĝ-ku3-ge šu mu-un-tag-[tag] Akk.: *i-na up-pi eb-bi ba-lam-gi el-li u2-la-pa-tu-ši* / 45. Sum.: gala ri-a mu-un-na-zi-zi e-ne-ra ᵈNin-in-si-na Akk.: GALA.MEŠ *i-na tak-rib-ti šu-a-ti ša* ᵈNin-kar-ra-a[k] / 46. Sum.: An ᵈEn-lil2 ᵈEn-ki ᵈNin-mah-e mu-un-huĝ-ĝa2-e-da Akk.: ᵈA-nu ᵈEn-lil2 ᵈE-a u3 ᵈNIN.DIGIR.MEŠ *nu-uh-h[u]* ...) / 47. Sum.: nin-mah-e e2-gal-mah-ne-a ki-tuš mi-ni-ib-du10-ga-ta Akk.: *iš-tu ru-ba-tu ṣir-ti i-na* e2-gal-mah *šub-ta uš-ṭib-bu* / 48. Sum.: lugal-e gu4 mu-un-na-ab-gaz-e udu mu-un-na-ab-šar2-re Akk.: *šar-ru* GU4ᵐᵉˢ *u2-pa-laq-ši* UDU ᵐᵉˢ*u2-da-aš2-ša-ši*). For *takribtu* rather than *taqribtu* in 45, see Gabbay 2011:71–73.

[132] 5 gin2 kuš gu4 u2-hab2 zu2 kak ĝiš ga-bu ᵈNin-he-nun-na.

[133] Limet 1960:223, 'gold strips'. Possibly granulation: RlA 3:530 (Boese/Rüss, *Gold).

[134] niĝ2-su3-a ku3-sig17 ᵈNin-he-nun-na ba-ra-[x].

The survivors of catastrophe, sent by Enlil after destruction of his temple, aim to pacify the god's wrath:

> (The chief lamenter ...) let seven balangs cover the ground (in a circle) like the base of the sky for seven days (and) seven nights.[135] In their midst sounded up meze, lilis, shem [percussion instruments] for him [Enlil] like the weather-god. An old woman did not cease with 'Oh, my city'. An old man did not cease with 'Oh, its people'. A lamenter did not cease with 'Oh, Ekur' [Enlil's temple].[136]

<u>44</u> UET 8 79 Inscription of Warad-Sin or Rim-Sin I of Larsa (PHG:99).

> For my life and the life of my own father, Kudur-Mabuk I, fashioned for him/her a bronze kettledrum balang.[137]

<u>45</u> HAV 13 rev. V 12'–15'. Kramer 1985:115n1; PHG:86, 141n568, 153n662.

A passage laments changes in the cult of Nin-Isina, partly in terms of Akkadian words replacing Sumerian ones. The hitherto unexplained Akkadian correspondence of kašbir with *ma-zu2-um* was recognized by Sallaberger (personal communication).

> (Now) her bread is *akalum*, her beer is *šikarum*, her pressed beer is *mazûm*, her balang is *gerrānum*.[138] The up-drum of my lady had become a kettledrum balang.[139]

<u>46</u> BIN 9 312:8 = P236322.
> One kid hide (for) balang.[140]

---

[135] Cooper 1983:59 translates "as if they stood at heaven's base;" PHG:16n9: "The image here refers to the performance of the balag instrument during dawn," translating (178n210) "for seven days and seven nights, (the lamenters) placed seven balaĝ instruments on earth like (i.e., at the time of) the standing horizon."

[136] u4 7 ĝi6 7-še3 balaĝ 7-e an ur2 gub-ba-gim ki mu-un-ši-ib-us2 ub3 me-ze2 li-li-is3 šem3 ᵈIškur-gim ša3-ba mu-na-an-du12 um-ma a uru2-mu nu-ĝa2-ĝa2 ab-ba a lu2-bi nu-ĝa2-ĝa2 gala-e a e2-kur nu-ĝa2-ĝa2.

[137] nam-ti-mu-še3 u3 nam-ti Ku-du-ur-ma<-bu>-uk a-a ugu x x balaĝ [l]i-li-is3 zabar mu-na-dim2. Gabbay understands balaĝ as a determinative.

[138] See 23d3.

[139] ninda-a-ni *a-ka-lu-um-ma* kaš-a-ni *ši-ka-ru-um-ma* kašbir-a-ni *ma-zu2-um-ma* balaĝ-a-ni gi4-er2-ra-an-um-ma ga-ša-an-ĝa2 ᵏᵘšub3-a-ni balaĝ li-li-is3-am3.

[140] 1 kuš maš2 balaĝ.

47 Ishtar Rituals from OB Mari. Dossin 1938; FM 3 no. 2 and 3; FM 9:55–64, including a model of the arrangement of participants and furnishings, with the Balang-harp (Ziegler's lyre) in central position.

47a FM 3 no. 2 I 3'–11'.

> [If] the king so wishes, he sleeps [in the b]ed of Ishtar. In the morning they make him rise earlier than normal and Ishtar is served breakfast. They thoroughly clean the house of Ishtar and they place Ningizippara vis-à-vis Ishtar. The lamenter[(s)] left of Ningigizippara ...[141]

The following lines describe the position taken by other participants, including craftsmen and hairdressers with their tools. A table sprinkled with flour and a pitcher of water is set before Ishtar. Latarak and other servant-gods take their seats to her left, the identities of those to her right are lost in a break. The emblems of goddesses are brought from their shrines, the king takes his seat behind the lamenters, the servants take their places, and "the lamenters sing the Uru'amma'irabi of the beginning of the month" (II 19'–20').[142]

At this point something is said about the behavior of an ecstatic. Lines 24'–25' are read and restored by Durand and Guichard to mean "after they (the lamenters) have reached (the words) ĝa2-e u2-re-[men2], the overseers let the singers go. If (the ecstatic) gets [into trance, they sing] ĝa2-e u2-re-m[en2]." These are the words that follow the fifth section (ki-ru-gu2) of the OB version of the oratorio Uru'amma'irabi.

After four missing lines at the head of the third column, a foot race is mentioned and the lamenters are said to be singing i-gi-it-te-en di-ba-x(-x). As the race ends in the temple of Ishtar, they sing the song AN-nu-wa-še, the king gets up and one of the lamenters sings an ershema to Enlil to the accompaniment of the halhallatum drum ([i]-na ha-al-ha-la-tim er-se-[m]a-kam a-na ᵈEn-lil2 i-za-mu-ur).

47b FM 3 no. 3 I 21'–22'.

> [ᵈNin]-gi-zi-pa-ra
> [   ] li-li-si-im

The two lines appear to confirm that the harp-god is not identical with the kettledrum.

---

[141] [bi]bil libbi šarrim [ina ma]yyal Ištar ittêl [ina k]aṣātišu eli ša k[a]yyantim ušahrapūma niĝ2-gub Ištar iššakkan bīt Ištar uštanazzakūma ᵈNin-gi-zi-ip-pa-ra ina mehret Ištar ušazzūma ka-l[u-u2 ina š]umēl ᵈNin-gi-zi-ip-pa-ra [ ] u3 šitru [ina i]mitti ...

[142] ka-lu-u2 u2-ru-am-ma-da-ru-bi re-eš wa-ar-hi i-z[a-a]m-mu-r[u].

48 VS 10 216: 4–8 Catalogue of liturgical texts (Krecher 1966:33; Löhnert 2009:16 [Hinweis Gabbay]).

"'Oh IllaLUM, Oh IllaLUM' 1 [(leather)] balang of Sin. 'The Lord, the ... of the Lord in his Land' 1 incantation song of [Suen], (altogether) 1 (leather) balang and 1 incantation song of Suen."[143]

The meaning of balang is clearly the lyrics of a song. The determinative indicates that the instrument identifies the song.

49 Examples from laments of temple-mistresses about loss of their home, including the venue of balang performances.

49a Balang composition *Uruhulake of Gula* according to CLAM 256 (for difficult parallel lines from VS 2 25 see Krecher 1966:151; line a+47 is obscure).

> Gula laments:
> a+45 The foremost city, my foremost balang-porch,
> a+46 the house of bitter tears, my house of tears, defiled.
> a+47 The Arali, my princely bowl bull,
> a+48 the balang-porch, my porch of the princely balang.[144]

49b Balang composition CT 36 46 III 5–9.

> Ishtar laments:
> 5 The shining gate, my house of ladyship,
> 6 the outer court, my judgment place,
> 7 my aurochs-like jostling balang-gate,[145]
> 8 my mighty portal of Mullil,
> 9 my netherworld portal, eye of the land.[146]

The image in line 7 could refer to gate sculptures, the bovidity of the balang, or the throng of the congregation at occasions when the balang strikes up.

50 CT 36 41:16–20 (Cohen 1981:104 [reference courtesy of Gabbay]). Gula laments disuse of cherished implements and musical instruments:

---

[143] [a] il-la-L[UM] a il-la-LUM [1 ᵏᵘˢ]balaĝ ᵈSuen u3-mu-un x-x-ti u3-mu-un-na kur-ra-na 1 šir3 nam-šu-ub ᵈ[Suen] 1 ᵏᵘˢbalaĝ 1 šir3 n[am-šu-ub ᵈ]Suen.

[144] a+45 uru2 saĝ-ĝa2 ma balaĝ saĝ-ĝa2-mu | a+46 e2 er2-gig e2 er2-ra pel-la2-mu | a+47 a-ra-li gu4 bur nun-na-mu | a+48 ma balaĝ-ĝa2 ma balaĝ nun-na-mu.

[145] The same and grammatically uncorrupted version is found in the description of the harp porch in the temple of Ningirsu in Girsu (21).

[146] 5 ka2 ku3 e2 na-aĝ2-ga-ša-an-na-mu | 6 kisal bar-ra ki di ku5-ru-mu | 7 ka2 balaĝ-ĝa2 am-gim du7-du7-mu | 8 abul-mah ᵈmu-ul-lil2-la2-mu | 9 abul ganzir i-bi2 kur-ra-mu.

16	My shining cup that poured no water,
17	my shining up-drum that no one placed,
18	my shining balang that no one played,
19	my shining tambour that gave no sound,
20	my shining meze instrument that did no good.[147]

51 CLAM 420 a+36–a+41.

Late text of the penultimate section of an unidentified balang composition (see Maul 1999:297n53; PHG:81–82 and 85). The section has an explanatory character rather than being lyrics of an oratorio:

a+36	Sum: That day the god [enters?] the house in balang and lament.
	Akk.: The god [enters] the house in balang (and) prayer.
a+37	Sum.: The lamenter who sang for him <<in>> a song,
	Akk.: The lamenters sing songs,
a+38	Sum.: the lamenter who sang for him <<in>> a song of lordship,
	Akk.: the lamenters (sing) a song of lordship,
a+39	Sum.: the lamenter (who sang for him) <<in>> a song of balang,
	Akk.: The lamenters (sing) a song of balang
a+40	Sum.: (who played for him) the shining up-drum, the shining kettledrum,
	Akk.: with the shining up-drum, the shining kettledrum,
a+41	Sum.: (who played for him) tambour, meze, shining balang.
	Akk.: [ ] the tambour and meze, shining balang.[148]

52 Late lexical series HAR-RA *hubullu* V 105–107 (MSL 6, 60).

ĝiš gur2 a2-la2	MIN (= *kip-pa-tum*) *a-le-e*	ring of alu drum
ĝiš gur2 balaĝ	MIN (= *kip-pa-tum*) *ba-la-an-gi*	hoop of Balang-harp

[147] 16 ti-lim-da ku3-ga a nu-de2-a-mu | 17 ᵏᵘˇub ku3-ga nu-mu-un-ĝar-ra-mu | 18 balaĝ ku3-ga nu-mu-un-du24-a-mu | 19 šem3 ku3-ga ad nu-ša4-ša4-mu | 20 me-ze2 ku3-ga nu-ze2-ze2-ba-mu.

[148] a+36 Sum.: e2-e dim3-me-er balaĝ er2-ra u4-de3 [ ] Akk.: *ana E2 i-lu ina ba-lag-gu tak-r[ib-tu2/ tes-li-tu2*] | a+37 Sum.: gala-e šir3-ra mu-un-na-an-du12-a Akk.: *ka-lu-u2 za-ma-ri i-za-am-mu-ru* | a+38 Sum.: gala-e šir3-ra nam-en-na mu-un-na-an-du12-a Akk.: *ka-lu-u2 za-mar be-lu-ti* | a+39 Sum.: [gala]-e šir3-ra balaĝ-ĝa2 mu-un- Akk.: *ka-lu-u2 za-mar ba-la-ag-gi* | a+40 Sum.: ᵏᵘˇub3-ku3 li-li-is3-ku3 mu-un- Akk. *ina up-pi el-lim ina li-li-is el-li* | a+41 Sum.: šem3 me-ze2 balaĝ ku3-ga mu-un- Akk.: [*h*]*al-hal-la-ti u ma-an-zi-i ba-la-ag2-ga el-li.*

ĝiš gur2 dub2-di   MIN (= kip-pa-tum) tim-bu-u2-ti   ring of *timbutu* instrument.

53 'Balang bulls' (GU4.BALAĜ) servant-gods in the Late god-list An:Anum (Litke 1998).[149]

	name of balang	translation	master-god
I 70	ᵈ ᵍᶦˢĜidri-si-sa2	Just Scepter	Nin-Shubura
I 71	ᵈEš-bar-an-na	An's/Heaven's Decision	Nin-Shubura
I 75	Diĝir-du-ru-na[150]	Sitting gods	An

In the OB version of the oratorio Elum Gusun, the gods are exhorted to go to the place called 'Sitting Gods', where the first fruits (nesaĝ) of the New Year were served (VS 2 11 II 12'–14'). Löhnert's interpretation of Elum Gusun as being connected with the maintenance of irrigation works (Löhnert 2009:56) fits the timing, as the threat of downpours flooding fields during the barley harvest coincides with the Babylonian New Year. The term Sitting Gods is also found in *Enuma Elish* I 24, designating a location where the younger gods made merry, thus enraging the older ones and leading to war between the generations. The netherworld gods had their own occasion for Sitting Gods. In an incantation prayer to Enmeshara, the netherworld is called *markas*, 'link, center' of 'Sitting Gods' (Ambos 2004: 120.44).

I 76	ᵈU3-tu-ud	Creator	An
I 77	ᵈLu2-an-na	Heaven's/An's Man	An
I 78	ᵈKa-tar-an-na	Heaven's/An's Fame	An
I 79	ᵈMul-1-iku	One-acre Star	An

The One-acre constellation consists of alpha, beta, gamma of Pegasus, and alpha of Andromeda. The constellation leads the stars of the path of An as they rise at the beginning of the year (RlA 5:45 [Hunger, *Ikû]). The four stars were matched with the lands of the four cardinal points expressed as the lands of Assyria, Akkad, Elam, and Amurru (RlA 4:412–413 [Hunger, *Himmelsgeographie]). The One-acre Star oratorio would have been performed at night, the first half of the Babylonian twelve-hour day.

---

[149] See also Gabbay's (PHG:103–109) analysis of names indicating the adviser role of GU4.BALAĜ; cf. Franklin, p30_33.

[150] The plural verb in the phrase ki AN dur2-ru-na in the OB version of the oratorio Elum Gusun (VS 2 11 II 13') indicates that the sign AN does not write the DN An. The Late version nevertheless translates: "place where Anum [dwells]" (SBH 21 rev. 34). This understanding was accepted by Horowitz 1998:225. Krecher 1966:99n268 translates "wo die Götter sitzen" (diĝir dur2-ru-na).

I 80	ᵈAn-ta-sur-ra	Dropped from Sky	An

A sanctuary of this name was located in the territory of Lagash, probably at its northwestern border (Gabbay 2013:19–20). The name was translated "Vom Himmel herabgetropft (dripped down from sky)" by Falkenstein 1966: 164, "Twinkles from Heaven" by George 1993:68. Perhaps it was a shrine built over a meteorite.

I 81	ᵈKi-gul-la	Ruin	An

The literal meaning is 'destroyed place'. The term also designates a type of person. B. Landsberger contrasted it with ki-sikil 'pure place' = '(virgin) girl' and understood it as the designation of a raped girl (ap. Jacobsen ap. Gordon 1959:477). The standard translation is 'waif'. The literal meaning fits the present context.

I 264	ᵈBalaĝ-ᵈEn-lil2	Enlil Balang	[Enlil]
I 265	ᵈNin-lil2-da gal-di	Greatly Speaking with Ninlil	[Enlil]
I 267	ᵈGu3-du10-ga	Good Voice	[Ninlil]
I 268	ᵈUr-ᵈZa-ba4-ba4	Divine Urzababa	Ninurta

Ur-Zababa was the last king of Kish at the turn from the ED III to the OAkk. periods. FM 9:53, an OB letter from Mari of a music instructor of Yasmah-Adad, king of Mari, mentions musical instruments and singles out MA2.TUR *ur-za-ba-bi-tum* [*Sa-a*]*m-si-Ya-as2-ma-ah*-ᵈ*Adad*. The editor N. Ziegler suggests that MA2.TUR designates the soundbox of the named instrument. The name means 'My-sun-Yasmah-Addu'. The association with Ninurta and the use of the instrument by the singer (nar) is attested in lexical texts (CAD s.v. *urzababītum*).

I 269	ᵈU3-ma-ni-sa2-di	Achieving his Triumph	Ninurta

The name appears to refer to a victory celebration as told in the 'long song' (šir3 gid2-da) of Ninurta (see 18).

I 270	ᵈU4-gu3-nun-di	... -voiced-Storm	Ninurta

The adjective nun is conventionally translated 'princely' according to the substantive nun, 'prince'; but, as here, the actual meaning of the adjective must be different.

I 272	ᵈBalaĝ-e-diri	Excellent through Balang	Nusku
I 273	ᵈAd-he-nun	Sound of Plenty	Sadarnuna

I 302	ᵈUn-ga-ša6-ga	Good among the People	Nissaba
I 303	ᵈHa-mun-an-na	Heaven's Harmony	Nissaba
II 92	ᵈSaĝ šu-ta-šub-šub-ba	Heads-fallen-from-Hands	Dingirmah
II 93	ᵈKiri3-zal šu-KID-DU.DU	... Splendor	Dingirmah
II 94	ᵈAd-gi4-gi4	Adviser	Dingirmah
II 95	ᵈ ᵐⁱⁿGU4.BALAĜ	ditto: Balang Bull	Dingirmah
II 96	ᵈE2-kur-eš3-diri	Excellent Sanctuary Ekur	Dingirmah
II 97	ᵈNin-A-ru-ru	Lady Aruru	Dingirmah
II 99	ᵈŠa3-tur3-nun-ta-e3	Sprung from Princely Womb	Ashgi
II 100	ᵈAš-pa4-huš	Fierce ...	Panigara
II 256	ᵈĜanun-he2-du7	Ornament ganun (room)	Marduk
II 257	ᵈEn-nun-daĝal-la	Wide Watch	Marduk
II 259	ᵈGašan-šud3-an-na	Lady Heaven's Prayer	Zarpanitu
II 310	ᵈNin-ezen	Festival Lady	Enki
II 311	ᵈNin-ezen-balaĝ	Balang Festival Lady	Enki
II 312	ᵈEš(4xAŠ)-ĝa2/ga/qa	?	Enki
II 315	ᵈA-ru6	Sister-in-law	Damgalnuna

A-ru6 is mentioned in connection with Damgalnuna as 'lady of the Abzu' (ga-ša-an Ab-zu) in lamentations, for example in the OB version of the Oratorio Elum Gusun (Nies 1315 I 26 [Langdon 1919:208]).

II 316	ᵈUr2-a-ru6	Sister-in-law Lap	Damgalnuna
II 343	ᵈNig2-na	Censer	Gibil
II 344	ᵈGi-izi-la2	Torch	Gibil

Censer and torch are examples of controlled fire and thus apt names for balang that control the fire god Gibil.

III 49	An-šar2-a2-mu/ gu-an-na/Ša3-an-ba		?Nanna
III 50	ᵈUri2ᵏⁱ-kiri3-zal	Splendor (City of) Ur	Nanna
III 51	ᵈAmar-ᵈSin	Bull Calf of Sin	Nanna

SbTU 3 (von Weiher 1988) 107 has ᵈAmar-ZA.MUŠ2 = ᵈAmar-šuba, 'Jasper Calf', instead of ᵈAmar-ᵈSin. Krebernik (RlA 8:365, *Mondgott §3.3), suggests that this is the name of the third king of Ur. It would be an example of an instrument named after a king in addition to Urzababitum. Yet the harp Calf of Sin is likely in direct reference to the moon-god. Another divinity ᵈAmar-ᵈSin is one of two calves of the weather-god (An:Anum III 254).

III 52	ᵈNanna-ušum-mah	Grand Dragon Nanna	Nanna
III 53	ᵈU4-men-an-na	Heaven's Crown Day	Nanna
III 54	ᵈU4-kiri3-zal-an-na	Heaven's Splendor Day	Nanna
III 55	ᵈU4-e2-zi-an-na	Heaven's good House Day	Nanna

Wiggermann 1992:169–172 treats the concept of personified days, the 'ud-beings', especially the demonic personifications of bad days, among them a group of seven that attack Nanna, the moon. The three balang-gods may well have been active on bad days, lamenting them and hoping for the return of the good days the balang-gods represent. Another balang-god named after a day serves Adad (III 261).

III 56	ᵈAn-na-hi-li-bi/ba	Heaven's Endearment	Nanna
III 59	ᵈNin-da-gal-zu[151]	Knowing well the Lady	Ningal
III 60	ᵈNin-da-mah-di	Grandly speaking with the Lady	Ningal
III 62	ᵈMiṭṭu	Club	Ningublaga
III 63	ᵈA2-mah-tuku	Strong-armed	Ninugblaga
III 85	ᵈEreš-an-zu	Eagle Queen	Nin-MAR.KI
III 153	ᵈDu11-ga-na-ga-ti	Let me live by his Word	Utu
III 154	ᵈDi-ku5-an-ki	Judge of Sky and Earth	Utu
III 155	ᵈEš-bar-an-ki	Decision of Sky and Earth	Utu
III 156	ᵈDi-ku5-si-sa2	Just Judge	Utu
III 157	ᵈKalam ša3-kuš2-u3	Homeland Consultant	Utu
III 158	ᵈŠa3-kuš2-u3-kalam-ma	Consultant of the Homeland	Utu

KAV 64. 5 secondary balangs of Utu (5 balaĝ us2 ᵈUtu-ke4 5 re-du-u2 ᵈŠa2-maš).

IV 12	ᵈA-ša3-ila2-na	Water on his risen heart
IV 13	ᵈAb2 ša3-ila2-na	Cow of his risen heart
IV 14	ᵈŠul-zi-mah-na	Youth of his mighty raising
IV 15	ᵈAd-pa-zi-mah-na	... sound of his mighty raising

The pacification of the 'risen heart' was the main task of a balang-god. The semantic difference between il2 in IV 12–13 and zi(g) in IV 14 and 15 is unclear to me and so is the sense of the names in IV 14 and 15.

IV 16	ᵈHa-mun-an-na	Heaven's Harmony

---

[151] Nindagalzu is entered after the balang Ninigizibara in the Mari god-list (Lambert 1985:183, lines 94–95).

The names Harmony (ᵈHa-mun in III 166) and Adviser (ᵈAd-gi4-gi4 in III 167) of servant-gods in the temple Ebabbar are typical balang-god names and could be secondary balang-gods, yet only divine caretakers (udug) and attendants (gubba) are identified by temple name in An:Anum.

A deified instrument ᵈGiš-ha-mun is mentioned in 23b2.

III 260	ᵈSur9-gal	Great Suru[152]	Adad
III 261	ᵈU4-sur9-ra	Day of the Suru	Adad
III 262	ᵈUg/piriĝ3-gu3-du10-ga	Panther of Good Voice	Adad
III 263	ᵈUr5-ša4-ni [x]	X his Thunder	Adad
III 264	ᵈŠeg10 mu-un-gi4-gi4	He Roars	Adad
III 265	ᵈKiri3-zal-kalam-ma	Splendor of Homeland	Adad
IV 73[153]	ᵈNin-igi-zi-[bar-ra]	Well regarded Lady	Inana
IV 74	[ᵈNin-si-ĝar-an-na]	[Lady Heaven's Bolt]	Inana
V 17	ᵈKur-gul-gul	Mountainland Destroyer	Lugalbanda
V 18[154]	ᵈAb2-ar2-he2-en-ĝal2	Cow Wealth Praise	Ninsun
V 30	ᵈU6-nir-si-sa2	Just Temple Tower	Lugal-Marada
V 31	ᵈŠu-ni-dugud	Heavy his Hand	Lugal-Marada
V 100	ᵈUšum-ur-saĝ-kur-ra-dib-dib-be2	Hero Dragon passing through the Mountainland	Ningirsu
V 100	ᵈUšum-ur-saĝ-kur-ra-dib-dib-be2	Hero Dragon passing through the Mountainland	Ningirsu
V 101	ᵈGaba-huš-gu2-Zubi abzu	Fierce Breast Groundwater Ocean Zubi (River) Bank	Ningirsu
V 102	ᵈU2-šum-bar/ba-ra ge-eš-pu e2-ninnu	Dragon of the Outback Grapple-hook of Eninnu	Ningirsu
V 103	ᵈKur-ra-huš-a-ni-nu-kuš2-u3	Unrelenting his Terror in the Mountainland	Ningirsu
V 104	ᵈDu11-ga-lugal-a-ni-ša3-hun-ĝa2	Spoken Words heart-soothing for his King	Ningirsu
V 105	ᵈNita-zi	Good Man	Ningirsu
V 106	ᵈKa-ga-ni zi	Good his Mouth	Ningirsu
V 107	ᵈSaĝ šu nu-ba	?	Baba
V 108	ᵈNin-gal-([x])-KU	?	Baba
V 109	ᵈNin-[x x)]-na	?	Baba
V 110	ᵈU4-men-x-šu-ĝal	?	Baba
V 168	ᵈMA2-x-ba	?	Damu

[152] The suru was a type of lamenter (see Section 3b).
[153] IV 73 and 74 are restored from Emesal Vocabulary I 87–88 (MSL 4:9).
[154] For the reading of the balang-gods of Lugalbanda and Ninsun see PHG:111n281.

Balang-Gods

V 186	ᵈNin-gal	Great Lady	Gula
V 187	ᵈNin-he-nun-na	Lady of Plenty	Gula
V 199	ᵈUp-lum	Louse (Akk.)	Manungal
V 200	ᵈMIN-Eh	the same: Louse (Sum.)	Manungal
V 279	ᵈUšum-ur-saĝ	Hero Dragon	Tishpak
V 291	ᵈQa-ad-ma	The One from Before	Ishtaran

The entry ᵈQa-ad-ma is preceded by names of the master-god Ishtaran and his vizier Qudma. Qudma and Qadma are also listed as 'bull gods' (diĝir gu4) in An:Anum VI 208–209. Little is known of their master-god Ishtaran. His word guided the Early Dynastic ruler En-Metena of Lagash at the erection of a boundary marker (RIME 1 9.5.1 I 10), and Ningirsu, the city-god of Girsu, refers to him as model administrator of city law (Gudea Cylinders A 10.24–26). He was the city-god of Der and ranked with Anu (see Lambert in RlA 5:211 [*Ishtaran]). The hinterland of Der at the foot of the Pusht-i-Kuh could well have been a habitat of aurochsen.

54 An:Anum I 362

"The Greater Dada, the man sitting by the harp. May he sing forever of the majesty of the gods!"[155]

The entry is found in two manuscripts, one unprovenanced, the other N-A from Nineveh. The entry is unparalleled in An:Anum for making a statement in the form of a sentence. Gabbay (PHG:90) would understand it as a quotation from a literary text. I believe the scribe of the original of the two manuscripts was a lamenter who took the liberty to make an epitaph for his divine forefather, the "greater Dada." The latter may have been the well-attested lamenter Dada of the Ur III period (Heimpel 1997). Michalowski described his career and characterized him as "impresario" and "an exceptional figure in the Ur III elite hierarchy."[156]

The scribe used Emesal Sumerian, the language used in oratorios, and produced an interesting verbal form. For the precative he used the Emesal form with /t/ instead of /ḫ/. The verbal preformative tu is phonetically good Emesal, albeit in unusual orthography for normal tu15. The reduplication of the base probably expresses continued success of his wish. The ending -a was perhaps meant to mark end of statement.

The designation "person sitting by(?) a balang (instrument?)" has a surprising, probably accidental, parallel from an Ur III record of a roll call of craftsmen of the royal workshops in the kingdom of Ur III (UET 3 1476), where

---

[155] ᵈDa-da gu-la lu2 balag-ga tuš-a nam-mah diĝir-e-<ne> tu-mu-un-du12-du12-a.
[156] Michalowski 2006:49–50.

two silversmiths (ku3-dim2) are titled with the occupation 'sitting balang' (ᵍⁱˢbalaĝ-tuš-a see n129 above and 34c).

<u>55</u> An:Anum II 304–307

II 304	ᵈDu-un-ga NAR | diĝir nar-a-ke4 | *ilu ša2 na-a-ri*
II 305	ᵈDu-un-ga SAĜ | MIN | MIN
II 306	ᵈGu3-du10-ga-lal3-bi | dam-bi-sal
II 307	ᵈLum-ha BALAĜ | diĝir gala-ke4

These entries mean that 'Dunga' is the pronunciation of the signs NAR and SAĜ when writing the name of the god of the singer. That-Honey-good-Voice (ᵈGu3-du10-ga-lal3-bi) is the name of his wife, and Lumha is the pronunciation of the sign BALAĜ when designating the name of the god of the lamenter.

Bibliography

Abel, E. 1891. *Scholia recentia in Pindari epinicia, vol. 1.* Berlin.
Ackerman, S. 2001. *Under Every Green Tree: Popular Religion in Sixth-Century Judah.* Winona Lake.
Adang, C. 1996. *Muslim Writers on Judaism and the Hebrew Bible: From Ibn Rabban to Ibn Hazm.* Leiden.
Ahl, F. 1985. *Metaformations: Soundplay and Wordplay in Ovid and Other Classical Poets.* Ithaca.
Aign, B. 1963. *Die Geschichte der Musikinstrumente des ägäischen Raumes bis um 700 vor Christus.* Frankfurt am Main.
Ainian, A. M. 1999. "Reflections on Hero Cults." In *Ancient Greek Hero Cult: Proceedings of the Fifth International Seminar on Ancient Greek Cult, Organized by the Department of Classical Archaeology and Ancient History, Göteborg University, 21-23 April 1995,* ed. R.-E. Hägg, 9-36. Stockholm.
Akurgal, E. 1962. *The Art of the Hittites.* New York.
Al-Fouadi, A. H. 1976. "Bassetki Statue with an Old Akkadian Royal Inscription of Naram-Sîn of Agade." *Sumer* 32:63-77.
Albertz, R. 1994. *A History of Israelite Religion in the Old Testament Period.* Louisville.
Albright, W. F. 1927. "Another Case of Egyptian û = Coptic ê." *Zeitschrift für ägyptische Sprache und Altertumskunde* 62:64.
———. 1934. *The Vocalization of the Egyptian Syllabic Orthography.* New Haven.
———. 1938. Review of J. Lassus, *Inventaire archéologique de la région au nord-est de Hama* (Damas 1935). *American Journal of Archaeology* 42:592-593.
———. 1940. "Islam and the Religions of the Ancient Orient." *Journal of the American Oriental Society* 60/3:283-301.
———. 1956. *Archaeology and the Religion of Israel.* 4th ed. Baltimore.
———. 1964. *History, Archaeology, and Christian Humanism.* New York.
Alexander, P. S. 1992. "Targum, Targumim." In Freedman 1992 6:320-331.
Alexiou, M. 2002. *The Ritual Lament in Greek Tradition.* 2nd rev. ed. Greek Studies: Interdisciplinary Approaches. Lanham.
Aliquot, J. 2009. *La Vie religieuse au Liban sous l'Empire romain.* Beirut.
Allen, T. W. 1924. *Homer: The Origins and the Transmission.* Oxford.

Bibliography

Allen, W. S. 1987. *Vox Graeca: A Guide to the Pronunciation of Classical Greek*. 3rd ed. Cambridge.
Alp, S. 1972. *Konya civarinda karahöyük kazılarında bulunan silindir ve damga mühürleri*. Ankara.
———. 2000. *Song, Music, and Dance of Hittites: Grapes and Wines in Anatolia During the Hittite Period*. Ankara.
Alster, B. and T. Oshima. 2007. "Sargonic Dinner at Kaneš: The Old Assyrian Sargon Legend." *Iraq* 69:1–20.
Amadasi, M. G. 1967. *Le Iscrizioni fenicie e puniche delle colonie in Occidente*. Rome.
———. 1982. "Influence directe de la Mésopotamie sur les inscriptions en Phénicien." In *Mesopotamien und seine Nachbarn: Politische und kulturelle Wechselbeziehungen im alten Vorderasien vom 4. bis 1. Jahrtausend v. Chr.* (2 vols.), ed. H.-J. Nissen and J. Renger, 2:383–394. Berliner Beiträge zum Vorderen Orient 1. Berlin.
Amadasi, M. G. and V. Karageorghis. 1977. *Fouilles de Kition III. Inscriptions phéniciennes*. Nicosia.
Ambos, C. 2004. *Mesopotamische Baurituale aus dem 1. Jahrtausend v. Chr.* Dresden.
Anastasiades, A. 2009. "Behind Masks: The Artists of Dionysos in Ptolemaic Cyprus." *Report of the Department of Antiquities of Cyprus* 2009:195–204.
Aneziri, S. 1994. "Zwischen Musen und Hof: Die dionysischen Techniten auf Zypern." *Zeitschrift für Papyrologie und Epigraphik* 104:179–198.
Aravantinos, V. L. 1996. "New Archaeological and Archival Discoveries at Mycenaean Thebes." *Bulletin of the Institute of Classical Studies* 41:135–136.
Aravantinos, V. L. et al. 2001. *Thèbes: Fouilles de la Cadmée. I. Les Tablettes en linéaire B de la Odos Pelopidou*. Pisa.
———. 2002. *Thèbes: Fouilles de la Cadmée. III. Corpus des documents d'archives en linéaire B de Thèbes (1-433)*. Pisa.
Archi, A. 1977. "I Poteri della dea Ištar ḫurrita-ittita." *Oriens Antiquus* 16:297–311.
———. 1978-1979. "Les Dieux d'Ebla au IIIe millénaire avant J. C. et les dieux d'Ugarit." *Annales Archéologiques Arabes Syriennes* 29/30:167–171.
———. 1986a. "The Archives of Ebla." In *Cuneiform Archives and Libraries*, ed. K. R. Veenhof, 72–86. Istanbul.
———. 1986b. "Die ersten zehn Könige von Ebla." *Zeitschrift für Assyriologie* 76:213–217.
———. 1987. "Ebla and Eblaite." In *Eblaitica 1*, ed. C. H. Gordon et al., 7–17. Winona Lake.
———. 1988a. "Cult of the Ancestors and Tutelary God at Ebla." In *Fucus: A Semitic/Afrasian Gathering in Remembrance of Albert Ehrman*, ed. Y. L. Arbeitman, 103–112. Amsterdam.

———. 1988b. "Les Noms de personnes mariotes à Ebla (IIIème millénaire)." *MARI, Annales de Recherches Interdisciplinaires* 4:53–58.

———, ed. 1988c. *Eblaite Personal Names and Semitic Name-Giving. Papers of a Symposium Held in Rome, July 15-17, 1985.* Rome.

———. 1992. "Transmission of the Mesopotamian Lexical and Literary Texts from Ebla." In Fronzaroli 1992:1–29 and pl. 21–10.

———. 1993. "How a Pantheon Forms: The Cases of Hattian-Hittite Anatolia and Ebla of the Third Millennium BC." In *Religionsgeschichtliche Beziehungen zwischen Kleinasien, Nordsyrien und dem Alten Testament,* ed. B. Janowski et al., 1–18. Orbis Biblicus et Orientalis 129. Freiburg.

———. 1994. "Studies in the Pantheon of Ebla." *Orientalia* 63:249–256.

———. 2001. "The King-Lists from Ebla." In *Historiography in the Cuneiform World I,* ed. T. Abusch, 1–13. Bethesda.

———. 2006. "Ebla in Its Geographical and Historical Context." In *The Akkadian Language in Its Semitic Context: Studies in the Akkadian of the Third and Second Millennium BC,* ed. G. Deutscher and N. J. C. Kouwenberg, 96–109. Leiden.

Archi, A. et al. 1988. "Studies in Eblaite Prosopography." In Archi 1988c:205–306.

Arnaud, D. 1986. *Recherches au pays d'Aštata. Emar VI. Tome 3: Textes sumériens et accadiens.* Synthèse 18. Paris.

———. 1987. *Recherches au pays d'Astata. Emar VI. Tome 4: Textes de la bibliothèque, transcriptions et traductions.* Synthèse no. 28. Paris.

———. 1994. "Relecture de la liste sacrificielle RS 26.142." *Studi Micenei ed Egeo-Anatolici* 34:107–109.

———. 1998. "Prolégomènes à la rédaction d'une histoire d'Ougarit II: Les Bordereaux de rois divinisés." *Studi Micenei ed Egeo-Anatolici* 41:153–173.

———. 2001. "Textes administratifs religieux et profanes." In *Les Textes alphabétiques en ougaritique,* ed. P. Bordreuil and D. Pardee, 323–332. Ras Shamra-Ougarit 14. Paris.

———. 2010. "Textes du Levant en sumérien et en babylonien (IIIe-IIe millénaires): Lectures et relectures." *Aula Orientalis* 28/2:157–179.

Artzy, M. et al. 1976. "Alasiya of the Amarna Letters." *Journal of Near Eastern Studies* 35:171–182.

Asher-Greve, J. M. and Westenholz, J. G. 2013. *Goddesses in Context: On Divine Powers, Roles, Relationships and Gender in Mesopotamian Textual and Visual Sources.* Orbis Biblicus et Orientalis 259. Fribourg.

Assemani, J. S., ed. 1732–1746. *Sancti patris nostri Ephraem Syri opera omnia quae exstant.* 3 vols. Rome.

Astour, M. C. 1964. "Second Millennium B.C. Cypriot and Cretan Onomastica Reconsidered." *Journal of the American Oriental Society* 84/3:240–254.

———. 1965. *Hellenosemitica: An Ethnic and Cultural Study in West Semitic Impact on Mycenaean Greece*. Leiden.

———. 1966. "Some New Divine Names from Ugarit." *Journal of the American Oriental Society* 86:277–284.

Åström, P., ed. 1992. *Acta Cypria: Acts of an International Congress on Cypriote Archaeology Held in Göteborg on 22-24 August, 1991*. 3 vols. Studies in Mediterranean Archaeology and Literature Pocket-Book 107, 117, 120. Jonsered.

Atallah, W. 1966. *Adonis dans la littérature et l'art grecs*. Paris.

Attinger, P. 1993. *Eléments de linguistique sumérienne: La Construction de du11/e/di 'dire'*. Göttingen.

Attinger, P. and M. Krebernik. 2005. "L'Hymne à Hendursaga (Hendursaga A)." In Rollinger 2005:21–104.

Attridge, H. W. and R. A. Oden. 1981. *Philo of Byblos, The Phoenician History. Introduction, Critical Text, Translation, Notes*. Washington, DC.

Aubet, M. 1993. *The Phoenicians and the West: Politics, Colonies and Trade*. Cambridge.

Aupert, P. 2000. *Guide to Amathus*. Nicosia.

Aupert, P. and M.-C. Hellmann, eds. 1984. *Amathonte I. Testimonia 1, Auteurs anciens, monnayage, voyageurs, fouilles, origines, géographie*. Paris.

Austin, J. L. 1962. *How to Do Things with Words*. The William James Lectures 1955. Cambridge, MA.

Averett, E. W. 2002–2004. "Drumming for the Divine: A Female Tympanon Player from Cyprus." *Muse* 36–38:14–28.

Avigad, N. 1978. "The King's Daughter and the Lyre." *Israel Exploration Journal* 28/3:146–151.

Avioz, M. 2015. *Josephus' Interpretation of the Book of Samuel*. Library of Second Temple Studies 86. London

Bachvarova, M. R. 2008. "The Poet's Point of View and the Prehistory of the *Iliad*." In Collins et al. 2008:93–106.

———. 2008. "Sumerian *Gala* Priests and Eastern Mediterranean Returning Gods: Tragic Lamentation in Cross-Cultural Perspective." In Suter 2008:18–52.

———. 2013. "Adapting Mesopotamian Myth in Hurro-Hittite Rituals at Hattuša: IŠTAR, the Underworld, and the Legendary Kings." In *Beyond Hatti: A Tribute to Gary Beckman*, ed. B. J. Collins and P. Michalowski, 23–44. Atlanta.

———. Forthcoming. *From Homer to Hittite: The Anatolian Background of Ancient Greek Epic*. Cambridge.

Badalì, E. 1991. *Strumenti musicali, musici e musica nella celebrazione delle feste ittite*. Heidelberg.

Baethgen, F. 1888. *Beiträge zur semitischen Religionsgeschichte: der Gott Israels und die Götter der Heiden*. Berlin.

Baldacci, M. 1992. *Partially Published Eblaite Texts*. Dipartimento di Studi Asiatici, Series Minor 40. Naples.

Bardet, G. et al., eds. 1984. *Archives administratives de Mari*. Archives Royales de Mari 23. Paris.

Barnett, R. D. 1935. "The Nimrud Ivories and the Art of the Phoenicians." *Iraq* 2/2:179-210.

———. 1939. "Phoenician and Syrian Ivory Carving." *Palestine Exploration Quarterly* 1939:4-19.

———. 1969. "New Facts about Musical Instruments from Ur." *Iraq* 31/2:96-103.

Barr, J. 1974. "Philo of Byblos and His Phoenician History." *Bonner Jahrbücher des rheinischen Landesmuseums* 57:17-68.

Bartoněk, A. 2003. *Handbuch des mykenischen Griechisch*. Heidelberg.

Bass, G. F. 1986. "A Bronze Age Shipwreck at Ulu Burun (Kaş): 1984 Campaign." *American Journal of Archaeology* 90.3:269-296.

Baudissin, W. W. 1911. *Adonis und Esmun: Eine Untersuchung zur Geschichte des Glaubens an Auferstehungsgötter und an Heilgötter*. Leipzig.

———. 1912. "Tammuz bei den Harranern." *Zeitschrift der Deutschen Morgenländischen Gesellschaft* 66:171-188.

Bauer, J. 1967. *Altsumerische Wirtschaftstexte aus Lagasch*. PhD diss., Julius-Maximilians-Universität Würzburg.

Baur, P. V. C. and M. I. Rostovtzeff, ed. 1929-1952. *The Excavations at Dura-Europos. Preliminary Report*. 9 vols. New Haven.

Baumgarten, A. 1981. *The Phoenician History of Philo of Byblos: A Commentary*. Leiden.

Baurain, C. 1975-1976. "Kinyras de Chypre, légende ou réalité historique." *Mélanges de l'Université Saint-Joseph* 49:521-540.

———. 1980a. "Kinyras. Une Étymologie obscure." *Onomata* 5:7-12.

———. 1980b. "Kinyras. La Fin de l'Age du Bronze à Chypre et la tradition antique." *Bulletin de Correspondance Hellénique* 104:277-308.

———. 1981. "KINURAS et KERAMOS." *L'Antiquité Classique* 50:23-37.

———. 1981. "Un Autre nom pour Amathonte de Chypre?" *Bulletin de Correspondance Hellénique* 105:361-372.

———. 1984. "Réflexions sur les origines de la ville d'après les sources littéraires." In *Amathonte I. Testimonia 1, Auteurs anciens, monnayage, voyageurs, fouilles, origines, géographie*, ed. P. Aupert and M.-C. Hellmann, 109-117. Etudes Chypriotes 4. Paris.

Bayer, B. 1968. "The Biblical Nebel." *Yuval: Studies of the Jewish Music Research Center* 1:89-131.

———. 1982. "The Finds That Could Not Be." *Biblical Archaeology Review* 8/1:20-33.

Beal, R. H. 1992. "The Location of Cilician Ura." *Anatolian Studies* 42:65-73.

Bibliography

———. 2002. "Dividing a God." In *Magic and Ritual in the Ancient World*, ed. P. A. Mirecki and M. W. Meyer, 197–208. Leiden.
Beazley, J. D. 1928. *Greek Vases in Poland*. Oxford.
Bechtel, F. 1921–1924. *Die griechischen Dialekte*. Berlin.
Beckman, G. M. 1998. "Ištar of Nineveh Reconsidered." *Journal of Cuneiform Studies* 50:1–10.
———. 2002a. "Babyloniaca Hethitica: The 'babilili-Ritual' from Bogazköy (CTH 718)." In *Recent Developments in Hittite Archaeology and History: Papers in Memory of Hans G. Güterbock*, ed. H. A. Hoffner, 35–41. Winona Lake.
———. 2002b. "'My Sun-God': Reflections of Mesopotamian Conceptions of Kingship among the Hittites." In *Ideologies as Intercultural Phenomena*, ed. A. Panaino and G. Pettinato, 37–43. Melammu Symposia 3. Milan.
———. 2010. "Mesopotamian Forerunners to the 'Babilili Ritual' from Bogazköy?" In *Acts of the VIIth International Congress of Hittitology, Corum, August 25–31, 2008*, ed. Y. Hazirlayan and A. Süel. 2 vols. 1:109–120. Ankara.
———. 2014. *The babilili-Ritual from Hattusa*. Mesopotamian Civilizations 19. Winona Lake.
Beckman, G. M. et al. 2011. *The Ahhiyawa Texts*. Atlanta.
Beckman, G. M. and H. A. Hoffner. 1985. "Hittite Fragments in American Collections." *Journal of Cuneiform Studies* 37/1:1–60.
———. 1999. *Hittite Diplomatic Texts*. 2nd ed. Writings from the Ancient World 7. Atlanta.
Begg, C. T. 1997. "David's Transfer of the Ark according to Josephus." *Bulletin for Biblical Research* 7:11–36.
Beekes, R. S. P. 2009. *Etymological Dictionary of Greek*. Leiden.
Behn, F. 1954. *Musikleben im Altertum und frühen Mittelalter*. Stuttgart.
Bell, J. M. 1984. "God, Man, and Animal in Pindar's Second Pythian." In *Greek Poetry and Philosophy: Studies in Honour of Leonard Woodbury*, ed. D. E. Gerber, 1–31. Chico.
Bellia, A. 2012. *Il Canto delle vergini locresi: La Musica a Locri Epizefrii nelle fonti scritte e nelle documentazione archeologica (secoli VI-II a.C)*. Pisa.
Bendall, L. M. 2003. "A Reconsideration of the Northeastern Building at Pylos: Evidence for a Mycenaean Redistributive Center." *American Journal of Archaeology* 107/2:181–231.
Benz, F. L. 1972. *Personal Names in the Phoenician and Punic Inscriptions. A Catalog, Grammatical Study, and Glossary of Elements*. Rome.
Betancourt, P. P. and S. C. Ferrence, eds. 2011. *Metallurgy: Understanding How, Learning Why. Studies in Honor of James D. Muhly*. Philadelphia.
Bietak, M. 2005. "The Setting of the Minoan Wall Paintings at Avaris." In *Aegean Wall Painting: A Tribute to Mark Cameron*, ed. L. Morgan, 83–90. London.

Biga, M. G. 2003. "A Ritual from Archive L.2712 of Ebla." In s.n. 2003:54–69.

———. 2006. "La Musique à Ebla." *Les Dossiers d'Archéologie* 310:24–31.

———. 2011. "La Fête à Ébla (Syrie, XXIVe siècle av J.-C.)." *Journal Asiatique* 299/2:479–494.

Biga, M. G. and A. M. G. Capomacchia. 2012. "I Testi di Ebla di ARET XI: Una Rilettura alla luce dei testi paralleli." *Revue d'Assyriologie et d'Archéologie Orientale* 106:19–32.

Biga, M. G. and F. Pomponio. 1987. "Išar-Damu, roi d'Ebla." *Nouvelles Assyriologiques Brèves et Utilitaires* 1987/4:60–61 no. 106.

Billigmeier, J.-C. and A. S. Dusing. 1981. "The Origin and Function of the *Naukrâroi* at Athens." *Transactions of the American Philological Association* 111:11–16.

Bing, J. D. 1971. "Tarsus: A Forgotten Colony of Lindos." *Journal of Near Eastern Studies* 30/2:99–109.

Birney, K. J. 2007. *Sea Peoples or Syrian Peddlers? The Late Bronze-Iron I Aegean Presence in Syria and Cilicia.* PhD diss., Harvard University.

Black, J. A. 1991. "Eme-sal Cult Songs and Prayers." In *Velles Paraules. Ancient Near Eastern Studies in Honor of Miguel Civil*, ed. P. Michalowski et al., 23–36. Aula Orientalis 9. Barcelona.

Black, J. A. and A. Green. 1992. *Gods, Demons and Symbols of Ancient Mesopotamia: An Illustrated Dictionary.* London.

Blades, J. 1984. *Percussion Instruments and Their History.* Rev. ed. London.

Blakely, S. 2006. *Myth, Ritual, and Metallurgy in Ancient Greece and Recent Africa.* Cambridge.

Blau, J. 1977. "'Weak' Phonetic Change and the Hebrew Sîn." *Hebrew Annual Review* 1:67–119.

Blau, J. and J. C. Greenfield. 1970. "Ugaritic Glosses." *Bulletin of the American Schools of Oriental Research* 200:11–17.

Blegen, C. W. and M. Lang. 1958. "The Palace of Nestor Excavations of 1957." *American Journal of Archaeology* 62/2:175–191.

Blegen, C. W. et al. 1966. *The Palace of Nestor at Pylos in Western Messenia.* 4 vols. Princeton.

Bleibtreu, E. 1980. *Die Flora der neuassyrischen Reliefs.* Vienna.

Blinkenberg, C. 1924. *Le Temple de Paphos.* Copenhagen.

———. 1931. *Lindos. Fouilles et recherches, 1902-1914. I. Les Petits objets.* Berlin.

Boardman, J. 1971. "THEIOS AOIDOS." *Report of the Department of Antiquities of Cyprus* 1971:37–42, pl. XVII–XVIII.

———. 1980. *The Greeks Overseas.* 2nd ed. London.

———. 1990. "The Lyre-Player Group of Seals: An Encore." *Archäologischer Anzeiger* 1990:1–17.

Bibliography

Boehmer, R.-M. 1965. *Die Entwicklung der Glyptik während der Akkad-Zeit. Untersuchungen zur Assyriologie und vorderasiatischen Archäologie.* Berlin.

Boisacq, E. 1938. *Dictionnaire étymologique de la langue grecque.* Heidelberg.

Boissonade, J. F. 1829–1833. *Anecdota Graeca: E codicibus regiis.* 5 vols. Paris.

Bömer, F. 1969–1986. *P. Ovidius Naso, Metamorphosen: Kommentar.* 2 vols. Heidelberg.

Bonechi, M. 1992. "Relations amicales syro-palestiniennes: Mari et Hazor au XVIIIe siècle av. J.C." In *Recueil d'études en l'honneur de Michel Fleury*, ed. J.-M. Durand, 9–22. Mémoires de NABU 2/Florilegium Marianum 1. Paris.

Bonnet, C. 1993. "Existe-t-il un BʻL GBL à Byblos?" *Ugarit-Forschungen* 25:25–34.

———. 1996. *Astarté. Dossier documentaire et perspectives historiques.* Collezione di Studi Fenici 37. Rome.

———. 2009. "De la prostitution sacrée dans l'Antiquité, et du bon usage de la démonstration en histoire." *Les Études Classiques* 77:171–177.

Bordreuil, P. 1973. "Une Inscription phénicienne champlevée des environs de Byblos." *Semitica* 27:23–27.

Bordreuil, P., ed. 1991. *Une Bibliotheque au sud de la ville: Les Textes de la 34e campagne (1973).* Ras Shamra-Ougarit 7. Paris.

Bordreuil, P. and D. Pardee. 1982. "Le Rituel funéraire ougaritique RS 34.126." *Syria* 59:121–128.

Borgeaud, P. 1975. "L'Absence d'Héphaïstos." In *Chypre des origines au moyen-âge: Séminaire interdisciplinaire, semestre d'été 1975*, ed. D. van Berchem, 156–158. Geneva.

Borger, R. 1956. *Die Inschriften Asarhaddons, Königs von Assyrien.* Graz.

———. 2004. *Mesopotamisches Zeichenlexikon.* Münster.

Bos, G. et al. 2001. *Hermetis Trismegisti Astrologica et Diuinatoria.* Corpus Christianorum. Continuatio Mediaevalis 144C. Turnhout.

Boscawen, W. S. C. 1893–1894. "The Hebrew Legend of Civilisation in the Light of Recent Discovery." *The Expository Times* 5:351–356.

Boson, G. 1936. *Tavolette cuneiformi sumere.* Milan.

Botterweck, G. J. and H. Ringgren. 1997–2006. *Theological Dictionary of the Old Testament.* Grand Rapids.

Bounni, A. 1981. "Les Représentations d'Apollon en Palmyrene et dans le millieu Syrien." In *Mythologie gréco-romaine, mythologies périphériques: Études d'iconographie: Paris, 17 mai 1979*, ed. Kahil, L. and C. Augé, 107–112. Colloques internationaux du Centre national de la recherche scientifique 593. Paris.

Bowersock, G. W. 1983. *Roman Arabia.* Cambridge, MA.

———. 2000. *Selected Papers on Late Antiquity.* Bari.

Bowra, C. M. 1964. *Pindar.* Oxford.

Bratke, E. 1899. *Das sogenannte Religionsgespräch am Hof der Sasaniden*. Texte und Untersuchungen zur Geschichte der altchristlichen Literatur 19/3 (= n.F 4/3). Leipzig.

Braun, J. 1997. "Musical Instruments." In Meyers 1997 4:70–79.

Braun-Holzinger, E. A. 1991. *Mesopotamische Weihgaben der frühdynastischen bis altbabylonischen Zeit*. Heidelberg.

Braune, G. 1997. *Küstenmusik in Südarabien: Die Lieder und Tänze an den jemenitischen Künsten des Arabischen Meeres*. Frankfurt am Main.

Breasted, J. H. 1906–1907. *Ancient Records of Egypt: Historical Documents from the Earliest Times to the Persian Conquest*. 4 vols. Chicago.

Brehm, A. 1911–1920. *Die Vögel, Erster Band. Neubearbeitung von William Marshall, vollendet von F. Hempelmann und O. zur Strassen. Brehm's Tierleben. Vierte, vollständig neubearbeitete Auflage*. 4 vols. Leipzig.

Brillante, C. 1995. "Amore senza χάρις: Pind. 'Pyth'. II 42–48." *Quaderni Urbinati di Cultura Classica* n.s. 49/1:33–38.

Brinkman, J. A. 1989. "The Akkadian Words for 'Ionia' and 'Ionian'." In *Daidalikon: Studies in Memory of Raymond V. Schoder, S. J.*, ed. R. F. Sutton, 53–72. Wauconda, Illinois.

Brinner, W. M. 2002. *Lives of the Prophets as Recounted by Abū Isḥāq Aḥmad ibn Muḥammad ibn Ibrāhīm al-Thaʿlabī*. Leiden.

Brisch, N., ed. 2008. *Religion and Power. Divine Kingship in the Ancient World and Beyond*. Chicago.

Brison, O. 2014. "Nudity and Music in Anatolian Mythological Seduction Scenes and Iconographic Imagery." In Maurey et al. 2014:185–200.

Brock, S. P. 2004. "Without Mushê of Nisibis, Where Would We Be? Some Reflections on the Transmission of Syriac Literature." *Journal of Eastern Christian Studies* 56.1–4:15–24.

Brockelmann, C. 1899. *Syrische Grammatik mit Litteratur, Chrestomathie und Glossar*. Berlin.

———. 1966. *Lexicon Syriacum*. Hildesheim.

Bron, F. 1979. *Recherches sur les inscriptions phéniciennes de Karatepe*. Geneva.

Brooke, A. E. and N. McLean, eds. 1906–1940. *The Old Testament in Greek, according to the Text of Codex Vaticanus*. Cambridge.

Brown, E. L. 1981. "The Origin of the Constellation Name 'Cynosura'." *Orientalia* n.s. 50:384–402.

Brown, F. et al. 1962. *A Hebrew and English Lexicon of the Old Testament, with an Appendix Containing the Biblical Aramaic*. Oxford.

Brown, J. P. 1965. "Kothar, Kinyras, and Kythereia." *Journal of Semitic Studies* 10:197–219.

Bibliography

———. 1968. "Literary Contexts of the Common Hebrew-Greek Vocabulary." *Journal of Semitic Studies* 13:163–191.

———. 1995. *Israel and Hellas*. Beihefte zur Zeitschrift für die alttestamentliche Wissenschaft 231. Berlin.

Brown, J. P. and S. Levin. 1986. "The Ethnic Paradigm as a Pattern for Nominal Forms in Greek and Hebrew." *General Linguistics* 26/2:71–105.

Brown, M. L. 1998. "Was There a West Semitic Asklepios?" *Ugarit-Forschungen* 30:133–154.

Brunke, H. and W. Sallaberger. 2010. "Aromata für Duftöl." In *Why Should Someone Who Knows Something Conceal It? Cuneiform Studies in Honor of David I. Owen on His 70th Birthday*, ed. A. Kleinerman and J. Sasson, 41–74. Bethesda.

Bryce, T. R. 2002. *Life and Society in the Hittite World*. Oxford.

Bubenik, M. 1974. "Evidence for Alasija in Linear B Texts." *Phoenix* 28:245–250.

Buccellati, G. 1966. *The Amorites of the Ur III period*. Naples.

Buchholz, H.-G. 1966. "Tönerne Rasseln aus Zypern." *Archäologischer Anzeiger* 1966:140–151.

———. 1990. "Kyprische Eulenrasseln." *Archaeologia Cypria (Κυπριακή Ἀρχαιολογία)* 2:33–51.

Buchholz, H. G. and J. Wiesner. 1977. *Kriegswesen*. Archaeologia Homerica 1.E. Göttingen.

Buchner, G. and J. Boardman. 1966. "Seals from Ischia and the Lyre-player Group." *Jahrbuch des Deutschen Archäologischen Instituts* 81:1–62.

Buchner, G. and D. Ridgway. 1993. *Pithekoussai I*. 1 vol. in 3. Rome.

Budge, E. A. W. 1886. *The Book of the Bee, the Syriac Text Edited from the Manuscripts in London, Oxford, and Munich, with an English Translation*. Oxford.

———. 1927. *Ma'arrath gazzē. The Book of the Cave of Treasures*. London.

Budin, S. L. 2002. "Creating a Goddess of Sex." In *Engendering Aphrodite: Women and Society in Ancient Cyprus*, ed. D. Bolger and N. Serwint, 315–324. Boston.

———. 2003. *The Origin of Aphrodite*. Bethesda.

———. 2008. *The Myth of Sacred Prostitution*. New York.

Bundy, E. L. 1962. *Studia Pindarica*. Berkeley.

Bunnens, G. 1979. *L'Expansion phénicienne en méditerranée. Essai d'interprétation fondé sur une analyse des traditions littéraires*. Brussels.

Buonocore, M. 1989. "Regium Iulium." *Supplementa Italica* 5:29–84.

Burchardt, M. 1909–1910. *Die altkanaanäischen Fremdworte und Eigennamen im Aegyptischen*. Leipzig.

Burgh, T. W. 2004. "'Who's the Man?' Sex and Gender in Iron Age Musical Performance." *Near Eastern Archaeology* 67/3:128–136.

———. 2006. *Listening to the Artifacts: Music Culture in Ancient Palestine*. New York.

Burke, B. 2008. "Mycenaean Memory and Bronze Age Lament." In Suter 2008:70–92.
Burkert, W. 1972a. *Lore and Science in Ancient Pythagoreanism.* Cambridge, MA.
———. 1972b. "Die Leistung eines Kreophylos. Kreophyleer, Homeriden und die archaische Heraklesepik." *Museum Helveticum* 29:74–85.
———. 1992. *The Orientalizing Revolution: Near Eastern Influence on Greek Culture in the Early Archaic Age.* Cambridge, MA.
———. 1994. "Orpheus, Dionysos, und die Euneiden in Athen: Das Zeugnis von Euripides' Hypsipyle." In *Orchestra. Drama, Mythos, Bühne,* ed. A. Bierl and P. von Möllendorff, 44–49. Stuttgart.
———. 1995. "Lydia between East and West or How to Date the Trojan War: A Study in Herodotus." In Carter and Morris 1995:139–148.
———. 2004. *Babylon, Memphis, Persepolis: Eastern Contexts of Greek Culture.* Cambridge, MA.
Burzik, M. 1995. *Quellenstudien zu europäischen Zupfinstrumentenformen: Methodenprobleme, kunsthistorische Aspekte und Fragen der Namenszuordnung.* Kölner Beiträge zur Musikforschung 187. Kassel.
Cagni, L. 1969. *L'Epopea di Erra.* Studi Semitici 34. Rome.
Calder, W. M. 1928. *Monumenta Asiae Minoris antiqua I.* Manchester.
Çambel, H. 1999. *Corpus of Hieroglyphic Luwian Inscriptions. Volume 2: Karatepe-Aslantaş: The Inscriptions: Facsimile Edition.* Berlin.
Cameron, A. 2004. *Greek Mythography in the Roman World.* New York.
Caminos, R. A. 1954. *Late-Egyptian Miscellanies.* London.
Campbell, A. F. 1975. *The Ark Narrative, 1 Sam 4-6, 2 Sam 6: A Form-Critical and Traditio-Historical Study.* Society of Biblical Literature Dissertation Series 16. Missoula.
Campbell, D. 1982-1993. *Greek Lyric.* 5 vols. Loeb Classical Library:142–144, 461, 476. Cambridge, MA.
Cannavo, A. 2011. *Histoire de Chypre à l'époque archaïque.* PhD diss., Université de Lyon.
Capomacchia, A. M. G. 1984. "Il Mito di Myrrha: Aspetti del rapporto tra cultura classica ed Oriente." In s.n. 1984:95–102.
Caquot, A. 1976. "La Tablette RS 24.252 et la question des Rephaim ougaritiques." *Syria* 53:295–304.
———. 1979. "La Littérature ugaritique." In *Dictionnaire de la Bible. Supplément,* ed. H. Cazelles and A. Feuillet, 9:1361–1417. Paris.
———. 1985. "Une Nouvelle interprétation de KTU 1.19 (1–19)." *Studi Epigrafici e Linguistici sul Vicino Oriente Antico* 2:93–114.
Caquot, A. and M. Sznycer. 1980. *Ugaritic Religion.* Leiden.

Caquot, A. et al. 1974. *Textes ougaritiques. I: Mythes et légendes*. Littératures Anciennes du Proche-Orient 7. Paris.
Carlucci, G. 2009. "L'Ipsa dello pseudo-Artemidoro." *Quaderni di Storia* 70:387–407.
Carratelli, G. P. 1939-1940. "Per la storia delle associazioni in Rodi antica." *Annuario della Regia Scuola Archeologica di Atene e delle Missioni Italiane in Oriente* 1–2:147–200.
Carruba, O. 1968. "Contributo alla storia di Cipro nel II millennio." *Studi Classici e Orientali* 17:5–29.
Carter, J. B. and S. P. Morris, eds. 1995. *The Ages of Homer. A Tribute to Emily Townsend Vermeule*. Austin.
Cassio, A. C. 2000. "Esametri orfici, dialetto attico e musica dell'asia minore." In *Synaulía: Cultura musicale in Grecia e contatti mediterranei*, ed. A. C. Cassio et al., 97–110. Annali dell'Istituto Universitario Orientale di Napoli. Sezione Filologico-Letteraria. Quaderni 5. Naples.
———. 2012. "Kypris, Kythereia and the Fifth Book of the *Iliad*." In *Homeric Contexts: Neoanalysis and the Interpretation of Oral Poetry*, ed. Montanari, F. et al., 413–426.
Cassuto, U. 1943. "The Reception of Ba'al in the Ugaritic Tablet V AB." *Bulletin of the Jewish Palestine Exploration Society* 10:47–54.
———. 1961. *A Commentary on the Book of Genesis*. 2 vols. Jerusalem.
———. 1971. *The Goddess Anath: Canaanite Epics of the Patriarchal Age*. Jerusalem.
Castellino, G. R. 1972. *Two Šulgi Hymns (BC)*. Rome.
Catagnoti, A. 1989. "I NE.DI nei testi amministrativi degli archivi di Ebla." *Miscellanea Eblaitica* 2:149–201.
Catagnoti, A. and M. Bonechi. 1998. "Magic and Divination at III Millennium Ebla, 1. Textual Typologies and Preliminary Lexical Approach." *Studi Epigrafici e Linguistici sul Vicino Oriente Antico* 15:17–39.
Cataudella, M. R. 1971. *Ka-Ma. Studi sulla società agraria micenea*. Rome.
Catling, H. W. 1963. "Patterns of Settlement in Bronze Age Cyprus." *Opuscula Atheniensia* 4:129–169.
———. 1964. *Cypriot Bronzework in the Mycenaean World*. Oxford.
———. 1971. "A Cypriot Bronze Statuette in the Bomford Collection." In Schaeffer 1971:14–32.
Caubet, A. 1987. "La Musique à Ougarit." *Comptes Rendus de l'Académie des Inscriptions et Belles-Lettres* 131/4:731–754.
———. 1987. "Chante en l'honneur de Ba'al." *Le Monde de la Bible* 48:33.
———. 1994. "La Musique du Levant au bronze récent." In *La Pluridisciplinarité en archéologie musicale. IVe Rencontres internationales d'archéologie musicale de l'ICTM, Saint-Germain-en-Laye, 8-12 octobre 1990*, ed. s.n., 129–135. Paris.

———. 1996. "La Musique à Ougarit: Nouveaux témoignages matériels." In Wyatt et al. 1996:9–31.

———. 1999. "Chantes et devins: Deux cas de pratiques de la musique à Ougarit." In *'Schnittpunkt' Ugarit*, ed. M. Kropp and A. Wagner, 9–29. Frankfurt am Main.

———. 2014. "Musical Practices and Instruments in Late Bronze Age Ugarit (Syria)." In Maurey et al. 2014:172–184.

Cavigneaux, A. 1998. "Sur le balag Urumma'irabi et le Rituel de Mari." *Nouvelles Assyriologiques Brèves et Utilitaires* 1998/2:46 no. 43.

Cayla, J.-B. 2001. "À propos de Kinyras. Nouvelle lecture d'une épiclèse d'Apollon à Chypre." *Cahiers du Centre d'Études Chypriotes* 31:69–81.

———. 2005. "Apollon ou la vie sauvage: À propos de quelques épiclèses d'Apollon à Chypre." In *Nommer les dieux: Théonymes, épithètes, épiclèses dans l'antiquité*, ed. N. Belayche, 227–240. Turnhout.

Cerchiai, L. and M. L. Nava. 2008–2009. "Uno Scarabeo del Lyre-Player Group da Monte Vetrano (Salerno)." *AION. Annali dell'Istituto Universitario Orientali di Napoli* 15–16:101–108.

Cesnola, L. P. di. 1877. *Cyprus, Its Ancient Cities, Tombs, and Temples: A Narrative of Researches and Excavations during Ten Years' Residence as American Consul in that Island*. London.

———. 1885. *A Descriptive Atlas of the Cesnola Collection of Cypriote Antiquities in the Metropolitan Museum of Art, New York. 1. Sculpture*. New York.

———. 1894. *A Descriptive Atlas of the Cesnola Collection of Cypriote Antiquities in the Metropolitan Museum of Art, New York. 2. Terracotta*. New York.

———. 1903. *A Descriptive Atlas of the Cesnola Collection of Cypriote Antiquties in the Metropolitan Museum of Art, New York. 3. Alabaster, Bronze, Faience, Glass, Inscription, Seals, etc.* New York.

Chabot, J. B., ed. 1899–1924. *Chronique de Michel le Syrien, Patriarche Jacobite d'Antioche (1166-1199)*. Paris.

———. 1918. "Punica." *Journal Asiatique* 1918:249–302.

———. 1940–1941. *Recueil des inscriptions libyques; Rédigé et publié*. Paris.

Chadwick, J. 1975. "Who Was E-ke-ra2-wo?" In *Le Monde grec: Pensée, littérature, histoire, documents: Hommages à Claire Préaux*, ed. J. Bingen et al., 450–453. Brussels.

Chaniotis, A. 1990. "Zur Frage der Spezialisierung im griechischen Theater des Hellenismus und der Kaiserzeit." *Ktema: Civilisations de l'Orient, de la Grèce et de Rome Antique* 15:89–108.

———. 2013. "Memories of Early Crete." In *Kreta in der geometrischen und archaischen Zeit. Akten des Internationalen Kolloquiums am Deutschen*

Archäologischen Institut, Abteilung Athen, 27.29. Januar 2006, Berlin, ed. W.-D. Niemeier et al., 1–18. Munich.

Chantraine, P. 1968. *Dictionnaire étymologique de la langue grecque.* Paris.

Charlesworth, J. H., ed. 1997. *The Dead Sea Scrolls: Hebrew, Aramaic, and Greek Texts with English Translations. Volume 4A, Pseudepigraphic and Non-Masoretic Psalms and Prayer.* Princeton Theological Seminary Dead Sea Scrolls Project. Tübingen.

Charpin, D. 1978. "Recherches sur la Dynastie de Mananâ (I): Essai de localisation et de chronologie." *Revue d'Assyriologie et d'Archéologie Orientale* 72:13–40.

Charpin, D. and N. Ziegler. 2003. *Mari et le proche-orient à l'époque amorrite: Essai d'historie politique.* Florilegium Marianum 5. Paris.

Chatzēiōannou, K. 1971–2001. *Hē archaia Kypros eis tas Hellēnikas pēgas.* 5 vols. in 7. Leukosia.

Chatzis, A. 1914. *Der Philosoph und Grammatiker Ptolemaios Chennos. Leben, Schriftstellerei und Fragmente, mit Ausschluss der Aristotelesbiographie.* Paederborn.

Chavane, M.-J. and M. Yon. 1978. *Testimonia Salaminia 1. Première, deuxième et troisième parties.* Salamine de Chypre 10. Paris.

Cheng, J. 2001. *Assyrian Music as Represented and Representations of Assyrian Music.* PhD diss., Harvard University.

Chiera, F. 1929. *Sumerian Lexical Texts from the Temple School of Nippur.* Oriental Institute Publications 11. Chicago.

Chilton, B. D. 1990. *The Isaiah Targum.* The Aramaic Bible 11. Collegeville.

Chuvin, P. 1991. *Mythologie et géographie dionysiaques: Recherches sur l'œuvre de Nonnos de Panopolis.* Clermont-Ferrand.

Chwolsohn, D. 1856. *Die Ssabier und der Ssabismus.* St. Petersburg.

Civil, M. 1987a. "An Inscription of Ishbi-Erra." *Nouvelles Assyriologiques Brèves et Utilitaires* 1987/2:14–15 no. 28.

———. 1987b. "The Tigidlu and a Musical Instrument." *Nouvelles Assyriologiques Brèves et Utilitaires* 1987/2:27 no. 48.

———. 1989. "The Texts from Meskene-Emar." *Aula Orientalis* 7:5–25.

———. 2004. *The Series DIRI = (w)atru.* Materials for the Sumerian Lexicon 15. Rome.

———. 2008. *The Early Dynastic Practical Vocabulary A: Archaic HAR-ra A.* Archivi Reali di Ebla, Studi 4. Rome.

———. 2010. *The Lexical Texts in the Schøyen Collection.* Bethesda.

Clapham, L. R. 1969. *Sanchuniathon: The First Two Cycles.* PhD diss., Harvard University.

Clare, R. J. 2002. *The Path of the Argo: Language, Imagery and Narrative in the Argonautica of Apollonius Rhodius.* Cambridge Classical Studies. Cambridge.

Clauss, J. J. 1993. *The Best of the Argonauts: The Redefinition of the Epic Hero in Book 1 of Apollonius's Argonautica.* Hellenistic Culture and Society 10. Berkeley.
Clay, D. 2004. *Archilochos Heros: The Cult of Poets in the Greek Polis.* Washington, DC.
Clemen, C. 1939. *Die phönikische Religion nach Philo von Byblos.* Leipzig.
Clemens, D. M. 1993. "KTU 1.108.3-5 (RS 24.252): dyšr. wyd̲mr ..." *Ugarit-Forschungen* 25:63-74.
Clermont-Ganneau, C. 1885-1907. *Recueil d'archéologie orientale.* 8 vols. Paris.
Cline, E. H. 1994. *Sailing the Wine-Dark Sea: International Trade and the Late Bronze Age Aegean.* British Archaeological Reports, International Series 591. Oxford.
———. 2005. "Cyprus and Alashiya: One and the Same!" *Archaeology Odyssey* September/October:41-44.
———. 2007. "Rethinking Mycenaean International Trade with Egypt and the Near East." In Galaty and Parkinson 2007:190-200.
———. 2014. *1177 B.C.: The Year Civilization Collapsed.* Princeton.
Cochavi-Rainey, Z. 2003. *The Alashia Texts from the 14th and 13th Centuries BCE: A Textual and Linguistic Study.* Alter Orient und Altes Testament 289. Münster.
Cogan, M. 2000. *1 Kings: A New Translation with Introduction and Commentary.* The Anchor Bible 10. New York.
Cogan, M. and I. Eph'al, eds. 1991. *Ah, Assyria: Studies in Assyrian History and Ancient Near Eastern Historiography Presented to Hayim Tadmor.* Jerusalem.
Cohen, C. 1979. "Neo-Assyrian Elements in the First Speech of the Biblical Rab-Saqê." *Israel Oriental Studies* 9:32-48.
Cohen, M. E. 1974. *Balag-Compositions: Sumerian Lamentation Liturgies of the Second and First Millennium B.C.* Sources from the Ancient Near East 1, 2. Malibu.
———. 1981. *Sumerian Hymnology: The Eršemma.* Hebrew Union College Annual, Supplements 2. Cincinnati.
———. 1993. *The Cultic Calendars of the Ancient Near East.* Bethesda.
Cohen, Y. 2010. "The "Second Glosses' in the Lexical Lists from Emar: West Semitic or Akkadian?" In *Language in the Ancient Near East: Proceedings of the 53e Rencontre assyriologique internationale. Volume 1, Part 2,* ed. L. Kogan et al., 813-839. Winona Lake.
Coldstream, J. N. 1986. *The Originality of Ancient Cypriot Art.* Nicosia.
———. 1989. "Status Symbols in Cyprus in the Eleventh Century BC." In Peltenburg 1989:325-335.
———. 1994. "What Sort of Aegean Migration?" In Karageorghis 1994:143-147.
Coletti, M. L. 1996-1998. "Cinara." In *Enciclopedia oraziana,* ed. s.n., 1:689-670. Rome.
Collins, B. J. 2007. *The Hittites and Their World.* Atlanta.

Bibliography

Collins, B. J. et al., eds. 2008. *Anatolian Interfaces: Hittites, Greeks and Their Neighbors in Ancient Anatolia.* Oxford.

Collon, D. 1982. *The Alalakh Cylinder Seals.* British Archaeological Reports, International Series 132. Oxford.

———. 1987. *First Impressions: Cylinder Seals in the Ancient Near East.* Chicago.

———. 2006. "La Musique en Mésopotamie." *Les Dossiers d'Archéologie* 310:6–14.

Connelly, J. B. 1991. "Continuity and Change: The Cypriot Votive Tradition and the Hellenistic Koine." In Vandenabeele and Laffineur 1991:93–100 and pl. XIX-XXI.

———. 2011. "Ritual Movement Through Greek Sacred Space: Towards an Archaeology of Performance." In *Ritual Dynamics in the Ancient Mediterranean: Agency, Emotion, Gender, Reception*, ed. A. Chaniotis, 313–346. Stuttgart.

Constantinides, C. N. and R. Browning. 1993. *Dated Greek Manuscripts from Cyprus to the Year 1570.* Dumbarton Oaks Studies 30. Washington, D. C.

Conti, G. 1988. "Osservazioni sulla sezione KA della lista lessicale bilingue eblaita." *Miscellanea Eblaitica* 1:35–77.

———. 1990. *Il Sillabario della quarta fonte della lista lessicale bilingue eblaita.* Miscellanea Eblaitica 3. Florence.

Cooper, A. 1981. "Divine Names and Epithets in the Ugaritic Texts." In *Ras Shamra Parallels III: The Texts from Ugarit and the Hebrew Bible*, ed. L. R. Fisher, 3:333–469. Rome.

Cooper, J. S. 1978. *The Return of Ninurta to Nippur.* Analecta Orientalia 52. Rome.

———. 1983. *The Curse of Agade.* Baltimore.

———. 1993. "Sacred Marriage and Popular Cult in Early Mesopotamia." In Matsushima 1993:81–96.

———. 2006. "Genre, Gender, and the Sumerian Lamentation." *Journal of Cuneiform Studies* 58:39–47.

Corrigan, K. A. 1992. *Visual Polemics in the Ninth-Century Byzantine Psalters.* Cambridge.

Cosgrove, C. H. 2006. "Clement of Alexandria and Early Christian Music." *Journal of Early Christian Studies* 14/3:255–282.

Costa, V. 2004. "I Frammenti di Filocoro tràditi da Boccaccio e da Natale Conti." In *Ricerche di antichità e tradizione classica*, ed. E. Lanzillotta, 117–147. Rome.

Courtois, J.-C. 1971. "Le Sanctuaire du Dieu au Lingot d'Enkomi-Alasia." In Schaeffer 1971:151–362.

Courtois, J.-C. and Webb, J. M. 1987. *Les Cylindres-sceaux d'Enkomi: fouilles françaises 1957-1970.* Nicosia.

Creese, D. E. 2010. *The Monochord in Ancient Greek Harmonic Science.* Cambridge.

Cross, F. L. and Livingstone, E. A., eds. 1997. *The Oxford Dictionary of the Christian Church.* 3rd ed. Oxford.

Cross, F. M. 1972. "An Interpretation of the Nora Stone." *Bulletin of the American Schools of Oriental Research* 208:13–19.

———. 1973. *Canaanite Myth and Hebrew Epic: Essays in the History of the Religion of Israel.* Cambridge, MA.

———. 1974. "Prose and Poetry in the Mythic and Epic Texts from Ugarit." *Harvard Theological Review* 67:1–15.

———. 1998. *From Epic to Canon: History and Literature in Ancient Israel.* Baltimore.

Cross, F. M. and D. N. Freedman. 1955. "The Song of Miriam." *Journal of Near Eastern Studies* 14/4:237–250.

Crowley, J. L. 2013. *The Iconography of Aegean Seals.* Leuven.

Csapo, E. 2004. "The Politics of the New Music." In *Music and the Muses. The Culture of 'Mousikê' in the Classical Athenian City*, ed. P. Murray and P. Wilson, 207–248. Oxford.

Culican, W. 1982. "Cesnola 4555 and other Phoenician Bowls." *Rivista di Studi Fenici* 10:13–32.

Cureton, W. 1855. *Spicilegium Syriacum, Containing Remains of Bardesan, Meliton, Ambrose, and Mara bar Serapion.* London.

Currie, B. 2005. *Pindar and the Cult of Heroes.* Oxford.

Currie, G. I. Forthcoming. "Representations of Musical Instruments in Byzantine and Post-Byzantine Iconography." In *Musical Instruments in Greece from Antiquity to the Modern Era*, ed. A. Voutira. Athens.

Curtiss, S. I. 1903. *Ursemitische Religion im Volksleben des heutigen Orients: Forschungen und Funde aus Syrien und Palästina.* Leipzig.

D'Agostino, F. 1988. "Die ersten 14 Zeilen des sog. 'z à-m e'-Textes aus Abu Salabikh und die Bedeutung des Wortes z à-m e." *Oriens Antiquus* 27:75–83.

D'Albiac, C. 1992. "Some Aspects of the Sphinx in Cyprus: Status and Character." In Ioannides 1992:285–290 and pl. LI–LIII.

D'Acunto, M. 2009. "Efesto e le sue creazioni nel XVIII libro dell' Iliade." *Annali dell'Istituto Universitario Orientale di Napoli. Sezione Filologico-Letteraria* 31:145–198.

Dahood, M. 1963. "An Allusion to Koshar in Ezekiel 33, 32." *Biblica* 44:531–532.

———. 1966–1970. *Psalms. Introduction, Tanslation, and Notes.* Garden City.

Dalley, S. 1987. "Near Eastern Patron Deities of Mining and Smelting in the Late Bronze and Early Iron Ages." *Report of the Department of Antiquities of Cyprus* 1987:60–66.

Dalley, S. et al. 1998. *The Legacy of Mesopotamia.* Oxford.

Damon, C. 1999. "The Trial of Cn. Piso in Tacitus' Annals and the Senatus Consultum de Cn. Pisone Patre: New Light on Narrative Technique." *American Journal of Philology* 120/1:143–162.

Danthine, H. 1937. *Le Palmier-dattier et les arbres sacrés dans l'iconographie de l'Asie occidentale ancienne*. Bibliothèque Archéologique et Historique 25. Paris.

Daszewski, W. A. et al. 1988. *Mosaic Floors in Cyprus*. Biblioteca di 'Felix Ravenna' 3. Ravenna.

Davies, N. de G. 1908. *The Rock Tombs of El Amarna. Part VI. Tombs of Parennefer, Tutu, and Aÿ*. London.

de Martino, S. 1987. "Il Lessico musicale ittita II: GIŠ ^{d}INANNA = cetra." *Oriens Antiquus* 26:171–185.

———. 1992. *Die mantischen Texte*. Corpus der hurritischen Sprachdenkmäler I/7. Rome.

———. 2002. "Song and Singing in the Hittite Literary Evidence." In Hickmann et al. 2002:623–629.

de Moor, J. C. 1969. "Studies in the New Alphabetic Texts from Ras Shamra I." *Ugarit-Forschungen* 1:167–188.

———. 1970. "The Semitic Pantheon of Ugarit." *Ugarit-Forschungen* 2:187–228.

de Sarzec, E. 1884–1912. *Découvertes en Chaldée*. 2 vols. Paris.

de Vaux, R. 1961. *Ancient Israel: Its Life and Institutions*. London.

Deger-Jalkotzy, S. 1994. "The Post-Palatial Period of Greece: An Aegean Prelude to the 11th Century BC in Cyprus." In Karageorghis 1994:11–30.

Deimel, A. 1922. *Liste der archaischen Keilschriftzeichen*. Wissenschaftliche Veröffentlichungen der Deutschen Orient-Gesellschaft 40. Leipzig.

———. 1924. *Die Inschriften von Fara III: Wirtschaftstexte aus Fara*. Wissenschaftliche Veröffentlichung der Deutschen Orient-Gesellschaft 45. Leipzig.

del Olmo Lete, G. 1984. *Interpretación de la mitología cananea: estudios de semántica ugarítica*. Valencia.

———. 1992. *La Religion cananea segun la liturgia de Ugarit*. Aula Orientalis Supplementa 3. Barcelona.

———. 1999. *Canaanite Religion according to the Liturgical Texts of Ugarit*. Bethesda.

Desideri, P. and A. M. Jasink. 1990. *Cilicia: dall'età di Kizzuwatna alla conquista macedone*. Turin.

Dessenne, A. 1957. *Le Sphinx; Étude iconographique 1. Les Origines à la fin du Second Millénaire*. Paris.

Detienne, M. 1994. *The Gardens of Adonis: Spices in Greek Mythology*. 2nd ed. Princeton.

DeVale, S. C. 1988. "Musical Instruments and Ritual: A Systematic Approach." *Journal of the American Musical Instrument Society* 14:126–160.

Dever, W. G. 2005. *Did God Have a Wife? Archaeology and Folk Religion in Ancient Israel*. Grand Rapids.

Diakonoff, I. M. 1990. "The Importance of Ebla for History and Linguistics." In *Eblaitica 2*, ed. C. H. Gordon and G. A. Rendsburg, 2:3–30. Winona Lake.

Dickey, E. 2007. *Ancient Greek Scholarship*. Oxford.

Diehl, E. 1940. "FUERUNT ANTE HOMERUM POETAE." *Rheinisches Museum für Philologie* 89/2:81–114.

Dietrich, B. C. 1978. "Some Evidence from Cyprus of Apolline Cult in the Bronze Age." *Rheinisches Museum für Philologie* 121:1–18.

Dietrich, M. and O. Loretz. 1966. "Die soziale Struktur von Alalaḫ und Ugarit I: Berufsbezeichnungen mit der hurritischen Endung -ḫuli." *Die Welt des Orients* 3:188–205.

———. 1969a. "Die soziale Struktur von Alalaḫ und Ugarit V: Die Weingärten des Gebiets von Alalaḫ im 15. Jahrhundert." *Ugarit-Forschungen* 1:37–64.

———. 1969b. "Beschriftete Lungen, und Leber-Modelle aus Ugarit." In *Ugaritica* 6 (eds. C. F.-A. Schaeffer and A. Parrot):165–179. Paris.

———. 1981. "Neue Studien zu den Ritualtexten aus Ugarit." *Ugarit-Forschungen* 13:63–100.

———. 1989. "Rapi'u und Milku aus Ugarit: Neuere historisch-geographische Thesen zu *rpu mlk 'lm* (KTU 1.108:1) und *mt rpi* (KTU 1.17 I 1)." *Ugarit-Forschungen* 21:123–131.

Dijkstra, M. 1979. "Some Reflections on the Legend of Aqhat." *Ugarit-Forschungen* 11:199–210.

Dijkstra, M. and J. C. de Moor. 1975. "Problematical Passages in the Legend of Aqhâtu." *Ugarit-Forschungen* 7:171–215.

Dikaios, P. 1936–1937. "An Iron Age Painted Amphora in the Cyprus Museum." *Annual of the British School at Athens* 37:56–72 and pl. 57–58.

———. 1961. *A Guide to the Cyprus Museum*. Nicosia.

———. 1962. "The Bronze Statue of a Horned God from Enkomi." *Archäologischer Anzeiger* 1962:1–40.

———. 1969–1971. *Enkomi: Excavations 1948-1958*. Mainz am Rhein.

Diller, A. 1935. "The Text History of the Bibliotheca of Pseudo-Apollodorus." *Transactions of the American Philological Association* 66:296–313.

Dindorf, W. 1835–1838. *Aristophanis comœdiæ*. 4 vols. Oxford.

Dirven, L. 1999. *The Palmyrenes of Dura-Europos: A Study of Religious Interaction in Roman Syria*. Leiden.

Donceel, R. 1966. "Recherches et travaux archéologiques récents au Liban." *L'Antiquité Classique* 35:222–261.

Dossin, G. 1938. "Un Rituel du culte d'Ištar provenant de Mari." *Revue d'Assyriologie et d'Archéologie Orientale* 35:1–13.

Bibliography

———. 1969. "Trois inscriptions cunéiformes de Byblos." *Mélanges de l'Université Saint-Joseph* 45:243–255.
Dossin, G. et al. 1964. *Textes divers. Transcrits, traduits et commentés*. Archives Royales de Mari 13. Paris.
Dothan, M. 1970. "The Musicians of Ashdod." *Archaeology* 23:310–311.
———. 1971. *Ashdod II-III: The Second and Third Seasons of Excavations: 1963, 1965, Soundings in 1967*. 2 vols. 'Atiqot, English Series 9–10. Jerusalem.
Dothan, T. 1982. *The Philistines and Their Material Culture*. New Haven.
Dothan, T. and M. Dothan. 1992. *People of the Sea: The Search for the Philistines*. New York.
Doubleday, V. 1999. "The Frame Drum in the Middle East: Women, Musical Instruments and Power." *Ethnomusicology* 43/1:101–134.
Dover, K. J. 1968. *Aristophanes Clouds*. Oxford.
Draffkorn (Kilmer), A. 1959. *Hurrians and Hurrian at Aalaḫ: An Ethno-Linguistic Analysis*. PhD diss., University of Pennsylvania.
Drijvers, H. J. W. 1966. *Bardaisan of Edessa*. Assen.
Drower, E. S. 1937. *The Mandaeans of Iraq and Iran*. Leiden.
Drower, E. S. and R. Macuch. 1963. *A Mandaic Dictionary*. Oxford.
Duchesne-Guillemin, M. 1969. "La Harpe à plectre iranienne: Son origine et sa diffusion." *Journal of Near Eastern Studies* 28:109–115.
———. 1989. "Sur la lyre-kithara géante." In *Archaeologia Iranica et Orientalis: Miscellanea in honorem Louis Vanden Berghe*, ed. L. de Meyer and E. Haerinck, 128–134. Gent.
———. 1999. "L'Animal sur la cithare: Nouvelle lumière sur l'origine sumérienne de la cithare grecque." *Acta Iranica* 34:203–237.
Dué, C. 2006. *The Captive Woman's Lament in Greek Tragedy*. Austin.
Duentzer, H. 1848. *De Zenodoti studiis Homericis*. Göttingen.
Dugand, J.-E. 1973. *Chypre et Cana'an: Essai sur l'élément oriental à Chypre dans l'antiquite, notamment en matière de toponymie*. Nice.
———. 1974. "Aphrodite-Astarté (de l'étymologie du nom d'Aphrodite)." In *Hommage à Pierre Fargues: Philologie, littératures et histoire anciennes*, ed. s.n., 73–98. Annales de la Faculté des lettres et sciences humaines de Nice 21. Paris.
Dumbrill, R. J. 2000. *The Musicology and Organology of the Ancient Near East*. 2nd ed. London.
Dumbrill, R. J. and I. L. Finkel, eds. 2010. *ICONEA 2008: Proceedings of the International Conference of Near Eastern Archaeomusicology Held at the British Museum December 4, 5, and 6, 2008*. London.

Du Mesnil du Buisson, R. 1962. *Les Tessères et les monnaies de Palmyre: Un Art, une culture et une philosophie grecs dans les moules d'une cité et d'une religion sémitiques.* Paris.

Dunbabin, T. J. 1948. *The Western Greeks: The History of Sicily and South Italy from the Foundation of the Greek Colonies to 480 B.C.* Oxford.

Dunn-Vaturi, A.-E. 2003. "Dancers in the Louvre: The Iranian and Cypriot Collections." *Near Eastern Archaeology* 66/3:106–110.

Dupont-Sommer, A. 1974. "Les Phéniciens à Chypre." *Report of the Department of Antiquities of Cyprus* 1974:75–94.

Dupont-Sommer, A. and J. Starcky. 1958. *Les Inscriptions araméennes de Sfiré, stèles I et II.* Extraits des Mémoires Présentés par Divers Savants à l'Académie des Inscriptions et Belles-Lettres 15. Paris.

Durand, J.-M. 1983. *Textes administratifs des salles 134 et 160 du Palais de Mari.* Archives Royales de Mari 21. Paris.

———. 1988. *Archives épistolaires de Mari 1/1.* Archives Royales de Mari 26. Paris.

———. 1992. "Unité et diversité au Proche-Orient à l'époque amorrite." In *La Circulation des biens, des personnes et des idées dans le Proche-Orient ancien: Actes de la XXXVIIIe Rencontre assyriologique internationale (Paris, 8-10 juillet 1991)* (eds. D. Charpin and F. Joannès) 97–128. Paris.

———. 1997. *Les Documents épistolaires du palais de Mari.* 3 vols. Littératures Anciennes du Proche-Orient 16–18. Paris.

Durand, J.-M. and J.-R. Kupper, eds. 1985. *Miscellanea babylonica: Mélanges offerts à Maurice Birot.* Paris.

Durante, M. 1971–1974. *Sulla preistoria della tradizione poetica greca.* 2 vols. Incunabula Graeca 50, 64. Rome.

Durrell, L. 1959. *Bitter Lemons.* New York.

Dussaud, R. 1945. *Les Religions des Hittites et des Hourrites, des Phéniciens et des Syriens.* Paris.

———. 1950. "Kinyras. Étude sur les anciens cultes chypriotes." *Syria* 27:57–81.

———. 1954. "Review of H. Otten, 'Ein kanaanäischer Mythus aus Bogazköy'," *Mitteilungen des Instituts für Orientforschung* 1 (1953), 124–150. *Syria* 31:145–147.

Dyson, J. T. 1998–1999. "Myrrha's Catabasis." *The Classical Journal* 94/2:163–167.

Ebeling, E. 1919. *Keilschrifttexte aus Assur religiösen Inhalts.* Leipzig.

———. 1922. "Ein Hymnen-Katalog aus Assur." *Berliner Beiträge zur Keilschriftforschung* 1/3:1–32.

Eck, W. et al. 1996. *Das Senatus consultum de Cn. Pisone patre.* Munich.

Edgerton, W. F. and J. A. Wilson. 1936. *Historical Records of Ramses III.* Chicago.

Edwards, R. B. 1979. *Kadmos the Phoenician: A Study in Greek Legends of the Mycenaean Age.* Amsterdam.

Bibliography

Egetmeyer, M. 2010. "The Recent Debate on Eteocypriote People and Language." *Pasiphae* 3:69–90.

———. 2012. "'Sprechen Sie Golgisch?' Anmerkungen zu einer übersehenen Sprache." In *Études mycéniennes 2010. Actes du XIIIe colloque international sur les textes égéens, Sèvres, Paris, Nanterre, 20-23 septembre 2010*, ed. P. Carlier, 427-434. Biblioteca di Pasiphae 10. Pisa.

Egetmeyer, M. and A. Hintze. 1992. *Wörterbuch zu den Inschriften im kyprischen Syllabar*. Berlin.

Ego, B. 1996. *Targum scheni zu Ester: Übersetzung, Kommentar und theologische Deutung*. Texte und Studien zum Antiken Judentum 54. Tübingen.

Eichmann, R. 1988. "Zur Konstruktion und Spielhaltung der altorientalischen Spießlauten. Von den Anfängen bis in die seleukidisch-parthische Zeit." *Baghdader Mitteilungen* 19:583–625.

———. 1994. *Koptische Lauten. Eine musikarchäologische Untersuchung von sieben Langhalslauten des 3.-9. Jh. n. Chr. aus Ägypten*. Deutsches Archäologisches Institut, Abteilung Kairo, Sonderschrift 27. Mainz am Rhein.

———. 2001. "Musik und Migration." In *Migration und Kulturtransfer. Der Wandel vorder- und zentralasiatischer Kulturen im Umbruch vom 2. Zum 1. vorchristlichen Jahrtausend*, ed. R. Eichmann and H. Parzinger, 473–483. Bonn.

Ellenbogen, M. 1962. *Foreign Words in the Old Testament: Their Origin and Etymology*. London.

Ellermeier, F. 1970. "Beiträge zur Frühgeschichte altorientalischer Saiteninstrumenten." In *Archäologie und Altes Testament: Festschrift für Kurt Galling*, ed. A. Kuschke and E. Kutsch, 75–90. Tübingen.

Elayi, J. 2009. *Byblos, cité sacrée (8e-4e s. av. J.-C.)*. Transeuphratène supplément 15. Paris.

Ellis, R. S. 1968. *Foundation Deposits in Ancient Mesopotamia*. New Haven.

Emerit, S., ed. 2013. *Le Statut du musicien dans la Méditerranée ancienne: Égypte, Mésopotamie, Grèce, Rome. Actes de la table ronde internationale tenue a Lyon Maison de l'Orient et de la Méditerranée (université Lumière Lyon 2) les 4 et 5 juillet 2008, Lyon*. Bibliothèque d'étude 159. Paris.

Emerton, J. A. 1982. "Some Notes on the Ugaritic Counterpart of the Arabic ghain." In *Studies in Philology in Honour of Ronald James Williams: A Festschrift*, ed. G. E. Kadish and G. E. Freeman, 31–50. Toronto.

Engel, C. 1870. *The Music of the Most Ancient Nations*. London.

Engel, W. H. 1841. *Kypros: Eine Monographie*. 2 vols. Berlin.

Englund, R. and R. M. Boehmer. 1994. *Archaic Administrative Texts from Uruk: The Early Campaigns*. Archaische Texte aus Uruk 5. Berlin.

Englund, R. and H. Nissen. 1993. *Die lexikalischen Listen der archaischen Texte aus Uruk*. Archaische Texte aus Uruk 3. Berlin.

Erickson, K. 2011. "Apollo-Nabû: the Babylonian Policy of Antiochus I." In *Seleucid Dissolution: the Sinking of the Anchor*, ed. K. Erickson and G. Ramsey, 51–65. Philippika 50. Wiesbaden.

Esin, U. 2002. "Darstellungen von zwei Musikinstrumenten aus Anatolien im 2. Jahrtausend v. Chr." In Hickmann et al. 2002:513–518.

Etter, A., ed. 1986. *O-o-pe-ro-si: Festschrift für Ernst Risch zum 75. Geburtstag*. Berlin.

Evans, A. 1921–1936. *The Palace of Minos*. 3 vols. London.

Falkenstein, A. 1956. *Die neusumerischen Gerichtsurkunden*. 3 vols. Abhandlungen, Bayerische Akademie der Wissenschaften, Philosophisch-Historische Klasse, n.F. 39, 40, 44. Munich.

———. 1959. *Sumerische Götterlieder*. Abhandlungen der Heidelberger Akademie der Wissenschaften, Philosophisch-Historische Klasse 1959/1. Heidelberg.

———. 1966. *Die Inschriften Gudeas von Lagaš. I: Einleitung*. Analecta Orientalia 30. Rome.

Falkenstein, A. and L. Matouš. 1934. "Zur 3. Tafel der Serie diri = DIR = siạku = watru." *Zeitschrift für Assyriologie* 42:144–151.

Falkenstein, A. and W. von Soden. 1953. *Sumerische und akkadische Hymnen und Gebete*. Zürich.

Falsone, G. 1988. "La Fenicia come centro di lavorazione del bronzo nell'età del Ferro." *Dialoghi di Archeologia* 6:79–110.

Faraone, C. A. and D. Obbink. 2013. *The Getty Hexameters: Poetry, Magic, and Mystery in Ancient Selinous*. Oxford.

Fariselli, A. C. 2007. "Musica e danza in contesto fenicio e punico." *Itineraria* 6:9–46.

———. 2010. "Danze 'regali' e danze 'popolari' fra Levante fenicio e Occidente punico." In *Per una storia dei popoli senza note. Atti dell'Atelier del Dottorato di ricerca in Musicologia e Beni musicali (F. A. Gallo, Ravenna, 15-17 ottobre 2007)*, ed. P. Dessì, 13–28. Bologna.

Farmer, H. G. 1928. "Ibn Khurdādhbih on Musical Instruments." *Journal of the Royal Asiatic Society of Great Britain and Ireland* 3:509–518.

———. 1929. *A History of Arabian Music to the XIIIth Century*. London.

Farnell, L. R. 1896–1909. *The Cults of the Greek States*. 5 vols. Oxford.

———. 1921. *Greek Hero Cults and Ideas of Immortality*. Oxford.

———. 1930–1932. *The Works of Pindar*. 3 vols. London.

Faucounau, J. 1994. "The Cypro-Minoan Scripts: A Reappraisal Fifty Years after John F. Daniel's Paper." *Archaeologia Cypria (Κυπριακή Ἀρχαιολογία)* 3:93–106.

Feliu, L. 2003. *The God Dagan in Bronze Age Syria*. Culture and History of the Ancient Near East 19. Leiden.

Févrer, J.-G. 1956. "La Grande inscription dédicatoire de Mactar." *Semitica* 6:15–31.

Bibliography

Finkel, I. L. and M. J. Geller, eds. 1997. *Sumerian Gods and Their Representation.* Cuneiform Monographs 7. Groningen.

Finkelberg, M. 1991. "Royal Succession in Heroic Greece." *Classical Quarterly* 41:303–316.

———. 2005. *Greeks and Pre-Greeks: Aegean Prehistory and Greek Heroic Tradition.* Cambridge.

———. 2011. *The Homer Encyclopedia.* Oxford.

Finkelstein, J. J. 1955. "Subartu and Subarians in Old Babylonian Sources." *Journal of Cuneiform Studies* 9/1:1–7.

———. 1966. "The Genealogy of the Hammurapi Dynasty." *Journal of Cuneiform Studies* 20:95–118.

Fisher, L. R. 1963. "The Temple Quarter." *Journal of Semitic Studies* 34–41.

Fitzmyer, J. A. 1995. *The Aramaic Inscriptions of Sefire.* Rev. ed. Rome.

Fleming, D. E. 1992. *The Installation of Baal's High Priestess at Emar: A Window on Ancient Syrian Religion.* Atlanta.

Flinker, N. 1980. "Cinyras, Myrrha, and Adonis: Father-Daughter Incest from Ovid to Milton." *Milton Studies* 14:59–74.

Flourentzos, P. 1992. "Wind Musical Instruments from Ancient Cyprus." In Åström 1992 1:41–47.

———. 1996. *Cyprus Heritage: The Art of Ancient Cyprus as Exhibited at The Cyprus Museum.* Limassol.

Flower, M. A. 1994. *Theopompus of Chios: History and Rhetoric in the Fourth Century B.C.* Oxford.

Fontenrose, J. E. 1981. *Orion: The Myth of the Hunter and the Huntress.* Classical Studies 23. Berkeley.

Forbes Irving, P. M. C. 1990. *Metamorphosis in Greek Myths.* Oxford.

Ford, A. 1992. *Homer: The Poetry of the Past.* Ithaca.

Fortin, M. 1980. "Fondation de villes grecques à Chypre: Légendes et decouvertes archéologiques." In *Mélanges d'études anciennes offerts à Maurice Lebel*, ed. J.-B. Caron et al., 25–44. St-Jean-Chrysostôme.

Foster, B. R. 1993. *Before the Muses: An Anthology of Akkadian Literature.* 2 vols. Bethesda.

———. 2005. *Before the Muses: An Anthology of Akkadian Literature.* 3rd ed. Bethesda.

Foster, K. P. 1979. *Aegean Faience of the Bronze Age.* New Haven.

Fournet, A. 2013. *The Eteocypriot Languages and Hurrian.* Lille.

Fourrier, S. and G. Grivaud, eds. 2006. *Identités croisées en un milieu méditerranéen: Le Cas de Chypre (antiquité-Moyen Âge).* Mont-Saint-Aignan.

Foxvog, D. A. 2011. "Aspects of Name-Giving in Presargonic Lagash." In Heimpel 2011:59–97.

Foxvog, D. A. and A. D. Kilmer. 1979-1988. "Music." In *The International Standard Bible Encyclopedia* (ed. G. W. Bromiley) 4 vols. 3:436-449. Grand Rapids.

Franceschetti, A. 2008. "Musici e strumenti musicali alle corti micenee." In Sacconi et al. 2008:309-321.

Frankfort, H. 1948. *Kingship and the Gods. A Study of Ancient Near Eastern Religion as the Integration of Society and Nature.* Chicago.

———. 1970. *The Art and Architecture of the Ancient Orient.* New York.

Franklin, J. C. 2002a. "Diatonic Music in Greece: A Reassessment of Its Antiquity." *Mnemosyne* 56/1:669-702.

———. 2002b. "Harmony in Greek and Indo-Iranian Cosmology." *Journal of Indo-European Studies* 30/1-2:1-25.

———. 2002c. *Terpander: The Invention of Music in the Orientalizing Period.* PhD diss., University College London.

———. 2003. "The Language of Musical Technique in Greek Epic Diction." *Gaia* 7:295-307.

———. 2006a. "Lyre Gods of the Bronze Age Musical Koine." *Journal of Ancient Near Eastern Religions* 6.2:39-70.

———. 2006b. "The Wisdom of the Lyre: Soundings in Greece, Cyprus and the Ancient Near East." In Hickmann et al. 2006:379-398.

———. 2008. "'A Feast of Music'. The Greco-Lydian Musical Movement on the Assyrian Periphery." In Collins et al. 2008:193-204.

———. 2010. "Remembering Music in Early Greece." In *The Historiography of Music in Global Perspective*, ed. S. Mirelman, 9-50. Piscataway.

———. 2011a. "Music." In Finkelberg 2011: s.v.

———. 2011b. "Phorminx." In Finkelberg 2011: s.v.

———. 2012. "The Lesbian Singers: Towards a Reconstruction of Hellanicus' Karneian Victors." In *Poesia, musica e agoni nella Grecia antica*, ed. D. Castaldo et al., 2 vols., 720-764. Galatina.

———. 2013. "'Song-Benders of Circular Choruses': Dithyramb and the 'Demise of Music'." In *Dithyramb in Context*, ed. P. Wilson and B. Kowalzig, 213-236. Oxford.

———. 2014. "Greek Epic and Kypriaka: Why 'Cyprus Matters'." In Maurey et al. 2014:213-247.

———. Forthcoming. "Kinyras and the Musical Stratigraphy of Early Cyprus." In *Musical Traditions in the Middle East: Reminiscences of a Distant Past*, ed. G. van den Berg and T. Krispijn. Piscataway.

———. Forthcoming. *The Middle Muse: Mesopotamian Echoes in Early Greek Music.*

———. Forthcoming. *The Stormy Seas of Cyprus: The Poetics of Eastern Wandering in Greek Epic.*

Bibliography

Franzmann, M. 1991. *The Odes of Solomon: An Analysis of the Poetical Structure and Form*. Göttingen.
Fraser, P. M. 1979. "Lycophron on Cyprus." *Report of the Department of Antiquities of Cyprus* 1979:328–343.
Frayne, D. R. 1998. "New Light on the Reign of Ishme-Dagan." *Zeitschrift für Assyriologie* 88:6–44.
Frazer, J. G. 1914. *The Golden Bough: A Study in Magic and Religion. Part IV. Adonis Attis Osiris*. 3rd ed. 2 vols. London.
———. 1921. *Apollodorus. The Library*. 2 vols. Loeb Classical Library. Cambridge, MA.
Freedman, D. N. 1976. "Divine Names and Titles in Early Hebrew Poetry." In *Magnalia Dei, the Mighty Acts of God: Essays on the Bible and Archaeology in Memory of G. Ernest Wright*, ed. F. M. Cross et al., 55–107. Garden City.
Freedman, D. N., ed. 1992. *The Anchor Bible Dictionary*. 6 vols. New York.
Freedman, H. and M. Simon. 1983. *Midrash Rabbah*. London.
Friedman, R. E. 1980. "The Mrzh Tablet from Ugarit." *Maarav* 2/2:187–206.
———. 1987. *Who Wrote the Bible?* Englewood Cliffs.
Friedrich, J. H. and W. Röllig. 1970. *Phönizisch-Punische Grammatik*. 2nd ed. 2 vols. Analecta Orientalia 46. Rome.
Friedrich, J. H. et al. 1999. *Phönizisch-punische Grammatik*. 3rd ed. Analecta Orientalia 55. Rome.
Frisk, H. 1960. *Griechisches etymologisches Wörterbuch*. Heidelberg.
Fritz, V. 1978. "Kinneret und Ginnosar: Voruntersuchung für eine Ausgrabung auf dem Tell el-'Orēme am See Genezareth." *Zeitschrift des deutschen Palästina-Vereins* 94:32–45.
Frontisi-Ducroux, F. 1975. *Dédale: Mythologie de l'artisan en Grèce ancienne*. Paris.
Fronzaroli, P. 1980. "Un Verdetto reale." *Studi Eblaiti* 3/3–4:33–52.
———. 1984. "Eblaic Lexicon: Problems and Appraisal." *Quaderni di Semitistica* 13:117–157.
———. 1988. "Il Culto dei re defunti in ARET 3.178." *Miscellanea Eblaitica* 1:1–33.
———. 1989. "A proposito del culto dei re defunti a Ebla." *Nouvelles Assyriologiques Brèves et Utilitaires* 1989/1:1–2 no. 2.
———. 1991. "Noms de fonction dans les textes rituels d'Ebla." *Nouvelles Assyriologiques Brèves et Utilitaires* 1991/2:32–34 no. 49.
———. 1992. "The Ritual Texts of Ebla." In Fronzaroli 1992:163–185.
———. 1997. "Divinazione a Ebla (TM.76.G.86)." *Miscellanea Eblaitica* 4:1–22.
Fronzaroli, P., ed. 1992. *Literature and Literary Language at Ebla*. Florence.
Fronzaroli, P. and A. Catagnoti. 1993. *Testi rituali della regalità (archivio L.2769)*. Archivi Reali di Ebla, Testi 11. Rome.
Fujii, T. 2013. *Imperial Cult and Imperial Representation in Roman Cyprus*. Stuttgart.

Furley, W. D. and J. M. Bremer. 2001. *Greek Hymns: Selected Cult Songs from the Archaic to the Hellenistic Period*. 2 vols. Tübingen.

Gabbay, U. 2008. "The Akkadian Word for 'Third Gender:' The *kalû* (gala) Once Again." In *Proceedings of the 51st Rencontre assyriologique internationale*, ed. R. D. Biggs et al., 49–56. Chicago.

———. 2010. "The Ancient Mesopotamian Sistrum and Its References in Cuneiform Literature: The Identification of the SEM and MEZE." In Dumbrill and Finkel 2010:23–28.

———. 2011. "Laments in Garšana." In *Ĝaršana Studies*, ed. D. I. Owen, 67–74. Cornell Studies in Assyriology and Sumerology 6. Bethesda.

———. 2013. "'We Are Going to the House in Prayer'. Theology, Cultic Topography, and Cosmology in the Emesal Prayers of Ancient Mesopotamia." In *Heaven on Earth: Temples, Ritual and the Cosmic Symbolism in the Ancient World*, ed. D. Ragavan, 223–244. Chicago.

———. 2014. "The Balaĝ Instrument and Its Role in the Cult of Ancient Mesopotamia." In Maurey et al. 2014:128–147.

Gaber, P. Forthcoming. "The Iconography of Goddess Worship in the Ancient Near East." In *"Better is a Book than a Well-built House." Essays in Honor of James M. Weinstein*, ed. J. Zorn.

Gadotti, A. 2010. "The Nar and Gala in Sumerian Literary Texts." In Shehata and Pruzsinszky 2010:51–65.

Gaifman, M. 2008. "The Aniconic Image of the Roman Near East." In *The Variety of Local Religious Life in the Near East in the Hellenistic and Roman Periods*, ed. T. Kaizer, 37–72. Leiden.

———. 2012. *Aniconism in Greek Antiquity*. Oxford.

Galaty, M. L. and W. A. Parkinson, eds. 2007. *Rethinking Mycenaean Palaces II*. Rev. and exp. 2nd ed. Los Angeles.

Gallavotti, C. 1961. "Note sul lessico miceneo." *Rivista di Filologia e di Istruzione Classica* 39:160–179.

———. 1976. "Alasios e Kuprios nei documenti micenei." In *Studi ciprioti e rapporti di scavo 2*, ed. s.n., 51–58. Rome.

Galpin, F. W. 1936. *The Music of the Sumerians and Their Immediate Successors the Babylonians and Assyrians*. Cambridge.

Gantz, T. 1993. *Early Greek Myth: A Guide to Literary and Artistic Sources*. Baltimore.

Gantz, T. N. 1978. "Pindar's Second Pythian: The Myth of Ixion." *Hermes* 14–26.

Gantzert, M. 2008. *Emar Lexical Texts*. PhD diss., University of Leiden.

Gardiner, A. H. 1937. *Late-Egyptian Miscellanies*. Brussels.

Garland, R. 2001. *The Greek Way of Death*. 2nd ed. Ithaca.

Garr, W. R. 1985. *Dialect Geography of Syria-Palestine, 1000–586 B.C.E.* Philadelphia.

Gaster, T. H. 1936–1937. "Notes on the 'Song of the Sea'." *The Expository Times* 48:45.

———. 1961. *Thespis: Ritual, Myth, and Drama in the Ancient Near East*. 2nd rev. ed. Garden City.

Gelb, I. J. 1952. *Materials for the Assyrian Dictionary 1. Sargonic Texts from the Diyala Region*. Chicago.

———. 1961. "The Early History of the West Semitic Peoples." *Journal of Cuneiform Studies* 15/1:27–47.

———. 1975. "Homo Ludens in Early Mesopotamia." *Studia Orientalia* 46:43–76.

Gelb, I. J. 1980. *Computer-Aided Analysis of Amorite*. Chicago.

Gelb, I. J. and B. Kienast. 1990. *Die Altakkadischen Königsinschriften des dritten Jahrtausends v. Chr.* Freiburger Altorientalische Studien 7. Stuttgart.

Gelb, I. J. et al. 1989–1991. *Earliest Land Tenure Systems in the Near East: Ancient Kudurrus*. 2 vols. Oriental Institute Publications 104. Chicago.

Genz, H. 2010. "Reflections on the Early Bronze Age IV in Lebanon." In *Proceedings of the 6th International Congress on the Archaeology of the Ancient Near East, May 5th–10th 2008, "Sapienza"-Università di Roma*, ed. P. Matthiae et al., 2:205–217. Wiesbaden.

Gentili, B. 1992. "'Pindarica' III. La 'Pitica' 2 e il carme iporchematico di Castore (fr. 105 a-b Maehler)." *Quaderni Urbinati di Cultura Classica* n.s. 40/1:49–55.

George, A. R. 1993. *House Most High: The Temples of Ancient Mesopotamia*. Mesopotamian Civilizations 5. Winona Lake.

———. 2003. *The Babylonian Gilgamesh Epic: Introduction, Critical Edition and Cuneiform Texts*. 2 vols. Oxford.

Georges, P. 1994. *Barbarian Asia and the Greek Experience*. Baltimore.

Gérard-Rousseau, M. 1968. *Les Mentions religieuses dans les tablettes mycéniennes*. Rome.

Gesche, H. 1974. "Nikokles von Paphos und Nikokreon von Salamis." *Chiron* 4:103–123.

Gese, H. et al. 1970. *Die Religionen Altsyriens, Altarabiens und der Mandäer*. Stuttgart.

Gildersleeve, B. L. 1907. *Pindar: The Olympian and Pythian Odes*. London.

Gilula, D. 2000. "Stratonicus, the Witty Harpist." In *Athenaeus and His World*, ed. D. Braund and J. Wilkins, 423–433. Exeter.

Ginsberg, H. L. 1935. "The Victory of the Land-God over the Sea-God." *Journal of the Palestinian Oriental Society* 15:327–333.

———. 1938. "Women Singers and Wailers among the Northern Canaanites." *Bulletin of the American Schools of Oriental Research* 72:13–15.

Giovino, M. 2007. *The Assyrian Sacred Tree: A History of Interpretations*. Fribourg.

Giuffrida, M. 1996. "Echi ciprioti in Pindaro." *Kokalos* 42:283–301.

Given, M. 1998. "Inventing the Eteocypriots: Imperialist Archaeology and the Manipulation of Ethnic Identity." *Journal of Mediterranean Archaeology* 11.1:3–29.

Gjerstad, E. 1944. "The Colonization of Cyprus in Greek Legend." *Opuscula Archaeologica* 3:107–123.

———. 1946. "Decorated Metal Bowls from Cyprus." *Opuscula Archaeologica* 4:1–18.

———. 1948. *The Cypro-Geometric, Cypro-Archaic and Cypro-Classical Periods*. Swedish Cyprus Expedition 4/2. Stockholm.

Glover, S. 1981. "The Cults of Apollo in Cyprus: A Preliminary Study." In *Studies in Cypriote Archaeology*, ed. J. Biers and D. Soren, 145–151. Los Angeles.

Goetze, A. 1928. "Madduwattaš." *Mitteilungen der Vorderasiatisch-Aegyptischen Gesellschaft* 32/1:36–37 and 140.

———. 1958. "Remarks on Some Names Occurring in the Execration Texts." *Bulletin of the American Schools of Oriental Research* 151:28–33.

Goldhill, S. 1991. *The Poet's Voice: Essays on Poetics and Greek Literature*. Cambridge.

Goldman, H. 1935. "Preliminary Expedition to Cilicia, 1934, and Excavations at Gözlü Kule, Tarsus, 1935." *American Journal of Archaeology* 39/4:526–549.

Gomi, T. 1981. "Neo-Sumerian Administrative Tablets in the British Museum, II." *Acta Sumerologica* 3:149–184.

Good, R. M. 1991. "On RS 24.252." *Ugarit-Forschungen* 23:155–160.

Gordon, C. H. 1965a. *Ugaritic Textbook*. Rome.

———. 1965b. *The Common Background of Greek and Hebrew Civilizations*. New York.

———. 1966. *Ugarit and Minoan Crete: The Bearing of Their Texts on the Origins of Western Culture*. New York.

———. 1997. "Ugaritic Phonology." In *Phonologies of Asia and Africa*, ed. A. S. Kaye, 49–54. Winona Lake.

Gordon, E. I. 1959. *Sumerian Proverbs: Glimpses of Everyday Life in Ancient Mesopotamia*. Philadelphia.

Goren, Y. et al. 2003. "The Location of Alashiya: New Evidence from Petrographic Investigation of Alashiyan Tablets from El-Amarna and Ugarit." *American Journal of Archaeology* 107/2:233–255.

Görg, M. 1981. "Die Königstochter und die Leier." *Biblische Notizen* 14:7–10.

Gorman, J. 2003. *Reading and Theorizing Women's Sexualities: The Representation of Women in the Acts of Xanthippe and Polyxena*. PhD diss., Temple University.

Gostoli, A. 1990. *Terpandro: Introduzione, testimonianze, testo critico, traduzione e commento*. Rome.

Gow, A. S. F. 1965. *Machon*. Cambridge.

Grainger, J. D. 1991. *Hellenistic Phoenicia*. Oxford.

Green, L. 1992. "Asiatic Musicians and the Court of Akhenaten." In *Contacts between Cultures: West Asia and North Africa, Selected Papers from the 33rd Congress of Asian and North African Studies, Toronto, August 15-25, 1990*, ed. K. I. Koppedrayer et al., 215–220. Lewiston.

Green, M. W. and H. J. Nissen. 1987. *Zeichenliste der archaischen Texte aus Uruk*. Archaische Texte aus Uruk 2/Ausgrabungen der Deutschen Forschungsgemeinschaft in Uruk-Warka 11. Berlin.

Green, P. 1991. *Alexander of Macedon, 356-323 B.C.: A Historical Biography*. Berkeley.

Greenberg, M. 1983. *Ezekiel 1-20. A New Translation, Introduction and Commentary*. The Anchor Bible 22. Garden City.

Greenfield, J. C. 1965. "Stylistic Aspects of the Sefire Treaty Inscriptions." *Acta Orientalia* 29:1–18.

———. 1973. "Un Rite religieux araméen et ses parallèles." *Revue Biblique* 80:46–52.

———. 1974. "The Marzeah as a Social Institution." *Acta Antiqua Academiae Scientiarum Hungaricae* 22:423–435.

———. 1987. "Larnax tēs Lapethou III Revisited." In Lipiński 1987:391–401.

Grinsell, L. V. 1990. "Some Sacred Trees and Rag-Bushes in Cyprus." *Folklore* 101 2:228.

Grivaud, G. 1998. *Villages désertés à Chypre (fin XIIe - fin XIXe siècle)*. Meletai kai Ipomnimata 3. Nicosia.

Gröndahl, F. 1967. *Die Personennamen der Texte aus Ugarit*. Rome.

Groom, N. 1981. *Frankincense and Myrrh: A Study of the Arabian Incense Trade*. London.

Grottanelli, C. 1984. "Da Myrrha alla mirra: Adonis e il profumo dei re siriani." In s.n. 1984:35–60.

Gruppe, O. 1906. *Griechische Mythologie und Religionsgeschichte*. München.

Guillemin, M. and J. Duchesne. 1935. "Sur l'origine asiatique de la cithare grecque." *L'Antiquité Classique* 4:117–124.

Güntert, H. 1914. *Über Reimwortbildungen im Arischen und Altgriechischen: Eine sprachwissenschaftliche Untersuchung*. Heidelberg.

Gurney, O. R. 1962. "Tammuz Reconsidered: Some Recent Developments." *Journal of Semitic Studies* 7:147–160.

———. 1977. *Some Aspects of Hittite Religion*. Oxford.

Güterbock, H. G. 1948. "Hittite Version of the Hurrian Kumarbi Myths: Oriental Forerunners of Hesiod." *American Journal of Archaeology* 52/1:123–134.

———. 1951. "The Song of Ullikummi: Revised Text of the Hittite Version of a Hurrian Myth." *Journal of Cuneiform Studies* 5/4:135–161.

———. 1960. "An Outline of the Hittite AN.TAḪ.ŠUM Festival." *Journal of Near Eastern Studies* 19/2:80–89.

———. 1967. "The Hittite Conquest of Cyprus Reconsidered." *Journal of Near Eastern Studies* 26/2:73–81.

———. 1995. "Reflections on the Musical Instruments *arkammi*, *galgalturi*, and *ḫuḫupal* in Hittite." In *Studio historiae ardens. Ancient Near Eastern Studies Presented to Philo H. J. Houwink ten Cate on the Occcasion of his 65th Birthday*, ed. T. P. J. van den Hout and J. de Roos, 57–72. Istanbul.

Güterbock, H. G. and T. Jacobsen, eds. 1965. *Studies in Honor of Benno Landsberger on his Seventy-Fifth Birthday April 21, 1965*. Assyriological Studies 16. Chicago.

Haas, V. 1982. *Hethitische Berggötter und hurritische Steindämonen. Riten, Kulte und Mythen. Eine Einführung in die altkleinasiatischen religiösen Vorstellungen*. Mainz am Rhein.

———. 1984. *Die Serien itkaḫi und itkalzi des AZU-Priesters: Rituale für Tašmišarri und Tatuḫepa sowie weitere Texte mit Bezug auf Tašmišarri*. Corpus der hurritischen Sprachdenkmäler I/1. Rome.

———. 1994. *Geschichte der hethitische Religion*. Leiden.

Haas, V. and I. Wegner. 1988. *Die Rituale der Beschwörerinnen SALŠU.GI*. 2 vols. Corpus der hurritischen Sprachdenkmäler I/5. Rome.

Haas, V. and G. Wilhelm. 1974. *Hurritische und luwische Riten aus Kizzuwatna*. Kevelaer.

Hadas, M. 1953. *Three Greek Romances*. Garden City.

Hadjikyriakou, G. N. 2007. *Aromatic and Spicy Plants in Cyprus from Antiquity to Present Day*. Nicosia.

Hadjioannou, K. 1971. "On the Identification of the Horned God of Engomi-Alasia." In Schaeffer 1971:33–42.

Hadjisavvas, S. 1992. "Olive Oil Production and Divine Protection." In Åström 1992 3:233–249.

———. 1993. *Olive Oil Processing in Cyprus: From the Bronze Age to the Byzantine Period*. Nicosia.

———. 1996. "Alassa: A Regional Center of Alasia?" In *Late Bronze Age Settlement in Cyprus: Function and Relationship*, ed. P. Åström and E. Herscher, 23–38. Studies in Mediterranean Archaeology and Literature Pocket-Book 126. Jonsered.

Hagel, S. 2005. "Is Nid Qabli Dorian?" *Baghdader Mitteilungen* 36:287–348.

———. 2009. *Ancient Greek Music: A New Technical History*. Cambridge.

Hägg, T. 1973. "Photius at Work: Evidence from the *Bibliotheca*." *Greek, Roman, and Byzantine Studies* 14:213–222.

———. 1975. *Photios als Vermittler antiker Literatur: Untersuchungen zur Technik des Referierens und Exzerpierens in der Bibliotheke*. Studia Graeca Upsaliensia 8. Stockholm.

Hall, E. 1989. *Inventing the Barbarian: Greek Self-Definition through Tragedy*. Oxford.

Hall, J. M. 1997. *Ethnic Identity in Greek Antiquity*. Cambridge.
Hallo, W. W. 1963. "Royal Hymns and Mesopotamian Unity." *Journal of Cuneiform Studies* 17:112–118.
Halpern, B. 2004. *David's Secret Demons: Messiah, Murderer, Traitor, King*. Grand Rapids.
Halton, T. 1983. "Clement's Lyre: A Broken String, a New Song." *The Second Century. A Journal of Early Christian Studies* 3:177–199.
Hammond, N. G. L. 1983. *Three Historians of Alexander the Great: The So-Called Vulgate Authors, Diodorus, Justin, and Curtius*. Cambridge.
Hardie, P. 1985. "Imago mundi: Cosmological and Ideological Aspects of the Shield of Achilles." *Journal of Hellenic Studies* 105:11–31.
Harrington, D. J., ed. 1976. *Pseudo-Philo. Liber antiquitatum biblicarum*. Paris.
Harris, Z. S. 1936. *A Grammar of the Phoenician Language*. New Haven.
———. 1939. *Development of the Canaanite Dialects: An Investigation in Linguistic History*. New Haven.
Harrison, T., ed. 2008. *Cyprus, the Sea Peoples and the Eastern Mediterranean: Regional Perspectives of Continuity and Change*. Scripta Mediterranea 27–28. Toronto.
Hartmann, H. 1960. *Die Musik der sumerischen Kultur*. Frankfurt am Main.
Hava, J. G. 1964. *al-Faraid Arabic-English Dictionary*. Beirut.
Hawkins, J. D. 2000. *Corpus of Hieroglyphic Luwian Inscriptions*. Volume 1. Berlin.
———. 2009. "Cilicia, the Amuq, and Aleppo: New Light on a Dark Age." *Near Eastern Archaeology* 72/4:164–173.
Head, B. V. et al. 1911. *Historia numorum: A Manual of Greek Numismatics*. Oxford.
Healey, J. F. 1978. "MLKM/RP'UM and the Kispum." *Ugarit-Forschungen* 10:89–91.
Heckel, W. 2006. "Mazaeus, Callisthenes, and the Alexander Sarcophagus." *Historia* 55:385–396.
Heckel, W. and J. C. Yardley. 1997. *Epitome of the Philippic History of Pompeius Trogus: Books 11–12, Alexander the Great*. Oxford.
Heimpel, W. 1981. "The Nanshe Hymn." *Journal of Cuneiform Studies* 33:65–139.
———. 1995. "Plow Animal Inspection Records from Ur III Girsu and Umma." *Bulletin on Sumerian Agriculture* 8:71–171.
———. 1996. "The Gates of Eninnu." *Journal of Cuneiform Studies* 48:17–29.
———. 1997. "A Famous Harpist." *Nouvelles Assyriologiques Brèves et Utilitaires* 1997/4:126 no. 137.
———. 1998. "A Circumambulation Rite." *Acta Sumerologica* 20:13–16.
———. 1998. "Harp Gods." Unpublished paper circulated by author.
———. 2009. *Workers and Construction Work at Garšana*. Cornell Studies in Assyriology and Sumerology 5. Bethesda.
———. 2014. "LAK 41 and Sb 41." *Nouvelles Assyriologiques Brèves et Utilitaires* 2014/1:1–2 no. 1.

Heimpel, W., ed. 2011. *Strings and Threads: A Celebration of the Work of Anne Draffkorn Kilmer*. Winona Lake.

Helck, W. 1955. *Urkunden der 18. Dynastie, Heft 17. Historische Inschriften Thutmosis' III. und Amenophis' II.* Leipzig.

———. 1971. *Die Beziehungen Ägyptens zu Vorderasien im 3. und 2. Jahrtausend vor Christus.* 2nd ed. Wiesbaden.

———. 1989. "Grundsätzliches zur sog. 'Syllabischen Schreibung'." *Studien zur altägyptischen Kultur* 16:121–143.

Helm, R. 1984. *Die Chronik des Hieronymus*. Berlin.

Heltzer, M. 1982. *The Internal Organization of the Kingdom of Ugarit: Royal Service-System, Taxes, Royal Economy, Army and Administration*. Wiesbaden.

Hemmerdinger, B. 1970. "De la méconnaissance de quelques étymologies grecques." *Glotta* 48:40–66.

Henry, W. B. 2005. *Pindar's Nemeans: A Selection*. Munich.

Henshaw, R. A. 1993. *Female and Male: The Cultic Personnel, the Bible and the Rest of the Ancient Near East*. Princeton Theological Monograph Series 31. Allison Park.

Hercher, R. 1851. "Zu Apollodors Bibliothek." *Philologus* 6:571–575.

Herdner, A. 1963. *Corpus des tablettes en cunéiformes alphabétiques découvertes à Ras Shamra-Ugarit de 1929 à 1939*. Mission de Ras Shamra 10/Bibliotheque Archeologique et Historique 79. Paris.

———. 1978. "Nouveaux textes alphabétiques de Ras-Shamra—XXIVe campagne." In *Ugaritica 7*, ed. A.-I.-F. Al-Ouche, 1–74. Paris.

Hermary, A. 1989. *Musee du Louvre. Catalogue des antiquités de Chypre. Sculptures*. Paris.

Herrmann, W. 1973. "'ttrt-ḫr." *Die Welt des Orients* 7/1:135–136.

Herzog, R. 1899. *Koische Forschungen und Funde*. Leipzig.

Hespel, R. and R. Draguet. 1981–1982. *Livre des scolies: Recension de Séert*. Louvain.

Heubeck, A. 1958. "Griech. βασιλεύς und das Zeichen Nr. 16 in Linear B." *Indogermanische Forschungen* 63:113–138.

———. 1959. *Lydiaka: Untersuchungen zu Schrift, Sprache und Götternamen der Lyder*. Erlangen.

———. 1961. *Praegraeca: Sprachliche Untersuchungen zum vorgriechisch-indogermanischen Substrat*. Erlangen.

Heubner, H. 1963–1982. *P. Cornelius Tacitus. Die Historien: Kommentar.* 5 vols. Heidelberg.

Heyden, K. 2006. "Die christliche Geschichte des Philippos von Side: Mit einem kommentierten Katalog der Fragmente." In *Julius Africanus und die christliche Weltchronistik*, ed. M. Wallraff, 209–243. Berlin.

Heyne, C. G. 1803. *Ad Apollodori Bibliothecam observationes*. Göttingen.

Bibliography

Hickmann, E. et al., eds. 2000. *Musikarchäologie früher Metallzeiten: Vorträge des 1. Symposiums der International Study Group on Music Archaeology im Kloster Michaelstein, 18-24 Mai 1998*. Rahden.

Hickmann, E. et al., eds. 2002. *Archäologie früher Klangerzeugung und Tonordnungen*. Archäologie früher Klangerzeugung und Tonordnungen. Rahden.

Hickmann, E. et al., eds. 2006. *Musikarchäologie im Kontext: Archäologische Befunde, historische Zusammenhänge, soziokulturelle Beziehungen*. Studien zur Musikarchäologie 5/Orient-Archäologie 20. Rahden.

Hickmann, H. 1954a. "Dieux et déesses de la musique." *Cahiers d'Histoire Égyptienne* 6/1:31-59.

———. 1954b. "Le Métier de musicien." *Cahiers d'Histoire Égyptienne* 6/5-6:299-314.

———. 1961. "Ägypten und Vorderasien im musikalischen Austausch." *Zeitschrift der Deutschen Morgenländischen Gesellschaft* 111:23-41.

———. 1970. "Die Musik des arabisch-islamischen Bereichs." In Spuler 1970:1-134

Hicks, E. L. 1891. "Inscriptions from Western Cilicia." *Journal of Hellenic Studies* 12:225-273.

Higgins, R. A. and R. P. Winnington-Ingram. 1965. "Lute-Players in Greek Art." *Journal of Hellenic Studies* 85:62-71.

Hiller, S. 1979. "Ka-ko na-wi-o: Notes on Interdependence of Temple and Bronze in the Aegean Late Bronze Age." In Ernst and Mühlestein 1979:189-193.

Hiller von Gaertringen, F. et al., eds. 1906. *Inschriften von Priene*. Berlin.

Himmelhoch, L. 1990-1991. "The Use of the Ethnics a-ra-si-jo and ku-pi-ri-jo in Linear B Texts." *Minos* 25-26:91-104.

Hoch, J. E. 1994. *Semitic Words in Egyptian Texts of the New Kingdom and Third Intermediate Period*. Princeton.

Hoffman, G. 1896. "Aramäische Inschriften aus Nêrab bei Aleppo. Neue und alte Götter." *Zeitschrift für Assyriologie* 9:237-292.

Hoffner, H. A. 1967. "Second Millennium Antecedents to the Hebrew ʾÔḆ." *Journal of Biblical Literature* 86/4:385-401.

———. 1988. "The Song of Silver: A Member of the Kumarbi Cycle of 'Songs'." In *Documentum Asiae Minoris antiquae: Festschrift für Heinrich Otten zum 75. Geburtstag*, ed. E. Neu and C. Rüster, 143-166. Wiesbaden.

Hoffner, H. A. and G. M. Beckman. 1998. *Hittite Myths*. 2nd ed. Writings from the Ancient World 2. Atlanta.

Hofstra, S. 2000. *Small Things Considered: The Finds from LH IIIB Pylos in Context*. PhD diss., University of Texas at Austin.

Hoftijzer, J. and K. Jongeling. 1995. *Dictionary of the North-West Semitic Inscriptions*. Leiden.

Hogarth, D. G. 1889. *Devia Cypria: Notes of an Archaeological Journey in Cyprus in 1888*. London.

———. 1896. *A Wandering Scholar in the Levant*. 2nd ed. London.
Holmes, Y. L. 1971. "The Location of Alashiya." *Journal of the American Oriental Society* 91:426–429.
Holst-Warhaft, G. 1992. *Dangerous Voices: Women's Laments and Greek Literature*. London.
Honeyman, A. M. 1938. "*Larnax tēs Lapethou*: A Third Phoenician Inscription." *Le Muséon* 51:285–298.
Hopkins, D. 1985. "Nature's Laws and Man's: The Story of Cinyras and Myrrha in Ovid and Dryden." *The Modern Language Review* 80/4:786–801.
Horowitz, W. 1998. *Mesopotamian Cosmic Geography*. Mesopotamian Civilizations 8. Winona Lake.
———. 2006. "A Late Babylonian Tablet with Concentric Circles from the University Museum (CBS 1766)." *Journal of the Ancient Near Eastern Society* 30:37–53.
Horowitz, W. and S. Shnider. 2009. "Return to CBS 1766." *Nouvelles Assyriologiques Brèves et Utilitaires* 2009/1:7–9 no. 6.
Howard-Carter, T. 1987. "Dilmun: At Sea or Not at Sea?" *Journal of Cuneiform Studies* 39:57–117.
Hrozny, B. 1917. *Die Sprache der Hethiter: Ihr Bau und ihre Zugehörigkeit zum indogermanischen Sprachstamm: Ein Entzifferungsversuch*. Leipzig.
Houwink ten Cate, P. H. J. 1961. *The Luwian Population Groups of Lycia and Cilicia Aspera during the Hellenistic Period*. Leiden.
Hübner, U. 1992. "Der Tanz um die Ascheren." *Ugarit-Forschungen* 24:121–132.
Huehnergard, J. 2008. *Ugaritic Vocabulary in Syllabic Transcription*. Rev. ed. Winona Lake.
Huffmon, H. B. 1965. *Amorite Personal Names in the Mari Texts: A Structural and Lexical Study*. Baltimore.
Hutchinson, G. O. 2006. *Propertius, Elegies Book IV*. Cambridge.
Huxley, G. L. 1960. "Theopompos and Melia." *La Parola del Passato* 15:57–58.
———. 1966. *The Early Ionians*. New York.
Iacovou, M. 1988. *The Pictorial Pottery of Eleventh Century B.C. Cyprus*. Göteborg.
———. 1999. "The Greek Exodus to Cyprus: The Antiquity of Hellenism." *Mediterranean Historical Review* 14/2:1–28.
———. 2005. "Cyprus at the Dawn of the First Millenium BC: Cultural Homogenisation versus the Tyranny of Ethnic Identifications." In *Archaeological Perspectives on the Transmission and Transformation of Culture in the Eastern Mediterranean*, ed. J. Clarke, 125–134. Oxford.
———. 2006a. "From the Mycenaean QA-SI-RE-U to the Cypriote PA-SI-LE-WO-SE: The Basileus in the Kingdoms of Cyprus." In *Ancient Greece: From*

the Mycenaean Palaces to the Age of Homer, ed. S. Deger-Jalkotzy and I. S. Lemos, 315–335. Edinburgh.

———. 2006b. "'Greeks', 'Phoenicians' and 'Eteocypriots': Ethnic Identities in the Cypriote Kingdoms." In *'Sweet Land ... ': Lectures on the History and Culture of Cyprus*, ed. J. Chrysostomides and C. Dendrinos, 27–59. Camberley.

———. 2008. "Cyprus: From Migration to Hellenisation." In *Greek Colonization: An Account of Greek Colonies and Other Settlements Overseas*, ed. G. R. Tsetskhladze, 2:219–288. Leiden.

Ingholt, H. et al. 1955. *Recueil des tessères de Palmyre*. Bibliothèque archéologique et historique 58. Paris.

Ioannides, G. C., ed. 1992. *Studies in Honour of Vassos Karageorghis*. Leuosia.

Ivanov, V. V. 1999. "An Ancient Name of the Lyre." *Archiv Orientální* 67:585–600.

Jacobsen, T. 1973. "Notes on Nintur." *Orientalia* n.s. 42:274–298.

———. 1975. "Religious Drama in Ancient Mesopotamia." In *Unity and Diversity: Essays in the History, Literature, and Religion of the Ancient Near East*, ed. H. Goedicke and J. J. M. Roberts, 65–97. Baltimore.

———. 1987. *The Harps that Once ... Sumerian Poetry in Translation*. New Haven.

Jacobson, H. 1996. *A Commentary on Pseudo-Philo's Liber Antiquitatum Biblicarum: With Latin Text and English Translation*. Leiden.

Jager, R. M. 2000. "Traditionelle Musik auf Zypern." In *Zypern: Insel im Brennpunkt der Kulturen*, ed. S. Rogge, 269–284. Schriften des Instituts für Interdisziplinare Zypern-Studien 1. Münster.

James, M. R., ed. 1893. *Apocrypha anecdota: A Collection of Thirteen Apocryphal Books and Fragments Now First Edited from Manuscripts*. Texts and Studies: Contributions to Biblical and Patristic Literature 2.3. Cambridge.

James, P. and M. A. van der Sluijs. 2012. "'Silver': A Hurrian Phaethon." *Journal of Ancient Near Eastern Religions* 12/2:237–251.

Jan, K. von 1882. *Die griechischen Saiteninstrumente*. Leipzig.

Janko, R. 1982. *Homer, Hesiod, and the Hymns*. Cambridge.

Jasink, A. M. 2001. "Presenze micenee e greche nella Cilicia preclassica." In *ΠΟΙΚΙΛΜΑ, Studi in onore di Michele Cataudella*, ed. M. R. Cataudella and S. Bianchetti, 599–620. La Spezia.

———. 2010. "The Role of Cyprus and the Mycenaean/Greek Presence in the Island from the End of the Bronze Age to the First Phases of the Iron Age." *Studi Micenei ed Egeo-Anatolici* 52:149–167.

———. 2013. "The Göksu River Valley from Late Bronze to Iron Age: Local Cultures, External Influences, and Relations with Foreign Peoples." In *Rough Cilicia: New Historical and Archaeological Approaches*, ed. M. C. Hoff and R. F. Townsend, 12–26. Oxford.

Jasink, A. M. and M. Marino. 2007. "The West Anatolian Origins of the Que Kingdom Dynasty." *Studi Micenei ed Egeo-Anatolici* 49:407-426.
Jaussen, A. and R. Savignac. 1909-1920. *Mission archéologique en Arabie: Mars-mai 1907*. Paris.
Jean, C.-F. 1923. *Sumer et Akkad. Contribution a l'histoire de la civilisation dans la Basse-Mésopotamie*. Paris.
———. 1931. *La Religion sumérienne, d'après les documents sumériens antérieurs à la dynastie d'Isin (-2186)*. Paris.
Jenkins, J. 1969. "A Short Note on African Lyres in Use Today." *Iraq* 31/2:103 and pl. XVIII.
Jidejian, N. 1968. *Byblos through the Ages*. Beirut.
Jirku, A. 1960. "Gab es eine palästinisch-syrische Gottheit Kinneret?" *Zeitschrift für die alttestamentliche Wissenschaft* 72:69.
———. 1963. "Der kyprische Heros Kinyras und der syrische Gott Kinaru(m)." *Forschungen und Fortschritte* 37:211.
———. 1965. "Rapa'u, der Fürst der Rapa'uma-Rephaim." *Zeitschrift für die alttestamentliche Wissenschaft* 77:82-83.
Joannès, F. 1985. "Nouveaux mémorandums." In Durand and Kupper 1985:97-113.
Johnson, J. 1980. *Maroni de Chypre*. Studies in Mediterranean Archaeology 59. Göteborg.
Johnson, T. 2004. *A Symposion of Praise: Horace Returns to Lyric in Odes IV*. Madison.
Johnston, S. I., ed. 2004. *Religions of the Ancient World: A Guide*. Cambridge, MA.
Jones, G. H. 1990. *The Nathan Narratives*. Journal for the Study of the Old Testament, Supplement Series 80. Sheffield.
Jones, I. H. 1992. "Music and Musical Instruments." In Freedman 1992 4:930-939.
Jones, P. 2003. "Embracing Inana: Legitimation and Mediation in the Ancient Mesopotamian Sacred Marriage Hymn Iddin-Dagan A." *Journal of the American Oriental Society* 123/2:291-302.
Jones, T. B. and J. W. Snyder. 1961. *Sumerian Economic Texts from the Third Ur Dynasty*. Minneapolis.
Jost, M. 1985. *Sanctuaires et cultes d'Arcadie*. Paris.
Jouan, F. 1966. *Euripide et les legends des chants cypriens*. Paris.
Jugie, M. 1929-1930. "Poésies rhythmiques de Nicéphore Calliste Xanthopoulos." *Byzantion. Revue Internationale des Études Byzantines* 5:362-390.
K. Lawson Younger, J., ed. 2007. *Ugarit at Seventy-Five*. Winona Lake.
Kaizer, T. 2008. *The Variety of Local Religious Life in the Near East in the Hellenistic and Roman Periods*. Religions in the Graeco-Roman world 164. Leiden.
Kammenhuber, A. 1990. "Marduk und Santa in der hethitischen Überlieferung des 2. Jt.s v. Chr." *Orientalia* 59:188-195.
Kapera, Z. J. 1966. "Terakotowa flota Kinyrasa." *Filomata* 194:195-202.

Bibliography

———. 1969. "Die Terrakottaflotte des Kinyras." *Bibliotheca Classica Orientalis* 14:45–46.

———. 1970. "A Terracotta Model of a Sea-Barge." *Rozprawy i Sprawozdiana Muzeum Norodowego w Krakowie* 10:39–51.

———. 1971. "Kinyras and the Son of Mygdalion. Two Remarks on the Ancient Cypriot Onomastica." *Folia Orientalia* 13:130–142.

———. 1972. "Remarks on the Early History of the Kingdom of Paphos." In Karageorghis and Christodoulos 1972:191–199.

Karageorghis, J. 1977. *La Grande déesse de Chypre et son culte à travers l'iconographie de l'époque néolithique au VIème s.a.C.* Lyon.

———. 1988. "L'Apport des gloses à notre connaissance du dialecte chyprien ancien." In Karageorghis and Masson 1988:181–198.

———. 2005. *Kypris: The Aphrodite of Cyprus. Ancient Sources and Archaeological Evidence.* Nicosia.

Karageorghis, J. and V. Karageorghis. 2002. "The Great Goddess of Cyprus or the Genesis of Aphrodite in Cyprus." In Parpola and Whiting 2002 1:263–282.

Karageorghis, J. and O. Masson, eds. 1988. *The History of the Greek Language in Cyprus: Proceedings of an International Symposium sponsored by the Pierides Foundation, Larnaca, Cyprus, 8–13 September 1986.* Nicosia.

Karageorghis, V. 1960. "Chronique des fouilles à Chypre." *Bulletin de Correspondance Hellénique* 84/1:242–299.

———. 1967. *Excavations in the Necropolis of Salamis.* Salamis Volume 3. Nicosia.

———. 1969. *Salamis: Recent Discoveries in Cyprus.* New York.

———. 1976a. *The Civilization of Prehistoric Cyprus.* Athens.

———. 1976b. *Kition: Mycenaean and Phoenician Discoveries in Cyprus.* London.

———. ed. 1979. *Acts of the International Archaeological Symposium 'The Relations Between Cyprus and Crete, ca. 2000-500 B.C.': Nicosia, 16th April-22nd April 1978.* Nicosia.

———. 1980a. "Fouilles à l'Ancienne-Paphos de Chypre: Les Premiers colons grecs." *Comptes Rendus de l'Académie des Inscriptions et Belles-Lettres* 124/1:122–136.

———. 1980b. "Kypriaka V." *Report of the Department of Antiquities of Cyprus* 1980:128–135 and pl. 117–119.

———, ed. 1986. *Acts of the International Archaeological Symposium 'Cyprus between the Orient and the Occident,' Nicosia, 8–14 September 1985.* Nicosia.

———. 1993. "Erotica from Salamis." *Rivista di Studi Fenici* 21, Supplement:7–13.

———, ed. 1994. *Cyprus in the 11th Century B.C. Proceedings of the International Symposium Held at Nicosia, 30–31 October 1993.* Nicosia.

———. 1998. *Greek Gods and Heroes in Ancient Cyprus.* Athens.

———. 1999a. "A Cypriot Silver Bowl Reconsidered. I. The Iconography of the Decoration." *Metropolitan Museum Journal* 34:13–20.

———. 1999b. *Excavating at Salamis in Cyprus, 1952-1974*. Athens.

———. 2002a. *Ancient Art from Cyprus in the Collection of George and Nefeli Giabra Pierides*. Nicosia.

———. 2002b. *Early Cyprus, Crossroads of the Mediterranean*. Los Angeles.

———. 2003. *The Cyprus Collections in the Medelhavsmuseet*. Nicosia.

Karageorghis, V. and A. Christodoulos, eds. 1972. *Acts of the First International Congress of Cypriot Studies. Nicosia. April 14-19, 1969*. Nicosia.

Karageorghis, V. et al. 2000. *Ancient Art from Cyprus. The Cesnola Collection in The Metropolitan Museum of Art*. New York.

Karageorghis, V. and G. Papasavvas. 2001. "A Bronze Ingot-Bearer from Cyprus." *Oxford Journal of Archaeology* 20/4:339–354.

Kauhanen, T. 2012. *The Proto-Lucianic Problem in 1 Samuel*. Göttingen.

Kebede, A. 1968. "The Krar." *Ethiopian Observer* 11/3:154–161.

———. 1977. "The Bowl-Lyre of Northeast Africa. Krar: The Devil's Instrument." *Ethnomusicology* 21:379–395.

Keel, O. 1997. *Corpus der Stempelsiegel-Amulette aus Palästina/Israel: Von den Anfängen bis zur Perserzeit*. Orbis Biblicus et Orientalis 13. Freiburg.

———. 1998. *Goddesses and Trees, New Moon and Yahweh: Ancient Near Eastern Art and the Hebrew Bible*. Journal for the Study of the Old Testament Supplement Series 261. Sheffield.

Keel, O. and C. Uehlinger. 1998. *Gods, Goddesses, and Images of God in Ancient Israel*. Edinburgh.

Kern, O. 1922. *Orphicorum fragmenta*. Berlin.

Keswani, P. S. 1989. "Dimensions of Social Hierarchy in Late Bronze Age Cyprus: An Aanalysis of the Mortuary Data from Enkomi." *Journal of Mediterranean Archaeology* 2/1:49–86.

———. 1993. "Models of Local Exchange in Late Bronze Age Cyprus." *Bulletin of the American Schools of Oriental Research* 292:73–83.

———. 1996. "Hierarchies, Heterarchies, and Urbanization Processes: The View from Bronze Age Cyprus." *Journal of Mediterranean Archaeology* 9:211–250.

Khatzēiōannou, K. 1971–2001. *Hē arkhaia Kypros eis tas Hellēnikas pēgas*. Leukosia.

Killebrew, A. E. and G. Lehmann, eds. 2012. *The Philistines and Other 'Sea Peoples' in Text and Archaeology*. Archaeology and Biblical Studies 15. Atlanta.

Killen, J. T. 2000–2001. "A Note on Pylos Tablet Un1482." *Minos* 35–6:385–390.

———. 2008. "Mycenaean Economy." In *A Companion to Linear B: Mycenaean Greek Texts and Their World*, ed. Y. Duhoux and A. M. Davies, 159–200. Louvain-la-Neuve.

Bibliography

Kilmer, A. D. 1965. "The Strings of Musical Instruments: Their Names, Numbers and Significance." In Güterbock and Jacobsen 1965:261–268.

———. 1971. "The Discovery of an Ancient Mesopotamian Theory of Music." *Proceedings of the American Philosophical Society* 115:131–149.

Kimmel-Clauzet, F. 2013. *Morts, tombeaux et cultes des poètes grecs: Étude de la survie des grands poètes des époques archaïque et classique en Grèce ancienne.* Bordeaux.

Kindiy, O. 2008. *Christos Didaskalos: The Christology of Clement of Alexandria.* Saarbrücken.

King, P. J. 1989. "The Marzeah: Textual and Archaeological Evidence." *Eretz-Israel: Archaeological, Historical and Geographical Studies* 20:98–106.

Kinlaw, D. F. 1967. *A Study of the Personal Names in the Akkadian Texts from Ugarit.* PhD diss., Brandeis University.

Kirk, G. S. 1954. *Heraclitus: The Cosmic Fragments.* Cambridge.

Kirst, S. 1956. "Kinyras, König von Kypros, und El Schöpfer der Erde." *Forschungen und Fortschritte* 30:185–189.

Kitchen, K. A. 1977. "The King List of Ugarit." *Ugarit-Forschungen* 9:131–142.

———. 2008. *Ramesside Inscriptions Translated & Annotated. Vol. V: Setnakht, Ramesses III and Contermporaries.* Oxford.

Klein, J. 1981. *Three Šulgi Hymns. Sumerian Royal Hymns Glorifying King Šulgi of Ur.* Ramat-Gan.

———. 1990. "Šulgi and Išmedagan: Originality and Dependence in Sumerian Royal Hymnology." In Klein and Skaist 1990:65–136.

———. 1993. "Additional Notes to 'The Marriage of Martu'." In *kinattūtu ša dārâti. Raphael Kutscher Memorial Volume*, ed. A. F. Rainey, 93–106. Tel Aviv.

———. 1996. "The Marriage of Martu. The Urbanization of 'Barbaric' Nomads." In *Mutual Influences of Peoples and Cultures in the Ancient Near East*, ed. M. Malul, 83–96. Haifa.

———. 1997. "The God Martu in Sumerian Literature." In Finkel and Geller 1997:99–116.

Klein, J. and A. Skaist, eds. 1990. *Bar-Ilan Studies in Assyriology Dedicated to Pinhas Artzi.* Ramat-Gan.

Kleingünther, A. 1933. *Prōtos Heuretēs.* Philologus Supplementband 27. Leipzig.

Kleinig, J. W. 1993. *The Lord's Song: The Basis, Function, and Significance of Choral Music in Chronicles.* Sheffield.

Klinger, J. 1996. *Untersuchungen zur Rekonstruktion der hattischen Kultschicht.* Wiesbaden.

Knapp, A. B. 1979. *A Re-examination of the Interpretation of Cypriote Material Culture in the MCIII-LCI Period in the Light of Textual Data.* PhD diss., University of California, Berkeley.

———. 1980. "KBo I 26: Alašiya and Hatti." *Journal of Cuneiform Studies* 32:43–47.

———. 1983. "An Alashiyan Merchant at Ugarit." *Tel Aviv* 10:38–45.

———. 1985. "Alashiya, Caphtor/Keftiu, and Eastern Mediterranean Trade: Recent Studies in Cypriote Archaeology and History." *Journal of Field Archaeology* 12/2:231–250.

———. 1986. "Production, Exchange and Socio-Political Compexity on Bronze Age Cyprus." *Oxford Journal of Archaeology* 5:53–60.

———. 1986. *Copper Production and Divine Protection: Archaeology, Ideology, and Social Complexity on Bronze Age Cyprus*. Göteborg.

———. 1988. "Copper Production and Eastern Mediterranean Trade: The Rise of Complex Society on Cyprus." In *State and Society: The Emergence and Development of Social Hierarchy and Political Centralization*, ed. J. Gledhill et al., 149–169. London.

———. 1991. "Spice, Drugs, Grain, and Grog: Organic Goods in Bronze Age East Mediterranean Trade." In *Bronze Age Trade in the Aegean*, ed. N. H. Gale, 21–68. Jonsered.

———. 1993. "Thalassocracies in Bronze Age Eastern Mediterranean Trade: Making and Breaking a Myth." *World Archaeology* 24/3:332–347.

———. 1997. *The Archaeology of Late Bronze Age Cypriot Society: The Study of Settlement, Survey and Landscape*. Glasgow.

———. 2006. "Orientalization and Prehistoric Cyprus: The Social Life of Oriental Goods." In *Debating Orientalization. Multidisciplinary Approaches to Change in the Ancient Mediterranean*, ed. C. Riva and N. C. Vella, 48–68. Monographs in Mediterranean Archaeology 10. London.

———. 2011. "Sound of Silence: Music and Musical Practice in Late Bronze-Iron Age Cyprus." In Heimpel 2011:121–132.

———. 2011. "Cyprus, Copper and Alashiya." In Betancourt and Ferrence 2011:249–254.

———. 2013. *The Archaeology of Cyprus: From Earliest Prehistory through the Bronze Age*. Cambridge.

Knapp, A. B. and A. Marchant. 1982. "Cyprus, Cypro-Minoan, and Hurrians." *Report of the Department of Antiquities of Cyprus* 1982:15–30.

Knudtzon, J. A. 1907–1915. *Die El-Amarna-Tafeln*. 2 vols. Vorderasiatische Bibliothek 2. Leipzig.

Köcher, F. 1963–1980. *Die babylonisch-assyrische Medizin in Texten und Untersuchungen*. 6 vols. Berlin.

Köhler, L. and W. Baumgartner. 1994–2000. *The Hebrew and Aramaic Lexicon of the Old Testament*. Leiden.

Koitabashi, M. 1992. "The Deification of the 'Lyre' in Ancient Ugarit." *Orient* 28:106–110.

Bibliography

———. 1992. "Significance of Ugaritic msltm 'Cymbals' in the Anat Text." In *Cult and Ritual in the Ancient Near East*, ed. T. Mikasa, 1–5. Wiesbaden.

———. 1996. "Musicians in the Ugaritic Texts." In *Essays on Ancient Anatolia and Syria in the Second and Third Millenium B.C.*, ed. T. Mikasa, 221–232. Wiesbaden.

———. 1998. "Music in the Texts from Ugarit." *Ugarit-Forschungen* 30:363–396.

———. 2012. "Ashtart in the Mythological and Ritual Texts of Ugarit." *Bulletin of the Society for Near Eastern Studies in Japan* 55/2:53–62.

Kolotourou, K. 2002. "Images of Sound: Music Performances and the Lyre Player Motif in Early Iron Age Art." In *SOMA 2001. Symposium on Mediterranean Archaeology. Proceedings of the Fifth Annual Meeting of Postgraduate Researchers, The University of Liverpool, 23-25 February 2001*, ed. G. Muskett et al., 215–222. British Archaeological Reports, International Series 1040. Oxford.

———. 2005. "Music and Cult: The Significance of Percussion and the Cypriote Connection." In *Cyprus: Religion and Society from the Late Bronze Age to the End of the Archaic Period: Proceedings of an International Symposium on Cypriote Archaeology, Erlangen, 23-24 July 2004*, ed. V. Karageorghis et al., 183–204. Möhnesee.

———. 2007. "Rattling Jewellery and the Cypriot Coroplast." *Archaeologia Cypria (Κυπριακή Ἀρχαιολογία)* 5:79–99.

Kouremenos, T. et al. 2006. *The Derveni Papyrus*. Florence.

Krahmalkov, C. R. 2000. *Phoenician-Punic Dictionary*. Leuven.

———. 2001. *A Phoenician-Punic Grammar*. Leiden.

Kramer, S. N. 1963. "Cuneiform Studies and the History of Literature: The Sumerian Sacred Marriage Texts." *Proceedings of the American Philosophical Society* 107:485–527.

———. 1969. *The Sacred Marriage Rite. Aspects of Faith, Myth, and Ritual in Ancient Sumer*. London.

———. 1981. "BM 29616: The Fashioning of the Gala." *Acta Sumerologica* 3:1–11.

———. 1985. "BM 86535: A Large Extract of a Diversified Balag-Composition." In Durand and Kupper 1985:115–135.

———. 1987. "By the Rivers of Babylon: A Balag-Liturgy of Inanna." *Aula Orientalis* 5:71–90.

———. 1990. "The Marriage of Martu." In Klein and Skaist 1990:11–27.

———. 1991. "Solomon and Šulgi: A Comparative Portrait." In Cogan and Eph'al 1991:189–195.

Krappe, A. H. 1941–1942. "The Birth of Adonis." *Review of Religion* 6:3–17.

Krauss, S. 1910–1912. *Talmudische Archäologie*. Leipzig.

Krebernik, M. 1983. "Zu Syllabar und Orthographie der lexikalischen Texte aus Ebla. Teil 2." *Zeitschrift für Assyriologie* 73:1–47.

———. 1986. "Die Götterlisten aus Fara." *Zeitschrift für Assyriologie* 76:161–204.

Krecher, J. 1966. *Sumerische Kultlyrik*. Wiesbaden.

Krencker, D. and W. Zschietzschmann. 1938. *Römische Tempel in Syrien, nach Aufnahmen und Untersuchungen von Mitgliedern der Deutschen Baalbekexpedition 1901-1904*. Berlin.

Krispijn, T. J. H. 1990. "Beitrage zur altorientalischen Musikforschung 1. Šulgi und die Musik." *Akkadica* 70:1–27.

———. 2010. "Musical Ensembles in Ancient Mesopotamia." In Dumbrill and Finkel 2010:125–150.

———. 2011. "The Acceptance of Pop Music in Mesopotamia: The Mesopotamian Lute of the Second Millennium B.C. and Its Socio-Cultural Context." In *Proceedings of the International Conference of Near Eastern Archaeomusicology held at Senate House, University of London, December 1, 2 and 3, 2011*, ed. R. Dumbrill and I. L. Finkel, 113–126. London.

Kronasser, H. 1963. *Die Umsiedelung der schwarzen Gottheit: Das hethitische Ritual KUB XXIX 4 (des Ulippi)*. Vienna.

Kuhrt, A. 1995. *The Ancient Near East*. 2 vols. London.

Kurke, L. 1991. *The Traffic in Praise: Pindar and the Poetics of Social Economy*. Ithaca.

Kurtz, D. C. and J. Boardman. 1971. *Greek Burial Customs*. London.

Kushnareva, K. 2000. "Some Evidence of Musical Instruments in Bronze Age Caucasus." In Hickmann et al. 2000:103–112. Rahden.

Lafont, B. and F. Yildiz. 1989. *Tablettes cunéiformes de Tello au Musée d'Istanbul: Datant de l'époque de la IIIe Dynastie d'Ur. Tome I*. Uitgaven van het Nederlands Historisch-Archaeologisch Instituut te İstanbul 65. Leiden.

Lambert, R. 1984. *Beloved and God: The Story of Hadrian and Antinous*. New York.

Lambert, W. G. 1982. "The Hymn to the Queen of Nippur." In *Zikir Šumim: Assyriological Studies Presented to F. R. Kraus on the Occasion of His Seventieth Birthday*, ed. G. van Driel, 173–218. Leiden.

———. "A List of Gods' Names." In Durand and Kupper 1985:181–189.

———. 1990. "Ancient Mesopotamian Gods: Superstition, Philosophy, Theology." *Revue de l'Histoire des Religions* 207:115–130.

Landi, C. 1930. *Demogòrgone. Con saggio di nuova edizione delle "Genologie [sic] deorum gentilium" del Boccaccio e silloge dei frammenti di Teodonzio*. Palermo.

Lane, E. W. 1980. *An Arabic-English Lexicon*. Beirut.

Lane Fox, R. 1980. *The Search for Alexander*. Boston.

Lanfranchi, G. B. 2005. "The Luwian-Phoenician Bilingual of Çineköy and the Annexation of Cilicia to the Assyrian Empire." In Rollinger 2005:481–496.

Lang, M. 1969. *The Palace of Nestor at Pylos, II. The Frescoes*. Princeton.

Bibliography

Langdon, S. 1919. "Two Sumerian Liturgical Texts." *Revue d'Assyriologie et d'Archéologie Orientale* 16/4:207–209.

———. 1931. *The Mythology of All Races. V. Semitic*. Boston.

———. 1935. *Babylonian Menologies and the Semitic Calendars*. London.

Lapinkivi, P. 2004. *The Sumerian Sacred Marriage in the Light of Comparative Evidence*. State Archives of Assyria Studies 15. Helsinki.

Lardinois, A. P. 2001. "Keening Sappho: Female Speech Genre's in Sappho's Poetry." In *Making Silence Speak: Women's Voices in Greek Literature and Society*, ed. A. Lardinois and L. McClure, 75–92. Princeton.

Laroche, E. 1948. "Teššub, Ḫebat et leur cour." *Journal of Cuneiform Studies* 2:113–136.

———. 1955. "Études de vocabulaire V." *Revue Hittite et Asianique* 13/57:72–74.

———. 1968. "Documents en langue hourrite provenant de Ras Shamra." In Nougayrol et al. 1968:447–544.

———. 1976-1977. "Glossaire de la langue hourrite." *Revue Hittite et Asianique* 34–35:13–161, 159–323.

Lassus, J. 1935. *Inventaire archéologique de la région au nord-est de Hama*. 2 vols. Documents d'Études Orientales 4. Damas.

Latte, K. 1953–1956. *Hesychii Alexandrini Lexicon*. Copenhagen.

Lavagnini, B. 1950. *Studi sul romanzo greco*. Messina.

Lawergren, B. 1984. "The Cylinder Kithara in Etruria, Greece, and Anatolia." *Imago Musicae* 1:147–174.

———. 1985. "A Lyre Common to Etruria, Greece, and Anatolia: The Cylinder Kithara." *Acta Musicologica* 57:25–33.

———. 1993. "Lyres in the West (Italy, Greece) and the East (Egypt, the Near East), ca. 2000–400 b.c." *Opuscula Romana* 19/6:55–76.

Lawergren, B. and O. R. Gurney. 1987. "Sound Holes and Geometrical Figures: Clues to the Terminology of Ancient Mesopotamian Harps." *Iraq* 49:37–52.

Lawson, G. 2004. "Music, Intentionality, and Tradition: Identifying Purpose, and Continuity of Purpose, in the Music-Archaeological Record." In *Music Archeological Sources: Artifacts, Oral Tradition, Written Evidence*, ed. E. Hickmann and R. Eichmann, 61–97. Studien zur Musikarchäologie 4/Orient-Archäologie 15. Rahden.

———. 2006. "Sites, Landscapes and 'Portable Antiquities'. The Nature and Value of Context in the Music-Archaeological Record." In Hickmann et al. 2006:3–14.

———. 2008. "Conserving the Future of Music's Distant Past Some Thoughts on the Development of Music-Archaeological Conservation." In *Challenges and Objectives in Music Archaeology. Papers from the 5th Symposium of the International Study Group on Music Archaeology at the Ethnological Museum,*

State Museums Berlin, 19–23 September, 2006, ed. E. Hickmann et al., 389–400. Studien zur Musikarchäologie 6/Orient-Archäologie 22. Rahden.

Laymon, C. M., ed. 1971. *The Interpreter's One Volume Commentary on the Bible*. Nashville.

Leaf, W. 1900–1902. *The Iliad. Edited, with Apparatus Criticus, Prolegomena, Notes, and Appendices*. 2 vols. London and New York.

Lebek, W. D. 1973. "Ein Hymnus auf Antinoos (Mitford, the Inscriptions of Kourion No. 104)." *Zeitschrift für Papyrologie und Epigraphik* 12:101–137.

Lee, A. W. 2004. "Dryden's 'Cinyras and Myrrha'." *Explicator* 62/3:141–144.

Lefèvre-Novaro, D. 2007. "La Danse dans les modèles réduits des âges du Bronze et du Fer en Égée et à Chypre." *Ktema: Civilisations de l'Orient, de la Grèce et de Rome Antique* 32:57–63.

Leibovitch, J. 1960. "The Statuette of an Egyptian Harper and String-Instruments in Egyptian Statuary." *Journal of Egyptian Archaeology* 46:53–59.

Leigh, M. 1994. "Servius on Vergil's *Senex Corycius*: New Evidence." *Materiali e Discussioni per l'Analisi dei Testi Classici* 33:181–195.

Leithart, P. J. 2003. *From Silence to Song: The Davidic Liturgical Revolution*. Moscow, Idaho.

Lejeune, M. 1958. *Memoires de philologie mycénienne. Première série (1955–1957)*. Paris.

———. 1964. *Index inverse du grec mycénien*. Paris.

Lemaire, A. 1996. "Les Textes prophétiques de Mari dans leurs relations avec l'Ouest." In *Amurru 1. Mari, Ebla et les Hourrites: Dix ans de travaux. Actes du colloque international (Paris, mai 1993)*, ed. J.-M. Durand, 427–438. Paris.

Lemerle, P. 1986. *Byzantine Humanism: The First Phase: Notes and Remarks on Education and Culture in Byzantium from Its Origins to the 10th Century*. Canberra.

Lenchantin, M. 1932. "Nuovi frammenti di Filocoro." *Rivista di Filologia e di Istruzione Classica* 10:41–58.

Lenormant, F. 1871–1872. *Lettres assyriologiques sur l'histoire et les antiquités de l'Asie antérieure*. 2 vols. Paris.

Leonhard, C. 2001. "Ishodad of Merw's Exegesis of the Psalms 119 and 139–147." Corpus scriptorum Christianorum Orientalium 585, Subsidia 107. Louvain.

Leukart, A. 1979. "Autour de ka-ko na-wi-jo: Quelques critères." In Risch and Mühlestein 1979:183–188.

———. 1994. *Die frühgriechischen Nomina auf -tās und -ās: Untersuchungen zu ihrer Herkunft und Ausbreitung (unter Vergleich mit den Nomina auf -eús)*. Vienna.

Leumann, M. 1950. *Homerische Wörter*. Basel.

Levaniouk, O. 1999. "Penelope and the *Pênelops*." In *Nine Essays on Homer*, ed. M. Carlisle and O. Levaniouk, 95–136. Lanham.

Levenson, J. D. 1985. "A Technical Meaning for nʿm in the Hebrew Bible." *Vetus Testamentum* 35/1:61–67.
Levine, B. A. 1963a. "The Netînîm." *Journal of Biblical Literature* 82/2:207–212.
———. 1963b. "Ugaritic Descriptive Rituals." *Journal of Cuneiform Studies* 17/4:105–111.
———. 1983. "The Descriptive Ritual Texts from Ugarit: Some Formal and Functional Features of the Genre." In *The Word of the Lord Shall Go Forth: Essays in Honor of David Noel Freedman in Celebration of his Sixtieth Birthday*, ed. C. L. Meyers and M. O'Connor, 467–475. Winona Lake.
Levine, B. A. and J.-M. de Tarragon. 1984. "Dead Kings and Rephaim: The Patrons of the Ugaritic Dynasty." *Journal of the American Oriental Society* 104/4:649–659.
Levy, M. A. 1864. "Die palmyrenischen Inschriften." *Zeitschrift der Deutschen Morgenländischen Gesellschaft* 18:66–117.
Lewis, T. 1989. *Cults of the Dead in Ugarit and Israel*. Harvard Semitic Monographs 39. Atlanta.
Lewy, H. 1895. *Die semitischen Fremdwörter im Griechischen*. Berlin.
Li Castro, E. and P. Scardina. 2011. "The Double Curve Enigma." *Music in Art* 36/1–2:203–217.
Lichtenstein, M. H. 1972. "Psalm 68:7 Revisited." *Journal of the Ancient Near Eastern Society* 4/2:97–112.
Lichtheim, M. 1945. "The Songs of the Harpers." *Journal of Near Eastern Studies* 4/3:178–212.
———. 1973. *Ancient Egyptian Literature: A Book of Readings*. Berkeley.
Lieberman, S. 1942. *Greek in Jewish Palestine: Studies in the Life and Manners of Jewish Palestine in the II-IV Centuries C.E.* New York.
Liebowitz, H. A. 1967. "Horses in New Kingdom Art and the Date of an Ivory from Megiddo." *Journal of the American Research Center in Egypt* 6:129–134.
Lightfoot, J. L. 1999. *Parthenius of Nicaea: The Poetical Fragments and the Erōtika pathēmata*. Oxford.
———. 2004. "The Apology of Ps.-Meliton." *Studi Epigrafici e Linguistici sul Vicino Oriente Antico* 24:59–110.
———. 2009. "Ps.-Meliton and the Cults of the Roman Near East." In *Les Religions orientales dans le monde grec et romain: Cent ans après Cumont (1906-2006). Bilan historique et historiographique; Colloque de Rome, 16-18 Novembre 2006*, ed. C. Bonnet et al., 387–400. Brussels.
———. 2014. *Dionysius Periegetes: Description of the Known World*. Oxford.
Limet, H. 1960. *Le Travail du métal au pays de Sumer au temps de la IIIe dynastie d'Ur*. Bibliothèque de la Faculté de Philosophie et Lettres de l'Université de Liège, fasc. 155. Paris.

———. 1976. *Textes administratifs de l'époque des šakkanakku*. Archives Royales de Mari 19. Paris.

———. 1986. *Textes administratifs relatifs aux métaux*. Archives Royales de Mari 25. Paris.

Linssen, M. J. H. 2004. *The Cults of Uruk and Babylon The Temple Ritual Texts as Evidence for Hellenistic Cult Practice*. Leiden.

Lipiński, E. 1977. "An Ugaritic Letter to Amenophis III concerning Trade with Alašiya." *Iraq* 39:213–217.

———. 1978. "Ditanu." In *Studies in the Bible and the Ancient Near East Presented to Samuel E. Loewenstamm on his Seventieth Birthday*, ed. Y. Avishur and J. Blau, 2 vols. 1:91–110. Jerusalem.

———, ed. 1987a. *Phoenicia and the East Mediterranean in the First Millennium B.C.* Orientalia Lovaniensia Analecta 22/Studia Phoenicia 5. Leuven.

———. 1987b. "Resheph Amyklos." In Lipiński 1987a:87–99.

———. 1991. "The Cypriot Vassals of Esarhaddon." In Cogan and Eph'al 1991:58–64.

———. 2004. *Itineraria Phoenicia*. Leuven.

———. 2009. *Resheph: A Syro-Canaanite Deity*. Orientalia Lovaniensia Analecta 181/Studia Phoenicia 19. Leuven.

Litke, R. L. 1998. *A Reconstruction of the Assyro-Babylonian God-Lists, AN:dA-nu-um and AN:Anu šá amēli*. New Haven.

Liverani, M. 1971. "Sydyk e Misor." In *Studi in onore di Edoardo Volterra*, ed. s.n., 6 vols. 6:55–74. Milan.

———. 1990. *Prestige and Interest: International Relations in the Near East ca. 1600-1100 B.C.* History of the Ancient Near East. Studies 1. Padua.

———. 1997. "Bronze Production in Byblos." *Nouvelles Assyriologiques Brèves et Utilitaires* 1997/4:122–123 no. 131.

Livingstone, A. 1986. *Mystical and Mythological Explanatory Works of Assyrian and Babylonian Scholars*. Oxford.

———. 1989. *Court Poetry and Literary Miscellanea*. State Archives of Assyria 3. Helsinki.

Llewellyn-Jones, L. 2013. *King and Court in Ancient Persia, 559 to 331 BCE*. Edinburgh.

Lloyd-Jones, H. 1973. "Modern Interpretation of Pindar: The Second Pythian and Seventh Nemean Odes." *Journal of Hellenic Studies* 93:109–137.

Löhnert, A. 2009. *"Wie die Sonne tritt heraus": Eine Klage zum Auszug Enlils mit einer Untersuchung zu Komposition und Tradition sumerischer Klagelieder in altbabylonischer Zeit*. Alter Orient und Altes Testament 365. Münster.

Lokkegaard, F. 1954. "Some Comments on the Sanchuniathon Tradition." *Studia Theologica* 8/1:51–76.

Long, C. R. 1974. *The Haghia Triadha Sarcophagus*. Studies in Mediterranean Archaeology 41. Göteborg.

López-Ruiz, C. 2009. "Mopsos and Cultural Exchange between Greeks and Locals in Cilicia." In *Ancient Myth. Media, Transformations and Sense-Constructions*, ed. U. Dill and C. Walde, 487–501. Berlin.

———. 2010. *When the Gods Were Born: Greek Cosmogonies and the Near East*. Cambridge, MA.

Loretz, O. 1984. "adn come epiteto di Baal e i suoi rapporti con Adonis e Adonaj." In s.n. 1984:25–33.

Lorimer, H. 1950. *Homer and the Monuments*. London.

Loucas-Durie, E. 1989. "Kinyras et la sacralisation de la fonction technique à Chypre." *Métis* 4/1:117–127.

Loud, G. 1936. "News from Armageddon." *The Illustrated London News, 20 June* 1008–1111.

———. 1939. *The Megiddo Ivories*. Chicago.

Lowenstamm, S. 1969. "'The Lord is my Strength and my Glory'." *Vetus Testamentum* 19:464–470.

Ludwig, M.-C. 1990. *Untersuchungen zu den Hymnen des Isme-Dagan von Isin*. Santag 2. Wiesbaden.

Lupack, S. 2007. "Palaces, Sanctuaries, and Workshops: The Role of the Religious Sector in Mycenaean Economics." In Galaty and Parkinson 2007:54–65.

———. 2008a. "The Northeast Building of Pylos and An 1281." In Sacconi et al. 2008:467–484.

———. 2008b. *The Role of the Religious Sector in the Economy of Late Bronze Age Mycenaean Greece*. British Archaeological Reports, International Series 1858. Oxford.

Lyne, R. O. A. M. 1978. *Ciris: A Poem Attributed to Vergil*. Cambridge.

Machinist, P. 1983a. "Rest and Violence in the Poem of Erra." *Journal of the American Oriental Society* 103:221–226.

———. 1983b. "Assyria and Its Image in the First Isaiah." *Journal of the American Oriental Society* 103:719–737.

———. 1993. "Assyrians on Assyria in the First Millennium B.C." In *Anfänge politischen Denkens in der Antike: Die nahöstlichen Kulturen und die Griechen*, ed. K. Raaflaub, 135–144. Munich.

———. 2000. "Biblical Traditions: The Philistines and Israelite History." In Oren 2000:53–83. Philadelphia.

Maeda, T. 1981. "'King of Kish' in Pre-Sargonic Sumer." *Orient* 17:1–17.

Maier, F. G. 1974. "Excavations at Kouklia (Palaepaphos)." *Report of the Department of Antiquities of Cyprus* 1974:132–138.

———. 1979. "The Paphian Shrine of Aphrodite and Crete." In Karageorghis 1979:228–234.

———. 1983. "New Evidence for the Early History of Palaepaphos-Skales." In *Palaepaphos-Skales: An Iron Age Cemetery in Cyprus*, ed. V. Karageorghis, 229–233. Constance.

———. 1985. "Factoids in Ancient History: The Case of Fifth-Century Cyprus." *Journal of Hellenic Studies* 105:32–39.

———. 1986. "Kinyras and Agapenor." In Karageorghis 1986:311–320.

———. 1989. "Priest Kings in Cyprus." In Peltenburg 1989:376–391.

———. 1996. "History from the Earth: The Kingdom of Paphos in the Achaemenid Period." *Transeuphratène* 12:376–391.

Malamat, A. 1999. "Amorrite Musicians at Mari." *Nouvelles Assyriologiques Brèves et Utilitaires* 1999/2:49–50 no. 46.

———. 2003. "Musicians from Hazor and Mari." In s.n. 2003:355–357.

Malbran-Labat, F. 1999. "Nouvelles donées épigraphiques sur Chypre et Ougarit." *Report of the Department of Antiquities of Cyprus* 1999:121–123.

Maliaras, N. 2007. Βυζαντινά μουσικά όργανα. Athens.

Malkin, I. 1998. *The Returns of Odysseus: Colonization and Ethnicity*. Berkeley.

Mallowan, M. E. L. 1966. *Nimrud and Its Remains*. 2 vols. London.

Mander, P. 1988. "Sumerian Personal Names in Ebla." *Journal of the American Oriental Society* 108/3:481–483.

Manniche, L. 1971. "Les Scènes de musique sur les talatat du IXe pylone de Karnak." *Kêmi* 21:155–164.

———. 1976. *Musical Instruments from the Tomb of Tut'ankhamūn*. Tut'ankhamūn's Tomb Series VI. Oxford.

———. 1978. "Symbolic Blindness." *Chronique d'Égypte* 53:13–21.

———. 1989. "À la cour d'Akhenaton et de Nefertiti." *Les Dossiers d'Archéologie* 142:24–32.

———. 2000. "Musical Practises at the Court of Akhenaten and Nefertiti." In Hickmann et al. 2000:233–238.

———. 2006. "Angular Harps of the Amarna Period." *Journal of Egyptian Archaeology* 92:248–249.

Marcetteau, M. 2010. "A Queen's Orchestra at the Court of Mari: New Perspectives on the Archaic Instrumentarium in the Third Millennium." In Dumbrill and Finkel 2010:67–75.

Marchesi, G. and N. Marchetti. 2011. *Royal Statuary of Early Dynastic Mesopotamia*. Mesopotamian Civilizations 14. Winona Lake.

Margalit, B. 1972. "The Kôšārôt/kṯrt: Patroness-Saints of Women." *Journal of the Ancient Near Eastern Society* 4/1:52–61.

Bibliography

———. 1984. "Lexicographical Notes on the Aqht Epic (Part II: KTU 1.19)." *Ugarit-Forschungen* 16:119–179.

———. 1989. *The Ugaritic Poem of AQHT: Text, Translation, Commentary*. Berlin.

Markoe, G. 1988. "A Funerary Ritual on Two Cypriot Vases." *Report of the Department of Antiquities of Cyprus* 1988:19–24 and pl. VI.12.

———. 2003. "Phoenician Metalwork Abroad: A Question of Export or On-site Production?" In *Ploes/Sea Routes: Interconnections in the Mediterranean, 16th-6th c. BC. Proceedings of the International Symposium held at Rethymnon, Crete, September 29th-October 2nd, 2002*, ed. N. C. Stampolidis and V. Karageorghis, 209–216. Athens.

Markou, E. 2006. "Problèmes iconographiques du monnoyage d'or des derniers rois de Salamine au IVe siècle avant J.-C." In Fourrier and Grivaud 2006:135–152.

Marquand, A. 1887. "A Silver Patera from Kourion." *American Journal of Archaeology and the History of the Fine Arts* 3:322–337.

Marshall, K., ed. 1993. *Rediscovering the Muses: Women's Musical Traditions*. Boston.

Martelli, M. C. 1988. "La Stipe votive di Jalisos: Un Primo bilancio." In *Archaeology in the Dodecannese*, ed. S. Dietz and I. Papachristodoulou, 104–120. Copenhagen.

Martin, R. P. 1984. "Hesiod, Odysseus and the Instruction of Princes." *Transactions of the American Philological Association* 114:29–48.

———. 1989. *The Language of Heroes: Speech and Performance in the Iliad*. Ithaca.

———. 2003. "The Pipes are Brawling: Conceptualizing Musical Performance in Athens." In *The Cultures within Ancient Greek Culture: Contact, Conflict, Collaboration*, ed. C. Dougherty and L. Kurke, 153–180. Cambridge.

Martinelli, M. C. et al. 2009. *La Musa dimenticata: Aspetti dell'esperienza musicale greca in età ellenistica*. Pisa.

Mas Latrie, L. de 1852–1861. *Histoire de l'île de Chypre sous le règne des princes de la maison de Lusignan*. Paris.

Masson, D. 1958. *Le Coran et la révélation judéo-chrétienne: Études comparées*. 2 vols. Paris.

Masson, E. 1974. *Cyprominoica. Répertoires, documents de Ras Shamra, essais d'interprétation*. Studies in Mediterranean Archaeology 31.2. Göteborg.

Masson, O. 1968. "L'Émission de Nikokles de Paphos au type d'Apollon sur l'omphalos." *Opuscula Atheniensia* 8:116–118.

———. 1973. "Remarques sur les cultes chypriotes à l'époque du Bronze Recent." In *The Mycenaeans in the Eastern Mediterranean. Acts of the International Archaeological Symposium*, ed. V. Karageorghis, 110–121. Nicosia.

———. 1980. "Une Nouvelle inscription de Paphos concernant le roi Nikoklès." *Kadmos* 19:65–80.

———. 1986. "Vocabulaire grec et épigraphie: ἀρχός, 'chef, archonte'." In Etter 1986:450–457.

———. 1988a. "Le Dialecte de Paphos." In Karageorghis and Masson 1988:19–30.

———. 1988b. "L'Inscription syllabique en paphien recent du village de Tala (Paphos)." *Report of the Department of Antiquities of Cyprus* 1988:63–68.

———. 1991. "Notes de numismatique chypriote." *Revue Numismatique* 33:60–70.

———. 1992. "Encore les royaumes chypriotes dans la liste d'Essarhaddon." *Cahiers du Centre d'Études Chypriotes* 18:27–30.

Masson, O. and M. Sznycer. 1972. *Recherches sur les Phéniciens à Chypre*. Geneva.

Mathews, E. G. 1998. *The Armenian Commentary on Genesis Attributed to Ephrem the Syrian*. Corpus scriptorum Christianorum Orientalium 572–573/Scriptores Armeniaci 23–24. Louvain.

Matsushima, E., ed. 1993. *Official Cult and Popular Religion in the Ancient Near East*. Heidelberg.

———. 1993. "Divine Statues in Ancient Mesopotamia: Their Fashioning and Clothing and Their Interaction with the Society." In Matsushima 1993:209–219.

Matthäus, H. 1985. *Metallgefässe und Gefässuntersätze der Bronzezeit, der geometrischen und archaischen Periode auf Cypern*. Munich.

Matthews, V. J. 1974. *Panyassis of Halikarnassos: Text and Commentary*. Mnemosyne Supplement 33. Leiden.

———. 1996. *Antimachus of Colophon: Text and Commentary*. Mnemosyne Supplement 155. Leiden.

Matthiae, P. 1989. *Ebla: Un Impero ritrovato. Dai primi scavi alle ultime scoperte*. 2nd ed. Torino.

Maul, S. 1999. "Gottesdienst im Sonnenheiligtum zu Sippar." In *Munuscula Mesopotamica. Festschrift für Johannes Renger*, ed. B. Böck et al., 285–316. Alter Orient und Altes Testament 267. Münster.

———. 2005. "Bilingual (Sumerian-Akkadian) Hymns from the Seleucid-Arsacid Period." In *Corpus of Cuneiform Texts in the Metropolitan Museum of Art 2. Literary and Scholastic Texts of the First Millennium B.C.*, ed. I. Spar and W. G. Lambert, 11–116. New York.

Maurey, Y. et al., eds. 2014. *Music in Antiquity: The Near East and the Mediterranean*. Jerusalem.

Mavrogordato, J. 1956. *Digenes Akrites*. Oxford.

Mayer, W. 1996. "The Hurrian Cult at Ugarit." In Wyatt et al. 1996:205–211.

Mayrhofer, M. 1956–1976. *Kurzgefasstes etymologisches Wörterbuch des Altindischen*. Heidelberg.

Mazar, A. 2003. "Ritual Dancing the Iron Age." *Near Eastern Archaeology* 66/3:126–127.

Mazar, B. 1974. *Kenaʾan ve-Yiśraʾel: Meḥkarim hisṭoriyim*. Jerusalem.
McCallum, L. R. 1987. *Decorative Program in the Mycenaean Palace of Pylos: The Megaron Frescoes*. PhD diss., University of Pennsylvania.
McCarter, P. K. 1984. *II Samuel. A New Translation with Introduction, Notes and Commentary*. The Anchor Bible 9. Garden City.
McGeough, K. M. and M. S. Smith. 2011. *Ugaritic Economic Tablets: Text, Translation, and Notes*. Leuven.
McKinnon, J. W. 1968. "Musical Instruments in Medieval Psalm Commentaries and Psalters." *Journal of the American Musicological Society* 21/1:3–20.
McLaughlin, J. 1991. "The Marzeah at Ugarit: A Textual and Contextual Study." *Ugarit-Forschungen* 23:266–281.
———. 2001. *The Marzēaḥ in the Prophetic Literature: References and Allusions in Light of the Extra-Biblical Evidence*. Vetus Testamentum Supplements 86. Leiden.
Meekers, M. 1987. "The Sacred Tree on Cypriote Cylinder Seals." *Report of the Department of Antiquities of Cyprus* 1987:67–76.
Meerschaert, C. 1991. "Les Musiciens dans la coroplastie chypriote de l'époque archaïque." In Vandenabeele and Laffineur 1991:183–193, pl. 143–144.
Meier-Brügger, M. 2006. "Sprachliche Beobachtungen." In *Die neuen Linear B-Texte aus Theben: Ihr Aufschlusswert für die mykenische Sprache und Kultur*, ed. S. Deger-Jalkotzy and O. Panagl, 111–118. Vienna.
Meineke, A. 1843. *Analecta Alexandrina: Sive, Commentationes de Euphorione Chalcidensi, Rhiano Cretensi, Alexandro Aetolo, Parthenio Nicaeno*. Berlin.
Meissner, B. 1940. *Studien zur assyrischen Lexikographie IV*. Mitteilungen der altorientalischen Gesellschaft 13/2. Leipzig.
Mekouria, T. T. 1994. "L'Influence du roi David et de son Psautier en Ethiopie." In *Actes de la Xème Conférence Internationale des études ethiopiennes (1988)*, ed. C. Lepage, 1:145–153. Paris.
Melchert, H. C. 1994. *Anatolian Historical Phonology*. Leiden Studies in Indo-European 3. Amsterdam.
Melena, J. L. 1975. *Studies on Some Mycenaean Inscriptions from Knossos Dealing with Textiles*. Salamanca.
———. 2000–2001. "63 Joins and Quasi-joins of Fragments in the Linear B Tablets from Pylos." *Minos* 35–36:371–384.
———. 2001. *Textos griegos micénicos comentados*. Vitoria-Gasteiz.
Merrillees, R. S. 1987. *Alashia Revisited*. Cahiers de la Revue Biblique 22. Paris.
———. 1992. "The Government of Cyprus in the Late Bronze Age." In Åström 1992 3:310–328.
Merrillees, R. S. and A. S. Gilbert. 2011. "Alashiya: A Scientific Quest for Its Location." In Betancourt and Ferrence 2011:255–264.

Mertzenfeld, C. D. de 1954. *Inventaire commenté des ivoires phéniciens et apparentés découverts dans le proche-orient*. 2 vols. Paris.

Mettinger, T. N. D. 1976–1977. "'The Last Words of David.' A Study of Structure and Meaning in II Samuel 23:1–7." *Svensk Exegetisk Årsbook* 41/42:147–156.

———. 2001. *The Riddle of Resurrection: 'Dying and Rising Gods' in the Ancient Near East*. Stockholm.

Metzger, B. M. and M. D. Coogan. 1993. *The Oxford Companion to the Bible*. Oxford.

Meyer, E. 1877. "Über einige semitische Götter." *Zeitschrift der Deutschen Morgenländischen Gesellschaft* 31:716–741.

Meyers, C. L. 1991. "Of Drums and Damsels: Women's Performance in Ancient Israel." *Biblical Archaeologist* 54/1:16–27.

———. 1993. "The Drum-Dance-Song Ensemble: Women's Performance in Biblical Israel." In Marshall 1993:49–67, 234–238.

Meyers, E. M., ed. 1997. *The Oxford Encyclopedia of Archaeology in the Near East*. New York.

Michaelides, D. 1992. *Cypriot Mosaics*. 2nd rev. ed. Department of Antiquities, Cyprus, Picture Book 7. Nicosia.

Michaelides, S. 1978. *The Music of Ancient Greece: An Encyclopaedia*. London.

Michaelidou-Nicolaou, I. 1976. "Literary, Epigraphic, and Numismatic Evidence on Nikokles, King of Paphos." *Kypriakai Spoudai* 40:15–28.

———. 1987. "Repercussions of the Phoenician Presence in Cyprus." In Lipiński 1987:331–338.

Michalowski, P. 1983. "History as Charter: Some Observations on the Sumerian King List." *Journal of the American Oriental Society* 103:237–248.

———. 1985. "Third Millennium Contacts: Observations on the Relationships Between Mari and Ebla." *Journal of the American Oriental Society* 105:293–302.

———. 1986. "Mental Maps and Ideology: Reflections on Subartu." In *The Origins of Cities in Dry-Farming Syria and Mesopotamia in the Third Millennium B.C.*, ed. W. Harvey, 129–156. Guilford.

———. 1989. *The Lamentation over the Destruction of Sumer and Ur*. Mesopotamian Civilizations 1. Winona Lake.

———. 1992. "The Early Mesopotamian Incantation Tradition." In Fronzaroli 1992:305–326.

———. 1993. "Memory and Deed: The Historiography of the Political Expansion of the Akkad State." In *Akkad. The First World Empire. Structure, Ideology, Traditions*, ed. M. Liverani, 69–90. Padova.

———. 1999. "Sumer Dreams of Subartu: Politics and the Geographical Imagination." In *Languages and Cultures in Contact: At the Crossroads of Civilizations in the Syro-Mesopotamian Realm*, ed. V. L. Karel, 305–315. Leuven.

———. 2005. "Literary Works from the Court of King Ishbi-Erra of Isin." In *"An Experienced Scribe Who Neglects Nothing": Ancient Near Eastern Studies in Honor of Jacob Klein*, ed. Y. Sefati et al., 199–212. Bethesda.

———. 2006. "Love or Death? Observations on the Role of the Gala in Ur III Ceremonial Life." *Journal of Cuneiform Studies* 58:49–61.

———. 2008. "The Mortal Kings of Ur: A Short Century of Divine Rule in Ancient Mesopotamia." In Brisch 2008:33–46.

———. 2009. "Aššur during the Ur III Period." In *Here & There across the Ancient Near East: Studies in Honour of Krystyna Łyczkowska*, ed. O. Drewnowska, 149–156. Warszawa.

———. 2010a. "Learning Music: Schooling, Apprenticeship, and Gender in Early Mesopomia." In Shehata and Pruzsinszky 2010:199–239.

———. 2010b. "Traveler's Tales: Observations on Musical Mobility in Mesopotamia and Beyond." In Dumbrill and Finkel 2010:117–124.

———. 2011. *The Correspondence of the Kings of Ur: An Epistolary History of an Ancient Mesopotamian Kingdom*. Winona Lake.

Mierse, W. E. 2012. *Temples and Sanctuaries from the Early Iron Age Levant: Recovery After Collapse*. Winona Lake.

Miglio, A. 2013. *Tribe and State: The Dynamics of International Politics and the Reign of Zimri-Lim*. Piscataway.

Mildenberg, L. 1984. *The Coinage of the Bar Kokhba War*. Aarau.

Milik, J. T. 1972. *Dédicaces faites par des dieux (Palmyre, Hatra, Tyr) et des thiases sémitiques à l'époque romaine*. Bibliothèque archéologique et historique 92. Paris.

Millar, F. 1993. *The Roman Near East, 31 B.C.-A.D. 337*. Cambridge, MA.

Miller, J. I. 1969. *The Spice Trade of the Roman Empire, 29 B.C. to A.D. 641*. Oxford.

Miller, J. L. 2004. *Studies in the Origins, Development and Interpretation of the Kizzuwatna Rituals*. Wiesbaden.

———. 2008. "Setting up the Goddess of the Night Separately." In Collins et al. 2008:67–72.

Miller, M. 1971. *The Thalassocracies*. Albany.

Miller, S. G. 1988. "The Theorodokoi of the Nemean Games." *Hesperia* 57/2:147–163.

———. 2004. *Ancient Greek Athletics*. New Haven.

Mirelman, S. 2010. "The gala Musician Dada and the si-im Instrument." *Nouvelles Assyriologiques Brèves et Utilitaires* 2010/2:40–41 no. 33.

———. 2014. "The ala-Instrument: Its Identification and Role." In Maurey et al. 2014:148–171.

———. Forthcoming. "Birds, Balags and Snakes (K.4206+)." *Journal of Cuneiform Studies*.

Mitchell, S. et al. 1982. *Regional Epigraphic Catalogues of Asia Minor II: The Ankara District. The Inscriptions of North Galatia*. British Archaeological Reports, International Series 135. Oxford.

Mitford, T. B. 1947. "Some Published Inscriptions from Roman Cyprus." *Annual of the British School at Athens* 42:201–237.

———. 1953. "Seleucus and Theodorus." *Opuscula Atheniensia* 1:130–171.

———. 1960a. "Paphian Inscriptions of Hoffman nos. 98 and 99." *Bulletin of the Institute of Classical Studies* 7:1–10.

———. 1960b. "Unpublished Syllabic Inscriptions of the Cyprus Museum." *Opuscula Atheniensia* 3:177–213.

———. 1960c. "A Cypriot Oath of Allegiance to Tiberius." *Journal of Roman Studies* 50:75–79.

———. 1961a. "Further Contributions to the Epigraphy of Cyprus." *American Journal of Archaeology* 65/2:93–151.

———. 1961b. *Studies in the Signaries of South-Western Cyprus*. Bulletin of the Institute of Classical Studies Supplement 10. London.

———. 1990. "The Cults of Roman Cyprus." *Aufstieg und Niedergang der Römischen Welt* 18/3:2176–2211.

Mlynarczyk, J. 1980. "The Paphian Sanctuary of Apollo Hylates." *Report of the Department of Antiquities of Cyprus* 1980:239–252.

———. 1983. "Sur le Theios Aoidos de J. Boardman." *Travaux du Centre d'Archéologie Méditerranéenne de l'Académie Polonaise des Sciences* 24:110–115.

Molina, M. 1991. "Tablillas sargónicas del Museo de Montserrat, Barcelona." *Aula Orientalis* 9:137–154.

Monloup, T. 1984. *Les Figurines de terre cuite de tradition archaïque*. Salamine de Chypre 12. Paris.

———. 1994. *Les Terres cuites classiques: Un Sanctuaire de la grand déesse*. Salamine de Chypre 14. Paris.

Montecchi, B. 2011. "Allotments of HORD and VIN to carpenters (te-ka-ta-si) at Thebes (TH Fq 247, Gp 112, 114, 147, 175)." *Studi Micenei ed Egeo-Anatolici* 53:171–187.

Moortgat, A. 1955. *Tell Halaf 3: Die Bildwerke*. Berlin.

Moran, W. L. 1992. *The Amarna Letters*. Baltimore.

Morpurgo (Davies), A. 1963. *Mycenaeae Graecitatis Lexicon*. Incunabula Graeca 3. Rome.

———. 1960. "KTILOS (Pind., Pyth. II,17)." *Rivista di Cultura Classica e Medioevale* 2:30–40.

Morris, S. P. 1992. *Daidalos and the Origins of Greek Art*. Princeton.

———. 1997. "Homer and the Near East." In *A New Companion to Homer*, ed. I. Morris and B. Powell, 599–623. Leiden.

———. 1998. "Daidalos and Kothar: The Future of Their Relationship." In *The Aegean and the Orient in the Second Millennium: Proceedings of the 50th Anniversary Symposium, Cincinnati, 18-20 April 1997*, ed. E. H. Cline and D. Harris-Cline, 281–289. Liège.

Mosca, P. G. and J. Russell. 1987. "A Phoenician Inscription from Cebel Ire Daği in Rough Cilicia." *Epigraphica Anatolica* 9:1–28.

Moscati, S. 2001. *The Phoenicians*. London.

Moulton, C. 1977. *Similes in the Homeric Poems*. Göttingen.

Movers, F. C. 1841–1856. *Die Phönizier*. 2 vols. in 4. Bonn.

Mühlestein, H. 1981. "Der homerische Phoinix und sein Name." *Živa Antika* 31:85–91.

Muhly, J. D. 1972. "The Land of Alashiya: References to Alashiya in the Texts of the Second Millennium B.C. and the History of Cyprus in the Late Bronze Age." In Karageorghis and Christodoulos 1972:201–219.

———. 1979. "Cypriote Copper: Some Geological and Metallurgical Problems." In Karageorghis 1979:87–100 and pl. IV-VII.

———. 1980. "Bronze Figurines and Near Eastern Metalwork." *Israel Exploration Journal* 30:148–161.

———. 1986. "The Role of Cyprus in the Economy of the Eastern Mediterranean during the Second Millennium B.C." In Karageorghis 1986:45–62.

———. 1989. "The Organisation of the Copper Industry in Late Bronze Age Cyprus." In Peltenburg 1989:298–314.

———. 1996. "The Significance of Metals in the Late Bronze Age Economy of Cyprus." In *The Development of the Cypriot Economy: From the Prehistoric Period to the Present Day* (eds. V. Karageorghis and D. Michaelides) 45–60. Nicosia.

Muhly, J. D. et al. 1980. "The Oxhide Ingots from Enkomi and Mathiati and Late Bronze Age Copper Smelting on Cyprus." *Report of the Department of Antiquities of Cyprus* 1980:84–99.

Mullen, E. T. 1980. *The Divine Council in Canaanite and Early Hebrew Literature*. Harvard Semitic Monographs 24. Chico.

Murray, A. S. et al. 1900. *Excavations in Cyprus: Bequest of Miss E. T. Turner to the British Museum*. London.

Murray, R. 2004. *Symbols of Church and Kingdom: A Study in Early Syriac Tradition*. Rev. ed. Piscataway.

Murray, W. M. 1995. "Ancient Sailing Winds in the Eastern Mediterranean: The Case for Cyprus." In *Proceedings of the International Symposium Cyprus and the Sea*, ed. V. Karageorghis and D. Michaelides, 33–44. Nicosia.

Muscarella, O. W. 1981. *Ladders to Heaven: Art Treasures from Lands of the Bible*. Toronto.

Muss-Arnolt, W. 1892. "On Semitic Words in Greek and Latin." *Transactions of the American Philological Association* 23:35–156.

Myers, J. M. 1965. *I Chronicles. Introduction, Translations, and Notes*. The Anchor Bible 12. Garden City.

Myres, J. L. 1906. "On the 'List of Thalassocracies' in Eusebius." *Journal of Hellenic Studies* 26:84–130.

———. 1914. *Handbook of the Cesnola Collection*. New York.

Na'aman, N. 1990. "On Gods and Scribal Traditions in the Amarna Letters." *Ugarit-Forschungen* 22:248–250.

Nagy, G. 1973. "Phaethon, Sappho's Phaon, and the White Rock of Leukas." *Harvard Studies in Classical Philology* 77:137–177.

———. 1979. *The Best of the Achaeans: Concepts of the Hero in Archaic Greek Art and Poetry*. Baltimore.

———. 1990. *Pindar's Homer: The Lyric Possession of an Epic Past*. Baltimore.

———. 2007. "Lyric and Greek Myth." In *The Cambridge Companion to Greek Mythology*, ed. R. D. Woodard, 19–51. Cambridge.

Nakassis, D. 2012. "Prestige and Interest: Feasting and the King at Mycenaean Pylos." *Hesperia* 81:1–30.

———. 2013. *Individuals and Society in Mycenaean Pylos*. Leiden.

Naoumides, M. 1968. "New Fragments of Ancient Greek Poetry." *Greek, Roman, and Byzantine Studies* 9/3:267–290.

Neil, R. A., ed. 1901. *The Knights of Aristophanes*. Cambridge.

Nelson, H. H. et al. 1930. *Medinet Habu I: Earlier Historical Records of Ramses III*. Oriental Institute Publications 8. Chicago.

Neri, D. 2000. *Le Coppe fenicie della tomba Bernardini nel Museo di Villa Giulia*. La Spezia.

Nettl, B. 1985. *The Western Impact on World Music: Change, Adaptation, and Survival*. New York.

Neu, E. 1970. *Ein althethitisches Gewitterritual*. Studien zu den Bogazköy-Texten Heft 12. Wiesbaden.

Neumann, G. 1961. *Untersuchungen zum Weiterleben hethitischen und luwischen Sprachgutes in hellenistischer und römischer Zeit*. Wiesbaden.

Newberry, P. E. 1893. *Beni Hasan Part I*. London.

Nicolaou, I. 1964. "Inscriptiones Cypriae alphabeticae." *Report of the Department of Antiquities of Cyprus* 1964:189–219 and pl. XIX–XXI.

Nikoloudis, S. 2008. "Multiculturalism in the Mycenaean World." In Collins et al. 2008:45–56.

Nissinen, M. 2008. "Song of Songs and Sacred Marriage." In Nissinen and Uro 2008:173–218.

Nissinen, M. et al. 2003. *Prophets and Prophecy in the Ancient Near East*. Writings from the Ancient World 12. Atlanta.
Nissinen, M. and R. Uro, eds. 2008. *Sacred Marriages: The Divine-Human Sexual Metaphor from Sumer to Early Christianity*. Winona Lake.
Nketia, J. H. K. 1963. *Drumming in Akan Communities of Ghana*. Edinburgh.
Nöldeke, T. 1875. *Mandäische Grammatik*. Halle.
———. 1881. "ASSURIOS SURIOS SUROS." *Hermes* 5:443–468.
Noreña, C. F. 2011. *Imperial Ideals in the Roman West: Representation, Circulation, Power*. Cambridge.
Norris, H. T. 1983. "Fables and Legends in Pre-Islamic and Early Islamic Times." In *The Cambridge History of Arabic Literature. Arabic Literature to the End of the Umayyad Period*, ed. A. F. L. Beeston, 374–386. Cambridge.
North, R. 1964. "The Cain Music." *Journal of Biblical Literature* 83/4:373–389.
Nougayrol, J. 1956. *Le Palais royal d'Ugarit IV: Textes accadiens des archives sud*. Paris.
———. 1957. "Nouveaux textes d'Ugarit en cunéiforms babyloniens (20e campagne, 1956)." *Comptes Rendus de l'Académie des Inscriptions et Belles-Lettres* 101/1:77–86.
———. 1968. "Textes suméro-accadiens des archives et bibliothèques privées d'Ugarit." In Nougayrol et al. 1968:1–446.
Nougayrol, J. et al., ed. 1968. *Ugaritica 5*. Paris.
Obermann, J. 1947. "How Baal Destroyed a Rival. A Mythological Incantation Scene." *Journal of the American Oriental Society* 67:195–208.
Oded, B. 1979. *Mass Deportations and Deportees in the Neo-Assyrian Empire*. Wiesbaden.
Oden, R. A. 1977. *Studies in Lucian's De Syria Dea*. Missoula.
———. 1978. "Philo of Byblos and Hellenistic Historiography." *Palestine Exploration Quarterly* 115–126.
Oettinger, N. 2008. "The Seer Mopsos (Muksas) as a Historical Figure." In Collins et al. 2008:63–66.
Ohnefalsch-Richter, M. H. 1893. *Kypros, the Bible, and Homer. Oriental Civilization, Art and Religion in Ancient Times*. London.
Olivetti, P. 2010. *Uses and Interpretations of Ritual Terminology: Goos, Oimoge, Threnos, and Linos in Ancient Greek Literature*. PhD diss., University of Birmingham.
Olivier, J.-P. 1960. *À propos d'une 'liste' de desservants de sanctuaire dans les documents en linéaire B de Pylos*. Brussels.
Olivier, J.-P. et al. 1973. *Index généraux du linéaire B*. Rome.
———. 1996. *Corpus hieroglyphicarum inscriptionum Cretae*. Paris.
Oren, E. D., ed. 2000. *The Sea Peoples and Their World: A Reassessment*. University Museum Monograph 108. Philadelphia.

Otten, H. 1953. "Ein kanaanäischer Mythus aus Bogazköy." *Mitteilungen des Instituts für Orientforschung* 1:124–150.

———. 1958. *Hethitische Totenrituale*. Berlin.

———. 1963. "Neue Quellung zum Ausklang des hethitischen Reiches." *Mitteilungen der Deutschen Orient-Gesellschaft* 94:1–23.

———. 1971. *Ein hethitisches Festritual (KBo XIX 128)*. Wiesbaden.

Otto, J. K. T. von 1872. *Corpus apologetarum Christianorum saeculi secundi 9. Hermiae philosophi Irrisio gentilium philosophorum: Apologetarum quadrati Aristidis, Aristonis, Miltiadis, Melitonis, Apollinaris reliquiae*. Jena.

Ovadiah, R. and A. Ovadiah. 1987. *Hellenistic, Roman and Early Byzantine Mosaic Pavements in Israel*. Rome.

Owen, D. I. 1982. *Neo-Sumerian Archival Texts primarily from Nippur*. Winona Lake.

Owuor, H. A. 1983. "Contemporary Lyres in Eastern Africa." *African Musicology* 1/2:18–33.

Özgüç, T. 1988. *İnandıktepe: An Important Cult Center in the Old Hittite Period*. Ankara.

Pade, M. 1997. "The Fragments of Theodontius in Boccaccio's *Genealogie deorum gentilium libri*." In *Avignon & Naples: Italy in France, France in Italy in the Fourteenth Century*, ed. M. Pade et al., 149–182. Rome.

Palagia, O. 2000. "Hephaestion's Pyre and the Royal Hunt of Alexander." In *Alexander the Great in Fact and Fiction*, ed. A. B. Bosworth and E. J. Baynham, 167–206. New York.

Palaima, T. G. 1988. *The Scribes of Pylos*. Rome.

———. 1991. "Maritime Matters in the Linear B Tablets." In *Thalassa: L'Egée préhistorique et la mer: Actes de la troisième Rencontre égéenne internationale de l'Université de Liège, Station de recherches sous-marines et océanographiques (StaReSO), Calvi, Corse, 23–25 avril 1990*, eds. R. Laffineur and L. Basch, 273–309. Liège.

———. 1995a. "The Last Days of the Pylos Polity." In *Politeia: Society and State in the Aegean Bronze Age*, ed. R. Laffineur and W.-D. Niemeier, 623–637. Liège.

———. 1995b. "The Nature of the Mycenaean *Wanax*: Non-Indo-European Origins and Priestly Functions." In *The Role of the Ruler in the Prehistoric Aegean*, ed. P. Rehak, 119–138 and pl. XLI–XLII. Liège.

Palaima, T. G. and J. C. Wright. 1985. "Ins and Outs of the Archives Rooms at Pylos." *American Journal of Archaeology* 89:251–262.

Paleocosta, E. 1998. "L'Iconographie des joueurs de lyre à Chypre du VIIIe au Ve s. av. J.-C." *Cahiers du Centre d'Études Chypriotes* 28:45–66 and pl. I–XI.

Palmer, A. 1993. "'A Lyre without a Voice': The Poetics and the Politics of Ephrem the Syrian." *ARAM* 5:371–399.

Palmer, L. R. 1955. "Observations on the Linear 'B' Tablets from Mycenae." *Bulletin of the Institute of Classical Studies* 2:36–45.

———. 1963. *The Interpretation of Mycenaean Greek Texts*. Oxford.
Panagides, A. 1946. *Treis kyprioi titanes (Kinyras—Euagoras—Zēnōn)*. Cyprus (s.n.).
Papadopoulos, T., ed. 2004. *Estienne de Lusignan. Chorograffia/Description de toute l'isle de Cypre*. 2 vols. Kypriologikē Bibliothēkē 10A/10B. Nicosia.
Papadopoulos-Kerameus, A. 1904. *Theodoros Studites, Μεγάλη κατήχησις*. St. Petersburg.
Papantonio, G. 2012. *Religion and Social Transformations in Cyprus: From the Cypriot Basileis to the Hellenistic Strategos*. Leiden.
Papasavvas, G. 2001. *Chalkinoi hypostates apo tēn Kypro kai tēn Krētē: Tripodikoi kai tetrapleuroi hypostates apo tēn Hysterē Epochē tou Chalkou heōs tēn Prōimē Epochē tou Sidērou*. Nicosia.
———. 2004. "Cypriot Bronze Stands and Their Mediterranean Perspective." *Revista d'Arqueologia de Ponent* 14:31–59.
———. 2011. "From Smiting to Smithing: The Transformation of a Cypriot God." In Betancourt and Ferrence 2011:59–66.
Papathomopoulos, M. 1968. *Antoninus Liberalis. Les Métamorphoses*. Collection des Universités de France. Paris.
Pardee, D. 1988a. "An Evaluation of the Proper Names from Ebla from a West Semitic Perspective: Pantheon Distribution according to Genre." In Archi 1988:119–158.
———. 1988b. *Ugaritic and Hebrew Poetic Parallelism: A Trial Cut ('nt I and Proverbs 2)*. Leiden.
———. 1992. "RS 24.643: Texte et structure." *Syria* 69:153–170.
———. 1996a. "L'Ougaritique et le hourrite dans les textes rituels de Ras Shamra-Ougarit." In *Mosaïque de langues, mosaïque culturelle: Le Bilinguisme dans le Proche-Orient ancien. Actes de la table-ronde du 18 novembre 1995 organisée par l'URA 1062 'Etudes sémitiques'*, ed. F. Briquel-Chatonnet, 63–80. Paris.
———. 1996b. "*Marziḥu, Kispu,* and the Ugaritic Funerary Cult: A Minimalist View." In Wyatt et al. 1996:273–287.
———. 1997. Review of G. J. Brooke, ed., *Ugarit and the Bible* (Münster 1994). *Journal of the American Oriental Society* 117:375–378.
———. 2000. "Ugaritic Studies at the End of the 20th Century." *Bulletin of the American Schools of Oriental Research* 320:49–86.
———. 2007. "Preliminary Presentation of a New Ugaritic Song to ʿAttartu (RIH 98/02)." In Younger 2007:27–40.
———. 2008. "Ugaritic." In *The Ancient Languages of Syria-Palestine and Arabia*, ed. R. G. Woodard, 5–35. Cambridge.
Paribeni, R. 1908. "Sarcofago dipinto di Haghia Triada." *Monumenti Antichi pubblicati per cura della Reale Accademia dei Lincei* 19 coll. 5–86.
Parker, S. B. 1970. "The Feast of Râpi'u." *Ugarit-Forschungen* 2:243–249.

———. 1971. "Exodus XV 2 Again." *Vetus Testamentum* 21/3:373–379.
———. 1972. "The Ugaritic Deity Rapi'u." *Ugarit-Forschungen* 4:97–104.
———. ed. 1997. *Ugaritic Narrative Poetry.* Atlanta.
Parpola, S. 1997. *Assyrian Prophecies.* State Archives of Assyria 9. Helsinki.
———. 2004. "National and Ethnic Identity in the Neo-Assyrian Empire and Assyrian Identity in Post Empire Times." *Journal of Assyrian Academic Studies* 18/2:5–40.
Parpola, S. and K. Watanabe. 1988. *Neo-Assyrian Treaties and Loyalty Oaths.* State Archives of Assyria 2. Helsinki.
Parpola, S. and R. M. Whiting, eds. 2002. *Sex and Gender in the Ancient Near East: Proceedings of the 47th Rencontre assyriologique internationale, Helsinki, July 2-6, 2001.* 2 vols. Helsinki.
Parrot, A. 1967. *Mission archéologique de Mari. III: Les Temples d'Ishtarat et de Ninnizaza.* Paris.
Parry, H. 1982. "Hieron and Ares, Kinyras and Aphrodite. Pindar's second Pythian." In *Mélanges offerts en hommage au Révérend père Étienne Gareau,* ed. s.n., 25–34. Ottawa.
Patai, R. 1964. "Lilith." *The Journal of American Folklore* 77/No. 306:295–314.
Paton, L. B. 1919–1920. "Survivals of Primitive Religion in Modern Palestine." *The Annual of the American School of Oriental Research in Jerusalem* 1:51–65.
Patzek, B. 2003. "Homer and the Near East. The Case of Assyrian Historical Epic and Prose Narrative." *Gaia* 63–74.
Pearson, A. C. 1917. *The Fragments of Sophocles.* 2 vols. Cambridge.
Pearson, L. 1955. "The Diary and the Letters of Alexander the Great." *Historia* 3:429–455.
Pecchioli Daddi, F. 1982. *Mestieri, professioni e dignità nell'Anatolia ittita.* Rome.
Peckham, B. 1968. "Notes on a Fifth-Century Phoenician Inscription from Kition, Cyprus (CIS 86)." *Orientalia* n.s. 37:304–324.
Peek, W. 1955. *Griechische Vers-Inschriften I. Grab-Epigramme.* Berlin.
Peltenburg, E. J. 1968. *Western Asiatic Glazed Vessels of the Second Millennium.* PhD diss., University of Birmingham.
———. 1972. "On the Classification of Faience Vases from Late Bronze Age Cyprus." In Karageorghis and Christodolou 1972:129–136.
———. 1986. "Ramesside Egypt and Cyprus." In Karageorghis 1986:149–179.
———, ed. 1989. *Early Society in Cyprus.* Edinburgh.
———. 2007. "Hathor, Faience, and Copper on Late Bronze Age Cyprus." *Cahiers du Centre d'Études Chypriotes* 37:373–394.
Pelzel, S. 1977. "Dating the Early Dynastic Votive Plaques from Susa." *Journal of Near Eastern Studies* 36:1–15.

Pentiuc, E. J. 2001. *West Semitic Vocabulary in the Akkadian Texts from Emar.* Winona Lake.

Perpillou, J.-L. 1978. "Autour du locatif des thèmes en -i-." *Bulletin de la Société de Linguistique de Paris* 73/1:293–299.

Petit, T. 1998. "Amathousiens, Ethiopiens et Perses." *Cahiers du Centre d'Études Chypriotes* 28:73–86.

———. 1999. "Eteocypriot Myth and Amathusian Reality." *Journal of Mediterranean Archaeology* 12/1:108–120.

———. 2001. "The First Palace of Amathus and the Cypriot Poleogenesis." In *The Royal Palace Institution in the First Millennium BC: Regional Development and Cultural Interchange between East and West*, ed. I. Nielsen, 53–75. Athens.

Petruševski, M. D. 1955. "Golemoto otkritie na M. Ventris = La grande découverte de M. Ventris." *Živa Antika* 5:387–401.

Pettinato, G. 1979. *Culto ufficiale ad Ebla durante il regno di Ibbi-Sipis.* Orientis Antiqui Collectio 16. Rome.

———. 1982. *Testi lessicali bilingui della biblioteca L. 2769.* Materiali Epigrafici di Ebla 4. Naples.

———. 1992. *Il Rituale per la successione al trono ad Ebla.* Studi Semitici n.s. 9. Rome.

Pfister, F. 1909–1912. *Der Reliquienkult im Altertum.* 2 vols. Giessen.

Picard, C. 1955. "El, Kinyras, ou quelque guerrier chypriote?" *Revue Archéologique* 45:48–49.

Pinches, T. G. 1908. *The Amherst Tablets. An Account of the Babylonian Inscriptions in the Collection of Lord Amherst of Hackney.* London.

Pirenne-Delforge, V. 1994. *L'Aphrodite grecque: Contribution à l'étude de ses cultes et de sa personnalité dans le panthéon archaïque et classique.* Athènes.

Pitard, W. T. 1992. "A New Edition of the 'Rāpiʾūma' Texts: KTU 1.20–22." *Bulletin of the American Schools of Oriental Research* 285:33–77.

Pitra, J.-B. 1854. *Spicilegium Solesmense. Tome II.* Paris.

Plumley, G. A. 1976. *El Tanbur: The Sudanese Lyre or the Nubian Kissar.* Cambridge.

Poethig, E. B. 1985. *The Victory Song Tradition of the Women of Israel.* PhD diss., Union Theological Seminary.

Pöhlmann, E. and M. L. West. 2001. *Documents of Ancient Greek Music.* Oxford.

Polin, C. C. J. 1974. *Music of the Ancient Near East.* Westport.

Pomponio, F. 1978. *Nabû: Il Culto e la figura di un dio del pantheon babilonese ed assiro.* Studi Semitici 51. Roma.

Pomponio, F. et al. 2006. *Tavolette cuneiformi di Adab delle collezioni della Banca d'Italia.* 2 vols. Rome.

Pomponio, F. and P. Xella. 1997. *Les Dieux d'Ebla: Étude analytique des divinités éblaïtes à l'époque des archives royales du IIIe millénaire.* Alter Orient und Altes Testament 245. Münster.

Pomponius Laetus, I. 1544. *Iulii Pomponii Sabini Grammatici Eruditissimi, In omnia quae quidem extant, P. Vergilii Maronis opera, Commentarii, varia multarum rerum cognitione referti, nuncque primum in lucem editi; cum rerum & verborum in hisce memorabilium locupletissimo indice.* Basel.

Poncy, H. et al. 2001. "Sceaux du Musee d'Adana." *Anatolia Antiqua* 9:9–37.

Pongratz-Leisten, B. 1994. *Ina Šulmi Īrub: Die kulttopographische und ideologische Programmatik der akītu-Prozession in Babylonien und Assyrien im I. Jahrtausend v. Chr.* Mainz.

———. 2008. "Sacred Marriage and the Transfer of Divine Knowledge: Alliances between the Gods and the King in Ancient Mesopotamia." In Nissinen and Uro 2008:43–74.

Pongratz-Leisten, B. 2011. "Comments on the Translatability of Divinity: Cultic and Theological Responses to the Presence of the Other in the Ancient Near East." In *Les Représentations des dieux des autres. Colloque de Toulouse, 9-11 décembre 2010*, ed. C. Bonnet et al., 83–111. Caltanissetta.

Pope, M. H. 1955. *El in the Ugaritic Texts.* Leiden.

———. 1979-1980. "Le MRZH à Ougarit et ailleurs." *Annales Archéologiques Arabes Syriennes* 29–30:141–143.

———. 1981. "The Cult of the Dead at Ugarit." In *Ugarit in Retrospect. Fifty Years of Ugarit and Ugaritic*, ed. G. D. Young, 159–179. Winona Lake.

Pope, M. H. and Röllig, W. 1965. "Die Mythologie der Ugariter und Phönizier." In *Wörterbuch der Mythologie. 1. Abt., Die alten Kulturvölker Bd. 1. Götter und Mythen im Vorderen Orient*, ed. Haussig, H. W., 217–312. Stuttgart.

Popham, M. 1995. "An Engraved Near Eastern Bronze Bowl from Lefkandi." *Oxford Journal of Archaeology* 14/1:103–107.

Popko, M. 1978. *Kultobjekte in der hethitischen Religion (nach keilschriftlichen Quellen).* Warsaw.

Porada, E. 1947. *Seal Impressions of Nuzi.* New Haven.

———. 1948. "The Cylinder Seals of the Late Cypriote Bronze Age." *American Journal of Archaeology* 52/1:178–198.

———. 1956. "A Lyre Player from Tarsus and His Relations." In *The Aegean and the Near East. Studies Presented to Hetty Goldman*, ed. S. S. Weinberg, 185–211. Locust Valley.

———. 1980. "A Cylinder Seal Showing a Harpist." In *Music and Civilisation*, ed. T. C. Mitchell, 29–31. The British Museum Yearbook 4. London.

———. 1981. "The Cylinder Seals Found at Thebes in Boeotia." *Archiv für Orientforschung* 28:1–70, 77.

Porter, J. R. 1954. "The Interpretation of 2 Samuel VI and Psalm CXXXII." *Journal of Theological Studies* 5:161–173.

Bibliography

Pouilloux, J. 1976. "Chypriotes à Delphes." *Report of the Department of Antiquities of Cyprus* 1976:158–167.
Powell, J. E. 1939. "The Sources of Plutarch's Alexander." *Journal of Hellenic Studies* 59/2:229–240.
Power, E. 1929. "The Ancient Gods and Language of Cyprus Revealed by the Accadian Inscriptions of Amathus." *Biblica* 10:129–169.
Power, T. 2010. *The Culture of Kitharoidia*. Cambridge, MA.
———. 2012. "A Piping Odysseus in Ptolemy the Quail." In *Donum natalicium digitaliter confectum Gregorio Nagy septuagenario a discipulis collegis familiaribus oblatum*, ed. V. Bers et al. http://nrs.harvard.edu/urn-3:hlnc.essay:PowerT.A_Piping_Odysseus_in_Ptolemy_the_Quail.2012.
Price, M. and B. L. Trell. 1977. *Coins and Their Cities: Architecture on the Ancient Coins of Greece, Rome, and Palestine*. London.
Priebatsch, H. Y. 1980. "Spiranten und Aspiratae in Ugaritic, AT und Hellas." *Ugarit-Forschungen* 12:317–333.
Provenza, A. 2014. "Soothing Lyres and ἐπῳδαί. Music Therapy and the Cases of Orpheus, Empedocles, David." In Maurey et al. 2014:298–339.
Pruzsinszky, R. 2010. "Die königlichen Sänger der Ur III-Zeit." In Shehata and Pruzsinszky 2010:95–118.
———. 2013. The Social Positions of NAR-Musicians of the Ur III Period at the End of the IIIrd Millennium BC." In Emerit 2013:31–46.
Pulak, C. 1998. "The Uluburun Shipwreck: An Overview." *The International Journal of Nautical Archaeology* 27/3:188–224.
Putnam, M. C. J. 1986. *Artifices of Eternity: Horace's Fourth Book of Odes*. Ithaca.
Quasten, J. 1930. *Musik und Gesang in den Kulten der Heidnischen Antike und Christlichen Fruhzeit*. Münster in Westfalen.
———. 1951. *Patrology*. Westminster, Maryland.
Raaflaub, K. 2000. "Influence, Adaptation, and Interaction: Near Eastern and Early Greek Political Thought." In *The Heirs of Assyria*, ed. S. Aro and R. M. Whiting, 51–64. Melammu Symposia 1. Helsinki.
Radner, K. 2005. *Die Macht des Namens: Altorientalische Strategien zur Selbsterhaltung*. Wiesbaden.
Rainey, A. F. 1978. *El-Amarna tablets, 359-379: Supplement to J. A. Knudtzon, Die El-Amarna-Tafeln*. 2nd rev. ed. Alter Orient und Altes Testament 8. Kevelaer.
Ramelli, I. L. E. 2009. *Bardaisan of Edessa: A Reassessment of the Evidence and a New Interpretation*. Piscataway.
Rashid, S. A. 1995. "Untersuchungen zum Musikinstrumentarium Assyriens." In *Beiträge zur Kulturgeschichte Vorderasiens, Festschrift für Rainer Michael Boehmer*, ed. U. Finkebeiner et al., 573-595. Mainz am Rhein.
Rattray, R. S. 1923. *Ashanti*. Oxford.

Redfield, J. M. 2003. *The Locrian Maidens: Love and Death in Greek Italy.* Princeton.
Redford, D. B. 1990. "The Sea and the Goddess." In *Studies in Egyptology Presented to Miriam Lichtheim,* ed. S. Israelit-Groll, 824–835. Jerusalem.
Rehak, P., ed. 1995. *The Role of the Ruler in the Prehistoric Aegean.* Liège.
Reiner, E. 1938. *Die rituelle Totenklage der Griechen.* Stuttgart.
———. 1958. *Šurpu: A Collection of Sumerian and Akkadian Incantations.* Archiv für Orientforschung, Beihefte 11. Graz.
Reinhold, G. G. G., ed. 2008. *Die Zahl Sieben im Alten Orient: Studien zur Zahlensymbolik in der Bibel und ihrer altorientalischen Umwelt.* Frankfurt am Main.
Renan, E. 1864. *Mission de Phénicie.* Paris.
Reyes, A. T. 1994. *Archaic Cyprus. A Study of the Textual and Archaeological Evidence.* Oxford.
———. 2001. *The Stamp-Seals of Ancient Cyprus.* Oxford.
Ribichini, S. 1981. *Adonis. Aspetti "orientali" di un mito greco.* Studi Semitici 55. Rome.
———. 1982. "Kinyras di Cipro." *Religioni e Civiltà* 3:479–500.
Richards, L. O. 1985. *Expository Dictionary of Bible Words.* Grand Rapids.
Richardson, H. N. 1971. "The Last Words of David. Some Notes on II Sam 23:1–7." *Journal of Biblical Literature* 90:257–266.
Richardson, N. J. 1991. "Homer and Cyprus." In *The Civilizations of the Aegean and Their Diffusion in Cyprus and the Eastern Mediterranean, 2000-600 BC: Proceedings of an International Symposium, 18-24 September 1989,* ed. V. Karageorghis, 124–128. Larnaca.
Ridder, A. de 1908. *Collection de Clercq. V. Les Antiquités chypriotes.* Paris.
Rimmer, J. 1969. *Ancient Musical Instruments of Western Asia in the Department of Western Asiatic Antiquities, the British Museum.* London.
Risch, E. 1966. "Les Différences dialectales dans le mycénien." In *Proceedings of the Cambridge Colloquium on Mycenaean Studies,* ed. L. R. Palmer and J. Chadwick, 150–157. Cambridge.
———. 1974. "À propos de l'origine des masculins grecs en -ᾱΣ." *Bulletin de la Société de Linguistique de Paris* 69:109–119.
———. 1988. "Le Développement du chypriote dans le cadre des dialectes grecs anciens." In Karageorghis and Masson 1988:67–80.
Risch, E. and H. Mühlestein, eds. 1979. *Colloquium Mycenaeaum. The Sixth International Congress on the Aegean and Mycenaean Texts at Chaumont sur Neuchâtel, September 7-13, 1975.* Geneva.
Rizzo, M. A. 2007. "I Sigilli del 'Gruppo del Suonatore di Lira' dalla stipe dell'Athenaion di Jalysos." *Annuario della Scuola archeologica di Atene e delle missioni italiane in Oriente* 2007:33–82.

———. 2008-2009. "I Sigilli del Gruppo del Suonatore di Lira in Etruria e nell'Agro Falisco." *Annali di Archeologia e Storia antica* 15-16:105-142.
Roaf, M. 1990. *Cultural Atlas of Mesopotamia and the Ancient Near East*. New York.
Robert, C. 1883. "Die Phaethonsage bei Hesiod." *Hermes* 18/3:434-441.
Robert, L. 1940. *Les Gladiateurs dans l'Orient grec*. Paris.
Roberts, A. et al. 1885-1896. *The Ante-Nicene Fathers. Translations of the Writings of the Fathers down to A.D. 325*. Buffalo.
Robkin, A. L. H. 1979. "The Agricultural Year, the Commodity SA and the Linen Industry of Mycenaean Pylos." *American Journal of Archaeology* 89/4:469-474.
Robson, J. and H. G. Farmer, eds. 1938. *Ancient Arabian Musical Instruments as Described by ... Ibn Salama ... in the Kitāb al-malāhi*. Collection of Oriental Writers on Music 4. Glasgow.
Rochette, R. 1848. *Mémoires d'archéologie comparée, asiatique, grecque et étrusque*. Paris.
Rohde, E. 1914. *Der griechische Roman und seine Vorläufer*. Wiesbaden.
Rollinger, R., ed. 2005. *Von Sumer bis Homer: Festschrift für Manfred Schretter zum 60. Geburtstag am 25. Februar 2004*. Münster.
Rollinger, R. 2006. "The Terms 'Assyria' and 'Syria' Again." *Journal of Near Eastern Studies* 65.4:283-287.
Römer, W. H. P. 1965. *Sumerische Königshymnen der Isin-Zeit*. Leiden.
———. 1983. "Sumerische Emesallieder." *Bibliotheca Orientalis* 40:566-592.
———. 1989. "Miscellanea Sumerologica I: Zur sumerischen Dichtung 'Heirat des Gottes Mardu'." *Ugarit-Forschungen* 21:319-334.
Roscher, W. H. 2003. *Beiträge zur Zahlensymbolik der Griechen und anderer Völker*. Hildesheim.
Rosól, R. 2013. *Frühe semitische Lehnwörter im Griechischen*. Frankfurt am Main.
Roth, M. T. 1983. "The Slave and the Scoundrel: CBS 10467, A Sumerian Morality Tale?" *Journal of the American Oriental Society* 103: 275-282.
Rowley, H. H. 1939. "Zadok and Nehushtan." *Journal of Biblical Literature* 58:113-141.
Roy, J. 1987. "Pausanias, VIII, 5, 2-3 and VIII, 53, 7: Laodice Descendant of Agapenor; Tegea and Cyprus." *L'Antiquité Classique* 56:192-200.
Rudolf, M. 1965. *Handbook of Classical and Modern Mandaic*. Berlin.
Ruijgh, C. J. 1962. *Tabellae Mycenenses selectae*. Leiden.
———. 1967. *Études sur la grammaire et le vocabulaire du grec mycénien*. Amsterdam.
———. 1988. "Sur le vocalisme du dialecte chypriote au premier millénaire av. J.-C." In Karageorghis and Masson 1988:131-151.
Ruipérez, M. S. 1956. "Une Charte royale de partage des terres à Pylos." *Minos* 4:146-164.

Rupp, D. W. 1985. "Prolegomena to a Study of Stratification and Social Organisation in Iron Age Cyprus." In *Status, Social Organisation, and Stratification: Current Archaeological Reconstructions*, eds. M. Thompson et al., 119–130. Calgary.

Rutten, M. 1939. "Deux vases chypriotes du Musée du Louvre." In *Mélanges syriens offerts à Monsieur René Dussaud*, ed. s.n., 2 vols. 435–449. Paris.

s.n., ed. 1909. *Hilprecht Anniversary Volume. Studies in Assyriology and Archaeology Dedicated to Hermann V. Hilprecht ... by his Colleagues, Friends, and Admirers*. Leipzig.

s.n., ed. 1984. *Adonis: Relazioni del colloquio in Roma, 22-23 maggio 1981*. Collezione di Studi Fenici 18. Rome.

s.n., ed. 2003. *Semitic and Assyriological Studies Presented to Pelio Fronzaroli by Pupils and Colleagues*. Wiesbaden.

Sacconi, A. et al., eds. 2008. *Colloquium Romanum: Atti del XII colloquio internazionale di micenologia, Roma, 20-25 febbraio 2006*. Pisa.

Sachs, C. 1943. *The Rise of Music in the Ancient World East and West*. New York.

Saghieh, M. 1983. *Byblos in the Third Millennium B.C.: A Reconstruction of the Stratigraphy and a Study of the Cultural Connections*. Warminster.

Sallaberger, W. 1993. *Der kultische Kalender der Ur III-Zeit*. 2 vols. Untersuchungen zur Assyriologie und vorderasiatischen Archäologie 7. Berlin.

———. 1999. "Ur III-Zeit." In *Mesopotamien: Akkade-Zeit und Ur III-Zeit*, ed. W. Sallaberger and Å. Westenholz, 119–414. Freiburg.

———. 2000. "Das Erscheinen Marduks als Vorzeichen: Kultstatue und Neujahrsfest in der Omenserie Šumma ālu." *Zeitschrift für Assyriologie* 90:227–262.

Salviat, F. 1962. "Lions d'ivoire orientaux à Thasos." *Bulletin de Correspondance Hellénique* 86/1:95–116.

Salviat, F. and J. Servais. 1964. "Stèle indicatrice thasienne trouvée au sanctuaire d'Aliki." *Bulletin de Correspondance Hellénique* 88/1:267–287.

Sanmartín, J. 1980. "Glossen zum ugaritischen Lexicon (IV)." *Ugarit-Forschungen* 12:335–339.

———. 1991. "Isoglosas morfoléxicas eblaítico-ugaríticas: La Trampa lexicográfica." *Aula Orientalis* 9:165–217.

Sarna, N. M. 1993. *Songs of the Heart: An Introduction to the Book of Psalms*. New York.

Sasson, J. M. 1968. "Instances of Mobility among Mari Artisans." *Bulletin of the American Schools of Oriental Research* 190:46–54.

Sayce, A. H. 1898. *Lectures on the Origin and Growth of Religion as Illustrated by the Religion of the Ancient Babylonians*. London.

Bibliography

Scardina, P. 2010. "I Sigilli del Lyre Player Group: Tracce di archeologia musicale tra l'Etruria e il Mediterraneo orientale." In *La Musica in Etruria: Atti del convegno internazionale, Tarquinia 18/20 Settembre 2009*, ed. M. Carrese et al., 67–78. Tarquinia.

Schadewaldt, W. 1928. *Der Aufbau des Pindarischen Epinikion*. Halle.

Schaeffer, C. F.-A. 1952. *Enkomi-Alasia: Nouvelles missions en Chypre, 1946-1950*. Paris.

———. 1965. "An Ingot God from Cyprus." *Antiquity* 39:56–57.

———, ed. 1971. *Alasia I*. Paris.

———. 1983. *Corpus des cylindres-sceaux de Ras Shamra-Ugarit et d'Enkomi-Alasia. Tome 1*. Mission Archéologique de Ras Shamra-Ugarit et d'Enkomi-Alasia. Synthèse no. 13. Paris.

Scharff, A. 1922. *Aegyptische Sonnenlieder*. Berlin.

Schmidt, B. B. 1994. *Israel's Beneficent Dead: Ancestor Cult and Necromancy in Ancient Israelite Religion and Tradition*. Tübingen.

Schmidt-Colinet, C. 1981. *Die Musikinstrumente in der Kunst des Alten Orients: Archäologisch-philologische Studien*. Abhandlungen zur Kunst-, Musik- und Literaturwissenschaft 312. Bonn.

Schneider, N. 1932. *Die Drehem- und Dioha-Texte im Kloster Montserrat (Barcelona), in Autographie und mit systematischen Wörterverzeichnissen*. Analecta Orientalia 7. Rome.

Schoene, A. 1967. *Eusebi Chronicorum libri duo*. 2nd ed. Dublin.

Scholem, G. 1974. *Kabbalah*. New York.

Schott, S. 1934. "Der Gott des Harfenspiels." In *Mélanges Maspero I. Orient ancien*, ed. s.n., 457–464. Cairo.

Schretter, M. K. 1974. *Alter Orient und Hellas: Fragen der Beeinflussung griechischen Gedankengutes aus altorientalischen Quellen, dargestellt an den Göttern Nergal, Rescheph, Apollon*. Innsbruck.

———. 1990. *Emesal-Studien. Sprach- und literaturgeschichtliche Untersuchungen zur sogenannten Frauensprache des Sumerischen*. Innsbruck.

Schroeder, O. 1915. "Ueber den Namen des Tamūz von Byblos in der Amarnazeit." *Orientalistische Literaturzeitung* 18:292–293.

Schuller, E. M. 1986. *Non-Canonical Psalms from Qumran: A Pseudepigraphic Collection*. Harvard Semitic Studies 28. Atlanta.

Schwartz, B. 1938. "The Hittite and Luwian Ritual of Zarpiya of Kezzuwatna." *Journal of the American Oriental Society* 58/2:334–353.

Schwartz, E. 1931. "Einiges über Assyrien, Syrien und Koilesyrien." *Philologus* 86:373–399.

Segal, C. 1962. "Gorgias and the Psychology of the Logos." *Harvard Studies in Classical Philology* 66:99–155.

———. 1998. *Aglaia: The Poetry of Alcman, Sappho, Pindar, Bacchylides, and Corinna*. Lanham.
Segert, S. 1984. *Basic Grammar of the Ugaritic Language*. Berkeley.
Seibert, J. 1976. "Zur Bevölkerungsstruktur Cyperns." *Ancient Society* 7:1–28.
Sellers, O. R. 1941. "Musical Instruments of Israel." *Biblical Archaeologist* 4:33–47.
Selz, G. J. 1995. *Untersuchungen zu Götterwelt des altsumerischen Stadtstaates von Lagaš*. Occasional Publications of the Samuel Noah Kramer Fund 13. Philadelphia.
———. 1997. "'The Holy Drum, the Spear, and the Harp': Towards an Understanding of the Problems of Deification in Third Millennium Mesopotamia." In Finkel and Geller 1997:167–213.
———. 2008. "The Divine Prototypes." In Brisch 2008:13–31.
Sendrey, A. 1969. *Music in Ancient Israel*. New York.
———. 1974. *Music in the Social and Religious Life of Antiquity*. Rutherford.
Seow, C. L. 1989. *Myth, Drama, and the Politics of David's Dance*. Harvard Semitic Monographs 44. Atlanta.
Serghidou, A. 2006. "Discours ethnographique et quêtes identitaires en Chypre ancienne." In Fourrier and Grivaud 2006:165–186.
Servais-Soyez, B. 1977. *Byblos et la fête des Adonies*. Études Préliminaires aux Religions Orientales dans l'Empire Romain 60. Leiden.
———. 1984. "Musique et Adonies. Apport archéologique à la connaissance du rituel adonidien." In s.n. 1984:61–72. Rome.
Sethe, K. 1926. *Die Ächtung feindlicher Fürsten, Völker und Dinge auf altägyptischen Tongefässcherben des mittleren Reiches: Nach den Originalen im Berliner Museum*. Berlin.
Seznec, J. 1953. *The Survival of the Pagan Gods*. New York.
Shedid, A. G. 1994. *Die Felsgräber von Beni Hassan in Mittelägypten*. Mainz am Rhein.
Shehata, D. 2006a. "On the Mythological Background of the Lamentation Priest." In Hickmann et al. 2006:119–127.
———. 2006b. "Some Observations on the /alĝarsur/." In Hickmann et al. 2006:367–378.
———. 2009. *Musiker und ihr vokales Repertoire: Untersuchung zu Inhalt und Organisation von Musikerberufen und Liedgattugen in altbabylonischer Zeit*. Göttinger Beiträge zum Alten Orient 3. Göttingen.
———. 2013. "Status and Organization of the Babylonian Lamentation Priests." In Emerit 2013:69–84.
Shehata, D. and R. Pruzsinszky, eds. 2010. *Musiker und Tradierung: Studien zur Rolle von Musikern bei der Verschriftlichung und Tradierung von literarischen Werken*. Wiener Offene Orientalistik 8. Vienna.

Shelmerdine, C. W. 1984. "The Perfumed Oil Industry at Pylos." In Shelmerdine and Palaima 1984:81–95.

———. 1985. *The Perfume Industry of Mycenaean Pylos.* Göteborg.

———. 2008. "The Palace and Its Operations." In *Sandy Pylos: An Archaeological History from Nestor to Navarino,* ed. J. L. Davis et al., 2nd ed., 81–96. Princeton.

Shelmerdine, C. W. and T. G. Palaima, eds. 1984. *Pylos Comes Alive: Industry + Administration in a Mycenaean Palace.* New York.

Sherratt, E. S. 1992. "Immigration and Archaeology: Some Indirect Reflections." In Åström 1992 2:316–347.

———. 1994. "Commerce, Iron and Ideology: Metallurgical Innovation in 12th–11th Century Cyprus." In Karageorghis 1994:59–108.

Shiloah, A. 1972. "The Simsimiyya: A Stringed Instrument of the Red Sea Area." *Asian Music* 4/1:15–26.

———. 1993. *The Dimension of Music in Islamic and Jewish Culture.* Aldershot.

———. 1995. *Music in the World of Islam: A Socio-Cultural study.* Detroit.

Shipp, R. M. 2002. *Of Dead Kings and Dirges: Myth and Meaning in Isaiah 14:4b–21.* Leiden.

Shnider, S. 2010. "Some Comments on W. Horowitz, 'A Late Babylonian Tablet with Concentric Circles'." *Journal of the Ancient Near Eastern Society* 32:133–137.

Shrimpton, G. S. 1991. *Theopompus the Historian.* Montreal.

Siegelová, J. 1971. *Appu-Märchen und Hedammu-Mythus.* Studien zu den Bogazköy-Texten 14. Wiesbaden.

Sigrist, M. 1984a. *Les Sattukku dans l'Ešumeša durant la période d'Isin et Larsa.* Bibliotheca Mesopotamica 11. Malibu.

———. 1984b. *Neo-Sumerian Account Texts in the Horn Archaeological Museum.* Andrews University Cuneiform Texts 1. Berrien Springs, Michigan.

———. 1999. "Livraisons et depenses royales durant la Troisieme Dynastie d'Ur." In *Ki Baruch Hu: Ancient and Near Eastern, Biblical and Judaic Studies in Honor of Baruch A. Levine* (eds. R. Chazan et al.) 111–152. Winona Lake.

Sigrist, M. and T. Gomi. 1991. *The Comprehensive Catalogue of Published Ur III Tablets.* Bethesda.

Simmons, S. D. 1960. "Early Old Babylonian Tablets from Harmal and Elsewhere (Continued)." *Journal of Cuneiform Studies* 14/3:75–87.

Singer, I. 1983–1984. *The Hittite KI.LAM Festival.* 2 vols. Studien zu den Bogazköy-Texten 27–28. Wiesbaden.

———. 2006. "Ships Bound for Lukka: A New Interpretation of the Companion Letters RS 94.2530 and RS 94.2523." *Altorientalische Forschungen* 33:242–262.

Sivan, D. 1984. *Grammatical Analysis and Glossary of the Northwest Semitic Vocables in Akkadian Texts of the 15th–13th c. B.C. from Canaan and Syria.* Kevelaer.

———. 2001. *A Grammar of the Ugaritic Language*. Leiden.
Sivan, D. and Z. Cochavi-Rainey. 1992. *West-Semitic Vocabulary in Egyptian Script of the 14th to the 10th Centuries BCE*. Beer-Sheva.
Sjöberg, Å. W. 1965. "Beiträge zum sumerischen Wörterbuch." In Güterbock and Jacobsen 1965:63–70.
———, ed. 1984-. *The Sumerian Dictionary of the University Museum of the University of Pennsylvania*. Philadelphia.
Sjöberg, Å. W. and E. Bergmann. 1969. *The Collection of the Sumerian Temple Hymns*. Texts from Cuneiform Sources 3. Locust Valley.
Smith, J. S. 2008. "Cyprus, the Phoenicians, and Kition." In *Beyond the Homeland: Markers in Phoenician Chronology*, ed. C. Sagona, 261–303. Leuven.
———. 2009. *Art and Society in Cyprus from the Bronze Age into the Iron Age*. Cambridge.
Smith, M. S. 1984. "The Magic of Kothar in KTU 1.6 VI 49–50." *Revue Biblique* 91:377–380.
———. 1990. *The Early History of God: Yahweh and the Other Deities in Ancient Israel*. San Francisco.
———. 1994. *The Ugaritic Baal Cycle. Vol. I, Introduction with Text, Translation and Commentary of KTU/CAT 1.1–1.2*. Leiden.
———. 2001. *The Origins of Biblical Monotheism: Israel's Polytheistic Background and the Ugaritic Texts*. Oxford.
———. 2008. "Sacred Marriage in the Ugaritic Texts? The Case of KTU/CAT 1.23 (Rituals and Myths of the Goodly Gods)." In Nissinen and Uro 2008:93–113.
———. 2014. "'Athtart in Late Bronze Age Syrian Texts." In *Transformation of a Goddess: Ishtar, Astarte, Aphrodite*, ed. D. T. Sugimoto, 33–85. Fribourg.
Smith, M. S. and W. T. Pitard. 2009. *The Ugaritic Baal Cycle. Vol. 2, Introduction with Text, Translation and Commentary of KTU/CAT 1.3–1.4*. Leiden.
Snell, D. C. 1986. "The Rams of Lagash." *Acta Sumerologica* 8:133–218.
Snodgrass, A. 1994. "Gains, Losses, and Survivals: What We Infer for the 11th Century B.C." In Karageorghis 1994:167–176.
Sollberger, E. 1959/1960. "Byblos sous les rois d'Ur." *Archiv für Orientforschung* 19:120–122.
Sollberger, E. and C. Walker. 1985. "Hammu-rāpī à Mari et à Sippar." In Durand and Kupper 1985:257–264.
Solomon, J. 2011. *Giovanni Boccaccio: Genealogy of the Pagan Gods, Volume I, Books I–IV*. Cambridge, MA.
———. 2013. "Gods, Greeks, and Poetry." In *Boccaccio: A Critical Guide to the Complete Works*, ed. V. Kirkham et al., 235–244. Chicago.
Sommer, F. 1921. "Ein hethitisches Gebet." *Zeitschrift für Assyriologie* 33:85–102.

Sophocleous, S. 1985. *Atlas des représentations chypro-archaic des divinités.* Studies in Mediterranean Archaeology Pocket-Book 33. Göteborg.

South, A. K. 1984. "Kalavasos-Ayios Dhimitrios and the Late Bronze Age of Cyprus." In *Cyprus at the Close of the Late Bronze Age,* ed. V. Karageorghis and J. D. Muhly, 11–17. Nicosia.

Spuler, B., ed. 1970. *Handbuch der Orientalistik. Erste Abteilung, Nahe und der Mittlere Osten. Ergänzungsband 4.* Leiden.

Spycket, A. 1972. "La Musique instrumentale mesopotamienne." *Journal des Savants* July–Sept.:153–209.

Spyridakis, K. 1935. *Euagoris I. von Salamis; Untersuchungen zur Geschichte des kyprischen Königs.* Stuttgart.

———. 1963. *Kyprioi vasileis tou 4. ai. p.Kh. (411-311/10 p.Kh.): Meta eisagōgēs peri tou Hellēnikou kharaktēros tēs Arkhaias Kypriakēs historias.* Leukosia.

Stadelmann, R. 1967. *Syrisch-palästinensische Gottheiten in Ägypten.* Probleme der Ägyptologie 5. Leiden.

Staubli, T. 1991. *Das Image der Nomaden im alten Israel und in der Ikonographie seiner sesshaften Nachbarn.* Freiburg.

Stauder, W. 1957. *Die Harfen und Leiern der Sumerer.* Frankfurter am Main.

———. 1961. *Die Harfen und Leiern Vorderasiens, in babylonischer und assyrischer Zeit.* Frankfurt am Main.

———. 1970. "Die Musik der Sumerer, Babylonier und Assyrer." In Spuler 1970:171–243.

———. 1973. *Alte Musikinstrumente in ihrer vieltausendjährigen Entwicklung und Geschichte.* Braunschweig.

Steel, L. 1998. "The Social Impact of Mycenaean Imported Pottery in Cyprus." *Annual of the British School at Athens* 93:285–296.

———. 2004. *Cyprus before History: From the Earliest Settlers to the End of the Bronze Age.* London.

Steele, P. M. 2011. "Eteocypriot: Linguistic and Archaeological Evidence." In *Cyprus: An Island Culture. Society and Social Relations from the Bronze Age to the Venetian Period,* ed. A. Georgiou, 122–132. Oxford.

———, ed. 2012. *Syllabic Writing on Cyprus and Its Context.* Cambridge.

———. 2013. *A Linguistic History of Ancient Cyprus: The Non-Greek Languages and Their Relations with Greek, c.1600–300 BC.* Cambridge.

Stefanis, I. E. 1986. *Dionysiakoi tekhnitai: Symboles stēn prosōpographia tou theatrou kai tēs mousikēs tōn arkhaiōn Hellēnōn.* Iraklion.

Steiner, G. 1962. "Neue Alašija-Texts." *Kadmos* 1/2:130–138.

Steinkeller, P. 1987. "The Administrative and Economic Organization of the Ur III State: The Core and the Periphery." *Studies in Ancient Oriental Civilization* 46:19–41.

---. 1992. *Third-Millennium Legal and Administrative Texts in the Iraq Museum, Baghdad*. Mesopotamian Civilizations 4. Winona Lake.

---. 1993. "Observations on the Sumerian Personal Names in Ebla Sources and on the Onomasticon of Mari and Kish." In *The Tablet and the Scroll. Near Eastern Studies in Honor of William W. Hallo*, ed. M. E. Cohen et al., 236–245. Bethesda.

---. 1999. "On Rulers, Priests and Sacred Marriage: Tracing the Evolution of Early Sumerian Kingship." In *Priests and Officials in the Ancient Near East*, ed. K. Watanabe, 103–137. Heidelberg.

---. 2006. "New Light on Marhaši and Its Contacts with Makkan and Babylonia." *Journal of Magan Studies* 1:1–17.

Stella, L. A. 1958. "La Religione greca nei testi micenei." *Numen* 5/1:18–57.

---. 1965. *La Civiltà micenea nei documenti contemporanei*. Rome.

Stephens, S. A. 2002. "Linus Song." *Hermathena* 173/174:13–28.

Stieglitz, R. R. 1990. "Ebla and the Gods of Canaan." In *Eblaitica 2*, ed. C. H. Gordon and G. A. Rendsburg, 79–89. Winona Lake.

---. 2002. "The Deified Kings of Ebla." In *Eblaitica 4*, ed. C. H. Gordon and G. A. Rendsburg, 215–222. Winona Lake.

Stiehle, R. 1853. "Die kyklischen Nosten." *Philologus* 8:49–77.

Stökl, J. 2012. *Prophecy in the Ancient Near East: A Philological and Sociological Comparison*. Leiden.

Stoneman, R. 2008. *Alexander the Great: A Life in Legend*. New Haven.

Strack, H. L. 1983. *Introduction to the Talmud and Midrash*. New York.

Strange, J. 1980. *Caphtor/Keftiu: A New Investigation*. Leiden.

Strauss, R. 2006. *Reinigungsrituale aus Kizzuwatna: Ein Beitrag zur Erforschung hethitischer Ritualtradition und Kulturgeschichte*. Berlin.

Stutley, M. and J. Stutley. 1977. *Harper's Dictionary of Hinduism: Its Mythology, Folklore, Philosophy, Literature, and History*. New York.

Suter, A., ed. 2008. *Lament: Studies in the Ancient Mediterranean and Beyond*. Oxford.

Suter, C. E. 2000. *Gudea's Temple Building*. Groningen.

Sweet, R. F. G. 1994. "A New Look at the 'Sacred Marriage' in Ancient Meospotamia." In *Corolla Torontonensis: Studies in Honour of Ronald Morton Smith*, ed. E. Robbins and S. Sandahl, 85–104. Toronto.

Szemerényi, O. 1964. *Syncope in Greek and Indo-European and the Nature of Indo-European Accent*. Naples.

---. 1968. Review of E. Masson, *Recherches sur les plus anciens emprunts sémitiques en grec* (Paris, 1967). *Indogermanische Forschungen* 73:192–197.

---. 1974. "The Origins of the Greek Lexicon: *Ex Oriente lux*." *Journal of Hellenic Studies* 94:144–157.

———. 1981. Review of P. Chantraine, *Dictionnaire étymologique de la langue grecque. Histoire des mots. Tome IV* (Paris 1980). *Gnomon* 53/2:113–116.

———. 1986. "Etyma Graeca V (30–32): Vocabula maritima tria." In Etter 1986:425–450.

Tadmor, H. 1982. "Treaty and Oath in the Ancient Near East." In *Humanizing America's Iconic Book*, ed. G. M. Tucker and D. A. Knight, 127–152. Chico.

Talbert, R. J. A. 1984. *The Senate of Imperial Rome*. Princeton.

———. 1999. "Tacitus and the Senatus Consultum de Cn. Pisone Patre." *American Journal of Philology* 120/1:89–97.

———. 2010. *Rome's World: The Peutinger Map Reconsidered*. Cambridge.

Taylor, J. 2001. "A New OB Proto-Lu-Proto-Izi Combination Tablet." *Orientalia* n.s. 70:209–234.

Taylor, P. 2008. "The GALA and the Gallos." In Collins et al. 2008:173–180.

Teeter, E. 1993. "Female Musicians in Pharaonic Egypt." In Marshall 1993:68–91.

Tegyey, I. 1984. "The Northeast Workshop at Pylos." In Shelmerdine and Palaima 1984:65–79.

Teixidor, J. 1977. *The Pagan God: Popular Religion in the Greco-Roman Near East*. Princeton.

Tekoglu, R. and A. Lemaire. 2000. "La Bilingue royale louvito-phénicienne de Çineköy." *Comptes Rendus de l'Académie des Inscriptions et Belles-Lettres* 144/3:961–1006.

Thackston, W. M. 1978. *The Tales of the Prophets of al-Kisaʾi*. Boston.

Thalmann, W. G. 1984. *Conventions of Form and Thought in Early Greek Epic Poetry*. Baltimore.

Thomas, R. 1981. "Cinna, Calvus, and the Ciris." *Classical Quarterly* 31: 371–374.

Thompson, D. A. W. 1936. *A Glossary of Greek Birds*. London.

Thompson, E. M. 1893. *Handbook of Greek and Latin Palaeography*. New York.

Thubron, C. 1987. *The Hills of Adonis: A Journey in Lebanon*. Rev. ed. Harmondsworth.

Thureau-Dangin, F. 1903. *Recueil des tablettes chaldéennes*. Paris.

———. 1907. *Die sumerischen und akkadischen Königsinschriften*. Leipzig.

———. 1921. *Rituels accadiens*. Paris.

———. 1922. *Tablettes d'Uruk: À l'usage des prêtres du Temple d'Anu au temps des Séleucides*. Textes Cunéiformes. Musées du Louvre 6. Paris.

———. 1939. "Tablettes hourrites provenant de Mari." *Revue d'Assyriologie et d'Archéologie Orientale* 36:1–28.

Tischler, J. et al. 1977. *Hethitisches etymologisches Glossar*. Innsbrucker Beiträge zur Sprachwissenschaft 20. Innsbruck.

Todd, I. A. and A. K. South. 1992. "The Late Bronze Age in the Vasilikos Valley: Recent Research." In Ioannides 1992:191–204.

Tomberg, K.-H. 1968. *Die Kaine Historia des Ptolemaios Chennos: Eine literarhistorische und quellenkritische Untersuchung*. Bonn.
Tonietti, M. V. 1988. "La Figura del nar nei testi di Ebla. Ipotesi per una cronologia delle liste di nomi presenti nei testi economici." *Miscellanea Eblaitica* 1:79–119.
———. 1989. "Aggiornamento alla cronologia dei nar." *Miscellanea Eblaitica* 2:117–129.
———. 1997. "Nar Directly Connected to a Temple in Ebla." *Nouvelles Assyriologiques Brèves et Utilitaires* 1997/1:37–38 no. 39.
———. 1998. "The Mobility of the NAR and the Sumerian Personal Names in Pre-Sargonic Mari Onomasticon." *Subartu* 4/2:83–101.
———. 2010. "Musicians in the Ebla Texts: A Third-Millennium Local Source for Northern Syria." In Shehata and Pruzsinszky 2010:67–93.
Trémouille, M.-C. 2005. *Texte verschiedenen Inhalts*. Corpus der hurritischen Sprachdenkmäler I/8. Rome.
Tropper, J. 1994. "Is Ugaritic a Canaanite Language?" In *Ugarit and the Bible*, ed. G. J. Brooke, 343–353. Münster.
Tsablē, E. 2009. Κινύρας. Μελέτη στον αρχαίο κυπριακό μύθο. PhD diss., Πανεπιστήμιο Αθηνών.
Tsukimoto, A. 1985. *Untersuchungen zur Totenpflege (kispum) im alten Mesopotamien*. Kevelaer.
Tsumura, D. T. 1973. *The Ugaritic Drama of the Good Gods: A Philological Study*. PhD diss., Brandeis University.
Tubb, J. N. 2003. "Phoenician Dance." *Near Eastern Archaeology* 66/3:122–125.
Tuplin, C. 1996. *Achaemenid Studies*. Stuttgart.
Ulbrich, T. 1906. "Die pseudo-melitonische Apologie." In *Kirchengeschichtliche Abhandlungen*, ed. M. Sdralek, 4:67–148. Breslau.
Ulrich, E. G. 1978. *The Qumran Text of Samuel and Josephus*. Missoula.
———. 1989. "Josephus' Biblical Text for the Books of Samuel." In *Josephus, the Bible, and History*, ed. L. H. Feldmna and G. Hata, 81–96. Leiden.
Untersteiner, M. 1954. *The Sophists*. New York.
Utley, F. L. 1941. "The One Hundred and Three Names of Noah's Wife." *Speculum* 16/4:426–452.
van de Mieroop, M. 2005. *King Hammurabi of Babylon: A Biography*. Malden.
van den Branden, A. 1956. "Notes phéniciennes." *Bulletin du Musée de Beyrouth* 13:87–95.
———. 1968. *Grammaire phénicienne*. Beyrouth.
van der Ploeg, J. 1963. "Notes sur le Psaume XLIX." *Oudtestamentische Studiën* 13:137–172.

van der Sluijs, M. A. 2008. "On the Wings of Love." *Journal of Ancient Near Eastern Religions* 8/2:219–251.
van der Valk, M. 1949. *Textual Criticism of the Odyssey*. Leiden.
———. 1963. *Researches on the Text and Scholia of the Iliad*. Leiden.
———. 1971–1987. *Commentarii ad Homeri Iliadem pertinentes ad fidem codicis Laurentiani editi*. Leiden.
van Dijk, J. 1983. *Lugal Ud Me-Lám-bi Nir-Gál*. Leiden.
van Meurs, J. 1675. *Creta, Rhodus, Cyprus, sive De nobilissimarum harum insularum rebus & antiquitatibus, commentarii postumi, nunc primum editi*. 3 vols. Amsterdam.
van Selms, A. 1979. "The Root *k-ṯ-r* and Its Derivatives in Ugaritic Literature." *Ugarit-Forschungen* 11:739–744.
van Soldt, W. H. 1991. *Studies in the Akkadian of Ugarit: Dating and Grammar*. Kevelaer.
———. 1995. "Babylonian Lexical, Religious and Literary Texts and Scribal Education at Ugarit and its Implications for the Alphabetic Literary Texts." In *Ugarit: Ein ostmediterranes Kulturzentrum im Alten Orient: Ergebnisse und Perspektiven der Forschung*, ed. M. Dietrich and O. Loretz, 171–212. Münster.
Vandenabeele, F. and R. Laffineur, eds. 1991. *Cypriote Terracottas: Proceedings of the First International Conference of Cypriote Studies, Brussels-Liège-Amsterdam, 29 May–1 June 1989*. Brussels.
Vandervondelen, M. 1994. "Danseuses inédites du British Museum." In *Cypriote Stone Sculpture. Proceedings of the Second International Conference of Cypriote Studies, Brussels-Liège, 17–19 May, 1993*, ed. F. Vandenabeele and R. Laffineur, 149–152 and pl. XLIV–XLV. Brussels-Liège.
Vanschoonwinkel, J. 1990. "Mopsos: Legendes et réalité." *Hethitica* 10:185–211.
———. 1994. "La Présence grecque à Chypre au XIe siècle av. J.-C." In Karageorghis 1994:109–132.
Veldhuis, N. C. 1996. "The Ugarit Lexical Text RS 13.53 (PRU III, Planche X)." *Die Welt des Orients* 27:25–29.
———. 1997. *Elementary Education at Nippur: The Lists of Trees and Wooden Objects*. PhD diss., Rijksuniversiteit Groningen.
———. 1997–1998. "The Sur9-Priest, the Instrument gišAl-gar-sur9, and the Forms and Uses of a Rare Sign." *Archiv für Orientforschung* 44–45:115–128.
———. 2000. "Kassite Exercises: Literary and Lexical Extracts." *Journal of Cuneiform Studies* 52:67–94.
———. 2004. *Religion, Literature, and Scholarship: The Sumerian Composition "Nanše and the Birds."* Cuneiform Monographs 22. Leiden.
Vella, N. Forthcoming. "'Phoenician' Metal Bowls: Boundary Objects in the Archaic Period." In *Punic Interactions: Cultural, Technological and Economic*

Exchange between Punic and Other Cultures in the Mediterranean. Proceedings of the XVII International Congress of Classical Archaeology, Rome, ed. A. Wilson and J. Quinn.

Vellay, C. 1957. *Les Légendes du cycle troyen*. Monaco.

Vermes, G. 2011. *The Complete Dead Sea Scrolls in English*. Rev. ed. London.

Vermeule, E. 1979. *Aspects of Death in Early Greek Art and Poetry*. Sather Classical Lectures 46. Berkeley.

Virolleaud, C. 1929. "Les Inscriptions cunéiformes de Ras Shamra." *Syria* 10:304–310.

———. 1968. "Les Nouveaux textes mythologiques et liturgiques de Ras Shamra (XXIVe Campagne, 1961)." In Nougayrol et al. 1968:545–595.

Volk, K. 1988. "Eine bemerkenswerte nach-Fara-zeitliche Urkunde." *Orientalia* 57:206.

———. 2006. "'Inannas Tischlein Deck' Dich'. Vorläufiger Bericht zur Rekonstruktion der 17. Tafel von úru àm-ma-ir-ra-bi." *Baghdader Mitteilungen* 37:91–116.

von Hornbostel, E. M. and C. Sachs, 1914. "Systematik der Musikinstrumente. Ein Versuch." *Zeitschrift für Ethnologie* 46.4–5:553–590.

von Kamptz, H. 1956. *Homerische Personennamen: Sprachwissenschaftliche und historische Klassifikation*. Göttingen.

von Lieven, A. 2008. "Native and Foreign Elements in the Musical Life of Ancient Egypt." In Hickmann et al. 2008:155–160.

von Soden, W. 1988. "Musikinstrumente in Mari." *Nouvelles Assyriologiques Brèves et Utilitaires* 1988/3:42–43 no. 59.

von Weiher, E. 1988. *Spätbabylonische Texte aus Uruk 3*. Ausgrabungen der Deutschen Forschungsgemeinschaft in Uruk-Warka 12. Berlin.

Vorreiter, L. 1972/1973. "Westsemitische Urformen von Saiteninstrumenten." *Mitteilungen der Deutschen Gesellschaft für Musik des Orients (Berlin)* 11:71–77.

Voyatzis, M. E. 1985. "Arcadia and Cyprus: Aspects of Their Interrelationship Between the Twelfth and Eighth Centuries B.C." *Report of the Department of Antiquities of Cyprus* 1985:155–163.

Wace, A. J. B. 1902–1903. "Apollo Seated on the Omphalos: A Statue at Alexandria." *Annual of the British School at Athens* 9:211–242.

Waerzeggers, C. and R. Siebes. 2007. "An Alternative Interpretation of the Seven-Pointed Star on CBS 1766." *Nouvelles Assyriologiques Brèves et Utilitaires* 2007/2:43–45 no. 40.

Wagensonner, K. 2008. "Nin-Isina(k)s Journey to Nippur Reconsidered." *Wiener Zeitschrift für die Kunde des Morgenlandes* 98:277–294.

Wagner, R. 1891. *Epitoma Vaticana ex Apollodori Bibliotheca*. Leipzig.

———, ed. 1894. *Apollodori Bibliotheca*. Leipzig.
Walcot, P. 1966. *Hesiod and the Near East*. Cardiff.
Ward, W. A. and M. S. Joukowsky, eds. 1992. *The Crisis Years: The 12th Century B.C. from beyond the Danube to the Tigris*. Dubuque.
Watkins, C. 1995. *How to Kill a Dragon: Aspects of Indo-European Poetics*. New York.
Watson, W. G. E. 1994. "Aspects of Style in KTU 123." *Studi Epigrafici e Linguistici sul Vicino Oriente Antico* 11:3–8.
———. 1996. "Comments on Some Ugaritic Lexical Items." *Journal of Northwest Semitic Languages* 22:73–84.
Watt, J. W. 1986. *The Fifth Book of the Rhetoric of Antony of Tagrit*. 2 vols. Louvain.
Webb, J. M. 1992. "Cypriote Bronze Age Glyptic: Style, Function and Social Context." In *Eikon: Aegean Bronze Age Iconography: Shaping Methodology*, ed. R. Laffineur and J. L. Crowley, 113–121. Liège.
———. 1999. *Ritual Architecture, Iconography and Practice in the Late Cypriot Bronze Age*. Studies in Mediterranean Archaeology and Literature Pocket-Book 75. Jonsered.
———. 2001. "The Sanctuary of the Ingot God at Enkomi: A New Reading of Its Construction, Use, and Abandonment." In *Contributions to the Archaeology and History of the Bronze and Iron Ages in the Eastern Mediterranean: Studies in Honour of Paul Åström*, ed. P. M. Fischer, 69–82. Vienna.
———. 2002. "Device, Image, and Coercion: The Role of Glyptic in the Political Economy of Late Bronze Age Cyprus." In *Script and Seal Use on Cyprus in the Bronze and Iron Ages*, ed. J. S. Smith, 111–154. Boston.
———. 2003. "From Ishtar to Aphrodite: The Transformation of a Goddess." In *From Ishtar to Aphrodite: 3200 Years of Cypriot Hellenism: Treasures from the Museums of Cyprus*, ed. S. Hadjisavvas et al., 15–20. New York.
Webster, T. B. L. 1954. "Pylos Aa, Ab Tablets—Pylos E Tablets—Additional Homeric Notes." *Bulletin of the Institute of Classical Studies* 1:11–16.
———. 1964. *From Mycenae to Homer*. 2nd ed. New York.
Wegner, I. 1981. *Gestalt und Kult der Ištar-Šawuška in Kleinasien*. Alter Orient und Altes Testament 36/Hurritologische Studien 3. Kevelaer.
———. 2007. *Einführung in die hurritische Sprache*. 2nd ed. Wiesbaden.
Wegner, M. 1949. *Das Musikleben der Griechen*. Berlin.
———. 1950. *Die Musikinstrumente des alten Orients*. Münster.
Weidner, E. F. 1939. "The Inscription from Kythera." *Journal of Hellenic Studies* 59:137–138.
———. 1957–1958. "Neue Endeckungen in Ugarit." *Archiv für Orientforschung* 18:167–170.
Weitzman, S. 1997. *Song and Story in Biblical Narrative: The History of a Literary Convention in Ancient Israel*. Bloomington.

Wellhausen, J. 1871. *Der Text der Bücher Samuelis*. Göttingen.
Werner, E. 1957. "Musical Aspects of the Dead Sea Scrolls. For Curt Sachs on His 75th Birthday." *Musical Quarterly* 43:21-37.
West, M. L. 1966. *Hesiod Theogony*. Oxford.
———. 1990. "Notes on Sappho and Alcaeus." *Zeitschrift für Papyrologie und Epigraphik* 80:1-8.
———. 2000. "The Name of Aphrodite." *Glotta* 76:134-138.
———. 2001. *Studies in the Text and Transmission of the Iliad*. Munich.
———. 2003. *Greek Epic Fragments from the Seventh to the Fifth Centuries BC*. Loeb Classical Library 497. Cambridge, MA.
———. 2013. *The Epic Cycle: A Commentary on the Lost Troy Epics*. Oxford.
Westenholz, Å. 1999. "The Old Akkadian Period: History and Culture." In *Mesopotamien: Akkade-Zeit und Ur III-Zeit*, ed. W. Sallaberger and Å. Westenholz, 17-117. Freiburg.
Westenholz, J. G. 1997. *Legends of the Kings of Akkade. The Texts*. Mesopotamian Civilizations 7. Winona Lake.
———. 2007. "Notes on the Old Assyrian Sargon Legend." *Iraq* 69:21-27.
———. 2011. "The Transmission and Reception of the Sargonic Sagas in the Hittite World." In *Hethitische Literatur: Überlieferungsprozesse, Textstrukturen, Ausdrucksformen und Nachwirken. Akten des Symposiums vom 18. bis 20. Februar 2010 in Bonn*, ed. M. Hutter and S. Hutter-Braunsar, 285-304. Münster.
Westenholz, J. G. and A. Westenholz, 2006. *Cuneiform Inscriptions in the Collection of the Bible Lands Museum Jerusalem: The Old Babylonian Inscriptions*. Cuneiform Monographs 33. Leiden.
Westermann, A. 1843. *Mythographoi: Scriptores poeticae historiae Graeci*. Brunswick.
Wheeler, B. M. 2002. *Prophets in the Quran: An Introduction to the Quran and Muslim Exegesis*. London.
White, H. G. E. 1932. *The Monasteries of the Wâdi 'n Natrûn, Part II: The History of the Monasteries of Nitria and of Scetis*. New York.
Whittaker, G. 2002. "Linguistic Anthropology and the Study of Emesal as (a) Women's Language." In Parpola and Whiting 2002 2:633-644.
Wiggermann, F. A. M. 1992. *Mesopotamian Protective Spirits: The Ritual Rexts*. Cuneiform Monographs 1. Groningen.
Wijngaarden, G. J. 2002. *Use and Appreciation of Mycenaean Pottery in the Levant, Cyprus, and Italy (ca. 1600-1200 BC)*. Amsterdam.
Wilamowitz-Möllendorff, U. von. 1900. "Lesefrüchte." *Hermes* 35/3:533-566.
Wilcke, C. 1973. "Sumerische literarische Texte in Manchester und Liverpool." *Archiv für Orientforschung* 24:1-17.
———. 1987. "Die Inschriftenfunde der 7. und 8. Kampagnen (1983 und 1984)." In *Isin-Išān Baḥrīyāt III: Die Ergebnisse der Ausgrabungen 1983-1984*, ed. B.

Bibliography

Hrouda, 83–120 and Tafeln 133–144. Abhandlungen, Bayerische Akademie der Wissenschaften, Philosophisch-Historische Klasse, n.F. 94. Munich.

———. 2011. "Eine Weihinschrift Gudeas von Lagaš mit altbabylonischer Übersetzung." In *Cuneiform Royal Inscriptions and Related Texts in the Schøyen Collection*, ed. A. R. George and M. Civil, 29–47. Cornell Studies in Assyriology and Sumerology 17. Bethesda.

Wilhelm, G. 1989. *The Hurrians*. Warminster.

Williamson, M. 1969. "Les Harpes sculptees du temple d'Ishtar à Mari." *Syria* 46:209–224 and pl. XVII.

Wilson, E. J. 1996. *The Cylinders of Gudea: Transliteration, Translation and Index*. Alter Orient und Altes Testament 244. Neukirchen-Vluyn.

Wilson, N. G. 1983. *Scholars of Byzantium*. Baltimore.

Wilson, P. 1999. "The Aulos in Athens." In *Performance Culture and Athenian Democracy*, ed. S. D. Goldhill and R. Osborne, 58–95. Cambridge.

———. 2009. "Thamyris the Thracian: The Archetypal Wandering Poet?" In *Wandering Poets in Ancient Greek Culture: Travel, Locality and Panhellenism*, ed. R. Hunter and I. Rutherford, 117–187. Cambridge.

Wimber, M. 2009. "Makers of Meaning: Plays and Processions in Goddess Cults of the Near East." In *Pageants and Processions: Images and Idiom as Spectacle*, ed. H. du Toit, 3–24. Newcastle.

Winkler, J. J. 1990. *The Constraints of Desire. The Anthropology of Sex and Gender in Ancient Greece*. New York.

Winter, I. J. 1976. "Phoenician and North Syrian Ivory Carving in Historical Context: Questions of Style and Distribution." *Iraq* 38/1:1–22.

———. 1987. "Is There a South Syrian Style of Ivory Carving in the First Millennium B.C.?" *Iraq* 43:101–130.

———. 1988. "North Syria as a Bronze-Working Centre in the Early First Millennium B.C.: Luxury Commodities at Home and Abroad." In *Bronzeworking Centres of Western Asia c.1000–539 B.C.*, ed. J. E. Curtis, 193–225. London.

———. 1990. Review of G. Markoe, *Phoenician Bronze and Silver Bowls from Cyprus and the Mediterranean* (Berkeley 1985). *Gnomon* 62/3:236–241.

———. 1995. "Homer's Phoenicians: History, Ethnography, or Literary Trope?" In Carter and Morris 1995:247–271.

———. 1997. "Art in Empire: The Royal Image and the Visual Dimensions of Assyrian Ideology." In *Assyria 1995. Proceedings of the 10th Anniversary Symposium of the Neo-Assyrian Text Corpus Project, Helsinki, September 7-11, 1995*, ed. S. Parpola and R. M. Whiting, 359–381. Helsinki.

Wiseman, T. P. 1974. *Cinna the Poet, and Other Roman Essays*. Leicester.

———. 1985. "Who Was Crassicius Pansa?" *Transactions of the American Philological Association* 115:187–196.
Woodbury, L. 1978. "The Gratitude of the Locrian Maiden: Pindar, Pyth. 2.18–20." *Transactions of the American Philological Association* 108:285–299.
Wright, D. P. 2001. *Ritual in Narrative: The Dynamics of Feasting, Mourning, and Retaliation Rites in the Ugaritic Tale of Aqhat.* Winona Lake.
Wyatt, N. 2001. *Space and Time in the Religious Life of the Near East.* Sheffield.
———. 2007. "The Religious Role of the King in Ugarit." In Younger 2007:41–74.
Wyatt, N. et al., eds. 1996. *Ugarit, Religion, and Culture: Proceedings of the International Colloquium on Ugarit, Religion and Culture, Edinburgh, July 1994: Essays Presented in Honour of Professor John C. L. Gibson.* Ugaritisch-Biblische Literatur 12. Münster.
Wypustek, A. 2013. *Images of Eternal Beauty in Funerary Verse Inscriptions of the Hellenistic and Greco-Roman Periods.* Leiden.
Xella, P. 1976. "Il Dio siriano Kothar." In *Magia: Studi di storia delle religioni in memoria di Raffaela Garosi*, ed. P. Xella, 111–126. Rome.
———. 1979–1984. "Remarques sur le vocabulaire sacrificiel d'Ugarit." *Comptes Rendus du Groupe Linguistique d'Études Chamito-sémitiques* XXIV–XXVIII:467–487.
Yadin, Y. 1971. *Bar-Kokhba: The Rediscovery of the Legendary Hero of the Second Jewish Revolt against Rome.* New York.
Yakubovich, I. 2010. *Sociolinguistics of the Luvian Language.* Leiden.
Yamauchi, E. M. 1973. "Cultic Prostitution: A Case Study in Cultural Diffusion." In *Occident and Orient. Essays Presented to Cyrus H. Gordon on the Occasion of this Sixty-fifth Birthday*, ed. H. A. Hoffner, 213–222. Kevelaer.
Yasur-Landau, A. 2008. "A Message in a Jug: Canaanite, Philistine, and Cypriot Iconography and the 'Orpheus Jug'." In *Studies in the Archaeology of Israel and the Levant during the Bronze and Iron Ages in Honour of Israel Finkelstein*, ed. A. Fantalkin and A. Yasur-Landau, 213–229. Bene Israel.
Yon, M. 1974. *Un Dépôt de sculptures archaïques (Ayios Varnavas, site A).* Salamine de Chypre 5. Paris.
———. 1999. "Chypre et Ougarit à la fin du Bronze Récent." *Report of the Department of Antiquities of Cyprus* 1999:113–119.
———. 2004. *Kition dans les textes. Testimonia littéraires et épigraphiques et Corpus des inscriptions.* Paris.
Yon, M. and A. Caubet, 1988. "Un Culte populaire de la Grand Déesse à Lapithos." *Report of the Department of Antiquities of Cyprus* 1988/2:1–16 and pl. I–IV.
Yon, M. and M. Sznycer, 1991. "Une Inscription phénicienne royale de Kition (Chypre)." *Comptes Rendus de l'Académie des Inscriptions et Belles-Lettres* 135/4:791–823.

Bibliography

Younger, J. G. 1998. *Music in the Aegean Bronze Age.* Jonsered.

Younger, K. L., ed. 2007. *The Late Bronze Age/Iron Age Transition and the Origins of the Aramaeans.* Ugarit at Seventy-Five. Winona Lake.

Zaccagnini, C. 1973. *Lo Scambio dei doni nel Vicino Oriente durante i secoli XV–XIII.* Rome.

———. 1983a. "On Gift Exchange in the Old Babylonian Period." In *Studi orientalistici in ricordo di Franco Pintore,* ed. O. Carruba et al., 189–253. Pavia.

———. 1983b. "Patterns of Mobility among Ancient Near Eastern Craftsmen." *Journal of Near Eastern Studies* 42/4:245–264.

———. 1987. "Aspects of Ceremonial Exchange in the Near East During the Late Second Millennium BC." In *Centre and Periphery in the Ancient World,* ed. M. Rowlands et al., 57–65. Cambridge.

Zarmas, P. 1975. *Studien zur Volksmusik Zyperns.* Baden-Baden.

Zettler, R. 1987. "Sealings as Artifacts of Institutional Administration in Ancient Mesopotamia." *Journal of Cuneiform Studies* 39:197–240.

Ziegler, N. 1999. "Le Harem du vaincu." *Revue d'Assyriologie et d'Archéologie Orientale* 93:1–26.

———. 2006a. "Die 'internationale' Welt der Musik anhand der Briefe aus Mari (Syrien, 18. Jhd. v. Chr.)." In Hickmann et al. 2006:345–354.

———. 2006b. "Les Musiciens de la cour de Mari." *Les Dossiers d'Archéologie* 310:32–38.

———. 2010. "Teachers and Students: Conveying Musical Knowledge in the Kingdom of Mari." In Shehata and Pruzsinszky 2010:119–133.

Zimmerle, W. Forthcoming. *'Spices of All Kinds': South Arabian and Arabianizing Censers in Cultural Motion from Mesopotamia to the Mediterranean in the First Millennium B.C.* PhD diss., University of Pennsylvania.

Index Locorum

I have distributed the sources into four broad groups: Near Eastern Sources; Cypriot Inscriptions; Greek/Latin; Medieval and Early Modern. The first is subdivided by language and/or region, with classical authors included when relevant (Berossos resides in Mesopotamia, Josephus among Biblical/Judaica, and Philo of Byblos with Phoenician/Punic). Cypriot Inscriptions, in keeping with the book's Cyprocentric outlook, consolidates Greek, Phoenician, and 'Eteocypriot' material; further Phoenician and Greek examples are located respectively in Near Eastern Sources (Phoenician/Punic) and Greek/Latin (Inscriptions). Cross-references are provided to help navigation. Professor Heimpel's sources could not be not fully indexed; but my own citations of his Catalogue texts have been given in Near Eastern Sources (Mesopotamia).

Near Eastern Sources

Alalakh
AT 172.7, 54n41, 98n54; 385.2, 440n108

Arabic and Arabia
Arabian Nights 182, 543n32
CIS 2 268, 542n23 (Mada'in Saleh, Saudi Arabia, Nabataean)
Ibn 'Abd Rabbihi, 44n8
Ibn Ḫurdāḏbih, 543n29
Ibn Salama, Al-Mufaḍḍal, *Kitāb al-malāhī* (*Book of Instruments*), 301n127
'Iqd al-Farīd, 183n196
al-Kalbī, Hisham ibn, 312
al-Mas'ūdî, 60n88
Quran 17.55, 182n192; 21.79, 183n193; 21.81, 183n195; 27.15, 182n192; 27.16–45, 183n195; 34.10, 183n193; 34.12–14, 183n195; 38.18, 183n194; 38.36, 183n195
al-Tha'labī, 183

Biblical/Judaica
Acts 2:30, 175n153
Amos 5:21–23, 139n164; 6:4–7, 139n164; 6:5, 158n59
'Arakin 10a, 117n35; 10b, 155n39; 13b, 58n69, 117n36
Berakhot 3b 182n186
1 Chronicles 2:6, 152n23, 156n45,

Index Locorum

(1 Chronicles, *cont.*)
  177n161; 6:1–32, 149n1, 155n38; 6:22, 174n147; 9:19, 174n147; 9:31, 174n147; 9:33, 116n25; 13:8, 116n25; 117n35; 15–16, 168n103; 15:16, 116n25; 15:16–22, 117n35; 15:16–24, 149n1, 155n38, 164n86; 15:19, 117n34; 15:19–21, 116n24; 15:22, 157n55; 15:26, 170n119, 171n124; 15:27, 169n116; 15:28, 155n38; 15:29, 169n108; 16:5, 117n33, 117n35; 17:1, 151n13; 17:6, 151n13; 22:4, 151n13; 23:5, 158n59; 25:1, 164n86; 25:1–31, 149n1, 155n38; 25:3–6, 164n86; 25:6, 117n35; 26:29, 157n57
2 Chronicles 5:3, 172n133; 5:11, 172n133; 5:12, 164n86; 5:12–13, 116n25; 7:6, 155n38, 158n59, 173n141; 20:19, 174n147; 20:21–23, 164n86; 20:22–23, 164n87; 29:21–28, 172n134; 29:25, 155n38, 173n142; 29:26, 158n59; 29:27–28, 172n135
Dead Sea Scrolls 1Q33 4:5, 58n68; 1QH-a col. XIX, 301n128; 4Q162.6–10, 157n50; 4Q381 fr. 24.4, 178n168; 4Q381 fr. 31.4, 178n168; 4Q381 fr. 33.8, 178n168; 4Q427 1:4–5, 301n128; 4QSam, 168n105
Deuteronomy 31:19–22, 164n86; 32, 156n41
Ecclesiastes 2:8, 154n28
Exodus 15, 156n41; 15:2, 176n158, 177n161; 15:20, 126n90; 15:20–21, 164n86
Ezekiel 8:14–15, 470; 26:13, 43n3; 27:7, 323n15; 33:32, 445n11; 40:44–46, 164n86
Ezra 2:41, 155n38; 2:64, 155n38; 3:7, 151n13; 3:10, 117n35; 3:10–13, 155n38; 6:4, 151n13

Genesis 4:19–22, 44n5; 4:21, 129n104, 312n188; 4:21 (LXX), 215n164, 312n188; 4:22, 454n73; 4:23–24, 312n187; 10:3–4, 514n124, 514n127; 10:4–5, 10n44; 10:22–31, 43n3; 11:11–26, 43n3; 25:20, 43n3; 31:20, 43n4; 31:27, 43n4; 38:12–30, 404n26
Isaiah 5:11–12, 138n164, 157n50, 293n79; 12:2, 176n158, 177n161; 14:10–11, 43n3, 146n206; 16:10–11, 301n125; 23:15–16, 43n3, 302n130, 538n9; 24:8, 300n120; 36:1–2, 154n30
Jeremiah 9:17 and 20, 293n77; 31:4, 126n90; 34:5, 283n25
Josephus
  Against Apion 1.106–127, 407n45; 2.38–42, 47n19
  Antiquities of the Jews 3.12, 155n39; 5.180, 452n64; 5.183, 452n64; 6.166, 540n8; 6.168, 540n8; 7.12, 153n24; 7.78–89, 168n103 and 106–107; 7.80–81, 170n117; 7.85, 170n118, 540n8; 7.85–89, 169n108; 7.305, 158n59, 158n61; 7.306, 58n64, 540n8; 8.94, 149n1, 155n38, 158n61; 8.176, 149n1, 155n38, 158n61; 19.94, 284n35
Judges 3:8, 452n64; 3:10 (and LXX), 452n64; 5, 126n90, 156n41; 11:34, 126n90
Kelim 15 (*BT* 17.75) 302n131
1 Kings 4, 151n15; 4:22–28, 151n16; 4:30, 151n17; 4:31–34, 151n18; 5, 151n13; 5:6–10, 151n13; 5:18, 151n13; 6:15–16, 151n13; 6:37–38, 151n12; 7:2, 151n13; 7:2–3, 151n13; 7:11–12, 151n13; 7:27–37, 390n109; 8:2, 172n133; 9:10–14, 151n13; 9:11, 151n12; 10:1–3, 151n17; 10:11–25, 150n9;

10:12, 158n61; 10:23–25, 151n16, 151n16; 11:1–3, 154n31; 11:4–8, 154n34; 16:9–20, 138n162; 18, 146n207

2 Kings 3:13–20, 165n88; 18:13–37, 154n30; 24:13–25:21, 150n7

1 Maccabees 4:54, 215n164

Matthew 1:1–17, 180n174

Midrash Rabbah Numbers 15.11, 58n69; 15.16, 182n186

Nehemiah 7:1, 301n123; 7:67, 301n123; 7:73, 301n123; 12:27, 181n184; 12:27–47, 155n38, 301n123; 12:36, 158n59

Numbers 9:14, 152n23; 10:1–10, 155n39; 16:1–11, 174n147; 23–24, 156n41; 24:17, 180n176; 25:14, 138n162

[Philo] *Biblical Antiquities* 2.8, 215n164

Proverbs 7:17, 283n27

Psalms 3–9, 178n166; 4:1, 162n80; 5:1–2, 162n80; 8, 161n76; 11–32, 178n166; 18, 174n147, 178n166; 29, 174n148; 33:1–3, 58n67, 162n80; 34–41, 178n166; 34:1, 162n80; 42, 174n147; 44–49, 174n147; 47:1, 162n80; 49:1–4, 162; 49:2–5, 164n86; 51–70, 178n166; 57:8–9, 444n7; 61:1–2, 162n80; 68:25, 116n26; 77:1, 162n80; 78:2–3, 162n81; 80:1, 162n80; 81, 161n76; 81:1–2, 129n104, 162n80; 83:1, 162n80; 84, 161n76; 84–5, 174n147; 86, 178n166; 86:1, 162n80; 87–88, 174n147; 88, 152n23; 88:1–2, 162n80; 89:1, 162n80; 92:1–3, 162n80; 95:1–2, 162n80; 96:1–2, 162n80; 98:1–2, 162n80; 98:4–6, 179n169; 101, 178n166; 101:1, 162n80; 102:1–2, 162n80; 103, 178n166; 105:1–2, 162n80; 108:1–3, 163, 181; 109–110, 178n166; 116:1–2, 162n80; 118:14, 176n158, 177n161; 120:1, 162n80; 122, 178n166; 124, 178n166; 130:1–2, 162n80; 131, 178n166; 132, 168n103, 175; 133, 178n166; 135:3, 129n104; 137:1–4, 300n121; 138–145, 178n166; 141:1, 162n80; 142:1–2, 162n80; 143:1, 162n80; 144–145, 178n166; 144:9, 58n67; 147:1, 129n104, 162n80; 148:7–10, 179n179; 149, 179n170; 149:1, 162n80; 149:3, 179n171; 150, 179n171; 150:1–6, 162n80; 150:4, 117n35; 151 LXX, 178n166, 194n43; 151:2 LXX, 58n66; 151:3 LXX, 158n59

Psalms of Solomon, 152n20

Revelation 18:22, 300n120

1 Samuel 8:20, 150n6; 10:5–6, 45n11, 157n48, 265n105; 10.5, 157n53; 16:10, 172n132; 16:14, 166n94; 16:14–23, 166n95; 16:16, 166n96; 16:18, 167n98; 16:23, 58n66, 158n58, 540n8; 18:6, 126n90, 126n92; 19:20–24, 164n86; 19:36, 154n28; 27:1–6, 161n76; 31:10, 378n48

2 Samuel 1:17–27, 175n150, 301n126; 3:33–4, 175n150; 6, 168n103; 6:5, 117n35, 155n38, 169n115, 170n117; 6:5 LXX, 169n115, 214n154; 6:13, 171n124; 6:13–14 LXX, 170n121; 6:13–17, 169n109; 6:15, 155n38; 6:15 LXX, 169n115; 6:16, 169n108; 6:16 LXX, 170n121; 6:20–23, 169n108; 6:21, 174n146; 7:2, 151n13; 7:7, 151n13; 18:33, 301n126, 312n190; 22, 174n147; 23:1, 129n104–105, 178; 23:1–2, 175n152; 23:1–7, 174n147, 178n166

Sanhedrin 16a, 182n186; 38b, 180n177

Shabbath 56b, 154n36

Index Locorum

Sirach 45:9, 129n104
Song of Songs, 152, 154n34; 5:13, 283n27
Targum Sheni to Esther 1:3, 183n198
Zechariah 12:11, 485n154

Ebla

ARET 3 44 V.1, 66n28
ARET 11 1 §11, 68n42; 1 §13, 68n42; 1 §32, 68n42; 1 §63–65, 69n45; 1 §75–77, 69n50; 1 §85, 68n41; 1 §88, 68n41; 1§ 91, 68n41; 2, 68n40; 2 §16, 68n42; 2 §66, 68n43; 2 §66–68, 69n45; 2 §79–81, 69n50; 2 §89, 68n41; 2 §92, 68n41; 2 §95, 68n41; 3 §11–14, 68n40; 3 §12, 68n42, 69n50
ARET 12 709 I.3–4, 66n28; 773 I.1–2, 66n28; 874 XIV.11–12, 66n28
ARET 15.1 23 obv. VII.14–15 (§34), 66n24; 25 obv. VII.1 (§24), 65n23
Ebla Vocabulary §571, 66n32; §572, 54n35
TM.75.G.1672, 67n34; TM.75.G.1823+, 67n34; TM.75.G.1939+, 67n34; TM 75.G.2337 obv. VII 47, 71n62; TM 75.2365 rev. XII.17–20, 66n24

Egypt

Aten Hymns, 110n127
El-Amarna Letters EA 23, 373n11; 31, 323n15; 33–40, 11n45, 323n11; 33.16–18, 324n20; 34, 323n15; 34.18, 324n20; 34.24, 50–51, 330n63; 35, 372, 396n134; 35.10-15, 324n20, 372n1; 35.25, 330n63; 35.26, 373n8; 35.27–29, 326n34; 35.30–36, 12n58; 35.35–39, 372n1; 35.37, 324n20; 35.43, 323n11; 36.5–7, 12–14, 324n20; 37.9, 324n20; 39.10–20, 12n58, 326n34; 40.7–8, 13–20, 323n15, 324n20, 326n34; 77, 482n137; 84.33, 483n144; 101, 55n51; 114, 55n51, 481n134; 116, 55n51; 129.51, 483n146; 138.6, 55n51; 269.16, 199n71
Execration Texts 441, 452n62 and 64, 478n119
Medinet Habu Inscription (Ramesses III), 13n66
Papyrus Anastasi, 56n55, 106
Tale of Wen-Amun, 14, 105n101, 354, 481, 514n129

Emar

Ḫḫ VI.10–12, 78–79, 206n106
Installation of Baal's High Priestess, 171

Hittite, Hurro-Hittite, Neo-Hittite/Luwian

Çineköy inscription (Cilicia). *See* Phoenician/Punic
CTH 105, 12n54; 121, 13n64; 141, 376n38; 147, 13n64, 348n63; 321, 98n51; 344, 97n50; 345, 92n10; 348, 92n10; 364, 103n88; 481 (*Establishing a New Temple for the Goddess of the Night*), 100; 483, 376n35; 716, 376n31; 718, 329n52, 330n60; 771, 102n80
Karatepe inscriptions. *See* Phoenician/Punic (KAI 26)
KBo 1.52 obv. i.15–16, 98n55, 116n30; 2.9, 100n68, 376n31; 4.13, 94n21; 11.60 rev. 7'–15', 95n32; 12.38, 13n64; 12.39, 12n56, 376n38; 12.88.5–10, 32n92; 14.142 i.20–33, 103n86; 17.74, 94n23; 19.128, 94n23; 20.85 rev. iv.1–5, 95n27; 21.34 ii.9–10, 95n26; 23.42 + 27.119 rev. iv.24'–25', 94n25; 26.137, 2, 32n92; 33.109 right col. line 6, 99n60; 33.167 rev. iv.16'–20', 94n25, 101n79; 34.68, 95n31; 39.4.25, 95n31; 629, 99n58

Near Eastern Sources

KUB 1.1+ iii.28-30, 12n56; 9.31, 509n88; 10.82 rev. v.4-10, 94n21; 14.1 rev. 84-90, 13n64, 348n63; 14.14 obv. 16-22, 12n56; 15.34 i.48-65, 376n35; 15.35, 100n68, 376n31; 20.19, 95n26; 21.17 ii.5-8, 100n72; 23.1 iv.1-7, 12n54; 25.1 rev. v.11-16, 93n14; 25.37+, 102n80; 30.15, 95n35; 30.23, 95n35; 30.25, 95n31; 32.133 i.1-7, 100n71; 39.13 ii.5, 95n35; 39.19.17-20, 95n35; 39.71++ obv. ii.18-30, 329n52; 39.71++ rev. iv.9-21, 329n52; 45.45, 99n58; 47.40 obv. 10, 99n58; 51.87 rev. iv.12'-14', 95n26; 56.46 + ii.3'-7', 95n28
Kumarbi Cycle, 92n10, 97, 103
Ritual and Prayer to Ishtar of Nineveh, 100, 474
Song of Hedammu, 92n10
Song of Silver, 103, 506
Song of Ullikummi, 92n10
Tale of Illuyanka, 98

Mesopotamia

Abzu Pelam (The Defiled Apsu), 84n87
Amherst (Pinches 1908) 82 rev. 19, 483n141
An:Anum, 29n68; I 268, 35n114; II 343-344, 124n82; III 51, 36n118; III 153-158, 21n18, 507n72; V 100-106, 29n68; V 168, 485n159; V 291, 21n18
ARAB 1 §756, 300n119; 2 §186, 353n88; 2 §312, 154n30; 2 §319, 328n41; 2 §690, 14n73, 360n131, 546n9
ARM 13 20, 54n41, 76n25; 21 298, 76n28; 23 180, 76n26; 23 213, 76n28; 25 547, 76n27; 25 566, 84n81
Assyrian King List, 83
Babylonian Erra Myth, 25
Berossos FGH 680 F 4, 462n14
Curse of Agade, 41
Diri, 79, 122; III.43-45 (Assur), 79n49, 34n106; III.49, 36n115
Early Dynastic Practical Vocabulary B_2 = MS 2340+ 22:20', 54n37, 87
Elum Gusun (Honored One, Wild Ox), 27n60
Enegi temple-hymn, 140n169
Enki's Journey to Nippur, 34n107
Enmerkar and the Lord of Aratta, 474n96
Epic of Gilgamesh, 462n16; vi.24-79, 474n97
The Fashioning of the Gala, 29n72
FM 4 37, 82n69; 4 42.4-5, 77n29; 9 11, 74n10; 9 21, 75n22; 9 45-46, 75n21; 9 52.8'-9', 82n68; 9 53, 76n25, 86n85; 9 59, 81n63
Genealogy of the Hammurabi Dynasty, 83.
Gudea Cylinders A 5.2-10, 393n123; 6.6-8, 393n123; 6.24-7.6, 28n64; 7.9-8.1, 28n64; 7.25, 30n81; 9.24, 27n55; 15.19-25, 27n56; 18.10-19.2, 393n123; 18.18, 532n10; 20.24-21.12, 393n123; 22.20, 27n57; 28.17, 534n16; 28.18, 532n9, 532n10; B 6.11-23, 27n58; 6.24-7.11, 27n59; 7.12-21, 27n57; 8.10-22, 30n82; 10.9-15, 28n67; 10.16-11.2, 29n70; 15.19-16.2, 28n67, 32n96; 15.20, 532n10; 18.22-19.1, 28n67; 19.1, 532n10; 24.17, 26n49
Heimpel, "Balang Gods" Catalogue 4b, 66n26; 4c, 54n37, 65n22, 77n35; 4d and 4e, 71n65; 4g, 531n2; 9 and 11, 20n5, 41n152; 12, 20n5; 13, 20n5-6; 15, 20n5; 17b, 21n19; 17f, 20n5; 20a-20b, 20n5; 23, 84n83-84; 23a1, 22n21; 23b, 485n158; 23f, 84n86, 102n81, 291n69, 380n62, 485n158; 23g, 76n27; 23g2, 84n81; 27, 414n81;

719

Index Locorum

(Heimpel, *cont.*)
>34c, 76n27; 37, 41n152; 40, 36n119; 42a, 30n78; 42c, 76n27; 43, 41n150 and 152; 44, 84n78; 47, 84n85; 47a, 485n158; 49, 84n87; 53, 21n18, 29n68, 35n114, 36n118, 485n159, 507n72; 54, 30n79, 124n82

Ḫg 169 (MSL 6, 142), 36n115
Ḫh (HAR.ra/ur5-ra), 78n39, 79n50; 79–80, 36n115
Hymn to the Queen of Nippur, 78
Iddin-Dagan A, 37n125, 39n135, 39n136
Inanna's Descent to the Netherworld, 29n72, 145n197
In the Desert by the Early Grass, 140n170
Ishme-Dagan A + V, 81n61
Ishtar Ritual (OB Mari), 85n88
K 4806, 24n39
KAR 50, 24n34; 60, 24n37; 158, 97n47
Lilissu ritual, 23–24, 30n79
Lugalbanda and the Anzud Bird, 474n96
Lugal-e (*Exploits of Ninurta*), 25n46, 380
Marriage of Martu, 80
Martu A, 80n58; Martu A/B, 80n57
Metal List, 19, 580n21
RIME 1 10.12.3, 73n3; 2 1.4.10, 33n101, 37n123; 3/1 1.1.7 CylA/B, 26n51; 3/1 1.1.7 (3), 21n19; 3/1 1.1.7 (6), 27n56; 3/1 1.1.7.StB v.1–4, 29n75; 3/1 1.1.7.StE iv.12–14, 22n20; 3/2 1.1.2–8, 393n123; 3/2 1.2.1–34, 393n123; 3/2 1.3.3–9, 393n123; 3/2 1.3.14–17, 393n123; 4 1.1.1 lines 13–14, 36n119; 4 2.13.1002, 84n78; 4 3.6.2, 506n70; 4 3.6.10, 8, 87n100; 4 3.6.11, 86n99; 4 3.6.12, 506n70

The Rites of Egašankalamma, 283n26
Shulgi A, 39n133, 382n72; Shulgi B, 34n107, 38n129, 38n130, 38n131; Shulgi C, D, 37n125; Shulgi E, 37n125, 34n107; Shulgi G, P, Q, R, 37n125; Shulgi X, 37n125, 39n132

Sumerian Temple Hymns (no. 14), 140n169
Šurpu, 21n14
TSA (de Genouillac 1909) 1 ix.12–14, 41n149
Ur-Nammu A, 37n121, 144n194
Uru'amma'irabi (*That City Which has Been Pillaged*), 84–85, 291, 585, 588, 594–595, 611, 614, 619, 623
Uruhulake of Gula (*She of the Ruined City*), 84n87
VAT 8247, 24n34; 10101, 97n47

Phoenician/Punic

Mokhos of Sidon FGH 784 F 4, 445n13
Philo of Byblos 790 F 1 (20–22), 123n75; F 1 (21), 446n16; 790 F 2 (11), 446n19, 510n106; F 2 (13), 509n95, 510n107; F 2 (14), 510n106; F 2 (15–16, 24), 123n74; F 2 (15), 314n203; F 2 (22), 481n133; F 2 (25), 510n108; F 2 (31), 378n48; F 2 (35), 472n84, 481n133; F 2 (38), 511n109; F 10, 477n114
Inscriptions (excluding Cyprus: *v. infra*)
>Cebel Ires Daği inscription, 202n90
Chabot 1940–1941 no. 232, 452n60
Çineköy inscription, 3n11, 199n67, 252n49
KAI 1, 315n209; 4, 483n146, 510n100; 5–7, 407n45; 10, 407n45, 510n100; 13.1–2, 407n45; 14, 407n45; 26, 252n50; 26 A.I.12–13, 512n116; 26 A.II.19–20, 507n75; 26 A III.2–3, 507n75; 26 C.IV.20, 507n75; 46, 315n210, 344n38; 139.1 and 145.40, 452n60

Syriac and Syria
(including Aramaic)

Anton of Tagrit *Rhetoric* 5.10, 542n23
Book of the Bee 18, 455n79; 19, 455n78
St. Ephraim
   Commentary on Genesis 4:21
      (Armenian trans.), 454n76
   Commentary on 2 Kings 3:15, 165n89, 219
   Hymns, 61, 163n83, 182, 210, 216
Isaac of Antioch, 471n81
KAI 214.15-22 (Zincirli), 136n151; 222 (Sefire steles), 154, 300
Lassus 1935:33 no. 14 (Hama, Syria), 443n2
[Meliton] *Apology* 44.12-22, 470n73; 44.34-36, 496n7
Michael the Syrian *Chronicle* 1.6, 215n164, 454n76; 3.8, 378n52
Odes of Solomon, 152n21; 6.1, 542n23; 14.8, 542n23; 26.3, 542n23
Theodore Bar Koni *Liber Scholiorum, Mimrā* 2.97, 45n11, 455n78; 4.38, 471n79; 11.4, 471n79

Ugarit

CTA 6.6.54-55, 152n23
KTU/CAT 1.1 iii.1 and 18-19, 447n23; 1.1 iii.27-28, 447n24; 1.2 iii.2-3, 447n23; 1.2 iii.7-11, 447n24; 1.1 iii.27-28, 447n24; 1.2 iv.11-15, 447n26; 1.2 iv.11-27, 122n71; 1.3 i.18-22, 117n31, 128n97; 1.3 iii.4-5, 126n88; 1.3 vi.14-16, 447n23; 1.4 i.23-43, 447n25; 1.4 v.41-vi.38, 447n24; 1.4 vi.16-33, 150n11; 1.6 vi.51-53, 447n22; 1.7.22-24, 126n88; 1.17 v.10-28, 447n26; 1.17 vi.20-25, 447n26; 1.17 vi.26-32, 131n120; 1.17 vi.32, 129n101; 1.17 vi.34-38, 131n126; 1.17 vi.45-1.18 i.19, 132n128; 1.18 iv.14, 133n129; 1.18 iv.19, 133n129; 1.18 iv.30, 133n129; 1.18 iv.39, 133n130; 1.19 i.5, 133n132; 1.19 iv.22-31, 135n140, 144n192; 1.23, 113n5, 115n16, 128n100; 1.41, 283n20; 1.47, 4n18; 1.101.16-19, 125n87; 1.101.17, 126n88; 1.106.15-17, 113n5; 1.108, 117n31, 135n142, 256n69, 265n105, 456n81; 1.112, 113n5; 1.113, 141n177; 1.118, 4n19; 1.119, 139n166; 1.123, 509n97; 1.141, 373n13; 1.148, 5n22, 97n48, 120n51, 377n42; 1.161, 143n191; 2.42, 12n58, 374n17; 4.102, 441n115; 4.168, 114n10, 383n77; 4.352, 330n64; 4.360, 115n14; 4.399, 115n17; 4.410, 115n14; 4.609, 114n9; 4.610, 115n18
RIH 98/02, 52n26, 102n82, 114n13
RS 1.003.20, 283n20; 1.017, 4n18; 2.002, 113n5, 115n16, 128n100; 2.[004], 129n101, 131n120, 447n26; 2.[008]+, 150n11, 447n24, 447n25; 2.[009] + 5.155, 447n22; 2.[014] + 3.363, 117n31, 126n88, 128n97, 447n23; 3.322+, 135n140, 144n192; 3.346, 447n23, 447n24; 3.361, 447n23, 447n24; 3.367, 122n71, 447n26; 5.180 + 5.198, 126n88; 11.857, 441n115; 13.006, 5, 283n20; 13.53, 121n59; 15.82, 114n10, 383n77; 17.352, 12n56, 377n43; 18.42, 330n64; 18.050, 115n14; 18.056.22, 283n20; 18.113A, 12n58, 326n34, 374n17; 18.119, 326n34; 18.138, 115n17; 18.250A+B, 115n14; 19.16, 114n9, 167n100, 441n117; 19.017, 115n18; 20.18, 11n45; 20.19, 440n109; 20.024, 4n19, 235n100; 20.123+, 443n2, 449n35; 20.168, 11n45, 12n55; 20.238, 11n45,

Index Locorum

(RS, *cont.*)
12n55; 24.245, 125n87, 126n88; 24.250+, 113n5; 24.252, 117n31, 129n108, 134–135n142, 177n161, 256n69, 265n105, 374n17, 448n33, 456n81; 24.256, 113n5; 24.257, 134n139, 141–147, 177, 204n96; 24.264 + 24.280, 4n19; 24.266, 139n166; 24.271, 509n97; 24.274, 102n84, 374n15; 24.325, 373n13;

24.643, 5n22, 97n48, 120–121, 123n74, 139n166, 377n42; 26.142, 121n58, 121n61; 34.126, 143n191; 34.152, 12n58; 92.2004, 120n51, 121n56–58; 94.2177+, 12n62; 94.2475, 12n55; 94.2518, 139n166, 141n177

RSL 1, 11n45

Cypriot Inscriptions ('Eteocypriot', Greek, Phoenician)

Amadasi and Karageorghis 1977 C1, 57n58, 116n23, 262n98
DGAC 10, 349n70; 123, 349n70; 148–149, 349n70; 166.6, 412n70; 171.1, 284n30; 249, 349n70
ExcCyp 6, 402n5; 46, 409n54; 101, 421n119; 105, 420n116; 124, 234n88, 420n116
GIBM IV.2 975, 287n46
HIOP 1, 409n54; 32, 418n100; 40, 418n102; 70, 420n111; 99, 205n102, 420n116; 103–104, 420n115; 105, 234n88
Honeyman 1938, 339n11
ICS 1, 409n49 and 51, 412n70; 2, 409n49 and 53, 422n126; 3, 409n49 and 53, 422n126; 4.1, 407n44; 6, 407n44, 409n49; 7, 407n44, 409n49; 8, 414n85; 16.2, 407n44; 17.1, 412n70; 17.4, 407n44; 39, 230n66; 40, 230n66; 41, 230n66; 43, 230n66; 44, 230n66; 90, 407n44, 409n49 and 52; 91, 407n44, 409n49; 183, 349n70; 190–196, 349n66; 194.4, 404n25; 216, 229n61, 372n6; 220, 372n6

IGRom. 3:941, 402n5
I.Kourion 4, 244n7; 6, 287n46; 41, 230n67; 104, 213n152, 318–319
I.Paphos 1, 409n54; 9, 418n102; 19, 420n111; 64, 412–414; 66, 418n100; 72–73, 420n115; 79, 420n116; 82, 234n88; 148, 402n5; 151, 205n103; 181, 421n119
I.Rantidi 2.1, 284n30, 413n76; 14, 230n66
KAI 32–34, 344n38; 37, 116n23; 39, 344n38, 372n6; 41, 344n38
LBW 801, 287n46; 2798, 418n100
Masson and Sznycer 1972:p81–86, 271n129
Nicolaou 1964 23a, 412–414
SEG 13:586, 213n151; 18:578, 205n103; 18:586, 409n51; 20:114, 411n64; 20:225, 284n30, 413n76; 20:251, 409n51; 23:639, 412–414; 40:1365, 421n119; 51:1896, 205n103; 53:1747bis, 319n236; 55:1534, 205n103

Greek/Latin

Linear B

Knossos (KN) B 800.3, 434n67; C 954.1, 435n68; Da 1134, 435n68; Db 1279, 434n67; Fh 347, 331n68; Fh 361, 331n68; Fh 371, 331n68; Fh 372, 331n68; L 588.1, 439n102; Mc 4459, 435n68; Sc 238, 432n49; U 736.2, 437n90; V 52.2, 439n104; V 60, 432n49; V 831, 434n66; V 831.1, 434n65; X 1024.1, 435n69; Xd 7702, 432n49

Mycenae (MY) Ge 602.4, 429n16; Go 610+, 435n68

Pylos (PY) An 19.7, 435n69; An 340, 435n69; An 519.10, 439n102 and 104; An 654.14, 439n104; An 656, 439n102-104; An 724, 432n48 and 49; Aq 218, 431n42, 432n49; Aq 64.14, 431n42; Cn 131.4, 435n68; Cn 719.9, 435n68; Ep 705, 434n65; Er 880, 430n27; Fr 1225, 331n69; Jn series, 394n127; Jn 310.3, 435n68; Jn 320.3, 436n77; Jn 389, 437n92; Jn 829, 437n92; Jo 438, 435n68; Ma and Na tablets, 428n7; N- series, 437n86; Na 248 and 252, 437n87; Na 568, 437n86; Nn 228, 437n86; Qa series, 428n6; Qa 1259, 427n4; Qa 1289, 431n39; Qa 1290, 428n10, 432n51; Qa 1291, 428n12; Qa 1292, 432n51; Qa 1293, 432n51; Qa 1294, 428n10; 432n44; Qa 1295, 432n51; Qa 1297, 432n51; Qa 1298, 432n51; Qa 1300, 429n18, 431n39; Qa 1302, 428n12; Qa 1304, 428n10, 432n51; Qa 1305, 428n12, 431n37; Qa 1306, 428n12; Qa 1307, 431n37; Qa 1309, 428n12; Qa 1310, 428n12; Qa 1311, 428n12; Qa 1312, 428n12; Qa 1441, 427n4, 428n12; Sh 736, 322n9; Sn 64.4, 434n67; Tn 316, 423n129; Un 219, 431n36 and 38; Un 249, 331n67; Un 443.1, 436n78; Un 718, 431n36; Un 1482, 428n8; Vn 865, 436-438; Xa 1335, 429n23

Thebes (TH) Av 106.7, 434n62

Traditional Sources and Papyri

Abydenos FGH 685 F 2b-3b, 462n14

Acts of Xanthippe and Polyxena, 209n124

Ailianos
  On the Nature of Animals 9.36, 237n46, 290n63
  Various History 9.38, 196n53

Aiskhylos
  Libation Bearers 609, 233n83
  Persians 895, 355n103
  Seven against Thebes 26n49; 835-839, 295n95; 866-870, 233n83; Σ 122, 214n156
  Suppliants 694-697, 227n50

Alexander Romance, 303

Alexandros of Aphrodisias,
  Commentary on Aristotle's Metaphysics 3.2 (p220.22), 286n41

Alexandros Polyhistor FGH 273 F 31, 337n3

Alkaios 130.34, 411n68; 307c, 434n61; p507 Voigt, 271, 274-276

Alkidamas *Odysseus* 20-21, 1n1, 343n32

Alkman 3.71 PMGF, 1n3, 220n7, 330n61, 432n52; 26, 192n32; 41, 255n59; 140, 434n61

Index Locorum

Ammianus Marcellinus 14.8.3, 508n81; 19.1.10–11, 306n154, 311n184
Ammonios *On Similar and Different Words* 178, 310n177; 321, 209n125
Anakreon 361 PMG, 329n56, 515
Analecta Hymnica Graeca
  Canones Novembris, Day 30 Canon 44 Ode 7.8, 182n189
  Canones Decembris, Day 26 Canon 51 Ode 5.16–17, 182n187; Day 26 Canon 51 Ode 8.56–58, 182n187, 209n127
  Canones Januarii, Day 25 Canon 30 (1) Ode 6.46, 182n187; Day 27 Canon 34 Ode 4.3–7, 210n133
Androkles FGH 751 F 1, 337n3, 516n135
Anecdota Graeca (Bachmann 1828–1829) 1:278, 47n18, 188n7, 195n48; 1:304, 210n128
Anecdota Graeca (Cramer 1839–1841) 4:35.10–11, 197n55; 4:35.13–14, 197n55, 198n52; 4:36.20, 47n18; 4:274.5–6, 193n36; 4:183.15, 467n52
Antimachos fr. 92 Matthews (102 West IEG), 284n34, 290n63
Antiphanes fr. 200 PCG, 284n31, 491n14
Antoninos Liberalis *Metamorphoses* 34, 281n10, 284n37, 286n41, 287n47, 288n54, 467n56; 39, 281n10
Appendix Proverbiorum 4.68, 224n34, 504n59
Apion FGH 616 F 51 (= 48 Neitzel), 197n55
Apollodoros FGH 244 F 277, 197n55
[Apollodoros]
  Epitome 3.4–5, 1n2; 3.9, 1n2, 343n32, 344n34; 3.12, 359n124; 6.15, 359n126; 6.17, 340n20
  Library 1.3.2, 193n37; 1.3.3, 325n24; 1.6.3, 98n51; 1.9.5, 492n20; 2.1.2, 340n16, 558n8; 2.1.3, 343n30; 2.1.4, 354n100, 516n137; 2.1.5, 515n130; 2.5.11, 373n10; 3.8.1, 308n166; 3.9.1, 365n161, 511n115; 3.9.2, 343n31; 3.10.3, 492n20; 3.10.8, 359n125; 3.11.1, 333n81; 3.12.2, 434n67; 3.14.3, 250n41, 287n46, 290n63, 333n84 and 85, 344n37, 355n107, 356n109 and 113, 404n24, 477n113, 504n60, 511n115, 545n3; 3.14.3–4, 281n12, 288n56; 3.14.4, 284n32 and 37, 287n46, 313n194, 317n225, 467n50 and 52, 502n47
Apollonios of Rhodes 1.26–27, 193n37; 1.292, 200n77; 1.882–885, 200n73 and 75, 232n81; 3.259, 201n81; 3.664, 201n81; 4.611–618, 294n91; 4.1063, 201n86.
  Scholia (Σ) 1.292, 188n6, 197n55; 1.882–885; 3.1186, 325n24
Apollonios Sophistes *Homeric Lexicon* s.v. θυμαρέα, 512n119; κινυρή, 188n7
Apuleius *Golden Ass* 11.2, 287n46
Aristokles of Rhodes *On Poetry*, 310n177
Aristonikos Grammaticus *On the Signs of the Iliad* p168 Friedlander, 208n116
Aristophanes
  Clouds 595, 233n84; 749–750, 103n91
  Knights 8–12, 202n89, 214n156, 295n95. Σ 9, 295n95
  Lysistrata, 284
  fr. 325 PCG, 315n213
Aristotle
  Constitution of the Athenians 26.3, 356n108
  Metaphysics 388b18, 286n41; 389a14, 286n41
  On the Soul 407b–408a, 210n129

Greek/Latin

fr. 526–527 Rose (*Constitution of the Cypriots*), 382n70, 499n30
[Aristotle] *Peplos* fr. 640 §8 Rose, 355n103; §30, 359n126
Aristoxenos fr. 80 Wehrli, 295n95; fr. 97, 275n147 and 150
Arkhilokhos 1 West IEG, 255n59; 54.11, 434n61; 93a.5, 434n61
Arnobius *Against the Pagans* 6.6, 289n58, 419n106, 561n29; 6.22, 289n58
Arrian
  Anabasis of Alexander 2.20.3, 491n16, 493n29; 5.6.5, 515n130; 6.22.4, 286n41
  Events after Alexander FGH 156 F 10 §6, 414n82
Artemidoros *Interpretation of Dreams* 4.72, 434n62
Asklepiades of Cyprus FGH 752, 337n3
Athenaios 174a–185a, 275n148; 174f, 145n200, 190n19, 225n40, 567n66; 180d, 293n75; 182f, 275n150; 255c–257d, 491n14; 256b, 355n103; 256b–c, 366n165, 458n88; 257d, 284n31; 337e–f, 212n144; 346e, 363n150; 349e–f, 212n142; 352d, 212n142; 456a, 290n63, 313n192; 515e, 222n16; 531a–d, 212n143; 574a, 286n41; 619c, 309n172; 619f, 305n147; 633f, 456n81 634c–637f, 275n148; 636b, 275n150; 637b, 274n144; 638a, 211n140; 638b, 234n93; 681d, 309n174
Augustine
  City of God 15.17.35, 215n164, 540n9
  Commentary on Psalm 32, Sermon 1.4–5, 540n9
  Confessions 3.8.32, 540n9; 9.12.25 and 10.33, 541n14
Ausonius
  Epigrams 62.7, 299n111

Letters 14.42–43, 299n111
Basilios of Caesarea *Commentary on Isaiah* 5.155 (Trevisan), 293n79
Berossos. *See* Mesopotamia
Bion *Lament for Adonis* 24, 467n52; 42, 299n113; 65–66, 500n31; 91, 299n113, 432n52, 449n42; 91–95, 449n42
Boios *Creation of Birds*, 192
Carmina popularia 34 (Linos-song, PMG 800), 307n163
Catullus 68.51–52, 315n213; 95, 286n38
John Chrysostomus *Exposition of Psalm 41*, 540n5
[John Chrysostomus] *On the Adoration of the Precious Cross* PG 62:752.72, 214n155
Cicero *On the Laws* 1.5, 346n50
Cinna *Zmyrna*, 334n91, 386n38; fr. 6 Courtney FLP, 286n40, 502n49; fr. 8, 286n40
Clement of Alexandria
  Tutor 2.4.43, 540n5; 3.11.80, 540n6
  Exhortation 1, 210n130; 1.5.4, 210n131; 2.13.4–5, 222n15, 312n2; 2.14, 219n1; 2.15.3, 102n80, 540n6; 2.24.1, 540n6; 2.33, 219n1, 474n99; 3.45, 321n2, 419n106, 561n29; 4.49.2, 319n236; 4.57.3, 561n28; 12.119.2–120.2, 540n6. Σ 2.13.4, 321n2
  Miscellanies 1.21, 321n2, 449n43
Clement of Rome *Homilies* 5.15.2 (PG 2:184C–185D), 227n53
Columella *On Agriculture* 10.1.1, 286n41
Constantine Mannases *Chronicle* 4687–4688, 193n40
Constantine Porphyrogenitus
  On the Themes 1.15, 350n74, 516n134
  On Virtues and Vices 1 (55.16–22, Büttner-Wobst/Roos), 170n118

Index Locorum

Curtius Rufus 4.1, 490n6, 491n12
Cyril of Alexandria *Commentary on Isaiah* (PG 70:440C), 284n37
John of Damascus *Sermon on the Birth of Christ* 9, 216n167, 538
Damaskios
    Life of Isidore fr. 348 Zintzen, 511n111
    On First Principles 125c (1.323 Ruelle), 445n13
Demetrios of Salamis FGH 756 F 1, 337n3
Demodokos fr. 1-2, 497n17
[Demodokos] fr. 3 PLG/IEG, 497n15
Demosthenes 12.10, 353n92
Derveni Papyrus col. 6.1-11, 449n39
Digenes Akrites 4.396-435 (cod. Grottaferrata), 255n59
Diktys of Crete *Journal of the Trojan War* 6.8, 334n93
Dio Chrysostomus 8.28, 323n10; 33.47, 509n93
Diodoros Siculus 2.16.6, 327n35, 328n40, 547n13; 2.49.2, 286n41; 4.37.2, 365n163; 5.74.5, 229n56; 7 fr. 11, 327n36; 14.39, 347n56; 14.98, 347n53, 352n84; 15.2.4, 347n55, 493n26; 16.46.3, 493n28; 17.47.1-6, 490n6; 19.59.1, 416n94; 19.62, 416n94; 19.79.4-5, 416n94; 20.21.2-3, 417n96, 491n17; 20.47.2, 545n5
Diogenes Laertios 1.4, 308n165; 2.57, 566n65; 2.59, 566n63 and 65
Diogenianos 8.53, 323n10
Dionysios of Halicarnassus *On Thucydides* 5.1, 356n113
Dionysios the Periegete 508-509, 327n36, 403n16, 498n20
    Scholia (Σ) 509, 290n63, 321n2, 333n84, 350n74, 355n107, 356n114, 404n24, 406n49, 468n59, 498n23

[Dionysios the Periegete] fr. 1 (Heitsch), 545n4; fr. 2, 545n2
Dioskourides *On Medical Material* 1.24.1, 1.64.1, 1.66.1, 286n41; 3.39.1, 332n75
Ephoros FGH 70 F 4, 274n144
Epikharmos in Athenaios 681d, 309n174
Eratosthenes
    Amathousia (FGH 241 F 25), 337n3, 340n19, 546n8
    Hermes, 340n19
    fr. III B 91 Berger (130 Roller), 327n35
Etymologicum Genuinum s.v. Ἀῷος, 356n114; ἀμφικινυρόμεναι, 200n73, 232n81
Etymologicum Gudianum s.v. κίθαρις, 197n55; κινύρα, 200n78, 334n94; ὕμνος, 232n76
Etymologicum Magnum s.v. ἀμφικινυρόμεναι, 200n73, 232n81; Ἄφακα, 464n28; Ἀῷος, 356n114, 467n52, 500n33; Κίρρις, 315n211; Κύπρος, 516n135
Etymologicum Symeonis s.v. ἀμφικινυρόμεναι, 200n73, 232n81
Euripides
    Alkestis 445-447, 298n104; 583, 231n73
    Cyclops 489-490, 233n83
    Helen 144-150, 355n103; 167-178, 311n180; 371, 233n83; 1469-1470, 294n90
    Herakles 348-351, 309n172; 694, 232n80
    Hippolytos 454-455, 505n64
    Iphigeneia among the Taurians 1089-1093, 233n83; 1129, 232n80
    Iphigeneia at Aulis 1211-1212, 193n37
    Medea 190-200, 311n180; 668, 412n69

Orestes 1395–1399, 311n182
fr. 759a.1622–1623 TGF, 255n59
Eusebios
  Chronicle 1:35 Schoene, 520n161; 1:177, 558n8; 1:225, 327n36, 2:34, 378n52
  Commentaries on the Psalms PG 23:73A, 170n123
  In Praise of Constantine 8.5–9, 465n39
  Life of Constantine 3.55.1–3, 465n39
  Preparation for the Gospel 1.9.20–22, 123n75; 1.10.11–12, 446n19; 2.3.12, 222n15; 2.3.15, 222n15; 2.6.6, 419n106
Eustathios
  on Dionysios the Periegete 11, 348n60; 498, 478n121; 508–509, 323n13, 327n36, 403n16; 508–512, 350n74; 912, 466n48, 516n134
  on Homer *Iliad* 2.780–785, 503n56; 3.24, 196n53; 3.54, 196n53; 10.269, 478n121; 10.409, 514n124; 11.20–23, 1n1, 3n13, 187n3, 321n2, 322n6, 323n10 and 13, 343n32, 345n41, 346n47, 432n52, 466n49; 17.5, 188n7, 292n70; 18.613, 1n1; 19.129, 295n95.
  on Homer *Odyssey* 17.442–443, 342n28
  on Lykophron *Alexandra* 447, 516n135
Festus *On the Meaning of Words*, 404n19.
FGH 755, 337n3, 565n60
Firmicus Maternus *On the Error of Profane Religions* 10.1, 222n15; 18.1, 102n80
Fulgentius *Mythologies* 3.8, 283n27, 284n37, 286n41, 288n53
Gorgias DK 82 B 11–11a, 343n32
Greek Anthology 5.237.1 (Agathias Scholasticus), 191n27; 5.289.8 (Agathias Scholasticus), 299n109; 6.25 (Julian of Egypt), 329n55; 6.26 (Julian of Egypt), 329n55; 7.210.5 (Antipatros of Sidon), 191n27; 7.365.3–4 (Zonas of Sardis), 299n110; 7.407.7 (Dioskourides), 299n109; 11.236 ([Demodokos]), 497n15; 11.347.4 (Philip of Thessalonica), 554n30; 16.49 (Apollonides), 335n99
Gregory of Nazianzus *Orations* 14 (PG 35:873B), 295n95; 43 (PG 36:596B), 182n188
Gregory of Nyssa *Against Eunomios* 11 (PG 45.865D; 3.9.25 Jaeger), 295n95
Harpokration *Lexicon of the Ten Orators* s.v. ἄνακτες καὶ ἄνασσαι, 382n70; Χύτροι, 341n23
Herodian *De prosodia catholica* 89.20 Lentz, 378n52; 200.2, 350n74, 558n11, 559n12; 204.4, 350n74, 516n134; 242.34, 349n68, 350n74, 406n49, 559n12; 294.4, 349n68; 358.19, 350n74, 558n11, 559n12
Hellanikos FGH 4 F 5b, 345n43, 356n113; F 31, 348n60; F 36, 343n30; F 57, 337n3, 356n113, 506n67, 545n3, 553n28, 559n12; F 154a, 506n67; 756 F 1, 337n3, 506n67
Herakleitos 22 B 51 DK, 229n56
Hermesianax 7.2 CA, 325n24; 7.45–46, 284n34
Herodotos 1.105, 378n48, 478n121; 1.131, 378n50; 1.132.3, 449n39; 1.199.5, 222n16; 2.48–49, 305n142; 2.79, 304n141; 2.116–117, 467n55; 2.141, 154n30; 3.107.1, 275n146; 3.111.2, 275n146; 4.154.1–155.1, 333n82; 4.192, 274n144; 5.58, 348n60; 5.113, 340n16; 6.47, 379n54; 7.90, 340n15, 355n103, 359n126, 365n160, 506n67; 7.91,

Index Locorum

(Herodotos, *cont.*)
253n53, 340n18; 7.134, 423n128; 7.158, 224n28

Hesiod
Theogony 31-32, 411n68; 94-95, 310n175; 134-135, 288n52; 188-200, 330n59, 376n37; 191-193, 480n127; 192-193, 476n107; 194-195, 396n133; 371-374, 288n52; 986-991, 505n64
fr. 139 M-W, 313n194, 317n225; 141.16, 342n27; 305, 211n135, 316n218, 306n153; 306, 307n159

Hesykhios s.v. Ἀβώβας, 145n201, 502n46; ἀγήτωρ, 420n116; ἀερία, 403n13; ἀοῖα, 502n50; Ἀφρόδιτος, 315n213; ἀχαιομάντεις, 405n34; Ἄωοι, 503n53; γῆς ὀμφαλός, 204n99, 412n69, 416n91; Δαματρίζειν, 234n87, 287n46; Ἔγχειος, 375n22; ἐντροπίδες, 437n91; ἐντροπῶσαι, 437n91; Ἰοίην, 502n47; θαμυρίζει, 235n98; θάμυρις, 235n98; κάρπωσις, 287n46; κιναρύζεσθαι, 198n63; κιννυρίδες, 191n28; κινούρας, 197n55; κινύρα, 47n18, 195n48, 302n133; Κινυράδαι, 214n158, 420n111; Κινύρας, 227n54, 321n2, 504n59, 512n117; κινύρεσθαι, 188n6; κινυρή, 188n7, 214n158; κινυρίδες, 214n158; Κίρις, 315n211; κιχητός, 413n76; Κύβαβος, 462n16; λυροφοίνιξ, 274n144; μυρίκη, 284n37; νάβλα, 52n26; Πυγμαίων, 315n210; Ῥοίκου κριθοπομπία, 546n8; Ταμιράδαι, 404n23; φοιβητεύειν, 430n31; χλουνάζειν, 188n6

Hippokrates *On the Sacred Disease* 1.69 and 1.77, 103n91

Homer
Iliad 1.30, 340n16; 1.38, 342n27; 1.79, 340n16; 1.119, 340n16; 1.328, 411n68; 1.452, 342n27; 2.107-108, 340n16; 2.557-558, 355n102; 2.572, 339n14; 2.599-600, 411n68; 2.603-614, 359n124; 3.54, 196n53, 458n90; 3.82-83, 340n16; 3.187, 322n7; 4.228, 333n85; 5, 403n16; 6.478, 342n27; 8.114, 333n85; 8.498, 411n68; 9.114-161, 317n221; 9.185-189, 141n176; 9.189, 255n59, 318n233; 9.413, 318n233; 9.485-495, 317n227; 9.494-495, 317n227; 9.497-501, 316n219; 9.561-564, 191n25; 9.603, 317n221; 9.612, 207n112; 11.19-23, 1n1, 220n7, 322n5; 11.19-28, 409n47; 11.20, 321n2, 432n52; 11.24-28, 322n8, 447n25; 11.154-155, 340n16; 11.620, 333n85; 12.100-108, 322n7; 13.730-731, 255n59, 316n218; 14.172-174, 331n69; 17.4-6, 188n7; 17.5, 197n55, 318n234; 17.211, 439n104; 18.51, 293n75; 18.316, 293n75; 18.486-492, 308n167; 18.567-572, 308n168; 18.570, 306n151, 309n172; 19.301-302, 298n103; 22.254-255, 21n17, 211n136; 23.12-13, 292n72, 293n75, 411n68; 23.296-297, 322n6; 23.740-750, 322n9; 23.743, 199n71; 24.128, 207n112; 24.720-722, 292n73; 24.723, 293n75
Scholia (Σ) 2.494-877, 355n102; 9.612, 208n116; 11.20, 321n2, 322n6, 323n10, 466n49; 17.5, 188n6; 18.570, 306n153 and 155, 308n169, 309n173; 19.5, 286n41
Odyssey 1.159, 316n218; 1.243, 208n119; 2.23, 207n112; 3.267-272, 74n13; 4.10-12, ß33n81; 4.81-85, 104n98; 4.81-89, 323n12; 4.83-84, 339n8, 506n67;

4.100, 207n112; 4.477, 515n130;
4.581, 515n130; 4.602, 342n27;
4.615–619, 322n9; 5.247–248 and
361–362, 211n136; 8.224–228,
190n17; 8.267, 232n78; 8.285–288,
476n106; 8.359–366, 474n95;
8.360–366, 331n69; 8.362–363,
413n76; 9.13, 208n119; 11.134,
535n6; 11.214, 208n119; 11.305,
423n129; 12.158, 411n68; 14.40,
207n112; 14.258, 515n130; 15.103,
333n81; 15.115–119, 322n9;
15.242, 435n69; 15.425, 199n71,
322n9; 16.195, 208n119; 17.427,
515n130; 17.442–443, 342n26;
19.109–114, 387n99; 19.407–409,
333n81; 21.406, 211n135,
316n218; 21.406–413, 229n56,
255n59, 387n99; 21.411, 309n173;
24.58–61, 293n76 and 81
  Scholia (Σ) 17.442–443, 342n28
[Homer] *Margites* fr. 1.3 West IEG,
  434n61
Homeric Hymn to Aphrodite 58–59,
  413n76; 59–62, 331n69; 69–74,
  396n133; 80, 208n120; 112,
  342n27;
Homeric Hymn to Apollo 131, 229n56;
  181, 342n27; 194–203, 231n73;
  201, 208n120; 388–544, 190n17;
  514–517, 308n171; 515, 208n120.
Homeric Hymn to Demeter 385, 413n76
Homeric Hymn to Hermes 17, 208n120;
  38, 6n32; 39–51, 449n43; 54,
  309n173; 420–421, 6n32; 411n68;
  422, 434n61; 424, 208n120; 432,
  208n120, 316n218; 442, 6n32; 447,
  6n32; 449, 294n88; 455, 208n120;
  475, 208n120; 480–482, 294n88;
  482–484, 6n32, 307n159; 502,
  309n173; 510, 208n120; 515, 229n56
Homeric Hymns (Lesser) 6.18, 477n111;
  7.1–2, 232n78; 10.1, 476n106,
  477n111; 10.4–5, 345n42, 410n62,
  477n111; 19.1, 232n78; 22.1,
  232n78; 33.1, 232n78
Horace
  Epistles 1.7.28 and 1.14.33, 537n1
  Odes 3.9.9–10, 537n3; 4.1.3–4, 537n1;
    4.13.7, 537n3; 4.13.21–23, 537n1
  Satires 1.2.1, 454n76, 538n5
Hyginus
  Astronomica 2.6, 287n46
  Fabulae 56, 373n10; 58, 190n19,
    284n37, 288n54, 467n51, 507n76;
    242, 284n37, 288n54, 350n74,
    467n51; 248, 284n37, 514n127;
    251, 284n37, 288n56; 270, 335n99,
    350n74, 467n51; 271, 284n37; 275,
    284n37, 350n74, 406n39
Isidore *Origines* 4.12.8, 332n73; 15.1.48,
  503n54; 17.9.14, 332n73
Isidore of Pelusium *Epistles* 1.90 (PG
  78:244D–245A), 542n20
Isokrates 2, 358n123; 9.1, 212n143;
  9.18, 355n103; 9.18–19, 354n94;
  9.19–20, 351n80; 9.30–32, 347n54;
  9.54, 353n92; 9.57, 353n90; 10,
  343n32
Istros FGH 334 F 45, 350n74, 480n128,
  516n134
Jerome (Eusebios *Chronicle*), 378n52,
  551, 558
Josephus. *See* Biblical/Judaica
Juba FGH 275 F 15, 274n144; F 16,
  145n198
Julian *Epistles* 82, 323n10
Justin *Epitome (of Pompeius Trogus)*
  11.10.8–9, 490n6; 18.5, 222n16,
  281n13; 21.3, 221n13; 44.3,
  366n165
Juvenal *Satires* 3.62–65, 538n8
Kallimakhos *Hymns* 2.18–21, 235n101,
  318n233; 2.20, 201n86; 2.42–46,
  229n56

Index Locorum

Khariton 8.2.8-9, 413n77
Kharon of Lampsakos *Laws of Minos*, 357n120
Klearkhos fr. 19 Wehrli, 355n103, 491n14; fr. 43a, 222n16
Kleitarkhos FGH 137 F 3, 284n36, 492n23; F 9, 335n99, 467n52
Kollouthos 216, 201n86
Konon *Narrations* FGH 26 F 1 (45), 193n37
Kreon FGH 753, 337n3
Ktesias FGH 688 F 1b, 328n40, 547n13; F 30, 547n14
Kypria T 3-4 EGF/PEG 1 and 3, 211n139; T 7-9 EGF/PEG 7-9, 211n139; T 11 EGF/PEG, 211n139; fr. 4.1-6 EGF/PEG, 331n69; fr. 16 EGF/21 PEG, 317n226
[Lactantius Placidus] *Summaries of Ovidian Tales* 6.1, 281n7; 10.9, 288n54
Lexica Segueriana s.v. κινύρα, 195n48
Libanios
  Epistles 503.3, 323n10; 515.4, 323n10; 571.2, 323n10; 1197.5, 323n10; 1221.5, 323n10; 1400.3, 323n10
  Orations 1.273, 323n10; 25.23, 323n10; 47.31, 323n10; 55.21, 323n10; 63.6, 323n10; 61.20, 295n95
Linos-song, PMG 800 (*Carmina popularia* 34), 307n163
Lucian
  The Ignorant Book-Collector 3, 464n30; 11, 295n93
  On Dancing 58, 284n37, 466n46, 467n52
  On Funerals 20, 293
  On the Syrian Goddess 1, 461n8 and 10-11; 2, 462n19; 3-5, 463n20; 6, 298n101, 463n24; 6-9, 463n21; 7, 316n214, 516n136; 9, 464n26; 11, 461n11; 12, 462n14; 14, 237n109; 14-15, 461n8; 15, 315n213; 32, 461n8; 33, 237n109; 35-37, 495n2; 49, 509n93; 54, 237n109; 60, 461n10-11
  Professor of Public Speaking 11.9, 323n10, 335n99
  A True Story 2.25, 335n99; 2.26, 348n60
John Lydus *On the Months* 4.65, 221n10
Lykophron *Alexandra* 97-101, 196n52; 139-140, 196n54; 447, 516n135; 448, 286n38; 450-478, 355n103; 479-493, 359n126; 484-485, 364n151; 494-534, 340n20; 586-587, 340n18; 586-591, 340n17; 828-830, 284n37, 467n57; 831-832, 467n58; 859, 317n228
  Scholia (Σ) 447, 516n135; 450, 354n93, 511n115; 484-485, 364n151; 586, 340n17; 829, 283n28, 284n37, 467n52; 831, 284n37, 321n2, 467n52; 831-832, 467n58
Lyrica Adespota 37 CA, 224n33, 323n10
Macrobius
  Commentary on the Dream of Scipio 2.3.8, 193n38
  Saturnalia 1.17.66-68, 496n8; 3.8.2, 315n213
Makarios 7.100 (CPG 2:214-215), 325n29
Makhon 156-162 (11 Gow), 212n142
John Malalas *Chronography* 5.29 (Thurn), 355n103
Manilius *Astronomica* 4.579-581, 476n106
Martial 8.28.13, 236n108
Menandros of Ephesus FGH 783 F 1, 407n45; F 4, 337n3; FHG 4.448 fr. 7, 337n3
Mnaseas FHG 3.155 fr. 32, 363n150
Mokhos of Sidon. *See* Phoenician/Punic

[Moskhos] *Lament for Bion* 26, 294n91; 37-44, 191n27; 43, 191n30, 201n87, 298n107; 46-49, 191n27; 51-56, 298n108; 116-126, 298n108
Mythographi Vaticani 1.34, 332n73; 1.60, 284n37; 2.182, 332n73
Neanthes FGH 84 F 31 (191), 348n60
Nemesianus *Cynegetica* 26-29, 284n37
Nikandros fr. 64 (Gow/Schofield), 192n35
Nikephoros Basilakes *Orations* 1.608, 182n189
Nikephoros Kallistos *Carmina* 4, 214n155
Nikolaos of Damascus FGH 90 F 18, 363n150
Nikomakhos *Manual of Harmonics* 4 (MSG 243.15-17), 543n25
[Nikomakhos] *Excerpts* 1 (MSG:266), 295n93, 306n150, 492n21
Nonnos *Dionysiaka* 1.485-505, 492n21; 2.157, 201n86; 2.663-666, 492n21; 3.109-111, 476n106, 477n115; 4.199, 201n86; 5.614, 498n21; 13.432-463, 351n76; 13.432-433, 339n10; 13.441, 498n21; 13.444, 545n4; 13.451-452, 432n52, 545n5; 13.455, 545n4; 13.456-460, 501n36; 13.459, 286n38; 13.460, 284n37; 13.461-462, 355n103; 13.463, 345n42; 29.372, 498n21; 32.30, 284n37; 32.220, 284n37; 33.4-8, 331n69; 42.346, 284n37; 48.267, 284n37
Nymphis FGH 432 F 5, 305n147
Oppian *Halieutika, Scholia* (Σ) 3.403, 467n52; 3.407, 467n52
Oribasios *Collectiones medicae* 12Σ35 and 57, 286n41
Origen *Selecta in Ezechielem* PG 13.797D-800A, 470n77
[Orpheus] *Argonautika* 261-262, 193n37

Ovid
Amores 3.9.23-24, 294n91, 312n186
Art of Love 1.285-288, 282n17, 286n41; 2.607-608, 238n112; 3.315-316, 538n10
Ibis 361, 282n17
Metamorphoses 5.294-678, 191n31; 6.83-85, 280n4; 6.98-100, 280n5; 6.392-394, 295n95; 8.534-546, 191n31; 10.40-49, 294n92; 10.141-142, 294n91; 10.196-219, 294n90; 10.220, 396n133; 10.220-237, 498n20, 516n135; 10.238-242, 281n8; 10.243-297, 289n58; 10.270-273, 554n34; 10.295, 554n33; 10.297-298, 350n74, 499n28; 10.298-502, 2n8, 282n17; 10.299, 322n10; 10.311-314, 288n56; 10.354-355, 334n90; 10.360, 287n44; 10.361-362, 287n44; 10.369, 288n51; 10.387, 287n44; 10.396-399, 288n56; 10.400, 323n10; 10.406, 287n44; 10.419, 287n44; 10.435, 190n19; 10.476-480, 287n50; 10.478, 286n42; 10.500-501, 287n44; 10.509, 287n44; 10.514, 287n44; 10.531, 396n133; 10.717-720, 476n106; 11.44-53, 295n93; 11.410-748, 286n43; 13.600-622, 191n30; 14.698-764, 281n10
Remedy for Love 99-100, 282n17
Oxyrhynchus Papyri (Pap.Oxy.) 1795.32, 224n33, 323n10; 2688.4-13, 350n74, 499n30; 3000 with Σ, 505
Paion of Amathous FGH 757, 337n3; F 1, 315n213; F 2, 471n82
Palaiphatos of Abydos FGH 44 T 3, 337n3
Panyassis fr. 22ab EGF (27 PEG), 284n32, 467n50, 467n52, 502n47; fr. 25 Kinkel, Matthews (fr. 22c EGF, PEG), 502n47

Parthenios fr. 29 (Lightfoot) 316n214, 500n33, 500n35; fr. 42, 516n136
Paul of Aegina 7.3.10, 286n41
Paulinus *Carmina* 20.30–61, 210n133; 20.41–42, 180n175
Paulus Diaconus *Epitome of Festus* 18.23 (Lindsay), 404n19
Pausanias 1.3.2, 353n91, 355n103; 1.14.7, 378n48, 378n50; 2.19.8, 308n164; 2.27.7, 492n20; 3.1.3, 492n20; 3.12.9, 434n67; 4.33.3, 325n24; 6.20.18, 193n38; 6.23.3, 298n102; 7.3.1–2, 353n89; 7.23.7–8, 511n112; 8.1.3, 359n124; 8.5.2, 359n126, 359n127, 365n157; 8.5.3, 364n154, 364n155; 8.32.4, 409n51; 8.34.5, 230n64; 8.53.7, 359n126, 365n157; 9.29.6, 307n161; 9.29.6–7, 304n141, 306n151; 9.29.7, 308n169; 9.29.7–9, 305n143; 9.29.8, 307n156, 310n179; 9.29.8–9, 307n162; 9.29.9, 306n150; 10.12.11, 345n43; 10.14.6, 345n43; 10.24.3, 345n43; 10.26.4, 317n226, 333n81
Pausanias of Damascus FHG 4:469 fr. 4, 514n124
Petronius *Satyricon* 74.13 538n5
Phanokles 1.11–22 CA, 295n93
Pherekydes FGH 3 F 21, 325n24
Phileas fr. 7–12 (Gisinger), 503n57; fr. 12, 356, 500
Philip of Side *Christian History* fr. 3.2, 216n167, 538
Phillis of Delos FHG 4.476 fr. 2, 275n150
[Philo]. *See* Biblical/Judaica
Philo of Byblos. *See* Phoenician/Punic
Philokhoros FGH 328 F 92, 356n115; F 207, 306n151, 307n162, 307n163; F 214, 192n35; F 226, 551n16; F 228, 551n16

Philostephanos FHG 3:30–31 fr. 1, 348n60; fr. 10–14, 337n3; fr. 11, 350n74, 516n134; fr. 12, 340n17; fr. 13, 289n58, 561n28
Philostratos
Imagines 1.11.3, 295n95
On Heroes 53.10, 317n228
Photios
Lexicon s.v. Ἀφρόδιτος, 315n213; κινύρα, 47n18, 195n48; κινύρεσθαι, 188n6; κινυρή, 188n7; μουσικά, 210n128
Library 12b30, 348n60; 72a33, 348n60; 72b20–42, 547n14; 120a6–14, 346n51; 120a20–22, 2n7, 347n58; 120b8–13, 347n57; 120b17–18, 346n52; 121a35–41, 346n50; 146a40–153b29, 535n1; 146b41–147a2, 535n5; 147b34–36, 535n6; 148a410–411, 536n7; 149a5–8, 536n7; 150a12–19, 535n6; 151b5–7, 315n213, 535n5; 152b20–25, 536n7; 152b32–36, 536n7; 153a1–5, 196n53, 536n7; 153a11–23, 535n5
Pindar
Isthmian 1.52–54, 232n78; 5.47–48, 232n78; 8.56–62, 293n76
Nemean 4.46–47, 355n103 and 105; 8.1–18, 224n30; 8.17–18, 2n4, 223n27, 323n10, 329n53, 334n88; 8.19–22, 220n9; 9.54, 232n78; 9.7, 411n68
Scholia (Σ) 4.76–77, 355n103; 8.32c, 227n48
Olympian 1.1–12, 255n59; 1.9–10, 232n78; 2.1–2, 232n76, 78 and 80; 6.88, 232n78; 7.10–12, 227n50; 8.31, 333n85; 10.79–81, 232n78, 232n80
Scholia (Σ) 6.158a, 223n22
Pythian 1.1–4, 235n101; 1.92–98, 225n36; 2.13–20, 2n4, 221n11,

321n2; 334n87, 409n46; 2.56, 224n31; 2.58, 223n24; 2.58–61, 224n32; 2.62–63, 226n43, 232n78; 2.67–71, 225n37; 2.72–82, 220n4; 2.80, 226n44; 2.89–92, 220n4; 3.47–53, 510n108; 11.10, 232n78
  Scholia (Σ) 2.27 (Abel 1891), 223n25, 323n10; 2.27a, 227n54, 350n74, 499n29; 2.27b, 206n110, 222n20, 421n122; 2.27d, 231n75; 2.27e, 225n41; 2.28, 333n85, 350n74, 406n39, 499n25; 2.30g (Abel 1891), 229n55, 448n27; 2.31b, 231n70; 2.36bc, 221n13; 2.38, 221n13
  fr. 52g.1, 411n68; 105–106, 226n44; 122.3, 286n41; 128c5–6, 310n179; 128eb.7, 233n83; 129, 296n98
Plato
  Laws 656e–657f, 104n95; 659d–e, 449n40; 660e, 323n10, 432n52; 804d, 255n59
  Kratylos 404e–405d, 229n56
  Republic 364b, 449n40
  Symposium 202e, 449n40
Plato Comicus fr. 3 PCG, 290n63, 313n192, 321n2
Pliny the Elder *Natural History* 5.31.35, 516n135; 5.35.129, 349n68; 5.35.130, 545n1; 7.48.154, 329n56, 561n32; 7.56.195, 325n26, 450n45; 7.56.209, 327n39; 7.198, 552n20; 10.121, 451n51; 13.2.4–18, 330n61; 13.10, 553n26; 13.19, 332n77; 21.93.163, 332n75; 21.163, 553n26; 34.2.2–4, 324n23, 404n19; 36.60, 332n77
Pliny the Younger *Letters* 17.3, 434n62
Plutarch
  Alexander 15, 196n53; 29.1–6, 212n144
  Aratos 53, 296n97
  Cato the Younger 35, 420n117

  Lykourgos 21.4, 255n59
  Moralia 238b, 255n59; 310f, 286n43, 432n52; 310f–311a, 286n43, 432n52; 331d, 196n53; 340c–e, 490; 357b, 407n45; 357e–f, 305n145 and 148; 384b, 286n41
  Perikles 37.2–5, 356n108
  Solon 26, 340n20
[Plutarch]
  On Music 1136c, 295n95; 1145f, 255n59
Pollux *Onomastikon* 4.54–55, 305n147–148; 4.72–75, 295n95; 4.76, 202n92, 317n229; 4.78–79, 295n95; 6.105, 489n1
Polyainos *Stratagems* 8.48, 417n96, 491n17
Polybios 15.25.14–15, 419n105; 18.55.6–9, 419n105
Pompeius Trogus. *See* Justin
Porphyry *On Abstinence from Animal Food* 2.5, 413n76; 2.5.1–2, 286n41; 2.5.3–5, 284n29; 2.6.4, 286n41
Posidonius FGH 87 F 114, 286n41
Pratinas PMG 708, 231n73
[Probus]
  on Vergil *Eclogues* 10.18, 290n63, 460n4, 467n50
  on Vergil *Georgics* 1.399, 192n35, 286n43
Proklos *Chrestomathy* 80 (EGF:31.25–27, PEG:39.18–20), 1n2; 277 (EGF:67.23–24, PEG:95.15–16), 317n226
Prokopios *On the Wars* 4.6.30–31, 215n162, 303n134
Propertius 4.1.99–102, 538n6
Ptolemy of Ascalon (Heylbut 1887) 402.11–12, 209n125
Ptolemy Khennos *Novel History*, 192, 196n53, Appendix B
Ptolemy of Megalopolis FGH 161 F 1, 419n106

Quintilian *Institutio Oratoria* 10.4.4, 286n38
Quintus Smyrnaeus 6.81 and 7.335, 201n86
Religionsgespräch am Hof der Sasaniden, 216n167, 538
Sappho 5.1 and 18, 330n59; 44.26–27, 411n68; 44.30, 275n146; 44.33, 434n61; 103.9, 434n61; 140a, 307n156, 476n106; 140b, 307n156; 168, 307n156; 208, 434n61
Seneca
  Hercules Furens 569–572, 193n37
  Hercules Oetaeus 196, 286n41
  Medea 228–229, 193n37
Servius Auctus
  on Vergil *Aeneid* 1.28, 551n10; 1.693, 331n71, 552n18; 5.72, 284n37, 289n57
  on Vergil *Eclogues* 8.37, 237n110, 290n65; 9.35, 286n38 10.18, 250n41, 281n14, 284n37, 288n52, 321n2, 465n36, 498n22, 500n31, 513n120, 560n24
  on Vergil *Georgics* 1.288, 502n49; 2.64, 499n30; 3.5, 373n10
Skamon FGH 476 F 4, 274n144
[Skylax] 103 (GGM 1:78), 339n11, 349n65 and 69
Sophokles *Ajax* 582, 449n42
Sozomenos *Ecclesiastical History* 2.5.5, 465n42
Stephanos of Byzantium s.v. Ἄδανα, 508n85; Ἀμαθοῦς, 316n214, 349n68, 350n74, 406n39, 516n136, 559n12; Ἀπολλωνία, 308n166; Ἀσκάλων, 363n150; Βύβλος, 316n214, 516n136; Γολγοί, 339n14; Εὐρυμέδων, 499n27; Ἰδάλιον, 339n13; Καρπασία, 545n2–3, 553n28, 559n12; Κούριον, 350n74, 558n11; Κύθηρα, 478n121; Κύπρος, 350n74, 516n134–135; Μάριον, 350n74, 502n45, 559n12; Σφήκεια, 516n135; Χύτροι, 341n23
Stesikhoros 278.2 PMGF, 434n61
Stobaios *Anthology* 3.7.52, 196n53; 4.10.1, 432n52; 4.20.71, 286n43; 40.20.73, 284n36, 335n99, 467n52, 492n23
Strabo 1.2.32, 1n1, 12n59, 204n98; 14.4.3, 252n51, 340n18; 14.5.1, 507n76; 14.5.4, 565n58; 14.5.8, 356n110, 520n161, 520n161; 14.5.10, 356n110, 405n33; 14.6.3, 340n16–17, 340n20, 355n103, 359n126, 416n92, 565n55; 14.6.5, 327n35 and 39; 16.1.2, 3n11; 16.2.18, 466n47
Suda s.v. ἀμφιανακτίζειν, 232n79; ἄνακτες καὶ ἄνασσαι, 382n70; Θεόδωρος, 286n43; Ἴστρος, 515n133; καταγηρᾶσαι, 224n34, 321n2, 323n10; 504n59 κινύρα, 47n18, 195n48, 197n55, 302n133; Κινύρας, 334n94; κινυρή, 188n7; κινυρόμεθα, κινυρομένη, 188n6; Ξενοφῶν, 284n37, 337n3, 565n60, 566n61; Ξυναυλίαν πενθήσωμεν, Οὐλύμπου νόμον, 295n95; Ῥύκου κριθοπομπία, 546n8; Σαρδανάπαλος, 323n10
Suetonius
  Caligula 57, 284n35
  Nero 27, 538n5
  On Grammarians 18, 286n38
  Titus 5, 401n1
Synesios
  Epistles 4.14, 295n95
  Hymns 9.1–15, 541n13
Synkellos 185.14 Mosshammer, 378n52
Tabula Peutingeriana, 204n100

Tacitus
  Annals 3.60, 402n4; 3.62, 355n103, 402n3
  Histories 2.3, 99n62, 393n124, 401n2, 413n75, 449n43, 481n129
Terpandros 2 (Gostoli), 233n84; 4, 232n80; 5, 255n59
Themistios *Orations* 4.54a and 16.201c, 1n1
Theodontius. *See* Boccaccio (under "Medieval and Early Modern", below)
Theodoros SH 749, 284n37, 286n43, 288n56; SH 750, 192n35, 286n43
Theodoros Hyrtakenos *Anecdota Graeca*, Boissonade 1829–1833 1:263, 1n1
Theodoros Metokhites *Philosophical and Historical Miscellanies* p304 Müller, 295n95
Theodoros of Stoudios *Great Catechism* 91, 539n2, 541n17
Theodoros II Doukas Laskaris *Epistles* 195.19, 215n163
Theokritos *Idylls* 15, 308n170; 15.100–143, 293n78; 15.106, 403n16; 17.36, 403n16; 22.24, 226n44, 480n126
  Scholia (Σ) 1.109, 227n54, 284n37, 287n46, 288n55, 290n63; 3.48, 287n46
Theophrastos
  On Piety fr. 2 Pötscher (584A Fortenbaugh), 284n29, 286n41, 413n76
  History of Plants 4.4.12, 286n41; 5.8.1, 327n35; 7.6.3, 286n41; 9.1.2, 4, 286n41
Theophylaktos Simokates *Epistles* (p19.1 Zanetto), 295n95
Theopompos FGH 115 T 28a, 346n49; F 25–26, 346n49; F 75, 346n50; F 103, 2n7, 191n23, 214n158, 328n47, 347n53 and 57–58, 546n6, 564n51; F 114, 212n143
Thomas Magister *Anecdota Graeca*, Boissonade 1829–1833 2.212, 323n10
Thucydides 1.9, 359n124
Timomakhos FGH 754 F 1, 211n140; F 1–2, 337n3
Tragica Adespota 5d TGF, 284n35; 53, 295n95
Triphiodoros 430, 201n86
Tyrtaios 12.6 West IEG, 2n6, 323n10, 432n52
John Tzetzes
  Exegesis of Homer's Iliad, Σ 435.5–15 (Papathomopoulos), 335n99, 467n50
  Khiliades 3.77–88, 215n162, 303n134; 7.99, 215n161; 8.195, 535n2; 11.380, 191n27
Vergil
  Aeneid 1.416–417, 413n76; 1.619–622, 323n13, 354n99, 355n103, 379n57; 1.677–678, 331n70; 1.692–694, 331n72; 2.64, 289n57; 5.72, 284n37; 10.186, 537n2
[Vergil] *Ciris* 237–238, 286n42; 238–240, 286n42; 258–262, 288n56; 524–526, 334n91
Vita S. Theodori A (PG 99:167B–C) and *B* (PG 99:273C), 541n16
Xanthos FGH 765 F 8, 363n150; F 17a, 363n150
Xenophon
  Anabasis 1.2.15, 348n60; 4.1.1, 348n60
  Hellenika 4.3.10–12, 347n56
Xenagoras FGH 240 F 26, 516n135; F 27, 341n23
Zoïlos of Cedasa in *Etymologicum Genuinum* s.v. Ἀῶιος, 500n33
Zonaras *Epitome Historiarum* 1.116.3:58n64, 155n38

[Zonaras] *Lexicon* s.v. Αἰθιόπιον, 508n82
Zosimos *New History* 1.58, 465n42

Greek/Latin Inscriptions (excluding Cyprus: *V. Supra*)

Calder 1928 319 (Gözlu, Galatia), 201n87
Carratelli 1939–1940 19 (Ialysos, Rhodes), 234n91
CIL 6 1826 (Rome), 334n95
Herzog 1899 133 (Cos), 335n96
Hicks 1891 24 (Corycian Cave, Cilicia), 501n37
I.Thess.I 15 (Kierion), 334n95; 43B (Ktiri), 201n87
IG I^3 113, 353n92; II^2 20, 353n92; II^2 716, 353n92; IV 382, 334n95; IX.1 880, 412n71; XII.1, 680, 234n91; XII.3 1190, 412n71
Mitchell et al. 1982: 149e (Meyildere, Galatia), 202n87
Nemea Inv. I 85 (Miller 1988), 213n149
Parian Marble A 26 (FGH 239), 355n103; B 17, 492n18
Peek 1955 694 (Thessalian Thebes), 202n87
Priene inscription (FGH 115 F 305), 347n57
SEG 6:290, 201n87; 17:599, 335n100; 20:200, 566n65; 28:515, 201n87; 29:1202, 201n87; 32:503, 234n95, 235n98, 405n31; 34:24, 353n92; 49:697, 234n91; 55:562, 234n96
Senatus Consultum de Cn. Pisone Patre, 402n8

Medieval/Early Modern

John Adorno, 348n62, 362n139, 563n41.
Boccaccio *Genealogy of the Pagan Gods* Preface 1.4–5, 10, 560n22; 2.2–59, 554n31; 2.47–49, 550n4; 2.50–53, 3n10, 280n5, 281n7, 288n53, 350n74, 467n51, 550n5, 559n17; 2.55, 560n24; 2.269, 559n18; 3.19, 553n24; 4.20, 551n16; 4.23, 503n55; 8.8, 555n38; 10.7, 552n22; 10.11, 552n23; 13.1, 550n9; 15.6, 549n2, 552n22
Florio Bustron *Historia overo commentarii de Cipro* p7, 559n15; p12, 559n15–16; p14, 280n5, 281n7, 559n17–18
Ludolf of Suchen, 348n62, 563n42
Étienne de Lusignan
   Chorograffia (et breve historia universale) p2 (§1), 325n27, 404n19, 558n7; p6 (§4), 560n21; p6a (§6), 361n137; p7–8 (§9–10), 562n34; p8 (§10), 562n35; p9 (§12), 349n68, 547n12; p10 (§15), 558n7; p12 (§20), 559n12; p12a (§22), 558n8; p13a (§28), 325n24, 325n28, 450n45; p14a (§37), 325n28, 450n45; p16a (§42), 339n13, 558n11; p17 (§43), 547n16, 558n11, 560n21; p17 (§45), 565n55; p17 (§47), 558n8; p19a (§66), 332n79, 558n11, 561n27, 565n56; p19a–20 (§67), 558n8, 561n28; p19a–21 (§67–76), 560n20; p20 (§68), 453n66; p20a (§69–70), 560n24; p20a (§71–72), 325n28, 361n134, 558n11, 560n21, 562n34–35, 563n40; p20a (§73), 361n134, 560n24; p20a–21 (§74–75), 561n26 and 29; p21 (§76),

332n79; p22 (§87), 565n56; p28a (§157), 335n99, 558n7, 560n23; p35a–36 (§180), 361n133, 340n17, 349n68, 558n7, 558n8, 560n20 and 23, 561n30 and 32, 562n33; p87 (§590), 325n28, 450n45; p91 (§608), 558n10; p123a–124 (§610–611), 558n6

Description (de tout l'isle de Cypre) p1–1a, 558n7; p2a, 404n19; p15a, 361n138; p16, 403n11; p20a, 547n12; p27a, 450n45; p28, 325n28, 563; p30a, 450n45; p33a, 547n16, 565n55; p34–34a, 339n14; p37a–38, 339n14, 453n69, 558n8; p38a-39, 332n79, 361n134, 558n11, 560n24, 562n37; p39a, 558n7; p42a, 565n57; p80, 325n28; p91, 547n12; 91a–92, 339n13; p92–92a, 563n46; p213a, 561n32; p224a, 450n45; p468, 325n28; 557n2, 561n32

Paul of Perugia, 549

Theodontius. *See* Boccaccio

General Index

Abdalonymos/Abd-elonim of Sidon, 334, 488–494; transfer of tale to Paphos, 491–492
Abdastart: *see* Straton
Abd-elonim of Sidon: *see* Abdalonymos
Abdymon of Tyre/Kition, 347, 351
Abel, 454
Abî-shar, 44
Absalom, lament for, 301, 312
Abū Ṣalābīḫ, 19
Achaeans/*Akhai(w)oí*, 1, 10, 187, 317, 339–340, 342, 356, 363, 369; *akhaiománteis*, 405; beach of, 355; embassy to Kinyras, 211, 343–346; Half-Achaeans, Cilicia, 253, 520; receive lyre, 492n23. *See also* Ahhiyawa; Hiyawa
Achilles: laments for, 293–294, 298, 317; Linos, 318; lyre, 141, 254, 318; lyre silenced, 294; Patroklos, 292n72, 293n75, 333; Phoinix, 207, 280, 316–318; shield, 308, 318, 322; wrath, 316
Adana, 508, 519; Adanos, eponym, 508
Adonis: 'Assyrian', 467; *Abṓbas*, 502; *Adōniá*, 145, 221n10, 312–313, 505; *alter ordo fabulae*, Donatus/Servius, 513–515; alternative Cypriot names, 315, 467, 500–502; anointing rites, 283, 287;

Antinoos, 319; Aoios, 500–502; Aphaka, 463–465; Aphrodite, 145, 287n46, 290, 299, 313, 473–474, 498, 501–502; as honorand in Cypro-Phoenician symposium bowls, 145, 293; as storm-god, evidence limited, 465, 473, 484, 514; beauty, 335, 382, 484; birth, 2, 287; Byblos, 290, 298, 459–487, 501; —Byblian Baal, 473; —tomb at, 468, 498; Cyprus, 313–316; death while hunting, 290, 463–464, 470–471, 498, 504, 514; death while hunting, Levantine mytheme, 314, 466, 514n158; divine abduction, 499; etymology, 314, 464, 484; Gingras, 145, 202; Kinyras doublet, 313–316; Kinyras father, 233, 284, 289–290, 299, 312–316, 418, 447, 464, 468, 496, 504; lamentation, 289–290, 299, 312–317, 463–464, 468–473, 482–485, 514; —as incantation, 449; —traced to BA at Byblos, 485–486, 594; Levantine pastiche, 314, 464, 503; lyrist, 145, 313; metamorphosis into flower, 500; Osiris, 316, 516; Persephone, 287n46, 299n112; Phoinix father, 313, 317, 464n29; reigns on Cyprus, 500, 515, 560–562,

739

General Index

(Adonis, *cont.*)
564; resurrection, 290, 298, 314, 463, 484, 515; Sappho, 293, 307; sepulchral epigrams, 299; slain by Muses, 467; Tammuz equated, 464, 467, 470; Theias father, 464, 466–468, 502. *See also* Ao, Aoios, Dumuzi, Gauas, Kirris, Osiris, Tammuz.

Aegean migrations, 2, 4, 13–16, 98, 250–253; archaeological record —Cilicia, 250n44, 251–253, 405, 520; —Cyprus, 14, 253–258, 341, 368; —Philistia, 250, 255; circular migration, 230n64, 365–366, 378n49; confrontation with pre-Greek gods, 230, 250, 255, 363 and n147, 364, 367, 378, 380n58, 399, 405, 459, 503; Cyprocentricity, 204; duration, 14; involvement of western Anatolia, 13, 252, 341, 457; metals as stimulus, 339, 363–364, 475; migration/foundation legends, 8, 321, 337–369; — coexistence with Kinyras' family, 350–351. *See also* Great Collapse; lyres and lyric iconography

Aegina, 355

Aeneas, 287

Aeolian harp, 181

Aeos: *see* Aoios, hero

Aerias, 401–404, 406, 475–476. *See also* Ingot God

African parallels, 22, 23n25, 57, 62, 456n81. *See also* Ethiopia

afterlife, 134–141, 144, 296, 305, 328. *See also* underworld

Agamemnon: Achilles, 207, 311, 317; Aegean migrations, 2; Agapenor/Arcadians, 359; breastplate of Kinyras, 1, 322, 341, 344, 369, 409, 447; Great King, 11, 322, 409; invasion of Cyprus, 190, 310, 346–349, 359; singer of, 74; terracotta fleet, curses Kinyras, 187, 190, 328, 343–346, 369

Agapenor, 253, 329n57, 340–341, 343, 348, 350n75, 359–368, 406; as Kinyras, 364, 367; founds New Paphos, 359, 361–362, 364; Laodike, daughter, 364–368; metal-hunter, 364; old Cypriot legend, 359–360; Old Paphos, 362–363, 406; temple-builder, 359, 362–363, 406; *vis-à-vis* Kinyradai, 360–364, 367–368

Agenor, 317, 325n24, 354, 492, 516, 550

Agriopa or Argiope, mother/father of Kinyras, 325, 558n9, 563n39

Ahaz, 172

Ahhiyawa, 11, 251, 322. *See also* Achaeans/*Akhai(w)oí*; Hiyawa; Half-Achaeans

Aiakos, 224n30

Aigyptos, 515n130

Aithiopia (legendary), 505, 508; Cyprus, 506

Ajax son of Telamon, 354–355

Ajax son of Teukros, 356n110, 405

Akamas: hero, 340–341, 355, 498; peninsula, 501

Akhenaten, 107–111, 247, 250

Akitu-festival, 171

Akkad, 33, 41, 86, 101, 150, 393

Alalakh, 63; Alashiya, 324, 440; harp, 90, 392; Hurrians, 96, 98, 435, 440; ˡúkinnāruḫuli, 98; PNs, 98, 435, 440; —Kin(n)ar[-, 54, 98, 435, 440, 452; —resident Alashiyans, 440

Alashiya, Alashiyan, 10–14, 326; Ahhiyawa/Mycenae, 348 ; —PN *A-ra-si-jo*, Lin. B, 435, 440; Alalakh, 324, 440; —PN *A-la-ši-ia*, 440; Alashiya texts, 11–12, 104, 323–324, 326, 371, 399, 440; Alassa, 11, 399, 400; Apollo *Alasiṓtas*, 229, 372; Babylon, 324;

740

General Index

Byblos, 481–482; copper, 10–11, 323–324, 326, 372, 396n134, 397, 473–479, 482; decline and fall, 13, 321, 335, 400, 476; Egypt, 11–12, 104, 323–324, 326, 330, 371, 440; Elisha, son of Javan, eponym, 10n44; emulation of Mesopotamian music ideology, 392; exiles to, 12, 377; extent, 11; gods, 102, 372–375; —'all the gods of Alashiya', 374; —'god of Alashiya', 374; —Astarte/Ishtar, 104, 374–382, 392, 473–482; —engagement with mainland cults, 371–400; Great Kingdom, 10–14, 322; Hittites, 12–13, 104, 371, 376–377, 400, 440, 474; identified with Cyprus, 10–11; Kalavasos, 11, 399; Kushmeshusha, king, 12; Mari, 324; Paphos as religious center, 11, 400; PNs, 245, 350, 374, 440–441; Sargon legend, 324; scribal culture, 12; seafaring, 326–327, 479; Ugarit, 11–12, 104, 330, 372–375, 399–440, 459; —Alashiyan residents, 441. *See also* Astarte; Cyprus; Bomford Goddess; Great Goddess of Cyprus; Ingot God; Kinyras; Kothar; Kythereia; PNs

Alassa, 350, 399–400

Albright, W. F., 5, 124, 152, 166n92, 478n119

Alea (Athena), 364

Aleppo, 64, 74–75, 82, 96, 99, 103, 300, 461

Alexander the Great, 198, 212, 284, 303, 328, 409, 414, 542; Abdalonymos of Sidon, 488–494; Cyprus, 491

Alkaios, 271, 274–276

Alkidamas, 343n32, 357

Alkman, 1, 191, 330–331, 345, 436

Al-Mina, 199, 519

Amaracus, 289, 331–332, 350n75, 552–553

Amarna, 11, 92, 104, 107–111, 154, 507; Amarna letters, 12, 106, 150, 154, 373; —Alashiya, 10, 104, 245, 324, 326, 372, 399; —Byblos, 481, 483

Amar-Suen, Ur, 36, 393, 483

Amathous, Amathousian, 236, 287n46, 337n3, 340n19, 350, 402, 404, 406, 414, 420n116, 440n110, 471n82, 564n48; *Amathousía*, 349, 546; Aphroditos, 315, cf. 535; Cerastae, 498n20, 516n135; eponymous founders, 350, 402, 406; Kinyras, 328, 347–349, 358, 360–361, 557, 564; Kinyreia, 'lost site', 546–547; model boats, 328; Osiris, 315, 516; Persia, 352, 506n67; Phoenicians, 16; pre-Greek character, 14, 316n214, 328, 349, 352, 360; resists Euagoras, 352, 358–359. *See also* Eteocypriot; Kerastis/Kerastia; Propoetides

ambubaiae, Syrian pipe-girls, 454n76, 537–538; Akk. *embūbu*/Ebl. *na-bu-bù-um*, 55n44, 145n201

Amenhotep II, 106

Amenhotep III, 373, 374n17

Ametoridai, Crete, 234, 423n128

Ammianus Marcellinus, 508

Ammistamru II, Ugarit, 377

Ammon, 154, 164

'Ammurapi of Ugarit, 35, 119, 144, 383

Amorites, Amorite, 79–87, 96; divinized instruments, 83–88, 122, 482; in Mesopotamia, 73, 80, 87, 482; —Mesopotamian cult, 80, 86–88, 482; musical traditions, 82–83; PNs, 80–81, 138, 441, 452, 509; prophecy, 88n106; Ugaritian dynasty, 377; use of term, 73n2. *See also* Martu

741

Amphion, 193, 210
Amuq, 199, 440n107; Amyke, princess, 440n107
Amurru, 12–13, 374, 376
Amyklai: Amyklas, eponym, 365; Apollo *Ámyklos*, 294n90, 372n6
Amyntor, 317
AN.TAḪ.ŠUM festival, 94
An/Anu, 80, 403
Anakreon, 329, 515
Anat, 55n52, 135, 461; Anatu-goddesses, 450; Aqhat, 131–134, 140; —laments Aqhat, 133; gods of Alashiya, 374–375; sings to lyre, 125–126, 129–130, 133–134
Anatolia, Anatolian, 96, 119, 366, 499; Aegean migrations, 13, 252, 341; Apollo, 230; cymbals, 117; harps, 90, 92; interfaces, Cyprus, 104, 457, 500–501, 503; —Greece, 97, 252, 457–458; —Mesopotamia/Kanesh, 324; Ishtar cults, 375; lamentation, 201–204, 303n137, 305, 311; —*kinýresthai*, 204n97; Mopsos problem, 251–253; PNs, 202, 440, 508, 511; veneration of cult-objects, 101n77. *See also* Attis; Bormos song; Cilicia; Hittites; Hurrians; Kizzuwatna; Kybele; Lesbos; Lydia; Phrygia
Anaxarete, 281
Andromakhe, 275, 292, 293n75
anger: *see* grief or wrath, divine
angle-harps: *see* harps
Anglo-Saxon burials, lyres in, 3n14, 141
aniconism, 236, 481
animals: adorning instruments, 60, 269, 390n108; animal musicians, 153, 301; communication with, 151, 161, 183; lyrist and, 72, 126, 153, 159–160, 165, 179, 192–194, 229–230, 517, 522–528; parts used for instrument, 23, 248, 258n76, 274–275n144, 326, 449n43, 595; piper and, 144–145n197. *See also* birds; bull-lyre; lion; Orpheus
Ankaios, father of Agapenor, 343
Ankhises/Anchises, 287, 434n67, 474
anointing rites, 68, 94, 101–102, 283, 287; myrrh, 282
Antigonos, 416
Antimakhos of Colophon, 284, 313
Antinoos, 318–319
Antioch, 503
Antoninus Liberalis, 467, 468
Ao, 315, 502. *See also* Aoios
Aoia: wife of Theias, 502
Aoios (hero), 315, 356, 498–503, 512; Adonis doublet, 500–502; dialect forms, 502–503; first king of Cyprus, 500; Kephalos father, 498; Levantine kingship, 503, 505; Paphos doublet, 500–501, 503, 505; solar etymology, 145n201, 500–501, 503, 505; Typhon father, founder of Paphos, 503
Aoios (mountain in Cyprus), 500–501
Aoios (river), 503
Apamaea, 508
Aphaka, 456n80, 461–466, 464n28; Adonis, 463–465; —tomb, 468; Balthi, Tammuz, Kauthar, 314, 468–473; divination, 465; history of site, 465–466; Kinyras, 314, 461–466; lamentation, 468–473; oral tradition, 464–466; Theias, 467
Apheidas, 343, 365
Aphrodite (sometimes used loosely for Great Goddess of Cyprus, *q.v.*): apples, 290; birth, 376, 401, 480, 564; doves, 236, 290; dressing scene, 323n15, 331; grief/wrath, 281n13, 288, 291, 313, 315, 473; —anger at Kinyras' daughters, 250,

281, 288–289, 504; Julio-Claudians, 205, 402; Lyros son, 434n67; master-god to Kinyras, 291, 398; mother of Kypros, 480, 515–516; muse, 39, 307, 310, 313, 345; myrtle, 289; mysteries, 238n112; patroness of divination, Paphos, 383, 412, 414; patroness of sailors, 330, 375, 481; Pygmalion, 289; 'sacred prostitution', 221–222; Sappho, 310; *thymiatḗrion*, Paphos, 413; Venus, 281, 331, 402, 513–514; Zeus, 403n16
—Aphrodite, cult locations: Amathous, 287, 402; Aphaka, 463; Baths of Aphrodite, 501–502; Byblos, 464; Idalion, 331; Locri, 221; Kythera, 478; Paphos, 2, 124, 206, 222, 226, 284, 350n74, 366, 393, 401, 404, 411–412, 420; Salamis, 345, 410n62; Tegea, 230n64, 365
—Aphrodite, lovers: Adonis, 145, 287n46, 290, 299, 313, 473–474, 498, 501–502; Ares, 474; Kinyras, beloved priest, 1, 7, 36, 40, 89, 93, 102, 115, 219, 221, 223–224, 226, 291, 313, 375, 380, 382, 403, 409, 475; Phaethon, 474, 505; polyamorous, 474
—Aphrodite, parallel figures: Astarte, etymology, 380n58, 464, 481; Baalat Gebal, 463; Dione, 403, 481, 498; Ishara, 375; Syrian Goddess, 461
—Aphrodite, titles: *Akraía*, 205; *Énkheios*, 375; *Kýpris/Kypría*, 403; *Kythéreia*, 396, 404, 476–479; Ourania, 307, 378, 403, 463, 478
Aphroditos, 315, cf. 535
Apollo, absorption of rival cults, 189, 226; as sun, Sidon, 511; bearded, Samaria, 495; bow and lyre, 229–230; Delian, 290n65; Delphic, 204, 230; *kitharōidós*, 210–211n135, 230, 232–233, 496; —enacted by *kitharōidoí*, 233; —patron of singers, 6, 232, 310; Hyakinthios, 226n46, 227, 294; Jesus, 180, 210; Kadmos, 492n21; lamenting, 210, 294, 296, 312; Linos, 306, 308–309, 312; lyre invoked, 235, 318n233; Marsyas, 189–190n19, 212n146, 536; Nabu, 495–496; Paiawon, 190; Pharnake, 512; Seleucids, 415n88, 495; Sydyk, Eshmoun/Asklepios, 511–512; Syrian, Hierapolis, 462, 464, 495–496, 507
—Apollo, Cyprus: antiquity of cult, arrival to island, 190, 230; Cypriot cult-titles, 229, 230n64; —*Alasiṓtas*, 229, 372; —*Ámyklos*, 294n90, 372n6; —*Hylátēs*, 205, 229n62–230, 260n80, 386n91, 409–410, 415n86, 422n126; —*Kenyristḗs*, see below under Apollo, Kinyras; —*Kereátas*, 396n134; Kourion hymn, 319; —*Lýkios*, 308; Nikokles of Paphos, 410, 415; Resheph, 229, 372
—Apollo, Kinyras: Kinyras beloved, 1, 219, 221, 223, 226–231, 314, 448; Kinyras better referent in Lyre-Player Group of Seals, 527; Kinyras slain, 187, 189–192, 289, 306, 310; Kinyras son, 227, 314, 410, 512; *kenyristḗs* Apollo, 8, 98, 204–206, 210–213 and n135, 217, 226, 230–236, 241, 274, 319, 371, 402, 410, 423, 438
Apollodoros, pseudo, 250, 337, 354, 356, 359, 504–512; Achaean embassy to Kinyras, 343; Arcadian royal house, 343, 365; Egyptian Detour, 512–517

General Index

Apollonios of Rhodes, 200–201
Aqhat, 128, 131–134, 140, 142, 144, 172, 229, 443, 447
'Aqiba, 180
Arabic, Arabic tradition, 61n89, 129, 137–138, 543; *Arabian Nights*, 182; David and Solomon, 160, 181–183, 301; djinn, 61, 183; Herodotos, 378n50; Lamk, 312, 454; linguistic points, 138n160, 434n67, 443n2, 448n28, 460n3; *miʿzafa*, 301; myrrh, 282; Myrrha flees to Arabia, 286n42, 287, 467n54; *qānūn*, 544; Quran, 182–183; Quranic exegesis, 183; Saudi Arabia, 62; Tammuz lament, 471n79. See also *knr*, *kinnāru(m)*
Arachne, 280
Aramaean, Aramaic: Amuq, 199; Aram, Biblical eponym, 43n3; Bardaisan, 61; Cyprus, 272; dialects, 60; Kothar/Khauthar, 441, 443n1, 460n3; Laban, Bible, 43; linguistic points, 3n11, 138n160, 199, 202n93, 434n67, 460n3, 511; loyalty oaths, 300n119; parallelism, 156n41; PNs, 441, 443n2, 452; Sam'al/Zincirli, 136; targums, 216, 302. See also *knr*, *kinnāru(m)*; Sefire steles; St. Ephraim; Syria; Syriac sources
Arcadia, Arcadian, 230n64, 253, 308, 359–360n129, 364n154, 365n159, 409n51, 465; Agapenor, 359–368; Arkas, eponym, 329n57n16, 343, 365; Cyprus, 359–368; royal house (myth), 343, 365
Arcado-Cypriot dialect group, 14, 253, 340, 360
archery: *see* bow
Ares, 470, 474; Aphrodite, 474
Argos, Argive: 'conquest' of Cyprus, 343, 558n8, 561n32; Argos, eponym, 340n16, 343; Iasos, 343; Kourion foundation, 340, 350n74; Linos, 308; Mycenae, 340, 343
Ariadne, 471
Arion, 210, 233
Aristarkhos, 207–208, 309, 318
Aristonikos, 207, 316
Aristophanes, 202
Aristotle, 286, 334
Aristoxenos: on foreign instruments, 275
Ark, 40, 155, 167–175; Ark-narrative, 169, 172
Arkhòs tôn Kinyradôn, Paphos, 418. See also Kinyradai; *Kinýrarkhos*
Armenian, 61, 454n76
Arnaud, D., 121n58, 485–486
Arnobius, 419
Arpad, 300
Artaxerxes, 352–353, 547
Artemis, 226n46, 461, 504; *Agrotéra*, 409, 412n70; Artemides, 123n74, 445n11, 477, 510; Diana, 191, 513–514
Artists of Dionysos, 296n97; Cyprus, 212n148, 213
Asaph, 117–118, 156n46, 164n86
Ascalon, 378; Askalos, eponymous hero, 363n150; Mopsos, 364
Ascanius, 331
Ashdod, 157, 250
Asherah, 60, 375, 447n23, 461, 481
Ashlakka, 76
ashlar, 324, 330
Ashtoreth: *see* Astarte
Ashurbanipal, library, 23
Asklepios, 423n128, 492n20; calque for Eshmoun, 510–511; shrine, Achaea, 511
Assur: city, 23, 79, 121n61, 245; god, 38
Assurnerari V, 300

744

Aššuwa, 458
Assyria, Assyrian, 160n71, 266n115, 273, 326, 378, 461; *Assyrian King List*, 83; Kinyras, 3, 122, 281n7, 284, 288, 406, 467; lexical texts, 79; merchant colony, Kanesh, 92n10, 93n16, 324, 508; musical processions, 171; N-A expansion to West, Cilicia, 520; —Cyprus, 16, 327, 353, 407n43; —Israel/Judah, 146, 154, 178, 301; —Lydia, 275n147, 357n119; —palace musicians, 154, 178, 301; —peripheral responses, 407n43; —Syria/Phoenicia, 3n11, 153, 262; N-A prophecy texts, 38, 383; Theias, 284, 467; versus Syria, 3n11, 461, 467
Astarte, 135n145, 378, 461, 463, 481; Alashiya/LBA Cyprus, 104, 374–382, 392, 473–482; Aphrodite, etymology 380n58, 464; as form of Ishtar, 376, 486; as honorand in Cypro-Phoenician symposium bowls, 115, 145, 262, 293, 486, 523; Byblos, 407, 463, 471, 481, 486; Karkemish, 462; Kition temple, 116, 262, 315; mythological contexts, 7, 114, 377; Paphian, 270n129; patroness of sailors, 330, 481; royal cults, 7, 40, 114, 154, 376–377, 381–383, 407, 473–479, 492; Sidon, 376, 382, 407, 462n16, 463, 492; Solomon, 154, 382; Tyre, 376, 407; Ugarit, 7, 114, 374, 376, 407; —Astarte-of-the-Hurrian-Land, 376, 377; —Astarte-of-the-Steppe, 120, 377; —Singer(s) of, 40, 114, 383. *See also* Inanna/Ishtar
Asterias or Asteria, child of Teukros, 514n125
Astynoos, 504, 506, 511

Atargatis: *see* 'Syrian Goddess'
Aten, 107, 110; Aten-hymns, 110
Athena, 226n46, 280, 281n7, 461; Alea (Tegea), 364, 366; Ialysos, 520; Lindos, 520n161; Minerva, 513; Tarsus, 520n161
Athens, Athenian: *Adōniá*, 312; Ajax and Trojan War, 355; Atthidographers, 356, 497; Cypriot foundation legends, 341, 498, 506n67; Euneidai, 234; Kinyras, 355–356, 358, 497–498, 504; New Music, 190n19; Pamphos, 307n156; political relations, Cilicia, 497; —Cyprus, 341, 355, 497; —Cypriot Salamis and Euagoras, 353–356; —Saronic Salamis, 354–356; royal house (myth), 355, 498, 504; threnodic legislation, 294
Athienou, 378
'Attanu, Chief Priest, Ugarit, 152n23
Attis, 102, 315n213
aulós: *see* double-pipes
Axiothea, wife of Nikokles, 416
Ayia Irini, 378, 390
Azag, 25
Azatiwatas, Karatepe, 251, 507n75, 512

Baal: Adonis, 314, 473, 482–485; Anat, 125–126, 129, 132–133; Aqhat, 128, 131–134; Byblos, 314, 407n45, 473, 482–485; Damu, 482–485; death and return, 143, 484–485; Emar, priestess, 171; Haddu, 483; Kothar, 122, 443–444, 447–448; *Krntryš*, Karatepe, 507n75; lamentation, 143, 482–485; Marqod, 152n22; mountaintops, 374, 465, 467, 484, 514; praise-singing, 125–134, 137, 152; Rāp'iu, 135; royal cult, 135, 468, 503; singer of, 126–131,

(Baal, *cont.*)
   137, 152, 176; Ugarit, 4, 120n53, 125–132, 135n145; weapons of, 122, 443–444, 448; Yahweh, 158, 169, 484; Yamm, 122, 125, 128, 153, 447. *See also* Aoios; Belos
Baalat Gebal, 463, 483, 486; as Astarte/Ishtar, 463, 485; Balthi, ps.-Meliton, 470; Cypriot goddess compared, 375, 480–481; patroness of sailors, 375, 481; royal cult, 481
Babylon, 30n83, 74, 83, 86, 101, 313, 326, 495, 496; Akitu festival, 171; Alashiya, 324; Babylonian Exile, 181, 300; Crete, 479; sack of (1595), 96
Bakkhylides, 219
Balaam, Oracles of, 156n41
balang, 55, 83; BALAĜ dedicated by Hammurabi, 86–87, 152; BALAĜ.DI, 66–71, 92n10, 124, 304, 435; bull/GU4.BALAĜ, 30–31, 36, 84, 531; compositions, 81, 84, 380; destruction as lamentative trope, 84, 291, 596; divinized, 9, 20–21, 24, 26–33, 35–36, 88, 122, 167, 279, 291, 380, 388, 390–391, 423, 450, 485, 507; function and use, 26–33, 42, 84–85, 118, 279, 391, 414; hall/shrine, 30n83, 84, 531, 534; in PNs, 98, 435; instrument of NAR/NAR.BALAĜ, 28, 66, 163, 531; lamentation, 22, 29–30, 29n75, 65, 81, 84–85, 279, 291, 485, 486; LÚ.BALAĜ, 65–66; lunar/solar cult, 41n152, 584–585; lute?, 20, 576; seven-magic, 29n68, 41, 585; stringed instrument, 19, 20n4, 65, 87, 121, 531–534, 573–580; use of term outside Mesopotamia, 54, 65–67, 121, 486; —Byblos, Ur III period, 486; — = *kinnāru(m)*, 54, 65–67,

71, 77, 87, 121, 435, 486, 531; year names, 21–22, 28. *See also* divinized-instruments: as counselors; master- and servant-gods; Lugal-igi-ḫuš; Ninigizibara; Ur-zababa/*urzababîtum*; Ušumgal-kalama; royal ideology
Balthi, ps.-Meliton, 468–473; as Inanna/Ishtar/Astarte type, 473–479; conflates Baalat Gebal and Cypriot goddess, 470, 472, 480–481; Syrian phonology, 470
Bar Kokhba revolt, 180; coins, 59, 180–181; Davidic precedent, 181
Bar Koni, Theodore, 454–455, 470–475, 480, 486
Barama, 63, 68
bárbitos/n, 319, 543
Bardaisan, 61
Barnett, R. D., 384, 386
Baruch, 181
Baths of Aphrodite, 501–502
Bau: balang of, 22n20
Baurain, C., 3, 6, 438–439
beauty: Adonis, 335, 382, 484; ancient 'god-men' of Cyprus, 335n99, 560–561; David and Solomon, 382; Dumuzi, 35, 382; goddess, 281, 288, 471; king, 35, 382; Kinyras, 335, 382; Theias, 335
Beckman, G., 377
begena, 58n65, 111, 167, 456n81
Beirut, 510–511
Belisarios, 303
Belos, 354, 357n119, 379, 467–468
Beni Hassan painting, 44, 82, 105, 454
Benjaminites, 75, 82
Bes, 246–247, 248
Biga, M. G., 67
bi-musicality, 71, 215
birds, 100, 134, 151, 179, 183, 328, 521–522, 526n191; adorning instruments, 178, 247, 390n112;

General Index

doves, 100, 236, 284, 290; eagle-diviner, 373; goddess, 236, 521; halcyon, 187, 191–192, 289, 330; Iÿnx as 'melodious *kinýra*', 191n27; lamentation, 191–192, 289; lyrist and, 126, 159, 183, 192, 246, 517, 522–528; Memnonides, 191n30; metamorphoses, 192; peacock, 514–515; sacrifice, 102n83, 144; symbolizing epiphany, 126, 192, 517. *See also* Erinoma; Meleagrides; Memnonides; Peleia/Pelia; Pierides

Bit Bachiani, 153

Bithynia, 378

Blegen, C. W., 427

blindness, 110, 234, 312, 318, 405

Blinkenberg, C., 518

Boardman, J., 238, 519–522, 527

boats, model, 211, 328–329, 343–346; Hurrians, 328; Mesopotamia, 328–329. *See also* Kinyras: terracotta fleet

Boccaccio, 199, 499, 503, 517, 549–555, 559–562

Bömer, F., 283

Bomford Goddess, 394–396, 404, 475, 479. *See also* copper: divine protection; Ingot God

Book of Jashar, 175

Bormos song, Mariandynoi, 305n147

Bousiris, 373

bow, 190n17; and lyre, 131–134, 196n54, 229–30, 255, 387n99, 415; Aqhat, 131–134; Kinyras, 229, 447; Kothar, 131, 229, 443, 447; Resheph, 229; royal symbol, 131n118, 255, 387n99

Bowra, M., 225

Braisia, daughter of Kinyras, 281, 333, 504, 513

brothers motif, 43–46, 130, 229, 445–456, 480, 509–511

Brown, E. L., 196, 274

Brown, J. P., 4, 189, 443, 447, 456, 509

Buchner, G., 519, 521, 527

bull, 170, 172, 229; balang, 30–31, 36, 84; bull-lyres, 52, 72, 78, 125; in *lilissu* ritual, 24, 595

Bustron, Florio, 549, 554, 559–561, 563

Byblos, 105n101, 130, 283, 452; Adonis, 290, 298, 314, 459–487, 501; —laments traced to BA, 485–486, 594; —tomb, 468, 498; Astarte, 407, 463, 471, 481, 486; Baal of, 314, 482–485; Balthi/Tammuz/Kauthar, 9, 453, 468; Canaanite Shift, 55, 459–461; copper, 473–479, 482; Ebla, 63, 483; Egypt, 481–482; —Amarna letters, 481–483; eponym, father of Kypros, 480, 515–516; Ibdâdi/Abd-(H)addi, 483; Ishtar, 486; Kinyras, 57, 88, 123, 290, 358, 380, 406, 459–487, 496; —fused with Kothar/Khousor, 472–473, 486; —Byblos his most ancient capital, 466, 473; Myrrha, 283–284, 460, 466–468, 492, 502; Osiris, 316n214, 516; Rib-Hadda, 481, 485–486, 485; royal cult, 481–485, 484; Yahimilk, 510. *See also* Baalat Gebal; Aphaka; Philo of Byblos.

—Byblos and Cyprus, 354, 372, 459, 468–482, 486, 515–516; Alashiya, 481–482; Byblos not distinguished in IA Phoenician colonial movement, 476; 'gods of Byblos' inscription, 476n103; Paphos, 460; —agreement of Paphian and Byblian legend about Kinyras/Kauthar/Khousor, 475–476, 487

—Byblos and Mesopotamia, 482–483; cuneiform texts, 483, 485–486; theological influence, 482–485; —Byblian Kinyras and, 485–486;

747

(Byblos, *cont.*)
—Damu, 482–485; —mi2-nar, female balang-player, Ur III period, 486; Ur III dynasty, 88, 483
Cain, 43, 454; Abel, 454; folk etymology, 44n5
Cainan, 454–455
Cainites, 46n11, 454
Calcol, 151–152, 177n161
Canaan, Canaanite, 82, 160, 376, 378; cultural background, Biblical world, 43, 56, 152, 154n34, 155–159, 163, 166, 173; dialect zone, 55–57, 441, 459; —Canaanite Shift, 55–57, 273, 445n12, 456n84; —other linguistic points, 199n71, 273, 344n38, 434n63, 478n118; frame-drumming, 126n91; LBA Aegean and, 326, 379; LBA Cyprus and, 104, 369n179; material culture, 159–161, 246, 248, 255, 322; musical traditions, 105n101, 106, 152, 155–161, 173, 248, 250, 257, 260n80, 315, 386n91; —Canaanite orchestra, 46, 157, 250, 272; New Year ritual, 169; other cult, 465, 467, 477, 480; PNs, 44, 138, 273n138, 440–441, 452; under Egypt, 104, 106, 138, 481–483; use of term, 12n61, 55, 378; words in Egyptian sources, 55–56, 106, 273. *See also* brothers motif; lyres; Kinyras: Canaanite derivation of name; *kinýra*: Canaanite derivation; *knr*; Astarte: royal cults
Capomacchia, A. M. G., 67, 283
Cappadocia, 216, 508
captive musicians, 76, 106, 154, 178, 249, 300–301, 384n87
Caria, Carian, 4n15, 225n40, 457; Gingras, 202–204; Mopsos, 347, 353
Cassio, A. C., 360, 476

Cassuto, U., 129
Catalogue of Ships: *see* Homer
catharsis: *see* purification rites
Catling, H., 384, 386, 394, 396
Cato the Younger, 420
Caubet, A., 383
Cayla, J.-B., 8, 205, 233, 410, 412–413
Cebel Ires Daği, 405, 512
Cenchreis, 190n19, 287–288n54
Censer: *see* Divine Censer
center and periphery, various points: 37, 79, 92, 104, 121, 224, 276, 347, 371, 387, 416
Cerastae: *see* Kerastis/Kerastia
Ceres, 287
chariot, chariotry, 19, 27, 131, 219, 323–333, 388, 427, 431, 506
Chenaniah, 157, 169, 173, 381
Chief Singer, 28n65, 31, 158; David and Saul, 158; Leader of the Kinyradai, 418, 421–424; Mari, 35, 74–75, 114, 422. *See also* Agamemnon: singer; Chenaniah; Ibbi-Ilabrat; nar/NAR/*nâru*; Rishiya; singers; Warad-Ilishu
Chnumhotep, 45
chorus, choral, 294; Ark procession, 170; Biblical world, 152; circular, 231, 233; Cypro-Phoenician symposium bowls, 191, 222, 232, 262, 289, 293; Cyprus —Cypriot figurines, 231, 237, 398; —Kinyras, 222, 225, 231–236, 289, 525; —lyric choruses, 212n143, 222, 225, 231–236, 256, 398, 525; female, 95, 191, 222, 232, 262, 265, 289, 293; funerary/mortuary, 256, 293, 294n90, 298n104, 299n113, 306; Hittites, 95; lamentation/threnody, 29, 289, 293–294, 299n113, 306, 308, 311n180; led by lyrist, 191, 211n135, 231–237, 294, 298n104, 308, 398; Pindar,

General Index

225, 231–236, 525; seven-magic, 170. *See also* dance
Christian: contexts, 210n129, 215; —continuity of pagan cult, 466, 563–564; —lyre, 4, 180, 182, 189, 193–194, 209–210, 215–217, 539–544; hymnography, 61, 182, 210n133, 541; polemic, 123, 222n15, 465n39, 469, 474; reception of David/Solomon, 181, 193. *See also* Jesus: lyrist
Chronicler, 116–118, 149, 156, 169–170, 173
Cilicia, Cilician, 95–96, 98, 199, 334, 347, 375, 386, 405; Aegean migrations, 250, 356, 405; Aoios, 498–503; Half-Achaeans (*Hypakhaioí*), 253, 520; Hurrian influence, 96, 495; Kinyras, 3, 9, 57, 98, 104, 123, 199, 355–356, 367, 404, 406, 459, 461, 496–512, 517; Mopsos, 251–252, 508, 520; Paphian extispicy, 99, 373, 401, 405, 497; Paphian Zeus, 501; Phoenicians, 5n27, 9, 199, 202, 405, 461, 512, 517; revolt from Assyria, 705, 520; Rhodes, 356, 520; Sandas *vel sim.*, 508–509; Tamiras, Tamiradai, 404–406, 497. *See also* Cilix; Hiyawa; Karatepe; Kizzuwatna; Lyre-Player Group of Seals; lyres and lyric iconography
Cilicia, Rough, 405, 500, 507
Cilix, eponym: Appendix F, 559–560
Cinara, courtesan-muse in Horace, 199, Appendix C
Cinaras, Étienne de Lusignan, 2, 325, 332, 351, 361, 450, Appendix G; anonymous brother, 452–453; Cinaras II, 361, 561–564; Khousor compared, 452–453, 455; numbered among the gods, 289, 561–562; Syrian phonology doubtful, 199, 554–555; when this form used in study, 3n10
Cinna, 286, 288, 334
Cinyras, slave of Acastus, Diktys, 334
Cinyria: *see* Kinyreia
circumambulation rites, 84, 171
citharodes: see *kithára*
clarinets, double, Egypt, 104
Clement of Alexandria, 419
coins: as propaganda, 180, 415–416; Bar Kokhba revolt, 59, 180–181; Byblos, 481n129; Cyprus, 221n10, 230, 236, 403n16, 413, 415, 481n129; —Nikokles of Paphos, 414–416; —Salamis, 410n62; Samarian, 495; Sidon, 493; Tarsus, 508
Collon, D., 52n30, 522
colonization: Aegean, Cyprus, use of term, 14, 368; British, Cyprus, 349n65; Egyptian, Cyprus (legendary), 512–517; Greek, western, 338; Phoenician, western, 262, 274, 378. *See also* Aegean migrations; Cyprus: Greek conquest myths; Phoenician colonization of Cyprus
Colophon, 353
Community of Cyprus, 205, 402
concubines: *see* harem
Constantine, emperor, 465
Cooper, A., 159
copper: Aegean migrations, 339, 363–364, 475; Aerias, 403, 475; Agapenor, 364; Alashiya/LBA Cyprus, 10–11, 323–324, 326, 372, 394, 396–397, 473–479, 482; Byblos, 473–479, 482; deforestation, 327; divine protection, 330, 363–364, 394–396, 473–479, 482; Kinyras, 2, 323–326, 394, 447, 450, 452; name of Cyprus,

749

General Index

(copper, *cont.*)
403; Ninhursag, 396n134; oxhide ingots, 326, 394; —ingot-bearer, 384, 392; —talents of Kinyras, 326, 392; —votive, 396; Phoenician colonization of Cyprus, 16, 270, 475–476; Ugarit/Crete, 479. *See also* Bomford Goddess; Ingot God
Coptic, 60
Corycian Cave, 500–503
cosmogony, 23, 103, 124, 169n114, 445. *See also* theogony
cosmopolitanism
— cosmopolitanism, general: LBA Cyprus, 12, 104, 245, 326, 371, 382, 460, 487; Mycenaean world, 440; Ugarit, 119; United Monarchy, 150-151. *See also* Uluburun wreck
— cosmopolitanism, musical, 43, 301; Alalakh, 392; Ebla, 63; Hittites, 90, 392; LBA Cyprus, 245–250, 382; Mari, 73–75, 77, 82, 154, 155; NK Egypt, 104–111, 137, 154, 391; Solomon, 155; Ur III, 36–37, 73, 152; women, 106, 108, 249. *See also* harem
— cosmopolitanism, theological, 101, 372, 374, 396, 459, 464, 481, 483, *et passim*. *See also* syncretism, theological
counselor: *see* divinized instruments
craftsman-musician twins mytheme, 43–46, 453–456
craftsmen: *see* mobility
Crassicius Pansa, 286
Crete, 190, 204n101, 234, 262, 333n82, 478n120; bronze stands, 384; Cypro-Phoenician symposium bowls, 260–261, 266, 268; Kommos, 271; Kothar, 447, 478; Linos, 308; Ugarit, Mari, and Babylon, 479

Croton, 317n228
cult-objects: *see* divinized cult-objects
cult-transfer: *see* mobility
culture drift, 52
Cureton, W., 469, 470
Currie, B., 221–222
Curtius Rufus, 489
cylinder seals, 21, 71, 131n118, 160, 241, 250, 256, 393, 396–397, 517
cymbals, 32, 93–95, 115–118, 128–130, 134, 144, 155n39, 157, 164, 168, 170, 172, 241, 397, 444; Heb. *meṣiltayīm*, 116, 155; Hitt. *galgalturi*, 100–101; Sum. sim, 32; Ug. *mṣlm*, 115, 117n31
Cyprocentricity, 204, 211, 348, 373, 436, 440. *See also* Cyprus
Cypro-Minoan script, tablets, 12–13, 327n38, 349n66, 404n21; Hurrian?, 440. *See also* Cypro-Syllabic; Eteocypriot
Cypro-Phoenician (ethnicity), 204n97, 229, 275, 315n210, 322n9, 345, 352, 358, 368–369. *See also* Phoenician colonization of Cyprus
Cypro-Phoenician symposium bowls, 46, 57, 77, 105, 115–116, 134n139, 143n189, 145, 157, 191, 222, 232, 244, 248–249, 258–274n144, 276, 279, 289, 302, 486, 521–522, 525; analysis of lyre morphology, 244–245, 267–272; Astarte/'Adonis', 115, 145, 262, 293, 486, 523; lyric threnody, 145; North Syrian versus Phoenician traditions, 260, 267–268, 272, 458; production centers, Cyprus, 262, 269, 272; —Phoenicia, 260; temple orchestras, 145, 249, 279, 314, 422
Cypro-Syllabic script, 13n63, 262, 270, 404n21, 410n63; digraphic inscriptions, Paphos, 410. *See also*

750

General Index

Cypro-Minoan; Eteocypriot
Cyprus: Adonis, 313–316; Alexander the Great, 491; Anatolian interface, 104, 457, 500–501, 503; ancient histories of island, 337n3; Arcadia, 359–368; as seen from Aegean, 9, 345, 359–360n129, 365, 368, 409–410, 438, 474; Byblos, 354, 372, 459, 468–482, 486, 515–516; control claimed by Ramses III, 14, 354; early forests and smelting, 327; earthquakes, 361, 362n139; Greek conquest myths, 342–343, 346–349, 360–361, 368; Hurrian influence, 12, 96, 98, 104, 349n66, 386, 440; intermarriage of Greeks and pre-Greeks, 365–366, 368, 514; lyric threnody, 304–316; model boats, 328–329; musical interaction with Aegean, 211–213, 276, 476 (*see also* epic poetry, Greek: Cypriot branch); name connected with copper, 403; oil industry, 330–332; oral tradition, 3, 348, 360–362, 364–365, 378, 380, 404, 406, 419, 453, 475, 501, Appendix G; production centers, symposium bowls, 262, 269, 272; Ptolemaic period, 416–420; Roman period, 205, 401–407, 420–421, 499; seafaring, 326–330, 491; strategic location, 414, 417; thalassocracy lists, 327; wealth, 2, 323, 327n36, 345, 414, 418. *See also* Aegean migrations; Alashiya; copper; Eteocypriot; lyres and lyric iconography; Phoenician colonization of Cyprus; pre-Greek languages; syncretism, theological
—Cyprus in LBA: as Golden Age, 223, 321, 335, 369, 476; —center of maritime networks, 326–327, 479; —cosmopolitanism, 12, 104, 245, 371, 382, 460, 487; —music iconography, 371, 383–391, 393; —political configuration, 10–14, 399, 475; —sanctuary design, 377, 394
Cyrus the Great, 151n13, 490

D'Albiac, C., 390
Dada, 30n79, 631
Dagan, Dagon, 4, 63, 65n18, 78, 84n81, 120n53, 123n74
Damaskios, 511
Damu, 485; as dying-and-rising-god, 484–485; balang counselor of, 485; Dumuzi, 484; greater Levant, 485n154; lamentation, 485; royal cult, Byblos, 482–485; —Mesopotamia, 485; Ur III–OB zenith, 485
dance, 64–65, 77, 92, 105, 119n45, 135n140, 152–153, 156, 169–170, 173–174, 183, 191, 222, 231 and n73, 232–238, 241–242, 244n12, 246–248, 250, 253, 265, 294n90, 310, 315n209, 386, 397–398, ḪÚB, Ebla, 63; NE.DI, Ebla, 63. *See also* chorus
Danel, 144
Danunians, 251
Darda, 151–152, 177n161
David, 3, 8, 63, 149–184, 193, 490; Arabic tradition, 160, 182–183; builds instruments, 158, 173; controls natural world, 182–183; covenant with Yahweh, 177, 179, 468; cult-leader, 40, 118, 167–174, 381; dying words, 175–178; enacts Yahweh, 169, 173, 175, 177; epitome of Jewish musical tradition, 149; Ethiopian tradition, 62; Great Kingship,

751

General Index

(David, *cont.*)
150–155; harmonious realm, 153, 383, 387; Kinyras compared, 3, 36, 119, 150, 166n92, 381–382, 393, 468; lamentation, 175, 301, 312, 381, 393; legacy, 174–184, 543–544; legends reflect period propaganda, 169, 393; lyre, kingly virtue of, 166–167, 176, 381; —role of in rise to kingship, 165–174, 381; —seven-stringed, 58–59; —shelters ideas about Divine Lyre, 165, 178, 381–182, 393; messianism, 179; Michal, 169, 173–174; musical guilds, 116–117, 149, 155–158, 164–165, 168; *ne̔ˁîm*, 129, 142, 175–178; Orpheus, 193; performing role, 172, 178, 381; praise-singer of Yahweh, 36, 129, 149, 176, 382; prophetic, 161, 167, 178, 182, 383; psalms, 152, 161, 166, 174–175, 178, 182–183, 383; Saul, 31, 126, 135n145, 158, 166–167, 169, 173; shepherd motif, 194n43. See also enactment; *kinnōr*
Dea Syria: see Syrian Goddess
de Moor, J. C., 450
Dead Sea Scrolls, 43, 58, 157n50, 168, 178, 301
Deborah, song of, 156n41
Deger-Jalkotzky, S., 244, 256
Deinomenes of Syracuse, 222
Delos, 290
Delphi: as center of world, 204, 411, 416; contests, 211–212n148, 223, 536; Cypriots at, 211, 212n148, 230; hexametric oracles, 450
Demeter, 223; Adonis, 284n35; Ceres, 287n46, 396n133; Cypriot, 223n22, 234, 287, 396
Demodokos of Leros, 497
Demokrates son of Ptolemy, 418
Demophon, 340, 355

Derketo, 461
descriptive: see rituals
Deukalion, 462
Devale, S. C., 22
diatonic: see heptatonic/diatonic; tuning: Mesopotamian system
Digenes Akrites, 255n59, 564
Dijkstra, M., 144
Dikaios, P., 245, 247
Diodoros, 337, 352, 357–358, 365, 493; Abdalonymos, 489–490; demise of Nikokles, 416–417
Dione, 403, 463, 481, 498
Dionysios the Periegete, 498
Dionysos, 213n150; Adonis, 313n192; Artists of, 212n148, 213, 296n97
Dioskouroi, 206, 225, 226n44, 232n78, 510–511; as 'the Castors', 451; Cypriot, 205, 480n126; *kitharistaí*, 226n44, 480n126; Kastor-song, 225–226
distribution lists, 64, 67, 74, 114–115, 330, 427
Ditānu/Didānu, 83
divination, 23, 446; divination-priest, 98, 115, 401, 417, 429–430, 449, 508; —lúḪAL, 376; Ea/Enki, 449; eagle-diviner, 373; extispicy, 99, 120, 373, 383, 401, 405, 413–414, 418, 449n43, 497; incense, 413; Kinyras, 99, 383, 393, 412; lamentation, 38, 99; liver-models, liver-omens, 99, 120, 373, 383, 414; lyre, 99, 383, 414, 449; Shulgi, 35, 38, 393; water, Aphaka, 465. See also prophecy; Kinyradai of Paphos
Divine Censer (*utḫatu*), Ugarit, 5, 103, 120n53, 121–122, 124, 512n119; Myrrha, 124, 283
diviners: see divination: divination-priest
divine couples: Aerias/*Aeria?, 401,

752

475; An/Antu, 403n15; An/Inanna, 403; Aphrodite/Aphroditos, 315; Aphrodite/Zeus, 403n16; Baal/Baalat Gebal, 483; Bomford Goddess/Ingot God, 396, 474–476, 479; Khousor/Khousarthis?, 511; Kothar/Kythereia, 396, 404, 476; Ugaritic god-pairs, 450–451, 454, 509–511; Zeus/Dione, 403, 481
divine determinative, 4–5, 19, 21n12, 71, 101, 123, 141, 468, 486
Divine Heptad, 25n45, 26, 40
Divine Kings, Ugarit, 5, 124, 136, 139, 141–146, 423
divine kingship: *see* royal ideology
Divine Lyre: *see* Kinnaru; Kinyras; divinized musical instruments
divinized cult-objects, 6, 19–26; as familiars of master-gods, 27, 282, 291; divinization rituals, 22, 279, 445; Hurro-Hittite, 102, 122, 495; Kinyras, 279–291; lamentation, 27; manifestation of divinity, 20; mythogenic, 25, 282, 382; naming rituals, 23, 25, 122, 444; narrative contexts, 7, 25, 26–33, 103, 113, 122, 380–381, 444; nature of, 20; offerings to, 19–20, 22–23n29, 41, 71, 84, 94, 97, 101–103, 119–122, 139n166, 291n67, 377 (*see also* anointing rites)
divinized instruments, 7, 507; Amorite world, 83–88, 482; as counselors, 30, 36, 102, 485, 521–527, 593; best evidence BA, 57, 321; Byblos, Ur III period?, 486; communication with divine, 26–33, 41, 84–85, 158, 163, 173, 382, 450; construction rituals, 22–25; Damu, 485; Dumuzi, 84, 485; Ebla?, 71–72; Egypt?, 60, 390n112, 485; epiphany in guise of musician, 32, 163, 167, 388, 390, 444, 522–528; Hittites, 94, 101–102; Hurrian, 101–102; international phenomenon, 43; lamentation, 22–25, 28–30, 32, 84–85, 143, 279, 291; names, 23, 25, 29–30, 35–36, 86, 94, 122, 124; not played?, 32, 85, 102, 291; oaths on, 20, 21n14, 211n136; self-activated, 32, 85, 182n186. *See also* balang; divinized cult-objects; *kinnōr*; Kinnaru; Kinyras; Ninigizibara; Ušumgal-kalama; year-names
djinn, 61, 183
Dmetor, 342–343, 358n121
Donatus/Servius, 513–515
double-pipes, 105n101, 106, 111n129, 115, 117n35, 134, 141, 143n188, 144, 157, 169n115, 190n19–191, 202n89, 210, 212n148, 231, 242n1, 265, 269n121, 293n79, 295n95, 303n136, 311, 398, 444, 445n11, 454, 525, 540, 542; *Adōniá*, 145, 313; Akk. *embūbu*/Ebl. *na-bu-bù-um*, 55n44, 145n201; and lyre (Gk. *synaulía*), 295 (*see also* Cypro-Phoenician symposium bowls); central musician, 242; Dorion, 212n144; *gíngras*, 190n19, 202, 317; Ismenias, 303; lamentative, 143–145, 294, 296, 298, 303; Libyan, 310; Odysseus, 536; Olympos, 202, 295; spirits in, 455; Ug. *ṯlb*/Akk. *šulpu*, 134n139
doves: *see* birds
Dravidian dialects, 61
drinking rituals, 83, 94–96, 118n40, 131, 134, 136, 138, 144, 147, 160, 254, 256, 265n101, 266n107, 270–271, 302, 305, 338, 388, 525n183, 541; Mesopotamian iconography, 525. See also *marzeaḥ/marziḥu*

753

General Index

Dryopes, 365
Dumuzi, 39, 77n31, 140, 291, 382, 467, 483n144, 484–485; Damu, 484; death, lamentation, 84, 140n170, 144–145n197, 484–486; Inanna, 35, 37, 39; pre-Sargonic antiquity, 485; royal cult, Mesopotamia, 35, 37, 485. *See also* Adonis; Tammuz
Dura Europos, 496
Dussaud, R., 348
dying-and-rising gods, 140, 290, 314; influence on Baals of Ugarit and Byblos, 482–485

Ea/Enki, 23, 30n83, 63, 92, 509; creates lamentation-priest, 29, 291, 451, 591; divination, 449; Ea-Creator string, 451; incantations, 449n35; Kothar, 5, 448, 451; music, 5, 449; Zannaru, goddess, 78n45
Eanna complex, 19, 393
Early Iron Age (EIA), defined, 10n40
Eastern Wandering, Greek epic motif, 1, 204, 323, 338–339n8, 343n32, 355, 409, 467, 506n67
Ebla, 8, 45, 54, 63–73, 172; BALAĜ.DI, 66–71, 124, 304, 435; BALANG as *kinnārum*, 54, 65–67, 71, 77, 87, 121, 435, 486; Byblos, 63, 483; É.NUN, cultic chapel, 66–67; Ebla king list, 71; *Ebla Vocabulary*, 65, 67, 435; lamentation, 66, 145, 304; management of musicians, 63; Mari, 63, 74; royal ancestor cult, 67–71, 83; Ugarit, 63; Ur III dynasty, 483; women, 64
Edom, 154, 165
Egypt, 245, 282, 318, 327, 354, 373, 478; afterlife, 137, 328; Alashiya, 12, 104, 323–324, 330, 371, 440; anointing rites, 283; Byblos, 463, 481, 482; divinized instruments?, 60, 390n112, 485; foreign musicians/instruments, 104–111, 249; harp-songs, 304–305; Helen and Menelaos, 204, 310, 339; Herodotos, 304, 461; Illahun, 'Asiatic' musicians at, 105; Kinyras' daughters, 281, 497, 504, 512–517; Kothar, 478; lamentation, 145, 280, 304, 311, 316; Lucian, 462; lutes, 248; MK, 56, 105–106, 110, 137, 305, 441; modern lyres, 62; NK, 11, 56, 61, 77, 92, 104–111, 354, 372; Odysseus, 342; OK, 104; Solomon, 151, 154; surviving lyres, 106; Tentnau, songstress, Byblos, 105n101; women, 56, 61, 105n101, 106–108, 110–111, 154
Eichmann, R., 248
Ekhepolos of Sicyon, 322
El, 4, 102, 120n53, 132, 135n145, 374, 445, 468, 481, 511; Elioun, 123n74; *el-ku-ni-ir-ša*, 5n27, 447n21; Elos, 123n74
Elam, Elamite, 75, 92n8, 101, 328; 'Elamite orchestra', 384n87. *See also* Susa
Elatos son of Arkas, 329n57, 365–368, 514
Elis, 298, 317n228
Elisha, prophet, 165
Elisha, son of Javan, eponym, 10n44
Emar, 54, 63–64, 78, 137, 172, 206n106; lexical texts, 79, 121n59; priestess of Baal, 171; processions, 171–172; seven-magic, 40, 171; singers, 171 and n126
embodiment: *see* enactment
Emesal, 29, 99, 103, 171, 289
Emeslam, 86
enactment, instantiation, embodiment, mimesis: of Aphrodite, 310; of Apollo, 233; of divine lyrist by priest or king, 142, 173, 381–383; of divinized instrument by priest

754

or king, 32–33, 35–36, 381–383, 388, 522; of Kinyras, 231–236, 282, 291, 298–299, 319, 381–383, 423, 473, 522 (*see also* Kinyras: lamentation/threnody); of Linos, 308–310; of master-gods by divinized cult-objects, 20; of mourning by lamentation-priest, 24n40; of Yahweh by psalmodist, 163

Enegi, 140

Engel, W. H., 145, 190n19

Enki: *see* Ea/Enki

Eninnu, 25n46, 27–28

Enkherr'awon (king of Pylos?), 430–431

Enkomi, 378, 394, 396; Alashiya problem, 11, 348, 399; Horned God, 230n64, 396n134, 516n135; Salamis, 349, 354, 398, 460; sanctuary, 378, 394; —west adyton for goddess, 394, 398, 474; —votive figurines, 242, 250, 398. *See also* Bomford goddess, Ingot God.

Enlil, 24n39, 28, 36, 38, 41, 80

enthronement, 67, 92, 143–144, 146, 171, 256; musician, 72, 143, 153, 177, 229, 383–391, 495, 522–528. *See also* throne

entry ritual, 114, 120, 377

Enyalios, 439

Eos, 288n52, 499–500, 504–505, 507

Ephraim, St., 61, 182, 210, 216

epic poetry

—epic poetry, ANE: Amorite (?), 83; Gilgamesh, 474; Hebrew, 156; Hurro-Hittite, 103; Neo-Sumerian, 474; Ugarit, 122, 140, 447. *See also* Baal Cycle in Index Locorum

—epic poetry, Greek: Cypriot branch, 211, 253–255, 333, 338–339, 341–342, 345, 359–360, 368, 409, 476; —Salamis, 345, 477; diction, 6, 133, 201n86, 229, 316, 318, 338, 411, 476, 498n51; —lyre vocabulary and parallel lyric traditions, 6, 234, 318, 433, 457–458; —*theîos aoidós*, 6, 238, 309, 468, 527; epic cycle, 337–338, 369; figure-eight shield, 254; formulaic theme, 343; imperishable fame, 141, 227, 318; *kypriaká*, 323, 331, 339, 343–346, 359–360, 403, 474, 476–477, 481; —Kinyras versus Dmetor, 342–343; *nóstoi*, 204, 253, 323, 338–342; —'returns of Odysseus', 338; warrior-singer, 254–255n59. *See also* Achaeans/*Akhai(w)oí*; Eastern Wandering; Homer; Kinyras; *Kypria*; Kythereia; *Nostoi*; Troy/Trojan War

Epidauros, 492n20

Epigeios Autokhthon, 123n74

epiphany, 32–33, 39, 126, 167, 192, 235, 517, 522–528

epitaphs and sepulchral epigrams, 201n87, 298–299, 334–335n100

Epiuotasterius (corrupt), 514

Eratosthenes, 326, 337, 340, 364; Hermes, 505

Erekhtheus, 226n46

Eremboi, 506n67

Ereshkigal, 29, 140, 484, 591

Eridu, 393

Erinoma, 513–515

Erra, 25

Esagil, 30n83

Esarhaddon prism inscription, 14, 360, 407, 546

Eshmoun, Esmounos, 511

Eshnunna, 74, 140, 479

Essenes: *see* Dead Sea Scrolls

Eteocypriot: culture, 281, 316n214, 344; language, inscriptions, 14, 274, 328, 349–350, 360, 404, 434n63; use of term, 349. *See also* pre-Greek languages

General Index

Ethan, 117–118, 151–152, 156, 177n161
Ethiopia, Ethiopic, 61–62, 111; David, 58n65, 62, 167. *See also* African parallels; *begena*
ethnomusicology: bi-musicality, 71, 215; 'museum effect' (i.e. 'temple effect'), 93n13; musical syncretism, 272, 314; parallels for divinized instruments, 22
Étienne de Lusignan, 2, 199, 289, 325, 332, 351, 359–360, 450, 452–453, 480, Appendix E, G
Etruria, 260–262, 270, 519–521
Euagoras I, Salamis, 221n10, 346–347, 351–359; Athenian citizenship, 353–354; Athenian Kinyras, 355–356, 497; career, 346–347, 547; daughter of Kinyras, 321, 353–359, 362, 365, 493; in Cilicia, 347, 356; philhellenism, 351–352, 358; Phoenicia, 321, 347, 358, 493
Euagoras II, Salamis and Sidon, 410n62, 493
Euboea, Euboean, 255, 308, 519, 521
Eue, Eune, Eunoe, daughter of Kinyras, 354, 511, 514n125
Euhemeros, euhemerism, 123, 289, 419, 469, 499, 550, 553, 560
Euklees or Euklous, Cypriot prophet, 345, 356n113
Eumolpidai, Eleusis, 234, 423n128
Euneidai, Athens, 234
Euripides, 310–311
Europa, 378–379n52, 463, 492
Eurydike, 141
Eurymedon: hero, 333, 499; region near Tarsus, 499; river, 499
Eusebios, 123, 170, 378, 446, 487
Eustathios, 3, 4, 187–193, 280, 292, 298–299, 322–323, 342–343, 345, 466, 473, Appendix B
Execration Texts, 441, 452n62, 478n119

Ezekiel, 470

faience, 245–250, 323, 326
Fāra, 19
Fariselli, A. C., 244
Fates, 461
feasting, feasts, 23, 39, 63, 106, 108, 128, 131–133, 177, 252, 265, 293n79, 296, 305–306, 387n99–388, 525
festivals, 63–64, 67, 90, 93–94, 105, 107–108, 171, 212, 222, 231, 249, 262, 265, 279, 287, 294, 296, 298, 306, 308, 312, 318, 416, 461–462; AN.TAḪ.ŠUM, 95; KI.LAM, 95, 171n130, 387
figurines: basket-bearers, foundation deposits, 393n123; bull-masked, Amathous, 516n135; goddess, 375, 377; ritual use, 23, 103. *See also* Bomford Goddess, Ingot God
—figurines, musicians and dancers: Canaanite, 126n91, 134n139, 260n80; Cyprus, 126n91, 134n139, 231, 237, 241–242, 258, 269; —Enkomi, 242, 250, 393, 398; —Cypriote lyre shapes, 258; Egyptian tombs, 137n154; Philistia, 251; Ugarit, 134n139
Finkelberg, M., 366
First Temple: *see* Jerusalem
fish, fishing, 151, 159, 246, 329, 330n60, 384, 387n99, 446, 447n23; lyrist and, 330, 526
flutes, 37n121, 104, 144n194, 145
Follet, S., 412
foreign musicians: *see* mobility: musicians
foundation deposits, 393n123
foundation legends: *see* Aegean migrations
frame-drum, 77, 94–95, 115, 118, 126n92, 141, 143, 147, 157,

168–169, 242n1, 265, 293n79, 444, 525; duo with lyre, 77, 95, 525; Sem. *tp* and cognates (including Gk. *týmpanon*), 126n91, 157, 434n67, 538n8; women's art, 46, 61, 92, 126, 145, 191, 242, 265, 313, 525. *See also* Cypro-Phoenician symposium bowls; figurines
Frazer, J. G., 3, 38, 283, 309, 367, 382, 467, 484
Fronzaroli, P., 69
funeral rites, 29n75, 64, 95, 143–144, 146–147, 175, 256, 308; Achilles, 293; double-pipes, 143–145; gala, 29, 70; Greek world, 306; —*próthesis, ekphorá, góoi, thrênoi*, 292–298; Hektor, 292–293, 306; Hittite world, 95, 304; lamentation, 70, 145, 207; lyre, 95, 143; Minoan, 295; versus mortuary cult, 70n53. *See also* lamentation; threnody, lyric
Furies, 286, 288n56, 294

Gabbay, U., 24, 30–31, 291
Gaia/Ge, 123n74, 508
gala/*kalû*: *see* lamentation-priests
Gallavotti, C., 436
Galloi, 315, 462
Gantzert, M., 78
Gauas, 315, 467, 502
Gaza, 105n101, 193
Gelaw, Melaku, 167
Gelimer, Vandal king, 302
Gelon of Syracuse, 223
gender-blurring, 111, 126n94, 265n99, 315, 535. *See also* third gender
Gerginoi, Gergina, Gergitha, 366n165, 457
Gibeath-elohim, 156
Gibil, 124
gift, 37, 81, 131, 151, 316; gift-exchange, 1, 12, 64, 75, 150, 225, 262, 270, 272, 322, 344, 409
Gilgamesh, 462n16, 474
Gingras (name of Adonis and double-pipes), 145, 190, 202, 299, 567
Ginsberg, H. L., 456
Girsu, 41, 485
Gjerstad, E., 266n109, 338, 341, 355, 365
Goddess of the Night, 100–102, 329. *See also* Inanna/Ishtar
god-lists, 20, 28n68, 30, 35, 84, 86, 119–122, 373, 485; Hurro-Hittite *kaluti*, 102, 124. *See also* An:Anum in Index Locorum; Heimpel
gold, 322–323, 326; adornment, instruments, 76, 84–85, 106, 235, 309n172; Canaanite loanword in Greek, 273, 478n119; Kinyras, 325, 450
The Golden Bough: *see* Frazer
Goldman, H., 518
Golgoi, 236, 260n80, 266, 269, 345n46; Golgos, eponym, 339; undeciphered language, 270, 339, 350
Gorgias, 343n32
Graces, 220; dressing Aphrodite, 323n15, 331; lamenting Adonis, 299n113, 449n42
Great Collapse, 4, 13–16, 400
Great Dragon of the Land: *see* Ušumgal-kalama
Great Goddess of Cyprus, 7, 236, 239, 270, 279–280, 315, 365–366, 375, 380n58, 411, 470, 477, 480; as honorand in Cypro-Phoenician symposium bowls, 262, 293; Baalat Gebal compared, 480–481; Bomford Goddess, 404; Demeter, 223n22, 287, 396n133; reinterpretation as Ishtar-type, LBA, 380, 392; *Wánassa*, 380, 382n70, 407, 472. *See also* Aphrodite; Inanna/

General Index

Ishtar: Alashiya; Kythereia
Great Kingship, 1, 10–14, 110, 150, 322, 373; Aegean world, 387n99; Agamemnon, 409; David and Solomon, 150–155; Kinyras, 321–324, 333, 341, 409; poetics of, 11n50
grief or wrath, divine, 289; Achilles, 316; Alexander, 303; Aphrodite/Venus, 250, 280–281, 288–291, 313, 315, 504, 513–514; Apollo, 289, 306; Artemis/Diana, 504; Astarte/Baalat Gebal/Cypriot goddess, 468–473; Athena, 280; Hera/Juno, 514; Inanna/Ishtar, 29, 84–85, 291, 485–486; Kauthar, 473; Kinyras myth-cycle, 280, 289, 315; —Kinyras himself, 282, 291, 310, 473; lamentation soothes, 23, 25, 279, 282, 291, 593–594; Muses, 467; Nintu, 68, 69; Sun, 288, 506; Thetis, 317n228; Yahweh, 168, 169; Zeus/Jupiter, 514
grief, human, 70, 144, 292–293, 299, 486; lyreless (*ályros*), 294, 296, 298, 301, 304, 313
Grottanelli, C., 283
gryphon: *see* sphinx or gryphon
Gudea, 21, 26–33, 86, 113, 382, 393; Cylinders, 22, 26–33, 118, 279, 282, 380, 391, 393, 450; steles, 26
guilds, musical, 115–118; Artists of Dionysos, 296n97; —on Cyprus, 212n148, 213; Bible, 45, 116–117, 137n159, 152, 155–158, 168, 174, 381, 397, 422; Canaanite, 149, 152, 173, 250; cymbalists, 115–118, 155, 168, 397; implied by Cypro-Phoenician symposium bowls, 157, 249, 265–266, 422; kinship, 45, 115, 117, 155, 422; Kinyradai, Paphos, 421–424; Kition temple singers, 116, 262, 315; lyric,

Greece, 234, 405; names derived from eponymous ancestors, 234, 423; Philistines, 157; prominence of lyres, 93, 115–118, 164–165, 265, 421–424; prophecy, 156–157, 164–165, 422–424; Saul, 156–157; singers as umbrella term, 28, 115–118; Ugarit, 46, 113–119, 149, 155, 157, 249, 265, 381, 397, 422
Guzana/Tell Halaf, 153, 301

Haas, V., 103
Hadda, Hadad, Haddu, etc., 63, 135n145–136, 483, 485n154; as Damu, Byblos, 484
Hadrian, 180, 318–319
halcyons: *see* birds
Half-Achaeans (*Hypakhaioí*), Cilicia, 253, 520. *See also* Achaeans/*Akhai(w)oí*; Ahhiyawa; Hiyawa
Hamath, Hama, 63, 441, 460n3
Hammurabi of Babylon, 73, 86–87, 152
harem, 64, 74; Akhenaten, 107–108, 110, 247; Mari, 75–76; Solomon, 154; use of term, 74n8. *See also* women
Harmonia (heroine), 492
harps, 21n14, 90; Alalakh, 47n21, 90; angle-harps, 92, 107–108, 391; bow-harp, 26n52; Cycladic, 435n73; defined, versus lyre, 3n14; Egyptian curved, 104, 107–108; Gk. *paktís*, 275; Gk. *trígōnos*, 275; harp-songs, Egypt, 304–305; Hittite, 47n21, 95n35, 390n112, 392; horizontal, 76n28; LBA Cyprus, 47n21, 245, 383–391, 405; Mesopotamianizing, 47n21, 90, 108, 245, 388, 391–392; —as vehicle for Mesopotamian music ideology?, 90, 392; Nuzi, 92n8. *See also* balang

758

General Index

Harran, 63, 471n81, 496
harvest song: *see* vintage or harvest song
Hathor, 463
Hattian, Hattic, 90; cultic substrate, 93–94, 101; cult-music, 90, 93–94. *See also* lyres and lyric iconography; *zinar*
Hattusha, 93–94, 99, 245. *See also* Hittites
Hattusili I, 93
Hattusili III, 100
Hazor, 55, 74, 82
Hazzi: *see* mountains
Hebrew psalmody, 35, 44n6, 161–164, 178–179, 301, 310; Qumran, 178, 301
Hedammu, 103
Hegesandros, 502
Hegesias or Hegesinos, Salamis, 211, 345
Heimpel, W., 9, 20, 29–31, 41, 486
Hektor, 275, 292–293, 306
Hekuba, 292
Helen, 1, 292, 310, 339, 359, 467; at Paphos, 348; Gorgias, Isokrates, 343n32; Kinyras, 1, 329, 335n99, 409
Heliopolis/Baalbek, 463
Helios: *see* sun
Hellanikos, 337, 343, 350, 356, 506n67, 545n3, 553, 559n12
Heman, 117–118, 151–152, 156, 164n86, 177n161
Ḫendursanga, divinized scepter, 25
Hepat, 103
hepatoscopy: *see* divination
Hephaistion, Companion of Alexander, 491
Hephaistos, 308n167; Aerias, 475–476; Aphrodite, 474; as Khousor in Philo of Byblos, 446; calque for indigenous Cypriot metals-god, not Kinyras/Kothar, in Syriac sources, 404, 470–471, 473–476; early absence from Cyprus, 473
heptad: *see* Divine Heptad
heptatonic/diatonic, 40, 58–59, 171, 225. *See also* tuning: Mesopotamian system
Hera: Babylonian/Assyrian, 216, 461; Juno, 281n7, 514; Paphos, 409
Herakles, 357n119, 414, 471; Linos, 306; Melqart, 471; Sandas, 509
Hercher, R., 507
Hermes, 499, 501, 504; Eratosthenes, 340n19, 505; lyre, 6n32, 235n101, 307n159, 411n68, 449n43, 492n21; Mercury, 514
hero-cult: *see* mortuary cult
Herodotos, 312, 459; Cypriot lore, 222n16, 340n15, 365n160, 378, 506; Egypt, 304–306, 311, 461; Half-Achaeans (*Hypakhaioí*), Cilicia, 253; Kinyras and Adonis, 312; Linos-Song, 8, 145, 279–300, 304–316; Magi, 449; Maneros, 304–306, 311; model for Lucian, 461; Phoenician lyre, 274; 'sacred prostitution', 222n16
Herse, 355, 498, 504
Hesiod: Adonis, 313, 317; *Kythéreia* and Kythera, 476, 480; Linos, 306–308, 311; Phaethon, 505; succession myth, 97, 376
Hesione, 354
ḫešti temple (Hittites), 94
Hezekiah: cult-music, 172–173; Davidic precedent, 172–173; palace musicians, 154, 178, 301; psalms attributed to, 178, 383; restores Temple, 172
Hierapolis, 126n91, 236, 460n2–464, 495–496, 507, 509n93
hierogamy: *See* Sacred Marriage (so-called)

759

General Index

Hieron of Syracuse, 219–226, 227
Hiram of Tyre, 150
Hittites, Hittite, 89–96, 457; adopted cults, 90, 93, 99, 154; Ahhiyawa, 12, 252; Alashiya, 12, 104, 371, 376–377, 440, 474; —control of Alashiya, 13, 400; AN.TAḪ.ŠUM festival, 95; anointing rites, 283; *dammara* > Tamiradai?, 405; divination-priest (lúḪAL), 376; funeral rites, 95, 304; Great Collapse/Sea Peoples, 13; Great Kingdom, 10–11; Hurro-Hittite contexts/sources, 43, 90, 92n10, 96–104, 116, 124, 373, 375–376n36, 380, 448, 506, 508; incantation-priest (AZU), 98; Ishtar goddesses, 100–102, 375–377, 474; KI.LAM festival, 95, 171n130, 387; king and queen in cult, 94–95, 98, 118n40, 166, 381, 387, 422; —king as high priest of Ishtar-Shaushka, 383; lamentation-priests, 95; mortuary cult, 95, 304, 509; musical cosmopolitanism, 47n21, 392; —multilingual cult-music, 90; processions, 96, 171–172, 501; ritual silence, 95, 144, 304; royal ancestor cult, 94; royal succession, OK, 367; seven-magic, 26n49; singers, 95, 329, 509; Solomon, 154; sun in royal ideology, 175, 507; Ugarit, 12, 115; Ura, 507; Zarpiya ritual, 508–509. *See also* Hurrians; Inanna-instrument; lyres and lyric iconography; neo-Hittite sphere; *zinar*
Hiyawa, 251, 252n49, 508, 514n127, 520. *See also* Achaeans/*Akhai(w)oí*; Ahhiyawa; Cilicia; Half-Achaeans
Hoffman, G., 447, 470
Homer, 10, 213, 232, 405; Apollo, 189; bow and lyre, 133; Catalogue of Ships, 322n7, 339n14–340, 355, 359–360, 362; Cypriot birth, 345; —descendant of Cypriot prophet Euklees/Euklous, 356n113; Eastern Wandering motif, 204, 338; halcyon, 191; Kinyras, 1, 3, 187, 318, 321–322, 345, 409, 475, 480; *kinyrízōn*, variant, 207–208, 316–318; lamentation, 292–293, 306; Linos, 307–310, 312; lyre kings, 141, 254, 387; Panhellenism, 211, 348; Paris as lyrist, 196; Phoenicians, 275, 317, 345; scholia, 188; Solon, 355–356; Teukros, 354. *See also* epic poetry, Greek; Troy/Trojan War
Homeridai, Chios, 234, 423
Hubbard amphora, 232, 256, 258, 269, 525
Hugo IV of Cyprus, 503, 549, 559–560
Humbaba, 462n16
Hurrians, Hurrian, 96–104; Alalakh, 96, 98, 435, 440; Cilicia/Kizzuwatna, 96, 104, 375, 495; Cyprus, 12, 96, 98, 104, 349n66, 386, 440; divinized cult-objects, 102, 122, 495; god-list, Ugarit, 373; Hurro-Hittite contexts/sources, 43, 90, 92n10, 96–104, 116, 124, 373, 375–376n36, 380, 448, 506, 508; language, 96; Mesopotamian influence, 97, 375; model boats, 328; PNs, 440; succession myth, 97, 376; Syro-Hurrian contexts, 7, 9, 96–104, 329, 400, 444, 495, 517; Ugarit, 96, 104, 120
—Hurrian musical traditions, 76, 96; hymnography, 90, 97–98, 103, 119–120, 377; —hymns from Ugarit, 35, 59, 97, 383, 392, 451; incantations, 96, 98, 100, 376;

—lyres, *kinnāru*, 96–104, 414; *zinzabuššiya* (song-genre), 100
Hurro-Hittite: *see* Hurrians
Hyakinthos, 226n46, 227, 294, 296, 335, 492n20
hybridity, 14, 53, 97–98, 194, 255, 258, 260–261, 341, 358, 363–364, 366, 368, 375, 384, 435, 460, 469–471, 484
Hyksos, 105
Hylátēs: *see* Apollo
Hyon, 498, 504, 513–515 and n127
Hypakhaioí: *see* Half-Achaeans
Hyria, 504, 507, 512. *See also* Ura

Iacovou, M., 14n72, 363
Iapetos, 508
Iasos: Arcadian, son of Lykourgos, 343; Argive, son of Phoroneus or Argos, 343
Iawium of Kish, 84
Ibbi-Ilabrat: Chief Singer of Shamshi-Addu, 74n7
Ibbi-Sin, 22, 84, 86
Ibdâdi/Abd-(H)addi of Byblos, 483
iconography, musical (methodological points), 242; (un)reliability, 47, 57, 59, 273; correlating with lexical evidence, 46; variability, 47, 59
Idalion, 14n68, 16, 206n106, 236, 248, 262n92, 266, 269n122, 270, 331–332, 339, 349–350n75, 515; folk etymology, 339, 364; Kinyras, 350n75
Iddin-Dagan of Isin, 39–40
Ig-Alima, divinized door, 27, 282
Illahun, 'Asiatic' musicians at, 105
Illuyanka, 98
Ilshu-Ibbishu, musical instructor, Mari, 75
Immerum of Sippar, 83
Inandık vase, 90, 93, 105, 108, 111, 381–382
Inanna/Ishtar, 22, 37, 78; Alashiya/LBA Cyprus, 104, 375–382; Astarte as 376, 486; cult-music, 100–102, 373, 380–381, 574; —cult/divinized instruments, 100–102, 104, 380–381, 486 (*see also* Inanna-instrument); —playing harp, 92; Hittites, 100–102, 375–376; international profile, 101, 375–377, 380, 486, 584; Ishtar of Šamuḫa, 100; lamentation, 29, 84–85, 94, 291, 451, 482–485; muse, 38–39, 383; other forms of, 94, 100–102, 329, 375–376, 462, 486; prophecy, 38; royal cults, 37–40, 84–85, 93, 104, 375–376, 381–383, 386, 392, 473–479, 482–485; Ugarit, 376–377, 486; Zannaru, 78. *See also* Astarte; Goddess of the Night; Great Goddess of Cyprus; Ishara; Ninigizibara; Shaushka; Syrian Goddess
Inanna-instrument, 89, 100, 102, 381, 574(?); = *kinnāru/zannāru*, 55, 77–79, 88–89, 92, 99, 121–122, 291, 380, 391; ^{giš}za.^{d}Inanna, *vel sim.*, 78; harp, 92, 391; Kinyras, 291, 380–381; large and small, Hattian/Hittite, 90; theological implications, 88; variability of reference, 90, 92, 391–392. *See also* Ninigizibara
incantations: Asklepios, 510n108; Ea/Enki, 449n35; Ebla, 63; Greek conception, *epōidaí*, 210, 448–449; Hittite, 94, 98; Hurrian, 96, 98, 100, 376; incantation-priest, 94, 98, 329; Kothar/Khousor, 446, 448–449, 473, 510; lamentation as, 24, 449; Mesopotamian, 21, 23–24, 63, 329; Shaushka, 100

General Index

incense, 19, 23, 102, 124, 144, 145n197, 249, 275, 282–283, 316, 373n9, 512n119; balang, 414; divination, 413; Paphos, 124, 413, 418. *See also* Divine Censer

incest, 220, 282–283, 288, 367, 404n26

India, Indic, 328; dialects, 61; Kinnara gods, 61n93

Ingot God, 242, 394–396, 398–399, 404, 475, 479; consort at Enkomi, 394, 398, 474; Resheph, 372. *See also* Aerias; Bomford Goddess; copper: divine protection

instantiation: *see* enactment

instruction, musical, 34, 75–76, 82

instruments, construction: David, 158, 173; Mari, 74, 76, 158; Solomon, 158. See also *lilissu*

instruments, various (by language of source): Akkadian: *embūbu*, 55n44, 145n201; —*ḪASKALLATUM*, 101; —*paraḫsitu/parašitu*, 76; —*sammû*, 34, 40, 537; —*šulpu*, 134n139; —*tilmuttu*, 76; Arabic: *miʾzafa*, 301; *qānūn*, 544; Eblaitic: *na-bu-bù-um*, 55n44, 145n201; Egyptian; *dʒdʒt*, 106; Greek: *kanṓn*, 544; Hebrew: *ḥalil*, 157; Hittite: *arkammi*, 101–102; —*galgalturi*, 100–101; —*ḫuḫupal*, 101; Sumerian: adab, 34; —ala, 32, 84, 532; —alĝar, 28, 34, 39; —gudi, 34; —ḫarḫar, 34, 81; —miritum, 28, 34, 36; —sabitum, 34, 36, 81; —sa-eš, 34, 81; —sim, 32, 532n9; —tigi, 28, 34, 39, 41; —ub, 19; —zami, 34, 40; Syriac: *abbūba*, 145n201; Ugaritic: *ṯlb*, 134n139. *See also* balang; *bárbitos/n*; *begena*; cymbals; double-pipes; frame-drum; harps; Inanna-instrument; *kinnāru*; *kinýra*; kissar; *kithára*; knr; krar; lutes; *lýra*; lyres and lyric iconography; nbl; panpipes; percussion; *phórminx*; *sambŷkai*; trumpets; Ur-zababa/*urzababîtum*; *zannāru*; zinar

international style: *see* cosmopolitanism

invocation: citharodic formula, 232–233n84, 311; of divine lyrist, by lyrists, 232–234, 306–309, 319; of gods, by lyrists, 162, 232, 310; —of Ishtar, by lyrist, 100; of Rāpʾiu, by lyrist, 139; of lyre itself, 163, 231–236, 318n233

Ionian: ANE usage, 10n44, 514n127; Hyon?, 513–515; Ionian revolt, 352, 355; Javan, 10n44, 514

Ipemedeja (Mycenaean goddess), 423n129

Iphis, 281

Isaiah, 146–147, 157n50; harlot of Tyre, 61, 77, 302; Moab oracle, 301; Rephaim, 146–147; Targum, 302

Ishara, 375

Ishbi-Erra, Isin, 36, 81n62

Ishme-Dagan, Isin, 35, 80–81, 113, 178, 387, 391–393; *zannāru*, 81, 391

Ishtar: *see* Inanna/Ishtar

Ishum, servant-god, 25

Isidore of Seville, 503

Isin, Isin dynasty, 33–37n121, 39, 80–81n62, 83, 485. *See also* Ishbi-Erra; Iddin-Dagan; Ishme-Dagan

Isis, 145, 305, 375, 463

Islam, Islamic, 61, 126n91, 182–183, 214, 466, 543

Ismenias, Theban aulete, 303

Isokrates, 343n32, 351, 353–354, 358

Israel, Israelite, 43–46, 156, 158, 165, 168, 174–184, 260, 456n81

Issos, battle, 489, 491

Istros, 480, 515–516

Italy, 260–262, 270, 519–521

Iter-Piša, Isin, 83

General Index

Ithaca, 387
Itkalzi series, purification rites, 98
Itur-Šamaš of Kisurra, 83
Ixion, 220

Jabal, 44
Jacob, 44
Jacobsen, T., 37
Jahaziel, 164
James, P., 506, 509
Jan, K. von, 456
Jason, 200
Javan, 10n44, 514
Jebusite hypothesis, 156n43
Jeduthun, 156n46, 164
Jehoram, 165
Jehoshaphat, 164
Jeremiah, 181
Jerusalem, 3, 157n50, 265, 485n154;
    First Temple, 45, 149–150,
    155–158, 164, 172; —instruments
    hidden, 181; —sack (586), 150,
    158, 181, 300; —Jebusite hypothesis, 156n46; Second Temple,
    58, 149, 155n38, 181, 302; —sack
    (70CE), 155, 180, 401; Tammuz-
    laments, 470; transfer of Ark, 40,
    155, 167–174
Jesus: birth celebrated by muses and
    kinyrístriai, 216, 538; Davidic
    descent, 180n174; *kinýra* of the
    mysteries, 210n133; lyrist, 180,
    209–210; the 'new song', 210
Jirku, A., 159
Jonathan: lament for, 175, 301
Josephus, 149, 168, 194; David, 153,
    169; Solomon, 158; strings, 58
Jubal, 43–46, 82, 155, 312, 453–456
Judaea, 401
Judah, 43, 147, 158, 164–165, 175,
    178–179; eponym, 156n45, 404n26
Jupiter temple, Jerusalem, 180
justice, 21, 27, 282, 333, 366, 387n99;
    solar associations, 506–507,
    509–511
Justin, 221, 489

Kabeiroi, 511
Kadmos, 378–379, 463, 550; lyre, 492
Kaineus, 454n75
Kalavasos, 11, 330, 350, 399
Kallimakhos, 515
Kaloriziki, 255, 258
kalû/gala: *see* lamentation-priests
kaluti (Hurro-Hittite divine-circles),
    103
Kanesh: Hittite homeland, 93; OA
    merchant colony, 324, 508; —
    as conduit for Mesopotamian
    music and/or cult, 92n10, 93n16;
    Sandas, 508; Sargon legend,
    Alashiya, 324
Kapara of Bit Bachiani, 153
Kaptara (Crete), 447, 478
Karageorghis, J., 377; —V., 328, 363
Karatepe, 5n27, 199n67, 251, 253,
    272n132, 507n75, 512, 514n127,
    519–520
Karkemish, 13, 63, 74, 462, 508n83
Karnak, 108
Karpass, Karpasia, 6, 355–356n113,
    545, 553, 548
Kasios: *see* mountains
Kassandra, 196, 364
Kassites, Kassite, 326, 384n87,
    388n104
Kastor: *see* Dioskouroi
katábasis: *see* underworld
Kauthar, ps.-Meliton: at Aphaka/
    Byblos, father of Tammuz,
    314, 447, 460, 464, 468–473;
    controls Cyprus, 404, 460, 469,
    473–479; doublet of Kinyras in
    Paphian/Byblian foundation
    myth, 475–476; glosses Kinyras/
    Khousor fusion at Byblos, 465,

763

General Index

(Kauthar, *cont.*)
472, 486; Khousor compared, 470; Kinyras compared, 404, 447, 460, 470; lamentation compared with Philo's musicalized Khousor, 473; metals, 475, 482; Syrian phonology, 470. *See also* Kothar; Khousor; Khousoros

Kebede, A., 167
Kelenderis, 504, 507, 512; Baal *Krntryš*, Karatepe, 507n75
kenyristḗs: *see* Apollo
Kephalos, 355–356, 497–500, 504–505, 514, 517
Kepheus, 340
Kerastis/Kerastia, 498, 513, 516; Cerastae, 498n51, 516n135
Keret, 142
Keryneia, 205, 345n46, 416, 564n48
Kettes, eponym for Kition, 498, 514–516; emendation, 498n22
key-system, Greek, 58, 540, 542
Khalkanor, Idalion, 339, 364
Khauthar, PN, Hamath, 441, 443n2
Khousarthis, 477, 511
Khousor
—Khousor in Philo of Byblos: anonymous brother, 450–451, 480, 510; Cinaras compared, 452–453, 455; Kauthar compared, 470; Kinyras compared, 445–452, 470; Kothar of Ugarit compared, 445–452, 470; —less musical than Philo's Khousor, 450; mariner, 446–447, 510; musical and mantic qualities, 130, 448–450, 477, 510–511; phonetic shape of name, 445n12; Zeus Meilikhios, 448
—Khousor beyond Philo of Byblos: connection with Byblos consolidated by ps.-Meliton, lamentation added, 472–473; fused with Kinyras at Byblos, 472–473, 479–482. *See also* Kauthar; Kothar; Khousoros

Khousoros, Mokhos of Sidon, 445. *See also* Kauthar; Kothar; Khousor
Khytroi, 14n73, 345n46, 355, 498; eponym Khytros, 341
Kimon, 341
kínaris, 198, 457–458
kinarýzesthai, 198, 209n125, 458
Kinesias, 284
king: *see* Great Kingship; royal ideology
King James Version, 47, 176
King of Kish instrument: *see* Ur-zababa/*urzababîtum*
Kinnara gods, Hindu mythology, 61n93
Kinnaru, god/divine
—Ugarit: discovery, 4–5, 348, 438, 456, 527; Divine Censer grouped with, 103, 121, 124, 283; divine determinative, 5; —Theias, 123, 468; Divine Kings grouped with, 139; formally indistinguishable from other gods, 122; Kothar, 139, 443–445; (lack of) Mesopotamian equivalent in pantheon texts, 121–122, 451; narrative contexts?, 7, 113, 130, 139, 443–445, 517; offerings to, 97, 119–122, 377; only instrument divinized at Ugarit, 102, 118, 130–131, 139, 266, 391; servant-god, 161, 451
—implied beyond Ugarit: Amorite period?, 87, 122, 441; compared with Biblical *kinnōr*, 159; craftsman-musician twins mytheme, 453; epitome of Syro-Levantine lyric culture, not limited to Ugarit, 7–8, 57, 103, 131, 148, 184, 371, 391, 439, 495,

764

General Index

517; Hierapolis, 462, 495–496; Kothar, coalescence with, 136, 441, 451, 453; Lyre-Player Group of Seals, 522–528; Ugaritian god not exclusive ancestor of Kinyras, 459–461, 482, 486, 517
—possible functions, 7, 130, 143, 165, 382, 392, 485; lamentation of Baal, 143; musical director, 118, 131, 391, 444; praise-singer of Baal, 130; projection by professional musicians, 423

kinnāru(m): see *knr, kinnāru(m)*

kinnōr (Heb.), 149–184, 273, 301; Bar Kokhba coins, 180; Canaanite ancestor, 56; divine qualities, 158, 167–174; folk etymology, 44n5, 454n75; hereditary guilds, 45, 117, 155, 164, 169, 265; implied in psalms, 152, 179, 301; 'instrument of song', 116; invocation of, 163, 181; Jubal inventor, 43–46, 82, 312, 454; lyre not harp, 43, 46–53; mediation with divinity, 161, 164–165, 173; musical cognition, 161–165; musical prophecy, 157, 161, 164, 178, 383, 422, 450; narratological device in Samuel, 165–174; of lamentation, 301; of salvation, 301; overview, 43; plucked/picked, 58, 196n54; problem of stringing/tuning, 58–59; purification rites, 159, 165–166, 174, 381, 422; Rephaim, 147; royal ideology, 149, 153, 165–174, 381, 393; self-activated, 181; silence of, 300–301; song-acts, 164–165, 167–174; threnodic contexts, 300–302; transition to lute-class, 543; translated by *kinýra*, 3, 170, 182, 193–194, 213, 215; —by *kithára*, 47, 215–216; —by *psaltḗrion/psalterium*, 58n66,

182, 194n43, 215n164–216, 275n147; vocalization, 55. See also *kinnāru(m)*; *kinýra*; *knr*, lyres and lyric iconography; *zannāru*; *zinar*

kinnyrídes (birds, poetic), 191, 214n158

kinýra (Gk.): absence from Phoenician contexts in Greek sources, 274–276; *amphikinyrómenai*, 200; ancient etymological associations, with Kinyras, 3, 5, 140, 187, 217, 298–303; —with *kinýresthai*, 145, 188–189; — false, 197n55; Canaanite derivation, 57, 196, 199, 274, 276, 438, 440, 459; Christian contexts: '*kinýra* of the holy spirit', 182; —'of the mysteries', 210n133; cognate with *lýra*?, 434n63; currency/peripheral presence at Myc. Pylos, 433; joyful contexts, 210, 231–236; *kinýras* = '*kinýra*-man', 255, 422, 432–436, 438; *kithára* conceals, 211; *kithára* glosses, 195; *kithára* replaced by in Syro-Levantine contexts, 215; *pròs kynoûra*, Lykophron, 196; threnodic contexts, 201, 207–208, 233, 279, 291–292, 298–303, 316–318; translates Heb. *kinnōr*, 3, 170, 182, 193; umbrella term concealing linguistic variety, 189, 213–216, 292n70, 461; variants with -nn-, 210, 213–215. See also *kinnāru(m)*; *kinnōr*; *kinyrízein*; *knr*, lyres and lyric iconography; *zannāru*; *zinar*

— *kinýra*, historical link with Cyprus, 8, 53, 194–199, 204–206, 213, 241, 257, 291, 319, 435; —distinguished from Gk. *kithára*, 211, 276; —Cypriot lyre morphology, 276; —Kinyradai of Paphos, 421–424; —Kinýrarkhos, 421; *kinýra*-

765

General Index

(*kinýra*, cont.)
  players celebrate/enact Kinyras, 232–234; predates Septuagint, 194–199, 216; pre-Greek prototype proposed for LBA, 272–276, 433, 438; short upsilon versus *kinýresthai* and Semitic cognates, 199, 274, 298–303. See also *Arkhòs tôn Kinyradôn*; Apollo: *Kenyristḗs*; *Kinyradai*; *Kinýrarkhos*
Kinyra, maenad, 334n94
Kinyradai of Paphos, 401–417; Archaic period, 407–409; descent from Kinyras, 2, 124, 140, 223, 341, 360, 421–422, 468; divination, 383, 412–414, 420, 422, 449; —Cilician extispicy, 99, 373, 497; dynastic link to Apollo?, 227; end of monarchy, 416; high priests of goddess, 124, 239, 345, 380, 407, 410, 417, 422; island-wide prestige, 345, 416; Leader of, 418, 420–424; —role of king, 422–423; mortuary cult, 124, 136, 140, 310, 419, 423; musical function reflected in *kenyristḗs* Apollo, 234; musical implications of name, 265, 291; —connection with *kinýra*, 421–424; nature of continuity from LBA, 8, 363–364, 407, 423–24; —from monarchic period, 413, 417–419, 421, 492; Nikokles, 407–417; Paphian patriotism, promotion of virtuous Kinyras, 324, 345, 400; priestly costume, 407n43; Ptolemaic period, 413, 417–420; Roman period, 420–421; self-conception in *thyapolía* inscription, 412–414; Sostratos, Kinyrad diviner, 401; synchronic versus diachronic implications of name, 421–422; tombs in sanctuary, 136, 310, 382, 419; *vis-à-vis* Agapenor, 360–364, 367–368; *vis-à-vis* Tamiradai, 367, 401, 404–406. See also Nikokles; Paphos
Kinýrarkhos, Paphos, 421
Kinyras
—Kinyras, linguistic points: Canaanite derivation of name, 57, 214, 440, 459–461, 465, 468; form conceals linguistic variety, 213–216; shape in Greek, 366, 422; —Greek dialect forms, 432; —variant with -*nn*-, 213–215. See also Cinaras
—Kinyras, musical qualities: ancient etymology, 3–5, 187–188, 193, 214, 217, 280, 299, 432–436; Apollo, musical contest with, 189–192, 227, 289; —Kinyras son, 227, 314, 410, 512; —Kinyras beloved, 221, 226–230; David compared, 3, 36, 119, 150, 166n92, 381–382, 393, 468; *kinýras* = 'kinýra-man', 422, 432–436; Inanna-instrument, 291, 380–381; *kenyristḗs* as gloss, 210, 410, 438; lamentation/thrēnody, 143, 188, 191, 197n55, 279–319, 335, 472–473; Lyre-Player Group of Seals, 522–528; metamusicality develops, 6, 187, 329, 371, 388, 392–400, 427, 438–441, 447, 451, 480; musician, 3, 8, 187–194, 231–236, 298, 321, 512; outplays Orpheus and Thamyris, 192–194; performing role, musical, 231–236, 279, 298–299, 381–383, 388, 422; PN at Pylos, cultic agent, 427–432. See also Apollo: *Kenyristḗs*; Kinyradai; thrēnody, lyric.
—Kinyras, divine or cultic qualities, 9, 204–206, 231, 291, 410–411, 419, 423, 468, 517–528; Aphrodite's beloved priest, 1, 7, 36, 40, 89,

93, 102, 115, 219, 221, 223–224, 226, 291, 313, 375, 380, 382, 403, 409, 475; as master-god, 291, 391; as servant-god, 36, 102, 239, 279, 291, 380–382, 391, 398, 401, 526; cult-objects in myth-cycle, 280–291; Cypriot cult-narratives, 226, 231–236, 279–291, 304–316; divination, 99, 312, 383, 393, 403, 412, 414, 449 (*see also* Kinyradai); dwindling from divinity, 423; fused with Kothar/Khousor at Byblos, 472–473, 479–482, 486, 510; hieratic dimension not secondary, 409, 438–439; Kauthar compared, 404, 447, 460, 470; Khousor compared, 445–452; Kinnaru of Ugarit not exclusive ancestor, 459–461; Kothar of Ugarit compared, 4, 9, 229, 323, 396, 443–458; mortuary cult, 124, 140, 310, 419, 423; mysteries, 238; nature of continuity from LBA, 392–400, 423–424; performing role, royal, 348, 364, 381–383, 388, 400, 422; ram?, 221n10; roses?, 500; secondary stratum in Paphian cult, 401–407, 473–479, 473–479; sexual rites (real or alleged), 222n15, 238n112, 281; temple-builder, 222, 363, 380, 381, 393, 401, 439, 447, 464, 505; tomb in Paphos sanctuary, 2, 136, 310, 382, 419

—Kinyras, family and familiars: Adonis, doublet, 313–316; —son, 233, 284, 289–290, 299, 312–316, 418, 447, 464, 468, 496, 504; Amaracus?, 289, 331–332, 350n75; anonymous brother of Cinaras, 453; Apollo father, 227, 314, 410, 512; daughter marries Teukros, 351–359; daughters metamorphosed into temple steps, 280, 298; halcyon daughters, 187, 191–192, 289, 330; Kypros, son/daughter, 350, 515–517; Laodike, daughter, 365–368; Melus and Peleia/Pelia, 290; Myrrha, 2, 282–289, 367, 506; Pygmalion grandfather, 289, 369, 499; Pygmalion father-in-law, 344, 356, 358, 367, 369, 404, 497, 498, 504, 512, 517; Sandokos father, 367n170, 477, 504, 507–512; solar descent, 288, 504–512; son of Skintharos, 329, 335n99; speaking-names of children, 333, 366, 511; Theias, doublet or father, 123, 187, 284, 288n52, 335n99, 460, 464, 465, 466–468, 467n50, 486, 492, 502. *See also* Braisia; Cenchreis; Eue; Koureus; Laogore; Marieus; Metharme/Thymarate; Myrrha; Orsedike; Oxyporos; Paphia; Paphos, eponym

—Kinyras, extra-Cypriot associations: (As)syria, 3, 9, 57, 98, 122, 281n7, 284, 288, 406, 461, 467, 495–496, 504–512; 'Athenian' Kinyras, 356, 358, 497–498, 504; Cilicia, 3, 9, 57, 98, 104, 123, 199, 355–356, 367, 404, 459, 461, 496–512; Egypt, 250, 281, 497, 504, 512–517; multiformity of traditions, 57, 459–461; Phoenicia, 3, 57, 88, 369, 459–487, 493; — Aphaka/Byblos, 9, 57, 123, 284, 290, 358, 380, 406, 459–487 (Hellenizing gloss?, 464), 496; —Phoenician colonization of Cyprus, chronological implications, 313–316, 369, 476; —Sidon?, 9, 57, 334, 358, 406, 488–494, 496; —virtual Phoenician in some Greek myths, 225, 345

767

General Index

—Kinyras, Cypriot cultural associations (general): Amathous, 328, 347–349, 358, 360–361; immigrant to Cyprus, 336, 369, 371–400, 406, 459–487, 475, 495–528, 512; Kinyrad toponyms, 349–351; Lapethos, 325, 563, 350n75; Paphos, founder, 504; — Nikokles of Paphos, 407–417; — secondary stratum in cult, 401–407, 473–479, 473–479; proposed for LBA Cyprus, 8, 9, 16, 241, 321, 349, 369, 371–400, 380, 400, 476, 480; —Alashiyan ideology, 16, 321–324, 358, 371–400; PN at Pylos, Cypriot connotations, 435–436; Salamis, Euagoras, 351–359, 493; Tamassos, 325, 350n75, 563; totalizing cultural symbol of pre-Greek period, 8, 10, 321, 335, 349, 368–369, 371, 392–393, 400; —pan-Cypriot, 223, 324, 358, 369, 460; —popular character, 393. See also Appendix G

—Kinyras, industry and wealth (especially Cyprus): Alashiyan industries, 321, 323; building materials, 323–325, 393, 447, 450, 452; ceramics, 323–325, 330, 450, 452; copper/metallurgy, 2, 322–326, 364, 394, 447, 450, 452; gold, 325, 450; mariner, 223–224, 226, 323, 326–330, 439, 447, 510, 526; —fishing?, 329, 446, 526; —PN at Pylos, shipwright, 436–438; oil, 1, 283, 323, 330–32, 436; talents of (oxhide ingots), 326, 392; wealth, 1, 2, 187, 223–225, 226, 322–323, 334, 448; —poverty, 329, 490, 491. See also Appendix G

—Kinyras, in Greek and Greco-Cypriot epic and myth: Achaean embassy, 211, 343–346; Aegean migration legends, 8, 10, 337–369; Agamemnon's breastplate, 1, 322, 344, 409, 447; Agamemnon's curse, 2, 187, 190, 343, 369; Agapenor, 359–368; Alkidamas' 'Defense of Kinyras', 343n32, 357; Homer, 1, 3, 187, 318, 321–322, 345, 409, 475, 480; Liar King, 329, 333, 343–346, 357, 400; myth-cycle, 7, 227, 279, 280, 290, 291, 315, 380; terracotta fleet, 187, 190, 211, 220n7, 328, 343–346, 369, 439 (*see also* model boats); Trojan War, 1, 187, 343–346; unthroning by Agamemnon, 2, 190, 310, 346–349, 351–359, 360, 361, 369. See also Appendix G

—Kinyras, other: archer, 229, 447; beauty, 335, 382; Great Kingship, 321–324, 333, 341; Hellenistic tragedy, 284, 334; Hieron of Syracuse, 219–226; *kháris*, 1, 219–222, 225–226, 322, 330, 436, 448; longevity, 329, 365, 515; pantomime, 466; PN, 329, 334–335, 427–442, 452, 497; —at Pylos, 9, 274, 323, 392, 443, 451, 480; —relationship to mythical Kinyras, 438–441; virtuous, 223–225, 358, 369, 400, 491, 493, 497. See also Appendix G

Kinyreia, 'lost site', 351, Appendix E

kinýresthai, 191; *amphikinyrómenai*, 200; Anatolian associations, 201–204; ancient etymological association with *kinýra*, Kinyras, 143, 145, 188, 216, 280, 292, 298–299; Hellenistic interest, 191, 201; inscriptions, 201–204, 298–299; long upsilon versus *kinýra*, *kinyrízein*, Kinyras, 188n6–189, 199, 292n70; non-lamentative sense, 200, 233; *synaulía* of

General Index

Olympos, 295; threnody primary, wailing secondary, 298, 299; variant with -nn-, 213
kinyrístriai, 216
kinyrízein, 199, 206–211, 316–318, Appendix D; Homeric variant *kinyrízōn* in same verse position as *kitharízōn*, 208
kinýrō (false form?), 200
kinyrós (adj.), 188, 201n86, 280, 288, 433; variant with -nn-, 213
Kirris, 315
Kish, 35, 63–64, 84, 101. See also Ur-zababa/*urzababîtum*
kispu ritual, 70n54, 83
kissar, 456n81
Kisseus, 515n130
kithára: 'Asiatic', 458; cognate with *knr*?, 456; cradle, 269n126; currency of word on Cyprus, 213, 319; 'cylinder' *kithára*, 270n126; Dioskouroi, 480n126; distinguished from Cypriot *kinýra*, 211, 276; emulates tortoiseshell shape, 275n144; etymological link with Kothar?, 456–458; glosses *kinýra*, 195; *kítharis*, 198, 318–319, 456–458; *kitharistḗs*, 211n135; *kitharízōn* in same verse position as Homeric variant *kinyrízōn*, 208; *kitharōidoí*, 191, 210–213, 232, 234, 306, 496; —enacting Apollo, 233; lyric threnody, 296n97, 306, 309n172; morphological influence in Cyprus, 212, 278; replaces *kinýra* etc., 216; transition to lute-class, 543; translates Heb. *kinnōr*, 47
kítharis: see *kithára*
Kition, 57n58, 206n106, 236, 344, 347, 349, 352, 363, 416; Astarte temple, singers, 116, 262, 315; eponymous founders (Kittim, Kettes), 514–516; Kittia, princess, 440n107, 514n155; LBA, 14n68, 378, 394, 514; Milkyaton inscription, 357; Persians, 352; resists Euagoras, 352–353, 357–359; Sargon stele, 16, 353, 407n43; siege by Kimon, 341; Tyre, 16, 337n3
Kittim, eponym for Kition, 514, 558n6
Kizzuwatna, 9, 96, 98–100, 102, 123–124, 329, 371, 375, 400, 460, 495, 517; Kummanni, 508. See also Cilicia
Klearkhos, 222n16
Kleitarkhos, 284, 489–490, 492
Klytaimnestra, 74, 347
Knidos, battle of, 347, 353
Knossos, 432, 435
knr, kinnāru(m), etc.: overview of lexical evidence 43–62; partial identification with iconography, 46–53; —variability of reference, 53, 256, 272, 276, 391; peripheral diffusion, general, Chapter 6, Chapter 9, 272–276, Chapter 17; —LBA Cyprus, 89, 245, 249, 272–276, 435–436, 440–441; —Mycenaean world?, 435; problem of stringing and tuning, 57–60; root-form, when used in study, 8n38; —WS or areal?, 54; = Sum. BALANG, 54, 65–67, 71, 77, 87, 121, 435, 531; = *zannāru*/Inanna-instrument, 55, etc. See also Inanna-instrument; lyres and lyric iconography; *zannāru*; zinar
—*knr, kinnāru(m)*, forms attested, Syria, Mesopotamia, Anatolia: Alalakh (*Kin(n)ar[-*, ˡúkinnāruḫuli), 98; Arabic, 61, 543n32; Aramaic, 43, 60, 199, 216, 300–301; —Sefire steles, 300; —St. Ephraim, 61, 216; Ebla, 65–67, 145, 435; Hurrian and

769

General Index

(*knr*, cont.)
    Hurro-Hittite contexts, 98–100 (ᴸᵁ*kinirtallaš*, ᴸᵁ*kinnāruḫuli*, *ki-na-ra-a-i*, *ki-in-na-a-ri*); Mari, 76–79; Ugarit, 113–148. *See also* Cinaras; *kínaris*; *kinarýzesthai*
—*knr*, forms attested or assumed of Canaanite derivation: Can. *kinnōru or *kinnūru: 43, 56, 106, 196, 199, 274, 276, 439–440, 452, 456n83, 459–461, 465, 468; — represented by Egyptian *kn-nù-rú*, 106; Gk. *kinýra* and Kinyras, 57, etc.; Heb. *kinnōr*, 56, etc.; Phoen: *kinnūr, 57, 196–197, 199, 214, 273, 275, 302, 314, 472. *See also kinnōr*; *kinnyrídes*; *kinýra*; Kinyras; *kinýresthai*; *kinyrístriai*; *kinyrízein*; *kinýrō*; *kinyrós*

Koitabashi, M., 7
Kolotourou, K., 397
Kombabos, Hieropolitan myth, 462
Kommos, Crete, 271
Konon, 353
Konya-Karahöyük, 92
Korah, 174n147
Kothar (Ugarit and wider Syro-Levantine figure): absorbed by Kinyras on Cyprus, 443, 452–453, 479–482, 486; Amorites, 441, 452; as king, 167n100, 441, 452, 468–473 (*see also* Kauthar); Baal's weapons, 122, 443, 444, 447, 448; bowyer, 131, 229, 443, 447; builder, 447, 468–473; Byblos, 9, 453, 459–487; craftsman-musician twins mytheme, 453; equated with Ea, 5, 448, 451; etymology, 448; etymology of *kithára*?, 456–458; fused with Kinyras at Byblos, 472–473, 479–482; 'goodly companions of', 135, 139, 443–445; Kaptara (Crete), 447–478; Khousor compared, 445–452; *kinnāru* created by?, 444, 449; Kinnaru, god, 139, 443–445; —coalescence with, 136, 441, 451, 453; Kinyras compared, 4, 9, 229, 323, 396, 443–458; Kothar-wa-Hasis, 450; Kythera, island, 478–479; Kythereia, goddess (as form of Astarte/Ishtar), 396, 404, 476–479; LBA Cyprus, 473–479; maritime dimension, 447; musicality at Ugarit?, 130, 443–445; musicalization outside of Ugarit, 450, 451; name used for both Ugaritian and wider Syro-Levantine figure, 443n2; offerings to, 374, 443; phonology, 443n2, 460n3, 477–478; theophoric names, 441, 452; Ugaritian god distinguished from cognates, 451. *See also* Kauthar; Khousor; Khousoros

Kotharat goddesses, 123n74, 445n11, 477, 510
Kouklia: *see* Paphos; —Kouklia kalathos, 253–255, 258, 364
Koureus/'Curio', son of Kinyras, 350, 361, 558–559, 561–562, 564
Kourion, 14n68 and n73, 255, 262, 266, 270, 280, 349–350, 386n91, 410, 480; Antinoos lament, 318–319; Argive foundation, 340, 350n75; Kinyras, 350, 361; sacral kingship?, 410. *See also* Koureus/'Curio'; stands, bronze
krar, 58n65, 61n92, 167n101, 456n81
Kreophylidai, Samos, 234
Kroisos, 2, 224, 323
Kronos, 123n74, 481, 508, 511
Ktesias, 327, 547
Kubaba, 462, 508n83
Kültepe: *see* Kanesh
Kumarbi, 97, 103, 374

General Index

Kummanni, capital of Kizzuwatna, 508
Kuntillet 'Ajrud, 60
Kura, 63, 68
Kushmeshusha of Alashiya, 12
Kutha, Nergal temple, 86
Kwšr, Amorite royal name, 441
Kybele, 101, 126n91, 315, 462
Kynortas, Kynortion, 492n20
Kypria (lost epic), 1, 190, 211, 337, 344–345, 409, 476. *See also* Index Locorum
Kyprios, bronze-worker, Pylos, 436
Kypros: daughter of Byblos/Aphrodite, 480, 515–517; son/daughter of Kinyras, 350, 515–517
Kythera, island, 476, 478–480
Kythereia, goddess, 396, 404, 476–479, 478n119; 'Assyrian', Byblos, 477; connection with Cyprus, 477; Levantine paralells, 477; phonology, 476–478
Kytheros son of Phoinix, eponym, 478–479

Laban, 43n3
Laconia: *see* Sparta
Lagash, 19, 21, 25n43, 26, 30, 41n149, 86, 393n123
Lamech, 43–46, 312n187, 454; Lamk and invention of lamenting lute, Arabic tradition, 312, 454
lamentation: Adonis, 289–290, 298, 308, 312–317, 463–464, 484, 514; Anatolia, 303n137, 305, 311 (*see also* Attis, Galloi); —*kinýresthai*, 201–204; Antinoos, 318–319; Aphaka/Byblos, 468–473; —traced to BA, 485–486; apotropaic, 30, 70, 279, 282, 303; as incantation, 449; birds, 191–192, 289; Caria, 202–204; choral, 29, 289, 293–294, 299n113, 306, 308, 311n180; chronic versus acute, 30, 279, 282; city-lament, 292, 303, 310–311n138; Damu, 485; —Byblos, 482–485, 594; divinized cult-objects and instruments, 22–25, 27–30, 32, 84–85, 143, 279, 291; Dumuzi, 84, 144, 485–486; Ebla, 64, 66–71, 304; Egypt, 145, 280, 304, 311, 316; father-daughter motif, 191, 471, 473; father-son motif, 144, 233, 289, 299, 304, 311–319, 464, 471, 473, 482; female, 29, 46, 64, 133, 144–145, 200–201, 292–293, 296, 298, 312, 470, 486; —by goddess, 25, 84–85, 290–291, 299, 468–473, 484–485, 514; Gk. *góos*, 292–294, 296, 299; Gk. *thrênos*, 292–293, 295–296, 298–299, 306, 310; industrial, 22–25, 30, 279, 282, 394, 435, 532–534; Kinyras, 8, 143, 188, 191, 197n55, 279–319, 335, 473; mother-son motif, 317n228, 471, 473, 486; Nabu, 496; Osiris, 144, 316, 318; Phoenicia, 145, 315n209, 485n154; psychology, 298; royal contexts, 34–35, 67–71, 85, 94, 141–146, 175, 301, 311, 316–318, 382, 393, 468–473, 472–473, 482–485; Tammuz, 468–473; where performed, 30, 282. *See also* Achilles; David; funeral rites, Linos-Song; threnody, lyric
lamentation-priest, 5, 30, 41, 85; created by Enki/Ea, 29, 291, 451; enactment of mourning, 24n40, 291, 298; gala/*kalû*, 23–24, 28–30, 29n75, 66, 70, 141, 282, 291, 315, 451, 462; —Galloi, 315; Hittites, 95. *See also* third gender
Lamk, 312, 454
Lampsacius: 549–555

771

General Index

Laodike, daughter of Agapenor or Kinyras, 329, 333, 359–368, 511
Laogore, daughter of Kinyras, 281, 333, 504, 513
Lapethos, 234, 236, 242n2, 339–340, 416; Kinyras, 325, 350n75, 563; Phoenicians, 16, 260, 339, 349; —Ṣdqmlk, 'Sydyk-is-king', 510
Larsa, 83, 393n123, 414, 485
Lawergren, B., 47, 52–53, 244, 257, 267, 273
Lawson, G., 3n14, 141
Lebanon, Mount: *see* mountains; Aphaka
Ledroi, 14n73, 345n46, 411–412n70; identification, 411n64; Litros, eponym, 339
Lefkandi, 159n68, 255, 262, 266
Lelwani, 94–95
Lemnian women, 200–202
Lesbos, Lesbian, 140, 271, 275, 295n93, 458. *See also* Alkaios; Sappho; Terpandros
Levites, Levitical, 156–158, 164n86, 173, 302n131
Lewis, T., 142
Lewy, H., 456, 492
Li Castro, E., 517
Libya, Libyan, 274; double-pipes, 310; eponymous princess, 354; PNs, 57n58, 452n60
Lightfoot, J., 469n71, 472n86, 501, 566n64
lilissu, 32, 83, 87; construction rituals, 23, 41, 103, 595
Limassol, 361, 557, 564
Linear A, 13
Linear B, 2, 206n106, 230, 252, 273, 330, 360, 387n100, 411n67, 418, 423, 427–442
Linos: Adonis, 307, 312–316; *aílinon*, 309, 310; Apollo laments, 294, 311; —slays, 189, 306; death, 145, 306; Kinyras compared, 309–310; linen, 189, 306, 309; lyrist, 145, 306; lyrists invoke, 306–307, 311; lyrists reenact, 145, 308–310; Oito-Linos, 307; Ourania mother, 307; Pamphos, 307n156; regional cults, 307–308; resurrected through performance, 310; royal cult, 311; Shield of Achilles, 308, 318; wisdom figure, 307. *See also* Linos-Song
Linos-Song: Aegean, 306–310; bittersweet flavor, 70n55, 308; Cyprus, Phoenicia, Egypt, 145, 279, 300, 304–306, 315n209; —Cypriot, 8, 304–316; LBA antiquity, 308; traditional lyric genre, 296, 306, 318. *See also* Kinyras: lamentation/threnody; Maneros
lion, 390; and goddess, Lyre-Player Group of Seals, 521; and musician, 72, 159, 194, 388; as lyrist, 153, 301, Figure 5.4k; lyre adornment?, 269
Litros, 339
liver models and omens: *see* divination
Livingstone, A., 25, 282
Locri, 221; Locrian maidens, 220–222, 232
Lucian: Adonis laments, Byblos, 463, 472, 484n151; Attis, 315n213; autopsy and priestly informants, 461–464; Herodotean model, 461; Kinyras, and Myrrha, 466; —at Aphaka, 460, 461–466; —son of Skintharos, 329, 335n99; Osiris, Byblos, 316n214; Syrian Apollo, 462, 464, 495–496, 507; Syrian Goddess, 236, 461–462; threnodes, 293, 296
Lugal-igi-ḫuš, balang god of Ningirsu, 28

Lugalsisa, servant-god of Ningirsu, 30–31
Lumḫa, balang god, 24
Lupack, S., 435
Lusignan: *see* Étienne de Lusignan
lutes: anthropomorphic, 312; balang?, 20; Egypt, 106–108, 111, 247–248, 391; evanescence of lyre, 276, 312, Appendix D; Hittite/Neo-Hittite, 93, 247; lamenting, 312, 454; Mesopotamia, 21n14, 34; *skindapsós*, 535
tortoiseshell, 248, 326
Luwians, Luwian, 3n11, 90, 96, 102n80, 199, 251–252, 371, 405, 508–509
Luxor, 108
Lycia, Lycian, 202, 551n16; —Apollo *Lýkios*, 308
Lydia, Lydian, 201n87, 275n147, 330, 357n119, 368n177, 407n43, 457–458, 508
Lykaon, 308
Lykophron, 196–197, 201–202, 337, 340, 359, 363–364, 467
lýra, 211, 294n90–91, 295n93, 434 and n62; —constellation, 61n89, 196n54; transition to lute-class, 543
'Lyre of the Divinity' (Hittite text), 93
Lyre-Player Group of Seals, 9, 95, 272n132, 330, 386, 388, 390, 497, 517–528; iconographic analysis, 521–527; overview, late eighth-century Cilician origin, 518–521; uses, contexts, 521; —amuletic function, 521
lyres and lyric iconography: Aegean and Aegean diaspora, 47, 157, 242, 244, 250–258, 519–520 (*see also* round-based *below*); Anatolia, 270n126, 251–252, 256–258, 457–458, 517–518; Anglo-Saxon burials, 141; Aramaean, Aramaic, 43, 153, 300 (*see also* Syria and Syro-Anatolian *below*); Biblical world, 149–184; bull-lyres, 52, 72, 78, 125 and n86; Canaanite, 56, 248, 255, 257, 272; Christian contexts, 4, 180, 182, 189, 193–194, 209–210, 215–217, Appendix D; Cilicia, 250–253, 256–257, 386, 388, 497, 517–528; city-foundation rituals, 233; Cyprus, 53, 178, 229–230, 236–239, 241–278, 457, 517; —floral decor, 269, 278; —LBA, 8, 245–250, 258, 272, 276–278; —size and pitch, 269; dedicated at graves, 296; defined, versus harp, 3n14; divination, 99, 383, 414, 449; eastern and western, as defined by Lawergren, 52, 256–258, 267–272, 278; Ebla, 65–67; Egypt, 52, 56, 104–111, 178, 247–248, 275n144; giant, 108, 110–111, 456 (see also *begena*); Greek morphological influence in ANE, 59, 180, 194, 542; Hattian/Hittite, 32, 52, 55, 78, 89–96, 116, 178, 247, 381, 495, 525 (*see also* Syro-Anatolian *below*); Hurrians and Syro-Hurrian, 96–104, 495–496; invoked, 163, 231–236, 318n233; kingly virtue, 166–167, 176; living traditions, 62; lyre as teacher, 6n32; lyre/frame-drum duo, 77, 95, 525; Mari, 76–79; massed lyres, 94, 117n35, 118, 169, 172, 265, 314, 422; mediation with divinity, 32, 156, 161, 164–165, 173, 236–239, 517–258; Minoan, 108n120, 255, 295, 387n99, 435n73; mortuary cult, 67–71, 95, 134–147, 177, 423; Mycenaean, 255, 387; origin

773

General Index

(lyres and lyric iconography, *cont.*)
   in North Syria?, 52; Philistines, 157, 159, 244, 250–251, 255; Phoenician, 242, 244, 257–272, 274–276, 278, 300, 302 (see also *knr*, *kinnāru[m]*); 'Phoenician' *phoínix*, etc., 271, 274–276; prominence, 93, 102, 115, 118, 139, 143, 147, 164–165, 170, 178–179, 265, 291, 421–424, 525; purification rites, 99, 165–166, 174, 183, 233, 329; rectangular, 52, 105, 153, 543–544; round-based (Aegean, Cyprus, Cilicia, Philistia), 52, 108n120, 157, 242, 244–245, 250–258, 266n107, 267, 269n126, 272, 276, 278, 519, 521; royal contexts, 34, 36, 45, 67–71, 76, 81, 102, 134–147, 153, 167–174, 251–253, 316–318, 380–382, 400, 421–424, 468, 522–528; self-activated, 141, 181, 295 (see also sympathetic vibration; divinized instruments: self-activated); silence of, 85, 95, 141–147, 279–319 (see also silence, ritual); surviving specimens, Egypt, 106; Syria, 248, 268, 274, 276, 495–496; Syro-Anatolian/Neo-Hittite, 60, 253, 256, 258, 276, 520; thick and thin, as defined by Lawergren, 52; tortoiseshell, 258n76, 275n144, 298n104, 450n43; two 'lyrasts', Myc. Thebes, 434; Ugarit, 113–148; zigzag arms, 255–257, 260, 517. *See also* animals; balang; *bárbitos/n*; birds; Inanna-instrument; *kinnāru*; *kinýra*; *kissar*; *kithára*; *knr*; *krar*; *lýra*; *nbl*; *phórminx*; prophecy; threnody, lyric; women; *zannāru*; zinar

Lyros, son of Aphrodite and Ankhises, 434n67

Maas, M., 244
Magi, 449, 496; Magos, father of Misor and Sydyk, 507n78
Mahol, 151–152
Maier, F. G., 351–352, 363
Malachi, 510
management of musicians, 397; Bible, 154–158; Ebla, 63; Mari, 75–76; Paphos, 421–424; Ugarit, 113–119. *See also* guilds, musical
Manana of Urum/Ilip, 84
Manbog: *see* Hierapolis
Mandaean, Mandaic, 60; 'lyre of lust', 61, 538
Maneros, 304–306, 311, 313
Mannaseh, 178, 383
Marash, 60
Mardin, 517
Marduk, 495, 509, 511; lamentation for, 496n10
Mari, 8, 22, 45, 54, 64, 73–88, 106, 114, 155, 245, 291, 304, 422, 485; Alashiya, 324; Crete, 479; destruction by Hammurabi, 73, 152; Ebla, 63, 74; *kinnāru*, 76–79; 'Mari-lyre' (miritum), 34, 36; *mummum*, 'conservatory', 74; musical cosmopolitanism, 73–75, 77, 82, 154–155; pre-Sargonic, 485; Shakkanakku period, 74; Sumerian influence, 73, 81; Ur III dynasty, 483; women, harem, 74–77, 82, 85, 154, 292
Mariandynoi, 305n147
Marieus, son of Kinyras, 350, 502
Marion, 14n68, 229–230, 350, 414, 502; Marieus, eponym, 350, 502; population deported to Paphos, 416–417
Markoe, G., 256, 266n109, 268
Maroni, 248
marriage, 63, 67; dynastic, 74, 82, 92, 106, 154–155, 366–367

774

General Index

Marsyas, 189, 190n19
Martu, 80, 87. *See also* Amorites
marzeaḥ/marziḫu, 138n164, 293n79, 452n60
Masoretic Text (MT), 55, 168, 170n119, 175, 178
master- and servant-gods, 20–21, 26–33, 36, 84–86, 118, 122, 164, 167, 239, 279, 291, 382, 386, 388, 401, 485; in Lyre-Player Group of Seals, 526; servant reflects master in name and/or quality, 25, 36n116, 88, 124, 507; servants as familiars, 27, 282, 291; Ugarit, 130–131. *See also* Kinyras, divine or cultic qualities; Ninigizibara
Mati'el of Arpad, 300
matrilineal succession, 283, 366–367
Megassares of Hyria, 504, 507
Megiddo, 53, 59, 105, 159, 255, 386, 517; etching, 47n21, 53; plaque, 126
Meilikhios, Zeus, 446, 448
Meleagros, 207, 316; Meleagrides, 191
Melena, J., 428
Meliton, pseudo, 404, 447, 468–477, 480, 482, 487, 495; overview, 469
Melos, 378, 379
Melqart, 471n82
Melus/Melos, friend of Adonis, familiar of Kinyras, apple-tree, 290
Memnon, Memnonides, 191n30, 298, 505
Menelaos, 188n7, 204, 323, 333n81, 339, 344, 369, 467, 506n67
Menophanes, 346
Merneptah, 13
Mesopotamian tuning system: *see* tuning
messianism, 58, 175n153, 179–181
metals, metallurgy: *see* Aegean migrations; Agapenor; Bomford Goddess; copper; gold; Hephaistos; industry and wealth; Ingot God; Kauthar; Khalkanor; Kinyras, silver
metamorphoses: connection with cult-objects, 279–291, 381; Hellenistic popularity, 189, 192, 286. *See also* Amaracus; Anaxarete; birds; Erinoma; Meleagrides; Melus; Myrrha; Peleia/Pelia; Pierides; Propoetides
Metharme, wife of Kinyras, 290n63, 356, 367, 497, 504, 512n119, 513, 515; variant Thymarete, 512
Mettinger, T., 483–485
Meyer, E., 508
Michal, 169, 173–174
Michalowski, P., 55n46, 77
Midas, 2, 224, 323
migrations, migration legends: *see* Aegean migrations
Milku, 135, 138
Milkyaton, Kition, 344, 358; inscription, 357
Millar, F., 495
Milku: *see* Rāp'iu
mimesis: *see* enactment
mimation, 54
Minoans, Minoan: Cypro-Minoan script, 13; frescoes, Avaris, 447n23; Hagia Triada sarcophagus, 295; Kothar and Crete, 478; Kythera, 479; Minos, eponym, 432; royal ideology, 387n99; trade with Ugarit, Mari, Babylon, 479. *See also* pre-Greek languages; lyres and lyric iconography
Minyans, Orkhomenos, 432
Miriam, Song of, 156n41
Misor, Philo of Byblos, 509; Misharum and Kittum, 510

General Index

Mitanni, 10, 92, 96, 106, 108, 373, 375–376, 440; glyptic, 386, 397; Ugarit, 97
Mitford, T. B., 205–206, 362, 411
Mlynarczyk, J., 239, 410, 413, 417
Moab, 154, 164–165, 301
mobility: craftsmen, 12, 74, 261; cult-musicians, 102, 154, 373, 380, 405; cult-specialists and techniques, 373; diviners, 449; gods/cult, 100, 154, 364–368, 371–400, 380, 479–482; musical instruments, 37, 248; musicians, 37, 59, 63, 74, 82, 105n101 (*see also* captive musicians); objects, 247–248, 260, 270–272, 275, 326; ritual division of god, 100–102, 380. *See also* pilgrimage/tourism; tuning: Mesopotamian system
Mohammed, 182
Mokhos of Sidon, 445, 470, 477
moon, 97, 103; in magic, 41, 103; Kušuḫ, 99; lunar calendar and balang-cult, 41n152, 584–585; Selene, 461; Suen/Sin as master-god, 36
Mopsos, Moxos, Mukšaš, Mpš, 340n18, 346n50, 353, 363n150, 508, 520; Ascalon, 364n150; daughters, 346n50; historical individual?, 252n51; Meliac War, 347, 351
Morphou, 390
Morris, S., 379
mortuary cult: Greek world, 294, 296, 317; Hittite world, 95, 304; lyres, 67–71, 95, 134–147, 177, 189, 296, 423; royal ancestor cult, Alashiya, 382; —Byblos, 484; —Ebla, 67–71, 83, 175; —Hittites, 94, 509; —IA Paphos, 382, 401–417; —incense offerings, 283; —Mesopotamia, 83, 140, 485; —Sam'al/Zincirli, 136; —Ugarit, 5, 71, 83, 124, 134–147, 175, 177, 256, 313, 423, 484, Rephaim 146–147; versus funeral rites, 70n54
Moses, 379n52, 490; instruments from time of preserved in First Temple, 155n39; musical prophecy, 164n86; silver trumpets, 155n39; Song of, 156n41
mountains: Aoios, Cyprus, 500–501; Baal cult, Bible, 465; conjunction of mountain and river, 461–466, 468, 500–501; divinized, LBA, 465, 501; echo David's songs, 183; Ishtar-cults, Anatolia, 375n29; Kasios/Saphon/Hazzi, Baal, 120, 125, 374, 465; —gods of Ugarit, 120; —Teshup, 465; —Adonis, 465, 514; —Kasos, eponym, 440n107; Lebanon, Adonis, 463, 467, 501, 514; —Belos/Oreithuia, 467; —goddess of, 464; —Tammuz, 470–471; mountainous regions culturally conservative, 465; mountaintop shrines, 465; Troodos, 11, 16, 270, 324. *See also* storm-gods
Movers, F. C., 404, 513–514
Mowinckel, S., 169
Mursili I, 96
muse(s), 6, 126n89, 191, 211n135, 234–235, 293–294, 305, 307, 310, 383, 405; Aphrodite as, 39, 307, 310, 313, 345; Inanna/Ishtar as, 38–39; lyre as, 6n32; *Mousaïstaí*, 234; sing at Christ's birth with *kinyrístriai*, 216; slay Adonis, 467
Mushe of Nisibis, 469
musical cognition, 35–36, 41, 86, 161–165, 383–391, 521–527; epiphany in guise of musician, 26–33, 522–528

General Index

musical therapy, 140, 166, 174, 183, 233, 455. *See also* purification rites
Mycenae, Mycenaean, 322; Agamemnon, 74, 190, 347–348; Ahhiyawa, 10, 251; Alashiya, 348; Arcado-Cypriot dialect group, 360; Argos, Argives, 340; contact with Cyprus, 435–436; —chariot kraters, 388; —western margin of *knr*-culture?, 435; Cilicia, LH IIIC pottery, 250; Great Collapse, 13; international trade, 326–327, 330; Kythera, 478; lamentation, 292n71; linguistic points, 206n106, 252, 273–274, 380n58, 387n99, 407, 432–436, 451, 478; Linos-Song, 308; Melos/Phylakopi, 379; PNs, 428, 431–439; PNs, musical, 434n67; —non-Greek, 439; sub-Mycenaean, 255; —Cyprus, 253, 255, 258, 341, 368; —Philistia, 159; two 'lyrasts', Thebes, 434. *See also* Ahhiyawa; Hiyawa; Linear B; lyres and lyric iconography; Pylos
Mygdalion, son of, 344–345
Mykale, battle, 341
myrrh, 2, 124, 199n71, 275, 286n41, 331; anointing rites, 283; —Adonis, 287; aphrodisiac, 283; divinized at Byblos?, 283; royal burials, 283; sap-drops as tears, traditional idea, 286; sun, 288; Tammuz, 283; Ugaritian ritual, 282; uses, 282–283; where produced, 282, 287
Myrrha: 'numbered among the gods', 289; ancient literary treatments, 284–286; —Cinna's *Zmyrna*, 286; —Hellenistic tragedy, 284, 334; —Ovid, 2, 286–288; Byblos, 283, 460, 466–468, 492, 502; Divine Censer, 124, 283; incest motif, 220, 283, 367; *katábasis?*, 287; Kinyras, 282–289, 310, 492n20, 513; *mýron*, perfumed oil, 283–284; myrrh, 2, 124, 282–283, 331; myrtle, 288; phonology, 274, 477; ritual poetics, 282–283, 418; Sun, 288, 506; tears, 2, 282, 286, 288; wrath of Aphrodite, 288–289
Myrrhina, 284
Myrtion, 492n20
myrtle, 288
Myrtou, 378
mysteries, mysticism: Eleusis, 234; *kinýra* of, 210n133; Kinyras, 238; Kybele and Attis, 101; *lilissu* ritual, 24; Linos, 307; musical, seven-numerology, 40; N-A Tammuz ritual, 283; Orphism, 296
myth: reflection of ritual, 25, 33, 103, 282, 382, 393. *See also* divinized cult-objects: mythogenic

Naamah, 44, 46, 129n104
Nabataeans, Nabataean, 60, 542n23, 543n32
nábla(s): see *nbl*
Nabu, 462, 495–496
Nagar, 64
Nagy, G., 310
Nahr 'Ibrahim: *see* rivers
Nakassis, D., 438
naming rituals: *see* divinized cult-objects
Nanna, 84
Nanshe, 27
nar/NAR/*nâru*, 28n65, 66n30; balang, 28, 66; —Ušumgal-kalama, 28, 531–532; Byblos, mi2-nar, 486, 594; defined, 28; Ebla, 63, 65–67; —NAR.MAḪ, NAR.MÍ, NAR.TUR, 64; Hittites, lú.mešNAR, 100; —lúNAR, 329; —lúNAR-*aš*,

777

(nar, *cont.*)
    100; —ˡᵘNAR-*aš* = ˡᵘ*kinirtallaš* = '*kinnāru*-singer', 98, 116; Mari, 66n30, 73–74; —MUNUS.NAR.GAL, MUNUS.NAR.TUR, 75n23; —NAR.GAL, NAR.MÍ, *nargallum*, 74; Ugarit, NAR= *šr*, 116. See also Chief Singer; singers
Naram-Sin, Akkad, 33, 37, 41, 65, 131n118, 393
Naram-Sin, Eshnunna, 479
nbl: Gk. *nábla(s)*, 52n26, 58, 275, 538; Heb. *nēbel*, 52–53, 58, 116–117, 155, 157, 163–164, 169, 172, 180, 215n164; Lat. *nablium*, 538; Ug. *nbl*, 52n26, 102n82, 114
Nebuchadnezzar, 150
Nemesis, 461
Nenaš, 68
Neo-Hittite sphere, 60, 247, 519; persistence of Hittite royal ideology, 517. See also Cilicia; Karkemish; lyres and lyric iconography: Syro-Anatolian/Neo-Hittite; Mopsos
Nereids, 293–294
Nergal, 86–87; Alashiya, 372–373, 396n134; calque, 372; Resheph, 372, 396n134
netherworld: *see* underworld
New Year rituals, 169, 171
Nicolaou, I., 412–413
Nicosia: *see* Ledroi
Nikokles, Paphos, 230n69, 407–417; building program, 362, 409–410, 413; —(re)founds New Paphos, 362, 409, 416; rewalls Old Paphos, 409, 414; fall of, 416–417, 491; links Kinyras to Apollo?, 410, 415; Panhellenizing tendency, 409–410; proposed restoration in *thyapolía* inscription, 412–414; traditional Kinyrad stance, 410–414; wars of the Successors, 414–417

Nikokles, Salamis, 212
Nikokreon, Salamis, 212n144, 414, 416n95, 417, 491
Nile: *see* rivers
Nimrud: ivories, 248, 260, 268; symposium bowls, 260–261
Ninazu, 140, 304
Nineveh, 23, 328; Ishtar of, 100, 373, 375–376, 474
Ningal/Nikkal, 30n83, 97, 383
Ningirsu, 22n20, 26, 29n75, 30, 32, 42, 66, 118, 122, 163, 167, 279, 282, 382, 393, 444, 450; seven balang-gods, 29n68
Ninhursag, 396n134
Ninigizibara, balang-god, 22, 84–85, 292, 304, 383, 485; spouse or lover of Inanna/Ishtar, 84, 102, 291, 380
Ninos, 357n119, 547, 557–558n8
Nintu, 68–69
Ninurta, 25–26, 86, 122
Nippur, 30n83, 40n147, 393
Niqmaddu III, Ugarit, 143, 146
Nirar, 64
Noah, 44
nomad, nomadic, 44, 80–82
Nonnos, 337, 339, 351, 477, 501–502
Norborg, A., 47
Nostoi (lost Greek epic), 317n226, 337
notation, musical: Greek, 58; of Hurrian hymns, 59, 97, 119, 448
Nougayrol, J., 4, 120
Nubia, Nubian, 105, 326
Numidian PNs, 57n58, 452n60
Nuzi, 92n8, 154

oaths, 21n17, 205, 329; on musical instruments, 20–21, 211n136. See also treaties
Odysseus, 255, 328n49, 333, 338, 342, 343n32, 344, 369, 387n99, 536
offerings: *see* divinized cult-objects
offering-scenes, iconography, 262,

383–391, 525; ambiguity between human and divine, 265, 387, 525; offering of harp?, 398
oil, 249; anointing, 101, 144n197, 282; divine protection, 330; offerings, 20, 41, 69, 120, 139n166, 331n69; perfumed, 120, 249, 282, 284, 330, 413n76, 436; —Adonis, 283n25; —Aphrodite, 331; —Kinyras, 1, 283, 323, 330–332, 436; —Pylos, 330–331. *See also* Amaracus; myrrh; Myrrha
Oito-Linos, 307
Olbe, 356n110, 405
Old Testament, 43, 164, 450
Olymbros, 508
Olympia, 266, 271–272, 298
Olympian gods, 189, 226–227, 230, 234n87, 362, 409, 415, 459, 473, 475, 495
Olympos, Phrygian aulete, 202, 295
Opheltas *obelós*, 14, 253
oral tradition: Amorite, 83; at sanctuaries, 380, 401–407, 460–462, 472, 475, 487; —Byblos/Aphaka, 464–466, 472; Hurrianization of Akkadian musical terms, 97; Jewish folklore in Arabic sources, 182; transmission of Syro-Levantine cult-music, 448. *See also* Cyprus: oral tradition; epic poetry; parallelism
order, symbolized by music, 37, 41, 72, 86–87, 147, 152–154, 252, 300–301, 381, 383–391
Oreithuia, 'oread' of Mount Lebanon, 467
Orontes, 507, 538n8
Orpheus: animals, 229, 517; Argiope, 325n24; David, 179, 193; Eukleés/Euklous, Cypriot prophet, 345n43, 356n113; Hermes, 492n21; Hierapolis, 462, 496;

Jesus, 210; *katábasis*, 298n108; *kinýra* of, 215; Kinyras, 192–194; lyric threnody, 141, 294; Orâfî, Harran, 496; Orpheus Jug, 159–161, 163, 165, 179, 183, 194, 255, 386; Orphism, 296; Ovid's *Metamorphoses*, 281n7, 553; purifications through lyre, 166n97; Rāp'iu, 140
Orsedike, daughter of Kinyras, 281, 333, 504, 511, 513
Osiris, 305, 316, 318; Amathous, 516; Byblos, 316n214, 516
Ostasos, 508
Oulomos, Mokhos of Sidon, 445
Ourania: Aphrodite, 307, 378, 403, 463; —Kythera, 478; muse, 306–307
Ouranos, 97, 403, 508
Ovid: Apollo the Lamenter, 294, 311; Cinna, 286, 288; etymology of Kinyras, 188, 280; Kinyras the Lamenter, 188, 280–282, 291, 298, 300; Myrrha and Cinyras, 2, 282, 286–288, 334–335; Pygmalion-Paphos-Kinyras, 289, 499, 503; relationship between Ovid's two Cinyras scenes, *Metamorphoses*, 288
Oxyporos, son of Kinyras, 333, 497–498, 504, 512–513, 515

Pacific parallels, 22
Pahlavi, 61
Paiawon, 190
Palestine: *see* Canaan; Israel; Judah; Philistia
Palmer, A. N., 162
Palmyra, Palmyrene, 60, 496
Pamphos, 307n156
Pamphylia, 202, 335n100, 347, 499; *Abṓbas*, 145n201, 502
Panammuwas I, Sam'al, 136
Panchaea, 286n42, 287, 467n54

General Index

Pandion, 498–499, 505
Panhellenism, 189, 227, 230, 338, 341, 348, 359–360, 410
panpipes (sŷrinx), 298n108, 310
pantomime: Kinyras and Myrrha, 466
Panyassis, 284, 467–468, 492, 502
Papageorghiou, S., 501
Papasavvas, G., 384, 394
Paphia: mother of Kinyras, 350, 406n39, 499
Paphos, 3, 14n73, 99, 205, 211, 217, 226–227, 229–230, 319, 341, 348, 350, 360–361, 365–367, 438, 474, 501; Abdalonymos wrongly relocated, 491–492; abduction of Helen, gathering of Greek fleet, 348; absorbs Marion, 416–417; Agapenor, 359–368; *Basiliastaí*, 234; dual kingship traditions, 363–364, 367, 401, 404–406; earliest attestation of Greek, 14, 253, 360; earthquakes, 362; Eteocypriot inscriptions, 349; LBA contact with mainland, 379; LBA metalworking, 324; Nile resurfaces, 501; Paphian Zeus, 501; Salamis, alliance with Euagoras, 357; —rivalry in Archaic period?, 345, 357, 400; Roman period, emperor cult, 402; —metropolis of Cyprus, 499, 554; royal decadence trope, 284, 490, 493. See also Agapenor; Apollo: *Kenyristḗs*; Kinyradai of Paphos; Kouklia kalathos
—Paphos, foundation legends (city/sanctuary): Aerias, 401–407, 475–476, 487; Agapenor, 253, 341, 359, 362–363; Aoios, 503; Kinyras, 2, 222, 356, 363, 380, 393, 401–407, 475–476, 487, 504; Phoinix, 378–379, 487
—Paphos, sanctuary, 226, 345, 378; aniconism, 236, 481; *Adōniá*, 221n10, 505; *arkhiereús*, 420; Astarte, Paphian 271n129; bloodless sacrifice, 124, 283, 413; Byblian and Paphian legend agree, 460, 475–476, 487; Chalcolithic figurines, 375; cult-continuity LBA–IA, 8, 363–364, 407, 423–424; design, 378; fame of, 360, 365, 400–401, 416; —center of world, 204, 411, 416; incense/perfumed oil, 124, 331, 418; —*myroworgós*, Rantidi, 283; island-wide *panḗgyris*, 416; Kinyradai, 401–417; *mantiárkhēs*, 420; monumentalization, 363, 375, 380, 487; never rained upon, 505; oral tradition, 402, 404, 406, 475, 487; sacred site for Alashiya?, 11, 400; sexual rites (real or alleged), 94, 222; *thyapolía*, 124, 412–414; tombs of Kinyras and Kinyradai, 2, 136, 310, 382, 419; wealth of, 418
—Paphos, eponym, father or mother of Kinyras, 350, 356, 406n39, 453, 498–503, 512, 514; Aoios doublet, 500, 503–504
—Paphos, New, 287n46; administrative capital, Ptolemaic period, 418; Agapenor founds (myth), 359, 361–362; Artists of Dionysos, 212n148, 213; House of Aion, 212n146; tenth-century tombs, Iskender/Ktima, 362
parallelism, poetic, 128, 156, 162–163, 176, 444
paramythological texts, 26–33, 113, 115, 120, 125, 128, 138, 146, 313; defined, 7
Pardee, D., 114, 122–124, 137–138, 142
Paris, 1, 202, 329, 339, 409

Parsons, P. J., 505
Parthenios, 286, 500–503
Patroklos, 188n7, 292n72, 333, 335
Paul of Perugia, 549
Pausanias, 307–308, 337, 353, 359–360, 362, 364, 366, 378, 511; Theopompos, 353, 362
peace: *see* order
peg-wizards, 393n123
Peleia/Pelia, 237, 290. *See also* birds: doves
Peleset: *see* Philistines
Peloponnese, Peloponnesian, 340–341, 343, 360
percussion, 41, 46, 115–116, 118n38, 143n189, 144, 242n1, 265, 397; clappers, 135, 144, 313, 444; —Gk. *krótala*, 145; rattles, 241, 397; scrapers, 241. *See also* cymbals; frame-drum; instruments, various; sistrum
Perdikkas, 414
Perga, 502
Perikles' citizenship law, 356
perfume: *see* oil
Persephone, 223, 298n108; Adonis, 287, 299n112
Perseus, 506n67, 508
Persia, Persian, 196n50, 339n11, 378n50, 490, 508n83; Amathous, 352, 506n67; Cyprus, 16, 328, 351, 491; Euagoras, 347, 352; Euagoras II, 493; Ibn Ḫurdāḏbih, 60n88; Ionian revolt, 352; Kition, 352; Magi, 449; Middle Persian, 60; Mykale, 341; Perseus, 506n67; Persian Wars, 223; Pharnake, 507; PNs, 508n83
Phaethon, 103, 474, 504–506
Phaleron, eponym Phaleros, 341, 355
Pharnake, mother of Kinyras, 367n170, 504, 507; Apollo, 512
Philammon of Delphi, 325n24

Phileas, Athenian geographer, 356, 500, 502–503
Philip of Macedon, 284, 346–347
Philip V of Macedon, 346
Philistia, Philistine, 14, 363n150; Amuq, 199; Ark, 169; David among, 161n76; David and Saul, 126; instrument of Gath?, 161n76; Mopsos, 363n150; musical guilds, 157; Ramses III, 13, 354; religion, 250, 378. *See also* lyres and lyric iconography
Philo of Byblos, 45, 443n2, 445–452, 470, 507n78; Baaltis/Baalat Gebal, 472, 481; Byblian bias?, 446, 472; methodology, 446, 510; Sankhuniathon, 123; Ugaritian pantheon, 123n74
Philostephanos, 337, 340, 364, 515–516
Phoenicia, Phoenician: Alexander the Great in, 212, 284, 488–494; Cilicia, 5n27, 9, 199n67, 202, 405, 461, 512, 517; cultural history in Philo of Byblos, 446; dialect pressure, Cyprus, 206n106, 460; Greek usage, 3n11, 55; Homer, 275, 317, 345; in Aegean, 275, 378; —Kythera, 478; —Kommos, Crete, 271; Kinyras, 3, 57, 369, 459–487; linguistic points, 196n54, 199, 206n106, 214, 275–276, 282, 339n11, 372n6, 445n12, 472, 478n118; —Phoenician Shift, 273, 445; music and dance, 244; mythical foundations, 378–379, 478, 487, 516; N-A control, 262; Pindar, 225; PNs, 57n68, 452, 509; production centers, symposium bowls, 260; versus 'Canaanite', 12n61, 55. *See also* Adonis; Astarte: royal cults; Baal; Byblos; *knr*, *kinnāru(m)*; lamentation; lyres

General Index

(Phoenicia, Phoenician, *cont.*)
    and lyric iconography; Philo of Byblos; Sidon; Tyre
—Phoenician colonization of Cyprus, 16, 327n37; Adonis problem and chronology of Kinyras, 313–316, 369, 476; copper as stimulus, 16, 270, 475–476; lyric morphology, 242, 258–272, 276, 278, 457; other theological issues, 272, 373, 375; Tyre versus Byblos, 16, 476. *See also* Cypro-Phoenician (ethnicity); Cypro-Phoenician symposium bowls; Cyprus; Lapethos; Kition
Phoinix: Greek hero, 207, 280, 316–318; Phoenician eponym, 313, 317, 378–379, 478, 487; — Adonis son, 313, 317, 464n29; — Kytheros son, 478;
phórminx, 207, 211, 235, 269–270n126, 311, 318, 433, 458, 541
Phoroneus, 343
Photios, 210, 346–347, 511
Phrasios, Cypriot *mántis*, 373
Phrygia, Phrygian, 101, 202, 305n147, 311
Phylakopi: *see* Melos
Pierides, 191
pilgrimage/tourism, 348n62, 416n92, 462, 511
Pindar, 1, 8, 215, 217, 219–239, 241–242, 310, 321, 329, 334–345, 355, 360, 409, 410n59, 475, 525; lyric threnody, 293, 296; scholia, 187, 219, 241 (*see also* Index Locorum)
pipes: *see* double-pipes; single-pipe
Plato, 104, 449; Comicus, 312; cosmic harmony, 210
plectrum, 58, 309n172
Pliny, 324–325, 332, 351, 450, 452, 545–546, 552–553, 558, 560, 563

plucking, 47n17, 58, 196n54, 537, 540; Gk. *psállein*, 69, 210, 303, 537n3, 539–541; —*psaltōidoí*, 116; —*psaltḗrion*/Lat. *psalterium*, 58n66, 182, 194n43, 215n164, 216, 275n147, 540. *See also* Hebrew psalmody; plectrum
Plutarch, 305, 337; Abdalonymos, 489–491
PNs: Alalakh, 98, 435, 440, 452; Alashiya, 245, 350, 374, 440–441; Amorite, 80–81, 138, 441, 452, 509; Anatolia, 202, 252, 440, 508, 511; Aramaean, 441, 443, 452; Biblical, 138, 509; Canaanite, 44, 138, 273n138, 440–452; Hittite, 440; Hurrian, 245, 440; Libyan/Numidian, 57n58, 452nn60 and 64; Mycenaean/Linear B, 9, 252, 428, 431–439; —musical, 434n67; —non-Greek, 439; Persian, 508n83; Phoenician/Punic, 57n58, 452, 509; Sumerian, 98, 435; Syria, 78n45; Ugarit, 56n53, 167n100, 273n138, 377, 441, 452, 509
Pnytagoras, Salamis, 493
Polyainos, 417
Pompeius Trogus, 221, 490
Pompey, 199
Pomponius Laetus, Julius (Sabinus), 332, 552
Poncy, H., 519
Pongratz-Leisten, B., 38
Pope, M. H., 7, 130
Porada, E., 21, 518–522, 526
Poseidon, 226n46, 333n85, 354, 423n129, 431
Potnia, Potnian, 331n69, 429–430; bronze-workers, 394n127; Potnia Hippeia, 431; unguent boiler, 331
Power, T., 536

782

General Index

power, song as, 37, 41, 72, 86–87, 137–139, 147, 152–154, 175–178, 252, 301, 383–391
Praxandros, 340
pre-Greek languages: Aegean, 198, 274, 434n63; —Minoan, 198, 434n63; LBA Cyprus, 245, 272–276, 434n63, 436, 439–440, 477–478. *See also* Cypro-Minoan; Cypro-Syllabic; Eteocypriot; Minoans
prescriptive: *see* rituals
presentation scenes, 33
Priebatsch, H. Y., 478
Prittlewell Prince, 141
processions: Aegean, 294, 295n94, 387n99; Assyria, 171; Babylonia, 30, 32–33, 171; Biblical world, 43, 44n6, 118, 167–175, 178 (*see also* Ark); Canaanite/Phoenician, 115, 160, 173, 248, 265, 486; Cyprus, LBA, 250, 382, 388, 397; —Paphos, 416; Emar, 171–172; Hittites, 96, 171–172, 501; North Syria, 248
prophecy: ecstatic, 38, 43, 85, 88, 156–157, 383; musical, lyre, 43, 156–157, 161–165, 296, 345, 383, 414, 422, 450; N-A texts, 38, 383. *See also* divination; Kinyradai
Propoetides of Amathous, 281
prostitution, 266n113; harlot of Tyre, 61, 77, 302; 'sacred', 222n15, 238n112, 250n41, 281n13, 313n195, 463n24; —Babylon, 313n195; —Cyprus, 222n16, 281; —Kinyras, 222n15; —Locrian maidens, 221–222; *sambŷkai*, 537; Syrian *musiciennes* in Rome, 199, Appendix C. *See also* Propoetides of Amathous; sexual rites (real or alleged)
psállein, psaltḗrion, psalterium: *see* plucking
psalmody: *see* Hebrew psalmody

Psaroudakes, S., 248
Ptolemies: Cyprus, 321, 328, 414–417, 416n92, 417–420; —New Paphos administrative center, 418; —*stratēgía*, 417, 419–420; Demokrates son of Ptolemy, 418; dynastic cult, 213, 234, 420; influence on Istros?, 516; Kinyradai under, 410, 413, 417–420, 422; Ptolemy Epiphanes, 419; Ptolemy Euergetes II Physkon, 419; Ptolemy I and Nikokles of Paphos, 414–417; Ptolemy IV Philopator, 418–419; Ptolemy IX Soter II (Lathyros), 420; Ptolemy of Megalopolis on Kinyras and Kinyradai, 419; Ptolemy V Epiphanes, 418
Ptolemy Khennos, 192, Appendix B
Pumayyaton, Kition, 344, 358
Pummay/Pygmaion/*pmy*, 315 and n210, 344n38
Punic, 57, 274, 452
Punt, 282
purification rites, 68, 449; eagle-diviner?, 373; Itkalzi series, 98; lyre, 99, 158–159, 165, 298, 329, 381; model boats, 328–329. *See also* musical therapy
Puzrish-Dagan/Drehem, 483
Pygmaion: *see* Pummay
Pygmalion, 369n179; Bousiris, 373; Cilix father, 339n14, Appendix F, 559–560; conquest of Cyprus, 327n37, Appendix F, 559–560, 561n32; divinized statues, hierogamy, 289, 499; founder, Golgoi, 339n14; —Karpasia, 356n113; Kinyras' father-in-law, 344, 356, 358, 367, 369, 404, 497–498, 504, 512, 517; Sicyonian dynasty, 339n14; son/daughter Paphos, grandson Kinyras, 289, 369,

General Index

(Pygmalion, *cont.*)
    499, 503, Appendix F, G. *See also* Pummay
pygmies, 105
Pylos, 394n127, Chapter 17; Cypriot contacts, 330, 435–436; Northeast Building, 427; —cultic function?, 431, 435; oil industry, 436; PN Kinyras, 9, 274, 323, 392, Chapter 17, 451, 478, 480; Qa series, 427–432; Throne Room fresco, 387n99
Pyrodes, son of Cilix, 552–553
Pythagoreanism: cosmic harmony, 210; purifications through lyre, 166; seven-magic, 40n141
Pythian games: *see* Delphi
Pythias, cultic agent, Pylos, 430

Qatna, 74, 82
Queen of Sheba, 151
Qumran: *see* Dead Sea Scrolls
Quran: *see* Arabic, Arabic tradition; Index Locorum

Rabbinic tradition, 43, 59, 117, 155, 177, 181, 183, 462n14
rag-bushes: *see* trees
Ramses II, 14n68
Ramses III, 13–14, 354
Rantidi, 284
Rāp'iu, 130, 134–142, 144, 147, 177–178, 256, 265, 273, 444, 451; etymology, 135; identity, 135; Orpheus, 140; plays *kinnāru*?, 137–146, 143, 177, 304
Rapa'ūma, 134–141, 146, 484; identity, 136
Rašap: *see* Resheph
Rawson, M., 427
Rephaim, 43n3, 146–147, 484

Resheph, 63, 71, 229, 373n7, 396n134; *'lhyts*, 372; Alashiya, 372; Ebla, 372; Mikal, 372n3; NK Egypt, 372; Ugarit, 372
Rhea, 315n213, 461, 481, 508
Rhodes, 234, 356n110, 518–520
Rib-Hadda of Byblos, 481, 485–486
Ribichini, S., 6, 9, 143, 314
Rim-Sin of Larsa, 393n123
Rishiya, Chief Singer, Mari, 74n7, 75
ritual: descriptive, 172; prescriptive, 67, 120–121, 136, 171–172; prescriptive versus descriptive, 67n35; reflected in myth, 25, 33, 103, 282, 382, 393; ritual poetics, 26, 35–36, 92, 101, 164, 172, 177, 204, 282–283, 289, 292, 298, 301, 306, 381–382, 418, 485 *See also* divination; divinized cult-objects: naming rituals and construction rituals; drinking rituals; entry ritual; funeral rites; processions; prophecy; purification rites; sexual rites (real or alleged); silence
rivers: Adonis, modern Nahr 'Ibrahim, 463–464, 466, 468, 498, 501, 503; Aoios, 500–503; Aplieus, 500–502; *Cisseum fluvium*, 515; conjunction of mountain and river, 461–466, 468, 500–501; Diarrhizos, Old Paphos, 502; Euphrates, 73, 78, 97; Eurymedon, 499; Hebros, 295; Khabur, 96; Nile, 13, 105, 318, 325n24, 515n130; —resurfaces at Paphos, 501; of Babylon, 300; Orontes, 503; Pyramus, 501; Setrakhos, 500–502; Tigris, 328; underground, 500–503; —Cypriot folk belief, 501
Rizzo, M. A., 520

Rome, Roman: Cyprus, 205, 499; —annexation 58 BCE, 420; —Kinyradai of Paphos, 420–421; —sanctuaries, 401–407; emperor cult, 205, 402, 469; Judaea, 180–181, 401; Kinyras and Myrrha story, 286; Syria, Syrian *musiciennes*, 199, Appendix C
rose(s), 500
royal ancestor cult: *see* mortuary cult
royal hymns, Neo-Sumerian, 34, 37–38, 81, 392
royal ideology: covenant metaphors, 177, 179, 468; Damu, 484–485; divine kingship, 5, 33–34, 37n123, 114, 468; divinized instruments, 21–22, 31–33, 35–36, 84–85, 390; Dumuzi, 35, 37, 39, 382, 484–485; king and sun, 507; king as musician, 33–35, 38–39, 178, 383; —as shepherd, 35, 37n125; —as totalizing cultural symbol, 35, 151–152, 381, 392; king empowered by goddess or queen, 366–367, 383–391, 400, 407, 473–479, 506; king in cult, 166–167; —as high priest, 124, 223, 239, 345, 380, 383, 405, 407, 410, 417, 422, 492, 501; —as praise-singer of master god(dess), 36, 129, 149, 176, 382–383; —as sole or leading agent, 32–33, 39–40, 113, 118, 167–174, 381, 422–423; lamentation, 34–35, 85, 141–146, 482–485; LBA Aegean, 387; popular memory, 366, 392–400, 418; projection to public, 26, 153, 167–174, 251–253, 393–394, 397–399, 415–416, 491, 493; Ruler's Truth, Indo-European tradition, 387n99; storm-god patron, 135, 169, 468, 501, 503.
See also beauty; justice; lyres and lyric iconography: royal contexts; mortuary cult: royal ancestor cult; Sacred Marriage (so-called); temple-builder/building
Sabaeans, 287
Sabians, 471n81, 496
Sacred Marriage (so-called), 35, 37–40, 42, 68n37, 93, 128, 154n34, 265, 289, 382, 410–411n63, 418, 506; controversy, 38. *See also* sexual rites (real or alleged)
Sadykos: *see* Sydyk
Salamis: Cypriot, 5, 11, 14n68, 16, 211, 227, 236, 253, 266, 281, 287, 321, 341, 346–347, 350–359, 362, 402, 410n62; —Enkomi, 349, 354, 398, 460; —epic school and Kinyras as Liar King, 345, 357, 400; —Gerginoi, 457; —sacral kingship?, 410; Saronic, 287n45, 354–355. *See also* Enkomi; Teukros, Teukrid
Sam'al/Zincirli, 136, 253n52
Sambykai, *sambŷkai*, 537
Samsi-Yasmah-Addu, divinized *urzababîtum*, 86
Samuel, 149–150, 156, 165–174, 381. *See also* Index Locorum
Šamuḫa, 100
Sandas, Sandes, Sandon, Sandan, Šantaš, 508–509, 511; as Herakles, 509; as Marduk, 509, 511
Sandokos, father of Kinyras, 367n367, 477, 504, 507–512, 552; reflects Sandas *vel sim.*?, 508–509, 511–512; reflects *Ṣdq vel sim*?, 509–512
Sankhuniathon, 123
Saphon: *see* mountains
Sappho, 275, 293, 307–308, 310
Sardanapalos, 2, 224, 323
Sargon, Akkad, 19, 35, 37, 65, 151n151, 324, 393, 490

785

General Index

Sargon, Assyria, 146n205, 262, 327n37, 520; Kition stele, 353, 407n43

Saul, 126, 149, 173, 381; band of prophets, 156–157, 164, 175n153, 265; evil spirit, 31, 158, 166–167; lament for, 175, 301; Michal, 169

Scardina, P., 517, 520

scribal culture/practice: Alashiya, 12; Assur, 79; Biblical, 150–151; Byblos, 483, 485; Canaan, 12, 440, 511; Ebla, 63–66, 71, 87; Egypt, 56, 197, 273, 440, 483; Emar, 79, 121n59; Greek, Myc. Pylos, 427, 431; —Syro-Levantine influence, Byzantine period 213–216, 433n53; Hittite, 90, 92, 99; Mari, 81; Mesopotamia, 4, 63–65, 71, 77–79, 89, 151, 291; —musical texts, 59; —Nabu, 495; peripheral Akkadian, 12, 78–79, 329, 483; —Shulgi, 35; Minoans, 13; Tyre, 440; Ugarit, 4, 12, 54, 59, 79, 119, 121n59–122, 152n23, 197n56, 440, 448

Ṣdqmlk, 'Sydyk-is-king', Lapethos, 510

Sea Peoples, 10, 354, 481; use of term, 13. *See also* Aegean migrations; Great Collapse; Philistia, Philistine; Ramses III; Tjekkeru

Sebettu: *see* Divine Heptad

Second Temple: *see* Jerusalem

Sefire steles, 154, 300

Seleucia Tracheia: *see* Hyria; Ura

Seleucids, 418, 507; Apollo, 415n88, 495; Nabu, 495

Selz, G. J., 19

Semiramis, 327, 547, 566n64

Sennacherib, 154, 178, 301, 328, 520

Seow, C. L., 169

Septuagint, 3, 47, 116, 157, 176–177, 178; *kinýra*, 194–196, 198, 214;

Samuel, versus Josephus, MT and Qumran, 168, 170; transfer of Ark, 167–174

servant-gods: *see* master- and servant-gods

Servius: Adonis, *alter ordo fabulae*, 513–515; Amaracus, 331–332, 550–552; Melus, Adonis laments, etc., 290; Myrrha, 288

Sesostris II, 105

Setrakhos/Satrakhos: *see* rivers

seven-magic: balangs, 29n68, 41, 585; Biblical world, 150, 170–173; Divine Heptad, 26, 40; Ebla, 68; Emar, 171; heptatonic/diatonic tuning, 40, 171; Hittites, 26n49; Hurro-Hittite, 101; in *lilissu* ritual, 24n39; Mesopotamia, 40–41; music, 39–41, 170–73; Pythagoreanism, 40n141; seven-gated Thebes, 26n49, 193; Ugarit, 128, 143

sexual rites (real or alleged), 38, 93, 221–222, 238n112, 282–283, 465; Cyprus, 222n15, 281; Paphos, 94. *See also* Inandık vase; Sacred Marriage (so-called)

Shakkanakku period, Mari, 74

Shamshi-Addu, 74n7, 75–76n23

Shargaz, divinized weapon, 27

Sharur, divinized mace, 25–27

Shaushgamuwa of Amurru, 12, 376

Shaushka (Ishtar of Nineveh), 92n10, 100, 103, 373, 375–376, 383, 474. *See also* Inanna/Ishtar

shepherd motif, 19, 35, 37n125, 145n197, 194n43, 471

Shibtu, Mari, 82

shrines, model, 236–239, 386

Shulgi, Ur, 33–37; building materials, 393; divination, 35, 38, 393; lamentation-priest, 34–35,

393; musical cosmopolitanism, 36–37, 73, 391; musician, 33–37, 40, 81, 86, 152, 167, 178, 381, 387, 391–393; Sacred Marriage (so-called), 38–39, 93; sole or leading agent, 38–39, 113; standard measures, 392; temple-builder, 33, 393; totalizing cultural symbol, 152, 381, 392; *zannāru*, 34, 36, 81, 391

Sicyon, 322, 339 and n14

Sidon, 138n162, 151n13, 275; Astarte, 154, 376, 382, 407, 462n16, 463, 492; Belos, 354, 379; Canaanite Shift, 55; Damu, 485n154; Eshmoun/Asklepios, 511; Kinyras?, 9, 57, 334, 358, 406, 488–494, 496; Paris and Helen, 339; Salaminian dynasty, 493; Solomon, 154; Straton, 212. *See also* Abdalonymos; Astarte: royal cults; Mokhos; Straton

silence, ritual, 85, 95, 141–147, 279, 291–298, 304

silver, 103, 262, 323, 521; adornment, instruments, 39, 76n27, 84–85, 95, 106, 155n39; Cypriot, 327; Kothar-is-king, silversmith, Ugarit, 167n100, 441; seven-magic, 171n125; *Song of Silver*, 103, 122, 380, 506

Simeon the Pious, 181

Simonides: lyric threnody, 293, 296

singers: Ebla, 63–64, 66; Egypt, 105, 110; Emar, 171; Gk. *aoidós*, 6, 126n89, 211n135, 238, 292–293, 306, 309, 468, 527; Gk. *psaltōidoí*, 116; Hittites, 94–95, 98, 100, 329, 509; Kition temple singers, 116, 262, 315; Mari, 73, 75–76; Mesopotamia, 26, 28, 31, 35, 39, 41, 73; Ugarit, 113–119; —Singer of Ugarit, 114; —Singer(s) of Astarte, 40, 114, 383; —*šrm*, 115; umbrella term, 28, 115–117, 155, 383; —lyre implied, 116, 383. *See also* Chief Singer; epic poetry; *kithára*: *kitharōidoí*; nar/NAR/ *nâru*; psalmody, Hebrew

single-pipe, 145n197, 265n104

sistrum, 104, 110, 126n92, 169n115

Sisythes: *see* Ziusudra

Skindapsos (lute and eponymous inventor), 535

Skylax, pseudo, 349

Smith, M. S., 444

smiting-god type, 372, 394, 474n94

Smyrna: *see* Myrrha

Snyder, J., 244

Soloi: Cilician, 347, 356n110, 520; Cypriot, 14n68, 222n16, 340–341, 352, 355, 359, 414, 498; —resists Euagoras, 352; —Solon, 341

Solomon: Arabic tradition, 160, 182–183; Astarte, 154, 382; attribution of works to, 152, 174, 178, 383; bronze stands, 390; builds instruments, 158, 381; djinn, demons, spirits, Lilin, 183; Egypt, 151, 154–155; —pharaoh's daughter, 155; First Temple, 149–150, 155, 173; —transfers Ark, 172; Great Kingship, 150–155; harem, 154; management of musicians, 154; musical activity, 151–152, 159, 178, 381, 383, 387, 393; speaks with animals, 151, 183; totalizing cultural symbol, 151–152, 392; —Shulgi compared, 152, 381, 393; wisdom, 151–152, 159

Solomon of Akhlat, 455

Solon, 294, 341, 355–356

song-acts, 27, 164–165, 167–174, 172

General Index

Sostratos, Kinyradai diviner, 401
Sparta, Spartan/Laconian, 191, 196, 266, 294, 298n104, 317n228, 330, 348, 353, 357n119, 423n128, 432–433n52, 492n20
sphinx or gryphon, 269, 388, 390, 522, 527; and lyrist, 390, 522–528
spirit: evil, banished by pipes, 455; — in pipes, 455; —Saul, 31, 158–159, 166; not evil, in instrument, 32, 61, 163, 455; 'lyre of the spirit', 182, 209–210; 'spirit of the Lord', 157, 165–166
St. Maria Deipara, convent, Wadi El Natrun, 469
Standard of Ur, 73
stands, bronze, 241, 245–255, 383–391, 398, 405, 441, 443, 451, 480, 526
Stasinos, Salamis, 211, 269, 345
statues: anointing, 282; Astarte, Bar Koni, 471; Euagoras, 353; Ishtar of Nineveh, 373, 376; metamorphosis into, 281; offerings, 19, 71; oracular lyre-player, Hierapolis, 495; processions, 84, 486; Pygmalion, 289, 499; royal, Paphos, 407
—statues, divinized, 19, 22; attributa, 25–26, 94, 101; construction, repair, 23, 30, 101, 282; investiture, 114; lamentation, 30, 282; manifestation of divinity, 20, 22, 25, 373; mouth-washing ritual, 23; mythogenic, 25, 282; Pygmalion, 289
Stesandros or Stasandros, Salamis, 211, 269, 345
storm-gods: Adonis as, evidence limited, 465, 473, 484, 514; Aerias?, 403; Baal of Ugarit, 125–132, 403, 465, 484; dying-and-rising pattern secondary, 484; Haddu, Baal of Byblos, 483–485; Jupiter, 514; mountaintops, 465, 467, 484, 501, 514; royal cult, 135, 169, 468, 501, 503; Storm God of Zippalanda, 95; Tarhunzas, 507n75; Teshup, 92n10, 103, 465; Yahweh, 484; Zeus, 403
Strabo, 204, 326, 337, 340, 362, 416, 466, 473, 558, 565–567
Straton/Abdastart of Sidon, 212, 407n45, 462n16, 489–493
Stratonike, Hierapolitan myth, 462
Stratonikos, citharode, 211
strings: anthropomorphic conception as sinews, 312; decorative treatment of ends, 247n28, 388n104; Josephus on, 58; Kadmos', broken by Apollo, 492n21; linen, Linos, 189, 306, 309; lyre versus harp, 3; number of, 57–60, 58n65, 167, 229; —Rabbinic speculation, 58; sheep-gut, Greece, 449–450n43. *See also* heptatonic/diatonic; tuning; plucking, plectrum
Subarian, 76
succession myth, 97, 376
Suen/Sin, 36
Šulšaga, son of Ningirsu, 27
sun, 183; Akhenaten, 107, 110, 175, 507; ANE kingship, justice, 501, 506–507, 509–511; balang-cult, 21, 507, 584–585; Ebla, 68; etymology of Idalion, 339, 364; Hammurabi and Shamash, 506; Helios, 506n70; —of Hierapolis, 495, 507; Hittite king, 175, 501; in magic, 103; 'Lyre of the Divinity of the Father of the Sun God', 94n24; Lyre-Player Group of Seals, 522; Misharum and Kittum, servants of Shamash, 510; Myrrha, 288, 506; Phaethon, *Song of Silver*, 506; Phoenician Apollo, 511; royal

title, 507; Sandas, 509; Šapšu, Ugarit, 143, 374; *Ṣdq* and *Mšr*, 509–511; solar descent of Kinyras, 288, 504–512, 505; Sun Goddess of Arinna, 94; Utu as master-god, 21, 507; 'Yasmah-Addu is my Sun', divinized *urzababîtum*, 86. *See also* Aoios; Eos
Suppiluliuma I, 108n120
Suppiluliuma II, 13
Susa, 101, 507n74. *See also* Elam, Elamite
Sydyk, Philo of Byblos, 477, 509–511; as Apollo, 511–512; seven sons, 511
sympathetic magic, 25, 40, 165
sympathetic vibration, 85, 182
symposium: *see* drinking rituals
synaulía, 202, 295
syncretism, musical, 272, 314; theological, 459; —Aegean royal ideology, 387n99; —Apollo and epichoric rivals, 189; —Baal and Damu, Byblos, 482–85; —Cypriot and mainland gods/cult, 272, 373–375, 377–380; —Cyprus and Byblos, 475, 480–481; —Kothar and Kinyras, 9, 139, 229, 323, 396, 443–458
Syracuse, 219–226
Syria, Syrian: Kinyras, 3, 9, 57, 98, 122, 406, 461, 504–512, 517; PNs, 78n45; Roman annexation, 199, Appendix C; scented oil at Paphos, 284; Syro-Hurrian, defined, 96; versus Assyria, 3n11, 461, 467. *See also* Aramaean; Cypro-Phoenician symposium bowls; Hierapolis; Hurrians; Karkemish; Sefire steles; Sam'al; Syriac sources; 'Syrian Goddess'
Syriac sources, 2, 60–61, 216, 454–455, 460, 463, 468–473, 543n23

'Syrian Goddess', 126n91, 236, 363–364n150, 461–462, 521
Taautos, 448, 477, 510, 511
Tabernacle, 155, 169
Table of Nations, 43, 514, 558n7
Tacitus, 401–407, 413, 417–418, 420–422, 475
Talthybios, 344, 369; Talthybiadai, 423n128
Tamar, 404–405n26
Tamassos, 229, 236, 339, 372, 515; Kinyras, 325, 350n75, 563; Phoenicians, 16
Tamiras, Tamiradai, 401, 404–406, 497; proposed etymologies, 404–405; *vis-à-vis* Kinyradai, 367, 401, 404–406
Tammuz, 483n144; Adonis equated, 464, 467, 470; Aphaka/Byblos, 314, 464, 468–475; —tomb, 470; lamentation, 468–473; —Jerusalem, 470; myrrh as semen, 283. *See also* Adonis; Dumuzi
targums, 183, 216, 302
Tarhunzas, 507n75
Tarsus, 250n44, 256n72, 499, 517–521; destruction 696 BCE, 520; Sandan, Perseus, 508, 511
Tašmišari: *see* Tudhaliya III
Tattam, H., 469
teachers: *see* instruction, musical
Tegea, 230n64, 359, 364–365
Telamon, 354–355, 366n165
temple-builder/building, 366; Agapenor, 359, 362–363; Bar Kokhba, 180; David and Solomon, 150, 172, 381; Gudea, 26–33, 393; Kauthar, 468–473; Kinyras, 222, 363, 380–381, 393, 401, 439, 464, 505; lamentation, 279; Nikokles, Paphos, 409–410; Pylos?, 437; Ur III dynasty, 33, 393

Tentnau, Egyptian songstress, Byblos, 105n101
Terpandros, 232n80, 233
Teshup, 92n10, 103, 374, 465, 514
Teukros, Teukrid, 253, 340–341, 348–349, 351–360, 365, 366n165, 368, 379, 514; Asterias/Asteria, son/daughter, 514n125; 'Athenian', 354; banishment, foundation of Cypriot Salamis, 355, 359; Cilicia, 356; —priesthood at Olbe, 356n110, 405; Gerginoi, 458; marriage Eue/Eune/Eunoe, daughter of Kinyras, 353–354; multiformity, 354; Salaminian Zeus, 402. *See also* Tjekkeru
thalassocracy-lists, 327
Thamyris, 192–194, 234, 318, 325n24, 405, 411n68; Tamiras, Tamiradai?, 405; *Thamyríddontes*, Thespiai, 234–235, 405
Thasos, 379
Thebes, Egyptian, 106
Thebes, Greek: Ismenias, aulete, 303; Linos, 306n150, 307; Mycenaean period, 387n100; —two 'lyrasts', 434n62; Pindar as Theban *kinýra*, 215; seven-gated, 26n49, 193
Theia: wife of Hyperion, 288n52
Theias: Adonis son, 466–468; Aphaka, 467; 'Assyrian', 467n52, 502; beauty, 335n99; Belos father, 467, 468; divine determinative?, 123, 468; Greek gloss, of El?, 468; —of Kinyras cognate?, 465, 468, 486; Kinyras doublet, 284, 288n52, 460, 464, 466–468, 486, 492, 502; Kinyras son, 187, 466; Oreithuia mother, 467; wife Aoia, 502
Theodontius, 199, 499, 517, Appendix F, 559–561
Theodoros Studites, Appendix D

Theodosios, 465
theogony, 449. *See also* cosmogony
Theokritos, 308
Theophrastos, 286, 315n213, 413–414n76
Theopompos, 212; compared with Étienne de Lusignan, 361, 557, 564; Mopsos, 346n50, 347; Pausanias, 353, 362; unthroning of Kinyras, 190, 346–348, 351–361
Thera, 378–379
therapy: *see* musical therapy
Theseus, 340–341, 471n82
Thespiai, 234, 405
Thilo, G., 513
third gender, 29, 315, 462. *See also* gender-blurring
Thoth, 448, 477, 510
threnody, lyric, 43, 67–71, 83, 141, 145, 188–189, 199–200, 202, 207–208, 233, 279–319; female, 289, 293, 295; harlot of Tyre, 302; Hebrew psalmody, 301; Homer, 292–293; 'leaders', 293; legislation against, 294, 299; mythological repertoire, 293–296, 307, 311; Pindar and Simonides, 293, 296; seasonal cult, 294–296, 304–316
throne, 102, 143–144, 146, 150, 180, 209, 507. *See also* enthronement
Thutmosis III, 105
Thymarete, wife of Kinyras, 290n63, 404, 497–498, 512–513n119, 515; variant Metharme, 512
Tiberius, 205, 402, 423
Tibullus, 294
Timarkhos, Paphos, 236n108, 410n62, 411
Titans, Titanids, 123n74, 508, 510
Tithonos, 329n57, 504–505
Titus, 401, 420
Tjekkeru, 13, 354. *See also* Teukros, Teukrid

transgender: *see* third gender
treaties, 21, 300–301, 376–377.
    See also oaths
trees: *aoîa*, cuttings dedicated to Aphrodite, 502; apple-tree, Melus, 290; cedar, 27, 124n82, 147, 151, 179, 462n16; —Cedar Deities, 376; charmed by lyrist, 193; date-palm, 384; —Tamar, 404; early Cyprus, 327; elder-tree, 332; hanging from, 290, 300, 312; joining in lyric praise of Yahweh, 179; Mitannian glyptic, 386; musician and, 159, 246, 253, 383–388, 405, 522–528; offerings/blessings when used for instrument, 23; palm and ibex, 160; rag-bushes, 466, 563–564; representing sacred grove, 386, 397; Sacred Tree, 159, 160n71, 383–388, 386n92, 390, 391, 404, 522–528; —representing goddess, 386, 391, 522, 526; Solomon's wisdom, 151; sphinx or gryphon, 390, 522. *See also* myrrh
Troad, 317n228, 354, 457–458
Troodos: *see* mountains
Troy/Trojan War, 141, 204, 253, 275, 322–323, 338–340, 342, 347, 354–355; Arcadian contingent, 359; chronographic boundary, 379, 516n135, 560–563; Helen abducted from Paphos, fleet gathers there, 348; honeymoon escapade of Paris and Helen, 1, 339; Kinyras and, 1, 187, 343–346; lamentation of/at Troy, 292, 303, 311n183. *See also* Aegean migrations: migration/foundation legends; Cyprus: Greek conquest myths; epic poetry, Greek: *nóstoi*
trumpets, 118n38, 155, 164, 168, 169n115, 170, 172, 179, 212n148; Heb. *shofar*, 155; —Tutankhamun, 155n39
Tubal-Cain, 44, 453–456
Tudhaliya I/II, 100
Tudhaliya III, 99
Tudhaliya IV, 12–13, 376, 501
tuning: Mesopotamian system, 40, 57–60, 97, 119, 171, 392, 451; problem of, 57–60; Shulgi, 34. *See also* heptatonic/diatonic
Tushratta, 373, 375
Tutankhamun: tomb, trumpets, 155n39
Tuttul, 64, 78n45, 84, 483
twins: *see* brothers motif; Dioskouroi
Typhon, 98, 500, 503
Tyre, 43–44n3, 150, 275, 347, 446, 462, 490, 502; Astarte, 376, 407; Cyprus, Kition, 16, 337–338n3, 352, 476; Damu, 485n154; Euagoras, 347, 493; Isaiah oracle, harlot, 61, 77, 302; LBA, 440, 482; siege, 491, 493

Ugarit, Ugaritic, 4, 45, 113–148; Alashiya, 11–12, 104, 372–373, 399, 440, 459; —Alashiyan gods, 373–375; —Alashiyan residents, 441; —Alashiyan/Cypriot oil, 330; —'god of Ugarit', 374; Amorite dynasty and past, 83, 377; Astarte, 7, 114, 374, 376–377, 407, 486; —Singer(s) of, 40, 383; Baal, 131–132, 403, 465, 484; —and kingship, 468; Crete, 479; Damu, 485n154; destruction, 13, 459; Ebla, 63; Enkomi, 460; female singers?, 115; god-pairs, 450–451, 454, 509–511; Hittites, 12, 115; Hurrian influence, 96; —hymnography, 35, 59, 97–98, 103, 119–120, 377, 383, 392, 451; —Hurrian priest, House of 120;

General Index

(Ugarit, *cont.*)
  king in cult, 113, 166, 173, 381, 422; lexical texts, 79, 121n59; linguistic points, 137–139 and n162, 199n71, 443n2, 478n118, 479; —Canaanite Shift, 55, 459; Mesopotamian tuning system, 59, 97, 119, 171, 392, 451; Mitanni, 97; *n'm*, 128–129, 132, 141–143, 149, 175–178; pantheon texts, 4, 79, 103, 119–122, 235, 283, 377, 451; PNs, 56n53, 167n100, 273n138, 377, 441, 452, 509; royal ancestor cult, 5, 71, 124, 256, 313, 423, 484; *Ṣdq* and *Mšr*, 509–511; Singer of Ugarit, 114; Ura, 507, 512. *See also* Anat; Aqhat; Baal; guilds, musical; Kinnaru, god; PNs; seven-magic
Ullikummi, 103
Uluburun wreck, 248, 326, 479
underworld: Adonis, Persephone, 287, 299n112, 484; Dumuzi/Tammuz, 283, 484; Inanna, gala, 29, 141, 145n197; Isaiah, Rephaim, 146–147; *katábasis*, 147, 287, 298n108–299; Kinyras, 335n99; Lelwani, 94; musician figurines, Egypt, 137n154; Ninazu, 140, 304; Odysseus, 328n49; Orpheus, 141, 294; Rāp'iu/Milku and royal mortuary cult, Ugarit, 134–142, 256, 304. *See also* Nergal
Ur, 30n83, 37, 97, 393, 485; 'royal cemetery', 19; Ur III dynasty, 22, 28n65, 33–37, 73, 84, 86, 150, 152, 393, 485; —Byblos, 88, 483; —Ebla, 483; —Mari, 483. *See also* Amar-Suen; Ibbi-Sin; Shulgi; Ur-Nammu
Ura, 507, 512. *See also* Hyria
Urikina, 100
Urikki of Que/Hiyawa, 520

Ur-Nammu, Ur, 33, 393
Ur-Nanshe, 73
Uruk, 19, 23, 84, 393; Uruk period, 19; Uruk vase, 37
Ur-zababa/*urzababîtum*, 34–36, 76n27, 85–86
Ušumgal-kalama, 21, 28, 32, 66, 531–532; conceived as musical director, 28, 33, 118, 444; counselor, 30–31
Utu, 21, 507. *See also* sun

van der Sluijs, M. A., 506, 509
vanishing-god motif, 316, 376; faithless goddess, 474. *See also* grief or wrath, divine
Vellay, C., 190
Vergil, 331, 354, 379, 490, 513
Vespasian, 401
victory, performance context, 30, 43, 126, 128, 164, 169, 173–174, 178n166, 201
vintage or harvest song, 300–301, 308–310

Wánassa: *see* Aphrodite; Great Goddess of Cyprus
Warad-Ilishu, Chief Singer, Mari, 74
Warad-Sin, Larsa, 83
Webb, J., 394, 397
wedding: *see* marriage
Wegner, I., 376
Wen-Amun, 14, 105n101, 354, 481, 514nn129
West, M. L., 422–423, 476
Winter, I., 520
wisdom, 30n83; and lyre, 6n32, 72, 307; Canaanite traditions, 152, 156; David, 183; Hebrew psalmody, 162–163; Linos, 307; musical activity, 152; Solomon, 151–152

General Index

women: *Adōniá*, 145, 311n184, 312–313; chorus, 95, 191, 222, 232, 262, 265, 289, 293; cult-musicians, 171n126, 249, 262, 265, 302, 311n184, 486; Cypriot figurines, 242, 258n76, 260n80, 269n122, 394; double-pipes, 105n101; Egypt, 56, 61, 105n101, 106–111, 154; captive musicians, 106; harp, 76n28, 90, 107–108; lamentation, 29, 46, 64, 133, 144–145, 200–201, 292–293, 296, 298, 312, 470, 486; Lemnian, 200–202; lute, 248; lyre, 60–61, 77, 107–108, 110, 126, 191, 216, 222, 236n105, 242n1, 245–250, 258n76, 260n80, 265, 269n122, 302, 486; lyric threnody, 289, 293, 295; —harlot of Tyre, 302; musical cosmopolitanism, 106, 108, 249; palace musicians, David/Solomon, 154; —Ebla, 64; Egypt, 106–111; —Hezekiah, 154; Mari, 74–77, 82, 85, 154, 292; prophecy, 38; Ugarit, 115; victory song, 126, 201. *See also* Cypro-Phoenician symposium bowls; frame-drum; harem; lamentation: female; prostitution; royal ideology: king empowered by goddess or queen

wrath, divine: *see* grief or wrath, divine

Wyatt, N., 140, 142, 159, 164

Xenophon of Cyprus (?), 565–567

Yahimilk, Byblos, 510
Yahweh, 36, 147, 174, 179, 445; Asherah, 60; Baal, 169; cult-music, 156, 158, 172, 180; David, praise-singer of, 129, 149, 173, 176–178, 180, 382; —Davidic covenant, 177, 179, 468; —David enacts, 169, 173, 175, 177; —David favored, 167; lyre, 60, 163, 166, 182; —invocation of Yahweh by psalmodists, 162; —lyres of God, St. Ephraim, 61; —Yahweh creates, 167; —Yahweh's voice channeled by singer, 36, 161–165, 175, 177–178, 310; prophets as couriers of, 161; solar justice, 510; storm-god, 169, 484
Yamhad, 82, 96
Yamm: *see* Baal
Yarim-Lim, Yamhad, 82
Yasmah-Addu, Mari, 35–36, 74–75, 82, 84–86
Yasur-Landau, A., 159
Yazılıkaya, 501
year-names from divinized instruments, 21–22, 27–28, 83, 86
Yeronisos, 386n91
Yigriš-Halab, Ebla, 63
Yirkab-Damu, Ebla, 63
Yiš'ar-Damu, Ebla, 63
Yon: *see* Hyon

Zababa, 84
Zadok, 156n43
zannāru, 55, 77; = *kinnāru*/Inanna-instrument, 55, 77–79, 88–90, 92, 99, 121–122, 291, 380, 391; Ishme-Dagan, 81, 391; Ninazu, 140, 304; Shulgi, 34, 36, 81, 391; ZA as phonetic gloss, 78; Zannaru, goddess, 78; *zinar*, 55, 90. *See also* Inanna-instrument; *kinnāru*; *kinnōr*; *kinýra*; *knr*; lyres and lyric iconography; *zinar*
Zarpiya ritual, 508–509
Zedekiah, 181
Zenodotos, 207–208, 309, 316
Zerah, Sons of, 152n23, 177n161

793

Zeus, 373, 439; Aerias, Aerios, 403; Aigina, 224n30; Amathous, 516n135; Aphrodite, 403n16; Dione, 403, 481; Jupiter, 402, 514–515; Meilikhios, 446, 448; Ouranios, 403; Paphian, 501; Salaminian, 206, 402; Typhon, 98, 503
Zeuxis, a.k.a. Kinyras, gladiator, 335
zigzag arms: *see* lyres and lyric iconography
Zillah, 44
Zimri, name element: Bible, 138, 152n23, 177n161; Canaanite/Amorite, 138; —Zimri-Lim, Mari, 74–76, 82, 85–87, 96, 310n179

zinar, 89–96, 98; Caucasian cognates, 61; cult devotions, 94; derivation, 90n4; generalized to 'music', 93; *ḫun-zinar*, 90, 93; *ippi-zinar*, 90, 93; *kinnāru/zannāru*, Inanna-instrument, 55, 90, 92, 99, 380; umbrella term including *kinnāru*, 99. *See also* Inanna-instrument; *kinnāru*; *kinnōr*; *kinýra*; *knr*; lyres and lyric iconography; *zannāru*
Zincirli: *see* Sam'al
Ziusudra/Sisythes, flood hero, 462
Zoïlos of Cedasa (?), 502
Zosimos, 465

www.ingramcontent.com/pod-product-compliance
Lightning Source LLC
Chambersburg PA
CBHW052306300426
44110CB00035B/1938